2025 대비 최신개정판

해커스공무원
7개년
기출문제집
영어

문제집

해커스공무원

여러분의 합격을 응원하는
해커스공무원의 특별 혜택

FREE 공무원 영어
특강

해커스공무원(gosi.Hackers.com) 접속 후 로그인 ▶
상단의 [무료강좌] 클릭 ▶
[교재 무료특강] 클릭하여 이용

A 공무원 보카 어플
이용권

GOSIVOCA7GICHOOL

구글 플레이스토어/애플 앱스토어에서
'해커스공무원 기출보카' 검색 ▶ 어플 설치 후 실행 ▶
'인증코드 입력하기' 클릭 ▶ 위 인증코드 입력

* 등록 후 30일간 사용 가능
* 해당 자료는 [해커스공무원 기출 보카 4000+] 교재 내용으로 제공되는 자료로,
공무원 시험 대비에 도움이 되는 유용한 자료입니다.

A 핵심 기출
단어암기장(PDF)

회독용 답안지
(PDF)

해커스공무원(gosi.Hackers.com) 접속 후 로그인 ▶ 상단의 [교재·서점 → 무료 학습 자료] 클릭 ▶
본 교재의 [자료받기] 클릭하여 이용

해커스공무원 온라인 단과강의 **20% 할인쿠폰**

7B544ABC4F299E48

해커스공무원(gosi.Hackers.com) 접속 후 로그인 ▶ 상단의 [나의 강의실] 클릭 ▶
좌측의 [쿠폰등록] 클릭 ▶ 위 쿠폰번호 입력 후 이용

* 등록 후 7일간 사용 가능(ID당 1회에 한해 등록 가능)

무료 모바일 자동 채점 + 성적 분석 서비스
교재 내 수록되어 있는 문제의 채점 및 성적 분석 서비스를 제공합니다.

* 세부적인 내용은 해커스공무원(gosi.Hackers.com)에서 확인 가능합니다.

바로 이용하기 ▶

쿠폰 이용 관련 문의 **1588-4055**

단기 합격을 위한
해커스공무원 커리큘럼

입문

▼

기본+심화

▼

기출+예상 문제풀이

▼

동형문제풀이

▼

최종 마무리

▼

PASS

탄탄한 기본기와 핵심 개념 완성!

누구나 이해하기 쉬운 개념 설명과 풍부한 예시로 부담없이 쌩기초 다지기

TIP 베이스가 있다면 **기본 단계**부터!

필수 개념 학습으로 이론 완성!

반드시 알아야 할 기본 개념과 문제풀이 전략을 학습하고
심화 개념 학습으로 고득점을 위한 응용력 다지기

문제풀이로 집중 학습하고 실력 업그레이드!

기출문제의 유형과 출제 의도를 이해하고 최신 출제 경향을 반영한
예상문제를 풀어보며 본인의 취약영역을 파악 및 보완하기

동형모의고사로 실전력 강화!

실제 시험과 같은 형태의 실전모의고사를 풀어보며 실전감각 극대화

시험 직전 실전 시뮬레이션!

각 과목별 시험에 출제되는 내용들을 최종 점검하며 실전 완성

* 커리큘럼 및 세부 일정은 상이할 수 있으며,
자세한 사항은 해커스공무원 사이트에서 확인하세요.

**단계별 교재 확인 및
수강신청은 여기서!**

gosi.Hackers.com

해커스공무원

7개년
기출문제집
영어

문제집

해커스공무원

"기출문제" 그냥
풀어보기만 하면 될까?

—

합격자들이 모두 강조하니까 풀어봐야 할 것 같긴 한데
문제를 풀고 채점한 후 무엇을 더 해야 할지 모르겠어요.
틀린 문제를 다시 풀어보면 또 틀리기까지 해요···

기출문제, 그냥 풀어보기만 하면 되나요?

해커스는 자신 있게 대답합니다.

기출문제는 단순히 풀고 채점하는 것으로 끝나서는 안 됩니다. 기출문제 풀이를 통해 실제 시험의 문제 유형과 정답
및 오답의 출제 포인트를 이해하고, 자신이 취약한 부분을 파악 및 보완하여 실전에 대비할 수 있는 진짜 실력을 키
워야 합니다.

『해커스공무원 7개년 기출문제집 영어』는
한 문제를 풀어도 완벽히 이해할 수 있도록 꼼꼼한 해설을 제공합니다.

확실하게 실전에 대비하기 위해서는 기출문제의 출제 포인트와 정답 및 오답의 근거를 완벽히 이해할 수 있도록 해
야 합니다. 『해커스공무원 7개년 기출문제집 영어』는 한 문제를 풀어도 '출제 포인트 + 정답 해설 + 오답 분석 + 연
관 개념 정리'까지 포함하는 꼼꼼한 해설을 제공하여 확실한 실전 대비에 도움이 됩니다.

문제 유형에 맞는 풀이 비법을 익힐 수 있도록 기출로 보는 유형별 필승 비법을 제공합니다.

실제 시험장에서 정해진 시간 내에 모든 문제를 신속하고 정확하게 풀어내기 위해서는 각 문제 유형에 맞는 문제 풀이
전략을 알고 있어야 합니다. 『해커스공무원 7개년 기출문제집 영어』는 <기출로 보는 유형별 필승 비법>을 제공하여
기출 문제의 영역별 문제 유형들을 파악하고 각각의 유형에 맞는 문제풀이 비법을 익힐 수 있게 했습니다.

합격이 보이는 기출문제 풀이,
해커스가 여러분과 함께 합니다.

CONTENTS

회독을 통한 취약 부분 완벽 정복
다회독에 최적화된 **회독용 답안지** (PDF)
해커스공무원(gosi.Hackers.com) ▶ 사이트 상단의 '교재·서점' ▶ 무료학습자료

기출문제집과 함께 공부하면 효과는 2배
어휘 잡는 **핵심 기출 단어암기장** (PDF)
해커스공무원(gosi.Hackers.com) ▶ 사이트 상단의 '교재·서점' ▶ 무료학습자료

공무원 기출문제 무료 강의로 실전 대비
점수를 올려주는 **기출분석강의 (gosi.Hackers.com)**
해커스공무원(gosi.Hackers.com) ▶ 무료강좌 ▶ 기출문제 해설특강

기출문제집도 해커스가 만들면 다릅니다!

01 꼼꼼한 해설로 기출문제에 대한 **완벽한 이해**가 가능합니다!

> '끊어읽기 해석 + 정답 해설 + 오답 분석 + 이것도 알면 합격'까지, 꼼꼼한 해설을 통해 문제를 완벽히 이해하여 자신의 실력을 향상시킬 수 있습니다.

> 해설집의 취약영역 분석표를 통해 약점을 진단하고 해당 영역을 집중 보완할 수 있습니다.

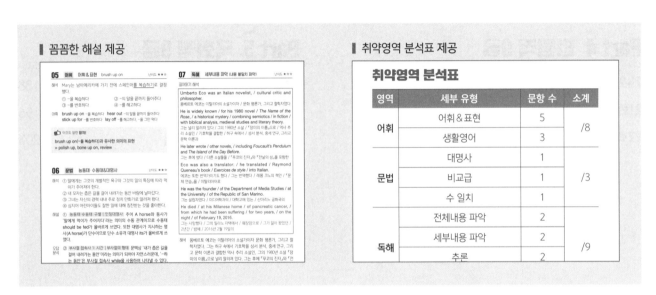

02 최신 출제 경향을 완벽하게 분석하여 **전략적 학습**이 가능합니다!

> 매년 달라지는 출제 경향을 직급/직렬별로 완벽하게 분석한 '최신 출제 경향 분석자료'를 통해 최신 출제 경향을 파악할 수 있습니다.

> 직렬별 출제 경향에 따라 영역별로 제시된 맞춤 학습 방법을 통해 취약한 부분을 효율적으로 보완하고 전략적으로 시험에 대비할 수 있습니다.

▌최신 출제 경향 분석자료 제공

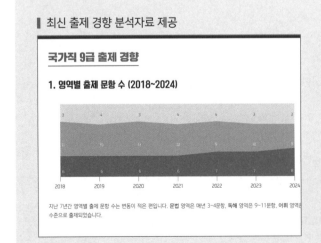

▌출제 경향에 따른 학습 방법 제공

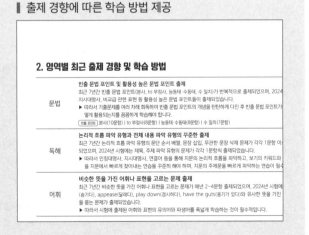

03 기출문제의 유형을 확실히 파악하여 **실전대비**가 가능합니다!

> 다양한 직렬의 7개년 기출문제를 통해 풍부한 실전 경험을 쌓아 실전에 대비할 수 있습니다.
> 매 회차를 끝낸 직후 해당 시험의 정답을 모바일 페이지에서 입력하고 채점결과 및 성적 분석 서비스를 이용할 수 있도록, 각 회차마다 QR 코드를 삽입하였습니다.
> 유형별 필승 비법을 통해 각 문제의 유형을 파악하고 비법을 곧바로 적용하여 빠르고 정확하게 풀이할 수 있습니다.

┃ 7개년(2018-2024) 기출문제 수록

┃ 기출로 보는 유형별 필승 비법

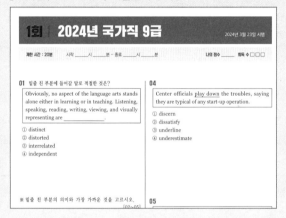

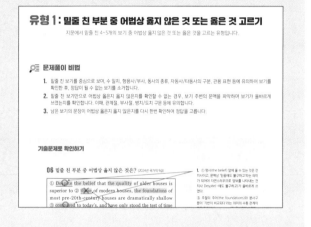

04 <어휘 잡는 핵심 기출 단어암기장>으로 **핵심 기출 어휘를 학습**할 수 있습니다!

> 시험에 나온 단어 중 가장 핵심적인 단어를 추린 <어휘 잡는 핵심 기출 단어암기장>으로 부족한 어휘를 반복해서 암기할 수 있습니다.
> 간단한 퀴즈를 통해 <어휘 잡는 핵심 기출 단어암기장>의 어휘와 표현을 확실히 암기했는지 확인할 수 있습니다.

┃ 핵심 기출 어휘 제공

┃ 어휘 Quiz 제공

공무원 영어 이렇게 출제된다!

01 공무원 영어 **시험 출제 영역**

공무원 영어 시험은 직렬에 따라 20문항 또는 25문항으로 구성되며, 크게 문법/독해/어휘 3개의 영역으로 나눌 수 있습니다. 국가직·지방직·서울시·국회직 9급 영어 시험은 총 20문항이며, 독해 영역이 약 50%를 차지하고 나머지 50%는 문법과 어휘 영역으로 구성됩니다. 이때 어휘 영역의 경우 세부적으로 어휘 및 표현, 생활영어로 구분됩니다. 한편, 법원직 9급 영어 시험은 총 25문항이며, 독해 영역이 약 80%를 차지하고 나머지 20%는 문법 영역으로 구성됩니다.

시험 구분	영역별 출제 문항 수		
	문법	독해	어휘
국가직·지방직 9급	3~4문항	9~11문항	4~5문항
서울시 9급*	3~5문항	9~12문항	5~6문항
법원직 9급	3~5문항	20~21문항	0~1문항
국회직 9급	3~5문항	7~13문항	4~8문항

*서울시 9급 영어 과목 시험은 2020년부터 지방직과 동일하게 인사혁신처에서 출제했습니다.

02 최근 7개년 **공무원 영어 출제 경향**

난이도 하락세

지난 7년간 공무원 영어의 문제 유형에는 큰 변화가 없었으나, 최근 시험에 인사혁신처에서 발표한 2025년 대비 출제 기조 전환과 관련된 새로운 소재의 문제들이 출제되거나 전반적인 난도가 하락세를 보이는 변화가 있었습니다. 문법 영역에서는 빈출 포인트가 반복 출제되고, 독해 영역에서는 실생활이나 직무 관련 소재의 지문이 자주 출제되고, 어휘 영역에서는 평이한 어휘가 주로 출제되고 있어, 수험생들의 체감 난도가 낮아지고 있습니다.

독해 영역 다양한 소재의 지문 출제

독해 영역의 경우, 사회 이슈와 환경, 역사나 사회 과학에 대한 지식을 다루는 지문의 출제 비중이 높습니다. 최근에는 안내문이나 정책 등 실생활과 관련된 소재나 직무 관련 소재가 출제되기도 했습니다. 문제 유형은 빈칸 완성, 주제·제목·요지·목적 파악 유형 등 빈출 유형의 문제들이 고르게 출제되고 있으며, 문장 삽입, 무관한 문장 삭제 등 논리적 흐름 파악 유형이 증가하고 있는 추세입니다.

문법 영역 빈출 포인트 반복 출제

문법에서는 분사, 수 일치, 병치·도치·강조 구문 등 빈출 개념들이 반복 출제되고 있습니다. 최근에는 문법 포인트에 밑줄을 그어 어떤 어법을 묻고 있는지 명확히 하는 문제가 출제되고 있으며, 지엽적인 문법 포인트보다는 활용성 높은 어법이 출제되는 추세입니다.

03 공무원 영어 **영역별 출제 경향 및 수험 대책**

문법

출제 경향

문법 영역에서는 분사, 수 일치, 병치·도치·강조 구문 등을 묻는 문제가 자주 출제됩니다. 최근에는 빈출 포인트가 반복 출제되고 한 문제에서 여러 보기 혹은 모든 보기가 동일한 문법 요소에 대해 묻는 문제가 출제되고 있습니다.

수험 대책

① 해커스공무원 영어 기본서로 기본 개념을 탄탄히 다진 후 **기출문제를 통해 문법 포인트가 어떻게 활용되는지 학습**하며 실력을 쌓아야 합니다.
② 틀린 문제의 경우, **오답분석을 통해 해당 문제의 핵심 개념을 확실히 정리**하고 회독을 통해 해당 포인트를 확실히 암기하고 넘어가야 합니다.
③ 자주 틀리는 문법 포인트의 경우, **기본서를 통해 반드시 복습**하고 넘어가야 합니다.

독해

출제 경향

독해 영역에서는 **빈칸 완성, 주제·제목·요지·목적 파악, 내용 일치·불일치 파악, 문단 순서 배열**의 출제 비중이 높은 편이며, **문장 삽입, 무관한 문장 삭제** 등 논리적 흐름 파악 유형의 출제가 증가하고 있습니다. 최근에는 지문이 이메일, 웹 페이지 등의 형태로 출제되는 등 실용문의 성격을 띤 문제도 출제되고 있습니다.

수험 대책

① 해설집의 **'끊어읽기 해석'**을 통해 문제를 풀면서 해석이 어려웠던 부분의 문장 구조와 정답의 힌트를 확인하여 지문을 빠르게 분석하고 정확히 정답을 찾는 훈련을 해야 합니다.
② 새로운 형식의 지문에 익숙해질 필요가 있으므로 해커스공무원 영어 기본서로 **다양한 유형별 지문과 풀이 전략**을 학습하여 실전에 대비하고, 언제나 **시간제한을 두고 문제를 푸는 연습**을 하여 시간 배분에 익숙해져야 합니다.
③ 틀린 문제의 경우, **'기출로 보는 유형별 필승 비법'**(12p)을 통해 세부 유형별 **문제풀이 비법**을 다시 한번 확인한 후 비법을 적용해보며 **문제풀이 노하우**를 쌓아야 합니다.

어휘

출제 경향

어휘 영역에서는 **어휘, 표현, 생활영어** 문제가 고르게 출제되며 유의어 찾기 유형의 비중이 높은 편입니다. 지문과 보기에 사용된 어휘의 수준은 **수능 영어 수준에서부터 고난도 수준까지 매우 다양**하나, 최근에는 conceal과 같은 수능 영어 수준 어휘의 출제 비중이 높습니다.

수험 대책

① 어휘를 암기할 때 유의어, 반의어 및 파생어를 폭넓게 학습하고, **형태는 비슷하지만 의미는 다른 표현**들을 정리하여 암기해야 합니다.
② 구동사 및 표현을 암기할 때는 **예문을 통해 의미를 익히고**, 표현에 전치사가 포함된 경우 **전치사에 유의하여 암기**해야 합니다.
③ 그동안 출제되었던 핵심 어휘와 표현을 모아 수록한 <**어휘 잡는 핵심 기출 단어암기장**>을 활용해 풍부한 어휘력을 키워야 합니다.

공무원시험전문 해커스공무원
gosi.Hackers.com

기출로 보는 유형별
필승 비법

문법

유형 1 : 밑줄 친 부분 중 어법상 옳지 않은 것 또는 옳은 것 고르기

지문에서 밑줄 친 4~5개의 보기 중 어법상 옳지 않은 것 또는 옳은 것을 고르는 유형입니다.

🔍 문제풀이 비법

1. 밑줄 친 보기를 중심으로 보며, 수 일치, 형용사/부사, 동사의 종류, 자동사/타동사의 구분, 관용 표현 등에 유의하여 보기를 확인한 후, 정답이 될 수 없는 보기를 소거합니다.

2. 밑줄 친 보기만으로 어법상 옳은지 옳지 않은지를 확인할 수 없는 경우, 보기 주변의 문맥을 파악하며 보기가 올바르게 쓰였는지를 확인합니다. 이때, 관계절, 부사절, 병치/도치 구문 등에 유의합니다.

3. 남은 보기의 문장이 어법상 옳은지 옳지 않은지를 다시 한번 확인하여 정답을 고릅니다.

기출문제로 확인하기

06 밑줄 친 부분 중 어법상 옳지 않은 것은? (2024년 국가직 9급)

① Despite the belief that ② the quality of older houses is superior to ② those of modern houses, the foundations of most pre-20th-century houses are dramatically shallow ③ compared to today's, and have only stood the test of time due to the flexibility of ④ their timber framework or the lime mortar between bricks and stones.

해석 p.7

1. ① 명사(the belief) 앞에 올 수 있는 것은 전치사이고, 문맥상 '믿음에도 불구하고'라는 의미가 되어야 자연스러우므로 양보를 나타내는 전치사 Despite(~에도 불구하고)가 올바르게 쓰였다.

③ 주절의 주어(the foundations)와 분사구문이 '기반이 비교되다'라는 의미의 수동 관계이므로 과거분사 compared가 올바르게 쓰였다.

2. ④ 명사(timber framework) 앞에서 소유의 의미를 나타내기 위해서는 소유격 대명사가 와야 하고, 대명사가 지시하는 명사(the foundations)가 복수이므로 복수 소유격 대명사 their가 올바르게 쓰였다.

3. ② 대명사가 지칭하는 명사(the quality)가 단수이므로 복수 지시대명사 those를 단수 지시대명사 that으로 고쳐야 한다.

유형 2 : 어법상 옳은 문장 또는 옳지 않은 문장 고르기

주어진 4~5개의 영어 문장 중 어법상 옳은 문장 또는 옳지 않은 문장을 고르는 유형입니다. 밑줄 없이 문장만 제시되는 문제와, 묻고 있는 문법 포인트에 밑줄이 그어져 있는 문제가 출제됩니다.

🔍 문제풀이 비법

1. 주어진 문장에 밑줄이 없는 경우, 주어진 보기들의 문장 구조를 파악한 후 수 일치, 형용사와 부사, 동사의 종류, 관계절 등 의미를 파악하지 않고도 한눈에 알 수 있는 문법 요소들을 중심으로 문장이 어법상 올바르게 쓰였는지 확인합니다. 주어진 문장에 밑줄이 그어져 있는 경우, 밑줄 친 보기를 중심으로 분사, 수 일치, 병치·도치·강조 구문 등 빈출 포인트에 유의하여 어법상 옳거나 옳지 않은 보기를 소거합니다.

2. 어법상 옳거나 옳지 않은 것을 한눈에 파악할 수 없는 보기의 경우, 문맥을 고려하여 문장이 어법상 올바르게 쓰였는지 확인합니다.

3. 남은 보기의 문장이 어법상 옳은지 옳지 않은지를 다시 한번 확인하여 정답을 고릅니다.

기출문제로 확인하기

07 밑줄 친 부분이 어법상 옳지 않은 것은? (2024년 지방직 9급)

① You must plan <u>not to spend</u> too much on the project.

② My dog <u>disappeared</u> last month and hasn't been seen since.

③ I'm sad that the people <u>who</u> daughter I look after are moving away.

④ I bought a book on my trip, and it was <u>twice as expensive as</u> it was at home.

1. ① to 부정사(to spend)의 부정형은 to 부정사 앞에 not을 붙이므로 not to spend가 올바르게 쓰였다.

2. ② 문장에 시간 표현 last month(지난달)가 왔고 문맥상 '지난달에 사라졌다'라는 과거의 동작을 표현하고 있으므로 과거 시제 disappeared가 올바르게 쓰였다. 또한, 동사 disappear는 '사라지다'라는 의미일 때 목적어를 취하지 않는 자동사이며 수동태로 쓸 수 없으므로 능동태로 올바르게 쓰였다.

④ 문맥상 '본국에서 사는 것보다 두 배만큼 비쌌다'라는 의미가 되어야 자연스러운데, '두 배만큼 비쌌다'는 '배수사 + as + 원급 + as'의 형태로 나타낼 수 있으므로 twice as expensive as가 올바르게 쓰였다.

3. ③ 선행사(the people)가 사람이고, 관계절 내에서 daughter가 누구의 딸인지 나타내므로, 주격 관계대명사 who를 사람을 가리키는 소유격 관계대명사 whose로 고쳐야 한다.

해석 p.73

유형 3 : 우리말을 영어로 잘 옮긴 것 또는 잘못 옮긴 것 고르기

주어진 우리말을 영어로 잘 옮긴 것 또는 잘못 옮긴 것을 고르는 유형입니다. 각 보기마다 우리말 문장과 영어 문장이 하나씩 제시되는 문제, 그리고 우리말 문장 1개와 영어 문장 4~5개가 주어지는 문제가 있습니다.

🔍 문제풀이 비법

1. 제시된 우리말과 영어 문장이 의미상 일치하거나 일치하지 않는 보기를 소거합니다.

2. 남은 보기들의 문장 구조를 파악하여 어법상 올바르게 쓰였는지를 확인합니다.

3. 남은 보기의 문장이 제시된 우리말의 의미와 부합하는지 부합하지 않는지, 어법상 옳은지 옳지 않은지를 다시 한번 확인하여 정답을 고릅니다.

기출문제로 확인하기

07 우리말을 영어로 잘못 옮긴 것은? (2023년 국가직 9급)

① 내 고양이 나이는 그의 고양이 나이의 세 배이다.
　→ My cat is three times as old as his.

② 우리는 그 일을 이번 달 말까지 끝내야 한다.
　→ We have to finish the work until the end of this month.

③ 그녀는 이틀에 한 번 머리를 감는다.
　→ She washes her hair every other day.

④ 너는 비가 올 경우에 대비하여 우산을 챙고 가는 게 낫겠다.
　→ You had better take an umbrella in case it rains.

1. ① '세 배이다'는 '배수사 + as + 원급 + as'의 형태로 나타낼 수 있으므로 three times as old as가 올바르게 쓰였다.

③ '이틀에 한 번 머리를 감는다'라는 반복되는 동작을 표현하고 있으므로 현재 시제 washes가 올바르게 쓰였다.

2. ④ 조동사처럼 쓰이는 표현 had better (~하는 게 좋겠다) 뒤에는 동사원형이 와야 하므로 동사원형 take가 올바르게 쓰였다.

3. ② '이번 달 말까지 끝내야 한다'라는 정해진 시점(이번 달 말)까지 완료되는 상황을 나타내고 있으므로, '특정 시점까지 어떤 행동이나 상황이 계속되는 것'을 의미하는 전치사 until을 '정해진 시점까지 어떤 행동이나 상황이 완료되는 것'을 의미하는 전치사 by(~까지)로 고쳐야 한다.

유형 4 : 빈칸에 적절한 것 고르기

어법상 빈칸에 들어갈 가장 적절한 보기를 고르는 유형입니다. 빈칸이 하나인 문제가 가장 많이 출제되며, 빈칸이 2~4개인 문제가 출제되기도 합니다.

🔍 문제풀이 비법

1. 문장의 전체 구조를 파악한 후, 빈칸이 문장 내에서 하는 역할을 확인하여 정답 후보를 고릅니다.

2. 보기에 공통적으로 제시된 어휘나 표현이 있는지 확인하고, 그것이 문맥상 어떤 의미로 사용되어야 하는지 파악합니다.

3. 정답 후보들 간의 어법상 차이를 파악하고 문맥상 빈칸에 가장 적절한 보기를 정답으로 고릅니다.

기출문제로 확인하기

04 밑줄 친 부분에 들어갈 표현으로 적절한 것은?

(2023년 국회직 9급)

Kind neighbors, a fund-raising campaign organized and sponsored by local corporate leaders, _____ its first benefit event for Kalamazoo Hospital this past Sunday. Held at the Kalamazoo Convention Center, the event drew an energetic crowd of over 800 supporters.

① jump-starts

② will jump-start

③ jump-started

④ was jump-started

⑤ has jump-started

해석 p.230

1. 특정 과거 시점을 나타내는 표현(this past Sunday)이 왔고, 주어(Kind neighbors)와 동사가 "다정한 이웃'이 자선 행사를 시작했다'라는 의미의 능동 관계이다.

2. 빈칸에는 과거시제와 능동태를 나타내는 jump-started가 들어가야 적절하다. 따라서 ③번이 정답이다.

유형 1 : 전체내용 파악하기 ① 주제, 제목, 요지, 목적 파악

지문의 중심 내용을 파악하여 지문의 주제, 제목, 요지, 목적을 고르는 유형입니다.

🔍 문제풀이 비법

1. 지문의 처음 또는 마지막에 중심 내용이 나오는 경우가 많으므로, 지문의 처음과 마지막을 먼저 읽고 대략적인 글의 중심 내용을 파악합니다.

2. 지문의 처음 또는 마지막에서 파악한 중심 내용과 맞지 않는 보기를 소거합니다.

3. 이후 남은 보기들 중 지문의 중심 내용을 가장 잘 표현한 보기를 정답으로 고릅니다. 이때, 보기의 내용이 지문과 관련된 내용이라고 할지라도 지문의 중심 내용이 아닌 경우에는 정답이 될 수 없다는 점에 유의합니다.

기출문제로 확인하기

14 다음 글의 주제로 적절한 것은? (2024년 국가직 9급)

It seems incredible that one man could be responsible for opening our eyes to an entire culture, but until British archaeologist Arthur Evans successfully excavated the ruins of the palace of Knossos on the island of Crete, the great Minoan culture of the Mediterranean was more legend than fact. Indeed its most famed resident was a creature of mythology: the half-man, half-bull Minotaur, said to have lived under the palace of mythical King Minos. But as Evans proved, this realm was no myth. In a series of excavations in the early years of the 20th century, Evans found a trove of artifacts from the Minoan age, which reached its height from 1900 to 1450 B.C.: jewelry, carvings, pottery, altars shaped like bull's horns, and wall paintings showing Minoan life.

① King Minos' successful excavations
② Appreciating artifacts from the Minoan age
③ Magnificence of the palace on the island of Crete
④ Bringing the Minoan culture to the realm of reality

해석 p.10

1. 지문 처음에서 고고학자 Arthur Evans가 크노소스 궁전의 유적을 발굴하기 전까지 미노아 문화는 사실이라기보다는 더 전설이었다고 하고 있으므로 '미노아 문화는 전설이 아니라 사실이다'라는 것이 글의 중심 내용이라는 것을 파악할 수 있다.

2. 지문에서 파악한 중심 내용은 미노아 문화에 대한 내용이므로, 미노스 왕의 성공적인 발굴에 대한 내용인 ①번은 정답이 될 수 없다.

3. ②번은 미노아 시대의 유물 감상에 대한 내용이고, ③번은 크레타섬에 있는 궁전의 웅장함에 대한 내용으로, 지문의 중심 내용이 아니므로 정답이 될 수 없다.

따라서 글의 주제를 '미노아 문화를 현실의 영역으로 끌어들이기'라고 표현한 ④번이 정답이다.

유형 1 : 전체내용 파악하기 ② 문단 요약

전체 지문을 요약한 문장의 빈칸을 완성하는 유형입니다. 한 개의 빈칸을 채우는 문제와 두 개 이상의 빈칸을 채우는 문제가 출제됩니다.

문제풀이 비법

1. 전체 지문을 요약한 제시된 문장을 읽으며 핵심적인 키워드를 확인하면서 빈칸에 필요한 정보가 무엇인지 파악합니다.

2. 제시된 문장의 키워드가 지문에서 언급된 부분을 찾습니다. 키워드가 지문에 그대로 등장하는 경우도 있지만 다르게 바꾸어 표현되는 경우도 있으므로 이에 유의합니다.

3. 지문에서 키워드가 등장한 부분 및 그 앞뒤 문맥을 통해 지문의 내용을 파악하여 빈칸에 적절한 정답을 고릅니다.

기출문제로 확인하기

02 다음 글의 내용을 한 문장으로 요약하고자 한다. 빈칸 (A), (B)에 들어갈 말로 가장 적절한 것은? (2022년 법원직 9급)

In India, approximately 360 million people—one-third of the population—live in or very close to the forests. More than half of these people live below the official poverty line, and consequently they depend crucially on the resources they obtain from the forests. The Indian government now runs programs aimed at improving their lot by involving them in the commercial management of their forests, in this way allowing them to continue to obtain the food and materials they need, but at the same time to sell forest produce. If the programs succeed, forest dwellers will be more prosperous, but they will be able to preserve their traditional way of life and culture, and the forest will be managed sustainably, so the wildlife is not depleted.

↓

The Indian government is trying to ___(A)___ the lives of the poor who live near forests without ___(B)___ the forests.

(A)	(B)	(A)	(B)
① improve	ruining	② control	preserving
③ improve	limiting	④ control	enlarging

해석 p.213

1. 제시된 문장을 통해 빈칸에 인도 정부가 숲을 어떻게 하는 것 없이 숲 근처에 사는 가난한 사람들의 삶을 어떻게 하려고 하고 있는지에 대한 내용이 나와야 한다는 것을 알 수 있다.

2. 제시된 문장의 키워드인 The Indian government(인도 정부)와 forests(숲)와 관련된 지문 주변의 내용을 확인한다.

3. 키워드와 관련된 지문 주변의 내용에서 인도 정부는 지역의 가치를 높이는 것을 목적으로 하는 프로그램을 운영하고 있는데, 그 프로그램이 성공하면 숲은 지속 가능하게 관리된다고 설명하고 있으므로, (A)와 (B)에는 인도 정부가 숲을 파괴하는 것(ruining) 없이 숲 근처에 사는 가난한 사람들의 삶을 개선하려(improve) 하고 있다는 내용이 와야 적절하다.

유형 1 : 전체내용 파악하기 ③ 글의 감상

전체적인 글의 흐름을 파악하여 글의 종류, 분위기, 전개방식, 또는 필자나 등장인물의 어조, 태도, 상황 등을
고르는 유형입니다.

문제풀이 비법

1. 문제와 보기를 먼저 확인하여 문제에서 묻는 것이 무엇인지를 정확히 파악합니다.

2. 문제에서 묻는 것에 대한 단서가 있는 부분을 찾아가며 지문을 읽습니다. 예를 들어, 문제에서 묻는 것이 등장인물의 상황
   이라면 특정한 상황을 나타나는 단서들에 유의하여 지문을 읽고, 정답을 고릅니다.

기출문제로 확인하기

20 다음 글에 나타난 Johnbull의 심경으로 가장 적절한 것은?

(2021년 국가직 9급)

In the blazing midday sun, the yellow egg-shaped rock stood
out from a pile of recently unearthed gravel. Out of curiosity,
sixteen-year-old miner Komba Johnbull picked it up and
fingered its flat, pyramidal planes. Johnbull had never seen
a diamond before, but he knew enough to understand that
even a big find would be no larger than his thumbnail. Still,
the rock was unusual enough to merit a second opinion.
Sheepishly, he brought it over to one of the more experienced
miners working the muddy gash deep in the jungle. The pit
boss's eyes widened when he saw the stone. "Put it in your
pocket," he whispered. "Keep digging." The older miner
warned that it could be dangerous if anyone thought they had
found something big. So Johnbull kept shoveling gravel until
nightfall, pausing occasionally to grip the heavy stone in his
fist. Could it be?

① thrilled and excited
② painful and distressed
③ arrogant and convinced
④ detached and indifferent

해석 p.39

1. 문제와 보기를 통해 trilled and excited(흥
분하고 신이 난)와 같은 '화자의 심경'을 묻는 문
제임을 알 수 있다.

2. 지문에서 필자는 어린 광부 Johnbull이 자
갈들 사이에서 우연히 발견한 특이한 돌이 어
쩌면 엄청나게 큰 다이아몬드일지도 모른다는
것을 알게 되는 일화를 소개하고 있다. 따라서
Johnbull의 심경을 '흥분하고 신이 난'이라고
표현한 ①번이 정답이다.

유형 2 : 세부내용 파악하기 ① 내용 일치·불일치 파악

지문의 세부내용을 파악하여 지문의 내용과 일치 혹은 일치하지 않는 보기를 고르는 유형입니다.

문제풀이 비법

1. 보기에 제시된 키워드가 지문에서 언급된 부분을 순서대로 찾아가며 각각의 보기가 정답이 될 수 있는지 확인합니다. 이때, 보기에서 쓰인 어휘 및 표현 등을 지문 내에서 다르게 표현할 수도 있으므로 이에 유의합니다.

2. 정답이 될 수 없는 보기들을 걸러내고 난 뒤, 남은 보기의 키워드가 지문에서 언급된 부분을 다시 한번 확인하며 정답을 고릅니다.

기출문제로 확인하기

12 Northeastern Wildlife Exposition에 관한 다음 글의 내용과 일치하는 것은? (2024년 국가직 9급)

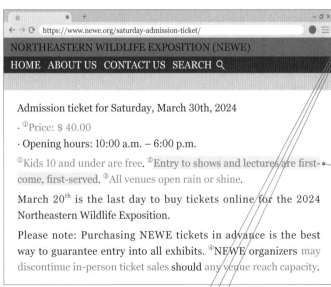

https://www.newe.org/saturday-admission-ticket/

NORTHEASTERN WILDLIFE EXPOSITION (NEWE)

HOME ABOUT US CONTACT US SEARCH 🔍

Admission ticket for Saturday, March 30th, 2024

· ①Price: $ 40.00

· Opening hours: 10:00 a.m. – 6:00 p.m.

①Kids 10 and under are free. ②Entry to shows and lectures are first-come, first-served. ③All venues open rain or shine.

March 20th is the last day to buy tickets online for the 2024 Northeastern Wildlife Exposition.

Please note: Purchasing NEWE tickets in advance is the best way to guarantee entry into all exhibits. ④NEWE organizers may discontinue in-person ticket sales **should** any venue reach capacity.

① 10세 어린이는 입장료 40불을 지불해야 한다.

② 공연과 강연의 입장은 선착순이다.

③ 비가 올 경우에는 행사장을 닫는다.

④ 입장권은 온라인으로만 구매할 수 있다.

해석 p.9

1. ① 10세 이하의 어린이는 무료라고 했으므로, 10세 어린이는 입장료 40불을 지불해야 한다는 것은 지문의 내용과 다르다.

③ 모든 행사장은 비가 오든 날이 개든 문을 연다고 했으므로, 비가 올 경우에는 행사장을 닫는다는 것은 지문의 내용과 다르다.

④ 행사장 수용 인원에 도달할 경우 NEWE 주최 측이 현장 입장권 판매를 중단할 수 있다고 언급한 내용을 통해 현장에서도 입장권을 판매한다는 것을 알 수 있으므로, 입장권은 온라인으로만 구매할 수 있다는 것은 지문의 내용과 다르다.

2. 공연 및 강의 입장은 선착순이라고 했다. 따라서 ②번이 지문의 내용과 일치한다.

유형 2 : 세부내용 파악하기 ② 지칭 대상 파악

밑줄 친 부분이 가리키는 것이 무엇인지 찾거나, 여러 개의 밑줄 중 가리키는 대상이 다른 하나를 찾는 문제 유형입니다.

문제풀이 비법

1. 밑줄이 있는 문장을 읽고, 지문에서 찾아야 하는 것이 무엇인지 파악합니다. 밑줄 친 부분이 가리키는 것이 나머지와 다른 하나를 찾는 문제인 경우, 첫 번째 밑줄 친 부분이 가리키는 것이 무엇인지 먼저 파악합니다.

2. 밑줄 친 부분이 가리키는 것을 찾고, 가장 적절한 보기를 정답으로 선택합니다. 밑줄 친 부분이 가리키는 것이 나머지와 다른 하나를 찾는 문제인 경우, 첫 번째 밑줄 친 부분과 나머지 밑줄 친 부분들을 비교하며 지문을 읽고, 가리키는 것이 나머지와 다른 것을 정답으로 선택합니다.

기출문제로 확인하기

12 밑줄 친 부분이 지칭하는 대상이 다른 것은? (2019년 서울시 9급)

Dracula ants get their name for the way they sometimes drink the blood of their own young. But this week, ① the insects have earned a new claim to fame. Dracula ants of the species *Mystrium camillae* can snap their jaws together so fast, you could fit 5,000 strikes into the time it takes us to blink an eye. This means ② the blood-suckers wield the fastest known movement in nature, according to a study published this week in the journal *Royal Society Open Science*. Interestingly, the ants produce their record-breaking snaps simply by pressing their jaws together so hard that ③ they bend. This stores energy in one of the jaws, like a spring, until it slides past the other and lashes out with extraordinary speed and force— reaching a maximum velocity of over 200 miles per hour. It's kind of like what happens when you snap your fingers, only 1,000 times faster. Dracula ants are secretive predators as ④ they prefer to hunt under the leaf litter or in subterranean tunnels.

해석 p.158

1. 지문을 처음부터 읽으며 첫 번째 밑줄 친 부분이 가리키는 것이 무엇인지 먼저 파악한다. 지문 처음에 Dracula ants(드라큘라 개미)가 있으므로, the insects(이 곤충들)는 드라큘라 개미를 지칭하는 것임을 알 수 있다.

2. 지문 처음에서 드라큘라 개미가 그들이 때때로 자기 새끼들의 피를 먹어서 그 이름을 얻게 되었다고 했고, 지문 마지막에서 드라큘라 개미들이 낙엽이나 지하 터널 안에서 사냥하는 것을 선호하기 때문에 비밀스러운 포식자들이라고 했으므로 ②번의 the blood-suckers(그 흡혈 동물들)와 ④번의 they(그들)는 드라큘라 개미들을 지칭하는 것임을 알 수 있다.

3. ③번 보기가 포함된 문장에서 밑줄 친 they(그것들) 앞부분에 그 개미들은 그들의 턱(their jaws)을 함께 매우 세게 누른다는 내용이 있고, 그렇게 해서 그것들(they)이 구부러지도록 한다고 했으므로 밑줄 친 they는 개미들의 턱을 지칭한다는 것을 알 수 있다. 따라서 ③ they가 정답이다.

유형 3 : 추론하기 ① 빈칸 완성 – 단어·구·절

빈칸 앞뒤 지문의 흐름을 자연스럽게 연결하는 보기를 골라 빈칸을 완성하는 유형입니다.

🔍 문제풀이 비법

1. 빈칸이 있는 문장을 읽으며 빈칸 앞뒤에 제시되는 키워드를 통해 빈칸에 필요한 정보가 무엇인지 파악합니다.
2. 빈칸 주변이나 중심 내용을 위주로 지문을 읽고 문맥상 빈칸에 가장 적절한 정답을 고릅니다.

기출문제로 확인하기

04 다음 빈칸에 들어갈 말로 가장 적절한 것은? (2024년 법원직 9급)

The understandings that children bring to the classroom can already be quite powerful in the early grades. For example, some children have been found to hold onto their preconception of a flat earth by imagining a round earth to be shaped like a pancake. This construction of a new understanding is guided by a model of the earth that helps the child explain how people can stand or walk on its surface. Many young children have trouble giving up the notion that one-eighth is greater than one-fourth, because 8 is more than 4. If children were blank slates, just telling them that the earth is round or that one-fourth is greater than one-eighth would be _____. But since they already have ideas about the earth and about numbers, those ideas must be directly addressed in order to transform or expand them.

① familiar
② adequate
③ improper
④ irrelevant

해석 p.184

1. 빈칸에 만약 아이들이 백지상태라면 지구가 둥글다거나 4분의 1이 8분의 1보다 크다고 말하는 것이 어떨 것인지에 대한 내용이 나와야 적절하다는 것을 알 수 있다.

2. 빈칸 뒤 문장에서 그들(아이들)은 이미 지구와 숫자에 대한 개념을 가지고 있기 때문에 그것들을 변형하거나 확장하기 위해서는 그 개념들이 직접적으로 다뤄져야 한다고 설명하고 있으므로, 만약 아이들이 백지상태라면 지구가 둥글다거나 4분의 1이 8분의 1보다 크다고 말하는 것만으로도 '충분할' 것이라고 한 ②번이 정답이다.

유형 3 : 추론하기 ② 빈칸 완성 – 연결어

지문에 제시된 빈칸에 들어가기에 가장 적절한 연결어를 고르는 문제 유형입니다.

🔍 문제풀이 비법

1. 빈칸 앞뒤에 있는 문장을 읽고 두 문장 사이의 논리적 관계를 파악합니다.

2. 빈칸 앞뒤 문장 사이의 논리적 관계를 가장 잘 표현한 정답을 고릅니다. 보기로 자주 등장하는 연결어들을 파악해 두면 쉽게 정답을 고를 수 있습니다.

기출문제로 확인하기

19 (A)와 (B)에 들어갈 말로 가장 적절한 것은? (2021년 지방직 9급)

Ancient philosophers and spiritual teachers understood the need to balance the positive with the negative, optimism with pessimism, a striving for success and security with an openness to failure and uncertainty. The Stoics recommended "the premeditation of evils," or deliberately visualizing the worst-case scenario. This tends to reduce anxiety about the future: when you soberly picture how badly things could go in reality, you usually conclude that you could cope. _____(A)_____, they noted, imagining that you might lose the relationships and possessions you currently enjoy increases your gratitude for having them now. Positive thinking, _____(B)_____, always leans into the future, ignoring present pleasures.

	(A)	(B)
①	Nevertheless	in addition
②	Furthermore	for example
③	Besides	by contrast
④	However	in conclusion

해석 p.103

1. (A) 빈칸 앞 문장은 당신이 얼마나 나쁘게 상황이 흘러갈지 상상함으로써 미래에 대한 염려를 줄일 수 있다는 내용으로 '불행에 대한 계획'에 관해서 설명하는 내용이다. (A) 빈칸 뒤 문장은 현재 누리고 있는 것들을 잃을지도 모른다고 상상하는 것이 현재 갖고 있는 것에 대한 감사함을 증가시킨다는 내용으로 '불행에 대한 계획'에 관한 추가적인 설명이다. 따라서 (A)에는 Furthermore(게다가) 또는 Besides(게다가)가 나와야 적절하다.

2. (B) 빈칸 뒤 문장은 긍정적인 생각이 현재의 기쁨을 무시하고 미래에만 의지하게 하므로 부정적인 결과를 낳는다는 내용이고 (B) 빈칸 앞 문장은 가진 것들을 모두 잃는다는 부정적인 생각이 현재 갖고 있는 것들에 대한 감사함을 증가시킨다는 긍정적인 결과를 낳는다는 내용으로 앞 문장과 대조된다. 따라서 (B)에는 by contrast(대조적으로)가 나와야 적절하다.

유형 4 : 논리적 흐름 파악하기 ① 문단 순서 배열

지문의 논리적 흐름을 파악하여 지문의 흐름이 자연스럽게 연결되도록 주어진 문단의 순서를 적절하게 배열하는 유형입니다.

필승 비법

해커스공무원 7개년 기출문제집 영어

🔍 문제풀이 비법

1. 첫 문장이 제시된 경우, 첫 문장을 통해 주제를 파악하고 앞으로 전개될 내용에 대해 예상합니다.

2. 제시된 문단들에서 연결어나 지시대명사 등을 통해 지문의 논리적 흐름을 파악하고, 그에 따라 문단의 순서를 배열합니다.

3. 배열된 순서대로 문단을 다시 읽으며 논리적 연결이 자연스러운지 확인하여 정답을 고릅니다.

기출문제로 확인하기

17 주어진 글 다음에 이어질 글의 순서로 가장 적절한 것은?

(2023년 지방직 9급)

> Just a few years ago, every conversation about artificial intelligence (AI) seemed to end with an apocalyptic prediction.

(A) More recently, however, things have begun to change. AI has gone from being a scary black box to something people can use for a variety of use cases.

(B) In 2014, an expert in the field said that, with AI, we are summoning the demon, while a Nobel Prize winning physicist said that AI could spell the end of the human race.

(C) This shift is because these technologies are finally being explored at scale in the industry, particularly for market opportunities.

① (A) – (B) – (C)

② (B) – (A) – (C)

③ (B) – (C) – (A)

④ (C) – (A) – (B)

해석 p.85

1. 제시된 문장을 통해 인공지능에 대한 예측과 관련된 내용이 전개될 것임을 예상할 수 있다.

2. 주어진 문장에서 불과 몇 년 전만 해도 인공지능에 대한 모든 대화는 종말론적 예측으로 끝나는 것처럼 보였다고 설명한 후, (B)에서 이 분야(인공지능)의 한 전문가와 노벨상을 수상한 한 물리학자는 우리가 AI로 악마를 소환하고 있고, AI가 인류의 종말을 가져올 수 있다고 말했다고 언급하고 있다. 이어서 (A)에서 하지만 (however) 더 최근에는 상황이 바뀌기 시작했다고 설명하고, 마지막으로 (C)에서 이러한 변화(This shift)는 이러한 기술(AI)이 마침내 업계에서 대규모로 탐구되고 있기 때문이라고 설명하고 있다. 따라서 ② (B) – (A) – (C)가 정답이다.

3. 배열된 순서대로 문단을 다시 읽으며 논리적 연결이 자연스러운지 확인하여 정답을 고른다.

유형 4 : 논리적 흐름 파악하기 ② 문장 삽입

지문의 흐름이 자연스럽게 연결되도록 주어진 문장이 들어갈 적절한 위치를 고르는 유형입니다.

문제풀이 비법

1. 제시된 문장에 키워드가 있는지를 확인하여 글의 흐름상 제시된 문장 앞뒤에 나올 수 있는 정보가 무엇일지 예상합니다.

2. 지문을 읽으며 제시된 문장 앞뒤에 나올 것으로 예상했던 내용이 있는지 확인하고 제시된 문장이 들어갈 위치를 고릅니다.

기출문제로 확인하기

14 글의 흐름으로 보아, 주어진 문장이 들어가기에 가장 적절한 곳은? (2022년 법원직 9급)

The effect, however, was just the reverse.

How we dress for work has taken on a new element of choice, and with it, new anxieties. (①) The practice of having a "dress-down day" or "casual day," which began to emerge a decade or so ago, was intended to make life easier for employees, to enable them to save money and feel more relaxed at the office. (②) In addition to the normal workplace wardrobe, employees had to create a "workplace casual" *wardrobe. (③) It couldn't really be the sweats and T-shirts you wore around the house on the weekend. (④) It had to be a selection of clothing that sustained a certain image—relaxed, but also serious.

* wardrobe : 옷, 의류

해석 p.220

1. 제시된 문장의 키워드를 통해 제시된 문장의 뒤에 어떤 것과 반대되는 효과에 대한 내용이 나올 것임을 예상할 수 있다.

2. ②번 뒤 문장에 직원들은 '직장 평상복' 옷을 만들어 낼 필요가 있었다는 처음 의도(직원들의 돈을 절약할 수 있게 하고 사무실에서 더 편안함을 느낄 수 있도록 하는 것)와 반대되는 내용이 있으므로 ②번 자리에 주어진 문장이 나와야 지문이 자연스럽게 연결된다. 따라서 ②번이 정답이다.

유형 4 : 논리적 흐름 파악하기 ③ 무관한 문장 삭제

보기로 제시된 문장들 중 지문의 흐름이 맞지 않는 것을 선택하는 문제 유형입니다.

문제풀이 비법

1. 첫 문장의 내용을 정확히 파악하여 이어질 지문의 내용이 무엇인지 예상합니다.
2. 지문을 읽으며 지문의 첫 문장이나 중심 내용과 관련이 없거나 흐름상 어색한 보기를 정답으로 고릅니다.

기출문제로 확인하기

10 다음 글의 흐름상 가장 어색한 문장은?　(2021년 국가직 9급)

The term burnout refers to a "wearing out" from the pressures of work. Burnout is a chronic condition that results as daily work stressors take their toll on employees. ① The most widely adopted conceptualization of burnout has been developed by Maslach and her colleagues in their studies of human service workers. Maslach sees burnout as consisting of three interrelated dimensions. The first dimension—emotional exhaustion—is really the core of the burnout phenomenon. ② Workers suffer from emotional exhaustion when they feel fatigued, frustrated, used up, or unable to face another day on the job. The second dimension of burnout is a lack of personal accomplishment. ③ This aspect of the burnout phenomenon refers to workers who see themselves as failures, incapable of effectively accomplishing job requirements. ④ Emotional labor workers enter their occupation highly motivated although they are physically exhausted. The third dimension of burnout is depersonalization. This dimension is relevant only to workers who must communicate interpersonally with others (e.g. clients, patients, students) as part of the job.

해석 p.34

1. 지문의 첫 문장을 통해 번아웃의 특징에 대한 내용이 이 지문의 중심 내용이라는 것을 파악할 수 있다.

2. 지문 전반에 걸쳐 번아웃의 의미와 특징에 대해 설명하고 있으므로 모두 첫 문장과 관련이 있지만, ④번은 감정적인 노동자들은 신체적으로 지쳤는데도 의욕을 가지고 일을 한다는 내용으로 지문의 내용과 관련이 없다.

어휘

유형 1 : 비슷한 뜻을 가진 어휘/표현 고르기

밑줄 친 부분의 어휘/표현과 비슷한 의미를 가진 것을 보기에서 고르는 유형입니다.

🔍 문제풀이 비법

1. 밑줄 친 어휘/표현을 먼저 확인하고, 그 의미를 이미 알고 있다면 보기에서 바로 정답을 고릅니다.

2. 밑줄 친 어휘/표현을 알지 못한다면 해당 어휘/표현이 문장 내에서 어떤 의미를 나타내는지 문맥에서 유추하여 정답을 고릅니다.

기출문제로 확인하기

03 밑줄 친 부분의 의미와 가장 가까운 것을 고르시오.

(2020년 국가직 9급)

> He's the best person to tell you how to get there because he knows the city inside out.

① eventually

② culturally

③ thoroughly

④ tentatively

해석 p.40

1. inside out(속속들이)의 의미를 이미 알고 있는 경우 보기에서 '완전히'라는 의미의 정답 ③ thoroughly를 고른다.

2. 그가 너에게 그곳에 가는 방법(how to get there)을 알려줄 최적의 사람이라고 했으므로, 그 도시를 '속속들이' 안다라는 의미의 inside out의 유의어인 ③ thoroughly(완전히)가 가장 적절하다.

유형 2 : 빈칸에 들어갈 어휘/표현 고르기

보기에 주어진 어휘/표현 중 문장의 빈칸에 들어갈 적절한 것을 고르거나, 두 개의 빈칸에 공통으로 들어갈 것을 고르는 유형입니다.

문제풀이 비법

1. 빈칸이 하나인 경우, 빈칸이 있는 문장과 주변 문맥을 확인하여 빈칸과 관련된 정보를 파악합니다. 빈칸이 두 개인 경우 제시된 문장들을 하나씩 읽으며 문맥상 두 빈칸에 공통으로 들어가기 적절한 의미가 무엇일지 예상합니다.

2. 문맥의 흐름상 가장 적절한 보기를 확인하여 정답을 고릅니다. 빈칸이 두 개인 경우 주어진 보기 중에서 제시된 문장들의 문맥과 모두 어울리는 정답을 고릅니다.

기출문제로 확인하기

02 밑줄 친 부분에 들어갈 말로 가장 적절한 것을 고르시오.

(2021년 지방직 9급)

Globalization leads more countries to open their markets, allowing them to trade goods and services freely at a lower cost with greater _____.

① extinction
② depression
③ efficiency
④ caution

해석 p.97

1. 빈칸 주변 문맥을 통해 더 많은 나라들이 상품과 서비스를 더 낮은 가격에 자유롭게 거래할 수 있다는 것을 파악할 수 있다.

2. 따라서 '상품과 서비스를 더 낮은 가격에 더 좋은 _____로 자유롭게 거래할 수 있게 한다'라는 문맥에서 allowing them to trade goods and services freely at a lower cost with greater _____의 빈칸에는 '효율'이라는 의미가 들어가야 자연스럽다. 따라서 ③ efficiency(효율)가 정답이다.

유형 3 : 대화의 빈칸에 들어갈 문장 고르기

대화의 전체적인 흐름과 빈칸 앞뒤 문맥을 고려하여 대화의 빈칸에 들어갈 알맞은 말을 고르는 유형입니다.

🔍 문제풀이 비법

1. 대화의 전체적인 흐름을 파악하고, 키워드를 바탕으로 빈칸에 들어갈 적절한 말을 예상하며 대화를 읽습니다.

2. 주어진 보기 중 대화의 흐름상 빈칸에 들어가기 가장 적절한 보기를 정답으로 고릅니다.

기출문제로 확인하기

04 밑줄 친 부분에 들어갈 말로 가장 적절한 것은?

(2019년 국가직 9급)

A: Would you like to try some dim sum?
B: Yes, thank you. They look delicious. What's inside?
A: These have pork and chopped vegetables, and those have shrimps.
B: And, um, _____?
A: You pick one up with your chopsticks like this and dip it into the sauce. It's easy.
B: Okay. I'll give it a try.

① how much are they
② how do I eat them
③ how spicy are they
④ how do you cook them

1. 빈칸 뒤에서 A가 B에게 먹는 방법을 알려주고 있으므로 빈칸에는 어떻게 먹는지에 대해 묻는 내용이 들어가야 함을 예상할 수 있다.

2. 주어진 보기 중 '내가 그것들은 어떻게 먹으면 돼'라고 묻는 표현이 빈칸에 가장 적절하므로 ① how do I eat them이 정답이다.

해석 p.51

유형 4 : 대화 내용 중 가장 어색한 것 고르기

두 사람 간의 대화로 이루어진 4~5개의 보기 중 대화의 내용이 가장 어색한 것을 고르는 유형입니다.

🔍 문제풀이 비법

1. 각각의 대화를 읽을 때, 앞서 말한 사람의 말에 대한 대답으로 어떤 내용이 나올 것인지를 예상하며 각각의 대화를 읽습니다.

2. 앞서 말한 사람의 말과 대답이 가장 어울리지 않는 보기를 확인하여 정답을 고릅니다. 문장에서 사용된 표현의 의미를 알지 못할 경우, 사용된 어휘들의 의미를 조합하면서 해당 표현의 의미를 유추합니다.

기출문제로 확인하기

11 두 사람의 대화 중 자연스럽지 않은 것은? (2023년 지방직 9급)

① A: How would you like your hair done?
  B: I'm a little tired of my hair color. I'd like to dye it.

② A: What can we do to slow down global warming?
  B: First of all, we can use more public transportation.

③ A: Anna, is that you? Long time no see! How long has it been?
  B: It took me about an hour and a half by car.

④ A: I'm worried about Paul. He looks unhappy. What should I
    do?
  B: If I were you, I'd wait until he talks about his troubles.

해석 p.82

1. A는 B에게 너무 오랜만이라며 이게 얼마 만이냐고 묻고 있으므로, B의 대답으로 반가움에 대한 반응이 나와야 함을 예상할 수 있다.

2. 따라서 B의 대답 It took me about an hour and a half by car(차로 한 시간 반 정도 걸렸어요)는 어울리지 않으므로 ③번이 정답이다.

EVERYTHING COMES TO HIM
WHO HUSTLES WHILE HE WAITS.

THOMAS A. EDISON

성공은 열심히 노력하며 기다리는 사람에게 찾아온다.
토마스 A. 에디슨

Part 1
국가직 9급

문제 유형	4지선다형
총 문항 수	20문항
경쟁률 (2024년 4월, 일반행정)	56.7:1
합격선 (2024년 4월, 일반행정)	90.00점
시험 안내	사이버국가고시센터 (https://gosi.kr)

01 밑줄 친 부분에 들어갈 말로 적절한 것은?

> Obviously, no aspect of the language arts stands alone either in learning or in teaching. Listening, speaking, reading, writing, viewing, and visually representing are _____.

① distinct
② distorted
③ interrelated
④ independent

※ 밑줄 친 부분의 의미와 가장 가까운 것을 고르시오.
[02~05]

02

> The money was so cleverly concealed that we were forced to abandon our search for it.

① spent
② hidden
③ invested
④ delivered

03

> To appease critics, the wireless industry has launched a $ 12 million public-education campaign on the drive-time radio.

① soothe
② counter
③ enlighten
④ assimilate

04

> Center officials play down the troubles, saying they are typical of any start-up operation.

① discern
② dissatisfy
③ underline
④ underestimate

05

> She worked diligently and had the guts to go for what she wanted.

① was anxious
② was fortunate
③ was reputable
④ was courageous

06 밑줄 친 부분 중 어법상 옳지 않은 것은?

> ① Despite the belief that the quality of older houses is superior to ② those of modern houses, the foundations of most pre-20th-century houses are dramatically shallow ③ compared to today's, and have only stood the test of time due to the flexibility of ④ their timber framework or the lime mortar between bricks and stones.

07 밑줄 친 부분이 어법상 옳지 않은 것은?

① They are not interested in reading poetry, <u>still more</u> in writing.

② <u>Once confirmed</u>, the order will be sent for delivery to your address.

③ <u>Provided that</u> the ferry leaves on time, we should arrive at the harbor by morning.

④ Foreign journalists hope to cover as <u>much news</u> as possible during their short stay in the capital.

08 우리말을 영어로 바르게 옮긴 것은?

① 지원자 수가 증가하고 있어서 우리는 기쁘다.
→ We are glad that the number of applicants is increasing.

② 나는 2년 전에 그에게서 마지막 이메일을 받았다.
→ I've received the last e-mail from him two years ago.

③ 어젯밤에 그가 잔 침대는 꽤 편안했다.
→ The bed which he slept last night was quite comfortable.

④ 그들은 영상으로 새해 인사를 교환했다.
→ They exchanged New Year's greetings each other on screen.

※ 밑줄 친 부분에 들어갈 말로 적절한 것을 고르시오.
[09~11]

09

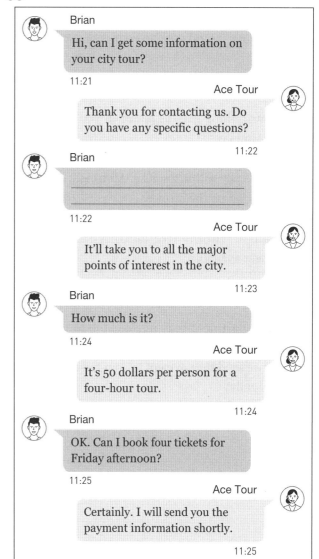

Brian
Hi, can I get some information on your city tour?
11:21

Ace Tour
Thank you for contacting us. Do you have any specific questions?
11:22

Brian
_____
11:22

Ace Tour
It'll take you to all the major points of interest in the city.
11:23

Brian
How much is it?
11:24

Ace Tour
It's 50 dollars per person for a four-hour tour.
11:24

Brian
OK. Can I book four tickets for Friday afternoon?
11:25

Ace Tour
Certainly. I will send you the payment information shortly.
11:25

① How long is the tour?
② What does the city tour include?
③ Do you have a list of tour packages?
④ Can you recommend a good tour guide book?

10

A: Thank you. We appreciate your order.

B: You are welcome. Could you send the goods by air freight? We need them fast.

A: Sure. We'll send them to your department right away.

B: Okay. I hope we can get the goods early next week.

A: If everything goes as planned, you'll get them by Monday.

B: Monday sounds good.

A: Please pay within 2 weeks. Air freight costs will be added on the invoice.

B: _____

A: I am afraid the free delivery service is no longer available.

① I see. When will we be getting the invoice from you?

② Our department may not be able to pay within two weeks.

③ Can we send the payment to your business account on Monday?

④ Wait a minute. I thought the delivery costs were at your expense.

11

A: Have you found your phone?

B: Unfortunately, no. I'm still looking for it.

A: Have you contacted the subway's lost and found office?

B: _____.

A: If I were you, I would do that first.

B: Yeah, you are right. I'll check with the lost and found before buying a new phone.

① I went there to ask about the phone

② I stopped by the office this morning

③ I haven't done that yet, actually

④ I tried searching everywhere

12 Northeastern Wildlife Exposition에 관한 다음 글의 내용과 일치하는 것은?

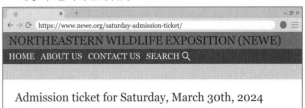

Admission ticket for Saturday, March 30th, 2024

· **Price:** $40.00

· **Opening hours:** 10:00 a.m. – 6:00 p.m.

Kids 10 and under are free. Entry to shows and lectures are first-come, first-served. All venues open rain or shine.

March 20th is the last day to buy tickets online for the 2024 Northeastern Wildlife Exposition.

Please note: Purchasing NEWE tickets in advance is the best way to guarantee entry into all exhibits. NEWE organizers may discontinue in-person ticket sales should any venue reach capacity.

① 10세 어린이는 입장료 40불을 지불해야 한다.

② 공연과 강연의 입장은 선착순이다.

③ 비가 올 경우에는 행사장을 닫는다.

④ 입장권은 온라인으로만 구매할 수 있다.

13 다음 글의 내용과 일치하지 않는 것은?

The tragedies of the Greek dramatist Sophocles have come to be regarded as the high point of classical Greek drama. Sadly, only seven of the 123 tragedies he wrote have survived, but of these perhaps the finest is *Oedipus the King*. The play was one of three written by Sophocles about Oedipus, the mythical king of Thebes (the others being *Antigone* and *Oedipus at Colonus*), known collectively as the Theban plays. Sophocles conceived each of these as a separate entity, and they were written and produced several years apart and out of chronological order. *Oedipus the King* follows the established formal structure and it is regarded as the best example of classical Athenian tragedy.

① A total of 123 tragedies were written by Sophocles.
② *Antigone* is also about the king Oedipus.
③ The Theban plays were created in time order.
④ *Oedipus the King* represents the classical Athenian tragedy.

14 다음 글의 주제로 적절한 것은?

It seems incredible that one man could be responsible for opening our eyes to an entire culture, but until British archaeologist Arthur Evans successfully excavated the ruins of the palace of Knossos on the island of Crete, the great Minoan culture of the Mediterranean was more legend than fact. Indeed its most famed resident was a creature of mythology: the half-man, half-bull Minotaur, said to have lived under the palace of mythical King Minos. But as Evans proved, this realm was no myth. In a series of excavations in the early years of the 20th century, Evans found a trove of artifacts from the Minoan age, which reached its height from 1900 to 1450 B.C.: jewelry, carvings, pottery, altars shaped like bull's horns, and wall paintings showing Minoan life.

① King Minos' successful excavations
② Appreciating artifacts from the Minoan age
③ Magnificence of the palace on the island of Crete
④ Bringing the Minoan culture to the realm of reality

15 다음 글의 제목으로 적절한 것은?

Currency debasement of a good money by a bad money version occurred via coins of a high percentage of precious metal, reissued at lower percentages of gold or silver diluted with a lower value metal. This adulteration drove out the good coin for the bad coin. No one spent the good coin, they kept it, hence the good coin was driven out of circulation and into a hoard. Meanwhile the issuer, normally a king who had lost his treasure on interminable warfare and other such dissolute living, was behind the move. They collected all the good old coins they could, melted them down and reissued them at lower purity and pocketed the balance. It was often illegal to keep the old stuff back but people did, while the king replenished his treasury, at least for a time.

① How Bad Money Replaces Good
② Elements of Good Coins
③ Why Not Melt Coins?
④ What Is Bad Money?

16 다음 글의 흐름상 어색한 문장은?

In spite of all evidence to the contrary, there are people who seriously believe that NASA's Apollo space program never really landed men on the moon. These people claim that the moon landings were nothing more than a huge conspiracy, perpetuated by a government desperately in competition with the Russians and fearful of losing face. ① These conspiracy theorists claim that the United States knew it couldn't compete with the Russians in the space race and was therefore forced to fake a series of successful moon landings. ② Advocates of a conspiracy cite several pieces of what they consider evidence. ③ Crucial to their case is the claim that astronauts never could have safely passed through the Van Allen belt, a region of radiation trapped in Earth's magnetic field. ④ They also point to the fact that the metal coverings of the spaceship were designed to block radiation. If the astronauts had truly gone through the belt, say conspiracy theorists, they would have died.

17 주어진 문장이 들어갈 위치로 적절한 것은?

Tribal oral history and archaeological evidence suggest that sometime between 1500 and 1700 a mudslide destroyed part of the village, covering several longhouses and sealing in their contents.

From the village of Ozette on the westernmost point of Washington's Olympic Peninsula, members of the Makah tribe hunted whales. (①) They smoked their catch on racks and in smokehouses and traded with neighboring groups from around the Puget Sound and nearby Vancouver Island. (②) Ozette was one of five main villages inhabited by the Makah, an Indigenous people who have been based in the region for millennia. (③) Thousands of artifacts that would not otherwise have survived, including baskets, clothing, sleeping mats, and whaling tools, were preserved under the mud. (④) In 1970, a storm caused coastal erosion that revealed the remains of these longhouses and artifacts.

18 주어진 글 다음에 이어질 글의 순서로 적절한 것은?

Interest in movie and sports stars goes beyond their performances on the screen and in the arena.

(A) The doings of skilled baseball, football, and basketball players out of uniform similarly attract public attention.

(B) Newspaper columns, specialized magazines, television programs, and Web sites record the personal lives of celebrated Hollywood actors, sometimes accurately.

(C) Both industries actively promote such attention, which expands audiences and thus increases revenues. But a fundamental difference divides them: What sports stars do for a living is authentic in a way that what movie stars do is not.

① (A) – (C) – (B) ② (B) – (A) – (C)
③ (B) – (C) – (A) ④ (C) – (A) – (B)

※ 밑줄 친 부분에 들어갈 말로 적절한 것을 고르시오.
[19~20]

19

_____. Nearly every major politician hires media consultants and political experts to provide advice on how to appeal to the public. Virtually every major business and special-interest group has hired a lobbyist to take its concerns to Congress or to state and local governments. In nearly every community, activists try to persuade their fellow citizens on important policy issues. The workplace, too, has always been fertile ground for office politics and persuasion. One study estimates that general managers spend upwards of 80% of their time in verbal communication — most of it with the intent of persuading their fellow employees. With the advent of the photocopying machine, a whole new medium for office persuasion was invented—the photocopied memo. The Pentagon alone copies an average of 350,000 pages a day, the equivalent of 1,000 novels.

① Business people should have good persuasion skills

② Persuasion shows up in almost every walk of life

③ You will encounter countless billboards and posters

④ Mass media campaigns are useful for the government

20

It is important to note that for adults, social interaction mainly occurs through the medium of language. Few native-speaker adults are willing to devote time to interacting with someone who does not speak the language, with the result that the adult foreigner will have little opportunity to engage in meaningful and extended language exchanges. In contrast, the young child is often readily accepted by other children, and even adults. For young children, language is not as essential to social interaction. So-called 'parallel play', for example, is common among young children. They can be content just to sit in each other's company speaking only occasionally and playing on their own. Adults rarely find themselves in situations where _____.

① language does not play a crucial role in social interaction

② their opinions are readily accepted by their colleagues

③ they are asked to speak another language

④ communication skills are highly required

정답·해석·해설 p. 6

1회 2024년 국가직 9급
모바일 자동 채점 + 성적 분석 서비스 바로 가기

QR코드를 이용해 모바일로 간편하게 채점하고 나의 실력이 어느 정도인지,
취약 부분이 어디인지 바로 파악해 보세요.

(p.212에서 전체 정답표를 확인하실 수 있습니다)

※ 밑줄 친 부분의 의미와 가장 가까운 것을 고르시오.

[01~04]

01

Jane wanted to have a small wedding rather than a fancy one. Thus, she planned to invite her family and a few of her intimate friends to eat delicious food and have some pleasant moments.

① nosy
② close
③ outgoing
④ considerate

02

The incessant public curiosity and consumer demand due to the health benefits with lesser cost has increased the interest in functional foods.

① rapid
② constant
③ significant
④ intermittent

03

Because of the pandemic, the company had to hold off the plan to provide the workers with various training programs.

① elaborate
② release
③ modify
④ suspend

04

The new Regional Governor said he would abide by the decision of the High Court to release the prisoner.

① accept
② report
③ postpone
④ announce

05 밑줄 친 부분 중 어법상 옳지 않은 것은?

While advances in transplant technology have made ① it possible to extend the life of individuals with end-stage organ disease, it is argued ② that the biomedical view of organ transplantation as a bounded event, which ends once a heart or kidney is successfully replaced, ③ conceal the complex and dynamic process that more ④ accurately represents the experience of receiving an organ.

06 어법상 옳지 않은 것은?

① All assignments are expected to be turned in on time.
② Hardly had I closed my eyes when I began to think of her.
③ The broker recommended that she buy the stocks immediately.
④ A woman with the tip of a pencil stuck in her head has finally had it remove.

07 우리말을 영어로 잘못 옮긴 것은?

① 내 고양이 나이는 그의 고양이 나이의 세 배이다.
→ My cat is three times as old as his.

② 우리는 그 일을 이번 달 말까지 끝내야 한다.
→ We have to finish the work until the end of this month.

③ 그녀는 이틀에 한 번 머리를 감는다.
→ She washes her hair every other day.

④ 너는 비가 올 경우에 대비하여 우산을 갖고 가는 게 낫겠다.
→ You had better take an umbrella in case it rains.

08 다음 글의 내용과 일치하지 않는 것은?

Are you getting enough choline? Chances are, this nutrient isn't even on your radar. It's time choline gets the attention it deserves. A shocking 90 percent of Americans aren't getting enough choline, according to a recent study. Choline is essential to health at all ages and stages, and is especially critical for brain development. Why aren't we getting enough? Choline is found in many different foods but in small amounts. Plus, the foods that are rich in choline aren't the most popular: think liver, egg yolks and lima beans. Taylor Wallace, who worked on a recent analysis of choline intake in the United States, says, "There isn't enough awareness about choline even among health-care professionals because our government hasn't reviewed the data or set policies around choline since the late '90s."

① A majority of Americans are not getting enough choline.

② Choline is an essential nutrient required for brain development.

③ Foods such as liver and lima beans are good sources of choline.

④ The importance of choline has been stressed since the late '90s in the U.S.

09 다음 글의 내용과 일치하는 것은?

Around 1700 there were, by some accounts, more than 2,000 London coffeehouses, occupying more premises and paying more rent than any other trade. They came to be known as penny universities, because for that price one could purchase a cup of coffee and sit for hours listening to extraordinary conversations. Each coffeehouse specialized in a different type of clientele. In one, physicians could be consulted. Others served Protestants, Puritans, Catholics, Jews, literati, merchants, traders, Whigs, Tories, army officers, actors, lawyers, or clergy. The coffeehouses provided England's first egalitarian meeting place, where a man chatted with his tablemates whether he knew them or not.

① The number of coffeehouses was smaller than that of any other business.

② Customers were not allowed to stay for more than an hour in a coffeehouse.

③ Religious people didn't get together in a coffeehouse to chat.

④ One could converse even with unknown tablemates in a coffeehouse.

※ 밑줄 친 부분에 들어갈 말로 알맞은 것을 고르시오.

[10~11]

10

A: I got this new skin cream from a drugstore yesterday. It is supposed to remove all wrinkles and make your skin look much younger.

B: _____

A: Why don't you believe it? I've read in a few blogs that the cream really works.

B: I assume that the cream is good for your skin, but I don't think that it is possible to get rid of wrinkles or magically look younger by using a cream.

A: You are so pessimistic.

B: No, I'm just being realistic. I think you are being gullible.

① I don't buy it.
② It's too pricey.
③ I can't help you out.
④ Believe it or not, it's true.

11

A: I'd like to go sightseeing downtown. Where do you think I should go?

B: I strongly suggest you visit the national art gallery.

A: Oh, that's a great idea. What else should I check out?

B: _____

A: I don't have time for that. I need to meet a client at three.

B: Oh, I see. Why don't you visit the national park, then?

A: That sounds good. Thank you!

① This is the map that your client needs. Here you go.
② A guided tour to the river park. It takes all afternoon.
③ You should check it out as soon as possible.
④ The checkout time is three o'clock.

12 두 사람의 대화 중 자연스럽지 않은 것은?

① A: He's finally in a hit movie!
   B: Well, he's got it made.
② A: I'm getting a little tired now.
   B: Let's call it a day.
③ A: The kids are going to a birthday party.
   B: So, it was a piece of cake.
④ A: I wonder why he went home early yesterday.
   B: I think he was under the weather.

13 다음 글의 제목으로 알맞은 것은?

The feeling of being loved and the biological response it stimulates is triggered by nonverbal cues: the tone in a voice, the expression on a face, or the touch that feels just right. Nonverbal cues—rather than spoken words—make us feel that the person we are with is interested in, understands, and values us. When we're with them, we feel safe. We even see the power of nonverbal cues in the wild. After evading the chase of predators, animals often nuzzle each other as a means of stress relief. This bodily contact provides reassurance of safety and relieves stress.

① How Do Wild Animals Think and Feel?
② Communicating Effectively Is the Secret to Success
③ Nonverbal Communication Speaks Louder than Words
④ Verbal Cues: The Primary Tools for Expressing Feelings

There are times, like holidays and birthdays, when toys and gifts accumulate in a child's life. You can use these times to teach a healthy nondependency on things. Don't surround your child with toys. Instead, arrange them in baskets, have one basket out at a time, and rotate baskets occasionally. If a cherished object is put away for a time, bringing it out creates a delightful remembering and freshness of outlook. Suppose your child asks for a toy that has been put away for a while. You can direct attention toward an object or experience that is already in the environment. If you lose or break a possession, try to model a good attitude ("I appreciated it while I had it!") so that your child can begin to develop an attitude of nonattachment. If a toy of hers is broken or lost, help her to say, "I had fun with that."

① building a healthy attitude toward possessions
② learning the value of sharing toys with others
③ teaching how to arrange toys in an orderly manner
④ accepting responsibility for behaving in undesirable ways

Many parents have been misguided by the "self-esteem movement," which has told them that the way to build their children's self-esteem is to tell them how good they are at things. Unfortunately, trying to convince your children of their competence will likely fail because life has a way of telling them unequivocally how capable or incapable they really are through success and failure. Research has shown that how you praise your children has a powerful influence on their development. Some researchers found that children who were praised for their intelligence, as compared to their effort, became overly focused on results. Following a failure, these same children persisted less, showed less enjoyment, attributed their failure to a lack of ability, and performed poorly in future achievement efforts. Praising children for intelligence made them fear difficulty because they began to equate failure with stupidity.

① Frequent praises increase self-esteem of children.
② Compliments on intelligence bring about negative effect.
③ A child should overcome fear of failure through success.
④ Parents should focus on the outcome rather than the process.

16 밑줄 친 부분에 들어갈 말로 알맞은 것은?

In recent years, the increased popularity of online marketing and social media sharing has boosted the need for advertising standardization for global brands. Most big marketing and advertising campaigns include a large online presence. Connected consumers can now zip easily across borders via the internet and social media, making it difficult for advertisers to roll out adapted campaigns in a controlled, orderly fashion. As a result, most global consumer brands coordinate their digital sites internationally. For example, Coca-Cola web and social media sites around the world, from Australia and Argentina to France, Romania, and Russia, are surprisingly _____. All feature splashes of familiar Coke red, iconic Coke bottle shapes, and Coca-Cola's music and "Taste the Feeling" themes.

① experimental
② uniform
③ localized
④ diverse

17 다음 글의 흐름상 어색한 문장은?

In our monthly surveys of 5,000 American workers and 500 U.S. employers, a huge shift to hybrid work is abundantly clear for office and knowledge workers. ① An emerging norm is three days a week in the office and two at home, cutting days on site by 30 % or more. You might think this cutback would bring a huge drop in the demand for office space. ② But our survey data suggests cuts in office space of 1 % to 2 % on average, implying big reductions in density not space. We can understand why. High density at the office is uncomfortable and many workers dislike crowds around their desks. ③ Most employees want to work from home on Mondays and Fridays. Discomfort with density extends to lobbies, kitchens, and especially elevators. ④ The only sure-fire way to reduce density is to cut days on site without cutting square footage as much. Discomfort with density is here to stay according to our survey evidence.

18 주어진 문장이 들어갈 위치로 알맞은 것은?

They installed video cameras at places known for illegal crossings, and put live video feeds from the cameras on a Web site.

Immigration reform is a political minefield. (①) About the only aspect of immigration policy that commands broad political support is the resolve to secure the U.S. border with Mexico to limit the flow of illegal immigrants. (②) Texas sheriffs recently developed a novel use of the Internet to help them keep watch on the border. (③) Citizens who want to help monitor the border can go online and serve as "virtual Texas deputies." (④) If they see anyone trying to cross the border, they send a report to the sheriff's office, which follows up, sometimes with the help of the U.S. Border Patrol.

19 주어진 글 다음에 이어질 글의 순서로 알맞은 것은?

All civilizations rely on government administration. Perhaps no civilization better exemplifies this than ancient Rome.

(A) To rule an area that large, the Romans, based in what is now central Italy, needed an effective system of government administration.

(B) Actually, the word "civilization" itself comes from the Latin word *civis*, meaning "citizen."

(C) Latin was the language of ancient Rome, whose territory stretched from the Mediterranean basin all the way to parts of Great Britain in the north and the Black Sea to the east.

① (A) – (B) – (C)　　② (B) – (A) – (C)
③ (B) – (C) – (A)　　④ (C) – (A) – (B)

20 밑줄 친 부분에 들어갈 말로 알맞은 것은?

Over the last fifty years, all major subdisciplines in psychology have become more and more isolated from each other as training becomes increasingly specialized and narrow in focus. As some psychologists have long argued, if the field of psychology is to mature and advance scientifically, its disparate parts (for example, neuroscience, developmental, cognitive, personality, and social) must become whole and integrated again. Science advances when distinct topics become theoretically and empirically integrated under simplifying theoretical frameworks. Psychology of science will encourage collaboration among psychologists from various sub-areas, helping the field achieve coherence rather than continued fragmentation. In this way, psychology of science might act as a template for psychology as a whole by integrating under one discipline all of the major fractions/factions within the field. It would be no small feat and of no small import if the psychology of science could become a model for the parent discipline on how to combine resources and study science _____.

① from a unified perspective
② in dynamic aspects
③ throughout history
④ with accuracy evidence

정답 · 해석 · 해설 p. 14

2회 2023년 국가직 9급
모바일 자동 채점 + 성적 분석 서비스 바로 가기

QR코드를 이용해 모바일로 간편하게 채점하고 나의 실력이 어느 정도인지, 취약 부분이 어디인지 바로 파악해 보세요.

(p.212에서 전체 정답표를 확인하실 수 있습니다)

제한 시간 : 20분　　시작 _____시 _____분 ~ 종료 _____시 _____분　　나의 점수 _____　회독 수 ☐ ☐ ☐

※ 밑줄 친 부분의 의미와 가장 가까운 것을 고르시오.

[01~03]

01

For years, detectives have been trying to unravel the mystery of the sudden disappearance of the twin brothers.

① solve　　　　② create
③ imitate　　　④ publicize

02

Before the couple experienced parenthood, their four-bedroom house seemed unnecessarily opulent.

① hidden　　　② luxurious
③ empty　　　 ④ solid

03

The boss hit the roof when he saw that we had already spent the entire budget in such a short period of time.

① was very satisfied
② was very surprised
③ became extremely calm
④ became extremely angry

※ 밑줄 친 부분에 들어갈 말로 가장 적절한 것을 고르시오.

[04~05]

04

A mouse potato is the computer _____ of television's couch potato: someone who tends to spend a great deal of leisure time in front of the computer in much the same way the couch potato does in front of the television.

① technician　　② equivalent
③ network　　　④ simulation

05

Mary decided to _____ her Spanish before going to South America.

① brush up on　　② hear out
③ stick up for　　 ④ lay off

06 어법상 옳은 것은?

① A horse should be fed according to its individual needs and the nature of its work.
② My hat was blown off by the wind while walking down a narrow street.
③ She has known primarily as a political cartoonist throughout her career.
④ Even young children like to be complimented for a job done good.

---

07 다음 글의 내용과 일치하지 않는 것은?

Umberto Eco was an Italian novelist, cultural critic and philosopher. He is widely known for his 1980 novel *The Name of the Rose*, a historical mystery combining semiotics in fiction with biblical analysis, medieval studies and literary theory. He later wrote other novels, including *Foucault's Pendulum* and *The Island of the Day Before*. Eco was also a translator: he translated Raymond Queneau's book *Exercices de style* into Italian. He was the founder of the Department of Media Studies at the University of the Republic of San Marino. He died at his Milanese home of pancreatic cancer, from which he had been suffering for two years, on the night of February 19, 2016.

① *The Name of the Rose* is a historical novel.
② Eco translated a book into Italian.
③ Eco founded a university department.
④ Eco died in a hospital of cancer.

08 밑줄 친 부분 중 어법상 옳지 않은 것은?

To find a good starting point, one must return to the year 1800 during ① underline{which} the first modern electric battery was developed. Italian Alessandro Volta found that a combination of silver, copper, and zinc ② underline{were} ideal for producing an electrical current. The enhanced design, ③ underline{called} a Voltaic pile, was made by stacking some discs made from these metals between discs made of cardboard soaked in sea water. There was ④ underline{such} talk about Volta's work that he was requested to conduct a demonstration before the Emperor Napoleon himself.

09 다음 글의 제목으로 가장 적절한 것은?

Lasers are possible because of the way light interacts with electrons. Electrons exist at specific energy levels or states characteristic of that particular atom or molecule. The energy levels can be imagined as rings or orbits around a nucleus. Electrons in outer rings are at higher energy levels than those in inner rings. Electrons can be bumped up to higher energy levels by the injection of energy—for example, by a flash of light. When an electron drops from an outer to an inner level, "excess" energy is given off as light. The wavelength or color of the emitted light is precisely related to the amount of energy released. Depending on the particular lasing material being used, specific wavelengths of light are absorbed (to energize or excite the electrons) and specific wavelengths are emitted (when the electrons fall back to their initial level).

① How Is Laser Produced?
② When Was Laser Invented?
③ What Electrons Does Laser Emit?
④ Why Do Electrons Reflect Light?

10 다음 글의 흐름상 가장 어색한 문장은?

Markets in water rights are likely to evolve as a rising population leads to shortages and climate change causes drought and famine. ① But they will be based on regional and ethical trading practices and will differ from the bulk of commodity trade. ② Detractors argue trading water is unethical or even a breach of human rights, but already water rights are bought and sold in arid areas of the globe from Oman to Australia. ③ Drinking distilled water can be beneficial, but may not be the best choice for everyone, especially if the minerals are not supplemented by another source. ④ "We strongly believe that water is in fact turning into the new gold for this decade and beyond," said Ziad Abdelnour. "No wonder smart money is aggressively moving in this direction."

11

A: I heard that the university cafeteria changed their menu.
B: Yeah, I just checked it out.
A: And they got a new caterer.
B: Yes. Sam's Catering.
A: _____?
B: There are more dessert choices. Also, some sandwich choices were removed.

① What is your favorite dessert
② Do you know where their office is
③ Do you need my help with the menu
④ What's the difference from the last menu

12

A: Hi there. May I help you?
B: Yes, I'm looking for a sweater.
A: Well, this one is the latest style from the fall collection. What do you think?
B: It's gorgeous. How much is it?
A: Let me check the price for you. It's $120.
B: _____.
A: Then how about this sweater? It's from the last season, but it's on sale for $50.
B: Perfect! Let me try it on.

① I also need a pair of pants to go with it
② That jacket is the perfect gift for me
③ It's a little out of my price range
④ We are open until 7 p.m. on Saturdays

13

① 우리가 영어를 단시간에 배우는 것은 결코 쉬운 일이 아니다.
  → It is by no means easy for us to learn English in a short time.
② 우리 인생에서 시간보다 더 소중한 것은 없다.
  → Nothing is more precious as time in our life.
③ 아이들은 길을 건널 때 아무리 조심해도 지나치지 않다.
  → Children cannot be too careful when crossing the street.
④ 그녀는 남들이 말하는 것을 쉽게 믿는다.
  → She easily believes what others say.

14

① 커피 세 잔을 마셨기 때문에, 그녀는 잠을 이룰 수 없다.
  → Having drunk three cups of coffee, she can't fall asleep.
② 친절한 사람이어서, 그녀는 모든 이에게 사랑받는다.
  → Being a kind person, she is loved by everyone.
③ 모든 점이 고려된다면, 그녀가 그 직위에 가장 적임인 사람이다.
  → All things considered, she is the best-qualified person for the position.
④ 다리를 꼰 채로 오랫동안 앉아 있는 것은 혈압을 상승시킬 수 있다.
  → Sitting with the legs crossing for a long period can raise blood pressure.

Beliefs about maintaining ties with those who have died vary from culture to culture. For example, maintaining ties with the deceased is accepted and sustained in the religious rituals of Japan. Yet among the Hopi Indians of Arizona, the deceased are forgotten as quickly as possible and life goes on as usual.   (A)   , the Hopi funeral ritual concludes with a break-off between mortals and spirits. The diversity of grieving is nowhere clearer than in two Muslim societies one in Egypt, the other in Bali. Among Muslims in Egypt, the bereaved are encouraged to dwell at length on their grief, surrounded by others who relate to similarly tragic accounts and express their sorrow.   (B)   , in Bali, bereaved Muslims are encouraged to laugh and be joyful rather than be sad.

	(A)	(B)
①	However	Similarly
②	In fact	By contrast
③	Therefore	For example
④	Likewise	Consequently

Scientists have long known that higher air temperatures are contributing to the surface melting on Greenland's ice sheet. But a new study has found another threat that has begun attacking the ice from below: Warm ocean water moving underneath the vast glaciers is causing them to melt even more quickly. The findings were published in the journal Nature Geoscience by researchers who studied one of the many "ice tongues" of the Nioghalvfjerdsfjorden Glacier in northeast Greenland. An ice tongue is a strip of ice that floats on the water without breaking off from the ice on land. The massive one these scientists studied is nearly 50 miles long. The survey revealed an underwater current more than a mile wide where warm water from the Atlantic Ocean is able to flow directly towards the glacier, bringing large amounts of heat into contact with the ice and _____ the glacier's melting.

① separating
② delaying
③ preventing
④ accelerating

Do people from different cultures view the world differently? A psychologist presented realistic animated scenes of fish and other underwater objects to Japanese and American students and asked them to report what they had seen. Americans and Japanese made about an equal number of references to the focal fish, but the Japanese made more than 60 percent more references to background elements, including the water, rocks, bubbles, and inert plants and animals. In addition, whereas Japanese and American participants made about equal numbers of references to movement involving active animals, the Japanese participants made almost twice as many references to relationships involving inert, background objects. Perhaps most tellingly, the very first sentence from the Japanese participants was likely to be one referring to the environment, whereas the first sentence from Americans was three times as likely to be one referring to the focal fish.

① Language Barrier Between Japanese and Americans
② Associations of Objects and Backgrounds in the Brain
③ Cultural Differences in Perception
④ Superiority of Detail-oriented People

Thus, blood, and life-giving oxygen, are easier for the heart to circulate to the brain.

People can be exposed to gravitational force, or g-force, in different ways. It can be localized, affecting only a portion of the body, as in getting slapped on the back. It can also be momentary, such as hard forces endured in a car crash. A third type of g-force is sustained, or lasting for at least several seconds. (①) Sustained, body-wide g-forces are the most dangerous to people. (②) The body usually withstands localized or momentary g-force better than sustained g-force, which can be deadly because blood is forced into the legs, depriving the rest of the body of oxygen. (③) Sustained g-force applied while the body is horizontal, or lying down, instead of sitting or standing tends to be more tolerable to people, because blood pools in the back and not the legs. (④) Some people, such as astronauts and fighter jet pilots, undergo special training exercises to increase their bodies' resistance to g-force.

19 다음 글의 요지로 가장 적절한 것은?

If someone makes you an offer and you're legitimately concerned about parts of it, you're usually better off proposing all your changes at once. Don't say, "The salary is a bit low. Could you do something about it?" and then, once she's worked on it, come back with "Thanks. Now here are two other things I'd like..." If you ask for only one thing initially, she may assume that getting it will make you ready to accept the offer (or at least to make a decision). If you keep saying "and one more thing...," she is unlikely to remain in a generous or understanding mood. Furthermore, if you have more than one request, don't simply mention all the things you want A, B, C, and D; also signal the relative importance of each to you. Otherwise, she may pick the two things you value least, because they're pretty easy to give you, and feel she's met you halfway.

① Negotiate multiple issues simultaneously, not serially.
② Avoid sensitive topics for a successful negotiation.
③ Choose the right time for your negotiation.
④ Don't be too direct when negotiating salary.

20 주어진 글 다음에 이어질 글의 순서로 가장 적절한 것은?

Today, Lamarck is unfairly remembered in large part for his mistaken explanation of how adaptations evolve. He proposed that by using or not using certain body parts, an organism develops certain characteristics.

(A) There is no evidence that this happens. Still, it is important to note that Lamarck proposed that evolution occurs when organisms adapt to their environments. This idea helped set the stage for Darwin.

(B) Lamarck thought that these characteristics would be passed on to the offspring. Lamarck called this idea inheritance of acquired characteristics.

(C) For example, Lamarck might explain that a kangaroo's powerful hind legs were the result of ancestors strengthening their legs by jumping and then passing that acquired leg strength on to the offspring. However, an acquired characteristic would have to somehow modify the DNA of specific genes in order to be inherited.

① (A) – (C) – (B)   ② (B) – (A) – (C)
③ (B) – (C) – (A)   ④ (C) – (A) – (B)

정답 · 해석 · 해설 p. 23

3회 2022년 국가직 9급
모바일 자동 채점 + 성적 분석 서비스 바로 가기

QR코드를 이용해 모바일로 간편하게 채점하고 나의 실력이 어느 정도인지, 취약 부분이 어디인지 바로 파악해 보세요.

(p.212에서 전체 정답표를 확인하실 수 있습니다)

제한 시간 : 20분   시작 _____시 _____분 ~ 종료 _____시 _____분   나의 점수 _____   회독 수 □□□

※ 밑줄 친 부분의 의미와 가장 가까운 것을 고르시오.

[01~03]

01

Privacy as a social practice shapes individual behavior in conjunction with other social practices and is therefore central to social life.

① in combination with   ② in comparison with
③ in place of   ④ in case of

02

The influence of Jazz has been so pervasive that most popular music owes its stylistic roots to jazz.

① deceptive   ② ubiquitous
③ persuasive   ④ disastrous

03

This novel is about the vexed parents of an unruly teenager who quits school to start a business.

① callous   ② annoyed
③ reputable   ④ confident

04 밑줄 친 부분에 들어갈 말로 가장 적절한 것은?

A group of young demonstrators attempted to _____ the police station.

① line up   ② give out
③ carry on   ④ break into

05 다음 글의 내용과 일치하는 것은?

The most notorious case of imported labor is of course the Atlantic slave trade, which brought as many as ten million enslaved Africans to the New World to work the plantations. But although the Europeans may have practiced slavery on the largest scale, they were by no means the only people to bring slaves into their communities: earlier, the ancient Egyptians used slave labor to build their pyramids, early Arab explorers were often also slave traders, and Arabic slavery continued into the twentieth century and indeed still continues in a few places. In the Americas some native tribes enslaved members of other tribes, and slavery was also an institution in many African nations, especially before the colonial period.

① African laborers voluntarily moved to the New World.
② Europeans were the first people to use slave labor.
③ Arabic slavery no longer exists in any form.
④ Slavery existed even in African countries.

06 어법상 옳은 것은?

① This guide book tells you where should you visit in Hong Kong.

② I was born in Taiwan, but I have lived in Korea since I started work.

③ The novel was so excited that I lost track of time and missed the bus.

④ It's not surprising that book stores don't carry newspapers any more, doesn't it?

08 밑줄 친 부분 중 어법상 옳지 않은 것은?

Urban agriculture (UA) has long been dismissed as a fringe activity that has no place in cities; however, its potential is beginning to ① be realized. In fact, UA is about food self-reliance: it involves ② creating work and is a reaction to food insecurity, particularly for the poor. Contrary to ③ which many believe, UA is found in every city, where it is sometimes hidden, sometimes obvious. If one looks carefully, few spaces in a major city are unused. Valuable vacant land rarely sits idle and is often taken over—either formally, or informally—and made ④ productive.

07 다음 글의 제목으로 가장 적절한 것은?

Warming temperatures and loss of oxygen in the sea will shrink hundreds of fish species—from tunas and groupers to salmon, thresher sharks, haddock and cod—even more than previously thought, a new study concludes. Because warmer seas speed up their metabolisms, fish, squid and other water-breathing creatures will need to draw more oxygen from the ocean. At the same time, warming seas are already reducing the availability of oxygen in many parts of the sea. A pair of University of British Columbia scientists argue that since the bodies of fish grow faster than their gills, these animals eventually will reach a point where they can't get enough oxygen to sustain normal growth. "What we found was that the body size of fish decreases by 20 to 30 percent for every 1 degree Celsius increase in water temperature," says author William Cheung.

① Fish Now Grow Faster than Ever

② Oxygen's Impact on Ocean Temperatures

③ Climate Change May Shrink the World's Fish

④ How Sea Creatures Survive with Low Metabolism

09 주어진 문장이 들어갈 위치로 가장 적절한 것은?

> For example, the state archives of New Jersey hold more than 30,000 cubic feet of paper and 25,000 reels of microfilm.

Archives are a treasure trove of material: from audio to video to newspapers, magazines and printed material—which makes them indispensable to any History Detective investigation. While libraries and archives may appear the same, the differences are important. (①) An archive collection is almost always made up of primary sources, while a library contains secondary sources. (②) To learn more about the Korean War, you'd go to a library for a history book. If you wanted to read the government papers, or letters written by Korean War soldiers, you'd go to an archive. (③) If you're searching for information, chances are there's an archive out there for you. Many state and local archives store public records—which are an amazing, diverse resource. (④) An online search of your state's archives will quickly show you they contain much more than just the minutes of the legislature—there are detailed land grant information to be found, old town maps, criminal records and oddities such as peddler license applications.

※ treasure trove: 귀중한 발굴물(수집물)
※ land grant: (대학·철도 등을 위해) 정부가 주는 땅

10 다음 글의 흐름상 가장 어색한 문장은?

The term burnout refers to a "wearing out" from the pressures of work. Burnout is a chronic condition that results as daily work stressors take their toll on employees. ① The most widely adopted conceptualization of burnout has been developed by Maslach and her colleagues in their studies of human service workers. Maslach sees burnout as consisting of three interrelated dimensions. The first dimension—emotional exhaustion—is really the core of the burnout phenomenon. ② Workers suffer from emotional exhaustion when they feel fatigued, frustrated, used up, or unable to face another day on the job. The second dimension of burnout is a lack of personal accomplishment. ③ This aspect of the burnout phenomenon refers to workers who see themselves as failures, incapable of effectively accomplishing job requirements. ④ Emotional labor workers enter their occupation highly motivated although they are physically exhausted. The third dimension of burnout is depersonalization. This dimension is relevant only to workers who must communicate interpersonally with others (e.g. clients, patients, students) as part of the job.

※ 밑줄 친 부분에 들어갈 말로 가장 적절한 것을 고르시오.
[11~12]

11

> A: Were you here last night?
> B: Yes. I worked the closing shift. Why?
> A: The kitchen was a mess this morning. There was food spattered on the stove, and the ice trays were not in the freezer.
> B: I guess I forgot to go over the cleaning checklist.
> A: You know how important a clean kitchen is.
> B: I'm sorry. _____

① I won't let it happen again.
② Would you like your bill now?
③ That's why I forgot it yesterday.
④ I'll make sure you get the right order.

12

> A: Have you taken anything for your cold?
> B: No, I just blow my nose a lot.
> A: Have you tried nose spray?
> B: _____
> A: It works great.
> B: No, thanks. I don't like to put anything in my nose, so I've never used it.

① Yes, but it didn't help.
② No, I don't like nose spray.
③ No, the pharmacy was closed.
④ Yeah, how much should I use?

13 다음 글의 내용과 일치하지 않는 것은?

> Deserts cover more than one-fifth of the Earth's land area, and they are found on every continent. A place that receives less than 25 centimeters (10 inches) of rain per year is considered a desert. Deserts are part of a wider class of regions called drylands. These areas exist under a "moisture deficit," which means they can frequently lose more moisture through evaporation than they receive from annual precipitation. Despite the common conceptions of deserts as hot, there are cold deserts as well. The largest hot desert in the world, northern Africa's Sahara, reaches temperatures of up to 50 degrees Celsius (122 degrees Fahrenheit) during the day. But some deserts are always cold, like the Gobi Desert in Asia and the polar deserts of the Antarctic and Arctic, which are the world's largest. Others are mountainous. Only about 20 percent of deserts are covered by sand. The driest deserts, such as Chile's Atacama Desert, have parts that receive less than two millimeters (0.08 inches) of precipitation a year. Such environments are so harsh and otherworldly that scientists have even studied them for clues about life on Mars. On the other hand, every few years, an unusually rainy period can produce "super blooms," where even the Atacama becomes blanketed in wildflowers.

① There is at least one desert on each continent.
② The Sahara is the world's largest hot desert.
③ The Gobi Desert is categorized as a cold desert.
④ The Atacama Desert is one of the rainiest deserts.

14

① 나는 너의 답장을 가능한 한 빨리 받기를 고대한다.
  → I look forward to receive your reply as soon as possible.

② 그는 내가 일을 열심히 했기 때문에 월급을 올려 주겠다고 말했다.
  → He said he would rise my salary because I worked hard.

③ 그의 스마트 도시 계획은 고려할 만했다.
  → His plan for the smart city was worth considered.

④ Cindy는 피아노 치는 것을 매우 좋아했고 그녀의 아들도 그랬다.
  → Cindy loved playing the piano, and so did her son.

15

① 당신이 부자일지라도 당신은 진실한 친구들을 살 수 없다.
  → Rich as if you may be, you can't buy sincere friends.

② 그것은 너무나 아름다운 유성 폭풍이어서 우리는 밤새 그것을 보았다.
  → It was such a beautiful meteor storm that we watched it all night.

③ 학위가 없는 것이 그녀의 성공을 방해했다.
  → Her lack of a degree kept her advancing.

④ 그는 사형이 폐지되어야 하는지 아닌지에 대한 에세이를 써야 한다.
  → He has to write an essay on if or not the death penalty should be abolished.

16

Social media, magazines and shop windows bombard people daily with things to buy, and British consumers are buying more clothes and shoes than ever before. Online shopping means it is easy for customers to buy without thinking, while major brands offer such cheap clothes that they can be treated like disposable items— worn two or three times and then thrown away. In Britain, the average person spends more than £1,000 on new clothes a year, which is around four percent of their income. That might not sound like much, but that figure hides two far more worrying trends for society and for the environment. First, a lot of that consumer spending is via credit cards. British people currently owe approximately £670 per adult to credit card companies. That's 66 percent of the average wardrobe budget. Also, not only are people spending money they don't have, they're using it to buy things _____. Britain throws away 300,000 tons of clothing a year, most of which goes into landfill sites.

① they don't need
② that are daily necessities
③ that will be soon recycled
④ they can hand down to others

17

Excellence is the absolute prerequisite in fine dining because the prices charged are necessarily high. An operator may do everything possible to make the restaurant efficient, but the guests still expect careful, personal service: food prepared to order by highly skilled chefs and delivered by expert servers. Because this service is, quite literally, manual labor, only marginal improvements in productivity are possible. For example, a cook, server, or bartender can move only so much faster before she or he reaches the limits of human performance. Thus, only moderate savings are possible through improved efficiency, which makes an escalation of prices _____. (It is an axiom of economics that as prices rise, consumers become more discriminating.) Thus, the clientele of the fine-dining restaurant expects, demands, and is willing to pay for excellence.

① ludicrous ② inevitable
③ preposterous ④ inconceivable

18 주어진 글 다음에 이어질 글의 순서로 가장 적절한 것은?

To be sure, human language stands out from the decidedly restricted vocalizations of monkeys and apes. Moreover, it exhibits a degree of sophistication that far exceeds any other form of animal communication.

(A) That said, many species, while falling far short of human language, do nevertheless exhibit impressively complex communication systems in natural settings.

(B) And they can be taught far more complex systems in artificial contexts, as when raised alongside humans.

(C) Even our closest primate cousins seem incapable of acquiring anything more than a rudimentary communicative system, even after intensive training over several years. The complexity that is language is surely a species-specific trait.

① (A) – (B) – (C) ② (B) – (C) – (A)
③ (C) – (A) – (B) ④ (C) – (B) – (A)

19 다음 글의 주제로 가장 적절한 것은?

During the late twentieth century socialism was on the retreat both in the West and in large areas of the developing world. During this new phase in the evolution of market capitalism, global trading patterns became increasingly interlinked, and advances in information technology meant that deregulated financial markets could shift massive flows of capital across national boundaries within seconds. 'Globalization' boosted trade, encouraged productivity gains and lowered prices, but critics alleged that it exploited the low-paid, was indifferent to environmental concerns and subjected the Third World to a monopolistic form of capitalism. Many radicals within Western societies who wished to protest against this process joined voluntary bodies, charities and other non-governmental organizations, rather than the marginalized political parties of the left. The environmental movement itself grew out of the recognition that the world was interconnected, and an angry, if diffuse, international coalition of interests emerged.

① The affirmative phenomena of globalization in the developing world in the past

② The decline of socialism and the emergence of capitalism in the twentieth century

③ The conflict between the global capital market and the political organizations of the left

④ The exploitative characteristics of global capitalism and diverse social reactions against it

20 다음 글에 나타난 Johnbull의 심경으로 가장 적절한 것은?

In the blazing midday sun, the yellow egg-shaped rock stood out from a pile of recently unearthed gravel. Out of curiosity, sixteen-year-old miner Komba Johnbull picked it up and fingered its flat, pyramidal planes. Johnbull had never seen a diamond before, but he knew enough to understand that even a big find would be no larger than his thumbnail. Still, the rock was unusual enough to merit a second opinion. Sheepishly, he brought it over to one of the more experienced miners working the muddy gash deep in the jungle. The pit boss's eyes widened when he saw the stone. "Put it in your pocket," he whispered. "Keep digging." The older miner warned that it could be dangerous if anyone thought they had found something big. So Johnbull kept shoveling gravel until nightfall, pausing occasionally to grip the heavy stone in his fist. Could it be?

① thrilled and excited

② painful and distressed

③ arrogant and convinced

④ detached and indifferent

정답·해석·해설 p. 31

4회 2021년 국가직 9급
모바일 자동 채점 + 성적 분석 서비스 바로 가기

QR코드를 이용해 모바일로 간편하게 채점하고 나의 실력이 어느 정도인지, 취약 부분이 어디인지 바로 파악해 보세요.

(p.212에서 전체 정답표를 확인하실 수 있습니다)

5회 | 2020년 국가직 9급

2020년 7월 11일 시행

제한 시간 : 20분   시작 _____시 _____분 ~ 종료 _____시 _____분   나의 점수 _____   회독 수 ☐ ☐ ☐

※ 밑줄 친 부분의 의미와 가장 가까운 것을 고르시오.
[01~04]

01

Extensive lists of microwave oven models and styles along with candid customer reviews and price ranges are available at appliance comparison websites.

① frank
② logical
③ implicit
④ passionate

02

It had been known for a long time that Yellowstone was volcanic in nature and the one thing about volcanoes is that they are generally conspicuous.

① passive
② vaporous
③ dangerous
④ noticeable

03

He's the best person to tell you how to get there because he knows the city inside out.

① eventually
② culturally
③ thoroughly
④ tentatively

04

All along the route were thousands of homespun attempts to pay tribute to the team, including messages etched in cardboard, snow and construction paper.

① honor
② compose
③ publicize
④ join

05 어법상 옳은 것은?

① The traffic of a big city is busier than those of a small city.
② I'll think of you when I'll be lying on the beach next week.
③ Raisins were once an expensive food, and only the wealth ate them.
④ The intensity of a color is related to how much gray the color contains.

06 우리말을 영어로 가장 잘 옮긴 것은?

① 몇 가지 문제가 새로운 회원들 때문에 생겼다.
→ Several problems have raised due to the new members.

② 그 위원회는 그 건물의 건설을 중단하라고 명했다.
→ The committee commanded that construction of the building cease.

③ 그들은 한 시간에 40마일이 넘는 바람과 싸워야 했다.
→ They had to fight against winds that will blow over 40 miles an hour.

④ 거의 모든 식물의 씨앗은 혹독한 날씨에도 살아남는다.
→ The seeds of most plants are survived by harsh weather.

07 우리말을 영어로 잘못 옮긴 것은?

① 인간은 환경에 자신을 빨리 적응시킨다.
→ Human beings quickly adapt themselves to the environment.

② 그녀는 그 사고 때문에 그녀의 목표를 포기할 수밖에 없었다.
→ She had no choice but to give up her goal because of the accident.

③ 그 회사는 그가 부회장으로 승진하는 것을 금했다.
→ The company prohibited him from promoting to vice-president.

④ 그 장난감 자동차를 조립하고 분리하는 것은 쉽다.
→ It is easy to assemble and take apart the toy car.

08 다음 글의 요지로 가장 적절한 것은?

Listening to somebody else's ideas is the one way to know whether the story you believe about the world—as well as about yourself and your place in it—remains intact. We all need to examine our beliefs, air them out and let them breathe. Hearing what other people have to say, especially about concepts we regard as foundational, is like opening a window in our minds and in our hearts. Speaking up is important. Yet to speak up without listening is like banging pots and pans together: even if it gets you attention, it's not going to get you respect. There are three prerequisites for conversation to be meaningful: 1. You have to know what you're talking about, meaning that you have an original point and are not echoing a worn-out, hand-me-down or pre-fab argument; 2. You respect the people with whom you're speaking and are authentically willing to treat them courteously even if you disagree with their positions; 3. You have to be both smart and informed enough to listen to what the opposition says while handling your own perspective on the topic with uninterrupted good humor and discernment.

① We should be more determined to persuade others.

② We need to listen and speak up in order to communicate well.

③ We are reluctant to change our beliefs about the world we see.

④ We hear only what we choose and attempt to ignore different opinions.

The future may be uncertain, but some things are undeniable: climate change, shifting demographics, geopolitics. The only guarantee is that there will be changes, both wonderful and terrible. It's worth considering how artists will respond to these changes, as well as what purpose art serves, now and in the future. Reports suggest that by 2040 the impacts of human-caused climate change will be inescapable, making it the big issue at the centre of art and life in 20 years' time. Artists in the future will wrestle with the possibilities of the post-human and post-Anthropocene — artificial intelligence, human colonies in outer space and potential doom. The identity politics seen in art around the #MeToo and Black Lives Matter movements will grow as environmentalism, border politics and migration come even more sharply into focus. Art will become increasingly diverse and might not 'look like art' as we expect. In the future, once we've become weary of our lives being visible online for all to see and our privacy has been all but lost, anonymity may be more desirable than fame. Instead of thousands, or millions, of likes and followers, we will be starved for authenticity and connection. Art could, in turn, become more collective and experiential, rather than individual.

① What will art look like in the future?
② How will global warming affect our lives?
③ How will artificial intelligence influence the environment?
④ What changes will be made because of political movements?

The Second Amendment of the U.S. Constitution states: "A well-regulated Militia, being necessary to the security of a free State, the right of the people to keep and bear Arms, shall not be infringed." Supreme Court rulings, citing this amendment, have upheld the right of states to regulate firearms. However, in a 2008 decision confirming an individual right to keep and bear arms, the court struck down Washington, D.C. laws that banned handguns and required those in the home to be locked or disassembled. A number of gun advocates consider ownership a birthright and an essential part of the nation's heritage. The United States, with less than 5 percent of the world's population, has about 35~50 percent of the world's civilian-owned guns, according to a 2007 report by the Switzerland-based Small Arms Survey. It ranks number one in firearms per capita. The United States also has the highest homicide-by-firearm rate among the world's most developed nations. But many gun-rights proponents say these statistics do not indicate a cause-and-effect relationship and note that the rates of gun homicide and other gun crimes in the United States have dropped since highs in the early 1990's.

① In 2008, the U.S. Supreme Court overturned Washington, D.C. laws banning handguns.
② Many gun advocates claim that owning guns is a natural-born right.
③ Among the most developed nations, the U.S. has the highest rate of gun homicides.
④ Gun crimes in the U.S. have steadily increased over the last three decades.

11 두 사람의 대화 중 가장 어색한 것은?

① A: When is the payment due?
   B: You have to pay by next week.
② A: Should I check this baggage in?
   B: No, it's small enough to take on the plane.
③ A: When and where shall we meet?
   B: I'll pick you up at your office at 8:30.
④ A: I won the prize in a cooking contest.
   B: I couldn't have done it without you.

12 밑줄 친 부분에 들어갈 말로 가장 적절한 것은?

A: Thank you for calling the Royal Point Hotel Reservations Department. My name is Sam. How may I help you?
B: Hello, I'd like to book a room.
A: We offer two room types: the deluxe room and the luxury suite.
B: _____?
A: For one, the suite is very large. In addition to a bedroom, it has a kitchen, living room and dining room.
B: It sounds expensive.
A: Well, it's $200 more per night.
B: In that case, I'll go with the deluxe room.

① Do you need anything else
② May I have the room number
③ What's the difference between them
④ Are pets allowed in the rooms

13 밑줄 친 (A), (B)에 들어갈 말로 가장 적절한 것은?

Advocates of homeschooling believe that children learn better when they are in a secure, loving environment. Many psychologists see the home as the most natural learning environment, and originally the home was the classroom, long before schools were established. Parents who homeschool argue that they can monitor their children's education and give them the attention that is lacking in a traditional school setting. Students can also pick and choose what to study and when to study, thus enabling them to learn at their own pace. ___(A)___, critics of homeschooling say that children who are not in the classroom miss out on learning important social skills because they have little interaction with their peers. Several studies, though, have shown that the home-educated children appear to do just as well in terms of social and emotional development as other students, having spent more time in the comfort and security of their home, with guidance from parents who care about their welfare. ___(B)___, many critics of homeschooling have raised concerns about the ability of parents to teach their kids effectively.

	(A)	(B)
①	Therefore	Nevertheless
②	In contrast	In spite of this
③	Therefore	Contrary to that
④	In contrast	Furthermore

14 다음 글의 주제로 가장 적절한 것은?

For many people, work has become an obsession. It has caused burnout, unhappiness and gender inequity, as people struggle to find time for children or passions or pets or any sort of life besides what they do for a paycheck. But increasingly, younger workers are pushing back. More of them expect and demand flexibility—paid leave for a new baby, say, and generous vacation time, along with daily things, like the ability to work remotely, come in late or leave early, or make time for exercise or meditation. The rest of their lives happens on their phones, not tied to a certain place or time—why should work be any different?

① ways to increase your paycheck
② obsession for reducing inequity
③ increasing call for flexibility at work
④ advantages of a life with long vacations

15 주어진 글 다음에 이어질 글의 순서로 가장 적절한 것은?

Past research has shown that experiencing frequent psychological stress can be a significant risk factor for cardiovascular disease, a condition that affects almost half of those aged 20 years and older in the United States.

(A) Does this mean, though, that people who drive on a daily basis are set to develop heart problems, or is there a simple way of easing the stress of driving?

(B) According to a new study, there is. The researchers noted that listening to music while driving helps relieve the stress that affects heart health.

(C) One source of frequent stress is driving, either due to the stressors associated with heavy traffic or the anxiety that often accompanies inexperienced drivers.

① (A) − (C) − (B)　　② (B) − (A) − (C)
③ (C) − (A) − (B)　　④ (C) − (B) − (A)

16 다음 글의 흐름상 가장 어색한 문장은?

When the brain perceives a threat in the immediate surroundings, it initiates a complex string of events in the body. It sends electrical messages to various glands, organs that release chemical hormones into the bloodstream. Blood quickly carries these hormones to other organs that are then prompted to do various things. ① The adrenal glands above the kidneys, for example, pump out adrenaline, the body's stress hormone. ② Adrenaline travels all over the body doing things such as widening the eyes to be on the lookout for signs of danger, pumping the heart faster to keep blood and extra hormones flowing, and tensing the skeletal muscles so they are ready to lash out at or run from the threat. ③ The whole process is called the fight-or-flight response, because it prepares the body to either battle or run for its life. ④ Humans consciously control their glands to regulate the release of various hormones. Once the response is initiated, ignoring it is impossible, because hormones cannot be reasoned with.

17 주어진 문장이 들어갈 위치로 가장 적절한 것은?

It was then he remembered his experience with the glass flask, and just as quickly, he imagined that a special coating might be applied to a glass windshield to keep it from shattering.

In 1903 the French chemist, Edouard Benedictus, dropped a glass flask one day on a hard floor and broke it. (①) However, to the astonishment of the chemist, the flask did not shatter, but still retained most of its original shape. (②) When he examined the flask he found that it contained a film coating inside, a residue remaining from a solution of collodion that the flask had contained. (③) He made a note of this unusual phenomenon, but thought no more of it until several weeks later when he read stories in the newspapers about people in automobile accidents who were badly hurt by flying windshield glass. (④) Not long thereafter, he succeeded in producing the world's first sheet of safety glass.

18 다음 글의 내용과 일치하지 않는 것은?

Dubrovnik, Croatia, is a mess. Because its main attraction is its seaside Old Town surrounded by 80-foot medieval walls, this Dalmatian Coast town does not absorb visitors very well. And when cruise ships are docked here, a legion of tourists turn Old Town into a miasma of tank-top-clad tourists marching down the town's limestone-blanketed streets. Yes, the city of Dubrovnik has been proactive in trying to curb cruise ship tourism, but nothing will save Old Town from the perpetual swarm of tourists. To make matters worse, the lure of making extra money has inspired many homeowners in Old Town to turn over their places to Airbnb, making the walled portion of town one giant hotel. You want an "authentic" Dubrovnik experience in Old Town, just like a local? You're not going to find it here. Ever.

① Old Town은 80피트 중세 시대 벽으로 둘러싸여 있다.
② 크루즈 배가 정박할 때면 많은 여행객이 Old Town 거리를 활보한다.
③ Dubrovnik 시는 크루즈 여행을 확대하려고 노력해 왔다.
④ Old Town에서는 많은 집이 여행객 숙소로 바뀌었다.

19 밑줄 친 (A), (B)에 들어갈 말로 가장 적절한 것은?

When an organism is alive, it takes in carbon dioxide from the air around it. Most of that carbon dioxide is made of carbon-12, but a tiny portion consists of carbon-14. So the living organism always contains a very small amount of radioactive carbon, carbon-14. A detector next to the living organism would record radiation given off by the carbon-14 in the organism. When the organism dies, it no longer takes in carbon dioxide. No new carbon-14 is added, and the old carbon-14 slowly decays into nitrogen. The amount of carbon-14 slowly ____(A)____ as time goes on. Over time, less and less radiation from carbon-14 is produced. The amount of carbon-14 radiation detected for an organism is a measure, therefore, of how long the organism has been ____(B)____. This method of determining the age of an organism is called carbon-14 dating. The decay of carbon-14 allows archaeologists to find the age of once-living materials. Measuring the amount of radiation remaining indicates the approximate age.

	(A)	(B)
①	decreases	dead
②	increases	alive
③	decreases	productive
④	increases	inactive

20 밑줄 친 부분에 들어갈 말로 가장 적절한 것은?

All creatures, past and present, either have gone or will go extinct. Yet, as each species vanished over the past 3.8-billion-year history of life on Earth, new ones inevitably appeared to replace them or to exploit newly emerging resources. From only a few very simple organisms, a great number of complex, multicellular forms evolved over this immense period. The origin of new species, which the nineteenth-century English naturalist Charles Darwin once referred to as "the mystery of mysteries," is the natural process of speciation responsible for generating this remarkable _____ with whom humans share the planet. Although taxonomists presently recognize some 1.5 million living species, the actual number is possibly closer to 10 million. Recognizing the biological status of this multitude requires a clear understanding of what constitutes a species, which is no easy task given that evolutionary biologists have yet to agree on a universally acceptable definition.

① technique of biologists
② diversity of living creatures
③ inventory of extinct organisms
④ collection of endangered species

정답·해석·해설 p. 40

5회 2020년 국가직 9급
모바일 자동 채점 + 성적 분석 서비스 바로 가기

QR코드를 이용해 모바일로 간편하게 채점하고 나의 실력이 어느 정도인지, 취약 부분이 어디인지 바로 파악해 보세요.

(p.212에서 전체 정답표를 확인하실 수 있습니다)

제한 시간 : 20분   시작 _____시 _____분 ~ 종료 _____시 _____분   나의 점수 _____ 회독 수 ☐☐☐

※ 밑줄 친 부분의 의미와 가장 가까운 것을 고르시오.
[01~02]

01

Natural Gas World subscribers will receive accurate and reliable key facts and figures about what is going on in the industry, so they are fully able to discern what concerns their business.

① distinguish
② strengthen
③ undermine
④ abandon

02

Ms. West, the winner of the silver in the women's 1,500m event, stood out through the race.

① was overwhelmed
② was impressive
③ was depressed
④ was optimistic

03 두 사람의 대화 중 가장 어색한 것은?

① A: I'm traveling abroad, but I'm not used to staying in another country.
  B: Don't worry. You'll get accustomed to it in no time.
② A: I want to get a prize in the photo contest.
  B: I'm sure you will. I'll keep my fingers crossed!
③ A: My best friend moved to Sejong City. I miss her so much.
  B: Yeah. I know how you feel.
④ A: Do you mind if I talk to you for a moment?
  B: Never mind. I'm very busy right now.

04 밑줄 친 부분에 들어갈 말로 가장 적절한 것은?

A: Would you like to try some dim sum?
B: Yes, thank you. They look delicious. What's inside?
A: These have pork and chopped vegetables, and those have shrimps.
B: And, um, _____?
A: You pick one up with your chopsticks like this and dip it into the sauce. It's easy.
B: Okay. I'll give it a try.

① how much are they
② how do I eat them
③ how spicy are they
④ how do you cook them

※ 우리말을 영어로 잘못 옮긴 것을 고르시오. [05~06]

05

① 제가 당신께 말씀드렸던 새로운 선생님은 원래 페루 출신입니다.
  → The new teacher I told you about is originally from Peru.
② 나는 긴급한 일로 자정이 5분이나 지난 후 그에게 전화했다.
  → I called him five minutes shy of midnight on an urgent matter.
③ 상어로 보이는 것이 산호 뒤에 숨어 있었다.
  → What appeared to be a shark was lurking behind the coral reef.
④ 그녀는 일요일에 16세의 친구와 함께 산 정상에 올랐다.
  → She reached the mountain summit with her 16-year-old friend on Sunday.

..

06

① 개인용 컴퓨터를 가장 많이 가지고 있는 나라는 종종 바뀐다.

→ The country with the most computers per person changes from time to time.

② 지난여름 나의 사랑스러운 손자에게 일어난 일은 놀라웠다.

→ What happened to my lovely grandson last summer was amazing.

③ 나무 숟가락은 아이들에게 매우 좋은 장난감이고 플라스틱 병 또한 그렇다.

→ Wooden spoons are excellent toys for children, and so are plastic bottles.

④ 나는 은퇴 후부터 내내 이 일을 해 오고 있다.

→ I have been doing this work ever since I retired.

※ 밑줄 친 부분 중 어법상 옳지 않은 것을 고르시오.

[07~08]

07

Domesticated animals are the earliest and most effective 'machines' ① available to humans. They take the strain off the human back and arms. ② Utilizing with other techniques, animals can raise human living standards very considerably, both as supplementary foodstuffs (protein in meat and milk) and as machines ③ to carry burdens, lift water, and grind grain. Since they are so obviously ④ of great benefit, we might expect to find that over the centuries humans would increase the number and quality of the animals they kept. Surprisingly, this has not usually been the case.

08

A myth is a narrative that embodies—and in some cases ① helps to explain—the religious, philosophical, moral, and political values of a culture. Through tales of gods and supernatural beings, myths ② try to make sense of occurrences in the natural world. Contrary to popular usage, myth does not mean "falsehood." In the broadest sense, myths are stories—usually whole groups of stories—③ that can be true or partly true as well as false; regardless of their degree of accuracy, however, myths frequently express the deepest beliefs of a culture. According to this definition, the *Iliad* and the *Odyssey*, the Koran, and the Old and New Testaments can all ④ refer to as myths.

09 다음 글의 제목으로 가장 적절한 것은?

Mapping technologies are being used in many new applications. Biological researchers are exploring the molecular structure of DNA ("mapping the genome"), geophysicists are mapping the structure of the Earth's core, and oceanographers are mapping the ocean floor. Computer games have various imaginary "lands" or levels where rules, hazards, and rewards change. Computerization now challenges reality with "virtual reality," artificial environments that stimulate special situations, which may be useful in training and entertainment. Mapping techniques are being used also in the realm of ideas. For example, relationships between ideas can be shown using what are called concept maps. Starting from a general or "central" idea, related ideas can be connected, building a web around the main concept. This is not a map by any traditional definition, but the tools and techniques of cartography are employed to produce it, and in some ways it resembles a map.

① Computerized Maps vs. Traditional Maps

② Where Does Cartography Begin?

③ Finding Ways to DNA Secrets

④ Mapping New Frontiers

10 다음 글의 요지로 가장 적절한 것은?

When giving performance feedback, you should consider the recipient's past performance and your estimate of his or her future potential in designing its frequency, amount, and content. For high performers with potential for growth, feedback should be frequent enough to prod them into taking corrective action, but not so frequent that it is experienced as controlling and saps their initiative. For adequate performers who have settled into their jobs and have limited potential for advancement, very little feedback is needed because they have displayed reliable and steady behavior in the past, knowing their tasks and realizing what needs to be done. For poor performers—that is, people who will need to be removed from their jobs if their performance doesn't improve—feedback should be frequent and very specific, and the connection between acting on the feedback and negative sanctions such as being laid off or fired should be made explicit.

① Time your feedback well.
② Customize negative feedback.
③ Tailor feedback to the person.
④ Avoid goal-oriented feedback.

11 다음 글의 내용과 일치하지 않는 것은?

Langston Hughes was born in Joplin, Missouri, and graduated from Lincoln University, in which many African-American students have pursued their academic disciplines. At the age of eighteen, Hughes published one of his most well-known poems, "Negro Speaks of Rivers." Creative and experimental, Hughes incorporated authentic dialect in his work, adapted traditional poetic forms to embrace the cadences and moods of blues and jazz, and created characters and themes that reflected elements of lower-class black culture. With his ability to fuse serious content with humorous style, Hughes attacked racial prejudice in a way that was natural and witty.

① Hughes는 많은 미국 흑인들이 다녔던 대학교를 졸업하였다.
② Hughes는 실제 사투리를 그의 작품에 반영하였다.
③ Hughes는 하층 계급 흑인들의 문화적 요소를 반영한 인물을 만들었다.
④ Hughes는 인종편견을 엄숙한 문체로 공격하였다.

12 밑줄 친 부분 중 글의 흐름상 가장 어색한 것은?

In 2007, our biggest concern was "too big to fail." Wall Street banks had grown to such staggering sizes, and had become so central to the health of the financial system, that no rational government could ever let them fail. ① Aware of their protected status, banks made excessively risky bets on housing markets and invented ever more complicated derivatives. ② New virtual currencies such as bitcoin and ethereum have radically changed our understanding of how money can and should work. ③ The result was the worst financial crisis since the breakdown of our economy in 1929. ④ In the years since 2007, we have made great progress in addressing the too-big-to-fail dilemma. Our banks are better capitalized than ever. Our regulators conduct regular stress tests of large institutions.

13 다음 글의 주제로 가장 적절한 것은?

Imagine that two people are starting work at a law firm on the same day. One person has a very simple name. The other person has a very complex name. We've got pretty good evidence that over the course of their next 16 plus years of their career, the person with the simpler name will rise up the legal hierarchy more quickly. They will attain partnership more quickly in the middle parts of their career. And by about the eighth or ninth year after graduating from law school the people with simpler names are about seven to ten percent more likely to be partners—which is a striking effect. We try to eliminate all sorts of other alternative explanations. For example, we try to show that it's not about foreignness because foreign names tend to be harder to pronounce. But even if you look at just white males with Anglo-American names—so really the true in-group, you find that among those white males with Anglo names they are more likely to rise up if their names happen to be simpler. So simplicity is one key feature in names that determines various outcomes.

① the development of legal names
② the concept of attractive names
③ the benefit of simple names
④ the roots of foreign names

※ 밑줄 친 부분의 의미와 가장 가까운 것을 고르시오.

[14~15]

14

Schooling is compulsory for all children in the United States, but the age range for which school attendance is required varies from state to state.

① complementary
② systematic
③ mandatory
④ innovative

15

Although the actress experienced much turmoil in her career, she never disclosed to anyone that she was unhappy.

① let on
② let off
③ let up
④ let down

16 밑줄 친 (A), (B)에 들어갈 말로 가장 적절한 것은?

Visionaries are the first people in their industry segment to see the potential of new technologies. Fundamentally, they see themselves as smarter than their opposite numbers in competitive companies—and, quite often, they are. Indeed, it is their ability to see things first that they want to leverage into a competitive advantage. That advantage can only come about if no one else has discovered it. They do not expect, (A) , to be buying a well-tested product with an extensive list of industry references. Indeed, if such a reference base exists, it may actually turn them off, indicating that for this technology, at any rate, they are already too late. Pragmatists, (B) , deeply value the experience of their colleagues in other companies. When they buy, they expect extensive references, and they want a good number to come from companies in their own industry segment.

	(A)	(B)
①	therefore	on the other hand
②	however	in addition
③	nonetheless	at the same time
④	furthermore	in conclusion

17 주어진 문장이 들어갈 위치로 가장 적절한 것은?

> Some of these ailments are short-lived; others may be long-lasting.

For centuries, humans have looked up at the sky and wondered what exists beyond the realm of our planet. (①) Ancient astronomers examined the night sky hoping to learn more about the universe. More recently, some movies explored the possibility of sustaining human life in outer space, while other films have questioned whether extraterrestrial life forms may have visited our planet. (②) Since astronaut Yuri Gagarin became the first man to travel in space in 1961, scientists have researched what conditions are like beyond the Earth's atmosphere, and what effects space travel has on the human body. (③) Although most astronauts do not spend more than a few months in space, many experience physiological and psychological problems when they return to the Earth. (④) More than two-thirds of all astronauts suffer from motion sickness while traveling in space. In the gravity-free environment, the body cannot differentiate up from down. The body's internal balance system sends confusing signals to the brain, which can result in nausea lasting as long as a few days.

18 밑줄 친 부분에 들어갈 말로 가장 적절한 것은?

> Why bother with the history of everything? _____. In literature classes you don't learn about genes; in physics classes you don't learn about human evolution. So you get a partial view of the world. That makes it hard to find *meaning* in education. The French sociologist Emile Durkheim called this sense of disorientation and meaninglessness *anomie*, and he argued that it could lead to despair and even suicide. The German sociologist Max Weber talked of the "disenchantment" of the world. In the past, people had a unified vision of their world, a vision usually provided by the origin stories of their own religious traditions. That unified vision gave a sense of purpose, of meaning, even of enchantment to the world and to life. Today, though, many writers have argued that a sense of meaninglessness is inevitable in a world of science and rationality. Modernity, it seems, means meaninglessness.

① In the past, the study of history required disenchantment from science

② Recently, science has given us lots of clever tricks and meanings

③ Today, we teach and learn about our world in fragments

④ Lately, history has been divided into several categories

19 다음 글의 내용과 일치하지 <u>않는</u> 것은?

The earliest government food service programs began around 1900 in Europe. Programs in the United States date from the Great Depression, when the need to use surplus agricultural commodities was joined to concern for feeding the children of poor families. During and after World War II, the explosion in the number of working women fueled the need for a broader program. What was once a function of the family—providing lunch—was shifted to the school food service system. The National School Lunch Program is the result of these efforts. The program is designed to provide federally assisted meals to children of school age. From the end of World War II to the early 1980s, funding for school food service expanded steadily. Today it helps to feed children in almost 100,000 schools across the United States. Its first function is to provide a nutritious lunch to all students; the second is to provide nutritious food at both breakfast and lunch to underprivileged children. If anything, the role of school food service as a replacement for what was once a family function has been expanded.

① The increase in the number of working women boosted the expansion of food service programs.

② The US government began to feed poor children during the Great Depression despite the food shortage.

③ The US school food service system presently helps to feed children of poor families.

④ The function of providing lunch has been shifted from the family to schools.

20 주어진 문장 다음에 이어질 글의 순서로 가장 적절한 것은?

South Korea boasts of being the most wired nation on earth.

(A) This addiction has become a national issue in Korea in recent years, as users started dropping dead from exhaustion after playing online games for days on end. A growing number of students have skipped school to stay online, shockingly self-destructive behavior in this intensely competitive society.

(B) In fact, perhaps no other country has so fully embraced the Internet.

(C) But such ready access to the Web has come at a price as legions of obsessed users find that they cannot tear themselves away from their computer screens.

① (A) – (B) – (C)　　② (A) – (C) – (B)
③ (B) – (A) – (C)　　④ (B) – (C) – (A)

정답 · 해석 · 해설 p. 50

6회 2019년 국가직 9급
모바일 자동 채점 + 성적 분석 서비스 바로 가기

QR코드를 이용해 모바일로 간편하게 채점하고 나의 실력이 어느 정도인지, 취약 부분이 어디인지 바로 파악해 보세요.

(p.212에서 전체 정답표를 확인하실 수 있습니다)

제한 시간 : 20분　　시작 _____시 _____분 ~ 종료 _____시 _____분　　　나의 점수 _____　회독 수 ☐☐☐

※ 밑줄 친 부분에 들어갈 말로 가장 적절한 것을 고르시오.
[01~02]

01

> A: Can I ask you for a favor?
> B: Yes, what is it?
> A: I need to get to the airport for my business trip, but my car won't start. Can you give me a lift?
> B: Sure. When do you need to be there by?
> A: I have to be there no later than 6 : 00.
> B: It's 4 : 30 now. _____. We'll have to leave right away.

① That's cutting it close
② I took my eye off the ball
③ All that glitters is not gold
④ It's water under the bridge

02

> Fear of loss is a basic part of being human. To the brain, loss is a threat and we naturally take measures to avoid it. We cannot, however, avoid it indefinitely. One way to face loss is with the perspective of a stock trader. Traders accept the possibility of loss as part of the game, not the end of the game. What guides this thinking is a portfolio approach; wins and losses will both happen, but it's the overall portfolio of outcomes that matters most. When you embrace a portfolio approach, you will be _____ because you know that they are small parts of a much bigger picture.

① less inclined to dwell on individual losses
② less interested in your investments
③ more averse to the losses
④ more sensitive to fluctuations in the stock market

03 다음 글의 제목으로 가장 적절한 것은?

> Over the last years of traveling, I've observed how much we humans live in the past. The past is around us constantly, considering that, the minute something is manifested, it is the past. Our surroundings, our homes, our environments, our architecture, our products are all past constructs. We should live with what is part of our time, part of our collective consciousness, those things that were produced during our lives. Of course, we do not have the choice or control to have everything around us relevant or conceived during our time, but what we do have control of should be a reflection of the time in which we exist and communicate the present. The present is all we have, and the more we are surrounded by it, the more we are aware of our own presence and participation.

① Travel: Tracing the Legacies of the Past
② Reflect on the Time That Surrounds You Now
③ Manifestation of a Hidden Life
④ Architecture of a Futuristic Life

04 밑줄 친 부분 중 어법상 옳지 <u>않은</u> 것은?

> It would be difficult ① to imagine life without the beauty and richness of forests. But scientists warn we cannot take our forest for ② granted. By some estimates, deforestation ③ has been resulted in the loss of as much as eighty percent of the natural forests of the world. Currently, deforestation is a global problem, ④ affecting wilderness regions such as the temperate rainforests of the Pacific.

05 밑줄 친 부분의 의미와 가장 가까운 것은?

Robert J. Flaherty, a legendary documentary filmmaker, tried to show how indigenous people gathered food.

① native
② ravenous
③ impoverished
④ itinerant

06 밑줄 친 부분에 들어갈 말로 가장 적절한 것은?

Listening to music is _____ being a rock star. Anyone can listen to music, but it takes talent to become a musician.

① on a par with
② a far cry from
③ contingent upon
④ a prelude to

07 다음 글의 흐름상 가장 어색한 문장은?

Biologists have identified a gene that will allow rice plants to survive being submerged in water for up to two weeks—over a week longer than at present. Plants under water for longer than a week are deprived of oxygen and wither and perish. ① The scientists hope their discovery will prolong the harvests of crops in regions that are susceptible to flooding. ② Rice growers in these flood-prone areas of Asia lose an estimated one billion dollars annually to excessively waterlogged rice paddies. ③ They hope the new gene will lead to a hardier rice strain that will reduce the financial damage incurred in typhoon and monsoon seasons and lead to bumper harvests. ④ This is dreadful news for people in these vulnerable regions, who are victims of urbanization and have a shortage of crops. Rice yields must increase by 30 percent over the next 20 years to ensure a billion people can receive their staple diet.

08 밑줄 친 부분에 들어갈 말로 가장 적절한 것은?

A: Do you know how to drive?
B: Of course. I'm a great driver.
A: Could you teach me how to drive?
B: Do you have a learner's permit?
A: Yes, I got it just last week.
B: Have you been behind the steering wheel yet?
A: No, but I can't wait to _____.

① take a rain check
② get my feet wet
③ get an oil change
④ change a flat tire

09 다음 글의 내용과 일치하는 것은?

Sharks are covered in scales made from the same material as teeth. These flexible scales protect the shark and help it swim quickly in water. A shark can move the scales as it swims. This movement helps reduce the water's drag. Amy Lang, an aerospace engineer at the University of Alabama, studies the scales on the shortfin mako, a relative of the great white shark. Lang and her team discovered that the mako shark's scales differ in size and in flexibility in different parts of its body. For instance, the scales on the sides of the body are tapered—wide at one end and narrow at the other end. Because they are tapered, these scales move very easily. They can turn up or flatten to adjust to the flow of water around the shark and to reduce drag. Lang feels that shark scales can inspire designs for machines that experience drag, such as airplanes.

① A shark has scales that always remain immobile to protect itself as it swims.
② Lang revealed that the scales of a mako shark are utilized to lessen drag in water.
③ A mako shark has scales of identical size all over its body.
④ The scientific designs of airplanes were inspired by shark scales.

10 밑줄 친 부분 중 어법상 옳지 <u>않은</u> 것은?

Focus means ① <u>getting stuff done</u>. A lot of people have great ideas but don't act on them. For me, the definition of an entrepreneur, for instance, is someone who can combine innovation and ingenuity with the ability to execute that new idea. Some people think that the central dichotomy in life is whether you're positive or negative about the issues ② <u>that interest or concern you</u>. There's a lot of attention ③ <u>paying to this question</u> of whether it's better to have an optimistic or pessimistic lens. I think the better question to ask is whether you are going to do something about it or just ④ <u>let life pass you by</u>.

11 밑줄 친 부분 중 글의 흐름상 가장 어색한 것은?

Most people like to talk, but few people like to listen, yet listening well is a ① <u>rare</u> talent that everyone should treasure. Because they hear more, good listeners tend to know more and to be more sensitive to what is going on around them than most people. In addition, good listeners are inclined to accept or tolerate rather than to judge and criticize. Therefore, they have ② <u>fewer</u> enemies than most people. In fact, they are probably the most beloved of people. However, there are ③ <u>exceptions</u> to that generality. For example, John Steinbeck is said to have been an excellent listener, yet he was hated by some of the people he wrote about. No doubt his ability to listen contributed to his capacity to write. Nevertheless, the result of his listening didn't make him ④ <u>unpopular</u>.

12 다음 글의 주제로 가장 적절한 것은?

Worry is like a rocking horse. No matter how fast you go, you never move anywhere. Worry is a complete waste of time and creates so much clutter in your mind that you cannot think clearly about anything. The way to learn to stop worrying is by first understanding that you energize whatever you focus your attention on. Therefore, the more you allow yourself to worry, the more likely things are to go wrong! Worrying becomes such an ingrained habit that to avoid it you consciously have to train yourself to do otherwise. Whenever you catch yourself having a fit of worry, stop and change your thoughts. Focus your mind more productively on what you do want to happen and dwell on what's already wonderful in your life so more wonderful stuff will come your way.

① What effects does worry have on life?
② Where does worry originate from?
③ When should we worry?
④ How do we cope with worrying?

13 다음 글의 내용과 일치하지 <u>않는</u> 것은?

Students at Macaulay Honors College (MHC) don't stress about the high price of tuition. That's because theirs is free. At Macaulay and a handful of other service academies, work colleges, single-subject schools and conservatories, 100 percent of the student body receive a full tuition scholarship for all four years. Macaulay students also receive a laptop and $7,500 in "opportunities funds" to pursue research, service experiences, study abroad programs and internships. "The most important thing is not the free tuition, but the freedom of studying without the burden of debt on your back," says Ann Kirschner, university dean of Macaulay Honors College. The debt burden, she says, "really compromises decisions students make in college, and we are giving them the opportunity to be free of that." Schools that grant free tuition to all students are rare, but a greater number of institutions provide scholarships to enrollees with high grades. Institutions such as Indiana University Bloomington offer automatic awards to high-performing students with stellar GPAs and class ranks.

① MHC에서는 모든 학생이 4년간 수업료를 내지 않는다.
② MHC에서는 학생들에게 컴퓨터 구입 비용과 교외활동 비용을 합하여 $7,500를 지급한다.
③ 수업료로 인한 빚 부담이 있으면 학생들이 자유롭게 공부할 수 없다고 Kirschner 학장은 말한다.
④ MHC와 달리 학업 우수자에게만 장학금을 주는 대학도 있다.

※ 밑줄 친 부분의 의미와 가장 가까운 것을 고르시오.
[14~15]

14

The police spent seven months working on the crime case but were never able to determine the identity of the <u>malefactor</u>.

① culprit ② dilettante
③ pariah ④ demagogue

15

While at first glance it seems that his friends are just leeches, they prove to be the ones he can depend on <u>through thick and thin</u>.

① in no time
② from time to time
③ in pleasant times
④ in good times and bad times

16 주어진 문장이 들어갈 위치로 가장 적절한 것은?

Some remain intensely proud of their original accent and dialect words, phrases and gestures, while others accommodate rapidly to a new environment by changing their speech habits, so that they no longer "stand out in the crowd."

Our perceptions and production of speech change with time. (①) If we were to leave our native place for an extended period, our perception that the new accents around us were strange would only be temporary. (②) Gradually, we will lose the sense that others have an accent and we will begin to fit in—to accommodate our speech patterns to the new norm. (③) Not all people do this to the same degree. (④) Whether they do this consciously or not is open to debate and may differ from individual to individual, but like most processes that have to do with language, the change probably happens before we are aware of it and probably couldn't happen if we were.

17 다음 글의 내용과 일치하지 <u>않는</u> 것은?

Insomnia can be classified as transient, acute, or chronic. Transient insomnia lasts for less than a week. It can be caused by another disorder, by changes in the sleep environment, by the timing of sleep, severe depression, or by stress. Its consequences such as sleepiness and impaired psychomotor performance are similar to those of sleep deprivation. Acute insomnia is the inability to consistently sleep well for a period of less than a month. Acute insomnia is present when there is difficulty initiating or maintaining sleep or when the sleep that is obtained is not refreshing. These problems occur despite adequate opportunity and circumstances for sleep and they can impair daytime functioning. Acute insomnia is also known as short term insomnia or stress related insomnia. Chronic insomnia lasts for longer than a month. It can be caused by another disorder, or it can be a primary disorder. People with high levels of stress hormones or shifts in the levels of cytokines are more likely than others to have chronic insomnia. Its effects can vary according to its causes. They might include muscular weariness, hallucinations, and/or mental fatigue. Chronic insomnia can also cause double vision.

* cytokines: groups of molecules released by certain cells of the immune system

① Insomnia can be classified according to its duration.
② Transient insomnia occurs solely due to an inadequate sleep environment.
③ Acute insomnia is generally known to be related to stress.
④ Chronic insomnia patients may suffer from hallucinations.

18 밑줄 친 부분에 들어갈 말로 가장 적절한 것은?

Kisha Padbhan, founder of Everonn Education, in Mumbai, looks at his business as nation-building. India's student-age population of 230 million (kindergarten to college) is one of the largest in the world. The government spends $83 billion on instruction, but there are serious gaps. "There aren't enough teachers and enough teacher-training institutes," says Kisha. "What children in remote parts of India lack is access to good teachers and exposure to good-quality content." Everonn's solution? The company uses a satellite network, with two-way video and audio _____

_____.

It reaches 1,800 colleges and 7,800 schools across 24 of India's 28 states. It offers everything from digitized school lessons to entrance exam prep for aspiring engineers and has training for job-seekers, too.

① to improve the quality of teacher training facilities
② to bridge the gap through virtual classrooms
③ to get students familiarized with digital technology
④ to locate qualified instructors across the nation

19 주어진 문장 다음에 이어질 글의 순서로 가장 적절한 것은?

> A technique that enables an individual to gain some voluntary control over autonomic, or involuntary, body functions by observing electronic measurements of those functions is known as biofeedback.

> (A) When such a variable moves in the desired direction (for example, blood pressure down), it triggers visual or audible displays—feedback on equipment such as television sets, gauges, or lights.
> (B) Electronic sensors are attached to various parts of the body to measure such variables as heart rate, blood pressure, and skin temperature.
> (C) Biofeedback training teaches one to produce a desired response by reproducing thought patterns or actions that triggered the displays.

① (A) – (B) – (C)
② (B) – (C) – (A)
③ (B) – (A) – (C)
④ (C) – (A) – (B)

20 우리말을 영어로 잘못 옮긴 것은?

① 그 연사는 자기 생각을 청중에게 전달하는 데 능숙하지 않았다.
　→ The speaker was not good at getting his ideas across to the audience.

② 서울의 교통 체증은 세계 어느 도시보다 심각하다.
　→ The traffic jams in Seoul are more serious than those in any other city in the world.

③ 네가 말하고 있는 사람과 시선을 마주치는 것은 서양 국가에서 중요하다.
　→ Making eye contact with the person you are speaking to is important in western countries.

④ 그는 사람들이 생각했던 만큼 인색하지 않았다는 것이 드러났다.
　→ It turns out that he was not so stingier as he was thought to be.

정답 · 해석 · 해설 p. 59

7회 2018년 국가직 9급
모바일 자동 채점 + 성적 분석 서비스 바로 가기

QR코드를 이용해 모바일로 간편하게 채점하고 나의 실력이 어느 정도인지, 취약 부분이 어디인지 바로 파악해 보세요.

(p.212에서 전체 정답표를 확인하실 수 있습니다)

*IF I ONLY HAD AN HOUR TO CHOP DOWN A TREE,
I WOULD SPEND THE FIRST 45 MINUTES
SHARPENING MY AXE.*

ABRAHAM LINCOLN

**만약 내게 나무를 베는 데 한 시간이 주어진다면,
나는 도끼를 가는 데 45분을 쓸 것이다.**
에이브러햄 링컨

Part 2
지방직 9급

문제 유형	4지선다형
총 문항 수	20문항
경쟁률 (2024년 6월, 행정직군)	평균: 23.4:1 최고: 100.5:1 (광주) *서울시: 22.7:1
합격선 (2024년 6월, 행정직군)	평균: 80점 최고: 90점 (대구, 광주) *서울시: 88점
시험 안내	사이버국가고시센터 (https://gosi.kr) 자치단체 통합 인터넷원서접수센터 (https://local.gosi.go.kr)

제한 시간 : 20분   시작 _____시 _____분 ~ 종료 _____시 _____분   나의 점수 _____   회독 수 ☐☐☐

※ 밑줄 친 부분의 의미와 가장 가까운 것을 고르시오.
[01~04]

01

> While Shakespeare's comedies share many similarities, they also differ <u>markedly</u> from one another.

① softly
② obviously
③ marginally
④ indiscernibly

02

> Jane poured out the strong, dark tea and <u>diluted</u> it with milk.

① washed
② weakened
③ connected
④ fermented

03

> The Prime Minister is believed to have <u>ruled out</u> cuts in child benefit or pensions.

① excluded
② supported
③ submitted
④ authorized

04

> If you <u>let on</u> that we are planning a surprise party, Dad will never stop asking you questions.

① reveal
② observe
③ believe
④ possess

05 밑줄 친 부분에 들어갈 말로 가장 적절한 것은?

> Automatic doors in supermarkets _____ the entry and exit of customers with bags or shopping carts.

① ignore
② forgive
③ facilitate
④ exaggerate

06 밑줄 친 부분 중 어법상 옳지 않은 것은?

> One of the many ① <u>virtues</u> of the book you are reading ② <u>is</u> that it provides an entry point into *Maps of Meaning*, ③ <u>which</u> is a highly complex work ④ <u>because of</u> the author was working out his approach to psychology as he wrote it.

07 밑줄 친 부분이 어법상 옳지 않은 것은?

① You must plan <u>not to spend</u> too much on the project.

② My dog <u>disappeared</u> last month and hasn't been seen since.

③ I'm sad that the people <u>who</u> daughter I look after are moving away.

④ I bought a book on my trip, and it was <u>twice as expensive as</u> it was at home.

08 우리말을 영어로 잘못 옮긴 것은?

① 그는 이곳에서 일하는 것이 흥미롭다는 것을 알았다.
→ He found it exciting to work here.

② 그녀는 나에게 일찍 떠날 것이라고 언급했다.
→ She mentioned me that she would be leaving early.

③ 나는 그가 오는 것을 원하지 않았다.
→ I didn't want him to come.

④ 좀 더 능숙하고 경험 많은 선생님이었다면 그를 달리 대했을 것이다.
→ A more skillful and experienced teacher would have treated him otherwise.

※ 밑줄 친 부분에 들어갈 말로 가장 적절한 것을 고르시오.
[09~11]

09

A: Charles, I think we need more chairs for our upcoming event.

B: Really? I thought we already had enough chairs.

A: My manager told me that more than 350 people are coming.

B: _____

A: I agree. I am also a bit surprised.

B: Looks like I'll have to order more then. Thanks.

① I wonder if the manager is going to attend the event.

② I thought more than 350 people would be coming.

③ That's actually not a large number.

④ That's a lot more than I expected.

10

A: Can I get the document you referred to at the meeting yesterday?

B: Sure. What's the title of the document?

A: I can't remember its title, but it was about the community festival.

B: Oh, I know what you're talking about.

A: Great. Can you send it to me via email?

B: I don't have it with me. Mr. Park is in charge of the project, so he should have it.

A: _____

B: Good luck. Hope you get the document you want.

① Can you check if he is in the office?

② Mr. Park has sent the email to you again.

③ Are you coming to the community festival?

④ Thank you for letting me know. I'll contact him.

11

A: Hello, can I ask you a question about the presentation next Tuesday?

B: Do you mean the presentation about promoting the volunteer program?

A: Yes. Where is the presentation going to be?

B: Let me check. It is room 201.

A: I see. Can I use my laptop in the room?

B: Sure. We have a PC in the room, but you can use yours if you want.

A: _____

B: We can meet in the room two hours before the presentation. Would that work for you?

A: Yes. Thank you very much!

① A computer technician was here an hour ago.

② When can I have a rehearsal for my presentation?

③ Should we recruit more volunteers for our program?

④ I don't feel comfortable leaving my laptop in the room.

12 다음 이메일의 내용과 일치하지 않는 것은?

To	reserve@metropolitan.com
From	BruceTaylor@westcity.com
Date	June 22, 2024
Subject	Venue facilities

Dear Sir,

I am writing to ask for information about Metropolitan Conference Center.

We are looking for a venue for a three-day conference in September this year. We need to have enough room for over 200 delegates in your main conference room, and we would also like three small conference rooms for meetings. Each conference room needs wi-fi as well. We need to have coffee available mid-morning and mid-afternoon, and we would also like to book your restaurant for lunch on all three days.

In addition, could you please let me know if there are any local hotels with discount rates for Metropolitan clients or large groups? We will need accommodations for over 100 delegates each night.

I look forward to hearing from you.

Best regards,
Bruce Taylor, Event Manager

① 주 회의실은 200명 이상의 대표자를 수용할 수 있어야 한다.
② wi-fi가 있는 작은 회의실 3개가 필요하다.
③ 3일간의 저녁 식사를 위한 식당 예약이 필요하다.
④ 매일 밤 100명 이상의 대표자를 위한 숙박시설이 필요하다.

13 다음 글의 내용과 일치하지 않는 것은?

According to the historians, neckties date back to 1660. In that year, a group of soldiers from Croatia visited Paris. These soldiers were war heroes whom King Louis XIV admired very much. Impressed with the colored scarves that they wore around their necks, the king decided to honor the Croats by creating a military regiment called the Royal Cravattes. The word *cravat* comes from the word *Croat*. All the soldiers in this regiment wore colorful scarves or cravats around their necks. This new style of neckwear traveled to England. Soon all upper class men were wearing cravats. Some cravats were quite extreme. At times, they were so high that a man could not move his head without turning his whole body. The cravats were made of many different materials from plaid to lace, which made them suitable for any occasion.

① A group of Croatian soldiers visited Paris in 1660.
② The Royal Cravattes was created in honor of the Croatian soldiers wearing scarves.
③ Some cravats were too uncomfortable for a man to move his head freely.
④ The materials used to make the cravats were limited.

14 다음 글의 주제로 적절한 것은?

In recent years Latin America has made huge strides in exploiting its incredible wind, solar, geothermal and biofuel energy resources. Latin America's electricity sector has already begun to gradually decrease its dependence on oil. Latin America is expected to almost double its electricity output between 2015 and 2040. Practically none of Latin America's new large-scale power plants will be oil-fueled, which opens up the field for different technologies. Countries in Central America and the Caribbean, which traditionally imported oil, were the first to move away from oil-based power plants, after suffering a decade of high and volatile prices at the start of the century.

① booming oil industry in Latin America
② declining electricity business in Latin America
③ advancement of renewable energy in Latin America
④ aggressive exploitation of oil-based resources in Latin America

15 다음 글의 제목으로 적절한 것은?

Every organization has resources that it can use to perform its mission. How well your organization does its job is partly a function of how many of those resources you have, but mostly it is a function of how well you use the resources you have, such as people and money. You as the organization's leader can always make the use of those resources more efficient and effective, provided that you have control of the organization's personnel and agenda, a condition that does not occur automatically. By managing your people and your money carefully, by treating the most important things as the most important, by making good decisions, and by solving the problems that you encounter, you can get the most out of what you have available to you.

① Exchanging Resources in an Organization
② Leaders' Ability to Set up External Control
③ Making the Most of the Resources: A Leader's Way
④ Technical Capacity of an Organization: A Barrier to Its Success

16 다음 글의 흐름상 어색한 문장은?

Critical thinking sounds like an unemotional process but it can engage emotions and even passionate responses. In particular, we may not like evidence that contradicts our own opinions or beliefs. ① If the evidence points in a direction that is challenging, that can rouse unexpected feelings of anger, frustration or anxiety. ② The academic world traditionally likes to consider itself as logical and free of emotions, so if feelings do emerge, this can be especially difficult. ③ For example, looking at the same information from several points of view is not important. ④ Being able to manage your emotions under such circumstances is a useful skill. If you can remain calm, and present your reasons logically, you will be better able to argue your point of view in a convincing way.

17 주어진 글 다음에 이어질 글의 순서로 적절한 것은?

Computer assisted language learning (CALL) is both exciting and frustrating as a field of research and practice.

(A) Yet the technology changes so rapidly that CALL knowledge and skills must be constantly renewed to stay apace of the field.

(B) It is exciting because it is complex, dynamic and quickly changing — and it is frustrating for the same reasons.

(C) Technology adds dimensions to the domain of language learning, requiring new knowledge and skills for those who wish to apply it into their professional practice.

① (A) – (C) – (B)
② (B) – (A) – (C)
③ (B) – (C) – (A)
④ (C) – (B) – (A)

18 주어진 문장이 들어갈 위치로 적절한 것은?

But she quickly popped her head out again.

The little mermaid swam right up to the small window of the cabin, and every time a wave lifted her up, she could see a crowd of well-dressed people through the clear glass. Among them was a young prince, the handsomest person there, with large dark eyes. (①) It was his birthday, and that's why there was so much excitement. (②) When the young prince came out on the deck, where the sailors were dancing, more than a hundred rockets went up into the sky and broke into a glitter, making the sky as bright as day. (③) The little mermaid was so startled that she dove down under the water. (④) And look! It was just as if all the stars up in heaven were falling down on her. Never had she seen such fireworks.

※ 밑줄 친 부분에 들어갈 말로 적절한 것을 고르시오.

[19~20]

19

Javelin Research noticed that not all Millennials are currently in the same stage of life. While all Millennials were born around the turn of the century, some of them are still in early adulthood, wrestling with new careers and settling down. On the other hand, the older Millennials have a home and are building a family. You can imagine how having a child might change your interests and priorities, so for marketing purposes, it's useful to split this generation into Gen Y.1 and Gen Y.2. Not only are the two groups culturally different, but they're in vastly different phases of their financial life. The younger group is financial beginners, just starting to show their buying power. The latter group has a credit history, may have their first mortgage and is raising young children. The _____ in priorities and needs between Gen Y.1 and Gen Y.2 is vast.

① contrast
② reduction
③ repetition
④ ability

20

Cost pressures in liberalized markets have different effects on existing and future hydropower schemes. Because of the cost structure, existing hydropower plants will always be able to earn a profit. Because the planning and construction of future hydropower schemes is not a short-term process, it is not a popular investment, in spite of low electricity generation costs. Most private investors would prefer to finance _____, leading to the paradoxical situation that although an existing hydropower plant seems to be a cash cow, nobody wants to invest in a new one. Where public shareholders/owners (states, cities, municipalities) are involved, the situation looks very different because they can see the importance of the security of supply and also appreciate long-term investments.

① more short-term technologies
② all high technology industries
③ the promotion of the public interest
④ the enhancement of electricity supply

정답·해석·해설 p. 72

8회 2024년 지방직 9급
모바일 자동 채점 + 성적 분석 서비스 바로 가기

QR코드를 이용해 모바일로 간편하게 채점하고 나의 실력이 어느 정도인지, 취약 부분이 어디인지 바로 파악해 보세요.

(p.212에서 전체 정답표를 확인하실 수 있습니다)

※ 밑줄 친 부분의 의미와 가장 가까운 것을 고르시오.
[01~04]

01

> Further explanations on our project will be given in subsequent presentations.

① required
② following
③ advanced
④ supplementary

02

> Folkways are customs that members of a group are expected to follow to show courtesy to others. For example, saying "excuse me" when you sneeze is an American folkway.

① charity
② humility
③ boldness
④ politeness

03

> These children have been brought up on a diet of healthy food.

① raised
② advised
③ observed
④ controlled

04

> Slavery was not done away with until the nineteenth century in the U.S.

① abolished
② consented
③ criticized
④ justified

05 밑줄 친 부분에 들어갈 말로 가장 적절한 것은?

> Voters demanded that there should be greater _____ in the election process so that they could see and understand it clearly.

① deception
② flexibility
③ competition
④ transparency

06 밑줄 친 부분 중 어법상 옳지 않은 것은?

> One reason for upsets in sports—① in which the team ② predicted to win and supposedly superior to their opponents surprisingly loses the contest—is ③ what the superior team may not have perceived their opponents as ④ threatening to their continued success.

07 밑줄 친 부분이 어법상 옳지 않은 것은?

① I should have gone this morning, but I was feeling a bit ill.

② These days we do not save as much money as we used to.

③ The rescue squad was happy to discover an alive man.

④ The picture was looked at carefully by the art critic.

08 우리말을 영어로 잘못 옮긴 것은?

① 우리는 그의 연설에 감동하게 되었다.
  → We were made touching with his speech.

② 비용은 차치하고 그 계획은 훌륭한 것이었다.
  → Apart from its cost, the plan was a good one.

③ 그들은 뜨거운 차를 마시는 동안에 일몰을 보았다.
  → They watched the sunset while drinking hot tea.

④ 과거 경력 덕분에 그는 그 프로젝트에 적합하였다.
  → His past experience made him suited for the project.

※ 밑줄 친 부분에 들어갈 말로 가장 적절한 것을 고르시오.
[09~10]

09

> A: Pardon me, but could you give me a hand, please?
> B: _____
> A: I'm trying to find the Personnel Department. I have an appointment at 10.
> B: It's on the third floor.
> A: How can I get up there?
> B: Take the elevator around the corner.

① We have no idea how to handle this situation.

② Would you mind telling us who is in charge?

③ Yes. I could use some help around here.

④ Sure. Can I help you with anything?

10

> A: You were the last one who left the office, weren't you?
> B: Yes. Is there any problem?
> A: I found the office lights and air conditioners on this morning.
> B: Really? Oh, no. Maybe I forgot to turn them off last night.
> A: Probably they were on all night.
> B: _____

① Don't worry. This machine is working fine.

② That's right. Everyone likes to work with you.

③ I'm sorry. I promise I'll be more careful from now on.

④ Too bad. You must be tired because you get off work too late.

11 두 사람의 대화 중 자연스럽지 않은 것은?

① A: How would you like your hair done?
   B: I'm a little tired of my hair color. I'd like to dye it.

② A: What can we do to slow down global warming?
   B: First of all, we can use more public transportation.

③ A: Anna, is that you? Long time no see! How long has it been?
   B: It took me about an hour and a half by car.

④ A: I'm worried about Paul. He looks unhappy. What should I do?
   B: If I were you, I'd wait until he talks about his troubles.

12 다음 글의 제목으로 가장 적절한 것은?

Well-known author Daniel Goleman has dedicated his life to the science of human relationships. In his book *Social Intelligence* he discusses results from neuro-sociology to explain how sociable our brains are. According to Goleman, we are drawn to other people's brains whenever we engage with another person. The human need for meaningful connectivity with others, in order to deepen our relationships, is what we all crave, and yet there are countless articles and studies suggesting that we are lonelier than we ever have been and loneliness is now a world health epidemic. Specifically, in Australia, according to a national Lifeline survey, more than 80 % of those surveyed believe our society is becoming a lonelier place. Yet, our brains crave human interaction.

① Lonely People
② Sociable Brains
③ Need for Mental Health Survey
④ Dangers of Human Connectivity

13 다음 글의 주제로 가장 적절한 것은?

Certainly some people are born with advantages (e.g., physical size for jockeys, height for basketball players, an "ear" for music for musicians). Yet only dedication to mindful, deliberate practice over many years can turn those advantages into talents and those talents into successes. Through the same kind of dedicated practice, people who are not born with such advantages can develop talents that nature put a little farther from their reach. For example, even though you may feel that you weren't born with a talent for math, you can significantly increase your mathematical abilities through mindful, deliberate practice. Or, if you consider yourself "naturally" shy, putting in the time and effort to develop your social skills can enable you to interact with people at social occasions with energy, grace, and ease.

① advantages some people have over others
② importance of constant efforts to cultivate talents
③ difficulties shy people have in social interactions
④ need to understand one's own strengths and weaknesses

14 다음 글의 요지로 가장 적절한 것은?

Dr. Roossinck and her colleagues found by chance that a virus increased resistance to drought on a plant that is widely used in botanical experiments. Their further experiments with a related virus showed that was true of 15 other plant species, too. Dr. Roossinck is now doing experiments to study another type of virus that increases heat tolerance in a range of plants. She hopes to extend her research to have a deeper understanding of the advantages that different sorts of viruses give to their hosts. That would help to support a view which is held by an increasing number of biologists, that many creatures rely on symbiosis, rather than being self-sufficient.

① Viruses demonstrate self-sufficiency of biological beings.
② Biologists should do everything to keep plants virus-free.
③ The principle of symbiosis cannot be applied to infected plants.
④ Viruses sometimes do their hosts good, rather than harming them.

15 다음 글의 내용과 일치하지 않는 것은?

The traditional way of making maple syrup is interesting. A sugar maple tree produces a watery sap each spring, when there is still lots of snow on the ground. To take the sap out of the sugar maple tree, a farmer makes a slit in the bark with a special knife, and puts a "tap" on the tree. Then the farmer hangs a bucket from the tap, and the sap drips into it. That sap is collected and boiled until a sweet syrup remains—forty gallons of sugar maple tree "water" make one gallon of syrup. That's a lot of buckets, a lot of steam, and a lot of work. Even so, most of maple syrup producers are family farmers who collect the buckets by hand and boil the sap into syrup themselves.

① 사탕단풍나무에서는 매년 봄에 수액이 생긴다.
② 사탕단풍나무의 수액을 얻기 위해 나무껍질에 틈새를 만든다.
③ 단풍나무시럽 1갤론을 만들려면 수액 40갤론이 필요하다.
④ 단풍나무시럽을 만들기 위해 기계로 수액 통을 수거한다.

16 다음 글의 흐름상 어색한 문장은?

I once took a course in short-story writing and during that course a renowned editor of a leading magazine talked to our class. ① He said he could pick up any one of the dozens of stories that came to his desk every day and after reading a few paragraphs he could feel whether or not the author liked people. ② "If the author doesn't like people," he said, "people won't like his or her stories." ③ The editor kept stressing the importance of being interested in people during his talk on fiction writing. ④ Thurston, a great magician, said that every time he went on stage he said to himself, "I am grateful because I'm successful." At the end of the talk, he concluded, "Let me tell you again. You have to be interested in people if you want to be a successful writer of stories."

17 주어진 글 다음에 이어질 글의 순서로 가장 적절한 것은?

Just a few years ago, every conversation about artificial intelligence (AI) seemed to end with an apocalyptic prediction.

(A) More recently, however, things have begun to change. AI has gone from being a scary black box to something people can use for a variety of use cases.

(B) In 2014, an expert in the field said that, with AI, we are summoning the demon, while a Nobel Prize winning physicist said that AI could spell the end of the human race.

(C) This shift is because these technologies are finally being explored at scale in the industry, particularly for market opportunities.

① (A) — (B) — (C)
② (B) — (A) — (C)
③ (B) — (C) — (A)
④ (C) — (A) — (B)

18 주어진 문장이 들어갈 위치로 가장 적절한 것은?

Yet, requests for such self-assessments are pervasive throughout one's career.

The fiscal quarter just ended. Your boss comes by to ask you how well you performed in terms of sales this quarter. How do you describe your performance? As excellent? Good? Terrible? (①) Unlike when someone asks you about an objective performance metric (e.g., how many dollars in sales you brought in this quarter), how to subjectively describe your performance is often unclear. There is no right answer. (②) You are asked to subjectively describe your own performance in school applications, in job applications, in interviews, in performance reviews, in meetings—the list goes on. (③) How you describe your performance is what we call your level of self-promotion. (④) Since self-promotion is a pervasive part of work, people who do more self-promotion may have better chances of being hired, being promoted, and getting a raise or a bonus.

※ 밑줄 친 부분에 들어갈 말로 가장 적절한 것을 고르시오.
[19~20]

19

We live in the age of anxiety. Because being anxious can be an uncomfortable and scary experience, we resort to conscious or unconscious strategies that help reduce anxiety in the moment—watching a movie or TV show, eating, video-game playing, and overworking. In addition, smartphones also provide a distraction any time of the day or night. Psychological research has shown that distractions serve as a common anxiety avoidance strategy. _____, however, these avoidance strategies make anxiety worse in the long run. Being anxious is like getting into quicksand—the more you fight it, the deeper you sink. Indeed, research strongly supports a well-known phrase that "What you resist, persists."

① Paradoxically
② Fortunately
③ Neutrally
④ Creatively

20

How many different ways do you get information? Some people might have six different kinds of communications to answer—text messages, voice mails, paper documents, regular mail, blog posts, messages on different online services. Each of these is a type of in-box, and each must be processed on a continuous basis. It's an endless process, but it doesn't have to be exhausting or stressful. Getting your information management down to a more manageable level and into a productive zone starts by _____.
Every place you have to go to check your messages or to read your incoming information is an in-box, and the more you have, the harder it is to manage everything. Cut the number of in-boxes you have down to the smallest number possible for you still to function in the ways you need to.

① setting several goals at once
② immersing yourself in incoming information
③ minimizing the number of in-boxes you have
④ choosing information you are passionate about

정답·해석·해설 p.80

9회 2023년 지방직 9급
모바일 자동 채점 + 성적 분석 서비스 바로 가기

QR코드를 이용해 모바일로 간편하게 채점하고 나의 실력이 어느 정도인지, 취약 부분이 어디인지 바로 파악해 보세요.

(p.212에서 전체 정답표를 확인하실 수 있습니다)

제한 시간 : 20분　　시작 ＿＿＿ 시 ＿＿＿ 분 ~ 종료 ＿＿＿ 시 ＿＿＿ 분　　나의 점수 ＿＿＿　회독 수 ☐ ☐ ☐

※ 밑줄 친 부분의 의미와 가장 가까운 것을 고르시오.
[01~03]

01

> School teachers have to be underline flexible to cope with different ability levels of the students.

① strong
② adaptable
③ honest
④ passionate

02

> Crop yields vary, improving in some areas and falling in others.

① change
② decline
③ expand
④ include

03

> I don't feel inferior to anyone with respect to my education.

① in danger of
② in spite of
③ in favor of
④ in terms of

04 밑줄 친 부분에 들어갈 말로 가장 적절한 것은?

> Sometimes we ＿＿＿＿＿ money long before the next payday.

① turn into
② start over
③ put up with
④ run out of

※ 어법상 옳지 않은 것을 고르시오.
[05~06]

05

① He asked me why I kept coming back day after day.
② Toys children wanted all year long has recently discarded.
③ She is someone who is always ready to lend a helping hand.
④ Insects are often attracted by scents that aren't obvious to us.

06

① You can write on both sides of the paper.
② My home offers me a feeling of security, warm, and love.
③ The number of car accidents is on the rise.
④ Had I realized what you were intending to do, I would have stopped you.

※ 우리말을 영어로 잘못 옮긴 것을 고르시오.
[07~08]

07

① 나는 단 한 푼의 돈도 낭비할 수 없다.
→ I can afford to waste even one cent.
② 그녀의 얼굴에서 미소가 곧 사라졌다.
→ The smile soon faded from her face.
③ 그녀는 사임하는 것 외에는 대안이 없었다.
→ She had no alternative but to resign.
④ 나는 5년 후에 내 사업을 시작할 작정이다.
→ I'm aiming to start my own business in five years.

08

① 식사를 마치자마자 나는 다시 배고프기 시작했다.
→ No sooner I have finishing the meal than I started feeling hungry again.

② 그녀는 조만간 요금을 내야만 할 것이다.
→ She will have to pay the bill sooner or later.

③ 독서와 정신의 관계는 운동과 신체의 관계와 같다.
→ Reading is to the mind what exercise is to the body.

④ 그는 대학에서 의학을 공부했으나 결국 회계 회사에서 일하게 되었다.
→ He studied medicine at university but ended up working for an accounting firm.

09 두 사람의 대화 중 가장 어색한 것은?

① A: I like this newspaper because it's not opinionated.
B: That's why it has the largest circulation.

② A: Do you have a good reason for being all dressed up?
B: Yeah, I have an important job interview today.

③ A: I can hit the ball straight during the practice but not during the game.
B: That happens to me all the time, too.

④ A: Is there any particular subject you want to paint on canvas?
B: I didn't do good in history when I was in high school.

10 밑줄 친 부분에 들어갈 말로 가장 적절한 것은?

A: Hey! How did your geography test go?
B: Not bad, thanks. I'm just glad that it's over! How about you? How did your science exam go?
A: Oh, it went really well. _____.
   I owe you a treat for that.
B: It's my pleasure. So, do you feel like preparing for the math exam scheduled for next week?
A: Sure. Let's study together.
B: It sounds good. See you later.

① There's no sense in beating yourself up over this
② I never thought I would see you here
③ Actually, we were very disappointed
④ I can't thank you enough for helping me with it

11 주어진 글 다음에 이어질 글의 순서로 가장 적절한 것은?

For people who are blind, everyday tasks such as sorting through the mail or doing a load of laundry present a challenge.

(A) That's the thinking behind Aira, a new service that enables its thousands of users to stream live video of their surroundings to an on-demand agent, using either a smartphone or Aira's proprietary glasses.

(B) But what if they could "borrow" the eyes of someone who could see?

(C) The Aira agents, who are available 24/7, can then answer questions, describe objects or guide users through a location.

① (A) — (B) — (C)　　② (A) — (C) — (B)
③ (B) — (A) — (C)　　④ (C) — (A) — (B)

12 주어진 문장이 들어갈 위치로 가장 적절한 곳은?

> The comparison of the heart to a pump, however, is a genuine analogy.

An analogy is a figure of speech in which two things are asserted to be alike in many respects that are quite fundamental. Their structure, the relationships of their parts, or the essential purposes they serve are similar, although the two things are also greatly dissimilar. Roses and carnations are not analogous. (①) They both have stems and leaves and may both be red in color. (②) But they exhibit these qualities in the same way; they are of the same genus. (③) These are disparate things, but they share important qualities: mechanical apparatus, possession of valves, ability to increase and decrease pressures, and capacity to move fluids. (④) And the heart and the pump exhibit these qualities in different ways and in different contexts.

13 다음 글의 제목으로 가장 적절한 것은?

One of the areas where efficiency can be optimized is the work force, through increasing individual productivity—defined as the amount of work (products produced, customers served) an employee handles in a given time. In addition to making sure you have invested in the right equipment, environment, and training to ensure optimal performance, you can increase productivity by encouraging staffers to put an end to a modern-day energy drain: multitasking. Studies show it takes 25 to 40 percent longer to get a job done when you're simultaneously trying to work on other projects. To be more productive, says Andrew Deutscher, vice president of business development at consulting firm The Energy Project, "do one thing, uninterrupted, for a sustained period of time."

① How to Create More Options in Life
② How to Enhance Daily Physical Performance
③ Multitasking is the Answer for Better Efficiency
④ Do One Thing at a Time for Greater Efficiency

14 글의 흐름상 가장 어색한 문장은?

The skill to have a good argument is critical in life. But it's one that few parents teach to their children. ① We want to give kids a stable home, so we stop siblings from quarreling and we have our own arguments behind closed doors. ② Yet if kids never get exposed to disagreement, we may eventually limit their creativity. ③ Children are most creative when they are free to brainstorm with lots of praise and encouragement in a peaceful environment. ④ It turns out that highly creative people often grow up in families full of tension. They are not surrounded by fistfights or personal insults, but real disagreements. When adults in their early 30s were asked to write imaginative stories, the most creative ones came from those whose parents had the most conflict a quarter-century earlier.

15

Christopher Nolan is an Irish writer of some renown in the English language. Brain damaged since birth, Nolan has had little control over the muscles of his body, even to the extent of having difficulty in swallowing food. He must be strapped to his wheelchair because he cannot sit up by himself. Nolan cannot utter recognizable speech sounds. Fortunately, though, his brain damage was such that Nolan's intelligence was undamaged and his hearing was normal; as a result, he learned to understand speech as a young child. It was only many years later, though, after he had reached 10 years, and after he had learned to read, that he was given a means to express his first words. He did this by using a stick which was attached to his head to point to letters. It was in this 'unicorn' manner, letter-by-letter, that he produced an entire book of poems and short stories, *Dam-Burst of Dreams*, while still a teenager.

① Christopher Nolan은 뇌 손상을 갖고 태어났다.
② Christopher Nolan은 음식을 삼키는 것도 어려웠다.
③ Christopher Nolan은 청각 장애로 인해 들을 수 없었다.
④ Christopher Nolan은 10대일 때 책을 썼다.

16

In many Catholic countries, children are often named after saints; in fact, some priests will not allow parents to name their children after soap opera stars or football players. Protestant countries tend to be more free about this; however, in Norway, certain names such as Adolf are banned completely. In countries where infant mortality is very high, such as in Africa, tribes only name their children when they reach five years old, the age in which their chances of survival begin to increase. Until that time, they are referred to by the number of years they are. Many nations in the Far East give their children a unique name which in some way describes the circumstances of the child's birth or the parents' expectations and hopes for the child. Some Australian aborigines can keep changing their name throughout their life as the result of some important experience which has in some way proved their wisdom, creativity or determination. For example, if one day, one of them dances extremely well, he or she may decide to re-name him/herself 'supreme dancer' or 'light feet'.

① Children are frequently named after saints in many Catholic countries.
② Some African children are not named until they turn five years old.
③ Changing one's name is totally unacceptable in the culture of Australian aborigines.
④ Various cultures name their children in different ways.

17 다음 글의 요지로 가장 적절한 것은?

In one study, done in the early 1970s when young people tended to dress in either "hippie" or "straight" fashion, experimenters donned hippie or straight attire and asked college students on campus for a dime to make a phone call. When the experimenter was dressed in the same way as the student, the request was granted in more than two-thirds of the instances; when the student and requester were dissimilarly dressed, the dime was provided less than half the time. Another experiment showed how automatic our positive response to similar others can be. Marchers in an antiwar demonstration were found to be more likely to sign the petition of a similarly dressed requester and to do so without bothering to read it first.

① People are more likely to help those who dress like themselves.
② Dressing up formally increases the chance of signing the petition.
③ Making a phone call is an efficient way to socialize with other students.
④ Some college students in the early 1970s were admired for their unique fashion.

18 (A)와 (B)에 들어갈 말로 가장 적절한 것은?

Duration shares an inverse relationship with frequency. If you see a friend frequently, then the duration of the encounter will be shorter. Conversely, if you don't see your friend very often, the duration of your visit will typically increase significantly. (A) _____, if you see a friend every day, the duration of your visits can be low because you can keep up with what's going on as events unfold. If, however, you only see your friend twice a year, the duration of your visits will be greater. Think back to a time when you had dinner in a restaurant with a friend you hadn't seen for a long period of time. You probably spent several hours catching up on each other's lives. The duration of the same dinner would be considerably shorter if you saw the person on a regular basis. (B) _____, in romantic relationships the frequency and duration are very high because couples, especially newly minted ones, want to spend as much time with each other as possible. The intensity of the relationship will also be very high.

	(A)	(B)
①	For example	Conversely
②	Nonetheless	Furthermore
③	Therefore	As a result
④	In the same way	Thus

※ 밑줄 친 부분에 들어갈 말로 가장 적절한 것을 고르시오.
[19~20]

19

One of the most frequently used propaganda techniques is to convince the public that the propagandist's views reflect those of the common person and that he or she is working in their best interests. A politician speaking to a blue-collar audience may roll up his sleeves, undo his tie, and attempt to use the specific idioms of the crowd. He may even use language incorrectly on purpose to give the impression that he is "just one of the folks." This technique usually also employs the use of glittering generalities to give the impression that the politician's views are the same as those of the crowd being addressed. Labor leaders, businesspeople, ministers, educators, and advertisers have used this technique to win our confidence by appearing to be _____.

① beyond glittering generalities
② just plain folks like ourselves
③ something different from others
④ better educated than the crowd

20

As a roller coaster climbs the first lift hill of its track, it is building potential energy—the higher it gets above the earth, the stronger the pull of gravity will be. When the coaster crests the lift hill and begins its descent, its potential energy becomes kinetic energy, or the energy of movement. A common misperception is that a coaster loses energy along the track. An important law of physics, however, called the law of conservation of energy, is that energy can never be created nor destroyed. It simply changes from one form to another. Whenever a track rises back uphill, the cars' momentum—their kinetic energy—will carry them upward, which builds potential energy, and roller coasters repeatedly convert potential energy to kinetic energy and back again. At the end of a ride, coaster cars are slowed down by brake mechanisms that create _____ between two surfaces. This motion makes them hot, meaning kinetic energy is changed to heat energy during braking. Riders may mistakenly think coasters lose energy at the end of the track, but the energy just changes to and from different forms.

① gravity
② friction
③ vacuum
④ acceleration

정답 · 해석 · 해설 p. 88

10회 2022년 지방직 9급
모바일 자동 채점 + 성적 분석 서비스 바로 가기

QR코드를 이용해 모바일로 간편하게 채점하고 나의 실력이 어느 정도인지, 취약 부분이 어디인지 바로 파악해 보세요.

(p.213에서 전체 정답표를 확인하실 수 있습니다)

제한 시간 : 20분　시작 _____시 _____분 ~ 종료 _____시 _____분　나의 점수 _____　회독 수 □□□

01 밑줄 친 부분의 의미와 가장 가까운 것은?

> For many compulsive buyers, the act of purchasing, rather than what they buy, is what leads to gratification.

① liveliness
② confidence
③ tranquility
④ satisfaction

※ 밑줄 친 부분에 들어갈 말로 가장 적절한 것을 고르시오.
[02~04]

02

> Globalization leads more countries to open their markets, allowing them to trade goods and services freely at a lower cost with greater _____.

① extinction
② depression
③ efficiency
④ caution

03

> We're familiar with the costs of burnout: Energy, motivation, productivity, engagement, and commitment can all take a hit, at work and at home. And many of the _____ are fairly intuitive: Regularly unplug. Reduce unnecessary meetings. Exercise. Schedule small breaks during the day. Take vacations even if you think you can't afford to be away from work, because you can't afford not to be away now and then.

① fixes
② damages
③ prizes
④ complications

04

> The government is seeking ways to soothe salaried workers over their increased tax burdens arising from a new tax settlement system. During his meeting with the presidential aides last Monday, the President _____ those present to open up more communication channels with the public.

① fell on
② called for
③ picked up
④ turned down

05 밑줄 친 부분의 의미와 가장 가까운 것은?

> In studying Chinese calligraphy, one must learn something of the origins of Chinese language and of how they were originally written. However, except for those brought up in the artistic traditions of the country, its aesthetic significance seems to be very difficult to apprehend.

① encompass
② intrude
③ inspect
④ grasp

※ 우리말을 영어로 잘못 옮긴 것을 고르시오. [06~07]

06

① 그의 소설들은 읽기가 어렵다.
→ His novels are hard to read.

② 학생들을 설득하려고 해 봐야 소용없다.
→ It is no use trying to persuade the students.

③ 나의 집은 5년마다 페인트칠된다.
→ My house is painted every five years.

④ 내가 출근할 때 한 가족이 위층에 이사 오는 것을 보았다.
→ As I went out for work, I saw a family moved in upstairs.

07

① 경찰 당국은 자신의 이웃을 공격했기 때문에 그 여성을 체포하도록 했다.
→ The police authorities had the woman arrested for attacking her neighbor.

② 네가 내는 소음 때문에 내 집중력을 잃게 하지 말아라.
→ Don't let me distracted by the noise you make.

③ 가능한 한 빨리 제가 결과를 알도록 해 주세요.
→ Please let me know the result as soon as possible.

④ 그는 학생들에게 모르는 사람들에게 전화를 걸어 성금을 기부할 것을 부탁하도록 시켰다.
→ He had the students phone strangers and ask them to donate money.

08 어법상 옳은 것은?

① My sweet-natured daughter suddenly became unpredictably.

② She attempted a new method, and needless to say had different results.

③ Upon arrived, he took full advantage of the new environment.

④ He felt enough comfortable to tell me about something he wanted to do.

09 다음 글의 제목으로 가장 적절한 것은?

The definition of 'turn' casts the digital turn as an analytical strategy which enables us to focus on the role of digitalization within social reality. As an analytical perspective, the digital turn makes it possible to analyze and discuss the societal meaning of digitalization. The term 'digital turn' thus signifies an analytical approach which centers on the role of digitalization within a society. If the linguistic turn is defined by the epistemological assumption that reality is constructed through language, the digital turn is based on the assumption that social reality is increasingly defined by digitalization. Social media symbolize the digitalization of social relations. Individuals increasingly engage in identity management on social networking sites(SNS). SNS are polydirectional, meaning that users can connect to each other and share information.

※ epistemological: 인식론의

① Remaking Identities on SNS

② Linguistic Turn Versus Digital Turn

③ How to Share Information in the Digital Age

④ Digitalization Within the Context of Social Reality

10 주어진 글 다음에 이어질 글의 순서로 가장 적절한 것은?

> Growing concern about global climate change has motivated activists to organize not only campaigns against fossil fuel extraction consumption, but also campaigns to support renewable energy.

(A) This solar cooperative produces enough energy to power 1,400 homes, making it the first large-scale solar farm cooperative in the country and, in the words of its members, a visible reminder that solar power represents "a new era of sustainable and 'democratic' energy supply that enables ordinary people to produce clean power, not only on their rooftops, but also at utility scale."

(B) Similarly, renewable energy enthusiasts from the United States have founded the Clean Energy Collective, a company that has pioneered "the model of delivering clean power-generation through medium-scale facilities that are collectively owned by participating utility customers."

(C) Environmental activists frustrated with the UK government's inability to rapidly accelerate the growth of renewable energy industries have formed the Westmill Wind Farm Co-operative, a community-owned organization with more than 2,000 members who own an onshore wind farm estimated to produce as much electricity in a year as that used by 2,500 homes. The Westmill Wind Farm Co-operative has inspired local citizens to form the Westmill Solar Co-operative.

① (C) — (A) — (B) ② (A) — (C) — (B)
③ (B) — (C) — (A) ④ (C) — (B) — (A)

11 밑줄 친 부분에 들어갈 말로 가장 적절한 것은?

> A: Did you have a nice weekend?
> B: Yes, it was pretty good. We went to the movies.
> A: Oh! What did you see?
> B: *Interstellar*. It was really good.
> A: Really? _____
> B: The special effects. They were fantastic. I wouldn't mind seeing it again.

① What did you like the most about it?
② What's your favorite movie genre?
③ Was the film promoted internationally?
④ Was the movie very costly?

12 두 사람의 대화 중 가장 어색한 것은?

① A: I'm so nervous about this speech that I must give today.
   B: The most important thing is to stay cool.

② A: You know what? Minsu and Yujin are tying the knot!
   B: Good for them! When are they getting married?

③ A: A two-month vacation just passed like one week. A new semester is around the corner.
   B: That's the word. Vacation has dragged on for weeks.

④ A: How do you say 'water' in French?
   B: It is right on the tip of my tongue, but I can't remember it.

13 다음 글의 내용과 일치하지 않는 것은?

Women are experts at gossiping, and they always talk about trivial things, or at least that's what men have always thought. However, some new research suggests that when women talk to women, their conversations are far from frivolous, and cover many more topics (up to 40 subjects) than when men talk to other men. Women's conversations range from health to their houses, from politics to fashion, from movies to family, from education to relationship problems, but sports are notably absent. Men tend to have a more limited range of subjects, the most popular being work, sports, jokes, cars, and women. According to Professor Petra Boynton, a psychologist who interviewed over 1,000 women, women also tend to move quickly from one subject to another in conversation, while men usually stick to one subject for longer periods of time. At work, this difference can be an advantage for men, as they can put other matters aside and concentrate fully on the topic being discussed. On the other hand, it also means that they sometimes find it hard to concentrate when several things have to be discussed at the same time in a meeting.

① 남성들은 여성들의 대화 주제가 항상 사소한 것들이라고 생각해 왔다.
② 여성들의 대화 주제는 건강에서 스포츠에 이르기까지 매우 다양하다.
③ 여성들은 대화하는 중에 주제의 변환을 빨리한다.
④ 남성들은 회의 중 여러 주제가 논의될 때 집중하기 어렵다.

14 다음 글의 흐름상 적절하지 않은 문장은?

There was no divide between science, philosophy, and magic in the 15th century. All three came under the general heading of 'natural philosophy'. ① Central to the development of natural philosophy was the recovery of classical authors, most importantly the work of Aristotle. ② Humanists quickly realized the power of the printing press for spreading their knowledge. ③ At the beginning of the 15th century Aristotle remained the basis for all scholastic speculation on philosophy and science. ④ Kept alive in the Arabic translations and commentaries of Averroes and Avicenna, Aristotle provided a systematic perspective on mankind's relationship with the natural world. Surviving texts like his *Physics*, *Metaphysics*, and *Meteorology* provided scholars with the logical tools to understand the forces that created the natural world.

15 어법상 옳지 않은 것은?

① Fire following an earthquake is of special interest to the insurance industry.
② Word processors were considered to be the ultimate tool for a typist in the past.
③ Elements of income in a cash forecast will be vary according to the company's circumstances.
④ The world's first digital camera was created by Steve Sasson at Eastman Kodak in 1975.

16

The slowing of China's economy from historically high rates of growth has long been expected to _____ growth elsewhere. "The China that had been growing at 10 percent for 30 years was a powerful source of fuel for much of what drove the global economy forward", said Stephen Roach at Yale. The growth rate has slowed to an official figure of around 7 percent. "That's a concrete deceleration", Mr. Roach added.

① speed up   ② weigh on
③ lead to   ④ result in

17

As more and more leaders work remotely or with teams scattered around the nation or the globe, as well as with consultants and freelancers, you'll have to give them more _____. The more trust you bestow, the more others trust you. I am convinced that there is a direct correlation between job satisfaction and how empowered people are to fully execute their job without someone shadowing them every step of the way. Giving away responsibility to those you trust can not only make your organization run more smoothly but also free up more of your time so you can focus on larger issues.

① work   ② rewards
③ restrictions   ④ autonomy

18 다음 글의 요지로 가장 적절한 것은?

"In Judaism, we're largely defined by our actions," says Lisa Grushcow, the senior rabbi at Temple Emanu-El-Beth Sholom in Montreal. "You can't really be an armchair do-gooder." This concept relates to the Jewish notion of tikkun olam, which translates as "to repair the world." Our job as human beings, she says, "is to mend what's been broken. It's incumbent on us to not only take care of ourselves and each other but also to build a better world around us." This philosophy conceptualizes goodness as something based in service. Instead of asking "Am I a good person?" you may want to ask "What good do I do in the world?" Grushcow's temple puts these beliefs into action inside and outside their community. For instance, they sponsored two refugee families from Vietnam to come to Canada in the 1970s.

① We should work to heal the world.
② Community should function as a shelter.
③ We should conceptualize goodness as beliefs.
④ Temples should contribute to the community.

19 (A)와 (B)에 들어갈 말로 가장 적절한 것은?

Ancient philosophers and spiritual teachers understood the need to balance the positive with the negative, optimism with pessimism, a striving for success and security with an openness to failure and uncertainty. The Stoics recommended "the premeditation of evils," or deliberately visualizing the worst-case scenario. This tends to reduce anxiety about the future: when you soberly picture how badly things could go in reality, you usually conclude that you could cope. ____(A)____, they noted, imagining that you might lose the relationships and possessions you currently enjoy increases your gratitude for having them now. Positive thinking, ____(B)____, always leans into the future, ignoring present pleasures.

(A)	(B)
① Nevertheless	in addition
② Furthermore	for example
③ Besides	by contrast
④ However	in conclusion

20 주어진 문장이 들어갈 위치로 가장 적절한 것은?

And working offers more than financial security.

Why do workaholics enjoy their jobs so much? Mostly because working offers some important advantages. (①) It provides people with paychecks—a way to earn a living. (②) It provides people with self-confidence; they have a feeling of satisfaction when they've produced a challenging piece of work and are able to say, "I made that". (③) Psychologists claim that work also gives people an identity; they work so that they can get a sense of self and individualism. (④) In addition, most jobs provide people with a socially acceptable way to meet others. It could be said that working is a positive addiction; maybe workaholics are compulsive about their work, but their addiction seems to be a safe—even an advantageous—one.

정답·해석·해설 p. 97

11회 2021년 지방직 9급
모바일 자동 채점 + 성적 분석 서비스 바로 가기

QR코드를 이용해 모바일로 간편하게 채점하고 나의 실력이 어느 정도인지, 취약 부분이 어디인지 바로 파악해 보세요.

(p.213에서 전체 정답표를 확인하실 수 있습니다)

제한 시간 : 20분   시작 _____시 _____분 ~ 종료 _____시 _____분   나의 점수 _____   회독 수 ☐☐☐

01 밑줄 친 부분에 들어갈 말로 가장 적절한 것은?

> The issue with plastic bottles is that they're not _____, so when the temperatures begin to rise, your water will also heat up.

① sanitary
② insulated
③ recyclable
④ waterproof

※ 밑줄 친 부분의 의미와 가장 가까운 것을 고르시오.
[02~04]

02

> Strategies that a writer adopts during the writing process may alleviate the difficulty of attentional overload.

① complement
② accelerate
③ calculate
④ relieve

03

> The cruel sights touched off thoughts that otherwise wouldn't have entered her mind.

① looked after
② gave rise to
③ made up for
④ kept in contact with

04

> The school bully did not know what it was like to be shunned by the other students in the class.

① avoided
② warned
③ punished
④ imitated

05 어법상 옳은 것은?
① Of the billions of stars in the galaxy, how much are able to hatch life?
② The Christmas party was really excited and I totally lost track of time.
③ I must leave right now because I am starting work at noon today.
④ They used to loving books much more when they were younger.

06 밑줄 친 부분의 의미와 가장 가까운 것은?

> After Francesca made a case for staying at home during the summer holidays, an uncomfortable silence fell on the dinner table. Robert was not sure if it was the right time for him to tell her about his grandiose plan.

① objected to
② dreamed about
③ completely excluded
④ strongly suggested

07 밑줄 친 부분 중 어법상 옳지 않은 것은?

Elizabeth Taylor had an eye for beautiful jewels and over the years amassed some amazing pieces, once ① declaring "a girl can always have more diamonds." In 2011, her finest jewels were sold by Christie's at an evening auction ② that brought in $115.9 million. Among her most prized possessions sold during the evening sale ③ were a 1961 bejeweled timepiece by Bulgari. Designed as a serpent to coil around the wrist, with its head and tail ④ covered with diamonds and having two hypnotic emerald eyes, a discreet mechanism opens its fierce jaws to reveal a tiny quartz watch.

08 우리말을 영어로 잘못 옮긴 것은?

① 보증이 만료되어서 수리는 무료가 아니었다.
  → Since the warranty had expired, the repairs were not free of charge.

② 설문지를 완성하는 누구에게나 선물카드가 주어질 예정이다.
  → A gift card will be given to whomever completes the questionnaire.

③ 지난달 내가 휴가를 요청했더라면 지금 하와이에 있을 텐데.
  → If I had asked for a vacation last month, I would be in Hawaii now.

④ 그의 아버지가 갑자기 작년에 돌아가셨고, 설상가상으로 그의 어머니도 병에 걸리셨다.
  → His father suddenly passed away last year, and, what was worse, his mother became sick.

09 밑줄 친 (A), (B)에 들어갈 말로 가장 적절한 것은?

Assertive behavior involves standing up for your rights and expressing your thoughts and feelings in a direct, appropriate way that does not violate the rights of others. It is a matter of getting the other person to understand your viewpoint. People who exhibit assertive behavior skills are able to handle conflict situations with ease and assurance while maintaining good interpersonal relations. _____(A)_____, aggressive behavior involves expressing your thoughts and feelings and defending your rights in a way that openly violates the rights of others. Those exhibiting aggressive behavior seem to believe that the rights of others must be subservient to theirs. _____(B)_____, they have a difficult time maintaining good interpersonal relations. They are likely to interrupt, talk fast, ignore others, and use sarcasm or other forms of verbal abuse to maintain control.

	(A)	(B)
①	In contrast	Thus
②	Similarly	Moreover
③	However	On one hand
④	Accordingly	On the other hand

10 다음 글의 주제로 가장 적절한 것은?

The e-book applications available on tablet computers employ touchscreen technology. Some touchscreens feature a glass panel covering two electronically-charged metallic surfaces lying face-to-face. When the screen is touched, the two metallic surfaces feel the pressure and make contact. This pressure sends an electrical signal to the computer, which translates the touch into a command. This version of the touchscreen is known as a resistive screen because the screen reacts to pressure from the finger. Other tablet computers feature a single electrified metallic layer under the glass panel. When the user touches the screen, some of the current passes through the glass into the user's finger. When the charge is transferred, the computer interprets the loss in power as a command and carries out the function the user desires. This type of screen is known as a capacitive screen.

① how users learn new technology
② how e-books work on tablet computers
③ how touchscreen technology works
④ how touchscreens have evolved

11 밑줄 친 부분에 들어갈 말로 가장 적절한 것은?

A: Oh, another one! So many junk emails!
B: I know. I receive more than ten junk emails a day.
A: Can we stop them from coming in?
B: I don't think it's possible to block them completely.
A: _____?
B: Well, you can set up a filter on the settings.
A: A filter?
B: Yeah. The filter can weed out some of the spam emails.

① Do you write emails often
② Isn't there anything we can do
③ How did you make this great filter
④ Can you help me set up an email account

12 우리말을 영어로 잘못 옮긴 것은?

① 나는 네 열쇠를 잃어버렸다고 네게 말한 것을 후회한다.
  → I regret to tell you that I lost your key.
② 그 병원에서의 그의 경험은 그녀의 경험보다 더 나빴다.
  → His experience at the hospital was worse than hers.
③ 그것은 내게 지난 24년의 기억을 상기시켜준다.
  → It reminds me of the memories of the past 24 years.
④ 나는 대화할 때 내 눈을 보는 사람들을 좋아한다.
  → I like people who look me in the eye when I have a conversation.

13 두 사람의 대화 중 가장 자연스러운 것은?

① A: Do you know what time it is?

　B: Sorry, I'm busy these days.

② A: Hey, where are you headed?

　B: We are off to the grocery store.

③ A: Can you give me a hand with this?

　B: OK. I'll clap for you.

④ A: Has anybody seen my purse?

　B: Long time no see.

14 다음 글의 제목으로 가장 적절한 것은?

Louis XIV needed a palace worthy of his greatness, so he decided to build a huge new house at Versailles, where a tiny hunting lodge stood. After almost fifty years of labor, this tiny hunting lodge had been transformed into an enormous palace, a quarter of a mile long. Canals were dug to bring water from the river and to drain the marshland. Versailles was full of elaborate rooms like the famous Hall of Mirrors, where seventeen huge mirrors stood across from seventeen large windows, and the Salon of Apollo, where a solid silver throne stood. Hundreds of statues of Greek gods such as Apollo, Jupiter, and Neptune stood in the gardens; each god had Louis's face!

① True Face of Greek Gods

② The Hall of Mirrors vs. the Salon of Apollo

③ Did the Canal Bring More Than Just Water to Versailles?

④ Versailles: From a Humble Lodge to a Great Palace

15 글의 흐름상 가장 어색한 문장은?

Philosophers have not been as concerned with anthropology as anthropologists have with philosophy. ① Few influential contemporary philosophers take anthropological studies into account in their work. ② Those who specialize in philosophy of social science may consider or analyze examples from anthropological research, but do this mostly to illustrate conceptual points or epistemological distinctions or to criticize epistemological or ethical implications. ③ In fact, the great philosophers of our time often drew inspiration from other fields such as anthropology and psychology. ④ Philosophy students seldom study or show serious interest in anthropology. They may learn about experimental methods in science, but rarely about anthropological fieldwork.

16 밑줄 친 부분에 들어갈 말로 가장 적절한 것은?

All of us inherit something: in some cases, it may be money, property or some object—a family heirloom such as a grandmother's wedding dress or a father's set of tools. But beyond that, all of us inherit something else, something ＿＿＿＿＿＿ ＿＿＿＿＿＿＿＿＿, something we may not even be fully aware of. It may be a way of doing a daily task, or the way we solve a particular problem or decide a moral issue for ourselves. It may be a special way of keeping a holiday or a tradition to have a picnic on a certain date. It may be something important or central to our thinking, or something minor that we have long accepted quite casually.

① quite unrelated to our everyday life

② against our moral standards

③ much less concrete and tangible

④ of great monetary value

17 다음 글의 요지로 가장 적절한 것은?

Evolutionarily, any species that hopes to stay alive has to manage its resources carefully. That means that first call on food and other goodies goes to the breeders and warriors and hunters and planters and builders and, certainly, the children, with not much left over for the seniors, who may be seen as consuming more than they're contributing. But even before modern medicine extended life expectancies, ordinary families were including grandparents and even great-grandparents. That's because what old folk consume materially, they give back behaviorally— providing a leveling, reasoning center to the tumult that often swirls around them.

① Seniors have been making contributions to the family.
② Modern medicine has brought focus to the role of old folk.
③ Allocating resources well in a family determines its prosperity.
④ The extended family comes at a cost of limited resources.

18 주어진 글 다음에 이어질 글의 순서로 가장 적절한 것은?

Nowadays the clock dominates our lives so much that it is hard to imagine life without it. Before industrialization, most societies used the sun or the moon to tell the time.

(A) For the growing network of railroads, the fact that there were no time standards was a disaster. Often, stations just some miles apart set their clocks at different times. There was a lot of confusion for travelers.

(B) When mechanical clocks first appeared, they were immediately popular. It was fashionable to have a clock or a watch. People invented the expression "of the clock" or "o'clock" to refer to this new way to tell the time.

(C) These clocks were decorative, but not always useful. This was because towns, provinces, and even neighboring villages had different ways to tell the time. Travelers had to reset their clocks repeatedly when they moved from one place to another. In the United States, there were about 70 different time zones in the 1860s.

① (A) – (B) – (C)
② (B) – (A) – (C)
③ (B) – (C) – (A)
④ (C) – (A) – (B)

19 주어진 문장이 들어갈 위치로 가장 적절한 것은?

> But there is also clear evidence that millennials, born between 1981 and 1996, are saving more aggressively for retirement than Generation X did at the same ages, 22~37.

> Millennials are often labeled the poorest, most financially burdened generation in modern times. Many of them graduated from college into one of the worst labor markets the United States has ever seen, with a staggering load of student debt to boot. ① Not surprisingly, millennials have accumulated less wealth than Generation X did at a similar stage in life, primarily because fewer of them own homes. ② But newly available data providing the most detailed picture to date about what Americans of different generations save complicates that assessment. ③ Yes, Gen Xers, those born between 1965 and 1980, have a higher net worth. ④ And that might put them in better financial shape than many assume.

20 다음 글의 내용과 일치하지 않는 것은?

> Carbonate sands, which accumulate over thousands of years from the breakdown of coral and other reef organisms, are the building material for the frameworks of coral reefs. But these sands are sensitive to the chemical make-up of sea water. As oceans absorb carbon dioxide, they acidify—and at a certain point, carbonate sands simply start to dissolve. The world's oceans have absorbed around one-third of human-emitted carbon dioxide. The rate at which the sands dissolve was strongly related to the acidity of the overlying seawater, and was ten times more sensitive than coral growth to ocean acidification. In other words, ocean acidification will impact the dissolution of coral reef sands more than the growth of corals. This probably reflects the corals' ability to modify their environment and partially adjust to ocean acidification, whereas the dissolution of sands is a geochemical process that cannot adapt.

① The frameworks of coral reefs are made of carbonate sands.

② Corals are capable of partially adjusting to ocean acidification.

③ Human-emitted carbon dioxide has contributed to the world's ocean acidification.

④ Ocean acidification affects the growth of corals more than the dissolution of coral reef sands.

정답·해석·해설 p. 105

12회 2020년 지방직 9급
모바일 자동 채점 + 성적 분석 서비스 바로 가기

QR코드를 이용해 모바일로 간편하게 채점하고 나의 실력이 어느 정도인지, 취약 부분이 어디인지 바로 파악해 보세요.

(p.213에서 전체 정답표를 확인하실 수 있습니다)

제한 시간 : 20분   시작 _____시 _____분 ~ 종료 _____시 _____분   나의 점수 _____   회독 수 ☐ ☐ ☐

※ 밑줄 친 부분의 의미와 가장 가까운 것을 고르시오. [01~02]

01

I came to see these documents as relics of a sensibility now dead and buried, which needed to be <u>excavated</u>.

① exhumed   ② packed
③ erased   ④ celebrated

02

Riding a roller coaster can be a joy ride of emotions: the nervous anticipation as you're strapped into your seat, the questioning and regret that comes as you go up, up, up, and the <u>sheer</u> adrenaline rush as the car takes that first dive.

① utter   ② scary
③ occasional   ④ manageable

03 두 사람의 대화 중 가장 어색한 것은?

① A: What time are we having lunch?
   B: It'll be ready before noon.
② A: I called you several times. Why didn't you answer?
   B: Oh, I think my cell phone was turned off.
③ A: Are you going to take a vacation this winter?
   B: I might. I haven't decided yet.
④ A: Hello. Sorry I missed your call.
   B: Would you like to leave a message?

04 밑줄 친 부분에 들어갈 말로 가장 적절한 것은?

A: Hello. I need to exchange some money.
B: Okay. What currency do you need?
A: I need to convert dollars into pounds. What's the exchange rate?
B: The exchange rate is 0.73 pounds for every dollar.
A: Fine. Do you take a commission?
B: Yes, we take a small commission of 4 dollars.
A: _____?
B: We convert your currency back for free. Just bring your receipt with you.

① How much does this cost
② How should I pay for that
③ What's your buy-back policy
④ Do you take credit cards

05 밑줄 친 부분 중 어법상 옳지 않은 것은?

Each year, more than 270,000 pedestrians ① <u>lose</u> their lives on the world's roads. Many leave their homes as they would on any given day never ② <u>to return</u>. Globally, pedestrians constitute 22% of all road traffic fatalities, and in some countries this proportion is ③ <u>as high as</u> two thirds of all road traffic deaths. Millions of pedestrians are non-fatally ④ <u>injuring</u>—some of whom are left with permanent disabilities. These incidents cause much suffering and grief as well as economic hardship.

06 어법상 옳은 것은?

① The paper charged her with use the company's money for her own purposes.

② The investigation had to be handled with the utmost care lest suspicion be aroused.

③ Another way to speed up the process would be made the shift to a new system.

④ Burning fossil fuels is one of the lead cause of climate change.

07 주어진 글 다음에 이어질 글의 순서로 가장 적절한 것은?

There is a thought that can haunt us: since everything probably affects everything else, how can we ever make sense of the social world? If we are weighed down by that worry, though, we won't ever make progress.

(A) Every discipline that I am familiar with draws caricatures of the world in order to make sense of it. The modern economist does this by building *models*, which are deliberately stripped down representations of the phenomena out there.

(B) The economist John Maynard Keynes described our subject thus: "Economics is a science of thinking in terms of models joined to the art of choosing models which are relevant to the contemporary world."

(C) When I say "stripped down," I really mean stripped down. It isn't uncommon among us economists to focus on one or two causal factors, exclude everything else, hoping that this will enable us to understand how just those aspects of reality work and interact.

① (A) — (B) — (C)　　② (A) — (C) — (B)

③ (B) — (C) — (A)　　④ (B) — (A) — (C)

08 다음 글의 내용과 일치하는 것은?

Prehistoric societies some half a million years ago did not distinguish sharply between mental and physical disorders. Abnormal behaviors, from simple headaches to convulsive attacks, were attributed to evil spirits that inhabited or controlled the afflicted person's body. According to historians, these ancient peoples attributed many forms of illness to demonic possession, sorcery, or the behest of an offended ancestral spirit. Within this system of belief, called *demonology*, the victim was usually held at least partly responsible for the misfortune. It has been suggested that Stone Age cave dwellers may have treated behavior disorders with a surgical method called *trephining*, in which part of the skull was chipped away to provide an opening through which the evil spirit could escape. People may have believed that when the evil spirit left, the person would return to his or her normal state. Surprisingly, trephined skulls have been found to have healed over, indicating that some patients survived this extremely crude operation.

※ convulsive: 경련의　※ behest: 명령

① Mental disorders were clearly differentiated from physical disorders.

② Abnormal behaviors were believed to result from evil spirits affecting a person.

③ An opening was made in the skull for an evil spirit to enter a person's body.

④ No cave dwellers survived trephining.

09 다음 글의 주제로 가장 적절한 것은?

As the digital revolution upends newsrooms across the country, here's my advice for all the reporters. I've been a reporter for more than 25 years, so I have lived through a half dozen technological life cycles. The most dramatic transformations have come in the last half dozen years. That means I am, with increasing frequency, making stuff up as I go along. Much of the time in the news business, we have no idea what we are doing. We show up in the morning and someone says, "Can you write a story about (pick one) tax policy/immigration/climate change?" When newspapers had once-a-day deadlines, we said a reporter would learn in the morning and teach at night—write a story that could inform tomorrow's readers on a topic the reporter knew nothing about 24 hours earlier. Now it is more like learning at the top of the hour and teaching at the bottom of the same hour. I'm also running a political podcast, for example, and during the presidential conventions, we should be able to use it to do real-time interviews anywhere. I am just increasingly working without a script.

① a reporter as a teacher
② a reporter and improvisation
③ technology in politics
④ fields of journalism and technology

10 글의 흐름상 가장 어색한 문장은?

Children's playgrounds throughout history were the wilderness, fields, streams, and hills of the country and the roads, streets, and vacant places of villages, towns, and cities. ① The term *playground* refers to all those places where children gather to play their free, spontaneous games. ② Only during the past few decades have children vacated these natural playgrounds for their growing love affair with video games, texting, and social networking. ③ Even in rural America few children are still roaming in a free-ranging manner, unaccompanied by adults. ④ When out of school, they are commonly found in neighborhoods digging in sand, building forts, playing traditional games, climbing, or playing ball games. They are rapidly disappearing from the natural terrain of creeks, hills, and fields, and like their urban counterparts, are turning to their indoor, sedentary cyber toys for entertainment.

※ 밑줄 친 부분의 의미와 가장 가까운 것을 고르시오. [11~12]

11

Time does seem to slow to a trickle during a boring afternoon lecture and race when the brain is engrossed in something highly entertaining.

① enhanced by
② apathetic to
③ stabilized by
④ preoccupied with

12

These daily updates were designed to help readers keep abreast of the markets as the government attempted to keep them under control.

① be acquainted with
② get inspired by
③ have faith in
④ keep away from

※ 밑줄 친 (A), (B)에 들어갈 말로 가장 적절한 것을 고르시오. [13~14]

13

In the 1840s, the island of Ireland suffered famine. Because Ireland could not produce enough food to feed its population, about a million people died of ___(A)___; they simply didn't have enough to eat to stay alive. The famine caused another 1.25 million people to ___(B)___; many left their island home for the United States; the rest went to Canada, Australia, Chile, and other countries. Before the famine, the population of Ireland was approximately 6 million. After the great food shortage, it was about 4 million.

	(A)	(B)
①	dehydration	be deported
②	trauma	immigrate
③	starvation	emigrate
④	fatigue	be detained

14

Today the technology to create the visual component of virtual-reality (VR) experiences is well on its way to becoming widely accessible and affordable. But to work powerfully, virtual reality needs to be about more than visuals. ___(A)___ what you are hearing convincingly matches the visuals, the virtual experience breaks apart. Take a basketball game. If the players, the coaches, the announcers, and the crowd all sound like they're sitting midcourt, you may as well watch the game on television—you'll get just as much of a sense that you are "there." ___(B)___, today's audio equipment and our widely used recording and reproduction formats are simply inadequate to the task of re-creating convincingly the sound of a battlefield on a distant planet, a basketball game at courtside, or a symphony as heard from the first row of a great concert hall.

	(A)	(B)
①	If	By contrast
②	Unless	Consequently
③	If	Similarly
④	Unless	Unfortunately

15 주어진 문장이 들어갈 위치로 가장 적절한 것은?

The same thinking can be applied to any number of goals, like improving performance at work.

The happy brain tends to focus on the short term. (①) That being the case, it's a good idea to consider what short-term goals we can accomplish that will eventually lead to accomplishing long-term goals. (②) For instance, if you want to lose thirty pounds in six months, what short-term goals can you associate with losing the smaller increments of weight that will get you there? (③) Maybe it's something as simple as rewarding yourself each week that you lose two pounds. (④) By breaking the overall goal into smaller, shorter-term parts, we can focus on incremental accomplishments instead of being overwhelmed by the enormity of the goal in our profession.

16 우리말을 영어로 잘못 옮긴 것은?

① 혹시 내게 전화하고 싶은 경우에 이게 내 번호야.
  → This is my number just in case you would like to call me.
② 나는 유럽 여행을 준비하느라 바쁘다.
  → I am busy preparing for a trip to Europe.
③ 그녀는 남편과 결혼한 지 20년 이상 되었다.
  → She has married to her husband for more than two decades.
④ 나는 내 아들이 읽을 책을 한 권 사야 한다.
  → I should buy a book for my son to read.

17

In the nineteenth century, the most respected health and medical experts all insisted that diseases were caused by "miasma," a fancy term for bad air. Western society's system of health was based on this assumption: to prevent diseases, windows were kept open or closed, depending on whether there was more miasma inside or outside the room; it was believed that doctors could not pass along disease because gentlemen did not inhabit quarters with bad air. Then the idea of germs came along. One day, everyone believed that bad air makes you sick. Then, almost overnight, people started realizing there were invisible things called microbes and bacteria that were the real cause of diseases. This new view of disease brought sweeping changes to medicine, as surgeons adopted antiseptics and scientists invented vaccines and antibiotics. But, just as momentously, the idea of germs gave ordinary people the power to influence their own lives. Now, if you wanted to stay healthy, you could wash your hands, boil your water, cook your food thoroughly, and clean cuts and scrapes with iodine.

① In the nineteenth century, opening windows was irrelevant to the density of miasma.
② In the nineteenth century, it was believed that gentlemen did not live in places with bad air.
③ Vaccines were invented after people realized that microbes and bacteria were the real cause of diseases.
④ Cleaning cuts and scrapes could help people to stay healthy.

18

Followers are a critical part of the leadership equation, but their role has not always been appreciated. For a long time, in fact, "the common view of leadership was that leaders actively led and subordinates, later called followers, passively and obediently followed." Over time, especially in the last century, social change shaped people's views of followers, and leadership theories gradually recognized the active and important role that followers play in the leadership process. Today it seems natural to accept the important role followers play. One aspect of leadership is particularly worth noting in this regard: Leadership is a social influence process shared among all members of a group. Leadership is not restricted to the influence exerted by someone in a particular position or role; followers are part of the leadership process, too.

① For a length of time, it was understood that leaders actively led and followers passively followed.
② People's views of subordinates were influenced by social change.
③ The important role of followers is still denied today.
④ Both leaders and followers participate in the leadership process.

※ 밑줄 친 부분에 들어갈 말로 가장 적절한 것을 고르시오.
[19~20]

19

Language proper is itself double-layered. Single noises are only occasionally meaningful: mostly, the various speech sounds convey coherent messages only when combined into an overlapping chain, like different colors of ice-cream melting into one another. In birdsong also, _____: the sequence is what matters. In both humans and birds, control of this specialized sound-system is exercised by one half of the brain, normally the left half, and the system is learned relatively early in life. And just as many human languages have dialects, so do some bird species: in California, the white-crowned sparrow has songs so different from area to area that Californians can supposedly tell where they are in the state by listening to these sparrows.

① individual notes are often of little value
② rhythmic sounds are important
③ dialects play a critical role
④ no sound-system exists

20

Nobel Prize-winning psychologist Daniel Kahneman changed the way the world thinks about economics, upending the notion that human beings are rational decision-makers. Along the way, his discipline-crossing influence has altered the way physicians make medical decisions and investors evaluate risk on Wall Street. In a paper, Kahneman and his colleagues outline a process for making big strategic decisions. Their suggested approach, labeled as "Mediating Assessments Protocol," or MAP, has a simple goal: To put off gut-based decision-making until a choice can be informed by a number of separate factors. "One of the essential purposes of MAP is basically to _____ intuition," Kahneman said in a recent interview with *The Post*. The structured process calls for analyzing a decision based on six to seven previously chosen attributes, discussing each of them separately and assigning them a relative percentile score, and finally, using those scores to make a holistic judgment.

① improve
② delay
③ possess
④ facilitate

정답·해석·해설 p. 114

13회 2019년 지방직 9급
모바일 자동 채점 + 성적 분석 서비스 바로 가기

QR코드를 이용해 모바일로 간편하게 채점하고 나의 실력이 어느 정도인지, 취약 부분이 어디인지 바로 파악해 보세요.

(p.213에서 전체 정답표를 확인하실 수 있습니다)

※ 밑줄 친 부분의 의미와 가장 가까운 것을 고르시오.

[01~02]

01

> The paramount duty of the physician is to do no harm. Everything else—even healing—must take second place.

① chief　　　　　② sworn

③ successful　　　④ mysterious

02

> It is not unusual that people get cold feet about taking a trip to the North Pole.

① become ambitious　　② become afraid

③ feel exhausted　　　　④ feel saddened

03 밑줄 친 부분 중 어법상 옳지 않은 것은?

> I am writing in response to your request for a reference for Mrs. Ferrer. She has worked as my secretary ① for the last three years and has been an excellent employee. I believe that she meets all the requirements ② mentioned in your job description and indeed exceeds them in many ways. I have never had reason ③ to doubt her complete integrity. I would, therefore, recommend Mrs. Ferrer for the post ④ what you advertise.

04 우리말을 영어로 잘못 옮긴 것은?

① 모든 정보는 거짓이었다.
　→ All of the information was false.

② 토마스는 더 일찍 사과했어야 했다.
　→ Thomas should have apologized earlier.

③ 우리가 도착했을 때 영화는 이미 시작했었다.
　→ The movie had already started when we arrived.

④ 바깥 날씨가 추웠기 때문에 나는 차를 마시려 물을 끓였다.
　→ Being cold outside, I boiled some water to have tea.

05 밑줄 친 부분의 의미와 가장 가까운 것은?

> The student who finds the state-of-the-art approach intimidating learns less than he or she might have learned by the old methods.

① humorous　　　② friendly

③ convenient　　　④ frightening

06 밑줄 친 부분에 들어갈 말로 가장 적절한 것은?

> Since the air-conditioners are being repaired now, the office workers have to _____ electric fans for the day.

① get rid of　　　② let go of

③ make do with　　④ break up with

07 어법상 옳은 것은?

① Please contact to me at the email address I gave you last week.

② Were it not for water, all living creatures on earth would be extinct.

③ The laptop allows people who is away from their offices to continue to work.

④ The more they attempted to explain their mistakes, the worst their story sounded.

08 우리말을 영어로 옳게 옮긴 것은?

① 그는 며칠 전에 친구를 배웅하기 위해 역으로 갔다.
→ He went to the station a few days ago to see off his friend.

② 버릇없는 그 소년은 아버지가 부르는 것을 못 들은 체했다.
→ The spoiled boy made it believe he didn't hear his father calling.

③ 나는 버팔로에 가본 적이 없어서 그곳에 가기를 고대하고 있다.
→ I have never been to Buffalo, so I am looking forward to go there.

④ 나는 아직 오늘 신문을 못 읽었어. 뭐 재미있는 것 있니?
→ I have not read today's newspaper yet. Is there anything interested in it?

09 다음 글의 흐름상 가장 어색한 문장은?

The Renaissance kitchen had a definite hierarchy of help who worked together to produce the elaborate banquets. ① At the top, as we have seen, was the *scalco*, or steward, who was in charge of not only the kitchen, but also the dining room. ② The dining room was supervised by the butler, who was in charge of the silverware and linen and also served the dishes that began and ended the banquet—the cold dishes, salads, cheeses, and fruit at the beginning and the sweets and confections at the end of the meal. ③ This elaborate decoration and serving was what in restaurants is called "the front of the house." ④ The kitchen was supervised by the head cook, who directed the undercooks, pastry cooks, and kitchen help.

10 다음 글의 요지로 가장 적절한 것은?

My students often believe that if they simply meet more important people, their work will improve. But it's remarkably hard to engage with those people unless you've already put something valuable out into the world. That's what piques the curiosity of advisers and sponsors. Achievements show you have something to give, not just something to take. In life, it certainly helps to know the right people. But how hard they go to bat for you, how far they stick their necks out for you, depends on what you have to offer. Building a powerful network doesn't require you to be an expert at networking. It just requires you to be an expert at something. If you make great connections, they might advance your career. If you do great work, those connections will be easier to make. Let your insights and your outputs—not your business cards—do the talking.

① Sponsorship is necessary for a successful career.

② Building a good network starts from your accomplishments.

③ A powerful network is a prerequisite for your achievement.

④ Your insights and outputs grow as you become an expert at networking.

11 밑줄 친 부분에 들어갈 말로 가장 적절한 것은?

A: My computer just shut down for no reason. I can't even turn it back on again.

B: Did you try charging it? It might just be out of battery.

A: Of course, I tried charging it.

B: _____

A: I should do that, but I'm so lazy.

① I don't know how to fix your computer.

② Try visiting the nearest service center then.

③ Well, stop thinking about your problems and go to sleep.

④ My brother will try to fix your computer because he's a technician.

12 다음 글에 나타난 화자의 심경으로 가장 적절한 것은?

My face turned white as a sheet. I looked at my watch. The tests would be almost over by now. I arrived at the testing center in an absolute panic. I tried to tell my story, but my sentences and descriptive gestures got so confused that I communicated nothing more than a very convincing version of a human tornado. In an effort to curb my distracting explanation, the proctor led me to an empty seat and put a test booklet in front of me. He looked doubtfully from me to the clock, and then he walked away. I tried desperately to make up for lost time, scrambling madly through analogies and sentence completions. "Fifteen minutes remain," the voice of doom declared from the front of the classroom. Algebraic equations, arithmetic calculations, geometric diagrams swam before my eyes. "Time! Pencils down, please."

① nervous and worried
② excited and cheerful
③ calm and determined
④ safe and relaxed

13 주어진 문장 다음에 이어질 글의 순서로 가장 적절한 것은?

Devices that monitor and track your health are becoming more popular among all age populations.

(A) For example, falls are a leading cause of death for adults 65 and older. Fall alerts are a popular gerotechnology that has been around for many years but have now improved.

(B) However, for seniors aging in place, especially those without a caretaker in the home, these technologies can be lifesaving.

(C) This simple technology can automatically alert 911 or a close family member the moment a senior has fallen.

* gerotechnology: 노인을 위한 양로 기술

① (B) – (C) – (A)　　② (B) – (A) – (C)
③ (C) – (A) – (B)　　④ (C) – (B) – (A)

※ 밑줄 친 부분에 들어갈 말로 가장 적절한 것을 고르시오.
[14~15]

14

A: Where do you want to go for our honeymoon?
B: Let's go to a place that neither of us has been to.
A: Then, why don't we go to Hawaii?
B: _____

① I've always wanted to go there.
② Isn't Korea a great place to live?
③ Great! My last trip there was amazing!
④ Oh, you must've been to Hawaii already.

15

The secret of successful people is usually that they are able to concentrate totally on one thing. Even if they have a lot in their head, they have found a method that the many commitments don't impede each other, but instead they are brought into a good inner order. And this order is quite simple: _____. In theory, it seems to be quite clear, but in everyday life it seems rather different. You might have tried to decide on priorities, but you have failed because of everyday trivial matters and all the unforeseen distractions. Separate off disturbances, for example, by escaping into another office, and not allowing any distractions to get in the way. When you concentrate on the one task of your priorities, you will find you have energy that you didn't even know you had.

① the sooner, the better
② better late than never
③ out of sight, out of mind
④ the most important thing first

With the help of the scientist, the commercial fishing industry has found out that its fishing must be done scientifically if it is to be continued. With no fishing pressure on a fish population, the number of fish will reach a predictable level of abundance and stay there. The only fluctuation would be due to natural environmental factors, such as availability of food, proper temperature, and the like. If a fishery is developed to take these fish, their population can be maintained if the fishing harvest is small. The mackerel of the North Sea is a good example. If we increase the fishery and take more fish each year, we must be careful not to reduce the population below the ideal point where it can replace all of the fish we take out each year. If we fish at this level, called the *maximum sustainable yield*, we can maintain the greatest possible yield, year after year. If we catch too many, the number of fish will decrease each year until we fish ourselves out of a job. Examples of severely overfished animals are the blue whale of the Antarctic and the halibut of the North Atlantic. Fishing just the correct amount to maintain a maximum annual yield is both a science and an art. Research is constantly being done to help us better understand the fish population and how to utilize it to the maximum without depleting the population.

① Say No to Commercial Fishing
② Sea Farming Seen As a Fishy Business
③ Why Does the Fishing Industry Need Science?
④ Overfished Animals: Cases of Illegal Fishing

Does terrorism ever work? 9/11 was an enormous tactical success for al Qaeda, partly because it involved attacks that took place in the media capital of the world and the actual capital of the United States,   (A)   ensuring the widest possible coverage of the event. If terrorism is a form of theater where you want a lot of people watching, no event in human history was likely ever seen by a larger global audience than the 9/11 attacks. At the time, there was much discussion about how 9/11 was like the attack on Pearl Harbor. They were indeed similar since they were both surprise attacks that drew America into significant wars. But they were also similar in another sense. Pearl Harbor was a great *tactical* success for Imperial Japan, but it led to a great *strategic* failure: Within four years of Pearl Harbor the Japanese empire lay in ruins, utterly defeated.   (B)   , 9/11 was a great tactical success for al Qaeda, but it also turned out to be a great strategic failure for Osama bin Laden.

	(A)	(B)
①	thereby	Similarly
②	while	Therefore
③	while	Fortunately
④	thereby	On the contrary

18 다음 글의 내용과 일치하지 <u>않는</u> 것은?

We entered a new phase as a species when Chinese scientists altered a human embryo to remove a potentially fatal blood disorder—not only from the baby, but all of its descendants. Researchers call this process "germline modification." The media likes the phrase "designer babies." But we should call it what it is, "eugenics." And we, the human race, need to decide whether or not we want to use it. Last month, in the United States, the scientific establishment weighed in. A National Academy of Sciences and National Academy of Medicine joint committee endorsed embryo editing aimed at genes that cause serious diseases when there is "no reasonable alternative." But it was more wary of editing for "enhancement," like making already-healthy children stronger or taller. It recommended a public discussion, and said that doctors should "not proceed at this time." The committee had good reason to urge caution. The history of eugenics is full of oppression and misery.

* eugenics: 우생학

① Doctors were recommended to immediately go ahead with embryo editing for enhancement.
② Recently, the scientific establishment in the U.S. joined a discussion on eugenics.
③ Chinese scientists modified a human embryo to prevent a serious blood disorder.
④ "Designer babies" is another term for the germline modification process.

19 주어진 문장이 들어갈 위치로 가장 적절한 것은?

If neither surrendered, the two exchanged blows until one was knocked out.

The ancient Olympics provided athletes an opportunity to prove their fitness and superiority, just like our modern games. (①) The ancient Olympic events were designed to eliminate the weak and glorify the strong. Winners were pushed to the brink. (②) Just as in modern times, people loved extreme sports. One of the favorite events was added in the 33rd Olympiad. This was the pankration, or an extreme mix of wrestling and boxing. The Greek word *pankration* means "total power." The men wore leather straps with metal studs, which could make a terrible mess of their opponents. (③) This dangerous form of wrestling had no time or weight limits. In this event, only two rules applied. First, wrestlers were not allowed to gouge eyes with their thumbs. Secondly, they could not bite. Anything else was considered fair play. The contest was decided in the same manner as a boxing match. Contenders continued until one of the two collapsed. (④) Only the strongest and most determined athletes attempted this event. Imagine wrestling "Mr. Fingertips," who earned his nickname by breaking his opponents' fingers!

20 밑줄 친 부분에 들어갈 말로 가장 적절한 것은?

In our time it is not only the law of the market which has its own life and rules over man, but also the development of science and technique. For a number of reasons, the problems and organization of science today are such that a scientist does not choose his problems; the problems force themselves upon the scientist. He solves one problem, and the result is not that he is more secure or certain, but that ten other new problems open up in place of the single solved one. They force him to solve them; he has to go ahead at an ever-quickening pace. The same holds true for industrial techniques. The pace of science forces the pace of technique. Theoretical physics forces atomic energy on us; the successful production of the fission bomb forces upon us the manufacture of the hydrogen bomb. We do not choose our problems, we do not choose our products; we are pushed, we are forced—by what? By a system which has no purpose and goal transcending it, and which _____.

① makes man its appendix
② creates a false sense of security
③ inspires man with creative challenges
④ empowers scientists to control the market laws

정답 · 해석 · 해설 p. 124

14회 2018년 지방직 9급
모바일 자동 채점 + 성적 분석 서비스 바로 가기

QR코드를 이용해 모바일로 간편하게 채점하고 나의 실력이 어느 정도인지, 취약 부분이 어디인지 바로 파악해 보세요.

(p.213에서 전체 정답표를 확인하실 수 있습니다)

DIFFICULTIES ARE MEANT TO ROUSE, NOT DISCOURAGE
THE HUMAN SPIRIT IS TO GROW STRONG BY CONFLICT.

WILLIM ELLERY CHANNING

어려움은 낙담이 아니라 분발하기 위한 것이다
인간의 정신은 갈등을 통해 강해진다.
월리엄 엘러리 채닝

Part 3
서울시 9급

문제 유형	4지선다형
총 문항 수	20문항
경쟁률 (2024년 2월, 건축)	10.6:1
합격선 (2024년 2월, 건축)	54점
시험 안내	서울시인터넷원서접수센터 (https://gosi.seoul.go.kr)

※ 서울시 9급 영어 과목 시험은 2020년부터 지방직과 동일하게 인사혁신처에서 출제했습니다.

제한 시간 : 20분　　시작 _____시 _____분 ~ 종료 _____시 _____분　　나의 점수 _____　회독 수 ☐ ☐ ☐

※ 밑줄 친 부분의 의미와 가장 가까운 것은? [01~03]

01

> After receiving an attractive job offer from a renowned company, she finally chose to spurn it in order to pursue her dream of starting her own business.

① contemplate　　② postpone

③ decline　　④ denounce

02

> Ever since the Red Sox traded Babe Ruth to the Yankees in 1918, Boston sports fans have learned to take the good with the bad. They have seen more basketball championships than any other city but haven't boasted a World Series title in over 75 years.

① waived　　② yielded

③ renounced　　④ bragged

03

> Nell has a singular talent for getting into trouble; the other morning, she managed to break her leg, insult a woman at the post office, drop some eggs at the grocery store, paint her bedroom green, and cut down the big maple tree in the next-door neighbor's front yard.

① conventional　　② exceptional

③ martial　　④ plural

※ 밑줄 친 부분에 들어갈 말로 가장 적절한 것은? [04~05]

04

> Instead of giving us an innovative idea on the matter in hand, the keynote speaker brought up a(n) _____ which was lengthy and made us feel tedium for quite a while.

① brainstorming　　② witticism

③ epigraph　　④ platitude

05

> It has rained so little in California for the last six years that forest rangers need to be especially _____ in watching for forest fires.

① vigilant　　② relaxed

③ indifferent　　④ distracted

※ 밑줄 친 부분에 들어갈 말로 가장 적절한 것은? [06~07]

06

> A: Sorry to keep you waiting, Ms. Krauss.
> B: Well, I see that you've got a lot on your plate today. I won't keep you any longer.
> A: Don't worry, Ms. Krauss. We'll get your order done on time.
> B: Should I give you a call?
> A: _____

① Well, you're a good customer. Let me see what I can do.

② No need for that. Come at 11:00 and I'll have your documents ready.

③ Tomorrow morning? No sweat. Can you get the documents to me before noon?

④ I'm afraid that might be difficult. I've got a lot of orders to complete this morning.

07

A: Did you see Emily's new haircut?
B: Yes, she chopped it all off _____!
A: I was so surprised. It's so different from before.
B: She said she needed a change.
A: Well, it definitely suits her.
B: Agreed, she looks fantastic!

① over the moon
② out of the blue
③ up in the air
④ under the weather

08 밑줄 친 부분 중 어법상 가장 옳은 것은?

① Despite the inconsistent and fairly sparse laboratory data regarding groupthink, the theory has been believed to have explanatory potential. ② Some of this continued confidence undoubtedly stems in part from a series of creative historical analysis that have been advanced to substantiate the model's various hypotheses. ③ Surely, we must be careful of such historical analysis for several reasons, as we cannot be certain that contradictory examples have not overlook. ④ Such case studies, however, do have the virtue of looking at cases which the antecedent conditions were strong enough to create the conditions deemed necessary by the model.

※ 밑줄 친 부분 중 어법상 가장 옳지 않은 것은? [09~10]

09

Research shows that tea drinkers can ① enjoy greater protection from heart disease, cancer, and stress, ② no matter how type of brew they choose. Experts say the antioxidants in tea leaves confer major health benefits. ③ That's why we admire how some creative cooks went beyond the cup to ④ find tasty ways to meld tea with their appetizers, meals, and desserts.

10

The rise of the modernist novel and poetry ① were accompanied between 1910 and 1930 by the rise of literary criticism ② as we know it. This is a kind of literary criticism ③ very different from the one that had existed in the nineteenth century, ④ not only in attitude but in vocation too, as criticism became increasingly academic and technical.

11 〈보기〉의 문장 다음에 이어질 글의 순서로 가장 적절한 것은?

─── 〈보기〉 ───
During the first few times you choose to celebrate the achievements of members of the group, you may want to explain your thinking behind the small ceremony. By simply stating your intention to thank members of the group for their courage or hard work, people become aware of the meaning of the celebration and are less apt to dismiss it.

(A) It is quite possible as you begin this process that the member of the group being honored will feel self-conscious and awkward.

(B) Coupled with the fact that the event being celebrated is based on authentic achievement, it is likely that the members of the group will feel encouraged to participate in future celebrations.

(C) This is a natural response, especially in groups that do not know each other well or in organizations in which celebration is not a part of the culture.

① (B) – (A) – (C)   ② (B) – (C) – (A)
③ (C) – (A) – (B)   ④ (C) – (B) – (A)

12 글의 내용과 일치하지 <u>않는</u> 것은?

The work of human body's immune system is carried out by the body's trillions of immune cells and specialized molecules. The first line of defense lies in the physical barriers of the skin and mucous membranes, which block and trap invaders. A second, the innate system, is composed of cells including phagocytes, whose basic job is to eat the invaders. In addition to these immune cells, many chemical compounds respond to infection and injury, move in to destroy pathogens, and begin repairing tissue. The body's third line of defense is a final, more specific response. Its elite fighting units are trained on the job; that is, they are created in response to a pathogen that the body has not seen before. Once activated in one part of the body, the adaptive system functions throughout, and it memorizes the antigens (a substance that provokes an immune system response). The next time they come along, the body hits back quicker and harder.

* mucous membranes 점막, phagocytes 포식세포
pathogens 병원체, antigens 항원

① 면역체계의 첫 번째 방어선은 피부와 점막의 물리적 장벽에 있다.
② 면역체계의 두 번째 방어선의 기본 역할은 침입자를 소멸시키는 것이다.
③ 면역체계의 세 번째 방어선은 몸에 이전부터 지니고 있던 병원체에 반응한다.
④ 몸의 적응 시스템은 항원을 기억하여 차후 이 항원에 대해 더 빠르고 강하게 반격한다.

※ 〈보기〉의 문장이 들어갈 위치로 가장 적절한 것은?
[13~14]

13

— 〈보기〉 —

International management is applied by managers of enterprises that attain their goals and objectives across unique multicultural, multinational boundaries.

The term management is defined in many Western textbooks as the process of completing activities efficiently with and through other individuals. (①) The process consists of the functions or main activities engaged in by managers. These functions or activities are usually labeled planning, organizing, staffing, coordinating(leading and motivating), and controlling. (②) The management process is affected by the organization's home country environment, which includes the shareholders, creditors, customers, employees, government, and community, as well as technological, demographic, and geographic factors. (③) These business enterprises are generally referred to as international corporations, multinational corporations(MNCs), or global corporations. (④) This means that the process is affected by the environment where the organization is based, as well as by the unique culture, including views on ethics and social responsibility, existing in the country or countries where it conducts its business activities.

14

This kind of development makes us realize that removing safety hazards is far better than creating alarms to detect them.

Spinoff technology can help to make our homes and communities safer and more comfortable places to live. Most people are aware that carbon monoxide(CO) buildup in our homes can be very dangerous. This may come from a faulty furnace or fireplace. (①) Consequently, some people have carbon monoxide detectors in their homes, but these detectors only alert them if the level of carbon monoxide is unsafe. (②) However, using space technology, NASA developed an air-conditioning system that can not only detect dangerous amounts of carbon monoxide, but actually oxidizes the toxic gases into harmless carbon dioxide. (③) In addition to helping people to have clean air, having access to clean water is also of major importance for everyone. NASA engineers have been working with private companies to create better systems for clean, drinkable water for astronauts in space. (④) These systems, which have been developed for the astronauts, can quickly and affordably cleanse any available water. This is a major advantage to the people on Earth who live in remote or developing areas where water is scarce or polluted.

15 (A)와 (B)에 들어갈 말로 가장 적절한 것은?

Antibiotics are among the most commonly prescribed drugs for people. Antibiotics are effective against bacterial infections, such as strep throat, some types of pneumonia, eye infections, and ear infections. But these drugs don't work at all against viruses, such as those that cause colds or flu. Unfortunately, many antibiotics prescribed to people and to animals are unnecessary. _____(A)_____, the overuse and misuse of antibiotics help to create drug-resistant bacteria. Here's how that might happen. When used properly, antibiotics can help destroy disease-causing bacteria. _____(B)_____, if you take an antibiotic when you have a viral infection like the flu, the drug won't affect the viruses making you sick.

	(A)	(B)
①	However	Instead
②	Furthermore	Therefore
③	On the other hand	For example
④	Furthermore	However

16

The assumption that politics and administration could be separated was ultimately disregarded as utopian. Wilson and Goodnow's idea of apolitical public administration proved unrealistic. A more realistic view—the so-called "politics school"—is that politics is very much a part of administration. The politics school maintains that in a pluralistic political system in which many diverse groups have a voice, public administrators with considerable knowledge play key roles. Legislation, for instance, is written by public administrators as much as by legislators. The public bureaucracy is as capable of engendering support for its interests as any other participant in the political process, and public administrators are as likely as any to be part of a policymaking partnership. Furthermore, laws are interpreted by public administrators in their execution, which includes many and often unforeseen scenarios.

① How to Cope with Unpredictable Situations in Politics
② Public Administrators' Surprising Influence in a Political System
③ Repetitive Attempts to Separate the Politics from Administration
④ Loopholes of the View that Politics and Administration are Inseparable

17

We are living in perhaps the most exciting times in all human history. The technological advances we are witnessing today are giving birth to new industries that are producing devices, systems, and services that were once only reflected in the realm of science fiction and fantasy. Industries are being completely restructured to become better, faster, stronger, and safer. You no longer have to settle for something that is "close enough," because customization is reaching levels that provide you with exactly what you want or need. We are on the verge of releasing the potential of genetic enhancement, nanotechnology, and other technologies that will lead to curing many diseases and maybe even slowing the aging process itself. Such advances are due to discoveries in separate fields to produce these wonders. In the not so distant future, incredible visions of imagination such as robotic surgeons that keep us healthy, self-driving trucks that deliver our goods, and virtual worlds that entertain us after a long day will be commonplace. If ever there were a time that we were about to capture perfection, it is now—and the momentum is only increasing.

① The Era of Unprecedented Technological Advancements
② Struggles with Imperfect Solutions in Modern Industries
③ Historical Perspectives on Technological Progress
④ The Stagnant State of Contemporary Industries

18

Emotional strength isn't about maintaining a stiff upper lip, being stoic or never showing emotion—actually, it's the opposite. "Emotional strength is about having the skills you need to regulate your feelings," says psychotherapist Amy Morin. "You don't need to chase happiness all the time. Instead, you can develop the courage you need to work through uncomfortable feelings, like anxiety and sadness." Someone with emotional strength, for instance, will know when to shift their emotional state, says Morin. "If their anxiety isn't serving them well, they have strategies they can use to calm themselves. They also have the ability to tolerate difficult emotions, but they do so by _____ them, not suppressing them. They don't distract themselves from painful feelings, like loneliness."

① exaggerating   ② pursuing
③ embracing   ④ ignoring

19

Like many small organisms, fungi are often overlooked, but their planetary significance is outsize. Plants managed to leave water and grow on land only because of their collaboration with fungi, which acted as their root systems for millions of years. Even today, roughly 90 percent of plants and nearly all the world's trees depend on fungi, which supply crucial minerals by breaking down rock and other substances. They can also be a scourge, eradicating forests and killing humans. At times, they even seem to _____ . When Japanese researchers released slime molds into mazes molded on Tokyo's streets, the molds found the most efficient route between the city's urban hubs in a day, instinctively recreating a set of paths almost identical to the existing rail network. When put in a miniature floor map of Ikea, they quickly found the shortest route to the exit.

① gather   ② breed
③ enjoy   ④ think

20

Species (or higher taxa) may go extinct for two reasons. One is "real" extinction in the sense that the lineage has died out and left no descendants. For modern species, the meaning is unambiguous, but for fossil real extinction has to be distinguished from *pseudoextinction*. Pseudoextinction means that the taxon appears to go extinct, but only because of an error or artifact in the evidence, and not because the underlying lineage really ceased to exist. For instance, _____ _____ . As a lineage evolves, later forms may look sufficiently different from earlier ones that a taxonomist may classify them as different species, even though there is a continuous breeding lineage. This may be because the species are classified phonetically, or it may be because the taxonomist only has a few specimens, some from early in the lineage and some from late in the lineage such that the continuous lineage is undetectable.

① clues for extinction are found in many regions
② a lineage may disappear temporarily from the fossil record
③ a continuously evolving lineage may change its taxonomic name
④ some divergent lineages have been fully identified

정답 · 해석 · 해설 p. 136

15회 2024년 서울시 9급 (2월 추가)
모바일 자동 채점 + 성적 분석 서비스 바로 가기

QR코드를 이용해 모바일로 간편하게 채점하고 나의 실력이 어느 정도인지, 취약 부분이 어디인지 바로 파악해 보세요.

(p.213에서 전체 정답표를 확인하실 수 있습니다)

※ 밑줄 친 부분의 의미와 가장 가까운 것은? [01~02]

01

> Norwegians led by Roald Amundsen arrived in Antarctica's Bay of Whales on January 14, 1911. With dog teams, they prepared to race the British to the South Pole. Amundsen's ship, *Fram*, loaned by renowned Arctic explorer Fridtjof Nansen, was the elite polar vessel of her time.

① famous   ② intrepid
③ early   ④ notorious

02

> In her presentation, she will give a lucid account of her future plan as a member of this organization.

① loquacious   ② sluggish
③ placid   ④ perspicuous

※ 밑줄 친 부분에 들어갈 말로 가장 적절한 것은? [03~05]

03

> People need to _____ skills in their jobs in order to be competitive and become successful.

① abolish   ② accumulate
③ diminish   ④ isolate

04

> Manhattan has been compelled to expand skyward because of the _____ of any other direction in which to grow. This, more than any other thing, is responsible for its physical majesty.

① absence   ② decision
③ exposure   ④ selection

05

> _____ is using someone else's exact words or ideas in your writing, and not naming the original writer or book, magazine, video, podcast, or website where you found them.

① citation   ② presentation
③ modification   ④ plagiarism

06 두 사람의 대화 중 가장 어색한 것은?

① A: I need to ask you to do me a favor.
   B: Sure thing, what is it?

② A: I'm afraid I have to close my account.
   B: OK, please fill out this form.

③ A: That was a beautiful wedding.
   B: I'll say. And the wedding couple looked so right for each other.

④ A: I bought this jacket last Monday and already the zipper was broken. I'd like a refund.
   B: OK, I will fix the zipper.

07 어법상 가장 옳은 것은?

① The poverty rate is the percentage of the population which family income falls below an absolute level.

② Not surprisingly, any college graduate would rather enter the labor force in a year of economic expansion than in a year of economic contraction.

③ It is hard that people pick up a newspaper without seeing some newly reported statistic about the economy.

④ Despite the growth is continued in average income, the poverty rate has not declined.

08 어법상 가장 옳지 않은 것은?

① With nothing left, she would have to cling to that which had robbed her.

② Send her word to have her place cleaning up.

③ Alive, she had been a tradition, a duty, and a care.

④ Will you accuse a lady to her face of smelling bad?

09 어법상 가장 옳지 않은 것은?

① An ugly, old, yellow tin bucket stood beside the stove.

② It is the most perfect copier ever invented.

③ John was very frightening her.

④ She thought that he was an utter fool.

10

People have opportunities to behave in sustainable ways every day when they get dressed, and fashion, when ① creating within a broad understanding of sustainability, can sustain people as well as the environment. People have a desire to make ② socially responsible choices regarding the fashions they purchase. As designers and product developers of fashion, we are challenged to provide responsible choices. We need to stretch the perception of fashion to remain ③ open to the many layers and complexities that exist. The people, processes, and environments ④ that embody fashion are also calling for new sustainable directions. What a fabulous opportunity awaits!

11

Newspapers, journals, magazines, TV and radio, and professional or trade publications ① provide further ② information that may help interpret the facts ③ given in the annual report or on developments since the report ④ published.

12

Tropical forests are incredibly rich ecosystems, which provide much of the world's biodiversity. ① However, even with increased understanding of the value of these areas, excessive destruction continues. There are a few promising signs, however. ② Deforestation in many regions is slowing as governments combat this practice with intensive tree planting. Asia, for example, has gained forest in the last decade, primarily due to China's large-scale planting initiatives. ③ One part of this challenge is to allow countries a more equitable share of the revenue from pharmaceutical products originating in the tropical forests. Moreover, the number of reserves designated for conservation of biodiversity is increasing worldwide with particularly strong gains in South America and Asia. ④ Unfortunately, despite these gains, the capacity for humans to destroy forests continues to appear greater than their ability to protect them.

13

In the early 1980s, a good friend of mine discovered that she was dying of multiple myeloma, an especially dangerous, painful form of cancer. I had lost elderly relatives and family friends to death before this, but I had never lost a personal friend. ① I had never watched a relatively young person die slowly and painfully of disease. It took my friend a year to die, and ② I got into the habit of visiting her every Saturday and taking along the latest chapter of the novel I was working on. This happened to be *Clay's Ark*. With its story of disease and death, it was thoroughly inappropriate for the situation. But my friend had always read my novels. ③ She insisted that she no longer wanted to read this one as well. I suspect that neither of us believed she would live to read it in its completed form— ④ although, of course, we didn't talk about this.

14 글의 요지로 가장 적절한 것은?

From computers to compact-disc players, railway engines to robots, the origins of today's machines can be traced back to the elaborate mechanical toys that flourished in the eighteenth century. As the first complex machines produced by man, automata represented a proving ground for technology that would later be harnessed in the industrial revolution. But their original uses were rather less utilitarian. Automata were the playthings of royalty, both as a form of entertainment in palaces and courts across Europe and as gifts sent from one ruling family to another. As a source of amusement, the first automata were essentially scaled-down versions of the elaborate mechanical clocks that adorned cathedrals. These clocks provided the inspiration for smaller and increasingly elaborate automata. As these devices became more complicated, their time-keeping function became less important, and automata became first and foremost mechanical amusements in the form of mechanical theaters or moving scenes.

① The history of machine has less to do with a source of amusement.
② Modern machine has a non-utilitarian origin.
③ Royalty across Europe was interested in toy industry.
④ The decline of automata is closely associated with the industrial revolution.

15 글의 내용과 가장 일치하지 않는 것은?

When Ali graduated, he decided he didn't want to join the ranks of commuters struggling to work every day. He wanted to set up his own online gift-ordering business so that he could work from home. He knew it was a risk but felt he would have at least a fighting chance of success. Initially, he and a college friend planned to start the business together. Ali had the idea and Igor, his friend, had the money to invest in the company. But then just weeks before the launch, Igor dropped a bombshell: he said he no longer wanted to be part of Ali's plans. Despite Ali's attempts to persuade him to hang fire on his decision, Igor said he was no longer prepared to take the risk and was going to beat a retreat before it was too late. However, two weeks later Igor stole a march on Ali by launching his own online gift-ordering company. Ali was shell-shocked by this betrayal, but he soon came out fighting. He took Igor's behaviour as a call to arms and has persuaded a bank to lend him the money he needs. Ali's introduction to the business world has certainly been a baptism of fire, but I'm sure he will be really successful on his own.

① 본래 온라인 선물주문 사업은 Ali의 계획이었다.
② Igor가 먼저 그 사업에서 손을 떼겠다고 말했다.
③ Igor가 Ali보다 앞서서 자기 소유의 선물주문 회사를 차렸다.
④ Ali는 은행을 설득하여 Igor에게 돈을 빌려주게 했다.

※ (A)와 (B)에 들어갈 말로 가장 적절한 것은? [16~17]

16

Scientists are working on many other human organs and tissues. For example, they have successfully generated, or grown, a piece of liver. This is an exciting achievement since people cannot live without a liver. In other laboratories, scientists have created a human jawbone and a lung. While these scientific breakthroughs are very promising, they are also limited. Scientists cannot use cells for a new organ from a very diseased or damaged organ. (A) _____, many researchers are working on a way to use stem cells to grow completely new organs. Stem cells are very simple cells in the body that can develop into any kind of complex cells, such as skin cells or blood cells and even heart and liver cells. (B) _____, stem cells can grow into all different kinds of cells.

	(A)	(B)
①	Specifically	For example
②	Additionally	On the other hand
③	Consequently	In other words
④	Accordingly	In contrast

17

To speak of 'the aim' of scientific activity may perhaps sound a little (A) _____; for clearly, different scientists have different aims, and science itself (whatever that may mean) has no aims. I admit all this. And yet it seems that when we speak of science we do feel, more or less clearly, that there is something characteristic of scientific activity; and since scientific activity looks pretty much like a rational activity, and since a rational activity must have some aim, the attempt to describe the aim of science may not be entirely (B) _____.

	(A)	(B)
①	naive	futile
②	reasonable	fruitful
③	chaotic	acceptable
④	consistent	discarded

18 〈보기〉의 문장 다음에 이어질 글의 순서로 가장 적절한 것은?

─── 〈보기〉 ───

The child that is born today may possibly have the same faculties as if he had been born in the days of Noah; if it be otherwise, we possess no means of determining the difference.

(A) That development is entirely under the control of the influences exerted by the society in which the child may chance to live.

(B) If such society be altogether denied, the faculties perish, and the child grows up a beast and not a man; if the society be uneducated and coarse, the growth of the faculties is early so stunted as never afterwards to be capable of recovery; if the society be highly cultivated, the child will be cultivated also, and will show, more or less, through life the fruits of that cultivation.

(C) Hence each generation receives the benefit of the cultivation of that which preceded it.

(D) But the equality of the natural faculties at starting will not prevent a vast difference in their ultimate development.

① (A) – (B) – (D) – (C)
② (A) – (D) – (B) – (C)
③ (D) – (A) – (B) – (C)
④ (D) – (B) – (A) – (C)

19

It is quite clear that people's view of what English should do has been strongly influenced by what Latin does. For instance, there is (or used to be — it is very infrequently observed in natural speech today) a feeling that an infinitive in English should not be split. What this means is that you should not put anything between the to which marks an infinitive verb and the verb itself: you should say to go boldly and never to boldly go. This 'rule' is based on Latin, where the marker of the infinitive is an ending, and you can no more split it from the rest of the verb than you can split -ing from the rest of its verb and say goboldlying for going boldly. English speakers clearly do not feel that to and go belong together _____ go and -ing. They frequently put words between this kind of to and its verb.

① less closely than
② as closely as
③ more loosely than
④ as loosely as

20

A company may be allowed to revalue non-current assets. Where the fair value of non-current assets increases this may be reflected in an adjustment to the value of the assets shown in the statement of financial position. As far as possible, this should reflect the fair value of assets and liabilities. However, the increase in value of a non-current asset does not necessarily represent _____ for the company. A profit is made or realized only when the asset is sold and the resulting profit is taken through the income statement. Until this event occurs prudence — supported by common sense — requires that the increase in asset value is retained in the balance sheet. Shareholders have the right to any profit on the sale of company assets, so the shareholders' stake (equity) is increased by the same amount as the increase in asset valuation. A revaluation reserve is created and the balance sheet still balances.

① the fair value
② an actual cost
③ an immediate profit
④ the value of a transaction

정답 · 해석 · 해설 p. 146

16회 2022년 서울시 9급 (2월 추가)
모바일 자동 채점 + 성적 분석 서비스 바로 가기

QR코드를 이용해 모바일로 간편하게 채점하고 나의 실력이 어느 정도인지, 취약 부분이 어디인지 바로 파악해 보세요.

(p.213에서 전체 정답표를 확인하실 수 있습니다)

제한 시간 : 20분 시작 _____시 _____분 ~ 종료 _____시 _____분 나의 점수 _____ 회독 수 ☐ ☐ ☐

※ 밑줄 친 부분의 의미와 가장 가까운 것은? [01~02]

01

> At least in high school she made one decision where she finally <u>saw eye to eye</u> with her parents.

① quarreled　　　② disputed

③ parted　　　　④ agreed

02

> Justifications are accounts in which one accepts responsibility for the act in question, but denies the <u>pejorative</u> quality associated with it.

① derogatory　　　② extrovert

③ mandatory　　　④ redundant

※ 밑줄 친 부분에 들어갈 말로 가장 적절한 것은? [03~05]

03

> Tests ruled out dirt and poor sanitation as causes of yellow fever, and a mosquito was the _____ carrier.

① suspected　　　② uncivilized

③ cheerful　　　　④ volunteered

04

> Generally speaking, people living in 2018 are pretty fortunate when you compare modern times to the full scale of human history. Life expectancy _____ at around 72 years, and diseases like smallpox and diphtheria, which were widespread and deadly only a century ago, are preventable, curable, or altogether eradicated.

① curtails　　　② hovers

③ initiates　　　④ aggravates

05

> To imagine that there are concrete patterns to past events, which can provide _____ for our lives and decisions, is to project on to history a hope for a certainty which it cannot fulfill.

① hallucinations　　　② templates

③ inquiries　　　　　④ commotion

06 대화 중 가장 어색한 것은?

① A : What was the movie like on Saturday?

　B : Great. I really enjoyed it.

② A : Hello. I'd like to have some shirts pressed.

　B : Yes, how soon will you need them?

③ A : Would you like a single or a double room?

　B : Oh, it's just for me, so a single is fine.

④ A : What time is the next flight to Boston?

　B : It will take about 45 minutes to get to Boston.

※ 밑줄 친 부분 중 어법상 가장 옳지 않은 것은? [07~10]

07

> Inventor Elias Howe attributed the discovery of the sewing machine ① <u>for</u> a dream ② <u>in which</u> he was captured by cannibals. He noticed as they danced around him ③ <u>that</u> there were holes at the tips of spears, and he realized this was the design feature he needed ④ <u>to solve</u> his problem.

08

By 1955 Nikita Khrushchev ① had been emerged as Stalin's successor in the USSR, and he ② embarked on a policy of "peaceful coexistence" ③ whereby East and West ④ were to continue their competition, but in a less confrontational manner.

09

Squid, octopuses, and cuttlefish are all ① types of cephalopods. ② Each of these animals has special cells under its skin that ③ contains pigment, a colored liquid. A cephalopod can move these cells toward or away from its skin. This allows it ④ to change the pattern and color of its appearance.

10

There is a more serious problem than ① maintaining the cities. As people become more comfortable working alone, they may become ② less social. It's ③ easier to stay home in comfortable exercise clothes or a bathrobe than ④ getting dressed for yet another business meeting!

11 글의 제목으로 가장 적절한 것은?

Economists say that production of an information good involves high fixed costs but low marginal costs. The cost of producing the first copy of an information good may be substantial, but the cost of producing(or reproducing) additional copies is negligible. This sort of cost structure has many important implications. For example, cost-based pricing just doesn't work: a 10 or 20 percent markup on unit cost makes no sense when unit cost is zero. You must price your information goods according to consumer value, not according to your production cost.

① Securing the Copyright
② Pricing the Information Goods
③ Information as Intellectual Property
④ The Cost of Technological Change

12 밑줄 친 부분이 지칭하는 대상이 다른 것은?

Dracula ants get their name for the way they sometimes drink the blood of their own young. But this week, ① the insects have earned a new claim to fame. Dracula ants of the species *Mystrium camillae* can snap their jaws together so fast, you could fit 5,000 strikes into the time it takes us to blink an eye. This means ② the blood-suckers wield the fastest known movement in nature, according to a study published this week in the journal *Royal Society Open Science*. Interestingly, the ants produce their record-breaking snaps simply by pressing their jaws together so hard that ③ they bend. This stores energy in one of the jaws, like a spring, until it slides past the other and lashes out with extraordinary speed and force—reaching a maximum velocity of over 200 miles per hour. It's kind of like what happens when you snap your fingers, only 1,000 times faster. Dracula ants are secretive predators as ④ they prefer to hunt under the leaf litter or in subterranean tunnels.

13 밑줄 친 부분에 들어갈 말로 가장 옳은 것은?

I am writing to you from a train in Germany, sitting on the floor. The train is crowded, and all the seats are taken. However, there is a special class of "comfort customers" who are allowed to make those already seated _____ their seats.

① give up   ② take
③ giving up   ④ taken

14

A country's wealth plays a central role in education, so lack of funding and resources from a nation-state can weaken a system. Governments in sub-Saharan Africa spend only 2.4 percent of the world's public resources on education, yet 15 percent of the school-age population lives there. _____, the United States spends 28 percent of all the money spent in the world on education, yet it houses only 4 percent of the school-age population.

① Nevertheless   ② Furthermore
③ Conversely   ④ Similarly

15

"Highly conscientious employees do a series of things better than the rest of us," says University of Illinois psychologist Brent Roberts, who studies conscientiousness. Roberts owes their success to "hygiene" factors. Conscientious people have a tendency to organize their lives well. A disorganized, unconscientious person might lose 20 or 30 minutes rooting through their files to find the right document, an inefficient experience conscientious folks tend to avoid. Basically, by being conscientious, people _____ they'd otherwise create for themselves.

① deal with setbacks
② do thorough work
③ follow norms
④ sidestep stress

16

Climate change, deforestation, widespread pollution and the sixth mass extinction of biodiversity all define living in our world today—an era that has come to be known as "the Anthropocene". These crises are underpinned by production and consumption which greatly exceeds global ecological limits, but blame is far from evenly shared. The world's 42 wealthiest people own as much as the poorest 3.7 billion, and they generate far greater environmental impacts. Some have therefore proposed using the term "Capitalocene" to describe this era of ecological devastation and growing inequality, reflecting capitalism's logic of endless growth and _____.

① the better world that is still within our reach
② the accumulation of wealth in fewer pockets
③ an effective response to climate change
④ a burning desire for a more viable future

17 글의 흐름상 빈칸에 들어갈 말로 가장 적절한 것은?

Ever since the time of ancient Greek tragedy, Western culture has been haunted by the figure of the revenger. He or she stands on a whole series of borderlines: between civilization and barbarity, between _____ and the community's need for the rule of law, between the conflicting demands of justice and mercy. Do we have a right to exact revenge against those who have destroyed our loved ones? Or should we leave vengeance to the law or to the gods? And if we do take action into our own hands, are we not reducing ourselves to the same moral level as the original perpetrator of murderous deeds?

① redemption of the revenger from a depraved condition
② divine vengeance on human atrocities
③ moral depravity of the corrupt politicians
④ an individual's accountability to his or her own conscience

18 글의 흐름상 가장 적절하지 <u>않은</u> 문장은?

It seems to me possible to name four kinds of reading, each with a characteristic manner and purpose. The first is reading for information—reading to learn about a trade, or politics, or how to accomplish something. ① <u>We read a newspaper this way, or most textbooks, or directions on how to assemble a bicycle.</u> ② <u>With most of this material, the reader can learn to scan the page quickly, coming up with what he needs and ignoring what is irrelevant to him, like the rhythm of the sentence, or the play of metaphor.</u> ③ <u>We also register a track of feeling through the metaphors and associations of words.</u> ④ <u>Courses in speed reading can help us read for this purpose, training the eye to jump quickly across the page.</u>

19 〈보기〉의 문장이 들어갈 위치로 가장 적절한 것은?

──── 〈보기〉 ────

In this situation, we would expect to find less movement of individuals from one job to another because of the individual's social obligations toward the work organization to which he or she belongs and to the people comprising that organization.

Cultural differences in the meaning of work can manifest themselves in other aspects as well. (①) For example, in American culture, it is easy to think of work simply as a means to accumulate money and make a living. (②) In other cultures, especially collectivistic ones, work may be seen more as fulfilling an obligation to a larger group. (③) In individualistic cultures, it is easier to consider leaving one job and going to another because it is easier to separate jobs from the self. (④) A different job will just as easily accomplish the same goals.

20 글을 문맥에 가장 어울리는 순서대로 배열한 것은?

㉠ To navigate in the dark, a microbat flies with its mouth open, emitting high-pitched squeaks that humans cannot hear. Some of these sounds echo off flying insects as well as tree branches and other obstacles that lie ahead. The bat listens to the echo and gets an instantaneous picture in its brain of the objects in front of it.

㉡ Microbats, the small, insect-eating bats found in North America, have tiny eyes that don't look like they'd be good for navigating in the dark and spotting prey.

㉢ From the use of echolocation, or sonar, as it is also called, a microbat can tell a great deal about a mosquito or any other potential meal. With extreme exactness, echolocation allows microbats to perceive motion, distance, speed, movement, and shape. Bats can also detect and avoid obstacles no thicker than a human hair.

㉣ But, actually, microbats can see as well as mice and other small mammals. The nocturnal habits of bats are aided by their powers of echolocation, a special ability that makes feeding and flying at night much easier than one might think.

① ㉠-㉢-㉡-㉣
② ㉡-㉣-㉠-㉢
③ ㉡-㉢-㉣-㉠
④ ㉠-㉣-㉢-㉡

정답·해석·해설 p. 155

17회 2019년 서울시 9급
모바일 자동 채점 + 성적 분석 서비스 바로 가기

QR코드를 이용해 모바일로 간편하게 채점하고 나의 실력이 어느 정도인지, 취약 부분이 어디인지 바로 파악해 보세요.

(p.213에서 전체 정답표를 확인하실 수 있습니다)

제한 시간 : 20분　　시작 _____시 _____분 ~ 종료 _____시 _____분　　나의 점수 _____　회독 수 □□□

※ 밑줄 친 부분과 의미가 가장 가까운 것은? [01~03]

01

> Man has continued to be disobedient to authorities who tried to muzzle new thoughts and to the authority of long-established opinions which declared a change to be nonsense.

① express
② assert
③ suppress
④ spread

02

> Don't be pompous. You don't want your writing to be too informal and colloquial, but you also don't want to sound like someone you're not—like your professor or boss, for instance, or the Rhodes scholar teaching assistant.

① presumptuous
② casual
③ formal
④ genuine

03

> Surgeons were forced to call it a day because they couldn't find the right tools for the job.

① initiate
② finish
③ wait
④ cancel

04 대화 중 가장 어색한 것은?

① A: I'd like to make a reservation for tomorrow, please.
  B: Certainly. For what time?
② A: Are you ready to order?
  B: Yes, I'd like the soup, please.
③ A: How's your risotto?
  B: Yes, we have risotto with mushroom and cheese.
④ A: Would you like a dessert?
  B: Not for me, thanks.

05 밑줄 친 부분 중 어법상 가장 옳지 않은 것은?

> His survival ① over the years since independence in 1961 does not alter the fact that the discussion of real policy choices in a public manner has hardly ② never occurred. In fact, there have always been ③ a number of important policy issues ④ which Nyerere has had to argue through the NEC.

06 밑줄 친 부분 중 어법상 가장 옳은 것은?

> More than 150 people ① have fell ill, mostly in Hong Kong and Vietnam, over the past three weeks. And experts ② are suspected that ③ another 300 people in China's Guangdong province had the same disease ④ begin in mid-November.

07 글의 흐름상 빈칸에 들어갈 단어로 가장 옳은 것은?

Social learning theorists offer a different explanation for the counter-aggression exhibited by children who experience aggression in the home. An extensive research on aggressive behavior and the coercive family concludes that an aversive consequence may also elicit an aggressive reaction and accelerate ongoing coercive behavior. These victims of aggressive acts eventually learn via modeling to _____ aggressive interchanges. These events perpetuate the use of aggressive acts and train children how to behave as adults.

① stop

② attenuate

③ abhor

④ initiate

08 밑줄 친 인물(Marcel Mauss)에 대한 설명으로 가장 옳지 않은 것은?

Marcel Mauss (1872-1950), French sociologist, was born in Épinal (Vosges) in Lorraine, where he grew up within a close-knit, pious, and orthodox Jewish family. Emile Durkheim was his uncle. By the age of 18 Mauss had reacted against the Jewish faith; he was never a religious man. He studied philosophy under Durkheim's supervision at Bordeaux; Durkheim took endless trouble in guiding his nephew's studies and even chose subjects for his own lectures that would be most useful to Mauss. Thus Mauss was initially a philosopher (like most of the early Durkheimians), and his conception of philosophy was influenced above all by Durkheim himself, for whom he always retained the utmost admiration.

① He had a Jewish background.

② He was supervised by his uncle.

③ He had a doctrinaire faith.

④ He was a sociologist with a philosophical background.

09 글의 문맥에 가장 어울리는 순서대로 배열한 것은?

ⓐ Today, however, trees are being cut down far more rapidly. Each year, about 2 million acres of forests are cut down. That is more than equal to the area of the whole of Great Britain.

ⓑ There is not enough wood in these countries to satisfy the demand. Wood companies, therefore, have begun taking wood from the forests of Asia, Africa, South America, and even Siberia.

ⓒ While there are important reasons for cutting down trees, there are also dangerous consequences for life on earth. A major cause of the present destruction is the worldwide demand for wood. In industrialized countries, people are using more and more wood for paper.

ⓓ There is nothing new about people cutting down trees. In ancient times, Greece, Italy, and Great Britain were covered with forests. Over the centuries those forests were gradually cut back. Until now almost nothing is left.

① ⓐ – ⓑ – ⓒ – ⓓ

② ⓓ – ⓐ – ⓑ – ⓒ

③ ⓑ – ⓐ – ⓒ – ⓓ

④ ⓓ – ⓐ – ⓒ – ⓑ

10 글의 흐름상 빈칸에 들어갈 표현으로 가장 옳은 것은?

Contemporary art has in fact become an integral part of today's middle class society. Even works of art which are fresh from the studio are met with enthusiasm. They receive recognition rather quickly—too quickly for the taste of the surlier culture critics. _____, not all works of them are bought immediately, but there is undoubtedly an increasing number of people who enjoy buying brand new works of art. Instead of fast and expensive cars, they buy the paintings, sculptures and photographic works of young artists. They know that contemporary art also adds to their social prestige. _____, since art is not exposed to the same wear and tear as automobiles, it is a far better investment.

① Of course – Furthermore

② Therefore – On the other hand

③ Therefore – For instance

④ Of course – For example

11 밑줄 친 부분과 의미가 가장 먼 것은?

As a prerequisite for fertilization, pollination is essential to the production of fruit and seed crops and plays an important part in programs designed to improve plants by breeding.

① crucial   ② indispensable

③ requisite   ④ omnipresent

12 글의 흐름상 빈칸에 들어갈 단어로 가장 옳은 것은?

Mr. Johnson objected to the proposal because it was founded on a _____ principle and also was _____ at times.

① faulty – desirable

② imperative – reasonable

③ conforming – deplorable

④ wrong – inconvenient

※ 밑줄 친 부분 중 어법상 가장 옳지 않은 것은? [13~14]

13

I'm ① pleased that I have enough clothes with me. American men are generally bigger than Japanese men so ② it's very difficult to find clothes in Chicago that ③ fits me. ④ What is a medium size in Japan is a small size here.

14

Blue Planet II, a nature documentary ① produced by the BBC, left viewers ② heartbroken after showing the extent ③ to which plastic ④ affects on the ocean.

15 글의 흐름상 빈칸에 들어갈 가장 적절한 문장은?

What became clear by the 1980s, however, as preparations were made for the 'Quincentenary Jubilee', was that many Americans found it hard, if not impossible, to see the anniversary as a 'jubilee'. There was nothing to celebrate the legacy of Columbus. _____

① According to many of his critics, Columbus had been the harbinger not of progress and civilization, but of slavery and the reckless exploitation of the environment.

② The Chicago World's Fair of 1893 reinforced the narrative link between discovery and the power of progress of the United States.

③ This reversal of the nineteenth-century myth of Columbus is revealing.

④ Columbus thus became integrated into Manifest Destiny, the belief that America's progress was divinely ordained.

16 글의 흐름상 빈칸에 들어갈 단어로 가장 옳지 <u>않은</u> 것은?

Following his father's imprisonment, Charles Dickens was forced to leave school to work at a boot-blacking factory alongside the River Thames. At the run-down, rodent-ridden factory, Dickens earned six shillings a week labeling pots of "blacking," a substance used to clean fireplaces. It was the best he could do to help support his family. Looking back on the experience, Dickens saw it as the moment he said goodbye to his youthful innocence, stating that he wondered "how he could be so easily cast away at such a young age." He felt _____ by the adults who were supposed to take care of him.

① abandoned   ② betrayed
③ buttressed   ④ disregarded

17 글의 내용과 일치하는 것은?

A family hoping to adopt a child must first select an adoption agency. In the United States, there are two kinds of agencies that assist with adoption. Public agencies generally handle older children, children with mental or physical disabilities, or children who may have been abused or neglected. Prospective parents are not usually expected to pay fees when adopting a child from a public agency. Fostering, or a form of temporary adoption, is also possible through public agencies. Private agencies can be found on the Internet. They handle domestic and international adoption.

① Public adoption agencies are better than private ones.
② Parents pay huge fees to adopt a child from a foster home.
③ Children in need cannot be adopted through public agencies.
④ Private agencies can be contacted for international adoption.

18 글의 흐름상 빈칸에 들어갈 단어로 가장 옳은 것은?

Moths and butterflies both belong to the order Lepidoptera, but there are numerous physical and behavioral differences between the two insect types. On the behavioral side, moths are _____ and butterflies are diurnal (active during the day). While at rest, butterflies usually fold their wings back, while moths flatten their wings against their bodies or spread them out in a "jet plane" position.

① nocturnal   ② rational
③ eternal   ④ semi-circular

19 글의 흐름상 빈칸에 들어갈 표현으로 가장 옳은 것은?

The idea of clowns frightening people started gaining strength in the United States. In South Carolina, for example, people reported seeing individuals wearing clown costumes, often hiding in the woods or in cities at night. Some people said that the clowns were trying to lure children into empty homes or the woods. Soon, there were reports of threatening-looking clowns trying to frighten both children and adults. Although there were usually no reports of violence, and many of the reported sightings were later found to be false, this _____.

① benefited the circus industry
② promoted the use of clowns in ads
③ caused a nationwide panic
④ formed the perfect image of a happy clown

20 글의 내용과 가장 부합하는 속담은?

It is one thing to believe that our system of democracy is the best, and quite another to impose it on other countries. This is a blatant breach of the UN policy of non-intervention in the domestic affairs of independent nations. Just as Western citizens fought for their political institutions, we should trust the citizens of other nations to do likewise if they wish to. Democracy is also not an absolute term—Napoleon used elections and referenda to legitimize his hold on power, as do leaders today in West Africa and Southeast Asia. States with partial democracy are often more aggressive than totally unelected dictatorships which are too concerned with maintaining order at home. The differing types of democracy make it impossible to choose which standards to impose. The U.S. and European countries all differ in terms of restraints on government and the balance between consensus and confrontation.

① The grass is always greener on the other side of the fence.
② One man's food is another's poison.
③ There is no rule but has exceptions.
④ When in Rome, do as the Romans do.

정답·해석·해설 p. 163

18회 2018년 서울시 9급
모바일 자동 채점 + 성적 분석 서비스 바로 가기

QR코드를 이용해 모바일로 간편하게 채점하고 나의 실력이 어느 정도인지, 취약 부분이 어디인지 바로 파악해 보세요.

(p.213에서 전체 정답표를 확인하실 수 있습니다)

제한 시간 : 20분　　시작 _____시 _____분 ~ 종료 _____시 _____분　　나의 점수 _____　회독 수 ☐☐☐

※ 밑줄 친 부분과 의미가 가장 가까운 것은? [01~02]

01

> Leadership and strength are inextricably bound together. We look to strong people as leaders because they can protect us from threats to our group.

① inseparably
② inanimately
③ ineffectively
④ inconsiderately

02

> Prudence indeed will dictate that governments long established should not be changed for light and transient causes.

① transparent
② momentary
③ memorable
④ significant

※ 밑줄 친 부분 중 어법상 가장 옳지 않은 것은? [03~04]

03

> The idea that justice ① in allocating access to a university has something to do with ② the goods that ③ universities properly pursue ④ explain why selling admission is unjust.

04

> Strange as ① it may seem, ② the Sahara was once an expanse of grassland ③ supported the kind of animal life ④ associated with the African plains.

05 대화의 흐름으로 보아 빈칸에 들어갈 가장 적절한 것은?

> A: Do you think we can get a loan?
> B: Well, it depends. Do you own any other property? Any stocks or bonds?
> A: No.
> B: I see. Then you don't have any _____. Perhaps you could get a guarantor—someone to sign for the loan for you.

① investigation
② animals
③ collateral
④ inspiration

06 다음 글의 주제로 가장 적절한 것은?

In 1782, J. Hector St. John De Crèvecoeur, a French immigrant who had settled in New York before returning to Europe during the Revolutionary War, published a series of essays about life in the British colonies in North America, *Letters from an American Farmer*. The book was an immediate success in England, France, and the United States. In one of its most famous passages, Crèvecoeur describes the process by which people from different backgrounds and countries were transformed by their experiences in the colonies and asks, "What then is the American?" In America, Crèvecoeur suggests, "individuals of all nations are melted into a new race of men, whose labors and posterity will one day cause great changes in the world." Crèvecoeur was among the first to develop the popular idea of America as that would come to be called "melting pot."

① Crèvecoeur's book became an immediate success in England.
② Crèvecoeur developed the idea of melting pot in his book.
③ Crèvecoeur described and discussed American individualism.
④ Crèvecoeur explained where Americans came from in his book.

※ 빈칸에 들어갈 가장 적절한 단어는? [07~08]

07

Again and again we light on words used once in a good, but now in an unfavorable sense. Until the late Eighteenth century this word was used to mean serviceable, friendly, very courteous and obliging. But a(n) _____ person nowadays means a busy uninvited meddler in matters which do not belong to him/her.

① servile   ② officious
③ gregarious   ④ obsequious

08

A faint odor of ammonia or vinegar makes one-week-old infants grimace and _____ their heads.

① harness   ② avert
③ muffle   ④ evoke

09 밑줄 친 부분 중 어법상 가장 옳지 <u>않은</u> 것은?

The first coffeehouse in western Europe ① <u>opened not</u> in ② <u>a center of</u> trade or commerce but in the university city of Oxford, ③ <u>in which</u> a Lebanese man ④ <u>naming Jacob</u> set up shop in 1650.

10 다음 문장 중 어법상 가장 옳지 <u>않은</u> 것은?

① John promised Mary that he would clean his room.
② John told Mary that he would leave early.
③ John believed Mary that she would be happy.
④ John reminded Mary that she should get there early.

11 대화의 흐름으로 보아 빈칸에 들어갈 가장 적절한 것은?

A: Why don't you let me treat you to lunch today, Mr. Kim?
B: _____.

① No, I'm not. That would be a good time for me
② Good. I'll put it on my calendar so I don't forget
③ OK. I'll check with you on Monday
④ Wish I could but I have another commitment today

12 글의 흐름으로 보아 빈칸에 들어갈 단어를 순서대로 고른 것은?

For centuries, people gazing at the sky after sunset could see thousands of vibrant, sparkling stars. But these days, you'll be lucky if you can view the Big Dipper. The culprit: electric beams pouring from homes and street lamps, whose brightness obscures the night sky. In the U.S., so-called light pollution has gotten so bad that by one estimate, 8 out of 10 children born today will never encounter a sky _____ enough for them to see the Milky Way. There is hope, however, in the form of astrotourism, a small but growing industry centered on stargazing in the worlds' darkest places. These remote sites, many of them in national parks, offer views for little more than the cost of a campsite. And the people who run them often work to reduce light pollution in surrounding communities. _____ astrotourism may not be as luxurious as some vacations, travelers don't seem to mind.

① dark – Although
② bright – Because
③ dark – Since
④ bright – In that

13 다음 글을 문맥에 맞게 순서대로 배열한 것은?

㉠ Millions of people suffering from watery and stinging eyes, pounding headaches, sinus issues, and itchy throats, sought refuge from the debilitating air by scouring stores for air filters and face masks.

㉡ The outrage among Chinese residents and the global media scrutiny impelled the government to address the country's air pollution problem.

㉢ Schools and businesses were closed, and the Beijing city government warned people to stay inside their homes, keep their air purifiers running, reduce indoor activities, and remain as inactive as possible.

㉣ In 2013, a state of emergency in Beijing resulting from the dangerously high levels of pollution led to chaos in the transportation system, forcing airlines to cancel flights due to low visibility.

① ㉡ – ㉠ – ㉣ – ㉢
② ㉡ – ㉢ – ㉣ – ㉠
③ ㉣ – ㉡ – ㉢ – ㉠
④ ㉣ – ㉢ – ㉠ – ㉡

※ 글의 흐름으로 보아 빈칸에 들어갈 가장 적절한 것은?
[14~16]

14

Both novels and romances are works of imaginative fiction with multiple characters, but that's where the similarities end. Novels are realistic; romances aren't. In the 19th century, a romance was a prose narrative that told a fictional story dealt with its subjects and characters in a symbolic, imaginative, and nonrealistic way. _____, a romance deals with plots and people that are exotic, remote in time or place from the reader, and obviously imaginary.

① Typically
② On the other hand
③ Nonetheless
④ In some cases

15

Definitions are especially _____ to children. There's an oft-cited 1987 study in which fifth graders were given dictionary definitions and asked to write their own sentences using the words defined. The results were discouraging. One child given the word erode wrote "Our family erodes a lot," because the definition given was "eat out, eat away."

① beneficial   ② disrespectful
③ unhelpful   ④ forgettable

16

Modern banking has its origins in ancient England. In those days people wanting to safeguard their gold had two choices—hide it under the mattress or turn it over to someone else for safekeeping. The logical people to turn to for storage were the local goldsmiths, since they had the strongest vaults. The goldsmiths accepted the gold for storage, giving the owner a receipt stating that the gold could be redeemed at a later date. When a payment was due, the owner went to the goldsmith, redeemed part of the gold and gave it to the payee. After all that, the payee was very likely to turn around and give the gold back to the goldsmith for safekeeping. Gradually, instead of taking the time and effort to physically exchange the gold, business people _____.

① began to exchange the goldsmith's receipts as payment
② saw the potential for profit in this arrangement
③ warned the depositors against redeeming their gold
④ lent the gold to somebody else for a fee

17 빈칸에 공통으로 들어갈 가장 적절한 것은?

In some cultures, such as in Korea and Egypt, politeness norms require that when someone is offered something to eat or drink, it must be refused the first time around. However, such a refusal is often viewed as a rejection of someone's hospitality and thoughtlessness in other cultures, particularly when no _____ is made for the refusal. Americans and Canadians, for instance, expect refusals to be accompanied by a reasonable _____.

① role   ② excuse
③ choice   ④ situation

18 다음 주어진 문장이 들어갈 가장 적절한 곳은?

Instead, these employees spoke first of the sincerity of the relationships at work, that their work culture felt like an extension of home, and that their colleagues were supportive.

(①) There is a clear link between job satisfaction and productivity. However, job satisfaction also depends on the service culture of an organization. (②) This culture comprises the things that make a business distinctive and make the people who work there proud to do so. (③) When employees of the "Top 10 Best Companies to Work For" were asked by *Fortune* magazine why they loved working for these companies, it was notable that they didn't mention pay, reward schemes, or advancing to a more senior position. (④)

19 다음 글의 내용과 일치하는 것은?

Why Orkney of all places? How did this scatter of islands off the northern tip of Scotland come to be such a technological, cultural, and spiritual powerhouse? For starters, you have to stop thinking of Orkney as remote. For most of history, Orkney was an important maritime hub, a place that was on the way to everywhere. It was also blessed with some of the richest farming soils in Britain and a surprisingly mild climate, thanks to the effects of the Gulf Stream.

① Orkney people had to overcome a lot of social and natural disadvantages.

② The region was one of the centers of rebellion that ultimately led to the annihilation of the civilization there.

③ Orkney did not make the best of its resources because it was too far from the mainland.

④ Orkney owed its prosperity largely to its geographical advantage and natural resources.

20 다음 글의 제목으로 가장 적절한 것은?

Initially, papyrus and parchment were kept as scrolls that could be unrolled either vertically or horizontally, depending on the direction of the script. The horizontal form was more common, and because scrolls could be quite long, a scribe would typically refrain from writing a single line across the entire length, but instead would mark off columns of a reasonable width. That way the reader could unroll one side and roll up the other while reading. Nevertheless, the constant need to re-roll the scroll was a major disadvantage to this format, and it was impossible to jump to various places in the scroll the way we skip to a particular page of a book. Moreover, the reader struggled to make notes while reading since both hands (or weights) were required to keep the scroll open.

① The inconvenience of scrolls

② The evolution of the book

③ The development of writing and reading

④ The ways to overcome disadvantages in scrolls

정답 · 해석 · 해설 p. 171

19회 2017년 서울시 9급
모바일 자동 채점 + 성적 분석 서비스 바로 가기

QR코드를 이용해 모바일로 간편하게 채점하고 나의 실력이 어느 정도인지,
취약 부분이 어디인지 바로 파악해 보세요.

(p.214에서 전체 정답표를 확인하실 수 있습니다)

ENERGY AND PERSISTENCE
CONQUER ALL THINGS.

BENJAMIN FRANKLIN

에너지와 끈기는 모든 것을 이겨낸다.
벤자민 프랭클린

Part 4
법원직 9급

문제 유형	4지선다형
총 문항 수	25문항
경쟁률 (2024년 6월, 법원사무)	8.8:1
합격선 (2024년 6월, 법원사무)	76점
시험 안내	대한민국 법원 시험정보 (https://exam.scourt.go.kr)

제한 시간 : 25분　　시작 _____시 _____분 ~ 종료 _____시 _____분　　나의 점수 _____　회독 수 ☐☐☐

01 주어진 글 다음에 이어질 글의 순서로 가장 적절한 것은?

Now we stand at the edge of a turning point as we face the rise of a coming wave of technology that includes both advanced AI and biotechnology. Never before have we witnessed technologies with such transformative potential, promising to reshape our world in ways that are both awe-inspiring and daunting.

(A) With AI, we could create systems that are beyond our control and find ourselves at the mercy of algorithms that we don't understand. With biotechnology, we could manipulate the very building blocks of life, potentially creating unintended consequences for both individuals and entire ecosystem.

(B) With biotechnology, we could engineer life to tackle diseases and transform agriculture, creating a world that is healthier and more sustainable. But on the other hand, the potential dangers of these technologies are equally vast and profound.

(C) On the one hand, the potential benefits of these technologies are vast and profound. With AI, we could unlock the secrets of the universe, cure diseases that have long eluded us and create new forms of art and culture that stretch the bounds of imagination.

> * daunt 겁먹게(기죽게) 하다
> ** elude (사물이) ~에게 이해되지 않다

① (B) - (A) - (C)
② (B) - (C) - (A)
③ (C) - (A) - (B)
④ (C) - (B) - (A)

02 다음 빈칸에 들어갈 말로 가장 적절한 것은?

Controversy over new art-making technologies is nothing new. Many painters recoiled at the invention of the camera, which they saw as a debasement of human artistry. Charles Baudelaire, the 19th-century French poet and art critic, called photography "art's most mortal enemy." In the 20th century, digital editing tools and computer-assisted design programs were similarly dismissed by purists for requiring too little skill of their human collaborators. What makes the new breed of A.I. image generating tools different is not just that they're capable of producing beautiful works of art with minimal effort. It's how they work. These tools are built by scraping millions of images from the open web, then teaching algorithms to recognize patterns and relationships in those images and generate new ones in the same style. That means that artists who upload their works to the internet may be unwittingly _____ _____ .

> * unwittingly 자신도 모르게, 부지불식간에

① helping to train their algorithmic competitors
② sparking a debate over the ethics of A.I.-generated art
③ embracing digital technology as part of the creative process
④ acquiring the skills of utilizing internet to craft original creations

03 Duke Kahanamoku에 관한 다음 글의 내용과 가장 일치하지 않는 것은?

> Duke Kahanamoku, born August 26, 1890, near Waikiki, Hawaii, was a Hawaiian surfer and swimmer who won three Olympic gold medals for the United States and who for several years was considered the greatest freestyle swimmer in the world. He was perhaps most widely known for developing the flutter kick, which largely replaces the scissors kick. Kahanamoku set three universally recognized world records in the 100-yard freestyle between July 5, 1913, and September 5, 1917. In the 100-yard freestyle Kahanamoku was U.S. indoor champion in 1913, and outdoor titleholder in 1916-17 and 1920. At the Olympic Games in Stockholm in 1912, he won the 100-metre freestyle event, and he repeated that triumph at the 1920 Olympics in Antwerp, Belgium, where he also was a member of the victorious U.S. team in the 800-metre relay race. Kahanamoku also excelled at surfing, and he became viewed as one of the icons of the sport. Intermittently from the mid-1920s, Kahanamoku was a motion-picture actor. From 1932 to 1961 he was sheriff of the city and county of Honolulu. He served in the salaried office of official greeter of famous personages for the state of Hawaii from 1961 until his death.
>
> * intermittently 간헐적으로 ** sheriff 보안관

① 하와이 출신의 서퍼이자 수영 선수로 올림픽 금메달리스트이다.

② 그는 플러터 킥을 대체하는 시저스 킥을 개발한 것으로 널리 알려져 있다.

③ 벨기에 앤트워프 올림픽의 800미터 계주에서 우승한 미국 팀의 일원이었다.

④ 그는 1920년대 중반부터 간헐적으로 영화배우로도 활동했다.

04 다음 빈칸에 들어갈 말로 가장 적절한 것은?

> The understandings that children bring to the classroom can already be quite powerful in the early grades. For example, some children have been found to hold onto their preconception of a flat earth by imagining a round earth to be shaped like a pancake. This construction of a new understanding is guided by a model of the earth that helps the child explain how people can stand or walk on its surface. Many young children have trouble giving up the notion that one-eighth is greater than one-fourth, because 8 is more than 4. If children were blank slates, just telling them that the earth is round or that one-fourth is greater than one-eighth would be _____. But since they already have ideas about the earth and about numbers, those ideas must be directly addressed in order to transform or expand them.

① familiar
② adequate
③ improper
④ irrelevant

05 Urban farming에 관한 다음 글의 내용과 가장 일치하지 않는 것은?

Urban farming, also known as urban agriculture, involves growing food within city environments, utilizing spaces like rooftops, abandoned buildings, and community gardens. This sustainable practice is gaining traction in cities across the world, including New York, Chicago, San Francisco, London, Amsterdam, and Berlin, as well as in many African and Asian cities where it plays a crucial role in food supply and local economies. Urban farming not only helps reduce carbon footprints by minimizing transport emissions but also increases access to fresh, healthy food in urban areas. It bolsters local economies by creating jobs and keeping profits within the community. Additionally, urban farms enhance cityscapes, improve air quality, conserve water, provide educational opportunities, promote biodiversity, connect people with nature, and improve food security by producing food locally, making cities more resilient to disruptions like natural disasters.

* traction 흡입력, 견인력   ** bolster 강화시키다

① 옥상, 버려진 건물, 그리고 공동체 정원과 같은 공간을 활용하여 도시 환경 내에서 식량을 재배하는 것이다.

② 지속 가능한 관행으로 식량 공급과 지역 경제에서 중요한 역할을 하는 많은 아프리카와 아시아를 포함한 세계의 도시들에서 인기를 얻고 있다.

③ 운송 배출을 최소화하여 탄소 발자국을 줄이는 것을 도울 뿐만 아니라 도시 지역에서 신선하고 건강한 식량에 대한 접근성을 증가시킨다.

④ 생물 다양성을 촉진하고, 지역에서 식량을 생산함으로써 식량의 안정성을 향상시키나, 자연 재해와 같은 혼란에 대한 도시의 회복력은 약화시킨다.

06 밑줄 친 "unfinished animals."가 다음 글에서 의미하는 바로 가장 적절한 것은?

Ideas or theories about human nature have a unique place in the sciences. We don't have to worry that the cosmos will be changed by our theories about the cosmos. The planets really don't care what we think or how we theorize about them. But we do have to worry that human nature will be changed by our theories of human nature. Forty years ago, the distinguished anthropologist said that human beings are "unfinished animals." What he meant is that it is human nature to have a human nature that is very much the product of the society that surrounds us. That human nature is more created than discovered. We "design" human nature, by designing the institutions within which people live. So we must ask ourselves just what kind of a human nature we want to help design.

① stuck in an incomplete stage of development

② shaped by society rather than fixed by biology

③ uniquely free from environmental context

④ born with both animalistic and spiritual aspect

07 다음 글의 내용을 한 문장으로 요약하고자 한다. 빈칸 (A), (B)에 들어갈 말로 가장 적절한 것은?

Passive House is a standard and an advanced method of designing buildings using the precision of building physics to ensure comfortable conditions and to deeply reduce energy costs. It removes all guesswork from the design process. It does what national building regulations have tried to do. Passive House methods don't affect "buildability", yet they close the gap between design and performance and deliver a much higher standard of comfort and efficiency than government regulations, with all their good intentions, have managed to achieve. When we use Passive House methods, we learn how to use insulation and freely available daylight, in the most sensible way and in the right amounts for both comfort and energy efficiency. This is, I believe, fundamental to good design, and is the next step we have to make in the evolution of our dwellings and places of work. The improvements that are within our grasp are potentially transformative for mankind and the planet.

Passive House utilizes precise building physics to ensure comfort and energy efficiency, ___(A)___ traditional regulations and offering transformative potential for ___(B)___ design.

	(A)	(B)
①	persisting	sustainable
②	persisting	unsustainable
③	surpassing	unsustainable
④	surpassing	sustainable

08 다음 글의 밑줄 친 부분 중 문맥 상 낱말의 쓰임이 가장 적절하지 않은 것은?

Today, there is only one species of humans, Homo sapiens, left in the world. But that one species, despite the fact that it is over 99.9 percent genetically ① identical, has adapted itself to a wide array of disparate environments. And while some degree of human genetic variation results from each society's adaptation to its own unique environment, the cultural adaptations that each society makes in so adjusting itself will, in their turn, exact some further degree of ② variation on that society's genetic makeup. In other words, we are so entangled with our local ecologies that not only do we humans ③ transform the environment as we cull from it the various resources upon which we come to depend but also the environment, which we have so transformed, transforms us in its turn: at times exerting upon us profound biological pressures. In those regions of the world, for example, where our environmental exploitation has included the domestication of cattle-northern Europe, for instance, or East Africa human populations have ④ reduced adult lactose tolerance: the ability to digest milk past infancy.

* lactose 유당, 젖당

09 주어진 글 다음에 이어질 글의 순서로 가장 적절한 것은?

> Briefly consider a metaphor that plays a significant role in how we live our daily lives: Time Is Money.

(A) We often speak of time as if it were money—for example, in everyday expressions such as "You're wasting my time," "This device will save you hours of work," "How will you spend your weekend?" and "I've invested a lot of time in this relationship."

(B) Every metaphor brokers what is made visible or invisible; this one highlights how time is like money and obscures ways it is not. Time thus becomes something that we can waste or lose, and something that diminishes as we grow older. It is abstracted in a very linear, orderly fashion.

(C) This metaphor, however, fails to disclose important phenomenological aspects of time, such as how it may speed up or slow down, depending on our engagement with what we are doing. We may instead conceive of time as quite fluid—as a stream, for example—thought we lose sight of this to the extent that we have adopted the worldview of Time Is Money.

* obscure 모호하게 하다

① (A) - (B) - (C)
② (A) - (C) - (B)
③ (B) - (A) - (C)
④ (C) - (B) - (A)

10 다음 글의 밑줄 친 부분 중, 어법상 틀린 것은?

His last thought were for his wife. "He is afraid she would ① hardly be able to bear it," he said to Burnet, the bishop who was allowed to be with him the last few days. Tears came into his eyes when he spoke of her. The last day came, and Lady Russell brought the three little children to say good-bye for ever to their father. "Little Fubs" was only nine, her sister Catherine seven, and the baby three years old, too young to realize his loss. He kissed them all ② calmly, and sent them away. His wife stayed and they ate their last meal together. Then they kissed in silence, and silently she left him. When she had gone, Lord Russel broke down completely. "Oh, what a blessing she has been to me!" he cried. "It is a great comfort to me to leave my children in such a mother's care; she has promised me to take care of ③ her for their sake; she will do it," he added resolutely. Lady Russell returned heavy-hearted to the sad home ④ to which she would never welcome him again. On July 21st, 1683, she was a widow, and her children fatherless. They left their dreary London house, and went to an old abbey in the country.

* bishop 주교(성직자)

11 The gig economy에 관한 다음 글의 내용과 가장 일치하지 않는 것은?

The gig economy, referring to the workforce of people engaged in freelance and side-hustle work, is growing rapidly in the United States, with 36% of employed participants in a 2022 McKinsey survey identifying as independent workers, up from 27% in 2016. This workforce includes a wide range of jobs from highly-paid professionals like lawyers to lower-earning roles like delivery drivers. Despite the flexibility and autonomy it offers, most independent workers desire more stable employment; 62% prefer permanent positions due to concerns over job security and benefits. The challenges faced by gig workers include limited access to healthcare, housing, and other basic needs, with a significant reliance on government assistance. Technological advancements have facilitated the rise in independent work, making remote and freelance jobs more accessible and appealing. The trend reflects broader economic pressures such as inflation and job market dynamics, influencing individuals to choose gig work for survival, flexibility, or enjoyment.

* side-hustle work 부업

① 조사에 참가한 사람들 중 독립 근로자의 비율이 2016년의 27%에서 36%까지 상승하였다.
② 대부분의 독립 근로자들은 안정적인 고용보다는 직업이 제공하는 유연성과 자율성을 선호하고 있다.
③ 근로자들이 직면한 어려움에는 의료, 주거 및 기타 기본 요구 사항에 대한 제한된 접근성이 포함된다.
④ 기술 발전은 독립 근로의 증가를 촉진하여 원격 및 프리랜서 일자리를 접근하기 쉽고 매력적인 것으로 만들고 있다.

12 주어진 글 다음에 이어질 글의 순서로 가장 적절한 것은?

We come to know and relate to the world by way of categories.

(A) The notion of an animal species, for instance, might in one setting best be thought of as described by folklore and myth, in another as a detailed legal construct, and in another as a system of scientific classification.

(B) Ordinary communication is the most immediate expression of this faculty. We refer to things through sounds and words, and we attach ideas to them that we call concepts.

(C) Some of our categories remain tacit; others are explicitly governed by custom, law, politics, or science. The application of category systems for the same things varies by context and in use.

* tacit 암묵적인, 무언의

① (B) - (A) - (C)
② (B) - (C) - (A)
③ (C) - (A) - (B)
④ (C) - (B) - (A)

13 다음 글에 나타난 화자의 심경으로 가장 적절한 것은?

It's three in the morning, and we are making our way from southern to northern Utah, when the weather changes from the dry chill of the desert to the freezing gales of an alpine winter. Ice claims the road. Snowflakes flick against the windshield like tiny insects, a few at first, then so many the road disappears. We push forward into the heart of the storm. The van skids and jerks. The wind is furious, the view out the window pure white. Richard pulls over. He says we can't go any further. Dad takes the wheel, Richard moves to the passenger seat, and Mother lies next to me and Audrey on the mattress. Dad pulls onto the highway and accelerates, rapidly, as if to make a point, until he has doubled Richard's speed. "Shouldn't we drive slower?" Mother asks. Dad grins. "I'm not driving faster than our angels can fly." The van is still accelerating. To fifty, then to sixty. Richard sits tensely, his hand clutching the armrest, his knuckles bleaching each time the tires slip. Mother lies on her side, her face next to mine, taking small sips of air each time the van fishtails, then holding her breath as Dad corrects and it snakes back into the lane. She is so rigid, I think she might shatter. My body tenses with hers; together we brace a hundred times for impact.

* gale 강풍, 돌풍 ** skid 미끄러지다 *** jerk 홱 움직이다
**** fishtail(차량)뒷부분이 좌우로 미끄러지다

① excited and thrilled
② anxious and fearful
③ cautious but settled
④ comfortable and relaxed

14 글의 흐름으로 보아, 주어진 문장이 들어가기에 가장 적절한 곳은?

However, there are now a lot of issues with the current application of unmanned distribution.

The city lockdown policy during COVID-19 has facilitated the rapid growth of numerous takeaways, vegetable shopping, community group buying, and other businesses. (①) Last-mile delivery became an important livelihood support during the epidemic. (②) At the same time, as viruses can be transmitted through aerosols, the need for contactless delivery for last-mile delivery has gradually increased, thus accelerating the use of unmanned logistics to some extent. (③) For example, the community space is not suitable for the operation of unmanned delivery facilities due to the lack of supporting logistics infrastructure. (④) In addition, the current technology is unable to complete the delivery process and requires the collaboration of relevant space as well as personnel to help dock unmanned delivery nodes.

* last-mile delivery 최종 단계의 배송

15 주어진 글 다음에 이어질 글의 순서로 가장 적절한 것은?

> People are too seldom interested in having a genuine exchange of points of view where a desire to understand takes precedence over the desire to convince at any price.

(A) Yet conflict isn't just an unpopular source of pressure to act. There's also a lot of energy inherent to it, which can be harnessed to create positive change, or, in other words, improvements, with the help of a skillful approach. Basically, today's misery is the starting shot in the race towards a better future.

(B) A deviating opinion is quickly accompanied by devaluation, denigration, insults, or even physical confrontations. If you look at the "discussions" taking place on social media networks, you don't even have to look to such hot potatoes as the refugee crisis or terrorism to see a clear degradation in the way people exchange opinions.

(C) You probably know this from your own experience, too, when you have succeeded in finding a constructive solution to a conflict and, at the end of an arduous clarification process, realize that the successful outcome has been worth all the effort.

    * denigration 명예훼손 ** arduous 몹시 힘든, 고된

① (B) - (A) - (C)
② (B) - (C) - (A)
③ (C) - (A) - (B)
④ (C) - (B) - (A)

16 다음 중 Belus Smawley에 대한 내용과 가장 일치하지 않는 것은?

> Belus Smawley grew up on a farm with his parents and six siblings. In his freshman years, he was tall and able to jump higher than any other boy, trying to improve his leaping ability by touching higher and higher limbs of the oak tree on their farm. This is where his first jump shot attempt is said to have taken place. When Belus Smawley started using his shot regularly, he became the leading scorer. At the age of 18, he got accepted for a position on an AAU18 basketball team. He finished high school afterwards and got an All-American athletic scholarship for Appalachian State University (majoring in history and physical education). He became player-coach until he went to the Navy. He started playing in their basketball team and refined his jump shot. He got married and either worked as a high school teacher and basketball coach or further pursued his NBA basketball career playing fulltime for several teams. Eventually he focused on family and his teaching career, becoming the principal of a junior high school.

① 부모님과 여섯 형제와 함께 농장에서 자랐다.
② 나무의 더 높은 가지를 만지면서 점프 연습을 하였다.
③ 애팔래치아 주립대학교에서 전미 체육 장학금을 받았다.
④ 결혼 후 NBA 농구 선수로서 한 팀에서 활동했다.

17 글의 흐름으로 보아, 주어진 문장이 들어가기에 가장 적절한 곳은?

> It might be understandable, then, for us to want to expect something similar from our machines: to know not only what they think they see but where, in particular, they are looking.

Humans, relative to most other species, have distinctly large and visible sclera—the whites of our eyes—and as a result we are uniquely exposed in how we direct our attention, or at the very least, our gaze. (①) Evolutionary biologists have argued, via the "cooperative eye hypothesis," that this must be a feature, not a bug: that it must point to the fact that cooperation has been uncommonly important in our survival as a species, to the point that the benefits of shared attention outweigh the loss of a certain degree of privacy or discretion. (②) This idea in machine learning goes by the name of "saliency": the idea is that if a system is looking at an image and assigning it to some category, then presumably some parts of the image were more important or more influential than others in making that determination. (③) If we could see a kind of "heat map" that highlighted these critical portions of the image, we might obtain some crucial diagnostic information that we could use as a kind of sanity check to make sure the system is behaving the way we think it should be. (④)

* sclera (눈의) 공막 ** outweigh 보다 더 크다
*** discretion 신중함 **** saliency 특징, 중요점

18 다음 (A), (B), (C) 중, 어법상 옳은 것끼리 고른 것은?

The climate of the irrigated plains can be glimpsed in the murals. The summer sun beats down on the hard ground, and the king himself is shaded by a large umbrella. War, often present, is also carved in vivid detail. In or about 878 BC, three men are depicted (A) (fleeing / fled) from a city which has probably been captured. Dressed in long robes, they jump into the Euphrates River (B) (which / where) one is swimming while the others hug a lifebuoy to their chests. Like a long pillow, the lifebuoy consists of the skin of an animal, inflated with air. As the hands of the refugees (C) (is / are) clutching the inflated lifebuoy, and as much of their breath is expended in blowing air into it, they can only stay afloat by swimming with their legs. Whether they reached the opposite shore will never be known.

	(A)	(B)	(C)
①	fleeing	which	is
②	fleeing	where	are
③	fled	which	is
④	fled	where	are

19 다음 글의 내용과 가장 일치하지 않는 것은?

When the Dutch arrived in the 17th century in what's now New York City, their encounters with the indigenous peoples, known as the Lenape, were, at first, mostly amicable, according to historical records. They shared the land and traded guns, beads and wool for beaver furs. The Dutch even "purchased" Manahatta island from the Lenape in 1626. The transaction, enforced by the eventual building of wall around New Amsterdam, marked the very beginning of the Lenape's forced mass migration out of their homeland. The wall, which started showing up on maps in the 1660s, was built to keep out the Native Americans and the British. It eventually became Wall Street, and Manahatta became Manhattan, where part of the Lenape trade route, known as Wickquasgeck, became Brede weg, later Broadway. The Lenape helped shape the geography of modern-day New York City, but other traces of their legacy have all but vanished.

① 네덜란드인과 르나페 원주민들은 총과 동물의 털을 교환 하는 무역을 했다.
② 이후에 월스트리트가 된 지역에 지어진 벽은 르나페 원주 민이 영국인을 막기 위해 세웠다.
③ 르나페 원주민의 무역로의 일부가 나중에 브로드웨이가 되었다.
④ 르나페 원주민은 현대 뉴욕시의 지형을 형성하는데 도움 을 주었다.

20 다음 글의 밑줄 친 부분 중 어법상 가장 틀린 것은?

Today, we take for granted that the media and the celebrity culture it sustains have created new forms of publicness, ① through which we might have intimate relationships with people we have never met. Thanks to media technologies we ② are brought ever closer to the famous, allowing us to enjoy an illusion of intimacy with them. To a greater or lesser degree, we have internalized celebrities, unconsciously made them a part of our consciousness, just ③ as if they were, in fact, friends. Celebrities take up permanent residence in our inner lives as well, ④ become central to our reveries and fantasies, guides to action, to ambition. Now, indeed, celebrity culture can be permanently insinuated into our sensibilities, as many of us carry them, their traits, and our relationships with them around as part of our mental luggage.

* reverie 몽상 ** insinuate 암시하다, 일부가 되다

21 다음 글의 빈칸에 들어갈 말로 가장 적절한 것은?

Festivals are significant cultural events that showcase tradition, heritage and community spirit globally. They serve as platforms to celebrate diversity, with each festival reflecting unique traditions like Brazil's Carnival or India's Diwali. Festivals also commemorate historical moments, such as Independence Day in the US or Bastille Day in France. Additionally, they preserve customs and rituals that strengthen personal and cultural identity, while fostering strong community ties through shared activities. Festivals reflect societal values, promote local crafts and arts, enhance spirituality, and attract tourism, which facilitates cultural exchange and understanding. Seasonal festivals, like Holi in India, align with natural cycles, celebrating times of renewal. Ultimately, participating in festivals reinforces community and individual identity, contributing to a global narrative that _____ _____.

* commemorate 기념하다

① makes the participants forget their daily concerns and pains

② values diversity and encourages mutual respect and understanding

③ allows people to break the link between personal life and social life

④ keeps the festivals from determining how people think about themselves

22 밑줄 친 you've been thrown a curve ball이 다음 글에서 의미하는 바로 가장 적절한 것은?

Life is full of its ups and downs. One day, you may feel like you have it all figured out. Then, in a moment's notice, <u>you've been thrown a curve ball</u>. You're not alone in these feelings. Everyone has to face their own set of challenges. Learning how to overcome challenges will help you stay centered and remain calm under pressure. Everyone has their own preferences for how to face a challenge in life. However, there are a few good tips and tricks to follow when the going gets tough. There's no need to feel ashamed for asking for help. Whether you choose to rely on a loved one, a stranger, a mentor, or a friend, there are people who want to help you succeed. You have to be open and willing to accept support. People who come to your aid truly do care about you. Be open to receiving help when you need it.

① 어려운 상황에 직면하다.

② 흥미로운 상황을 맞이하게 되다.

③ 대안적인 방법을 적용하게 되다.

④ 정면 승부를 피하여 에둘러 가다.

23 다음 중 글에 설명된 사회적 지배력과 번식 성공 사이의 관계를 가장 잘 요약한 것은?

Social dominance refers to situations in which an individual or a group controls or dictates others' behavior primarily in competitive situations. Generally, an individual or group is said to be dominant when "a prediction is being made about the course of future interactions or the outcome of competitive situations". Criteria for assessing and assigning dominance relationships can vary from one situation to another. It is difficult to summarize available data briefly, but generally it has been found that dominant individuals, when compared to subordinate individuals, often have more freedom of movement, have priority of access to food, gain higher-quality resting spots, enjoy favorable grooming relationships, occupy more protected parts of a group, obtain higher-quality mates, command and regulate the attention of other group members, and show greater resistance to stress and disease. Despite assertions that suggest otherwise, it really is not clear how powerful the relationship is between an individual's dominance status and its lifetime reproductive success.

* dominance 지배, 우세

① 하위 개체에 비해 모든 지배적인 개체는 평생 동안 높은 번식 성공률을 보인다.
② 개체의 우세 상태와 평생 번식 성공 사이의 관계는 다면적이며 명확하게 정립되어 있다고 할 수는 없다.
③ 사회적 지배력을 갖춘 존재는 음식 및 짝과 같은 자원에 대한 접근을 통해 번식 성공에 영향을 미친다.
④ 하위 개체는 스트레스 수준이 높지 않기 때문에 평생 번식 성공률이 더 높은 경향이 있다.

24 다음 글의 주제로 가장 적절한 것은?

While mindfulness meditation is generally safe, concerns arise from its side effects like panic attacks and psychosis, which are seldom reported and poorly understood in academic studies. Critics argue the rapid adoption of mindfulness by organizations and educational systems may inappropriately shift societal issues to individuals, suggesting that personal stress is due to a lack of meditation rather than addressing systemic causes like environmental pollution or workplace demands. Critics like Professor Ronald Purser suggest that mindfulness may make individuals more compliant with adverse conditions instead of empowering them to seek change. Despite these concerns, the critique isn't against mindfulness itself but against its promotion as a universal solution by entities resistant to change. For a more thorough understanding of mindfulness' benefits and risks, long-term and rigorously controlled studies are essential.

* psychosis 정신 질환 ** compliant 순응하는

① the criticism regarding the safety and societal implications of the widespread adoption of mindfulness meditation
② the social and national measures which are taken to relieve personal stress and prevent social and cultural confusion
③ the basic elements of mindfulness that must precede the resolution of social problems rather than individual problems
④ the disadvantages that individuals and societies face due to the meditation performed improperly and the lack of meditation

25 Mike Mansfield에 관한 다음 글의 내용과 가장 일치하지 않는 것은?

A man of few words and great modesty, Mike Mansfield often said he did not want to be remembered. Yet, his fascinating life story and enormous contributions are an inspiration for all who follow. Mike Mansfield was born in New York City on March 16, 1903. Following his mother's death when Mike was 7, his father sent him and his two sisters to Great Falls, Montana, to be raised by an aunt and uncle there. At 14, he lied about his age in order to enlist in the U.S. Navy for the duration of World War I. Later, he served in the Army and the Marines, which sent him to the Philippines and China, awakening a lifelong interest in Asia. Mike Mansfield's political career was launched in 1942 when he was elected to the U.S. House of Representatives. He served five terms from Montana's 1st District. In 1952, he was elected to the U.S. Senate and re-elected in 1958, 1964 and 1970. His selection as Democratic Assistant Majority Leader was followed by election in 1961 as Senate Majority Leader. He served in that capacity until his retirement from the Senate in 1977, longer than any other Majority Leader in history.

* House of Representatives 하원 ** Senate 상원
*** Majority Leader 다수당 원내대표

① 말수가 적고 겸손했으며 자신이 기억되지 않기를 원했었다.
② 모친이 사망한 이후 친인척의 보살핌을 받았다.
③ 군 복무 중 아시아 파병을 계기로 아시아에 대한 관심이 커졌다.
④ 상원의원에 5번 당선되었으며 가장 긴 다수당 원내대표를 역임했다.

정답 · 해석 · 해설 p. 182

20회 2024년 법원직 9급
모바일 자동 채점 + 성적 분석 서비스 바로 가기

QR코드를 이용해 모바일로 간편하게 채점하고 나의 실력이 어느 정도인지, 취약 부분이 어디인지 바로 파악해 보세요.

(p.214에서 전체 정답표를 확인하실 수 있습니다)

01 Henry Molaison에 대한 다음 글의 내용과 가장 일치하지 않는 것은?

Henry Molaison, a 27-year-old man, suffered from debilitating *seizures for about a decade in the 1950s. On September 1, 1953, Molaison allowed surgeons to remove a section of tissue from each side of his brain to stop the seizures. The operation worked, but Molaison was left with permanent **amnesia, unable to form new memories. This tragic outcome led to one of the most significant discoveries in 20th century brain science: the discovery that complex functions like learning and memory are linked to specific regions of the brain. Molaison became known as "H.M." in research to protect his privacy. Scientists William Scoville studied Molaison and nine other patients who had similar surgeries, finding that only those who had parts of their ***medial temporal lobes removed experienced memory problems, specifically with recent memory. He discovered that a specific structure in the brain was necessary for normal memory. Molaison's life was a series of firsts, as he couldn't remember anything he had done before. However, he was able to acquire new motor skills over time. Studies of Molaison allowed neuroscientists to further explore the brain networks involved in conscious and unconscious memories, even after his death in 2008.

* seizure 발작
** amnesia 기억 상실증
*** medial temporal lobe 내측 측두엽

① 외과의사들이 발작을 멈추기 위해 그의 뇌의 양쪽에서 조직의 한 부분을 제거하게 했다.

② 수술 결과는 학습과 기억과 같은 복잡한 기능들이 뇌의 특정 영역과 연결되어 있다는 발견으로 이어졌다.

③ 살아가면서 이전에 한 일을 조금씩 기억할 수 있었지만, 시간이 지나면서 운동 능력이 약화되었다.

④ 그에 대한 연구는 의식적 기억 및 무의식적 기억과 관련된 뇌의 연결 조직을 더 탐구할 수 있게 하였다.

02 다음 글의 밑줄 친 부분 중, 어법상 가장 틀린 것은?

Humans have an inborn *affinity for nature that goes beyond the tangible benefits we derive from the microbes, plants, and animals of the **biomes ① in which we live. The idea that nature in the form of landscapes, plants, and animals ② are good for our well-being is old and can be traced to Charles Darwin or earlier. This idea was called biophilia by psychologist Erich Fromm and was studied by Harvard ant biologist Edward O. Wilson and Stephen Kellert. In 1984, Wilson published *Biophilia*, which was followed by another book, The Biophilia Hypothesis, ③ edited by Kellert and Wilson, in 1995. Their biophilia hypothesis is ④ that humans have a universal desire to be in natural settings.

* affinity 친밀감
** biome 생물군계(生物群系)

03 다음 글의 내용과 가장 일치하지 않는 것은?

Life on Earth faced an extreme test of survivability during the *Cryogenian Period, which began 720 million years ago. The planet was frozen over most of the 85 million-year period. But life somehow survived during this time called "Snowball Earth". Scientists are trying to better understand the start of this period. They believe a greatly reduced amount of the sun's warmth reached the planet's surface as its radiation bounced off the white ice sheets. Also, they said the fossils found in black shale and identified as seaweed are a sign that livable water environments were more widespread at the time than they once believed. The findings of some research support the idea that the planet was more of a "Slushball Earth" with melting snow. This enabled the earliest forms of complex life to survive in areas once thought to have been frozen solid. The researchers said the most important finding was that ice-free, open water conditions existed in place during the last part of so-called "the Ice Age". The findings demonstrate that the world's oceans were not completely frozen. It means areas of habitable refuge existed where multicellular organisms could survive.

* Cryogenian Period 크라이오제니아기

(600~850만년 전 시기)

① 지구는 8천 5백만 년의 대부분의 기간 동안 얼어 있었지만 생명체는 살아남았다.
② 과학자들은 "눈덩이 지구" 기간 동안에도 지구의 표면에 다다른 태양의 온기가 크게 감소하지 않았다고 믿고 있다.
③ "슬러시볼 지구"의 기간 동안에 초기 형태의 복잡한 생명체가 생존하는 것은 가능했다.
④ 연구결과 "빙하 시대" 후반기의 세계의 바다가 완전히 얼지 않았다는 것이 입증되었다.

04 다음 빈칸에 들어갈 말로 가장 적절한 것은?

As global temperatures rise, so do sea levels, threatening coastal communities around the world. Surprisingly, even small organisms like oysters _____.
Oysters are keystone species with *ripple effects on the health of their ecosystems and its inhabitants. Just one adult oyster can filter up to fifty gallons of water in a single day, making waterways cleaner. Healthy oyster reefs also provide a home for hundreds of other marine organisms, promoting biodiversity and ecosystem balance. As rising sea levels lead to pervasive flooding, oyster reefs act as walls to buffer storms and protect against further coastal erosion.

* ripple effect 파급효과

① can come to our defense
② can be the food for emergency
③ may be contaminated by microplastics
④ can increase the income of local residents

05 다음 글의 내용을 한 문장으로 요약하고자 한다. 빈칸 (A), (B)에 들어갈 말로 가장 적절한 것은?

The myth of the taste map, which claims that different sections of the tongue are responsible for specific tastes, is incorrect, according to modern science. The taste map originated from the experiments of German scientist David Hänig in the early 1900s, which found that the tongue is most sensitive to tastes along the edges and not so much at the center. However, this has been misinterpreted over the years to claim that sweet is at the front of the tongue, bitter is at the back, and salty and sour are at the sides. In reality, different tastes are sensed by *taste buds all over the tongue. Taste buds work together to make us crave or dislike certain foods, based on our long-term learning and association. For example, our ancestors needed fruit for nutrients and easy calories, so we are naturally drawn to sweet tastes, while bitterness in some plants serves as a warning of toxicity. Of course, different species in the animal kingdom also have unique taste abilities: carnivores do not eat fruit and therefore do not crave sugar like humans do.

* taste bud 미뢰

The claim that different parts of the tongue are responsible for specific tastes has been proven to be ____(A)____ by modern science, and the taste preferences are influenced by the ____(B)____ history.

	(A)		(B)
①	correct	…	evolutionary
②	false	…	evolutionary
③	false	…	psychological
④	correct	…	psychological

06 다음 글의 밑줄 친 부분 중 어법상 가장 틀린 것은?

Language is the primary means ① <u>by which</u> people communicate with one another. Although most creatures communicate, human speech is more complex, more creative, and ② <u>used</u> more extensively than the communication systems of other animals. Language is an essential part of what it means to be human and is a basic part of all cultures. Linguistic anthropology is concerned with understanding language and its relation to culture. Language is an amazing thing ③ <u>what</u> we take for granted. When we speak, we use our bodies—our lungs, vocal cords, mouth, tongue, and lips—to produce noises of varying tone and pitch. And, somehow, when we and others ④ <u>do</u> this together, we are able to communicate with one another, but only if we speak the same language. Linguistic anthropologists want to understand the variation among languages and how language is structured, learned, and used.

07 글의 흐름으로 보아, 주어진 문장이 들어가기에 가장 적절한 곳은?

> Healthcare chatbots have been purposed to solve this problem and ensure proper diagnosis and advice for people from the comfort of their homes.

> People have grown hesitant to approach hospitals or health centers due to the fear of contracting a disease or the heavy sum of consultation fees. (①) This leads them to self-diagnose themselves based upon unverified information sources on the Internet. (②) This often proves harmful effects on the person's mental and physical health if misdiagnosed and improper medicines are consumed. (③) Based upon the severity of the diagnosis, the chatbot prescribes over the counter treatment or escalates the diagnosis to a verified healthcare professional. (④) Interactive chatbots that have been trained on a large and wide variety of symptoms, risk factors, and treatment can handle user health queries with ease, especially in the case of COVID-19.

08 주어진 글 다음에 이어질 글의 순서로 가장 적절한 것은?

> Sports fan depression is a real phenomenon that affects many *avid sports fans, especially during times of disappointment or defeat.

> (A) Fans may experience a decrease in mood, appetite, and sleep quality, as well as an increase in stress levels and a heightened risk of developing anxiety or depression. There are many factors that can contribute to sports fan depression, including personal investment in a team's success, social pressures to support a particular team, and the intense media coverage and scrutiny that often accompanies high-profile sports events.
>
> (B) For many fans, their emotional investment in their favorite teams or athletes can be so intense that losing or failing to meet expectations can lead to feelings of sadness, frustration, and even depression. Research has shown that sports fan depression can have a range of negative effects on both mental and physical health.
>
> (C) To mitigate the negative effects of sports fan depression, it's important for fans to maintain a healthy perspective on sports and remember that they are ultimately just games. Engaging in self-care activities such as exercise, spending time with loved ones, and seeking support from a mental health professional can also be helpful.
>
> * avid 열심인

① (A) - (C) - (B)　　② (B) - (A) - (C)

③ (B) - (C) - (A)　　④ (C) - (B) - (A)

09 Roald Dahl에 관한 다음 글의 내용과 가장 일치하지 않는 것은?

Roald Dahl (1916-1990) was born in Wales of Norwegian parents. He spent his childhood in England and, at age eighteen, went to work for the Shell Oil Company in Africa. When World War II broke out, he joined the Royal Air Force and became a fighter pilot. At the age of twenty-six he moved to Washington, D.C., and it was there he began to write. His first short story, which recounted his adventures in the war, was bought by *The Saturday Evening Post*, and so began a long and illustrious career. After establishing himself as a writer for adults, Roald Dahl began writing children's stories in 1960 while living in England with his family. His first stories were written as entertainment for his own children, to whom many of his books are dedicated. Roald Dahl is now considered one of the most beloved storytellers of our time.

① 어린 시절을 영국에서 보냈고, 18세에 아프리카에서 일했다.
② 2차 세계대전이 발발했을 때는 공군에 입대하여 조종사가 되었다.
③ 전쟁에서 자신의 모험을 다룬 첫 번째 단편 소설을 썼다.
④ 성인을 위한 작가가 된 뒤 영국에서 가족과 떨어져 혼자 살면서 글을 썼다.

10 다음 글에서 전체 흐름과 가장 관계 없는 문장은?

One of the most interesting discoveries in the field of new sources of sustainable energy is bio-solar energy from jellyfish. Scientists have discovered that the fluorescent protein in this animal can be used to generate solar energy in a more sustainable way than current *photovoltaic energy. How is this energy generated? ① The process involves converting the jellyfish's fluorescent protein into a solar cell that is capable of generating energy and transferring it to small devices. ② There has been constant criticism that the natural environment is being damaged by reckless solar power generation. ③ The main advantage of using these living beings as a natural energy source is that they are a clean alternative that does not use fossil fuels or require the use of limited resources. ④ Although this project is still currently in the trial phase, the expectation is that this source of energy will be able to be expanded and become a green alternative for powering the type of small electronic devices that are becoming more and more common.

* photovoltaic 광전기성의

11 주어진 글 다음에 이어질 글의 순서로 가장 적절한 것은?

On the human level, a cow seems simple. You feed it grass, and it pays you back with milk. It's a trick whose secret is limited to cows and a few other mammals (most can't digest grass).

(A) A cow's complexity is even greater. In particular, a cow (plus a bull) can make a new generation of baby cows. This is a simple thing on a human level, but inexpressibly complex on a microscopic level.

(B) Seen through a microscope, though, it all gets more complicated. And the closer you look, the more complicated it gets. Milk is not a single substance, but a mixture of many. Grass is so complex that we still don't fully understand it.

(C) You don't need to understand the details to exploit the process: it's a straightforward transformation from grass into milk, more like chemistry — or *alchemy — than biology. It is, in its way, magic, but it's rational magic that works reliably. All you need is some grass, a cow and several generations of practical knowhow.

* alchemy 연금술

① (B) - (A) - (C)　　② (B) - (C) - (A)
③ (C) - (A) - (B)　　④ (C) - (B) - (A)

12 글의 흐름으로 보아, 주어진 문장이 들어가기에 가장 적절한 곳은?

But here it's worth noting that more than half the workforce has little or no opportunity for remote work.

COVID-19's spread flattened the cultural and technological barriers standing in the way of remote work. One analysis of the potential for remote work to persist showed that 20 to 25 percent of workforces in advanced economies could work from home in the range of three to five days a week. (①) This is four to five times more remote work than pre-COVID-19. (②) Moreover, not all work that can be done remotely should be; for example, negotiations, brainstorming, and providing sensitive feedback are activities that may be less effective when done remotely. (③) The outlook for remote work, then, depends on the work environment, job, and the tasks at hand, so *hybrid work setups, where some work happens on-site and some remotely, are likely to persist. (④) To unlock sustainable performance and well-being in a hybrid world, the leading driver of performance and productivity should be the sense of purpose work provides to employees, not compensation.

* hybrid 혼합체

13 Sigmund Freud에 관한 다음 글의 내용과 가장 일치하지 않는 것은?

Sigmund Freud was a doctor of psychology in Vienna, Austria at the end of the nineteenth century. He treated many patients with nervous problems through his "talk cure." For this type of treatment, Freud simply let his patients talk to him about anything that was bothering them. While treating his patients, he began to realize that although there were events in a patient's past that she or he might not remember consciously, these events could affect the person's actions in her or his present life. Freud called the place where past memories were hidden the unconscious mind. Images from the unconscious mind might show up in a person's dreams or through the person's actions. Freud wrote a book about his theories about the unconscious mind and dreaming in 1899. The title of the book was "The Interpretation of Dreams"

① 오스트리아의 정신과 의사였다.
② 신경 문제가 있는 환자들을 대화를 통해 치료했다.
③ 기억이 나지 않는 과거는 환자에게 영향을 미치지 못한다고 주장했다.
④ "꿈의 해석"이라는 책을 썼다.

14 다음 글의 요지로 가장 적절한 것은?

All emotions tell us something about ourselves and our situation. But sometimes we find it hard to accept what we feel. We might judge ourselves for feeling a certain way, like if we feel jealous, for example. But instead of thinking we should not feel that way, it's better to notice how we actually feel. Avoiding negative feelings or pretending we don't feel the way we do can *backfire. It's harder to move past difficult feelings and allow them to fade if we don't face them and try to understand why we feel that way. You don't have to dwell on your emotions or constantly talk about how you feel. Emotional awareness simply means recognizing, respecting, and accepting your feelings as they happen.

* backfire 역효과를 내다

① 부정적인 감정은 잘 조절해서 표현해야 한다.
② 과거의 부정적 감정은 되도록 빨리 극복해야 한다.
③ 감정을 수용하기 어렵다면 전문가의 도움을 받아야 한다.
④ 우리의 감정을 인식하고 존중하며 그대로 받아들여야 한다.

15 주어진 글 다음에 이어질 글의 순서로 가장 적절한 것은?

At the level of lawmaking, there is no reason why tech giants should have such an ironclad grip on technological resources and innovation.

(A) As the Daily Wire's Matt Walsh has pointed out, for example, if you don't buy your kid a smartphone, he won't have one. There is no need to put in his hand a device that enables him to indulge his every impulse without supervision.

(B) At the private and personal level, there's no reason why they should have control of your life, either. In policy, politics, and our personal lives, it should not be taken as "inevitable" that our data will be sold to the highest bidder, our children will be addicted to online games, and our lives will be lived in the metaverse.

(C) As a free people, we are entitled to exert absolute control over which kinds of digital products we consume, and in what quantities. Most especially, parents should control what tech products go to their kids.

① (B) - (A) - (C)   ② (B) - (C) - (A)
③ (C) - (A) - (B)   ④ (C) - (B) - (A)

16 글의 흐름으로 보아, 주어진 문장이 들어가기에 가장 적절한 곳은?

These may appear as challenges which may be impossible to address because of the uncertainty in our ability to predict future climate.

Global warming is a reality man has to live with. (①) This is a very important issue to recognize, because, of all the parameters that affect human existence, on planet earth, it is the food security that is of paramount importance to life on earth and which is most threatened by global warming. (②) Future food security will be dependent on a combination of the stresses, both biotic and *abiotic, imposed by climate change, variability of weather within the growing season, development of **cultivars more suited to different ***ambient conditions, and, the ability to develop effective adaptation strategies which allow these cultivars to express their genetic potential under the changing climate conditions. (③) However, these challenges also provide us the opportunities to enhance our understanding of soil-plant-atmosphere interaction and how one could utilize this knowledge to enable us achieve the ultimate goal of enhanced food security across all areas of the globe. (④)

* abiotic 비생물적인 ** cultivar 품종 *** ambient 주변의

17 다음 글의 밑줄 친 부분 중, 어법상 가장 틀린 것은?

Anthropologist Paul Ekman proposed in the 1970s that humans experience six basic emotions: anger, fear, surprise, disgust, joy, and sadness. However, the exact number of emotions ① disputing, with some researchers suggesting there are only four, and others counting as many as 27. Additionally, scientists debate whether emotions are universal to all human cultures or whether we're born with them or learn them through experience. ② Despite these disagreements, emotions are clear products of activity in specific regions of the brain. The *amygdala and the insula or **insular cortex are two representative brain structures most ③ closely linked with emotions. The amygdala, a paired, almond-shaped structure deep within the brain, integrates emotions, emotional behavior, and motivation. It interprets fear, helps distinguish friends from foes, and identifies social rewards and how to attain ④ them. The insula is the source of disgust. The experience of disgust may protect you from ingesting poison or spoiled food.

* amygdala 편도체

** insula cortex 대뇌 피질

18 다음 글의 주제로 가장 적절한 것은?

Do you want to be a successful anchor? If so, keep this in mind. As an anchor, the individual will be called upon to communicate news and information to viewer during newscasts, special reports and other types of news programs. This will include interpreting news events, adlibbing, and communicating breaking news effectively when scripts are not available. Anchoring duties also involve gathering and writing stories. The anchor must be able to deliver scripts clearly and effectively. Strong writing skills, solid news judgement and a strong sense of visual storytelling are essential skills. This individual must be a self-starter who cultivates sources and finds new information as a regular part of job. Live reporting skills are important, as well as the ability to adlib and describe breaking news as it takes place.

① difficulties of producing live news
② qualifications to become a news anchor
③ the importance of the social role of journalists
④ the importance of forming the right public opinion

19 다음 글의 내용과 가장 일치하지 않는 것은?

Modern sculpture is generally considered to have begun with the work of French sculptor Auguste Rodin. Rodin, often considered a sculptural Impressionist, did not set out to rebel against artistic traditions, however, he incorporated novel ways of building his sculpture that defied classical categories and techniques. Specifically, Rodin modeled complex, turbulent, deeply pocketed surfaces into clay. While he never self-identified as an Impressionist, the vigorous, gestural modeling he employed in his works is often likened to the quick, gestural *brush strokes aiming to capture a fleeting moment that was typical of the Impressionists. Rodin's most original work departed from traditional themes of mythology and **allegory, in favor of modeling the human body with intense realism, and celebrating individual character and physicality.

* brush stroke 붓놀림
** allegory 우화, 풍자

① 현대 조각은 일반적으로 로댕의 작품에서 시작된 것으로 여겨진다.
② 로댕은 고전적인 기술을 거부하며 조각품을 만드는 새로운 방법을 통합했다.
③ 로댕은 자신을 인상파라고 밝히며 인상파의 전형적인 붓놀림을 보여주었다.
④ 로댕의 가장 독창적인 작품은 신화와 우화의 전통적인 주제에서 벗어나고자 했다.

20 다음 글의 주제로 가장 적절한 것은?

Cosmetics became so closely associated with portraiture that some photography handbooks included recipes for them. American photographers also, at times, used cosmetics to retouch negatives and prints, enlivening women's faces with traces of rouge. Some customers with dark skin requested photographs that would make them look lighter. A skin lightener advertisement that appeared in an African American newspaper in 1935 referenced this practice by promising that its product could achieve the same look produced by photographers: a lighter skin Cop free of *blemishes. By drawing attention to the face and encouraging cosmetics use, portrait photography heightened the aesthetic valuation of smooth and often light-colored skin.

* blemish (피부 등의)티

① side effects of excessive use of cosmetics
② overuse of cosmetics promoted by photographers
③ active use of cosmetics to make the face look better
④ decreased use of cosmetics due to advances in photography

21 다음 글의 밑줄 친 부분 중 문맥 상 낱말의 쓰임이 가장 적절하지 않은 것은?

"Play is something done for its own sake." says psychiatrist Stuart Brown, author of "Play" He writes: "It's voluntary, it's pleasurable, it offers a sense of engagement, it takes you out of time. And the act itself is more important than the outcome." With this definition in mind, it's easy to recognize play's potential benefits. Play ① nurtures relationships with oneself and others. It ② relieves stress and increases happiness. It builds feelings of empathy, creativity, and collaboration. It supports the growth of *sturdiness and grit. When children are deprived of opportunities for play, their development can be significantly ③ enhanced. Play is so important that the United Nations High Commission on Human Rights declared it a ④ fundamental right of every child. Play is not **frivolous. It is not something to do after the "real work" is done. Play is the real work of childhood. Through it, children have their best chance for becoming whole, happy adults.

* sturdiness 강건함

** frivolous 경박한, 하찮은

22 다음 빈칸에 들어갈 말로 가장 적절한 것은?

Lewis Pugh is a British endurance swimmer, who is best known for his long-distance swims in cold and open waters. He swims in cold places as a way to draw attention to the urgent need to protect the world's oceans and waterways from the effects of climate change and pollution. In 2019, Pugh decided to swim in Lake Imja, which is located in the Khumbu region of Nepal, near Mount Everest. After a failed first attempt, Lewis had a *debrief to discuss the best way to swim at 5,300 meters above sea level. He is usually very aggressive when he swims because he wants to finish quickly and get out of the cold water. But this time he showed _____ and swam slowly.

* debrief 평가회의

① grief   ② anger   ③ humility   ④ confidence

23 다음 글에서 전체 흐름과 가장 관계 없는 문장은?

Fast fashion is a method of producing inexpensive clothing at a rapid pace to respond to the latest fashion trends. With shopping evolving into a form of entertainment in the age of fast fashion, customers are contributing to what sustainability experts refer to as a throwaway culture. This means customers simply discard products once they are deemed useless rather than recycling or donating them. ① The consumers are generally satisfied with the quality of fast fashion brand clothing. ② As a result, these discarded items add a huge burden to the environment. ③ To resolve the throwaway culture and fast fashion crisis, the concept of sustainability in fashion is brought to the spotlight. ④ Sustainable fashion involves apparel, footwear, and accessories that are produced, distributed, and utilized as sustainably as possible while taking into account socio-economic and environmental concerns.

24 다음 글의 요지로 가장 적절한 것은?

Wrinkles are a sure sign of aging, and may also hint that bone health is on the decline. Researchers at Yale School of Medicine found that some women with deepening and worsening skin wrinkles also had lower bone density, independent of age and factors known to influence bone mass. Skin and bones share a common building-block protein, type 1 collagen, which is lost with age, says study author Dr. Lubna Pal. Wrinkles between the eyebrows — the vertical lines above the bridge of the nose — appear to be the strongest markers of *brittle bones, she says. Long-term studies are needed, but it appears the skin reflects what's happening at the level of the bone, says Pal.

* brittle 잘 부러지는

① 나이가 들면서 주름이 생기는 것은 당연한 현상이다.
② 골밀도 감소와 주름 생성의 관계에 관해서는 연구가 더 필요하다.
③ 여성이 남성보다 주름이 더 많이 생기는 이유는 골밀도 차이 때문이다.
④ 주름은 단지 피부 노화와만 연관된 것이 아니라 뼈 건강 상태와도 연관이 있다.

25 다음 글의 내용과 가장 일치하지 않는 것은?

Meditation can improve your quality of life thanks to its many psychological and physical benefits. Mindfulness-based interventions, such as meditation, have been shown to improve mental health, specifically in the area of stress, according to a study in the Clinical Psychology Review. When faced with a difficult or stressful moment, our bodies create cortisol, the steroid hormone responsible for regulating stress and our natural fight-or-flight response, among many other functions. Chronic stress can cause sustained and elevated levels of cortisol, which can lead to other negative effects on your health, including *cardiovascular and immune systems and gut health. Meditation, which focuses on calming the mind and regulating emotion, can help to reduce chronic stress in the body and lower the risk of its side effects.

* cardiovascular 심혈관계의

① Meditation benefits us both mentally and physically.
② Cortisol is released in a stressful situation.
③ Stress does not usually affect our cardiovascular systems.
④ Meditation can help lower chronic stress in the body.

정답 · 해석 · 해설 p. 198

21회 2023년 법원직 9급
모바일 자동 채점 + 성적 분석 서비스 바로 가기

QR코드를 이용해 모바일로 간편하게 채점하고 나의 실력이 어느 정도인지, 취약 부분이 어디인지 바로 파악해 보세요.

(p.214에서 전체 정답표를 확인하실 수 있습니다)

제한 시간 : 25분　시작 _____ 시 _____ 분 ~ 종료 _____ 시 _____ 분　나의 점수 _____ 회독 수 ☐☐☐

01 (A), (B), (C)의 각 네모 안에서 어법에 맞는 표현으로 가장 적절한 것은?

The selection of the appropriate protective clothing for any job or task (A) is / are usually dictated by an analysis or assessment of the hazards presented. The expected activities of the wearer as well as the frequency and types of exposure, are typical variables that input into this determination. For example, a firefighter is exposed to a variety of burning materials. Specialized multilayer fabric systems are thus used (B) to meet / meeting the *thermal challenges presented. This results in protective gear that is usually fairly heavy and essentially provides the highest levels of protection against any fire situation. In contrast, an industrial worker who has to work in areas (C) where / which the possibility of a flash fire exists would have a very different set of hazards and requirements. In many cases, a flame-resistant coverall worn over cotton work clothes adequately addresses the hazard.

* thermal : 열의

	(A)	(B)	(C)
①	is	to meet	where
②	is	meeting	which
③	are	meeting	where
④	are	to meet	which

02 다음 글의 내용을 한 문장으로 요약하고자 한다. 빈칸 (A), (B)에 들어갈 말로 가장 적절한 것은?

In India, approximately 360 million people—one-third of the population—live in or very close to the forests. More than half of these people live below the official poverty line, and consequently they depend crucially on the resources they obtain from the forests. The Indian government now runs programs aimed at improving their lot by involving them in the commercial management of their forests, in this way allowing them to continue to obtain the food and materials they need, but at the same time to sell forest produce. If the programs succeed, forest dwellers will be more prosperous, but twhey will be able to preserve their traditional way of life and culture, and the forest will be managed sustainably, so the wildlife is not depleted.

⇒ The Indian government is trying to __(A)__ the lives of the poor who live near forests without __(B)__ the forests.

	(A)	(B)
①	improve	ruining
②	control	preserving
③	improve	limiting
④	control	enlarging

03 다음 글의 내용을 한 문장으로 요약하고자 한다. 빈칸 (A), (B)에 들어갈 말로 가장 적절한 것은?

In the absence of facial cues or touch during pandemic, there is a greater need to focus on other aspects of conversation, including more emphasis on tone and inflection, slowing the speed, and increasing loudness without sounding annoying. Many *nuances of the spoken word are easily missed without facial expression, so eye contact will assume an even greater importance. Some hospital workers have developed innovative ways to try to solve this problem. One of nurse specialists was deeply concerned that her chronically sick young patients could not see her face, so she printed off a variety of face stickers to get children to point towards. Some hospitals now also provide their patients with 'face-sheets' that permit easier identification of staff members, and it is always useful to reintroduce yourself and colleagues to patients when wearing masks.

*nuance : 미묘한 차이, 뉘앙스

Some hospitals and workers are looking for ____(A)____ ways to ____(B)____ conversation with patients during pandemic.

     (A)   (B)
① alternative – complement
② bothering   – analyze
③ effective   – hinder
④ disturbing   – improve

04 주어진 글 다음에 이어질 글의 순서로 가장 적절한 것은?

Once they leave their mother, primates have to keep on making decisions about whether new foods they encounter are safe and worth collecting.

(A) By the same token, if the sampler feels fine, it will reenter the tree in a few days, eat a little more, then wait again, building up to a large dose slowly. Finally, if the monkey remains healthy, the other members figure this is OK, and they adopt the new food.

(B) If the plant harbors a particularly strong toxin, the sampler's system will try to break it down, usually making the monkey sick in the process. "I've seen this happen," says Glander. "The other members of the troop are watching with great interest—if the animal gets sick, no other animal will go into that tree. There's a cue being given—a social cue."

(C) Using themselves as experiment tools is one option, but social primates have found a better way. Kenneth Glander calls it "sampling." When howler monkeys move into a new habitat, one member of the troop will go to a tree, eat a few leaves, then wait a day.

① (A) – (B) – (C)   ② (B) – (A) – (C)
③ (C) – (B) – (A)   ④ (C) – (A) – (B)

05 다음 글의 Zainichi에 관한 내용으로 가장 일치하지 않는 것은?

Following Japan's defeat in World War II, the majority of ethnic Koreans (1-1.4 million) left Japan. By 1948, the population of ethnic Koreans settled around 600,000. These Koreans and their descendants are commonly referred to as Zainichi (literally "residing in Japan"), a term that appeared in the immediate postwar years. Ethnic Koreans who remained in Japan did so for diverse reasons. Koreans who had achieved successful careers in business, the imperial bureaucracy, and the military during the colonial period or who had taken advantage of economic opportunities that opened up immediately after the war—opted to maintain their relatively privileged status in Japanese society rather than risk returning to an impoverished and politically unstable post-liberation Korea. Some Koreans who *repatriated were so repulsed by the poor conditions they observed that they decided to return to Japan. Other Koreans living in Japan could not afford the train fare to one of the departure ports, and among them who had ethnic Japanese spouses and Japanese-born, Japanese-speaking children, it made more sense to stay in Japan rather than to navigate the cultural and linguistic challenges of a new environment.

* repatriate : 본국으로 송환하다

① 주로 제2차 세계대전 이후에 일본에 남은 한국인들과 후손을 일컫는다.
② 전쟁 후에 경제적인 이득을 취한 사람들도 있었다.
③ 어떤 사람들은 한국에 갔다가 다시 일본으로 돌아왔다.
④ 한국으로 돌아갈 교통비를 마련하지 못한 사람들은 일본인과 결혼했다.

06 다음 빈칸에 들어갈 말로 가장 적절한 것은?

There are a few jobs where people have had to _____. We see referees and umpires using their arms and hands to signal directions to the players—as in cricket, where a single finger upwards means that the batsman is out and has to leave the *wicket. Orchestra conductors control the musicians through their movements. People working at a distance from each other have to invent special signals if they want to communicate. So do people working in a noisy environment, such as in a factory where the machines are very loud, or lifeguards around a swimming pool full of school children.

* wicket : (크리켓에서) 삼주문

① support their parents and children
② adapt to an entirely new work style
③ fight in court for basic human rights
④ develop their signing a bit more fully

Opponents of the use of animals in research also oppose use of animals to test the safety of drugs or other compounds. Within the pharmaceutical industry, it was noted that out of 19 chemicals known to cause cancer in humans when taken, only seven caused cancer in mice and rats using standards set by the National Cancer Instituted(Barnard and Koufman, 1997). For example, and antidepressant, nomifensin, had minimal toxicity in rats, rabbits, dogs, and monkeys yet caused liver toxicity and *anemia in humans. In these and other cases, it has been shown that some compounds have serious adverse reactions in humans that were not predicted by animal testing resulting in conditions in the treated humans that could lead to disability, or even death. And researchers who are calling for an end to animal research state that they have better methods available such as human clinical trials, observation aided by laboratory of autopsy tests.

* anemia : 빈혈

① 한 기관의 실험 결과 동물과 달리 19개의 발암물질 중에 7개는 인간에게 영향을 미쳤다.
② 어떤 약물은 동물 실험 때와 달리 인간에게 간독성과 빈혈을 일으켰다.
③ 동물 실험에서 나타난 결과가 인간에게는 다르게 작용될 수 있다.
④ 동물 실험을 반대하는 연구자들은 대안적인 방법들을 제시하고 있다.

Cold showers are any showers with a water temperature below 70°F. They may have health benefits. For people with depression, cold showers can work as a kind of gentle electroshock therapy. The cold water sends many electrical impulses to your brain. They *jolt your system to ① increase alertness, clarity, and energy levels. Endorphins, which are sometimes called happiness hormones, are also released. This effect leads to feelings of well-being and ② optimism. For people that are obese, taking a cold shower 2 or 3 times per week may contribute to increased metabolism. It may help fight obesity over time. The research about how exactly cold showers help people lose weight is ③ clear. However, it does show that cold water can even out certain hormone levels and heal the **gastrointestinal system. These effects may add to the cold shower's ability to lead to weight loss. Furthermore, when taken regularly, cold showers can make our circulatory system more efficient. Some people also report that their skin looks better as a result of cold showers, probably because of better circulation. Athletes have known this benefit for years, even if we have only ④ recently seen data that supports cold water for healing after a sport injury.

* jolt : 갑자기 덜컥 움직이다 ** gastrointestinal : 위장의

09 다음 글의 내용을 한 문장으로 요약하고자 한다. 빈칸 (A), (B)에 들어갈 말로 가장 적절한 것은?

Researchers have been interested in the habitual ways a single individual copes with conflict when it occurs. They've called this approach conflict styles. There are several apparent conflict styles, and each has its pros and cons. The collaborating style tends to solve problems in ways that maximize the chances that the best result is provided for all involved. The pluses of a collaborating style include creating trust, maintaining positive relationship, and building commitment. However, it's time consuming and it takes a lot of energy to collaborate with another during conflict. The competing style may develop hostility in the person who doesn't achieve their goals. However, the competing style tends to resolve a conflict quickly.

The collaborating style might be used for someone who put a great value in ___(A)___, while a person who prefers ___(B)___ may choose the competing style.

	(A)	(B)
①	financial ability	interaction
②	saving time	peacefulness
③	mutual understanding	time efficiency
④	effectiveness	consistency

10 주어진 글 다음에 이어질 글의 순서로 가장 적절한 것은?

The historical evolution of Conflict Resolution gained momentum in the 1950s and 1960s, at the height of the Cold War, when the development of nuclear weapons and conflict between the superpowers seemed to threaten human survival.

(A) The combination of analysis and practice implicit in the new ideas was not easy to reconcile with traditional scholarly institutions or the traditions of practitioners such as diplomats and politicians.

(B) However, they were not taken seriously by some. The international relations profession had its own understanding of international conflict and did not see value in the new approaches as proposed.

(C) A group of pioneers from different disciplines saw the value of studying conflict as a general phenomenon, with similar properties, whether it occurs in international relations, domestic politics, industrial relations, communities, or between individuals.

① (B) – (A) – (C)　　② (B) – (C) – (A)
③ (C) – (A) – (B)　　④ (C) – (B) – (A)

11 (A), (B), (C)의 각 네모 안에서 어법에 맞는 표현으로 가장 적절한 것은?

The key to understanding economics is accepting (A) that / what there are always unintended consequences. Actions people take for their own good reasons have results they don't envision or intend. The same is true with *geopolitics. It is doubtful that the village of Rome, when it started its expansion in the seventh century BC, (B) had / have a master plan for conquering the Mediterranean world five hundred years later. But the first action its inhabitants took against neighboring villages set in motion a process that was both constrained by reality and (C) filled / filling with unintended consequences. Rome wasn't planned, and neither did it just happen.

* geopolitics : 지정학

	(A)	(B)	(C)
①	that	had	filled
②	what	had	filling
③	what	have	filled
④	that	have	filling

12 다음 빈칸에 들어갈 말로 가장 적절한 것을 고르시오.

Water and civilization go hand-in-hand. The idea of a "*hydraulic civilization" argues that water is the unifying context and justification for many large-scale civilizations throughout history. For example, the various multi-century Chinese empires survived as long as they did in part by controlling floods along the Yellow River. One interpretation of the hydraulic theory is that the justification for gathering populations into large cities is to manage water. Another interpretation suggests that large water projects enable the rise of big cities. The Romans understood the connections between water and power, as the Roman Empire built a vast network of **aqueducts throughout land they controlled, many of which remain intact. For example, Pont du Gard in southern France stands today as a testament to humanity's investment in its water infrastructure. Roman governors built roads, bridges, and water systems as a way of _____.

* hydraulic : 수력학의 ** aqueduct : 송수로

① focusing on educating young people
② prohibiting free trade in local markets
③ concentrating and strengthening their authority
④ giving up their properties to other countries

13 주어진 글 다음에 이어질 글의 순서로 가장 적절한 것은?

Ambiguity is so uncomfortable that it can even turn good news into bad. You go to your doctor with a persistent stomachache. Your doctor can't figure out what the reason is, so she sends you to the lab for tests.

(A) And what happens? Your immediate relief may be replaced by a weird sense of discomfort. You still don't know what the pain was! There's got to be an explanation somewhere.

(B) A week later you're called back to hear the results. When you finally get into her office, your doctor smiles and tells you the tests were all negative.

(C) Maybe it is cancer and they've just missed it. Maybe it's worse. Surely they should be able to find a cause. You feel frustrated by the lack of a definitive answer.

① (B) – (A) – (C) ② (B) – (C) – (A)
③ (C) – (A) – (B) ④ (C) – (B) – (A)

14 글의 흐름으로 보아, 주어진 문장이 들어가기에 가장 적절한 곳은?

The effect, however, was just the reverse.

How we dress for work has taken on a new element of choice, and with it, new anxieties. (①) The practice of having a "dress-down day" or "casual day," which began to emerge a decade or so ago, was intended to make life easier for employees, to enable them to save money and feel more relaxed at the office. (②) In addition to the normal workplace wardrobe, employees had to create a "workplace casual" *wardrobe. (③) It couldn't really be the sweats and T-shirts you wore around the house on the weekend. (④) It had to be a selection of clothing that sustained a certain image—relaxed, but also serious.

* wardrobe : 옷, 의류

15 다음 글의 밑줄 친 부분 중, 어법상 가장 틀린 것은?

You should choose the research method ① that best suits the outcome you want. You may run a survey online that enables you to question large numbers of people and ② provides full analysis in report format, or you may think asking questions one to one is a better way to get the answers you need from a smaller test selection of people. ③ Whichever way you choose, you will need to compare like for like. Ask people the same questions and compare answers. Look for both similarities and differences. Look for patterns and trends. Deciding on a way of recording and analysing the data ④ are important. A simple self created spreadsheet may well be enough to record some basic research data.

16 다음 글의 요지로 가장 적절한 것은?

Some criminal offenders may engage in illegal behavior because they love the excitement and thrills that crime can provide. In his highly influential work *Seductions of Crime*, sociologist Jack Katz argues that there are immediate benefits to criminality that "seduce" people into a life of crime. For some people, shoplifting and *vandalism are attractive because getting away with crime is a thrilling demonstration of personal competence. The need for excitement may counter fear of apprehension and punishment. In fact, some offenders will deliberately seek out especially risky situations because of the added "thrill". The need for excitement is a significant predictor of criminal choice.

* vandalism : 기물 파손

① 범죄를 줄이기 위해서 재소자를 상대로 한 교육이 필요하다.
② 범죄 행위에서 생기는 흥분과 쾌감이 범죄를 유발할 수 있다.
③ 엄격한 형벌 제도와 법 집행을 통해 강력 범죄를 줄일 수 있다.
④ 세밀하고 꼼꼼한 제도를 만들어 범죄 피해자를 도울 필요가 있다.

17 다음 빈칸에 들어갈 말로 가장 적절한 것은?

In one classic study showing the importance of attachment, Wisconsin University psychologists Harry and Margaret Harlow investigated the responses of young monkeys. The infants were separated from their biological mothers, and two *surrogate mothers were introduced to their cages. One, the wire mother, consisted of a round wooden head, a mesh of cold metal wires, and a bottle of milk from which the baby monkey could drink. The second mother was a foam-rubber form wrapped in a heated terry-cloth blanket. The infant monkeys went to the wire mother for food, but they overwhelmingly preferred and spent significantly more time with the warm terry-cloth mother. The warm terry-cloth mother provided no food, but did provide _____ .

* surrogate : 대리의

① jobs   ② drugs
③ comfort   ④ education

18 다음 글의 밑줄 친 부분 중, 어법상 가장 틀린 것은?

I was released for adoption by my biological parents and ① spend the first decade of my life in orphanages. I spent many years thinking that something was wrong with me. If my own parents didn't want me, who could? I tried to figure out ② what I had done wrong and why so many people sent me away. I don't get close to anyone now because if I do they might leave me. I had to isolate ③ myself emotionally to survive when I was a child, and I still operate on the assumptions I had as a child. I am so fearful of being deserted ④ that I won't venture out and take even minimal risks. I am 40 years old now, but I still feel like a child.

19 다음 글의 밑줄 친 부분 중 어법상 가장 틀린 것은?

Music can have *psychotherapeutic effects that may transfer to everyday life. A number of scholars suggested people ① to use music as psychotherapeutic agent. Music therapy can be broadly defined as being 'the use of music as an adjunct to the treatment or rehabilitation of individuals to enhance their psychological, physical, cognitive or social ② functioning'. Positive emotional experiences from music may improve therapeutic process and thus ③ strengthen traditional cognitive/behavioral methods and their transfer to everyday goals. This may be partially because emotional experiences elicited by music and everyday behaviors ④ share overlapping neurological pathways responsible for positive emotions and motivations.

* psychotherapeutic : 심리 요법의

20 다음 빈칸에 들어갈 말로 가장 적절한 것은?

Cultural interpretations are usually made on the basis of _____ rather than measurable evidence. The arguments tend to be circular. People are poor because they are lazy. How do we "know" they are lazy? Because they are poor. Promoters of these interpretations rarely understand that low productivity results not from laziness and lack of effort but from lack of capital inputs to production. African farmers are not lazy, but they do lack soil nutrients, tractors, feeder roads, irrigated plots, storage facilities, and the like. Stereotypes that Africans work little and therefore are poor are put to rest immediately by spending a day in a village, where backbreaking labor by men and women is the norm.

① statistics
② prejudice
③ appearance
④ circumstances

21 글의 흐름으로 보아, 주어진 문장이 들어가기에 가장 적절한 곳은?

> But the demand for food isn't *elastic; people don't eat more just because food is cheap.

> The free market has never worked in agriculture and it never will. (①) The economics of a family farm are very different than a firm's: When prices fall, the firm can lay off people and idle factories. (②) Eventually the market finds a new balance between supply and demand. (③) And laying off farmers doesn't help to reduce supply. (④) You can fire me, but you can't fire my land, because some other farmer who needs more cash flow or thinks he's more efficient than I am will come in and farm it.
>
> * elastic : 탄력성 있는

22 다음 글의 주제로 가장 적절한 것은?

> Daily training creates special nutritional needs for an athlete, particularly the elite athlete whose training commitment is almost a fulltime job. But even recreational sport will create nutritional challenges. And whatever your level of involvement in sport, you must meet these challenges if you're to achieve the maximum return from training. Without sound eating, much of the purpose of your training might be lost. In the worst-case scenario, dietary problems and deficiencies may directly impair training performance. In other situations, you might improve, but at a rate that is below your potential or slower than your competitors. However, on the positive side, with the right everyday eating plan your commitment to training will be fully rewarded.

① how to improve body flexibility
② importance of eating well in exercise
③ health problems caused by excessive diet
④ improving skills through continuous training

23 다음 글의 주제로 가장 적절한 것은?

> A very well-respected art historian called Ernst Gombrich wrote about something called "the beholder's share". It was Gombrich's belief that a viewer "completed" the artwork, that part of an artwork's meaning came from the person viewing it. So you see—there really are no wrong answers as it is you, as the viewer who is completing the artwork. If you're looking at art in a gallery, read the wall text at the side of the artwork. If staff are present, ask questions. Ask your fellow visitors what they think. Asking questions is the key to understanding more—and that goes for anything in life—not just art. But above all, have confidence in front of an artwork. If you are contemplating an artwork, then you are the intended viewer and what you think matters. You are the only critic that counts.

① 미술작품의 가치는 일정 부분 정해져 있다.
② 미술 작품을 제작할 때 대중의 요구를 반영해야 한다.
③ 미술작품은 감상하는 사람으로 인하여 비로소 완성된다.
④ 미술 감상의 출발은 작가의 숨겨진 의도를 파악하는 것이다.

24 Argentina에 관한 다음 글의 내용과 가장 일치하지 않는 것은?

> Argentina is the world's eighth largest country, comprising almost the entire southern half of South America. Colonization by Spain began in the early 1500s, but in 1816 Jose de San Martin led the movement for Argentine independence. The culture of Argentina has been greatly influenced by the massive European migration in the late nineteenth and early twentieth centuries, primarily from Spain and Italy. The majority of people are at least nominally Catholic, and the country has the largest Jewish population (about 300,000) in South America. From 1880 to 1930, thanks to its agricultural development, Argentina was one of the world's top ten wealthiest nations.

① Jose de San Martin이 스페인으로부터의 독립운동을 이끌었다.
② 북미 출신 이주민들이 그 문화에 많은 영향을 끼쳤다.
③ 남미지역 중에서 가장 많은 유대인들이 살고 있는 곳이다.
④ 농업의 발전으로 한때 부유한 국가였다.

25 Sonja Henie에 관한 다음 글의 내용과 가장 일치하지 않는 것은?

> Sonja Henie is famous for her skill into a career as one of the world's most famous figure skaters—in the rink and on the screen. Henie, winner of three Olympic gold medals and a Norwegian and European champion, invented a thrillingly theatrical and athletic style of figure skating. She introduced short skirts, white skates, and attractive moves. Her spectacular spins and jumps raised the bar for all competitors. In 1936, Twentieth-Century Fox signed her to star in One in a Million, and she soon became one of Hollywood's leading actresses. In 1941, the movie 'Sun Valley Serenade' received three Academy Award nominations which she played as an actress. Although the rest of Henie's films were less acclaimed, she triggered a popular surge in ice skating. In 1938, she launched extravagant touring shows called Hollywood Ice Revues. Her many ventures made her a fortune, but her greatest legacy was inspiring little girls to skate.

① 피겨 스케이터와 영화배우로서의 업적으로 유명하다.
② 올림픽과 다른 대회들에서 좋은 성적을 거두었다.
③ 출연한 영화가 1941년에 영화제에서 3개 부문에 수상했다.
④ 어린 여자아이들에게 스케이트에 대한 영감을 주었다.

정답 · 해석 · 해설 p. 213

22회 2022년 법원직 9급
모바일 자동 채점 + 성적 분석 서비스 바로 가기

QR코드를 이용해 모바일로 간편하게 채점하고 나의 실력이 어느 정도인지, 취약 부분이 어디인지 바로 파악해 보세요.

(p.214에서 전체 정답표를 확인하실 수 있습니다)

OUR PATIENCE WILL ACHIEVE
MORE THAN OUR FORCE.

EDMUND BURKE

힘보다는 인내심으로 더 많은 것을 이룰 수 있다.
에드먼드 버크

Part 5
국회직 9급

문제 유형	5지선다형
총 문항 수	20문항
경쟁률 (2023년 8월, 속기)	58:1
합격선 (2023년 8월, 속기)	66점
시험 안내	국회채용시스템 (https://gosi.assembly.go.kr)

※ 밑줄 친 부분의 의미와 가까운 것을 고르시오. [01~03]

01

The app is designed to help users regulate their heart rhythms and mental well-being to achieve a state of "coherence," characterized by reduced stress, increased resilience, and better overall emotional health.

① benevolence   ② elasticity
③ suppression   ④ promotion
⑤ experience

02

It makes sense to think demand will inevitably rebound briskly, sending Brent and WTI higher in the year to come.

① necessarily   ② substantially
③ miraculously   ④ utterly
⑤ incredibly

03

The flippancy of the second graders was almost more than the substitute teacher could stand it.

① disrespect   ② humourlessness
③ seriousness   ④ stipend
⑤ verge

04 밑줄 친 부분에 들어갈 표현으로 적절한 것은?

Kind neighbors, a fund-raising campaign organized and sponsored by local corporate leaders, _____ its first benefit event for Kalamazoo Hospital this past Sunday. Held at the Kalamazoo Convention Center, the event drew an energetic crowd of over 800 supporters.

① jump-starts
② will jump-start
③ jump-started
④ was jump-started
⑤ has jump-started

05

The seventeenth and eighteenth centuries were the period of transition to the modern age of public finance. First in England and the Netherlands and then elsewhere, investors secured protections against arbitrary action by the sovereign. They established legislatures and parliaments, ① in which creditors were represented, to advise and consent to the state's fiscal policies. ② With checks and balances in place, interest rates came down, and borrowing became easier. Acquisition of these additional fiscal and administrative resources allowed the formation of larger territories, ③ leading to the emergence of the modern state system. Public debt played a substantial role in the advent of the nation-state and then, in the nineteenth century, ④ followed the Treaty of Vienna, in a declining incidence of interstate conflict. It is no coincidence ⑤ that England and the Netherlands, two countries that were early to develop markets in public debt, were in the vanguard of this process.

06

The organic molecules were found in Mars's Gale Crater, a large area ① that may have been a watery lake over three billion years ago. NASA's nuclear-powered rover Curiosity encountered traces of the molecule in rocks ② extracted from the area. The rocks also contain sulfur, ③ which scientists speculate ④ helping preserve the organics even when the rocks were exposed to the harsh radiation on the surface of the planet. Scientists are quick to state that the presence of these organic molecules is not sufficient evidence for ancient life on Mars, ⑤ as the molecules could have been formed by non-living processes. But it's still one of the most astonishing discoveries.

07 다음 글의 요지로 가장 적절한 것은?

Maps are imperfect projections of a three-dimensional globe onto a two-dimensional surface. Similarly, a mapmaker superimposes his own point of view upon the world he is visualizing. What he presents may seemingly appear objective, but it is to a considerable extent a product of his own cultural and political proclivities—and even of his imagination. The cartographer's projection of the outer world is therefore dependent on his own inner psychological state as his maps are based on an "act of seeing" rather than on "what was seen." Geographical maps reflect perceptions of space that are socially conditioned, and they are basically mental. They are "mediators" between a person's inner world and the physical world, and they "construct" the world rather than "reproduce" it. People tend to see what they describe, rather than vice versa. Conceptual categories, such as continents or oceans, emanate from the cartographer's intellect and are then applied to his maps just as constellations are formulated to provide a systematic vision of the skies.

① 지도 제작은 3차원 입체 형상의 정확한 투사를 요구한다.
② 지도의 종류에 따라 사람들의 공간에 대한 인식이 달라진다.
③ 지도는 제작자의 문화적·정치적 성향과 상상력의 산물이다.
④ 지도 제작자는 지도를 통해 세계를 객관적으로 보여주고자 한다.
⑤ 지도는 제작자가 물리적 세상을 건설한 것이라기보다는 재생산한 것이다.

08 글의 흐름상 가장 적절하지 않은 문장은?

According to Sigmund Freud, the Id, Ego, and Superego are the three components of personality. He contended that people are born with the Id. ① The Id contains basic human drives like hunger and thirst. It cares for nothing except that its needs are met immediately. It does not even care whether those needs are rational or harmful. ② Therefore, it is closely associated with the reality principle. ③ In contrast, the Ego develops as a person grows after birth. The Ego realizes that other people have needs as well. ④ It seeks to satisfy the Id's instinctual needs in realistic ways while simultaneously weighing those of other people. Last to develop is the Superego. The Superego functions as an individual's conscience. ⑤ It distinguishes between what is right and wrong.

09 다음 글의 내용과 일치하지 않는 것은?

Leucippus and Democritus taught that everything is composed of elementary objects in constant movement. This proposal did not meet with the approval of Plato or Aristotle, for if everything is made of corpuscles in motion, why are the forms of things so well preserved? The atomic theory could not account for the stability of nature or for the reappearance of organic forms generation after generation. All in all, atoms appeared to be a rather mechanical explication. This certainly did not appeal to those Greek philosophers who envisioned a world of underlying forms and ideals. All in all the Greeks preferred their elements. These were not actual physical substances—such as real fire or real water—but rather, nonmaterial essences out of which the whole world was created. Such ideas persisted in the West for well over 2,000 years, and, with the rise of alchemy, new principles, or elements, were added. The spirit Mercury, for example, is present in all that is volatile. Salt, which is unchanged by fire, represents that which is fixed, while sulfur is the principle of combustion.

① 원자론은 세대가 변해도 불변하는 자연의 안정성을 설명할 수 없었다.
② Democritus는 모든 것은 끊임없이 움직이는 기본 개체로 구성된다고 가르쳤다.
③ Plato와 Aristotle은 Democritus의 의견에 반대했다.
④ 그리스인들은 소금이 불에 의해서 변질이 되지 않는다고 믿었다.
⑤ 당대의 그리스 철학자들은 세계가 창조된 물질적 본질을 선호했다.

10 밑줄 친 부분 중 어법상 옳지 않은 것은?

We really cannot make in the schools adequate preparation for social life, for ① instilling the social point of view into the pupils and furnishing them with a social motive and purpose, ② until the schools themselves are somewhat differently equipped. The social spirit and motive is the product of people living together and doing certain things ③ in common, and sharing in each other's activities and each other's experiences because they have common ends and purposes. It is because people have something to do which ④ is interested to them and holds them all alike, and to the doing of which each makes his own contribution, that people become ⑤ permeated with the real social spirit.

11 다음 글의 내용과 일치하는 것은?

The system in which men have more value and more social and economic power than women is found throughout the history of the world. Women suffer both from structural oppression and from individual men. Too many movements for social justice accept the assumptions of male dominance and ignore the oppression of women, but patriarchy pervades both our political and personal lives. Feminism recognizes that no pattern of domination is necessary and seeks to liberate both women and men from the structures of dominance that characterize patriarchy.

① 역사적으로 동양 여성들은 서양 여성들보다 더 많이 억압받아 왔다.
② 여성에 대한 구조적 억압이 남성 개인들에 의한 억압보다 더욱 심각한 문제이다.
③ 사회적 정의를 추구하는 역사적 운동들도 여성 억압 현상을 경시했다.
④ 가부장제는 개인적 삶보다는 정치적 삶에 더 많이 퍼져 있다.
⑤ 여성주의 운동은 가부장제로부터 여성들을 우선적으로 해방시키려 한다.

12 밑줄 친 (A)와 (B)에 들어갈 표현으로 가장 적절한 것은?

Over the past four decades a fundamental shift has been occurring in the world economy. We have been moving away from a world in which national economies were relatively self-contained entities, _____(A)_____ each other by barriers to cross-border trade and investment; by distance, time zones, and language; and by national differences in government regulation, culture, and business systems. We are moving toward a world in which barriers to cross-border trade and investment are _____(B)_____; perceived distance is shrinking due to advances in transportation and telecommunications technology; material culture is starting to look similar the world over; and national economies are merging into an interdependent, integrated global economic system. The process by which this transformation is occurring is commonly referred to as globalization.

	(A)	(B)
①	introduced to	– fulfilling
②	taking care of	– escalating
③	converged with	– diminishing
④	winning on	– unfaltering
⑤	isolated from	– declining

13 밑줄 친 부분 중 어법상 옳지 않은 것은?

One of the most discussed causes of de-industrialisation has been the migration of jobs to newly industrialised countries. It has been ① <u>argued</u> that this represents the emergence of a new international division of labour in which the manufacturing functions of the inner areas of older industrial cities ② <u>have</u> been surpassed. This theory is able to ③ <u>account for</u> a number of major, worldwide economic developments. These include the de-industrialisation of Western cities, the growth of cities in newly industrialised countries and the growth of global cities as the control and command centres of an interconnected world economy. However, despite this, the explanatory scope of this theory, while not ④ <u>to be</u> incorrect, is limited. In relying ⑤ <u>so</u> heavily on economic processes it is able to say little about, for example, the social geographies of cities that are clearly related to economic change. This theory is able to offer only one-directional explanations of the relationship between economic change and urbanisation.

14 밑줄 친 부분에 들어갈 단어로 적절한 것은?

Usually you will find that each scene in a fictional narrative film uses an establishing shot; that is a shot that gives the setting in which the scene is to take place and enables the viewer to establish the spatial relationships between characters involved in the scene. But, although this is what might be known as the Hollywood standard and was certainly the expected norm throughout the period of Classical Hollywood, the practice of using an establishing shot has not always been followed by filmmakers. By _____ an establishing shot the viewer is put in the position of struggling to make sense of the relationship between the characters shown. We are effectively disorientated and this will be part of what the filmmakers are attempting to achieve; as well as perhaps defying the expected filmic norm and thereby challenging any presumption that there are certain correct (and therefore, certain incorrect) ways of making films.

① underestimating
② triggering
③ omitting
④ maintaining
⑤ controlling

15 밑줄 친 부분에 들어갈 단어로 가장 적절한 것은?

Without language, an individual or a group of individuals would have no way of explaining them to others, or of directing the actions of the participants in _____ enterprises toward the common goal.

① comprehensive
② collaborative
③ meaningless
④ competitive
⑤ harmful

16 다음 글의 요지로 적절한 것은?

The naive listener might assume a life story to be a truthful, factual account of the storyteller's life. The assumption is that the storyteller has only to penetrate the fog of the past and that once a life is honestly remembered, it can be sincerely recounted. But the more sophisticated listener understands that no matter how sincere the attempt, remembering the past cannot render it as it was, not only because memory is selective but because the life storyteller is a different person now than he or she was ten or thirty years ago; and he or she may not be able to, or even want to, imagine that he or she was different then. The problem of how much a person may change without losing his or her identity is the greatest difficulty facing the life storyteller, whose chief concern, after all, is to affirm his or her identity and account for it. So life storytelling is a fiction, a making, an ordered past imposed by a present personality on a disordered life.

① 전기(傳記)를 읽는 독자는 행간의 의미를 정확히 파악해야 한다.
② 수동적인 독자는 전기(傳記)를 사실 그대로의 기록으로 받아들인다.
③ 정확한 기억력과 변하지 않는 인격이 전기(傳記) 작가에게 요구된다.
④ 전기(傳記)는 무결(無缺)하지 않은 작가에 의해서 기록된 일종의 픽션이다.
⑤ 올바르게 전기(傳記)를 이해하기 위해서는 독자의 적극적인 역할이 중요하다.

17 밑줄 친 부분에 들어갈 표현으로 가장 적절한 것을 고르시오.

The problems which have preoccupied recent social anthropology are rather different to those which interested Herodotus and Tacitus. They were first formulated during the Enlightenment. Theories which attempt to resolve these problems were established at the same time. Until the seventeenth and eighteenth centuries, European kings had been believed to rule by Divine Right, and human society was supposed to reproduce, on a lower scale, the Divine society of Heaven. These assumptions were questioned during the Enlightenment. Once people considered themselves free to decide for themselves _____ according to natural rather than divine law it became possible to ask both how actual societies might be improved, and how present societies had diverged from the natural, or original human condition. Both the European past and more exotic but living, human societies were seen as sources of information that could help answer these questions.

① the truth of the assumptions underlying these social problems
② what was, or was not, proper social behaviour
③ the socialistic kind of governmental forms
④ the conflicts between citizens and kings
⑤ how society was to be degenerated

18 밑줄 친 부분에 들어갈 표현으로 가장 적절한 것을 고르시오.

Hunting big game would have likely been a dangerous activity in early times, especially before the invention of throwing spears about half a million years ago. Prior to this, hunting even small and medium-size game likely depended on thrusting spears (i.e., held in the hands while thrusting into the animal). Some have suggested that hunting may have occurred by chasing animals until they died from exhaustion. This technique is called persistence hunting and essentially means that a small group of people would simply chase a selected animal, perhaps for days, until the animal died from exhaustion. This makes sense to some since, while most game animals are quite quick over short distances, they usually cannot maintain the quickness over long distances. Bipedalism in humans, on the other hand, leads to _____. People may not be as quick as some animals over short distances, but they can outlast them over long distances.

① energy exhaustion
② comparative disadvantage
③ extended endurance
④ teamed play
⑤ delayed attack

19 다음 글의 내용과 일치하지 않는 것은?

Weather forecasts, market reports, cost-of-living indexes, and the results of public opinion polls are good examples. Statistical methods are employed extensively in the preparation of such reports. Reports that are based on sound statistical reasoning and the careful interpretation of conclusions are truly informative. Frequently, however, the deliberate or inadvertent misuse of statistics leads to erroneous conclusions and distortions of truth. For the general public, the basic consumers of these reports, some idea of statistical reasoning is essential to properly interpret the data and evaluate the conclusions that are drawn. Statistical reasoning provides criteria for determining the conclusions that are actually supported by data and those that are not.

① 통계학적 방법은 소비자 물가 지수와 여론 조사 결과 등에서 광범위하게 활용된다.
② 통계 리포트의 기본 소비자는 일반 대중이다.
③ 타당한 통계학적 추론에 근거한 리포트들은 유용하다.
④ 통계학적 추론은 통계 자료 해석의 기준을 제공해 준다.
⑤ 정확한 통계 자료는 실수에 의해서만 잘못된 결론으로 이어진다.

20 밑줄 친 부분에 들어갈 단어로 적절한 것은?

Text representations must be built up sequentially. It is not possible psychologically to construct and integrate a text representation for a whole book chapter or a whole lecture. The chapter and the lecture have to be processed word by word and sentence by sentence. As each text segment is processed, it is immediately integrated with the rest of the text that is currently being held in working memory. The immediate processing hypothesis generally holds, at least for lower-level processes in comprehension. Occasionally, however, readers use _____ strategies when dealing with potentially ambiguous syntactic constructions or they continue reading when constructing a situation model when they do not understand something, in the hope that the succeeding text will clarify their problem. But in general information in a text is processed as soon as possible. In the model this means that as each text element is processed and a new proposition is added to the text representation, it is immediately integrated with the text representation.

① social
② delay
③ clarification
④ retrospection
⑤ compensation

정답·해석·해설 p. 230

23회 2023년 국회직 9급
모바일 자동 채점 + 성적 분석 서비스 바로 가기

QR코드를 이용해 모바일로 간편하게 채점하고 나의 실력이 어느 정도인지, 취약 부분이 어디인지 바로 파악해 보세요.

(p.214에서 전체 정답표를 확인하실 수 있습니다)

※ 밑줄 친 부분의 의미와 가장 가까운 것을 고르시오.

[01~04]

01

When they erupt, they release large amounts of carbon dioxide into the atmosphere, thereby warming it.

① address
② decline
③ explode
④ endure
⑤ ponder

02

Meeting in Germany, leaders of the Group of Seven industrialized countries reiterated their commitment to helping Ukraine win the war this week and added new sanctions on Russia, including a cap on the price of Russian oil exports.

① embargoes
② provisions
③ commodities
④ commitments
⑤ engagements

03

In general, young people often develop antagonistic feelings toward each other when competing for grades.

① extravagant
② sympathetic
③ unbearable
④ aboriginal
⑤ hostile

04

Scientists attach great importance to the human capacity for spoken language. But we also have a parallel track of nonverbal communication, and those messages may reveal more than our carefully chosen words and sometimes be at odds with them.

① in harmony with
② incongruent with
③ indispensable to
④ indifferent to
⑤ in favor of

05 밑줄 친 부분에 들어갈 단어로 가장 적절한 것은?

Movies that are "restricted" to adult audiences are rated "R" and contain scenes with nudity and sex. The language in these movies contains _____, and the violence shown can be very graphic, usually filmed with blood and other disturbing special effects.

① profanity
② guidelines
③ penalties
④ warning
⑤ clichés

※ 밑줄 친 부분에 들어갈 표현으로 가장 적절한 것을 고르시오.

[06~07]

06

So far, around 130 students _____ suspensions, which means they are not allowed to use the library for up to 30 days.

① to give
② are given
③ have been given
④ have been giving
⑤ will have been given

07

For this reason, drones can be _____ than traditional aircraft.

① very smaller and more maneuverable
② much smaller and more maneuverable
③ much smaller and much maneuverable
④ much smaller and maneuverabler
⑤ very smaller and very maneuverable

※ 밑줄 친 부분 중 어법상 옳지 않은 것을 고르시오.

[08~09]

08

The whole issue about life on other worlds ① begs the question: What is life, and how would we recognize it? Certainly, living things are made of cells (or a cell) and share three critical processes that make them ② alive. They ingest energy, excrete waste energy, and pass on their genes through reproduction. But they also respond ③ to their environments. They maintain homeostasis, or internal balance. They evolve and adapt. Some living things even have evolved to the point ④ which they can walk and think about the universe that surrounds them. We are literally products of the universe. Most of the atoms and molecules in our bodies were created in the engines of stars, and the energy we receive that enables life ⑤ comes from our star: the Sun.

09

Validity is the most important consideration in test evaluation. The concept refers to the appropriateness, meaningfulness, and usefulness of the specific inferences ① made from test scores. Test validation is the process of accumulating evidence to back up such inferences. A variety of inferences may be made from scores produced by a ② given test, and there are many ways of accumulating evidence to ③ support any particular inference. Validity, however, is a unitary concept. Although evidence may be accumulated in many ways, validity always refers to the degree to which that evidence supports the inferences that ④ is made from the scores. The inferences ⑤ regarding specific uses of a test are validated, not the test itself.

10 밑줄 친 부분 중 문맥상 단어의 쓰임이 적절하지 않은 것은?

Databases provided an ① efficient way to store and search for data. Organized into fields of information, the database enabled marketers to rank or select various groups of individuals from its master list of customers—a practice called "modeling." Through this process, ② more mailings or calls needed to be made, resulting in a higher response rate and lower costs. In addition to isolating a company's most ③ profitable customers, marketers studied them, profiled them, and then used that profile to find ④ similar customers. This, of course, required not only information about existing customers, but the collection of data about ⑤ prospective customers as well.

11 다음 글의 내용과 일치하지 않는 것은?

Despite such losses, Germany as a country is rich, but a recent study from the European Central Bank suggests that the typical German household is not. Astonishingly, the median household's net assets, at €51,400, are less than those of the typical Italian, Spanish or even Greek household. These figures need careful interpretation. Households in Germany are smaller than in those countries, and their average is dragged down by the east, where 20 years ago no one had any assets to speak of. Moreover, the figures do not include pension promises. But the main reason for the poor showing is that far fewer people than in other European countries own their homes. Most households rent, and the housing stock is owned by a relatively small number of people, so Germany ends up with the most unequal distribution of household wealth in the euro zone.

① 전형적인 독일 가구가 부유하다는 최근 연구 결과가 있다.
② 한 연구에 따르면 전형적인 스페인 가구의 순자산은 독일 중위 가구의 순자산을 능가한다.
③ 유럽중앙은행의 연구가 제시한 수치는 신중한 해석이 필요하다.
④ 독일의 경우 자신의 집을 소유한 사람의 수는 다른 유럽 국가보다 적다.
⑤ 가구 재산의 분배에 있어 독일은 유로존에서 가장 불평등하다.

12 글의 흐름상 가장 어색한 문장은?

Now that we have some understanding of how language works, we can go back and try and answer the question of whether any animals have a true language. ① According to many leading scientists in the field, the answer is: maybe. Most scientists agree that human language is clearly the most complex, and that no other animal has a communication system that comes close. ② Many forms of animal communication do have some of the elements of human language. Some scientists believe that certain animals, such as primates and marine mammals, do use a type of language. ③ For example, vervet monkeys have different sounds for different predators. When an alarm call is given, the monkeys know whether they should be on the lookout for an eagle, leopard, or snake. ④ Monkeys aren't the only land mammals that have a complex communication system with elements of human language in it. ⑤ These monkeys are using arbitrary sounds that have agreed-upon meanings. This is a key element of language.

13

A 'cover' is typically defined as a recording of a song that was first recorded by someone else. Something like this is given in many dictionaries and by some scholars. _____(A)_____, Albin Zak provides a glossary entry defining a 'cover version' as "a recording of a song that has been recorded previously by another artist." Don Cusic writes, "the definition of a 'cover' song is one that has been recorded before." Consider the song 'Let It Be,' written by John Lennon and Paul McCartney. Their band, the Beatles, had a hit with it when they released their version in 1970. _____(B)_____, the first released recording of the song—by a few months—was by Aretha Franklin. A website which generates its descriptions automatically labels the Beatles' version as a cover of Franklin's, and that is just what the usual definition would suggest.

(A)	(B)
① For instance	Therefore
② In addition	Nevertheless
③ For example	However
④ For example	Consequently
⑤ Moreover	However

14

As the scale of economic activity has proceeded steadily upward, the scope of environmental problems triggered by that activity has transcended both _____(A)_____ and _____(B)_____ boundaries. When the environmental problems were smaller in scale, the nation-state used to be a sufficient form of political organization for resolving them, but is that still the case? Whereas each generation used to have the luxury of being able to satisfy its own needs without worrying about the needs of generations to come, intergenerational effects are now more prominent. Solving problems such as poverty, climate change, ozone depletion, and the loss of biodiversity requires international cooperation. Because future generations cannot speak for themselves, the current generation must speak for them. Current policies must incorporate our obligation to future generations, however difficult or imperfect that incorporation might prove to be.

(A)	(B)
① intercultural	economic
② geographic	generational
③ political	sociocultural
④ ecological	ethical
⑤ environmental	behavioral

15 밑줄 친 (A), (B), (C)에 들어갈 표현으로 가장 적절한 것은?

Why did communicative sound take so long to evolve? Bacterial and single-celled life existed for three billion years with no known sonic signals. Although all these cells could sense water motions and vibrations, none reached out to ____(A)____ with sound. The first three hundred million years of animal evolution, too, seem to have lacked any communicative signals. No known fossil from this time has a rasp or other sound-making structure. The expert paleontologists ____(B)____ advice I sought all said that they knew of no physical evidence of sound-making structures from animals until the first cricket-and cicada-like insects evolved. Of course, the fossil record is incomplete and some sound-making structures, such as the swim bladders of fish, leave ____(C)____ or no trace in rock, and so we hear imperfectly across these great stretches of time.

	(A)	(B)	(C)
①	other	whose	a little
②	other	what	little
③	others	whose	a little
④	others	what	a little
⑤	others	whose	little

16 다음 글의 제목으로 가장 적절한 것은?

Eating at home is the norm for most people on most days, yet traditions of eating out go back centuries, and the practice is typical. The French do not eat outside of the home as frequently as residents of some nations with a comparable standard of living, such as the United Kingdom. Nonetheless, the trend to take meals outside of the home increases perceptibly in France, if not as quickly as in some affluent nations. Between 1970 and 1990, household spending on eating out increased 0.25 percent, and expenditure for food to be eaten at home fell by a full 7 percent. An estimate from 2004 calculated 9 billion meals out taken annually. Of these people ate 3.7 billion meals in cafeterias and other collective settings and 4.6 billion in commercial restaurants, from fine restaurants to fast-food restaurants and chains.

① Gorgeous Restaurants in Europe
② Fast-food Chains in France
③ Traditional Food of France
④ Typical French Food
⑤ Eating Out in France

17 다음 글의 내용과 일치하는 것은?

Glass Beach was created by accident. Beginning in 1906, people were permitted to throw away their garbage in the ocean near the city. People threw away glass bottles, appliances, and even cars. In 1967, the local government made it illegal to throw away trash in the water. After this, there were many cleanup efforts to recycle the metal and the other non-biodegradable waste. However, most of the glass had already been broken into tiny pieces. The glass was too difficult to remove, so it was left in the water. Over time, the pounding waves caused the rough pieces of glass to become smooth. These green, white, and brown pieces of smooth glass began washing up on shore, creating Glass Beach.

① Glass Beach는 의도적으로 만들어졌다.
② 정부는 1906년에 바다에 쓰레기를 버리는 것을 금지했다.
③ 금속 폐기물을 재활용하기 위한 노력이 있었다.
④ 사람들은 바다에 남겨진 유리조각을 남김없이 치웠다.
⑤ 거대한 유리조각들이 Glass Beach를 관광명소로 만들었다.

18 주어진 글 사이에 들어갈 글의 순서로 가장 적절한 것은?

Some visual displays are meant only for members of an animal's own species. These include mating rituals and signals that tell a group when to move to a new location. Have you ever noticed that when a flock of birds takes off, they often all leave together?

(A) The only difference is that instead of using sound, one of the more dominant birds will signal to the rest of the birds using an action called an intention movement.
(B) In a typical "take off" signal, one bird will raise its wings and lift off the ground a few inches.
(C) It's almost as if one of them said, "Let's go." In fact, this is exactly what happens.

Seeing this, the birds around it will pick up the signal and pass it to the other members of the group. Within a few seconds, the whole flock lifts off and heads into the sky.

① (A) – (C) – (B)
② (B) – (A) – (C)
③ (B) – (C) – (A)
④ (C) – (A) – (B)
⑤ (C) – (B) – (A)

19

What counts as private information or as intrusion can vary among cultures and even within subcultures of a particular society. Whether an act is regarded as intrusion or comfortable familiarity depends on _____ _____. For example, knocking on doors and waiting to be granted permission to enter is one way that privacy is respected in some cultures. In other cultures, it is acceptable for people to walk unannounced through entranceways or to enter a friend's or family member's home without knocking.

① the circumstances and shared understandings of those involved
② the rights and responsibilities associated with privacy
③ people's ability to live a life without being interfered
④ the individual's control over personal information
⑤ the efficacy of the law to protect privacy

20

Researchers at Princeton University and the University of California, Los Angeles, found that students who handwrote lecture notes rather than typing them out retained more of the information precisely because they were slowed down. A quick keyboard transcription doesn't require critical thinking. The slower process of handwriting means not everything will be captured verbatim; instead, the brain is forced to exert more effort to capture the essence of what's important, thus _____ _____. Slowing down doesn't mean being slow; it just means taking a few minutes to absorb what we are seeing. Details, patterns, and relationships take time to register. Nuances and new information can be missed if we rush past them.

① distracting our attention for more information
② speeding up the whole process of imagination
③ assigning our mental resources to various tasks
④ inundating the memory with too much information
⑤ committing the information more effectively to memory

정답·해석·해설 p. 240

**24회 2022년 국회직 9급
모바일 자동 채점 + 성적 분석 서비스 바로 가기**

QR코드를 이용해 모바일로 간편하게 채점하고 나의 실력이 어느 정도인지, 취약 부분이 어디인지 바로 파악해 보세요.

(p.214에서 전체 정답표를 확인하실 수 있습니다)

제한 시간 : 20분　시작 _____시 _____분 ~ 종료 _____시 _____분　나의 점수 _____　회독 수 ☐☐☐

※ 밑줄 친 부분의 의미와 가장 가까운 것을 고르시오.
[01~02]

01

> These economic policies are inimical to the interests of society.

① amenable
② arduous
③ favorable
④ harmful
⑤ pertinent

02

> When a group of atoms is driven by an external source of energy and surrounded by a heat bath, it will often gradually restructure itself in order to dissipate increasingly more energy.

① conserve
② create
③ scatter
④ secure
⑤ utilize

03 어법상 옳지 않은 문장은?

① The question debated in Parliament yesterday was about the new tax.
② A man wearing a red vest is standing still on roller skates.
③ They knew the man who was going out with their daughter.
④ The list shows all articles that are belonging to the owner.
⑤ Authorities are afraid of people knowing the truth.

04 밑줄 친 부분에 들어갈 가장 적절한 표현은?

> Obviously, the educational process for jurors needs to be improved, and judges and lawyers need to become active participants in this educational process. They need to take the responsibility for informing jurors about the relevant legal issues in each case. They must educate jurors on the rules of law applicable to the cases at hand and in language they can understand. Some may argue that this system may be abused by lawyers who want to bias a jury in their favor. This is, of course, possible. But one must realize that _____. Each juror walks in with his or her own distinct set of values and beliefs. The lawyers are always trying to influence them to see their side. I would argue, however, that it is better to risk the possibility of some additional bias in order for the juries to be better informed. It is more desirable to have a knowledgeable jury, even at the risk of some bias, rather than to have a jury that is totally in the dark about the legal issues surrounding a particular case.

① juries are inherently biased
② juries will never change their mind
③ judges are always impartial
④ lawyers hardly succeed in persuading juries
⑤ judges are likely to dictate the court

05 밑줄 친 부분에 들어갈 가장 적절한 표현은?

One useful guideline for differentiating a dialect from a language is that different languages are not _____, whereas different dialects generally are. For example, if you are a monolingual speaker of Mandarin Chinese and you encounter a monolingual speaker of Cantonese Chinese, the two of you will have a great deal of difficulty communicating through language alone, since Mandarin and Cantonese are two different languages. On the other hand, if you are a native Dane and you encounter a native Norwegian, the similarities between your linguistic systems will far outweigh any differences; you will have little trouble communicating with each other, since Danish and Norwegian represent two different dialects of a single language.

① of the same ethnic background
② culturally comprehensible
③ officially used in a country
④ learned in the same way
⑤ mutually intelligible

06 Komodo dragons에 대한 다음 글의 내용과 일치하지 않는 것은?

Do dragons really exist? In Indonesia they do. Called Komodo dragons, they are the largest living members of the lizard family. They grow up to 10 feet long. They are part of a group of lizards known as monitors. According to legend, these lizards get the name "monitor" because they warn of the presence of crocodiles. Coincidentally, Indonesians call Komodo dragons "land crocodiles." They have armor-plated heads, thick forked tongues, claws that are sharp and long, and strong skin that looks like polished gravel. They don't breathe fire like the mythical dragons of European lore. But neither do they sit on logs all day sunning themselves like some lizards. During the hottest hours of the day, the giant lizards rest in caves that they've dug, storing up their energy for hunting in the evening and early morning. Their hunting tactics are a lot like a cat's. After hiding in a bush, they lunge at and surprise their prey, which includes deer, wild pigs, and even water buffalo. If carrion (the rotting flesh of dead animals) presents itself, they'll choose it over animals they have to kill themselves.

① 도마뱀과 중에서 가장 큰 살아있는 동물로 신화 속 용들처럼 불을 내뿜지는 않는다.
② 두껍고 갈라진 혀를 가지고 있으며 피부 표면이 거칠어 보인다.
③ 가장 더운 시간에는 직접 판 동굴에 들어가 나중의 사냥에 대비한다.
④ 덤불에 숨어있다가 갑자기 사냥감에 달려드는 사냥방식이 고양이와 비슷하다.
⑤ 죽은 동물과 직접 사냥해야 할 동물 중에서 죽은 동물을 선호한다.

07 밑줄 친 부분 중 어법상 옳지 않은 것은?

Most people know the phrase Stockholm Syndrome from the numerous high-profile kidnapping and hostage cases—usually involving women—① in which it has been cited. The term ② most associates with Patty Hearst, the Californian newspaper heiress who was kidnapped by revolutionary militants in 1974. She ③ appeared to develop sympathy with her captors and joined them in a robbery. She was eventually caught and received a prison sentence. But Hearst's defense lawyer Bailey claimed that the 19-year-old ④ had been brainwashed and was suffering from "Stockholm Syndrome"—a term that had been recently coined to explain the ⑤ apparently irrational feelings of some captives for their captors.

08 글의 흐름상 아래 문장이 들어가기에 가장 적절한 곳은?

Similarly, *television* gave rise to *televise*, *double-glazing* preceded *double-glaze*, and *baby-sitter* preceded *baby-sit*.

It is common in English to form a new lexeme by adding a prefix or a suffix to an old one. From *happy* we get *unhappy*; from *inspect* we get *inspector*. (①) Every so often, however, the process works the other way round, and a shorter word is derived from a longer one by deleting an imagined affix. (②) *Editor*, for example, looks as if it comes from *edit*, whereas the noun was in the language first. (③) Such forms are known as 'back-formations'. Each year sees a new crop of back-formations. (④) Some are coined because they meet a real need, as when a group of speech therapists in the 1970s felt they needed a new verb to describe what they did—to *therap*. Some are playful formations, as when a tidy person is described as *couth*, *kempt*, or *shevelled*. (⑤) Back-formations often attract criticism when they first appear, as happened in the late 1980s to *explete* ('to use an *expletive*') and *accreditate* (from *accreditation*).

09 밑줄 친 부분에 들어갈 가장 적절한 표현은?

Issues seem to become more and more complex as the world becomes more complex. In an interview, the actress Susan Sarandon, who has always been engaged with social issues, stated that in the mid- to late 1960s, when she was in college, the issues seemed simpler, more black and white. The issues at that time, for example, centered on civil rights and the Vietnam War. "We were blessed with clear-cut issues," she says. "We were blessed with clear-cut grievances.   ”

① Issues were never as clear as they are.
② We talked about politics more often than now.
③ We are now seeing the light at the end of the tunnel.
④ Truly, every cloud has a silver lining.
⑤ Things were not as gray as they are now.

10 밑줄 친 (A)와 (B)에 들어갈 가장 적절한 표현은?

Child psychologist Jean Piaget was one of the first to study questions of moral development. He suggested that moral development, like cognitive development, proceed in stages. The earliest stage is a broad form of moral thinking he called heteronomous morality, in which rules are seen as invariant and unchangeable. During this stage, which lasts from about age 4 to age 7, children play games rigidly, assuming that there is one, and only one, way to play and that every other way is wrong. At the same time, though, preschool-age children may not even fully grasp game rules. _____(A)_____, a group of children may be playing together, with each child playing according to a slightly different set of rules. Nevertheless, they enjoy playing with others. Piaget suggests that every child may "win" such a game _____(B)_____ winning is equated with having a good time, as opposed to truly competing with others.

	(A)	(B)
①	Consequently	because
②	For instance	although
③	In reality	whereas
④	However	by the time
⑤	In addition	in case

※ 밑줄 친 부분의 의미와 가장 가까운 것을 고르시오.
[11~12]

11

He lamented the public apathy that has led to the emergence of new COVID-19 clusters.

① anger
② anxiety
③ commotion
④ disorder
⑤ indifference

12

Altruistic people don't care about your skin color, or how much money you have in your bank account.

① cheerful
② ferocious
③ greedy
④ intolerant
⑤ unselfish

13 밑줄 친 부분에 들어갈 가장 적절한 표현은?

The slippery-slope fallacy is a scare tactic that suggests that _____, we will immediately be sliding down the slippery slope to disaster. This fallacy is sometimes introduced into environmental and abortion issues. If we allow loggers to cut a few trees, we will soon lose all the forests. Or if a woman is required to wait twenty-four hours to reconsider her decision to have an abortion, soon there will be so many restrictions that no one will be able to have an abortion. This fallacy is similar to the saying about the camel that gets into its nose in the tent. If we permit the nose today, we have the whole camel to deal with tomorrow. It is better not to start because disaster may result.

① even if we do everything we can to stay safe
② even though we believe everything is good that ends well
③ if we allow one thing to happen
④ if we try to scare others
⑤ if we do nothing to protect ourselves

14 밑줄 친 부분 중 어법상 옳지 않은 것은?

Learning to ① pose questions and receive information that is satisfying ② is a key social as well as intellectual experience in a child's development. Children who don't have a successful experience at this stage, or ③ who experience is frustrated or perverted, ④ stop participating in the learning process. They stop expressing their questions, and eventually may stop ⑤ thinking them up.

15 글의 흐름상 적절하지 않은 문장은?

Although parent-child conflicts are found in every culture, there does seem to be less conflict between parents and their teenage children in "traditional," preindustrial cultures. ① Teens in such traditional cultures also experience fewer mood swings and instances of risky behavior than do teens in industrialized countries. ② Why? The answer may relate to the degree of independence that adolescents expect and adults permit. In more industrialized societies, in which the value of individualism is typically high, independence is an expected component of adolescence. ③ Consequently, adolescents and their parents must negotiate the amount and timing of the adolescents' increasing independence—a process that often leads to strife. ④ Parent-child conflicts are more likely to occur during adolescence, particularly during the early stages. In contrast, in more traditional societies, individualism is not valued as highly, and therefore adolescents are less inclined to seek out independence. ⑤ With diminished independence-seeking on the part of adolescents, the result is less parent-child conflict.

16 밑줄 친 부분에 들어갈 가장 적절한 표현은?

Two kinds of evidence show that much of the behavioral differences among groups are _____. First, individual cross-cultural adoptees behave like members of their adopted culture, not the culture of their biological parents. Second, groups of people often change behavior much more rapidly than natural selection could change gene frequencies. These data are far too coarse to prove that there are no genetic differences between human groups, but we believe the evidence is sufficient to conclude that the cultural differences between groups are much larger than any genetic variation that might exist.

① not genetic
② inherent to human beings
③ linked to biological traits
④ explained in terms of evolution
⑤ unknowable

17 다음 글의 주제로 가장 적절한 것은?

Think about how you feel if somebody cuts you off, or makes an illegal left turn in front of you. If you are like most people you get annoyed, perhaps very annoyed, and want to punish the rule breaker, even though you know you'll never see the person again. Or, think about how you feel when someone cuts in line while you wait for a movie. Most people get quite angry, even if they are near the front of the line and are sure to get a good seat. Such emotions can give rise to voluntary, informal punishment of people who break social rules. But in complex societies, it's hard to know whether such punishment plays a significant role in maintaining social norms because police and courts also act to punish rule breakers. Many simple societies lack formal legal institutions, so the only kind of punishment is informal and voluntary. In small-scale societies, considerable ethnographic evidence suggests that moral norms are enforced by punishment.

① benefits and disadvantages of formal punishment
② the relationship between punishment and the scale of society
③ moral norms and their impacts on the society
④ the effect of harsh punishment on antisocial behaviors
⑤ the role of the legal system in safeguarding national security

18 어법상 옳지 않은 문장은?

① The average size of humans have fluctuated over the last million years.

② Before I made a decision about what to do, I had weighed all the alternatives.

③ Tom played so well that he received a standing ovation from the audience.

④ The local government addresses the problems of malnutrition in the state.

⑤ All members must agree to abide by the club regulations.

19 밑줄 친 부분의 의미와 가장 가까운 단어는?

Parents who are overly involved in the lives of their college-age children are the folks we love to scorn. A steady stream of articles and blog posts bristle with <u>indignation</u> over dads who phone the dean about a trivial problem or moms who know more than we think they should about junior's love life.

① argumentation

② contemplation

③ indulgence

④ resentment

⑤ quest

20 다음에 이어질 글의 순서로 가장 적절한 것은?

Dottie and I entered 1966 expecting another good year, but as it turned out, that was not to be, as our parents were hurting.

(A) We flew to Wichita and were met by my sisters. By the time we got to the hospital, Dad was responding to some new medicine. He recovered and was able to go home in a couple of weeks.

(B) We made some changes in his care, and after a couple of days, he was beginning to recover. We then received the call that Dad had gotten worse, his remaining kidney had stopped functioning, he had fallen into a coma, and that we should come.

(C) Mother had fallen and hurt her leg; then, in April, Dad had a kidney removed due to a tumor. At the same time, Dottie's father became very sick, and we flew to Tucson to be with him.

① (A) – (C) – (B) ② (B) – (A) – (C)

③ (B) – (C) – (A) ④ (C) – (A) – (B)

⑤ (C) – (B) – (A)

정답·해석·해설 p. 248

25회 2021년 국회직 9급
모바일 자동 채점 + 성적 분석 서비스 바로 가기

QR코드를 이용해 모바일로 간편하게 채점하고 나의 실력이 어느 정도인지, 취약 부분이 어디인지 바로 파악해 보세요.

(p.214에서 전체 정답표를 확인하실 수 있습니다)

gosi.Hackers.com

정답
한눈에 보기

1회 2024년 국가직 9급 p.32

01	③	11	③
02	②	12	②
03	①	13	③
04	④	14	④
05	④	15	①
06	②	16	④
07	①	17	③
08	①	18	②
09	②	19	②
10	④	20	①

2회 2023년 국가직 9급 p.38

01	②	11	②
02	②	12	③
03	④	13	③
04	①	14	①
05	③	15	②
06	④	16	②
07	②	17	③
08	④	18	③
09	④	19	③
10	①	20	①

3회 2022년 국가직 9급 p.44

01	①	11	④
02	②	12	③
03	④	13	②
04	②	14	④
05	①	15	②
06	①	16	④
07	④	17	④
08	②	18	④
09	①	19	①
10	③	20	③

4회 2021년 국가직 9급 p.50

01	①	11	①
02	②	12	②
03	②	13	④
04	④	14	④
05	④	15	②
06	②	16	①
07	③	17	②
08	③	18	③
09	④	19	④
10	④	20	①

5회 2020년 국가직 9급 p.57

01	①	11	④
02	④	12	③
03	③	13	②
04	①	14	③
05	④	15	③
06	④	16	④
07	③	17	④
08	②	18	③
09	①	19	①
10	④	20	②

6회 2019년 국가직 9급 p.64

01	①	11	④
02	②	12	②
03	④	13	③
04	②	14	④
05	②	15	①
06	①	16	③
07	②	17	④
08	④	18	③
09	④	19	②
10	③	20	④

7회 2018년 국가직 9급 p.70

01	①	11	④
02	①	12	④
03	②	13	②
04	③	14	①
05	①	15	④
06	②	16	④
07	④	17	②
08	②	18	②
09	②	19	③
10	③	20	④

8회 2024년 지방직 9급 p.78

01	②	11	②
02	②	12	③
03	①	13	④
04	①	14	③
05	②	15	③
06	④	16	③
07	③	17	③
08	②	18	④
09	④	19	①
10	④	20	①

9회 2023년 지방직 9급 p.84

01	②	11	③
02	④	12	②
03	①	13	②
04	①	14	④
05	④	15	④
06	③	16	④
07	③	17	②
08	①	18	②
09	④	19	①
10	③	20	③

10회 2022년 지방직 9급   p.90

01	②	11	③
02	①	12	③
03	④	13	④
04	④	14	③
05	②	15	③
06	②	16	③
07	①	17	①
08	①	18	①
09	④	19	②
10	④	20	②

11회 2021년 지방직 9급   p.96

01	④	11	①
02	③	12	③
03	①	13	②
04	②	14	②
05	④	15	③
06	④	16	②
07	②	17	④
08	②	18	①
09	④	19	③
10	①	20	②

12회 2020년 지방직 9급   p.102

01	②	11	②
02	④	12	①
03	②	13	②
04	①	14	④
05	③	15	③
06	④	16	③
07	④	17	①
08	②	18	③
09	①	19	④
10	③	20	④

13회 2019년 지방직 9급   p.108

01	①	11	④
02	①	12	①
03	④	13	③
04	③	14	④
05	④	15	④
06	②	16	③
07	②	17	①
08	②	18	③
09	②	19	①
10	④	20	②

14회 2018년 지방직 9급   p.114

01	①	11	②
02	②	12	①
03	④	13	②
04	④	14	①
05	④	15	④
06	③	16	③
07	②	17	①
08	①	18	①
09	③	19	④
10	②	20	①

15회 2024년 서울시 9급 (2월 추가)   p.122

01	③	11	①
02	④	12	③
03	②	13	③
04	④	14	③
05	①	15	④
06	②	16	②
07	②	17	①
08	①	18	②
09	②	19	④
10	①	20	③

16회 2022년 서울시 9급 (2월 추가)   p.128

01	①	11	④
02	④	12	③
03	②	13	③
04	①	14	②
05	④	15	④
06	④	16	③
07	②	17	①
08	②	18	③
09	③	19	②
10	①	20	③

17회 2019년 서울시 9급   p.134

01	④	11	②
02	①	12	③
03	①	13	①
04	②	14	③
05	②	15	④
06	④	16	②
07	①	17	④
08	①	18	③
09	③	19	③
10	④	20	②

18회 2018년 서울시 9급   p.138

01	③	11	④
02	①	12	④
03	②	13	③
04	③	14	④
05	②	15	①
06	③	16	③
07	④	17	④
08	③	18	①
09	④	19	③
10	①	20	②

19회 2017년 서울시 9급   p.143

01	①	11	④
02	②	12	①
03	④	13	④
04	③	14	①
05	③	15	③
06	②	16	①
07	②	17	②
08	②	18	④
09	④	19	④
10	③	20	①

20회 2024년 법원직 9급   p.150

01	④	11	②	21	②
02	①	12	②	22	①
03	②	13	②	23	②
04	②	14	③	24	①
05	④	15	①	25	④
06	②	16	④		
07	④	17	②		
08	④	18	②		
09	①	19	②		
10	③	20	④		

21회 2023년 법원직 9급   p.163

01	③	11	④	21	③
02	②	12	②	22	③
03	②	13	③	23	①
04	①	14	④	24	④
05	②	15	②	25	③
06	③	16	③		
07	③	17	①		
08	②	18	②		
09	④	19	③		
10	②	20	③		

22회 2022년 법원직 9급   p.175

01	①	11	①	21	③
02	①	12	③	22	②
03	①	13	①	23	③
04	③	14	②	24	②
05	④	15	④	25	③
06	④	16	②		
07	①	17	③		
08	③	18	①		
09	③	19	①		
10	④	20	②		

23회 2023년 국회직 9급   p.188

01	②	11	③
02	①	12	⑤
03	①	13	④
04	③	14	③
05	④	15	②
06	④	16	④
07	③	17	②
08	②	18	③
09	⑤	19	⑤
10	④	20	②

24회 2022년 국회직 9급   p.196

01	③	11	①
02	①	12	④
03	⑤	13	③
04	②	14	②
05	①	15	⑤
06	③	16	⑤
07	②	17	③
08	④	18	④
09	④	19	①
10	②	20	⑤

25회 2021년 국회직 9급   p.203

01	④	11	⑤
02	③	12	⑤
03	④	13	③
04	①	14	③
05	⑤	15	④
06	②	16	①
07	②	17	②
08	③	18	①
09	⑤	19	④
10	①	20	⑤

해커스공무원 7개년 기출문제집 영어

답안지

답안지 활용 방법

1. 맞은 것은 O, 찍었는데 맞은 것은 △, 틀린 것은 x를 문번에 표시하며 채점합니다.
2. △, x가 표시된 문제는 반드시 해설로 개념을 익히고, 회독을 통해 확실하게 학습합니다.
   회독을 할 때는 해커스공무원(gosi.Hackers.com) ▶ 사이트 상단의 [교재·서점] ▶ [무료학습자료]에서 회독용 답안지를 다운받아 진행하실 수 있습니다.
3. 점선을 따라 답안지를 잘라내어 사용하실 수도 있습니다.

___ 회

문번	제 2 과목			
01	①	②	③	④
02	①	②	③	④
03	①	②	③	④
04	①	②	③	④
05	①	②	③	④
06	①	②	③	④
07	①	②	③	④
08	①	②	③	④
09	①	②	③	④
10	①	②	③	④
11	①	②	③	④
12	①	②	③	④
13	①	②	③	④
14	①	②	③	④
15	①	②	③	④
16	①	②	③	④
17	①	②	③	④
18	①	②	③	④
19	①	②	③	④
20	①	②	③	④

O: 개 △: 개 X: 개

___ 회

문번	제 2 과목			
01	①	②	③	④
02	①	②	③	④
03	①	②	③	④
04	①	②	③	④
05	①	②	③	④
06	①	②	③	④
07	①	②	③	④
08	①	②	③	④
09	①	②	③	④
10	①	②	③	④
11	①	②	③	④
12	①	②	③	④
13	①	②	③	④
14	①	②	③	④
15	①	②	③	④
16	①	②	③	④
17	①	②	③	④
18	①	②	③	④
19	①	②	③	④
20	①	②	③	④

O: 개 △: 개 X: 개

___ 회

문번	제 2 과목			
01	①	②	③	④
02	①	②	③	④
03	①	②	③	④
04	①	②	③	④
05	①	②	③	④
06	①	②	③	④
07	①	②	③	④
08	①	②	③	④
09	①	②	③	④
10	①	②	③	④
11	①	②	③	④
12	①	②	③	④
13	①	②	③	④
14	①	②	③	④
15	①	②	③	④
16	①	②	③	④
17	①	②	③	④
18	①	②	③	④
19	①	②	③	④
20	①	②	③	④

O: 개 △: 개 X: 개

___ 회

문번	제 2 과목			
01	①	②	③	④
02	①	②	③	④
03	①	②	③	④
04	①	②	③	④
05	①	②	③	④
06	①	②	③	④
07	①	②	③	④
08	①	②	③	④
09	①	②	③	④
10	①	②	③	④
11	①	②	③	④
12	①	②	③	④
13	①	②	③	④
14	①	②	③	④
15	①	②	③	④
16	①	②	③	④
17	①	②	③	④
18	①	②	③	④
19	①	②	③	④
20	①	②	③	④

O: 개 △: 개 X: 개

___ 회

문번	제 2 과목			
01	①	②	③	④
02	①	②	③	④
03	①	②	③	④
04	①	②	③	④
05	①	②	③	④
06	①	②	③	④
07	①	②	③	④
08	①	②	③	④
09	①	②	③	④
10	①	②	③	④
11	①	②	③	④
12	①	②	③	④
13	①	②	③	④
14	①	②	③	④
15	①	②	③	④
16	①	②	③	④
17	①	②	③	④
18	①	②	③	④
19	①	②	③	④
20	①	②	③	④

O: 개 △: 개 X: 개

___ 회

문번	제 2 과목			
01	①	②	③	④
02	①	②	③	④
03	①	②	③	④
04	①	②	③	④
05	①	②	③	④
06	①	②	③	④
07	①	②	③	④
08	①	②	③	④
09	①	②	③	④
10	①	②	③	④
11	①	②	③	④
12	①	②	③	④
13	①	②	③	④
14	①	②	③	④
15	①	②	③	④
16	①	②	③	④
17	①	②	③	④
18	①	②	③	④
19	①	②	③	④
20	①	②	③	④

O: 개 △: 개 X: 개

___ 회

문번	제 2 과목			
01	①	②	③	④
02	①	②	③	④
03	①	②	③	④
04	①	②	③	④
05	①	②	③	④
06	①	②	③	④
07	①	②	③	④
08	①	②	③	④
09	①	②	③	④
10	①	②	③	④
11	①	②	③	④
12	①	②	③	④
13	①	②	③	④
14	①	②	③	④
15	①	②	③	④
16	①	②	③	④
17	①	②	③	④
18	①	②	③	④
19	①	②	③	④
20	①	②	③	④

O: 개 △: 개 X: 개

___ 회

문번	제 2 과목			
01	①	②	③	④
02	①	②	③	④
03	①	②	③	④
04	①	②	③	④
05	①	②	③	④
06	①	②	③	④
07	①	②	③	④
08	①	②	③	④
09	①	②	③	④
10	①	②	③	④
11	①	②	③	④
12	①	②	③	④
13	①	②	③	④
14	①	②	③	④
15	①	②	③	④
16	①	②	③	④
17	①	②	③	④
18	①	②	③	④
19	①	②	③	④
20	①	②	③	④

O: 개 △: 개 X: 개

해커스공무원 7개년 기출문제집 영어

답안지

답안지 활용 방법

1. 맞은 것은 O, 찍었는데 맞은 것은 △, 틀린 것은 x를 문번에 표시하며 채점합니다.
2. △, x가 표시된 문제는 반드시 해설로 개념을 익히고, 회독을 통해 확실하게 학습합니다.
   회독을 할 때는 해커스공무원(gosi.Hackers.com) ▶ 사이트 상단의 [교재·서점] ▶ [무료학습자료]에서 회독용 답안지를 다운받아 진행하실 수 있습니다.
3. 점선을 따라 답안지를 잘라내어 사용하실 수도 있습니다.

___ 회

문번	제 2 과목			
01	①	②	③	④
02	①	②	③	④
03	①	②	③	④
04	①	②	③	④
05	①	②	③	④
06	①	②	③	④
07	①	②	③	④
08	①	②	③	④
09	①	②	③	④
10	①	②	③	④
11	①	②	③	④
12	①	②	③	④
13	①	②	③	④
14	①	②	③	④
15	①	②	③	④
16	①	②	③	④
17	①	②	③	④
18	①	②	③	④
19	①	②	③	④
20	①	②	③	④
O: 개	△: 개	X: 개		

___ 회

문번	제 2 과목			
01	①	②	③	④
02	①	②	③	④
03	①	②	③	④
04	①	②	③	④
05	①	②	③	④
06	①	②	③	④
07	①	②	③	④
08	①	②	③	④
09	①	②	③	④
10	①	②	③	④
11	①	②	③	④
12	①	②	③	④
13	①	②	③	④
14	①	②	③	④
15	①	②	③	④
16	①	②	③	④
17	①	②	③	④
18	①	②	③	④
19	①	②	③	④
20	①	②	③	④
O: 개	△: 개	X: 개		

___ 회

문번	제 2 과목			
01	①	②	③	④
02	①	②	③	④
03	①	②	③	④
04	①	②	③	④
05	①	②	③	④
06	①	②	③	④
07	①	②	③	④
08	①	②	③	④
09	①	②	③	④
10	①	②	③	④
11	①	②	③	④
12	①	②	③	④
13	①	②	③	④
14	①	②	③	④
15	①	②	③	④
16	①	②	③	④
17	①	②	③	④
18	①	②	③	④
19	①	②	③	④
20	①	②	③	④
O: 개	△: 개	X: 개		

___ 회

문번	제 2 과목			
01	①	②	③	④
02	①	②	③	④
03	①	②	③	④
04	①	②	③	④
05	①	②	③	④
06	①	②	③	④
07	①	②	③	④
08	①	②	③	④
09	①	②	③	④
10	①	②	③	④
11	①	②	③	④
12	①	②	③	④
13	①	②	③	④
14	①	②	③	④
15	①	②	③	④
16	①	②	③	④
17	①	②	③	④
18	①	②	③	④
19	①	②	③	④
20	①	②	③	④
O: 개	△: 개	X: 개		

___ 회

문번	제 2 과목			
01	①	②	③	④
02	①	②	③	④
03	①	②	③	④
04	①	②	③	④
05	①	②	③	④
06	①	②	③	④
07	①	②	③	④
08	①	②	③	④
09	①	②	③	④
10	①	②	③	④
11	①	②	③	④
12	①	②	③	④
13	①	②	③	④
14	①	②	③	④
15	①	②	③	④
16	①	②	③	④
17	①	②	③	④
18	①	②	③	④
19	①	②	③	④
20	①	②	③	④
O: 개	△: 개	X: 개		

___ 회

문번	제 2 과목			
01	①	②	③	④
02	①	②	③	④
03	①	②	③	④
04	①	②	③	④
05	①	②	③	④
06	①	②	③	④
07	①	②	③	④
08	①	②	③	④
09	①	②	③	④
10	①	②	③	④
11	①	②	③	④
12	①	②	③	④
13	①	②	③	④
14	①	②	③	④
15	①	②	③	④
16	①	②	③	④
17	①	②	③	④
18	①	②	③	④
19	①	②	③	④
20	①	②	③	④
O: 개	△: 개	X: 개		

___ 회

문번	제 2 과목			
01	①	②	③	④
02	①	②	③	④
03	①	②	③	④
04	①	②	③	④
05	①	②	③	④
06	①	②	③	④
07	①	②	③	④
08	①	②	③	④
09	①	②	③	④
10	①	②	③	④
11	①	②	③	④
12	①	②	③	④
13	①	②	③	④
14	①	②	③	④
15	①	②	③	④
16	①	②	③	④
17	①	②	③	④
18	①	②	③	④
19	①	②	③	④
20	①	②	③	④
O: 개	△: 개	X: 개		

___ 회

문번	제 2 과목			
01	①	②	③	④
02	①	②	③	④
03	①	②	③	④
04	①	②	③	④
05	①	②	③	④
06	①	②	③	④
07	①	②	③	④
08	①	②	③	④
09	①	②	③	④
10	①	②	③	④
11	①	②	③	④
12	①	②	③	④
13	①	②	③	④
14	①	②	③	④
15	①	②	③	④
16	①	②	③	④
17	①	②	③	④
18	①	②	③	④
19	①	②	③	④
20	①	②	③	④
O: 개	△: 개	X: 개		

해커스공무원 7개년 기출문제집 영어

답안지

답안지 활용 방법

1. 맞은 것은 O, 찍었는데 맞은 것은 △, 틀린 것은 x를 문번에 표시하며 채점합니다.
2. △, x가 표시된 문제는 반드시 해설로 개념을 익히고, 회독을 통해 확실하게 학습합니다.
   회독을 할 때는 해커스공무원(gosi.Hackers.com) ▶ 사이트 상단의 [교재·서점] ▶ [무료학습자료]에서 회독용 답안지를 다운받아 진행하실 수 있습니다.
3. 점선을 따라 답안지를 잘라내어 사용하실 수도 있습니다.

___ 회

문번	제 2 과목			
01	①	②	③	④
02	①	②	③	④
03	①	②	③	④
04	①	②	③	④
05	①	②	③	④
06	①	②	③	④
07	①	②	③	④
08	①	②	③	④
09	①	②	③	④
10	①	②	③	④
11	①	②	③	④
12	①	②	③	④
13	①	②	③	④
14	①	②	③	④
15	①	②	③	④
16	①	②	③	④
17	①	②	③	④
18	①	②	③	④
19	①	②	③	④
20	①	②	③	④
O: 개 △: 개 X: 개				

___ 회

문번	제 2 과목			
01	①	②	③	④
02	①	②	③	④
03	①	②	③	④
04	①	②	③	④
05	①	②	③	④
06	①	②	③	④
07	①	②	③	④
08	①	②	③	④
09	①	②	③	④
10	①	②	③	④
11	①	②	③	④
12	①	②	③	④
13	①	②	③	④
14	①	②	③	④
15	①	②	③	④
16	①	②	③	④
17	①	②	③	④
18	①	②	③	④
19	①	②	③	④
20	①	②	③	④
O: 개 △: 개 X: 개				

___ 회

문번	제 2 과목			
01	①	②	③	④
02	①	②	③	④
03	①	②	③	④
04	①	②	③	④
05	①	②	③	④
06	①	②	③	④
07	①	②	③	④
08	①	②	③	④
09	①	②	③	④
10	①	②	③	④
11	①	②	③	④
12	①	②	③	④
13	①	②	③	④
14	①	②	③	④
15	①	②	③	④
16	①	②	③	④
17	①	②	③	④
18	①	②	③	④
19	①	②	③	④
20	①	②	③	④
O: 개 △: 개 X: 개				

___ 회

문번	제 2 과목			
01	①	②	③	④
02	①	②	③	④
03	①	②	③	④
04	①	②	③	④
05	①	②	③	④
06	①	②	③	④
07	①	②	③	④
08	①	②	③	④
09	①	②	③	④
10	①	②	③	④
11	①	②	③	④
12	①	②	③	④
13	①	②	③	④
14	①	②	③	④
15	①	②	③	④
16	①	②	③	④
17	①	②	③	④
18	①	②	③	④
19	①	②	③	④
20	①	②	③	④
O: 개 △: 개 X: 개				

___ 회

문번	제 2 과목			
01	①	②	③	④
02	①	②	③	④
03	①	②	③	④
04	①	②	③	④
05	①	②	③	④
06	①	②	③	④
07	①	②	③	④
08	①	②	③	④
09	①	②	③	④
10	①	②	③	④
11	①	②	③	④
12	①	②	③	④
13	①	②	③	④
14	①	②	③	④
15	①	②	③	④
16	①	②	③	④
17	①	②	③	④
18	①	②	③	④
19	①	②	③	④
20	①	②	③	④
O: 개 △: 개 X: 개				

___ 회

문번	제 2 과목			
01	①	②	③	④
02	①	②	③	④
03	①	②	③	④
04	①	②	③	④
05	①	②	③	④
06	①	②	③	④
07	①	②	③	④
08	①	②	③	④
09	①	②	③	④
10	①	②	③	④
11	①	②	③	④
12	①	②	③	④
13	①	②	③	④
14	①	②	③	④
15	①	②	③	④
16	①	②	③	④
17	①	②	③	④
18	①	②	③	④
19	①	②	③	④
20	①	②	③	④
O: 개 △: 개 X: 개				

___ 회

문번	제 2 과목			
01	①	②	③	④
02	①	②	③	④
03	①	②	③	④
04	①	②	③	④
05	①	②	③	④
06	①	②	③	④
07	①	②	③	④
08	①	②	③	④
09	①	②	③	④
10	①	②	③	④
11	①	②	③	④
12	①	②	③	④
13	①	②	③	④
14	①	②	③	④
15	①	②	③	④
16	①	②	③	④
17	①	②	③	④
18	①	②	③	④
19	①	②	③	④
20	①	②	③	④
O: 개 △: 개 X: 개				

___ 회

문번	제 2 과목			
01	①	②	③	④
02	①	②	③	④
03	①	②	③	④
04	①	②	③	④
05	①	②	③	④
06	①	②	③	④
07	①	②	③	④
08	①	②	③	④
09	①	②	③	④
10	①	②	③	④
11	①	②	③	④
12	①	②	③	④
13	①	②	③	④
14	①	②	③	④
15	①	②	③	④
16	①	②	③	④
17	①	②	③	④
18	①	②	③	④
19	①	②	③	④
20	①	②	③	④
O: 개 △: 개 X: 개				

해커스공무원 7개년 기출문제집 영어

답안지

답안지 활용 방법

1. 맞은 것은 O, 찍었는데 맞은 것은 △, 틀린 것은 x를 문번에 표시하며 채점합니다.
2. △, x가 표시된 문제는 반드시 해설로 개념을 익히고, 회독을 통해 확실하게 학습합니다. 회독을 할 때는 해커스공무원(gosi.Hackers.com) ▶ 사이트 상단의 [교재·서점] ▶ [무료학습자료]에서 회독용 답안지를 다운받아 진행하실 수 있습니다.
3. 점선을 따라 답안지를 잘라내어 사용하실 수도 있습니다.

___ 회

문번	제 2 과목			
01	①	②	③	④
02	①	②	③	④
03	①	②	③	④
04	①	②	③	④
05	①	②	③	④
06	①	②	③	④
07	①	②	③	④
08	①	②	③	④
09	①	②	③	④
10	①	②	③	④
11	①	②	③	④
12	①	②	③	④
13	①	②	③	④
14	①	②	③	④
15	①	②	③	④
16	①	②	③	④
17	①	②	③	④
18	①	②	③	④
19	①	②	③	④
20	①	②	③	④
O: 개	△: 개	X: 개		

___ 회

문번	제 2 과목			
01	①	②	③	④
02	①	②	③	④
03	①	②	③	④
04	①	②	③	④
05	①	②	③	④
06	①	②	③	④
07	①	②	③	④
08	①	②	③	④
09	①	②	③	④
10	①	②	③	④
11	①	②	③	④
12	①	②	③	④
13	①	②	③	④
14	①	②	③	④
15	①	②	③	④
16	①	②	③	④
17	①	②	③	④
18	①	②	③	④
19	①	②	③	④
20	①	②	③	④
O: 개	△: 개	X: 개		

___ 회

문번	제 2 과목			
01	①	②	③	④
02	①	②	③	④
03	①	②	③	④
04	①	②	③	④
05	①	②	③	④
06	①	②	③	④
07	①	②	③	④
08	①	②	③	④
09	①	②	③	④
10	①	②	③	④
11	①	②	③	④
12	①	②	③	④
13	①	②	③	④
14	①	②	③	④
15	①	②	③	④
16	①	②	③	④
17	①	②	③	④
18	①	②	③	④
19	①	②	③	④
20	①	②	③	④
O: 개	△: 개	X: 개		

___ 회

문번	제 2 과목			
01	①	②	③	④
02	①	②	③	④
03	①	②	③	④
04	①	②	③	④
05	①	②	③	④
06	①	②	③	④
07	①	②	③	④
08	①	②	③	④
09	①	②	③	④
10	①	②	③	④
11	①	②	③	④
12	①	②	③	④
13	①	②	③	④
14	①	②	③	④
15	①	②	③	④
16	①	②	③	④
17	①	②	③	④
18	①	②	③	④
19	①	②	③	④
20	①	②	③	④
O: 개	△: 개	X: 개		

___ 회

문번	제 2 과목			
01	①	②	③	④
02	①	②	③	④
03	①	②	③	④
04	①	②	③	④
05	①	②	③	④
06	①	②	③	④
07	①	②	③	④
08	①	②	③	④
09	①	②	③	④
10	①	②	③	④
11	①	②	③	④
12	①	②	③	④
13	①	②	③	④
14	①	②	③	④
15	①	②	③	④
16	①	②	③	④
17	①	②	③	④
18	①	②	③	④
19	①	②	③	④
20	①	②	③	④
O: 개	△: 개	X: 개		

___ 회

문번	제 2 과목			
01	①	②	③	④
02	①	②	③	④
03	①	②	③	④
04	①	②	③	④
05	①	②	③	④
06	①	②	③	④
07	①	②	③	④
08	①	②	③	④
09	①	②	③	④
10	①	②	③	④
11	①	②	③	④
12	①	②	③	④
13	①	②	③	④
14	①	②	③	④
15	①	②	③	④
16	①	②	③	④
17	①	②	③	④
18	①	②	③	④
19	①	②	③	④
20	①	②	③	④
O: 개	△: 개	X: 개		

___ 회

문번	제 2 과목			
01	①	②	③	④
02	①	②	③	④
03	①	②	③	④
04	①	②	③	④
05	①	②	③	④
06	①	②	③	④
07	①	②	③	④
08	①	②	③	④
09	①	②	③	④
10	①	②	③	④
11	①	②	③	④
12	①	②	③	④
13	①	②	③	④
14	①	②	③	④
15	①	②	③	④
16	①	②	③	④
17	①	②	③	④
18	①	②	③	④
19	①	②	③	④
20	①	②	③	④
O: 개	△: 개	X: 개		

___ 회

문번	제 2 과목			
01	①	②	③	④
02	①	②	③	④
03	①	②	③	④
04	①	②	③	④
05	①	②	③	④
06	①	②	③	④
07	①	②	③	④
08	①	②	③	④
09	①	②	③	④
10	①	②	③	④
11	①	②	③	④
12	①	②	③	④
13	①	②	③	④
14	①	②	③	④
15	①	②	③	④
16	①	②	③	④
17	①	②	③	④
18	①	②	③	④
19	①	②	③	④
20	①	②	③	④
O: 개	△: 개	X: 개		

해커스공무원 7개년 기출문제집 영어

답안지

답안지 활용 방법

1. 맞은 것은 O, 찍었는데 맞은 것은 △, 틀린 것은 x를 문번에 표시하며 채점합니다.
2. △, x가 표시된 문제는 반드시 해설로 개념을 익히고, 회독을 통해 확실하게 학습합니다.
   회독을 할 때는 해커스공무원(gosi.Hackers.com) ▶ 사이트 상단의 [교재·서점] ▶ [무료학습자료]에서 회독용 답안지를 다운받아 진행하실 수 있습니다.
3. 점선을 따라 답안지를 잘라내어 사용하실 수도 있습니다.

___ 회

문번	제 2 과목			
01	①	②	③	④
02	①	②	③	④
03	①	②	③	④
04	①	②	③	④
05	①	②	③	④
06	①	②	③	④
07	①	②	③	④
08	①	②	③	④
09	①	②	③	④
10	①	②	③	④
11	①	②	③	④
12	①	②	③	④
13	①	②	③	④
14	①	②	③	④
15	①	②	③	④
16	①	②	③	④
17	①	②	③	④
18	①	②	③	④
19	①	②	③	④
20	①	②	③	④
O: 개 △: 개 X: 개				

___ 회

문번	제 2 과목			
01	①	②	③	④
02	①	②	③	④
03	①	②	③	④
04	①	②	③	④
05	①	②	③	④
06	①	②	③	④
07	①	②	③	④
08	①	②	③	④
09	①	②	③	④
10	①	②	③	④
11	①	②	③	④
12	①	②	③	④
13	①	②	③	④
14	①	②	③	④
15	①	②	③	④
16	①	②	③	④
17	①	②	③	④
18	①	②	③	④
19	①	②	③	④
20	①	②	③	④
O: 개 △: 개 X: 개				

___ 회

문번	제 2 과목			
01	①	②	③	④
02	①	②	③	④
03	①	②	③	④
04	①	②	③	④
05	①	②	③	④
06	①	②	③	④
07	①	②	③	④
08	①	②	③	④
09	①	②	③	④
10	①	②	③	④
11	①	②	③	④
12	①	②	③	④
13	①	②	③	④
14	①	②	③	④
15	①	②	③	④
16	①	②	③	④
17	①	②	③	④
18	①	②	③	④
19	①	②	③	④
20	①	②	③	④
O: 개 △: 개 X: 개				

___ 회

문번	제 2 과목			
01	①	②	③	④
02	①	②	③	④
03	①	②	③	④
04	①	②	③	④
05	①	②	③	④
06	①	②	③	④
07	①	②	③	④
08	①	②	③	④
09	①	②	③	④
10	①	②	③	④
11	①	②	③	④
12	①	②	③	④
13	①	②	③	④
14	①	②	③	④
15	①	②	③	④
16	①	②	③	④
17	①	②	③	④
18	①	②	③	④
19	①	②	③	④
20	①	②	③	④
O: 개 △: 개 X: 개				

___ 회

문번	제 2 과목			
01	①	②	③	④
02	①	②	③	④
03	①	②	③	④
04	①	②	③	④
05	①	②	③	④
06	①	②	③	④
07	①	②	③	④
08	①	②	③	④
09	①	②	③	④
10	①	②	③	④
11	①	②	③	④
12	①	②	③	④
13	①	②	③	④
14	①	②	③	④
15	①	②	③	④
16	①	②	③	④
17	①	②	③	④
18	①	②	③	④
19	①	②	③	④
20	①	②	③	④
O: 개 △: 개 X: 개				

___ 회

문번	제 2 과목			
01	①	②	③	④
02	①	②	③	④
03	①	②	③	④
04	①	②	③	④
05	①	②	③	④
06	①	②	③	④
07	①	②	③	④
08	①	②	③	④
09	①	②	③	④
10	①	②	③	④
11	①	②	③	④
12	①	②	③	④
13	①	②	③	④
14	①	②	③	④
15	①	②	③	④
16	①	②	③	④
17	①	②	③	④
18	①	②	③	④
19	①	②	③	④
20	①	②	③	④
O: 개 △: 개 X: 개				

___ 회

문번	제 2 과목			
01	①	②	③	④
02	①	②	③	④
03	①	②	③	④
04	①	②	③	④
05	①	②	③	④
06	①	②	③	④
07	①	②	③	④
08	①	②	③	④
09	①	②	③	④
10	①	②	③	④
11	①	②	③	④
12	①	②	③	④
13	①	②	③	④
14	①	②	③	④
15	①	②	③	④
16	①	②	③	④
17	①	②	③	④
18	①	②	③	④
19	①	②	③	④
20	①	②	③	④
O: 개 △: 개 X: 개				

___ 회

문번	제 2 과목			
01	①	②	③	④
02	①	②	③	④
03	①	②	③	④
04	①	②	③	④
05	①	②	③	④
06	①	②	③	④
07	①	②	③	④
08	①	②	③	④
09	①	②	③	④
10	①	②	③	④
11	①	②	③	④
12	①	②	③	④
13	①	②	③	④
14	①	②	③	④
15	①	②	③	④
16	①	②	③	④
17	①	②	③	④
18	①	②	③	④
19	①	②	③	④
20	①	②	③	④
O: 개 △: 개 X: 개				

답안지

답안지 활용 방법

1. 맞은 것은 ○, 찍었는데 맞은 것은 △, 틀린 것은 ×를 문번에 표시하며 채점합니다.
2. △, × 가 표시된 문제는 반드시 해설로 개념을 익히고, 회독을 통해 확실하게 학습합니다.
   회독을 할 때는 해커스공무원(gosi.Hackers.com) ▶ 사이트 상단의 [교재·서점] ▶
   [무료학습자료]에서 회독용 답안지를 다운받아 진행하실 수 있습니다.
3. 점선을 따라 답안지를 잘라내어 사용하실 수도 있습니다.

___ 회

문번	제 2 과목
01	① ② ③ ④ ⑤
02	① ② ③ ④ ⑤
03	① ② ③ ④ ⑤
04	① ② ③ ④ ⑤
05	① ② ③ ④ ⑤
06	① ② ③ ④ ⑤
07	① ② ③ ④ ⑤
08	① ② ③ ④ ⑤
09	① ② ③ ④ ⑤
10	① ② ③ ④ ⑤
11	① ② ③ ④ ⑤
12	① ② ③ ④ ⑤
13	① ② ③ ④ ⑤
14	① ② ③ ④ ⑤
15	① ② ③ ④ ⑤
16	① ② ③ ④ ⑤
17	① ② ③ ④ ⑤
18	① ② ③ ④ ⑤
19	① ② ③ ④ ⑤
20	① ② ③ ④ ⑤
21	① ② ③ ④ ⑤
22	① ② ③ ④ ⑤
23	① ② ③ ④ ⑤
24	① ② ③ ④ ⑤
25	① ② ③ ④ ⑤

○: 개 △: 개 X: 개

(위와 동일한 답안 표가 총 8개 반복됨 — 4열 × 2행)

공무원 교육 1위* 해커스공무원
모바일 자동 채점 + 성적 분석 서비스

한눈에 보는 서비스 사용법

Step 1.

교재 구입 후 시간 내 문제 풀어보고
교재 내 수록되어 있는 QR코드 인식!

Step 2.

모바일로 접속 후 '지금 채점하기'
버튼 클릭!

Step 3.

OMR 카드에 적어놓은 답안과 똑같이
모바일 채점 페이지에 입력하기!

Step 4.

채점 후 내 석차, 문제별 점수, 회차별
성적 추이 확인해보기!

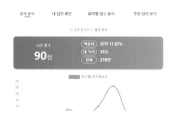

**실시간 성적 분석
결과 확인**

**문제별 정답률 및
틀린 문제 난이도 체크**

**회차별 나의 성적
변화 확인**

* [공무원 교육 1위 해커스공무원] 한경비즈니스 2024 한국품질만족도 교육(온·오프라인 공무원학원) 1위

해커스공무원 gosi.Hackers.com

바로 이용하기 ▶

회독 학습 점검표

_____월   _____일까지 회독 완료!

회독이 끝나면 □박스에 체크하고 틀린 문항의 번호는 적어서 복습해 보세요.

회차	다시 풀어볼 문항 체크		
	1 회독	2 회독	3 회독
예시	□ 5, 9, 10, 14	□ 5, 9	□ 9
1회	□	□	□
2회	□	□	□
3회	□	□	□
4회	□	□	□
5회	□	□	□
6회	□	□	□
7회	□	□	□
8회	□	□	□
9회	□	□	□
10회	□	□	□
11회	□	□	□
12회	□	□	□
13회	□	□	□
14회	□	□	□
15회	□	□	□

회차	다시 풀어볼 문항 체크		
	1 회독	2 회독	3 회독
16회	□	□	□
17회	□	□	□
18회	□	□	□
19회	□	□	□
20회	□	□	□
21회	□	□	□
22회	□	□	□
23회	□	□	□
24회	□	□	□
25회	□	□	□

해커스공무원

7개년
기출문제집
영어

CONTENTS

해커스공무원 7개년 기출문제집 영어

[책 속의 책] 문제집

국가직 9급 출제 경향

1. 영역별 출제 문항 수 (2018~2024)

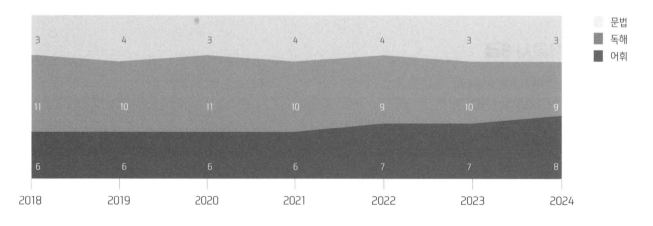

지난 7년간 영역별 출제 문항 수는 변동이 적은 편입니다. **문법** 영역은 매년 3~4문항, **독해** 영역은 9~11문항, **어휘** 영역은 6~8문항 수준으로 출제되었습니다.

Part 1
국가직 9급

2. 영역별 최근 출제 경향 및 학습 방법

문법

빈출 문법 포인트 및 활용성 높은 문법 포인트 출제

최근 7년간 빈출 문법 포인트(분사, to 부정사, 능동태·수동태, 수 일치)가 반복적으로 출제되었으며, 2024년 시험에는 지시대명사, 비교급 관련 표현 등 활용성 높은 문법 포인트들이 출제되었습니다.

▶ 따라서 기출문제를 여러 차례 회독하여 빈출 문법 포인트의 개념을 탄탄하게 다진 후 빈출 문법 포인트가 문맥에서 어떻게 활용되는지를 꼼꼼하게 학습해야 합니다.

빈출 포인트 분사(10문항) | to 부정사(8문항) | 능동태·수동태(8문항) | 수 일치(7문항)

독해

논리적 흐름 파악 유형과 전체 내용 파악 유형의 꾸준한 출제

최근 7년간 논리적 흐름 파악 유형의 문단 순서 배열, 문장 삽입, 무관한 문장 삭제 문제가 각각 1문항 이상 매년 출제되었으며, 2024년 시험에는 제목, 주제 파악 유형의 문제가 각각 1문항씩 출제되었습니다.

▶ 따라서 인칭대명사, 지시대명사, 연결어 등을 통해 지문의 논리적 흐름을 파악하고, 보기의 키워드와 관련된 부분을 지문에서 빠르게 찾아내는 연습을 꾸준히 해야 하며, 지문의 주제문을 빠르게 파악하는 연습이 필수적입니다.

어휘

비슷한 뜻을 가진 어휘나 표현을 고르는 문제 출제

최근 7년간 비슷한 뜻을 가진 어휘나 표현을 고르는 문제가 매년 2~4문항 출제되었으며, 2024년 시험에는 conceal (숨기다), appease(달래다), play down(경시하다), have the guts(용기가 있다)와 유사한 뜻을 가진 어휘와 표현을 묻는 문제가 출제되었습니다.

▶ 따라서 시험에 출제된 어휘와 표현의 유의어와 파생어를 폭넓게 학습하는 것이 필수적입니다.

정답

p.32

01	③ 어휘 - 어휘 & 표현	11	③ 어휘 - 생활영어
02	② 어휘 - 어휘 & 표현	12	② 독해 - 세부내용 파악
03	① 어휘 - 어휘 & 표현	13	③ 독해 - 세부내용 파악
04	④ 어휘 - 어휘 & 표현	14	④ 독해 - 전체내용 파악
05	④ 어휘 - 어휘 & 표현	15	① 독해 - 전체내용 파악
06	② 문법 - 대명사	16	④ 독해 - 논리적 흐름 파악
07	① 문법 - 비교급	17	③ 독해 - 논리적 흐름 파악
08	① 문법 - 수 일치	18	③ 독해 - 논리적 흐름 파악
09	② 어휘 - 생활영어	19	② 독해 - 추론
10	④ 어휘 - 생활영어	20	① 독해 - 추론

취약영역 분석표

영역	세부 유형	문항 수	소계
어휘	어휘&표현	5	/8
	생활영어	3	
문법	대명사	1	/3
	비교급	1	
	수 일치	1	
독해	전체내용 파악	2	/9
	세부내용 파악	2	
	추론	2	
	논리적 흐름 파악	3	
총계			/20

· 자신이 취약한 영역은 '공무원 영어, 이렇게 출제된다!'(문제집 p.8)를 통해 다시 한번 확인하고 학습하시기 바랍니다.

---

01 어휘 어휘&표현 interrelated   난이도 ★☆☆

해석 분명히, 언어 예술의 어떤 측면도 배움이나 가르침에 있어 분리되지 않는다. 듣기, 말하기, 읽기, 쓰기, 보기, 그리고 시각적으로 표현하기는 상호 연관되어 있다.

① 뚜렷한   ② 왜곡된
③ 상호 연관된   ④ 독립된

어휘 obviously 분명히, 확실히 aspect 측면
stand alone 분리되다, 혼자 떨어져 있다 visually 시각적으로
represent 표현하다, 나타내다 distinct 뚜렷한, 분명한
distorted 왜곡된, 비뚤어진 interrelated 상호 연관된
independent 독립된

👍 이것도 알면 **합격!**

interrelated(상호 연관된)의 유의어
= interdependent, related, complementary

---

02 어휘 어휘&표현 conceal = hide   난이도 ★☆☆

해석 그 돈은 너무 교묘하게 숨겨져서 우리는 그것을 찾는 것을 포기할 수밖에 없었다.

① 소비된   ② 숨겨진
③ 투자된   ④ 배달된

어휘 cleverly 교묘하게, 영리하게 conceal 숨기다, 감추다
abandon 포기하다, 그만두다 invest 투자하다

👍 이것도 알면 **합격!**

conceal(숨기다)의 유의어
= cover, disguise, obscure

---

03 어휘 어휘&표현 appease = soothe   난이도 ★★☆

해석 비평가들을 달래기 위해, 라디오 업계는 출퇴근 시간대 라디오에서 1,200만 달러의 공교육 캠페인을 시작했다.

① 달래다   ② 반박하다
③ 이해시키다   ④ 동화시키다

어휘 appease 달래다, 누그러뜨리다 wireless 라디오; 무선의
industry 업계, 산업 drive-time 출퇴근 시간대, 드라이브 타임
soothe 달래다 counter 반박하다 enlighten 이해시키다
assimilate 동화시키다, 완전히 이해하다

👍 이것도 알면 **합격!**

appease(달래다)의 유의어
= ease, calm, pacify, mitigate

---

04 어휘 어휘&표현 play down = underestimate   난이도 ★★☆

해석 센터 관계자들은 그 문제들이 신생 기업 운영의 전형이라고 말하며 그것들을 경시한다.

① 분간하다   ② 불만을 품게 하다
③ 강조하다   ④ 경시하다

어휘 official 관계자, 간부 play down 경시하다 typical 전형적인
start-up 신생 기업, 벤처 기업 operation 운영
discern 분간하다, 식별하다 dissatisfy 불만을 품게 하다
underline 강조하다 underestimate 경시하다, 과소평가하다

👍 이것도 알면 **합격!**

play down(경시하다)과 유사한 의미의 표현
= deemphasize, make light of, underrate

05 어휘 어휘&표현 | have the guts = be courageous | 난이도 ★★☆

해석 그녀는 부지런히 일했고 그녀가 원하는 것을 얻기 위해 애쓸 용기가 있었다.

① 불안해했다
② 운이 좋았다
③ 평판이 좋았다
④ 용기가 있었다

어휘 diligently 부지런히, 열심히 have the guts to ~할 용기가 있다
go for ~을 얻으려고 애쓰다 anxious 불안해하는
fortunate 운 좋은 reputable 평판이 좋은
courageous 용기가 있는

👍 **이것도 알면 합격!**

have the guts(용기가 있다)와 유사한 의미의 표현
= be bold, be brave, be audacious, be daring, be fearless

06 문법 대명사 | 난이도 ★☆☆

해석 오래된 주택의 품질이 현대 주택의 그것(품질)보다 뛰어나다는 믿음에도 불구하고, 대부분의 20세기 이전 주택의 기반은 오늘날의 것과 비교했을 때 극히 얕고, 단지 그것들의 목재 구조의 유연성이나 벽돌과 돌 사이의 석회 모르타르 덕분에 시간의 시험을 견뎌왔을 뿐이다.

해설 ② 지시대명사 대명사가 지칭하는 명사(the quality)가 단수이므로 복수 지시대명사 those를 단수 지시대명사 that으로 고쳐야 한다.

오답분석 ① 전치사 4: 양보 명사(the belief) 앞에 올 수 있는 것은 전치사이고, 문맥상 '믿음에도 불구하고'라는 의미가 되어야 자연스러우므로 양보를 나타내는 전치사 Despite(~에도 불구하고)가 올바르게 쓰였다.
③ 분사구문의 형태 주절의 주어(the foundations)와 분사구문이 '기반이 비교되다'라는 의미의 수동 관계이므로 과거분사 compared가 올바르게 쓰였다.
④ 인칭대명사 명사(timber framework) 앞에서 소유의 의미를 나타내기 위해서는 소유격 대명사가 와야 하고, 대명사가 지시하는 명사(the foundations)가 복수이므로 복수 소유격 대명사 their가 올바르게 쓰였다.

어휘 foundation 기반, 기초 shallow 얕은, 피상적인 timber 목재
mortar 모르타르(시멘트와 모래를 물로 반죽한 것)

👍 **이것도 알면 합격!**

지시대명사 those는 '~한 사람들'이라는 뜻으로 쓰일 수 있고, 이때 뒤에서 수식어(전치사구, 관계절, 분사)의 꾸밈을 받는다는 것을 알아두자.

(ex) (Those, ~~They~~) <u>interested in joining the club</u> should sign up
분사구
by Friday.
동아리 가입에 관심이 있는 사람들은 금요일까지 신청해야 한다.

07 문법 비교급 | 난이도 ★★☆

해석 ① 그들은 시를 읽는 것에 관심이 없고, 하물며 글쓰기에도 관심이 없다.
② 일단 확인되면, 주문품이 배송을 위해 당신의 주소로 발송될 것이다.

③ 여객선이 정시에 출발하는 경우에, 우리는 아침까지 항구에 도착해야 한다.
④ 외신 기자들은 수도에 머무는 짧은 기간 동안 가능한 한 많은 뉴스를 취재하기를 희망한다.

해설 ① 비교급 관련 표현 '하물며 글쓰기에도 관심이 없다'는 비교급 관련 표현 'still less'(하물며 ~ 아닌)를 사용하여 나타낼 수 있으므로 still more를 still less로 고쳐야 한다.

오답분석 ② 분사구문의 형태 주절의 주어(the order)와 분사구문이 '주문품이 확인되다'라는 의미의 수동 관계이므로 과거분사 confirmed가 올바르게 쓰였다. 참고로, '일단 확인되면'이라는 의미를 나타내기 위해 조건을 나타내는 부사절 접속사 Once(일단 ~하면)가 분사구문 앞에 올바르게 쓰였다.
③ 부사절 접속사 1: 조건 '여객선이 정시에 출발하는 경우에'라는 의미를 나타내기 위해 조건을 나타내는 부사절 접속사 Provided that(오직 ~하는 경우에)이 올바르게 쓰였다.
④ 원급 원급 표현 as ~ as 사이의 수량 형용사는 뒤의 명사에 따라 선택하는데, 뒤에 불가산 명사 news가 왔으므로 불가산 명사와 함께 쓰이는 수량 형용사 much가 올바르게 쓰였다.

어휘 poetry 시 confirm 확인하다, 확정하다 delivery 배송
ferry 여객선, 페리 harbor 항구 journalist 기자
cover 취재하다, 보도하다 capital 수도

👍 **이것도 알면 합격!**

비교급 관련 표현을 추가로 알아두자.

• much[still] less 하물며 ~ 아닌	• all the more 더욱더
• no longer 더 이상 ~ 않다	• no later than ~까지는
• other than ~ 외에, ~ 말고, ~ 않은	• no more than 단지 ~밖에 안 되는
• no sooner ~ than - ~하자마자 - 하다	
• more often than not 대개, 자주	

08 문법 수 일치 | 난이도 ★★☆

해설 ① 수량 표현의 수 일치 주어 자리에 단수 취급하는 수량 표현 'the number of + 명사'(the number of applicants)가 왔으므로 단수 동사 is가 올바르게 쓰였다.

오답분석 ② 과거 시제 문장에 시간 표현 two years ago(2년 전에)가 왔고, 문맥상 '이메일을 받았다'라며 과거의 동작을 표현하고 있으므로 현재완료 시제 have received를 과거 시제 received로 고쳐야 한다.
③ 전치사 + 관계대명사 완전한 절(he slept last night) 앞에는 '전치사 + 관계대명사'가 와야 하고, 문맥상 '침대에서 자다'라는 의미가 되어야 자연스러우므로 관계대명사 which를 전치사 in(~에서)이 관계대명사 which 앞에 쓰인 in which로 고쳐야 한다.
④ 기타 전치사 '새해 인사를 교환했다'는 전치사 숙어 표현 exchange A with B(A를 B와 교환하다)를 사용하여 나타낼 수 있으므로 exchanged New Year's greetings each other를 exchanged New Year's greetings with each other로 고쳐야 한다.

어휘 applicant 지원자 comfortable 편안한 greeting 인사

단수/복수 취급하는 수량 표현을 추가로 알아두자.

단수 취급하는 수량 표현	복수 취급하는 수량 표현
· one/each (+ 명사) · every/the number of/one of/neither of + 명사 · somebody, someone, something · anybody, anyone, anything · everybody, everyone, everything · nobody, no one, nothing	· many/several/few/both (+ of the) + 복수 명사 · a number of/a couple of/a range of/a variety of + 복수 명사

09 어휘 생활영어 What does the city tour include? 난이도 ★☆☆

해석
> Brian: 안녕하세요, 귀사의 시티 투어에 대한 정보를 좀 얻을 수 있을까요?
> Ace 관광: 연락해 주셔서 감사합니다. 구체적인 질문이 있으신가요?
> Brian: 시티 투어에는 무엇이 포함되나요?
> Ace 관광: 도시의 주요 명소를 모두 안내해 드립니다.
> Brian: 얼마인가요?
> Ace 관광: 4시간 투어에 1인당 50달러입니다.
> Brian: 알겠습니다. 금요일 오후 티켓 4장을 예매할 수 있나요?
> Ace 관광: 물론입니다. 곧 결제 정보를 보내드리겠습니다.

① 투어 시간은 얼마나 되나요?
② 시티 투어에는 무엇이 포함되나요?
③ 투어 패키지 목록이 있나요?
④ 좋은 여행 가이드북을 추천해 주실 수 있나요?

해설 구체적인 질문이 있냐고 묻는 Ace 관광 직원의 말에 Brian이 대답하고, 빈칸 뒤에서 Ace 관광 직원이 It'll take you to all the major points of interest in the city(도시의 주요 명소를 모두 안내해 드립니다)라고 말하고 있으므로, 빈칸에는 '② 시티 투어에는 무엇이 포함되나요?(What does the city tour include?)'가 오는 것이 자연스럽다.

어휘 contact 연락하다 specific 구체적인, 특정한
book 예매하다, 예약하다 include 포함하다
recommend 추천하다

여행사에 문의할 때 쓸 수 있는 다양한 표현을 알아두자.

· When will I receive my travel itinerary?
  여행 일정은 언제 받아볼 수 있나요?
· I need assistance with my booking confirmation.
  예약 확인에 도움이 필요해요.
· Can you help me with travel insurance?
  여행자 보험과 관련해서 도와주실 수 있나요?
· How do I book a guided tour?
  가이드 투어는 어떻게 예약하나요?
· What are some must-see attractions?
  꼭 가봐야 할 명소가 뭐가 있을까요?

10 어휘 생활영어 Wait a minute. I thought the delivery costs were at your expense. 난이도 ★★☆

해석
> A: 감사합니다. 주문해 주셔서 고맙습니다.
> B: 별말씀을요. 상품을 항공 화물로 보내주실 수 있나요? 저희가 그것들이 빨리 필요해서요.
> A: 물론이죠. 지금 바로 귀하의 부서로 보내드리겠습니다.
> B: 알겠습니다. 저희가 다음 주 초에 상품을 받을 수 있으면 좋겠습니다.
> A: 모든 일이 계획대로 진행되면, 월요일까지 받아 보실 수 있을 것입니다.
> B: 월요일이 좋은 것 같네요.
> A: 2주 이내에 결제해 주시기 바랍니다. 청구서에 항공 운송비가 추가될 것입니다.
> B: 잠시만요. 배송비는 귀사 부담인 줄 알았는데요.
> A: 죄송하지만 무료 배송 서비스는 더 이상 제공되지 않습니다.

① 그렇군요. 청구서는 언제 받을 수 있나요?
② 저희 부서에서는 2주 이내에 지불하지 못할 수도 있습니다.
③ 월요일에 귀하의 법인 계좌로 대금을 보내 드려도 될까요?
④ 잠시만요. 배송비는 귀사 부담인 줄 알았는데요.

해설 청구서에 항공 운송비가 추가될 것이라는 A의 말에 B가 대답하고, 빈칸 뒤에서 A가 I am afraid the free delivery service is no longer available(죄송하지만 무료 배송 서비스는 더 이상 제공되지 않습니다)이라고 말하고 있으므로, 빈칸에는 '④ 잠시만요. 배송비는 귀사 부담인 줄 알았는데요(Wait a minute. I thought the delivery costs were at your expense)'가 오는 것이 자연스럽다.

어휘 appreciate 고마워하다, 감사하다 goods 상품, 물품
air freight 항공 화물 invoice 청구서, 송장
business account 법인 계좌
at one's expense 부담으로, 비용으로

배송과 관련된 다양한 표현을 알아두자.

· parcel 소포	· express 속달
· shipment 수송품	· same-day 당일, 즉일
· handling 취급	· PO box 사서함
· dispatch 발송	

11 어휘 생활영어 I haven't done that yet, actually. 난이도 ★☆☆

해석
> A: 핸드폰을 찾으셨나요?
> B: 불행하게도, 아니요. 아직도 찾고 있어요.
> A: 지하철 분실물 센터에 연락해 보셨나요?
> B: 사실 아직 그건 안 했어요.
> A: 제가 당신이라면, 그것을 먼저 하겠어요.
> B: 네, 당신 말이 맞아요. 새 핸드폰을 사기 전에 분실물 센터에 확인해 볼게요.

① 핸드폰에 대해 물어보려고 그곳에 갔어요
② 오늘 아침에 사무실에 들렀어요
③ 사실 아직 그건 안 했어요
④ 모든 곳을 찾아봤어요

해설 지하철 분실물 센터에 연락해 봤냐는 A의 질문에 B가 대답하고, 빈칸 뒤에서 A가 If I were you, I would do that first(제가 당신이라면, 그것을 먼저 하겠어요)라고 말하고 있으므로, 빈칸에는 '③ 사실 아직 그건 안 했어요(I haven't done that yet, actually)'가 오는 것이 자연스럽다.

어휘 unfortunately 불행하게도, 유감스럽게도
lost and found office 분실물 센터 stop by 들르다, 잠깐 방문하다

👍 이것도 알면 **합격!**

분실물 센터에서 쓸 수 있는 다양한 표현을 알아두자.

· I'm here to claim a lost item.
분실물을 찾으러 왔습니다.

· Can I leave my contact information in case it's found?
혹시 그것이 발견될 경우를 대비해서 연락처를 남겨도 될까요?

· I'd like to turn in a found item.
찾은 물건을 돌려주려고 합니다.

· Here's my phone number. Please let me know if you find it.
제 전화번호입니다. 찾으시면 연락해 주세요.

---

12 독해 세부내용 파악 (내용 일치 파악) 난이도 ★☆☆

끊어읽기 해석

NORTHEASTERN WILDLIFE EXPOSITION (NEWE)
북동부 야생동물 박람회(NEWE)

Admission ticket for Saturday, March 30th, 2024
2024년 3월 30일 토요일 입장권

· Price: $ 40.00
가격: 40달러

· Opening hours: 10:00 a.m. – 6:00 p.m.
운영 시간: 오전 10시 – 오후 6시

①Kids 10 and under are free.
10세 이하의 어린이는 무료입니다

②Entry to shows and lectures are first-come, first-served.
공연 및 강의 입장은 선착순입니다

③All venues open / rain or shine.
모든 행사장은 문을 엽니다 / 비가 오든 날이 개든 (상관없이)

March 20th is the last day / to buy tickets online / for the 2024 Northeastern Wildlife Exposition.
3월 20일은 마지막 날입니다 / 입장권을 온라인에서 구매할 수 있는 / 2024 북동부 야생동물 박람회의

Please note: / Purchasing NEWE tickets in advance / is the best way / to guarantee entry / into all exhibits.
참고: / NEWE 입장권을 미리 구매하는 것이 / 가장 좋은 방법입니다 / 입장을 보장하는 / 모든 전시회의

④NEWE organizers may discontinue in-person ticket sales / should any venue reach capacity.
NEWE 주최 측은 현장 입장권 판매를 중단할 수 있습니다 / 행사장 수용 인원에 도달할 경우

해석 북동부 야생동물 박람회(NEWE)

2024년 3월 30일 토요일 입장권

· 가격: 40달러

· 운영 시간: 오전 10시 – 오후 6시

10세 이하의 어린이는 무료입니다. 공연 및 강의 입장은 선착순입니다. 모든 행사장은 비가 오든 날이 개든 (상관없이) 문을 엽니다.

3월 20일은 2024 북동부 야생동물 박람회 입장권을 온라인에서 구매할 수 있는 마지막 날입니다.

참고: NEWE 입장권을 미리 구매하는 것이 모든 전시회 입장을 보장하는 가장 좋은 방법입니다. NEWE 주최 측은 행사장 수용 인원에 도달할 경우 현장 입장권 판매를 중단할 수 있습니다.

해설 지문 처음에서 공연 및 강의 입장은 선착순이라고 했으므로, '② 공연과 강연의 입장은 선착순이다'는 지문의 내용과 일치한다.

오답 분석
① 첫 번째 문장에서 10세 이하의 어린이는 무료라고 했으므로 지문의 내용과 다르다.
③ 세 번째 문장에서 모든 행사장은 비가 오든 날이 개든 (상관없이) 문을 연다고 했으므로 지문의 내용과 다르다.
④ 마지막 문장에 NEWE 주최 측은 행사장 수용 인원에 도달할 경우 현장 입장권 판매를 중단할 수 있다고 언급한 내용을 통해 현장에서도 입장권을 판매한다는 것을 알 수 있으므로 지문의 내용과 다르다.

어휘 wildlife 야생동물 exposition 박람회
first-come, first-served 선착순의
venue (콘서트·스포츠 경기·회담 등의) 장소
rain or shine 비가 오든 날이 개든, 어떤 일이 있더라도
guarantee 보장하다 discontinue 중단하다
capacity 수용력, 용량

---

13 독해 세부내용 파악 (내용 불일치 파악) 난이도 ★★☆

끊어읽기 해석

The tragedies of the Greek dramatist Sophocles / have come to be regarded / as the high point of classical Greek drama.
그리스 극작가 소포클레스의 비극은 / 여겨지게 되었다 / 그리스 고전극의 정점으로

Sadly, / only seven of the 123 tragedies / he wrote / have survived, / but of these / perhaps the finest is *Oedipus the King*.
안타깝게도 / 123편의 비극 중 단지 7편만이 / 그가 쓴 / 살아남았다 / 하지만 그중에서 / 아마도 가장 훌륭한 것은 『오이디푸스 왕』일 것이다

The play was one of three / written by Sophocles / about Oedipus, / the mythical king of Thebes / (the others being *Antigone* and *Oedipus at Colonus*), / known collectively as / the Theban plays.
이 연극은 세 편 중 하나였다 / 소포클레스에 의해 쓰인 / 오이디푸스에 대해 / 테베의 신화 속 왕인 / (다른 것들은 『안티고네』와 『콜로노스의 오이디푸스』이다) / 집합적으로 알려져 있다 / 테베 연극으로

Sophocles conceived each of these / as a separate entity, / and / they were written and produced / several years apart / and / out of chronological order.
소포클레스는 이들 각각을 생각했다 / 별도의 실체로 / 그리고 / 그것들은 집필되고 제작되었다 / 몇 년 간격을 두고 / 그리고 / 연대순에서 벗어나서

Oedipus the King follows / the established formal structure / and / it is regarded / as the best example of classical Athenian tragedy.
『오이디푸스 왕』은 따른다 / 확립된 형식적 구조를 / 그리고 / 그것은 여겨진다 / 고전 아테네 비극의 가장 좋은 예로

해석 그리스 극작가 소포클레스의 비극은 그리스 고전극의 정점으로 여겨지게 되었다. 안타깝게도, 그가 쓴 123편의 비극 중 단지 7편만이 살아남았는데, 그중에서 아마도 가장 훌륭한 것은 『오이디푸스 왕』일 것이다. 이 연극은 소포클레스가 테베의 신화 속 왕인 오이디푸스에 대해 쓴 세 편(다른 것들은 『안티고네』와 『콜로노스의 오이디푸스』이다) 중 하나였고, 이는 집합적으로 테베 연극으로 알려져 있다. 소포클레스는 이들 각각을 별도의 실체로 생각했고, 그것들은 몇 년 간격을 두고 연대순에서 벗어나서 집필되고 제작되었다. 『오이디푸스 왕』은 확립된 형식적 구조를 따르며 고전 아

테네 비극의 가장 좋은 예로 여겨진다.
① 소포클레스는 총 123편의 비극을 썼다.
② 『안티고네』도 오이디푸스 왕에 관한 것이다.
③ 테베 연극은 시간 순서대로 만들어졌다.
④ 『오이디푸스 왕』은 고전적인 아테네 비극을 대표한다.

해설 지문 마지막에서 테베 연극들은 몇 년 간격을 두고 연대순에서 벗어나서 집필되고 제작되었다고 했으므로 '③ 테베 연극은 시간 순서대로 만들어졌다'는 지문의 내용과 일치하지 않는다.

어휘 tragedy 비극 dramatist 극작가 high point 정점
mythical 신화 속에 나오는, 가공의
collectively 집합적으로, 전체적으로 conceive 생각하다, 여기다
separate 별도의, 개별적인 entity 실체, 존재 out of ~에서 벗어나
chronological 연대순의 establish 확립하다, 설립하다
formal 형식적인, 정식의 structure 구조

---

③ 크레타섬에 있는 궁전의 웅장함
④ 미노아 문화를 현실의 영역으로 끌어들이기

해설 지문 앞부분에서 영국의 고고학자 Arthur Evans가 크노소스 궁전의 유적을 발굴하기 전까지 미노아 문화는 사실이라기보다는 더 전설이었다고 한 후, 지문 뒷부분에서 Evans가 미노아 시대의 유물 발굴품을 발견했다는 것을 설명하며 이 왕국은 신화가 아니었다고 하고 있다. 따라서 '④ 미노아 문화를 현실의 영역으로 끌어들이기'가 이 글의 주제이다.

어휘 archaeologist 고고학자 excavate ~을 발굴하다 ruin 유적
Mediterranean 지중해의 indeed 실제로, 정말로 famed 유명한
mythology 신화 bull 황소 realm 왕국, 영역
trove 발굴품, 귀중한 수집품 artifact 유물 carving 조각품
pottery 도자기 altar 제단 horn 뿔 appreciate 감상하다
magnificence 웅장함

---

14 독해 전체내용 파악 (주제 파악) 난이도 ★★☆

끊어읽기 해석

It seems incredible / that one man could be responsible for / opening our eyes / to an entire culture, / but until British archaeologist Arthur Evans successfully excavated / the ruins of the palace of Knossos / on the island of Crete, / the great Minoan culture of the Mediterranean / was more legend than fact.
믿을 수 없는 것처럼 보인다 / 한 사람이 책임을 질 수 있다는 것은 / 우리의 눈을 뜨게 하는 / 전체 문화에 대해 / 하지만 영국의 고고학자 Arthur Evans가 성공적으로 발굴하기 전까지 / 크노소스 궁전의 유적을 / 크레타섬에 있는 / 지중해의 위대한 미노아 문화는 / 사실이라기보다는 더 전설이었다

Indeed / its most famed resident / was a creature of mythology: / the half-man, half-bull Minotaur, / said to have lived / under the palace of mythical King Minos.
실제로 / 그곳의 가장 유명한 거주자는 / 신화 속의 생명체였다 / 반은 인간이고, 반은 황소인 미노타우로스는 / 살았다고 한다 / 신화 속 미노스 왕의 궁전 아래에서

But / as Evans proved, / this realm was no myth.
그러나 / Evans가 증명했듯이 / 이 왕국은 신화가 아니었다

In a series of excavations / in the early years of the 20th century, / Evans found a trove of artifacts / from the Minoan age, / which reached its height from 1900 to 1450 B.C.: / jewelry, / carvings, / pottery, / altars shaped like bull's horns, / and wall paintings / showing Minoan life.
일련의 발굴에서 / 20세기 초의 / Evans는 유물 발굴품을 발견했다 / 미노아 시대의 / 기원전 1900년에서 1450년 사이에 절정에 달했던 / 보석 / 조각품 / 도자기 / 황소 뿔 모양의 제단 / 그리고 벽화를 / 미노아의 삶을 보여주는

해석 한 사람이 전체 문화에 대해 우리의 눈을 뜨게 하는 책임을 질 수 있다는 것은 믿을 수 없는 것처럼 보이지만, 영국의 고고학자 Arthur Evans가 크레타섬에 있는 크노소스 궁전의 유적을 성공적으로 발굴하기 전까지 지중해의 위대한 미노아 문화는 사실이라기보다는 더 전설이었다. 실제로 그곳의 가장 유명한 거주자는 신화 속의 생명체였다. 반은 인간이고, 반은 황소인 미노타우로스는 신화 속 미노스 왕의 궁전 아래에서 살았다고 한다. 그러나 Evans가 증명했듯이, 이 왕국은 신화가 아니었다. 20세기 초의 일련의 발굴에서, Evans는 기원전 1900년에서 1450년 사이에 절정에 달했던 미노아 시대의 유물 발굴품인 보석, 조각품, 도자기, 황소 뿔 모양의 제단, 그리고 미노아의 삶을 보여주는 벽화를 발견했다.

① 미노스 왕의 성공적인 발굴
② 미노아 시대의 유물 감상

---

15 독해 전체내용 파악 (제목 파악) 난이도 ★★★

끊어읽기 해석

Currency debasement of a good money by a bad money version / occurred / via coins of a high percentage of precious metal, / reissued at lower percentages of gold or silver / diluted with a lower value metal.
악화 형태에 의한 양화의 화폐 가치 하락은 / 일어났다 / 귀금속 함량이 높은 동전을 통해 / 더 낮은 비율의 금 또는 은으로 재발행되었다 / 더 낮은 가치의 금속으로 희석된

This adulteration / drove out the good coin for the bad coin.
이렇게 불순물을 섞는 것은 / 양화를 악화로 몰아냈다

No one spent the good coin, / they kept it, / hence the good coin was driven out of circulation / and into a hoard.
누구도 양화를 쓰지 않았다 / 그들은 그것을 보관했다 / 따라서 양화는 유통에서 사라졌다 / 그리고 축적되었다

Meanwhile / the issuer, / normally a king / who had lost his treasure / on interminable warfare / and / other such dissolute living, / was behind the move.
한편 / 발행인은 / 대개 왕인 / 재산을 잃은 / 끝없는 전쟁으로 / 그리고 / 그 밖의 방탕한 생활로 / 이러한 움직임의 배후에 있었다

They collected all the good old coins they could, / melted them down / and / reissued them / at lower purity / and / pocketed the balance.
그들은 그들이 모을 수 있는 모든 양화들을 모았다 / 그것들을 녹였다 / 그리고 / 그것들을 재발행했다 / 낮은 순도로 / 그리고 / 차액을 횡령했다

It was often illegal / to keep the old stuff back / but / people did, / while the king replenished his treasury, / at least for a time.
종종 불법이었다 / 옛 물건들을 숨겨두는 것은 / 하지만 / 사람들은 그렇게 했다 / 왕이 국고를 다시 채우는 동안 / 적어도 한동안은

해석 악화 형태에 의한 양화의 화폐 가치 하락은 귀금속 함량이 높은 동전을 통해 일어났으며, 더 낮은 가치의 금속으로 희석된 더 낮은 비율의 금 또는 은으로 재발행되었다. 이렇게 불순물을 섞는 것은 양화를 악화로 몰아냈다. 누구도 양화를 쓰지 않고 보관했기 때문에, 양화는 유통에서 사라졌고 축적되었다. 한편, 대개 끝없는 전쟁과 그 밖의 방탕한 생활로 재산을 잃은 왕인 발행인이 이러한 움직임의 배후에 있었다. 그들은 그들이 모을 수 있는 모든 양화들을 모아서 그것들을 녹여 낮은 순도로 재발행했고, 차액을 횡령했다. 옛 물건들을 숨겨두는 것은 종종 불법이었지만, 왕이 국고를 다시 채우는 동안, 사람들이 적어도 한동안은 그렇게 했다.

① 악화가 어떻게 양화를 대체하는가
② 양화의 요소

③ 왜 동전을 녹이면 안 되는가?
④ 악화란 무엇인가?

해설 지문 처음에서 악화 형태에 의한 양화의 화폐 가치 하락은 귀금속 함량이 높은 동전을 통해 일어났다고 언급하고, 불순물을 섞는 것이 양화를 악화로 몰아냈다고 하면서 지문 전반에 걸쳐 양화가 유통에서 사라지게 된 이유를 설명하고 있으므로, '① 악화가 어떻게 양화를 대체하는가'가 이 글의 제목이다.

어휘 currency 화폐, 통화 debasement 가치 하락, 저하
good money 양화(좋은 품질의 화폐)
bad money 악화(나쁜 품질의 화폐) version 형태
occur 일어나다, 발생하다 via ~을 통해 precious metal 귀금속
reissue 재발행하다 dilute 희석하다 adulteration 불순물 섞기
drive out (of) ~에서 몰아내다, 사라지게 하다
circulation 유통, 순환 hoard 축적, 저장 issuer 발행인
treasure 재산, 보물 interminable 끝없는 warfare 전쟁
dissolute 방탕한, 타락한 purity 순도 pocket 횡령하다
balance 차액, 잔고 illegal 불법인 keep back 숨기다
replenish 다시 채우다, 보충하다 treasury 국고 element 요소

16 독해 논리적 흐름 파악 (무관한 문장 삭제) 난이도 ★★☆

끊어읽기 해석

In spite of all evidence to the contrary, / there are people / who seriously believe / that NASA's Apollo space program / never really landed men / on the moon.
반대되는 모든 증거에도 불구하고 / 사람들이 있다 / 진지하게 믿는 / NASA의 아폴로 우주 프로그램이 / 실제로 사람을 착륙시킨 적이 없다고 / 달에

These people claim / that the moon landings were nothing more than a huge conspiracy, / perpetuated by a government / desperately in competition with the Russians / and fearful of losing face.
이러한 사람들은 주장한다 / 달 착륙이 거대한 음모에 불과했다고 / 정부에 의해 지속된 / 러시아와 필사적으로 경쟁하는 / 그리고 체면을 잃을 것을 두려워하는

① These conspiracy theorists claim / that the United States knew / it couldn't compete with the Russians / in the space race / and / was therefore forced to fake a series of successful moon landings.
이 음모론자들은 주장한다 / 미국은 알았다고 / 그것(미국)이 러시아와 경쟁할 수 없다는 것을 / 우주 경쟁에서 / 그리고 / 그래서 일련의 성공적인 달 착륙을 가짜로 만들 수밖에 없었다고

② Advocates of a conspiracy / cite several pieces of what they consider evidence.
음모론의 옹호자들은 / 그들이 증거라고 생각하는 몇 가지를 인용한다

③ Crucial to their case / is the claim / that astronauts never could have safely passed through the Van Allen belt, / a region of radiation / trapped in Earth's magnetic field.
그들의 주장에서 결정적인 것은 / 주장이다 / 우주 비행사들이 밴앨런대를 결코 안전하게 통과할 수 없었을 것이라는 / 방사선의 지역인 / 지구의 자기장에 갇힌

④ They also point to the fact / that the metal coverings of the spaceship / were designed to block radiation.
그들은 또한 사실을 들먹인다 / 우주선의 금속 덮개가 / 방사선을 차단하도록 설계되었다는

If the astronauts had truly gone through the belt, / say conspiracy theorists, / they would have died.
만약 우주 비행사들이 진정으로 그 벨트를 통과했다면 / 음모론자들은 말한다 / 그들은 죽었을 것이라고

해석 반대되는 모든 증거에도 불구하고, NASA의 아폴로 우주 프로그램이 실제로 달에 사람을 착륙시킨 적이 없다고 진지하게 믿는 사람들이 있다. 이러한 사람들은 달 착륙이 러시아와 필사적으로 경쟁하며 체면을 잃을 것을 두려워하는 정부에 의해 지속된 거대한 음모에 불과했다고 주장한다. ① 이 음모론자들은 미국이 우주 경쟁에서 러시아와 경쟁할 수 없다는 것을 알았기 때문에 일련의 성공적인 달 착륙을 가짜로 만들 수밖에 없었다고 주장한다. ② 음모론의 옹호자들은 그들이 증거라고 생각하는 몇 가지를 인용한다. ③ 그들의 주장에서 결정적인 것은 우주 비행사들이 지구의 자기장에 갇힌 방사선의 지역인 밴앨런대를 결코 안전하게 통과할 수 없었을 것이라는 주장이다. ④ 그들은 또한 우주선의 금속 덮개가 방사선을 차단하도록 설계되었다는 사실을 들먹인다. 만약 우주 비행사들이 진정으로 그 벨트를 통과했다면, 그들은 죽었을 것이라고 음모론자들은 말한다.

해설 지문 처음에서 NASA의 아폴로 우주 프로그램이 실제로 달에 사람을 착륙시킨 적이 없다고 믿는 사람들에 대해 언급한 뒤, ①, ②, ③번에서 그들의 주장과 그 증거에 대해 설명하고 있으므로 모두 첫 문장과 관련이 있다. 그러나 ④번은 음모론의 옹호자들이 우주선의 금속 덮개가 방사선을 차단하도록 설계되었다는 사실을 들먹인다는 내용으로 아폴로 우주 프로그램이 달에 사람을 착륙시킨 적이 없다는 음모론자들의 주장에 대해 설명하는 지문 전반의 내용과 반대다. 따라서 ④번이 정답이다.

어휘 evidence 증거, 근거 contrary 반대의 것 land 착륙하다
claim 주장하다 conspiracy 음모
perpetuate 지속하다, ~을 영속하게 하다
desperately 필사적으로, 절실하게 lose face 체면을 잃다
fake 가짜로 만들다, 가장하다 advocate 옹호자 crucial 결정적인
case 주장, 진술 astronaut 우주 비행사 radiation 방사선
trap 가두다 magnetic field 자기장 spaceship 우주선

17 독해 논리적 흐름 파악 (문장 삽입) 난이도 ★★☆

끊어읽기 해석

Tribal oral history and archaeological evidence suggest / that sometime between 1500 and 1700 / a mudslide destroyed part of the village, / covering several longhouses and sealing in their contents.
부족의 구전 역사와 고고학적 증거는 암시한다 / 1500년에서 1700년 사이의 언젠가 / 진흙 사태가 그 마을의 일부를 파괴하여 / 여러 채의 전통 가옥을 뒤덮고 그 안에 있는 것들을 봉인했다는 것을

From the village of Ozette on the westernmost point of Washington's Olympic Peninsula, / members of the Makah tribe hunted whales.
워싱턴주 올림픽 반도의 가장 서쪽 지점에 위치한 오제트 마을에서 / 마카족의 사람들이 고래를 사냥했다

(①) They smoked their catch on racks and in smokehouses / and / traded with neighboring groups / from around the Puget Sound / and / nearby Vancouver Island.
그들은 선반 위와 훈제실에서 잡은 것들을 훈제했다 / 그리고 / 이웃 무리들과 거래했다 / 퓨젯 사운드에서 온 / 그리고 / 인근의 밴쿠버섬 주변에서

(②) Ozette was one of five main villages / inhabited by the Makah, / an Indigenous people / who have been based in the region / for millennia.
오제트는 다섯 개의 주요 마을 중 하나였다 / 마카족이 거주했던 / 토착민인 / 그 지역에 근거지를 두고 살아온 / 수천 년간

(③) Thousands of artifacts / that would not otherwise have survived, / including baskets, clothing, sleeping mats, and whaling tools, / were preserved / under the mud.

수천 개의 유물들이 / 그렇지 않았더라면 잔존하지 못했을 / 바구니, 옷, 수면 요, 그리고 고래잡이 도구를 포함하여 / 보존되었다 / 진흙 속에

(④) In 1970, / a storm caused coastal erosion / that revealed the remains of these longhouses and artifacts.
1970년에 / 한 폭풍이 해안 침식을 일으켰고 / 그것이 이 전통 가옥들과 유물들의 잔해를 드러냈다

해석　부족의 구전 역사와 고고학적 증거는 1500년에서 1700년 사이의 언젠가 진흙 사태가 그 마을의 일부를 파괴하여 여러 채의 전통 가옥을 뒤덮고 그 안에 있는 것들을 봉인했다는 것을 암시한다.

워싱턴주 올림픽 반도의 가장 서쪽 지점에 위치한 오제트 마을에서 마카족의 사람들이 고래를 사냥했다. (①) 그들은 선반 위와 훈제실에서 잡은 것을 훈제했고, 퓨젯 사운드와 인근의 밴쿠버섬 주변에서 온 이웃 무리들과 거래했다. (②) 오제트는 수천 년간 그 지역에 근거지를 두고 살아온 토착민인 마카족이 거주했던 다섯 개의 주요 마을 중 하나였다. (③) 바구니, 옷, 수면 요, 그리고 고래잡이 도구를 포함하여, 그렇지 않았더라면 잔존하지 못했을 수천 개의 유물들이 진흙 속에 보존되었다. (④) 1970년에, 한 폭풍이 해안 침식을 일으켰고, 그것이 이 전통 가옥들과 유물들의 잔해를 드러냈다.

해설　주어진 문장의 the village(그 마을)를 통해 주어진 문장 앞에는 마을에 대한 설명이 나오고, sealing in their contents(그 안에 있는 것들을 봉인했다)를 통해 주어진 문장 뒤에 진흙 속에 봉인되었던 것들에 대한 설명이 나올 것임을 예상할 수 있다. ③번 앞 문장에서 오제트가 마카족이 거주했던 다섯 개의 주요 마을 중 하나였다고 설명하고, ③번 뒤 문장에서 진흙이 봉인하지 않았더라면 잔존하지 못했을 수천 개의 유물들이 진흙 속에 보존되었다고 하고 있으므로 ③번 자리에 주어진 문장이 들어가야 글의 흐름이 자연스럽게 연결된다. 따라서 ③번이 정답이다.

어휘　tribal 부족의　oral 구전의, 구두의　archaeological 고고학적인
mudslide 진흙 사태　longhouse (미국 일부 원주민들의) 전통 가옥
seal 봉(인)하다　peninsula 반도　indigenous 토착의
coastal erosion 해안 침식

18　독해　논리적 흐름 파악 (문단 순서 배열)　난이도 ★☆☆

끊어읽기 해석

Interest in movie and sports stars / goes beyond their performances / on the screen and in the arena.
영화와 스포츠 스타에 대한 관심은 / 그들의 활약의 범위를 넘어선다 / 스크린과 경기장에서의

(A) The doings of skilled baseball, football, and basketball players / out of uniform / similarly attract public attention.
뛰어난 야구, 축구, 그리고 농구 선수들의 행동은 / 유니폼을 벗고 하는 / 비슷하게 대중의 관심을 끈다

(B) Newspaper columns, specialized magazines, television programs, and Web sites record / the personal lives / of celebrated Hollywood actors, / sometimes accurately.
신문 칼럼, 전문 잡지, 텔레비전 프로그램, 그리고 웹사이트는 기록한다 / 개인 생활을 / 유명 할리우드 배우들의 / 때로는 정확하게

(C) Both industries / actively promote such attention, / which expands audiences / and thus increases revenues.
두 업계 모두 / 이러한 관심을 적극적으로 홍보한다 / 이는 관객을 확장한다 / 그리고 따라서 수익도 증가시킨다

But a fundamental difference / divides them: / What sports stars do for a living is authentic / in a way that what movie

stars do is not.
그러나 근본적인 차이점이 / 그들을 나눈다 / 스포츠 스타가 생계를 위해 하는 일은 진짜이다 / 영화배우들이 하지 않는 방식으로

해석　영화와 스포츠 스타에 대한 관심은 스크린과 경기장에서의 그들의 활약의 범위를 넘어선다.
(B) 신문 칼럼, 전문 잡지, 텔레비전 프로그램, 그리고 웹사이트는 유명 할리우드 배우들의 개인 생활을 때로는 정확하게 기록한다.
(A) 뛰어난 야구, 축구, 그리고 농구 선수들이 유니폼을 벗고 하는 행동도 비슷하게 대중의 관심을 끈다.
(C) 두 업계 모두 이러한 관심을 적극적으로 홍보하는데, 이는 관객을 확장하고 따라서 수익도 증가시킨다. 그러나 근본적인 차이점이 그들을 나눈다. 스포츠 스타가 생계를 위해 하는 일은 영화배우들이 하지 않는 방식으로 진짜이다.

해설　주어진 문장에서 영화와 스포츠 스타에 대한 관심은 스크린과 경기장에서의 그들의 활약의 범위를 넘어선다고 하고, (B)에서 각종 매체들은 유명 배우들의 개인 생활을 기록한다고 설명하고 있다. 이어서 (A)에서 운동선수들이 경기 중이 아닐 때 하는 행동도 배우들과 비슷하게 대중의 관심을 끈다고 하고, (C)에서 배우와 운동선수 두 업계 모두 이러한 관심을 적극적으로 홍보한다고 설명하고 있다. 따라서 ② (B) – (A) – (C)가 정답이다.

어휘　arena 경기장, 시합장　attract 끌다, 유인하다　specialized 전문의
accurately 정확하게　actively 적극적으로
expand 확장하다, 확대하다　revenue 수익
fundamental 근본적인　divide 나누다　authentic 진짜의, 진정한

19　독해　추론 (빈칸 완성 - 절)　난이도 ★★☆

끊어읽기 해석

Persuasion shows up / in almost every walk of life.
설득은 나타난다 / 거의 모든 직업에서

Nearly every major politician / hires / media consultants and political experts / to provide advice / on how to appeal / to the public.
거의 모든 주요 정치인들은 / 고용한다 / 미디어 컨설턴트와 정치 전문가를 / 조언을 제공하기 위해 / 어떻게 호소할 것인지에 대해 / 대중들에게

Virtually every major business and special-interest group / has hired a lobbyist / to take its concerns / to Congress / or / to state and local governments.
거의 모든 주요 사업체와 특수 이익 단체들은 / 로비스트를 고용해 왔다 / 그들의 우려 사항을 전달하기 위해 / 의회에 / 또는 / 주정부 및 지방정부에

In nearly every community, / activists try to persuade / their fellow citizens / on important policy issues.
거의 모든 지역사회에서 / 활동가들은 설득하려고 노력한다 / 그들의 동료 시민들을 / 중요한 정책 문제에 대해

The workplace, too, has always been fertile ground / for office politics and persuasion.
직장 또한 항상 비옥한 땅이었다 / 사내 정치와 설득을 위한

One study estimates / that general managers spend upwards of 80% of their time / in verbal communication / — most of it with the intent / of persuading their fellow employees.
한 연구는 추정한다 / 일반 관리자들이 그들의 시간의 80퍼센트 이상을 소비한다고 / 언어적 의사소통에 / 이 중 대부분은 의도를 가지고 있다 / 그들의 동료 직원들을 설득하려는

With the advent of the photocopying machine, / a whole new medium for office persuasion was invented / —the photocopied memo.
복사기의 출현으로 / 설득을 위한 완전히 새로운 매체가 발명되었다 / 즉 복사된 메모

The Pentagon alone / copies / an average of 350,000 pages / a day, / the equivalent of 1,000 novels.
국방부에서만 / 복사한다 / 평균 35만 페이지를 / 하루에 / 이것은 소설 1,000권에 해당한다

해석 설득은 거의 모든 직업에서 나타난다. 거의 모든 주요 정치인들은 미디어 컨설턴트와 정치 전문가를 고용하여 대중들에게 어떻게 호소할 것인지에 대한 조언을 제공하게 한다. 거의 모든 주요 사업체와 특수 이익 단체들은 의회나 주정부 및 지방정부에 그들의 우려 사항을 전달하기 위해 로비스트를 고용해 왔다. 거의 모든 지역사회에서, 활동가들은 중요한 정책 문제에 대해 동료 시민들을 설득하려고 노력한다. 직장 또한 항상 사내 정치와 설득을 위한 비옥한 땅이었다. 한 연구는 일반 관리자들이 그들의 시간의 80퍼센트 이상을 언어적 의사소통에 소비한다고 추정하는데, 이 중 대부분은 그들의 동료 직원들을 설득하려는 의도를 가지고 있다. 복사기의 출현으로 사내 설득을 위한 완전히 새로운 매체, 즉 복사된 메모가 발명되었다. 국방부에서만 하루에 평균 35만 페이지를 복사하는데, 이것은 소설 1,000권에 해당한다.

① 사업가들은 뛰어난 설득 기술을 지녀야 한다.
② 설득은 거의 모든 직업에서 나타난다.
③ 당신은 수많은 광고판과 포스터를 만나게 될 것이다.
④ 대중 매체 캠페인은 정부에 유용하다.

해설 지문 전반에 걸쳐 정치인들은 대중들에게 호소하기 위한 조언을 받고, 사업체와 특수 이익 단체들은 그들의 우려 사항을 정부에 전달하고, 활동가들은 동료 시민들을 설득하고, 일반 관리자들은 동료 직원들을 설득하는 데 언어적 의사소통의 대부분을 사용하는 등 여러 분야에서 설득이 이루어지는 예시를 설명하고 있으므로, 빈칸에는 '② 설득은 거의 모든 직업에서 나타난다'는 내용이 들어가야 한다.

어휘 politician 정치인 hire 고용하다 appeal 호소하다
virtually 거의, 사실상 lobbyist 로비스트(특정 압력 단체의 이익을 위해 입법에 영향을 줄 목적으로 정당이나 의원을 상대로 활동하는 전문가)
congress 의회 activist 활동가 persuade 설득하다
fellow 동료 citizen 시민 fertile 비옥한 estimate 추정하다
upwards 이상의 intent 의도 advent 출현, 도래
photocopy 복사하다 pentagon 국방부, 펜타곤(미국 국방부 건물)
equivalent 해당하는, 맞먹는 walk of life 직업, 사회적 계급
encounter 만나다, 마주치다 countless 수많은
billboard 광고판, 게시판 mass media 대중 매체

20 독해 추론 (빈칸 완성 - 절) 난이도 ★★☆

끊어읽기 해석

It is important to note / that for adults, / social interaction mainly occurs / through the medium of language.
유의하는 것이 중요하다 / 성인의 경우 / 사회적 상호작용은 주로 발생한다 / 언어라는 매개체를 통해

Few native-speaker adults / are willing to devote time / to interacting with someone / who does not speak the language, / with the result / that the adult foreigner will have little opportunity / to engage in meaningful and extended language exchanges.
원어민인 성인은 거의 없다 / 기꺼이 시간을 할애하려는 / 누군가와 상호작용을 하는 데 / 해당 언어를 구사하지 않는 / 그 결과 / 성인 외국인은 기

회가 거의 없게 될 것이다 / 의미 있고 확장된 언어 교환에 참여할

In contrast, / the young child is often readily accepted / by other children, / and even adults.
대조적으로 / 어린아이는 종종 쉽게 받아들여진다 / 다른 아이들에게 / 그리고 심지어 어른들에게도

For young children, / language is not as essential / to social interaction.
어린아이들에게 / 언어는 그만큼 필수적인 것은 아니다 / 사회적 상호작용에서

So-called 'parallel play', / for example, / is common / among young children.
소위 '병행 놀이'는 / 예를 들어 / 흔하다 / 어린아이들 사이에서

They can be content / just to sit in each other's company / speaking only occasionally / and / playing on their own.
그들은 만족할 수 있다 / 서로의 친구와 앉아 있는 것만으로도 / 가끔만 이야기하는 것 / 그리고 / 혼자 노는 것

Adults rarely find themselves in situations / where language does not play a crucial role / in social interaction.
성인들은 상황에 처하는 경우가 거의 없다 / 언어가 중요한 역할을 하지 않는 / 사회적 상호작용에서

해석 성인의 경우, 사회적 상호작용은 주로 언어라는 매개체를 통해 발생한다는 점에 유의하는 것이 중요하다. 해당 언어를 구사하지 않는 사람과 상호작용을 하는 데 기꺼이 시간을 할애하려는 원어민인 성인은 거의 없으며, 그 결과 성인 외국인은 의미 있고 확장된 언어 교환에 참여할 기회가 거의 없게 될 것이다. 대조적으로, 어린아이는 종종 다른 아이들, 그리고 심지어 어른들에게도 쉽게 받아들여진다. 어린아이들에게, 언어는 사회적 상호작용에서 그만큼 필수적인 것은 아니다. 예를 들어, 소위 '병행 놀이'는 어린아이들 사이에서 흔하다. 그들은 가끔만 서로의 친구와 앉아서 이야기하고 혼자 노는 것만으로도 만족할 수 있다. 성인들은 언어가 사회적 상호작용에서 중요한 역할을 하지 않는 상황에 처하는 경우가 거의 없다.

① 언어가 사회적 상호작용에서 중요한 역할을 하지 않는다
② 그들의 의견은 그들의 동료들에게 쉽게 받아들여진다
③ 그들은 다른 언어를 말하도록 요청받는다
④ 의사소통 능력이 매우 요구된다

해설 지문 처음에서 성인의 경우 사회적 상호작용은 주로 언어라는 매개체를 통해 발생하기 때문에 해당 언어를 구사하지 않는 사람과 상호작용을 하는 데 기꺼이 시간을 할애하려는 원어민인 성인은 거의 없다고 했으므로, 빈칸에는 성인들은 '① 언어가 사회적 상호작용에서 중요한 역할을 하지 않는' 상황에 처하는 경우가 거의 없다는 내용이 들어가야 한다.

어휘 note 유의하다 medium 매개체 devote 할애하다, 헌신하다
engage in ~에 참여하다 meaningful 의미 있는
extended 확장된 readily 쉽게
parallel play 병행 놀이(유아가 같은 종류의 장난감을 사용해 나란히 앉아 독립적으로 노는 것) content 만족하는
occasionally 가끔, 때때로

정답
p.38

01	② 어휘 - 어휘 & 표현	11	② 어휘 - 생활영어
02	② 어휘 - 어휘 & 표현	12	③ 어휘 - 생활영어
03	④ 어휘 - 어휘 & 표현	13	③ 독해 - 전체내용 파악
04	① 어휘 - 어휘 & 표현	14	① 독해 - 전체내용 파악
05	③ 문법 - 수 일치	15	② 독해 - 전체내용 파악
06	④ 문법 - 동사의 종류	16	② 독해 - 추론
07	② 문법 - 전치사	17	③ 독해 - 논리적 흐름 파악
08	④ 독해 - 세부내용 파악	18	③ 독해 - 논리적 흐름 파악
09	④ 독해 - 세부내용 파악	19	③ 독해 - 논리적 흐름 파악
10	① 어휘 - 생활영어	20	① 독해 - 추론

취약영역 분석표

영역	세부 유형	문항 수	소계
어휘	어휘&표현	4	/7
	생활영어	3	
문법	수 일치	1	/3
	동사의 종류	1	
	전치사	1	
독해	전체내용 파악	3	/10
	세부내용 파악	2	
	추론	2	
	논리적 흐름 파악	3	
	총계		/20

· 자신이 취약한 영역은 '공무원 영어, 이렇게 출제된다!'(문제집 p.8)를 통해 다시 한번 확인하고 학습하시기 바랍니다.

---

01 어휘 어휘&표현 intimate = close 난이도 ★☆☆

해석 Jane은 화려한 결혼식보다는 작은 결혼식을 하고 싶었다. 그래서, 그녀는 맛있는 음식을 먹고 즐거운 시간을 보내기 위해 그녀의 가족과 몇몇 친한 친구들을 초대하기로 계획했다.

① 참견하기 좋아하는
② 친한
③ 사교적인
④ 사려 깊은

어휘 fancy 화려한 intimate 친한 nosy 참견하기 좋아하는
outgoing 사교적인, 외향적인 considerate 사려 깊은

👍 이것도 알면 합격!

intimate(친한)의 유의어
= personal, dearest, beloved, affectionate

02 어휘 어휘&표현 incessant = constant 난이도 ★★☆

해석 건강상의 이익과 더 낮은 가격으로 인한 끊임없는 대중의 호기심과 소비자의 수요가 기능성 식품에 대한 관심을 높였다.

① 급속한
② 끊임없는
③ 중요한
④ 간헐적인

어휘 incessant 끊임없는 curiosity 호기심 consumer 소비자
demand 수요 functional 기능성의
intermittent 간헐적인

👍 이것도 알면 합격!

incessant(끊임없는)의 유의어
= unceasing, continuous, perpetual, persistent

03 어휘 어휘&표현 hold off = suspend 난이도 ★★☆

해석 전세계적 유행병 때문에, 회사는 근로자들에게 다양한 훈련 프로그램을 제공하려는 계획을 미뤄야만 했다.

① 상세히 말하다
② 발표하다
③ 변경하다
④ 연기하다

어휘 pandemic 전세계적 유행병 hold off 미루다
elaborate 상세히 말하다 release 발표하다 modify 변경하다
suspend 연기하다

👍 이것도 알면 합격!

hold off(미루다)와 유사한 의미의 표현
= delay, postpone, put off, defer

04 어휘 어휘&표현 abide by = accept 난이도 ★★☆

해석 신임 지역 주지사는 수감자를 석방하라는 고등법원의 결정을 따르겠다고 말했다.

① 받아들이다
② 발표하다
③ 연기하다
④ 공표하다

어휘 abide by (법률·합의 등을) 따르다 release 석방하다
accept 받아들이다, 수락하다 postpone 연기하다
announce 공표하다

👍 이것도 알면 **합격!**

abide by(따르다)와 유사한 의미의 표현
= follow, observe, adhere to, comply with, conform to

---

05 문법 수 일치 난이도 ★★☆

해석 이식 기술의 발전이 말기의 장기 질환을 가진 개인의 수명을 연장하는 것을 가능하게 한 반면, 일단 심장이나 신장이 성공적으로 교체되면 끝나는 한정된 사건으로서의 장기 이식의 생물 의학적 관점은 장기를 받는 경험을 보다 정확하게 표현하는 복잡하고 역동적인 과정을 감춘다고 주장된다.

해설 ③ 주어와 동사의 수 일치 주어 자리에 단수 명사 the biomedical view가 왔으므로 복수 동사 conceal을 단수 동사 conceals로 고쳐야 한다. 참고로, 주어와 동사 사이의 수식어 거품(of ~ replaced)은 동사의 수 결정에 영향을 주지 않는다.

오답
분석
① 5형식 동사 | 목적어 자리 동사 make(made)는 5형식 동사로 쓰일 때 'make(made) + 목적어 + 목적격 보어(possible)' 형태를 취하며 '~을 -하게 만들다'라는 의미를 나타내는데, to 부정사구 목적어가 목적격 보어와 함께 오면 진짜 목적어(to 부정사구)를 목적격 보어 뒤로 보내고 목적어가 있던 자리에 가짜 목적어 it을 써서 '가짜 목적어 it + 목적격 보어(possible) + 진짜 목적어(to extend ~ disease)'의 형태가 되어야 하므로 목적어 자리에 it이 올바르게 쓰였다.
② 명사절 접속사 1: that | 가짜 주어 구문 완전한 절(the biomedical ~ receiving an organ)을 이끌며 동사 argue의 목적어 자리에 올 수 있는 명사절 접속사 that이 올바르게 쓰였다. 또한 that절(that ~ an organ)과 같이 긴 주어가 오면 진짜 주어인 that절을 맨 뒤로 보내고 가주어 it이 주어 자리에 대신해서 쓰이므로 진짜 주어 자리에 that절을 이끄는 that이 올바르게 쓰였다.
③ 부사 자리 동사(represent)를 앞에서 수식할 수 있는 것은 부사이므로 부사 accurately가 올바르게 쓰였다.

어휘 advance 발전 transplant 이식 extend 연장하다
end-stage 말기의 organ 장기, 기관 biomedical 생물 의학적인
bounded 한정된, 한계가 있는 kidney 신장 conceal 감추다
dynamic 역동적인 accurately 정확하게
represent 표현하다, 나타내다

👍 이것도 알면 **합격!**

동명사구·to 부정사구·명사절 주어에는 단수 동사가 와야 한다.

ex Jogging every morning (is, ~~are~~) good for your health.
동명사구 주어   단수 동사
매일 아침에 조깅을 하는 것은 건강에 좋다.

ex To learn a new language (requires, ~~require~~) dedication.
to 부정사구 주어   단수 동사
새로운 언어를 배우는 것은 헌신을 필요로 한다.

ex What you did (was, ~~were~~) unexpected.
명사절 주어   단수 동사
네가 한 일은 예상치 못한 것이었다.

---

06 문법 동사의 종류 난이도 ★★☆

해석 ① 모든 과제가 제시간에 제출될 것으로 기대된다.
② 나는 눈을 감자마자 그녀를 생각하기 시작했다.
③ 그 중개인은 그녀가 즉시 그 주식을 사야 한다고 추천했다.
④ 연필 끝이 머리에 박힌 여자는 마침내 그것을 제거했다.

해설 ④ 5형식 동사 사역동사 have(had)의 목적어(it)와 목적격 보어가 '그것이(연필 끝이) 제거되다'라는 의미의 수동 관계이므로 동사원형 remove를 과거분사 removed로 고쳐야 한다.

오답
분석
① 5형식 동사의 수동태 | to 부정사의 형태 to 부정사를 목적격 보어로 취하는 5형식 동사(expect)가 수동태가 되면, to 부정사는 수동태 동사(are expected) 뒤에 그대로 남아야 하고, to 부정사(to be turned in) 뒤에 목적어가 없고 to 부정사가 가리키는 명사(All assignments)와 to 부정사가 '과제가 제출되다'라는 의미의 수동 관계이므로 are expected 뒤에 to 부정사의 수동형 to be turned in이 올바르게 쓰였다.
② 도치 구문: 부사구 도치 1 부정을 나타내는 부사(Hardly)가 강조되어 문장 맨 앞에 나오면 주어와 조동사가 도치되어 '조동사 + 주어 + 동사'의 어순이 되어야 하므로 Hardly had I closed가 올바르게 쓰였다.
③ 조동사 should의 생략 주절에 제안을 나타내는 동사 recommend가 오면 종속절에는 '(should +) 동사원형'이 와야 하므로, 종속절에 동사원형 buy가 올바르게 쓰였다.

어휘 turn in ~을 제출하다 on time 제시간에 broker 중개인
stock 주식 immediately 즉시

👍 이것도 알면 **합격!**

제안·의무·요청·주장을 나타내는 동사·형용사가 주절에 나오면, 종속절에는 'should + 동사원형'이 와야 하며, 이때 should는 생략할 수 있다.

	request 요청하다	command 명령하다
동사	order 명령하다	insist 주장하다
	desire 요구하다	propose 제안하다
형용사	necessary 필수적인	imperative 필수적인
	essential 필수적인	important 중요한

---

07 문법 전치사 난이도 ★★★

해설 ② 전치사 2: 시점 '이번 달 말까지 끝내야 한다'라는 정해진 시점(이번 달 말)까지 완료되는 상황을 나타내고 있으므로, '특정 시점까지 어떤 행동이나 상황이 계속되는 것'을 의미하는 전치사 until을 '정해진 시점까지 어떤 행동이나 상황이 완료되는 것'을 의미하는 전치사 by(~까지)로 고쳐야 한다.

오답
분석
① 원급 '세 배이다'는 '배수사 + as + 원급 + as'의 형태로 나타낼 수 있으므로 three times as old as가 올바르게 쓰였다.
③ 현재 시제 '이틀에 한 번 머리를 감는다'라는 반복되는 동작을 표현하고 있으므로 현재 시제 washes가 올바르게 쓰였다. 참고로, every other day는 '이틀에 한 번'이라는 의미이다.
④ 조동사 관련 표현 조동사처럼 쓰이는 표현 had better(~하는 게 좋겠다) 뒤에는 동사원형이 와야 하므로 동사원형 take가 올바르게 쓰였다.

어휘 every other day 이틀에 한 번 in case ~할 경우에 대비해서

08 독해 세부내용 파악 (내용 불일치 파악) 난이도 ★☆☆

끊어읽기 해석

Are you getting enough choline?
당신은 콜린을 충분히 섭취하고 있는가?

Chances are, / this nutrient isn't even on your radar.
아마도, / 이 영양소는 당신의 관심사에도 없을 것이다

It's time / choline gets the attention / it deserves.
이제는 ~할 때이다 / 콜린이 주목을 받을 / 마땅히 받아야 할

A shocking 90 percent of Americans / aren't getting enough choline, / according to a recent study.
충격적인 90퍼센트의 미국인들이 / 콜린을 충분히 섭취하지 않고 있다 / 최근의 연구에 따르면

Choline is essential to health / at all ages and stages, / and is especially critical / for brain development.
콜린은 건강에 필수적이다 / 모든 연령과 단계에서 / 그리고 특히 중요하다 / 뇌 발달에

Why aren't we getting enough?
우리는 왜 충분히 섭취하지 않는가

Choline is found / in many different foods / but in small amounts.
콜린은 발견된다 / 많은 다양한 음식에서 / 하지만 소량이다

Plus, / the foods that are rich in choline / aren't the most popular: / think liver, egg yolks and lima beans.
게다가, / 콜린이 풍부한 음식은 / 가장 인기 있는 것이 아니다 / 간, 달걀노른자, 그리고 리마콩을 생각해 보라

Taylor Wallace, who worked on a recent analysis of choline intake in the United States, says, / "There isn't enough awareness about choline / even among health-care professionals / because our government hasn't reviewed the data / or set policies around choline / since the late '90s."
미국에서의 콜린 섭취에 대한 최근의 분석을 진행한 Taylor Wallace는 말한다 / "콜린에 대한 인식이 충분하지 않다 / 심지어 의료 전문가들 사이에서도 / 우리 정부가 자료를 검토하지 않았기 때문에 / 또는 콜린에 대한 정책을 수립하지 않거나 / 90년대 후반 이후로"

해석　당신은 콜린을 충분히 섭취하고 있는가? 아마도, 이 영양소는 당신의 관심사에도 없을 것이다. 이제는 콜린이 마땅히 받아야 할 주목을 받을 때이다. 최근의 연구에 따르면, 충격적인 90퍼센트의 미국인들이 콜린을 충분히 섭취하지 않고 있다. 콜린은 모든 연령과 단계에서 건강에 필수적이며, 특히 뇌 발달에 중요하다. 우리는 왜 충분히 섭취하지 않는가? 콜린은 많은 다양한 음식에서 발견되지만, 소량이다. 게다가, 콜린이 풍부한 음식은 가장 인기 있는 것이 아니다. 간, 달걀노른자, 그리고 리마콩을 생각해 보라. 미국에서의 콜린 섭취에 대한 최근의 분석을 진행한 Taylor Wallace는 "우리 정부가 90년대 후반 이후로 콜린에 대한 자료를 검토하거나 정책을 수립하지 않았기 때문에 심지어 의료 전문가들 사이에서도 콜린에 대한 인식이 충분하지 않다"고 말한다.

① 대다수의 미국인들은 콜린을 충분히 섭취하지 못하고 있다.
② 콜린은 뇌 발달에 필요한 필수적인 영양소이다.
③ 간과 리마콩과 같은 음식은 콜린의 좋은 공급원이다.

④ 미국에서는 90년대 후반부터 콜린의 중요성이 강조되어 왔다.

해설　지문 마지막에서 Taylor Wallace는 미국 정부가 90년대 후반 이후로 콜린에 대한 자료를 검토하거나 정책을 수립하지 않았기 때문에 심지어 의료 전문가들 사이에서도 콜린에 대한 인식이 충분하지 않다고 말한다고 했으므로 '④ 미국에서는 90년대 후반부터 콜린의 중요성이 강조되어 왔다'는 지문의 내용과 일치하지 않는다.

어휘　choline 콜린(비타민 B 복합체의 하나)　nutrient 영양소
radar 관심사, 탐지기　essential 필수적인　critical 중요한
liver 간　yolk 노른자　analysis 분석　intake 섭취
awareness 인식　policy 정책　majority 대다수　stress 강조하다

09 독해 세부내용 파악 (내용 일치 파악) 난이도 ★☆☆

끊어읽기 해석

①Around 1700 / there were, / by some accounts, / more than 2,000 London coffeehouses, / occupying more premises / and paying more rent / than any other trade.
약 1700년경에 / ~가 있었다 / 일부 기록에 따르면, / 2,000개 이상의 런던 커피하우스가 / 더 많은 부지를 차지하는 / 그리고 더 많은 임대료를 지불하는 / 다른 어떤 업종보다도

②They came to be known / as penny universities, / because / for that price / one could purchase a cup of coffee / and sit for hours / listening to extraordinary conversations.
그것들은 알려지게 되었다 / 페니 대학으로 / 왜냐하면 / 그 가격에 / 커피 한 잔을 구매할 수 있었다 / 그리고 몇 시간 동안 앉아있을 수 있었다 / 엄청난 대화를 들으면서

Each coffeehouse / specialized in a different type of clientele.
각 커피하우스는 / 서로 다른 유형의 고객을 전문으로 했다

In one, / physicians could be consulted.
한 곳에서는, / 의사와 상담할 수 있었다

③Others served / Protestants, Puritans, Catholics, Jews, literati, merchants, traders, Whigs, Tories, army officers, actors, lawyers, or clergy.
다른 곳에서는 주문을 받았다 / 신교도, 청교도, 가톨릭교도, 유대인, 지식인, 상인, 무역업자, 휘그당원, 토리당원, 육군 장교, 배우, 법조인, 또는 성직자의

④The coffeehouses provided / England's first egalitarian meeting place, / where a man chatted with his tablemates / whether he knew them or not.
그 커피하우스는 제공했다 / 영국 최초의 평등주의적 만남의 장소를 / 그곳에서 함께 식사하는 사람들과 대화를 나누었다 / 그들을 알든 모르든

해석　1700년경에, 일부 기록에 따르면, 2,000개 이상의 런던 커피하우스가 있었으며, 다른 어떤 업종보다도 더 많은 부지를 차지하고 더 많은 임대료를 지불했다. 그것들은 페니 대학으로 알려지게 되었는데, 그 가격에 커피 한잔을 구매하고 엄청난 대화를 들으면서 몇 시간 동안 앉아있을 수 있었기 때문이다. 각 커피하우스는 서로 다른 유형의 고객을 전문으로 했다. 한 곳에서는 의사와 상담할 수 있었다. 다른 곳에서는 신교도, 청교도, 가톨릭교도, 유대인, 지식인, 상인, 무역업자, 휘그당원, 토리당원, 육군 장교, 배우, 법조인, 또는 성직자의 주문을 받았다. 그 커피하우스는 영국 최초의 평등주의적 만남의 장소를 제공했으며, 그곳에서 함께 식사하는 사람들과 알든 모르든 대화를 나눴다.

① 커피하우스의 수는 다른 어떤 사업의 수보다도 적었다.
② 고객들은 커피하우스에서 한 시간 이상 머무를 수 없었다.
③ 종교인들은 대화를 나누기 위해 커피하우스에서 만나지 않았다.
④ 커피하우스에서는 심지어 알지 못하는 사람들과도 대화를 나눌 수 있었다.

해설 지문 마지막에서 커피하우스에서 함께 식사하는 사람들과 알든
모르든 대화를 나눴다고 했으므로, '④ 커피하우스에서는 심지어
알지 못하는 사람들과도 대화를 나눌 수 있었다'는 지문의 내용과
일치한다.

오답 ① 첫 번째 문장에서 커피하우스는 다른 어떤 업종보다도 더 많은
분석 부지를 차지하고 더 많은 임대료를 지불했다고 했으므로 지문
의 내용과 일치하지 않는다.
② 두 번째 문장에서 커피하우스는 커피 한잔을 구매하고 엄청난
대화를 듣는 동안 몇 시간 동안 앉아있을 수 있었다고 했으므
로 지문의 내용과 일치하지 않는다.
③ 다섯 번째 문장에서 커피하우스에서는 신교도, 청교도, 가톨릭
교도, 유대인 등의 사람들에게 주문을 받았다고 했으므로 지문
의 내용과 일치하지 않는다.

어휘 account 기록, 설명 occupy 차지하다 premises 부지
rent 임대료 trade 업종, 직업 extraordinary 엄청난, 특별한
clientele 고객 physician 의사 consult 상담하다
serve 주문을 받다, 시중들다 Protestant 신교도 Puritan 청교도
literati 지식인 merchant 상인 trader 무역업자, 상인
Whig 휘그당(원) Tory 토리당(원) army officer 육군 장교
clergy 성직자 egalitarian 평등주의적인

---

10 어휘 생활영어 I don't buy it.   난이도 ★☆☆

해석
A: 저는 어제 약국에서 이 새로운 피부 크림을 샀어요. 이것이
주름을 모두 없애 주고 피부를 훨씬 젊어 보이게 해준다고
해요.
B: 저는 그걸 믿지 않아요.
A: 왜 안 믿어요? 저는 몇몇 블로그에서 이 크림이 정말 효과
가 있다는 것을 읽었어요.
B: 저는 그 크림이 당신의 피부에 좋을 것이라고 생각하지만,
크림을 사용해서 주름을 없애거나 마법처럼 어려 보이는 것
은 가능하다고 생각하지 않아요.
A: 당신은 너무 비관적이에요.
B: 아니요, 저는 그냥 현실적인 거예요. 제 생각엔 당신이 잘 속
아 넘어가는 것 같아요.

① 저는 그걸 믿지 않아요.
② 그것은 너무 비싸요.
③ 저는 당신을 도와드릴 수 없어요.
④ 믿기 힘들겠지만, 그것은 사실이에요.

해설 새로 산 피부 크림이 주름을 모두 없애 주고 피부를 훨씬 젊어 보이
게 해준다고 말하는 A에게 B가 대답하고, 빈칸 뒤에서 A가
Why don't you believe it?(왜 안 믿어요?)이라고 말하고 있으
므로, 빈칸에는 '① 저는 그걸 믿지 않아요(I don't buy it)'가 오
는 것이 자연스럽다.

어휘 drugstore 약국 wrinkle 주름 assume 생각하다, 추정하다
pessimistic 비관적인 gullible 잘 속아 넘어가는 pricey 비싼

👍 이것도 알면 **합격!**
약국에서 사용할 수 있는 다양한 표현을 알아두자.
· I'm looking for something to relieve a headache.
  두통을 완화시킬 무언가를 찾고 있어요.
· What are the possible side effects of this medication?
  이 약의 가능한 부작용은 무엇인가요?
· What is the recommended dosage for this medication?
  이 약의 권장 섭취량은 어떻게 되나요?

---

11 어휘 생활영어 A guided tour to the river park. It takes all afternoon.   난이도 ★☆☆

해석
A: 저는 시내 관광을 하고 싶어요. 제가 어디를 가야 한다고 생
각하나요?
B: 국립 미술관에 방문하는 것을 강력히 추천해요.
A: 오, 그거 좋은 생각이에요. 제가 또 무엇을 봐야 할까요?
B: 강변 공원으로 가는 안내 투어요. 오후 내내 걸릴 거예요.
A: 그럴 시간은 없어요. 저는 3시에 고객을 만나야 해요.
B: 오, 그렇군요. 그렇다면 국립 공원을 방문해 보는 건 어때요?
A: 좋은 생각이에요. 감사합니다!

① 이것은 당신의 고객이 필요한 지도예요. 여기 있어요.
② 강변 공원으로 가는 안내 투어요. 오후 내내 걸릴 거예요.
③ 당신은 가능한 한 빨리 그것을 봐야 해요.
④ 퇴실 시간은 세시입니다.

해설 시내 관광을 할 때 또 무엇을 봐야 하는지 묻는 A의 말에 B가 대
답하고, 빈칸 뒤에서 A가 I don't have time for that(그럴 시간
은 없어요)이라고 말하고 있으므로, 빈칸에는 '② 강변 공원으로
가는 안내 투어요. 오후 내내 걸릴 거예요(A guided tour to the
river park. It takes all afternoon)'가 오는 것이 자연스럽다.

어휘 sightseeing 관광 downtown 시내 national 국립의

👍 이것도 알면 **합격!**
관광지에서 사용할 수 있는 다양한 표현을 알아두자.
· Where is the nearest tourist information center?
  가장 가까운 관광 안내 센터는 어디에 있나요?
· What are the opening hours of this museum?
  이 박물관의 운영 시간은 어떻게 되나요?
· Are there any souvenir shops nearby?
  근처에 기념품 가게가 있나요?

---

12 어휘 생활영어 It was a piece of cake.   난이도 ★☆☆

해석 ① A: 그는 마침내 흥행 영화에 출연했군요!
B: 음, 그는 이제 성공했네요.
② A: 이제 좀 피곤해지는군요.
B: 오늘은 이만합시다.
③ A: 아이들은 생일파티에 갈 거예요.
B: 그럼, 그것은 식은 죽 먹기였네요.
④ A: 그가 어제 왜 집에 일찍 갔는지 궁금하네요.
B: 아마 그는 몸이 좀 안 좋았던 것 같아요.

해설 ③번에서 A는 아이들이 생일파티에 갈 거라고 말하고 있으므로,
그것이 식은 죽 먹기였다고 말하는 B의 대답 So, it was a piece
of cake(그럼, 그것은 식은 죽 먹기였네요)은 어울리지 않는다. 따
라서 ③번이 정답이다.

어휘 hit movie 흥행 영화 a piece of cake 식은 죽 먹기

👍 이것도 알면 **합격!**
파티에서 사용할 수 있는 다양한 표현을 알아두자.
· What a cool party theme!
  파티 테마가 정말 멋지네요!
· You did a great job with the decorations!
  장식을 정말 잘했어요!
· Thank you all for coming and making this party special!
  모두 파티에 참석해 주시고 특별한 시간을 만들어 주셔서 감사해요!

끊어읽기 해석

> The feeling of being loved / and the biological response it stimulates / is triggered by nonverbal cues: / the tone in a voice, the expression on a face, or the touch that feels just right.
> 사랑을 받고 있다는 느낌은 / 그리고 그것이 촉진시키는 생물학적 반응은 / 비언어적인 신호에 의해 촉발된다 / 바로 목소리의 어조, 얼굴의 표정, 또는 딱 알맞은 느낌의 접촉이다
>
> Nonverbal cues—rather than spoken words— / make us feel / that the person we are with is / interested in, understands, and values us.
> 비언어적인 신호는 구어적인 말보다 / 우리가 느끼게 한다 / 우리와 함께 있는 사람이 / 우리에게 관심을 갖고, 이해하고, 중시하고 있다고
>
> When we're with them, / we feel safe.
> 우리가 그들과 함께 있을 때, / 우리는 안전하다고 느낀다
>
> We even see / the power of nonverbal cues / in the wild.
> 우리는 심지어 본다 / 비언어적인 신호의 힘을 / 야생에서
>
> After evading the chase of predators, / animals often nuzzle each other / as a means of stress relief.
> 포식자의 추적을 피한 후에, / 동물들은 종종 서로 코를 비빈다 / 스트레스 해소의 수단으로
>
> This bodily contact / provides / reassurance of safety / and relieves stress.
> 이 신체상의 접촉은 / 제공한다 / 안전에 대한 확신을 / 그리고 스트레스를 완화한다

해석　사랑을 받고 있다는 느낌과 그것이 촉진시키는 생물학적 반응은 비언어적인 신호에 의해 촉발된다. 바로 목소리의 어조, 얼굴의 표정, 또는 딱 알맞은 느낌의 접촉이다. 비언어적인 신호는 구어적인 말보다 우리가 함께 있는 사람이 우리에게 관심을 갖고, 이해하고, 중시하고 있다는 것을 느끼게 한다. 우리가 그들과 함께 있을 때, 우리는 안전하다고 느낀다. 우리는 심지어 야생에서 비언어적인 신호의 힘을 본다. 포식자의 추적을 피한 후에, 동물들은 종종 스트레스 해소의 수단으로 서로 코를 비빈다. 이 신체상의 접촉은 안전에 대한 확신을 제공하고 스트레스를 완화한다.

① 야생 동물들은 어떻게 생각하고 느끼는가?
② 효과적으로 의사소통하는 것은 성공의 비결이다
③ 비언어적 의사소통은 말보다 더 중요하다
④ 언어적 단서: 감정을 표현하는 주요 도구

해설　지문 전반에 걸쳐 비언어적인 신호는 사랑을 받고 있다는 느낌과 그것이 촉진시키는 생물학적 반응을 촉발하며, 구어적인 말보다 우리가 함께 있는 사람이 우리에게 관심을 갖고, 이해하고, 중시하고 있다는 것을 느끼게 한다고 설명하고 있다. 따라서 '③ 비언어적 의사소통은 말보다 더 중요하다'가 이 글의 제목이다.

어휘　**biological** 생물학적인　**response** 반응
stimulate 촉진시키다, 자극하다　**trigger** 촉발하다
nonverbal 비언어적인　**cue** 신호　**tone** 어조　**evade** 피하다
nuzzle 코를 비비다　**reassurance** 확신
primary 주요한

끊어읽기 해석

> There are times, / like holidays and birthdays, / when toys and gifts accumulate / in a child's life.
> ~ 때가 있다 / 명절이나 생일처럼 / 장난감과 선물이 쌓이는 / 아이의 삶에

> You can use these times / to teach a healthy nondependency / on things.
> 당신은 이러한 시간을 사용할 수 있다 / 건강한 비의존성을 가르치기 위해 / 물건에 대한
>
> Don't surround your child with toys.
> 당신의 아이를 장난감으로 둘러싸지 마라
>
> Instead, / arrange them in baskets, / have one basket out / at a time, / and rotate baskets occasionally.
> 대신, / 그것들을 바구니에 정리하라 / 한 개의 바구니만 꺼내 놓아라 / 한 번에 / 그리고 이따금 바구니들을 교대하라
>
> If a cherished object is put away for a time, / bringing it out / creates a delightful remembering / and freshness of outlook.
> 소중히 여기는 물건이 잠시 동안 치워지면, / 그것을 꺼내는 것은 / 즐거운 기억을 만들어 낸다 / 그리고 신선한 시각을
>
> Suppose your child asks for a toy / that has been put away for a while.
> 당신의 아이가 장난감을 요구한다고 가정해 보자 / 잠시 동안 치워져 있던
>
> You can direct attention / toward an object or experience / that is already in the environment.
> 당신은 주의를 유도할 수 있다 / 물건이나 경험으로 / 이미 그 환경에 있는
>
> If you lose or break a possession, / try to model a good attitude / ("I appreciated it while I had it!") / so that your child can begin to develop / an attitude of nonattachment.
> 당신이 소유물을 잃어버리거나 망가뜨린다면, / 좋은 태도를 모범으로 보여라 / ("내가 그것을 가지고 있는 동안 고맙게 생각했어!") / 당신의 아이가 발달시키기 시작할 수 있도록 / 애착을 갖지 않는 태도를
>
> If a toy of hers is broken or lost, / help her to say, / "I had fun with that."
> 만약 그녀의 장난감이 망가지거나 없어지면, / 그녀가 말할 수 있도록 도와주어라 / "그것과 함께 재미있었어."라고

해석　명절이나 생일처럼 아이의 삶에 장난감과 선물이 쌓이는 때가 있다. 당신은 이러한 시간을 물건에 대한 건강한 비의존성을 가르치기 위해 사용할 수 있다. 당신의 아이를 장난감으로 둘러싸지 마라. 대신, 그것들을 바구니에 정리하고, 한 번에 한 개의 바구니만 꺼내 놓고, 이따금 바구니들을 교대하라. 소중히 여기는 물건이 잠시 동안 치워지면, 그것을 꺼내는 것은 즐거운 기억과 신선한 시각을 만들어 낸다. 당신의 아이가 잠시 동안 치워져 있던 장난감을 요구한다고 가정해 보자. 당신은 이미 그 환경에 있는 물건이나 경험으로 주의를 유도할 수 있다. 당신이 소유물을 잃어버리거나 망가뜨린다면, 당신의 아이가 애착을 갖지 않는 태도를 발달시키기 시작할 수 있도록 좋은 태도를 ("내가 그것을 가지고 있는 동안 고맙게 생각했어!") 모범으로 보여라. 만약 그녀의 장난감이 망가지거나 없어지면, 그녀가 "그것과 함께 재미있었어."라고 말할 수 있도록 도와주어라.

① 소유물에 대한 건강한 태도 구축하기
② 다른 사람들과 장난감을 공유하는 것의 가치 배우기
③ 장난감을 질서정연하게 정리하는 법 가르치기
④ 바람직하지 않은 방식으로 행동하는 것에 대한 책임 받아들이기

해설　지문 처음에서 아이의 삶에 장난감과 선물이 쌓이는 시간을 물건에 대한 건강한 비의존성을 가르치기 위해 사용할 수 있다고 설명하고, 지문 전반에 걸쳐 바구니에 장난감을 정리하면서 그 소중히 여기는 물건을 잠시 치워 두는 방법을 사용하거나, 소유물을 잃어버리거나 망가뜨렸을 때 아이가 애착을 갖지 않는 태도를 발달시키기 시작할 수 있도록 소유물에 대한 좋은 태도를 모범으로 보이는 것에 대해 설명하고 있다. 따라서 '① 소유물에 대한 건강한 태도 구축하기'가 이 글의 주제이다.

어휘　**accumulate** 쌓이다, 축적하다　**nondependency** 비의존성

surround 둘러싸다 **arrange** 정리하다, 배열하다 **basket** 바구니
rotate 교대하다 **occasionally** 이따금, 때때로
cherish 소중히 여기다 **delightful** 즐거운 **outlook** 시각
possession 소유물 **orderly** 질서정연한 **responsibility** 책임
undesirable 바람직하지 않은

15 독해 전체내용 파악 (요지 파악) 난이도 ★★☆

끊어읽기 해석

> Many parents / have been misguided / by the "self-esteem movement," / which has told them / that the way to build their children's self-esteem / is to tell them / how good they are at things.
> 많은 부모들은 / 잘못된 방향으로 이끌어져 왔다 / '자존감 운동'에 의해 / 이것은 그들에게 말해왔다 / 아이들의 자존감을 쌓는 방법은 / 그들에게 알려주는 것이라고 / 그들이 얼마나 잘하는지를
>
> Unfortunately, / trying to convince your children / of their competence / will likely fail / because life has a way of telling them unequivocally / how capable or incapable they really are / through success and failure.
> 불행하게도, / 당신의 아이들에게 확신시키려 시도하는 것은 / 그들의 능력을 / 실패할 가능성이 높다 / 인생은 그들에게 명확하게 알려주는 방법이 있기 때문에 / 그들이 실제로 얼마나 유능한지 또는 무능한지를 / 성공과 실패를 통해
>
> Research has shown / that how you praise your children / has a powerful influence on their development.
> 연구는 보여주었다 / 당신이 아이들을 칭찬하는 방법은 / 그들의 발달에 강력한 영향을 미친다는 것을
>
> Some researchers found / that children who were praised for their intelligence, / as compared to their effort, / became overly focused on results.
> 일부 연구원들은 발견했다 / 지능에 대해 칭찬받은 아이들은 / 그들의 노력에 비교하여 / 결과에 과도하게 집중하게 되었다는 것을
>
> Following a failure, / these same children / persisted less, / showed less enjoyment, / attributed their failure to a lack of ability, / and performed poorly in future achievement efforts.
> 실패 이후에, / 이 동일한 아이들은 / 덜 지속했고, / 즐거움을 덜 보였고, / 그들의 실패를 능력 부족에 기인했다 / 그리고 미래의 성취 노력에서 저조한 성과를 거두었다
>
> Praising children for intelligence / made them fear difficulty / because they began to equate failure with stupidity.
> 아이들의 지능을 칭찬하는 것은 / 그들이 어려움을 두려워하게 만들었다 / 그들이 실패를 어리석음과 동일시하기 시작했기 때문에

해석 많은 부모들은 '자존감 운동'에 의해 잘못된 방향으로 이끌어져 왔는데, 이 운동은 그들에게 아이들의 자존감을 쌓는 방법은 그들이 얼마나 잘하는지 알려주는 것이라고 말해왔다. 불행하게도, 인생은 성공과 실패를 통해 그들이(아이들이) 실제로 얼마나 유능한지 혹은 무능한지를 명확하게 알려주는 방법이 있기 때문에 당신의 아이들에게 그들의 능력을 확신시키려고 시도하는 것은 실패할 가능성이 높다. 연구는 당신이 아이들을 칭찬하는 방법이 그들의 발달에 강력한 영향을 미친다는 것을 보여주었다. 일부 연구원들은 노력에 비교하여 지능에 대해 칭찬받은 아이들은 결과에 과도하게 집중하게 되었다는 것을 발견했다. 실패 이후에, 이 동일한 아이들은 덜 지속했고, 즐거움을 덜 보였으며, 그들의 실패를 능력 부족에 기인했고, 미래의 성취 노력에서 저조한 성과를 거두었다. 아이들의 지능을 칭찬하는 것은 그들이 실패를 어리석음과 동일시하기 시작했기 때문에 그들이 어려움을 두려워하게 만들었다.

① 잦은 칭찬은 아이들의 자존감을 높여준다.
② 지능에 대한 칭찬은 부정적인 효과를 가져온다.
③ 아이는 성공을 통해 실패에 대한 두려움을 극복해야 한다.
④ 부모는 과정보다 결과에 집중해야 한다.

해설 지문 처음에서 많은 부모들이 아이들에게 그들이 얼마나 잘하는지를 알려주는 방법인 '자존감 운동'에 의해 잘못된 방향으로 이끌어져 왔다고 하고, 지문 중간에서 아이들을 칭찬하는 방법이 그들의 발달에 강력한 영향을 미친다고 설명하고 있다. 또한, 일부 연구원들이 노력에 비교하여 지능에 대해 칭찬받은 아이들은 결과에 과도하게 집중하게 되었다는 것을 발견했고, 아이들의 지능을 칭찬하는 것은 그들이 어려움을 두려워하게 만들었다고 설명하고 있으므로, '② 지능에 대한 칭찬은 부정적인 효과를 가져온다'가 이 글의 요지이다.

어휘 **misguide** 잘못된 방향으로 이끌다 **self-esteem** 자존감 **competence** 능력 **unequivocally** 명확하게 **capable** 유능한 **incapable** 무능한 **praise** 칭찬하다 **intelligence** 지능 **persist** 지속하다 **attribute** 기인하다 **achievement** 성취 **equate** 동일시하다 **stupidity** 어리석음 **compliment** 칭찬 **bring about** ~을 가져오다

16 독해 추론 (빈칸 완성 - 단어) 난이도 ★★☆

끊어읽기 해석

> In recent years, / the increased popularity / of online marketing and social media sharing / has boosted the need / for advertising standardization / for global brands.
> 최근에, / 높아진 인기는 / 온라인 마케팅과 소셜 미디어 공유의 / 필요성을 북돋웠다 / 광고 표준화의 / 글로벌 브랜드에 대한
>
> Most big marketing and advertising campaigns / include a large online presence.
> 대부분의 대규모 마케팅과 광고 캠페인은 / 대규모의 온라인상에서의 존재감을 포함한다
>
> Connected consumers / can now zip easily across borders / via the internet and social media, / making it difficult for advertisers / to roll out adapted campaigns / in a controlled, orderly fashion.
> 연결된 소비자들은 / 이제 국경을 쉽게 넘나들 수 있다 / 인터넷과 소셜 미디어를 통해 / 광고주들을 어렵게 만든다 / 적합한 캠페인을 시작하는 것을 / 통제되고 질서정연한 방식으로
>
> As a result, / most global consumer brands / coordinate their digital sites / internationally.
> 결과적으로, / 대부분의 글로벌 소비자 브랜드는 / 그들의 디지털 사이트를 동등하게 한다 / 국제적으로
>
> For example, / Coca-Cola web and social media sites around the world, / from Australia and Argentina / to France, Romania, and Russia, / are surprisingly <u>uniform</u>.
> 예를 들어, / 전 세계의 코카콜라 웹 사이트와 소셜 미디어 사이트는 / 호주와 아르헨티나부터 / 프랑스, 루마니아, 그리고 러시아에 이르기까지 / 놀랍게도 <u>똑같다</u>
>
> All feature / splashes of familiar Coke red, / iconic Coke bottle shapes, / and Coca-Cola's music and "Taste the Feeling" themes.
> 전부 특징으로 한다 / 친숙한 코카콜라 빨간색의 물방울들을, / 상징적인 콜라병 모양 / 그리고 코카콜라의 음악과 '이 맛, 이 느낌' 테마를

해설 최근에, 온라인 마케팅과 소셜 미디어 공유의 높아진 인기는 글로벌 브랜드에 대한 광고 표준화의 필요성을 북돋웠다. 대부분의 대규모 마케팅과 광고 캠페인은 대규모의 온라인상에서의 존재감을 포함한다. 연결된 소비자들은 이제 인터넷과 소셜 미디어를 통해 국경을 쉽게 넘나들 수 있고, 이는 광고주들이 적합한 캠페인을 통제되고 질서정연한 방식으로 시작하는 것을 어렵게 만든다. 결과

적으로, 대부분의 글로벌 소비자 브랜드는 그들의 디지털 사이트를 국제적으로 동등하게 한다. 예를 들어, 호주와 아르헨티나부터 프랑스, 루마니아, 그리고 러시아에 이르기까지, 전 세계의 코카콜라 웹 사이트와 소셜 미디어 사이트는 놀랍게도 똑같다. 전부 친숙한 코카콜라 빨간색의 물방울들, 상징적인 콜라병 모양, 그리고 코카콜라의 음악과 '이 맛, 이 느낌' 테마를 특징으로 한다.

① 실험의　　　　　　② 똑같은
③ 국한된　　　　　　④ 다양한

해설 지문 처음에서 최근에 온라인 마케팅과 소셜 미디어 공유의 높아진 인기는 글로벌 브랜드에 대한 광고 표준화의 필요성을 북돋았다고 했고, 지문 마지막에서 대부분의 글로벌 소비자 브랜드는 그들의 디지털 사이트를 국제적으로 동등하게 하는데, 코카콜라 웹 사이트는 전부 친숙한 코카콜라 빨간색의 물방울들, 상징적인 콜라병 모양, 그리고 코카콜라의 음악과 '이 맛, 이 느낌' 테마를 특징으로 한다고 했으므로, 빈칸에는 전 세계의 코카콜라 웹 사이트와 소셜 미디어 사이트는 놀랍게도 '② 똑같다'는 내용이 들어가야 한다.

어휘 popularity 인기　advertising 광고　standardization 표준화
online presence 온라인상에서의 존재감, 영향력
consumer 소비자　border 국경
via (특정한 사람·시스템 등을) 통해　roll out 시작하다, 출시하다
adapted 적합한, 알맞은　fashion 방식
coordinate 동등하게 하다, 조정하다　feature ~을 특징으로 하다
iconic 상징적인　experimental 실험의　uniform 똑같은
localize ~을 국한시키다

17 독해　논리적 흐름 파악 (무관한 문장 삭제)　난이도 ★★☆

끊어읽기 해석

In our monthly surveys / of 5,000 American workers and 500 U.S. employers, / a huge shift to hybrid work is / abundantly clear / for office and knowledge workers.
월간 설문조사에서 / 5,000명의 미국인 근로자와 500명의 미국인 고용주를 대상으로 실시한 / 하이브리드 근무로의 대대적인 전환은 / 매우 분명하다 / 사무실 근로자 및 지식 근로자에게

① An emerging norm / is three days a week in the office / and two at home, / cutting days on site / by 30 % or more.
최근 생겨난 표준은 / 일주일에 3일은 사무실에서 근무하는 것으로 / 그리고 이틀은 집에서 / 현장에서의 일수를 단축하는 것이다 / 30퍼센트 이상

You might think / this cutback would bring a huge drop / in the demand for office space.
당신은 생각할지도 모른다 / 이 단축이 큰 감소를 가져올 수 있다고 / 사무실 공간에 대한 수요의

② But our survey data suggests / cuts in office space / of 1 % to 2 % on average, / implying big reductions / in density not space.
하지만 우리의 설문조사 자료는 보여준다 / 사무실 공간의 감소를 / 평균 1퍼센트에서 2퍼센트의 / 큰 감소를 의미한다 / 공간이 아닌 밀도에서의

We can understand why.
우리는 그 이유를 이해할 수 있다

High density at the office is uncomfortable / and many workers dislike crowds / around their desks.
사무실의 밀도가 높은 것은 불편하다 / 그리고 많은 근로자들은 모여 있는 사람들을 싫어한다 / 그들의 책상 주위에

③ Most employees / want to work from home / on Mondays and Fridays.
대부분의 직원들은 / 집에서 근무하기를 원한다 / 월요일과 금요일에

Discomfort with density / extends to lobbies, kitchens, and especially elevators.
밀도에 대한 불편함은 / 로비, 식당, 그리고 특히 엘리베이터까지 확장된다

④ The only sure-fire way / to reduce density / is to cut days on site / without cutting square footage as much.
단 하나의 확실한 방법은 / 밀도를 줄이기 위한 / 현장에서 근무하는 날을 단축하는 것이다 / 평방 피트를 많이 줄이지 않고

Discomfort with density / is here to stay / according to our survey evidence.
밀도에 대한 불편함은 / 계속 남아 있다 / 우리의 설문조사 증거에 따르면

해석 5,000명의 미국인 근로자와 500명의 미국인 고용주를 대상으로 실시한 월간 설문조사에서 사무실 근로자 및 지식 근로자에게 하이브리드 근무로의 대대적인 전환은 매우 분명하다. ① 최근 생겨난 표준은 일주일에 3일은 사무실에서 그리고 이틀은 집에서 근무하는 것으로, 현장에서의 근무 일수를 30퍼센트 이상 단축하는 것이다. 당신은 이 단축이 사무실 공간에 대한 수요의 큰 감소를 가져올 수 있다고 생각할지도 모른다. ② 하지만 우리의 설문조사 자료는 사무실 공간의 평균 1퍼센트에서 2퍼센트의 감소를 보여주며, 이는 공간이 아닌 밀도에서의 큰 감소를 의미한다. 우리는 그 이유를 이해할 수 있다. 사무실의 밀도가 높은 것은 불편하고 많은 근로자들은 그들의 책상 주위에 모여 있는 사람들을 싫어한다. ③ 대부분의 직원들은 월요일과 금요일에 집에서 근무하기를 원한다. 밀도에 대한 불편함은 로비, 식당, 그리고 특히 엘리베이터까지 확장된다. ④ 밀도를 줄이기 위한 단 하나의 확실한 방법은 평방 피트를 많이 줄이지 않고 현장에서 근무하는 날을 단축하는 것이다. 우리의 설문조사 증거에 따르면 밀도에 대한 불편함은 계속 남아 있다.

해설 지문 처음에서 하이브리드 근무로의 전환에 대해 언급한 뒤, ①, ②, ④번에서 하이브리드 근무의 정의와 하이브리드 근무로 사무실 공간의 밀도를 감소시킬 수 있는 방법에 대해 설명하고 있으므로 모두 첫 문장과 관련이 있다. 그러나 ③번은 대부분의 직원들이 월요일과 금요일에 집에서 근무하기를 원한다는 내용으로 하이브리드 근무가 사무실 공간의 밀도를 감소시킬 수 있는 방법이라고 설명하는 지문 전반의 내용과 관련이 없다.

어휘 abundantly 매우, 많이　emerging 최근 생겨난　norm 표준
cut 단축하다, 감축하다　on site 현장의　cutback 단축
demand 수요　imply 의미하다　reduction 감소
density 밀도　extend 확장하다
sure-fire 확실한, 성공할 것이 틀림없는

18 독해　논리적 흐름 파악 (문장 삽입)　난이도 ★★☆

끊어읽기 해석

They installed video cameras / at places known for illegal crossings, / and put live video feeds from the cameras / on a Web site.
그들은 비디오 카메라를 설치했다 / 불법 횡단로로 알려진 장소에 / 그리고 카메라의 생중계 영상 피드를 올렸다 / 웹 사이트에

Immigration reform is a political minefield.
이민 개혁은 정치적 지뢰밭이다

(①) About the only aspect of immigration policy / that commands broad political support / is the resolve to secure the U.S. border with Mexico / to limit the flow of illegal immigrants.
이민 정책의 거의 유일한 측면은 / 광범위한 정치적 지지를 받는 / 멕시코와의 미국 국경을 확보하려는 결의이다 / 불법 이민자의 유입을 제한하기 위해

(②) Texas sheriffs / recently developed / a novel use of the Internet / to help them keep watch on the border.

텍사스 보안관들은 / 최근에 개발했다 / 새로운 인터넷 사용 방법을 / 국경을 감시하는 데 도움이 되는

(③) Citizens who want to help monitor the border / can go online and serve as "virtual Texas deputies."
국경 감시를 돕고 싶은 시민들은 / 온라인에서 '가상 텍사스 대표' 역할을 할 수 있다

(④) If they see anyone / trying to cross the border, / they send a report to the sheriff's office, / which follows up, / sometimes with the help of the U.S. Border Patrol.
그들이 누군가를 보면 / 국경을 넘으려는 / 그들은 보안관 사무실로 보고서를 보낸다 / 그것은 후속 조치를 취한다 / 때때로 미국 국경 순찰대의 도움을 받아서

해석 이민 개혁은 정치적 지뢰밭이다. 광범위한 정치적 지지를 받는 이민 정책의 거의 유일한 측면은 불법 이민자의 유입을 제한하기 위해 멕시코와의 미국 국경을 확보하려는 결의이다. 텍사스 보안관들은 최근에 국경을 감시하는 데 도움이 되는 새로운 인터넷 사용 방법을 개발했다. ③ 그들은 불법 횡단로로 알려진 장소에 비디오 카메라를 설치했고, 웹 사이트에 카메라의 생중계 영상 피드를 올렸다. 국경 감시를 돕고 싶은 시민들은 온라인에서 '가상 텍사스 대표' 역할을 할 수 있다. 그들이 국경을 넘으려는 누군가를 보면, 그들은 보안관 사무실로 보고서를 보내고, 그곳(보안관 사무실)은 때때로 미국 국경 순찰대의 도움을 받아서 후속 조치를 취한다.

해석 ③번 앞 문장에 텍사스 보안관들이 최근에 국경을 감시하는 데 도움이 되는 새로운 인터넷 사용 방법을 개발했다는 내용이 있고, ③번 뒤 문장에 국경 감시를 돕고 싶은 시민들은 온라인에서 '가상 텍사스 대표' 역할을 할 수 있다는 내용이 있으므로, ③번 자리에 텍사스 보안관들이 불법 횡단로로 알려진 장소에 비디오 카메라를 설치했고, 웹 사이트에 카메라의 생중계 영상 피드를 올렸다는 내용의 주어진 문장이 나와야 지문이 자연스럽게 연결된다.

어휘 install 설치하다 illegal 불법의 crossing 횡단로
immigration 이민 reform 개혁 political 정치적인
minefield 지뢰밭 aspect 측면 command 받다 resolve 결의
secure 확보하다 border 국경 sheriff 보안관 novel 새로운
keep watch 감시하다, 망을 보다 citizen 시민 virtual 가상의
deputy 대표, 대리인 patrol 순찰대

19 독해 논리적 흐름 파악 (문단 순서 배열) 난이도 ★★☆

끊어읽기 해석

All civilizations rely on government administration.
모든 문명은 정부의 행정에 의존한다

Perhaps / no civilization better exemplifies this / than ancient Rome.
아마도 / 이것을 더 잘 보여주는 문명은 없을 것이다 / 고대 로마보다

(A) To rule an area that large, / the Romans, / based in what is now central Italy, / needed an effective system / of government administration.
그렇게 넓은 지역을 통치하기 위해, / 로마인들은 / 현재의 중부 이탈리아에 기반을 둔 / 효과적인 시스템이 필요했다 / 정부 행정의

(B) Actually, / the word "civilization" itself / comes from the Latin word civis, / meaning "citizen."
사실, / '문명'이라는 단어 자체는 / 라틴어 'civis'에서 왔다 / '시민'을 의미하는

(C) Latin was the language of ancient Rome, / whose territory stretched / from the Mediterranean basin / all the way to parts of Great Britain in the north / and the Black Sea to the east.
라틴어는 고대 로마의 언어였다 / 그들의 영토는 뻗어 있었다 / 지중해의 분지에서 / 북쪽의 그레이트브리튼 섬의 일부까지 / 그리고 동쪽의 흑해까지

해석 모든 문명은 정부의 행정에 의존한다. 아마도 고대 로마보다 이것을 더 잘 보여주는 문명은 없을 것이다.

(B) 사실, '문명'이라는 단어 자체는 '시민'을 의미하는 라틴어 'civis'에서 왔다.
(C) 라틴어는 고대 로마의 언어였는데, 그들의 영토는 지중해의 분지에서 북쪽의 그레이트브리튼 섬의 일부와 동쪽의 흑해까지 뻗어 있었다.
(A) 로마인들은 현재의 중부 이탈리아에 기반을 둔 그렇게 넓은 지역을 통치하기 위해, 효과적인 정부 행정 시스템이 필요했다.

해석 주어진 문장에서 고대 로마보다 문명이 정보의 행정에 의존하는 것을 잘 보여주는 문명은 없을 것이라고 하고, (B)에서 '문명'이라는 단어 자체가 '시민'을 의미하는 라틴어에서 왔다고 설명하고 있다. 이어서 (C)에서 라틴어는 고대 로마의 언어였는데, 그들의 영토가 지중해의 분지에서 동쪽의 흑해까지 뻗어 있었다고 하고, (A)에서 그렇게 넓은 지역을 통치하기 위해 로마인들은 효과적인 정부 행정 시스템이 필요했다고 설명하고 있다. 따라서 ③ (B) – (C) – (A)가 정답이다.

어휘 civilization 문명 administration 행정 exemplify 보여주다
ancient 고대의 rule 통치하다 effective 효과적인 territory 영토
stretch 뻗어 있다, 이르다 basin 분지

20 독해 추론 (빈칸 완성 - 구) 난이도 ★★★

끊어읽기 해석

Over the last fifty years, / all major subdisciplines in psychology / have become more and more isolated from each other / as training becomes increasingly specialized and narrow in focus.
지난 50년 동안, / 심리학의 모든 주요 하위 학문들은 / 서로 점점 더 고립되었다 / 훈련이 점점 더 전문화되고 초점이 좁혀짐에 따라

As some psychologists have long argued, / if the field of psychology is to mature and advance scientifically, / its disparate parts / (for example, neuroscience, developmental, cognitive, personality, and social) / must become whole and integrated again.
일부 심리학자들이 오랫동안 주장해 온 것처럼, / 심리학 분야가 과학적으로 성장하고 발전하려면, / 서로 다른 부분들이 / (예를 들어, 신경과학, 발달 심리학, 인지 심리학, 성격 심리학, 그리고 사회 심리학) / 완전해지고 다시 통합되어야 한다

Science advances / when distinct topics become theoretically and empirically integrated / under simplifying theoretical frameworks.
과학은 발전한다 / 서로 다른 주제가 이론적으로 그리고 경험적으로 통합될 때 / 단순화하는 이론적인 틀 아래에서

Psychology of science will encourage collaboration / among psychologists from various sub-areas, / helping the field achieve coherence / rather than continued fragmentation.
과학 심리학은 협업을 장려할 것이다 / 다양한 하위 영역의 심리학자들 간의 / 그 분야가 결합의 긴밀성을 달성하도록 도울 것이다 / 지속적인 분열보다

In this way, / psychology of science might act / as a template for psychology as a whole / by integrating under one discipline all of the major fractions/factions within the field.
이러한 방식으로, / 과학 심리학은 작용할지도 모른다 / 전체로써의 심리학의 본보기로 / 그 분야 내의 모든 주요 분파와 파벌을 하나의 학문 아래 통합함으로써

It would be no small feat / and of no small import / if the psychology of science could become a model / for the parent discipline / on how to combine resources and study science / from a unified perspective.
그것은 작지 않은 업적일 것이다 / 그리고 작지 않은 중요성이 있을 것이다 / 과학 심리학이 본보기가 될 수 있다면 / 모학문의 / 자원을 결합하고 과학을 연구하는 방법에 대한 / 통일된 관점에서

해석   지난 50년 동안, 심리학의 모든 주요 하위 학문들은 훈련이 점점 더 전문화되고 초점이 좁혀짐에 따라 서로 점점 더 고립되었다. 일부 심리학자들이 오랫동안 주장해 온 것처럼, 심리학 분야가 과학적으로 성장하고 발전하려면, 서로 다른 부분들이 (예를 들어, 신경과학, 발달 심리학, 인지 심리학, 성격 심리학, 그리고 사회 심리학) 완전해지고 다시 통합되어야 한다. 과학은 서로 다른 주제가 단순화하는 이론적인 틀 아래에서 이론적으로 그리고 경험적으로 통합될 때 발전한다. 과학 심리학은 다양한 하위 영역의 심리학자들 간의 협업을 장려하여 그 분야가 지속적인 분열보다는 결합의 긴밀성을 달성하도록 도울 것이다. 이러한 방식으로, 과학 심리학은 그 분야 내의 모든 주요 분파와 파벌을 하나의 학문 아래 통합함으로써 전체로써의 심리학의 본보기로 작용할지도 모른다. 과학 심리학이 자원을 결합하고 통일된 관점에서 과학을 연구하는 방법에 대한 모학문의 본보기가 될 수 있다면 그것은 작지 않은 업적일 것이고 작지 않은 중요성이 있을 것이다.

① 통일된 관점에서
② 역동적인 측면에서
③ 역사를 통틀어
④ 정확한 증거로

해설   지문 처음에서 심리학 분야가 과학적으로 성장하고 발전하려면, 서로 다른 부분들이 완전해지고 다시 통합되어야 한다고 했고, 지문 마지막에서 과학 심리학은 그 분야 내의 모든 주요 분파와 파벌을 하나의 학문 아래 통합함으로써 전체로써의 심리학의 본보기로 작용할지도 모른다고 했으므로, 빈칸에는 과학 심리학이 자원을 결합하고 '① 통일된 관점에서' 과학을 연구하는 방법에 대한 모학문의 본보기가 될 수 있다면 그것은 작지 않은 업적일 것이고 작지 않은 중요성이 있을 것이라는 내용이 들어가야 한다.

어휘   subdiscipline 하위 학문 psychology 심리학 isolate 고립시키다
mature 성장하다 disparate 서로 다른, 이질적인
neuroscience 신경과학 developmental 발달의
cognitive 인지적인 personality 성격 integrate 통합하다
theoretically 이론적으로 empirically 경험적으로
simplify 단순화하다 framework 틀
coherence 결합의 긴밀성, 일관성 fraction 분파
faction 파벌, 알력 feat 업적 import 중요(성), 수입
unified 통일된 aspect 측면 accurate 정확한

3회 | 2022년 국가직 9급

정답
p.44

01	① 어휘 – 어휘&표현	**11**	④ 어휘 – 생활영어
02	② 어휘 – 어휘&표현	**12**	③ 어휘 – 생활영어
03	④ 어휘 – 어휘&표현	**13**	② 문법 – 비교 구문
04	② 어휘 – 어휘&표현	**14**	④ 문법 – 분사
05	① 어휘 – 어휘&표현	**15**	② 독해 – 추론
06	① 문법 – 능동태·수동태&대명사	**16**	④ 독해 – 추론
07	④ 독해 – 세부내용 파악	**17**	③ 독해 – 전체내용 파악
08	② 문법 – 수 일치	**18**	④ 독해 – 논리적 흐름 파악
09	① 독해 – 전체내용 파악	**19**	① 독해 – 전체내용 파악
10	③ 독해 – 논리적 흐름 파악	**20**	③ 독해 – 논리적 흐름 파악

취약영역 분석표

영역	세부 유형	문항 수	소계
어휘	어휘&표현	5	/7
	생활영어	2	
문법	능동태·수동태&대명사	1	/4
	수 일치	1	
	비교 구문	1	
	분사	1	
독해	전체내용 파악	3	/9
	세부내용 파악	1	
	추론	2	
	논리적 흐름 파악	3	
	총계		**/20**

· 자신이 취약한 영역은 '공무원 영어, 이렇게 출제된다!'(문제집 p.8)를 통해 다시 한번 확인하고 학습하시기 바랍니다.

---

01 어휘 어휘&표현 unravel = solve 난이도 ★☆☆

해석 몇 년 동안, 형사들은 그 쌍둥이 형제의 갑작스러운 실종에 대한 수수께끼를 풀기 위해 노력해왔다.

① 풀다 ② 창조하다
③ 모방하다 ④ 알리다

어휘 detective 형사 unravel 풀다, 해결하다
disappearance 실종, 사라짐 solve 풀다, 해결하다
imitate 모방하다 publicize 알리다, 공표하다

👍 이것도 알면 **합격!**

unravel(풀다)의 유의어
= crack, resolve, figure out, puzzle out

02 어휘 어휘&표현 opulent = luxurious 난이도 ★★☆

해석 그 부부가 부모가 되는 것을 경험하기 전에, 그들의 침실 4개짜리 집은 불필요하게 호화로운 것처럼 보였다.

① 숨겨진 ② 호화로운
③ 비어 있는 ④ 단단한

어휘 opulent 호화로운 luxurious 호화로운, 사치스러운
solid 단단한, 견고한

👍 이것도 알면 **합격!**

opulent(호화로운)의 유의어
= lavish, palatial

03 어휘 어휘&표현 hit the roof = become extremely angry 난이도 ★★☆

해석 상사는 우리가 그렇게 단기간에 이미 모든 예산을 썼다는 것을 알게 되었을 때 머리끝까지 화가 났다.

① 매우 만족했다
② 매우 놀랐다
③ 극도로 침착해졌다
④ 극도로 화가 났다

어휘 hit the roof 머리끝까지 화가 나다 budget 예산 calm 침착한

👍 이것도 알면 **합격!**

hit the roof(머리끝까지 화가 나다)와 유사한 의미의 표현
= blow up, lose one's temper, hit the ceiling, go through the roof

04 어휘 어휘&표현 equivalent 난이도 ★★☆

해석 마우스 포테이토(컴퓨터 중독자)는 텔레비전의 카우치 포테이토(TV만 보는 사람)의 컴퓨터 상당어구인데, 카우치 포테이토가 텔레비전 앞에서 그러는 것과 거의 동일한 방식으로 컴퓨터 앞에서 많은 여가 시간을 보내는 경향이 있는 사람이다.

① 기술자 ② 상당어구
③ 통신망 ④ 모의실험

어휘 equivalent 상당어구, 동의어

👍 이것도 알면 **합격!**

equivalent(상당어구)의 유의어
= counterpart, equal

05 어휘 어휘&표현 brush up on 난이도 ★★☆

해석 Mary는 남아메리카에 가기 전에 스페인어를 복습하기로 결정했다.

① ~을 복습하다　　　② ~의 말을 끝까지 들어주다
③ ~를 변호하다　　　④ ~를 해고하다

어휘 brush up on ~을 복습하다 hear out ~의 말을 끝까지 들어주다
stick up for ~를 변호하다 lay off ~를 해고하다, ~을 그만 먹다

👍 이것도 알면 **합격!**

brush up on(~을 복습하다)과 유사한 의미의 표현
= polish up, bone up on, review

06 문법 능동태·수동태&대명사 난이도 ★★☆

해석 ① 말에게는 그것의 개별적인 욕구와 그것의 일의 특징에 따라 먹이가 주어져야 한다.
② 내 모자는 좁은 길을 걸어 내려가는 동안 바람에 날아갔다.
③ 그녀는 자신의 경력 내내 주로 정치 만화가로 알려져 왔다.
④ 심지어 어린아이들도 잘한 일에 대해 칭찬받는 것을 좋아한다.

해설 ① 능동태·수동태 구별 | 인칭대명사 주어 A horse와 동사가 '말에게 먹이가 주어지다'라는 의미의 수동 관계이므로 수동태 should be fed가 올바르게 쓰였다. 또한 대명사가 지시하는 명사(A horse)가 단수이므로 단수 소유격 대명사 its가 올바르게 쓰였다.

오답분석 ② 부사절 접속사 1: 시간 | 부사절의 형태 문맥상 '내가 좁은 길을 걸어 내려가는 동안'이라는 의미가 되어야 자연스러운데, '~하는 동안'은 부사절 접속사 while을 사용하여 나타낼 수 있다. 이때 while이 이끄는 부사절은 '부사절 접속사 + 주어 + 동사'의 형태가 되어야 하므로 while walking down ~을 while I walked ~나 while I was walking down ~으로 고쳐야 한다.

③ 능동태·수동태 구별 주어 She와 동사가 '그녀가 알려져 왔다'라는 의미의 수동 관계이므로 현재완료 시제의 능동태 has known을 수동태 has been known으로 고쳐야 한다.

④ 현재분사 vs. 과거분사 | 부사 자리 수식받는 명사 a job과 분사가 '일이 행해지다'라는 의미의 수동 관계이므로 과거분사 done이 쓰였는데, 이때 과거분사(done)를 수식할 수 있는 것은 형용사(good)가 아닌 부사(well)이므로 good을 well로 고쳐야 한다.

어휘 feed 먹이를 주다 individual 개별적인, 각각의 nature 특징, 본성
blow off ~을 바람에 날리다 narrow 좁은 primarily 주로
compliment 칭찬하다

👍 이것도 알면 **합격!**

능동태 문장의 목적어가 수동태 문장의 주어가 되므로, 목적어를 갖지 않는 자동사는 수동태가 될 수 없다.
(ex) The cruise ship ~~was arrived~~(→ arrived) at the harbor yesterday, exactly one week after departing.
출발한 지 정확히 1주 뒤인 어제 크루즈 배가 항구에 도착했다.

07 독해 세부내용 파악 (내용 불일치 파악) 난이도 ★☆☆

끊어읽기 해석

Umberto Eco was an Italian novelist, / cultural critic and philosopher.
움베르토 에코는 이탈리아의 소설가이자 / 문화 평론가, 그리고 철학자였다

He is widely known / for his 1980 novel / *The Name of the Rose*, / a historical mystery / combining semiotics / in fiction / with biblical analysis, medieval studies and literary theory.
그는 널리 알려져 있다 / 그의 1980년 소설 / 『장미의 이름』으로 / 역사 추리 소설인 / 기호학을 결합한 / 허구 속에서 / 성서 분석, 중세 연구, 그리고 문학 이론과

He later wrote / other novels, / including *Foucault's Pendulum* and *The Island of the Day Before*.
그는 후에 썼다 / 다른 소설들을 / 『푸코의 진자』와 『전날의 섬』을 포함한

Eco was also a translator: / he translated / Raymond Queneau's book / *Exercices de style* / into Italian.
에코는 또한 번역가이기도 했다 / 그는 번역했다 / 레몽 크노의 책인 / 『문체 연습』을 / 이탈리아어로

He was the founder / of the Department of Media Studies / at the University / of the Republic of San Marino.
그는 설립자였다 / 미디어학과의 / 대학교에 있는 / 산마리노 공화국의

He died / at his Milanese home / of pancreatic cancer, / from which he had been suffering / for two years, / on the night / of February 19, 2016.
그는 사망했다 / 그의 밀라노 자택에서 / 췌장암으로 / 그가 앓아 왔던 / 2년간 / 밤에 / 2016년 2월 19일의

해석 움베르토 에코는 이탈리아의 소설가이자 문화 평론가, 그리고 철학자였다. 그는 허구 속에서 기호학을 성서 분석, 중세 연구, 그리고 문학 이론과 결합한 역사 추리 소설인, 그의 1980년 소설 『장미의 이름』으로 널리 알려져 있다. 그는 후에 『푸코의 진자』와 『전날의 섬』을 포함한 다른 소설들을 썼다. 에코는 또한 번역가이기도 했는데, 그는 레몽 크노의 책인 『문체 연습』을 이탈리아어로 번역했다. 그는 산마리노 공화국의 대학교에 있는 미디어학과의 설립자였다. 그는 2016년 2월 19일의 밤에 그의 밀라노 자택에서 그가 2년간 앓아 왔던 췌장암으로 사망했다.

① 『장미의 이름』은 역사 소설이다.
② 에코는 책을 이탈리아어로 번역했다.
③ 에코는 대학 학과를 설립했다.
④ 에코는 병원에서 암으로 사망했다.

해설 ④번의 키워드인 cancer(암)가 그대로 언급된 지문 주변의 내용에서 에코는 2016년 2월 19일의 밤에 그의 밀라노 자택에서 그가 2년간 앓아 왔던 췌장암으로 사망했다고 했으므로, '④ 에코는 병원에서 암으로 사망했다'는 지문의 내용과 일치하지 않는다.

어휘 critic 평론가 semiotics 기호학 fiction 허구, 소설
biblical 성서의 analysis 분석 medieval 중세의 literary 문학의
pendulum 진자, 추 translator 번역가 founder 설립자
pancreatic 췌장의

08 문법 수 일치 난이도 ★★☆

해석 좋은 출발점을 찾기 위해서는 최초의 현대식 전기 배터리가 개발되었던 1800년으로 돌아가야 한다. 이탈리아의 알레산드로 볼타는 은, 구리, 그리고 아연의 조합이 전류를 만드는 데 이상적이라는 것을 발견했다. 볼타의 전지라고 불리는 이 향상된 디자인은 바닷물에 적신 판지로 만들어진 원반들 사이에 이 금속들로 만들어진 원반들을 쌓아 올림으로써 만들어졌다. 볼타의 업적에 대한 소문

이 퍼져서 그는 나폴레옹 황제 앞에서 직접 시연하라는 요청을 받았다.

해설 ② 주어와 동사의 수 일치 주어 자리에 단수 명사 a combination이 왔으므로 복수 동사 were를 단수 동사 was로 고쳐야 한다. 참고로 주어와 동사 사이의 수식어 거품(of silver ~ zinc)은 동사의 수 결정에 영향을 주지 않는다.

오답 분석
① 전치사 + 관계대명사 선행사 the year 1800가 사물이고 관계절 내에서 전치사 during의 목적어 역할을 하므로 목적격 관계대명사 which가 올바르게 쓰였다.
③ 현재분사 vs. 과거분사 수식받는 명사 The enhanced design과 분사가 '이 향상된 디자인이 ~이라고 불리다'라는 의미의 수동 관계이므로 과거분사 called가 올바르게 쓰였다.
④ 부사절 접속사 2: 기타 문맥상 '볼타의 업적에 대한 소문이 퍼져서 그는 ~ 요청을 받았다'라는 의미가 되어야 자연스러운데, '~해서 -하다'는 부사절 접속사 such ~ that을 사용하여 나타낼 수 있으므로 형용사 such가 명사 talk 앞에 올바르게 쓰였다.

어휘 combination 조합, 결합 copper 구리 zinc 아연 ideal 이상적인 electrical current 전류 pile 전지 stack 쌓아 올리다 disc 원반 soak 적시다, 담그다 conduct 하다, 행동하다 demonstration 시연, 설명

👍 **이것도 알면 합격!**

분사가 명사를 수식하는 경우, 수식받는 명사와 분사가 능동 관계이면 현재분사가, 수동 관계이면 과거분사가 와야 한다는 것을 알아두자.

(ex) The machine **designed** by the engineer was revolutionary when it was released.
그 엔지니어에 의해 설계된 기계는 출시되었을 때 획기적이었다.

09 독해 전체내용 파악 (제목 파악) 난이도 ★★☆

끊어읽기 해석

Lasers are possible / because of the way / light interacts / with electrons.
레이저는 가능하다 / 방식 때문에 / 빛이 상호작용하는 / 전자와

Electrons exist / at specific energy levels / or states / characteristic of that particular atom or molecule.
전자는 존재한다 / 특정 에너지 준위에서 / 또는 상태에서 / 그 특정한 원자나 분자의 특유한

The energy levels / can be imagined / as rings or orbits / around a nucleus.
에너지 준위는 / 생각될 수 있다 / 고리나 궤도로 / 핵 주변에 있는

Electrons in outer rings / are at higher energy levels / than those / in inner rings.
외부 고리 속의 전자는 / 더 높은 에너지 준위에 있다 / ~것보다 / 내부 고리 속에 있는

Electrons can be bumped up / to higher energy levels / by the injection / of energy /—for example, / by a flash of light.
전자는 올라갈 수 있다 / 더 높은 에너지 준위로 / 주입에 의해 / 에너지의 / 예를 들어 / 빛의 섬광과 같은

When an electron drops / from an outer / to an inner level, / "excess" energy / is given off / as light.
전자가 떨어질 때 / 외부에서 / 내부 준위로 / '여분의' 에너지는 / 발산된다 / 빛으로

The wavelength or color / of the emitted light / is precisely related / to the amount / of energy released.
파장이나 색상은 / 그 방출된 빛의 / 정확히 관련이 있다 / 양과 / 방출되는 에너지의

Depending on the particular lasing material / being used, / specific wavelengths / of light / are absorbed (to energize or excite the electrons) / and specific wavelengths / are emitted (when the electrons fall back / to their initial level).
특정한 레이저 방출 물질에 따라 / 사용되는 / 특유한 파장이 / 빛의 / 흡수되고 (전자를 활발하게 하거나 자극하기 위해) / 특유한 파장이 / 방출된다 (전자가 다시 떨어지면 / 그것들의 처음 (에너지) 준위로)

해석 레이저는 빛이 전자와 상호작용하는 방식 때문에 가능하다. 전자는 그 특정한 원자나 분자의 특유한 특정 에너지 준위 또는 상태에서 존재한다. 에너지 준위는 핵 주변에 있는 고리나 궤도로 생각될 수 있다. 외부 고리 속의 전자는 내부 고리 속에 있는 것들(전자)보다 더 높은 에너지 준위에 있다. 전자는 예를 들어, 빛의 섬광과 같은 에너지의 주입에 의해 더 높은 에너지 준위로 올라갈 수 있다. 전자가 외부에서 내부 준위로 떨어질 때, '여분의' 에너지는 빛으로 발산된다. 그 방출된 빛의 파장이나 색상은 방출되는 에너지의 양과 정확히 관련이 있다. 사용되는 특정한 레이저 방출 물질에 따라, (전자를 활발하게 하거나 자극하기 위해) 빛의 특유한 파장이 흡수되고 (전자가 그것들의 처음 (에너지) 준위로 다시 떨어지면) 특유한 파장이 방출된다.

① 레이저는 어떻게 만들어지는가?
② 레이저는 언제 발명되었는가?
③ 레이저는 어떤 전자를 방출하는가?
④ 전자는 왜 빛을 반사하는가?

해설 지문 처음에서 레이저는 빛이 전자와 상호작용하는 방식 때문에 가능하다고 했고, 지문 중간에서 전자는 빛의 섬광과 같은 에너지의 주입에 의해 더 높은 에너지 준위로 올라갈 수 있으며 전자가 외부에서 내부 준위로 떨어질 때 여분의 에너지가 빛으로 발산된다고 하였다. 이는 빛이 전자와 상호작용하여 레이저가 생성되는 원리에 관한 설명이므로 '① 레이저는 어떻게 만들어지는가?'가 이 글의 제목이다.

어휘 electron 전자
energy level 에너지 준위(원자나 분자가 갖는 에너지 값)
state 상태 characteristic of ~의 특유한 atom 원자
molecule 분자 orbit 궤도 nucleus (원자)핵, 중심
injection 주입, 투입 give off 발산하다 wavelength 파장
emit 방출하다 absorb 흡수하다 initial 처음의 reflect 반사하다

10 독해 논리적 흐름 파악 (무관한 문장 삭제) 난이도 ★☆☆

끊어읽기 해석

Markets in water rights / are likely to evolve / as a rising population leads to shortages / and climate change / causes drought and famine.
수리권 시장은 / 발달할 가능성이 있다 / 증가하는 인구가 (물) 부족을 초래함에 따라 / 기후 변화가 / 가뭄과 기근을 야기하고

① But they will be based / on regional and ethical trading practices / and will differ / from the bulk / of commodity trade.
그러나 그것들(시장)은 기초할 것이다 / 지역적이고 윤리적인 무역 관행에 / 그리고 다를 것이다 / 대부분과는 / 상품 무역의

② Detractors argue / trading water is unethical / or even a breach of human rights,/ but already water rights are bought and sold / in arid areas / of the globe / from Oman to Australia.
비방하는 사람들은 주장한다 / 물을 거래하는 것이 비윤리적이거나 / 심지어 인권 침해라고 / 하지만 이미 수리권은 구매되고 판매된다 / 건조한 지역

에서 / 지구의 / 오만에서 호주까지

③ Drinking distilled water / can be beneficial, / but may not be the best choice / for everyone, / especially if the minerals are not supplemented / by another source.
증류수를 마시는 것은 / 이로울 수 있다 / 하지만 최선의 선택은 아닐 수 있다 / 모든 사람들에게 / 특히 무기물이 보충되지 않는 경우에 그렇다 / 다른 공급원에 의해

④ "We strongly believe / that water is in fact / turning into the new gold / for this decade and beyond," / said Ziad Abdelnour.
"우리는 강하게 믿습니다 / 물이 사실상 / 새로운 금으로 변하고 있다고 / 지난 10년 동안 그리고 그 이후에" / 라고 Ziad Abdelnour가 말했다

"No wonder / smart money is / aggressively moving / in this direction."
"당연합니다 / 스마트 머니가 / 공격적으로 움직이는 것은 / 이런 방향으로"

해석 수리권 시장은 증가하는 인구가 (물) 부족을 초래하고 기후 변화가 가뭄과 기근을 야기함에 따라 발달할 가능성이 있다. ① 그러나 그 것들(시장)은 지역적이고 윤리적인 무역 관행에 기초할 것이고 상품 무역의 대부분과는 다를 것이다. ② 비방하는 사람들은 물을 거래하는 것이 비윤리적이거나 심지어 인권 침해라고 주장하지만, 이미 수리권은 오만에서 호주까지 지구의 건조한 지역에서 구매되고 판매된다. ③ 증류수를 마시는 것은 이로울 수 있지만, 모든 사람들에게 최선의 선택은 아닐 수 있는데, 특히 무기물이 다른 공급원에 의해 보충되지 않는 경우에 그렇다. ④ "우리는 물이 사실상 지난 10년 동안 그리고 그 이후에 새로운 금으로 변하고 있다고 강하게 믿습니다"라고 Ziad Abdelnour가 말했다. "스마트 머니가 이런 방향으로 공격적으로 움직이는 것은 당연합니다."

해설 지문 처음에서 인구 증가 및 기후 변화로 인해 수리권 시장이 발달할 가능성이 있다고 언급하고, ①, ②, ④번에서 수리권 시장의 특징, 수리권이 구매되고 판매되는 지역, 그리고 물이 새로운 금으로 변하고 있다는 주장에 대해 설명하고 있다. 그러나 ③번은 '증류수를 마시는 것'에 대한 내용으로, 지문 처음의 내용과 관련이 없다.

어휘 lead to ~을 초래하다 shortage 부족
climate change 기후 변화 famine 기근
be based on ~에 기초하다 regional 지역적인 ethical 윤리적인
practice 관행, 연습 the bulk of ~의 대부분 breach 침해, 위반
arid 건조한 distilled water 증류수 beneficial 이로운
supplement 보충하다; 보충(물)

11 어휘 생활영어 What's the difference from the last menu? 난이도 ★☆☆

해석
A: 대학 구내식당이 메뉴를 바꿨다고 들었어.
B: 응, 나는 방금 그것을 확인했어.
A: 그리고 그들이 새로운 음식 공급업체를 구했대.
B: 맞아. Sam's Catering이야.
A: 이전 메뉴와 다른 점이 뭐야?
B: 더 많은 디저트 종류가 있어. 게다가, 일부 샌드위치 종류가 없어졌어.

① 네가 가장 좋아하는 디저트는 뭐야
② 그들의 사무실이 어디 있는지 알아
③ 메뉴에 대해 내 도움이 필요하니
④ 이전 메뉴와 다른 점이 뭐야

해설 B가 대학 구내식당이 구한 새로운 음식 공급업체가 Sam's

Catering이라고 언급한 후, 빈칸 뒤에서 다시 There are more dessert choices. Also, some sandwich choices were removed(더 많은 디저트 종류가 있어. 게다가, 일부 샌드위치 종류가 없어졌어)라고 말하고 있으므로, 빈칸에는 '④ What's the difference from the last menu(이전 메뉴와 다른 점이 뭐야)'가 오는 것이 자연스럽다.

어휘 check out ~을 확인하다

👍 이것도 알면 **합격!**

식당에서 자주 쓰이는 표현

· Today's specials are ~ 오늘의 특선은 ~ 입니다.
· Gratuity is included. 팁이 포함되어 있습니다.
· The check is here when you're ready.
  준비되시면 계산서는 여기 있습니다.

12 어휘 생활영어 It's a little out of my price range. 난이도 ★☆☆

해석
A: 안녕하세요. 무엇을 도와드릴까요?
B: 네, 저는 스웨터를 찾고 있어요.
A: 음, 이건 이번 가을 컬렉션의 최신 스타일이에요. 어떤가요?
B: 멋져요. 얼마인가요?
A: 가격을 확인해볼게요. 120달러네요.
B: 제 가격대를 조금 벗어나요.
A: 그럼 이 스웨터는 어때요? 이건 지난 시즌 제품인데 50달러로 할인 중이에요.
B: 완벽해요! 한 번 입어볼게요.

① 저는 이것과 어울리는 바지 하나도 필요해요
② 그 재킷은 나를 위한 완벽한 선물이에요
③ 제 가격대를 조금 벗어나요
④ 우리는 토요일에 오후 7시까지 영업해요

해설 스웨터를 찾는다는 A의 말에 B가 120달러짜리 최신 스타일의 스웨터를 권하고, 빈칸 뒤에서 다시 A가 Then how about this sweater?(그럼 이 스웨터는 어때요?)라고 하면서 50달러로 할인 중인 지난 시즌 제품을 다시 권하고 있으므로, 빈칸에는 '③ It's a little out of my price range(제 가격대를 조금 벗어나요)'가 오는 것이 자연스럽다.

어휘 latest 최신의 on sale 할인 중인

👍 이것도 알면 **합격!**

쇼핑할 때 자주 쓰는 표현

· What's your return policy? 반품 정책이 어떻게 되나요?
· Do you have any ~ in stock? ~의 재고가 있나요?
· I'm just browsing. 저는 그냥 둘러보고 있어요.

13 문법 비교 구문 난이도 ★★☆

해설 ② 비교급 형태로 최상급 의미를 만드는 표현 'nothing ~ 비교급 + than'(다른 어떤 -도 ~보다 더 ~하지 않다)의 형태를 사용하여 비교급 형태로 최상급 의미를 만들 수 있으므로 as를 than으로 고쳐야 한다.

오답 ① to 부정사의 의미상 주어 문장의 주어(It)와 to 부정사의 행위
분석   주체(we)가 달라 to 부정사의 의미상 주어가 필요한 경우 'for

+ 목적격 대명사'를 to 부정사 앞에 써야 하므로 for us가 to learn 앞에 올바르게 쓰였다.

③ 조동사 관련 표현 '아무리 조심해도 지나치지 않다'는 조동사 관련 숙어 표현 cannot ~ too(아무리 -해도 지나치지 않다)의 형태로 나타낼 수 있으므로 cannot be too careful이 올바르게 쓰였다.

④ 명사절 접속사 3: 의문사 동사(say)의 목적어가 없는 불완전한 절(others say)을 이끌며 문장의 목적어 자리에 올 수 있는 명사절 접속사 what이 올바르게 쓰였다.

어휘 by no means 결코 ~이 아닌 precious 소중한

👍 이것도 알면 합격!

조동사 관련 표현

- would rather 차라리 ~하는 게 낫다
- may[might] as well ~하는 편이 더 낫다
- may well ~하는 게 당연하다
- cannot ~ too 아무리 -해도 지나치지 않다

14 문법 분사
난이도 ★★☆

해설 ④ 분사구문의 관용 표현 동시에 일어나는 상황은 'with + 명사 + 분사'의 형태로 나타낼 수 있는데, 명사(the legs)와 분사가 '다리가 꼬아지다'라는 의미의 수동 관계이므로 현재분사 crossing을 과거분사 crossed로 고쳐야 한다.

오답 분석 ① 분사구문의 형태 주절의 주어(she)와 동사가 '그녀가 마시다'라는 의미의 능동 관계이므로 현재분사가 와야 하고, 문맥상 '커피를 마신' 시점이 '그녀가 잠을 이룰 수 없는' 시점보다 이전에 일어난 일이므로 분사구문의 완료형 Having drunk가 올바르게 쓰였다.

② 분사구문의 역할 '친절한 사람이어서'라는 의미를 만들기 위해 이유를 나타내는 부사절 역할을 하는 분사구문 Being a kind person이 올바르게 쓰였다.

③ 분사구문의 의미상 주어 주절의 주어(she)와 분사구문의 주어(All things)가 달라 분사구문의 의미상 주어가 필요한 경우 명사 주어를 분사구문 앞에 써야 하므로 분사구문의 주어 All things가 과거분사 considered 앞에 올바르게 쓰였다.

어휘 blood pressure 혈압

👍 이것도 알면 합격!

분사구문의 의미상 주어는 '명사' 또는 '주격 대명사'를 분사구문 앞에 써서 나타낸다는 것을 함께 알아두자.

ex The roads getting icy, drivers began to slow down and drive carefully.
길이 미끄러워서, 운전자들은 천천히 그리고 조심해서 운전하기 시작했다.

15 독해 추론 (빈칸 완성 - 연결어)
난이도 ★☆☆

끊어읽기 해석

Beliefs about maintaining ties / with those who have died / vary from culture to culture.
유대 관계를 유지하는 것에 대한 생각은 / 죽은 사람들과의 / 문화마다 다르다

For example, / maintaining ties / with the deceased / is accepted and sustained / in the religious rituals of Japan.
예를 들어 / 유대 관계를 유지하는 것은 / 고인과의 / 받아들여지고 지속된다 / 일본의 종교의식에서

Yet / among the Hopi Indians of Arizona, / the deceased are forgotten / as quickly / as possible / and life goes on / as usual.
하지만 / 애리조나주의 호피족 인디언들 사이에서 / 고인은 잊힌다 / 빠르게 / 가능한 한 / 그리고 삶은 계속된다 / 평소처럼

(A) In fact, / the Hopi funeral ritual / concludes with a break-off / between mortals and spirits.
(A) 실제로 / 호피족의 장례 의식은 / 단절로 마무리된다 / 인간들과 영혼들 사이의

The diversity of grieving / is nowhere clearer / than in two Muslim societies / one in Egypt, / the other in Bali.
애도의 차이가 / 더 뚜렷한 곳은 없다 / 두 이슬람 사회보다 / 이집트와 / 발리에 있는

Among Muslims in Egypt, / the bereaved are encouraged / to dwell at length / on their grief, / surrounded by others / who relate / to similarly tragic accounts / and express their sorrow.
이집트의 이슬람교도들 사이에서 / 유족들은 격려된다 / 오랫동안 자세히 이야기하도록 / 자신들의 슬픔을 / 다른 사람들에 둘러싸여 / 언급하는 / 유사한 비극적 이야기에 대해 / 그리고 슬픔을 표하는

(B) By contrast, / in Bali, / bereaved Muslims are encouraged / to laugh / and be joyful / rather than be sad.
(B) 그에 반해 / 발리에서는 / 이슬람교도 유족은 격려된다 / 웃고 / 기뻐하도록 / 슬퍼하기보다는

해석 죽은 사람들과의 유대 관계를 유지하는 것에 대한 생각은 문화마다 다르다. 예를 들어, 고인과의 유대 관계를 유지하는 것은 일본의 종교의식에서 받아들여지고 지속된다. 하지만 애리조나주의 호피족 인디언들 사이에서, 고인은 가능한 한 빠르게 잊히고 삶은 평소처럼 계속된다. (A) 실제로, 호피족의 장례 의식은 인간들과 영혼들 사이의 단절로 마무리된다. 애도의 차이가 이집트와 발리에 있는 두 이슬람 사회보다 더 뚜렷한 곳은 없다. 이집트의 이슬람교도들 사이에서, 유족들은 유사한 비극적 이야기에 대해 언급하고 슬픔을 표하는 다른 사람들에 둘러싸여 자신들의 슬픔을 오랫동안 자세히 이야기하도록 격려된다. (B) 그에 반해, 발리에서는, 이슬람교도 유족은 슬퍼하기보다는 웃고 기뻐하도록 격려된다.

	(A)	(B)
①	하지만	비슷하게
②	실제로	그에 반해
③	그러므로	예를 들어
④	마찬가지로	그 결과

해설 (A) 빈칸 앞 문장은 애리조나주의 호피족 인디언들 사이에서 고인은 가능한 한 빨리 잊히고 삶은 평소처럼 계속된다는 내용이고, 빈칸 뒤 문장은 호피족의 장례 의식은 인간들과 영혼들 사이의 단절로 마무리된다고 강조하는 내용이다. 따라서 빈칸에는 강조를 나타내는 연결어인 In fact(실제로)가 들어가야 한다. (B) 빈칸 앞 문장은 이집트의 이슬람교도 유족들은 유사한 비극적 이야기에 대해 언급하고 슬픔을 표하는 다른 사람들에 둘러싸여 자신들의 슬픔을 오랫동안 자세히 이야기하도록 격려된다는 내용이고, 빈칸 뒤 문장은 발리의 이슬람교도 유족들은 슬퍼하기보다는 웃고 기뻐하도록 격려된다는 내용으로 앞 문장과 대조적인 내용이다. 따라서 빈칸에는 대조를 나타내는 연결어인 By contrast(그에 반해)가 들어가야 한다.

따라서 ② (A) In fact(실제로) - (B) By contrast(그에 반해)가 정답이다.

어휘 tie 유대 관계, 인연 vary 다르다 the deceased 고인 sustain 지속하다 ritual 의식 as usual 평소처럼

funeral 장례의; 장례식   conclude with ~으로 마무리되다
mortal 인간; 언젠가는 반드시 죽는   spirit 영혼
diversity 차이, 다양성   grieve 애도하다   the bereaved 유족
dwell on ~을 자세히 이야기하다   surround 둘러싸다
tragic 비극적인   account 이야기, 계좌   sorrow 슬픔

16 　독해 　추론 (빈칸 완성 - 단어)   난이도 ★★☆

끊어읽기 해석

Scientists have long known / that higher air temperatures / are contributing / to the surface melting / on Greenland's ice sheet.
과학자들은 오래전부터 알고 있었다 / 더 높은 기온이 / 원인이 되고 있다는 것을 / 표면이 녹는 것의 / 그린란드 대륙 빙하의

But / a new study / has found another threat / that has begun attacking / the ice / from below: / Warm ocean water / moving underneath the vast glaciers / is causing them to melt / even more quickly.
그러나 / 새로운 연구는 / 또 다른 위협을 발견했는데 / 공격하기 시작한 / 얼음을 / 아래에서 / 따뜻한 해수가 / 그 거대한 빙하 아래에서 움직이는 / 그것들(빙하)을 녹게 하고 있다 / 훨씬 더 빠르게

The findings / were published / in the journal Nature Geoscience / by researchers / who studied / one of the many "ice tongues" / of the Nioghalvfjerdsfjorden Glacier / in northeast Greenland.
이 연구 결과는 / 발표되었다 / 「Nature Geoscience」지에서 / 연구원들에 의해 / 연구한 / 여러 '빙설' 중 하나를 / Nioghalvfjerdsfjorden 빙하의 / 그린란드 북동부에 있는

An ice tongue / is a strip of ice / that floats on the water / without breaking off / from the ice / on land.
빙설은 / 길고 가느다란 얼음 조각이다 / 물 위에 떠 있는 / 분리되지 않은 채 / 얼음으로부터 / 육지의

The massive one / these scientists studied / is nearly 50 miles long.
그 거대한 것(빙설)은 / 이 과학자들이 연구한 / 길이가 거의 50마일이다

The survey / revealed an underwater current / more than a mile wide / where warm water from the Atlantic Ocean / is able to flow / directly towards the glacier, / bringing large amounts of heat into contact / with the ice / and accelerating the glacier's melting.
이 조사는 / 수중 해류를 밝혀냈다 / 폭이 1마일 이상인 / 대서양에서 온 따뜻한 물이 / 흐를 수 있는 / 빙하를 향해 직접 / 다량의 열을 접촉시킨다 / 얼음과 / 그리고 빙하가 녹는 것을 가속화한다

해석　과학자들은 더 높은 기온이 그린란드 대륙 빙하의 표면이 녹는 것의 원인이 되고 있다는 것을 오래전부터 알고 있었다. 그러나 새로운 연구는 얼음을 아래에서 공격하기 시작한 또 다른 위협을 발견했는데, 그 거대한 빙하 아래에서 움직이는 따뜻한 해수가 그것들(빙하)을 훨씬 더 빠르게 녹게 하고 있다. 이 연구 결과는 그린란드 북동부에 있는 Nioghalvfjerdsfjorden 빙하의 여러 '빙설' 중 하나를 연구한 연구원들에 의해 「Nature Geoscience」지에서 발표되었다. 빙설은 육지의 얼음으로부터 분리되지 않은 채 물 위에 떠 있는 길고 가느다란 얼음 조각이다. 이 과학자들이 연구한 그 거대한 것(빙설)은 길이가 거의 50마일이다. 이 조사는 대서양에서 온 따뜻한 물이 빙하를 향해 직접 흐를 수 있는 폭이 1마일 이상인 수중 해류를 밝혀냈는데, 이는 다량의 열을 얼음과 접촉시켜 빙하가 녹는 것을 가속화한다.

① 분리시키는
② 지연시키는
③ 막는
④ 가속화하는

해설　지문 중간에서 새로운 연구가 그린란드 대륙 빙하 아래에서 움직이는 따뜻한 해수가 빙하를 훨씬 더 빠르게 녹게 하고 있다고 했고, 지문 후반에서 대서양에서 온 따뜻한 물이 빙하를 향해 직접 흐를 수 있는 폭이 1마일 이상인 수중 해류가 밝혀졌다고 했으므로, 빈칸에는 수중 해류가 다량의 열을 얼음과 접촉시켜 빙하가 녹는 것을 '가속화한다'는 내용이 들어가야 한다. 따라서 ④번이 정답이다.

어휘　contribute to ~의 원인이 되다   threat 위협
vast 거대한, 어마어마한   glacier 빙하   publish 발표하다, 게재하다
break off 분리되다   massive 거대한, 대규모의   reveal 밝혀내다
current 해류   bring into contact 접촉시키다   delay 지연시키다
accelerate 가속화하다

17 　독해 　전체내용 파악 (제목 파악)   난이도 ★★☆

끊어읽기 해석

Do people from different cultures / view the world differently?
서로 다른 문화의 사람들은 / 세계를 다르게 보고 있을까?

A psychologist / presented realistic animated scenes / of fish and other underwater objects / to Japanese and American students / and asked them / to report / what they had seen.
한 심리학자는 / 사실적인 동영상으로 된 장면을 보여주고 / 물고기와 다른 수중 사물에 관한 / 일본인과 미국인 학생들에게 / 그리고 요청했다 / 보고하라고 / 그들이 본 것을

Americans and Japanese / made about an equal number of references / to the focal fish, / but the Japanese / made more than 60 percent more references / to background elements, / including the water, rocks, bubbles, and inert plants and animals.
미국인과 일본인은 / 거의 비슷한 수로 언급했다 / 중심의 물고기에 대해 / 하지만 일본인이 / 60퍼센트 이상 더 언급했다 / 배경 요소에 대해 / 물, 바위, 거품, 그리고 부동의 동식물을 포함한

In addition, / whereas / Japanese and American participants / made about equal numbers of references / to movement / involving active animals, / the Japanese participants / made almost twice as many references / to relationships involving inert, background objects.
또한 / 반면 / 일본인과 미국인 참가자가 / 거의 동일한 수로 언급한 / 움직임에 대해 / 활동적인 동물을 포함한 / 일본인 참가자들은 / 두 배 가까이 더 언급했다 / 관계에 대해 / 부동의 배경 사물을 포함한

Perhaps / most tellingly, / the very first sentence / from the Japanese participants / was likely to be one / referring to the environment, / whereas / the first sentence / from Americans / was three times as likely to be one / referring to the focal fish.
아마도 / 가장 강력하게, / 맨 처음 문장은 / 일본인 참가자의 / ~ 것일 가능성이 높았고 / 환경에 대해 언급하는 / 반면에 / 첫 번째 문장은 / 미국인의 / ~ 것일 가능성이 세 배 더 높았다 / 중심의 물고기에 대해 언급하는

해석　서로 다른 문화의 사람들은 세계를 다르게 보고 있을까? 한 심리학자는 일본인과 미국인 학생들에게 물고기와 다른 수중 사물에 관한 사실적인 동영상으로 된 장면을 보여주고 그들이 본 것을 보고하라고 요청했다. 미국인과 일본인은 중심의 물고기에 대해 거의 비슷한 수로 언급했지만, 일본인은 물, 바위, 거품, 그리고 부동의 동식물을 포함한 배경 요소에 대해 60퍼센트 이상 더 언급했다. 또한, 일본인과 미국인 참가자가 활동적인 동물을 포함한 움직임에 대해 거의 동일한 수로 언급한 반면, 일본인 참가자들은 부동의 배경 사물을 포함한 관계에 대해 두 배 가까이 더 언급했다. 아마도 가장 강력하게, 일본인 참가자의 맨 처음 문장은 환경에 대해 언급

하는 문장일 가능성이 높았고, 반면에 미국인의 첫 번째 문장은 중심의 물고기에 대해 언급하는 문장일 가능성이 세 배 더 높았다.

① 일본인과 미국인 사이의 언어 장벽
② 뇌에서의 사물과 배경의 연상
③ 인식에 있어서의 문화적인 차이점들
④ 세부내용 지향적인 사람들의 우월성

해설 지문 처음에서 서로 다른 문화의 사람들이 세계를 다르게 보고 있을지에 대해 의문을 제기하고, 지문 전반에 걸쳐 일본인과 미국인 학생들에게 물고기와 다른 수중 사물에 관한 사실적인 동영상으로 된 장면을 보여주고 그들이 본 것을 보고하라고 요청한 결과 일본인과 미국인의 답변에 차이가 있었다는 것을 설명하고 있으므로, '③ 인식에 있어서의 문화적인 차이점들'이 이 글의 제목이다.

어휘 present 보여주다 animated 동영상으로 된
make reference 언급하다 focal 중심의
inert 부동의, 자력으로 행동할 수 없는 participant 참가자
tellingly 강력하게, 효과적으로 refer to ~에 대해 언급하다
barrier 장벽 associations 연상 perception 인식
superiority 우월성

---

18 독해 논리적 흐름 파악 (문장 삽입) 난이도 ★★☆

끊어읽기 해석

Thus, / blood, and life-giving oxygen, / are easier / for the heart / to circulate / to the brain.
따라서 / 혈액이나 생명을 주는 산소를 / 더 쉽다 / 심장이 / 순환시키기가 / 뇌로

People / can be exposed / to gravitational force, or g-force, / in different ways.
사람들은 / 노출될 수 있다 / 중력에 / 다양한 방식으로

It can be localized, / affecting / only a portion / of the body, / as in getting slapped / on the back.
이것은 한 곳에 국한될 수 있다 / 영향을 주면서 / 일부에만 / 몸의 / 맞을 때처럼 / 등을

It can also be momentary, / such as hard forces / endured in a car crash.
이것은 또한 순간적일 수도 있다 / 강력한 힘과 같이 / 자동차 충돌사고에서 겪게 되는

A third type / of g-force / is sustained, / or lasting / for at least several seconds.
세 번째 유형의 / 중력은 / 지속되거나 / 유지된다 / 최소 몇 초간

(①) Sustained, / body-wide g-forces / are the most dangerous / to people.
지속되는 / 신체 범위의 중력이 / 가장 위험하다 / 사람에게

(②) The body usually withstands / localized or momentary g-force / better than sustained g-force, / which can be deadly / because blood is forced / into the legs, / depriving / the rest of the body / of oxygen.
신체는 보통 견뎌낼 수 있다 / 국한적이거나 순간적인 중력을 / 지속적인 중력보다 더 잘 / 이것은 치명적일 수 있다 / 왜냐하면 혈액이 밀려가게 한다 / 다리에 / 빼앗아서 / 나머지 몸의 / 산소를

(③) Sustained g-force applied / while the body is horizontal, / or lying down, / instead of sitting / or standing / tends to be more tolerable / to people, / because blood pools / in the back / and not the legs.
가해지는 지속적인 중력은 / 몸이 수평이 되거나 / 누워있는 동안 / 앉아있거나 / 일어나있는 대신 / 더 견딜 수 있는 경향이 있는데 / 사람에게 / 왜냐하면 혈액이 고이기 때문이다 / 등에 / 다리가 아닌

(④) Some people, / such as astronauts and fighter jet pilots, / undergo special training exercises / to increase their

bodies' resistance / to g-force.
어떤 사람들은 / 우주인이나 전투기 조종사와 같은 / 특별한 훈련을 받는다 / 몸의 저항력을 높이기 위해 / 중력에 대한

해설 사람들은 다양한 방식으로 중력에 노출될 수 있다. 이것은 등을 맞을 때처럼 몸의 일부에만 영향을 주면서 한 곳에 국한될 수 있다. 이것은 또한 자동차 충돌사고에서 겪게 되는 강력한 힘과 같이 순간적일 수도 있다. 세 번째 유형의 중력은 최소 몇 초간 지속되거나 유지된다. 지속되는 신체 범위의 중력이 사람에게 가장 위험하다. 신체는 보통 국한적이거나 순간적인 중력을 지속적인 중력보다 더 잘 견뎌낼 수 있는데, 이것은 다리에 혈액이 밀려가게 하여 나머지 몸의 산소를 빼앗기 때문에 치명적일 수 있다. 앉아있거나 일어나있는 대신에, 몸이 수평이 되거나 누워있는 동안 가해지는 지속적인 중력은 사람에게 더 견딜 수 있는 경향이 있는데, 왜냐하면 혈액이 다리가 아닌 등에 고이기 때문이다. ④ 따라서, 심장이 혈액이나 생명을 주는 산소를 뇌로 순환시키기가 더 쉽다. 우주인이나 전투기 조종사와 같은 어떤 사람들은 중력에 대한 몸의 저항력을 높이기 위해 특별한 훈련을 받는다.

해설 ④번 앞 문장에 몸이 수평이 되거나 누워있는 동안 가해지는 지속적인 중력이 더 견디기 쉬운 경향이 있다는 내용이 있으므로 ④번 자리에 따라서(Thus) 심장이 혈액이나 생명을 주는 산소를 뇌로 순환시키기가 더 쉽다는 내용의 주어진 문장이 나와야 지문이 자연스럽게 연결된다.

어휘 circulate 순환시키다 expose 노출하다
gravitational force(g-force) 중력 localize 국한시키다
portion 일부, 부분 slap 때리다 momentary 순간적인
endure 겪다, 견디다 sustain 지속하다 withstand 견뎌내다
deprive 빼앗다 apply 가하다, 적용하다
horizontal 수평의, 수평적인 lie down 눕다
tolerable 견딜 수 있는 pool 고이다; 웅덩이 undergo 받다, 겪다
resistance 저항력

---

19 독해 전체내용 파악 (요지 파악) 난이도 ★☆☆

끊어읽기 해석

If someone / makes you an offer / and you're legitimately concerned / about parts of it, / you're usually better off / proposing all your changes / at once.
만약 누군가가 / 당신에게 제안을 하고 / 당신이 정당하게 관심을 갖는다면 / 그것의 일부분에 대해 / 당신은 보통 더 낫다 / 당신의 모든 변경 사항을 제안하는 것이 / 동시에

Don't say, / "The salary is a bit low. / Could you do something / about it?" / and then, / once she's worked on it, / come back / with "Thanks. Now here are two other things / I'd like..."
말하지 말라 / "월급이 좀 적습니다. / 무엇인가를 해주시겠어요" / 그것에 대해 / 그런 다음 / 그녀가 그것에 노력을 들이자마자 / 되돌아가다 / "고맙습니다. 이제 다른 두 가지가 있는데요..."라는 말로 / 제가 바라는

If you ask for / only one thing initially, / she may assume / that getting it / will make you ready / to accept the offer / (or at least / to make a decision).
만약 당신이 요청한다면 / 처음에 한 가지만 / 그녀는 가정할지도 모른다 / 그것을 얻어내는 것이 / 당신이 준비가 되게 만들 것이라고 / 그 제안을 받아들일 / (혹은 최소한 / 결정을 내릴)

If you keep saying / "and one more thing...," / she is unlikely to remain / in a generous / or understanding mood.
만약 당신이 계속해서 말한다면 / "그리고 한 가지만 더요..."라고 / 그녀는 유지할 것 같지 않다 / 관대하거나 / 이해심 있는 기분을

Furthermore, / if you have / more than one request, / don't

simply mention / all the things / you want A, B, C, and D; / also signal / the relative importance of each to you.
더 나아가 / 만약 당신이 가지고 있다면 / 한 개 이상의 요구 사항을 / 단순히 언급만 하지 말고 / 모두를 / 당신이 원하는 A, B, C, D / 또한 암시하라 / 당신에게 있어 각각의 상대적 중요성을

Otherwise, / she may pick / the two things you value least, / because they're pretty easy / to give you, / and feel she's met you halfway.
그렇지 않으면 / 그녀는 고를지도 모르는데 / 당신이 가장 덜 가치 있게 여기는 두 가지를 / 이는 그것들은 꽤 쉽기 때문이며 / 당신에게 주기 / (그녀는) 당신을 어느 정도 만족시켰다고 느낄지도 모른다

해석 만약 누군가가 당신에게 제안을 하고 당신이 그것의 일부분에 대해 정당하게 관심을 갖는다면, 당신은 보통 당신의 모든 변경 사항을 동시에 제안하는 것이 더 낫다. "월급이 좀 적습니다. 그것에 대해 무엇인가를 해주시겠어요?"라고 말하지 말고, 그런 다음 그녀가 그것에 노력을 들이자마자, "고맙습니다. 이제 제가 바라는 다른 두 가지가 있는데요..."라고 되돌아가지도 말라. 만약 당신이 처음에 한 가지만 요청한다면, 그녀는 그것을 얻어내는 것이 당신이 그 제안을 받아들일 (혹은 최소한 결정을 내릴) 준비가 되게 만들 것이라고 가정할지도 모른다. 만약 당신이 계속해서 "그리고 한 가지만 더요..."라고 말한다면, 그녀는 관대하거나 이해심 있는 기분을 유지할 것 같지 않다. 더 나아가, 만약 당신이 한 개 이상의 요구 사항을 가지고 있다면, 당신이 원하는 A, B, C, D 모두를 단순히 언급만 하지 말고, 또한 당신에게 있어 각각의 상대적 중요성을 암시하라. 그렇지 않으면, 그녀는 당신이 가장 덜 가치 있게 여기는 두 가지를 고를지도 모르는데, 이는 그것들은 당신에게 주기 꽤 쉽기 때문이며, (그녀는) 당신을 어느 정도 만족시켰다고 느낄지도 모른다.

① 많은 문제들을 순차적으로가 아니라 동시에 협상하라.
② 성공적인 협상을 위해 민감한 주제를 피하라.
③ 당신의 협상에 적합한 시간을 선택하라.
④ 급여를 협상할 때 너무 단도직입적이지 말라.

해설 지문 전반에 걸쳐 누군가에게 여러 가지 요구 사항을 전달할 때는 동시에 모든 요구 사항들을 제안하고, 각 요구 사항들의 상대적 중요성을 암시하라고 설명하고 있다. 따라서 '① 많은 문제들을 순차적으로가 아니라 동시에 협상하라'가 이 글의 요지이다.

어휘 legitimately 정당하게, 합법적으로 at once 동시에, 바로
work on ~에 노력을 들이다 initially 처음에 assume 가정하다
generous 관대한 mood 기분, 분위기 mention 언급하다
signal 암시하다; 신호 relative 상대적인 halfway 어느 정도
negotiate 협상하다 multiple 많은 simultaneously 동시에
serially 순차적으로 sensitive 민감한

20 독해 논리적 흐름 파악 (문단 순서 배열)   난이도 ★☆☆

끊어읽기 해석

Today, / Lamarck is unfairly remembered / in large part / for his mistaken explanation / of how adaptations evolve.
오늘날 / Lamarck는 부당하게 기억되고 있다 / 대개 / 그의 잘못된 설명으로 인해 / 적응이 어떻게 전개되는지에 대한

He proposed / that by using or not using / certain body parts, / an organism develops / certain characteristics.
그는 제안했다 / 사용하거나 사용하지 않음으로써 / 특정 신체 부위들을 / 유기체가 발달시킨다고 / 특정 특성들을

(A) There is no evidence / that this happens.
증거는 없다 / 이것이 일어난다는

Still, / it is important to note / that Lamarck proposed /

that evolution occurs / when organisms adapt to their environments.
그럼에도 불구하고 / 주목하는 것은 중요하다 / Lamarck가 제안한 것에 / 진화가 일어난다고 / 유기체가 환경에 적응할 때

This idea helped / set the stage for Darwin.
이 개념은 도움이 되었다 / Darwin의 발판을 마련하는 데

(B) Lamarck thought / that these characteristics would be passed / on to the offspring.
Lamarck는 생각했다 / 이러한 특성들이 전해질 것이라고 / 자손에게

Lamarck called this idea / inheritance of acquired characteristics.
Lamarck는 이 개념을 불렀다 / 획득형질의 유전이라고

(C) For example, / Lamarck might explain / that a kangaroo's powerful hind legs / were the result of ancestors / strengthening their legs by jumping / and then / passing that acquired leg strength / on to the offspring.
예를 들어 / Lamarck는 설명할지도 모른다 / 캥거루의 강력한 뒷다리가 / 조상들의 결과였다고 / 뛰어다님으로써 다리를 강화시키고 / 그 후 / 획득된 다리 힘을 / 자손에게 물려준 것의

However, / an acquired characteristic / would have to somehow modify / the DNA of specific genes / in order to be inherited.
하지만 / 획득형질은 / 어떻게든 수정해야 할 것이다 / 특정 유전자의 DNA를 / 유전되기 위해

해석 | 오늘날, Lamarck는 대개 적응이 어떻게 전개되는지에 대한 그의 잘못된 설명으로 인해 부당하게 기억되고 있다. 그는 특정한 신체 부위들을 사용하거나 사용하지 않음으로써 유기체가 특정한 특성들을 발달시킨다고 제안했다.

(B) Lamarck는 이러한 특성들이 자손에게 전해질 것이라고 생각했다. Lamarck는 이 개념을 획득형질의 유전이라고 불렀다.

(C) 예를 들어, Lamarck는 캥거루의 강력한 뒷다리가 조상들이 뛰어다님으로써 다리를 강화시키고 그 후 획득된 다리 힘을 자손에게 물려준 것의 결과였다고 설명할지도 모른다. 하지만, 획득형질은 유전되기 위해 특정 유전자의 DNA를 어떻게든 수정해야 할 것이다.

(A) 이것이 일어난다는 증거는 없다. 그럼에도 불구하고, Lamarck가 유기체가 환경에 적응할 때 진화가 일어난다고 제안한 것에 주목하는 것은 중요하다. 이 개념은 Darwin의 발판을 마련하는 데 도움이 되었다.

해설 주어진 글에서 Lamarck가 특정 신체 부위들을 사용하거나 사용하지 않음으로써 유기체가 특정 특성들을 발달시킨다고 제안했다고 한 후, (B)에서 Lamarck는 이러한 특성들(these characteristics)이 자손에게 전해질 것이라고 생각했으며, 이 개념을 획득형질의 유전이라고 불렀다고 설명하고 있다. 이어서 (C)에서 예를 들어(For example) 그는 캥거루의 강력한 뒷다리가 조상들이 뛰어다님으로써 획득된 다리 힘을 자손에게 물려준 것의 결과였다고 설명할지도 모른다고 언급한 후, 획득형질은 유전되기 위해 특정 유전자의 DNA를 어떻게든 수정해야 할 것이라며 획득 형질이 유전되기 위해 필요한 조건을 언급하고 있다. 마지막으로, (A)에서 이것(this)이 일어난다는 증거는 없지만 그럼에도 불구하고 Lamarck의 제안에 주목하는 것이 중요하다고 하고 있다. 따라서 ③ (B) – (C) – (A)가 정답이다.

어휘 adaptation 적응, 각색 evolve 전개되다, 진화하다
evidence 증거 set the stage for ~의 발판을 마련하다
pass on to ~에게 전하다 offspring 자손, 새끼
inheritance 유전, 유산 acquired characteristics 획득형질
ancestor 조상 modify 수정하다

4회 | 2021년 국가직 9급

정답
p.50

01	① 어휘 - 어휘&표현	11	① 어휘 - 생활영어
02	② 어휘 - 어휘&표현	12	② 어휘 - 생활영어
03	② 어휘 - 어휘&표현	13	④ 독해 - 세부내용 파악
04	④ 어휘 - 어휘&표현	14	④ 문법 - 병치·도치·강조 구문
05	④ 독해 - 세부내용 파악	15	② 문법 - 부사절&어순
06	② 문법 - 시제	16	① 독해 - 추론
07	③ 독해 - 전체내용 파악	17	② 독해 - 추론
08	③ 문법 - 명사절	18	③ 독해 - 논리적 흐름 파악
09	④ 독해 - 논리적 흐름 파악	19	④ 독해 - 전체내용 파악
10	④ 독해 - 논리적 흐름 파악	20	① 독해 - 전체내용 파악

취약영역 분석표

영역	세부 유형	문항 수	소계
어휘	어휘&표현	4	/6
	생활영어	2	
문법	시제	1	/4
	명사절	1	
	병치·도치·강조 구문	1	
	부사절&어순	1	
독해	전체내용 파악	3	/10
	세부내용 파악	2	
	추론	2	
	논리적 흐름 파악	3	
총계			/20

· 자신이 취약한 영역은 '공무원 영어, 이렇게 출제된다!'(문제집 p.8)를 통해 다시 한번 확인하고 학습하시기 바랍니다.

---

01 어휘 어휘&표현 in conjunction with = in combination with 난이도 ★☆☆

해석 사회 관행으로서의 사생활은 다른 사회 관행들과 함께 개인의 행동을 형성하고, (사생활은) 그러므로 사회생활에서 가장 중요하다.

① ~과 짝지어　　　② ~에 비해
③ ~ 대신에　　　　④ ~한다면

어휘 privacy 사생활 social practice 사회 관행
in conjunction with ~과 함께 central 가장 중요한
in combination with ~과 짝지어 in comparison with ~에 비해
in place of ~ 대신에 in case of ~한다면

👍 이것도 알면 합격!

in conjunction with(~과 함께)와 유사한 의미의 표현
= alongside, together with, combined with, in addition to, as well as

02 어휘 어휘&표현 pervasive = ubiquitous 난이도 ★★☆

해석 재즈의 영향력은 너무 만연해서 대부분의 대중음악은 양식의 뿌리를 재즈에 두고 있다.

① 현혹하는　　　　② 어디에나 있는
③ 설득력 있는　　　④ 처참한

어휘 pervasive 만연하는 popular music 대중음악 stylistic 양식의
deceptive 현혹하는 ubiquitous 어디에나 있는
persuasive 설득력 있는 disastrous 처참한

👍 이것도 알면 합격!

pervasive(만연하는)의 유의어
= common, prevalent, persistent, omnipresent

03 어휘 어휘&표현 vexed = annoyed 난이도 ★★★

해석 이 소설은 사업을 시작하기 위해 학교를 그만두고 제멋대로 하는 한 10대의 성난 부모에 대한 것이다.

① 냉담한　　　　　② 화가 난
③ 평판이 좋은　　　④ 자신감 있는

어휘 vexed 화가 난 unruly 제멋대로 하는 callous 냉담한
annoyed 화가 난 reputable 평판이 좋은

👍 이것도 알면 합격!

vexed(성난)의 유의어
= annoyed, angry, irritated, upset

04 어휘 어휘&표현 break into 난이도 ★☆☆

해석 한 무리의 젊은 시위자들이 경찰서에 침입하려고 시도했다.

① 줄을 서다　　　　② 나눠 주다
③ 계속 가다　　　　④ 침입하다

어휘 demonstrator 시위자 line up 줄을 서다
give out 나눠 주다, (열·빛 등을) 발하다 carry on 계속 가다
break into 침입하다

👍 이것도 알면 합격!

break into(침입하다)와 유사한 의미의 표현
= breach, invade, raid, trespass, get into

practice 행하다 by no means 결코 ~이 아닌 institution 관습
colonial period 식민지 시대 voluntarily 자발적으로

05 독해 세부내용 파악 (내용 일치 파악) 난이도 ★☆☆

끊어읽기 해석

①The most notorious case / of imported labor / is of course
the Atlantic slave trade, / which brought as many as ten
million enslaved Africans / to the New World / to work the
plantations.
가장 악명 높은 사례는 / 수입 노동의 / 당연히 대서양 노예무역이다 / 이것
은 천만 명이나 되는 노예가 된 아프리카인들을 데려왔다 / 아메리카 대륙
으로 / 대규모 농장들을 운영하기 위해

②③But although the Europeans may have practiced slavery /
on the largest scale, / they were by no means the only people
/ to bring slaves / into their communities: / earlier, / the
ancient Egyptians used slave labor / to build their pyramids,
/ early Arab explorers were often also slave traders, / and
Arabic slavery continued / into the twentieth century / and
indeed still continues / in a few places.
하지만 비록 유럽인들이 노예제도를 행했을지도 모르지만 / 가장 큰 규모로
/ 그들은 결코 유일한 사람들이 아니었다 / 노예들을 데려온 / 그들의 지역
사회로 / 앞서 / 고대 이집트인들은 강제 노동자들을 이용했다 / 그들의 피
라미드를 짓기 위해 / 초창기의 아랍 탐험가들 또한 보통 노예 무역상들이
었다 / 그리고 아랍의 노예제도는 계속되었다 / 20세기까지 / 그리고 사실
여전히 계속된다 / 몇몇 지역에서

④In the Americas / some native tribes enslaved members of
other tribes, / and slavery was also an institution / in many
African nations, / especially before the colonial period.
아메리카 대륙에서 / 일부 원주민들은 다른 부족의 구성원들을 노예로 만들
었다 / 그리고 노예제도는 또한 하나의 관습이었다 / 많은 아프리카 국가
들에서 / 특히 식민지 시대 이전에

해석 수입 노동의 가장 악명 높은 사례는 당연히 대서양 노예무역이고,
이것은 대규모 농장을 운영하기 위해 아메리카 대륙으로 천만 명
이나 되는 노예가 된 아프리카인들을 데려왔다. 하지만 비록 유럽
인들이 가장 큰 규모로 노예제도를 행했을지도 모르지만, 그들은
결코 노예들을 그들의 지역 사회로 데려온 유일한 사람들이 아니
었다. 앞서, 고대 이집트인들은 그들의 피라미드를 짓기 위해 강제
노동자들을 이용했고, 초창기의 아랍 탐험가들 또한 보통 노예 무
역상들이었으며, 아랍의 노예제도는 20세기까지 지속되었고 사실
몇몇 지역에서는 여전히 계속된다. 아메리카 대륙에서 일부 원주
민들은 다른 부족의 구성원들을 노예로 만들었고, 특히 식민지 시
대 이전에 노예제도는 또한 많은 아프리카 국가들에서 하나의 관
습이었다.
① 아프리카인 노동자들은 자발적으로 아메리카 대륙으로 이주했다.
② 유럽인들은 강제 노동자들을 이용한 최초의 사람들이었다.
③ 아랍의 노예제도는 어떠한 형태로도 더 이상 존재하지 않는다.
④ 노예제도는 심지어 아프리카 대륙에서도 존재했다.

해설 지문 뒷부분에서 식민지 시대 이전에 노예제도는 많은 아프리카
국가들에서 관습이었다고 했으므로, '④ 노예제도는 심지어 아프
리카 대륙에서도 존재했다'는 지문의 내용과 일치한다.

오답 ① 첫 번째 문장에서 아프리카 노예들이 아메리카 대륙으로 이동
분석   한 것은 대서양 노예무역의 영향이라고 했으므로 지문의 내용
과 다르다.
② 두 번째 문장에서 유럽인들은 결코 노예들을 그들의 사회로 데
려온 유일한 사람들이 아니라고 했고, 앞서 고대 이집트인들과
아랍 탐험가들도 강제 노동자들을 이용했다는 내용이 있으므
로 지문의 내용과 다르다.
③ 세 번째 문장에서 아랍의 노예제도는 몇몇 지역에서 여전히 계
속된다고 했으므로 지문의 내용과 다르다.

어휘 notorious 악명 높은 import 수입하다 enslave 노예로 만들다
the New World 아메리카 대륙 plantation 대규모 농장

06 문법 시제 난이도 ★★☆

해석 ① 이 가이드북은 당신이 홍콩에서 어디를 방문해야 하는지를 알
려준다.
② 나는 대만에서 태어났지만, 내가 일을 시작한 이후로는 한국에
서 살아왔다.
③ 그 소설은 너무 흥미진진해서 나는 시간 가는 줄 몰랐고 버스를
놓쳤다.
④ 서점들이 더 이상 신문을 취급하지 않는다는 것이 놀랍지 않다,
그렇지 않은가?

해설 ② 시제 일치 현재완료 시제와 자주 함께 쓰이는 시간 표현
since가 왔으므로, 현재완료 시제 have lived가 올바르게 쓰였다.

오답 ① 의문문의 어순 의문문이 다른 문장 안에 포함된 간접 의문문
분석   은 '의문사 + 주어 + 동사'의 어순이 되어야 하므로 where
should you visit을 where you should visit으로 고쳐야 한다.
③ 3형식 동사의 수동태 감정을 나타내는 동사(excite)의 경우
주어가 감정의 원인이면 현재분사, 감정을 느끼는 주체이면
과거분사를 써야 하는데, 문맥상 '소설이 흥미진진했다'라는
의미로 주어(the novel)가 감정의 원인이 되어야 하므로 과거
분사 excited를 be 동사(was) 뒤에서 능동태를 완성하는 현
재분사 exciting으로 고쳐야 한다.
④ 의문문의 어순 평서문(It's not surprising ~ any more)에
be 동사(is)가 온 부정문이므로, 부정 부가 의문문 doesn't it
을 긍정 부가 의문문 is it으로 고쳐야 한다.

어휘 lose track of time 시간 가는 줄 모르다 carry 취급하다

👍 이것도 알면 합격!
부정문 뒤에는 긍정 부가 의문문을, 긍정문 뒤에는 부정 부가 의문문
을 써야 하며, 평서문의 동사가 일반동사일 경우 부가 의문문에는 do
동사를 쓰고, 평서문의 동사가 be 동사나 조동사인 경우에는 부가 의
문문에도 동일하게 be 동사나 조동사를 쓴다.

07 독해 전체내용 파악 (제목 파악) 난이도 ★★☆

끊어읽기 해석

Warming temperatures and loss of oxygen / in the sea / will
shrink hundreds of fish species / —from tunas and groupers
to salmon, thresher sharks, haddock and cod / —even more
than previously thought, / a new study concludes.
따뜻해지고 있는 온도와 산소의 부족이 / 바다에서 / 수백의 물고기 종을
줄어들게 할 것이라고 / 참치와 그루퍼에서 연어, 환도상어, 해덕과 대구까
지의 / 이전에 생각되었던 것보다 훨씬 더 / 한 새로운 연구는 결론 내린다

Because warmer seas speed up their metabolisms, / fish,
squid and other water-breathing creatures / will need to draw
more oxygen / from the ocean.
더 따뜻한 바다는 그것들의 신진대사를 촉진하기 때문에 / 물고기, 오징어
와 다른 수중 호흡을 하는 생물들은 / 더 많은 산소를 얻어야 할 것이다 /
바다에서

At the same time, / warming seas are already reducing / the
availability of oxygen / in many parts / of the sea.
동시에 / 따뜻해지고 있는 바다는 이미 감소시키고 있다 / 산소의 이용 가
능성을 / 많은 부분에서 / 바다의

A pair of University of British Columbia scientists argue / that

since the bodies of fish grow faster / than their gills, / these animals eventually will reach a point / where they can't get enough oxygen / to sustain normal growth.
두 명의 브리티시 컬럼비아 대학교의 과학자들은 주장한다 / 물고기의 몸통이 더 빨리 자라기 때문에 / 그것들의 아가미보다 / 이러한 동물들은 결국 한 시점에 이르게 될 것이다 / 그것들이 충분한 산소를 얻지 못하는 / 정상적인 성장을 지속하기 위한

"What we found / was that the body size of fish decreases / by 20 to 30 percent / for every 1 degree Celsius increase / in water temperature," / says author William Cheung.
"우리가 발견했던 것은 / 물고기의 몸통 크기가 줄어든다는 것이었다 / 20에서 30퍼센트만큼씩 / 섭씨 1도의 상승마다 / 물의 온도에서" / ~라고 저자 윌리엄 청은 말한다

해석 한 새로운 연구는 바다에서 따뜻해지고 있는 온도와 산소의 부족이 참치와 그루퍼에서 연어, 환도상어, 해덕과 대구까지의 수백의 물고기 종을 이전에 생각되었던 것보다 훨씬 더 줄어들게 할 것이라고 결론 내린다. 더 따뜻한 바다는 그것들의 신진대사를 촉진하기 때문에, 물고기, 오징어와 다른 수중 호흡을 하는 생물들은 바다에서 더 많은 산소를 얻어야 할 것이다. 동시에, 따뜻해지고 있는 바다는 이미 바다의 많은 부분에서 산소의 이용 가능성을 감소시키고 있다. 두 명의 브리티시 컬럼비아 대학교의 과학자들은 이러한 동물들은 그것들의 아가미보다 물고기의 몸통이 더 빨리 자라기 때문에, 결국 정상적인 성장을 지속하기 위한 충분한 산소를 얻지 못하는 한 시점에 이르게 될 것이라고 주장한다. "우리가 발견했던 것은 물의 온도에서 섭씨 1도의 상승이 있을 때마다 물고기의 몸통 크기가 20에서 30퍼센트만큼씩 줄어든다는 것이었다"라고 저자 윌리엄 청은 말한다.

① 이제 물고기들은 여느 때보다 더 빠르게 자란다
② 바다의 온도에 대한 산소의 영향
③ 기후 변화는 세계의 물고기들을 줄어들게 할 수도 있다
④ 바다 생물들은 어떻게 낮은 신진대사로 살아남는가

해설 지문 처음에서 바다의 따뜻해지는 온도와 산소의 부족이 수많은 물고기 종을 줄어들게 할 것이라고 했으므로, '③ 기후 변화는 세계의 물고기들을 줄어들게 할 수도 있다'가 이 글의 제목이다.

어휘 shrink 줄어들게 하다 cod (어류) 대구 metabolism 신진대사 draw from ~에서 얻다 availability 이용 가능성, 유용성 gill 아가미 sustain 지속하다 Celsius 섭씨

08 문법 명사절
난이도 ★★☆

해석 도시 농업(UA)은 도시에는 적절한 장소가 없는 비주류 활동으로 오랫동안 묵살되어 왔다. 하지만, 그것의 가능성이 실현되기 시작하고 있다. 사실, UA는 식량 자립에 관한 것으로, 그것은 일자리를 창출하는 것을 포함하고 특히 가난한 사람들을 위한 식량 불안정에 대한 반응이다. 많은 사람들이 믿는 것과 반대로, UA는 모든 도시에서 발견되는데, 그것은 때로는 숨겨져 있고, 때로는 대번에 알 수 있다. 어떤 사람이 주의 깊게 본다면, 대도시에서 사용되지 않는 공간은 거의 없다. 값비싸고 비어 있는 땅은 거의 사용되지 않는 상태로 방치되지 않고, 종종 공식적이거나 비공식적으로 인수되어 생산적이게 만들어진다.

해설 ③ 명사절 접속사 3: 의문사 목적어가 없는 불완전한 절(many believe)이 왔으므로 관계대명사 which를 전치사 to 뒤에서 목적어 역할을 하며 불완전한 절을 이끄는 명사절 접속사 what으로 고쳐야 한다.

오답 분석 ① to 부정사의 형태 주어(its potential)와 to 부정사가 '그것의 가능성이 실현되다'라는 의미의 수동 관계이므로, to 부정사의 수동형 to be realized가 올바르게 쓰였다.

② 동명사를 목적어로 취하는 동사 동사 involve는 동명사를 목적어로 취할 수 있으므로 동명사 creating이 올바르게 쓰였다.

④ 5형식 동사의 수동태 목적격 보어를 취하는 5형식 동사(make)가 수동태(is made)가 되면 목적격 보어 productive는 수동태 동사 뒤에 그대로 남아야 하므로 productive가 올바르게 쓰였다.

어휘 dismiss 묵살하다 fringe 비주류 potential 가능성 self-reliance 자립 reaction 반응 food insecurity 식량 불안정 vacant 비어 있는 sit 방치되어 있다 idle 사용되지 않는 take over 인수하다

👉 이것도 알면 합격!

동사 involve와 같이 동명사를 목적어로 취하는 동사들을 알아두자.

제안·고려를 나타내는 동사	recommend -ing -을 추천하다
	consider -ing -을 고려하다
중지·연기를 나타내는 동사	stop -ing -을 그만두다
	finish -ing -을 끝내다
	quit -ing -을 그만두다
	discontinue -ing -을 중지하다
	give up -ing -을 포기하다
	postpone -ing -을 연기하다
부정적 의미를 나타내는 동사	dislike -ing -을 싫어하다
	deny -ing -을 부인하다
	mind -ing -을 꺼리다
	avoid -ing -을 피하다

09 독해 논리적 흐름 파악 (문장 삽입)
난이도 ★☆☆

끊어읽기 해석

For example, / the state archives of New Jersey hold / more than 30,000 cubic feet of paper and 25,000 reels of microfilm.
예를 들어 / 뉴저지주의 주립 기록 보관소는 수용한다 / 3만 입방 피트 이상의 종이와 2만 5천 릴 이상의 마이크로필름을

Archives are a treasure trove / of material: / from audio to video to newspapers, magazines and printed material— / which makes them indispensable / to any History Detective investigation.
기록 보관소는 귀중한 발굴물이다 / 자료들의 / 오디오에서 비디오와 신문, 잡지와 인쇄물까지의 / 이것들은 그것들이 없어서는 안 되게 만든다 / 그 어떠한 역사 탐정 조사에 있어서

While libraries and archives may appear the same, / the differences are important.
도서관과 기록 보관소가 동일하게 보일지도 모르지만 / 그 차이점들은 중요하다

(①) An archive collection / is almost always made up of primary sources, / while a library contains secondary sources.
기록 보관소의 소장품은 / 거의 항상 최초의 자료들로 구성되어 있다 / 반면에 도서관은 부차적인 자료들을 포함하고 있다

(②) To learn more / about the Korean War, / you'd go to a library / for a history book.
더 알기 위해 / 한국 전쟁에 대해 / 당신은 도서관에 갈 것이다 / 역사책을 찾을 목적으로

If you wanted to read the government papers, / or letters / written by Korean War soldiers, / you'd go to an archive.
만약 당신이 정부 문서를 읽기를 원했다면 / 또는 편지들을 / 한국 전쟁 병사들에 의해 쓰여진 / 당신은 기록 보관소에 갈 것이다

(③) If you're searching for information, / chances are there's an archive out there / for you.
만약 당신이 정보를 찾고 있다면 / 아마 그곳에 기록 보관소가 있을 것이다 / 당신을 위한

Many state and local archives store public records / —which are an amazing, diverse resource.
많은 주와 지역의 기록 보관소들은 공문서를 보관한다 / 이것들은 놀랍고 다양한 자원이다

(④) An online search / of your state's archives / will quickly show you / they contain much more / than just the minutes of the legislature / —there are detailed land grant information to be found, / old town maps, criminal records and oddities / such as peddler license applications.
온라인 검색은 / 당신 주의 기록 보관소에 대한 / 당신에게 빠르게 보여줄 것이다 / 그것들이 훨씬 더 많은 것을 포함한다는 것을 / 입법 기관의 회의록뿐만 아니라 / 그곳에는 정부가 주는 상세한 땅 정보가 있다 / 옛 도시 지도, 전과 기록과 이상한 것들을 찾아볼 수 있다 / 예를 들면 행상인 면허 신청서와 같은

해석 기록 보관소는 오디오에서부터 비디오와 신문, 잡지와 인쇄물까지의 자료들로 이루어진 귀중한 발굴물이고, 이러한 자료들은 그 어떠한 역사 탐정 조사에 있어서 그것(기록 보관소)들이 없어서는 안 되게 만든다. 도서관과 기록 보관소가 동일하게 보일지도 모르지만, 그 차이점들은 중요하다. 기록 보관소의 소장품은 거의 항상 최초의 자료들로 구성되어 있는 반면에, 도서관은 부차적인 자료들을 포함하고 있다. 한국 전쟁에 대해 더 알기 위해, 당신은 역사책을 찾을 목적으로 도서관에 갈 것이다. 만약 당신이 정부 문서나 한국 전쟁 병사들에 의해 쓰여진 편지들을 읽기를 원한다면, 당신은 기록 보관소에 갈 것이다. 만약 당신이 정보를 찾고 있다면, 아마 그곳에 당신을 위한 기록 보관소가 있을 것이다. 많은 주와 지역의 기록 보관소들은 공문서를 보관하고, 이것들은 놀랍고 다양한 자원이다. ④ 예를 들어, 뉴저지주의 주립 기록 보관소는 3만 입방 피트 이상의 종이와 2만 5천 릴 이상의 마이크로필름을 수용한다. 당신 주의 기록 보관소에 대한 온라인 검색은 입법 기관의 회의록뿐만 아니라 그것들이 훨씬 더 많은 것을 포함한다는 것을 당신에게 빠르게 보여줄 것이다. 그곳에는 정부가 주는 상세한 땅 정보, 옛 도시 지도, 전과 기록과 예를 들면 행상인 면허 신청서와 같은 이상한 것들을 찾아 볼 수 있다.

해설 ④번 앞 문장에 많은 주와 지역의 기록 보관소들에 있는 공문서들이 놀랍고 다양한 자원이라는 내용이 있으므로, ④번 자리에 뉴저지 주의 기록 보관소가 많은 양의 자료를 수용한다는 내용의 주어진 문장이 나와야 지문이 자연스럽게 연결된다.

어휘 archives 기록 보관소 hold 수용하다 cubic feet 입방 피트
indispensable 없어서는 안 되는 important 중요한
chances are 아마 ~일 것이다 minutes 회의록
criminal record 전과 기록 peddler 행상인

10 독해 논리적 흐름 파악 (무관한 문장 삭제) 난이도 ★☆☆

끊어읽기 해석

The term burnout refers / to a "wearing out" / from the pressures of work.
번아웃이라는 용어는 나타낸다 / '지치는 것'을 / 일에 대한 압박으로 인해

Burnout is a chronic condition / that results / as daily work stressors take their toll on employees.
번아웃은 만성적인 상태이다 / 발생하는 / 매일의 업무 스트레스 요인이 직원들에게 타격을 줄 때

① The most widely adopted conceptualization of burnout / has been developed / by Maslach and her colleagues / in their studies / of human service workers.
번아웃에 대해 가장 널리 채택되는 개념적인 해석은 / 전개되어왔다 / Maslach와 그녀의 동료들에 의해 / 그들의 연구에서 / 사회 복지 근로자들에 대한

Maslach sees burnout / as consisting / of three interrelated dimensions.
Maslach는 번아웃을 본다 / 포함하는 것으로 / 세 가지의 밀접하게 연관된 요소들을

The first dimension / —emotional exhaustion / —is really the core / of the burnout phenomenon.
첫 번째 요소는 / 감정적인 소모는 / 실제로 핵심이다 / 번아웃 현상의

② Workers suffer / from emotional exhaustion / when they feel fatigued, frustrated, used up, / or unable to face another day / on the job.
근로자들은 고통받는다 / 감정적인 소모로부터 / 그들이 지쳤다고 느끼거나, 좌절감을 느끼거나, 녹초가 되었을 때 / 또는 후일을 직면할 수 없을 때 / 직장에서

The second dimension / of burnout / is a lack of personal accomplishment.
번아웃의 두 번째 요소는 / 개인적인 성취의 부족이다

③ This aspect / of the burnout phenomenon / refers to workers / who see themselves as failures, / incapable of effectively accomplishing job requirements.
이 번아웃 현상의 양상은 / 근로자들을 가리킨다 / 그들 자신들을 실패자라고 바라보는 / 효과적으로 임무 요건을 완수하기에 불가능한

④ Emotional labor workers / enter their occupation highly motivated / although they are physically exhausted.
감정 노동자들은 / 많은 의욕을 가지고 그들의 일을 시작한다 / 그들이 신체적으로는 지쳤음에도 불구하고

The third dimension of burnout / is depersonalization.
번아웃의 세 번째 요소는 / 비인격화이다

This dimension is relevant / only to workers / who must communicate interpersonally with others / (e.g. clients, patients, students) / as part of the job.
이 요소는 유의미하다 / 근로자들에게만 / 다른 사람들과의 대인 관계에서 의사소통을 해야 하는 / 예를 들어, 고객들, 환자들, 학생들과 / 일의 일부로서

해석 번아웃이라는 용어는 일에 대한 압박으로 인해 '지치는 것'을 나타낸다. 번아웃은 매일의 업무 스트레스 요인이 직원들에게 타격을 줄 때 발생하는 만성적인 상태이다. ① 번아웃에 대해 가장 널리 채택되는 개념적인 해석은 Maslach와 그녀의 동료들에 의해 사회 복지 근로자들에 대한 그들의 연구에서 전개되어왔다. Maslach는 번아웃을 세 가지의 밀접하게 연관된 요소들을 포함하는 것으로 본다. 첫 번째 요소, 즉 감정적인 소모는 실제로 번아웃 현상의 핵심이다. ② 근로자들은 그들이 지쳤다고 느끼거나, 좌절감을 느끼거나, 녹초가 되거나, 직장에서 후일을 직면할 수 없을 때 감정적인 소모로부터 고통받는다. 번아웃의 두 번째 요소는 개인적인 성취의 부족이다. ③ 이 번아웃 현상의 양상은 그들 자신들을 효과적으로 임무 요건을 완수하기에 불가능한 실패자라고 바라보는 근로자들을 가리킨다. ④ 감정 노동자들은 그들이 신체적으로는 지쳤음에도 불구하고 많은 의욕을 가지고 그들의 일을 시작한다. 번아웃의 세 번째 요소는 비인격화이다. 이 요소는 일의 일부로서 다른 사람들, 예를 들어, 고객들, 환자들, 학생들과의 대인 관계에서 의사소통을 해야 하는 근로자들에게만 유의미하다.

해설 첫 문장에서 번아웃의 증상에 대해 언급한 뒤, ①, ②, ③번에서 번아웃 해석에 기초가 되는 연구에서 구분한 번아웃의 세 가지 요소에 대해 설명하고 있으므로 모두 첫 문장과 관련이 있다. 그러나 ④번은 감정적인 노동자들이 신체적으로 지쳤는데도 의욕을 가지고 일을 한다는 내용으로 첫 문장의 내용과 관련이 없다.

어휘

refer 나타내다, 가리키다　wear out 지치다　pressure 압박
chronic 만성적인　stressor 스트레스 요인
take a toll on ~에 타격(피해)을 가져오다　adopt 채택하다
conceptualization 개념적인 해석　interrelated 밀접하게 연관된
dimension 요소　exhaustion 소모　fatigued 지친
frustrated 좌절감을 느끼다　used up 녹초가 된
occupation 일, 직업　motivated 의욕을 가진
depersonalization 비인격화　relevant 유의미한
interpersonally 대인 관계에서

---

11 어휘 생활영어 I won't let it happen again. 난이도 ★★☆

해석

A: 어젯밤에 여기 왔었나요?
B: 네. 저는 마감 교대 조로 일했어요. 왜 그러세요?
A: 오늘 아침에 부엌이 엉망이었어요. 레인지 위에 음식이 흩어져 떨어져 있었고, 제빙 그릇들은 냉동고 안에 없었어요.
B: 제 생각에 제가 청소 점검표를 검토하는 것을 잊은 것 같아요.
A: 당신은 깨끗한 주방이 얼마나 중요한지 알잖아요.
B: 죄송합니다. 이런 일이 다시 일어나지 않도록 할게요.

① 이런 일이 다시 일어나지 않도록 할게요.
② 지금 당신의 계산서를 원하시나요?
③ 그것이 어제 제가 그것을 잊어버린 이유입니다.
④ 주문하신 대로 옳게 받으실 수 있도록 하겠습니다.

해설 청소 점검표를 검토하는 것을 잊었다는 B의 말에 대해 빈칸 앞에서 A가 You know how important a clean kitchen is(당신은 깨끗한 주방이 얼마나 중요한지 알잖아요)라고 말하고 있으므로, 빈칸에는 '① 이런 일이 다시 일어나지 않도록 할게요(I won't let it happen again)'가 오는 것이 자연스럽다.

어휘 shift 교대 조　spatter 흩어져 떨어지다　stove 레인지
go over 검토하다　bill 계산서

👍 이것도 알면 **합격!**

직장에서 업무와 관련해서 사용할 수 있는 다양한 표현을 알아두자.

· That's not in my job description.
　그것은 제 업무가 아니에요.
· I've got to finish editing this report by tomorrow.
　내일까지 이 보고서를 수정하는 것을 끝내야 해요.
· Don't forget to update the schedule.
　일정을 업데이트하는 것을 잊지 마세요.

---

12 어휘 생활영어 No, I don't like nose spray. 난이도 ★☆☆

해석

A: 너 감기를 낫게 하기 위해 무엇을 좀 먹었니?
B: 아니, 그냥 코만 아주 많이 풀고 있어.
A: 너 코 스프레이를 사용해본 적 있니?
B: 아니, 난 코 스프레이를 좋아하지 않아.
A: 그거 효과가 좋아.
B: 아니, 괜찮아. 나는 내 코에 무언가를 넣는 것을 좋아하지 않아서 그걸 한 번도 사용해본 적이 없어.

① 응, 그런데 그것은 도움이 되지 않았어.
② 아니, 난 코 스프레이를 좋아하지 않아.
③ 아니, 약국이 문을 닫았어.
④ 응, 얼마나 많이 써야 해?

해설 코 스프레이를 사용해본 적이 있는지 묻는 A에게 B가 대답하고, 빈칸 뒤에서 A가 코 스프레이가 효과가 좋다고 하지만 다시 B가 No, thanks. I don't like to put anything in my nose, so I've never used it(아니, 괜찮아. 나는 내 코에 무언가를 넣는 것을 좋아하지 않아서 그걸 한 번도 사용해본 적이 없어)라고 말하고 있으므로, 빈칸에는 '② 아니, 난 코 스프레이를 좋아하지 않아(No, I don't like nose spray)'가 오는 것이 자연스럽다.

어휘 blow one's nose 코를 풀다　work 효과가 있다　help 도움이 되다

👍 이것도 알면 **합격!**

무언가를 권하거나 거절할 때 사용할 수 있는 다양한 표현을 알아두자.

· You should try this tablet.
　이 태블릿 한 번 써 봐.
· I don't prefer using herbal remedies.
　나는 한방 치료법을 좋아하지 않아.
· Eating vegetables is good for your health.
　야채를 먹는 것은 네 건강에 좋아.

---

13 독해 세부내용 파악 (내용 불일치 파악) 난이도 ★☆☆

끊어읽기 해석

Deserts cover more than one-fifth / of the Earth's land area, / and they are found / on every continent.
사막은 5분의 1 이상을 감싼다 / 지구 육지 면적의 / 그리고 그것들은 발견된다 / 모든 대륙에서

A place that receives less than 25 centimeters (10 inches) of rain / per year / is considered a desert.
비를 25센티미터(10인치)보다 더 적게 받는 장소는 / 매년 / 사막으로 여겨진다

Deserts are part / of a wider class of regions / called drylands.
사막은 일부이다 / 더 폭넓은 지역 종류의 / 건조 지역이라고 불리는

These areas exist / under a "moisture deficit," / which means / they can frequently lose more moisture / through evaporation / than they receive / from annual precipitation.
이러한 지역들은 존재한다 / '수분 부족' 하에 / 그리고 이것은 의미한다 / 그곳들이 자주 더 많은 수분을 잃을 수 있다는 것을 / 증발을 통해 / 그곳들이 받는 것보다 / 연간 강수량으로부터

Despite the common conceptions / of deserts / as hot, / there are cold deserts as well.
보통의 생각에도 불구하고 / 사막에 대한 / 덥다는 / 추운 사막들도 있다

The largest hot desert / in the world, / northern Africa's Sahara, / reaches temperatures / of up to 50 degrees Celsius (122 degrees Fahrenheit) / during the day.
가장 큰 더운 사막인 / 세계에서 / 아프리카 북부의 사하라 사막은 / 온도에 도달한다 / 섭씨 50도(화씨 122도)까지의 / 낮 동안에

But some deserts are always cold, / like the Gobi Desert in Asia / and the polar deserts / of the Antarctic and Arctic, which are the world's largest.
그러나 몇몇 사막들은 항상 춥다 / 아시아의 고비 사막과 같은 / 그리고 극지의 사막들은 / 남극과 북극의 / 그리고 이 극지의 사막들은 세계에서 가장 크다

Others are mountainous.
다른 곳들은 산이 많다

Only about 20 percent / of deserts / are covered by sand.
약 20퍼센트만이 / 사막의 / 모래로 덮여 있다

The driest deserts, / such as Chile's Atacama Desert, / have parts / that receive less than two millimeters (0.08 inches) / of precipitation a year.

가장 건조한 사막들은 / 칠레의 아타카마 사막과 같은 / 지역들이 있다 / 2밀리미터(0.08인치)보다 더 적은 / 1년에 강수량을 받는

Such environments are so harsh and otherworldly / that scientists have even studied them / for clues / about life on Mars.
그러한 환경은 너무 황량하고 비현실적이다 / 그래서 과학자들은 심지어 그곳들을 연구하기도 했다 / 실마리를 찾기 위해 / 화성에 사는 생물에 대한

On the other hand, / every few years, / an unusually rainy period can produce "super blooms," / where even the Atacama becomes blanketed / in wildflowers.
반면 / 몇 년마다 / 비정상적인 우기는 '슈퍼 블룸'을 초래할 수 있다 / 그리고 이 슈퍼 블룸은 아타카마 사막조차 완전히 뒤덮이게 한다 / 들꽃들로

해석 사막은 지구 육지 면적의 5분의 1 이상을 감싸고, 그것(사막)들은 모든 대륙에서 발견된다. 매년 비를 25센티미터(10인치)보다 더 적게 받는 장소는 사막으로 여겨진다. 사막은 건조 지역이라고 불리는 더 폭넓은 종류의 지역들 중 일부이다. 이러한 지역들은 '수분 부족' 하에 존재하고, 이것은 그곳들이 연간 강수량으로부터 받는 것보다 증발을 통해 더 많은 수분을 자주 잃을 수 있다는 것을 의미한다. 덥다는 사막에 대한 보통의 생각에도 불구하고, 추운 사막들도 있다. 세계에서 가장 큰 더운 사막인 아프리카 북부의 사하라 사막은 낮 동안에 섭씨 50도(화씨 122도)까지의 온도에 도달한다. 그러나 아시아의 고비 사막과 남극과 북극의 극지 사막과 같은 몇몇 사막은 항상 춥고, 이 극지의 사막들은 세계에서 가장 크다. 다른 곳(사막)들은 산이 많다. 사막의 약 20퍼센트만이 모래로 덮여 있다. 칠레의 아타카마 사막과 같은 가장 건조한 사막들은 1년에 2밀리미터(0.08인치)보다 더 적은 강수량을 받는 지역들이 있다. 그러한 환경은 너무 황량하고 비현실적이어서 과학자들은 심지어 화성에 사는 생물에 대한 실마리를 찾기 위해 그곳들을 연구하기도 했다. 반면, 몇 년마다 비정상적인 우기는 '슈퍼 블룸'을 초래할 수 있는데, 이것(슈퍼 블룸)은 아타카마 사막조차 들꽃들로 완전히 뒤덮이게 한다.

① 각 대륙에 최소 한 개의 사막이 있다.
② 사하라 사막은 세계에서 가장 큰 더운 사막이다.
③ 고비 사막은 추운 사막으로 분류된다.
④ 아타카마 사막은 비가 많이 오는 사막들 중의 하나이다.

해설 지문 뒷부분에서 칠레의 아타카마 사막은 가장 건조한 사막이라고 했으므로, '④ 아타카마 사막은 비가 많이 오는 사막들 중의 하나이다'는 지문의 내용과 다르다.

어휘 deficit 부족 evaporation 증발 conception 생각, 개념 mountainous 산이 많은 precipitation 강수량 harsh 황량한 otherworldly 비현실적인 blanket 완전히 뒤덮다 wildflower 들꽃 categorize 분류하다

---

14 **문법** 병치·도치·강조 구문 난이도 ★★☆

해설 ④ 도치 구문: 기타 도치 부사 so가 '~역시 그렇다'라는 의미로 쓰여 절 앞에 오면 주어와 조동사가 도치되어 '조동사(did) + 주어(her son)'의 어순이 되어야 하므로 so did her son이 올바르게 쓰였다. 참고로, 동사 love는 to 부정사와 동명사를 모두 목적어로 취하는 동사이므로 동명사를 목적어로 취한 loved playing이 올바르게 쓰였다.

오답분석 ① 동명사 관련 표현 '답장을 ~ 받기를 고대한다'는 동명사 관련 표현 'look forward to -ing'(-을 고대하다)로 나타낼 수 있으므로 동사원형 receive를 동명사 receiving으로 고쳐야 한다.
② 혼동하기 쉬운 자동사와 타동사 '월급을 올리다'는 타동사 raise를 써서 나타낼 수 있으므로 자동사 rise를 타동사 raise(떠오르다)로 고쳐야 한다.

---

③ 동명사 관련 표현 '고려할 만했다'는 동명사 관련 표현 'be worth -ing'(-할 만하다)로 나타낼 수 있으므로 과거분사 considered를 동명사 considering으로 고쳐야 한다.

어휘 look forward to ~을 고대하다 salary 월급

👍 이것도 알면 **합격!**

형태가 비슷해서 혼동하기 쉬운 자동사와 타동사를 알아두자.

자동사	타동사
lie-lay-lain 놓여있다, 눕다 lie-lied-lied 거짓말하다	lay-laid-laid ~을 놓다, ~을 두다, (알을) 낳다
sit-sat-sat 앉다	seat-seated-seated ~을 앉히다
rise-rose-risen 떠오르다	raise-raised-raised ~을 모으다, 올리다

---

15 **문법** 부사절 & 어순 난이도 ★★★

해설 ② 부사절 접속사 2: 기타 | 혼동하기 쉬운 어순 부사절 접속사 such ~ that(매우 ~해서 -하다)은 'such + 형용사/부사 + that + 주어(we) + 동사(watched)'의 형태로 쓰이고, such 뒤의 형용사가 명사를 수식할 때는 'such + a/an + 형용사(beautiful) + 명사(meteor storm)'의 어순으로 나타낼 수 있으므로 such a beautiful meteor storm that we watched 가 올바르게 쓰였다.

오답분석 ① 부사절 접속사 2: 양보 문맥상 '부자일지라도'는 양보의 부사절 접속사 as(비록 ~이지만)를 사용하여 나타낼 수 있으므로, as if를 부사절 접속사 as로 고쳐야 한다. 참고로, 양보의 부사절 내의 보어가 강조되어 as 앞에 나오면 '(As +) 보어(Rich) + as + 주어(you) + 동사(may be)'의 어순으로 쓰인다.
③ 전치사 숙어 표현 문맥상 '그녀의 성공을 방해했다(그녀가 성공하는 것을 방해했다)'는 목적어 뒤에 특정 전치사구와 함께 쓰이는 숙어 표현 'keep + 목적어(her) + from'(~을 -으로부터 막다)으로 나타낼 수 있으므로, kept her advancing을 kept her from advancing으로 고쳐야 한다. 참고로, 전치사 from 뒤에는 명사 역할을 하는 것이 와야 하므로 동명사 advancing이 쓰였다.
④ 명사절 접속사 2: if와 whether 명사절 접속사 if와 whether 모두 '~인지 아닌지'라는 의미이지만, if는 'if or not'의 형태로 쓰일 수 없고, if가 이끄는 명사절은 전치사 on의 목적어 자리에 올 수 없으므로 if를 whether로 고쳐야 한다.

어휘 as if 마치 ~인 것처럼 sincere 진실한, 성실한 meteor storm 유성 폭풍 degree 학위 advance 성공을 돕다 death penalty 사형 제도 abolish 폐지하다

👍 이것도 알면 **합격!**

전치사 from과 함께 쓰여 'A가 B하는 것을 막다'라는 의미를 나타내는 표현

· hinder A from B	· keep A from B
· prohibit A from B	· deter A from B
· prevent A from B	· restrain A from B

끊어읽기 해석

Social media, magazines and shop windows / bombard people daily / with things to buy, / and British consumers are buying / more clothes and shoes / than ever before.
소셜 미디어, 잡지와 상품진열창은 / 사람들에게 날마다 퍼붓는다 / 살 것들을 / 그리고 영국 소비자들은 사고 있다 / 더 많은 옷과 신발들을 / 이제까지보다

Online shopping means / it is easy for customers to buy / without thinking, / while major brands offer such cheap clothes / that they can be treated / like disposable items / —worn two or three times / and then thrown away.
온라인 쇼핑은 의미한다 / 소비자들이 사기 쉽다는 것을 / 생각하지 않고 / 동시에 주요한 브랜드들이 그러한 저렴한 옷들을 내놓아서 / 그것들이 대해질 수 있다 / 일회용 물건들처럼 / 두 번 혹은 세 번 입어진다 / 그리고 나서 버려진다

In Britain, / the average person spends more than £1,000 / on new clothes a year, / which is around four percent / of their income.
영국에서는 / 보통의 사람이 1,000파운드 이상을 소비한다 / 1년 동안 새로운 옷에 / 이것은 약 4퍼센트이다 / 그들의 수입의

That might not sound like much, / but that figure hides two far more worrying trends / for society / and for the environment.
그것은 많게 들리지 않을지도 모른다 / 그러나 그 수치는 두 가지의 훨씬 더 걱정스러운 경향들을 가린다 / 사회에 대한 / 그리고 환경에 대한

First, / a lot of that consumer spending / is via credit cards.
첫째로 / 그러한 소비자 지출의 상당수가 / 신용카드를 통한 것이다

British people currently owe / approximately £670 per adult / to credit card companies.
영국 사람들은 현재 빚지고 있다 / 각 성인당 약 670파운드를 / 신용카드 회사에

That's 66 percent / of the average wardrobe budget.
그것은 66퍼센트이다 / 평균 옷장 예산의

Also, not only are people spending money / they don't have, / they're using it / to buy things / they don't need.
또한 사람들이 돈을 소비하고 있을 뿐만 아니라 / 그들이 가지지 않은 / 그들은 그것을 사용하고 있다 / 물건들을 사기 위해 / 그들이 필요하지 않은

Britain throws away 300,000 tons of clothing / a year, / most of which goes into landfill sites.
영국은 30만 톤의 옷을 버리고 있다 / 1년에 / 그리고 그것의 대부분은 쓰레기 매립지로 들어간다

해석 소셜 미디어, 잡지와 상품진열창은 살 것들을 사람들에게 날마다 퍼붓고, 영국 소비자들은 이제까지보다 더 많은 옷과 신발들을 사고 있다. 주요한 브랜드들이 그러한 저렴한 옷들을 내놓아서 그것(옷)들이 일회용 물건들처럼 두 번 혹은 세 번 입혀지고 나서 버려질 수 있는 동시에, 온라인 쇼핑은 소비자들이 생각하지 않고 사기 쉽다는 것을 의미한다. 영국에서는, 보통의 사람이 1년 동안 새로운 옷에 1,000파운드 이상을 소비하며, 이것은 그들의 수입의 약 4퍼센트이다. 그것은 많게 들리지 않을지도 모르나, 그 수치는 사회와 환경 두 가지에 대한 훨씬 더 걱정스러운 경향들을 가린다. 첫째로, 그러한 소비자 지출의 상당수가 신용카드를 통한 것이다. 영국 사람들은 현재 각 성인당 약 670파운드를 신용카드 회사에 빚지고 있다. 그것은 평균 옷장 예산(평균적으로 옷에 소비하는 금액)의 66퍼센트이다. 또한 사람들이 그들이 가지지 않은 돈을 소비하고 있을 뿐만 아니라, 그들은 필요하지 않은 물건들을 사기 위해 그것(돈)을 사용하고 있다. 영국은 1년에 30만 톤의 옷을 버리고 있고, 그것의 대부분은 쓰레기 매립지로 들어간다.

① 그들이 필요하지 않은
② 매일의 필수품인
③ 곧 재활용될
④ 그들이 다른 사람들에게 물려줄 수 있는

해설 지문 초반에서 소비자들이 생각하지 않고 옷을 사기 쉽고, 주요한 브랜드들이 저렴한 옷들을 내놓아 옷이 일회용처럼 입고 버려진다고 설명하고 있다. 또한, 빈칸 뒷부분에서 1년에 30만 톤의 옷이 버려지는 영국의 예시를 들며 설명하고 있으므로, 빈칸에는 '① 그들이 필요하지 않은'이 들어가야 한다.

어휘 bombard with ~을 퍼붓다   disposable 일회용의   figure 수치
worrying 걱정스러운   spending 지출   via ~을 통하여
owe 빚지고 있다   wardrobe 옷장   budget 예산
landfill 쓰레기 매립지   necessity 필수품
hand down to ~을 물려주다

끊어읽기 해석

Excellence is the absolute prerequisite / in fine dining / because the prices charged / are necessarily high.
우수성은 절대적인 전제 조건이다 / 고급 식당에서 / 그 부과되는 가격이 ~ 때문이다 / 필연적으로 비싸다

An operator may do everything possible / to make the restaurant efficient, / but the guests still expect careful, personal service: / food prepared to order / by highly skilled chefs / and delivered by expert servers.
경영자는 가능한 모든 것을 할 것이다 / 레스토랑을 효율적이게 하기 위해 / 그러나 손님들은 여전히 세심하고 개인적인 서비스를 기대할 것이다 / 주문에 맞추어 준비된 음식 / 매우 실력 있는 주방장에 의해 / 전문적인 서버에 의해 전달되는

Because this service is, quite literally, manual labor, / only marginal improvements / in productivity / are possible.
이 서비스는 그야말로 육체노동이기 때문 / 겨우 미미한 개선만이 / 생산성에서 / 가능하다

For example, / a cook, server, or bartender can move / only so much faster / before she or he reaches / the limits of human performance.
예를 들어 / 요리사, 서빙하는 사람 또는 바텐더는 움직일 수 있다 / 오직 그 정도까지만 빠르게 / 그녀 또는 그가 이르기 전에 / 인간 성능의 한계에

Thus, only moderate savings are possible / through improved efficiency, / which makes an escalation of prices inevitable.
따라서 오직 그저 그런 절약만이 가능하다 / 향상된 효율성을 통해 / 그리고 이것은 가격의 상승을 불가피하게 한다

(It is an axiom of economics / that as prices rise, / consumers become more discriminating.)
이것은 경제학의 자명한 이치이다 / 가격이 상승함에 따라 / 소비자들이 더 안목 있게 된다

Thus, the clientele / of the fine-dining restaurant / expects, demands, and is willing to pay for excellence.
따라서 모든 고객들은 / 고급 레스토랑의 / 우수성을 예상하고 요구하며 기꺼이 지불한다

해석 고급 식당에서 우수성은 절대적인 전제 조건인데, 그 이유는 부과되는 가격이 필연적으로 비싸기 때문이다. 경영자는 레스토랑을 효율적이게 하기 위해 가능한 모든 것을 하겠지만, 손님들은 매우 실력 있는 주방장에 의해 주문에 맞추어 준비되고 전문적으로 서버에 의해 전달되는 음식과 같이 여전히 세심하고 개인적인 서비스를 기대할 것이다. 이 서비스는 그야말로 육체노동이기 때문에, 생산성에서 겨우 미미한 개선만이 가능하다. 예를 들어, 요리사, 서빙하는 사람 또는 바텐더는 오직 그녀 또는 그가 인간 성능의 한계에 이르기 전 그 정도까지만 빠르게 움직일 수 있다. 따라서 향상된 효율성

을 통해서는 오직 그저 그런 절약만이 가능하고, 이것은 가격의 상승을 불가피하게 한다. (가격이 상승함에 따라 소비자들이 더 안목 있게 된다는 것은 경제학의 자명한 이치이다.) 따라서 고급 레스토랑의 모든 고객들은 우수성을 예상하고 요구하며(그 우수성을 위해) 기꺼이 지불한다.

① 터무니없는   ② 불가피한
③ 말도 안 되는   ④ 상상도 할 수 없는

해설   지문 초반에서 식당의 경영자들은 세심하고 개인적인 서비스를 기대하는 손님들에 맞추기 위해 실력 있는 주방장과 전문적인 서버를 고용하지만, 육체노동인 서비스는 겨우 미미한 생산성 개선만이 가능하다고 설명했다. 또한, 빈칸 뒤에서 가격이 상승함에 따라 소비자들은 더 안목 있게 되고, 고급 레스토랑의 우수성을 기대하며 기꺼이 돈을 지불한다고 설명하고 있으므로, 빈칸에는 '② 불가피한'이 들어가야 한다.

어휘   excellence 우수성   absolute 절대적인   prerequisite 전제 조건
fine dining 고급 식당   necessarily 필연적으로   operator 경영자
efficient 효율적인   literally 그야말로   manual labor 육체노동
marginal 미미한   moderate 그저 그런   escalation 상승
axiom 자명한 이치   discriminating 안목 있는
clientele 모든 고객들   be willing to 기꺼이 ~하다
ludicrous 터무니없는   inevitable 불가피한
preposterous 말도 안 되는   inconceivable 상상도 할 수 없는

(C) 우리의 가장 가까운 영장류 사촌들조차 수년간의 집중적인 훈련 이후에도 가장 기초적인 의사소통 체계 이상의 무언가를 습득하는 것을 할 수 없는 것처럼 보인다. 언어라는 복잡성은 분명히 한 종에만 국한된 특성이다.

(A) 그렇긴 하지만, 많은 종들이 인간의 언어에 훨씬 미치지 못하는 반면, 그럼에도 불구하고 자연적인 환경에서 인상 깊게 복잡한 의사소통 체계를 보인다.

(B) 그리고 그들은 인간과 함께 길러졌을 때와 같이 인위적인 환경 속에서 훨씬 더 복잡한 체계들에 대한 가르침을 받을 수 있다.

해설   주어진 문장에서 인간의 언어가 원숭이와 유인원과 같은 다른 동물의 의사소통의 형태를 능가한다고 한 후, (C)에서 영장류 사촌들조차 기초 의사소통 체계 이상은 습득하지 못한다는 예시를 들며, 언어라는 복잡성이 분명히 인간에게만 국한되어 있다고 언급하고 있다. 이어서 (A)에서 그렇긴 하지만(That said) 자연적 환경에서 동물의 의사소통이 인상 깊게 복잡하다(complex)고 설명한 뒤, (B)에서 인위적인 환경 속에서 훨씬 더 복잡한(more complex) 체계를 배울 수 있음을 알려주고 있다.

어휘   stand out 두드러지다   decidedly 확실히   vocalization 발성
exhibit 보이다   sophistication 지적 교양   that said 그렇긴 하지만
fall short of ~에 미치지 못하다   artificial 인위적인
alongside ~와 함께   acquire 습득하다
rudimentary 가장 기초적인   intensive 집중적인
species-specific 한 종에만 국한된

18   독해   논리적 흐름 파악 (문단 순서 배열)   난이도 ★★☆

끊어읽기 해석

To be sure, / human language stands out / from the decidedly restricted vocalizations / of monkeys and apes.
틀림없이 / 인간의 언어는 두드러진다 / 확실히 제한된 발성으로부터 / 원숭이들과 유인원들의

Moreover, / it exhibits a degree of sophistication / that far exceeds any other form / of animal communication.
게다가 / 그것은 어느 정도의 지적 교양을 보인다 / 다른 어떤 형태를 훨씬 능가하는 / 동물의 의사소통의

(A) That said, / many species, / while falling far short of human language, / do nevertheless exhibit impressively complex communication systems / in natural settings.
그렇긴 하지만 / 많은 종들이 / 인간의 언어에 훨씬 미치지 못하는 반면 / 그럼에도 불구하고 인상 깊게 복잡한 의사소통 체계를 보인다 / 자연적인 환경에서

(B) And they can be taught / far more complex systems / in artificial contexts, / as when raised alongside humans.
그리고 그들은 가르침을 받을 수 있다 / 훨씬 더 복잡한 체계들에 대한 / 인위적인 환경 속에서 / 인간과 함께 길러졌을 때와 같이

(C) Even our closest primate cousins / seem incapable of acquiring anything / more than a rudimentary communicative system, / even after intensive training over several years.
우리의 가장 가까운 영장류 사촌들조차 / 무언가를 습득하는 것을 할 수 없는 것처럼 보인다 / 가장 기초적인 의사소통 체계 이상의 / 수년간의 집중적인 훈련 이후에도

The complexity / that is language / is surely a species-specific trait.
복잡성은 / 언어라는 / 분명히 한 종에만 국한된 특성이다

해석   틀림없이, 인간의 언어는 원숭이들과 유인원들의 확실히 제한된 발성으로부터 두드러진다. 게다가, 그것은 동물의 의사소통의 다른 어떤 형태를 훨씬 능가하는 어느 정도의 지적 교양을 보인다.

19   독해   전체내용 파악 (주제 파악)   난이도 ★★☆

끊어읽기 해석

During the late twentieth century / socialism was on the retreat / both in the West and in large areas of the developing world.
20세기 후반 동안에 / 사회주의는 후퇴 중이었다 / 서양과 개발도상국의 많은 지역들 모두에서

During this new phase / in the evolution of market capitalism, / global trading patterns became increasingly interlinked, / and advances in information technology meant / that deregulated financial markets could shift / massive flows of capital / across national boundaries / within seconds.
이 새로운 시기 동안에 / 시장 자본주의의 발전 속에서 / 세계적인 무역 거래 형태는 점점 더 연결되었다 / 그리고 정보 통신 기술의 발달은 의미했다 / 규제가 철폐된 금융 시장이 바꿀 수 있었다는 것을 / 거대한 자본의 흐름을 / 국경선을 가로질러 / 잠깐 사이에

'Globalization' boosted trade, / encouraged productivity gains / and lowered prices, / but critics alleged / that it exploited the low-paid, / was indifferent to environmental concerns / and subjected the Third World / to a monopolistic form of capitalism.
'세계화'는 무역을 증대시켰다 / 생산성 증가를 촉진했다 / 그리고 물가를 내렸다 / 그러나 비평가들은 주장했다 / 그것(세계화)은 임금이 적은 사람들을 착취했다고 / 환경적인 우려들에 무관심했다고 / 그리고 제3세계를 종속시켰다고 / 자본주의의 독점적인 형태에

Many radicals / within Western societies / who wished to protest against this process / joined voluntary bodies, charities and other non-governmental organizations, / rather than the marginalized political parties of the left.
많은 급진주의자들은 / 서양 사회 내의 / 이러한 과정에 대해 항의하고 싶어 했던 / 자발적인 조직, 자선 단체들과 다른 비정부단체들에 가입했다 / 사회적으로 무시 받는 좌파 정당들 대신

The environmental movement itself grew / out of the recognition / that the world was interconnected, / and an angry, / if diffuse, / international coalition of interests

emerged.
환경적인 움직임 그 자체는 발달했다 / 인식에서 / 세계가 상호 연결되어 있다는 / 그리고 성난 / 비록 분산되어 있지만 / 국제적인 이익 연합이 나타났다

해석 20세기 후반 동안에 사회주의는 서양과 개발도상국의 많은 지역들 모두에서 후퇴 중이었다. 이 새로운 시기 동안에 시장 자본주의의 발전 속에서, 세계적인 무역 거래 형태는 점점 더 연결되었고, 정보 통신 기술의 발달은 규제가 철폐된 금융 시장이 잠깐 사이에 국경을 가로질러 거대한 자본의 흐름을 바꿀 수 있었다는 것을 의미했다. '세계화'는 무역을 증대시켰고, 생산성 증가를 촉진했으며, 물가를 내렸으나, 비평가들은 그것(세계화)은 임금이 적은 사람들을 착취했고, 환경적인 우려들에 무관심했으며 제3세계를 자본주의의 독점적인 형태에 종속시켰다고 주장했다. 이러한 과정에 대해 항의하고 싶어 했던 서양 사회 내의 많은 급진주의자들은 사회적으로 무시 받는 좌파 정당들 대신 자발적인 조직들, 자선 단체들과 다른 비정부단체들에 가입했다. 환경적인 움직임 그 자체는 세계가 상호 연결되어 있다는 인식에서 발달했고, 비록 분산되어 있지만 성난 국제적인 이익 연합이 나타났다.

① 과거 개발도상국에서의 세계화에 대한 긍정적인 현상
② 20세기에 사회주의의 쇠퇴와 자본주의의 출현
③ 세계 자본 시장과 정치적인 좌파 조직들 사이의 갈등
④ 세계 자본주의의 착취적인 특징과 그것에 대항하는 다양한 사회적인 반발

해설 지문 중간의 but(그러나) 뒤에서 시장 자본주의는 저임금 노동자 착취, 환경에 대한 무관심 등과 같은 문제점을 가졌다고 비판한 뒤, 이에 대항하여 급진주의자들은 좌파 정당들 대신 자발적인 조직과 자선 단체, 그 밖의 비정부단체들에 가입했고, 환경적인 움직임과 국제적인 이익 연합이 나타났다고 그 결과를 설명하고 있으므로 '④ 세계 자본주의의 착취적인 특징과 그것에 대항하는 다양한 사회적인 반발'이 이 글의 주제이다.

어휘 socialism 사회주의 retreat 후퇴 developing world 개발도상국 interlink 연결되다 deregulate 규제를 철폐하다 boost 증대시키다 allege 주장하다 exploit 착취하다 indifferent 무관심한 subject 종속시키다; 주제 the Third World 제3세계 monopolistic 독점적인 capitalism 자본주의 radical 급진주의자; 급진적인 protest against ~에 대해 항의하다 voluntary 자발적 marginalize 사회적으로 무시하다 political party 정당 the left 좌파 grow out of ~에서 발달하다 diffuse 분산되다 coalition 연합 affirmative 긍정적인

---

20 **독해** **전체내용 파악 (글의 감상)** 난이도 ★★☆

끊어읽기 해석

In the blazing midday sun, / the yellow egg-shaped rock stood out / from a pile of recently unearthed gravel.
타는 듯이 더운 정오의 태양 아래에 / 노란 달걀 모양의 돌이 튀어나왔다 / 최근에 파내진 자갈 더미에서

Out of curiosity, / sixteen-year-old miner Komba Johnbull picked it up / and fingered its flat, pyramidal planes.
호기심에 / 16살의 광부 Komba Johnbull은 그것을 집어 들었다 / 그리고 그것의 납작하고 피라미드 같은 면을 손가락으로 만졌다

Johnbull had never seen a diamond before, / but he knew enough / to understand / that even a big find / would be no larger than his thumbnail.
Johnbull은 이전에 다이아몬드를 본 적이 없었다 / 그러나 그는 ~할 정도의 상식은 있었다 / 알 정도로 / 엄청난 발견이라도 / 그의 엄지손톱보다 더 크지 않을 것이라고

Still, / the rock was unusual enough / to merit a second opinion.
그런데도 / 그 돌은 충분히 특이했다 / 다른 의견의 가치가 있을 정도로

Sheepishly, / he brought it over / to one of the more experienced miners / working the muddy gash / deep in the jungle.
소심하게 / 그는 그것을 가지고 왔다 / 더 경험이 많은 광부들 중 한 명에게 / 진흙투성이의 갈라진 틈을 작업하고 있는 / 정글 깊숙한 곳에서

The pit boss's eyes widened / when he saw the stone.
현장 감독의 눈이 커졌다 / 그가 그 돌을 보자

"Put it in your pocket," / he whispered. // "Keep digging."
그것을 네 주머니에 넣어라 / 그가 속삭였다 // 땅 파는 것을 계속해라

The older miner warned / that it could be dangerous / if anyone thought / they had found something big.
나이가 더 많은 광부는 경고했다 / 위험할 수 있다는 것을 / 누군가가 생각한다면 / 그들이 엄청난 무언가를 발견했다고

So Johnbull kept shoveling gravel / until nightfall, / pausing occasionally / to grip the heavy stone / in his fist.
그래서 Johnbull은 자갈을 삽질하는 것을 계속했다 / 해 질 녘까지 / 가끔씩 멈추면서 / 그 무거운 돌을 움켜잡기 위해 / 그의 손에

Could it be?
이것이 그것일까?

해석 타는 듯이 더운 정오의 태양 아래에, 최근에 파내진 자갈 더미에서 노란 달걀 모양의 돌이 튀어나왔다. 호기심에, 16살의 광부 Komba Johnbull은 그것을 집어 들고 그것의 납작하고 피라미드 같은 면을 손가락으로 만졌다. Johnbull은 이전에 다이아몬드를 본 적이 없었으나, 그는 엄청난 발견이라도 그의 엄지손톱보다 더 크지 않을 것이라고 알 정도의 상식은 있었다. 그런데도, 그 돌은 다른 의견의 가치가 있을 정도로 충분히 특이했다. 소심하게, 그는 정글 깊숙한 곳에서 진흙투성이의 갈라진 틈을 작업하고 있는 더 경험이 많은 광부들 중 한 명에게 그것을 가지고 왔다. 그 돌을 보자 현장 감독의 눈이 커졌다. "그것을 네 주머니에 넣어라" 그가 속삭였다. "땅 파는 것을 계속해라." 나이가 더 많은 광부는 누군가가 그들이 엄청난 무언가를 발견했다고 생각한다면 위험할 수 있다는 것을 경고했다. 그래서 Johnbull은 그의 손에 그 무거운 돌(다이아몬드)을 움켜잡기 위해 가끔씩 멈추면서 해 질 녘까지 자갈을 삽질하는 것을 계속했다. 이것이 그것(다이아몬드)일까?

① 흥분하고 신이 난
② 고통스럽고 괴로워하는
③ 오만하고 확신하는
④ 무심하고 무관심한

해설 지문 전반에 걸쳐 어린 광부가 자갈 더미에서 색다른 돌을 발견했는데, 그 돌을 보고 놀란 다른 광부의 조언에 따라 발견한 것을 비밀로 하고 해 질 녘까지 삽질을 계속했다는 일화를 소개하고 있으므로, '① 흥분하고 신이 난'이 글에 나타난 화자의 심경으로 적절하다.

어휘 blazing 타는 듯이 더운 stand out 튀어나오다 unearth 파내다 gravel 자갈 miner 광부 finger 손가락으로 만지다 plane (평평한) 면 merit 가치가 있다 sheepishly 소심하게 pit boss 현장 감독 shovel 삽질하다 grip 움켜잡다 distressed 괴로워하는 arrogant 오만한 detached 무심한 indifferent 무관심한

정답

p.57

01	① 어휘 – 어휘&표현	11	④ 어휘 – 생활영어
02	④ 어휘 – 어휘&표현	12	③ 어휘 – 생활영어
03	③ 어휘 – 어휘&표현	13	② 독해 – 추론
04	① 어휘 – 어휘&표현	14	③ 독해 – 전체내용 파악
05	④ 문법 – 어순	15	③ 독해 – 논리적 흐름 파악
06	② 문법 – 조동사	16	④ 독해 – 논리적 흐름 파악
07	③ 문법 – 동명사	17	④ 독해 – 논리적 흐름 파악
08	② 독해 – 전체내용 파악	18	③ 독해 – 세부내용 파악
09	① 독해 – 전체내용 파악	19	① 독해 – 추론
10	④ 독해 – 세부내용 파악	20	② 독해 – 추론

취약영역 분석표

영역	세부 유형	문항 수	소계
어휘	어휘&표현	4	/6
	생활영어	2	
문법	어순	1	/3
	조동사	1	
	동명사	1	
독해	전체내용 파악	3	/11
	세부내용 파악	2	
	추론	3	
	논리적 흐름 파악	3	
	총계		**/20**

· 자신이 취약한 영역은 '공무원 영어, 이렇게 출제된다!'(문제집 p.8)를 통해 다시 한번 확인하고 학습하시기 바랍니다.

---

01 어휘 어휘&표현 candid = frank 난이도 ★☆☆

해석 솔직한 고객 리뷰, 가격대와 함께 전자레인지 모델과 스타일의 상세한 목록은 가전제품 비교 웹사이트에서 이용할 수 있다.

① 솔직한 ② 논리적인
③ 함축적인 ④ 열렬한

어휘 extensive 상세한, 대규모의 candid 솔직한
available 이용할 수 있는 appliance 가전제품 comparison 비교
frank 솔직한 logical 논리적인 implicit 함축적인
passionate 열렬한, 열정적인

👍 이것도 알면 **합격!**
candid(솔직한)의 유의어
= direct, honest, straightforward, forthright, plainspoken

02 어휘 어휘&표현 conspicuous = noticeable 난이도 ★★☆

해석 옐로우스톤이 본질적으로 화산 작용에 의해 만들어졌다는 것은 오랫동안 알려져 왔고, 화산에 대한 한 가지는 그것들이 일반적으로 눈에 잘 띈다는 것이다.

① 수동적인 ② 수증기가 가득한
③ 위험한 ④ 눈에 띄는

어휘 volcanic 화산 작용에 의해 만들어진 nature 본질, 천성
conspicuous 눈에 잘 띄는 vaporous 수증기가 가득한

👍 이것도 알면 **합격!**
conspicuous(눈에 잘 띄는)의 유의어
= obvious, distinct, visible, prominent, manifest

03 어휘 어휘&표현 inside out = thoroughly 난이도 ★☆☆

해석 그는 그 도시를 속속들이 알고 있기 때문에 너에게 그곳에 가는 방법을 알려줄 최적의 사람이다.

① 결국 ② 문화적으로
③ 완전히 ④ 머뭇거리며

어휘 inside out 속속들이, 완전히 thoroughly 완전히, 철저히
tentatively 머뭇거리며, 시험적으로

👍 이것도 알면 **합격!**
inside out(속속들이)과 유사한 의미의 표현
= completely, comprehensively, exhaustively, fully, through and through

04 어휘 어휘&표현 pay tribute to = honor 난이도 ★★☆

해석 두꺼운 종이, 눈 그리고 색 도화지에 새겨진 메시지들을 포함하여, 그 팀에게 경의를 표하는 수천 개의 투박한 노력들이 길을 따라서 있었다.

① 존경하다 ② 구성하다
③ 광고하다 ④ 참여하다

어휘 route 길, 경로 homespun 투박한, 손으로 만든
pay (a) tribute to ~에게 경의를 표하다, ~에게 찬사를 보내다
etched in ~에 새겨진 cardboard 두꺼운 종이
construction paper 색 도화지, 색판지

👍 이것도 알면 **합격!**
pay tribute to(~에게 경의를 표하다)의 유의어
= praise, salute, extol, hail

05 문법 어순

난이도 ★★☆

해석 ① 대도시의 교통은 소도시의 그것(교통)보다 더 붐빈다.
② 내가 다음 주에 해변에 누워있을 때 나는 너를 떠올릴 것이다.
③ 건포도는 한때 비싼 음식이어서, 부자들만 그것을 먹었다.
④ 색의 명도는 그 색이 얼마만큼 회색을 포함하고 있는지와 관련되어 있다.

해설 ④ 간접 의문문의 어순 전치사 to의 목적어 자리에 명사 역할을 하는 간접 의문문이 왔고, 의문문이 다른 문장 안에 포함된 간접 의문문은 '의문사(how much gray) + 주어(the color) + 동사(contains)'의 어순이 되어야 하므로 how much gray the color contains가 올바르게 쓰였다.

오답 ① 대명사 수 일치 대명사가 지시하는 명사가 단수 명사 the
분석 traffic(교통)이므로 복수 지시대명사 those를 단수 지시대명사 that으로 고쳐야 한다.
② 시간 부사절의 시제 시간을 나타내는 부사절(when ~ next week)에서 미래를 나타내기 위해 미래 시제 대신 현재 시제를 사용하므로 미래진행 시제 will be lying을 현재 시제 lie로 고쳐야 한다. 참고로, 현재진행 시제 am lying으로 고쳐도 맞다.
③ 정관사의 쓰임 문맥상 '부유한 사람(부자)들만 그것을 먹었다'라는 의미가 되어야 자연스럽고, '부유한 사람들'은 'the +형용사'(~한 사람들/것들)를 사용하여 나타낼 수 있으므로 명사 wealth(부, 다량)를 형용사 wealthy(부유한)로 고쳐야 한다.

어휘 raisin 건포도 intensity 명도, 강렬함 contain 포함하다

👍 이것도 알면 합격!

think, believe, imagine, suppose, suggest 등이 동사로 쓰인 의문문에 간접 의문문이 포함되면 의문사가 문장의 맨 앞으로 온다는 것을 알아두자.
ex) Do you think? + What is he talking about?
당신은 생각하나요? + 그가 무엇에 대해 말하고 있나요?
→ What do you think he is talking about?
당신은 그가 무엇에 대해 말하고 있다고 생각하나요?

06 문법 조동사

난이도 ★★☆

해설 ② 의무의 주절 뒤 종속절 동사 주절에 의무를 나타내는 동사 command가 오면 종속절에는 '(should +) 동사원형'이 와야 하므로, 종속절에 동사원형 cease가 올바르게 쓰였다.

오답 ① 능동태 vs. 수동태 주어(Several problems)와 동사가 '몇 가
분석 지 문제가 일어나게 되었다(생겼다)'라는 의미의 수동 관계이므로 능동태 have raised를 수동태 have been raised로 고쳐야 한다.
③ 시제 일치 주절의 시제가 과거(had)이므로 종속절에는 과거 시제가 쓰여야 한다. 따라서 미래 시제 will blow를 과거 시제 blew로 고쳐야 한다.
④ 능동태 vs. 수동태 주어(The seeds)와 동사가 '씨앗이 살아 남다'라는 의미의 능동 관계이므로 수동태 are survived by를 능동태 survive로 고쳐야 한다.

어휘 raise 일으키다 due to ~때문에 command 명령하다
cease 중단하다 harsh 혹독한

👍 이것도 알면 합격!

제안·의무·요청·주장을 나타내는 동사 중 suggest와 insist가 해야 할 것에 대한 제안과 주장의 의미가 아닌 '암시', '사실에 대한 주장'을 나타낼 때 종속절에 '(should +) 동사원형'이 아닌 일반동사가 쓰인다는 것을 알아두자.
ex) Kelly insisted I was wrong.
     일반동사
Kelly는 내가 틀렸다고 주장했다.

07 문법 동명사

난이도 ★★★

해설 ③ 동명사의 형태 동명사(promoting)의 의미상 주어인 him과 동명사가 '그가 승진이 되다'라는 의미의 수동 관계이므로 동명사의 능동형 promoting을 동명사의 수동형 being promoted로 고쳐야 한다.

오답 ① 재귀대명사의 쓰임 재귀대명사는 주어나 목적어를 강조할 때
분석 쓰이거나, 목적어가 지칭하는 대상이 주어와 동일할 때 쓰이는데, 제시된 문장에서 동사 adapt의 목적어 themselves가 지칭하는 대상이 주어 Human beings와 동일하므로, Human beings quickly adapt themselves ~가 올바르게 쓰였다.
② to 부정사 관련 표현 '포기할 수밖에 없었다'는 to 부정사 관련 표현 'have no choice but + to 부정사'(~할 수밖에 없다)를 사용하여 나타낼 수 있으므로 had no choice but to give up이 올바르게 쓰였다.
④ to 부정사의 역할 | 병치 구문 해당 문장은 가주어 It이 길이가 긴 진짜 주어 to 부정사구(to assemble ~ toy car) 대신 주어 자리에 쓰인 형태이므로, 진짜 주어 자리에 to 부정사구를 이끄는 to 부정사 to assemble이 올바르게 쓰였다. 또한, 접속사(and)로 연결된 병치 구문에서는 같은 구조끼리 연결되어야 하는데, and 앞에 to 부정사(to assemble)가 왔으므로 and 뒤에도 to 부정사가 와야 한다. 병치 구문에서 나온 두 번째 to는 생략될 수 있으므로 (to) take apart가 올바르게 쓰였다.

어휘 adapt 적응시키다 give up 포기하다
prohibit A from B A가 B하는 것을 금하다 assemble 조립하다
take apart 분리하다

👍 이것도 알면 합격!

②번 보기에 쓰인 'have no choice but + to 부정사'(~할 수밖에 없다)와 같은 다양한 to 부정사 관용 표현을 알아두자.
• too ~ to 너무 ~해서 -할 수 없다   • enough to ~하기에 충분히 -하다
• It takes ~ to -하는 데 ~이 걸리다   • can't afford to ~할 여유가 없다

08 독해 전체내용 파악 (요지 파악)

난이도 ★☆☆

끊어읽기 해석

Listening to somebody else's ideas / is the one way to know / whether the story / you believe about the world / —as well as about yourself and your place in it / —remains intact.
다른 사람들의 생각을 듣는 것은 / 아는 한 가지 방법이다 / 이야기가 ~인지 아닌지를 / 세상에 대해 당신이 믿는 / 자기 자신과 세상에서의 당신의 위치에 대해서뿐만 아니라 / 여전히 그대로인지

We all need to examine / our beliefs, / air them out / and let them breathe.

우리는 모두 고찰할 필요가 있다 / 우리의 신념을 / 그것들을 환기시킬 / 그리고 그것들을 숨쉬게 할

Hearing what other people have to say, / especially about concepts / we regard as foundational, / is like opening a window / in our minds and in our hearts.
다른 사람들이 말하는 것을 듣는 것은 / 특히 개념에 대해서 / 우리가 근본적이라고 여기는 / 창문을 여는 것과 같다 / 우리의 머리 속과 가슴 속의

Speaking up is important.
목소리를 내는 것이 중요하다

Yet to speak up / without listening / is like banging pots and pans together: / even if it gets you attention, / it's not going to get you respect.
그러나 목소리를 내는 것은 / 경청하지 않고 / 냄비와 팬을 함께 쾅쾅 두드리는 것과 같다 / 비록 그것은 당신이 주목 받게는 하겠지만 / 당신이 존경 받도록 하지는 않을 것이다

There are three prerequisites / for conversation to be meaningful:
세 가지 전제 조건이 있다 / 대화가 의미있기 위한

1. You have to know / what you're talking about, / meaning / that you have an original point / and are not echoing a worn-out, hand-me-down or pre-fab argument;
1. 당신은 알아야 한다 / 당신이 이야기 하고 있는 것을 / 그리고 이것은 의미한다 / 당신이 독창적인 의견이 있다는 것을 / 그리고 진부하거나 독창성 없거나 이미 만들어진 주장을 그대로 따라 하는 것이 아니라는 것을

2. You respect the people / with whom you're speaking / and are authentically willing to treat them courteously / even if you disagree / with their positions;
2. 당신은 사람들을 존중한다 / 당신과 이야기 하고 있는 / 그리고 진정으로 기꺼이 그들을 예의 바르게 대한다 / 비록 당신이 동의하지 않을지라도 / 그들의 입장에

3. You have to be both smart and informed / enough to listen to what the opposition says / while handling your own perspective / on the topic / with uninterrupted good humor and discernment.
3. 당신은 똑똑할 뿐만 아니라 잘 알아야 한다 / 상대방이 말하는 것에 충분히 귀 기울일 만큼 / 자신만의 관점을 논하는 동시에 / 그 주제에 대한 / 계속되는 좋은 유머와 안목으로

해석　다른 사람들의 생각을 듣는 것은 자기 자신과 세상에서의 당신의 위치에 대해서뿐만 아니라, 세상에 대해 당신이 믿는 이야기가 여전히 그대로인지 아닌지를 아는 한 가지 방법이다. 우리는 모두 우리의 신념을 고찰하고 그것들을 환기시키고 숨쉬게 할 필요가 있다. 다른 사람들이, 특히 우리가 근본적이라고 여기는 개념에 대해서, 말하는 것을 듣는 것은 우리의 머리 속과 가슴 속의 창문을 여는 것과 같다. 목소리를 내는 것이 중요하다. 그러나 경청하지 않고 목소리를 내는 것은 냄비와 팬을 함께 쾅쾅 두드리는 것과 같다. 비록 그것은 당신이 주목받게는 하겠지만, 당신이 존경받도록 하지는 않을 것이다. 대화가 의미있기 위한 세 가지 전제 조건이 있다. 1. 당신은 당신이 이야기 하고 있는 것을 알아야 하고, 이것이 당신이 독창적인 의견이 있으며 진부하거나 독창성이 없거나 이미 만들어진 주장을 그대로 따라 하는 것이 아니라는 것을 의미한다. 2. 당신은 당신과 이야기 하고 있는 사람들을 존중하고, 비록 그들의 입장에 당신이 동의하지 않을지라도 진정으로 기꺼이 그들을 예의 바르게 대한다. 3. 당신은 계속되는 좋은 유머와 안목으로 그 주제에 대한 자신만의 관점을 논하는 동시에 상대방이 말하는 것에 충분히 귀 기울일 만큼 똑똑할 뿐만 아니라 잘 알아야 한다.
① 우리는 다른 사람들을 설득하기 위해 더 단호해야 한다.
② 우리는 의사소통을 잘하기 위해 경청하고 목소리를 내야 할 필요가 있다.
③ 우리는 우리가 보는 세계에 대한 신념을 바꾸는 것을 꺼린다.
④ 우리는 우리가 선택하는 것만 듣고 다른 의견들은 애써 무시한다.

해설　지문 중간에서 목소리를 내는 것은 중요하지만, 경청하지 않고 목소리를 내는 것은 냄비와 팬을 함께 쾅쾅 두드리는 것과 같다고 하고, 대화가 의미있기 위해서는 독창적인 의견을 가지는 동시에 다른 사람들을 존중하고 그들의 의견에 귀 기울여야 한다고 했으므로, 이 글의 요지를 '우리는 의사소통을 잘하기 위해 경청하고 목소리를 내야 할 필요가 있다'라고 표현한 ②번이 정답이다.

어휘　intact (의견 등이) 그대로인, 변하지 않은　foundational 근본적인
speak up 목소리를 내다　bang 쾅쾅 두드리다
prerequisite 전제 조건　echo 그대로 따라하다; 울림
worn-out 진부한　hand-me-down 독창성이 없는
pre-fab 이미 만들어진　authentically 진정으로
courteously 예의 바르게　informed 잘 아는
uninterrupted 계속된　discernment 안목　determined 단호한
reluctant 꺼리는

09　독해　전체내용 파악 (제목 파악)　난이도 ★☆☆

끊어읽기 해석

The future may be uncertain, / but some things are undeniable: / climate change, shifting demographics, geopolitics.
미래는 불확실할지도 모른다 / 하지만 어떤 것들은 명백하다 / 기후 변화, 변화하는 인구 통계와 지정학과 같은

The only guarantee is / that there will be changes, / both wonderful and terrible.
유일하게 보장되는 것은 ~이다 / 변화가 있을 것이라는 것 / 훌륭하기도 하고 끔찍하기도 한

It's worth considering / how artists will respond / to these changes, / as well as what purpose art serves, / now and in the future.
생각해보는 것은 가치가 있다 / 예술가들이 어떻게 반응할 것인지를 / 이러한 변화에 / 예술이 어떤 목적을 수행할지 뿐만 아니라 / 현재와 미래에

Reports suggest / that by 2040 / the impacts of human-caused climate change / will be inescapable, / making it the big issue / at the centre of art and life / in 20 years' time.
보고서는 암시한다 / 2040년까지 / 인간이 야기한 기후 변화의 영향은 / 피할 수 없을 것이라고 / 그리고 그것이 큰 이슈가 될 것이다 / 예술과 삶의 중심에서 / 20년의 시간 후에

Artists in the future / will wrestle with the possibilities / of the post-human and post-Anthropocene / —artificial intelligence, human colonies in outer space and potential doom.
미래의 예술가들은 / 가능성과 씨름할 것이다 / 포스트휴먼과 포스트 인류세의 / 인공지능, 우주에 있는 인간 식민지 그리고 잠재적 파멸과 같은

The identity politics / seen in art / around the #MeToo and Black Lives Matter movements / will grow / as environmentalism, border politics and migration / come even more sharply into focus.
정체성 정치는 / 예술에서 보이는 / 미투와 블랙 라이브즈 매터(흑인의 목숨도 소중하다) 운동 주위의 / 성장할 것이다 / 환경 보호주의, 경계 정치학 그리고 이주가 ~에 따라 / 심지어 더 뚜렷이 주목 받는다

Art will become increasingly diverse / and might not 'look like art' / as we expect.
예술은 점점 더 다양해질 것이다 / 그리고 '예술처럼 보이지' 않을 수도 있다 / 우리가 예상하는 것처럼

In the future, / once we've become weary of / our lives being visible online / for all to see, / and our privacy has been all but lost, / anonymity may be more desirable / than fame.
미래에 / 우리는 싫증나게 되면 / 온라인에서 보여지는 우리의 삶이 / 모두가 볼 수 있는 / 그리고 우리의 사생활이 거의 없어진다면 / 익명성이 더 바람직할 지도 모른다 / 명성보다

Instead of thousands, or millions, of likes and followers, / we will be starved / for authenticity and connection.
수천 개 혹은 수백만 개의 좋아요와 팔로워들 대신에 / 우리는 갈망하게 될 것이다 / 진정성과 관계를

Art could, / in turn, / become more collective and experiential, / rather than individual.
예술은 ~할 수 있다 / 결국 / 더 집단적이고 경험적이게 된다 / 개인적이기 보다는

해석 미래는 불확실할지도 모르지만, 기후 변화, 변화하는 인구 통계와 지정학과 같은 어떤 것들은 명백하다. 유일하게 보장되는 것은 훌륭하기도 하고 끔찍하기도 한 변화가 있을 것이라는 것이다. 현재와 미래에 예술이 어떤 목적을 수행할지 뿐만 아니라, 예술가들이 이러한 변화에 어떻게 반응할 것인지를 생각해보는 것은 가치가 있다. 보고서는 2040년까지 인간이 야기한 기후 변화의 영향은 피할 수 없을 것이고, 20년의 시간 후에 예술과 삶의 중심에서 그것이 큰 이슈가 될 것이라고 암시한다. 미래의 예술가들은 인공지능, 우주에 있는 인간 식민지 그리고 잠재적 파멸과 같은 포스트휴먼과 포스트 인류세의 가능성과 씨름할 것이다. 미투와 블랙 라이브즈 매터(흑인의 목숨도 소중하다) 운동 주위의 예술에서 보여지는 정체성 정치는 환경 보호주의, 경계 정치학 그리고 이주가 심지어 더 뚜렷이 주목받음에 따라 성장할 것이다. 예술은 점점 더 다양해질 것이고 우리가 예상하는 것처럼 '예술처럼 보이지' 않을 수도 있다. 미래에, 우리는 모두가 볼 수 있는 온라인에서 보이는 우리의 삶이 싫증나게 되고 우리의 사생활이 거의 없어지면, 익명성이 명성보다 더 바람직할 지도 모른다. 수천 개 혹은 수백만 개의 좋아요와 팔로워들 대신에, 우리는 진정성과 관계를 갈망하게 될 것이다. 결국, 예술은 개인적이기보다는 더 집단적이고 경험적이게 될 수 있다.

① 미래에 예술은 어떤 모습일 것인가?
② 지구 온난화가 어떻게 우리 삶에 영향을 미칠 것인가?
③ 인공 지능이 환경에 어떻게 영향을 미칠 것인가?
④ 정치적 운동 때문에 어떤 변화들이 생길 것인가?

해설 지문 전반에 걸쳐 예술이 미래에 어떤 목적을 수행할 것인지 생각해보는 것은 가치가 있으며, 예술은 점점 더 다양해질 것이고, 우리가 예상하는 것처럼 보이지 않을 수도 있으며 더 집단적이고 경험적이게 될 수 있다고 설명하고 있다. 따라서 이 지문의 제목을 '미래에 예술은 어떤 모습일 것인가?'라고 표현한 ①번이 정답이다.

어휘 undeniable 명백한 demographics 인구 통계, 인구학의
geopolitics 지정학 inescapable 피할 수 없는
wrestle with ~과 씨름하다 post-human 포스트휴먼(현 인류보다 더 확장된 능력을 갖춘 존재, 또는 그런 존재가 사는 미래시대)
Anthropocene 인류세(인간의 활동이 지구의 환경을 바꾸는 지질 시대)
doom 파멸, 우울 identity politics 정체성 정치(여러 기준으로 분화된 집단이 각 집단의 권리를 주장하는 데 주력하는 정치)
migration 이주 weary of ~에 싫증난
for all to see 모두가 볼 수 있는 anonymity 익명성
desirable 바람직한 starve for ~을 갈망하다 authenticity 진정성
collective 집단적인 experiential 경험적인

10 독해 세부내용 파악 (내용 불일치 파악) 난이도 ★★☆

끊어읽기 해석

The Second Amendment / of the U.S. Constitution / states: / "A well-regulated Militia, / being necessary to the security of a free State, / the right of the people / to keep and bear Arms, / shall not be infringed."
수정 헌법 제2조는 / 미국 헌법의 / ~라고 명시한다 / 잘 통제된 민병대는 / 자유로운 주의 안보에 필수적이므로 / 국민의 권리는 / 무기를 소장하고 휴대하는 / 침해될 수 없다

Supreme Court rulings, / citing this amendment, / have upheld the right / of states / to regulate firearms.
대법원 판결은 / 이 수정 조항을 인용하면서 / 권리를 유지해 왔다 / 연방 주들의 / 총기를 규제하기 위한

However, / in a 2008 decision / confirming an individual right / to keep and bear arms, / the court struck down Washington, D.C. laws / that banned handguns / and required those in the home / to be locked or disassembled.
그러나 / 2008년 판결로 / 개인의 권리를 정당하다고 입증한 / 총기를 소장하고 휴대하는 / 법원은 워싱턴 주의 법을 폐지했다 / 권총을 금지했던 / 그리고 집에 있는 것들을 ~할 것을 명령했던 / 잠가놓거나 해체할 것을

A number of gun advocates / consider ownership a birthright / and an essential part / of the nation's heritage.
많은 총기 옹호자들은 / 소유권을 타고난 권리라고 여긴다 / 그리고 필수적인 부분이라고 / 국가 유산의

The United States, / with less than 5 percent of the world's population, / has about 35~50 percent / of the world's civilian-owned guns, / according to a 2007 report / by the Switzerland-based Small Arms Survey.
미국은 / 세계 인구의 5퍼센트보다 적은 / 약 35~50퍼센트를 차지한다 / 세계 민간인 총기 소지의 / 2007년 보고에 따르면 / 스위스에 근거지를 둔 스몰 암스 서베이에 의한

It ranks number one / in firearms per capita.
이것은 1위를 차지한다 / 1인당 총기 소지에서

The United States also has the highest homicide-by-firearm rate / among the world's most developed nations.
미국은 또한 총기에 의한 살인율이 가장 높다 / 세계의 선진국들 중에서

But many gun-rights proponents say / these statistics do not indicate a cause-and-effect relationship / and note / that the rates of gun homicide and other gun crimes / in the United States / have dropped / since highs in the early 1990's.
그러나 많은 총기 소유권 지지자들은 말한다 / 이러한 통계가 인과관계를 보여주지 않는다고 / 그리고 언급한다 / 총기에 의한 살인과 다른 총기 관련 범죄의 비율은 / 미국에서의 / 떨어져왔다고 / 1990년대 초반의 최고 수치 이후로

해석 미국 헌법의 수정 헌법 제2조는 잘 통제된 민병대는 자유로운 주의 안보에 필수적이므로, 무기를 소장하고 휴대하는 국민의 권리는 침해될 수 없다고 명시한다. 이 수정 조항을 인용하면서, 대법원 판결은 연방 주들의 총기를 규제하기 위한 권리를 유지해 왔다. 그러나, 총기를 소장하고 휴대하는 개인의 권리를 정당하다고 입증한 2008년의 판결로, 법원은 권총을 금지하고 집에 있는 것들을 잠가놓거나 해체할 것을 명령했던 워싱턴 주의 법을 폐지했다. 많은 총기 옹호자들은 소유권을 타고난 권리라고 여기며 국가 유산의 필수적인 부분이라고 여긴다. 세계 인구의 5퍼센트보다 적은 미국은, 스위스에 근거지를 둔 스몰 암스 서베이에 의한 2007년 보고에 따르면, 세계 민간인 총기 소지의 약 35~50퍼센트를 차지한다. 이것은 1인당 총기 소지에서 1위를 차지한다. 미국은 또한 세계의 선진국들 중에서 총기에 의한 살인율이 가장 높다. 그러나 많은 총기 소유권 지지자들은 이러한 통계가 인과관계를 보여주지 않는다고 말하며 미국에서의 총기에 의한 살인과 다른 총기 관련 범죄의 비율은 1990년대 초반의 최고 수치 이후로 떨어져왔다고 언급한다.

① 2008년에, 미국 대법원은 권총을 금지하는 워싱턴 주의 법안을 뒤집었다.
② 많은 총기 옹호자들은 총기를 소지하는 것은 타고난 권리라고 주장한다.
③ 선진국들 중에서, 미국은 총기 살인율이 가장 높다.
④ 미국에서의 총기 관련 범죄는 지난 30년 동안 꾸준히 증가해왔다.

해설 ④번의 키워드인 Gun crimes(총기 관련 범죄)가 그대로 언급된 지문 주변의 내용에서, 미국에서의 총기 관련 범죄의 비율은 1990년대 초반의 최고 수치 이후에 떨어져왔다고 했으므로, 미국

에서의 총기 관련 범죄가 지난 30년 동안 꾸준히 증가해왔다는 것은 지문의 내용과 다르다. 따라서 ④번이 정답이다.

어휘 amendment 수정 regulate 통제하다, 규제하다 infringe 침해하다
uphold 유지하다 firearm 총기, 화기 confirm 정당하다고 입증하다
strike down 폐지하다, 때려눕히다 ban 금지하다 handgun 권총
disassemble 해체하다 essential 필수적인 heritage 유산
per capita 1인당 homicide 살인 proponent 지지자
overturn 뒤집다, 번복하다 natural-born 타고난
steadily 꾸준히, 끊임없이

11 어휘 생활영어 I couldn't have done it without you. 난이도 ★☆☆

해석 ① A: 납부 기한이 언제예요?
B: 당신은 다음 주까지 지불해야 합니다.
② A: 이 짐을 부쳐야 하나요?
B: 아니요, 이건 비행기에 들고 탈 수 있을 정도로 충분히 작아요.
③ A: 우리는 언제 어디서 만날까요?
B: 제가 8시 30분에 당신의 사무실로 데리러 갈게요.
④ A: 요리 경연대회에서 상을 탔어요.
B: 당신 없이는 해낼 수 없었을 거예요.

해설 ④번에서 A는 요리 경연대회에서 입상했다고 말하고 있으므로, 당신 없이는 해낼 수 없었을 거라는 B의 대답 I couldn't have done it without you(당신 없이는 해낼 수 없었을 거예요)는 어울리지 않는다. 따라서 ④번이 정답이다.

어휘 payment due 납부 기한 check in (짐을) 부치다, 맡기다

👍 이것도 알면 합격!

공항에서 사용할 수 있는 다양한 표현을 추가로 알아두자.
· Do you have anything to declare? 세관에 신고하실 것이 있나요?
· Are you checking any bags? 짐을 부치시나요?
· Do you have any batteries in your suitcase?
여행가방에 배터리가 있나요?

12 어휘 생활영어 What's the difference between them? 난이도 ★☆☆

해석
A: Royal Point Hotel 예약 부서에 연락주셔서 감사드립니다.
제 이름은 Sam입니다. 무엇을 도와드릴까요?
B: 안녕하세요, 저는 방을 예약하고 싶습니다.
A: 저희는 두 가지 종류의 방을 제공하는데, 디럭스 룸과 고급
스위트 룸이 있습니다.
B: 그것들의 차이점이 무엇인가요?
A: 첫째로, 스위트 룸은 매우 넓습니다. 침실뿐만 아니라 부엌,
거실 그리고 다이닝룸이 있습니다.
B: 비쌀 것 같네요.
A: 음, 하룻밤에 200달러 더 비쌉니다.
B: 그렇다면, 저는 디럭스 룸으로 할게요.

① 다른 건 필요 없으신가요
② 객실 번호를 알려주시겠어요
③ 그것들의 차이점이 무엇인가요
④ 객실에 반려동물이 들어갈 수 있나요

해설 방을 예약하고 싶다는 B의 말에 A가 두 가지 종류의 방이 있다고
하고, 빈칸 뒤에서 스위트 룸에 대해서 설명하고 있으므로, 빈칸
에는 '그것들의 차이점이 무엇인가요'라는 의미가 들어가야 자연

스럽다. 따라서 ③ What's the difference between them이
정답이다.

어휘 reservation 예약 book 예약하다

👍 이것도 알면 합격!

호텔에서 예약할 때 사용할 수 있는 다양한 표현을 추가로 알아두자.
· I'd like a single room for one night.
저는 싱글룸으로 하룻밤 묵고 싶습니다.
· How long will you be staying? 얼마나 오래 머무르실 예정입니까?
· I have a reservation under the name Chris Neal.
Chris Neal이란 이름으로 예약했습니다.

13 독해 추론 (빈칸 완성 - 연결어) 난이도 ★★☆

끊어읽기 해석

Advocates of homeschooling believe / that children learn better / when they are in a secure, loving environment.
홈스쿨링을 옹호하는 사람들은 믿는다 / 아이들이 더 잘 학습한다고 / 그들이 안정되고 사랑이 넘치는 환경에 있을 때

Many psychologists see the home / as the most natural learning environment, / and originally the home was the classroom, / long before schools were established.
많은 심리학자들은 집을 ~로 생각한다 / 가장 자연스러운 학습 환경으로 / 그리고 원래 집은 교실이었다 / 학교가 설립되기 훨씬 전에

Parents who homeschool argue / that they can monitor their children's education / and give them the attention / that is lacking in a traditional school setting.
홈스쿨링을 하는 부모들은 주장한다 / 그들이 자녀들의 교육을 관리할수 있다고 / 그리고 주의를 그들에게 기울일 수 있다고 / 전통적인 학교 환경에서는 부족한

Students can also pick and choose / what to study and when to study, / thus enabling them to learn / at their own pace.
학생들은 또한 선택할 수 있다 / 무엇을 공부하고 언제 공부할지를 / 그러므로 이는 그들이 공부할 수 있도록 한다 / 그들만의 속도로

(A) In contrast, / critics of homeschooling say / that children / who are not in the classroom / miss out on learning important social skills / because they have little interaction / with their peers.
(A) 반대로 / 홈스쿨링을 비판하는 사람들은 말한다 / 아이들이 / 교실에 있지 않은 / 중요한 사회성 기술을 배우는 것을 놓친다고 / 그들은 상호작용이 거의 없기 때문에 / 그들의 또래와

Several studies, / though, / have shown / that the home-educated children / appear to do just as well / in terms of social and emotional development / as other students, / having spent more time / in the comfort and security / of their home, / with guidance from parents / who care about their welfare.
몇몇 연구에서는 / 하지만 / 보여주었다 / 집에서 교육받은 아이들이 / ~만큼 잘 하는 것처럼 보인다는 것을 / 사회적, 그리고 정서적인 발달의 관점에서 / 다른 학생들만큼 / 더 많은 시간을 보내왔기 때문에 / 편안함과 안도감 안에서 / 그들의 집의 / 부모님의 지도와 함께 / 그들의 행복에 관심을 가지는

(B) In spite of this, / many critics of homeschooling have raised concerns / about the ability of parents / to teach their kids effectively.
(B) 이것에도 불구하고 / 홈스쿨링을 비판하는 많은 사람들은 우려를 제기해왔다 / 부모들의 능력에 대해 / 그들의 자녀들을 효과적으로 가르칠 수 있는

해석 홈스쿨링을 옹호하는 사람들은 아이들이 안정되고 사랑이 넘치는 환경에 있을 때 더 잘 학습한다고 믿는다. 많은 심리학자들은 집을 가장 자연스러운 학습 환경으로 생각하고, 원래 집은 학교가 설립되기 훨씬 전에 교실이었다. 홈스쿨링을 하는 부모들은 그들이 자녀들의 교육을 관리할 수 있고 전통적인 학교 환경에서는 부족한 주의를 그들에게 기울일 수 있다고 주장한다. 학생들은 또한 무엇을 공부하고 언제 공부할지를 선택할 수 있으므로, 이는 그들이 그들만의 속도로 공부할 수 있도록 한다. (A) 반대로, 홈스쿨링을 비판하는 사람들은 교실에 있지 않은 아이들이 그들의 또래와 상호작용이 거의 없기 때문에 중요한 사회성 기술을 배우는 것을 놓친다고 말한다. 하지만, 몇몇 연구에서는 집에서 교육받은 아이들이 사회적, 그리고 정서적인 발달의 관점에서 다른 학생들만큼 잘 하는 것처럼 보인다는 것을 보여주었는데, 그들의 행복에 관심을 가지는 부모님의 지도와 함께, 그들의 집의 편안함과 안도감 안에서 더 많은 시간을 보냈기 때문이다. (B) 이것에도 불구하고, 홈스쿨링을 비판하는 많은 사람들은 그들의 자녀들을 효과적으로 가르칠 수 있는 부모들의 능력에 대해 우려를 제기해왔다.

	(A)	(B)
①	그러므로	그럼에도 불구하고
②	반대로	이것에도 불구하고
③	그러므로	그것과는 반대로
④	반대로	더욱이

해설 (A) 빈칸 앞부분은 홈스쿨링을 옹호하는 사람들이 생각하는 홈스쿨링의 이점에 대한 내용이고, 빈칸 뒤 문장은 홈스쿨링을 비판하는 사람들이 생각하는 홈스쿨링의 단점에 대한 설명으로 대조적인 내용이다. 따라서 대조를 나타내는 연결어인 In contrast(반대로)가 나와야 적절하다. (B) 빈칸 앞 문장은 홈스쿨링을 하는 아이들도 사회적 감정적 발달이 잘 되어 있고 그들의 부모님의 지도와 함께 편안함과 안도감 안에서 더 많은 시간을 보낸다는 내용이고, 빈칸 뒤 문장은 홈스쿨링을 비판하는 사람들이 아이들을 가르칠 수 있는 부모들의 능력에 대해 우려를 제기해왔다는 양보적인 내용이다. 따라서 양보를 나타내는 연결어 In spite of this(이것에도 불구하고)가 나와야 적절하다.

따라서 ② (A) In contrast(반대로) - (B) In spite of this(이것에도 불구하고)가 정답이다.

어휘 secure 안정된, 안심되는 establish 설립하다
monitor 관리하다, 관찰하다
pick and choose 선택하다, 까다롭게 고르다
miss out on ~을 놓치다 interaction 상호작용 welfare 행복, 복지

14 독해 전체내용 파악 (주제 파악) 난이도 ★☆☆

끊어읽기 해석

For many people, / work has become an obsession.
많은 사람들에게 / 일은 강박이 되어왔다

It has caused burnout, unhappiness and gender inequity, / as people struggle to find time / for children or passions or pets or any sort of life / besides what they do for a paycheck.
그것(일)은 극도의 피로, 불행 그리고 성 불평등을 야기시켜왔다 / 사람들은 시간을 내기 위해 고군분투하면서 / 아이들, 취미 활동, 반려동물 또는 어떤 종류의 삶을 위한 / 그들이 월급을 위해 하는 것 외에

But increasingly, / younger workers are pushing back.
그러나 점점 더 / 젊은 근로자들은 반발하고 있다

More of them expect and demand flexibility / —paid leave for a new baby, say, and generous vacation time, / along with daily things, / like the ability to work remotely, / come in late or leave early, / or make time for exercise or meditation.
그들 중 더 많은 사람들은 유연성을 기대하고 요구한다 / 이를테면 이제 막 태어난 아기를 위한 유급 휴가와 넉넉한 휴가 기간 같은 / 일상적인 것들과 더불어 / 원격으로 근무하는 것처럼 / 늦은 출근 이나 이른 퇴근 / 혹은 운동이나 명상을 위한 시간을 갖는 것

The rest of their lives happens / on their phones, / not tied to a certain place or time / —why should work be any different?
그들의 생활의 다른 것들은 일어난다 / 그들의 휴대폰에서 / 특정 장소나 시간에 묶여있지 않고 / 왜 일이라고 달라야 하는가?

해석 많은 사람들에게 일은 강박이 되어왔다. 사람들이 월급을 위해 하는 것 외에 아이들, 취미 활동, 반려동물 또는 어떤 종류의 삶을 위한 시간을 내기 위해 고군분투하면서, 그것(일)은 극도의 피로, 불행, 그리고 성 불평등을 야기시켜왔다. 그러나 젊은 근로자들은 점점 더 반발하고 있다. 그들 중 더 많은 사람들은 원격으로 근무하는 것, 늦은 출근이나 이른 퇴근, 혹은 운동이나 명상을 위한 시간을 갖는 것처럼 일상적인 것들과 더불어, 이를테면 이제 막 태어난 아기를 위한 유급 휴가와 넉넉한 휴가 기간 같은 유연성을 기대하고 요구한다. 그들의 생활의 다른 것들은 특정 장소나 시간에 묶여 있지 않고 그들의 휴대폰에서 일어나는데, 왜 일이라고 달라야 하는가?

① 당신의 월급을 인상시키는 방법
② 줄어드는 불평등에 대한 강박
③ 직장에서의 유연성에 대한 늘어나는 요구
④ 장기 휴가가 있는 삶의 장점

해설 지문 중간에서 젊은 근로자들이 점점 더 반발하고 있는데 그들은 원격으로 근무하는 것처럼 일상적인 것들과 더불어 넉넉한 휴가 기간 같은 유연성을 기대하고 요구한다고 설명하고 있다. 따라서 이 지문의 주제를 '직장에서의 유연성에 대한 늘어나는 요구'라고 표현한 ③번이 정답이다.

어휘 obsession 강박, 집착 burnout 극도의 피로 inequity 불평등
struggle 고군분투하다 passion (열정적으로 하는) 취미 활동, 열정
paycheck 월급 push back 반발하다 flexibility 유연성
paid leave 유급 휴가 remotely 원격으로, 멀리서
meditation 명상

15 독해 논리적 흐름 파악 (문단 순서 배열) 난이도 ★☆☆

끊어읽기 해석

Past research has shown / that experiencing frequent psychological stress / can be a significant risk factor / for cardiovascular disease, / a condition that affects almost half of those / aged 20 years and older in the United States.
과거 연구는 보여주었다 / 잦은 정신적인 스트레스를 경험하는 것은 / 상당한 위험 요소가 될 수 있다는 것을 / 심혈관 질병에 / ~인 사람들 중 거의 절반에게 영향을 끼치는 질환인 / 미국의 20세 이상인

(A) Does this mean, / though, / that people / who drive on a daily basis / are set to develop heart problems, / or is there a simple way / of easing the stress / of driving?
이것은 의미할까 / 하지만 / 사람들이 / 매일 운전하는 / 심장병이 생길 예정이라는 것을 / 혹은 간단한 방법이 있을까 / 스트레스를 푸는 / 운전으로 인한

(B) According to a new study, / there is.
새로운 연구에 따르면 / (그 방법이) 있다

The researchers noted / that listening to music / while driving / helps relieve the stress / that affects heart health.
연구원들은 언급했다 / 음악을 듣는 것이 / 운전하는 동안 / 스트레스를 줄이도록 돕는다고 / 심장 건강에 영향을 끼치는

(C) One source / of frequent stress / is driving, / either due

to the stressors / associated with heavy traffic / or the anxiety / that often accompanies / inexperienced drivers.
한 가지 원인은 / 잦은 스트레스의 / 운전이다 / 스트레스 요인 때문이든 / 극심한 교통량과 관련된 / 불안감 때문이든 / 종종 동반되는 / 미숙한 운전자들에게

해석　과거 연구는 잦은 정신적인 스트레스를 경험하는 것은 미국의 20세 이상인 사람들 중 거의 절반에게 영향을 끼치는 질환인 심혈관 질병에 상당한 위험 요소가 될 수 있다는 것을 보여주었다.

(C) 잦은 스트레스의 한 가지 원인은, 극심한 교통량과 관련된 스트레스 요인 때문이든 미숙한 운전자들에게 종종 동반되는 불안감 때문이든, 운전이다.
(A) 하지만, 이것은 매일 운전하는 사람들이 심장병이 생길 예정이라는 것을 의미할까? 혹은 운전으로 인한 스트레스를 푸는 간단한 방법이 있을까?
(B) 새로운 연구에 따르면 (그 방법이) 있다. 연구원들은 운전하는 동안 음악을 듣는 것이 심장 건강에 영향을 끼치는 스트레스를 줄이도록 돕는다고 언급했다.

해설　주어진 문장에서 잦은 정신적인 스트레스를 경험하는 것은 심혈관 질병에 엄청난 위험 요소(a significant risk factor)가 될 수 있다고 하고, (C)에서 잦은 스트레스의 한 가지 원인(One source of frequent stress)인 운전에 대해서 설명하고 있다. 이어서 (A)에서 운전으로 인한 스트레스(stress of driving)를 푸는 방법이 있는지에 대해 언급한 후, 이어서 (B)에서 그 방법으로 운전하는 동안 음악을 듣는 것에 대해서 이야기 하고 있다. 따라서 ③ (C) - (A) - (B)가 정답이다.

어휘　frequent 잦은, 빈번한　significant 상당한
cardiovascular 심혈관의　condition 질환
stressor 스트레스 요인　accompany 동반되다, 딸리다
inexperienced 미숙한

16　독해　논리적 흐름 파악 (무관한 문장 삭제)　난이도 ★★☆

끊어읽기 해석

When the brain perceives a threat / in the immediate surroundings, / it initiates / a complex string of events / in the body.
뇌가 위협을 인지하면 / 인접한 환경에서 / 그것은 일으킨다 / 복잡한 일련의 사건들을 / 신체에

It sends electrical messages / to various glands, / organs / that release chemical hormones / into the bloodstream.
그것(뇌)은 전기적 메시지를 보낸다 / 다양한 분비샘에 / 기관인 / 화학적 호르몬을 방출하는 / 혈류로

Blood quickly carries these hormones / to other organs / that are then prompted to do various things.
혈액은 이 호르몬들을 빠르게 이동시킨다 / 다른 기관들로 / 그 다음에 다양한 일들을 하도록 촉진되는

① The adrenal glands above the kidneys, / for example, / pump out adrenaline, / the body's stress hormone.
신장 위의 부신은 / 예를 들어 / 아드레날린을 분비한다 / 신체의 스트레스 호르몬인

② Adrenaline travels all over the body / doing things / such as widening the eyes / to be on the lookout / for signs of danger, / pumping the heart faster / to keep blood and extra hormones flowing, / and tensing the skeletal muscles / so they are ready / to lash out at or run from the threat.
아드레날린은 온몸을 돌아다닌다 / 일들을 하면서 / 눈을 크게 뜨는 것과 같은 / 세심히 살피기 위해 / 위험 신호들을 / 심장을 더 빠르게 펌프질하는 것 / 혈액과 부수적인 호르몬들이 계속 흘러가도록 / 그리고 골격근을 긴장시키는 것 / 그들이 준비를 하도록 / 위협에 대항하거나 그로부터 도망칠

③ The whole process is called / the fight-or-flight response, / because it prepares the body / to either battle or run for its life.
이 모든 과정은 ~라고 불린다 / 투쟁-도피 반응 / 이것이 신체를 준비시키기 때문에 / 생명을 구하기 위해 싸우거나 달아나도록

④ Humans consciously control their glands / to regulate the release of various hormones.
인간들은 분비샘들을 의식적으로 통제한다 / 다양한 호르몬의 분비를 조절하기 위해

Once the response is initiated, / ignoring it is impossible, / because hormones cannot be reasoned with.
일단 이 반응이 시작되고 나면 / 그것을 무시하는 것이 불가능하다 / 호르몬들은 논리적으로 설득될 수 없기 때문이다

해석　뇌가 인접한 환경에서 위협을 인지하면, 그것은 복잡한 일련의 사건들을 신체에 일으킨다. 그것(뇌)은 화학적 호르몬을 혈류로 방출하는 기관인 다양한 분비샘에 전기적 메시지를 보낸다. 혈액은 그 다음에 다양한 일들을 하도록 촉진되는 다른 기관들로 이 호르몬들을 빠르게 이동시킨다. ① 예를 들어, 신장 위의 부신은 신체의 스트레스 호르몬인 아드레날린을 분비한다. ② 아드레날린은 위험 신호들을 세심히 살피기 위해 눈을 크게 뜨는 것, 혈액과 부수적인 호르몬들이 계속 흘러가도록 심장을 더 빠르게 펌프질하는 것, 그리고 위협에 대항하거나 그로부터 도망칠 준비를 하도록 골격근을 긴장시키는 것과 같은 일들을 하면서 온몸을 돌아다닌다. ③ 이 모든 과정은 이것이 생명을 구하기 위해 싸우거나 달아나도록 신체를 준비시키기 때문에 투쟁-도피 반응이라고 불린다. ④ 인간들은 다양한 호르몬의 분비를 조절하기 위해 분비샘들을 의식적으로 통제한다. 일단 이 반응이 시작되고 나면, 그것을 무시하는 것이 불가능한데, 호르몬들은 논리적으로 설득될 수 없기 때문이다.

해설　첫 문장에서 뇌가 인접한 환경에서 위협을 인지하면 이것이 일련의 사건들을 신체에 일으킨다고 언급하고 있고, ①, ②, ③번에서 부신이 분비하는 스트레스 호르몬인 아드레날린이 온몸을 돌아다니며 여러 신체 반응들을 일으키고, 이러한 과정은 생명을 구하기 위해 신체를 준비시키는 투쟁-도피 반응이라고 설명하고 있다. 그러나 ④번은 인간이 호르몬 분비샘을 의식적으로 통제한다는 내용으로, 첫 문장의 내용과 관련이 없으므로 ④번이 정답이다.

어휘　immediate 인접한, 직접 접해 있는　initiate 일으키다, 시작하다
a string of 일련의　gland (분비)샘, 선(腺)
prompt 촉진하다, 자극하다　adrenal gland 부신　kidney 신장
be on the lookout 세심히 살피다　tense 긴장시키다; 긴장한
skeletal muscles 골격근　lash out at 대항하다, 대들다
consciously 의식적으로　regulate 조절하다
reason with 논리적으로 설득하다

17　독해　논리적 흐름 파악 (문장 삽입)　난이도 ★★★

끊어읽기 해석

It was then / he remembered his experience / with the glass flask, / and just as quickly, / he imagined / that a special coating might be applied to a glass windshield / to keep it from shattering.
바로 그때였다 / 그가 자신의 경험을 기억한 것은 / 유리 플라스크에 관한 / 그리고 재빨리 / 그는 생각했다 / 특수 코팅이 자동차 앞 유리에 적용될지도 모른다고 / 그것이 산산조각 나지 않게 하기 위해

In 1903 the French chemist, Edouard Benedictus, / dropped a glass flask one day / on a hard floor / and broke it.
1903년에 프랑스의 화학자 Edouard Benedictus는 / 어느 날 유리 플라스크를 떨어뜨렸다 / 딱딱한 바닥에 / 그리고 그것을 깨뜨렸다

(①) However, / to the astonishment of the chemist, / the flask did not shatter, / but still retained / most of its original shape.
하지만 / 그 화학자에게 놀랍게도 / 플라스크는 산산조각 나지 않았다 / 그리고 여전히 유지했다 / 그것의 원래 형태의 대부분을

(②) When he examined the flask / he found / that it contained a film coating inside, / a residue / remaining from a solution of collodion / that the flask had contained.
그가 플라스크를 살펴보았을 때 / 그는 알아냈다 / 필름 코팅이 안쪽에 들어 있다는 것을 / 잔여물인 / 콜로디온 용액으로부터 남아있는 / 플라스크가 담고 있었던

(③) He made a note of this unusual phenomenon, / but thought no more of it / until several weeks later / when he read stories in the newspapers / about people / in automobile accidents / who were badly hurt / by flying windshield glass.
그는 이 특이한 현상을 써 놓았다 / 하지만 그것에 대해 더 이상 생각하지 않았다 / 몇 주 뒤까지는 / 그가 이야기를 신문에서 읽었을 때 / 사람들에 대한 / 자동차 사고에서 / 심하게 다친 / 날아오는 자동차 앞 유리에 의해

(④) Not long thereafter, / he succeeded / in producing the world's first sheet of safety glass.
그 후 얼마 지나지 않아, / 그는 성공했다 / 세계 최초의 안전 유리를 생산하는 데

해석 1903년에 프랑스의 화학자 Edouard Benedictus는 어느 날 딱딱한 바닥에 유리 플라스크를 떨어뜨렸고, 그것을 깨뜨렸다. 하지만 그 화학자에게 놀랍게도, 플라스크는 산산조각 나지 않았고, 그것의 원래 형태의 대부분을 여전히 유지했다. 그가 플라스크를 살펴보았을 때 그는 플라스크가 담고 있었던 콜로디온 용액으로부터 남아있는 잔여물인 필름 코팅이 (플라스크) 안쪽에 들어있다는 것을 알아냈다. 그는 이 특이한 현상을 써 놓았지만, 몇 주 뒤 자동차 사고에서 날아오는 자동차 앞 유리에 의해 심하게 다친 사람들에 대한 이야기를 신문에서 읽었을 때까지는 그것(특이한 현상)에 대해 더 이상 생각하지 않았다. ④ 그가 유리 플라스크에 관한 자신의 경험을 기억한 것은 바로 그때였고, 그는 재빨리 특수 코팅이 그것(자동차 앞 유리)이 산산조각 나지 않게 하기 위해 자동차 앞 유리에 적용될지도 모른다고 생각했다. 그 후 얼마 지나지 않아, 그는 세계 최초의 안전 유리를 생산하는 데 성공했다.

해설 ④번 앞부분에서 Edouard Benedictus가 떨어뜨린 플라스크를 살펴보았을 때 그것이 담고 있었던 콜로디온 용액의 잔여물인 필름 코팅이 그것의 안쪽에 들어 있어 산산조각 나지 않았던 것을 알아낸 일을 기록해 두었지만, 자동차 사고에서 날아오는 자동차 앞 유리에 의해 심하게 다친 사람들에 대한 이야기를 신문에서 읽었을 때까지는 그것에 대해 생각하지 않았다고 이야기하고 있다. 이어서, ④번 뒤 문장에서 그 후 얼마 지나지 않아 그가 안전 유리 생산에 성공했다고 말하고 있으므로, ④번에 그가 그때 유리 플라스크에 관한 자신의 경험을 기억했고, 특수 코팅이 자동차 앞 유리에 적용될지도 모른다고 생각했다는 내용의 주어진 문장이 나와야 지문이 자연스럽게 연결된다. 따라서 ④번이 정답이다.

어휘 windshield (자동차 등의) 앞 유리
shatter 산산조각 나다, 산산이 부서지다   astonishment 놀람, 경악
retain 유지하다   contain ~이 들어 있다, ~을 담고 있다
residue 잔여물, 찌꺼기   solution 용액, 해결책
make a note of ~을 써 놓다   thereafter 그 후에

---

18 독해   세부내용 파악 (내용 불일치 파악)   난이도 ★★☆

끊어읽기 해석

Dubrovnik, Croatia, is a mess.
Croatia의 Dubrovnik는 엉망진창이다

Because its main attraction is its seaside Old Town / surrounded by 80-foot medieval walls, / this Dalmatian Coast town does not absorb visitors very well.
그것의 주요 명소가 해안가의 Old Town이기 때문에 / 80피트의 중세 시대 벽돌로 둘러싸인 / 이 달마티아식 해안 도시는 방문객들을 잘 받아들이지 못한다

And when cruise ships are docked here, / a legion of tourists turn Old Town / into a miasma of tank-top-clad tourists / marching down the town's limestone-blanketed streets.
그리고 크루즈선들이 이곳에 정박할 때 / 다수의 여행객들은 Old Town을 바꾸어 놓는다 / 탱크톱을 입은 관광객들로 이루어진 불건전한 분위기로 / 그 마을의 석회암으로 뒤덮인 거리를 걷는

Yes, / the city of Dubrovnik has been proactive / in trying to curb cruise ship tourism, / but nothing will save Old Town / from the perpetual swarm of tourists.
그렇다 / Dubrovnik 시는 적극적이다 / 크루즈선 관광을 억제하기 위해 노력하는 것에 / 하지만 어떤 것도 Old Town을 구할 수 없을 것이다 / 끊임없는 관광객 무리로부터

To make matters worse, / the lure of making extra money / has inspired many homeowners in Old Town / to turn over their places to Airbnb, / making the walled portion of town / one giant hotel.
설상가상으로 / 여분의 돈을 버는 것의 유혹은 / Old Town의 많은 집주인들을 자극했다 / 그들의 거처를 Airbnb로 바꾸도록 / 그러면서 마을의 벽으로 둘러싸인 부분을 ~로 만들었다 / 하나의 거대한 호텔로

You want / an "authentic" Dubrovnik experience in Old Town, / just like a local?
당신은 원하는가 / Old Town에서 '진정한' Dubrovnik를 경험하기를 / 꼭 현지인들처럼?

You're not going to find it here. // Ever.
당신은 그것을 이곳에서 발견하지는 않을 것이다 // 절대로

해석 Croatia의 Dubrovnik는 엉망진창이다. 그것의 주요 명소가 80피트의 중세 시대 벽돌로 둘러싸인 해안가의 Old Town이기 때문에, 이 달마티아식 해안 도시는 방문객들을 잘 받아들이지 못한다. 그리고 크루즈선들이 이곳에 정박할 때, 다수의 여행객들은 Old Town을 그 마을의 석회암으로 뒤덮인 거리를 걷는 탱크톱을 입은 관광객들로 이루어진 불건전한 분위기로 바꾸어 놓는다. 그렇다, Dubrovnik 시는 크루즈선 관광을 억제하기 위해 노력하는 것에 적극적이지만, 어떤 것도 Old Town을 끊임없는 관광객 무리로부터 구할 수 없을 것이다. 설상가상으로, 여분의 돈을 버는 것의 유혹은 Old Town의 많은 집주인들이 그들의 거처를 Airbnb로 바꾸도록 자극했으며, 그러면서 마을의 벽으로 둘러싸인 부분을 하나의 거대한 호텔로 만들었다. 당신은 Old Town에서 꼭 현지인들처럼 '진정한' Dubrovnik를 경험하기를 원하는가? 당신은 그것을 이곳에서 발견하지는 않을 것이다. 절대로.

해설 지문 중간에서 Dubrovnik 시는 크루즈선 관광을 억제하기 위해 노력하는 것에 적극적이라고 했으므로, Dubrovnik 시가 크루즈 여행을 확대하려고 노력해 왔다는 것은 지문의 내용과 반대이다. 따라서 ③번이 정답이다.

어휘 mess 엉망진창, 혼란   attraction 명소   absorb 받아들이다
legion 다수   miasma 불건전한 분위기   clad ~을 입은
march (당당히) 걷다   limestone 석회암   blanket 뒤덮다
proactive 적극적인   curb 억제하다   perpetual 끊임없는
swarm 무리, 떼   lure 유혹   inspire 자극하여 ~할 마음을 품게 하다
wall 벽으로 둘러싸다   local 현지인

끊어읽기 해석

When an organism is alive, / it takes in carbon dioxide / from the air around it.
유기체가 살아있을 때 / 그것은 이산화탄소를 흡수한다 / 주변의 공기로부터

Most of that carbon dioxide / is made of carbon-12, / but a tiny portion consists of carbon-14.
그 이산화탄소의 대부분은 / 탄소 12로 이루어져 있다 / 하지만 아주 적은 부분은 탄소 14로 구성되어 있다

So the living organism always contains / a very small amount of radioactive carbon, carbon-14.
따라서 살아있는 유기체는 항상 포함한다 / 매우 적은 양의 방사성 탄소인 탄소 14를

A detector next to the living organism / would record radiation / given off by the carbon-14 / in the organism.
살아있는 유기체 옆의 탐지기는 / 방사능을 기록한다 / 탄소 14에 의해 방출된 / 그 유기체 안의

When the organism dies, / it no longer takes in carbon dioxide.
그 유기체가 죽으면 / 그것은 더 이상 이산화탄소를 흡수하지 않는다

No new carbon-14 is added, / and the old carbon-14 slowly decays / into nitrogen.
어떠한 새로운 탄소 14도 추가되지 않는다 / 그리고 기존의 탄소 14는 천천히 붕괴된다 / 질소로

The amount of carbon-14 slowly (A) decreases / as time goes on.
탄소 14의 양은 천천히 (A) 감소한다 / 시간이 지나면서

Over time, / less and less radiation from carbon-14 / is produced.
시간이 흐르면서 / 탄소 14로부터 점점 더 적은 방사능이 / 생산된다

The amount of carbon-14 radiation / detected for an organism / is a measure, / therefore, / of how long the organism has been (B) dead.
탄소 14의 방사능의 양이 / 유기체에서 감지되는 / 척도이다 / 따라서 / 그 유기체가 얼마나 오랫동안 (B) 죽어있었는지에 대한

This method / of determining the age of an organism / is called carbon-14 dating.
이러한 방식은 / 유기체의 연대를 결정하는 / 탄소 14 연대 측정법이라고 불린다

The decay of carbon-14 / allows archaeologists to find / the age of once-living materials.
탄소 14의 붕괴는 / 고고학자들이 알아내도록 한다 / 한때 살아있던 물질들의 연대를

Measuring the amount of radiation remaining / indicates the approximate age.
남아있는 방사능의 양을 측정하는 것은 / 대략적인 연대를 알려준다

해석 유기체가 살아있을 때, 그것은 주변의 공기로부터 이산화탄소를 흡수한다. 그 이산화탄소의 대부분은 탄소12로 이루어져 있지만, 아주 적은 부분은 탄소 14로 구성되어 있다. 따라서 살아있는 유기체는 항상 매우 적은 양의 방사성 탄소인 탄소14를 포함한다. 살아있는 유기체 옆의 탐지기는 그 유기체 안의 탄소14에 의해 방출된 방사능을 기록한다. 그 유기체가 죽으면 그것은 더 이상 이산화탄소를 흡수하지 않는다. 어떠한 새로운 탄소 14도 추가되지 않고, 기존의 탄소 14는 질소로 천천히 붕괴된다. 시간이 지나면서 탄소 14의 양은 천천히 (A) 감소한다. 시간이 흐르면서, 탄소 14로부터 점점 더 적은 방사능이 생산된다. 따라서, 유기체에서 감지되는 탄소 14의 방사능의 양이 그 유기체가 얼마나 오랫동안 (B) 죽어 있었는지에 대한 척도이다. 유기체의 연대를 결정하는 이러한 방식은 탄소 14 연대 측정법이라고 불린다. 탄소 14의 붕괴는 고고학

자들이 한때 살아있던 물질들의 연대를 알아내도록 한다. 남아있는 방사능의 양을 측정하는 것은 대략적인 연대를 알려준다.

(A)	(B)
① 감소하다	죽은
② 증가하다	살아있는
③ 감소하다	생산적인
④ 증가하다	활동하지 않는

해설 (A) 빈칸의 앞부분에서 유기체가 죽으면 더 이상 이산화탄소를 흡수하지 않으며, 새로운 탄소 14도 추가되지 않고 기존의 탄소 14는 질소로 천천히 붕괴된다고 했으므로, 빈칸에는 탄소 14의 양이 천천히 '감소한다' 내용이 나와야 적절하다. (B) 빈칸의 뒷부분에서 유기체의 연대를 결정하는 탄소 14 연대 측정법을 통해 고고학자들은 한때 살아있던 물질들의 연대를 알아낼 수 있고, 남아있는 방사능의 양을 측정하는 것이 대략적인 연대를 알려준다고 했으므로, 빈칸에는 유기체에서 감지되는 탄소 14의 방사능의 양이 그 유기체가 얼마나 오랫동안 '죽어'있었는지의 척도라는 내용이 나와야 적절하다.
따라서 ① (A) decreases(감소하다) - (B) dead(죽은)가 정답이다.

어휘 organism 유기체 take in 흡수하다, 섭취하다
carbon dioxide 이산화탄소 radioactive 방사성의
detector 탐지기 give off 방출하다
decay (방사성 물질이) 붕괴하다; 붕괴 nitrogen 질소
detect 감지하다, 발견하다 measure 척도 approximate 대략적인
inactive 활동하지 않는

끊어읽기 해석

All creatures, / past and present, / either have gone / or will go extinct.
모든 생명체들은 / 과거와 현재의 / 사라졌다 / 또는 멸종할 것이다

Yet, / as each species vanished / over the past 3.8-billion-year history / of life on Earth, / new ones inevitably appeared / to replace them / or to exploit newly emerging resources.
그러나 / 각각의 종들이 사라짐에 따라 / 38억 년 역사에 걸쳐 / 지구상 생물의 / 새로운 종들은 필연적으로 나타났다 / 그들을 대체하기 위해 / 또는 새롭게 생겨난 자원을 활용하기 위해

From only a few very simple organisms, / a great number of complex, multicellular forms evolved / over this immense period.
단지 몇몇의 매우 단순한 유기체로부터 / 엄청난 수의 복잡하고 다세포적인 형태가 진화했다 / 이 어마어마한 기간 동안

The origin of new species, / which the nineteenth-century English naturalist Charles Darwin once referred to / as "the mystery of mysteries," / is the natural process of speciation / responsible for generating this remarkable diversity of living creatures / with whom humans share the planet.
새로운 종의 기원 / 19세기 영국의 자연학자인 찰스 다윈이 옛날에 언급했던 / '미스터리 중의 미스터리'라고 / 종분화라는 자연적인 과정이다 / 이러한 놀라운 생명체들의 다양성을 만들어 내는 데 원인이 되는 / 인간이 지구를 함께 공유하는

Although taxonomists presently recognize / some 1.5 million living species, / the actual number is possibly closer / to 10 million.
비록 분류학자들이 현재 인지하고 있을지라도 / 약 150만의 생존하는 종들을 / 실질적 숫자는 아마도 더 가까울 것이다 / 천만에

Recognizing the biological status / of this multitude / requires a clear understanding / of what constitutes a species, / which

> is no easy task / given that evolutionary biologists have yet to agree / on a universally acceptable definition.
> 생물학적 상태를 인식하는 것은 / 이러한 다수의 / 명확한 이해를 요구한다 / 무엇이 하나의 종을 구성하는지에 대한 / 이것은 쉬운 일이 아니다 / 진화 생물학자들이 아직 합의하지 못한 것을 고려하면 / 보편적으로 수용될 수 있는 정의에 대해

해석 과거와 현재의 모든 생명체들은 사라졌거나 멸종할 것이다. 그러나, 지구상 생물의 38억 년 역사에 걸쳐 각각의 종들이 사라짐에 따라, 새로운 종들은 그들(사라진 종들)을 대체하기 위해 또는 새롭게 생겨난 자원을 활용하기 위해 필연적으로 나타났다. 단지 몇몇의 매우 단순한 유기체로부터, 엄청난 수의 복잡하고 다세포적인 형태가 이 어마어마한 기간 동안 진화했다. 19세기 영국의 자연학자인 찰스 다윈이 옛날에 '미스터리 중의 미스터리'라고 언급했던 새로운 종의 기원은, 인간이 지구를 함께 공유하는 이러한 놀라운 생명체들의 다양성을 만들어 내는 데 원인이 되는 종분화라는 자연적인 과정이다. 비록 분류학자들이 현재 약 150만의 생존하는 종들을 인지하고 있을지라도, 실질적 숫자는 아마도 천만에 더 가까울 것이다. 이러한 다수의 생물학적 상태를 인식하는 것은 무엇이 하나의 종을 구성하는지에 대한 명확한 이해를 요구하는데, 이것은 진화 생물학자들이 보편적으로 수용될 수 있는 정의에 대해 아직 합의하지 못한 것을 고려하면 쉬운 일이 아니다.

① 생물학자들의 기술
② 생명체들의 다양성
③ 멸종된 유기체들의 목록
④ 멸종 위기에 처한 종들의 모음

해설 빈칸이 있는 문장을 통해 빈칸에 새로운 종의 기원은 놀라운 무엇을 만들어 내는 데 원인이 되는 종분화라는 자연적인 과정인지에 대한 내용이 나와야 적절하다는 것을 알 수 있다. 빈칸 앞 문장에서 단지 몇몇의 매우 단순한 유기체로부터 엄청난 수의 복잡하고 다세포적 형태가 진화했다고 하고, 빈칸 뒤 문장에서는 분류학자들이 현재 약 150만의 생존하는 종들을 인지하고 있을지라도 실질적 숫자는 아마도 천만에 더 가까울 것이라는 내용이 있으므로, 새로운 종의 기원은 놀라운 '생명체들의 다양성'을 만들어 내는 원인이 되는 종분화라는 자연적인 과정이라고 한 ②번이 정답이다.

어휘 vanish 사라지다 inevitably 필연적으로 exploit 활용하다
immense 어마어마한, 엄청난 speciation 종분화(種分化)
responsible for ~의 원인이 되는 taxonomist 분류학자
multitude 다수 constitute 구성하다 given that ~을 고려하면
universally 보편적으로 inventory 목록
endangered 멸종 위기에 처한

정답 p.64

01	① 어휘 - 어휘&표현	11	④ 독해 - 세부내용 파악
02	② 어휘 - 어휘&표현	12	② 독해 - 논리적 흐름 파악
03	④ 어휘 - 생활영어	13	③ 독해 - 전체내용 파악
04	② 어휘 - 생활영어	14	③ 어휘 - 어휘&표현
05	② 문법 - 우리말과영작문의의미상불일치	15	① 어휘 - 어휘&표현
06	① 문법 - 우리말과영작문의의미상불일치	16	① 독해 - 추론
07	② 문법 - 분사	17	④ 독해 - 논리적 흐름 파악
08	④ 문법 - 능동태·수동태	18	③ 독해 - 추론
09	④ 독해 - 전체내용 파악	19	② 독해 - 세부내용 파악
10	③ 독해 - 전체내용 파악	20	④ 독해 - 논리적 흐름 파악

취약영역 분석표

영역	세부 유형	문항 수	소계
어휘	어휘&표현	4	/6
	생활영어	2	
문법	우리말과 영작문의 의미상 불일치	2	/4
	분사	1	
	능동태·수동태	1	
독해	전체내용 파악	3	/10
	세부내용 파악	2	
	추론	2	
	논리적 흐름 파악	3	
	총계		/20

· 자신이 취약한 영역은 '공무원 영어, 이렇게 출제된다!'(문제집 p.8)를 통해 다시 한번 확인하고 학습하시기 바랍니다.

---

01 어휘 어휘&표현 discern = distinguish · 난이도 ★★☆

해석 『Natural Gas World』 구독자들은 그 산업에서 무슨 일이 일어나고 있는지에 대한 정확하고 신뢰할 수 있는 주요 사실들과 수치들을 받게 될 것이므로, 그들은 그들의 사업에 관련된 것을 완전히 파악할 수 있다.

① 식별하다 　　　 ② 강화하다
③ 약화시키다 　　 ④ 버리다

어휘 subscriber 구독자 accurate 정확한 reliable 신뢰할 수 있는
figure 수치, 숫자 discern 파악하다, 알아차리다
concern 관련되다, 영향을 미치다 distinguish 식별하다, 구별하다
strengthen 강화하다 undermine 약화시키다, ~의 밑을 파다
abandon 버리다, 떠나다

👍 이것도 알면 **합격!**

discern(파악하다)과 유사한 의미의 표현
= recognize, determine, make out

---

02 어휘 어휘&표현 stand out = be impressive 난이도 ★★☆

해석 여자 1,500미터 경기의 은메달 수상자인 Ms. West는 경주 내내 눈에 띄었다.

① 압도되었다 　　　 ② 인상적이었다
③ 우울했다 　　　　 ④ 낙관적이었다

어휘 stand out 눈에 띄다, 두드러지다 overwhelmed 압도된
impressive 인상적인 depressed 우울한, 낙담한
optimistic 낙관적인

👍 이것도 알면 **합격!**

stand out(눈에 띄다)과 유사한 의미의 표현
= attract attention, be conspicuous, catch the eye

---

03 어휘 생활영어 I'm very busy right now. 난이도 ★☆☆

해석 ① A: 나는 해외 여행을 갈 건데, 다른 나라에서 지내는 것이 익숙하지 않아.
　　 B: 걱정하지마. 너는 그것에 곧 익숙해질 거야.
② A: 나는 그 사진 대회에서 상을 타고 싶어.
　　 B: 나는 네가 그럴 거라고 확신해. 행운을 빌게!
③ A: 나의 가장 친한 친구가 세종시로 이사했어. 나는 그녀가 너무 그리워.
　　 B: 그렇구나. 나도 네가 어떤 기분인지 알아.
④ A: 잠깐 이야기를 나눌 수 있을까?
　　 B: 괜찮아. 나는 지금 매우 바빠.

해설 ④번에서 A는 이야기를 나눌 수 있는지를 묻고 있으므로, 괜찮다고 한 후에 매우 바쁘다고 하는 B의 대답 Never mind. I'm very busy right now(괜찮아. 나는 지금 매우 바빠)는 어울리지 않는다. 따라서 ④번이 정답이다.

어휘 abroad 해외에서, 해외로 get accustomed to ~에 익숙해지다
in no time 곧, 당장에 keep one's fingers crossed 행운을 빌다

👍 이것도 알면 **합격!**

바쁜 상황을 나타내는 다양한 표현을 알아두자.

· I'm busy as a bee. 나는 아주 바빠. (나는 벌처럼 바빠.)
· I'm swamped with work. 나는 일 때문에 매우 바빠.
· I've got a lot on my plate. 나는 해야 할 일이 엄청 많아.

04 어휘 생활영어 how do I eat them   난이도 ★☆☆

해석

> A: 딤섬 좀 먹어볼래?
> B: 응, 고마워. 그것들은 맛있어 보인다. 안에 무엇이 들었어?
> A: 이것에는 돼지고기와 다진 야채가 있고, 저것에는 새우가 있어.
> B: 그러면, 음, 내가 그것들을 어떻게 먹으면 돼?
> A: 하나를 이렇게 젓가락으로 집어서 소스에 적시면 돼. 쉬워.
> B: 알겠어. 한번 시도해 볼게.

① 그것들은 얼마야
② 내가 그것들을 어떻게 먹으면 돼
③ 그것들은 얼마나 매워
④ 너는 그것들을 어떻게 요리해

해설 딤섬 안에 무엇이 들었냐는 B의 말에 A가 대답하고 빈칸 뒤에서 다시 A가 You pick one up with your chopsticks like this and dip it into the sauce(하나를 이렇게 젓가락으로 집어서 소스에 적시면 돼)라고 말하고 있으므로, 빈칸에는 '내가 그것들을 어떻게 먹으면 돼'라는 의미의 'how do I eat them'이 오는 것이 자연스럽다. 따라서 ②번이 정답이다.

어휘 chop 다지다 dip 적시다, 살짝 담그다

👍 이것도 알면 **합격!**

I'll give it a try(한번 시도해 볼게)와 유사한 의미의 표현
· I'll give it a go. 내가 한번 해 볼게.
· I'll give it a shot. 내가 한번 해 볼게.
· I'll make an attempt. 내가 시도해 볼게.

05 문법 우리말과 영작문의 의미상 불일치   난이도 ★★☆

해설 ② 우리말과 영작문의 의미상 불일치 '자정이 5분이나 지난 후'는 전치사 'past(~이 지나서)'를 사용하여 five minutes past midnight으로 나타낼 수 있으므로 'shy of'(~이 모자라는)를 past로 고쳐야 한다. 참고로, five minutes shy of midnight은 자정에서 5분이 모자라는, 즉 자정이 되기 5분 전을 의미한다.

오답분석 ① 주어 동사 수 일치 주어 자리에 단수 명사 The new teacher가 왔으므로 단수 동사 is가 올바르게 쓰였다. 주어와 동사 사이의 수식어 거품(I ~ about)은 동사의 수 결정에 영향을 주지 않는다. 참고로, 해당 문장은 선행사 The new teacher 뒤에 관계절(I ~ about)을 이끄는 목적격 관계대명사 whom 또는 that이 생략된 형태이다.
③ 명사절 접속사 | 주어 동사 수 일치 주어가 없는 불완전한 절 (appeared ~ shark)을 이끌며 문장의 주어 자리에 올 수 있는 명사절 접속사 What이 올바르게 쓰였고, 명사절 주어는 단수 취급하므로 단수 동사 was가 올바르게 쓰였다.
④ 수사 + 하이픈(-) + 단위 표현 '수사 + 하이픈(-) + 단위 표현'(16-year-old)이 명사(friend)를 수식하는 형용사로 쓰이는 경우, 단위 표현은 반드시 단수형이 되어야 하므로 16-year-old가 올바르게 쓰였다.

어휘 shy of (~에 대하여) ~이 모자라는 lurk 숨어 있다, 도사리다
summit 정상, 산꼭대기

👍 이것도 알면 **합격!**

①번 문장처럼 목적격 관계대명사는 생략할 수 있다는 것을 알아두자.
(ex) I forgot the name of the band (whom / that) you told me about. 나는 네가 나에게 말했던 밴드의 이름을 잊어버렸다.

06 문법 우리말과 영작문의 의미상 불일치   난이도 ★★☆

해설 ① 우리말과 영작문의 의미상 불일치 '개인용 컴퓨터'는 형용사 personal(개인용의)을 써서 나타낼 수 있으므로 computers per person을 personal computers로 고쳐야 한다. 참고로, 전치사 per는 '~당'이란 의미로 computers per person은 '개인 당 컴퓨터'라는 의미가 된다.

오답분석 ② 명사절 접속사 | 주어 동사 수 일치 주어가 없는 불완전한 절 (happened ~ summer)을 이끌며 문장의 주어 자리에 올 수 있는 명사절 접속사 What이 올바르게 쓰였고, 명사절 주어는 단수 취급하므로 단수 동사 was가 올바르게 쓰였다.
③ 도치 구문 부사 so가 '~역시 그렇다'라는 의미로 쓰여 절 앞에 오고, so 뒤에 be동사가 오면 주어와 be동사가 도치되어 'so + be동사(are) + 주어(plastic bottles)'의 어순이 되어야 하므로 so are plastic bottles가 올바르게 쓰였다.
④ 현재완료진행 시제 현재완료 시제와 자주 함께 쓰이는 시간 표현 'since + 과거시간 표현'(since I retired)이 왔고, '은퇴 후부터 내내 이 일을 해오고 있다'라는 과거에서 시작된 일이 현재까지 계속되는 것을 표현하고 있으므로, 현재완료진행 시제 I have been doing this work가 올바르게 쓰였다.

어휘 retire 은퇴하다

👍 이것도 알면 **합격!**

부정문에 대해 '~ 역시 그렇다'라는 의미를 나타낼 때는 so가 아닌 neither/nor가 쓰인다는 것을 알아두자.
(ex) I don't like horror movies and neither does my sister.
나는 공포영화를 싫어하고 내 여동생 역시 그렇다.

07 문법 분사   난이도 ★★☆

해석 길들여진 가축들은 인간들이 이용할 수 있는 가장 초기의 그리고 가장 효율적인 '기계'이다. 그들은 사람의 허리와 팔에서 부담을 덜어 준다. 다른 기술들과 함께 활용되어, 가축들은 (고기와 우유에 있는 단백질 같은) 추가 식량으로써 그리고 또 짐들을 옮기고, 물을 들어 올리고, 곡물을 가는 기계로써 인간의 생활 수준을 정말로 상당히 향상시킬 수 있다. 그들이 너무 명백하게 대단히 도움이 되기 때문에, 우리는 수 세기 동안 인간들이 그들이 기르는 가축들의 수와 품질을 증대시켰다는 것을 발견하기를 기대할지도 모른다. 놀랍게도, 이것은 실제로 대개 그렇지 않았다.

해설 ② 현재분사 vs. 과거분사 문맥상 주절의 주어 animals와 분사구문이 '가축들이 다른 기술들과 함께 활용되다'라는 의미의 수동 관계이므로 현재분사 Utilizing을 과거분사 Utilized로 고쳐야 한다.

오답분석 ① 형용사의 쓰임 문맥상 '이용할 수 있는 기계'라는 의미가 되어야 자연스러우므로 명사 machines를 뒤에서 수식할 수 있는 형용사 available이 올바르게 쓰였다.
③ to 부정사의 쓰임 '옮기는 기계'라는 의미를 표현하기 위해 형용사처럼 명사(machines)를 수식하는 to 부정사 to carry가 올바르게 쓰였다.

④ 보어 자리 be동사(are)는 주격 보어를 취하는 동사인데, 보어 자리에는 명사나 형용사 역할을 하는 것이 올 수 있으므로 형용사 역할을 하는 'of + 추상명사(benefit)'의 of가 올바르게 쓰였다.

어휘 domesticate 길들이다 take off 덜다, 없애다 strain 부담, 긴장
utilize 활용하다, 이용하다 considerably 상당히
supplementary 추가의, 보충의 foodstuff 식량 grind 갈다
obviously 명백하게

👍 이것도 알면 **합격!**

-able, -ible로 끝나는 형용사는 명사를 뒤에서 수식할 수 있으며, -where, -thing, -one, -body로 끝나는 명사는 항상 뒤에서 수식한다는 것을 알아두자.

08 문법 능동태·수동태 난이도 ★★☆

해석 신화는 한 문화의 종교적, 철학적, 도덕적, 그리고 정치적 가치를 담은, 그리고 어떤 경우에는 (그것들을) 설명하는 것을 돕는 이야기이다. 신들과 초자연적인 존재들의 이야기들을 통해, 신화는 자연 세계에서 발생하는 것들을 이해하려고 노력한다. 대중적인 (단어의) 용법과는 반대로, 신화는 '거짓말'을 의미하지 않는다. 가장 넓은 의미에서, 신화는 거짓인 것뿐만 아니라 사실일 수 있거나 부분적으로 사실일 수 있는 이야기들인, 통상적으로는 이야기의 전체 묶음이다. 하지만, 그것들의 정확도와는 상관없이, 신화는 종종 한 문화의 가장 뿌리 깊은 신념을 표현한다. 이러한 정의에 따르면, 『일리아드』와 『오디세이』, 코란과 구약 및 신약 성경은 모두 신화라고 지칭될 수 있다.

해설 ④ 능동태 vs. 수동태 주어(the Iliad ~ Testaments)와 동사가 '『일리아드』와 『오디세이』, 코란과 구약 및 신약 성경은 지칭될 수 있다'라는 의미의 수동 관계이므로 능동태 refer to as를 수동태 be referred to as로 고쳐야 한다.

오답 ① 동사의 쓰임 동사 help는 3형식 동사로 쓰일 때 to 부정사와
분석 원형부정사를 모두 목적어로 취할 수 있으므로 to 부정사를 목적어로 취한 helps to explain이 올바르게 쓰였다.
② 타동사의 쓰임 문맥상 '이해하려고 노력한다'라는 의미가 되어야 자연스러운데, '~하려고 노력하다'는 'try + to 부정사'를 사용하여 나타낼 수 있으므로 try to make가 올바르게 쓰였다.
③ 관계사 선택 선행사와 관계절 사이에 삽입절(usually whole groups of stories)이 있는 구조이다. 선행사(stories)가 사물이고, 관계절 내에서 동사 can be의 주어 역할을 하므로 주격 관계대명사 that이 올바르게 쓰였다.

어휘 myth 신화 narrative 이야기 embody 담다, 포함하다
supernatural 초자연적인 occurrence 발생하는 것
usage (단어의) 용법, 사용 falsehood 거짓말 accuracy 정확도
frequently 종종 definition 정의, 개념
refer to ~ as ~을 −라고 지칭하다

👍 이것도 알면 **합격!**

'refer to + 목적어 + as + 명사'(목적어를 명사라고 부르다)가 수동태가 되어 목적어(the Iliad ~ Testaments)가 주어가 된 경우, 자동사(refer)와 함께 쓰인 전치사(to)와 목적어 뒤에 쓰인 전치사(as) 모두 수동태 동사(be referred) 뒤에 그대로 남는다.

(ex) People can refer to the Iliad ~ New Testaments as myths.
　　　　　　　　　　목적어　　　　　　　　　as + 명사
→ The Iliad ~ New Testaments can be referred to as myths.

09 독해 전체내용 파악 (제목 파악) 난이도 ★☆☆

끊어읽기 해석

Mapping technologies are being used / in many new applications.
매핑기술은 사용되고 있다 / 많은 새로운 응용프로그램에

Biological researchers are exploring / the molecular structure of DNA / ("mapping the genome"), / geophysicists are mapping / the structure of the Earth's core, / and oceanographers are mapping / the ocean floor.
생물학 연구원들은 탐구하고 있다 / DNA의 분자 구조 / ('게놈을 지도화하기')를 / 지구 물리학자들은 지도화하고 있다 / 지구 중심부의 구조를 / 그리고 해양학자들은 지도화하고 있다 / 대양저를

Computer games have / various imaginary "lands" or levels / where rules, hazards, and rewards change.
컴퓨터 게임은 가지고 있다 / 다양한 가상의 '땅' 혹은 레벨들을 / 규칙, 위험, 그리고 보상이 변화하는

Computerization now challenges reality / with "virtual reality," / artificial environments / that stimulate special situations, / which may be useful / in training and entertainment.
컴퓨터화는 이제 현실에 도전한다 / '가상현실'로 / 인위적인 환경인 / 특별한 상황들을 자극하는 / 그리고 이것은 유용할 수도 있다 / 훈련과 오락에서

Mapping techniques are being used / also in the realm of ideas.
매핑기술은 사용되고 있다 / 관념의 영역에서도

For example, / relationships between ideas can be shown / using what are called concept maps.
예를 들어 / 생각들 사이의 관계는 보여질 수 있다 / 개념도라고 불리는 것을 사용하여

Starting from a general or "central" idea, / related ideas can be connected, / building a web / around the main concept.
일반적이거나 '중심적인' 생각에서 출발하여 / 관련된 생각들은 이어질 수 있다 / 망을 형성하며 / 주요 개념 주위에

This is not a map / by any traditional definition, / but the tools and techniques of cartography / are employed to produce it, / and in some ways / it resembles a map.
이것은 지도가 아니다 / 어느 전통적인 정의에 의한 / 하지만 지도제작의 도구들과 기술들은 / 그것을 생산하기 위해 사용된다 / 그리고 어떤 점에서는 / 그것은 지도와 유사하다

해석 매핑기술은 많은 새로운 응용프로그램에 사용되고 있다. 생물학 연구원들은 DNA의 분자 구조를 탐구하고 있고('게놈을 지도화하기'), 지구 물리학자들은 지구 중심부의 구조를 지도화하고 있고, 해양학자들은 대양저를 지도화하고 있다. 컴퓨터 게임은 규칙, 위험, 그리고 보상이 변화하는 다양한 가상의 '땅' 혹은 레벨들을 가지고 있다. 컴퓨터화는 이제 특별한 상황들을 자극하는 인위적인 환경인 '가상현실'로 현실에 도전하는데, 이것은 훈련과 오락에서 유용할 수도 있다. 매핑기술은 관념의 영역에서도 사용되고 있다. 예를 들어, 생각들 사이의 관계는 개념도라고 불리는 것을 사용하여 보여질 수 있다. 일반적이거나 '중심적인' 생각에서 출발하여 관련된 생각들은 주요 개념 주위에 망을 형성하며 이어질 수 있다. 이것은 어느 전통적인 정의에 의한 지도가 아니지만, 지도제작의 도구들과 기술들은 그것을 생산하기 위해 사용되고, 어떤 점에서는 그것은 지도와 유사하다.

① 컴퓨터화된 지도 vs. 전통적인 지도
② 지도제작은 어디에서 시작되었는가?
③ DNA의 비밀로 가는 방법 찾기
④ 새로운 분야를 지도화하기

해설 지문 처음에서 매핑기술이 새로운 응용프로그램에 사용된다고 하고, 이어서 생물학, 컴퓨터 게임, 관념의 영역에서 매핑기술이 어

떻게 사용되는지를 설명하고 있다. 따라서 이 지문의 제목을 '새로운 분야를 지도화하기'라고 표현한 ④번이 정답이다.

어휘 mapping technology 매핑기술(컴퓨터를 이용하여 지도를 만들고 데이터베이스화 하는 기술) molecular 분자의
genome 게놈(세포나 생명체의 유전자 총체)
geophysicist 지구 물리학자 core 중심부
oceanographer 해양학자 imaginary 가상의 hazard 위험
virtual 가상의 artificial 인위적인, 인공의 realm 영역
idea 관념, 생각 cartography 지도제작 resemble 유사하다
frontier 새로운 분야

10 독해 전체내용 파악 (요지 파악) 난이도 ★★☆

끊어읽기 해석

When giving performance feedback, / you should consider / the recipient's past performance / and your estimate / of his or her future potential / in designing its frequency, amount, and content.
성과에 대한 피드백을 줄 때 / 당신은 고려해야 한다 / 받는 사람의 과거 성과를 / 그리고 당신의 추정치를 / 그 혹은 그녀의 이후의 가능성에 대한 / 그것의 빈도, 양, 그리고 내용을 설계하는 데에 있어

For high performers / with potential for growth, / feedback should be frequent / enough to prod them / into taking corrective action, / but not so frequent / that it is experienced / as controlling / and saps their initiative.
고성과자들에게는 / 성장의 가능성이 있는 / 피드백은 자주 있어야 한다 / 그들을 자극할 만큼 충분히 / 교정 조치를 취하도록 / 하지만 너무 잦아서 / 그것(피드백)이 느껴져서는 안 된다 / 통제하는 것으로 / 그리고 그들의 진취적인 마음을 약화시켜서는 안 된다

For adequate performers / who have settled into their jobs / and have limited potential / for advancement, / very little feedback is needed / because they have displayed / reliable and steady behavior / in the past, / knowing their tasks / and realizing what needs to be done.
유능한 수행자들에게는 / 그들의 일자리에 자리를 잡은 / 그래서 한정된 가능성을 가진 / 발전의 / 매우 적은 피드백이 필요된다 / 왜냐하면 그들은 보여왔기 때문이다 / 믿을만하고 지속적인 행동을 / 과거에 / 그들의 업무를 알아서 / 그리고 완료될 필요가 있는 것을 알아차리면서

For poor performers / —that is, people / who will need to be removed / from their jobs / if their performance doesn't improve— / feedback should be frequent and very specific, / and the connection / between acting on the feedback and negative sanctions / such as being laid off or fired / should be made explicit.
낮은 성과자들에게는 / 즉, 사람들인 / 내보내질 필요가 있을 / 그들의 일자리로부터 / 그들의 성과가 나아지지 않으면 / 피드백은 자주 있어야 하고 매우 구체적이어야 한다 / 그리고 연관성이 / 피드백에 따라서 행동하는 것과 부정적인 제재들 사이의 / 일시 해고되는 것이나 해고되는 것과 같은 / 분명히 만들어져야 한다

해석 성과에 대한 피드백을 줄 때, 당신은 (피드백을) 받는 사람의 과거 성과와 그것의 빈도, 양, 그리고 내용을 설계하는 데에 있어 그 혹은 그녀의 이후의 가능성에 대한 당신의 추정치를 고려해야 한다. 성장의 가능성이 있는 고성과자들에게는, 피드백은 그들이 교정 조치를 취하도록 자극할 만큼 충분히 자주 있어야 하지만, 그것(피드백)이 너무 잦아서 통제하는 것으로 느껴지고 그들의 진취적인 마음을 약화시켜서는 안 된다. 그들의 일자리에 자리를 잡아서 한정된 발전 가능성을 가진 유능한 수행자들에게는, 매우 적은 피드백이 필요되는데, 왜냐하면 그들은 과거에 그들의 업무를 알고 완료될 필요가 있는 것을 알아차리면서 믿을만하고 지속적인 행동을 보여왔기 때문이다. 낮은 성과자들 즉, 그들의 성과가 나아지지 않

으면 그들의 일자리로부터 내보내질 필요가 있을 사람들에게는 피드백은 자주 있어야 하고 매우 구체적이어야 하며, 피드백에 따라서 행동하는 것과 일시 해고되는 것이나 해고되는 것과 같은 부정적인 제재들 사이의 연관성이 분명히 만들어져야 한다.

① 당신의 피드백의 시간을 잘 맞춰라.
② 부정적인 피드백을 사용자의 사정에 맞춰라.
③ 사람에 피드백을 맞추어라.
④ 목표 지향적인 피드백을 피해라.

해설 지문 처음에서 성과에 대한 피드백을 줄 때는 받는 사람의 과거 성과와 이후의 가능성에 대한 추정치를 고려해야 한다고 하고, 이어서 고성과자, 적절한 수행자, 낮은 성과자들에게 각각 다른 방식으로 피드백을 주는 것이 필요하다는 것을 설명하고 있으므로, 이 지문의 요지를 '사람에 피드백을 맞추어라'라고 표현한 ③번이 정답이다.

어휘 recipient 받는 사람 estimate 추정치 prod 자극하다
corrective 교정하는, 바로잡는 sap 약화시키다
initiative 진취적인 마음 adequate 유능한, 적절한
reliable 믿을만한 steady 지속적인
act on (주의 등에) 따라서 행동하다 sanction 제재
lay off 일시 해고하다 explicit 분명한
customize 사용자의 사정에 맞추다 tailor 맞추다

11 독해 세부내용 파악 (내용 불일치 파악) 난이도 ★☆☆

끊어읽기 해석

Langston Hughes was born / in Joplin, Missouri, / and graduated from Lincoln University, / in which many African-American students / have pursued their academic disciplines.
랭스턴 휴즈는 태어났다 / 미주리주 조플린에서 / 그리고 링컨대학교를 졸업했다 / 그곳에서 많은 아프리카계 미국인 학생들이 / 그들의 학문 분야를 추구했다

At the age of eighteen, / Hughes published / one of his most well-known poems, / "Negro Speaks of Rivers."
18세에 / 휴즈는 출간했다 / 그의 가장 유명한 시 중 하나인 「Negro Speaks of Rivers」를

Creative and experimental, / Hughes incorporated authentic dialect / in his work, / adapted traditional poetic forms / to embrace the cadences and moods of blues and jazz, / and created characters and themes / that reflected elements / of lower-class black culture.
창의적이고 실험적인 / 휴즈는 진짜 사투리를 포함했다 / 그의 작품에 / 전통적인 시의 형태들을 각색했다 / 블루스와 재즈의 리듬과 분위기를 이용하기 위해 / 그리고 인물들과 주제들을 만들어냈다 / 요소들을 반영한 / 하층 계급 흑인 문화의

With his ability / to fuse serious content / with humorous style, / Hughes attacked racial prejudice / in a way / that was natural and witty.
그의 능력으로 / 심각한 내용을 결합시키는 / 재미있는 방식으로 / 휴즈는 인종적 편견을 비난했다 / 방식으로 / 자연스럽고 재치 있는

해석 랭스턴 휴즈는 미주리주 조플린에서 태어났고, 링컨대학교를 졸업했는데, 그곳에서 많은 아프리카계 미국인 학생들이 그들의 학문 분야를 추구했다. 18세에, 휴즈는 그의 가장 유명한 시 중 하나인 「Negro Speaks of Rivers」를 출간했다. 창의적이고 실험적인 휴즈는 그의 작품에 진짜 사투리를 포함했고, 블루스와 재즈의 리듬과 분위기를 이용하기 위해 전통적인 시의 형태들을 각색했으며, 하층 계급 흑인 문화의 요소들을 반영한 인물들과 주제들을 만들어냈다. 재미있는 방식으로 심각한 내용을 결합시키는 그의 능력으로, 휴즈는 자연스럽고 재치 있는 방식으로 인종적 편견을 비난했다.

지문 뒷부분에서 휴즈는 자연스럽고 재치 있는 방식으로 인종적 편견을 비난했다는 내용이 있으므로, 인종편견을 엄숙한 문체로 공격했다는 것은 지문의 내용과 다르다. 따라서 ④번이 정답이다.

어휘 pursue 추구하다 publish 출간하다 experimental 실험적인
incorporate 포함하다, 혼합하다 authentic 진짜의, 정확한
dialect 사투리 adapt 각색하다 embrace 이용하다
cadence 리듬, 가락 fuse 결합시키다 prejudice 편견
witty 재치 있는

12 독해 논리적 흐름 파악 (무관한 문장 삭제) 난이도 ★★☆

끊어읽기 해석

In 2007, / our biggest concern was "too big to fail."
2007년에 / 우리의 가장 큰 걱정은 '파산하기에는 너무 크다'는 것이었다

Wall Street banks / had grown to such staggering sizes, / and had become so central / to the health of the financial system, / that no rational government / could ever let them fail.
월스트리트에 있는 은행들은 / 너무나도 엄청난 규모로 성장했다 / 그리고 매우 중요하게 되었다 / 금융제도의 안정에 / 그래서 어떤 이성적인 정부도 / 그들이 한 번이라도 파산하도록 방치할 수 없었다

① Aware of their protected status, / banks made excessively risky bets / on housing markets / and invented ever more complicated derivatives.
그들의 보호받는 상황을 깨달은 / 은행들은 극도로 위험한 베팅을 했다 / 주택 시장에 / 그리고 여태까지 없었던 더욱 더 복잡한 금융 파생 상품을 창안했다

② New virtual currencies / such as bitcoin and ethereum / have radically changed / our understanding / of how money can and should work.
새로운 가상화폐들은 / 비트코인과 이더리움 같은 / 급진적으로 바꿨다 / 우리의 이해를 / 어떻게 화폐가 영향을 미칠 수 있고 어떻게 영향을 미쳐야 하는지에 대한

③ The result was the worst financial crisis / since the breakdown of our economy / in 1929.
그 결과는 최악의 금융 위기였다 / 우리 경제의 붕괴 이후로 / 1929년의

④ In the years since 2007, / we have made great progress / in addressing the too-big-to-fail dilemma.
2007년 이후로는 / 우리는 엄청난 발전을 이루었다 / 파산하기에는 너무 큰 딜레마를 처리하는 데

Our banks are better capitalized than ever. // Our regulators conduct / regular stress tests / of large institutions.
우리의 은행들은 이전보다 더욱 잘 투자를 받는다 // 우리의 단속기관들은 시행한다 / 규칙적인 스트레스 테스트를 / 대형 단체들의

해석 2007년에, 우리의 가장 큰 걱정은 '파산하기에는 너무 크다' 는 것이었다. 월스트리트에 있는 은행들은 너무나도 엄청난 규모로 성장했고, 금융제도의 안정에 매우 중요하게 되어서, 어떤 이성적인 정부도 그들이 한 번이라도 파산하도록 방치할 수 없었다. ① 그들의 보호받는 상황을 깨달은 은행들은 주택 시장에 극도로 위험한 베팅을 했고 여태까지 없었던 더욱 더 복잡한 금융 파생 상품을 창안했다. ② 비트코인과 이더리움 같은 새로운 가상화폐들은 어떻게 화폐가 영향을 미칠 수 있고 어떻게 영향을 미쳐야 하는지에 대한 우리의 이해를 급진적으로 바꿨다. ③ 그 결과는 1929년의 우리 경제의 붕괴 이후로 최악의 금융 위기였다. ④ 2007년 이후로는, 우리는 파산하기에는 너무 큰 딜레마를 처리하는 데 엄청난 발전을 이루었다. 우리의 은행들은 이전보다 더욱 잘 투자를 받는다. 우리의 단속기관들은 대형 단체들의 규칙적인 스트레스 테스트를 시행한다.

해설 지문 앞부분에서 월스트리트에 있는 은행들이 엄청난 규모로 성장하면서 정부는 그들이 파산하도록 방치할 수 없었다고 한 뒤, ①번에서 은행들은 자신들이 보호받는다는 것을 깨닫고 주택 시장에 위험한 베팅을 했고 복잡한 금융 파생 상품을 창안했다고 하고, ③, ④번에서 그 결과는 최악의 금융 위기였으며, 2007년 이후로 은행의 규모로 인한 딜레마를 처리하는 데 엄청난 발전을 이루었다고 설명하고 있으므로 모두 지문의 흐름과 관련이 있다. 그러나 ②번은 새로운 가상화폐들이 화폐의 영향에 대한 우리의 이해를 바꿨다는 내용으로 월스트리트에 있는 은행들의 문제와는 관련이 없으므로 ②번이 정답이다.

어휘 concern 걱정, 관심사 staggering 엄청난, 막대한
rational 이성적인 complicated 복잡한
derivative 금융 파생 상품 virtual 가상의 radically 급진적으로
breakdown 붕괴 capitalize 투자하다 regulator 단속기관

13 독해 전체내용 파악 (주제 파악) 난이도 ★☆☆

끊어읽기 해석

Imagine / that two people are starting work / at a law firm / on the same day.
상상해보라 / 두 사람이 일을 시작하고 있는 것을 / 법률 사무소에서 / 같은 날에

One person has a very simple name. // The other person has a very complex name.
한 사람은 매우 단순한 이름을 갖고 있다 // 다른 사람은 매우 복잡한 이름을 갖고 있다

We've got pretty good evidence / that over the course of their next 16 plus years / of their career, / the person with the simpler name / will rise up the legal hierarchy / more quickly.
우리는 꽤 좋은 증거를 얻었다 / 이후 16년이 넘는 시간 동안 / 그들의 경력에서 / 더욱 단순한 이름을 가진 사람이 / 법조계의 지배층으로 승진할 것이라는 / 더욱 빠르게

They will attain partnership / more quickly / in the middle parts of their career.
그들은 동업자를 얻을 것이다 / 더욱 빠르게 / 그들의 경력의 중반에서

And by about the eighth or ninth year / after graduating from law school / the people with simpler names / are about seven to ten percent / more likely to be partners / —which is a striking effect.
그리고 대략 8년 혹은 9년 차까지 / 로스쿨에서 졸업한 후 / 더욱 단순한 이름을 가진 사람들은 / 대략 7-10퍼센트 정도 / 파트너가 될 가능성이 더 많다 / 그리고 이것은 놀랄만한 결과이다

We try to eliminate / all sorts of other alternative explanations.
우리는 없애려고 노력한다 / 모든 종류의 다른 새로운 설명들을

For example, / we try to show / that it's not about foreignness / because foreign names tend to be harder / to pronounce.
예를 들어 / 우리는 보여주려고 노력한다 / 그것은 외래성에 관한 것이 아니라는 것을 / 외국 이름들은 더욱 어려운 경향이 있기 때문에 / 발음하기

But even if you look at / just white males / with Anglo-American names / —so really the true in-group, / you find / that among those white males / with Anglo names / they are more likely to rise up / if their names happen to be simpler.
하지만 당신이 보더라도 / 그저 백인 남성들을 / 영국계 미국인의 이름을 가진 / 그래서 정말로 진정한 내집단에 속한 / 당신은 알게 된다 / 그 백인 남성들 중에서 / 영국계 이름을 가진 / 그들이 승진할 가능성이 더 많다 / 그들의 이름이 마침 더욱 간단하다면

So simplicity is one key feature / in names / that determines various outcomes.

그래서 간단함은 하나의 핵심적인 특징이다 / 이름에 관한 / 다양한 결과들을 결정하는

해석 두 사람이 같은 날에 법률 사무소에서 일을 시작하고 있는 것을 상상해보라. 한 사람은 매우 단순한 이름을 갖고 있다. 다른 사람은 매우 복잡한 이름을 갖고 있다. 우리는 그들의 경력에서 이후 16년이 넘는 시간 동안, 더욱 단순한 이름을 가진 사람이 법조계의 지배층으로 더욱 빠르게 승진할 것이라는 꽤 좋은 증거를 얻었다. 그들은 더욱 빠르게 그들의 경력의 중반에서 동업자를 얻을 것이다. 그리고 로스쿨에서 졸업한 후 대략 8년 혹은 9년 차까지 더욱 단순한 이름을 가진 사람들은 대략 7-10퍼센트 정도 파트너가 될 가능성이 더 많은데 이것은 놀랄만한 결과이다. 우리는 모든 종류의 다른 새로운 설명들을 없애려고 노력한다. 예를 들어, 우리는 외국 이름들은 발음하기 더욱 어려운 경향이 있기 때문에 그것은 외래성에 관한 것이 아니라는 것을 보여주려고 노력한다. 하지만 당신이 그저 영국계 미국인의 이름을 가져 정말로 진정한 내집단에 속한 백인 남성들을 보더라도, 영국계 이름을 가진 그 백인 남성들 중에서 그들의 이름이 마침 더욱 간단하다면 당신은 그들이 승진할 가능성이 더 많다는 것을 알게 된다. 그래서 간단함은 다양한 결과들을 결정하는 이름에 관한 하나의 핵심적인 특징이다.

① 법적 이름의 발전
② 매력적인 이름의 개념
③ 간단한 이름의 이점
④ 외국 이름의 뿌리

해설 지문 중간에서 더욱 단순한 이름을 가진 사람이 더욱 빠르게 법조계의 지배층으로 승진할 것이라고 하며, 그들은 더욱 빠르게 동업자를 얻고, 파트너가 될 가능성이 높다는 것을 설명하고 있으므로, 이 지문의 주제를 '간단한 이름의 이점'이라고 표현한 ③번이 정답이다.

어휘 hierarchy 지배층, 서열 attain 얻다, 획득하다 striking 놀랄만한 eliminate 없애다 alternative 새로운, 대안이 되는 foreignness 외래성, 이질성 simplicity 간단함 attractive 매력적인

14 어휘 어휘&표현 compulsory = mandatory 난이도 ★★☆

해석 학교 교육은 미국의 모든 어린이들에게 의무적이지만, 학교 출석이 요구되는 연령대는 주마다 다르다.

① 보완적인
② 체계적인
③ 의무적인
④ 획기적인

어휘 compulsory 의무적인, 강제적인 vary 다르다, 차이가 있다 complementary 보완적인 mandatory 의무적인, 명령의 innovative 획기적인

👍 이것도 알면 **합격!**

compulsory(의무적인)의 유의어
= obligatory, required, imperative, forced

15 어휘 어휘&표현 disclose = let on 난이도 ★★★

해석 비록 그 여배우는 그녀의 경력에서 큰 불안을 느꼈지만, 그녀는 결코 누구에게도 그녀가 불행하다고 밝히지 않았다.

① 털어놓다
② ~의 책임에서 해방하다
③ 약해지다
④ 실망시키다

어휘 turmoil 불안, 혼란 disclose 밝히다, 공개하다 let on 털어놓다, 말하다 let off ~의 책임에서 해방하다 let up 약해지다, 누그러지다 let down 실망시키다

👍 이것도 알면 **합격!**

disclose(밝히다)의 유의어
= admit, announce, proclaim

16 독해 추론 (빈칸 완성 - 연결어) 난이도 ★★☆

끊어읽기 해석

Visionaries are the first people / in their industry segment / to see the potential / of new technologies.
선지자들은 최초의 사람들이다 / 그들의 업종부문에서 / 잠재력을 알아보는 / 새로운 기술들의

Fundamentally, / they see themselves as smarter / than their opposite numbers / in competitive companies / —and, quite often, they are.
근본적으로 / 그들은 그들 자신을 더 똑똑하다고 여긴다 / 그들의 반대 집단들보다 / 경쟁 회사에 있는 / 그리고 상당히 자주 그들은 그렇다

Indeed, / it is their ability / to see things first / that they want to leverage / into a competitive advantage.
실제로 / 그들의 능력이다 / (~한) 것들을 먼저 발견하는 것이 / 그들이 활용하길 원하는 / 경쟁우위로

That advantage can only come about / if no one else has discovered it.
그 우위는 ~에만 생길 수 있다 / 다른 누구도 그것을 발견하지 않았을 경우에

They do not expect, / **(A)** underline{therefore}, / to be buying a well-tested product / with an extensive list / of industry references.
그들은 기대하지 않는다 / (A) 그러므로 / 시험이 잘된 상품을 사고 있는 것을 / 긴 목록이 있는 / 산업 증명서들의

Indeed, / if such a reference base exists, / it may actually turn them off, / indicating / that for this technology, / at any rate, / they are already too late.
실제로 / 만약 그러한 증명서 근거가 존재하면 / 그것은 실제로 그들이 흥미를 잃게 할지도 모른다 / 보여 주며 / 이 기술의 경우에는 / 어쨌든 / 그들이 이미 너무 늦었다는 것을

Pragmatists, / **(B)** on the other hand, / deeply value / the experience of their colleagues / in other companies.
실용주의자들은 / (B) 반면에 / 몹시 소중히 여긴다 / 그들의 동료들의 경험을 / 다른 회사에 있는

When they buy, / they expect extensive references, / and they want / a good number to come from companies / in their own industry segment.
그들이 구매할 때 / 그들은 긴 증명서를 기대한다 / 그리고 그들은 원한다 / 상당히 많은 (증명서들이) 회사들에서 오기를 / 그들 자신의 업종부문에 있는

해석 선지자들은 그들의 업종부문에서 새로운 기술들의 잠재력을 알아보는 최초의 사람들이다. 근본적으로, 그들은 경쟁 회사에 있는 그들의 반대 집단들보다 그들 자신을 더욱 똑똑하다고 여기고, 상당히 자주 그들은 그렇다. 실제로, 그들이 경쟁우위로 활용하길 원하는 것들을 먼저 발견하는 것이 그들의 능력이다. 그 우위는 다른 누구도 그것을 발견하지 않았을 경우에만 생길 수 있다. (A) 그러므로, 그들은 산업 증명서들의 긴 목록이 있는 시험이 잘된 상품을 사고 있는 것을 기대하지 않는다. 실제로, 만약 그러한 증명서 근거가 존재하면, 그것은 이 기술의 경우에는 어쨌든 그들이 이미 너무 늦었다는 것을 보여 주며, 실제로 그들의 흥미를 잃게 할지도 모른다. (B) 반면에, 실용주의자들은 다른 회사에 있는 그들의 동료들의 경험을 몹시 소중히 여긴다. 그들이 구매할 때, 그들은 긴 증명서를 기대하고, 그들은 그들 자신의 업종부문에 있는 회사들

에서 상당히 많은 증명서들이 오기를 원한다.

	(A)	(B)
①	그러므로	반면에
②	그러나	게다가
③	그럼에도 불구하고	동시에
④	게다가	결론적으로

해설 (A) 빈칸 앞 문장은 선지자들이 활용하길 원하는 경쟁 우위는 다른 누구도 그것을 발견하지 않았을 경우에 생긴다는 내용이고, 빈칸이 있는 문장은 그들이 긴 산업 증명서 목록이 있는 상품을 사는 것을 기대하지 않는다는 결론적인 내용이다. 따라서 결론을 나타내는 연결어인 therefore(그러므로)가 나와야 적절하다. (B) 빈칸 앞 문장은 선지자들은 증명서 근거가 있는 기술에 흥미를 잃는다는 내용이고, 뒤 문장은 실용주의자들은 다른 회사 동료들의 경험을 몹시 소중히 여겨 긴 증명서를 기대한다고 하는 대조적인 내용이다. 따라서 대조를 나타내는 연결어인 on the other hand(반면에)가 나와야 적절하다.

따라서 ① therefore(그러므로) – on the other hand(반면에)가 정답이다.

어휘 visionary 선지자, 공상가 segment 부문 number 집단
leverage 활용하다, 강화하다 competitive advantage 경쟁우위
come about 생기다 extensive 긴, 아주 넓은
turn off 흥미를 잃게 하다 pragmatist 실용주의자

17 독해 논리적 흐름 파악 (문장 삽입)   난이도 ★★☆

끊어읽기 해석

Some of these ailments / are short-lived; / others may be long-lasting.
이러한 질병들 중 몇몇은 / 일시적인 반면 / 다른 것들은 오래 지속될 수도 있다

For centuries, / humans have looked up at the sky / and wondered what exists / beyond the realm of our planet.
수세기 동안 / 인간들은 하늘을 올려다보았다 / 그리고 무엇이 존재하는지 궁금해했다 / 우리 행성의 영역 너머에는

(①) Ancient astronomers examined / the night sky / hoping to learn / more about the universe.
고대 천문학자들은 조사했다 / 밤하늘을 / 알게 되길 바라면서 / 우주에 대해 더 많이

More recently, / some movies explored / the possibility of sustaining human life / in outer space, / while other films have questioned / whether extraterrestrial life forms / may have visited our planet.
더욱 최근에는 / 몇몇 영화들이 탐구했다 / 인간의 삶을 살아가게 하는 것의 가능성을 / 우주 공간에서 / 동시에 다른 영화들은 의문을 가졌다 / 외계의 생물 형태가 / 우리의 행성에 방문했을 수도 있는지에 대해

(②) Since astronaut Yuri Gagarin became / the first man to travel / in space / in 1961, / scientists have researched / what conditions are like / beyond the Earth's atmosphere, / and what effects space travel has / on the human body.
우주 비행사 유리 가가린이 ~이 된 이후로 / 여행한 최초의 남성이 / 우주에서 / 1961년에 / 과학자들은 조사해왔다 / 환경이 어떠한지 / 지구 대기 너머의 / 그리고 어떤 영향들을 우주 여행이 미치는지 / 인간의 신체에

(③) Although most astronauts do not spend / more than a few months / in space, / many experience / physiological and psychological problems / when they return to the Earth.
비록 대부분의 우주 비행사들은 보내지 않지만 / 몇 개월 이상을 / 우주에서 / 많은 사람들은 경험한다 / 생리적이고 심리적인 문제들을 / 그들이 지구로 돌아올 때

(④) More than two-thirds of all astronauts / suffer from motion sickness / while traveling in space.
모든 우주 비행사들의 3분의 2 이상은 / 멀미로 고통받는다 / 우주에서 여행하는 동안

In the gravity-free environment, / the body cannot differentiate / up from down.
무중력 상태에서는 / 신체는 구별할 수 없다 / 올라가는 것을 내려가는 것과

The body's internal balance system / sends confusing signals / to the brain, / which can result in nausea / lasting as long as a few days.
신체 내부의 평형 장치는 / 혼란스러운 신호를 보낸다 / 뇌에 / 그런데 이것은 메스꺼움을 유발할 수 있다 / 며칠 동안 오래 지속되는

해석 수세기 동안 인간들은 하늘을 올려다보았고 우리 행성의 영역 너머에는 무엇이 존재하는지 궁금해했다. 고대 천문학자들은 우주에 대해 더 많이 알게 되길 바라면서 밤하늘을 조사했다. 더욱 최근에는, 몇몇 영화들이 인간의 삶을 우주 공간에서 살아가게 하는 것의 가능성을 탐구한 동시에, 다른 영화들은 외계의 생물 형태가 우리의 행성에 방문했을 수도 있는지에 대해 의문을 가졌다. 우주 비행사 유리 가가린이 1961년에 우주에서 여행한 최초의 남성이 된 이후로, 과학자들은 지구 대기 너머의 환경이 어떠한지, 그리고 우주 여행이 인간의 신체에 어떤 영향들을 미치는지 조사해왔다. 비록 대부분의 우주 비행사들은 몇 개월 이상을 우주에서 보내지 않지만, 많은 사람들은 그들이 지구로 돌아올 때 생리적이고 심리적인 문제들을 경험한다. ④ 이러한 질병들 중 몇몇은 일시적인 반면, 다른 것들은 오래 지속될 수도 있다. 모든 우주 비행사들의 3분의 2 이상은 우주에서 여행하는 동안 멀미로 고통받는다. 무중력 상태에서, 신체는 올라가는 것을 내려가는 것과 구별할 수 없다. 신체 내부의 평형 장치는 뇌에 혼란스러운 신호를 보내는데, 이것은 며칠 동안 오래 지속되는 메스꺼움을 유발할 수 있다.

해설 ④번 앞 문장에 우주 비행사들이 우주에서 지구로 돌아올 때 생리적이고 심리적인 문제들을 경험한다는 내용이 있으므로, ④번 자리에 이러한 질병들 중 몇몇(Some of these ailments)은 일시적인 반면, 다른 것들은 오래 지속될 수도 있다는 주어진 문장이 나와야 지문이 자연스럽게 연결된다. 따라서 ④번이 정답이다.

어휘 ailment 질병 realm 영역 astronomer 천문학자
sustain 살아가게 하다 extraterrestrial 외계의
atmosphere 대기, 분위기 physiological 생리적인
psychological 심리적인 motion sickness 멀미
differentiate 구별하다 nausea 메스꺼움

18 독해 추론 (빈칸 완성 - 절)   난이도 ★★☆

끊어읽기 해석

Why bother with / the history of everything?
왜 신경 쓸까 / 모든 것의 역사에

Today, / we teach and learn / about our world / in fragments.
오늘날 / 우리는 가르치고 배운다 / 우리의 세계에 대해 / 단편적으로

In literature classes / you don't learn about genes; / in physics classes / you don't learn about human evolution.
문학 수업에서 / 당신은 유전자에 대해 배우지 않는다 / 물리 수업에서 / 당신은 인간의 진화에 대해 배우지 않는다

So you get / a partial view of the world.
그래서 당신은 얻는다 / 세계에 대한 부분적인 시각을

That makes it hard / to find *meaning* / in education.
그것은 어렵게 만든다 / '의미'를 발견하는 것을 / 교육에서

The French sociologist Emile Durkheim called / this sense of disorientation and meaninglessness / *anomie*, / and he

argued / that it could lead / to despair and even suicide.
프랑스 사회학자 에밀 뒤르켐은 불렀다 / 이러한 방향 감각의 상실감과 무의미함의 감각을 / '아노미'라고 / 그리고 그는 주장했다 / 이것이 이어질 수 있다고 / 절망과 심지어는 자살로

The German sociologist Max Weber / talked of the "disenchantment" / of the world.
독일 사회학자 막스 베버는 / '환멸'에 대해 이야기했다 / 세계의

In the past, / people had a unified vision / of their world, / a vision / usually provided by the origin stories / of their own religious traditions.
과거에는 / 사람들은 그들의 통일된 시각이 있었다 / 세계에 대한 / 시각인 / 보통 근원설화들에 의해 제공되는 / 그들 자신의 종교적인 전통의

That unified vision gave / a sense of purpose, of meaning, even of enchantment / to the world and to life.
그 통일된 시각은 주었다 / 목적 의식, 의미에 대한 감각, 심지어 황홀감을 / 세상과 인생에

Today, / though, / many writers have argued / that a sense of meaninglessness is inevitable / in a world of science and rationality.
오늘날 / 하지만 / 많은 작가들은 주장해왔다 / 무의미함의 감각은 불가피하다고 / 과학과 합리성의 세계에서

Modernity, / it seems, means meaninglessness.
현대성은 / 무의미함을 의미하는 듯하다

해석 왜 모든 것의 역사에 신경을 쓸까? 오늘날, 우리는 우리의 세계에 대해 단편적으로 가르치고 배운다. 문학 수업에서 당신은 유전자에 대해 배우지 않는다. 물리 수업에서 당신은 인간의 진화에 대해 배우지 않는다. 그래서 당신은 세계에 대한 부분적인 시각을 얻는다. 그것은 교육에서 '의미'를 발견하는 것을 어렵게 만든다. 프랑스 사회학자 에밀 뒤르켐은 이러한 방향 감각의 상실감과 무의미함의 감각을 '아노미'라고 불렀고, 그는 이것이 절망과 심지어는 자살로 이어질 수 있다고 주장했다. 독일 사회학자 막스 베버는 세계의 '환멸'에 대해 이야기했다. 과거에는, 사람들은 보통 그들 자신의 종교적인 전통의 근원설화들에 의해 제공되는 시각인 그들의 세계에 대한 통일된 시각이 있었다. 그 통일된 시각은 목적 의식, 의미에 대한 감각, 심지어 황홀감을 세상과 인생에 주었다. 하지만, 오늘날, 많은 작가들은 과학과 합리성의 세계에서 무의미함의 감각은 불가피하다고 주장해왔다. 현대성은 무의미함을 의미하는 듯하다.

① 과거에는, 역사 연구는 과학으로부터 환멸을 요구했다
② 최근에, 과학은 우리에게 많은 현명한 속임수와 의미를 주었다
③ 오늘날, 우리는 우리의 세계에 대해 단편적으로 가르치고 배운다
④ 최근에, 역사는 몇몇 범주로 나누어졌다

해설 빈칸 뒤 문장에서 문학 수업에서 유전자에 대해 배우지 않고, 물리 수업에서 인간의 진화에 대해 배우지 않아서 세계에 대한 부분적인 시각을 얻는다는 내용이 있으므로, '오늘날, 우리는 우리의 세계에 대해 단편적으로 가르치고 배운다'라고 한 ③번이 정답이다.

어휘 bother 신경 쓰다 partial 부분적인
disorientation 방향 감각의 상실 anomie 아노미, 사회적 무질서
despair 절망 suicide 자살 disenchantment 환멸
enchantment 황홀 inevitable 불가피한 rationality 합리성
clever 현명한 fragment 단편

19 독해 세부내용 파악 (내용 불일치 파악) 난이도 ★★☆

끊어읽기 해석

The earliest government food service programs / began around 1900 in Europe.
가장 초기의 정부 식량 제공 프로그램은 / 1900년쯤에 유럽에서 시작했다

Programs in the United States / date from the Great Depression, / when the need / to use surplus agricultural commodities / was joined to concern / for feeding the children / of poor families.
미국의 프로그램들은 / 대공황부터 시작한다 / 그때 필요성이 / 잉여농산품을 사용할 / 우려와 결합되었다 / 아이들에게 식량을 공급하는 것에 대한 / 가난한 가정의

During and after World War II, / the explosion / in the number of working women / fueled the need / for a broader program.
2차 세계대전 동안과 후에 / 폭발적인 증가는 / 근로 여성 수의 / 필요성을 자극했다 / 더 광범위한 프로그램에 대한

What was once a function of the family / —providing lunch— / was shifted / to the school food service system.
한때 가족의 역할이었던 것은 / 점심을 제공하는 것 / 옮겨졌다 / 학교 급식 서비스 제도로

The National School Lunch Program / is the result of these efforts.
전국적인 학교 점심 프로그램은 / 이러한 노력의 결과이다

The program is designed / to provide federally assisted meals / to children of school age.
그 프로그램은 계획되었다 / 연방차원에서 지원되는 식사를 제공하기 위해 / 취학 연령의 아이들에게

From the end of World War II to the early 1980s, / funding for school food service / expanded steadily.
2차 세계대전 말부터 1980년대 초기까지 / 학교 급식 서비스를 위한 재정 지원은 / 꾸준히 확대되었다

Today / it helps / to feed children / in almost 100,000 schools / across the United States.
오늘날 / 그것은 돕는다 / 아이들에게 식량을 공급하는 것을 / 거의 10만 개의 학교에 있는 / 미국 전역에 걸쳐

Its first function is to provide / a nutritious lunch / to all students; / the second is to provide / nutritious food / at both breakfast and lunch / to underprivileged children.
그것의 첫 번째 역할은 제공하는 것이다 / 영양분이 많은 점심을 / 모든 학생들에게 / 두 번째는 제공하는 것이다 / 영양분이 많은 음식을 / 아침과 점심에 모두 / 혜택을 못 받는 아이들에게

If anything, / the role of school food service / as a replacement / for what was once a family function / has been expanded.
오히려 / 학교 급식 서비스의 역할은 / 대체물로써의 / 한때 가족의 역할이었던 것의 / 확대되었다

해석 가장 초기의 정부 식량 제공 프로그램은 1900년쯤에 유럽에서 시작했다. 미국의 프로그램들은 대공황부터 시작하는데, 그때 잉여 농산품을 사용할 필요성이 가난한 가정의 아이들에게 식량을 공급하는 것에 대한 우려와 결합되었다. 2차 세계대전 동안과 후에, 근로 여성 수의 폭발적인 증가는 더 광범위한 프로그램에 대한 필요성을 자극했다. 한때 가족의 역할이었던 점심을 제공하는 것은 학교 급식 서비스 제도로 옮겨졌다. 전국적인 학교 점심 프로그램은 이러한 노력의 결과이다. 그 프로그램은 취학 연령의 아이들에게 연방차원에서 지원되는 식사를 제공하기 위해 계획되었다. 2차 세계대전 말부터 1980년대 초기까지, 학교 급식 서비스를 위한 재정 지원은 꾸준히 확대되었다. 오늘날 그것은 미국 전역에 걸쳐 거의 10만 개의 학교에 있는 아이들에게 식량을 공급하는 것을 돕는다. 그것의 첫 번째 역할은 모든 학생들에게 영양분이 많은 점심을 제공하는 것이고, 두 번째는 혜택을 못 받는 아이들에게 영양분이 많은 음식을 아침과 점심에 모두 제공하는 것이다. 오히려, 한때 가족의 역할이었던 것의 대체물로써의 학교 급식 서비스의 역할은 확대되었다.

① 근로 여성 수의 증가는 식량 제공 프로그램의 확대를 뒷받침했다.

② 미국 정부는 식량부족에도 불구하고 대공황 중에 가난한 아이들에게 식량을 공급하기 시작했다.

③ 미국 학교 급식 서비스 제도는 현재 가난한 가정의 아이들에게 식량을 공급하도록 돕는다.

④ 점심을 제공하는 역할은 가정에서 학교로 옮겨졌다.

해설 지문 앞부분에서 대공황 때부터 시작한 미국의 식량 제공 프로그램들은 잉여농산품을 사용할 필요성이 가난한 가정의 아이들에게 식량을 공급하는 것에 대한 우려와 결합되었던 대공황 시기부터 시작되었다고 했으므로, 미국 정부가 식량부족에도 불구하고 대공황 중에 가난한 아이들에게 식량을 공급하기 시작했다는 것은 지문의 내용과 다르다. 따라서 ②번이 정답이다.

어휘 surplus 잉여의 agricultural commodity 농산품 join 결합하다 feed ~에게 식량을 공급하다 fuel 자극하다 federally 연방차원에서 assist 지원하다 expand 확대되다 steadily 꾸준히 underprivileged 혜택을 못 받는 replacement 대체물 boost 뒷받침하다 shortage 부족, 결핍

해설 주어진 문장에서 대한민국은 인터넷에 가장 잘 연결된 국가인 것을 자랑한다고 하고, (B)에서 다른 어떤 국가도 인터넷을 그렇게 완전히 수용하지는 않았을 것이라고 하며, (C)에서 하지만 그러한 웹으로의 편리한 접근(such ready access to the Web)에는 중독된 사용자들이라는 대가가 따랐다고 한 후, 이어서 (A)에서 이러한 중독(This addiction)은 국가적인 사안이 되었다고 설명하고 있다. 따라서 ④ (B) – (C) – (A)가 정답이다.

어휘 boast of ~을 자랑하다 wired (네트워크 등에) 연결된 addiction 중독 drop dead 급사하다 exhaustion 피폐 on end 계속 self-destructive 자멸적인 embrace 수용하다 ready 편리한, 쉽게 쓸 수 있는 come at a price 대가가 따르다 legion 많은 사람들, 군단, 부대 obsessed ~에 중독된 tear away 억지로 떼어내다

---

20 독해 논리적 흐름 파악 (문단 순서 배열) 난이도 ★★☆

끊어읽기 해석

South Korea boasts of / being the most wired nation / on earth.
대한민국은 자랑한다 / 인터넷에 가장 잘 연결된 국가인 것을 / 이 세상에서

(A) This addiction has become / a national issue / in Korea / in recent years, / as users started dropping dead / from exhaustion / after playing online games / for days on end.
이 중독은 ~이 되었다 / 국가적인 사안이 / 한국에서 / 최근에 몇 년 동안 / 사용자들이 급사하기 시작했기 때문에 / 피폐해져서 / 온라인 게임을 한 후에 / 며칠 동안 계속

A growing number of students / have skipped school / to stay online, / shockingly self-destructive behavior / in this intensely competitive society.
점점 더 많은 학생들은 / 학교를 가지 않았다 / 온라인에 접속해있기 위해 / 이것은 엄청나게 자멸적인 행동이다 / 이렇게 극도로 경쟁하는 사회에서

(B) In fact, / perhaps / no other country / has so fully embraced the Internet.
사실상 / 아마도 / 다른 어떤 국가도 / 인터넷을 그렇게 완전히 수용하지는 않았을 것이다

(C) But such ready access to the Web / has come at a price / as legions of obsessed users find / that they cannot tear themselves away / from their computer screens.
하지만 그러한 웹으로의 편리한 접근은 / 대가가 따랐다 / 많은 중독된 사용자들이 깨달으면서 / 그들은 그들 자신을 억지로 떼어낼 수 없는 것을 / 그들의 컴퓨터 화면으로부터

해석 대한민국은 이 세상에서 인터넷에 가장 잘 연결된 국가인 것을 자랑한다.

(B) 사실상, 아마도 다른 어떤 국가도 인터넷을 그렇게 완전히 수용하지는 않았을 것이다.

(C) 하지만 그러한 웹으로의 편리한 접근은 많은 중독된 사용자들이 그들 자신을 그들의 컴퓨터 화면으로부터 억지로 떼어낼 수 없는 것을 깨달으면서 대가가 따랐다.

(A) 이 중독은 사용자들이 온라인 게임을 며칠 동안 계속 한 후에 피폐해져서 급사하기 시작했기 때문에, 한국에서 최근에 몇 년 동안 국가적인 사안이 되었다. 점점 더 많은 학생들은 온라인에 접속해있기 위해 학교를 가지 않았고, 이것은 이렇게 극도로 경쟁하는 사회에서 엄청나게 자멸적인 행동이다.

정답

p.70

01	① 어휘 - 생활영어	**11**	④ 독해 - 논리적 흐름 파악
02	① 독해 - 추론	**12**	④ 독해 - 전체내용 파악
03	② 독해 - 전체내용 파악	**13**	② 독해 - 세부내용 파악
04	③ 문법 - 능동태·수동태	**14**	① 어휘 - 어휘&표현
05	① 어휘 - 어휘&표현	**15**	④ 어휘 - 어휘&표현
06	② 어휘 - 어휘&표현	**16**	④ 독해 - 논리적 흐름 파악
07	④ 독해 - 논리적 흐름 파악	**17**	④ 독해 - 세부내용 파악
08	② 어휘 - 생활영어	**18**	② 독해 - 추론
09	② 독해 - 세부내용 파악	**19**	③ 독해 - 논리적 흐름 파악
10	③ 문법 - 분사	**20**	④ 문법 - 비교 구문

취약영역 분석표

영역	세부 유형	문항 수	소계
어휘	어휘&표현	4	/6
	생활영어	2	
문법	능동태·수동태	1	/3
	분사	1	
	비교 구문	1	
독해	전체내용 파악	2	/11
	세부내용 파악	3	
	추론	2	
	논리적 흐름 파악	4	
총계			**/20**

· 자신이 취약한 영역은 '공무원 영어, 이렇게 출제된다!'(문제집 p.8)를 통해 다시 한번 확인하고 학습하시기 바랍니다.

---

01 어휘 생활영어 That's cutting it close.
난이도 ★★☆

해석
A: 부탁 하나 드려도 될까요?
B: 네, 무엇인가요?
A: 제가 출장 때문에 공항에 가야 하는데, 제 차가 시동이 걸리지 않아요. 저를 태워다 주실 수 있나요?
B: 물론이죠. 당신은 거기에 언제까지 가야 하나요?
A: 저는 그곳에 늦어도 6시까지는 가야 해요.
B: 지금이 4시 30분이에요. <u>시간이 촉박하네요.</u> 우리 당장 출발해야겠어요.

① 시간이 촉박하네요
② 중요한 것에서 눈을 뗐어요
③ 빛나는 것이 모두 금은 아니에요
④ 지나간 일이에요

해설 공항에 언제까지 가야 하는지 묻는 B의 질문에 A가 6시까지는 가야 한다고 답하고, 빈칸 뒤에서 다시 B가 We'll have to leave right away(우리 당장 출발해야겠어요)라고 말하고 있으므로, 빈칸에는 '시간이 촉박하네요'라는 의미가 들어가야 자연스럽다. 따라서 ① That's cutting it close가 정답이다.

어휘 cut it close 시간이 촉박하다, 아슬아슬하다
take one's eye off the ball 중요한 것에서 눈을 떼다
all that glitters is not gold 빛나는 것이 모두 금은 아니다
water under the bridge 지나간 일

👍 이것도 알면 **합격!**

'cut'을 포함하는 다양한 표현을 알아두자.
· cut it fine 시간이 빠듯하게 되다
· cut to the chase 바로 본론으로 들어가다
· be a cut above ~보다 훨씬 낫다
· be cut out for ~에 적합하다

---

02 독해 추론 (빈칸완성 - 구)
난이도 ★★☆

끊어읽기 해석

Fear of loss is a basic part / of being human.
손실에 대한 두려움은 기본적인 부분이다 / 인간의

To the brain, / loss is a threat / and we naturally take measures / to avoid it.
뇌에 있어서 / 손실은 위협이다 / 그리고 우리는 자연스럽게 조치를 취한다 / 그것을 피하기 위한

We cannot, / however, / avoid it indefinitely.
우리는 ~할 수 없다 / 그러나 / 그것을 무기한으로 피한다

One way / to face loss / is with the perspective of a stock trader.
한 가지 방법은 / 손실을 마주하는 / 주식 거래자의 관점을 갖는 것이다

Traders accept / the possibility of loss / as part of the game, / not the end of the game.
거래자들은 받아들인다 / 손실 가능성을 / 게임의 일부로 / 게임의 끝이 아닌

What guides this thinking / is a portfolio approach; / wins and losses will both happen, / but it's the overall portfolio of outcomes / that matters most.
이러한 사고를 이끄는 것은 / 포트폴리오 접근법이다 / 수익과 손실이 모두 발생할 것이다 / 하지만 결과의 전반적인 포트폴리오이다 / 가장 중요한 것은

When you embrace a portfolio approach, / you will be <u>less inclined to dwell on individual losses</u> / because you know / that they are small parts / of a much bigger picture.
당신이 포트폴리오 접근법을 수용하면 / 당신은 <u>개별적인 손실에 대해 덜 곱씹게 될 것</u>인데 / 당신이 알기 때문이다 / 그것들이 작은 부분들이라는 것을 / 훨씬 더 큰 그림의

해석 손실에 대한 두려움은 인간의 기본적인 부분이다. 뇌에 있어서, 손실은 위협이며 우리는 자연스럽게 그것을 피하기 위한 조치를 취한다. 그러나 우리는 그것을 무기한으로 피할 수 없다. 손실을 마주하는 한 가지 방법은 주식 거래자의 관점을 갖는 것이다. 거래자

들은 손실 가능성을 게임의 끝이 아닌 게임의 일부로 받아들인다. 이러한 사고를 이끄는 것은 포트폴리오 접근법이며, 수익과 손실이 모두 발생할 것이지만 가장 중요한 것은 결과의 전반적인 포트폴리오이다. 당신이 포트폴리오 접근법을 수용하면, 당신은 개별적인 손실에 대해 덜 곱씹게 될 것인데, 그것들이 훨씬 더 큰 그림의 작은 부분들이라는 것을 당신이 알기 때문이다.

① 개별적인 손실에 대해 덜 곱씹는
② 당신의 투자에 관심을 덜 갖는
③ 손실을 더 싫어하는
④ 주식 시장의 변동에 더 민감한

해설   빈칸이 있는 문장을 통해 빈칸에 포트폴리오 접근법을 수용하면 어떻게 되는지에 대한 내용이 나와야 적절하다는 것을 알 수 있다. 빈칸 앞 문장에서 포트폴리오 접근법에서는 수익과 손실이 모두 발생하지만 가장 중요한 것은 결과의 전반적인 포트폴리오라고 하고, 빈칸이 있는 문장에서 당신이 포트폴리오 접근법을 수용하면 그것들(개별적인 손실)이 훨씬 더 큰 그림의 작은 부분들이라는 것을 알기 때문에 ~하게 될 것이라고 했으므로, '개별적인 손실에 대해 덜 곱씹는'이라고 한 ①번이 정답이다.

어휘   take measure 조치를 취하다   indefinitely 무기한으로
perspective 관점   guide 이끌다
portfolio 포트폴리오(유가 증권 보유 일람표)   embrace 수용하다
dwell on 곱씹다   averse ~를 싫어하는   fluctuation 변동

---

03   독해   전체내용 파악 (제목 파악)   난이도 ★★☆

끊어읽기 해석

Over the last years of traveling, / I've observed / how much we humans live / in the past.
지난 수년간의 여행 동안 / 나는 관찰해왔다 / 우리 인간들이 얼마나 사는지를 / 과거에

The past is around us constantly, / considering that, / the minute something is manifested, / it is the past.
과거는 끊임없이 우리 주변에 있다 / ~을 고려해 볼 때 / 어떤 것이 나타나자마자 / 그것은 과거의 일이다

Our surroundings, our homes, our environments, our architecture, our products / are all past constructs.
우리 주위의 상황, 우리의 집, 우리의 환경, 우리의 건축물, 우리의 생산물은 / 모두 과거의 구성체들이다

We should live / with what is part of our time, / part of our collective consciousness, / those things that were produced / during our lives.
우리는 살아야 한다 / 우리 시대의 일부인 것과 함께 / 우리의 집단의식의 일부(인 것과 함께) / 생산된 그러한 것들(과 함께) / 우리의 생애 동안에

Of course, / we do not have the choice or control / to have everything / around us / relevant or conceived / during our time, / but what we do have control of / should be a reflection of the time / in which we exist / and communicate the present.
물론 / 우리는 선택권이나 통제권을 가지고 있지 않다 / 모든 것을 가질 / 우리 주위의 / 관련이 있거나 시작된 / 우리의 시대 동안에 / 그러나 우리가 통제권을 가지고 있는 것은 / 시대의 반영이어야 한다 / 우리가 존재하고 / 현재를 함께하는

The present is all we have, / and the more we are surrounded / by it, / the more we are aware of / our own presence and participation.
현재는 우리가 가진 모든 것이다 / 그리고 우리가 더 둘러싸여 있을수록 / 그것에 / 우리는 더 많이 알게 된다 / 우리의 존재와 참여에 대해

해석   지난 수년간의 여행 동안, 나는 우리 인간들이 얼마나 과거에 사는

지를 관찰해왔다. 어떤 것이 나타나자마자 그것은 과거의 일이라는 것을 고려해 볼 때, 과거는 끊임없이 우리 주변에 있다. 우리 주위의 상황, 우리의 집, 우리의 환경, 우리의 건축물, 우리의 생산물은 모두 과거의 구성체들이다. 우리는 우리 시대의 일부인 것, 우리의 집단의식의 일부인 것, 우리의 생애 동안에 생산된 그러한 것들과 함께 살아야 한다. 물론 우리는 우리의 시대 동안에 관련이 있거나 시작된 우리 주위의 모든 것을 가질 선택권이나 통제권을 가지고 있지 않지만, 우리가 통제권을 가지고 있는 것은 우리가 존재하고 현재를 함께하는 시대의 반영이어야 한다. 현재는 우리가 가진 모든 것이고, 우리가 그것에 더 둘러싸여 있을수록, 우리는 우리의 존재와 참여에 대해 더 많이 알게 된다.

① 여행: 과거의 유산 추적하기
② 현재 당신을 둘러싼 시간에 대해 숙고하라
③ 숨겨진 삶의 표명
④ 초현대적 삶의 건축

해설   지문의 중간에서 우리는 우리 시대의 일부인 것, 우리의 집단의식의 일부인 것, 우리의 생애 동안에 생산된 것들과 함께 살아야 한다고 하고, 지문 마지막에 우리가 현재에 더 둘러싸여 있을수록 우리는 우리의 존재와 참여에 대해 더 많이 알게 된다는 내용이 있다. 따라서 이 지문의 제목을 '현재 당신을 둘러싼 시간에 대해 숙고하라'라고 표현한 ②번이 정답이다.

어휘   constantly 끊임없이   manifest 나타내다, 명시하다
construct 구성체   collective consciousness 집단의식
conceive 시작하다, 창설하다   communicate 함께하다, 나누다
surround 둘러싸다   presence 존재   legacy 유산
manifestation 표명, 표시   futuristic 초현대적인, 미래의

---

04   문법   능동태·수동태   난이도 ★★☆

해석   숲의 아름다움과 풍요로움이 없는 삶을 상상하는 것은 어려울 것이다. 그러나 과학자들은 우리가 우리의 숲들을 당연히 여겨서는 안 된다고 경고한다. 몇몇 추정치에 따르면, 삼림벌채는 세계 자연 삼림의 80퍼센트에 달하는 양의 손실을 초래했다. 최근 삼림벌채는 전 세계적인 문제이며, 태평양의 온대 강우림과 같은 야생지역들에 영향을 미치고 있다.

해설   ③ 수동태로 쓸 수 없는 자동사 동사 result는 전치사 in과 함께 쓰여 '~을 초래하다'라는 의미로 쓰이는 자동사이므로 수동태로 쓸 수 없다. 따라서 수동태 has been resulted in을 능동태 has resulted in으로 고쳐야 한다.

오답   ① to 부정사의 역할 해당 문장은 가주어 it이 길이가 긴 진짜 주어 to 부정사구(to imagine ~ forests) 대신 주어 자리에 쓰인 형태이므로, 진짜 주어 자리에 to 부정사구를 이끄는 to 부정사 to imagine이 올바르게 쓰였다.
② 숙어 표현 문맥상 '우리의 숲들을 당연히 여겨서는 안 된다'라는 의미가 되어야 자연스러우므로 숙어 표현 take ~ for granted(~을 당연히 여기다)를 완성하는 granted가 올바르게 쓰였다.
④ 현재분사 분사 뒤에 목적어(wilderness regions)가 있고, 주절의 주어 deforestation과 분사구문이 '삼림벌채가 영향을 미친다'라는 의미의 능동 관계이므로, 현재분사 affecting이 올바르게 쓰였다.

어휘   richness 풍요로움   take ~ for granted ~을 당연히 여기다
deforestation 삼림벌채   result in ~을 초래하다
wilderness 야생지역   temperate rainforest 온대 강우림

👍 이것도 알면 **합격!**

③번에 쓰인 현재완료 시제(have p.p.)의 다양한 형태들을 잘 알아두자.

현재완료 진행	have been -ing ⓔⓧ You have been talking for a long time. 너는 오랫동안 이야기해왔다.
현재완료 수동	have been p.p. ⓔⓧ The young workers have been hired by the company. 그 젊은 근로자들은 회사에 의해 고용되었다.

---

05 어휘 **어휘&표현** indigenous = native   난이도 ★☆☆

해석 전설적인 기록 영화 제작자 로버트 플라어티는 토착 민족이 어떻게 식량을 모았는지를 보여주려고 했다.

① 토착의
② 탐욕스러운
③ 빈곤한
④ 떠돌아다니는

어휘 legendary 전설적인 indigenous 토착의, 지역 고유의
native 토착의, 원주민의 ravenous 탐욕스러운, 몹시 굶주린
impoverished 빈곤한 itinerant 떠돌아다니는

👍 이것도 알면 **합격!**

indigenous(토착의)의 유의어
= aboriginal, endemic

---

06 어휘 **어휘&표현** a far cry from   난이도 ★★★

해석 음악을 듣는 것은 록스타가 되는 것과는 전혀 다르다. 누구나 음악을 들을 수는 있지만, 음악가가 되는 데는 재능이 필요하다.

① ~와 동등한
② ~와는 전혀 다른
③ ~여하에 달린
④ ~의 서막

어휘 on a par with ~와 동등한 a far cry from ~와는 전혀 다른
contingent upon ~여하에 달린 a prelude to ~의 서막

👍 이것도 알면 **합격!**

a far cry from(~와는 전혀 다른)과 유사한 의미의 표현
= vastly different from, not similar to

---

07 독해 **논리적 흐름 파악 (무관한 문장 삭제)**   난이도 ★★☆

끊어읽기 해석

Biologists have identified / a gene / that will allow rice plants to survive / being submerged / in water / for up to two weeks / —over a week longer / than at present.
생물학자들은 찾아냈다 / 유전자를 / 벼가 생존할 수 있게 할 / 잠긴 채로 / 물속에 / 2주까지 / 일주일 이상 더 긴 / 현재보다

Plants / under water / for longer than a week / are deprived of oxygen / and wither and perish.
식물은 / 물에 잠긴 / 일주일 이상 / 산소를 빼앗긴다 / 그리고 시들어 죽는다

① The scientists hope / their discovery will prolong / the harvests of crops / in regions / that are susceptible to flooding.
과학자들은 희망한다 / 그들의 발견이 연장시키기를 / 작물의 수확을 / 지역에서의 / 홍수에 취약한

② Rice growers / in these flood-prone areas of Asia / lose an estimated one billion dollars annually / to excessively waterlogged rice paddies.
벼 재배자들은 / 이러한 홍수가 잦은 아시아 지역들의 / 매년 10억 달러로 추정되는 돈을 잃는다 / 과도하게 침수된 논으로 인해

③ They hope / the new gene will lead to a hardier rice strain / that will reduce the financial damage / incurred in typhoon and monsoon seasons / and lead to bumper harvests.
그들은 희망한다 / 새로운 유전자가 더 강인한 벼 품종을 가져오기를 / 재정적 손해를 줄일 / 태풍과 장마 시기에 발생하는 / 그리고 풍작을 가져오기를

④ This is dreadful news / for people / in these vulnerable regions, / who are victims of urbanization / and have a shortage of crops.
이것은 끔찍한 소식인데 / 사람들에게 / 이러한 취약한 지역의 / 이들은 도시화의 희생자이다 / 그리고 작물 부족을 겪는다

Rice yields must increase / by 30 percent / over the next 20 years / to ensure / a billion people can receive / their staple diet.
쌀 생산량은 증가해야 한다 / 30퍼센트만큼 / 다음 20년에 걸쳐 / 확실히 하기 위해 / 10억 명의 사람들이 얻을 수 있는 것을 / 그들의 주식을

해석 생물학자들은 벼가 현재보다 일주일 이상 더 긴 2주까지 물속에 잠긴 채로 생존할 수 있게 할 유전자를 찾아냈다. 일주일 이상 물에 잠긴 식물은 산소를 빼앗기고 시들어 죽는다. ① 과학자들은 그들의 발견이 홍수에 취약한 지역에서의 작물의 수확을 연장시키기를 희망한다. ② 이러한 홍수가 잦은 아시아 지역들의 벼 재배자들은 과도하게 침수된 논으로 인해 매년 10억 달러로 추정되는 돈을 잃는다. ③ 그들은 새로운 유전자가 태풍과 장마 시기에 발생하는 재정적 손해를 줄일 더 강인한 벼 품종과 풍작을 가져오기를 희망한다. ④ 이것은 이러한 취약한 지역의 사람들에게 끔찍한 소식인데, 이들은 도시화의 희생자이며 작물 부족을 겪는다. 쌀 생산량은 10억 명의 사람들이 그들의 주식을 얻을 수 있는 것을 확실히 하기 위해 다음 20년에 걸쳐 30퍼센트만큼 증가해야 한다.

해설 첫 문장에서 생물학자들이 벼가 물속에 잠긴 채 2주까지 생존할 수 있게 할 유전자를 찾아냈다고 언급하고, ①번에서 과학자들은 이 발견이 홍수에 취약한 지역의 작물 수확을 연장시키기를 희망한다고 했다. 이어서 ②, ③번에서 매년 침수된 논으로 인해 엄청난 손해를 입는 아시아 지역의 쌀 재배자들은 새로운 유전자가 이 손해를 줄일 더 강인한 벼 품종과 풍작을 가져오기를 희망한다고 설명하고 있으므로 모두 첫 문장과 관련이 있다. 그러나 ④번은 '도시화의 희생자이자 작물 부족을 겪는 취약 지역의 사람들에게 끔찍한 소식'이라는 내용으로 지문 전반의 내용과 관련이 없다. 따라서 ④번이 정답이다.

어휘 identify 찾아내다, 확인하다 submerge 물속에 잠그다, 물속에 넣다
deprive 빼앗다 wither 시들다 perish 죽다, 소멸하다
prolong 연장시키다 be susceptible to ~에 취약하다
flood-prone 홍수가 잦은 waterlogged 침수된 paddy 논
hardy 강인한 strain 품종 incur 발생시키다 monsoon 장마
bumper harvest 풍작 dreadful 끔찍한 vulnerable 취약한
urbanization 도시화 staple diet 주식

해석

> A: 너 운전하는 법 알아?
> B: 당연하지. 난 훌륭한 운전자야.
> A: 내게 운전하는 법을 가르쳐 줄 수 있어?
> B: 너 임시 운전 면허증은 있어?
> A: 응, 지난주에 막 땄어.
> B: 운전해 본 적은 있고?
> A: 아니, 하지만 <u>해보고 싶어서 못 견디겠어.</u>

① 다음을 기약하다
② (처음) 해보다
③ 엔진 오일을 교체하다
④ 펑크 난 타이어를 갈다

해설 지난주에 임시 운전 면허증을 땄다는 A에게 B가 운전해 본 적은 있는지 묻자, 빈칸 앞에서 A가 No, but I can't wait to(아니, 하지만 ~고 싶어서 못 견디겠어)라고 말하고 있으므로, 빈칸에는 '해보다'라는 의미가 들어가야 자연스럽다. 따라서 ② get my feet wet이 정답이다.

어휘 learner's permit 임시 운전 면허증
behind the steering wheel (자동차를) 운전하다, (배를) 조종하다
take a rain check 다음을 기약하다
get one's feet wet (처음) 해보다, 시작하다 flat tire 펑크 난 타이어

👍 **이것도 알면 합격!**

'신체 부위'를 포함하는 다양한 표현을 알아두자.
· cost an arm and a leg 엄청난 돈이 들다
· be all ears 열심히 귀를 기울이다
· Break a leg! 행운을 빌어!
· a sight for sore eyes 보기만 해도 좋은 사람(물건)

끊어읽기 해석

Sharks are covered / in scales / made from the same material / as teeth.
상어는 덮여있다 / 비늘로 / 동일한 물질로 만들어진 / 치아와

These flexible scales protect the shark / and help it swim quickly / in water.
이 유연성 있는 비늘은 상어를 보호한다 / 그리고 그것이 빠르게 헤엄치도록 돕는다 / 물속에서

①A shark can move the scales / as it swims.
상어는 비늘을 움직일 수 있다 / 헤엄칠 때

This movement helps / reduce the water's drag.
이 움직임은 돕는다 / 물의 항력을 줄이는 것을

Amy Lang, / an aerospace engineer / at the University of Alabama, / studies the scales / on the shortfin mako, / a relative of the great white shark.
Amy Lang은 / 항공 우주 공항자인 / 앨라배마 대학의 / 비늘을 연구한다 / 청상아리의 / 백상아리의 동족인

②③Lang and her team discovered / that the mako shark's scales differ / in size / and in flexibility / in different parts of its body.
Lang과 그녀의 팀은 발견했다 / 청상아리의 비늘이 다르다는 것을 / 크기가 / 그리고 유연성이 / 청상아리 몸의 다른 부분들에서

For instance, / the scales on the sides of the body / are tapered / —wide at one end / and narrow at the other end.
예를 들어 / 몸의 측면의 비늘은 / 점점 가늘어진다 / 한쪽 끝은 넓다 / 그리고 다른 한쪽 끝은 좁다

Because they are tapered, / these scales move very easily.
그것들이 점점 가늘어지기 때문에 / 이 비늘들은 매우 쉽게 움직인다

②They can turn up or flatten / to adjust / to the flow of water / around the shark / and to reduce drag.
그것들은 위로 젖히거나 평평해질 수 있다 / 맞추기 위해 / 물의 흐름에 / 상어 주변의 / 그리고 항력을 줄이기 위해

④Lang feels / that shark scales can inspire designs / for machines / that experience drag, / such as airplanes.
Lang은 생각한다 / 상어 비늘이 디자인에 영감을 줄 수 있다고 / 기계들의 / 항력을 받는 / 비행기와 같이

해석 상어는 치아와 동일한 물질로 만들어진 비늘로 덮여있다. 이 유연성 있는 비늘은 상어를 보호하고 그것이 물속에서 빠르게 헤엄치도록 돕는다. 상어는 헤엄칠 때 비늘을 움직일 수 있다. 이 움직임은 물의 항력을 줄이는 것을 돕는다. 앨라배마 대학의 항공 우주 공학자인 Amy Lang은 백상아리의 동족인 청상아리의 비늘을 연구한다. Lang과 그녀의 팀은 청상아리의 비늘이 청상아리 몸의 다른 부분들에서 크기와 유연성이 다르다는 것을 발견했다. 예를 들어, 몸의 측면의 비늘은 점점 가늘어지는데, 한쪽 끝은 넓고 다른 한쪽 끝은 좁다. 그것들이 점점 가늘어지기 때문에, 이 비늘들은 매우 쉽게 움직인다. 그것들은 상어 주변의 물의 흐름에 맞추고 항력을 줄이기 위해 위로 젖히거나 평평해질 수 있다. Lang은 상어 비늘이 비행기와 같이 항력을 받는 기계들의 디자인에 영감을 줄 수 있다고 생각한다.

① 상어는 헤엄칠 때 스스로를 보호하기 위해 항상 움직이지 않는 비늘을 가지고 있다.
② Lang은 청상아리의 비늘이 물속에서 항력을 줄이는 데 이용된다는 것을 밝혀냈다.
③ 청상아리는 그것들 몸 전체에 동일한 크기의 비늘을 가지고 있다.
④ 비행기의 과학적·디자인은 상어 비늘에 의해 영감을 받았다.

해설 지문 중간에서 Lang과 그녀의 팀은 청상아리의 비늘이 몸의 다른 부분에서 크기와 유연성이 다르다는 것을 발견했다고 하고, 지문 뒷부분에서 그것들(청상아리의 비늘)은 항력을 줄이기 위해 위로 젖히거나 평평해질 수 있다고 했으므로, Lang이 청상아리의 비늘을 물속에서 항력을 줄이는 데 이용된다는 것을 밝혀냈다는 것을 알 수 있다. 따라서 ②번이 정답이다.

오답 분석
① 상어는 헤엄칠 때 비늘을 움직일 수 있다고 했으므로, 상어가 항상 움직이지 않는 비늘을 가지고 있다는 것은 지문의 내용과 다르다.
③ Lang과 그녀의 팀은 청상아리의 비늘이 청상아리 몸의 다른 부분들에서 크기와 유연성이 다르다는 것을 발견했다고 했으므로, 청상아리가 몸 전체에 동일한 크기의 비늘을 가지고 있다는 것은 지문의 내용과 반대이다.
④ Lang은 상어 비늘이 비행기와 같이 항력을 받는 기계의 디자인에 영감을 줄 수 있다고 생각한다고는 했지만, 비행기의 과학적 디자인이 상어 비늘에 의해 영감을 받았는지는 알 수 없다.

어휘 scale 비늘 drag 항력 aerospace engineer 항공 우주 공학자
shortfin mako 청상아리 relative 동족, 친척 differ in ~이 다르다
flexibility 유연성 taper 점점 가늘어지다 flatten 평평해지다
immobile 움직이지 않는 utilize 이용하다 identical 동일한

해석 집중은 일을 완료하는 것을 의미한다. 많은 사람이 대단한 생각들을 가지고 있지만 그것들에 따라 행동하지는 않는다. 예를 들어,

나에게 기업가의 정의는 그 새로운 생각을 실행하는 능력으로 혁신과 창의력을 결합할 수 있는 사람이다. 어떤 사람들은 인생에서 가장 중요한 이분법은 당신을 흥미 있게 하거나 걱정시키는 문제들에 대해 당신이 긍정적인지 부정적인지라고 생각한다. 낙관적인 시각을 갖는 것이 나은지 비관적인 시각을 갖는 것이 나은지에 대한 이 질문에 많은 관심이 기울어져 있다. 나는 물어보기에 더 나은 질문은 당신이 무언가 행동을 취할 것인지 아니면 그저 인생이 당신을 스쳐 지나가게 할 것인지라고 생각한다.

해설 ③ 현재분사 vs. 과거분사 | 수식받는 명사(attention)와 분사가 '관심이 기울어지다'라는 의미의 수동 관계이므로 현재분사 paying을 과거분사 paid로 고쳐야 한다.

오답 분석 ① 동명사를 취하는 동사 | 동사 get의 쓰임 동사 mean(means)은 동명사를 목적어로 취할 수 있으므로 동명사 getting이 올바르게 쓰였다. 또한 동사 get(getting)은 목적어와 목적격 보어가 수동 관계일 때에는 목적격 보어로 과거분사를 취하는데, 목적어 stuff와 목적격 보어가 '일이 완료되다'라는 의미의 수동 관계이므로 과거분사 done이 올바르게 쓰였다.
② 관계대명사 선택 | 관계절 수 일치 선행사 the issues(문제들)가 사물이고 관계절 내에서 동사(interest, concern)의 주어 역할을 하므로 사물을 가리키는 주격 관계대명사 that이 올바르게 쓰였고, 관계절의 동사는 선행사에 수 일치시켜야 하는데 선행사가 복수 명사이므로 복수 동사 interest, concern이 올바르게 쓰였다.
④ 사역동사의 쓰임 | 어순 동사 let은 동사원형을 목적격 보어로 취하는 사역동사이므로 동사원형 pass가 목적격 보어 자리에 올바르게 쓰였고, '동사 + 부사'로 이루어진 구동사는 목적어가 대명사이면 '동사(pass) + 목적어(you) + 부사(by)'의 어순으로 쓰이므로 pass you by가 올바르게 쓰였다.

어휘 act on ~에 따라 행동하다 entrepreneur 기업가 ingenuity 창의력 execute 실행하다 dichotomy 이분법 optimistic 낙관적인 pessimistic 비관적인 pass by ~을 스쳐 지나가다

👍 이것도 알면 **합격!**

분사가 명사를 수식할 때, 수식받는 명사가 사람이 아닌 사물인 경우에도 '사물이 분사하다'라고 해석되는 능동 관계이면 현재분사가 온다.

ex) He sent an email calling off the afternoon meeting.
그는 오후 미팅을 취소하는 이메일을 보냈다.

11 독해 논리적 흐름 파악 (문맥상 부적절한 어휘) 난이도 ★☆☆

끊어읽기 해석

Most people like to talk, / but few people like to listen, / yet listening well is a ① rare talent / that everyone should treasure.
대부분의 사람들은 말하는 것을 좋아한다 / 하지만 듣는 것을 좋아하는 사람들은 거의 없다 / 그래도 잘 듣는 것은 ① 귀한 재능이다 / 모든 사람이 소중히 여겨야 하는

Because they hear more, / good listeners tend to know more / and to be more sensitive / to what is going on / around them / than most people.
그들이 더 많이 듣기 때문에 / 훌륭한 청자들은 더 많이 아는 경향이 있다 / 그리고 더 민감한 (경향이 있다) / 무슨 일이 일어나고 있는지에 대해 / 그들 주변에서 / 대부분의 사람들보다

In addition, / good listeners are inclined to accept or tolerate / rather than to judge and criticize.

게다가 / 훌륭한 청자들은 받아들이거나 참는 경향이 있다 / 판단하고 비판하기보다

Therefore, / they have ② fewer enemies / than most people.
그러므로 / 그들은 ② 더 적은 적을 가진다 / 대부분의 사람들보다

In fact, / they are probably / the most beloved of people.
사실 / 그들은 아마 ~일 것이다 / 사람들에게 가장 사랑을 받고 있는

However, / there are ③ exceptions / to that generality.
하지만 / ③ 예외가 있다 / 그러한 일반론에는

For example, / John Steinbeck is said to have been an excellent listener, / yet he was hated / by some of the people / he wrote about.
예를 들어 / 존 스타인벡은 뛰어난 청자였다고 전해진다 / 하지만 그는 미움을 받았다 / 일부 사람들에게 / 그가 글에 썼던

No doubt / his ability to listen / contributed to his capacity to write.
의심의 여지가 없다 / 경청하는 그의 능력이 / 그의 집필 능력에 기여했던 것은

Nevertheless, / the result of his listening / didn't make him ④ unpopular.
그럼에도 불구하고 / 그의 경청의 결과는 / 그를 ④ 인기 없게 만들지는 않았다

해석 대부분의 사람들은 말하는 것을 좋아하지만, 듣는 것을 좋아하는 사람들은 거의 없는데, 그래도 잘 듣는 것은 모든 사람이 소중히 여겨야 하는 ① 귀한 재능이다. 그들이 더 많이 듣기 때문에, 훌륭한 청자들은 대부분의 사람들보다 더 많이 알고 그들 주변에서 무슨 일이 일어나고 있는지에 대해 더 민감한 경향이 있다. 게다가, 훌륭한 청자들은 판단하고 비판하기보다 받아들이거나 참는 경향이 있다. 그러므로, 그들은 대부분의 사람들보다 ② 더 적은 적을 가진다. 사실, 그들은 아마 사람들에게 가장 사랑을 받고 있을 것이다. 하지만, 그러한 일반론에는 ③ 예외가 있다. 예를 들어, 존 스타인벡은 뛰어난 청자였다고 전해지지만, 그는 그가 글에 썼던 일부 사람들에게 미움을 받았다. 경청하는 그의 능력이 그의 집필 능력에 기여했던 것은 의심의 여지가 없다. 그럼에도 불구하고, 그의 경청의 결과는 그를 ④ 인기 없게 만들지는 않았다.

해설 지문 중간에서 훌륭한 청자들은 사람들에게 가장 사랑을 받지만 이러한 일반론에는 예외가 있다고 한 후, 존 스타인벡은 뛰어난 청자였지만 일부 사람들에게 미움을 받았다고 했으므로, 그의 경청의 결과가 그를 인기 없게(unpopular) 만들지는 않았다는 것은 문맥상 적절하지 않다. 따라서 ④ unpopular가 정답이다. 참고로, 주어진 unpopular를 대신할 수 있는 어휘로는 '인기 있는'이라는 의미의 popular, favored 등이 있다.

어휘 rare 귀한, 드문 treasure 소중히 여기다 sensitive 민감한 in addition 게다가 be inclined to ~ 하는 경향이 있다 tolerate 참다 be beloved of ~에게 사랑을 받고 있다 exception 예외 generality 일반론 capacity 능력

12 독해 전체내용 파악 (주제 파악) 난이도 ★☆☆

끊어읽기 해석

Worry is like a rocking horse.
걱정은 흔들 목마와 같다

No matter how fast you go, / you never move anywhere.
당신이 아무리 빨리 가더라도 / 당신은 결코 어디로도 움직이지 않는다

Worry is a complete waste of time / and creates so much clutter / in your mind / that you cannot think clearly / about anything.

걱정은 완전한 시간 낭비이다 / 그리고 너무 많은 혼란을 만들어서 / 당신의 마음속에 / 당신은 명확하게 생각할 수 없다 / 어떤 것에 대해서도

The way / to learn to stop worrying / is by first understanding / that you energize / whatever you focus your attention on.
방법은 / 걱정을 그만두는 것을 배우는 / 먼저 이해함에 의해서이다 / 당신이 ~에 동력을 준다는 것을 / 무엇이든 당신이 주의를 집중하는 것

Therefore, / the more you allow yourself to worry, / the more likely things are to go wrong!
그러므로 / 당신이 스스로에게 걱정하도록 허락할수록 / 일들이 잘못될 가능성이 더 많아진다!

Worrying becomes such an ingrained habit that / to avoid it / you consciously have to train yourself / to do otherwise.
걱정하는 것은 깊이 배어든 습관이 되어서 / 그것을 피하기 위해 / 당신은 의식적으로 스스로를 훈련해야 한다 / 다르게 행동하도록

Whenever you catch yourself / having a fit of worry, / stop and change your thoughts.
당신이 스스로를 발견할 때마다 / 걱정의 발작을 겪고 있는 / 멈추고 당신의 생각을 바꾸어라

Focus your mind more productively / on what you do want to happen / and dwell on what's already wonderful / in your life / so more wonderful stuff will come your way.
당신의 마음을 더 생산적으로 집중시켜라 / 당신이 정말로 일어나기를 바라는 일에 / 그리고 이미 멋진 것들에 대해 숙고하라 / 당신의 인생에서 / 더 멋진 일이 당신에게 일어나도록

해석 걱정은 흔들 목마와 같다. 당신이 아무리 빨리 가더라도, 당신은 결코 어디로도 움직이지 않는다. 걱정은 완전한 시간 낭비이고, 당신의 마음속에 너무 많은 혼란을 만들어서 당신은 어떤 것에 대해서도 명확하게 생각할 수 없다. 걱정을 그만두는 것을 배우는 방법은 무엇이든 당신이 주의를 집중하는 것에 당신이 동력을 준다는 것을 먼저 이해함에 의해서이다. 그러므로, 당신이 스스로에게 걱정하도록 허락할수록, 일들이 잘못될 가능성이 더 많아진다! 걱정하는 것은 깊이 배어든 습관이 되어서 그것을 피하기 위해 당신은 다르게 행동하도록 의식적으로 스스로를 훈련해야 한다. 당신이 걱정의 발작을 겪고 있는 스스로를 발견할 때마다, 멈추고 당신의 생각을 바꾸어라. 더 멋진 일이 당신에게 일어나도록 당신의 마음을 당신이 정말로 일어나기를 바라는 일에 더 생산적으로 집중시키고 당신의 인생에서 이미 멋진 것들에 대해 숙고하라.

① 걱정은 삶에 어떤 영향을 미치는가?
② 걱정은 어디에서 비롯되는가?
③ 우리는 언제 걱정해야 하는가?
④ 우리는 어떻게 걱정을 극복해야 하는가?

해설 지문 중간에서 걱정을 그만두는 것을 배우는 방법은 당신이 주의를 집중하는 것에 당신이 동력을 준다는 사실을 이해함에 의해서라고 하고, 이어서 걱정하는 습관을 피하기 위해서는 다르게 행동하도록 의식적으로 스스로를 훈련하고, 정말로 일어나기를 바라는 일에 마음을 집중시키며 당신의 인생에서 이미 멋진 것들에 대해 숙고하라고 설명하고 있다. 따라서 이 지문의 주제를 '우리는 어떻게 걱정을 극복해야 하는가?'라고 표현한 ④번이 정답이다.

어휘 rocking horse 흔들 목마 clutter 혼란
energize ~에 동력을 주다, 활기차게 하다 ingrained 깊이 배어든
consciously 의식적으로 fit (감정 등의) 발작, 격발
dwell on 숙고하다 come one's way ~에게 일어나다
cope with 극복하다, 대처하다

---

13 독해 세부내용 파악 (내용 불일치 파악)
난이도 ★☆☆

끊어읽기 해석

Students / at Macaulay Honors College (MHC) / don't stress / about the high price of tuition.
학생들은 / 매콜레이우등대학(MHC)의 / 스트레스를 받지 않는다 / 고액의 등록금에 대해

That's because theirs is free.
이는 그들의 것(등록금)이 무료이기 때문이다

At Macaulay and a handful of other service academies, work colleges, single-subject schools and conservatories, / 100 percent of the student body / receive a full tuition scholarship / for all four years.
매콜레이와 소수의 다른 군 사관학교, 직업 대학, 단과대학 그리고 음악 학교에서 / 전교생의 100퍼센트가 / 수업료 전액 장학금을 받는다 / 4년 내내

Macaulay students also receive / a laptop and $7,500 / in "opportunities funds" / to pursue research, service experiences, study abroad programs and internships.
매콜레이의 학생들은 또한 받는다 / 노트북과 7천 5백 달러를 / '기회 자금'으로 / 연구, 업무 경험, 해외 연수 프로그램 그리고 인턴십을 수행하기 위한

"The most important thing is not the free tuition, / but the freedom of studying / without the burden of debt on your back," / says Ann Kirschner, / university dean of Macaulay Honors College.
"가장 중요한 것은 무료 등록금이 아니라 / 공부할 자유입니다 / 빚의 부담을 짊어지지 않고" / 라고 Ann Kirschner는 말한다 / 매콜레이우등대학의 학장인

The debt burden, / she says, / "really compromises decisions / students make / in college, / and we are giving them / the opportunity / to be free of that."
빚의 부담은 / 그녀는 ~라고 말한다 / "결정들을 정말로 위태롭게 합니다 / 학생들이 내리는 / 대학에서 / 그리고 우리는 그들에게 제공하고 있습니다 / 기회를 / 그것으로부터 자유로워질"

Schools / that grant free tuition / to all students / are rare, / but a greater number of institutions / provide scholarships / to enrollees / with high grades.
학교는 / 무료 등록금을 수여하는 / 모든 학생들에게 / 드물다 / 하지만 더 많은 수의 기관들이 / 장학금을 제공한다 / 등록생들에게 / 높은 성적의

Institutions / such as Indiana University Bloomington / offer automatic awards / to high-performing students / with stellar GPAs and class ranks.
기관들은 / 인디애나대학교 블루밍턴 캠퍼스와 같은 / 자동적인 장학금을 제공한다 / 성취도가 높은 학생들에게 / 평점과 강의에서의 석차가 뛰어난

해석 매콜레이우등대학(MHC)의 학생들은 고액의 등록금에 대해 스트레스를 받지 않는다. 이는 그들의 것(등록금)이 무료이기 때문이다. 매콜레이와 소수의 다른 군 사관학교, 직업 대학, 단과대학, 그리고 음악 학교에서, 전교생의 100퍼센트가 4년 내내 수업료 전액 장학금을 받는다. 매콜레이의 학생들은 또한 연구, 업무 경험, 해외 연수 프로그램 그리고 인턴십을 수행하기 위한 '기회 자금'으로 노트북과 7천 5백 달러를 받는다. "가장 중요한 것은 무료 등록금이 아니라 빚의 부담을 짊어지지 않고 공부할 자유입니다"라고 매콜레이우등대학의 학장인 Ann Kirschner는 말한다. 그녀는 빚의 부담은 "학생들이 대학에서 내리는 결정들을 정말로 위태롭게 하며, 우리는 그들에게 그것으로부터 자유로워질 기회를 제공하고 있습니다."라고 말한다. 모든 학생에게 무료 등록금을 수여하는 학교는 드물지만, 더 많은 수의 기관들이 높은 성적의 등록생들에게 장학금을 제공한다. 인디애나대학교 블루밍턴 캠퍼스와 같은 기관들은 평점과 강의에서의 석차가 뛰어난 성취도가 높은 학생들에게 자동적인 장학금을 제공한다.

해설 지문 중간에서 매콜레이 학생들은 연구, 업무 경험, 해외 연수 프

로그램, 인턴십을 수행하기 위한 기회 자금으로 노트북과 7천 5백 달러를 받는다고 했으므로, MHC에서 학생들에게 컴퓨터 구입 비용과 교외활동 비용을 합하여 7천 5백 달러를 지급한다는 것은 지문의 내용과 다르다. 따라서 ②번이 정답이다.

어휘 tuition 등록금 service academy 군 사관학교
single-subject school 단과대학 conservatory 음악 학교
scholarship 장학금 pursue 수행하다 burden 부담 dean 학장
compromise 위태롭게 하다, 손상시키다
be free of ~으로부터 자유롭다 institution 기관
enrollee 등록생, 등록자 stellar 뛰어난 GPA 평점

14 어휘 어휘 & 표현 malefactor = culprit 난이도 ★★☆

해석 경찰은 그 범죄 사건을 수사하며 7개월을 보냈지만 그 범죄자의 신원을 결코 밝혀낼 수 없었다.

① 범죄자 　　　　　　　② 호사가
③ 부랑자 　　　　　　　④ 선동 정치가

어휘 work on (사건을) 수사하다, 노력을 들이다 determine 밝혀내다
identity 신원 malefactor 범죄자, 악인 culprit 범죄자
dilettante 호사가, 예술 애호가 pariah 부랑자, (사회에서) 버림받은 자
demagogue 선동 정치가

👍 이것도 알면 합격!

malefactor(범죄자)의 유의어
= criminal, convict, offender

15 어휘 어휘 & 표현 through thick and thin = in good times and bad times 난이도 ★★☆

해석 언뜻 보기에 그의 친구들은 그저 거머리 같은 사람들로 보이기는 하지만, 그들은 그가 좋을 때나 안 좋을 때나 의지할 수 있는 사람들로 판명된다.

① 즉시 　　　　　　　② 때때로
③ 즐거운 시기에 　　　　④ 좋을 때나 나쁠 때나

어휘 at first glance 언뜻 보기에 leech 거머리 같은 사람, 착취자
prove ~로 판명되다, ~임이 알려지다
through thick and thin 좋을 때나 안 좋을 때나
in no time 즉시, 당장 from time to time 때때로

👍 이것도 알면 합격!

through thick and thin(좋을 때나 안 좋을 때나)과 유사한 의미의 표현
= despite any obstacles, no matter what

16 독해 논리적 흐름 파악 (문장 삽입) 난이도 ★★☆

끊어읽기 해석

Some remain intensely proud / of their original accent and dialect words, phrases and gestures, / while others accommodate rapidly / to a new environment / by changing their speech habits, / so that they no longer "stand out in the crowd."

어떤 사람들은 계속 몹시 자랑스럽게 여긴다 / 그들의 원래 억양과 방언 어휘들, 구절들과 몸짓들을 / 반면, 다른 사람들은 빠르게 맞춘다 / 새로운 환경에 / 그들의 말하기 습관을 바꿈으로써 / 그들이 더 이상 '군중 속에서 두드러지지' 않도록

Our perceptions and production of speech / change / with time.
언어에 대한 우리의 인식과 창작은 / 변한다 / 시간에 따라

(①) If we were to leave our native place / for an extended period, / our perception / that the new accents / around us / were strange / would only be temporary.
만약 우리가 우리의 출생지를 떠나 있게 된다면 / 장기간에 걸친 시간 동안 / 우리의 인식은 / 새로운 억양이 / 우리 주변의 / 이상하다는 / 단지 일시적일 것이다

(②) Gradually, / we will lose the sense / that others have an accent / and we will begin to fit in / —to accommodate our speech patterns / to the new norm.
서서히 / 우리는 느낌을 잃을 것이다 / 다른 사람들이 억양을 갖고 있다는 / 그리고 우리는 적응하기 시작할 것이다 / 우리의 말투를 맞추기 위해 / 새로운 표준에

(③) Not all people do this / to the same degree.
모든 사람들이 이렇게 하는 것은 아니다 / 같은 정도로

(④) Whether they do this consciously or not / is open to debate / and may differ / from individual to individual, / but like most processes / that have to do with language, / the change probably happens / before we are aware of it / and probably couldn't happen / if we were.
그들이 이것을 의식적으로 하는지 아닌지는 / 논쟁의 여지가 있다 / 그리고 다를 수도 있다 / 개개인에 따라 / 하지만 대부분의 과정들처럼 / 언어와 관련이 있는 / 그 변화는 아마 일어난다 / 우리가 인식하기 전에 / 그리고 아마 일어나지 못했을 것이다 / 우리가 (인식)했다면

해석 언어에 대한 우리의 인식과 창작은 시간에 따라 변한다. 만약 우리가 장기간에 걸친 시간 동안 우리의 출생지를 떠나 있게 된다면, 우리 주변의 새로운 억양이 이상하다는 우리의 인식은 단지 일시적일 것이다. 서서히 우리는 다른 사람들이 억양을 갖고 있다는 느낌을 잃을 것이고, 우리의 말투를 새로운 표준에 맞추기 위해 적응하기 시작할 것이다. 모든 사람들이 같은 정도로 이렇게 하는 것은 아니다. ④ 어떤 사람들은 계속 그들의 원래 억양과 방언 어휘들, 구절들과 몸짓들을 몹시 자랑스럽게 여기는 반면, 다른 사람들은 그들이 더 이상 '군중 속에서 두드러지지' 않도록 그들의 말하기 습관을 바꿈으로써 새로운 환경에 빠르게 맞춘다. 그들이 이것을 의식적으로 하는지 아닌지는 논쟁의 여지가 있고 개개인에 따라 다를 수도 있지만, 언어와 관련이 있는 대부분의 과정들처럼 그 변화는 아마 우리가 인식하기 전에 일어나고, 만약 우리가 인식했다면 아마 일어나지 못했을 것이다.

해설 ④번 앞 문장에 모든 사람들이 같은 정도로 이렇게 하는 것(새로운 억양에 적응)은 아니라는 내용이 있으므로, ④번 자리에 어떤 사람들은 계속 그들의 원래 억양과 방언 어휘들, 구절들과 몸짓들을 몹시 자랑스럽게 여기는 반면, 다른 사람들은 그들이 더 이상 군중 속에서 두드러지지 않도록 그들의 말하기 습관을 바꿈으로써 새로운 환경에 빠르게 맞춘다는 주어진 문장이 나와야 지문이 자연스럽게 연결된다. 따라서 ④번이 정답이다.

어휘 intensely 격하게 accent 억양, 사투리 dialect 방언
accommodate 맞추다 perception 인식 native 출생지의
extended 장기간에 걸친 temporary 일시적인
gradually 점차적으로 fit in 적응하다, 어울리다 norm 표준
consciously 의식적으로

끊어읽기 해석

Insomnia can be classified / as transient, acute, or chronic.
불면증은 분류될 수 있다 / 일시적이거나, 급성이거나 만성적인 것으로

Transient insomnia lasts / for less than a week.
일시적인 불면증은 지속된다 / 일주일 미만 동안

It can be caused / by another disorder, / by changes in the sleep environment, / by the timing of sleep, severe depression, / or by stress.
그것은 야기될 수 있다 / 또 다른 질환에 의해 / 수면 환경의 변화에 의해 / 수면의 시기나 심한 우울증에 의해 / 혹은 스트레스에 의해

Its consequences / such as sleepiness and impaired psychomotor performance / are similar / to those of sleep deprivation.
그것의 결과들은 / 졸음과 약된 정신 운동 수행과 같은 / 비슷하다 / 수면 부족의 그것들(결과들)과

Acute insomnia is / the inability to consistently sleep well / for a period of less than a month.
급성 불면증은 ~이다 / 지속적으로 잠을 잘 수 없는 것 / 한 달 미만의 기간 동안

Acute insomnia is present / when there is difficulty / initiating or maintaining sleep / or when the sleep / that is obtained / is not refreshing.
급성 불면증은 존재한다 / 어려움이 있을 때 / 수면을 시작하거나 지속하는 데 / 혹은 수면이 ~일 때 / 취해진 / 상쾌하지 않

These problems occur / despite adequate opportunity and circumstances / for sleep / and they can impair / daytime functioning.
이 문제들은 발생한다 / 적절한 기회와 환경에도 불구하고 / 수면을 위한 / 그리고 그것들은 약화시킬 수 있다 / 낮 시간의 활동을

Acute insomnia is also known as / short term insomnia / or stress related insomnia.
급성 불면증은 또한 ~으로 알려져 있다 / 단기 불면증 / 혹은 스트레스 관련 불면증

Chronic insomnia lasts / for longer than a month.
만성 불면증은 지속된다 / 한 달 이상

It can be caused / by another disorder, / or it can be a primary disorder.
그것은 야기될 수 있다 / 또 다른 질환에 의해 / 또는 그것이 1차 질환일 수 있다

People / with high levels of stress hormones / or shifts in the levels of cytokines / are more likely / than others / to have chronic insomnia.
사람들은 / 높은 수치의 스트레스 호르몬을 갖고 있는 / 또는 시토킨 수치에 변화가 있는 / 가능성이 더 크다 / 다른 사람들보다 / 만성 불면증이 있을

Its effects can vary / according to its causes.
그것의 영향들은 다를 수 있다 / 그것의 원인들에 따라

They might include / muscular weariness, hallucinations, and/or mental fatigue.
그것들(영향들)은 포함할 수 있다 / 근육의 피로, 망상 그리고/혹은 정신적 피로를

Chronic insomnia can also cause / double vision.
만성 불면증은 또한 야기할 수 있다 / 복시를

해석   불면증은 일시적이거나, 급성이거나 만성적인 것으로 분류될 수 있다. 일시적 불면증은 일주일 미만 동안 지속된다. 그것은 또 다른 질환에 의해, 수면 환경의 변화에 의해, 수면의 시기나 심한 우울증에 의해 혹은 스트레스에 의해 야기될 수 있다. 졸음과 약화된 정신 운동 수행과 같은 그것의 결과들은 수면 부족의 그것들(결과들)과 비슷하다. 급성 불면증은 한 달 미만의 기간 동안 지속적으

로 잠을 잘 수 없는 것이다. 급성 불면증은 수면을 시작하거나 지속하는 데 어려움이 있을 때 혹은 취해진 수면이 상쾌하지 않을 때 존재한다. 이 문제들은 수면을 위한 적절한 기회와 환경에도 불구하고 발생하며, 그것들은 낮 시간의 활동을 약화시킬 수 있다. 급성 불면증은 또한 단기 불면증 혹은 스트레스 관련 불면증으로 알려져 있다. 만성 불면증은 한 달 이상 지속된다. 그것은 또 다른 질환에 인해 야기될 수 있거나, 그것이 1차 질환일 수 있다. 높은 수치의 스트레스 호르몬을 갖고 있거나 시토킨 수치에 변화가 있는 사람들은 다른 사람들보다 만성 불면증이 있을 가능성이 더 크다. 그것의 영향들은 그것의 원인들에 따라 다를 수 있다. 그것들(영향들)은 근육의 피로, 망상 그리고/혹은 정신적 피로를 포함할 수 있다. 만성 불면증은 또한 복시를 야기할 수 있다.

① 불면증은 그것의 지속기간에 따라 분류될 수 있다.
② 일시적인 불면증은 부적절한 수면 환경에 의해서만 발생한다.
③ 급성 불면증은 일반적으로 스트레스와 관련이 있다고 알려져 있다.
④ 만성 불면증 환자들은 망상에 시달릴 수도 있다.

해설   지문 앞부분에서 일시적인 불면증은 또 다른 질환, 수면 환경의 변화, 수면의 시기나 심한 우울증, 또는 스트레스에 의해 야기될 수 있다고 했으므로, 일시적인 불면증이 부적절한 수면 환경에 의해서만 발생한다는 것은 지문의 내용과 다르다. 따라서 ②번이 정답이다.

여휘   **insomnia** 불면증   **classify** 분류하다, 구분하다   **transient** 일시적인
acute 급성의, 극심한   **chronic** 만성적인   **disorder** 질환
severe 심한, 혹독한   **depression** 우울증   **impair** 약화시키다
psychomotor 정신 운동의   **deprivation** 부족, 결핍
initiate 시작하다   **adequate** 적절한   **shift** 변화   **vary** 다르다
muscular 근육의   **weariness** 피로, 권태   **hallucination** 망상
fatigue 피로   **double vision** 복시   **duration** 지속기간

끊어읽기 해석

Kisha Padbhan, / founder of Everonn Education, / in Mumbai, / looks at his business / as nation-building.
Kisha Padbhan은 / Everonn 교육의 창립자인 / 뭄바이의 / 그의 사업을 본다 / 국가 건설로

India's student-age population / of 230 million (kindergarten to college) / is one of the largest / in the world.
인도의 학생 연령 인구는 / 2억 3천만 명(유치원에서 대학까지)의 / 가장 많은 것 중 하나이다 / 세계에서

The government spends $83 billion / on instruction, / but there are serious gaps.
정부는 830억 달러를 쓴다 / 교육에 / 하지만 심각한 격차가 있다

"There aren't enough teachers and enough teacher-training institutes," / says Kisha.
"충분한 교사들과 충분한 교사 교육 기관들이 없습니다" / Kisha는 ~라고 말한다

"What children in remote parts of India lack / is access / to good teachers / and exposure / to good-quality content."
"인도의 외딴 지역의 아이들에게 부족한 것은 / 접근 기회입니다 / 훌륭한 선생님들에 대한 / 그리고 노출입니다 / 양질의 콘텐츠에 대한"

Everonn's solution? // The company uses a satellite network, / with two-way video and audio / to bridge the gap / through virtual classrooms.
Everonn의 해결책은 무엇일까? // 이 회사는 위성 네트워크를 사용한다 / 양방향 영상과 오디오를 갖춘 / 그 격차를 메우기 위해 / 가상 교실을 통해

It reaches 1,800 colleges and 7,800 schools / across 24 of India's 28 states.
그것은 1,800곳의 대학과 7,800곳의 학교에 닿는다 / 인도의 28개 주 가운데 24개 주의 전역에서

It offers everything / from digitized school lessons / to entrance exam prep / for aspiring engineers / and has training / for job-seekers, too.
그것은 모든 것을 제공한다 / 디지털화된 학교 수업에서부터 / 대학 입학 시험 준비까지 / 포부가 있는 기술자들을 위해 / 그리고 훈련 과정을 갖추고 있다 / 또한 구직자들을 위한

해석 뭄바이의 Everonn 교육의 창립자인 Kisha Padbhan은 그의 사업을 국가 건설로 본다. 인도의 2억 3천만 명(유치원에서 대학까지)의 학생 연령 인구는 세계에서 가장 많은 것 중 하나이다. 정부는 교육에 830억 달러를 쓰지만, 심각한 격차가 있다. "충분한 교사들과 충분한 교사 교육 기관들이 없습니다"라고 Kisha는 말한다. "인도의 외딴 지역의 아이들에게 부족한 것은 훌륭한 선생님들에 대한 접근 기회와 양질의 콘텐츠에 대한 노출입니다." Everonn의 해결책은 무엇일까? 이 회사는 가상 교실을 통해 그 격차를 메우기 위해 양방향 영상과 오디오를 갖춘 위성 네트워크를 사용한다. 그것은 인도의 28개 주 가운데 24개 주의 전역에서 1,800곳의 대학과 7,800곳의 학교에 닿는다. 그것은 포부가 있는 기술자들을 위해 디지털화된 학교 수업에서부터 대학 입학 시험 준비까지 모든 것을 제공하며, 구직자들을 위한 훈련 과정 또한 갖추고 있다.

① 교사 교육 시설의 질을 향상시키기 위해
② 가상 교실을 통해 그 격차를 메우기 위해
③ 학생들을 디지털 기술에 익숙하게 만들기 위해
④ 자격 있는 교육자를 전국에 배치하기 위해

해설 빈칸이 있는 문장을 통해 빈칸에 Everonn 교육 회사가 무엇을 위해 양방향 영상과 오디오를 갖춘 위성 네트워크를 사용하는지에 대한 내용이 나와야 적절하다는 것을 알 수 있다. 빈칸 앞 문장에 인도의 외딴 지역의 아이들에게 부족한 것은 훌륭한 선생님들에 대한 접근 기회와 양질의 콘텐츠에 대한 노출이라는 내용이 있고, 빈칸 뒤 문장에 그것(가상 교실)은 인도의 대다수 주의 대학과 학교에 닿으며 디지털화된 학교 수업, 대학 입시 시험 준비, 구직자를 위한 훈련 과정을 갖췄다는 내용이 있으므로, '가상 교실을 통해 그 격차를 메우기 위해'라고 한 ②번이 정답이다.

어휘 founder 창립자 instruction 교육 gap 격차, 틈 institute 기관 remote 외딴 lack ~이 부족하다 access 접근 기회 exposure 노출 good-quality 양질의 satellite 위성 two-way 양방향의 digitize 디지털화하다 aspiring 포부가 있는 job-seeker 구직자 bridge ~을 메우다 gap 격차 virtual 가상의 familiarize 익숙하게 만들다 qualified 자격 있는

19 독해 논리적 흐름 파악 (문단 순서 배열) 난이도 ★★☆

끊어읽기 해석

A technique / that enables an individual to gain some voluntary control / over autonomic, or involuntary, body functions / by observing electronic measurements / of those functions / is known / as biofeedback.
기술은 / 개인이 어떤 자발적인 제어력을 얻을 수 있게 하는 / 자율적이거나 본능적인 신체 기능들에 대한 / 전자기기의 측정값을 관찰함으로써 / 그러한 기능들에 대한 / 알려져 있다 / 생체 자기 제어로

(A) When such a variable moves / in the desired direction (for example, blood pressure down), / it triggers visual or audible displays / —feedback on equipment / such as television sets,

gauges, or lights.
그러한 변수가 움직일 때 / 바라던 방향으로(예를 들어, 혈압이 낮아지는) / 그것은 시각적 혹은 청각적 표시들을 촉발시킨다 / 기기들에서 나타나는 반응인 / 텔레비전 수상기, 측정기 또는 조명과 같은

(B) Electronic sensors are attached / to various parts of the body / to measure / such variables as heart rate, blood pressure, and skin temperature.
전자 감지기들은 부착된다 / 신체의 다양한 부분에 / 측정하기 위해 / 심장 박동수, 혈압 그리고 피부 온도와 같은 변수들을

(C) Biofeedback training teaches / one / to produce a desired response / by reproducing thought patterns or actions / that triggered the displays.
생체 자기 제어 훈련은 가르친다 / 사람에게 / 바라던 반응을 일으키는 법을 / 사고 패턴들이나 행동들을 재생산함으로써 / 그 표시들을 촉발시켰던

해석 개인이 자율적이거나 본능적인 신체 기능들에 대한 어떤 자발적인 제어력을, 그러한 기능들에 대한 전자기기의 측정값을 관찰함으로써 얻을 수 있게 하는 기술은 생체 자기 제어로 알려져 있다.

(B) 전자 감지기들은 심장 박동수, 혈압, 그리고 피부 온도와 같은 변수들을 측정하기 위해 신체의 다양한 부분에 부착된다.
(A) 그러한 변수가 바라던 방향으로(예를 들어, 혈압이 낮아지는) 움직일 때, 그것은 텔레비전 수상기, 측정기 또는 조명과 같은 기기들에서 나타나는 반응인 시각적 혹은 청각적 표시들을 촉발시킨다.
(C) 생체 자기 제어 훈련은 그 표시들을 촉발시켰던 사고 패턴들이나 행동들을 재생산함으로써 사람에게 바라던 반응을 일으키는 법을 가르친다.

해설 주어진 문장에서 개인이 신체 기능들에 대한 전자기기의 측정값(electronic measurements) 관찰을 통해 신체 기능들에 대한 자발적 제어력을 얻을 수 있게 하는 기술이 생체 자기 제어라고 하고, (B)에서 변수들을 측정하기 위해(to measure) 전자 감지기들이 신체에 부착된다고 설명하고 있다. 이어서 (A)에서 그러한 변수(such a variable)가 바라던 방향으로 움직이면 기기들에서 시각적 혹은 청각적 표시(visual or audible displays)들이 촉발된다고 하고, (C)에서 그 표시들(the displays)을 촉발시켰던 사고 패턴들이나 행동들을 재생산함으로써 사람이 바라던 반응을 일으키는 것을 가르치는 것이 생체 자기 제어 훈련이라고 설명하고 있다. 따라서 ③ (B) – (A) – (C)가 정답이다.

어휘 voluntary 자발적인 autonomic 자율적인 involuntary 본능적인 measurements 측정값 variable 변수 desired 바라던 trigger 촉발시키다 audible 청각의 display 표시 gauge 측정기 attach 부착하다 heart rate 심장 박동수

20 문법 비교 구문 난이도 ★★☆

해설 ④ 원급 표현 '사람들이 생각했던 만큼 인색하지 않았다는 것'은 두 대상의 동등함을 나타내는 원급 표현 'not as/so + 형용사/부사의 원급 + as'(~만큼 -하지 않은)를 사용하여 나타낼 수 있으므로 비교급 stingier를 원급 stingy로 고쳐야 한다.

오답분석 ① 전치사 뒤에 올 수 있는 것 전치사(at) 뒤에는 명사 역할을 하는 것이 와야 하므로 전치사 at 뒤에 동명사 getting이 올바르게 쓰였다.
② 비교급 표현 | 지시대명사의 쓰임 '세계 어느 도시보다 심각하다'는 비교급 형태로 최상급 의미를 만드는 표현 '비교급(more serious) + than any other + 단수 명사(city)'(다른 어떤 -보다 더 ~한)의 형태를 사용하여 나타내므로, more serious

than those in any other city가 올바르게 쓰였다. 또한, 지시
대명사(those)가 가리키는 명사 The traffic jams가 복수이
므로 복수 지시대명사 those가 올바르게 쓰였다.

③ 주어 동사 수 일치 동명사 주어(Making eye contact)는 단
수 취급하므로 단수 동사 is가 올바르게 쓰였다. 참고로, 해당
문장은 the person과 you 사이에 전치사 to의 목적어 역할을
하는 목적격 관계대명사 whom이 생략된 형태이다.

어휘 get ~ across ~를 전달하다 turn out ~인 것으로 드러나다
stingy 인색한

👍 이것도 알면 **합격!**

③번의 동명사구 주어와 마찬가지로 명사절 주어에도 단수 동사가
와야 한다.

ex What they want ~~are~~ some time to relax. (→ is)
그들이 원하는 것은 휴식을 취할 약간의 시간이다.

지방직 9급 출제 경향

1. 영역별 출제 문항 수 (2018~2024)

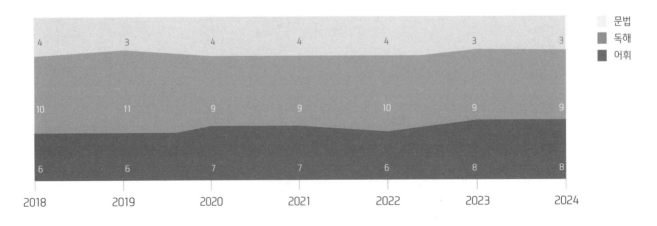

지방직 9급 시험의 영역별 출제 문항 수는 약간의 변동이 있는 편입니다. **문법** 영역은 3~4문항으로 변동이 없으나, 6~7문항씩 출제되었던 **어휘** 영역은 2023년과 2024년 시험에 8문항이 출제되었으며, 10~11문항씩 출제되었던 **독해** 영역은 각각 9문항이 출제되었습니다.

Part 2
지방직 9급

2. 영역별 최근 출제 경향 및 학습 방법

문법	**여러 문법 포인트가 복합된 문제와 다소 지엽적인 문제 출제** 최근 7년간 대부분의 시험에서 한 문장에 두 개 이상의 문법 포인트가 복합된 문제가 출제되었으며, 2024년 시험에는 3형식 동사인 mention의 쓰임을 묻는 다소 지엽적인 문제가 출제되었습니다. ▶ 따라서 빈출 포인트 외에도 다양한 문법 요소를 파악하며 문법 영역을 폭넓게 학습하는 것이 중요합니다. [빈출 포인트] 분사(8문항) ┃ 동사의 종류(8문항) ┃ 능동태·수동태(7문항) ┃ 수 일치(7문항)
독해	**논리적 흐름 파악 유형의 꾸준한 출제와 다양한 형식의 지문 출제** 최근 7년간 논리적 흐름 파악 유형의 문단 순서 배열, 문장 삽입, 무관한 문장 삭제 문제가 각각 1문항 이상 매년 출제되었으며, 2024년 시험에는 내용 일치 파악 문제가 이메일 형식으로 출제되는 등 새로운 형식의 지문이 출제되었습니다. ▶ 따라서 지시대명사, 연결어, 관사 등을 통해 지문의 논리적 흐름을 파악하고, 보기의 키워드와 관련된 부분을 지문에서 빠르게 찾아내는 연습을 꾸준히 해야 하며, 지문의 형식에 맞춰 전략적으로 학습하는 것이 중요합니다.
어휘	**평이한 어휘와 표현의 의미를 파악하는 문제 출제** 최근 3년간 flexible, vary와 같은 수능 수준의 평이한 어휘 및 표현들의 유의어를 찾는 문제가 출제되었으며, 2024년 시험에는 markedly(현저하게), rule out(배제하다)과 같은 어휘와 표현이 출제되었습니다. ▶ 따라서 시험에 출제된 어휘와 표현의 유의어와 파생어를 폭넓게 학습하는 것이 필요합니다.

정답

p.78

01	② 어휘 - 어휘 & 표현	11	② 어휘 - 생활영어
02	② 어휘 - 어휘 & 표현	12	③ 독해 - 세부내용 파악
03	① 어휘 - 어휘 & 표현	13	④ 독해 - 세부내용 파악
04	① 어휘 - 어휘 & 표현	14	③ 독해 - 전체내용 파악
05	③ 어휘 - 어휘 & 표현	15	③ 독해 - 전체내용 파악
06	④ 문법 - 부사절	16	③ 독해 - 논리적 흐름 파악
07	③ 문법 - 관계절	17	③ 독해 - 논리적 흐름 파악
08	② 문법 - 동사의 종류	18	④ 독해 - 논리적 흐름 파악
09	④ 어휘 - 생활영어	19	① 독해 - 추론
10	④ 어휘 - 생활영어	20	① 독해 - 추론

취약영역 분석표

영역	세부 유형	문항 수	소계
어휘	어휘 & 표현	5	/8
	생활영어	3	
문법	부사절	1	/3
	관계절	1	
	동사의 종류	1	
독해	전체내용 파악	2	/9
	세부내용 파악	2	
	추론	2	
	논리적 흐름 파악	3	
총계			/20

· 자신이 취약한 영역은 '공무원 영어, 이렇게 출제된다!'(문제집 p.8)를 통해 다시 한번 확인하고 학습하시기 바랍니다.

---

01 어휘 | 어휘&표현 markedly = obviously
난이도 ★☆☆

해석 셰익스피어의 희극은 많은 유사점을 공유하지만, 또한 서로 현저하게 다르기도 하다.
① 부드럽게
② 분명히
③ 미미하게
④ 분간할 수 없게

어휘 comedy 희극 share 공유하다 similarity 유사점, 공통점
differ 다르다 markedly 현저하게, 두드러지게
obviously 분명히, 명백히 marginally 미미하게, 조금만
indiscernibly 분간할 수 없게

👍 이것도 알면 **합격!**

markedly(현저하게)의 유의어
= noticeably, decidedly, distinctly, remarkably

02 어휘 | 어휘&표현 dilute = weaken
난이도 ★★☆

해석 Jane은 진하고 짙은 차를 따르고 그것을 우유로 희석했다.
① 씻다
② 묽게 하다
③ 연결하다
④ 발효시키다

어휘 pour 따르다, 붓다 strong (차가) 진한 dark (색이) 짙은, 어두운
dilute 희석하다, 묽게 하다 ferment ~을 발효시키다

👍 이것도 알면 **합격!**

dilute(희석하다)와 유사한 의미의 표현
= make weaker, thin out, water down

03 어휘 | 어휘&표현 rule out = exclude
난이도 ★★☆

해석 총리는 아동 수당이나 연금의 삭감을 배제했다고 여겨진다.
① 배제했다
② 지지했다
③ 제출했다
④ 인가했다

어휘 prime minister 총리, 수상 rule out 배제하다, 제외하다
cut 삭감, 인하 benefit 수당, 혜택 pension 연금
exclude 배제하다, 제외하다 submit 제출하다
authorize 인가하다, 승인하다

👍 이것도 알면 **합격!**

rule out(배제하다)의 유의어
= preclude, dismiss, reject

04 어휘 | 어휘&표현 let on = reveal
난이도 ★★☆

해석 우리가 깜짝 파티를 계획하고 있다고 털어놓으면, 아빠는 너에게 질문을 멈추지 않을 것이다.
① 밝히다
② 관찰하다
③ 믿다

④ 소유하다

어휘 let on 털어놓다, 폭로하다 reveal 밝히다, 드러내다
observe 관찰하다 possess 소유하다

👍 이것도 알면 **합격!**

let on(털어놓다)과 유사한 의미의 표현
= confess, disclose, give away, let out

05 **어휘** 어휘 & 표현 facilitate
난이도 ★★☆

해석 슈퍼마켓의 자동문은 가방이나 쇼핑 카트를 가진 고객의 출입을 용이하게 한다.
① 무시하다
② 용서하다
③ 용이하게 하다
④ 과장하다

어휘 automatic 자동의 entry and exit 출입
facilitate 용이하게 하다, 촉진하다 exaggerate 과장하다

👍 이것도 알면 **합격!**

facilitate(용이하게 하다)와 유사한 의미의 표현
= ease, make easy, enable, help

06 **문법** 부사절
난이도 ★☆☆

해석 당신이 읽고 있는 책의 많은 장점 중 하나는 그것이 『의미의 지도』에 대한 진입점을 제공한다는 점인데, 이것은 작가가 이 책을 쓰면서 심리학에 대한 그의 접근법을 연구하고 있었기 때문에 매우 복잡한 작품이다.

해설 ④ 부사절 자리와 쓰임 전치사(because of)의 목적어 자리에는 명사 역할을 하는 것이 와야 하는데, 뒤에 완전한 절(the author ~ it)이 왔으므로 전치사 because of를 완전한 절 앞에 올 수 있는 부사절 접속사 because로 고쳐야 한다.

오답 ① 수량 표현 수량 표현 One of(~ 중 하나)는 복수 명사 앞에 오
분석 는 수량 표현이므로 복수 명사 virtues가 올바르게 쓰였다.
② 수량 표현의 수 일치 주어 자리에 단수 취급하는 수량 표현 'One of + 명사'(One of the many virtues)가 왔으므로 단수 동사 is가 올바르게 쓰였다.
③ 관계대명사 선행사(Maps of Meaning)가 사물이고, 관계절 내에서 주어 역할을 하므로 주격 관계대명사 which가 올바르게 쓰였다.

어휘 virtue 장점, 덕목 provide 제공하다 entry point 진입점
approach 접근법 psychology 심리학

👍 이것도 알면 **합격!**

이유를 나타내는 부사절 접속사를 알아두자.

· because, as, since ~이기 때문에
· now (that) ~이니까
· in that ~이라는 점에서

07 **문법** 관계절
난이도 ★☆☆

해석 ① 그 프로젝트에 너무 많은 시간을 들이지 않도록 계획해야 한다.
② 나의 개는 지난달에 사라졌고 그 이후로 보이지 않는다.
③ 내가 돌보던 딸을 가진 사람들이 이사를 가서 슬프다.
④ 나는 여행에서 책을 샀는데, 본국에서 사는 것보다 두 배만큼 비쌌다.

해설 ③ 관계대명사 선행사(the people)가 사람이고, 관계절 내에서 daughter가 누구의 딸인지 나타내므로, 주격 관계대명사 who를 사람을 가리키는 소유격 관계대명사 whose로 고쳐야 한다.

오답 ① to 부정사의 형태 to 부정사(to spend)의 부정형은 to 부정사
분석 앞에 not을 붙이므로 not to spend가 올바르게 쓰였다.
② 과거 시제 | 수동태로 쓸 수 없는 동사 문장에 시간 표현 last month(지난달)가 왔고 문맥상 '지난달에 사라졌다'라는 과거의 동작을 표현하고 있으므로 과거 시제 disappeared가 올바르게 쓰였다. 또한, 동사 disappear는 '사라지다'라는 의미일 때 목적어를 취하지 않는 자동사이며 수동태로 쓸 수 없으므로 능동태로 올바르게 쓰였다.
④ 원급 문맥상 '본국에서 사는 것보다 두 배만큼 비쌌다'라는 의미가 되어야 자연스러운데, '두 배만큼 비쌌다'는 '배수사 + as + 원급 + as'의 형태로 나타낼 수 있으므로 twice as expensive as가 올바르게 쓰였다.

어휘 disappear 사라지다 expensive 비싼

👍 이것도 알면 **합격!**

'as + many/much/few/little + 명사 + as'는 '~만큼 많은/적은 ~'을 나타낸다는 것을 알아두자.
ex We packed **as many clothes as** we could fit into the suitcase.
우리는 여행 가방에 들어갈 수 있을 만큼 많은 옷을 챙겼다.

08 **문법** 동사의 종류
난이도 ★★☆

해설 ② 3형식 동사 that절을 목적어로 갖는 3형식 동사 mention 뒤에는 '사람(me)'이 혼자 올 수 없고 'to + 사람'(to me)의 형태로 와야 하므로 mentioned me that ~을 mention to me that ~으로 고쳐야 한다.

오답 ① 5형식 동사 | 목적어 자리 동사 find(found)는 5형식 동사
분석 로 쓰일 때 'find(found) + 목적어 + 목적격 보어(exciting)'를 취하며 '~이 -이라는 것을 알다'라는 의미를 나타내는데, to 부정사구 목적어가 목적격 보어와 함께 오면 진짜 목적어(to 부정사구)를 목적격 보어 뒤로 보내고 목적어가 있던 자리에 가짜 목적어 it을 써서 '가짜 목적어 it + 목적격 보어(exciting) + 진짜 목적어(to work here)'의 형태가 되어야 하므로 found it ~ to work here가 올바르게 쓰였다. 참고로, 감정을 나타내는 분사가 목적격 보어일 때 목적어가 감정의 원인인 경우 현재분사를 쓰고, 감정을 느끼는 대상인 경우 과거분사를 쓰는데, 목적어가 '이곳에서 일하는 것은 흥미롭다'라는 의미로 감정의 원인이므로 현재분사 exciting이 올바르게 쓰였다.
③ 5형식 동사 동사 want는 to 부정사를 목적격 보어로 취하는 5형식 동사이므로 want him to come이 올바르게 쓰였다.
④ 가정법 과거완료 | 부사 자리 '좀 더 능숙하고 경험 많은 선생님이었다면'이라며 과거의 상황을 반대로 가정하고 있으므로 가정법 과거완료 would have treated가 올바르게 쓰였다. 참고로, 해당 문장은 if절이 생략된 상태이며, 문맥이나 상황에

가정하는 내용이 명백하게 드러나는 경우에는 가정법 문장에서 if절이 생략될 수 있다. 또한, 부사(otherwise)는 동사를 수식할 때 '동사 + 목적어'의 뒤에 올 수 있으므로, '동사 + 목적어(treated him)' 뒤에 부사 otherwise가 올바르게 쓰였다.

어휘 mention 언급하다 skillful 능숙한, 숙련된 experienced 경험 많은
treat 대하다, 다루다
otherwise 달리, 만약 그렇지 않다면, 다른 상황에서는

👍 이것도 알면 **합격!**

목적어(that절/의문사절)를 하나만 가지는 3형식 동사와 목적어를 2개 가지는 4형식 동사를 구별해서 써야 한다는 것을 알아두자.

3형식 동사	say/mention/announce 말하다 suggest/propose/recommend 제안하다 explain/describe 설명하다	+ (to 사람)	+ 목적 (that절/ 의문사절)
4형식 동사	tell/inform/notify 말하다 assure/convince 확신시키다	+ 간접 목적어 (~에게)	+ 직접 목적어 (that절/ 의문사절)

---

09 어휘 생활영어 That's a lot more than I expected. 난이도 ★☆☆

해석
A: Charles, 다가오는 행사에 의자가 더 필요할 것 같아요.
B: 정말요? 의자가 이미 충분하다고 생각했는데요.
A: 부장님께서 350명 이상 올 거라고 말씀하셨어요.
B: 제가 예상했던 것보다 훨씬 더 많네요.
A: 동의해요. 저도 조금 놀랐어요.
B: 그럼 제가 더 주문해야 할 것 같네요. 감사해요.

① 부장님이 행사에 참석하실지 궁금해요.
② 350명 이상 올 거라고 생각했어요.
③ 그것은 사실 많은 숫자가 아니네요.
④ 제가 예상했던 것보다 훨씬 더 많네요.

해설 부장님이 350명 이상 올 거라고 말했다는 A의 말에 B가 대답하고, 빈칸 뒤에서 A가 I agree. I am also a bit surprised(동의해요. 저도 조금 놀랐어요)라고 말하고 있으므로, 빈칸에는 '④ 제가 예상했던 것보다 훨씬 더 많네요(That's a lot more than I expected)'가 오는 것이 자연스럽다.

어휘 upcoming 다가오는, 곧 있을 attend 참석하다
expect 예상하다, 기대하다

👍 이것도 알면 **합격!**

놀라움을 나타낼 때 쓸 수 있는 다양한 표현을 알아두자.

• What a surprise! 정말 놀랐어요!
• I'm astonished! 놀랐어요!
• No way! 말도 안 돼요!
• You must be kidding! 농담이죠!

---

10 어휘 생활영어 Thank you for letting me know. I'll contact him. 난이도 ★☆☆

해석
A: 어제 회의에서 말씀하신 서류를 받아볼 수 있을까요?
B: 물론이죠. 서류 제목이 어떻게 되나요?
A: 제목은 기억이 안 나는데, 지역사회 축제에 관한 내용이었어요.

B: 아, 무엇을 말씀하시는지 알겠어요.
A: 좋아요. 이메일로 보내주실 수 있나요?
B: 저는 가지고 있지 않아요. Park 씨가 프로젝트를 담당하고 있으니, 그가 가지고 있을 거예요.
A: 알려주셔서 감사해요. 그에게 연락해 볼게요.
B: 행운을 빌어요. 원하시는 서류를 꼭 받으시길 바라요.

① 그가 사무실에 있는지 확인해 주시겠어요?
② Park 씨가 당신에게 이메일을 다시 보냈어요.
③ 지역사회 축제에 오시나요?
④ 알려주셔서 감사해요. 그에게 연락해 볼게요.

해설 Park 씨가 프로젝트를 담당하고 있으니 그가 서류를 가지고 있을 거라는 B의 말에 A가 대답하고, 빈칸 뒤에서 B가 Good luck. Hope you get the document you want(행운을 빌어요. 원하시는 서류를 꼭 받으시길 바라요)라고 말하고 있으므로, 빈칸에는 '④ 알려주셔서 감사해요. 그에게 연락해 볼게요(Thank you for letting me know. I'll contact him)'가 오는 것이 자연스럽다.

어휘 document 서류, 문서 refer to 말하다, 참고하다
via ~을 통하여, ~에 의해 in charge of 담당하는, 책임이 있는

👍 이것도 알면 **합격!**

행운을 빌어줄 때 쓸 수 있는 다양한 표현을 알아두자.

• Best of luck! 행운을 빌어요!
• Wishing you all the best! 모든 일이 잘 되길 바라요!
• I'll keep my fingers crossed for you! 행운을 빌어요!
• I hope everything goes well! 모든 일이 잘 되길 바라요!

---

11 어휘 생활영어 When can I have a rehearsal for my presentation? 난이도 ★★☆

해석
A: 안녕하세요, 다음 주 화요일에 있을 발표에 관해 질문을 하나 해도 될까요?
B: 자원봉사 프로그램 홍보에 관한 발표 말씀이신가요?
A: 네. 발표는 어디에서 진행되나요?
B: 확인해 볼게요. 201호입니다.
A: 그렇군요. 방에서 제 노트북을 사용할 수 있나요?
B: 물론이죠. 방에 컴퓨터가 있지만, 원하시면 본인 것을 사용하셔도 돼요.
A: 발표 리허설은 언제 할 수 있나요?
B: 발표 두 시간 전에 방에서 만날 수 있어요. 괜찮으시겠어요?
A: 네. 정말 감사해요!

① 한 시간 전에 컴퓨터 기술자가 여기에 왔어요.
② 발표 리허설은 언제 할 수 있나요?
③ 우리 프로그램을 위해 더 많은 자원봉사자를 모집해야 할까요?
④ 제 노트북을 방에 두고 가는 것이 불편합니다.

해설 빈칸 뒤에서 B가 We can meet in the room two hours before the presentation(발표 두 시간 전에 방에서 만날 수 있어요)이라고 말하고 있으므로, 빈칸에는 '② 발표 리허설은 언제 할 수 있나요(When can I have a rehearsal for my presentation)'가 오는 것이 자연스럽다.

어휘 presentation 발표, 설명 promote 홍보하다, 촉진하다
volunteer 자원봉사 laptop 노트북 technician 기술자
rehearsal 리허설, 예행연습 recruit 모집하다, 채용하다
comfortable 편한, 편안한

이것도 알면 합격!

감사를 표현할 때 쓸 수 있는 다양한 표현을 알아두자.

- Thanks a lot! 정말 감사합니다!
- I appreciate it. 감사합니다.
- I'm deeply grateful. 진심으로 감사드립니다.
- I owe you one! 정말 고맙습니다! (당신에게 신세를 졌습니다!)
- I can't thank you enough. 얼마나 감사한지 몰라요.
- You've been very helpful. 많은 도움이 되었습니다.

---

12 독해 세부내용 파악 (내용 불일치 파악) 난이도 ★☆☆

끊어읽기 해석

To: reserve@metropolitan.com
수신: reserve@metropolitan.com

From: BruceTaylor@westcity.com
발신: BruceTaylor@westcity.com

Date: June 22, 2024
날짜: 2024년 6월 22일

Subject: Venue facilities
제목: 행사장 시설

Dear Sir,
담당자분께,

I am writing / to ask for information / about Metropolitan Conference Center.
저는 글을 씁니다 / 정보를 요청하기 위해 / 메트로폴리탄 컨퍼런스 센터에 대한

We are looking for a venue / for a three-day conference / in September / this year.
저희는 장소를 찾고 있습니다 / 3일간의 컨퍼런스를 위한 / 9월에 있을 / 올해

We need to have enough room / for over 200 delegates / in your main conference room, / and / we would also like three small conference rooms / for meetings.
저희는 충분한 공간이 필요합니다 / 200명 이상의 대표자들을 위한 / 주 회의실에 / 그리고 / 세 개의 작은 회의실도 필요합니다 / 회의용으로

Each conference room needs / wi-fi as well.
각 회의실은 필요합니다 / wi-fi도

We need to have coffee available / mid-morning and mid-afternoon, / and / we would also like to book your restaurant / for lunch / on all three days.
저희는 커피가 필요합니다 / 오전과 오후 중반에 / 그리고 / 귀사의 식당을 예약하고 싶습니다 / 점심 식사를 위해 / 3일 모두

In addition, / could you please let me know / if there are any local hotels / with discount rates / for Metropolitan clients or large groups?
또한 / 알려주실 수 있나요 / 현지 호텔이 있는지 / 할인율이 있는 / 메트로폴리탄 고객이나 대규모 그룹을 위한

We will need accommodations / for over 100 delegates / each night.
저희는 숙박시설이 필요합니다 / 100명 이상의 대표자를 위한 / 매일 밤

I look forward to hearing from you.
답장 기다리겠습니다

Best regards,
Bruce Taylor, Event Manager
행사 기획자 Bruce Taylor 드림

해석 수신: reserve@metropolitan.com
발신: BruceTaylor@westcity.com
날짜: 2024년 6월 22일
제목: 행사장 시설

담당자분께,

저는 메트로폴리탄 컨퍼런스 센터에 대한 정보를 요청하기 위해 글을 씁니다.

저희는 올해 9월에 있을 3일간의 컨퍼런스를 위한 장소를 찾고 있습니다. 주 회의실에 200명 이상의 대표자들이 사용할 수 있는 충분한 공간이 필요하며, 회의용으로 세 개의 작은 회의실도 필요합니다. 각 회의실에는 wi-fi도 필요합니다. 오전과 오후 중반에 커피가 필요하며, 3일 모두 점심 식사를 위해 귀사의 식당을 예약하고 싶습니다.

또한, 메트로폴리탄 고객이나 대규모 그룹을 위한 할인율이 있는 현지 호텔이 있는지 알려주실 수 있나요? 매일 밤 100명 이상의 대표자를 수용할 숙박시설이 필요합니다.

답장 기다리겠습니다.

행사 기획자 Bruce Taylor 드림

해설 지문 중간에서 3일 모두 점심 식사를 위해 식당을 예약하고 싶다고 했으므로 '③ 3일간의 저녁 식사를 위한 식당 예약이 필요하다'는 지문의 내용과 일치하지 않는다.

어휘 metropolitan 메트로폴리탄, 대도시의 venue 행사장, 장소 facility 시설, 설비 delegate 대표자, 사절 conference room 회의실 book 예약하다 discount 할인 client 고객 accommodation 숙박시설, 수용

---

13 독해 세부내용 파악 (내용 불일치 파악) 난이도 ★★☆

끊어읽기 해석

According to the historians, / neckties date back to 1660.
역사가들에 따르면 / 넥타이의 역사는 1660년까지 거슬러 올라간다

In that year, / a group of soldiers from Croatia / visited Paris.
그 해에 / 크로아티아에서 온 한 무리의 군인들이 / 파리를 방문했다

These soldiers were war heroes / whom King Louis XIV admired very much.
이 군인들은 전쟁 영웅들이었다 / 루이 14세가 매우 존경했던

Impressed with the colored scarves / that they wore around their necks, / the king decided to honor the Croats / by creating a military regiment / called the Royal Cravattes.
색깔이 있는 스카프에 감명을 받아서 / 그들이 목에 둘렀던 / 그 왕은 크로아티아인들을 기리기로 결정했다 / 군사 연대를 창설하여 / Royal Cravattes라고 불리는

The word *cravat* / comes from the word *Croat*.
'크라바트'라는 단어는 / 'Croat'라는 단어에서 왔다

All the soldiers in this regiment / wore colorful scarves or cravats / around their necks.
이 연대의 모든 군인들은 / 다채로운 스카프나 크라바트를 둘렀다 / 그들의 목에

This new style of neckwear / traveled to England.
이 새로운 스타일의 넥웨어는 / 영국으로 전파되었다

Soon / all upper class men were wearing cravats.
곧 / 모든 상류층 남성들이 크라바트를 맸다

Some cravats were quite extreme.
어떤 크라바트는 상당히 지나쳤다

At times, / they were so high / that a man could not move his head / without turning his whole body.

때때로 / 그것들은 너무 높아서 / 머리를 움직일 수 없었다 / 전신을 돌리지 않고는

The cravats were made of many different materials / from plaid to lace, / which made them suitable / for any occasion.
크라바트는 다양한 재료들로 만들어졌다 / 격자무늬 천부터 레이스까지 / 이는 그것들을 적합하게 만들었다 / 어떤 경우에도

해석　역사가들에 따르면, 넥타이의 역사는 1660년까지 거슬러 올라간다. 그 해에, 크로아티아에서 온 한 무리의 군인들이 파리를 방문했다. 이 군인들은 루이 14세가 매우 존경했던 전쟁 영웅들이었다. 그들이 목에 둘렀던 색깔이 있는 스카프에 감명을 받은 왕은 Royal Cravattes라고 불리는 군사 연대를 창설하여 크로아티아인들을 기리기로 결정했다. '크라바트'라는 단어는 'Croat'라는 단어에서 왔다. 이 연대의 모든 군인들은 목에 다채로운 스카프나 크라바트를 둘렀다. 이 새로운 스타일의 넥웨어는 영국으로 전파되었다. 곧 모든 상류층 남성들이 크라바트를 맸다. 어떤 크라바트는 상당히 지나쳤다. 때때로, 그것들은 너무 높아서 전신을 돌리지 않고는 머리를 움직일 수 없었다. 크라바트는 격자무늬 천부터 레이스까지 다양한 재료들로 만들어졌고, 이는 그것들을 어떤 경우에도 적합하게 만들었다.

① 1660년에 한 무리의 크로아티아 군인들이 파리를 방문했다.
② Royal Cravattes는 스카프를 맨 크로아티아 군인들을 기리기 위해 창설되었다.
③ 일부 크라바트는 머리를 자유롭게 움직이기에 너무 불편했다.
④ 크라바트를 만드는 데 사용된 재료들은 제한적이었다.

해설　④번의 키워드인 'materials(재료들)'가 그대로 언급된 지문 주변의 내용에서 크라바트는 격자무늬 천부터 레이스까지 다양한 재료들(many different materials)로 만들어졌다고 했으므로 '④ 크라바트를 만드는 데 사용된 재료들은 제한적이었다'는 지문의 내용과 일치하지 않는다.

어휘　historian 역사가, 사학자　necktie 넥타이
date back to ~까지 거슬러 올라가다　soldier 군인, 병사
admire 존경하다, 동경하다　impress 감명을 주다, 감동시키다
honor 기리다, 예우하다　military 군사의, 군대의
regiment (군사) 연대
cravat 크라바트(넥타이처럼 매는 남성용 스카프)
neckwear 넥웨어(넥타이·스카프 등 목에 두르는 물건들)
extreme (유행 등이) 지나친, 극심한　material 재료
plaid 격자무늬 천　lace 레이스　suitable 적합한
occasion 경우, 때　limited 제한적인, 한정된

14　독해　전체내용 파악 (주제 파악)　난이도 ★★☆

끊어읽기 해석

In recent years / Latin America has made huge strides / in exploiting / its incredible wind, solar, geothermal and biofuel energy resources.
최근 몇 년 동안 / 라틴 아메리카는 큰 진전을 이루었다 / 개발하는 데 / 엄청난 풍력, 태양열, 지열 및 바이오 연료 에너지 자원을

Latin America's electricity sector / has already begun to gradually decrease / its dependence on oil.
라틴 아메리카의 전력 부문은 / 이미 점차 낮추기 시작했다 / 그것의 석유에 대한 의존도를

Latin America is expected to / almost double its electricity output / between 2015 and 2040.
라틴 아메리카는 예상된다 / 그것의 전력 생산량을 거의 두 배로 늘릴 것으로 / 2015년과 2040년 사이에

Practically / none of Latin America's new large-scale power plants / will be oil-fueled, / which opens up the field / for different technologies.
사실상 / 라틴 아메리카의 새로운 대규모 발전소 중 어떤 것도 / 석유를 연료로 사용하지 않을 것이다 / 이는 장을 열어준다 / 다른 기술들을 위한

Countries in Central America and the Caribbean, / which traditionally imported oil, / were the first to move away / from oil-based power plants, / after suffering a decade of high and volatile prices / at the start of the century.
중앙아메리카와 카리브해 국가들은 / 전통적으로 석유를 수입했던 / 가장 먼저 벗어났다 / 석유 기반 발전소에서 / 10년 동안 높고 변동성이 큰 가격을 겪은 후에 / 금세기 초에

해석　최근 몇 년 동안 라틴 아메리카는 엄청난 풍력, 태양열, 지열 및 바이오 연료 에너지 자원을 개발하는 데 큰 진전을 이루었다. 라틴 아메리카의 전력 부문은 이미 석유에 대한 의존도를 점차 낮추기 시작했다. 라틴 아메리카는 2015년에서 2040년 사이에 전력 생산량을 거의 두 배로 늘릴 것으로 예상된다. 사실상 라틴 아메리카의 새로운 대규모 발전소 중 어떤 것도 석유를 연료로 사용하지 않을 것이고, 이는 다른 기술들을 위한 장을 열어준다. 전통적으로 석유를 수입했던 중앙아메리카와 카리브해 국가들은 금세기 초에 10년 동안 높고 변동성이 큰 가격을 겪은 후에 석유 기반 발전소에서 가장 먼저 벗어났다.

① 라틴 아메리카에서의 석유 산업 호황
② 라틴 아메리카에서의 전력 사업 감소
③ 라틴 아메리카에서의 재생 가능 에너지 발전
④ 라틴 아메리카에서의 석유 기반 자원의 적극적인 개발

해설　지문 전반에 걸쳐 라틴 아메리카는 풍력 등의 에너지 자원을 개발하는 데 큰 진전을 이루었으며, 이미 석유에 대한 의존도를 점차 낮추기 시작했고, 2015년에서 2040년 사이에 전력 생산량을 거의 두 배로 늘릴 것으로 예상된다고 설명하고 있다. 따라서 '③ 라틴 아메리카에서의 재생 가능 에너지 발전'이 이 글의 주제이다.

어휘　stride 진전, 발전　exploit 개발하다, 활용하다
incredible 엄청난, 믿을 수 없는　geothermal 지열의
biofuel 바이오 연료　electricity 전력, 전기　sector 부문, 분야
gradually 점차, 점진적으로　dependence 의존
output 생산량, 출력　practically 사실상, 실제로
power plant 발전소　import 수입하다
volatile 변동성이 큰, 변덕스러운　renewable 재생 가능한
aggressive 적극적인, 공격적인

15　독해　전체내용 파악 (제목 파악)　난이도 ★★☆

끊어읽기 해석

Every organization has resources / that it can use / to perform its mission.
모든 조직은 자원이 있다 / 사용할 수 있는 / 임무를 수행하는 데

How well your organization does its job / is partly a function of / how many of those resources you have, / but mostly / it is a function of / how well you use the resources you have, / such as people and money.
당신의 조직이 임무를 얼마나 잘 수행하는가는 / 부분적으로는 ~에 달려 있다 / 당신이 얼마나 많은 자원을 가지고 있느냐 / 하지만 대부분은 / ~에 달려 있다 / 당신이 가진 자원을 얼마나 잘 사용하느냐 / 인력과 돈과 같은

You as the organization's leader / can always make the use of those resources / more efficient and effective, / provided that / you have control of / the organization's personnel and agenda, / a condition / that does not occur automatically.
조직의 리더로서 당신이 / 항상 이러한 자원을 사용할 수 있다 / 더 효율적이고 효과적으로 / ~한 경우에 / 당신이 ~를 통제하는 / 조직의 인력과 의

제를 / 조건인 / 자동으로 발생하지 않는

By managing your people and your money carefully, / by treating the most important things as the most important, / by making good decisions, / and by solving the problems / that you encounter, / you can get the most out of / what you have available to you.
직원과 돈을 신중하게 관리함으로써 / 가장 중요한 문제를 가장 중요한 것으로 취급함으로써 / 올바른 결정을 내림으로써 / 그리고 문제를 해결함으로써 / 당신이 직면한 / 당신은 최대한 활용할 수 있다 / 당신이 이용할 수 있는

해석 모든 조직은 임무를 수행하는 데 사용할 수 있는 자원이 있다. 당신의 조직이 임무를 얼마나 잘 수행하는가는 부분적으로는 당신이 얼마나 많은 자원을 가지고 있느냐에 달려 있지만, 대부분은 당신이 가진 인력과 돈과 같은 자원을 얼마나 잘 사용하느냐에 달려 있다. 조직의 리더로서 당신이 자동으로 발생하지 않는 조건인 조직의 인력과 의제를 통제할 수 있는 경우에, 당신은 항상 이러한 자원을 더 효율적이고 효과적으로 사용할 수 있다. 직원과 돈을 신중하게 관리하고, 가장 중요한 것을 가장 중요한 것으로 취급하고, 올바른 결정을 내리고, 직면한 문제를 해결함으로써, 당신은 당신이 이용할 수 있는 것을 최대한 활용할 수 있다.

① 조직 내 자원의 교환
② 외부 통제를 설정하는 리더의 능력
③ 자원을 최대한 활용하기: 리더의 방법
④ 조직의 기술적 역량: 성공의 장벽

해설 지문 처음에서 조직이 임무를 얼마나 잘 수행하는가의 대부분은 가진 자원을 얼마나 잘 사용하느냐에 달려 있다고 했고, 지문 마지막에서 조직의 리더로서 직원과 돈을 신중하게 관리하고, 직면한 문제를 해결하는 등의 방법을 통해 이용할 수 있는 것을 최대한 활용할 수 있다고 했다. 따라서 '③ 자원을 최대한 활용하기: 리더의 방법'이 이 글의 제목이다.

어휘 organization 조직 resource 자원 mission 임무
partly 부분적으로 efficient 효율적인 effective 효과적인
personnel 인력, 직원 agenda 의제, 안건 condition 조건
occur 발생하다 automatically 자동으로
encounter 직면하다, 마주치다 external 외부의
technical 기술적인, 기술의 capacity 역량, 능력 barrier 장벽

16 독해 논리적 흐름 파악 (무관한 문장 삭제) 난이도 ★★☆

끊어읽기 해석

Critical thinking sounds / like an unemotional process / but it can engage emotions / and even passionate responses.
비판적 사고는 들린다 / 비감정적인 과정처럼 / 하지만 감정을 끌 수 있다 / 그리고 심지어 격렬한 반응을

In particular, / we may not like evidence / that contradicts our own opinions or beliefs.
특히 / 우리는 증거를 좋아하지 않을 수도 있다 / 우리 자신의 의견이나 신념과 모순되는

① If the evidence points in a direction / that is challenging, / that can rouse / unexpected feelings of anger, frustration or anxiety.
만약 그 증거가 방향을 가리키면 / 어려운 / 그것은 일으킬 수 있다 / 예상치 못한 분노, 좌절, 또는 불안의 감정을

② The academic world / traditionally likes to consider itself / as logical and free of emotions, / so / if feelings do emerge, / this can be especially difficult.
학계는 / 전통적으로 그 자체를 생각하기를 좋아한다 / 논리적이고 감정이 없다고 / 그래서 / 감정이 나타나면 / 이것은 특히 어려울 수 있다

③ For example, / looking at the same information / from several points of view / is not important.
예를 들어 / 같은 정보를 보는 것은 / 여러 관점에서 / 중요하지 않다

④ Being able to manage your emotions / under such circumstances / is a useful skill.
당신의 감정을 관리할 수 있는 것은 / 그러한 상황에서 / 유용한 기술이다

If you can remain calm, / and present your reasons logically, / you will be better able to argue your point of view / in a convincing way.
만약 당신이 침착함을 유지할 수 있다면 / 그리고 당신의 이유를 논리적으로 제시한다면 / 당신은 당신의 관점을 더 잘 주장할 수 있을 것이다 / 설득력 있는 방식으로

해석 비판적 사고는 비감정적인 과정처럼 들리지만, 감정과 심지어 격렬한 반응을 끌 수 있다. 특히, 우리는 우리 자신의 의견이나 신념과 모순되는 증거를 좋아하지 않을 수도 있다. ① 만약 그 증거가 어려운 방향을 가리키면, 그것은 예상치 못한 분노, 좌절, 또는 불안의 감정을 불러일으킬 수 있다. ② 학계는 전통적으로 그 자체를 논리적이고 감정이 없다고 생각하기를 좋아하기 때문에, 감정이 나타나면, 이것(비판적 사고)이 특히 어려울 수 있다. ③ 예를 들어, 같은 정보를 여러 관점에서 보는 것은 중요하지 않다. ④ 그러한 상황에서 당신의 감정을 관리할 수 있는 것은 유용한 기술이다. 만약 당신이 침착함을 유지하고, 당신의 이유를 논리적으로 제시할 수 있다면, 당신은 당신의 관점을 설득력 있는 방식으로 더 잘 주장할 수 있을 것이다.

해설 지문 처음에서 비판적 사고는 감정과 격렬한 반응을 끌 수 있다고 한 뒤, ①, ②, ④번에서 비판적 사고가 분노, 좌절, 불안과 같은 감정을 불러일으킬 수 있고, 감정이 나타나면 비판적 사고가 특히 어려울 수 있으며, 감정을 관리할 수 있는 것이 유용한 기술이라고 설명하고 있으므로 모두 첫 문장과 관련이 있다. 그러나 ③번은 같은 정보를 여러 관점에서 보는 것은 중요하지 않다는 내용으로 비판적 사고가 비감정적인 과정처럼 들리지만 감정을 수반할 수 있다는 지문 전반의 내용과 관련이 없다.

어휘 critical thinking 비판적 사고 unemotional 비감정적인, 이지적인
process 과정 engage (마음·주의 등을) 끌다, 관여하다
emotion 감정 passionate 격렬한, 열정적인 evidence 증거
contradict 모순되다 challenging 어려운, 도전적인
rouse 불러일으키다 anger 분노 frustration 좌절
anxiety 불안 academic world 학계 traditionally 전통적으로
logical 논리적인 emerge 나타나다, 떠오르다
circumstance 상황, 환경 convincing 설득력 있는, 그럴듯한

17 독해 논리적 흐름 파악 (문단 순서 배열) 난이도 ★★☆

끊어읽기 해석

Computer assisted language learning (CALL) / is both exciting and frustrating / as a field of research and practice.
컴퓨터 보조 언어 학습(CALL)은 / 흥미롭기도 하고 좌절감을 주기도 한다 / 연구 및 실습 분야로서

(A) Yet / the technology changes so rapidly / that CALL knowledge and skills / must be constantly renewed / to stay apace / of the field.
하지만 / 그 기술은 매우 빠르게 변화한다 / 그래서 CALL 지식과 기술은 / 지속적으로 새로 교체되어야 한다 / 발맞추어 나가기 위해 / 그 분야에

(B) It is exciting / because it is complex, dynamic and quickly changing / —and it is frustrating / for the same reasons.
그것은 흥미롭다 / 그것은 복잡하고, 역동적이며, 빠르게 변화하기 때문

에 / 그리고 그것은 좌절감을 준다 / 같은 이유로

(C) Technology adds dimensions / to the domain of language learning, / requiring new knowledge and skills / for those who wish to apply it / into their professional practice.
기술은 차원을 추가한다 / 언어 학습 영역에 / 새로운 지식과 기술을 요구한다 / 이를 적용하려는 사람들에게 / 그들의 전문적인 실습에

해석 | 컴퓨터 보조 언어 학습(CALL)은 연구 및 실습 분야로서 흥미롭기도 하고 좌절감을 주기도 한다.

(B) 그것은 복잡하고, 역동적이며, 빠르게 변화하기 때문에 흥미롭고, 같은 이유로 좌절감을 준다.
(C) 기술은 언어 학습 영역에 차원을 추가하여 이를 전문적인 실습에 적용하려는 사람들에게 새로운 지식과 기술을 요구한다.
(A) 하지만 그 기술은 매우 빠르게 변화하기 때문에 CALL 지식과 기술은 그 분야에 발맞추어 나가기 위해 지속적으로 새로 교체되어야 한다.

해설 주어진 문장에서 컴퓨터 보조 언어 학습(CALL)은 흥미롭기도 하고 좌절감을 주기도 한다고 하고, (B)에서 그것이(It) 복잡하고, 역동적이며, 빠르게 변화하기 때문에 흥미롭고 좌절감을 준다며 주어진 문장을 부연 설명하고 있다. 이어서 (C)에서 기술은 언어 학습 영역에 차원을 추가한다고 하면서 앞서 언급한 흥미로운 예시를 설명하고, (A)에서 하지만(Yet) 그 기술은 매우 빠르게 변화하기 때문에 지속적으로 새로 교체되어야 한다고 하며 좌절감을 주는 예시를 설명하고 있다. 따라서 ③ (B) – (C) – (A)가 정답이다.

어휘 assist 보조하다, 조력하다 frustrating 좌절감을 주는 field 분야 rapidly 빠르게 constantly 지속적으로, 끊임없이 renew 새로 교체하다, 갱신하다 apace 발맞추어 dynamic 역동적인 dimension 차원 domain 영역 require 요구하다 professional 전문적인, 직업적인

(③) The little mermaid was so startled / that she dove down / under the water.
인어공주는 너무 놀랐다 / 그녀는 뛰어들었다 / 물속으로

(④) And look!
그리고 보아라

It was just as if / all the stars up in heaven / were falling down / on her.
마치 ~인 것 같았다 / 하늘에 있는 모든 별들이 / 떨어지는 것 / 그녀 위로

Never had she seen such fireworks.
그녀는 그런 불꽃놀이를 본 적이 없었다.

해석 | 하지만 그녀는 재빨리 다시 고개를 내밀었다.

인어공주는 선실의 작은 창문으로 헤엄쳐 올라갔고, 파도가 그녀를 들어 올릴 때마다, 그녀는 투명한 유리를 통해 옷을 잘 차려입은 사람들의 무리를 볼 수 있었다. 그들 중에는, 크고 어두운 눈을 가진, 그곳에서 가장 잘생긴 사람인 어린 왕자가 있었다. (①) 그날은 그의 생일이었고, 그래서 신나는 일이 매우 많았다. (②) 어린 왕자가 선원들이 춤을 추고 있는 갑판으로 나왔을 때, 백 개가 넘는 로켓이 하늘로 솟아올라 반짝이는 불빛으로 부서져 하늘을 대낮처럼 밝게 만들었다. (③) 인어공주는 너무 놀라서 물속으로 뛰어들었다. (④) 그리고 보아라! 마치 하늘에 있는 모든 별들이 그녀 위로 떨어지는 것 같았다. 그녀는 그런 불꽃놀이를 본 적이 없었다.

해설 ④번 앞 문장에 인어공주가 물속으로 뛰어들었다는 내용이 있고, ④번 뒤 문장에 마치 하늘에 있는 모든 별들이 그녀 위로 떨어지는 것 같았다는 내용이 있으므로, ④번 자리에 하지만 그녀는 재빨리 다시 고개를 내밀었다는 내용의 주어진 문장이 나와야 지문이 자연스럽게 연결된다.

어휘 the little mermaid 인어공주 cabin (배의) 선실, 오두막 deck 갑판 sailor 선원 glitter 반짝이는 불빛 firework 불꽃놀이

---

18 독해 논리적 흐름 파악 (문장 삽입) 난이도 ★☆☆

끊어읽기 해석

But / she quickly popped her head out / again.
하지만 / 그녀는 재빨리 고개를 내밀었다 / 다시

The little mermaid swam right up / to the small window / of the cabin, / and / every time a wave lifted her up, / she could see a crowd / of well-dressed people / through the clear glass.
인어공주는 헤엄쳐 올라갔다 / 작은 창문으로 / 선실의 / 그리고 / 파도가 그녀를 들어 올릴 때마다 / 그녀는 무리를 볼 수 있었다 / 옷을 잘 차려입은 사람들의 / 투명한 유리를 통해

Among them was a young prince, / the handsomest person there, / with large dark eyes.
그들 중에는 어린 왕자가 있었다 / 그곳에서 가장 잘생긴 사람인 / 크고 어두운 눈을 가진

(①) It was his birthday, / and / that's why there was so much excitement.
그날은 그의 생일이었다 / 그리고 / 그래서 신나는 일이 매우 많았다

(②) When the young prince came out / on the deck, / where the sailors were dancing, / more than a hundred rockets / went up into the sky / and / broke into a glitter, / making the sky / as bright as day.
어린 왕자가 나왔을 때 / 갑판으로 / 선원들이 춤을 추고 있는 / 백 개가 넘는 로켓이 / 하늘로 솟아올랐다 / 그리고 / 불빛으로 부서졌다 / 하늘을 만들며 / 대낮처럼 밝게

---

19 독해 추론 (빈칸 완성 - 단어) 난이도 ★☆☆

끊어읽기 해석

Javelin Research noticed / that not all Millennials are currently in the same stage of life.
Javelin 리서치는 주목했다 / 모든 밀레니얼 세대가 현재 동일한 삶의 단계에 있는 것은 아니라는 점에

While all Millennials were born / around the turn of the century, / some of them are still in early adulthood, / wrestling with new careers / and / settling down.
모든 밀레니얼 세대는 태어났지만 / 세기가 바뀔 무렵에 / 그들 중 일부는 여전히 성인 초기에 있다 / 새로운 직업과 씨름하면서 / 그리고 / 정착하며

On the other hand, / the older Millennials have a home / and / are building a family.
반면에 / 더 나이가 많은 밀레니얼 세대는 집을 가지고 있다 / 그리고 / 가족을 이루고 있다

You can imagine / how having a child / might change your interests and priorities, / so / for marketing purposes, / it's useful to split this generation / into Gen Y.1 and Gen Y.2.
당신은 상상할 수 있다 / 아이를 갖는 것이 어떻게 / 당신의 관심사와 우선순위를 바꿀 수 있는지 / 그러므로 / 마케팅 목적으로 / 이 세대를 나누는 것이 유용하다 / Y.1 세대와 Y.2 세대로

Not only are the two groups culturally different, / but they're in vastly different phases / of their financial life.
두 그룹은 문화적으로 다를 뿐만 아니라 / 그들은 매우 다른 단계에 있다 / 그들의 경제적 생활에서

The younger group is financial beginners, / just starting to show their buying power.
더 어린 그룹은 금융 초보자이다 / 이제 막 그들의 구매력을 보여주기 시작하는

The latter group / has a credit history, / may have their first mortgage / and / is raising young children.
후자의 그룹은 / 신용 이력이 있다 / 그들의 첫 번째 주택 담보 대출을 가지고 있을 수 있다 / 그리고 / 어린아이들을 키우고 있다

The contrast in priorities and needs / between Gen Y.1 and Gen Y.2 / is vast.
우선순위와 필요한 것에 있어서의 차이는 / Y.1 세대와 Y.2 세대 사이의 / 엄청나다

해석   Javelin 리서치는 모든 밀레니얼 세대가 현재 동일한 삶의 단계에 있는 것은 아니라는 점에 주목했다. 모든 밀레니얼 세대는 세기가 바뀔 무렵에 태어났지만, 그들 중 일부는 여전히 성인 초기에 있으며, 새로운 직업과 씨름하면서 정착하고 있다. 반면에, 더 나이가 많은 밀레니얼 세대는 집을 가지고 있고 가족을 이루고 있다. 아이를 갖는 것이 관심사와 우선순위를 어떻게 바꿀 수 있는지 상상할 수 있으므로, 마케팅 목적으로 이 세대를 Y.1세대와 Y.2세대로 나누는 것이 유용하다. 두 그룹은 문화적으로 다를 뿐만 아니라, 그들은 경제적 생활에서 매우 다른 단계에 있다. 더 어린 그룹은 이제 막 그들의 구매력을 보여주기 시작하는 금융 초보자이다. 후자의 그룹은 신용 이력이 있고, 그들의 첫 번째 주택 담보 대출을 가지고 있을 수 있으며 어린아이들을 키우고 있다. Y.1 세대와 Y.2 세대 사이의 우선순위와 필요한 것에 있어서의 차이는 엄청나다.

① 차이
② 감소
③ 반복
④ 능력

해설   지문 처음에서 모든 밀레니얼 세대가 현재 동일한 삶의 단계에 있는 것은 아니라고 했고 지문 전반에 걸쳐 더 나이가 어린 밀레니얼 (Y.1) 세대와 더 나이가 많은 밀레니얼(Y.2) 세대의 문화적, 경제적 차이에 대해 설명하고 있으므로, 빈칸에는 Y.1 세대와 Y.2 세대 사이의 우선순위와 필요한 것에 있어서의 '① 차이'는 엄청나다는 내용이 들어가야 한다.

어휘   settle down 정착하다, 안정되다   priority 우선순위   split 나누다
generation 세대   vastly 매우   phase 단계
financial 금융의, 경제적인   buying power 구매력   latter 후자의
credit history 신용 이력   mortgage 주택 담보 대출
reduction 감소   repetition 반복

20   독해   추론 (빈칸 완성 - 구)   난이도 ★★★

끊어읽기 해석

Cost pressures / in liberalized markets / have different effects / on existing and future hydropower schemes.
비용 압박은 / 자유화된 시장에서의 / 서로 다른 영향을 미친다 / 기존 및 미래의 수력 발전 계획에

Because of the cost structure, / existing hydropower plants / will always be able to earn / a profit.
비용 구조 때문에 / 기존의 수력 발전소는 / 항상 얻을 수 있을 것이다 / 이익을

Because / the planning and construction / of future hydropower schemes / is not a short-term process, / it is not a popular investment, / in spite of low electricity generation costs.
~이기 때문에 / 구상과 건설은 / 미래 수력 발전 계획의 / 단기적인 과정

이 아니다 / 그것은 대중적인 투자가 아니다 / 낮은 전기 생산 비용에도 불구하고

Most private investors / would prefer to finance / more short-term technologies, / leading to / the paradoxical situation / that although an existing hydropower plant seems / to be a cash cow, / nobody wants to invest / in a new one.
대부분의 민간 투자자들은 / 자금을 조달하는 것을 선호할 것이다 / 더 단기적인 기술에 / 이는 이어진다 / 역설적인 상황으로 / 비록 기존 수력 발전소가 ~인 것처럼 보이지만 / 효자 사업 / 누구도 투자하고 싶어 하지 않는다는 / 새로운 것(수력 발전소)에

Where public shareholders/owners (states, cities, municipalities) are involved, / the situation looks very different / because they can see / the importance of the security of supply / and / also appreciate / long-term investments.
공공 주주/소유주(주, 도시, 지방 자치 단체)가 참여하는 경우 / 상황은 매우 다르게 보인다 / 그들이 인식할 수 있기 때문에 / 공급 보안의 중요성을 / 그리고 / 또한 이해한다 / 장기적인 투자를

해석   자유화된 시장에서의 비용 압박은 기존 및 미래의 수력 발전 계획에 서로 다른 영향을 미친다. 비용 구조 때문에, 기존의 수력 발전소는 항상 이익을 얻을 수 있을 것이다. 미래 수력 발전 계획의 구상과 건설은 단기적인 과정이 아니기 때문에, 낮은 전기 생산 비용에도 불구하고 대중적인 투자가 아니다. 대부분의 민간 투자자들은 더 단기적인 기술에 자금을 조달하는 것을 선호할 것이고, 이는 기존 수력 발전소가 효자 사업인 것처럼 보이지만, 누구도 새로운 수력 발전소에 투자하고 싶어 하지 않는다는 역설적인 상황으로 이어진다. 공공 주주/소유주(주, 도시, 지방 자치 단체)가 참여하는 경우, 공급 보안의 중요성을 인식하고 장기적인 투자를 이해할 수 있기 때문에 상황은 매우 다르게 보인다.

① 더 단기적인 기술
② 모든 첨단 기술 산업
③ 공익의 증진
④ 전력 공급의 강화

해설   빈칸 앞 문장에서 미래 수력 발전 계획의 구상과 건설은 단기적인 과정이 아니기 때문에 대중적인 투자가 아니라고 언급하고 있고, 빈칸이 있는 문장에서 기존 수력 발전소가 효자 사업인 것처럼 보이지만 누구도 새로운 수력 발전소에 투자하고 싶어 하지 않는 상황으로 이어진다고 설명하고 있으므로, 빈칸에는 대부분의 민간 투자자들은 '① 더 단기적인 기술'에 자금을 조달하는 것을 선호할 것이라는 내용이 들어가야 한다.

어휘   cost 비용, 가격   pressure 압박, 압력
liberalize 자유화하다, 완화하다   existing 기존의
hydropower 수력 발전력   scheme 계획, 기획   structure 구조
plant 발전소   earn 얻다   profit 이익   short-term 단기적인
investment 투자   private 민간의, 개인의   investor 투자자
paradoxical 역설적인, 모순적인
cash cow 효자 사업, 캐시 카우(시장점유율이 높아 꾸준한 수익을 가져다주지만 시장의 성장 가능성은 낮은 제품이나 산업)   shareholder 주주
municipality 지방 자치 단체   security 보안
appreciate 이해하다, 감사하다   long-term 장기적인
promotion 증진, 진흥   public interest 공익
enhancement 강화, 증대

정답

p.84

01	② 어휘 – 어휘 & 표현	11	③ 어휘 – 생활영어
02	④ 어휘 – 어휘 & 표현	12	② 독해 – 전체내용 파악
03	① 어휘 – 어휘 & 표현	13	② 독해 – 전체내용 파악
04	① 어휘 – 어휘 & 표현	14	④ 독해 – 전체내용 파악
05	④ 어휘 – 어휘 & 표현	15	④ 독해 – 세부내용 파악
06	③ 문법 – 명사절	16	④ 독해 – 논리적 흐름 파악
07	③ 문법 – 형용사와 부사	17	② 독해 – 논리적 흐름 파악
08	① 문법 – 능동태·수동태 & 분사	18	② 독해 – 논리적 흐름 파악
09	④ 어휘 – 생활영어	19	① 독해 – 추론
10	③ 어휘 – 생활영어	20	③ 독해 – 추론

취약영역 분석표

영역	세부 유형	문항 수	소계
어휘	어휘 & 표현	5	/8
	생활영어	3	
문법	명사절	1	/3
	형용사와 부사	1	
	능동태·수동태 & 분사	1	
독해	전체내용 파악	3	/9
	세부내용 파악	1	
	추론	2	
	논리적 흐름 파악	3	
총계			/20

· 자신이 취약한 영역은 '공무원 영어, 이렇게 출제된다!'(문제집 p.8)를 통해 다시 한번 확인하고 학습하시기 바랍니다.

---

01 어휘 어휘&표현 subsequent = following 난이도 ★☆☆

해석 우리의 프로젝트에 대한 추가 설명은 <u>다음의</u> 발표에서 제공될 것이다.
① 필요한
② 다음의
③ 진보한
④ 보충의

어휘 further 추가의 subsequent 다음의 supplementary 보충의

👍 이것도 알면 합격!

subsequent(다음의)의 유의어
= next, succeeding, latter, subsequential

---

02 어휘 어휘&표현 courtesy = politeness 난이도 ★☆☆

해석 관습은 한 집단의 구성원들이 다른 사람들에게 <u>예의</u>를 보이기 위해 따라야 하는 풍습이다. 예를 들어, 재채기를 할 때 "실례합니다"라고 말하는 것은 미국의 관습이다.
① 자선
② 겸손
③ 대담함
④ 예의

어휘 folkways 관습, 어떤 사회 집단의 관행적인 생활 양식·사고방식·행동 courtesy 예의 sneeze 재채기하다 charity 자선 humility 겸손 boldness 대담함 politeness 예의

👍 이것도 알면 합격!

courtesy(예의)의 유의어
= etiquette, civility, respect

---

03 어휘 어휘&표현 bring up = raise 난이도 ★☆☆

해석 이 아이들은 건강한 음식의 규정식을 먹고 <u>길러졌다</u>.
① 길러졌다
② 조언받았다
③ 관찰됐다
④ 통제됐다

어휘 bring up ~를 기르다, 양육하다 observe 관찰하다

👍 이것도 알면 합격!

bring up(~를 기르다)의 유의어
= rear, nurture, foster, parent

---

04 어휘 어휘&표현 do away with = abolish 난이도 ★★☆

해석 노예제도는 19세기까지 미국에서 <u>폐지되지</u> 않았다.
① 폐지되다
② 허가되다
③ 비난받다
④ 정당화되다

어휘 slavery 노예제도 do away with 폐지하다 abolish 폐지하다 consent 허가하다, 승낙하다 criticize 비난하다 justify 정당화하다

👍 이것도 알면 합격!

do away with(폐지하다)와 유사한 의미의 표현
= eliminate, remove, get rid of

05 어휘 어휘&표현 transparency　　　　　난이도 ★★☆

해석 유권자들은 선거 과정을 명확하게 보고 이해할 수 있도록 그것의 투명성을 높여야 한다고 요구했다.
① 기만
② 융통성
③ 경쟁
④ 투명성

어휘 voter 유권자 demand 요구하다 election 선거 deception 기만 flexibility 융통성 transparency 투명성

 이것도 알면 합격!

transparency(투명성)의 유의어
= clarity, clearness, visibility

06 문법 명사절　　　　　난이도 ★★☆

해석 스포츠에서의 뜻밖의 패배, 즉 승리할 것으로 예상되고 상대 팀보다 아마 우세할 것이라고 생각되는 팀이 예상외로 시합에서 지는 경우에 대한 한 가지 이유는, 더 우세한 팀이 그들의 상대 팀을 그들의 지속적인 성공을 위협하는 것으로 인식하지 않았을 수도 있다는 것이다.

해설 ③ what vs. that 완전한 절(the superior team ~ success)을 이끌며 be동사(is)의 보어 자리에 올 수 있는 것은 명사절 접속사 that이므로, 불완전한 절을 이끄는 명사절 접속사 what을 완전한 절을 이끄는 명사절 접속사 that으로 고쳐야 한다.

오답 분석
① 전치사 + 관계대명사 관계사 뒤에 완전한 절(the team ~ the contest)이 왔으므로 '전치사 + 관계대명사' 형태가 올 수 있다. '전치사 + 관계대명사'에서 전치사는 선행사 또는 관계절의 동사에 따라 결정되는데, 문맥상 '스포츠에서 승리할 것으로 예상되는 팀'이라는 의미가 되어야 자연스러우므로 전치사 in(~에서)이 관계대명사 which 앞에 온 in which가 올바르게 쓰였다.
② 현재분사 vs. 과거분사 수식받는 명사(the team)와 분사가 '팀이 승리할 것으로 예상되다'라는 의미의 수동 관계이므로, 과거분사 predicted가 올바르게 쓰였다.
④ 현재분사 vs. 과거분사 감정을 나타내는 분사(threatening)가 보충 설명하는 대상이 감정을 일으키는 주체인 경우 현재분사를 쓰고, 감정을 느끼는 대상인 경우 과거분사를 쓰는데, their opponents가 '그들의 상대 팀을 그들의 성공을 위협하는 것으로 인식하다'라는 의미로 감정을 일으키는 주체이므로 현재분사 threatening이 올바르게 쓰였다.

어휘 upset 뜻밖의 패배 supposedly 아마 opponent 상대 surprisingly 예상외로 superior 더 우세한 perceive 인식하다

 이것도 알면 합격!

감정을 나타내는 분사가 수식 또는 보충 설명하는 대상이 감정을 일으키는 주체인 경우 현재분사를 쓰고, 감정을 느끼는 대상인 경우 과거분사를 쓴다.
(ex) The essay that my sister wrote is interesting.
나의 언니가 쓴 수필은 흥미롭다.
The excited puppy wagged its tail eagerly.
신이 난 강아지가 꼬리를 열심히 흔들었다.

07 문법 형용사와 부사　　　　　난이도 ★★☆

해석 ① 나는 오늘 아침에 갔어야 했는데, 몸이 약간 좋지 않았다.
② 요즘 우리는 예전(에 저축한 것)만큼 많은 돈을 저축하지 않는다.
③ 구조대는 살아 있는 사람을 발견해서 기뻤다.
④ 그 그림은 미술 평론가에 의해 주의 깊게 살펴보아졌다.

해설 ③ 형용사 자리 형용사는 명사나 대명사를 수식하는 자리에 오거나 보어 자리에 오는데, alive(살아 있는)는 보어 자리에만 쓰이며 명사를 앞에서 수식할 수 없으므로, an alive man을 a man alive 또는 '살아 있는'이라는 의미의 형용사 living을 써서 a living man으로 고쳐야 한다.

오답 분석
① 조동사 관련 표현 문맥상 '오늘 아침에 갔어야 했다'라는 의미가 되어야 자연스러운데, '~했어야 했다'는 조동사 관련 표현 should have p.p.를 사용하여 나타낼 수 있으므로, should have gone이 올바르게 쓰였다.
② 원급 | 조동사 관련 표현 '예전만큼 많은 돈을 저축하지 않는다'에서 '예전만큼 많은 돈'은 '~만큼 많은 -'을 나타내는 'as + much + 명사 + as'로 나타낼 수 있으므로 as much money as가 올바르게 쓰였다. 또한 '예전(에 저축한 것)만큼'은 조동사 관련 표현 used to(~하곤 했다)를 써서 나타낼 수 있으므로 we used to가 올바르게 쓰였다.
④ 동사구의 수동태 '자동사 + 전치사'(look at) 형태의 동사구가 수동태가 되어 목적어(The picture)가 주어가 된 경우, 전치사 at이 수동태 동사 뒤에 그대로 남으므로 was looked at이 올바르게 쓰였다.

어휘 ill 몸이 안 좋은 rescue squad 구조대, 구호반 critic 평론가, 비평가

 이것도 알면 합격!

조동사 관련 숙어
• would rather 차라리 ~하는 게 낫다
• would like to ~하고 싶다
• may[might] as well ~하는 편이 더 낫겠다
• may well ~하는 게 당연하다
• cannot ~ too 아무리 ~해도 지나치지 않다
• cannot (help) but ~할 수밖에 없다 (= cannot help + -ing / have no choice but + to 동사원형)

08 문법 능동태·수동태 & 분사　　　　　난이도 ★★☆

해설 ① 5형식 동사의 수동태 | 현재분사 vs. 과거분사 목적격 보어를 갖는 5형식 동사 make(made)가 수동태가 되는 경우 목적격 보어는 수동태 동사 뒤에 남아야 하는데, 감정을 나타내는 분사가 보충 설명하는 대상이 감정을 느끼는 대상(We)이므로 현재분사 touching을 과거분사 touched로 고쳐야 한다. 참고로, 이 문장은 동사 make(made) 대신 be동사(were)를 쓰고, '~에 의해'라는 의미의 전치사 by를 써서 We were touched by his speech로 고치는 것이 가장 자연스럽다.

오답 분석
② 기타 전치사 | 부정대명사 one '비용을 차치하고'는 전치사 숙어 표현 apart from(~을 제외하고)을 사용하여 나타낼 수 있으므로 Apart from its cost가 올바르게 쓰였다. 또한 대명사가 지칭하는 명사(the plan)가 단수이므로 단수 부정대명사 one이 올바르게 쓰였다.
③ 분사구문의 형태 '뜨거운 차를 마시는 동안에'라는 의미를 만들기 위해 시간을 나타내는 부사절 역할을 하는 분사구문 while drinking hot tea가 올바르게 쓰였다. 참고로, 분사구

문의 의미를 분명하게 하기 위해 부사절 접속사 while이 분사구문 앞에 쓰였다.

④ **5형식 동사** 사역동사 make(made)는 목적어와 목적격 보어가 수동 관계일 때 과거분사를 목적격 보어로 취하는 5형식 동사인데, 목적어 him과 목적격 보어가 '그가 적합했다(적합하게 되었다)'라는 의미의 수동 관계이므로 과거분사 suited가 올바르게 쓰였다.

어휘 apart from ~을 차치하고, ~을 제외하고
suit 적합하게 하다, 어울리게 하다

👍 이것도 알면 **합격!**

get, 사역동사, 지각동사는 목적어와 목적격 보어가 수동 관계일 때 목적격 보어로 과거분사를 취할 수 있다. 단, 사역동사 let은 목적어와 목적격 보어가 수동 관계일 때 목적격 보어로 'be + p.p.' 형태를 취한다.

ex Jeremy had the wall ~~paint~~.(→ painted)
Jeremy는 벽이 페인트칠 되게 했다.
→ '페인트칠하다'가 아니라 '페인트칠 되게 하다'라는 의미의 수동 관계이므로 사역동사 have(had)의 목적격 보어로 과거분사(painted)가 온다.

ex He let his dog ~~photograph~~.(→ be photographed)
그는 그의 강아지가 사진 찍히도록 허락했다.
→ '사진을 찍다'가 아니라 '사진이 찍히다'라는 의미의 수동 관계이므로 사역동사 let의 목적격 보어로 'be + p.p.'형태(be photographed)가 온다.

09 **어휘** **생활영어**   Sure. Can I help you with anything?   난이도 ★☆☆

해석
A: 실례합니다, 좀 도와주시겠어요?
B: 물론이죠. 무엇을 도와드릴까요?
A: 저는 인사과를 찾으려고 합니다. 10시에 약속이 있어요.
B: 그것은 3층에 있어요.
A: 그곳에는 어떻게 올라가나요?
B: 모퉁이를 돌아서 엘리베이터를 타세요.

① 우리는 이 상황을 어떻게 처리해야 할지 모르겠습니다.
② 담당자가 누구인지 말씀해 주시겠습니까?
③ 네. 도움이 좀 필요합니다.
④ 물론이죠. 무엇을 도와드릴까요?

해설 도와줄 수 있냐고 묻는 A에게 B가 대답하고, 빈칸 뒤에서 A가 I'm trying to find the Personnel Department(저는 인사과를 찾으려고 합니다)라고 말하고 있으므로, 빈칸에는 '④ 물론이죠, 무엇을 도와드릴까요?(Sure. Can I help you with anything?)'가 오는 것이 자연스럽다.

어휘 personnel department (회사의) 인사과 handle 처리하다, 다루다
in charge 담당인

👍 이것도 알면 **합격!**

도움을 요청할 때 사용할 수 있는 다양한 표현을 알아두자.

· Could you lend me a hand?
저 좀 도와주실 수 있나요?
· Would you mind helping me out with this?
이것을 좀 도와주시겠어요?
· Can you offer some guidance?
안내 좀 해줄 수 있나요?
· I could use your help. Can you spare a few minutes?
당신의 도움이 필요해요. 몇 분만 시간을 내줄 수 있나요?

10 **어휘** **생활영어**   I'm sorry. I promise I'll be more careful from now on.   난이도 ★☆☆

해석
A: 당신이 어제 마지막으로 퇴근하셨죠, 맞아요?
B: 네. 무슨 문제라도 있나요?
A: 오늘 아침에 사무실 전등과 에어컨이 켜져 있는 것을 발견했어요.
B: 정말요? 이런. 제가 어젯밤에 끄는 걸 깜빡했나 봐요.
A: 아마 밤새 켜져 있었을 거예요.
B: 죄송해요. 앞으로 더 조심할 것을 약속할게요.

① 걱정하지 마세요. 이 기계는 잘 작동합니다.
② 맞아요. 모두가 당신과 함께 일하는 것을 좋아합니다.
③ 죄송해요. 앞으로 더 조심할 것을 약속할게요.
④ 안됐군요. 당신은 너무 늦게 퇴근해서 피곤하겠어요.

해설 A가 B에게 아침에 사무실 전등과 에어컨이 켜져 있는 것을 발견했다고 하고 B가 어젯밤에 끄는 것을 깜빡했나 보다고 대답한 후 A가 다시 아마 밤새 켜져 있었을 거라고 말하고 있으므로, 빈칸에는 '③ 죄송해요. 앞으로 더 조심할 것을 약속할게요(I'm sorry. I promise I'll be more careful from now on)'가 오는 것이 자연스럽다.

어휘 get off work 퇴근하다

👍 이것도 알면 **합격!**

직장에서 사용할 수 있는 다양한 표현을 알아두자.

· Let's get down to business.
본론으로 들어갑시다.
· Do you have a moment to discuss something?
잠시 의논할 시간이 있습니까?
· I'll follow up with an email.
이메일로 후속 조치를 취하겠습니다.
· Let's schedule a meeting to go over the details.
세부 사항을 검토하기 위해 회의 일정을 잡읍시다.
· I appreciate your hard work and dedication.
당신의 노고와 헌신에 감사드립니다.

11 **어휘** **생활영어**   It took me about an hour and a half by car.   난이도 ★★☆

해석
① A: 머리를 어떻게 해드릴까요?
B: 머리 색깔이 조금 지겨워요. 염색하고 싶어요.
② A: 지구 온난화를 늦추기 위해 우리가 할 수 있는 일은 무엇입니까?
B: 우선, 대중교통을 더 많이 이용할 수 있습니다.
③ A: Anna, 당신인가요? 너무 오랜만이에요! 이게 얼마 만인가요?
B: 차로 한 시간 반 정도 걸렸어요.
④ A: Paul이 걱정돼요. 그는 불행해 보여요. 제가 어떻게 해야 할까요?
B: 제가 당신이라면, 그가 문제에 대해 말할 때까지 기다릴 거예요.

해설 ③번에서 A는 B에게 너무 오랜만이라며 이게 얼마 만이냐고 묻고 있으므로, 차로 한 시간 반 정도 걸렸다는 B의 대답 '③ It took me about an hour and a half by car(차로 한 시간 반 정도 걸렸어요)'은 어울리지 않는다.

어휘 dye 염색하다 public transportation 대중교통 unhappy 불행한

미용실에서 사용할 수 있는 다양한 표현을 알아두자.

- Would you like a trim or a complete haircut?
  머리를 다듬어 드릴까요, 아니면 완전히 잘라 드릴까요?
- How would you like your bangs?
  앞머리는 어떻게 해드릴까요?
- I'd like to get highlights in my hair.
  머리에 부분 염색을 하고 싶어요.
- Can you give me a layered haircut?
  머리를 층이 있게 잘라줄 수 있나요?

③ 정신 건강 설문조사의 필요성
④ 인간 연결성의 위험성

해설 지문 처음에서 Goleman에 따르면 우리는 다른 사람과 관계를 맺을 때마다 다른 사람의 뇌에 이끌린다고 설명하고 있고, 지문 마지막에서 우리의 뇌는 인간의 상호작용을 갈망한다고 하고 있으므로 '② 사교적인 두뇌'가 이 글의 제목이다.

어휘 dedicate 바치다, 헌신하다 social intelligence 사회적 지능
neuro-sociology 신경 사회학 sociable 사교적인
engage with ~와 관계를 맺다 connectivity 연결(성)
crave 갈망하다 countless 수많은 epidemic 전염병
lifeline 생명의 전화, 생명선 interaction 상호작용

12 독해 전체내용 파악 (제목 파악) 난이도 ★★☆

끊어읽기 해석

Well-known author Daniel Goleman / has dedicated his life / to the science of human relationships.
유명한 작가 Daniel Goleman은 / 그의 인생을 바쳤다 / 인간관계의 과학에

In his book *Social Intelligence* / he discusses results / from neuro-sociology / to explain how sociable / our brains are.
그의 책 『사회적 지능』에서 / 그는 결과에 대해 논한다 / 신경 사회학의 / 얼마나 사교적인지 설명하기 위해 / 우리의 뇌가

According to Goleman, / we are drawn / to other people's brains / whenever we engage / with another person.
Goleman에 따르면, / 우리는 이끌린다 / 다른 사람의 뇌에 / 우리가 관계를 맺을 때마다 / 다른 사람과

The human need for meaningful connectivity with others, / in order to deepen our relationships, / is what we all crave, / and yet there are countless articles and studies / suggesting that we are lonelier / than we ever have been / and loneliness is now a world health epidemic.
다른 사람들과의 의미 있는 연결에 대한 인간의 욕구는 / 우리의 관계를 더 깊어지게 하기 위한 / 우리 모두가 갈망하는 것이다 / 하지만 수많은 기사와 연구들이 있다 / 우리가 더 외롭다는 것을 시사하는 / 우리가 그 어느 때 그랬던 것보다 / 그리고 외로움은 이제 세계적인 보건 전염병이라는 것을 (시사하는)

Specifically, / in Australia, / according to a national Lifeline survey, / more than 80 % of those surveyed believe / our society is becoming a lonelier place.
특히, / 호주에서는, / 국립 '생명의 전화' 설문조사에 따르면, / 조사 대상자의 80퍼센트 이상이 생각한다 / 우리 사회가 점점 더 외로운 공간이 되어가고 있다고

Yet, / our brains crave human interaction.
하지만, / 우리의 뇌는 인간의 상호작용을 갈망한다

해석 유명한 작가 Daniel Goleman은 인간관계의 과학에 그의 인생을 바쳤다. 그는 그의 책 『사회적 지능』에서 우리의 뇌가 얼마나 사교적인지 설명하기 위해 신경 사회학의 결과에 대해 논한다. Goleman에 따르면, 우리는 다른 사람과 관계를 맺을 때마다 다른 사람의 뇌에 이끌린다. 우리의 관계를 더 깊어지게 하기 위한 다른 사람들과의 의미 있는 연결에 대한 인간의 욕구는 우리 모두가 갈망하는 것이지만, 우리가 그 어느 때 그랬던 것보다 더 외롭다는 것과 외로움은 이제 세계적인 보건 전염병이라는 것을 시사하는 수많은 기사와 연구들이 있다. 특히, 호주에서는, 국립 '생명의 전화' 설문조사에 따르면, 조사 대상자의 80퍼센트 이상이 우리의 사회가 점점 더 외로운 공간이 되어가고 있다고 생각한다. 하지만, 우리의 뇌는 인간의 상호작용을 갈망한다.

① 외로운 사람들
② 사교적인 두뇌

13 독해 전체내용 파악 (주제 파악) 난이도 ★★★

끊어읽기 해석

Certainly / some people are born / with advantages / (e.g., physical size for jockeys, / height for basketball players, / an "ear" for music for musicians).
확실히 / 어떤 사람들은 태어난다 / 장점을 가지고 / (예를 들면, 기수들의 신체적 크기, / 농구 선수들의 키, / 음악가들의 '음감')

Yet / only dedication to mindful, deliberate practice / over many years / can turn those advantages into talents / and those talents into successes.
그러나 / 유념하고 신중한 연습에의 헌신만이 / 오랜 세월 동안의 / 이러한 장점들을 재능으로 바꿀 수 있다 / 그리고 그러한 재능들을 성공으로 바꿀 수 있다

Through the same kind of dedicated practice, / people who are not born / with such advantages / can develop talents / that nature put a little farther / from their reach.
같은 종류의 헌신적인 연습을 통해, / 태어나지 않은 사람들은 / 그러한 장점을 갖고 / 재능을 개발할 수 있다 / 자연이 조금 멀리 둔 / 그들이 닿을 수 있는 곳보다

For example, / even though you may feel / that you weren't born / with a talent for math, / you can significantly increase / your mathematical abilities / through mindful, deliberate practice.
예를 들어, / 비록 당신이 느낄지도 모르지만, / 당신이 태어나지 않았다고 / 수학에 대한 재능을 가지고 / 당신은 상당히 높일 수 있다 / 당신의 수학적인 능력을 / 유념하고 신중한 연습을 통해

Or, / if you consider yourself "naturally" shy, / putting in the time and effort / to develop your social skills / can enable you to interact with people / at social occasions / with energy, grace, and ease.
또는, / 만약 당신이 스스로를 '선천적으로' 수줍음이 많다고 생각한다면, / 시간과 노력을 들이는 것은 / 당신의 사회적 기술을 발전시키기 위해 / 당신이 사람들과 상호작용할 수 있도록 해줄 수 있다 / 사회적인 상황에서 / 에너지, 품위, 그리고 편안함을 가지고

해석 확실히 어떤 사람들은 장점을 가지고 태어난다. (예를 들면, 기수들의 신체적 크기, 농구 선수들의 키, 음악가들의 '음감') 그러나 오랜 세월 동안의 유념하고 신중한 연습에의 헌신만이 이러한 장점들을 재능으로, 그리고 그러한 재능들을 성공으로 바꿀 수 있다. 같은 종류의 헌신적인 연습을 통해, 그러한 장점을 갖고 태어나지 않은 사람들은 자연이 그들이 닿을 수 있는 곳보다 조금 멀리 둔 재능을 개발할 수 있다. 예를 들어, 비록 당신이 수학에 대한 재능을 가지고 태어나지 않았다고 느낄지도 모르지만, 당신은 당신의 수학적인 능력을 유념하고 신중한 연습을 통해 상당히 높일 수 있다. 또는, 만약 당신이 스스로를 '선천적으로' 수줍음이 많다고 생각한다면, 당신의 사회적 기술을 발전시키기 위해 시간과 노력을 들이는 것은 당신이 사회적인 상황에서 에너지, 품위, 그리고 편안함을

가지고 사람들과 상호작용할 수 있도록 해줄 수 있다.
① 어떤 사람들이 다른 사람들에 비해 가지고 있는 장점들
② 재능을 기르기 위한 끊임없는 노력의 중요성
③ 수줍은 사람들이 사회적 상호작용에서 겪는 어려움
④ 자신의 장점과 단점을 이해해야 할 필요성

해설 지문 처음에서 오랜 세월 동안 유념하고 신중한 연습에 헌신하는 것만이 선천적인 장점들을 재능으로, 그리고 그러한 재능들을 성공으로 바꿀 수 있다고 설명하고 있고, 지문 중간에서 장점을 갖고 태어나지 않은 사람들도 헌신적인 연습을 통해 재능을 기를 수 있다는 것에 대한 예시를 설명하고 있으므로, '② 재능을 기르기 위한 끊임없는 노력의 중요성'이 이 글의 주제이다.

어휘 physical 신체의 jockey (경마에서 특히 직업적으로 말을 타는) 기수
dedication 헌신 mindful 유념하는, 주의를 기울이는
deliberate 신중한 significantly 상당히, 현저하게
mathematical 수학적인 consider 생각하다, 고려하다
enable ~을 할 수 있게 하다 interact 상호작용하다, 교류하다
occasion 상황 grace 품위 ease 편안함 constant 끊임없는
cultivate 기르다, 계발하다

14 독해 전체내용 파악 (요지 파악) 난이도 ★★★

끊어읽기 해석

Dr. Roossinck and her colleagues / found by chance / that a virus increased resistance to drought / on a plant / that is widely used / in botanical experiments.
Roossinck 박사와 그녀의 동료들은 / 우연히 발견했다 / 바이러스가 가뭄에 대한 저항을 증가시켰다는 것을 / 식물에서 / 널리 사용되는 / 식물 실험에

Their further experiments with a related virus showed / that was true / of 15 other plant species, too.
관련된 바이러스에 대한 그들의 추가 실험은 보여주었다 / 그것이 적용되었다는 것을 / 15종의 다른 식물들에게도

Dr. Roossinck is now doing experiments / to study another type of virus / that increases heat tolerance / in a range of plants.
Roossinck 박사는 현재 실험을 하고 있다 / 또 다른 종류의 바이러스를 연구하기 위한 / 내열성을 높이는 / 다양한 식물에서

She hopes to extend her research / to have a deeper understanding / of the advantages / that different sorts of viruses give / to their hosts.
그녀는 그녀의 연구를 확장하기를 희망한다 / 더 깊이 이해하기 위해 / 이점들에 대해 / 다양한 종류의 바이러스가 주는 / 그들의 숙주에게

That would help to support a view / which is held by an increasing number of biologists, / that many creatures rely on symbiosis, / rather than being self-sufficient.
그것은 관점을 지지하는 데 도움이 될 것이다 / 점점 더 많은 생물학자들이 주장하는 / 많은 생물들이 공생에 의존한다는 / 자급자족하기보다는

해석 Roossinck 박사와 그녀의 동료들은 식물 실험에 널리 사용되는 식물에서 바이러스가 가뭄에 대한 저항을 증가시켰다는 것을 우연히 발견했다. 관련된 바이러스에 대한 그들의 추가 실험은 그것이 15종의 다른 식물들에게도 적용되었다는 것을 보여주었다. Roossinck 박사는 현재 다양한 식물에서 내열성을 높이는 또 다른 종류의 바이러스를 연구하기 위한 실험을 하고 있다. 그녀는 다양한 종류의 바이러스가 그들의 숙주에게 주는 이점들에 대해 더 깊이 이해하기 위해 그녀의 연구를 확장하기를 희망한다. 그것은 점점 더 많은 생물학자들이 주장하는, 많은 생물들이 자급자족하기보다는 공생에 의존한다는 관점을 지지하는 데 도움이 될 것이다.
① 바이러스는 생물학적 존재의 자급자족을 보여준다.

② 생물학자들은 식물을 바이러스가 없는 상태로 유지하기 위해 모든 것을 해야 한다.
③ 공생의 원리는 감염된 식물에게 적용될 수 없다.
④ 바이러스는 때때로 숙주에게 해를 끼치기보다는 이롭다.

해설 지문 처음에서 Roossinck 박사와 그녀의 동료들이 식물 실험에 널리 사용되는 식물에서 바이러스가 가뭄에 대한 저항을 증가시켰다는 것을 우연히 발견했다고 했고, 지문 마지막에서 Roossinck 박사는 다양한 종류의 바이러스가 그들의 숙주에게 주는 이점들에 대해 더 깊이 이해하기 위해 그녀의 연구를 확장하기를 희망한다고 설명하고 있다. 따라서 '④ 바이러스는 때때로 숙주에게 해를 끼치기보다는 이롭다'가 이 글의 요지이다.

어휘 colleague 동료 by change 우연히 resistance 저항
botanical 식물의 heat tolerance 내열성 a range of 다양한
host 숙주 symbiosis 공생 self-sufficient 자급자족하는
demonstrate 보여주다, 나타내다 principle 원리
infect 감염시키다

15 독해 세부내용 파악 (내용 불일치 파악) 난이도 ★★☆

끊어읽기 해석

The traditional way / of making maple syrup / is interesting.
전통적인 방법은 / 단풍나무시럽을 만드는 / 흥미롭다

A sugar maple tree produces a watery sap each spring, / when there is still lots of snow on the ground.
사탕단풍나무는 매년 봄에 물기를 머금은 수액을 생산한다 / 그때 땅에는 여전히 많은 눈이 있다

To take the sap / out of the sugar maple tree, / a farmer makes a slit / in the bark / with a special knife, / and puts a "tap" on the tree.
수액을 얻기 위해 / 사탕단풍나무에서 / 농부는 기다란 구멍을 낸다 / 나무 껍질에 / 특수한 칼로 / 그리고 나무에 '꼭지'를 끼운다

Then the farmer hangs a bucket from the tap, / and the sap drips into it.
그러고 나서 농부는 꼭지에 양동이를 매단다 / 그리고 수액은 그 안으로 떨어진다

That sap is collected and boiled / until a sweet syrup remains / —forty gallons of sugar maple tree "water" make / one gallon of syrup.
그 수액은 수집되어 끓여진다 / 달콤한 시럽이 남을 때까지 / 40갤런의 사탕단풍나무 '물'이 만든다 / 1갤런의 시럽을

That's a lot of buckets, a lot of steam, and a lot of work.
그것은 많은 양동이, 많은 열기, 그리고 많은 일이다

Even so, / most of maple syrup producers are family farmers / who collect the buckets by hand / and boil the sap into syrup themselves.
그럼에도 불구하고, / 대부분의 단풍나무시럽 생산자들은 가족 농부들이다 / 양동이를 직접 수거하고 / 수액을 시럽으로 직접 끓이는

해석 단풍나무시럽을 만드는 전통적인 방법은 흥미롭다. 사탕단풍나무는 매년 봄에 물기를 머금은 수액을 생산하는데, 그때 땅에는 여전히 많은 눈이 있다. 사탕단풍나무에서 수액을 얻기 위해, 농부는 특수한 칼로 나무껍질에 기다란 구멍을 내고, 나무에 '꼭지'를 끼운다. 그러고 나서 농부는 꼭지에 양동이를 매달고, 수액은 그 안으로 떨어진다. 그 수액은 수집되어 달콤한 시럽이 남을 때까지 끓여지는데, 40갤런의 사탕단풍나무 '물'이 1갤런의 시럽을 만든다. 그것은 많은 양동이, 많은 열기, 그리고 많은 일이다. 그럼에도 불구하고, 대부분의 단풍나무시럽 생산자들은 양동이를 직접 수거하고 수액을 시럽으로 직접 끓이는 가족 농부들이다.

해설 지문 마지막에서 대부분의 단풍나무시럽 생산자들은 양동이를 직접 수거하고 수액을 시럽으로 직접 끓이는 가족 농부들이라고 했으므로, '④ 단풍나무시럽을 만들기 위해 기계로 수액 통을 수거한다'는 것은 지문의 내용과 일치하지 않는다.

어휘 traditional 전통적인 watery 물기를 머금은 sap 수액
slit 기다란 구멍, 틈 bark 나무껍질 tap 꼭지 bucket 양동이
steam 열기

16 독해 논리적 흐름 파악 (무관한 문장 삭제) 난이도 ★☆☆

끊어읽기 해석

> I once took a course in short-story writing / and during that course / a renowned editor of a leading magazine / talked to our class.
> 나는 한때 단편 소설 쓰기 수업을 들은 적이 있다 / 그리고 그 수업에서 / 일류 잡지의 유명한 편집자가 / 우리 학급에 강연했다
>
> ① He said / he could pick up / any one of the dozens of stories / that came to his desk every day / and after reading a few paragraphs / he could feel / whether or not the author liked people.
> 그는 말했다 / 그는 고를 수 있다고 / 수십 개의 이야기들 중 아무거나 / 매일 그의 책상으로 오는 / 그리고 몇 단락을 읽고 나면 / 그는 느낄 수 있다고 / 그 작가가 사람을 좋아하는지 아닌지를
>
> ② "If the author doesn't like people," / he said, / "people won't like his or her stories."
> "만약 작가가 사람을 좋아하지 않는다면," / 그는 말했다 / "사람들은 그나 그녀의 이야기를 좋아하지 않을 것입니다."
>
> ③ The editor kept stressing / the importance of being interested in people / during his talk on fiction writing.
> 그 편집자는 계속 강조했다 / 사람들에게 관심을 갖는 것의 중요성을 / 그가 소설 쓰기에 대해 강연을 하는 동안
>
> ④ Thurston, a great magician, said that / every time he went on stage / he said to himself, / "I am grateful because I'm successful."
> 훌륭한 마술사인 Thurston은 말했다 / 그가 무대에 오를 때마다 / 혼잣말을 했다고 / "성공해서 감사합니다."라고
>
> At the end of the talk, / he concluded, / "Let me tell you again. / You have to be interested in people / if you want to be a successful writer of stories."
> 강연 말미에, / 그는 끝맺었다 / "다시 한번 말씀드리겠습니다 / 여러분은 사람들에게 관심을 가져야 합니다 / 여러분이 성공적인 이야기 작가가 되고 싶다면"

해석 나는 한때 단편 소설 쓰기 수업을 들은 적이 있는데, 그 수업에서 일류 잡지의 유명한 편집자가 우리 학급에게 강연했다. ① 그는 매일 그의 책상으로 오는 수십 개의 이야기들 중 아무거나 고를 수 있고, 몇 단락을 읽고 나면 그 작가가 사람을 좋아하는지 아닌지를 느낄 수 있다고 말했다. ② "만약 작가가 사람을 좋아하지 않는다면, 사람들은 그나 그녀의 이야기를 좋아하지 않을 것입니다."라고 그는 말했다. ③ 그 편집자는 소설 쓰기에 대해 강연을 하는 동안 사람들에게 관심을 갖는 것의 중요성을 계속 강조했다. ④ 훌륭한 마술사인 Thurston은 그가 무대에 오를 때마다 "성공해서 감사합니다."라고 혼잣말을 했다고 말했다. 강연 말미에, 그는 "다시 한번 말씀드리겠습니다. 여러분이 성공적인 이야기 작가가 되고 싶다면, 사람들에게 관심을 가져야 합니다."라며 끝맺었다.

해설 지문 처음에서 화자의 학급에서 유명한 편집자가 강연했다고 하고, 이어서 ①, ②, ③번에서 그 편집자가 소설 쓰기에 대해 강연하는 동안 사람들에게 관심을 갖는 것의 중요성에 대해 강조한 내용을 설명하고 있다. 그러나 ④번은 훌륭한 마술사가 무대에 오를 때마다 "성공해서 감사합니다."라고 혼잣말을 했다는 내용으로, 성공적인 이야기 작가가 되고 싶다면 사람들에게 관심을 가져야 한다고 강조한 편집자의 강연에 대한 지문 전반의 내용과 관련이 없다.

어휘 renowned 유명한 editor 편집자 leading 일류의, 선두적인
dozens of 수십의 paragraph 단락 stress 강조하다

17 독해 논리적 흐름 파악 (문단 순서 배열) 난이도 ★★☆

끊어읽기 해석

> Just a few years ago, / every conversation about artificial intelligence (AI) / seemed to end / with an apocalyptic prediction.
> 불과 몇 년 전만 해도, / 인공지능(AI)에 대한 모든 대화는 / 끝나는 것처럼 보였다 / 종말론적 예측으로
>
> (A) More recently, / however, / things have begun to change.
> 더 최근에는, / 하지만, / 상황이 바뀌기 시작했다
>
> AI has gone / from being a scary black box / to something people can use / for a variety of use cases.
> AI는 ~이 되었다 / 무서운 블랙박스에서 / 사람들이 사용할 수 있는 것 / 다양한 사용의 사례로
>
> (B) In 2014, / an expert in the field said that, / with AI, / we are summoning the demon, / while a Nobel Prize winning physicist said / that AI could spell the end of the human race.
> 2014년에, / 이 분야의 한 전문가가 말했다 / AI로 우리는 악마를 소환하고 있다고 / 반면 노벨상을 수상한 한 물리학자는 말했다 / AI가 인류의 종말을 가져올 수 있다고
>
> (C) This shift is because / these technologies are finally being explored / at scale / in the industry, / particularly for market opportunities.
> 이러한 변화는 왜냐하면 / 이러한 기술이 마침내 탐구되고 있기 때문이다 / 대규모로 / 업계에서 / 특히 시장 기회를 위해

해석
> 불과 몇 년 전만 해도, 인공지능(AI)에 대한 모든 대화는 종말론적 예측으로 끝나는 것처럼 보였다.

(B) 2014년에, 이 분야의 한 전문가가 우리는 AI로 악마를 소환하고 있다고 말한 반면 노벨상을 수상한 한 물리학자는 AI가 인류의 종말을 가져올 수 있다고 말했다.

(A) 하지만, 더 최근에는 상황이 바뀌기 시작했다. AI는 무서운 블랙박스에서 사람들이 다양한 사용의 사례로 사용할 수 있는 것이 되었다.

(C) 이러한 변화는 이러한 기술이 마침내 업계에서, 특히 시장 기회를 위해 대규모로 탐구되고 있기 때문이다.

해설 주어진 문장에서 불과 몇 년 전만 해도, 인공지능에 대한 모든 대화는 종말론적 예측으로 끝나는 것처럼 보였다고 설명한 후, (B)에서 이 분야(인공지능)의 한 전문가와 노벨상을 수상한 한 물리학자는 우리가 AI로 악마를 소환하고 있고, AI가 인류의 종말을 가져올 수 있다고 말했다고 언급하고 있다. 이어서 (A)에서 하지만(however) 더 최근에는 상황이 바뀌기 시작했다고 설명하고, 마지막으로 (C)에서 이러한 변화(This shift)는 이러한 기술(AI)이 마침내 업계에서 대규모로 탐구되고 있기 때문이라고 설명하고 있다. 따라서 ② (B) – (A) – (C)가 정답이다.

어휘 artificial intelligence 인공지능 apocalyptic 종말론적인
prediction 예측 expert 전문가 summon 소환하다
demon 악마 physicist 물리학자
spell ~을 가져오다, ~의 결과를 초래하다 shift 변화 industry 업계

끊어읽기 해석

Yet, / requests for such self-assessments are pervasive / throughout one's career.
그러나, / 이러한 자기 평가에 대한 요청은 만연하다 / 한 사람의 경력 전반에 걸쳐

The fiscal quarter just ended.
회계 분기가 막 끝났다

Your boss comes by / to ask you / how well you performed / in terms of sales / this quarter.
당신의 상사가 방문한다 / 당신에게 묻기 위해 / 당신이 얼마나 잘했는지 / 매출액 측면에서 / 이번 분기에

How do you describe your performance? As excellent? Good? Terrible?
당신은 당신의 성과를 어떻게 설명하는가? 훌륭하다고? 좋다고? 끔찍하다고?

(①) Unlike when someone asks you / about an objective performance metric / (e.g., how many dollars in sales / you brought in this quarter), / how to subjectively describe your performance / is often unclear.
누군가가 당신에게 질문하는 것과 달리 / 객관적인 성과 측정 기준에 대해 / (예를 들어, 얼마나 많은 매출액을 / 이번 분기에 당신이 가져왔는지) / 당신의 성과를 주관적으로 묘사하는 방법은 / 종종 불분명하다

There is no right answer.
정답은 없다

(②) You are asked / to subjectively describe / your own performance / in school applications, in job applications, in interviews, in performance reviews, in meetings—the list goes on.
당신은 요청받는다 / 주관적으로 묘사하도록 / 당신 자신의 성과를 / 학교 지원서, 입사 지원서, 면접, 성과 검토, 회의, 그리고 계속되는 목록에서

(③) How you describe your performance / is what we call / your level of self-promotion.
당신이 당신의 성과를 어떻게 묘사하느냐가 / 우리가 부르는 것이다 / 자기 홍보 수준이라고

(④) Since self-promotion is a pervasive part of work, / people who do more self-promotion / may have better chances / of being hired, being promoted, and getting a raise or a bonus.
자기 홍보는 일의 만연한 한 부분이기 때문에, / 자기 홍보를 더 많이 하는 사람들은 / 더 좋은 기회를 가질 수 있다 / 고용되고, 승진되고, 연봉 인상이나 상여금을 받을

해석 회계 분기가 막 끝났다. 당신의 상사가 당신에게 이번 분기에 매출액 측면에서 당신이 얼마나 잘했는지 묻기 위해 방문한다. 당신은 당신의 성과를 어떻게 설명하는가? 훌륭하다고? 좋다고? 끔찍하다고? 누군가가 당신에게 객관적인 성과 측정 기준(예를 들어, 이번 분기에 당신이 얼마나 많은 매출액을 가져왔는지)에 대해 질문하는 것과 달리, 당신의 성과를 주관적으로 묘사하는 방법은 종종 불분명하다. 정답은 없다. ② 그러나, 이러한 자기 평가에 대한 요청은 한 사람의 경력 전반에 걸쳐 만연하다. 당신은 학교 지원서, 입사 지원서, 면접, 성과 검토, 회의, 그리고 계속되는 목록에서 당신 자신의 성과를 주관적으로 묘사하도록 요청받는다. 당신이 당신의 성과를 어떻게 묘사하느냐가 우리가 자기 홍보 수준이라고 부르는 것이다. 자기 홍보는 일의 만연한 한 부분이기 때문에, 자기 홍보를 더 많이 하는 사람들은 고용되고, 승진되고, 연봉 인상이나 상여금을 받을 더 좋은 기회를 가질 수 있다.

해설 ②번 앞 문장에서 누군가가 당신에게 객관적인 성과 측정 기준에 대해 질문하는 것과 달리, 당신의 성과를 주관적으로 묘사하는 방법은 종종 불분명하다고 했고, ②번 뒤 문장에서 당신은 학교 지원서, 입사 지원서, 면접, 성과 검토, 회의, 그리고 계속되는 목록에서 당신 자신의 성과를 주관적으로 묘사하도록 요청받는다고 했다. 따라서 ②번에 그러나(Yet) 이러한 자기 평가에 대한 요청은 한 사람의 경력 전반에 걸쳐 만연하다는 내용의 주어진 문장이 들어가야 지문이 자연스럽게 연결된다.

어휘 self-assessment 자기 평가 pervasive 만연한
fiscal quarter 회계 분기 objective 객관적인 metric 측정 기준
subjectively 주관적으로 self-promotion 자기 홍보

끊어읽기 해석

We live / in the age of anxiety.
우리는 살고 있다 / 불안의 시대에

Because being anxious can be an uncomfortable and scary experience, / we resort to conscious or unconscious strategies / that help reduce anxiety in the moment / — watching a movie or TV show, eating, video-game playing, and overworking.
불안한 것은 불편하고 무서운 경험이 될 수 있기 때문에, / 우리는 의식적이거나 무의식적인 전략에 의존한다 / 그 순간 불안을 줄이는 데 도움이 되는 / 즉, 영화나 TV 쇼를 보거나, 먹거나, 비디오 게임을 하거나, 과로하는 것이다

In addition, / smartphones also provide a distraction / any time of the day or night.
게다가, / 스마트폰 또한 주의를 산만하게 한다 / 낮이나 밤의 어느 때라도

Psychological research has shown / that distractions serve as a common anxiety avoidance strategy.
심리학적 연구는 보여주었다 / 주의 산만이 일반적인 불안 회피 전략의 역할을 한다는 것을

Paradoxically, / however, / these avoidance strategies make anxiety worse / in the long run.
역설적으로, / 그러나, / 이러한 회피 전략은 불안을 더 악화시킨다 / 장기적으로

Being anxious is like getting into quicksand / —the more you fight it, the deeper you sink.
불안한 것은 유사에 빠지는 것과 같다 / 즉, 당신이 모래와 더 싸울수록 더 깊이 가라앉는다

Indeed, / research strongly supports a well-known phrase / that "What you resist, persists."
실제로, / 연구는 유명한 구절을 강력하게 지지한다 / '당신이 저항하는 것은 지속된다'라는

해석 우리는 불안의 시대에 살고 있다. 불안한 것은 불편하고 무서운 경험이 될 수 있기 때문에, 우리는 그 순간 불안을 줄이는 데 도움이 되는 의식적이거나 무의식적인 전략에 의존한다. 즉, 영화나 TV 쇼를 보거나, 먹거나, 비디오 게임을 하거나, 과로하는 것이다. 게다가, 스마트폰 또한 낮이나 밤의 어느 때라도 주의를 산만하게 한다. 심리학적 연구는 주의 산만이 일반적인 불안 회피 전략의 역할을 한다는 것을 보여주었다. 그러나 역설적으로, 이러한 회피 전략은 장기적으로 불안을 더 악화시킨다. 불안한 것은 유사에 빠지는 것과 같다. 즉, 당신이 모래와 더 싸울수록 더 깊이 가라앉는다. 실제로, 연구는 '당신이 저항하는 것은 지속된다'라는 유명한 구절을 강력하게 지지한다.

① 역설적으로
② 운 좋게
③ 중립적으로
④ 창조적으로

해설 빈칸 앞 문장에서 심리학적 연구는 주의 산만이 일반적인 불안 회피 전략의 역할을 한다는 것을 보여주었다고 하고, 빈칸이 있는 문장에서 그러나 이러한 회피 전략은 장기적으로 불안을 더 악화시킨다고 했으므로 빈칸에는 대조적인 의미를 나타내는 '① 역설적으로'가 들어가야 한다.

어휘 anxiety 불안 uncomfortable 불편한 conscious 의식적인
unconscious 무의식적인 strategy 전략
in the moment 그 순간에 overwork 과로하다
distraction 주의 산만 psychological 심리학적인
avoidance 회피 quicksand 유사(올라서면 빠져버리는 젖은 모래층)
resist 저항하다 persist 지속되다 paradoxically 역설적으로
neutrally 중립적으로

20 독해 추론 (빈칸 완성 - 구) 난이도 ★★☆

끊어읽기 해석

How many different ways / do you get information?
얼마나 많은 다른 방법으로 / 당신은 정보를 얻는가?

Some people might have six different kinds of communications / to answer / —text messages, voice mails, paper documents, regular mail, blog posts, messages on different online services.
일부 사람들은 여섯 가지 다른 종류의 통신 수단을 가질지도 모른다 / 응답해야 할 / 문자 메시지, 음성 메일, 종이 문서, 일반 메일, 블로그 게시물, 서로 다른 온라인 서비스의 메시지 등

Each of these is a type of in-box, / and each must be processed / on a continuous basis.
각 항목은 받은 편지함 유형이다 / 그리고 각각은 처리되어야 한다 / 지속적으로

It's an endless process, / but it doesn't have to be exhausting or stressful.
그것은 끝이 없는 과정이다 / 그러나 피곤해하거나 스트레스를 받을 필요는 없다

Getting your information management down / to a more manageable level / and into a productive zone / starts by minimizing the number of in-boxes you have.
당신의 정보 관리를 낮추는 것은 / 보다 관리하기 쉬운 수준으로 / 그리고 생산적인 영역으로 가져오는 것은 / 당신이 가진 받은 편지함의 수를 최소화하는 것부터 시작한다

Every place you have to go / to check your messages / or to read your incoming information / is an in-box, / and the more you have, / the harder it is to manage everything.
당신이 가야 하는 모든 곳은 / 메시지를 확인하기 위해 / 또는 들어오는 정보를 읽기 위해 / 받은 편지함이다 / 그리고 그것을 더 많이 가질수록 / 모든 것을 관리하기가 더 어렵다

Cut the number of in-boxes you have / down to the smallest number possible / for you still to function in the ways you need to.
당신이 가진 받은 편지함의 수를 / 가능한 한 최소로 줄여라 / 당신이 필요한 방식으로 계속 기능할 수 있도록

해석 당신은 얼마나 많은 다른 방법으로 정보를 얻는가? 일부 사람들은 문자 메시지, 음성 메일, 종이 문서, 일반 메일, 블로그 게시물, 서로 다른 온라인 서비스의 메시지 등 응답해야 할 여섯 가지 다른 종류의 통신 수단을 가질지도 모른다. 각 항목은 받은 편지함 유형이며, 각각은 지속적으로 처리되어야 한다. 그것은 끝이 없는 과정이지만, 피곤해하거나 스트레스를 받을 필요는 없다. 당신의 정보 관리를 보다 관리하기 쉬운 수준으로 낮추고 생산적인 영역으로 가져오는 것은 당신이 가진 받은 편지함의 수를 최소화하는 것부터 시작한다. 메시지를 확인하거나 들어오는 정보를 읽기 위해

당신이 가야 하는 모든 곳은 받은 편지함이며, 그것을 더 많이 가질수록 모든 것을 관리하기가 더 어렵다. 당신이 필요한 방식으로 계속 기능할 수 있도록 당신이 가진 받은 편지함의 수를 가능한 한 최소로 줄여라.

① 한 번에 여러 목표를 설정하는 것
② 들어오는 정보에 스스로 몰두하는 것
③ 당신이 가진 받은 편지함의 수를 최소화하는 것
④ 당신이 열정을 가지고 있는 정보를 선택하는 것

해설 빈칸 뒤 문장에서 메시지를 확인하거나 들어오는 정보를 읽기 위해 당신이 가야 하는 모든 곳은 받은 편지함이며, 그것을 더 많이 가질수록 모든 것을 관리하기가 더 어렵다고 설명하고, 당신이 필요한 방식으로 계속 기능할 수 있도록 당신이 가진 받은 편지함의 수를 가능한 한 최소로 줄이라고 하고 있다. 따라서 빈칸에는 당신의 정보 관리를 보다 관리하기 쉬운 수준으로 낮추고 생산적인 영역으로 가져오는 것은 '③ 당신이 가진 받은 편지함의 수를 최소화하는 것'부터 시작한다는 내용이 들어가야 한다.

어휘 document 문서 in-box 받은 편지함, 수신함
process 처리하다; 과정 continuous 지속적인
exhausting 피곤하게 하는 management 관리
productive 생산적인 immerse 몰두시키다

정답

p.90

01	② 어휘 – 어휘&표현	**11**	③ 독해 – 논리적 흐름 파악
02	① 어휘 – 어휘&표현	**12**	③ 독해 – 논리적 흐름 파악
03	④ 어휘 – 어휘&표현	**13**	④ 독해 – 전체내용 파악
04	④ 어휘 – 어휘&표현	**14**	③ 독해 – 논리적 흐름 파악
05	② 문법 – 수 일치&능동태·수동태	**15**	③ 독해 – 세부내용 파악
06	② 문법 – 전치사&병치·도치·강조 구문	**16**	③ 독해 – 세부내용 파악
07	① 문법 – 우리말과 영작문의 의미상 불일치	**17**	① 독해 – 전체내용 파악
08	① 문법 – 병치·도치·강조 구문&시제	**18**	① 독해 – 추론
09	④ 어휘 – 생활영어	**19**	② 독해 – 추론
10	④ 어휘 – 생활영어	**20**	② 독해 – 추론

취약영역 분석표

영역	세부 유형	문항 수	소계
어휘	어휘&표현	4	/6
	생활영어	2	
문법	수 일치&능동태·수동태	1	/4
	전치사&병치·도치·강조 구문	1	
	우리말과 영작문의 의미상 불일치	1	
	병치·도치·강조 구문&시제	1	
독해	전체내용 파악	2	/10
	세부내용 파악	2	
	추론	3	
	논리적 흐름 파악	3	
총계			**/20**

· 자신이 취약한 영역은 '공무원 영어, 이렇게 출제된다!'(문제집 p.8)를 통해 다시 한번 확인하고 학습하시기 바랍니다.

---

01 어휘 어휘&표현 flexible = adaptable 난이도 ★☆☆

해석 학교 교사들은 학생들의 서로 다른 능력 수준에 대응하기 위해 융통성 있어야 한다.
① 강경한
② 융통성 있는
③ 솔직한
④ 열정적인

어휘 flexible 융통성 있는, 유연한 cope with ~에 대응하다
adaptable 융통성 있는 passionate 열정적인

👍 이것도 알면 **합격!**

flexible(융통성 있는)의 유의어
= compatible, adjustable, versatile, malleable

---

02 어휘 어휘&표현 vary = change 난이도 ★☆☆

해석 농작물 수확량은 달라지며, 일부 지역에서는 개선되고 다른 지역에서는 줄어든다.
① 달라지다
② 줄어들다
③ 커지다
④ 포함하다

어휘 vary 달라지다 decline 줄어들다 expand 커지다, 확장하다
include 포함하다

👍 이것도 알면 **합격!**

vary(달라지다)의 유의어
= differ, fluctuate, alternate, digress

---

03 어휘 어휘&표현 with respect to = in terms of 난이도 ★★☆

해석 나는 내 교육에 관하여 어느 누구에게도 열등감을 느끼지 않는다.
① ~의 위험이 있는
② ~에도 불구하고
③ ~을 위하여
④ ~에 관하여

어휘 feel inferior 열등감을 느끼다 with respect to ~에 관하여
in favor of ~을 위하여 in terms of ~에 관하여

👍 이것도 알면 **합격!**

with respect to(~에 관하여)와 유사한 의미의 표현
= with regard to, in regards to, in connection with, on the subject of

---

04 어휘 어휘&표현 run out of 난이도 ★★☆

해석 때때로 우리는 다음 봉급일 훨씬 이전에 돈을 다 써버린다.
① ~으로 변하다
② 다시 시작하다
③ ~을 참고 견디다
④ ~을 다 써버리다

어휘 start over 다시 시작하다 put up with ~을 참고 견디다
run out of ~을 다 써버리다

👍 이것도 알면 **합격!**

run out of(~을 다 써버리다)와 유사한 의미의 표현
= be out of, finish up, exhaust one's supply of, deplete

05　문법　수 일치 & 능동태·수동태　난이도 ★★☆

해석　① 그는 나에게 왜 매일 같이 계속해서 돌아왔는지 물었다.

② 아이들이 일 년 내내 갖고 싶어 했던 장난감들이 최근에 버려졌다.

③ 그녀는 언제나 도와줄 준비가 되어 있는 사람이다.

④ 곤충들은 우리에게는 분명하지 않은 냄새에 종종 끌린다.

해설　② 주어와 동사의 수 일치 | 능동태·수동태 구별　주어(Toys)가 복수 명사이고, 주어와 동사 사이의 수식어 거품(children ~ long)은 동사의 수 결정에 영향을 주지 않으므로 단수 동사 has를 복수 동사 have로 고쳐야 한다. 또한, 주어(Toys)와 동사가 '장난감들이 버려지다'라는 의미의 수동 관계이므로 능동태 have recently discarded를 수동태 have recently been discarded로 고쳐야 한다. 참고로, 부사가 수동형 동사를 수식할 때 부사는 조동사와 과거분사의 사이나 과거분사의 뒤에 올 수 있으므로 능동태 have recently discarded를 수동태 have been recently discarded로 고쳐도 맞다.

오답 분석　① 의문문의 어순　의문문이 다른 문장 안에 포함된 간접 의문문은 '의문사 + 주어 + 동사'의 어순이 되어야 하므로 why I kept coming back ~이 올바르게 쓰였다. 참고로, 동사 keep은 동명사를 목적어로 취하는 동사이므로 kept 뒤에 coming이 쓰였다.

③ 주격 관계절의 수 일치　주격 관계절(who ~ hand) 내의 동사는 선행사(someone)에 수 일치시켜야 하므로 단수 동사 is가 올바르게 쓰였다.

④ 능동태·수동태 구별 | 주격 관계절의 수 일치　주어(Insects)와 동사가 '곤충들이 끌리다'라는 의미의 수동 관계이므로 수동태 are often attracted가 올바르게 쓰였다. 또한, 주격 관계절 (that ~ us) 내의 동사는 선행사(scents)에 수 일치시켜야 하므로 복수 동사 are의 부정형 aren't가 올바르게 쓰였다.

어휘　day after day 매일 같이　discard 버리다
lend a helping hand 도와주다　attract 끌다, 유인하다
scent 냄새, 향기　obvious 분명한

👍 이것도 알면 **합격!**

think, believe, imagine, suppose, suggest 등이 동사로 쓰인 의문문에 간접 의문문이 포함되면 의문사가 문장의 맨 앞으로 온다는 것을 알아두자.

(ex) Do you suppose? + What will they do about the problem?
　　당신은 생각하나요?　+ 그들은 그 문제에 대해 무엇을 할 것인가요?

　　→ What do you suppose they will do about the problem?
　　　당신은 그들이 그 문제에 대해 무엇을 할 것이라고 생각하나요?

06　문법　전치사 & 병치·도치·강조 구문　난이도 ★★☆

해석　① 당신은 그 종이의 양면에 글을 쓸 수 있다.

② 나의 집은 나에게 든든함, 따뜻함, 그리고 사랑의 느낌을 준다.

③ 자동차 사고의 수가 증가하고 있다.

④ 당신이 무엇을 할 생각인지 내가 알았더라면, 나는 당신을 말렸을 것이다.

해설　② 전치사 자리 | 병치 구문　전치사 뒤에는 명사 역할을 하는 것이 와야 하고, 접속사 and로 연결된 병치 구문에서는 같은 품사끼리 연결되어야 한다. and 앞과 뒤에 명사 security, love가 나열되고 있으므로 and 앞의 형용사 warm을 명사 warmth로 고쳐야 한다.

오답 분석　① 수량 표현　복수 취급하는 수량 표현 both 뒤에는 복수 명사가 와야 하므로 복수 명사 sides가 올바르게 쓰였다.

③ 수량 표현의 수 일치　주어 자리에 단수 취급하는 수량 표현 'the number of + 명사'(The number of car accidents)가 왔으므로 단수 동사 is가 올바르게 쓰였다.

④ 가정법 도치　if절에서 if가 생략되어 동사 Had가 주어(I) 앞으로 온 가정법 과거완료 구문 Had I realized ~가 왔으므로, 주절에도 가정법 과거완료를 만드는 '주어 + would + have p.p.'의 형태가 와야 한다. 따라서 I would have stopped가 올바르게 쓰였다.

어휘　security 든든함, 안정　on the rise 증가하는
intend ~하려고 생각하다, 의도하다

👍 이것도 알면 **합격!**

수량 표현 the number of와 a number of의 차이를 알아두자.

the number of (단수 취급하는 수량 표현)	+ 단수 명사/복수 명사/불가산 명사 + 단수 동사
a number of (복수 취급하는 수량 표현)	+ 복수 명사 + 복수 동사

07　문법　우리말과 영작문의 의미상 불일치　난이도 ★★☆

해설　① 우리말과 영작문의 의미상 불일치　동사 afford는 조동사 can의 부정형 cannot과 함께 'cannot + afford + to 부정사'의 형태로 '~할 수 없다, ~할 여력이 없다'라는 의미로 쓰인다. 따라서 '단 한 푼의 돈도 낭비할 수 없다'라는 의미를 만들기 위해서는 긍정형 조동사 can을 부정형 조동사 cannot으로 고쳐야 한다.

오답 분석　② 수동태로 쓸 수 없는 동사　동사 fade는 목적어를 갖지 않는 자동사이고 수동태로 쓸 수 없으므로 능동태 faded가 올바르게 쓰였다.

③ 조동사 관련 표현　조동사 관련 표현 have no alternative but(~외에는 대안이 없다) 뒤에는 to 부정사가 와야 하므로 to resign이 올바르게 쓰였다.

④ 현재진행 시제 | 전치사 1: 시간　현재진행 시제를 사용해 가까운 미래에 일어나기로 예정되어 있는 일이나 곧 일어나려고 하는 일을 표현할 수 있으므로 현재진행 시제 am aiming이 올바르게 쓰였다. 또한, 전치사 in은 숫자를 포함한 시간 표현 (five years) 앞에 쓰일 때 '~ 후에'라는 의미를 나타낼 수 있으므로 in five years가 올바르게 쓰였다.

어휘　afford ~할 수 있다　fade 사라지다　resign 사임하다
aim ~할 작정이다

👍 이것도 알면 **합격!**

수동태로 쓸 수 없는 자동사를 추가로 알아두자.

• remain ~인 채로 남아 있다	• emerge 나타나다, 부상하다
• arise 발생하다	• wait 기다리다
• occur 일어나다	• consist 이루어져 있다

08　문법　병치·도치·강조 구문 & 시제　난이도 ★★☆

해설　① 도치 구문: 부사구 도치 1 | 과거완료 시제　부정을 나타내는 부사구(No sooner)가 강조되어 문장 맨 앞에 나오면 주어와 조동사가 도치되어 '조동사 + 주어 + 동사'의 어순이 되어야 하는

데, 문맥상 '내가 식사를 마친' 시점이 '내가 다시 배고프기 시작한' 시점보다 더 이전에 일어난 일이므로 과거완료 시제가 쓰여야 한다. 따라서 No sooner I have finishing을 No sooner had I finished로 고쳐야 한다.

오답 분석
② 조동사 관련 표현 | 숙어 표현 조동사처럼 쓰이는 표현 have to(~해야 한다) 뒤에는 동사원형이 와야 하므로 동사원형 pay가 올바르게 쓰였다. 참고로, '조만간'은 부사 역할을 하는 숙어 표현 sooner or later(조만간)로 나타낼 수 있다.
③ 숙어 표현 '독서와 정신의 관계는 운동과 신체의 관계와 같다'는 A is to B what C is to D(A가 B인 것은 C가 D인 것과 관계와 같다)를 사용하여 나타낼 수 있으므로 Reading is to ~ to the body가 올바르게 쓰였다.
④ 동명사 관련 표현 '결국 일하게 되었다'는 동명사 관련 표현 end up -ing(결국 ~하게 되다)를 사용하여 나타낼 수 있으므로 ended up working ~이 올바르게 쓰였다.

어휘 sooner or later 조만간   medicine 의학   accounting 회계

👍 이것도 알면 **합격!**
부정과 제한을 나타내는 부사(구)가 강조되어 문장의 맨 앞에 나올 때 주어와 조동사가 도치되어 '조동사 + 주어 + 동사'의 어순이 된다는 것을 알아두자.
(ex) Rarely does the city experience flooding.
　　　　　 조동사　주어　　　동사
그 도시는 홍수를 거의 겪지 않는다.

09　어휘　생활영어　I didn't do good in history when I was in high school.　난이도 ★☆☆

해석 ① A: 나는 이 신문사가 자기 의견을 고집하지 않아서 좋아.
　　　　 B: 그래서 그곳이 판매 부수가 가장 많은 거야.
　　② A: 그렇게 차려입은 이유가 있니?
　　　　 B: 응, 나는 오늘 중요한 면접이 있어.
　　③ A: 나는 연습 중에는 공을 똑바로 칠 수 있지만 경기 중에는 그러지 못해.
　　　　 B: 나한테도 그런 일이 자주 일어나.
　　④ A: 캔버스에 그리고 싶은 어떤 특별한 주제가 있니?
　　　　 B: 나는 고등학교 때 역사 과목을 잘하지 못했어.

해설 ④번에서 A는 B에게 캔버스에 그리고 싶은 주제가 있는지 질문하고 있으므로, 고등학교 때 역사 과목을 잘하지 못했다는 B의 대답 '④ I didn't do good in history when I was in high school(나는 고등학교 때 역사 과목을 잘하지 못했어)'은 어울리지 않는다.

어휘 opinionated 자기 의견을 고집하는, 독선적인
　　 circulation 판매 부수, 순환   subject 주제, 과목

👍 이것도 알면 **합격!**
do를 포함하는 다양한 표현을 추가로 알아두자.
· do over ~을 다시 하다
· do without ~ 없이 해내다
· do something in ~을 다치게 하다
· do something up (단추 등을) 채우다, 잠그다

10　어휘　생활영어　I can't thank you enough for helping me with it.　난이도 ★★☆

해석
> A: 이봐! 지리 시험은 어땠어?
> B: 나쁘지 않았어, 고마워. 나는 그저 그게 끝나서 기뻐! 너는 어때? 과학 시험은 어땠어?
> A: 오, 그건 정말 결과가 좋았어. 네가 그걸 도와줘서 얼마나 고마운지 몰라. 그것 때문에 너한테 한턱내야 해.
> B: 도움이 되어서 나도 기뻐. 그러면, 다음 주에 예정된 수학 시험을 준비하지 않을래?
> A: 물론이지. 같이 공부하자.
> B: 좋은 생각이야. 나중에 보자.

① 이 일로 너 스스로 자책하는 건 무의미해
② 여기서 너를 만날 줄은 몰랐어
③ 사실, 우리는 매우 실망했어
④ 네가 그걸 도와줘서 얼마나 고마운지 몰라

해설 과학 시험이 어땠냐는 B의 질문에 대해 A가 정말 결과가 좋았다고 하며 B에게 자신이 한턱내야 한다고 대답하자, 빈칸 뒤에서 다시 B가 It's my pleasure(도움이 되어서 나도 기뻐)라고 말하고 있다. 따라서 빈칸에는 '④ I can't thank you enough for helping me with it(네가 그걸 도와줘서 얼마나 고마운지 몰라)'이 들어가야 자연스럽다.

어휘 geography 지리(학)   owe (남의 은혜를 입었으므로) ~해야 한다
　　 treat 한턱, 대접   beat oneself 자책하다   disappointed 실망한

👍 이것도 알면 **합격!**
고마움을 표현할 때 사용할 수 있는 표현
· Please accept my deepest thanks. 제 깊은 감사를 받아주세요.
· I'm really grateful for your support. 지지해주셔서 정말 감사해요.
· I'd like to express my gratitude. 제 감사함을 표현하고 싶어요.

11　독해　논리적 흐름 파악 (문단 순서 배열)　난이도 ★★☆

끊어읽기 해석

> For people who are blind, / everyday tasks / such as sorting through the mail or doing a load of laundry / present a challenge.
> 시각장애가 있는 사람들에게 / 일상적인 일들은 / 우편물을 분류하거나 빨래를 많이 하는 것과 같은 / 도전을 제기한다
>
> (A) That's the thinking behind Aira, / a new service that enables its thousands of users / to stream live video of their surroundings / to an on-demand agent, / using either a smartphone or Aira's proprietary glasses.
> 그것은 Aira의 이면에 있는 생각이다 / 그것의 수천 명의 사용자들이 할 수 있게 해주는 새로운 서비스인 / 그들 주변 환경의 실시간 영상을 스트리밍하는 것을 / 언제든지 에이전트에게 / 스마트폰이나 Aira의 전매 안경을 사용하여
>
> (B) But what if they could "borrow" the eyes of someone / who could see?
> 하지만 만약 그들이 누군가의 눈을 '빌릴' 수 있다면 어떻겠는가 / 앞을 볼 수 있는
>
> (C) The Aira agents, / who are available 24/7, / can then answer questions, describe objects / or guide users through a location.
> Aira 에이전트는 / 24시간 연중무휴로 이용할 수 있는 / 질문에 답하거나, 사물을 묘사할 수 있다 / 혹은 위치 추적을 통해 사용자들에게 길을 안내한다

해석 | 시각장애가 있는 사람들에게, 우편물을 분류하거나 빨래를 많이 하는 것과 같은 일상적인 일들은 도전을 제기한다.

(B) 하지만 만약 그들이 앞을 볼 수 있는 누군가의 눈을 '빌릴' 수 있다면 어떻겠는가?

(A) 그것은 수천 명의 사용자들이 스마트폰이나 Aira의 전매 안경을 사용하여 그들 주변 환경의 실시간 영상을 언제든지 에이전트에게 스트리밍할 수 있게 해주는 새로운 서비스인 Aira의 이면에 있는 생각이다.

(C) 24시간 연중무휴로 이용할 수 있는 Aira 에이전트는 질문에 답하거나, 사물을 묘사하거나, 위치 추적을 통해 사용자들에게 길을 안내할 수 있다.

해설 주어진 문장에서 우편물을 분류하는 것과 같은 일상적인 일들이 시각장애가 있는 사람들에게는 도전을 제기할 정도로 어려운 일이라고 설명한 후, (B)에서 만약 그들(they)이 앞을 볼 수 있는 누군가의 눈을 빌릴 수 있다면 어떠할 것 같은지에 대해 의문을 제기하고 있다. 이어서 (A)에서 그것(That)은 사용자들이 그들 주변 환경의 실시간 영상을 언제든지 에이전트에게 스트리밍할 수 있게 해주는 새로운 서비스인 Aira의 이면에 있는 생각이라고 설명하면서, 마지막으로 (C)에서 Aira의 기능에 대해 설명하고 있다. 따라서 ③ (B) – (A) – (C)가 정답이다.

어휘 sort 분류하다 enable ~을 할 수 있게 하다
stream 스트리밍하다(음악 파일이나 동영상 파일을 내려받거나 저장하여 재생하지 않고 인터넷에 연결된 상태에서 실시간으로 재생하다)
proprietary 전매의, 독점의 borrow 빌리다 describe 묘사하다
location 위치 추적

---

12 독해 논리적 흐름 파악 (문장 삽입)   난이도 ★★☆

끊어읽기 해석

The comparison of the heart to a pump, / however, / is a genuine analogy.
심장을 펌프에 비유하는 것은 / 그러나 / 진정한 비유이다

An analogy is a figure of speech / in which two things are asserted to be alike / in many respects that are quite fundamental.
비유란 수사적 표현이다 / 그것에서 두 개의 사물은 서로 비슷한 것으로 가정된다 / 상당히 근본적인 여러 측면에서

Their structure, the relationships of their parts, or the essential purposes they serve / are similar, / although the two things are also greatly dissimilar.
그것들의 구조, 그것들 일부의 관계, 혹은 그것들이 제공하는 본질적인 목적은 / 유사하다 / 하지만 그 두 가지 사물은 대단히 다른 것이기도 하다

Roses and carnations are not analogous.
장미와 카네이션은 비유적이지 않다

(①) They both have stems and leaves / and may both be red in color.
그것들은 둘 다 줄기와 잎을 가지고 있다 / 그리고 둘 다 빨간색일 수도 있다

(②) But they exhibit these qualities / in the same way; / they are of the same genus.
하지만 그것들은 이러한 특성을 보여준다 / 동일한 방식으로 / 그것들은 같은 속이다

(③) These are disparate things, / but they share important qualities: / mechanical apparatus, possession of valves, ability to increase and decrease pressures, / and capacity to move fluids.
이것들은 서로 다른 것들이다 / 하지만 그것들은 중요한 특성을 공유한다 /

기계 장치, 밸브의 보유, 압력을 증가시키고 감소시키는 능력 / 그리고 유체를 움직일 수 있는 능력

(④) And the heart and the pump exhibit these qualities / in different ways and in different contexts.
그리고 심장과 펌프는 이러한 특성들을 보여준다 / 다른 방식과 다른 맥락에서

해석 비유란 수사적 표현으로, 그것(비유)에서 두 개의 사물은 상당히 근본적인 여러 측면에서 서로 비슷한 것으로 가정된다. 그것들의 구조, 그것들 일부의 관계, 혹은 그것들이 제공하는 본질적인 목적은 유사하지만, 그 두 가지 사물은 대단히 다른 것이기도 하다. 장미와 카네이션은 비유적이지 않다. 그것들은 둘 다 줄기와 잎을 가지고 있고 둘 다 빨간색일 수도 있다. 하지만 그것들은 동일한 방식으로 이러한 특성을 보여주는 것이며, 이는 그것들이 같은 속이기 때문이다. ③ 그러나, 심장을 펌프에 비유하는 것은 진정한 비유이다. 이것들은 서로 다른 것들이지만, 그것들은 기계 장치, 밸브의 보유, 압력을 증가시키고 감소시키는 능력, 그리고 유체를 움직일 수 있는 능력과 같은 중요한 특성을 공유한다. 그리고 심장과 펌프는 다른 방식과 다른 맥락에서 이러한 특성들을 보여준다.

해설 ③번 앞부분에 비유에서 비슷한 것으로 가정되는 두 가지 사물은 본질적인 목적 등의 여러 측면에서 유사하지만, 대단히 다른 것이기도 하다고 설명한 후, 장미와 카네이션을 예시로 들며 그것들은 같은 속이기 때문에 비유적이지 않다는 내용이 있다. 또한 ③번 뒤 문장에 심장과 펌프는 서로 다른 것들(disparate things)이지만 중요한 특성을 공유하고, 다른 방식과 다른 맥락에서 이러한 특성들을 보여준다고 하며 두 가지 사물이 비유적이라고 설명하는 내용이 있다. 따라서 ③번에 그러나(however) 심장을 펌프에 비유하는 것은 진정한 비유라고 하는 내용의 주어진 문장이 들어가야 지문이 자연스럽게 연결된다.

어휘 comparison 비유, 비교 genuine 진정한, 진짜의 analogy 비유
similar 유사한, 비슷한 dissimilar 다른 analogous 비유적인
stem 줄기 exhibit 보여주다, 전시하다 genus 속, 종류
mechanical 기계의 apparatus 장치 possession 보유, 소유
fluid 유체 context 맥락

---

13 독해 전체내용 파악 (제목 파악)   난이도 ★★☆

끊어읽기 해석

One of the areas / where efficiency can be optimized / is the work force, / through increasing individual productivity / —defined as the amount of work (products produced, customers served) an employee handles / in a given time.
영역 중 하나는 / 효율성이 최적화될 수 있는 / 인력이다 / 개별 생산성을 늘림으로써 / 직원이 처리하는 작업량(생산된 제품, 고객 서비스)으로 정의되는 / 주어진 시간 내에

In addition to making sure you have invested / in the right equipment, environment, and training / to ensure optimal performance, / you can increase productivity / by encouraging staffers / to put an end to a modern-day energy drain: multitasking.
당신이 투자했는지를 확인하는 것에 더해 / 올바른 장비, 환경 및 교육에 / 최적의 성과를 보장하기 위해 / 당신은 생산성을 높일 수 있다 / 직원들을 장려함으로써 / 오늘날의 에너지 낭비인 한꺼번에 여러 일을 처리하는 것을 중단하도록

Studies show / it takes 25 to 40 percent longer / to get a job done / when you're simultaneously trying / to work on other projects.
연구들은 보여준다 / 25에서 40퍼센트 더 오래 걸린다는 것을 / 작업을 완료하는 데 / 당신이 동시에 ~하려 할 때 / 다른 프로젝트들을 수행하려고

To be more productive, / says Andrew Deutscher, / vice president of business development at consulting firm The Energy Project, / "do one thing, uninterrupted, / for a sustained period of time."
더 생산적이기 위해 / Andrew Deutscher는 말한다 / 컨설팅 회사인 The Energy Project의 사업 개발 담당 부사장인 / "한 가지 일을 하라, 중단 없이 / 지속적인 기간 동안"

해석 주어진 시간 내에 직원이 처리하는 작업량(생산된 제품, 고객 서비스)으로 정의되는 개별 생산성을 늘림으로써 효율성이 최적화될 수 있는 영역 중 하나는 인력이다. 최적의 성과를 보장하기 위해 당신이 올바른 장비, 환경 및 교육에 투자했는지를 확인하는 것에 더해, 당신은 직원들이 오늘날의 에너지 낭비인 한꺼번에 여러 일을 처리하는 것을 중단하도록 장려함으로써 생산성을 높일 수 있다. 연구들은 당신이 동시에 다른 프로젝트들을 수행하려고 할 때 작업을 완료하는 데 25에서 40퍼센트 더 오래 걸린다는 것을 보여준다. 더 생산적이기 위해, 컨설팅 회사인 The Energy Project의 사업 개발 담당 부사장인 Andrew Deutscher는 "지속적인 기간 동안 중단 없이 한 가지 일을 하라"고 말한다.

① 인생에서 어떻게 더 많은 선택지를 만드는지
② 매일의 신체적 기능을 어떻게 향상시키는지
③ 한꺼번에 여러 일을 처리하는 것은 더 나은 효율성을 위한 해결책이다
④ 더 좋은 효율성을 위해 한 번에 한 가지 일을 해라

해설 지문 중간에서 직원들이 한꺼번에 여러 일을 처리하는 것을 중단하도록 장려함으로써 생산성을 높일 수 있다고 언급하면서, 동시에 다른 프로젝트들을 수행할 경우 작업을 완료하는 데 시간이 더 걸린다는 연구 결과들을 설명하고 있고, 이어서 지문의 후반에서는 더 생산적이기 위해 지속적인 기간 동안 중단 없이 한 가지 일을 하라고 한 컨설팅 전문가의 말을 인용하고 있다. 따라서 '④ 더 좋은 효율성을 위해 한 번에 한 가지 일을 해라'가 이 글의 제목이다.

어휘 efficiency 효율성 optimize 최적화하다 productivity 생산성 handle 처리하다 ensure 보장하다 drain 낭비; 배수하다 multitask 한꺼번에 여러 일을 처리하다 simultaneously 동시에 uninterrupted 중단 없이 sustained 지속적인, 한결같은 enhance 향상시키다, 강화하다

14 독해 논리적 흐름 파악 (무관한 문장 삭제) 난이도 ★★☆

끊어읽기 해석

The skill to have a good argument is critical / in life.
좋은 논쟁을 하는 기술은 매우 중요하다 / 인생에서

But it's one / that few parents teach / to their children.
하지만 그것은 ~한 것이다 / 극소수의 부모들만이 가르치는 / 그들의 아이들에게

① We want to give kids a stable home, / so we stop siblings from quarreling / and we have our own arguments behind closed doors.
우리는 아이들에게 안정적인 가정을 만들어주고 싶어 한다 / 그래서 우리는 형제자매들이 언쟁하는 것을 막는다 / 그리고 우리 자신의 논쟁은 비밀로 한다

② Yet if kids never get exposed to disagreement, / we may eventually limit their creativity.
그러나 만약 아이들이 전혀 의견 차이에 노출되지 않는다면 / 우리는 결국 그들의 창의력을 제한하게 될지도 모른다

③ Children are most creative / when they are free to brainstorm / with lots of praise and encouragement / in a peaceful environment.

아이들은 가장 창의적이다 / 그들이 자유롭게 브레인스토밍을 할 수 있을 때 / 많은 칭찬과 격려로 / 평화로운 환경에서

④ It turns out / that highly creative people often grow up / in families full of tension.
밝혀졌다 / 대단히 창의적인 사람들은 대개 자라는 것으로 / 갈등이 넘치는 가정에서

They are not surrounded / by fistfights or personal insults, / but real disagreements.
그들은 둘러싸여 있지 않다 / 주먹다짐이나 인신공격적인 모욕으로 / 그것이 아니라 진정한 의견 차이로

When adults in their early 30s were asked / to write imaginative stories, / the most creative ones came / from those whose parents had the most conflict a quarter-century earlier.
30대 초반의 어른들이 요청을 받았을 때 / 상상의 이야기를 쓰라고 / 가장 창의적인 것들은 나왔다 / 25년 전에 부모가 가장 많은 갈등을 겪었던 사람들에게서

해석 좋은 논쟁을 하는 기술은 인생에서 매우 중요하다. 하지만 그것은 극소수의 부모만이 그들의 아이들에게 가르치는 것이다. ① 우리는 아이들에게 안정적인 가정을 만들어주고 싶어서, 형제자매들이 언쟁하는 것을 막고 우리 자신의 논쟁은 비밀로 한다. ② 그러나 만약 아이들이 전혀 의견 차이에 노출되지 않는다면, 우리는 결국 그들의 창의력을 제한하게 될지도 모른다. ③ 아이들은 평화로운 환경에서 많은 칭찬과 격려로 자유롭게 브레인스토밍을 할 수 있을 때 가장 창의적이다. ④ 대단히 창의적인 사람들은 대개 갈등이 넘치는 가정에서 자라는 것으로 밝혀졌다. 그들은 주먹다짐이나 인신공격적인 모욕이 아니라, 진정한 의견 차이로 둘러싸여 있다. 30대 초반의 어른들이 상상의 이야기를 쓰라고 요청을 받았을 때, 가장 창의적인 것들은 25년 전에 부모가 가장 많은 갈등을 겪었던 사람들에게서 나왔다.

해설 지문 처음에서 좋은 논쟁을 하는 기술이 인생에서 매우 중요하지만 이를 가르치는 부모가 거의 없다고 한 뒤, ①번에서 우리는 아이들에게 안정적인 가정을 만들어주기 위해 우리 자신의 논쟁을 숨긴다고 하며 그 이유를 설명하고 있다. 이어서 ②번에서 그러나(Yet) 만약 아이들이 전혀 의견 차이에 노출되지 않는다면, 결국 아이들의 창의력을 제한하게 될지도 모른다고 하고, ④번에서 대단히 창의적인 사람들은 대개 갈등이 넘치는 가정에서 자라는 것으로 밝혀졌다고 하며 그러한 사람들의 특징을 설명하고 있다. 그러나 ③번은 아이들이 평화로운 환경에서 많은 칭찬과 격려로 자유롭게 브레인스토밍을 할 때 가장 창의적이라는 내용으로, 좋은 논쟁을 하는 것이 창의력에 중요하다는 지문 전반의 내용과 관련이 없다.

어휘 argument 논쟁, 언쟁 stable 안정적인 behind closed doors 비밀로 disagreement 의견 차이 praise 칭찬 tension 갈등, 긴장 fistfight 주먹다짐 personal 인신공격적인, 개인의 insult 모욕 imaginative 상상의, 상상력이 풍부한 conflict 갈등

15 독해 세부내용 파악 (내용 불일치 파악) 난이도 ★☆☆

끊어읽기 해석

Christopher Nolan is an Irish writer / of some renown in the English language.
Christopher Nolan은 아일랜드의 작가이다 / 영문학에서 어느 정도 유명한

Brain damaged since birth, / Nolan has had little control / over the muscles of his body, / even to the extent of having difficulty in swallowing food.

태어날 때부터 뇌가 손상되어서 / Nolan은 거의 통제하지 못했다 / 몸의 근육을 / 음식을 삼키는 것조차 어려울 정도로

He must be strapped to his wheelchair / because he cannot sit up by himself.
그는 휠체어에 묶여 있어야 한다 / 그는 스스로 똑바로 앉아 있을 수 없기 때문에

Nolan cannot utter recognizable speech sounds.
Nolan은 알아들을 수 있는 말소리를 낼 수 없다.

Fortunately, though, / his brain damage was such / that Nolan's intelligence was undamaged / and his hearing was normal; / as a result, / he learned to understand speech / as a young child.
하지만 다행히도 / 그의 뇌 손상은 그러한 것이었다 / Nolan의 지능이 손상되지 않은 / 그리고 그의 청력은 정상이었다 / 그 결과 / 그는 말을 이해하는 법을 배웠다 / 어린아이였을 때

It was only many years later, though, / after he had reached 10 years, / and after he had learned to read, / that he was given a means / to express his first words.
그러나 수년이 지나고 나서야 / 그가 10살이 되고 / 그리고 그가 읽는 법을 배운 후에야 / 비로소 그에게 수단이 주어졌다 / 그의 첫마디를 표현할 수 있는

He did this / by using a stick / which was attached to his head / to point to letters.
그는 이것을 했다 / 막대기를 사용하여 / 그의 머리에 붙어있는 / 글자를 가리키기 위해

It was in this 'unicorn' manner, / letter-by-letter, / that he produced an entire book of poems and short stories, / *Dam-Burst of Dreams*, / while still a teenager.
그것은 이런 '유니콘' 방식이었다 / 한 글자씩 / 그가 시집과 단편소설을 만든 / 『댐-꿈의 폭발』 / 그가 아직 10대일 때

해석 Christopher Nolan은 영문학에서 어느 정도 유명한 아일랜드의 작가이다. 태어날 때부터 뇌가 손상되어서, Nolan은 음식을 삼키는 것조차 어려울 정도로 몸의 근육을 거의 통제하지 못했다. 그는 스스로 똑바로 앉아 있을 수 없기 때문에 휠체어에 묶여 있어야 한다. Nolan은 알아들을 수 있는 말소리를 낼 수 없다. 하지만 다행히도, 그의 뇌 손상은 Nolan의 지능이 손상되지 않은 정도였고 그의 청력은 정상이어서, 그 결과, 그는 어린아이였을 때 말을 이해하는 법을 배웠다. 그러나 그가 10살이 되고, 읽는 법을 배운 후 수년이 지나고 나서야, 비로소 그에게 그의 첫마디를 표현할 수 있는 수단이 주어졌다. 그는 글자를 가리키기 위해 그의 머리에 붙어있는 막대기를 사용하여 이것을 했다. 그가 아직 10대일 때 시집과 단편소설 『댐-꿈의 폭발』을 한 글자씩 만든 것은 이런 '유니콘' 방식이었다.

해설 지문 중간에서 그의 뇌 손상은 지능이 손상되지 않은 정도였고 그의 청력은 정상이었다고 했으므로, '③ Christopher Nolan은 청각 장애로 인해 들을 수 없었다'는 것은 지문의 내용과 다르다.

어휘 renown 유명한 swallow 삼키다 strap 묶다
utter (입으로 어떤 소리를) 내다
recognizable 알아들을 수 있는, 인식할 수 있는 attach 붙이다
manner 방식

16 **독해** 세부내용 파악 (내용 불일치 파악) 난이도 ★☆☆

끊어읽기 해석

In many Catholic countries, / children are often named after saints; / in fact, / some priests will not allow parents / to name their children / after soap opera stars or football players.
많은 가톨릭 국가에서 / 아이들은 종종 성인들의 이름을 따서 이름이 지어

진다 / 실제로 / 일부 성직자들은 부모들에게 허락하지 않을 것이다 / 그들 아이들의 이름을 짓는 것을 / 드라마 스타나 축구 선수의 이름을 따서

Protestant countries tend to be more free about this; / however, in Norway, / certain names such as Adolf are banned completely.
개신교 국가들은 이것에 대해 더 자유로운 경향이 있다 / 하지만 노르웨이에서는 / 아돌프와 같은 특정 이름들이 완전히 금지되어 있다

In countries where infant mortality is very high, / such as in Africa, / tribes only name their children / when they reach five years old, / the age in which their chances of survival begin to increase.
유아 사망률이 매우 높은 국가에서 / 아프리카와 같이 / 부족들은 오직 그들 아이들의 이름을 짓는다 / 그들이 다섯 살이 되었을 때 / 생존 가능성이 높아지기 시작하는 나이인

Until that time, / they are referred to / by the number of years they are.
그때까지 / 그들(아이들)은 불린다 / 그들의 나이 햇수로

Many nations in the Far East give their children a unique name / which in some way describes / the circumstances of the child's birth or the parents' expectations and hopes for the child.
극동의 많은 나라들은 그들의 자녀에게 독특한 이름을 지어준다 / 어떤 식으로든 묘사하는 / 아이의 출생 환경이나 아이에 대한 부모들의 기대와 희망을

Some Australian aborigines can keep changing their name / throughout their life / as the result of some important experience / which has in some way proved their wisdom, creativity or determination.
일부 호주 원주민들은 그들의 이름을 계속해서 바꿀 수 있다 / 그들의 일생 동안 / 몇몇 중요한 경험의 결과로 / 어떤 식으로든 그들의 지혜, 창의성 또는 결단력을 증명한

For example, / if one day, one of them dances extremely well, / he or she may decide / to re-name him/herself 'supreme dancer' or 'light feet'.
예를 들어 / 만약 어느 날 그들 중 한 명이 춤을 아주 잘 춘다면 / 그 사람은 결정할 수도 있다 / 자신의 이름을 '최고의 무용수'나 '가벼운 발로 다시 짓기로

해석 많은 가톨릭 국가에서, 아이들은 종종 성인들의 이름을 따서 이름이 지어지는데, 실제로, 일부 성직자들은 부모들이 그들 아이들의 이름을 드라마 스타나 축구 선수의 이름을 따서 짓는 것을 허락하지 않을 것이다. 개신교 국가들은 이것에 대해 더 자유로운 경향이 있지만, 노르웨이에서는 아돌프와 같은 특정 이름들이 완전히 금지되어 있다. 아프리카와 같이 유아 사망률이 매우 높은 국가에서, 부족들은 오직 그들(아이들)이 생존 가능성이 높아지기 시작하는 나이인 다섯 살이 되었을 때만 그들 아이들의 이름을 짓는다. 그때까지, 그들(아이들)은 그들의 나이 햇수로 불린다. 극동의 많은 나라들은 그들의 자녀에게 어떤 식으로든 아이의 출생 환경이나 아이에 대한 부모들의 기대와 희망을 묘사하는 독특한 이름을 지어준다. 일부 호주 원주민들은 어떤 식으로든 그들의 지혜, 창의성 또는 결단력을 증명한 몇몇 중요한 경험의 결과로 그들의 일생 동안 이름을 계속해서 바꿀 수 있다. 예를 들어, 만약 어느 날, 그들 중 한 명이 춤을 아주 잘 춘다면, 그 사람은 자신의 이름을 '최고의 무용수'나 '가벼운 발'로 다시 짓기로 결정할 수도 있다.

① 많은 가톨릭 국가에서 아이들은 종종 성인들의 이름을 따서 이름이 지어진다.

② 일부 아프리카 아이들은 다섯 살이 될 때까지 이름이 지어지지 않는다.

③ 이름을 바꾸는 것은 호주 원주민들의 문화에서 전혀 용납될 수 없다.

④ 다양한 문화들은 그들 자녀들의 이름을 서로 다른 방식으로 짓는다.

해설 지문의 후반에서 일부 호주 원주민들은 그들의 지혜, 창의성 등을 증명한 몇몇 중요한 경험의 결과로 그들의 일생 동안 이름을 계속해서 바꿀 수 있다고 했으므로, '③ 이름을 바꾸는 것은 호주 원주민들의 문화에서 전혀 용납될 수 없다'는 것은 지문의 내용과 다르다.

어휘 name after ~의 이름을 따서 이름을 짓다 saint 성인
protestant 개신교 ban 금지하다 infant 유아 mortality 사망률
tribe 부족 describe 묘사하다 aborigine 원주민 wisdom 지혜
determination 결단력 light 가벼운
unacceptable 용납될 수 없는

---

17 독해 전체내용 파악 (요지 파악)   난이도 ★★☆

끊어읽기 해석

> In one study, / done in the early 1970s / when young people tended to dress / in either "hippie" or "straight" fashion, / experimenters donned hippie or straight attire / and asked college students on campus / for a dime to make a phone call.
> 한 연구에서 / 1970년대 초에 행해진 / 젊은이들이 옷을 입는 경향이 있었던 / '히피'나 '일자형' 패션으로 / 실험자들은 히피나 일자형 복장을 입었다 / 그리고 대학 캠퍼스의 학생에게 달라고 부탁했다 / 전화를 걸기 위한 10센트짜리 동전을
>
> When the experimenter was dressed / in the same way as the student, / the request was granted / in more than two-thirds of the instances; / when the student and requester were dissimilarly dressed, / the dime was provided less than half the time.
> 실험자가 옷을 입었을 때 / 학생과 같은 방식으로 / 그 부탁은 받아들여졌다 / 사례 중 3분의 2 이상 / 학생과 부탁을 한 사람이 다르게 옷을 입었을 때 / 10센트짜리 동전은 절반 이하의 수로 주어졌다
>
> Another experiment showed / how automatic our positive response / to similar others can be.
> 또 다른 실험은 보여주었다 / 우리의 긍정적인 반응이 얼마나 무의식적일 수 있는지를 / 비슷한 다른 사람들에 대한
>
> Marchers in an antiwar demonstration / were found to be more likely to sign the petition / of a similarly dressed requester / and to do so / without bothering to read it first.
> 반전 시위에 참가한 시위자들은 / 탄원서에 서명할 가능성이 더 높은 것으로 밝혀졌다 / 비슷한 복장을 한 요청자의 / 그리고 그렇게 할 / 먼저 그것을 읽어보려고 애쓰지 않고

해석 젊은이들이 '히피'나 '일자형' 패션으로 옷을 입는 경향이 있었던 1970년대 초에 행해진 한 연구에서, 실험자들은 히피나 일자형 복장을 입고 대학 캠퍼스의 학생들에게 전화를 걸기 위한 10센트짜리 동전을 달라고 부탁했다. 실험자가 학생과 같은 방식으로 옷을 입었을 때, 그 부탁은 사례 중 3분의 2 이상 받아들여졌고, 학생과 부탁을 한 사람이 다르게 옷을 입었을 때, 10센트짜리 동전은 절반 이하의 수로 주어졌다. 또 다른 실험은 비슷한 다른 사람들에 대한 우리의 긍정적인 반응이 얼마나 무의식적일 수 있는지를 보여주었다. 반전 시위에 참가한 시위자들은 비슷한 복장을 한 요청자의 탄원서에 서명할 가능성이 더 높았고, 먼저 그것을 읽어보려고 애쓰지 않고 그렇게 할 가능성도 더 높은 것으로 밝혀졌다.

① 사람들은 그들 자신과 비슷하게 옷을 입는 사람들을 도울 가능성이 더 높다.
② 옷을 갖춰 입는 것은 청원서에 서명할 확률을 높인다.
③ 전화를 거는 것은 다른 학생들과 어울릴 수 있는 효율적인 방법이다.
④ 1970년대 초반의 일부 대학생들은 독특한 패션으로 동경 되었다.

해설 지문 처음에서 학생들에게 전화를 걸기 위한 10센트짜리 동전을 달라고 부탁했던 실험에 대해 언급하며, 실험자들이 학생들과 같은 방식으로 옷을 입었을 때 3분의 2 이상 그 부탁이 받아들여졌다고 설명하고 있다. 또한, 지문 후반에서 시위에 참가한 시위자들과 비슷한 복장을 입었을 때 탄원서에 서명할 가능성이 더 높았다는 또 다른 실험 결과에 대해 설명하고 있으므로, '① 사람들은 그들 자신과 비슷하게 옷을 입는 사람들을 도울 가능성이 더 높다'가 이 글의 요지이다.

어휘 straight 일자형의 experimenter 실험자 don (옷 등을) 입다
attire 복장 dime 10센트 request 부탁; 요구하다
grant (부탁·요청 등을) 받아들이다, 수여하다 instance 사례
dissimilarly 다르게 automatic 무의식적인, 자동의
marcher 시위자 demonstration 시위 petition 탄원서, 청원
bother 애쓰다, 괴롭히다 socialize 어울리다, 교제하다

---

18 독해 추론 (빈칸 완성 - 연결어)   난이도 ★★☆

끊어읽기 해석

> Duration shares an inverse relationship with frequency.
> 지속 시간은 빈도와 반비례 관계를 갖는다
>
> If you see a friend frequently, / then the duration of the encounter will be shorter.
> 만약 당신이 한 친구를 자주 만난다면 / 그렇다면 만남의 지속 시간은 더 짧을 것이다
>
> Conversely, / if you don't see your friend very often, / the duration of your visit will typically increase significantly.
> 반대로 / 만약 당신이 친구를 자주 보지 않는다면 / 당신의 만남의 지속 시간은 일반적으로 상당히 늘어날 것이다
>
> (A) For example, / if you see a friend every day, / the duration of your visits can be low / because you can keep up with / what's going on as events unfold.
> (A) 예를 들어 / 만약 당신이 매일 친구를 본다면 / 당신의 만남의 지속 시간이 저조할 수 있다 / 당신은 ~에 대해 계속 알 수 있기 때문에 / 일이 전개될 때 무엇이 일어나고 있는지
>
> If, however, you only see your friend / twice a year, / the duration of your visits will be greater.
> 그러나, 만약 당신이 오직 친구를 만난다면 / 일 년에 두 번 / 당신의 만남의 지속 시간은 더 커질 것이다
>
> Think back to a time / when you had dinner in a restaurant / with a friend you hadn't seen / for a long period of time.
> 때를 생각해 보아라 / 당신이 식당에서 저녁을 먹었던 / 당신이 보지 못했던 친구와 / 오랜 기간 동안
>
> You probably spent several hours / catching up on each other's lives.
> 당신은 아마도 몇 시간을 보냈을 것이다 / 서로의 삶에 대한 소식을 주고받는 데
>
> The duration of the same dinner would be considerably shorter / if you saw the person / on a regular basis.
> 같은 저녁 식사의 지속 시간은 상당히 짧아질 것이다 / 만약 당신이 그 사람을 본다면 / 정기적으로
>
> (B) Conversely, / in romantic relationships / the frequency and duration are very high / because couples, especially newly minted ones, want to spend / as much time with each other as possible.
> (B) 반대로 / 연인 관계에서 / 빈도와 지속 시간이 매우 높다 / 연인들, 특히 최근에 생겨난 연인들은 보내고 싶어 하기 때문에 / 가능한 한 많은 시간을 서로와
>
> The intensity of the relationship will also be very high.
> 관계의 강렬함 또한 매우 높을 것이다

해석 지속 시간은 빈도와 반비례 관계를 갖는다. 만약 당신이 한 친구를 자주 만난다면, 만남의 지속 시간은 더 짧을 것이다. 반대로, 만약 당신이 친구를 자주 보지 않는다면, 당신의 만남의 지속 시간은 일반적으로 상당히 늘어날 것이다. (A) 예를 들어, 만약 당신이 매일 친구를 본다면, 당신은 일이 전개될 때 무엇이 일어나고 있는지에 대해 계속 알 수 있기 때문에 만남의 지속 시간이 저조할 수 있다. 그러나, 만약 당신이 오직 일 년에 두 번 친구를 만난다면, 당신의 만남의 지속 시간은 더 커질 것이다. 당신이 오랜 기간 동안 보지 못했던 친구와 식당에서 저녁을 먹었던 때를 생각해 보아라. 당신은 아마도 서로의 삶에 대한 소식을 주고받는 데 몇 시간을 보냈을 것이다. 만약 당신이 그 사람을 정기적으로 본다면 같은 저녁 식사의 지속 시간은 상당히 짧아질 것이다. (B) 반대로, 연인 관계에서, 연인들, 특히 최근에 생겨난 연인들은 가능한 한 많은 시간을 서로와 보내고 싶어 하기 때문에 빈도와 지속 시간이 매우 높다. 관계의 강렬함 또한 매우 높을 것이다.

(A)	(B)
① 예를 들어	반대로
② 그럼에도 불구하고	게다가
③ 그러므로	결과적으로
④ 같은 방법으로	따라서

해설 (A) 빈칸 앞부분은 지속 시간이 빈도와 반비례 관계를 갖기 때문에 만약 당신이 친구를 자주 보지 않는다면 당신의 만남의 지속 시간은 일반적으로 상당히 늘어날 것이라는 내용이고, 빈칸 뒷부분은 만약 당신이 매일 친구를 본다면 무엇이 일어나고 있는지에 대해 계속 알 수 있기 때문에 만남의 지속 시간이 저조할 수 있다는 예시를 드는 내용이므로, (A)에는 For example(예를 들어)이 들어가야 한다. (B) 빈칸 앞부분은 오랜 기간 동안 보지 못했던 친구와 식사를 한다면 소식을 주고받는 데 몇 시간을 보내겠지만 만약 당신이 그 사람을 정기적으로 본다면 같은 저녁 식사의 지속 시간은 짧아질 것이라는 내용이고, 빈칸 뒷부분은 연인들, 특히 최근에 생겨난 연인들은 가능한 한 많은 시간을 서로와 보내고 싶어 하기 때문에 빈도와 지속 시간이 매우 높다는 대조적인 내용이므로, (B)에는 Conversely(반대로)가 들어가야 한다. 따라서 ①번이 정답이다.

어휘 duration 지속 시간 inverse 반비례의, 역의
frequency 빈도, 주파수 encounter 만남; 만나다, 접하다
keep up with ~에 대해 계속 알다, ~을 따라 잡다
unfold 전개되다, 펴다 catch up on 소식을 주고받다
minted 최근에 생겨난 intensity 강렬함, 격렬함

19 독해 추론 (빈칸 완성 - 구) 난이도 ★★☆

끊어읽기 해석

One of the most frequently used propaganda techniques / is to convince the public / that the propagandist's views reflect those of the common person / and that he or she is working / in their best interests.
가장 자주 사용되는 선전 기법 중 하나는 / 대중들에게 확신시키는 것이다 / 선전자의 관점이 일반적인 사람들의 그것(관점)을 반영하고 있다는 것을 / 그리고 그 사람이 일하고 있다는 것을 / 그들의 최선의 이익을 위해

A politician speaking / to a blue-collar audience / may roll up his sleeves, undo his tie, / and attempt to use the specific idioms of the crowd.
연설하는 정치인은 / 육체노동자인 청중에게 / 그의 소매를 걷어붙이고 넥타이를 풀 수도 있다 / 그리고 군중 특유의 언어를 사용하려고 시도한다

He may even use language incorrectly / on purpose / to give the impression / that he is "just one of the folks."
그는 심지어 말을 부정확하게 사용할 수도 있다 / 일부러 / 인상을 주기 위

해 / 그가 '민중의 한 명일 뿐'이라는

This technique usually also employs the use of glittering generalities / to give the impression / that the politician's views are the same / as those of the crowd being addressed.
이 기법은 대개 겉보기에는 그럴듯한 일반론도 사용한다 / 인상을 주기 위해 / 정치인의 관점이 같다는 / 연설의 대상이 되는 군중의 것과

Labor leaders, businesspeople, ministers, educators, and advertisers have used this technique / to win our confidence / by appearing to be just plain folks like ourselves.
노동 지도자, 사업가, 장관, 교육자 및 광고주는 이 기법을 사용해 왔다 / 우리의 신뢰를 얻기 위해 / 우리 같은 그저 평범한 민중들처럼 보임으로써

해석 가장 자주 사용되는 선전 기법 중 하나는 대중들에게 선전자의 관점이 일반적인 사람들의 그것(관점)을 반영하고 있고 그 사람이 그들의 최선의 이익을 위해 일하고 있다는 것을 확신시키는 것이다. 육체 노동자인 청중에게 연설하는 정치인은 그의 소매를 걷어붙이고 넥타이를 풀고서 군중 특유의 언어를 사용하려고 시도할 수 있다. 그는 심지어 그가 '민중의 한 명일 뿐'이라는 인상을 주기 위해 일부러 말을 부정확하게 사용할 수도 있다. 이 기법은 대개 정치인의 관점이 연설의 대상이 되는 군중의 것과 같다는 인상을 주기 위해 겉보기에는 그럴듯한 일반론도 사용한다. 노동 지도자, 사업가, 장관, 교육자 및 광고주는 우리 같은 그저 평범한 민중들처럼 보임으로써 우리의 신뢰를 얻기 위해 이 기법을 사용해 왔다.

① 겉보기에는 그럴듯한 일반론 이상인
② 우리 같은 그저 평범한 민중들
③ 다른 사람들과 다른 무언가
④ 군중보다 더 잘 교육받은

해설 지문의 처음에서 가장 자주 사용되는 선전 기법 중 하나가 대중들에게 선전자의 관점이 일반적인 사람들의 관점을 반영하고 있고 그 사람이 그들의 최선의 이익을 위해 일하고 있다는 것을 확신시키는 것이라고 한 뒤, 정치인이 육체노동자들에게 연설할 때 소매를 걷어붙이고 군중 특유의 언어를 사용하려고 시도하는 것을 예시로 들고 있다. 또한, 지문의 중간에서 정치인은 그도 민중의 한 명일 뿐이라는 인상을 주기 위해 일부러 말을 부정확하게 사용하거나 그의 관점이 군중의 것과 같다는 인상을 주기 위해 겉보기에는 그럴듯한 일반론도 사용한다고 설명하고 있다. 따라서 빈칸에는 노동 지도자, 사업가 등이 '② 우리 같은 그저 평범한 민중들'처럼 보임으로써 우리의 신뢰를 얻기 위해 이 기법을 사용해 왔다는 내용이 들어가야 한다.

어휘 propaganda 선전 convince 확신시키다 reflect 반영하다
common 일반적인, 흔한 blue-collar 육체노동자의
audience 청중 undo 풀다, 원상태로 하다
idiom (특정 시기·집단의) 언어, 관용구 on purpose 일부러
folk 민중들 employ 사용하다, 고용하다
glittering 겉보기에는 그럴듯한, 번지르르한
generality 일반론, 보편성 address 연설하다
confidence 신뢰, 자신감 plain 평범한

20 독해 추론 (빈칸 완성 - 단어) 난이도 ★★☆

끊어읽기 해석

As a roller coaster climbs the first lift hill of its track, / it is building potential energy / —the higher it gets above the earth, / the stronger the pull of gravity will be.
롤러코스터가 트랙의 첫 번째 오르막 경사로를 오를 때 / 그것은 위치 에너지를 만들고 있다 / 그것이 지면 위로 더 높이 올라갈수록 / 중력의 끌어당기는 힘은 더 강해질 것이다

When the coaster crests the lift hill / and begins its descent, /

its potential energy becomes kinetic energy, / or the energy of movement.
롤러코스터가 오르막 경사로의 꼭대기에 이를 때 / 그리고 하강을 시작하면 / 그것의 위치 에너지는 운동 에너지가 된다 / 즉 움직임의 에너지인

A common misperception is that a coaster loses energy / along the track.
일반적인 오해는 롤러코스터가 에너지를 잃는다는 것이다 / 트랙을 따라

An important law of physics, however, / called the law of conservation of energy, / is that energy can never be created nor destroyed.
그러나, 물리학의 중요한 법칙은 / 에너지 보존의 법칙이라고 불리는 / 에너지가 결코 생성되거나 파괴될 수 없다는 것이다

It simply changes / from one form to another.
그것(에너지)은 단순히 바뀐다 / 한 형태에서 다른 형태로

Whenever a track rises back uphill, / the cars' momentum— their kinetic energy— / will carry them upward, / which builds potential energy, / and roller coasters repeatedly convert potential energy to kinetic energy / and back again.
트랙이 오르막으로 되돌아올 때마다 / (롤러코스터) 차량의 운동 에너지인 가속도가 / 그것들을 위로 운반할 것이다 / 이것이 위치 에너지를 만든다 / 그리고 롤러코스터는 반복적으로 위치 에너지를 운동 에너지로 변환한다 / 그리고 다시 원래대로 되돌린다

At the end of a ride, / coaster cars are slowed down / by brake mechanisms that create <u>friction</u> / between two surfaces.
놀이기구가 끝날 때 / 롤러코스터 차량은 속도가 늦춰진다 / 마찰을 일으키는 제동 장치에 의해 / 두 표면 사이에

This motion makes them hot, / meaning kinetic energy is changed to heat energy / during braking.
이 운동은 그것들을 뜨겁게 만든다 / 이것은 운동 에너지가 열에너지로 바뀌는 것을 의미한다 / 제동 중에

Riders may mistakenly think / coasters lose energy / at the end of the track, / but the energy just changes / to and from different forms.
탑승자들은 잘못 생각할 수도 있다 / 롤러코스터가 에너지를 잃는다고 / 트랙의 끝에서 / 하지만 에너지는 단지 바뀌는 것뿐이다 / 다른 형태로 혹은 다른 형태에서

해석 롤러코스터가 트랙의 첫 번째 오르막 경사로를 오를 때, 그것은 위치 에너지를 만들고 있는데, 그것이 지면 위로 더 높이 올라갈수록, 중력의 끌어당기는 힘은 더 강해질 것이다. 롤러코스터가 오르막 경사로의 꼭대기에 이르러 하강을 시작할 때, 그것의 위치 에너지는 운동 에너지, 즉 움직임의 에너지가 된다. 일반적인 오해는 롤러코스터가 트랙을 따라 에너지를 잃는다는 것이다. 그러나, 에너지 보존의 법칙이라고 불리는 물리학의 중요한 법칙은 에너지가 결코 생성되거나 파괴될 수 없다는 것이다. 그것(에너지)은 단순히 한 형태에서 다른 형태로 바뀐다. 트랙이 오르막으로 되돌아올 때마다, (롤러코스터) 차량의 운동 에너지인 가속도가 그것들을 위로 운반할 것이고, 이것이 위치 에너지를 만들면, 롤러코스터는 반복적으로 위치 에너지를 운동 에너지로 변환하여 다시 원래대로 되돌린다. 놀이기구가 끝날 때, 롤러코스터 차량은 두 표면 사이에 <u>마찰</u>을 일으키는 제동 장치에 의해 속도가 늦춰진다. 이 운동은 그것들(롤러코스터 차량의 두 표면)을 뜨겁게 만드는데, 이것은 제동 중에 운동 에너지가 열에너지로 바뀌는 것을 의미한다. 탑승자들은 롤러코스터가 트랙의 끝에서 에너지를 잃는다고 잘못 생각할 수도 있지만, 에너지는 단지 다른 형태로 혹은 다른 형태에서 바뀌는 것뿐이다.

① 중력
② 마찰
③ 진공 상태
④ 가속도

해설 지문 중간에서 에너지는 결코 생성되거나 파괴될 수 없고 단순히 한 형태에서 다른 형태로 바뀐다고 하면서 롤러코스터 차량의 위치 에너지가 운동 에너지로 전환되었다가 다시 원래대로 되돌아오는 것을 예시로 들어 설명하고 있다. 이어서 빈칸이 있는 문장에서 롤러코스터 차량이 제동 장치에 의해 속도가 늦춰진다고 언급한 뒤, 빈칸 뒤 문장에서 이 운동(This motion)은 차량의 두 표면을 뜨겁게 만들고 제동 중에 운동 에너지가 열에너지로 바뀌는 것을 의미한다는 것을 설명하고 있으므로, 빈칸에는 '② 마찰'이 들어가야 한다.

어휘 potential energy 위치 에너지 gravity 중력
crest 꼭대기에 이르다 descent 하강 kinetic energy 운동 에너지
conservation 보존 destroy 파괴하다
momentum 가속도, 추진력 convert 변환하다
brake 제동; 속도를 줄이다 mechanism 장치, 방법 friction 마찰
vacuum 진공 (상태) acceleration 가속(도)

정답

p.96

01	④ 어휘 – 어휘&표현	11	① 어휘 – 생활영어
02	③ 어휘 – 어휘&표현	12	③ 어휘 – 생활영어
03	① 어휘 – 어휘&표현	13	② 독해 – 세부내용 파악
04	② 어휘 – 어휘&표현	14	② 독해 – 논리적 흐름 파악
05	④ 어휘 – 어휘&표현	15	③ 문법 – 주어·동사/목적어·보어/수식어
06	④ 문법 – 동사의 종류	16	② 독해 – 추론
07	② 문법 – 동사의 종류	17	④ 독해 – 추론
08	② 문법 – 병치·도치·강조 구문	18	① 독해 – 전체내용 파악
09	④ 독해 – 전체내용 파악	19	③ 독해 – 추론
10	① 독해 – 논리적 흐름 파악	20	② 독해 – 논리적 흐름 파악

취약영역 분석표

영역	세부 유형	문항 수	소계
어휘	어휘&표현	5	/7
	생활영어	2	
문법	동사의 종류	2	/4
	병치·도치·강조 구문	1	
	주어·동사/목적어·보어/수식어	1	
독해	전체내용 파악	2	/9
	세부내용 파악	1	
	추론	3	
	논리적 흐름 파악	3	
총계			/20

· 자신이 취약한 영역은 '공무원 영어, 이렇게 출제된다!'(문제집 p.8)를 통해 다시 한번 확인하고 학습하시기 바랍니다.

---

01 어휘 어휘&표현 gratification = satisfaction 난이도 ★★☆

해석 많은 충동 구매자들에게는 그들이 무엇을 사는지보다 구매의 행위가 만족감으로 이어지는 것이다.

① 활기 ② 자신감
③ 평온함 ④ 만족감

어휘 compulsive 충동적인 lead to ~로 이어지다, ~을 야기하다
gratification 만족감 liveliness 활기 tranquility 평온함

👍 이것도 알면 **합격!**

gratification(만족감)의 유의어
= satisfaction, fulfillment, enjoyment, pleasure

02 어휘 어휘&표현 efficiency 난이도 ★☆☆

해석 세계화는 더 많은 나라들이 그들의 시장을 개방하게 되고 그들이 상품과 서비스를 더 낮은 가격에 더 좋은 효율로 자유롭게 거래할 수 있게 한다.

① 멸종 ② 우울
③ 효율 ④ 경고

어휘 extinction 멸종 efficiency 효율

👍 이것도 알면 **합격!**

efficiency(효율)의 유의어
= efficacy, productivity, effectiveness

03 어휘 어휘&표현 fix 난이도 ★★☆

해석 우리는 번아웃에 대한 대가를 익히 안다. 활기, 동기 부여, 생산성, 참여, 그리고 헌신은 직장과 집 모두에서 타격을 입을 수 있다. 그리고 해결책들의 대다수는 꽤 직관적이다. 정기적으로 플러그를 뽑아라(책임과 의무에서 물러서라). 불필요한 회의들을 줄여라. 운동을 해라. 낮 동안에 짧은 휴식들을 계획해라. 당신은 이따금 자리를 비울 여유가 없을 수도 있기 때문에 당신이 직장에서 설사 자리를 비울 여유가 없다고 생각할지라도 휴가를 내라.

① 해결책들 ② 손해들
③ 포상들 ④ 문제들

어휘 be familiar with ~을 익히 알다 burnout 번아웃(극도의 피로)
motivation 동기 부여 productivity 생산성 engagement 참여
commitment 헌신 take a hit 타격을 입다 intuitive 직관적인
be away from ~에서 자리를 비우다 now and then 이따금, 때때로
fix 해결책 complication 문제

👍 이것도 알면 **합격!**

fix(해결책)의 유의어
= solution, repair, remedy

04 어휘 어휘&표현 call for 난이도 ★★☆

해석 정부는 새로운 세금 정산 체계로부터 발생하는 그들(급여 노동자들)의 증가한 조세 부담에 대해 급여 노동자들을 진정시키기 위한 방법들을 찾고 있다. 지난 월요일 대통령 보좌관들과 함께했던 그의 회의 동안, 대통령은 참석한 사람들에게 대중들과의 소통 경로들을 더 열 것을 요구했다.

① ~을 엄습했다 ② ~을 요구했다
③ ~을 듣게 되었다 ④ ~을 거절했다

어휘 **soothe** 진정시키다, 달래다 **arise from** ~로부터 발생하다
settlement 정산, 결산 **presidential aide** 대통령 보좌관
present 참석한 **fall on** ~을 엄습하다, ~의 책임이다
call for ~을 요구하다 **pick up** ~을 듣게 되다
turn down ~을 거절하다

📖 이것도 알면 **합격!**

call for(~을 요구하다)와 유사한 의미의 표현
= demand, request, ask for, suggest

05 어휘 | 어휘&표현 grasp = apprehend
난이도 ★☆☆

해석 중국의 서예를 공부하는 것에 있어서, 누구나 중국어의 기원과 그 것들이 원래 어떻게 쓰였는지에 대한 것을 배워야만 한다. 하지만, 그 나라의 예술적 전통(환경)에서 길러진 사람들을 제외하고는, 그 것의 미학적 의미는 매우 <u>파악하기</u> 어려운 것 같다.

① 포함하다
② 침범하다
③ 검사하다
④ 파악하다

어휘 **calligraphy** 서예 **bring up** 기르다 **aesthetic** 미학적
apprehend 파악하다 **encompass** 포함하다 **intrude** 침범하다
inspect 검사하다 **grasp** 파악하다

📖 이것도 알면 **합격!**

apprehend(파악하다)의 유의어
= understand, comprehend, absorb, catch

06 문법 | 동사의 종류
난이도 ★★☆

해설 ④ 5형식 동사 지각동사 see(saw)는 목적어와 목적격 보어가 능동 관계일 때 동사원형이나 현재분사를 목적격 보어로 취하는 5형식 동사인데, 주어진 문장에서 목적어(a family)와 목적격 보어가 '한 가족이 이사 오다'라는 의미의 능동 관계이므로 과거분사 moved를 동사원형 move나 현재분사 moving으로 고쳐야 한다.

오답 ① to 부정사의 역할 '읽기가 어렵다'를 나타내기 위해 부사처럼
분석 형용사(hard)를 꾸며줄 수 있는 to 부정사 to read가 올바르게 쓰였다.
② 동명사 관련 표현 '~해 봐야 소용없다'는 동명사구 관용 표현 'It's no use -ing'(~해도 소용없다)를 사용하여 나타낼 수 있으므로 It is no use trying ~이 올바르게 쓰였다.
③ 수량 표현 every(모든)는 일반적으로 단수 가산 명사를 수식하지만, 특정한 숫자와 함께 오면 '~마다 한 번씩'의 뜻으로 쓰여 복수 명사 앞에 올 수 있으므로, every five years가 올바르게 쓰였다.

어휘 **It's no use -ing** ~해도 소용없다 **persuade** 설득하다
move in 이사 오다

📖 이것도 알면 **합격!**

동명사구 관용 표현

· It's no use[good] -ing	· on[upon] -ing -하자마자
~해도 소용없다	· end up -ing 결국 -하다
· be busy -ing -하느라 바쁘다	· go -ing -하러 가다
· cannot help -ing	· be worth -ing -할 가치가 있다
-하지 않을 수 없다	

07 문법 | 동사의 종류
난이도 ★★★

해설 ② 5형식 동사 사역동사 let은 목적어와 목적격 보어가 수동 관계일 때 목적격 보어로 'be + p.p.' 형태를 취하는 5형식 동사인데, 목적어 me와 목적격 보어가 '내가 집중력을 잃게 되다'라는 의미의 수동 관계이므로 let me distracted를 let me be distracted로 고쳐야 한다.

오답 ① 5형식 동사 사역동사 have(had)는 목적어와 목적격 보어가
분석 수동 관계일 때 과거분사를 목적격 보어로 취하는 5형식 동사인데, 목적어 the woman과 목적격 보어가 '여자가 (경찰 당국에 의해) 체포되다'라는 의미의 수동 관계이므로 과거분사 arrested가 올바르게 쓰였다.
③ 5형식 동사 사역동사 let은 목적어와 목적격 보어가 능동 관계일 때 동사원형을 목적격 보어로 취하는 5형식 동사인데, 목적어 me와 목적격 보어가 '내가 알다'라는 의미의 능동 관계이므로, 동사원형 know가 올바르게 쓰였다.
④ 5형식 동사 사역동사 have(had)는 목적어와 목적격 보어가 능동 관계일 때 동사원형을 목적격 보어로 취하는 5형식 동사인데, 목적어 the students와 목적격 보어가 '학생들이 전화를 걸다'라는 의미의 능동 관계이므로, 동사원형 phone이 올바르게 쓰였다. 참고로, 접속사 and 앞에 동사원형 phone이 왔으므로 and 뒤에도 동사원형 ask가 올바르게 쓰였다.

어휘 **authorities** 당국 **distract** 집중력을 잃게 하다 **phone** 전화를 걸다

📖 이것도 알면 **합격!**

예외적으로 사역동사 let은 목적어와 목적격 보어가 수동 관계일 때 목적격 보어로 'be + p.p.' 형태를 취한다.
(ex) She lets her refrigerator (be used, ~~use~~) by her roommate.
그녀는 룸메이트가 그녀의 냉장고를 쓰도록 허락한다.
→ '쓰다'가 아니라 '쓰이다'라는 의미로 수동 관계이므로 사역동사 let의 목적격 보어로 'be + p.p.' 형태(be used)가 온다.

08 문법 | 병치·도치·강조 구문
난이도 ★★☆

해석 ① 나의 다정한 딸이 갑자기 예측할 수 없게 되었다.
② 그녀는 새로운 방법을 시도했고, 말할 것도 없이 다른 결과를 얻었다.
③ 도착하자마자, 그는 그 새로운 환경을 최대한 이용했다.
④ 그는 자신이 하고 싶었던 것에 대해 나에게 말할 정도로 충분히 편하게 느꼈다.

해설 ② 병치 구문 접속사(and)로 연결된 병치 구문에서는 같은 구조끼리 연결되어야 하는데, and 앞에 과거 시제 동사 attempted가 왔으므로 and 뒤에도 과거 시제 동사 had가 올바르게 쓰였다.

오답 ① 보어 자리 동사 become(became)은 주격 보어를 취하는 동
분석 사인데, 보어 자리에는 명사나 형용사 역할을 하는 것이 올 수 있으므로 부사 unpredictably를 형용사 unpredictable로 고쳐야 한다.
③ 동명사 관련 표현 문맥상 '도착하자마자'라는 의미가 되어야 자연스러운데, '-하자마자'는 동명사 관련 표현 'upon -ing'를 사용하여 나타낼 수 있으므로 과거분사 arrived를 동명사 arriving으로 고쳐야 한다. 참고로, 명사 arrival(도착)을 사용해 Upon arrival로 고쳐도 맞다.
④ 혼동하기 쉬운 어순 부사 enough는 형용사(comfortable)를 뒤에서 수식하므로, enough comfortable을 comfortable enough로 고쳐야 한다.

어휘 **sweet-natured** 다정한 **unpredictably** 예측할 수 없게
needless to say 말할 것도 없이
take full advantage of ~을 최대한 이용하다

이것도 알면 **합격!**

부사 enough의 다양한 어순

enough + 명사	ex It has enough problems already. 그것은 이미 충분한 문제들이 있다.
형용사/부사 + enough	ex He is busy enough. 그는 충분히 바쁘다.
형용사/부사 + enough + to 부정사	ex The book was long enough to take weeks to read. 그 책은 읽는데 몇 주가 걸릴 정도로 충분히 길었다.

---

09 독해 **전체내용 파악 (제목 파악)** 난이도 ★★☆

끊어읽기 해석

The definition of 'turn' casts the digital turn / as an analytical strategy / which enables us to focus / on the role of digitalization / within social reality.
'전환'의 정의는 디지털 전환을 묘사한다 / 분석적 전략으로서 / 우리가 집중할 수 있게 하는 / 디지털화의 역할에 / 사회적 현실 안에서

As an analytical perspective, / the digital turn makes it possible / to analyze and discuss the societal meaning of digitalization.
분석적인 관점에서 / 디지털 전환은 가능하게 한다 / 디지털화의 사회적인 의미를 분석하고 논의하는 것을

The term 'digital turn' thus signifies an analytical approach / which centers on the role of digitalization / within a society.
'디지털 전환'이라는 용어는 따라서 분석적인 접근을 의미한다 / 디지털화의 역할에 집중하는 / 사회 안에서

If the linguistic turn is defined / by the epistemological assumption / that reality is constructed through language, / the digital turn is based on the assumption / that social reality is increasingly defined by digitalization.
만약 언어론적 전환이 정의된다면 / 인식론의 가설에 의해 / 현실이 언어를 통해 구성된다는 / 디지털 전환은 가설에 기반한다 / 사회적 현실이 점점 더 디지털화에 의해 정의된다는

Social media symbolize the digitalization / of social relations.
소셜 미디어는 디지털화를 상징한다 / 사회적 관계들의

Individuals increasingly engage in identity management / on social networking sites(SNS).
개인들은 주체성 관리에 더욱더 관여한다 / 소셜 네트워킹 사이트(SNS)에서

SNS are polydirectional, / meaning / that users can connect to each other / and share information.
SNS는 다방향적이다 / 그리고 이것은 의미한다 / 사용자들이 서로와 연락할 수 있다는 것을 / 그리고 정보를 공유한다

해설 '전환'의 정의는 우리가 사회적 현실 안에서 디지털화의 역할에 집중할 수 있게 하는 분석적 전략으로서 디지털 전환을 묘사한다. 분석적인 관점에서, 디지털 전환은 디지털화의 사회적인 의미를 분석하고 논의하는 것을 가능하게 한다. '디지털 전환'이라는 용어는 따라서 사회 안에서 디지털화의 역할에 집중하는 분석적 접근을 의미한다. 만약 현실이 언어를 통해 구성된다는 인식론의 가설에 의해 언어론적 전환이 정의된다면, 디지털 전환은 사회적 현실이 점점 더 디지털화에 의해 정의된다는 가설에 기반한다. 소셜 미디어는 사회적 관계들의 디지털화를 상징한다. 개인들은 소셜 네트워킹 사이트(SNS)에서 주체성 관리에 더욱더 관여한다. SNS는 다방향적이고, 이것은 사용자들이 서로와 연락하고 정보를 공유할

수 있다는 것을 의미한다.
① SNS에서 주체성 다시 만들기
② 언어론적 전환 대 디지털 전환
③ 디지털 시대에 정보를 공유하는 방법
④ 사회적 현실의 맥락 안에서의 디지털화

해설 지문 중간에서 디지털 전환은 사회 안에서 디지털화의 역할에 초점을 맞추는 분석적인 접근이고, 사회적 현실이 점점 더 디지털화에 의해 정의된다는 가설에 기반한다고 설명하고 있다. 이어서 소셜 미디어가 사회적 관계들의 디지털화를 상징한다고 하면서 사회적 현실이 디지털화되는 예시를 들고 있으므로, '④ 사회적 현실의 맥락 안에서의 디지털화'가 이 글의 제목이다.

어휘 **cast** 묘사하다, 던지다 **analytical** 분석적인 **perspective** 관점
signify 의미하다 **assumption** 가설 **engage in** ~에 관여하다
identity 주체성, 신원 **polydirectional** 다방향적인
connect to ~와 연락하다

---

10 독해 **논리적 흐름 파악 (문단 순서 배열)** 난이도 ★☆☆

끊어읽기 해석

Growing concern / about global climate change / has motivated activists to organize / not only campaigns against fossil fuel extraction consumption, / but also campaigns to support renewable energy.
심해지는 걱정은 / 세계 기후 변화에 대해 / 활동가들이 조직하도록 동기를 부여해왔다 / 화석 연료 추출 소비에 반대하는 캠페인들뿐만 아니라 / 재생 가능한 에너지를 지지하는 캠페인을 또한

(A) This solar cooperative produces enough energy / to power 1,400 homes, / making it the first large-scale solar farm cooperative / in the country / and, in the words of its members, / a visible reminder / that solar power represents / "a new era of sustainable and 'democratic' energy supply / that enables ordinary people to produce clean power, / not only on their rooftops, / but also at utility scale."
이 태양열 협동조합은 충분한 에너지를 생산한다 / 천 4백 가구들에 동력을 공급하기에 / 그것(협동조합)을 첫 번째 대규모 태양열 농장 협동조합으로 만들면서 / 국내에서 / 그리고 그것(협동조합)의 회원들의 말을 빌리자면 / 뚜렷한 신호이다 / 태양열 발전이 대표한다는 / 지속 가능하고 '민주적인' 에너지 공급의 새 시대를 / 일반인들이 깨끗한 동력을 생산할 수 있게 하는 / 그들(일반인들)의 옥상들에서뿐만 아니라 / 공익사업 규모에서 또한

(B) Similarly, / renewable energy enthusiasts / from the United States / have founded the Clean Energy Collective, / a company that has pioneered / "the model of delivering clean power-generation / through medium-scale facilities / that are collectively owned / by participating utility customers."
마찬가지로 / 재생 가능한 에너지의 열렬한 지지자들은 / 미국 출신의 / Clean Energy Collective를 설립했다 / 개척해온 회사인 / 청정 전력 발전을 가져올 모델을 / 중간규모의 시설들로 / 공동으로 소유된 / 공익사업 고객들을 참여시킴으로써

(C) Environmental activists / frustrated with the UK government's inability / to rapidly accelerate the growth of renewable energy industries / have formed the Westmill Wind Farm Co-operative, / a community-owned organization / with more than 2,000 members / who own an onshore wind farm / estimated to produce as much electricity in a year as / that used by 2,500 homes.
환경 활동가들은 / 영국 정부의 무능함에 불만스러운 / 재생 가능한 에너지 사업의 성장을 빠르게 가속화시키는 것에 대한 / Westmill Wind Farm 협동조합을 만들었다 / 지역사회 소유 기관인 / 2천 명이 넘는 회원이 있는 / 육지의 풍력 발전소를 소유한 / 한 해 ~만큼의 전기를 생산한다고 추정되는 / 2천 5백 가구들에 의해 사용되는

The Westmill Wind Farm Co-operative / has inspired local citizens / to form the Westmill Solar Co-operative.
Westmill 풍력 발전소 협동조합은 / 지역 시민들에게 영감을 주었다 / Westmill 태양열 협동조합을 만들도록

해석   세계 기후 변화에 대해 심해지는 걱정은 활동가들이 화석 연료 추출 소비에 반대하는 캠페인들뿐만 아니라 재생 가능한 에너지를 지지하는 캠페인들 또한 조직하도록 동기를 부여해왔다.

(C) 재생 가능한 에너지 사업의 성장을 빠르게 가속화시키는 것에 대한 영국 정부의 무능함에 불만스러운 환경 활동가들은 한 해 2천 5백 가구들에 의해 사용되는 만큼의 전기를 생산한다고 추정되는 육지의 풍력 발전소를 소유하고 2천 명이 더 되는 회원이 있는 지역사회 소유 기관인 Westmill Wind Farm 협동조합을 만들었다. Westmill 풍력 발전소 협동조합은 Westmill 태양열 협동조합을 만들도록 지역 시민들에게 영감을 주었다.

(A) 이 태양열 협동조합은 국내에서 그것(협동조합)을 첫 번째 대규모 태양열 농장 협동조합으로 만들면서 천 4백 가구들에 동력을 공급하기에 충분한 에너지를 생산하고, 이는 그것(협동조합)의 회원들의 말을 빌리자면, 태양열 발전이 "일반인들이 그들의 옥상들에서뿐만 아니라 공익사업 규모에서도 또한 깨끗한 동력을 생산할 수 있게 하는 지속 가능하고 '민주적인' 에너지 공급의 새 시대"를 대표한다는 뚜렷한 신호이다.

(B) 마찬가지로, 미국 출신의 열렬한 재생 가능한 에너지의 지지자들은 공익사업 고객들을 참여시킴으로써 공동 소유된 중간규모의 시설들로 청정 전력 발전을 가져올 모델을 개척해온 회사인 Clean Energy Collective를 설립했다.

해설   주어진 문단에서 세계 기후 변화에 대한 커가는 걱정은 활동가들이 여러 캠페인들을 조직하도록 동기 부여한다고 한 뒤, (C)에서 이에 대한 예시로 영국의 환경 활동가들이 Westmill Wind Farm 협동조합을 만들었다고 하며 후에 이 풍력 발전소 협동조합이 태양열 협동조합을 만드는 데 영감을 주었다고 하고 있다. 이어서 (A)에서 Westmill Wind Farm에서 파생된 이 태양열 협동조합(This solar cooperative)이 생산하는 에너지와 그 규모에 대해 언급하고 있고, (B)에서 마찬가지로(Similarly) 재생 가능한 에너지와 관련된 미국의 회사인 Clean Energy Collective를 예시로 들며 설명하고 있다.

어휘   extraction 추출   consumption 소비   solar 태양열의   cooperative 협동조합   in the words of ~의 말을 빌리자면   visible 뚜렷한, 가시적인   reminder 신호, 암시   era 시대   utility 공익사업, 유용성   enthusiast 열렬한 지지자   pioneer 개척하다; 선구자   collectively 공동으로, 집단으로   accelerate 가속화시키다   wind farm 풍력 발전소   onshore 육지의

---

11   어휘   생활영어   What did you like the most about it?   난이도 ★☆☆

해석
A: 좋은 주말 보냈어?
B: 응, 정말 좋았어. 우리는 영화 보러 갔어.
A: 오! 뭐 봤어?
B: 「인터스텔라」. 매우 좋았어.
A: 정말? 그것의 어떤 점이 가장 좋았어?
B: 특수 효과. 정말 환상적이었어. 난 그것을 다시 봐도 괜찮을 것 같아.

① 그것의 어떤 점이 가장 좋았어?
② 네가 가장 좋아하는 영화 장르는 뭐야?
③ 그 영화는 국제적으로 홍보되었니?
④ 그 영화는 매우 비쌌니?

해설   영화가 매우 좋았다는 B의 말에 A가 질문하고, 빈칸 뒤에서 B가 다시 The special effects. They were fantastic(특수 효과. 정말 환상적이었어)이라고 대답하고 있으므로, 빈칸에는 '① 그것의 어떤 점이 가장 좋았어?(What did you like the most about it?)'가 오는 것이 자연스럽다.

어휘   special effect 특수 효과

👍 이것도 알면 **합격!**

영화에 대해 이야기할 때 쓸 수 있는 표현을 알아두자.
· It's one of my all-time favorites.
  이건 내가 항상 가장 좋아하는 것들 중 하나야.
· It's a good way to spend a couple hours.
  몇 시간을 보내는 데 좋은 방법이야.
· It lived up to my expectations. 이건 내 기대를 충족시켰어.
· It didn't live up to the hype. 이건 과대광고의 기대에 미치지 못했어.

---

12   어휘   생활영어   That's the word. Vacation has dragged on for weeks.   난이도 ★★☆

해석   ① A: 오늘 내가 해야만 하는 이번 연설이 너무 긴장돼.
       B: 가장 중요한 건 침착하게 행동하는 거야.
     ② A: 그거 아니? 민수와 유진이가 결혼한대!
       B: 잘됐다! 그들은 언제 결혼하니?
     ③ A: 두 달 방학이 마치 한 주처럼 지나갔어. 새 학기가 코앞이야.
       B: 내 말이 그 말이야. 방학이 몇 주 동안 느릿느릿 지나갔어.
     ④ A: 프랑스어로 '물'은 어떻게 말하니?
       B: 딱 생각이 날 듯 말 듯 한데, 그게 기억이 안 나.

해설   ③번에서 A가 두 달 방학이 한 주처럼 빠르게 지나갔다고 하며 시간이 빠르게 흘러갔다고 했으므로, 방학이 몇 주 동안 느릿느릿 지나갔다는 B의 대답 '③ That's the word. Vacation has dragged on for weeks(내 말이 그 말이야. 방학이 몇 주 동안 느릿느릿 지나갔어)'는 어울리지 않는다.

어휘   tie the knot 결혼하다   around the corner (일정이) 코앞인, 다가오는
That's the word 내 말이 그 말이야
drag on (시간이) 느릿느릿 지나가다, 질질 끌다
on the tip of one's tongue 생각이 날 듯 말 듯한

👍 이것도 알면 **합격!**

상대방의 의견에 동의하는 표현을 알아두자.
· Me (n)either. 나도 그래. (나도 그렇지 않아.)
· I agree with you. 너의 의견에 동의해.
· Exactly the same with me. 나도 마찬가지야.

---

13   독해   세부내용 파악 (내용 불일치 파악)   난이도 ★☆☆

끊어읽기 해석

Women are experts at gossiping, / and they always talk about trivial things, / or at least that's what men have always thought.
여자들은 수다 떠는 데 전문가들이다 / 그리고 그들은 항상 사소한 것들에 대해 이야기한다 / 혹은 그게 아니더라도 최소한 그것이 남자들은 항상 생각해 왔던 것이다

However, / some new research suggests / that when women talk to women, / their conversations are far from frivolous, / and cover many more topics (up to 40 subjects) / than when men talk to other men.

그러나 / 몇몇 새로운 연구는 시사한다 / 여자들이 여자들에게 이야기할 때 / 그들의 대화들은 사소한 것과는 거리가 멀다는 것을 / 그리고 더 많은 주제들을 다룬다(40개의 주제들까지) / 남자들이 다른 남자들에게 이야기할 때보다

Women's conversations range / from health to their houses, / from politics to fashion, / from movies to family, / from education to relationship problems, / but sports are notably absent.

여자들의 대화들은 ~에 걸친다 / 건강부터 그들의 집까지 / 정치에서 패션까지 / 영화에서 가족까지 / 교육에서 연애 문제들까지 / 하지만 스포츠는 눈에 띄게 없다.

Men tend to have a more limited range of subjects, / the most popular being work, sports, jokes, cars, and women.

남자들은 더 제한된 범위의 주제들을 가지는 경향이 있다 / 가장 대중적인 것은 일, 스포츠, 농담, 차, 그리고 여자이다

According to Professor Petra Boynton, / a psychologist who interviewed over 1,000 women, / women also tend to move quickly / from one subject to another / in conversation, / while men usually stick to one subject / for longer periods of time.

Petra Boynton 교수에 의하면 / 천 명이 넘는 여자들을 인터뷰한 심리학자인 / 여자들은 또한 빠르게 바꾸는 경향이 있다 / 한 주제에서 다른 것으로 / 대화 중에 / 남자들이 보통 한 주제를 고수하는 반면 / 더 긴 시간 동안

At work, / this difference can be an advantage for men, / as they can put other matters aside / and concentrate fully on the topic / being discussed.

직장에서 / 이 차이점은 남자들에게 이점일 수 있다 / 그들은 다른 일들을 제쳐놓을 수 있기 때문에 / 그리고 그 주제에 완전히 집중할 수 있기 때문에 / 논의되고 있는

On the other hand, / it also means / that they sometimes find it hard to concentrate / when several things have to be discussed / at the same time in a meeting.

반면에 / 이는 또한 의미한다 / 그들(남자들)이 가끔 집중하는 것을 어려워한다는 것을 / 몇 가지 일들이 논의되어야 할 때 / 회의에서 동시에

해석 여자들은 수다 떠는 데 전문가들이고 그들은 항상 사소한 것들에 대해 이야기하는데, 혹은 그게 아니더라도 최소한 그것은 남자들이 항상 생각해 왔던 것이다. 그러나 몇몇 새로운 연구는 여자들이 여자들에게 이야기할 때 그들의 대화들은 사소한 것과는 거리가 멀고, 남자들이 다른 남자들에게 이야기할 때보다 더 많은 주제들을(40개의 주제들까지) 다룬다는 것을 시사한다. 여자들의 대화들은 건강부터 그들의 집까지, 정치에서 패션까지, 영화에서 가족까지, 교육에서 연애 문제들까지 걸치지만, 스포츠는 눈에 띄게 없다. 남자들은 더 제한된 범위의 주제들을 가지는 경향이 있으며, 가장 대중적인 것은 일, 스포츠, 농담, 차, 그리고 여자이다. 천 명이 넘는 여자들을 인터뷰한 심리학자인 Petra Boynton 교수에 의하면, 남자들이 보통 더 긴 시간 동안 한 주제를 고수하는 반면, 여자들은 또한 대화 중에 한 주제에서 다른 것으로 빠르게 바꾸는 경향이 있다. 그들(남자들)은 다른 일들을 제쳐놓고 논의되고 있는 그 주제에 완전히 집중할 수 있기 때문에 직장에서 이 차이점은 남자들에게 이점일 수 있다. 반면에, 이는 또한 그들(남자들)이 회의에서 몇 가지 일들이 동시에 논의되어야 할 때 가끔 집중하는 것을 어려워한다는 것도 의미한다.

해설 지문 중간에서 여자들의 대화는 건강, 집, 정치 등 다양한 주제에 걸친다고 했지만 스포츠는 눈에 띄게 없다고 했으므로, '② 여성들의 대화 주제는 건강에서 스포츠에 이르기까지 매우 다양하다'는 지문의 내용과 다르다.

어휘 gossip 수다를 떨다 frivolous 사소한, 하찮은 range from A to B A에서 B에 걸치다 notably 눈에 띄게, 현저히 absent 없는, 부재한 psychologist 심리학자 stick to ~을 고수하다 put ~ aside ~을 제쳐놓다

14 독해 논리적 흐름 파악 (무관한 문장 삭제) 난이도 ★☆☆

끊어읽기 해석

There was no divide / between science, philosophy, and magic / in the 15th century.
차이점이 없었다 / 과학, 철학 그리고 마법 사이에 / 15세기에는

All three came under the general heading / of 'natural philosophy'.
세 가지 모두는 일반적인 주제에 포함되었다 / '자연철학'의

① Central to the development of natural philosophy / was the recovery of classical authors, / most importantly / the work of Aristotle.
자연철학의 발달에 중심이 되는 / 고전 작가들의 복구였다 / 가장 중요하게 / 아리스토텔레스의 작품이

② Humanists quickly realized / the power of the printing press / for spreading their knowledge.
인문주의자들은 빠르게 깨달았다 / 인쇄기의 힘을 / 그들의 지식을 퍼뜨리는 것에 있어서

③ At the beginning of the 15th century / Aristotle remained the basis / for all scholastic speculation / on philosophy and science.
15세기 초반에 / 아리스토텔레스는 기반으로 남아있었다 / 모든 학문적 고찰의 / 철학과 과학에서

④ Kept alive / in the Arabic translations and commentaries of Averroes and Avicenna, / Aristotle provided a systematic perspective / on mankind's relationship with the natural world.
명맥이 이어지면서 / Averroes와 Avicenna의 아랍어 번역과 논평에서 / 아리스토텔레스는 체계적인 시각을 제공했다 / 인류와 자연 세계의 관계에 대한

Surviving texts / like his *Physics*, *Metaphysics*, and *Meteorology* / provided scholars with the logical tools / to understand the forces / that created the natural world.
잔존한 서적들은 / 그의 물리학, 형이상학, 기상학과 같은 / 학자들에게 논리적인 도구들을 제공했다 / 물리력을 이해할 수 있는 / 자연 세계를 형성한

해석 15세기에는 과학, 철학 그리고 마법 사이에 차이점이 없었다. 세 가지 모두는 '자연철학'의 일반적인 주제에 포함되었다. ① 고전 작가들의 복구, 가장 중요하게 아리스토텔레스의 작품이 자연철학의 발달에 중심이 되었다. ② 인문주의자들 그들의 지식을 퍼뜨리는 것에 있어서 인쇄기의 힘을 빠르게 깨달았다. ③ 15세기 초반에 아리스토텔레스는 철학과 과학에서 모든 학문적 고찰의 기반으로 남아있었다. ④ Averroes와 Avicenna의 아랍어 번역과 논평에서 명맥이 이어지면서, 아리스토텔레스는 인류와 자연 세계의 관계에 대한 체계적인 시각을 제공했다. 그의 물리학, 형이상학, 기상학과 같은 잔존한 서적들은 학자들에게 자연 세계를 형성한 물리력을 이해할 수 있는 논리적인 도구들을 제공했다.

해설 지문 앞부분에서 15세기에 과학, 철학, 마법은 차이점이 없이 모두 '자연철학'의 일반적인 주제에 포함되었다고 설명하고, ①, ③, ④에서 자연철학의 발달에 가장 중심이 되는 아리스토텔레스가 학문 등에 미친 영향과 역할에 대해 설명하고 있다. 그러나 ②번은 인문주의자들이 그들의 지식을 퍼뜨리는 데에서 인쇄기의 힘을 깨달았다는 내용으로 지문 전체의 흐름과 어울리지 않는다.

어휘 come under 포함되다 speculation 고찰, 추측
keep alive 명맥을 이어가다 commentary 논평
Metaphysics 형이상학 Meteorology 기상학

15 문법 주어·동사/목적어/보어/수식어 난이도 ★★★

해석 ① 지진 후에 뒤따르는 화재는 보험 업계에게 특히 흥미가 있는 부분이다.
② 워드 프로세서는 과거에 타자수에게 최고의 도구로 여겨졌다.
③ 현금 예측에서 발생하는 소득의 요소들은 그 회사의 상황에 따라 달라질 것이다.
④ 세계 최초의 디지털카메라는 이스트먼 코닥에서 Steve Sasson에 의해 1975년에 만들어졌다.

해설 ③ 동사 자리 동사 자리에는 조동사(will) + 동사원형이 올 수 있는데, 동사원형 자리에 동사가 두 개(be, vary) 왔으므로 will be vary를 자동사 vary(달라지다)만 남긴 will vary로 고쳐야 한다.

오답 ① 형용사 자리 be 동사(is)는 주격 보어를 취하는 동사인데, 보
분석　　어 자리에는 명사나 형용사 역할을 하는 것이 올 수 있으므로 형용사 역할을 하는 'of + 추상명사'(of special interest)가 올바르게 쓰였다.
② 5형식 동사의 수동태 동사 consider는 목적어 뒤에 '(to be) + 명사/형용사'를 취하는 5형식 동사인데, consider가 수동태가 되면 '(to be) + 명사'(to be ~ tool)는 수동태 동사 뒤에 그대로 남아야 하므로 were considered to be ~ tool이 올바르게 쓰였다.
④ 능동태·수동태 구별 동사 create 뒤에 목적어가 없고, 주어(The world's first digital camera)와 동사가 '세계 최초의 디지털카메라가 만들어졌다'라는 의미의 수동 관계이므로 수동태 was created가 올바르게 쓰였다.

어휘 following ~후에, ~에 이어 ultimate 최고의, 궁극적인
vary 달라지다 circumstance 상황

👍 이것도 알면 **합격!**

동사 자리에는 수, 시제, 태가 적절한 동사가 와야 한다.

ⓔⓧ Flight attendants on the plane (are, is) trained in basic
　　복수 주어　　　　　　　　　　복수 동사
safety protocol.
그 비행기에 탄 승무원들은 기본적인 안전 수칙을 훈련받았다.

ⓔⓧ My salary last month (was, is) higher than usual.
　　　　　과거 시간 표현 과거 시제
지난달에 내 월급은 평소보다 더 높았다.

ⓔⓧ The new medicine (has undergone, undergoes) rigorous
　　　　　주어　　　　　수동태(받았다)
testing.
그 신약은 엄격한 검사를 받았다.

16 독해 추론 (빈칸 완성 - 구) 난이도 ★★☆

끊어읽기 해석

The slowing of China's economy / from historically high rates of growth / has long been expected / to weigh on growth elsewhere.
중국 경제의 둔화는 / 역사적으로 높은 성장률로부터 / 오랫동안 예상되어 왔다 / 다른 곳의 성장을 압박할 것으로

"The China that had been growing / at 10 percent for 30 years / was a powerful source of fuel / for much of what drove the global economy forward", / said Stephen Roach at Yale.

The growth rate has slowed / to an official figure of around 7 percent.
성장률은 더뎌졌다 / 공식적인 수치상 약 7퍼센트로

"That's a concrete deceleration", / Mr. Roach added.
그것은 명확한 감속이다 / Mr. Roach가 덧붙였다

해석 역사적으로 높은 성장률로부터 중국 경제의 둔화는 다른 곳(다른 나라들)의 성장을 압박할 것으로 오랫동안 예상되어 왔다. "30년 동안 10퍼센트 대로 성장해왔던 중국은 세계 경제를 앞으로 몰고 갔던 강력한 동력원이었다"라고 예일대의 Stephen Roach가 말했다. 성장률은 공식적인 수치상 약 7퍼센트로 더뎌졌다. "그것은 명확한 감속이다"라고 Mr. Roach가 덧붙였다.

① 속도를 높일 것으로　　　② ~을 압박할 것으로
③ ~로 이어질 것으로　　　④ ~을 야기할 것으로

해설 빈칸 뒤 문장에서 중국의 엄청난 성장이 세계 경제를 앞으로 몰고 갔던 강력한 동력원이었지만 그 성장률이 이제는 더뎌졌다고 했고, 빈칸이 있는 문장에서 오랫동안 높은 성장률을 보인 중국 경제가 둔화되는 것이 다른 곳에 미치는 영향에 대해 언급하고 있으므로, 빈칸에는 '② ~을 압박할 것으로'가 들어가야 적절하다.

어휘 figure 수치 concrete 명확한, 구체적인 deceleration 감속
weigh on ~을 압박하다 lead to ~로 이어지다
result in ~을 야기하다

17 독해 추론 (빈칸 완성 - 단어) 난이도 ★☆☆

끊어읽기 해석

As more and more leaders work remotely / or with teams / scattered around the nation or the globe, / as well as with consultants and freelancers, / you'll have to give them more autonomy.
점점 더 많은 리더들이 원격으로 일하면서 / 혹은 팀들과 함께 / 전국 또는 전 세계적으로 흩어져 있는 / 자문 위원들과 프리랜서들뿐만 아니라 / 당신은 그들에게 더 많은 자율성을 줘야 할 것이다

The more trust you bestow, / the more others trust you.
당신이 더 많은 신뢰를 줄수록 / 다른 사람들이 당신을 더 신뢰한다

I am convinced / that there is a direct correlation / between job satisfaction and how empowered people are / to fully execute their job / without someone shadowing them / every step of the way.
나는 확신한다 / 직접적인 상관관계가 있다는 것을 / 직업 만족도와 사람들이 권한을 얼만큼 부여받았는지 사이에 / 그들의 일을 완전히 수행하기 위해 / 그들을 따라다니는 누군가가 없이 / 그 일의 매 단계에

Giving away responsibility / to those you trust / can not only make your organization run more smoothly / but also free up more of your time / so you can focus on larger issues.
책임감을 나누어 주는 것은 / 당신이 신뢰하는 사람들에게 / 당신의 단체가 더 순조롭게 돌아갈 수 있게 할 뿐만 아니라 / 당신의 시간을 더 자유롭게 할 수도 있다 / 그래서 당신이 더 큰 문제들에 집중할 수 있도록

해석 점점 더 많은 리더들이 원격으로, 혹은 자문 위원들과 프리랜서들뿐만 아니라 전국 또는 전 세계적으로 흩어져 있는 팀들과 함께 일하면서, 당신은 그들에게 더 많은 자율성을 줘야 할 것이다. 당신이 더 많은 신뢰를 줄수록, 다른 사람들이 당신을 더 신뢰한다. 나는 직업 만족도와 사람들이 그 일의 매 단계에 그들을 따라다니는 누군가가 없이 그들의 일을 완전히 수행하기 위해 권한을 얼만큼 부여받았는지 사이에 직접적인 상관관계가 있다는 것을 확신한다. 당신이 신뢰하는 사람들에게 책임감을 나누어 주는 것은 당신의

단체가 더 순조롭게 돌아갈 수 있게 할 뿐만 아니라 당신의 시간을 더 자유롭게 해서 당신이 더 큰 문제들에 집중할 수 있도록 할 수도 있다.

① 일　　　　　　② 보상
③ 제한　　　　　④ 자율성

해설　빈칸 뒤 문장에서 당신이 더 많은 신뢰를 줄수록 다른 사람들이 당신을 더 신뢰한다고 했고, 사람들의 직업 만족도와 완전한 업무 수행을 위해 얼마나 권한을 부여받았는지 사이에는 직접적인 상관관계가 있다고 했으므로, 빈칸에는 '④ 자율성'이 들어가야 한다.

어휘　bestow 주다　correlation 상관관계　empower 권한을 부여하다
execute 수행하다　shadow (그림자처럼) 따라다니다
give away 나누어 주다　smoothly 순조롭게

18　독해　전체내용 파악 (요지 파악)　난이도 ★★☆

끊어읽기 해석

"In Judaism, / we're largely defined / by our actions," / says Lisa Grushcow, / the senior rabbi / at Temple Emanu-El-Beth Sholom / in Montreal.
유대교에서 / 우리는 대체로 정의된다 / 우리의 행동들에 의해 / 라고 Lisa Grushcow는 말한다 / 수석 율법학자인 / Emanu-El-Beth Sholom 신전에서 / 몬트리올의

"You can't really be / an armchair do-gooder."
당신은 실제로 될 수 없다 / 탁상공론적인 공상적 사회 개량가가

This concept relates / to the Jewish notion of tikkun olam, / which translates as "to repair the world."
이 개념은 관련된다 / 유대인의 tikkun olam 관념과 / 그런데 이것은 '세상을 바로잡는 것'을 뜻한다

Our job / as human beings, / she says, / "is to mend / what's been broken.
우리의 책임은 / 인간으로서 / 그녀는 말한다 / 고치는 것이다 / 망가진 것을

It's incumbent on us / to not only take care of ourselves and each other / but also to build a better world around us."
이것은 우리에게 의무로서 지워진다 / 우리 자신과 서로를 돌보는 것뿐만 아니라 / 우리 주위의 더 나은 세상을 만드는 것은

This philosophy conceptualizes goodness / as something based in service.
이 철학은 선량함을 개념화한다 / 봉사에 기반을 둔 무언가로

Instead of asking / "Am I a good person?" / you may want to ask / "What good do I do / in the world?"
묻는 것 대신에 / 내가 좋은 사람인가 / 당신은 묻기를 원할지도 모른다 / 내가 어떤 선을 행하는가 / 세상에서

Grushcow's temple / puts these beliefs into action / inside and outside their community.
Grushcow의 신전은 / 실행에 옮긴다 이러한 생각들을 / 그들의 지역 사회 안팎으로

For instance, / they sponsored two refugee families / from Vietnam / to come to Canada / in the 1970s.
예를 들어 / 그들은 두 난민 가족을 후원했다 / 베트남에서 온 / 캐나다로 오도록 / 1970년대에

해석　"유대교에서, 우리는 우리의 행동들에 의해 대체로 정의된다"라고 몬트리올의 Emanu-El-Beth Sholom 신전에서 수석 율법학자인 Lisa Grushcow는 말한다. "당신은 실제로 탁상공론적인 공상적 사회 개량가가 될 수 없다." 이 개념은 유대인의 tikkun olam 관념과 관련되는데, 이것은 '세상을 바로잡는 것'을 뜻한다. 그녀는 말한다. "인간으로서 우리의 책임은 망가진 것을 고치는 것이다. 우리 자신과 서로를 돌보는 것뿐만 아니라 우리 주위의 더 나은 세상

을 만드는 것은 우리에게 의무로서 지워진다." 이 철학은 선량함을 봉사에 기반을 둔 무언가로 개념화한다. "내가 좋은 사람인가?"라고 묻는 것 대신에 당신은 "내가 세상에서 어떤 선을 행하는가?"를 묻기를 원할지도 모른다. Grushcow의 신전은 이러한 생각들을 그들(유대인들)의 지역 사회 안팎으로 실행에 옮긴다. 예를 들어, 그들(유대인들)은 1970년대에 베트남에서 온 두 난민 가족이 캐나다로 오도록 후원했다.

① 우리는 세상을 치유하기 위해 노력해야 한다.
② 지역 사회는 피난처로서 기능해야 한다.
③ 우리는 선량함을 믿음으로 개념화해야 한다.
④ 신전들은 지역 사회에 기여해야 한다.

해설　지문 중간에서 유대인의 tikkun olam 관념은 '세상을 바로잡는 것'을 뜻한다고 한 뒤, 그 관념에 따르면 망가진 것을 고치고, 우리 자신을 돌보는 것뿐만 아니라 더 나은 세상을 만드는 것이 인간으로서 우리의 책임이라고 했으므로, '① 우리는 세상을 치유하기 위해 노력해야 한다'가 이 글의 요지이다.

어휘　Judaism 유대교　define 정의하다　rabbi 율법학자
armchair 탁상공론적인　do-gooder 공상적 사회 개량가
relate to ~과 관련되다　job 책임, 일　mend 고치다
incumbent on ~에게 의무로서 지워지는　conceptualize 개념화하다
goodness 선량함　put into action 실행에 옮기다
sponsor 후원하다　refugee 난민　contribute 기여하다

19　독해　추론 (빈칸 완성 - 연결어)　난이도 ★★☆

끊어읽기 해석

Ancient philosophers and spiritual teachers / understood the need / to balance the positive with the negative, / optimism with pessimism, / a striving for success and security / with an openness to failure and uncertainty.
고대 철학자들과 정신적인 스승들은 / 필요성을 알고 있었다 / 긍정적인 것과 부정적인 것의 균형을 이룰 / 낙관주의와 비관주의의 / 성공과 안전을 위해 분투하는 것과 / 실패와 불확실성에 대한 개방성의

The Stoics recommended "the premeditation of evils," / or deliberately visualizing / the worst-case scenario.
스토아 철학자들은 '불행의 계획'을 권했다 / 즉 의도적으로 상상하는 것 / 최악의 경우에 대비한 시나리오를

This tends to reduce anxiety / about the future: / when you soberly picture / how badly things could go in reality, / you usually conclude / that you could cope.
이것은 염려를 줄이는 경향이 있다 / 미래에 대한 / 당신이 진지하게 상상할 때 / 실제로 얼마나 나쁘게 상황이 흘러갈지를 / 당신은 대개 결론을 내린다 / 당신이 대처할 수 있을 것이라고

(A) Besides, / they noted, / imagining / that you might lose the relationships and possessions / you currently enjoy / increases your gratitude / for having them now.
(A) 게다가 / 그들은 주목했다 / 상상하는 것이 / 관계와 소유물들을 잃을지도 모른다고 / 당신이 현재 향유하는 / 감사를 증가시킨다는 것을 / 그것들을 현재 가지고 있는 것에 대한

Positive thinking, / (B) by contrast, / always leans into the future, / ignoring present pleasures.
긍정적인 생각은 / (B) 대조적으로 / 항상 미래에 의지한다 / 현재의 기쁨을 무시하면서

해석　고대 철학자들과 정신적인 스승들은 긍정적인 것과 부정적인 것, 낙관주의와 비관주의, 성공과 안전을 위해 분투하는 것과 실패와 불확실성에 대한 개방성의 균형을 이룰 필요성을 알고 있었다. 스토아 철학자들은 '불행의 계획,' 즉 의도적으로 최악의 경우에 대비한 시나리오를 상상하는 것을 권했다. 이것은 미래에 대한 염려

를 줄이는 경향이 있다. 당신이 실제로 얼마나 나쁘게 상황이 흘러갈지를 진지하게 상상할 때, 당신은 대처할 수 있을 것이라고 대개 결론을 내린다. (A) 게다가, 그들은 당신이 현재 향유하는 관계와 소유물들을 잃을지도 모른다고 상상하는 것이 그것들을 현재 가지고 있는 것에 대한 감사를 증가시킨다는 것을 주목했다. (B) 대조적으로, 긍정적인 생각은 현재의 기쁨을 무시하면서 항상 미래에 의지한다.

	(A)	(B)
①	그럼에도 불구하고	게다가
②	게다가	예를 들어
③	게다가	대조적으로
④	그러나	결론적으로

해설 (A) 앞부분에서 상황이 얼마나 나쁘게 흘러갈지를 상상할 때 그것에 대처할 수 있다고 결론 내릴 수 있다고 했고, (A) 뒤 문장은 현재 향유하는 관계와 소유를 잃을지도 모른다고 생각할 때 현재 가지는 것을 감사하게 된다는 추가적인 내용이므로, (A)에는 Besides(게다가)가 나와야 적절하다. (B) 뒤 문장은 긍정적인 생각은 미래에 의지한다는 대조적인 내용이므로, (B)에는 by contrast(대조적으로)가 나와야 적절하다.
따라서 ③ (A) Besides – (B) by contrast가 정답이다.

어휘 philosopher 철학자 optimism 낙관주의 pessimism 비관주의 strive 분투하다 openness 개방성 Stoic 스토아 철학자 premeditation 계획, 미리 생각하는 것 evil 불행 visualize 상상하다 worst-case 최악의 경우에 대비한 anxiety 염려 soberly 진지하게 conclude 결론을 내리다 cope 대처하다 gratitude 감사

말할 수 있다 / 일하는 것은 긍정적인 중독이라고 / 아마 워커홀릭들은 강박적일 것이다 / 그들의 일에 대해서 / 그러나 그들의 중독은 안전한 것처럼 보인다 / 심지어 유익한 / 것으로

해석 왜 워커홀릭들은 그들의 일을 그렇게 많이 즐길까? 대부분 일하는 것이 몇몇 중요한 이점들을 제공하기 때문이다. 그것은 사람들에게 생계를 유지하는 한 방법인 급료를 제공해 준다. ② 그리고 일하는 것은 금전적인 안정 이상을 제공한다. 그것은 사람들에게 자신감을 제공한다. 그들은 그들이 힘든 작업을 완성하고 '내가 저것을 해냈어'라고 말할 수 있을 때 만족감의 느낌을 갖는다. 심리학자들은 일은 또한 사람들에게 주체성을 준다고 주장한다. 그들은 그들이 자아의식과 개성을 얻을 수 있도록 일한다. 게다가 대부분의 일은 사람들에게 사회적으로 받아들여지는 다른 사람들을 만나기 위한 수단을 제공한다. 일하는 것은 긍정적인 중독이라고 말할 수 있다. 아마 워커홀릭들은 그들의 일에 대해서 강박적일 것이지만, 그들의 중독은 안전한, 심지어는 유익한 것처럼 보인다.

해설 ②번 앞 문장에서 일하는 것은 사람들에게 급료를 제공해 준다고 하고, ②번 뒤 문장에서는 그것은 사람들에게 자신감을 제공한다고 했으므로, ②번 자리에 일하는 것이 금전적인 안정 이상을 제공한다는 내용의 주어진 문장이 나와야 지문이 자연스럽게 연결된다.

어휘 paycheck 급료 earn a living 생계를 유지하다 individualism 개성 acceptable 받아들여지는 compulsive 강박적인 advantageous 유익한, 이로운

20 독해 논리적 흐름 파악 (문장 삽입) 난이도 ★☆☆

끊어읽기 해석

And working offers / more than financial security.
그리고 일하는 것은 제공한다 / 금전적인 안정 이상을

Why do workaholics enjoy / their jobs / so much?
왜 워커홀릭들은 즐길까 / 그들의 일을 / 그렇게 많이

Mostly because / working offers some important advantages.
대부분 ~때문이다 / 일하는 것이 몇몇 중요한 이점들을 제공한다

(①) It provides people with paychecks / —a way to earn a living.
그것은 사람들에게 급료를 제공해 준다 / 생계를 유지하는 한 방법인

(②) It provides people with self-confidence; / they have a feeling of satisfaction / when they've produced a challenging piece of work / and are able to say, / "I made that".
그것은 사람들에게 자신감을 제공한다 / 그들은 만족감의 느낌을 갖는다 / 그들이 힘든 작업을 완성했을 때 / 그리고 말할 수 있다 / '내가 저것을 해냈어'라고

(③) Psychologists claim / that work also gives people an identity; / they work / so that they can get / a sense of self and individualism.
심리학자들은 주장한다 / 일은 또한 사람들에게 주체성을 준다고 / 그들은 일한다 / 그들이 얻을 수 있도록 / 자아의식과 개성을

(④) In addition, / most jobs provide people with a socially acceptable way / to meet others.
게다가 / 대부분의 일은 사람들에게 사회적으로 받아들여지는 수단을 제공한다 / 다른 사람들을 만나기 위한

It could be said / that working is a positive addiction; / maybe workaholics are compulsive / about their work, / but their addiction seems to be a safe / —even an advantageous— / one.

12회 | 2020년 지방직 9급

정답
p.102

01	② 어휘 - 어휘&표현	11	② 어휘 - 생활영어
02	④ 어휘 - 어휘&표현	12	① 문법 - 동명사
03	② 어휘 - 어휘&표현	13	② 어휘 - 생활영어
04	① 어휘 - 어휘&표현	14	④ 독해 - 전체내용 파악
05	③ 문법 - 시제&명사와 관사	15	③ 독해 - 논리적 흐름 파악
06	④ 어휘 - 어휘&표현	16	③ 독해 - 추론
07	③ 문법 - 병치·도치 구문&수 일치	17	① 독해 - 전체내용 파악
08	② 문법 - 명사절	18	③ 독해 - 논리적 흐름 파악
09	① 독해 - 추론	19	④ 독해 - 논리적 흐름 파악
10	③ 독해 - 전체내용 파악	20	④ 독해 - 세부내용 파악

· 자신이 취약한 영역은 '공무원 영어, 이렇게 출제된다!'(문제집 p.8)를 통해 다시 한번 확인하고 학습하시기 바랍니다.

취약영역 분석표

영역	세부 유형	문항 수	소계
어휘	어휘&표현	5	/7
	생활영어	2	
문법	시제&명사와 관사	1	/4
	병치·도치 구문&수 일치	1	
	명사절	1	
	동명사	1	
독해	전체내용 파악	3	/9
	세부내용 파악	1	
	추론	2	
	논리적 흐름 파악	3	
총계			/20

---

01 어휘 어휘&표현 insulated 난이도 ★★☆

해석 플라스틱병의 문제는 그것들이 절연 처리가 되지 않는다는 것이어서 기온이 상승하기 시작하면, 당신의 물도 뜨거워질 것이다.
① 위생적인
② 절연 처리가 된
③ 재활용 가능한
④ 방수의

어휘 sanitary 위생적인 insulated 절연 처리가 된 waterproof 방수의

👍 이것도 알면 **합격!**

insulated(절연 처리가 된)의 유의어
= protected, covered, wrapped, shielded, encased, enveloped, coated

02 어휘 어휘&표현 alleviate = relieve 난이도 ★☆☆

해석 글을 쓸 때 작가가 채택하는 전략은 주의력 과부하의 어려움을 완화시킬 수도 있다.
① 보완하다
② 가속화하다
③ 계산하다
④ 완화시키다

어휘 adopt 채택하다, 입양하다 alleviate 완화시키다, 경감하다
overload 과부하 complement 보완하다
accelerate 가속화하다 calculate 계산하다

👍 이것도 알면 **합격!**

alleviate(완화시키다)의 유의어
= lesson, assuage, ease

03 어휘 어휘&표현 touch off = give rise to 난이도 ★★☆

해석 그 잔인한 광경은 그렇지 않았으면 그녀의 머리에 떠오르지 않았을 생각을 유발했다.
① 돌보았다
② 초래했다
③ 보상했다
④ 연락을 유지했다

어휘 cruel 잔인한, 괴로운 touch off 유발하다, 발사하다
give rise to 초래하다 make up for 보상하다, 보충하다
keep in contact with 연락을 유지하다

👍 이것도 알면 **합격!**

touch off(유발하다)의 유의어
= spark, kindle, provoke, stir, trigger

04 어휘 어휘&표현 shun = avoid 난이도 ★★☆

해석 학교의 불량배는 교실에서 다른 학생들에 의해 기피되는 것이 어떤 것인지 몰랐다.
① 회피되는
② 경고된
③ 처벌된
④ 모방된

어휘 **bully** 불량배, (약자를) 괴롭히는 사람; 괴롭히다
shun 기피하다, 멀어지다 **imitate** 모방하다

👍 **이것도 알면 합격!**

shun(기피하다)의 유의어
= spurn, reject, ignore

---

05 문법 시제&명사와 관사 난이도 ★★☆

해석 ① 은하계에 있는 수십억 개의 별 중에서, 얼마나 많은 별이 생명을 부화할 수 있을까?
② 크리스마스 파티가 매우 즐거워서 나는 전혀 시간 가는 줄 몰랐다.
③ 나는 오늘 정오에 일을 시작할 것이기 때문에 지금 떠나야만 한다.
④ 그들은 어렸을 때 훨씬 더 책을 좋아하곤 했다.

해설 ③ 미래 시제 | 불가산 명사의 쓰임 미래를 나타내는 시간 표현 at noon today(오늘 정오)가 쓰였고, 현재진행 시제를 사용해 미래에 일어나기로 예정되어 있는 일이나 곧 일어나려고 하는 일을 표현할 수 있으므로 현재진행 시제 am starting이 올바르게 쓰였다. 또한, 명사 work는 '일'이라는 의미로 쓰일 때 앞에 부정관사(a/an)를 쓰거나 복수형으로 쓸 수 없는 불가산 명사이므로 work가 올바르게 쓰였다.

오답 ① 대명사 수 일치 대명사 much가 지시하는 명사(stars)가 가
분석 산 복수 명사이므로, 불가산 대명사 much를 가산 복수 대명사 many로 고쳐야 한다.
② 감정동사의 분사 감정을 나타내는 동사(excite)의 경우 주어가 감정의 원인이면 현재분사를, 감정을 느끼는 주체이면 과거분사를 써야 하는데, 문맥상 '크리스마스 파티가 즐거웠다'라는 의미로 주어(The Christmas party)가 감정의 원인이 되어야 자연스러우므로 과거분사 excited를 현재분사 exciting으로 고쳐야 한다.
④ 조동사 표현 조동사처럼 쓰이는 표현 used to(~하곤 했다) 뒤에는 동사원형이 와야 하므로 loving을 동사원형 love로 고쳐야 한다.

어휘 **hatch** 부화하다 **lose track of time** 시간 가는 줄 모르다

👍 **이것도 알면 합격!**

다음 세 가지 표현을 혼동하지 않도록 구별하여 알아두자.
· be used to -ing ~에 익숙하다
· be used to + 동사원형 ~하는 데 사용되다
· used to(= would) + 동사원형 ~하곤 했다

---

06 어휘 어휘&표현 make a case for = strongly suggest 난이도 ★★★

해석 Francesca가 여름 휴가 동안 집에 있을 것을 주장한 후, 불편한 정적이 저녁 식탁을 엄습했다. Robert는 그녀에게 그의 거창한 계획에 대해 이야기하기에 적절한 때인지 확실하지 않았다.

① ~에 반대했다
② ~을 꿈꾸었다
③ 완전히 제외했다
④ 강력하게 제안했다

어휘 **make a case for** 주장하다 **uncomfortable** 불편한
silence 정적, 침묵 **fall on** ~을 엄습하다 **grandiose** 거창한, 과장된
object 반대하다 **exclude** 제외하다

👍 **이것도 알면 합격!**

make a case for(주장하다)의 유의어
= argue, contend, claim, maintain

---

07 문법 병치·도치 구문&수 일치 난이도 ★★☆

해석 엘리자베스 테일러는 아름다운 보석을 보는 안목이 있었고, 한 때 "여자는 항상 더 많은 다이아몬드를 가질 수 있습니다"라고 말하며 수년간 몇몇 멋진 보석들을 수집했다. 2011년에, 그녀의 가장 멋진 보석은 1억1천5백만 9천 달러의 수입을 얻은 Christie's의 저녁 경매에서 팔렸다. 그 저녁 경매 동안에 팔린 그녀의 가장 가치 있는 소유물 중에는 불가리의 보석으로 장식된 1961년식 시계가 있었다. 손목 주위를 휘감는 뱀처럼 디자인되어, 머리와 꼬리는 다이아몬드로 덮여있고, 최면을 거는 듯한 두 개의 에메랄드로 된 눈을 가진, 작아서 눈에 띄지 않는 기계는 그것의 사나운 턱을 열어젖혀서 작은 쿼츠식 시계를 드러낸다.

해설 ③ 도치 구문 | 주어·동사 수 일치 장소를 나타내는 부사구(Among ~ sale)가 강조되어 문장 맨 앞에 나오면 주어와 동사가 도치되어 '동사 + 주어(a 1961 bejeweled timepiece)'의 어순이 되어야 한다. 주어 자리에 단수 명사 a 1961 bejeweled timepiece가 왔으므로 복수 동사 were를 단수 동사 was로 고쳐야 한다.

오답 ① 현재분사 vs. 과거분사 주절의 주어(Elizabeth Taylor)와 분
분석 사구문이 '엘리자베스 테일러가 말했다'라는 의미의 능동 관계이므로 현재분사 declaring이 올바르게 쓰였다.
② 주격 관계대명사 선행사 an evening auction이 사물이고, 관계절 내에서 동사 brought의 주어 역할을 하므로 주격 관계대명사 that이 올바르게 쓰였다.
④ with + 목적어 + 분사 동시에 일어나는 상황은 'with + 목적어(its head and tail) + 분사'의 형태로 나타낼 수 있는데 목적어 its head and tail과 분사가 '그것의 머리와 꼬리는 덮여있다'라는 의미의 수동 관계이므로 과거분사 covered가 올바르게 쓰였다.

어휘 **have an eye for** 안목이 있다 **amass** 수집하다, 축적하다
auction 경매 **bring in** 수입을 얻다 **prized** 가치 있는, 소중한
possession 소유물, 재산 **bejewel** 보석으로 장식하다
timepiece 시계 **serpent** 뱀 **coil** 휘감다; 고리
hypnotic 최면을 거는 듯한 **discreet** (작아서) 눈에 띄지 않는
fierce 사나운, 험악한
quartz 쿼츠식의(수정의 압정 현상을 이용하는 방식)

👍 **이것도 알면 합격!**

동시에 일어나는 상황은 'with + 목적어 + 부사'로도 나타낼 수 있으며, 이때 '~한 채', '~하면서'라는 뜻으로 해석된다는 것을 기억하자.
(ex) She sometimes likes to watch movies **with the sound off**.
그녀는 가끔 소리를 끈 채로 영화 보는 것을 좋아한다.

---

08 문법 명사절 난이도 ★★☆

해설 ② 복합관계대명사의 쓰임 복합관계대명사의 격은 복합관계대명사가 이끄는 명사절 내에서 그것의 역할에 따라 결정된다. 주어가

없는 불완전한 절(completes the questionnaire)을 이끌며 동사(completes)의 주어 자리에 올 수 있는 것은 주격 복합관계대명사이므로 목적격 복합관계대명사 whomever를 주격 복합관계대명사 whoever로 고쳐야 한다.

오답 분석

① 과거완료 시제 | 수동태로 쓸 수 없는 자동사 '보증이 만료된' 것은 특정 과거 시점(수리는 무료가 아닌 시점)보다 이전에 일어난 일이고, 동사 expire는 '만료되다'라는 의미를 가질 때 목적어를 갖지 않는 자동사이므로 수동태로 쓰일 수 없다. 따라서, 과거완료 능동태 had expired가 올바르게 쓰였다.

③ 혼합 가정법 '지난달 내가 휴가를 요청했더라면 지금 하와이에 있을 텐데'는 과거의 상황을 반대로 가정했을 경우 그 결과가 현재에 영향을 미칠 때 쓰는 혼합 가정법을 사용하여 나타낼 수 있다. 혼합 가정법은 'If + 주어 + had p.p., 주어 + would/should/could/might + 동사원형'의 형태로 나타내므로 If I had asked ~, I would be in Hawaii now가 올바르게 쓰였다.

④ 과거 시제 | 숙어 표현 과거 시제와 자주 함께 쓰이는 시간 표현 'last + 시간 표현'(last year)이 왔으므로, 과거 시제 passed away, became이 올바르게 쓰였다. 또한, '설상가상으로'라는 의미의 숙어 표현 what is worse의 과거형인 what was worse도 올바르게 쓰였다.

어휘 warranty 보증, 품질 보증서　expire 만료되다, 끝나다
free of charge 무료의　questionnaire 설문지
pass away 돌아가시다, 사라지다　what is worse 설상가상으로

👍 이것도 알면 합격!

③번 보기에 쓰인 now처럼 혼합 가정법의 주절에는 '현재'임을 나타내는 단서가 함께 온다.

ex If I had done my homework, I could go to a movie today.
내가 숙제를 했더라면, 오늘 영화를 보러 갈 수 있을 텐데

09　독해　추론 (빈칸 완성 - 연결어)　난이도 ★★☆

끊어읽기 해석

Assertive behavior involves / standing up for your rights / and expressing your thoughts and feelings / in a direct, appropriate way / that does not violate the rights of others.
자기주장이 강한 행동은 포함한다 / 당신의 권리를 옹호하는 것을 / 그리고 당신의 생각과 감정을 표현하는 것을 / 직접적이고 적절한 방식으로 / 타인의 권리를 침해하지 않는

It is a matter / of getting the other person to understand / your viewpoint.
그것은 문제이다 / 다른 사람이 이해하도록 하는 것의 / 당신의 관점을

People / who exhibit assertive behavior skills / are able to handle conflict situations / with ease and assurance / while maintaining good interpersonal relations.
사람들은 / 자기주장이 강한 행동 기량을 보이는 / 갈등이 있는 상황을 다룰 수 있다 / 쉽고 자신감 있게 / 바람직한 대인관계를 유지하면서

(A) In contrast, / aggressive behavior involves / expressing your thoughts and feelings / and defending your rights / in a way / that openly violates the rights of others.
(A) 그에 반해서 / 공격적인 행동은 포함한다 / 당신의 생각과 감정을 표현하는 것을 / 그리고 당신의 권리를 옹호하는 것을 / ~한 방식으로 / 공공연하게 타인의 권리를 침해하는

Those exhibiting aggressive behavior / seem to believe / that the rights of others / must be subservient to theirs.
공격적인 행동을 보이는 사람들은 / 믿는 것 같다 / 타인의 권리는 / 그들의 것(권리)보다 덜 중요해야 한다고

(B) Thus, / they have a difficult time maintaining / good interpersonal relations.
(B) 따라서 / 그들은 유지하는 데 어려움을 겪는다 / 바람직한 대인관계를

They are likely to interrupt, talk fast, ignore others, and use / sarcasm or other forms of verbal abuse / to maintain control.
그들은 말을 끊고, 빨리 말하고, 타인을 무시하고 사용할 가능성이 있다 / 풍자나 언어폭력의 다른 형태를 / 지배권을 유지하기 위해

해석 자기주장이 강한 행동은 타인의 권리를 침해하지 않는 직접적이고 적절한 방식으로 당신의 권리를 옹호하고 당신의 생각과 감정을 표현하는 것을 포함한다. 그것은 다른 사람이 당신의 관점을 이해하도록 하는 것의 문제이다. 자기주장이 강한 행동 기량을 보이는 사람들은 바람직한 대인관계를 유지하면서 갈등이 있는 상황을 쉽고 자신감 있게 다룰 수 있다. (A) 그에 반해서, 공격적인 행동은 공공연하게 타인의 권리를 침해하는 방식으로 당신의 생각과 감정을 표현하고 당신의 권리를 옹호하는 것을 포함한다. 공격적인 행동을 보이는 사람들은 타인의 권리는 그들의 권리보다 덜 중요해야 한다고 믿는 것 같다. (B) 따라서, 그들은 바람직한 대인관계를 유지하는 데 어려움을 겪는다. 그들은 지배권을 유지하기 위해 말을 끊고, 빨리 말하고, 타인을 무시하고, 풍자나 언어폭력의 다른 형태를 사용할 가능성이 있다.

(A)	(B)
① 그에 반해서	따라서
② 마찬가지로	게다가
③ 하지만	한편
④ 그에 따라	반면에

해설 (A) 빈칸 앞부분은 자기주장이 강한 행동은 타인의 권리를 침해하지 않는 적절한 방식으로 자신의 권리를 옹호하고 생각과 감정을 표현한다는 내용이고, (A) 빈칸 뒤 문장은 공격적인 행동은 타인의 권리를 침해하는 방식으로 생각과 감정을 표현하고 자신의 권리를 옹호하는 것을 포함한다는 대조적인 내용이다. 따라서 대조를 나타내는 연결어인 In contrast(그에 반해서) 또는 However(하지만)가 나와야 적절하다. (B) 빈칸 앞 문장은 공격적인 행동을 보이는 사람들은 타인의 권리가 자신의 권리보다 덜 중요해야 한다고 믿는 것 같다는 내용이고, (B) 빈칸 뒤 문장은 그들(공격적인 행동을 보이는 사람들)이 바람직한 대인관계를 유지하는 데 어려움을 겪는다는 결론적인 내용이다. 따라서 결론을 나타내는 연결어인 Thus(따라서)가 나와야 적절하다.
따라서 ① In contrast(그에 반해서) - Thus(따라서)가 정답이다.

어휘 assertive 자기주장이 강한, 적극적인
stand up for ~을 옹호하다, 지키다　violate 침해하다, 위반하다
viewpoint 관점, 방향　exhibit 보이다, 드러내다
conflict 갈등, 마찰; 상충하다　assurance 자신감, 확신
interpersonal relation 대인관계　aggressive 공격적인
defend 옹호하다, 지키다　subservient 덜 중요한, 부차적인
sarcasm 풍자, 비꼼　verbal 언어의, 구두의

10　독해　전체내용 파악 (주제 파악)　난이도 ★☆☆

끊어읽기 해석

The e-book applications / available on tablet computers / employ touchscreen technology.
전자책 애플리케이션은 / 태블릿 컴퓨터에서 이용 가능한 / 터치스크린 기술을 이용한다

Some touchscreens feature a glass panel / covering two electronically-charged metallic surfaces / lying face-to-face.
일부 터치스크린은 유리판을 특징으로 한다 / 두 개의 전자 충전식 금속 표

면을 덮고 있는 / 마주 보고 있는

When the screen is touched, / the two metallic surfaces feel the pressure and make contact.
화면에 손을 대면 / 두 개의 금속 표면은 압력을 느끼고 접촉한다

This pressure sends an electrical signal / to the computer, / which translates the touch into a command.
이 압력은 전기 신호를 보낸다 / 컴퓨터에 / 이것은 그 접촉을 명령어로 전환한다

This version of the touchscreen is known / as a resistive screen / because the screen reacts to pressure / from the finger.
이러한 터치스크린의 형태는 알려져 있다 / 저항식 화면으로 / 화면이 압력에 반응하기 때문에 / 손가락의

Other tablet computers feature / a single electrified metallic layer / under the glass panel.
다른 태블릿 컴퓨터는 특징으로 한다 / 전기가 통하는 단일 금속판을 / 유리판 아래에 있는

When the user touches the screen, / some of the current / passes through the glass into the user's finger.
사용자가 화면을 가볍게 누르면 / 전류의 일부는 / 유리를 통과하여 사용자의 손가락으로 향한다

When the charge is transferred, / the computer interprets the loss in power / as a command / and carries out the function / the user desires.
전하(電荷)가 이동하면 / 컴퓨터는 에너지의 손실을 해석한다 / 명령어로 / 그리고 기능을 수행한다 / 사용자가 원하는

This type of screen is known / as a capacitive screen.
이러한 종류의 화면은 알려져 있다 / 정전식 화면으로

해석 태블릿 컴퓨터에서 이용 가능한 전자책 애플리케이션은 터치스크린 기술을 이용한다. 일부 터치스크린은 마주 보고 있는 두 개의 전자 충전식 금속 표면을 덮고 있는 유리판을 특징으로 한다. 화면에 손을 대면, 두 개의 금속 표면은 압력을 느끼고 접촉한다. 이 압력은 전기 신호를 컴퓨터에 보내는데, 이것은 그 접촉을 명령어로 전환한다. 이러한 터치스크린의 형태는 화면이 손가락의 압력에 반응하기 때문에 저항식 화면으로 알려져 있다. 다른 태블릿 컴퓨터는 유리판 아래에 있는, 전기가 통하는 단일 금속판을 특징으로 한다. 사용자가 화면을 가볍게 누르면, 전류의 일부는 유리를 통과하여 사용자의 손가락으로 향한다. 전하(電荷)가 이동하면, 컴퓨터는 에너지의 손실을 명령어로 해석하고 사용자가 원하는 기능을 수행한다. 이러한 종류의 화면은 정전식 화면으로 알려져 있다.

① 사용자들이 새로운 기술을 배우는 방법
② 전자책이 태블릿 컴퓨터에서 작동하는 방식
③ 터치스크린 기술이 작동하는 방식
④ 터치스크린이 발전해온 방식

해설 지문 전반에 걸쳐 태블릿 컴퓨터의 전자책 애플리케이션이 사용하는 두 가지 다른 특징을 가진 터치스크린이 어떻게 작동하는지에 대해 설명하고 있다. 따라서, 지문의 주제를 '터치스크린 기술이 작동하는 방식'이라고 표현한 ③번이 정답이다.

어휘 available 이용 가능한 employ 이용하다, 고용하다
feature 특징으로 하다 panel 판 electrical 전기의
translate 전환하다, 바꾸다 command 명령(어); 명령하다
resistive 저항식의, 저항력이 있는 electrified 전기가 통하는
current 전류, 흐름; 현재의 carry out 수행하다, 완수하다
capacitive 정전식의, 전기 용량의

---

11 어휘 생활영어 Isn't there anything we can do? 난이도 ★☆☆

해석
A: 아, 하나 더 있네! 스팸 메일들이 너무 많아!
B: 그러니까. 나도 하루에 10개도 넘는 스팸 메일을 받아.
A: 우리는 그것들이 오지 못하게 할 수 있을까?
B: 나는 그것들을 완전히 차단하는 것이 가능하다고 생각하진 않아.
A: 우리가 할 수 있는 것이 없을까?
B: 음, 너는 설정에서 필터를 설정할 수 있어.
A: 필터?
B: 응. 필터는 일부 스팸 메일을 추려낼 수 있어.

① 너는 이메일을 자주 작성해
② 우리가 할 수 있는 것이 없을까
③ 너는 이렇게 훌륭한 필터를 어떻게 만들었어
④ 이메일 계정 만드는 걸 도와줄 수 있어

해설 빈칸 앞에서 B가 스팸 메일을 완전히 차단하는 것이 가능하다고 생각하진 않는다고 했고 빈칸 뒤에서 Well, you can set up a filter on the settings(음, 너는 설정에서 필터를 설정할 수 있어)라고 말하고 있으므로, 빈칸에는 '우리가 할 수 있는 것이 없을까'라는 의미가 들어가야 자연스럽다. 따라서 ② Isn't there anything we can do가 정답이다.

어휘 block 차단하다, 막다 weed out 추려내다, 제거하다 account 계정

 이것도 알면 **합격!**

이메일과 관련된 표현을 알아두자.
· My inbox is always full of spam mails.
내 받은 편지함은 항상 스팸 메일로 꽉 차 있어.
· Please read the forwarded email below.
아래의 전달된 이메일을 읽어주시기 바랍니다.

---

12 문법 동명사 난이도 ★☆☆

해설 ① 동명사/to 부정사 목적어 구별 동사 regret은 동명사와 to 부정사를 둘 다 목적어로 취할 수 있는 동사인데, '~한 것을 후회하다'라는 과거의 의미를 나타낼 때는 동명사를 목적어로 취하므로 to 부정사 to tell을 동명사 telling으로 고쳐야 한다.

오답분석 ② 비교급 표현 | 병치 구문 '그녀의 경험보다 더 나빴다'는 비교급 표현 '형용사/부사의 비교급 + than'의 형태로 나타낼 수 있으므로 worse than이 올바르게 쓰였고, 비교 구문에서 비교 대상은 같은 품사나 구조끼리 연결되어야 하는데, than 앞의 명사(His experience)가 '소유격 + 대명사'의 형태이므로 than 뒤에도 '소유격 + 대명사'의 역할을 하는 소유대명사 hers가 올바르게 쓰였다.
③ 동사의 종류 동사 remind는 전치사 of와 함께 쓰여 'remind A of B(A에게 B를 상기시키다)'의 형태로 쓰이므로 reminds me of the memories가 올바르게 쓰였다.
④ 관계사 선택 | 숙어 표현 선행사 people이 사람이고, 관계절 내에서 동사 look의 주어 역할을 하므로 주격 관계대명사 who가 올바르게 쓰였다. 또한, '내 눈을 보는 사람들'은 숙어 표현 look A in the eye(A의 눈을 똑바로 쳐다보다)를 사용하여 나타낼 수 있으므로 look me in the eye가 올바르게 쓰였다.

어휘 look A in the eye[face] A의 눈[얼굴]을 똑바로 쳐다보다

👍 이것도 알면 **합격!**

다음은 동명사와 to 부정사를 둘 다 목적어로 취할 수 있는 동사이다. 동명사가 목적어일 때와 to 부정사가 목적어일 때 문장의 의미 변화를 구분하여 알아두자.

	+ -ing	+ to 부정사
remember	~한 것을 기억하다	~할 것을 기억하다
forget	~한 것을 잊다	~할 것을 잊다
try	(시험 삼아) ~해보다	~하려고 노력하다
regret	~한 것을 후회하다	~하게 되어 유감스럽다

13 어휘 생활영어   We are off to the grocery store.   난이도 ★★☆

해석 ① A: 지금이 몇시인줄 아니?
　　　 B: 미안, 나는 요즘 바빠.
　　 ② A: 이봐, 어디 가는 길이니?
　　　 B: 우리는 식료품점으로 가고 있어.
　　 ③ A: 이것 좀 도와줄 수 있어?
　　　 B: 그래. 너를 위해서 박수칠게.
　　 ④ A: 내 지갑 본 사람 있니?
　　　 B: 오랜만이야.

해설 ②번에서 A는 B에게 어디로 가고 있는지를 묻고 있으므로, 식료품점으로 가고 있다는 B의 대답 We are off to the grocery store(우리는 식료품점으로 가고 있어)는 자연스럽다. 따라서 ②번이 정답이다.

어휘 clap 박수치다

👍 이것도 알면 **합격!**

'~로 가다/향하다'라고 말할 때 쓸 수 있는 다양한 표현을 알아두자.

· The packages are en route to the city.
　그 택배는 도시로 가는 중이다.
· We are on the way to the theater.
　우리는 극장으로 가는 길이다.
· The tour group is going to the island.
　그 여행 단체는 섬으로 가고 있다.

14 독해 전체내용 파악 (제목 파악)   난이도 ★☆☆

끊어읽기 해석

Louis XIV needed a palace / worthy of his greatness, / so he decided to build / a huge new house at Versailles, / where a tiny hunting lodge stood.
루이 14세는 궁전이 필요했다 / 그의 위대함에 걸맞은 / 그래서 그는 짓기로 결정했다 / 새로운 거대한 저택을 베르사유에 / 그런데 그곳에는 작은 사냥꾼 오두막이 있었다

After almost fifty years of labor, / this tiny hunting lodge had been transformed / into an enormous palace, / a quarter of a mile long.
거의 50년간의 작업 후 / 이 작은 사냥꾼 오두막은 변했다 / 거대한 궁전으로 / 4분의 1마일이나 되는

Canals were dug / to bring water from the river / and to drain the marshland.
운하가 파였다 / 강에서 물을 길어오기 위해 / 그리고 습지대에서 물을 빼내기 위해

Versailles was full of elaborate rooms / like the famous Hall of

Mirrors, / where seventeen huge mirrors stood / across from seventeen large windows, / and the Salon of Apollo, / where a solid silver throne stood.
베르사유는 화려한 방으로 가득했다 / 그 유명한 거울의 방과 같은 / 그곳에는 17개의 거대한 거울이 있었다 / 17개의 큰 창문 맞은편에 / 그리고 아폴론의 방과 같은 / 그곳에는 순은으로 된 왕좌가 있었다

Hundreds of statues of Greek gods / such as Apollo, Jupiter, and Neptune / stood in the gardens; / each god had Louis's face!
수백 개의 그리스 신들의 조각상이 / 아폴론, 주피터, 그리고 넵튠과 같은 / 정원에 있었다 / 그리고 각 신은 루이의 얼굴을 하고 있었다!

해석 루이 14세는 그의 위대함에 걸맞은 궁전이 필요해서 새로운 거대한 저택을 베르사유에 짓기로 결정했는데, 그곳에는 작은 사냥꾼 오두막이 있었다. 거의 50년간의 작업 후에, 이 작은 사냥꾼 오두막은 4분의 1마일이나 되는 거대한 궁전으로 변했다. 강에서 물을 길어오고 습지대에서 물을 빼내기 위해 운하가 파였다. 베르사유는 17개의 거대한 거울이 17개의 큰 창문 맞은편에 있는 그 유명한 거울의 방과, 순은으로 된 왕좌가 있는 아폴론의 방과 같은 화려한 방들로 가득했다. 아폴론, 주피터, 그리고 넵튠과 같은 수백 개의 그리스 신들의 조각상이 정원에 있었고, 각 신은 루이의 얼굴을 하고 있었다!

① 그리스 신들의 진짜 얼굴
② 거울의 방 vs. 아폴론의 방
③ 운하가 베르사유에 물 이상의 것을 가져다주었나?
④ 베르사유: 초라한 오두막에서 거대한 궁전으로

해설 지문 초반에서 루이 14세가 베르사유에 자신의 위대함에 걸맞은 궁전을 짓기로 결정했다고 하고, 베르사유에 있던 작은 사냥꾼 오두막은 화려한 방이 가득한 거대한 궁전이 되었다고 설명하고 있다. 따라서 이 지문의 제목을 '베르사유: 초라한 오두막에서 거대한 궁전으로'라고 표현한 ④번이 정답이다.

어휘 lodge 오두막   enormous 거대한   canal 운하
　　 drain 물을 빼내다   marshland 습지대   elaborate 화려한, 정교한
　　 solid 순수한, 단단한   throne 왕좌, 왕위   statue 조각상
　　 humble 초라한, 변변찮은

15 독해 논리적 흐름 파악 (무관한 문장 삭제)   난이도 ★☆☆

끊어읽기 해석

Philosophers have not been as concerned / with anthropology / as anthropologists have / with philosophy.
철학자들은 관심을 가진 적이 없다 / 인류학에 / 인류학자들이 (관심을) 가진 만큼 / 철학에

① Few influential contemporary philosophers / take anthropological studies into account / in their work.
영향력 있는 현대 철학자들은 거의 없다 / 인류학 연구를 고려한다 / 그들의 연구에서

② Those who specialize in philosophy of social science / may consider or analyze examples from anthropological research, / but do this / mostly to illustrate conceptual points or epistemological distinctions / or to criticize epistemological or ethical implications.
사회 과학의 철학을 전공한 사람들은 / 인류학 연구의 사례를 검토하거나 분석할지도 모른다 / 하지만 이것을 한다 / 주로 개념의 요점이나 인식론적인 차이를 설명하기 위해 / 또는 인식론적이거나 윤리적 영향을 비판하기 위해

③ In fact, / the great philosophers of our time / often drew inspiration / from other fields / such as anthropology and psychology.

실제로 / 우리 시대의 위대한 철학자들은 / 종종 영감을 얻는다 / 다른 분야로부터 / 인류학과 심리학 같은

④ Philosophy students seldom / study or show serious interest in anthropology.
철학을 공부하는 학생들은 거의 ~하지 않는다 / (인류학을) 공부하거나 인류학에 대한 진지한 흥미를 보인다

They may learn / about experimental methods in science, / but rarely about anthropological fieldwork.
그들은 배울지도 모른다 / 과학의 실험 방법에 대해 / 하지만 인류학의 현장 연구에 대해서는 거의 배우지 않는다

해석 철학자들은 인류학자들이 철학에 관심을 가진 만큼 인류학에 관심을 가진 적이 없다. ① 그들의 연구에서 인류학 연구를 고려하는 영향력 있는 현대 철학자들은 거의 없다. ② 사회 과학의 철학을 전공한 사람들은 인류학 연구의 사례를 검토하거나 분석할지도 모르지만, 주로 개념의 요점이나 인식론적인 차이를 설명하기 위해 또는 인식론적이거나 윤리적 영향을 비판하기 위해 이것(인류학 연구의 사례를 검토하거나 분석하는 것)을 한다. ③ 실제로, 우리 시대의 위대한 철학자들은 종종 인류학과 심리학 같은 다른 분야로부터 영감을 얻는다. ④ 철학을 공부하는 학생들은 거의 인류학을 공부하지 않거나 인류학에 진지한 흥미를 보이지 않는다. 그들은 과학의 실험 방법에 대해 배울지도 모르지만, 인류학의 현장 연구에 대해서는 거의 배우지 않는다.

해설 첫 문장에서 철학자들은 인류학자들이 철학에 관심을 가진 만큼 인류학에 관심을 가진 적이 없다고 설명한 뒤, ①번에서 인류학 연구를 고려하는 영향력 있는 현대 철학자들은 거의 없다고 설명하고 있다. 이어서, ②번에서 사회 과학의 철학을 전공한 사람들은 특정한 목적을 위해서만 인류학 연구의 사례를 검토하거나 분석한다고 하고, ④번에서 철학을 공부하는 학생들은 거의 인류학을 공부하지 않거나 인류학에 흥미를 보이지 않는다고 설명하고 있으므로 모두 첫 문장과 관련이 있다. 그러나 ③번은 위대한 철학자들은 종종 인류학과 심리학 같은 다른 분야로부터 영감을 얻는다는 내용으로, 첫 문장의 내용과 반대된다. 따라서 ③번이 정답이다.

어휘 philosopher 철학자 anthropology 인류학
contemporary 현대의, 동시대의 specialize in ~을 전공하다
illustrate 설명하다 conceptual 개념의
epistemological 인식론적인 distinction 차이, 특별함
implications 영향, 결과 inspiration 영감 experimental 실험의
fieldwork 현장 연구

그것은 방식일 수도 있다 / 일상의 업무를 하는 / 또는 방식일 수 있다 / 우리가 특정한 문제를 해결하는 / 또는 도덕상의 문제를 결정하는 / 스스로

It may be a special way / of keeping a holiday or a tradition / to have a picnic / on a certain date.
그것은 특별한 방식일 수도 있다 / 휴가를 보내거나 전통을 지키는 / 소풍을 가는 전통을 / 특정한 날에

It may be something important or central / to our thinking, / or something minor / that we have long accepted / quite casually.
그것은 중요하거나 중심이 되는 것일 수도 있다 / 우리의 사고에 / 또는 사소한 것일 수도 있다 / 우리가 오랫동안 받아들여 온 / 정말 무심코

해석 우리 모두는 무언가를 물려받는다. 경우에 따라서 그것은 돈, 자산 또는 할머니의 웨딩드레스나 아버지의 공구 세트와 같은 집안의 가보인 어떤 물건일 수도 있다. 하지만 그것 이상으로, 우리 모두 무언가 다른 것을, 훨씬 덜 구체적이고 덜 실체적인 무언가를, 우리가 전혀 의식조차 하지 못할 수도 있는 어떤 것을 물려받는다. 그것은 일상의 업무를 하는 방식이거나, 우리가 특정한 문제를 해결하거나 스스로 도덕상의 문제를 결정하는 방식일 수도 있다. 그것은 휴가를 보내거나, 특정한 날에 소풍을 가는 전통을 지키는 특별한 방식일 수도 있다. 그것은 우리의 사고에 중요하거나 중심이 되는 것일 수도 있고, 또는 우리가 오랫동안 정말 무심코 받아들여 온 사소한 것일 수도 있다.

① 우리의 일상생활과 상당히 관련 없는
② 우리의 도덕적 규범에 반하는
③ 훨씬 덜 구체적이고 덜 실체적인
④ 엄청난 금전상의 가치가 있는

해설 빈칸이 있는 문장을 통해 빈칸에 우리는 어떤 것을 물려받는지에 대한 내용이 나와야 적절하다는 것을 알 수 있다. 빈칸이 있는 문장에서, 하지만 그것(돈, 자산 또는 집안의 가보인 어떤 물건) 이상으로 우리는 우리가 의식하지 못할 수도 있는 어떤 것을 물려받는다고 하며, 빈칸 뒷부분에서 그것은 일상의 업무나 문제를 해결하는 방식이거나, 전통을 지키거나 휴가를 보내는 특별한 방식, 또는 우리의 사고에 중심이 되는 것일 수도 있다는 내용이 있으므로, '훨씬 덜 구체적이고 덜 실체적인' 무언가를 물려받는다고 한 ③번이 정답이다.

어휘 inherit 물려받다 property 자산, 부동산 heirloom (집안의) 가보
moral 도덕상의, 도덕적인 central 중심이 되는 minor 사소한
casually 무심코, 아무 생각 없이 unrelated 관련 없는
concrete 구체적인, 사실에 의거한 tangible 실체적인
monetary 금전상의, 재정상의

---

16 독해 추론 (빈칸 완성 - 구) 난이도 ★★☆

끊어읽기 해석

All of us inherit something: / in some cases, / it may be money, property or some object / —a family heirloom / such as a grandmother's wedding dress or a father's set of tools.
우리 모두는 무언가를 물려받는다 / 경우에 따라서 / 그것은 돈, 자산 또는 어떤 물건일 수도 있다 / 집안의 가보인 / 할머니의 웨딩드레스나 아버지의 공구 세트와 같은

But beyond that, / all of us inherit something else, / something much less concrete and tangible, / something we may not even be fully aware of.
하지만 그것 이상으로, / 우리 모두 무언가 다른 것을 물려받는다 / 훨씬 덜 구체적이고 덜 실체적인 무언가를 / 우리가 전혀 의식조차 하지 못할 수도 있는 어떤 것을

It may be a way / of doing a daily task, / or the way / we solve a particular problem / or decide a moral issue / for ourselves.

---

17 독해 전체내용 파악 (요지 파악) 난이도 ★★☆

끊어읽기 해석

Evolutionarily, / any species / that hopes to stay alive / has to manage its resources carefully.
진화론적으로 / 어느 종이든 / 살아남기를 바라는 / 그것의 자원을 신중하게 관리해야 한다

That means / that first call / on food and other goodies / goes to the breeders and warriors and hunters and planters and builders and, certainly, the children, / with not much left over / for the seniors, / who may be seen as consuming / more than they're contributing.
그것은 의미한다 / 우선적인 요구는 / 음식과 다른 맛있는 것들에 대한 / 사육사, 전사, 사냥꾼, 농장 관리자, 건축업자 그리고 반드시 아이들에게 간다 / 많이 남아있지 않은 채로 / 노인들에게는 / 이들은 소비한다고 여겨질지도 모른다 / 그들이 기여하고 있는 것보다 더 많이

But even before / modern medicine extended life

expectancies, / ordinary families were including / grandparents and even great-grandparents.
그러나 ~하기 이전에도 / 현대 의학이 기대 수명을 연장했다 / 보통의 가정은 포함하고 있었다 / 조부모들과 심지어 증조부모까지

That's because / what old folk consume materially, / they give back behaviorally / —providing a leveling, reasoning center / to the tumult / that often swirls around them.
그것은 왜냐하면 / 노인들이 물질적으로 소비하는 것을 / 그들이 행동으로 되돌려주기 때문이다 / 공평하고 합리적인 중심을 제공하며 / 소란에 / 그들 주위에 종종 몰아치는

해석 진화론적으로, 살아남기를 바라는 어느 종이든 그것의 자원을 신중하게 관리해야 한다. 그것은 음식과 다른 맛있는 것들에 대한 우선적인 요구는 사육사, 전사, 사냥꾼, 농장 관리자, 건축업자 그리고 반드시 아이들에게 가고 그들이 기여하고 있는 것보다 더 많이 소비한다고 여겨질지도 모르는 노인들에게는 많이 남아있지 않은 채로 간다는 것을 의미한다. 그러나 현대 의학이 기대 수명을 연장하기 이전에도 보통의 가정은 조부모들과 심지어 증조부모까지 포함하고 있었다. 그것은 왜냐하면 노인들이 물질적으로 소비하는 것을 그들 주위에 종종 몰아치는 소란에 공평하고 합리적인 중심을 제공하며 행동으로 되돌려주기 때문이다.

① 노인들은 가족들에게 기여를 해왔다.
② 현대 의학은 노인들의 역할에 초점을 두어왔다.
③ 가정에서 자원을 잘 배분하는 것은 그것의 번영을 결정한다.
④ 대가족은 한정된 자원의 희생으로 이루어진다.

해설 지문 중간에서 노인들이 그들이 기여하고 있는 것보다 더 많이 소비한다고 여겨질지도 모른다고 설명한 뒤, 하지만 그들은 현대 의학이 기대 수명을 연장하기 이전에도 가정에 포함되어 있었는데, 왜냐하면 그들이 물질적으로 소비하는 것을 주위의 소란에 공평하고 합리적인 중심을 제공하며 행동으로 되돌려주기 때문이라고 설명하고 있으므로, 이 지문의 요지를 '노인들은 가족들에게 기여를 해왔다'라고 표현한 ①번이 정답이다.

어휘 evolutionarily 진화론적으로   stay alive 살아남다, 살아있다
call 요구; 요구하다   goody 맛있는 것   breeder 사육사
warrior 전사   life expectancy 기대 수명   old folk 노인
tumult 소란   swirl 몰아치다   allocate 배분하다   prosperity 번영

18 독해 논리적 흐름 파악 (문단 순서 배열)   난이도 ★★☆

끊어읽기 해석

Nowadays / the clock dominates our lives so much / that it is hard to imagine life / without it.
오늘날 / 시계는 우리의 생활을 너무 많이 지배해서 / 생활을 상상하기 힘들다 / 그것이 없는

Before industrialization, / most societies used the sun or the moon / to tell the time.
산업화 이전에는 / 대부분의 사회에서 해나 달을 이용했다 / 시간을 알리기 위해

(A) For the growing network of railroads, / the fact / that there were no time standards / was a disaster.
성장하는 철도망으로 인해 / 사실 / 표준 시간이 없다는 / 끔찍한 일이었다

Often, / stations just some miles apart / set their clocks / at different times.
종종 / 단지 몇 마일 떨어진 역들은 / 그들의 시계를 맞추었다 / 서로 다른 시간에

There was a lot of confusion / for travelers.
많은 혼란이 있었다 / 여행객들에게는

(B) When mechanical clocks first appeared, / they were immediately popular.
기계식 시계가 처음 나타났을 때 / 그것들은 바로 인기를 얻었다

It was fashionable / to have a clock or a watch.
유행이었다 / 시계나 손목시계를 갖는 것은

People invented / the expression "of the clock" or "o'clock" / to refer to this new way / to tell the time.
사람들은 만들어냈다 / 'of the clock'이나 'o'clock'과 같은 표현 / 이 새로운 방법을 지칭하기 위해 / 시간을 알리는

(C) These clocks were decorative, / but not always useful.
이러한 시계들은 장식용이었다 / 하지만 항상 유용하지는 않았다

This was because / towns, provinces, and even neighboring villages / had different ways / to tell the time.
그 이유는 ~이기 때문이었다 / 마을, 지방 그리고 심지어 이웃 마을까지도 / 다른 방법을 가지고 있었다 / 시간을 알리는

Travelers had to reset / their clocks repeatedly / when they moved / from one place to another.
여행객들은 다시 맞춰야만 했다 / 그들의 시계를 반복해서 / 그들이 이동할 때 / 한 장소에서 다른 장소로

In the United States, / there were about 70 different time zones / in the 1860s.
미국에서는 / 약 70개의 상이한 시간대가 있었다 / 1860년대에

해석   오늘날 시계는 우리의 생활을 너무 많이 지배해서 그것이 없는 생활을 상상하기 힘들다. 산업화 이전에는, 대부분의 사회에서 시간을 알리기 위해 해나 달을 이용했다.

(B) 기계식 시계가 처음 나타났을 때, 그것들은 바로 인기를 얻었다. 시계나 손목시계를 갖는 것은 유행이었다. 사람들은 시간을 알리는 이 새로운 방법을 지칭하기 위해 'of the clock'이나 'o'clock'과 같은 표현을 만들어냈다.
(C) 이러한 시계들은 장식용이었지만, 항상 유용하지는 않았다. 그 이유는 마을, 지방 그리고 심지어 이웃 마을까지도 시간을 알리는 다른 방법을 가지고 있었기 때문이었다. 여행객들은 그들이 한 장소에서 다른 장소로 이동할 때 그들의 시계를 반복해서 다시 맞춰야만 했다. 미국에서는, 1860년대에 약 70개의 상이한 시간대가 있었다.
(A) 성장하는 철도망으로 인해, 표준 시간이 없다는 사실은 끔찍한 일이었다. 종종, 단지 몇 마일 떨어진 역들은 그들의 시계를 서로 다른 시간에 맞추었다. 여행객들에게는 많은 혼란이 있었다.

해설 주어진 문장에서 산업화 이전에는 시간을 알리기 위해 해나 달을 이용했다고 언급한 뒤, (B)에서 기계식 시계(mechanical clocks)가 처음 나타났을 때 바로 인기를 얻었으며, 시계나 손목시계를 갖는 것은 유행이었다고 한 뒤, (C)에서 이러한 시계들(These clocks)은 시간을 알리는 방법이 달라 유용하지 않았으며, 미국에는 1860년대 70개의 상이한 시간대(time zones)가 있었다고 설명하고 있다. 이어서 (A)에서 성장하는 철도망으로 인해 표준 시간(time standards)이 없다는 사실은 끔찍한 일이었고, 몇 마일 떨어진 역들은 서로 다른 시간에 시계를 맞춰야 해서 많은 여행객들에게 혼란이 있었다고 설명하고 있다. 따라서 ③ (B) - (C) - (A)가 정답이다.

어휘 dominate 지배하다   industrialization 산업화   tell (시간을) 알리다
railroad 철도망   confusion 혼란
mechanical 기계식의, 기계로 작동되는   refer to 지칭하다
decorative 장식용의   province 지방   neighboring 이웃의

끊어읽기 해석

But there is also clear evidence / that millennials, / born between 1981 and 1996, / are saving more aggressively / for retirement / than Generation X did / at the same ages, 22~37.
그러나 분명한 근거도 있다 / 밀레니얼 세대가 / 1981년과 1996년 사이에 태어난 / 더 적극적으로 저축하고 있다는 / 은퇴를 대비하기 위해 / X세대가 그랬던 것보다 / 동일한 22~37살 시기에

Millennials are often labeled / the poorest, most financially burdened generation / in modern times.
밀레니얼 세대는 종종 ~라고 불린다 / 가장 가난하고 가장 재정적으로 부담을 지고 있는 세대 / 현대에 들어서

Many of them / graduated from college / into one of the worst labor markets / the United States has ever seen, / with a staggering load of student debt / to boot.
그들 중 많은 사람들은 / 대학을 졸업해서 / 최악의 노동 시장 중 하나로 (진입했다) / 미국이 이제까지 경험했던 / 충격적인 양의 학자금 대출과 함께 / 그것도

(①) Not surprisingly, / millennials have accumulated less wealth / than Generation X did / at a similar stage in life, / primarily because fewer of them own homes.
놀랄 것 없이 / 밀레니얼 세대는 부를 덜 축적했다 / X세대가 그랬던 것 보다 / 인생의 비슷한 단계에서 / 주로 그들 중 극소수가 집을 소유하고 있기 때문이다

(②) But newly available data / providing the most detailed picture / to date / about what Americans of different generations save / complicates that assessment.
그러나 새롭게 이용 가능한 자료는 / 가장 자세한 설명을 제공하는 / 지금까지 / 서로 다른 세대의 미국인들이 무엇을 저축하는지에 대해 / 그 평가를 더 복잡하게 만든다

(③) Yes, / Gen Xers, / those born between 1965 and 1980, / have a higher net worth.
그렇다 / X세대들은 / 1965년과 1980년 사이에서 태어난 사람들인 / 더 많은 순자산을 소유하고 있다

(④) And that might put them / in better financial shape / than many assume.
그리고 그것은 아마 그들을 이르게 할 수도 있다 / 더 나은 재정 상태에 / 많은 사람들이 추측하는 것보다

해석 밀레니얼 세대는 현대에 들어서 가장 가난하고 가장 재정적으로 부담을 지고 있는 세대라고 종종 불린다. 그들 중 많은 사람들은 대학을 졸업해서, 그것도 충격적인 양의 학자금 대출과 함께, 미국이 이제까지 경험했던 최악의 노동 시장 중 하나로 진입했다. 놀랄 것 없이, 밀레니얼 세대는 X세대가 인생의 비슷한 단계에서 그랬던(부를 축적했던) 것보다 부를 덜 축적했는데, 이는 주로 그들 중 극소수가 집을 소유하고 있기 때문이다. 그러나 지금까지 서로 다른 세대의 미국인들이 무엇을 저축한 지에 대해 가장 자세한 설명을 제공하는, 새롭게 이용 가능한 자료는 그 평가를 더 복잡하게 만든다. 그렇다, 1965년과 1980년 사이에서 태어난 사람들인 X세대들은 더 많은 순자산을 소유하고 있다. ④ 그러나 1981년과 1996년 사이에 태어난 밀레니얼 세대는 동일한 22~37살 시기에 X세대가 그랬던(저축했던) 것보다 은퇴를 대비하기 위해 더 적극적으로 저축하고 있다는 분명한 근거도 있다. 그리고 그것은 아마 많은 사람들이 추측하는 것보다 그들을 더 나은 재정 상태에 이르게 할 수도 있다.

해설 ④번 앞 문장에 X세대들이 밀레니얼 세대보다 더 많은 순자산을 소유하고 있다는 내용이 있고, ④번 뒤 문장에 그것(더 적극적으로 저축하는 것)이 그들(밀레니엄 세대)을 더 나은 재정 상태에 이르게 할 수도 있다는 내용이 있으므로, ④번 자리에 그러나(But)

밀레니얼 세대가 X세대보다 은퇴를 대비하기 위해 더 적극적으로 저축하고 있다는 분명한 근거도 있다는 내용의 주어진 문장이 나와야 지문이 자연스럽게 연결된다. 따라서 ④번이 정답이다.

어휘 aggressively 적극적으로, 공격적으로
label ~을 부르다, ~에 라벨을 붙이다 staggering 충격적인
to boot 그것도, 더구나 accumulate 축적하다 to date 지금까지
complicate (더) 복잡하게 만들다; 복잡한 net worth 순자산

끊어읽기 해석

Carbonate sands, / which accumulate over thousands of years / from the breakdown of coral and other reef organisms, / are the building material / for the frameworks of coral reefs.
탄산염 모래는 / 수천 년 이상 축적되는데 / 산호와 다른 암초 유기체의 분해로 / 건축 자재이다 / 산호초의 뼈대를 위한

But these sands are sensitive / to the chemical make-up / of sea water.
그러나 이 모래는 민감하다 / 화학적 구성 요소에 / 해수의

As oceans absorb carbon dioxide, / they acidify / —and at a certain point, / carbonate sands simply start to dissolve.
바다가 이산화탄소를 흡수할 때 / 그들은 산성화된다 / 그리고 특정 시점에서 / 탄산염 모래는 그저 용해되기 시작한다

The world's oceans have absorbed / around one-third / of human-emitted carbon dioxide.
세계의 바다는 흡수해왔다 / 약 3분의 1을 / 인간이 방출한 이산화탄소의

The rate / at which the sands dissolve / was strongly related to the acidity / of the overlying seawater, / and was ten times more sensitive / than coral growth / to ocean acidification.
비율은 / 모래가 용해되는 / 산성과 강력하게 연관되어 있었다 / 위에 있는 해수의 / 그리고 10배 더 민감했다 / 산호의 성장보다 / 해양 산성화에

In other words, / ocean acidification will impact / the dissolution of coral reef sands / more than the growth of corals.
다시 말하면 / 해양 산성화는 영향을 미칠 것이다 / 산호초 모래의 용해에 / 산호의 성장보다 더욱

This probably reflects the corals' ability / to modify their environment / and partially adjust to ocean acidification, / whereas the dissolution of sands / is a geochemical process / that cannot adapt.
이는 아마 산호의 능력을 반영하는 것이다 / 그들의 환경을 바꾸는 / 그리고 부분적으로 바다의 산성화에 적응하는 / 반면에 모래의 용해는 / 지구 화학적 과정이다 / 적응할 수 없는

해석 탄산염 모래는 산호와 다른 암초 유기체의 분해로 수천 년 이상 축적되는데, 이는 산호초의 뼈대를 위한 건축 자재이다. 그러나 이 모래는 해수의 화학적 구성 요소에 민감하다. 바다가 이산화탄소를 흡수할 때, 그들은 산성화되고 특정 시점에서, 탄산염 모래는 그저 용해되기 시작한다. 세계의 바다는 인간이 방출한 이산화탄소의 약 3분의 1을 흡수해왔다. 모래가 용해되는 비율은 위에 있는 해수의 산성과 강력하게 연관되어 있었고, 산호의 성장보다 해양 산성화에 10배 더 민감했다. 다시 말하면, 해양 산성화는 산호의 성장보다 산호초 모래의 용해에 더욱 영향을 미칠 것이다. 이는 아마 그들의 환경을 바꾸고 부분적으로 바다의 산성화에 적응하는 산호의 능력을 반영하는 것이고, 반면에 모래의 용해는 적응할 수 없는 지구 화학적 과정이다.
① 산호초의 뼈대는 탄산염 모래로 구성되어 있다
② 산호는 부분적으로 바다 산성화에 적응하는 것이 가능하다.
③ 인간에 의해 방출된 이산화탄소는 세계의 해양 산성화에 기여해 왔다.

④ 해양 산성화는 산호초 모래의 용해보다 산호의 성장에 더 영향을 끼친다.

해설 ④번의 키워드인 Ocean acidification(해양 산성화)이 그대로 언급된 지문 주변의 내용에서, 해양 산성화는 산호의 성장보다 산호초 모래의 용해에 더욱 영향을 미칠 것이라고 했으므로, 해양 산성화가 산호초 모래의 용해보다 산호의 성장에 더 영향을 끼친다는 것은 지문의 내용과 반대이다. 따라서 ④번이 정답이다.

어휘 carbonate sand 탄산염 모래 breakdown 분해
framework 뼈대 coral reef 산호초 make-up 구성 (요소)
carbon dioxide 이산화탄소 acidify 산성화되다
dissolve 용해되다, 녹다 emit 방출하다 acidity 산성
overlying 위에 놓인 acidification 산성화
geochemical 지구 화학적

정답   p.108

01	① 어휘 – 어휘＆표현	11	④ 어휘 – 어휘＆표현
02	① 어휘 – 어휘＆표현	12	① 어휘 – 어휘＆표현
03	④ 어휘 – 생활영어	13	③ 독해 – 추론
04	③ 어휘 – 생활영어	14	④ 독해 – 추론
05	④ 문법 – 분사	15	④ 독해 – 논리적 흐름 파악
06	② 문법 – 부사절	16	③ 문법 – 동사의 종류
07	② 독해 – 논리적 흐름 파악	17	① 독해 – 세부내용 파악
08	② 독해 – 세부내용 파악	18	④ 독해 – 세부내용 파악
09	② 독해 – 전체내용 파악	19	① 독해 – 추론
10	④ 독해 – 논리적 흐름 파악	20	② 독해 – 추론

취약영역 분석표

영역	세부 유형	문항 수	소계
어휘	어휘＆표현	4	/6
	생활영어	2	
문법	분사	1	/3
	부사절	1	
	동사의 종류	1	
독해	전체내용 파악	1	/11
	세부내용 파악	3	
	추론	4	
	논리적 흐름 파악	3	
총계			/20

· 자신이 취약한 영역은 '공무원 영어, 이렇게 출제된다!'(문제집 p.8)를 통해 다시 한번 확인하고 학습하시기 바랍니다.

---

01   어휘   어휘＆표현   excavated = exhumed   난이도 ★★★

해석   나는 이 문서들을 지금은 완전히 죽은 감성의 유물로 보았는데, 그것은 발굴되어야 한다.

① 발굴된   ② 포장된
③ 지워진   ④ 유명한

어휘   relic 유물, 유적   sensibility 감성, 감정
dead and buried 완전히 죽은   excavate 발굴하다, 파다
exhume 발굴하다, 파내다   pack 포장하다   erase 지우다, 없애다
celebrated 유명한

👍 이것도 알면 **합격!**

excavate(발굴하다)와 유사한 의미의 표현
= dig up, uncover, unearth

---

02   어휘   어휘＆표현   sheer = utter   난이도 ★★☆

해석   롤러코스터를 타는 것은 감정의 폭주일 수 있다. 당신이 좌석에 끈으로 묶여질 때의 불안한 예상, 위로 올라갈수록 생겨나는 의문과 후회 그리고 그 전차가 처음으로 급하강할 때 순수한 아드레날린이 돌진한다.

① 순전한   ② 무서운
③ 가끔의   ④ 처리하기 쉬운

어휘   joy ride 폭주, 난폭 운전   anticipation 예상, 기대
strap 끈으로 묶다   sheer 순수한, 순전한
utter 순전한, 완전한; 말하다   occasional 가끔의

👍 이것도 알면 **합격!**

sheer(순수한)의 유의어
= absolute, complete, pure

---

03   어휘   생활영어   Would you like to leave a message?   난이도 ★☆☆

해석   ① A: 우리는 몇 시에 점심을 먹을 건가요?
     B: 12시 전에는 준비될 거예요.
② A: 당신에게 여러 번 전화했어요. 왜 받지 않았나요?
     B: 오, 제 핸드폰이 꺼졌던 거 같아요.
③ A: 당신은 이번 겨울에 휴가를 가실 건가요?
     B: 갈지도 몰라요. 아직 결정을 내리지 않았어요.
④ A: 여보세요. 당신의 전화를 못 받아서 죄송해요.
     B: 메시지를 남기길 원하시나요?

해설   ④번에서 A는 전화를 못 받아서 죄송하다고 하고 있으므로 메시지를 남기길 원하는지를 묻는 B의 대답 Would you like to leave a message?(메시지를 남기길 원하시나요?)는 어울리지 않는다. 따라서 ④번이 정답이다.

어휘   turn off 끄다   decide 결정을 내리다

👍 이것도 알면 **합격!**

불확실한 것에 대해 말할 때 사용하는 표현을 알아두자.
· I'm still not sure. 나는 아직 확신이 없어.
· No decision has been made. 아직 결정이 나지 않았어.
· It's up in the air. 아직 미정이에요.
· No one knows for sure. 아무도 확실히 몰라요.

04 어휘 생활영어 What's your buy-back policy?
난이도 ★★★

해석

> A: 안녕하세요. 저는 돈을 좀 환전해야 해요.
> B: 알겠습니다. 어떤 화폐가 필요하신가요?
> A: 저는 달러를 파운드로 바꿔야 해요. 환율이 어떻게 되나요?
> B: 환율은 달러당 0.73 파운드입니다.
> A: 좋아요. 수수료를 받으시나요?
> B: 네, 우리는 4달러의 많지 않은 수수료를 받습니다.
> A: 당신의 환매 방침은 무엇인가요?
> B: 우리는 당신의 화폐를 무료로 다시 바꿔드립니다. 그저 영수증만 가져오세요.

① 이것은 얼마인가요
② 이것을 사려면 얼마를 지불해야 하나요
③ 당신의 환매 방침은 무엇인가요
④ 신용카드 받으시나요

해설 수수료가 있는지 묻는 A의 말에 B가 4달러라고 대답하고, 빈칸 뒤에서 B가 We convert your currency back for free(우리는 당신의 화폐를 무료로 다시 바꿔드립니다)라고 말하고 있으므로, 빈칸에 '당신의 환매 방침은 무엇인가요'라는 의미의 'What's your buy-back policy'가 들어가야 자연스럽다. 따라서 ③번이 정답이다.

어휘 exchange 환전하다, 교환하다 currency 화폐, 지폐 convert 바꾸다, 전환하다 commission 수수료 receipt 영수증

👍 이것도 알면 **합격!**

은행 업무를 볼 때 사용하는 다양한 표현을 알아두자.

· What's the interest? 이자율은 어떻게 되나요?
· Could you exchange this to dollars, please?
  이것을 달러로 환전해 주시겠어요?
· I'd like to withdraw money from my account.
  제 계좌에서 돈을 찾고 싶어요.

05 문법 분사
난이도 ★★☆

해석 매년, 27만 명 이상의 보행자들은 전 세계의 도로에서 그들의 목숨을 잃는다. 많은 사람들은 그들이 어떤 날이든 그러곤 했듯이 그들의 집을 나서고 결국 돌아오지 않는다. 세계적으로, 보행자들은 도로 교통 사망자 수 전체의 22퍼센트를 구성하고, 일부 국가들에서 이 비율은 도로 교통 사고사 전체의 3분의 2만큼이나 높다. 수백만 명의 보행자들은 치명상을 입지는 않으며, 그들 중 일부는 영구적인 장애가 남아 있다. 이러한 사고들은 경제적인 어려움뿐만 아니라 더 많은 고통과 슬픔의 원인이 된다.

해설 ④ 현재분사 vs. 과거분사 현재분사(injuring) 뒤에 목적어가 없고, 주어 Millions of pedestrians와 동사가 '수백만 명의 보행자들은 치명상을 입지 않는다'라는 의미의 수동 관계이므로, 현재분사 injuring을 be동사(are) 뒤에서 수동태를 완성하는 과거분사 injured로 고쳐야 한다.

오답분석 ① 주어 동사 수 일치 주어 자리에 복수 명사 pedestrians가 왔으므로 복수 동사 lose가 올바르게 쓰였다.
② to 부정사의 쓰임 문맥상 '결국 돌아오지 않는다'라는 의미가 되어야 자연스러우므로 부정어 never 뒤에 결과를 나타내는 to 부정사 to return이 올바르게 쓰였다.
③ 원급 표현 내 형용사/부사 원급 표현 'as + 형용사/부사의 원급 + as'(~만큼 -한)에서 as ~ as 사이가 형용사 자리인지 부

사 자리인지는 as, as를 지우고 구별할 수 있다. be동사(is)의 보어 자리에는 형용사 역할을 하는 것이 와야 하므로 형용사 high가 올바르게 쓰였다.

어휘 pedestrian 보행자 constitute 구성하다 fatality 치사율, 사망자 proportion 비율 permanent 영구적인 grief 슬픔

👍 이것도 알면 **합격!**

to 부정사가 결과를 나타낼 때는 to 부정사 앞에 only, never와 같은 부사를 써서 의도되지 않은 결과(only)나 부정(never)의 의미를 나타내기도 한다.

ex She visited the restaurant, **only to find** it closed.
그녀는 그 식당에 방문했으나, 결국 그곳이 문을 닫았음을 알게 되었다.

06 문법 부사절
난이도 ★★★

해석 ① 그 신문은 개인의 목적을 위해 회사의 돈을 사용한 것으로 그녀를 고소했다.
② 그 수사는 의혹을 불러일으키지 않도록 최대한 조심스럽게 다루어져야 한다.
③ 그 과정의 속도를 높이는 또 다른 방법은 새로운 시스템으로 전환하는 것이다.
④ 화석연료를 태우는 것은 기후 변화의 주된 원인 중 하나이다.

해설 ② 부사절 접속사 문맥상 '의혹을 불러일으키지 않도록'이라는 의미가 되어야 자연스러운데, '~하지 않도록'은 부사절 접속사 lest를 사용하여 나타낼 수 있고, 접속사 lest가 이끄는 절의 동사는 '(should) + 동사원형(be)'의 형태를 취하므로 lest suspicion be aroused가 올바르게 쓰였다.

오답분석 ① 전치사 뒤에 올 수 있는 것 전치사(with) 뒤에는 명사 역할을 하는 것이 와야 하므로 동사 use를 동명사 using으로 바꿔야 한다.
③ 능동태 vs. 수동태 동사(made) 뒤에 목적어 the shift가 있고, 문맥상 주어와 동사가 '또 다른 방법은 ~ 전환하는 것이다'라는 의미의 능동 관계이므로 과거분사 made를 동명사 making 또는 to 부정사 to make로 고쳐야 한다.
④ 수량 표현 | 형용사 자리 수량 표현 one of(~ 중 하나)는 복수 명사 앞에 오는 수량 표현이므로 단수 명사 cause를 복수 명사 causes로 고쳐야 한다. 또한, 명사(cause)를 수식하는 것은 형용사 역할을 하는 것이므로 명사 cause 앞의 동사 lead를 형용사 leading으로 고쳐야 한다.

어휘 charge 고소하다, 기소하다 investigation 수사, 조사 utmost 최대한의, 최고의 lest ~하지 않도록 suspicion 의혹, 의심 arouse 불러일으키다

👍 이것도 알면 **합격!**

부사절 접속사 lest(~하지 않도록)는 이미 부정의 의미를 포함하고 있으므로 부사절 내 동사에 다시 부정어를 쓰지 않아야 한다는 것을 알아두자.

ex Keep your eyes open **lest** you should ~~not~~ miss the exit road. 나가는 길을 놓치지 않도록 주의해라.

끊어읽기 해석

There is a thought / that can haunt us: / since everything probably affects / everything else, / how can we ever make sense of / the social world?
생각이 있다 / 우리를 괴롭힐 수 있는 / 모든 것이 대체로 영향을 주기 때문에 / 다른 모든 것에 / 우리가 도대체 어떻게 이해할 수 있을까 / 사회 세계를

If we are weighed down / by that worry, / though, / we won't ever make progress.
만약 우리가 억압된다면 / 그러한 걱정에 의해 / 하지만 / 우리는 절대로 앞으로 나아갈 수 없을 것이다

(A) Every discipline / that I am familiar with / draws caricatures of the world / in order to make sense of it.
모든 학문의 분야는 / 내가 익숙한 / 세계에 대한 캐리커쳐를 그린다 / 그것(세계)을 이해하기 위해

The modern economist does this / by building *models*, / which are deliberately stripped down representations / of the phenomena / out there.
현대 경제학자는 이것을 한다 / '모형들'을 만들어냄으로써 / 그것들(모형들)은 의도적으로 불필요한 것을 모두 뺀 묘사이다 / 현상들에 대한 / 세상의

(B) The economist John Maynard Keynes / described our subject thus: / "Economics is a science of thinking / in terms of models / joined to the art / of choosing models / which are relevant to the contemporary world."
경제학자 존 메이너드 케인스는 / 우리의 주제를 이와 같이 묘사했다 / "경제학은 생각의 과학이다 / 모형들에 있어서 / 기술과 결합된 / 모형들을 선택하는 / 현대 세계와 관련된"

(C) When I say "stripped down," / I really mean stripped down.
내가 '불필요한 것을 모두 뺀'이라고 말할 때는 / 나는 정말로 불필요한 것을 모두 뺀 것을 의미하는 것이다

It isn't uncommon / among us economists / to focus on one or two causal factors, / exclude everything else, / hoping that this will enable us to understand / how just those aspects of reality work and interact.
드문 일이 아니다 / 우리 경제학자들 사이에서 / 한두 가지의 원인 요소들에 집중하고 / 다른 모든 것을 배제하는 것은 / 이것이 우리가 이해할 수 있게 해 주기를 바라며 / 현실의 이러한 양상들이 어떻게 작동하고 상호작용하는지를

해석

> 우리를 괴롭힐 수 있는 생각이 있는데, 모든 것이 대체로 다른 모든 것에 영향을 주기 때문에, 우리가 도대체 어떻게 사회 세계를 이해할 수 있을까 하는 것이다. 하지만, 만약 우리가 그러한 걱정에 의해 억압된다면, 우리는 절대로 앞으로 나아갈 수 없을 것이다.

(A) 내가 익숙한 모든 학문의 분야는 세계를 이해하기 위해 그것에 대한 캐리커쳐를 그린다. 현대 경제학자는 '모형들'을 만들어냄으로써 이것을 하는데, 그것들(모형들)은 의도적으로 불필요한 것을 모두 뺀 세상의 현상들에 대한 묘사이다.

(C) 내가 '불필요한 것을 모두 뺀'이라고 말할 때는, 정말로 불필요한 것을 모두 뺀 것을 의미하는 것이다. 우리가 현실의 이러한 양상들이 어떻게 작동하고 상호작용하는지를 이해할 수 있게 해 주기를 바라며 한두 가지의 원인 요소에 집중하고 다른 모든 것을 배제하는 것은 우리 경제학자들 사이에서 드문 일이 아니다.

(B) 경제학자 존 메이너드 케인스는 우리의 주제를 이와 같이 묘사했다. "경제학은 현대 세계와 관련된 모형들을 선택하는 기술과 결합된 모형들에 있어서 생각의 과학이다."

해설   주어진 문장에서 모든 것이 다른 모든 것에 영향을 주기 때문에 사회 세계를 어떻게 이해해야(make sense of the social world) 할지에 대한 걱정이 우리를 괴롭힌다고 하고, (A)에서 모든 학문 분야는 세계를 이해하기 위해(in order to make sense of it) 그것에 대한 캐리커쳐(그림)를 그리는데, 경제학자들은 의도적으로 불필요한 것을 모두 뺀(stripped down) 묘사인 '모형들'을 만들어냄으로써 이것을 한다고 설명하고 있다. 이어서 (C)에서 불필요한 것을 모두 뺀(stripped down) 것을 다시 한 번 강조하며, 경제학자들은 현실의 양상들을 이해하기 위해 다른 모든 것을 배제하고 한두 가지의 원인 요소에만 집중한다고 한 뒤, (B)에서 경제학자 존 메이너드 케인스가 경제학에 대해 묘사한 것을 인용하고 있다. 따라서 ② (A) – (C) – (B)가 정답이다.

어휘   **haunt** 괴롭히다, 늘 따라다니다   **discipline** 학문의 분야, 규율
     deliberately 의도적으로
     stripped down 불필요한 것을 모두 뺀, 꼭 필요한 것만 남긴
     representation 묘사, 설명
     phenomenon 현상 (복수형 phenomena)
     relevant 관련된   **contemporary** 현대의, 동시대의
     uncommon 드문   **causal** 원인의, 인과 관계의
     exclude 배제하다   **interact** 상호작용하다

---

08 독해 세부내용 파악 (내용 일치 파악)   난이도 ★★☆

끊어읽기 해석

①Prehistoric societies / some half a million years ago / did not distinguish sharply / between mental and physical disorders.
선사시대의 사회들은 / 약 50만년 전의 / 뚜렷하게 구분하지 않았다 / 정신과 신체적 이상들을

②Abnormal behaviors, / from simple headaches to convulsive attacks, / were attributed to evil spirits / that inhabited or controlled / the afflicted person's body.
비정상적인 행동들은 / 단순한 두통에서 경련성 발작까지의 / 사악한 영혼들의 결과라고 생각되었다 / 존재했거나(그것을) 통제한 / 피해를 입은 사람의 신체에

According to historians, / these ancient peoples / attributed many forms of illness / to demonic possession, sorcery, or the behest / of an offended ancestral spirit.
역사학자들에 따르면 / 이러한 고대 민족들은 / 다수의 질병의 형태를 결과라고 생각했다 / 악령의 점유, 마법, 혹은 명령의 / 성난 조상 영혼의

Within this system of belief, / called *demonology*, / the victim was usually held at least partly responsible / for the misfortune.
이러한 신념의 체계 속에서 / '귀신론'이라 불리는 / 그 희생자는 보통 최소한 부분적으로 책임이 지워졌다 / 그 불운에

③It has been suggested / that Stone Age cave dwellers / may have treated behavior disorders / with a surgical method / called *trephining*, / in which part of the skull was chipped away / to provide an opening / through which the evil spirit could escape.
암시되었다 / 석기시대의 동굴에 살던 사람들은 / 행동 이상들을 다루었을지도 모른다고 / 수술의 과정으로 / '천공'이라 불리는 / 그런데 그 과정에서 두개골의 일부가 조금씩 깎였다 / 구멍이 생기게 하기 위해 / 사악한 영혼들이 새어나올 수 있는

People may have believed / that when the evil spirit left, / the person would return to his or her normal state.
사람들은 믿었을지도 모른다 / 그 사악한 영혼이 떠나면 / 그 사람이 본인의 평범한 상태로 돌아올 것이라고

④Surprisingly, / trephined skulls have been found / to have healed over, / indicating / that some patients survived / this extremely crude operation.
놀랍게도 / 천공된 두개골들은 밝혀졌다 / 치료되었던 것으로 / 이것은 나타낸다 / 몇몇 환자들이 생존했다는 것을 / 이렇게 극도로 허술한 수술에서

해석 약 50만년 전의 선사시대의 사회들은 정신과 신체적 이상들을 뚜렷하게 구분하지 않았다. 단순한 두통에서 경련성 발작까지의 비정상적인 행동들은 피해를 입은 사람의 신체에 존재했거나 그것을 통제한 사악한 영혼들의 결과라고 생각되었다. 역사학자들에 따르면, 이러한 고대 민족들은 다수의 질병의 형태를 악령의 점유, 마법, 혹은 성난 조상 영혼의 명령의 결과라고 생각했다. '귀신론'이라 불리는 이러한 신념의 체계 속에서, 그 희생자는 보통 그 불운에 최소한 부분적으로 책임이 지워졌다. 석기시대의 동굴에 살던 사람들은 행동 이상들을 '천공'이라 불리는 수술의 과정으로 다루었을지도 모른다고 암시되었는데, 그 과정에서 사악한 영혼들이 새어나올 수 있는 구멍이 생기게 하기 위해 두개골의 일부가 조금씩 깎였다. 사람들은 그 사악한 영혼이 떠나면 그 사람이 본인의 평범한 상태로 돌아올 것이라고 믿었을지도 모른다. 놀랍게도, 천공된 두개골들은 치료되었던 것으로 밝혀졌는데, 이것은 이렇게 극도로 허술한 수술에서 몇몇 환자들이 생존했다는 것을 나타낸다.

① 정신적 이상들은 신체적 이상들과 분명히 구분되었다.
② 비정상적인 행동들은 사람에게 영향을 미치는 사악한 영혼들로 인한 결과라고 믿어졌다.
③ 사악한 영혼이 사람의 신체에 들어가기 위해 두개골에 구멍이 만들어졌다.
④ 어떤 동굴에 살던 사람들도 천공으로 살아남지 못했다.

해설 ②번의 키워드인 Abnormal behaviors(비정상적인 행동들)가 그대로 언급된 지문 주변의 내용을 살펴보면, 비정상적인 행동들은 피해를 입은 사람의 신체에 존재했거나 그것을 통제한 사악한 영혼의 결과라고 생각되었다는 내용이 있으므로, 비정상적인 행동들은 사람에게 영향을 미치는 사악한 영혼들로 인한 결과라고 믿어졌다는 것을 알 수 있다. 따라서 ②번이 정답이다.

오답 분석
① 정신과 신체적 이상들을 뚜렷하게 구분하지 않았다고 했으므로 정신적 이상들은 신체적 이상들과 분명히 구분되었다는 것은 지문의 내용과 반대이다.
③ 사악한 영혼들이 새어나올 수 있는 구멍이 생기게 하기 위해 두개골의 일부가 조금씩 깎였다고 했으므로 사악한 영혼이 사람의 신체에 들어가기 위해 두개골에 구멍이 만들어졌다는 것은 지문의 내용과 반대이다.
④ 천공된 두개골들은 환자들이 생존했다는 것을 나타내며 치료되었던 것으로 밝혀졌다고 했으므로 어떤 동굴에 살던 사람들도 천공으로 살아남지 못했다는 것은 지문의 내용과 반대이다.

어휘 prehistoric 선사시대의 distinguish 구분하다
disorder 이상, 장애 abnormal 비정상적인
attribute ~ to - ~을 -의 결과라고 생각하다
inhabit 존재하다, 상주하다 control 통제하다
afflict 피해를 입히다, 괴롭히다 demonic 악령의
possession 점유, 소유 sorcery 마법, 요술 demonology 귀신론
hold ~ responsible ~에게 책임이 지워지다
surgical 수술의, 외과의 skull 두개골 chip away 조금씩 깎다
escape 새어나오다 crude 허술한 differentiate 구분하다

09 독해 전체내용 파악 (주제 파악)   난이도 ★★☆

끊어읽기 해석

As the digital revolution upends newsrooms / across the country, / here's my advice / for all the reporters.
디지털 혁명이 뉴스 편집실을 뒤엎기 때문에 / 전국에 걸쳐 / 여기에 나의 충고가 있다 / 모든 기자들을 위한

I've been a reporter / for more than 25 years, / so I have lived through / a half dozen technological life cycles.
나는 기자였다 / 25년 이상 동안 / 그래서 나는 겪었다 / 6번의 기술적 라이프 사이클을

The most dramatic transformations / have come in the last half dozen years.
가장 극적인 변화들은 / 지난 6년간 있었다

That means / I am, / with increasing frequency, / making stuff up / as I go along.
이것은 의미한다 / 내가 / 점점 더 빈번히 / 시시한 이야기를 지어내고 있다는 것을 / 내가 활동을 계속하면서

Much of the time / in the news business, / we have no idea / what we are doing.
대부분의 시간 / 뉴스 업무에서 / 우리는 모른다 / 우리가 무엇을 하고 있는지를

We show up in the morning / and someone says, / "Can you write a story / about (pick one) tax policy/immigration/climate change?"
우리는 아침에 나타난다 / 그리고 누군가 ~라고 말한다 / "기사를 써주시겠어요 / (하나 골라서) 세금 정책/이민/기후 변화에 대해?"

When newspapers had once-a-day deadlines, / we said / a reporter would learn in the morning / and teach at night / ―write a story / that could inform tomorrow's readers / on a topic / the reporter knew nothing / about 24 hours earlier.
신문들에 하루에 한 번 있는 마감 일자가 있었을 때 / 우리는 말했다 / 기자가 아침에 배울 것이라고 / 그리고 저녁에 가르칠 것이라고 / 기사를 써서 / 내일의 독자들에게 정보를 제공할 / 주제에 대해 / 그 기자가 전혀 알지 못했던 / 대략 24시간 전에는

Now it is more like learning / at the top of the hour / and teaching at the bottom of the same hour.
현재로서는 그것은 배우는 것에 더욱 가깝다 / 정시에 / 그리고 같은 시간의 30분에 가르치는 것과

I'm also running a political podcast, / for example, / and during the presidential conventions, / we should be able to use it / to do real-time interviews anywhere.
나는 또한 정치에 관한 팟캐스트를 운영하고 있다 / 예를 들어 / 그리고 대선 전당대회 동안 / 우리는 그것을 사용할 수 있어야 한다 / 어느 곳에서든지 실시간 인터뷰를 하기 위해

I am just increasingly working / without a script.
나는 단지 갈수록 더 일하고 있다 / 대본 없이

해설 디지털 혁명이 전국에 걸쳐 뉴스 편집실을 뒤엎기 때문에, 여기에 모든 기자들을 위한 나의 충고가 있다. 나는 25년 이상 동안 기자였어서, 6번의 기술적 라이프 사이클을 겪었다. 가장 극적인 변화들은 지난 6년간 있었다. 이것은 내가 활동을 계속하면서, 점점 더 빈번히, 시시한 이야기를 지어내고 있다는 것을 의미한다. 뉴스 업무에서 대부분의 시간, 우리는 우리가 무엇을 하고 있는지를 모른다. 우리는 아침에 나타나고 누군가 "(하나 골라서) 세금 정책/이민/기후 변화에 대해 기사를 써주시겠어요?"라고 말한다. 신문들에 하루에 한 번 있는 마감 일자가 있었을 때, 우리는 기자가 아침에 배워서 그 기자가 대략 24시간 전에는 전혀 알지 못했던 주제에 대해 내일의 독자들에게 정보를 제공할 기사를 써서 저녁에 가르칠 것이라고 말했다. 현재로서는 그것은 정시에 배워서 같은 시간의 30분에 가르치는 것에 더욱 가깝다. 예를 들어, 나는 또한 정치에 관한 팟캐스트를 운영하고 있고, 대선 전당대회 동안, 우리는 어느 곳에서든지 실시간 인터뷰를 하기 위해 그것을 사용할 수 있어야 한다. 나는 단지 갈수록 더 대본 없이 일하고 있다.

① 선생님으로서의 기자   ② 기자와 즉석에서 하기
③ 정치에서의 기술   ④ 언론계와 기술의 분야

해설 지문 전반에 걸쳐 디지털 혁명으로 인한 뉴스 편집실에 대한 변화에 대해 이야기하며, 신문에 마감 일자가 있었을 때는 기자들이 24시간 전 아침에 전혀 모르던 한 주제를 배워서 저녁에 독자들에게 기사를 통해 가르쳐 주었지만, 현재는 정시에 배워서 같은 시간의 30분에 가르치는 것에 가깝고, 실시간 인터뷰를 위한 팟캐스트

또한 사용한다고 설명하고 있다. 따라서 이 지문의 주제를 '기자와 즉석에서 하기'라고 표현한 ②번이 정답이다.

어휘 revolution 혁명 upend 뒤엎다, 거꾸로 하다 dramatic 극적인
transformation 변화 make up 지어내다 tax 세금
policy 정책 immigration 이민
at the top[bottom] of the hour 정시[30분]에
real-time 실시간의 improvisation 즉석에서 하기

10 독해 논리적 흐름 파악 (무관한 문장 삭제) 난이도 ★★☆

끊어읽기 해석

Children's playgrounds throughout history / were the wilderness, fields, streams, and hills of the country and the roads, streets, and vacant places of villages, towns, and cities.
역사를 통틀어 아이들의 운동장은 / 황무지, 들판, 개울과 시골의 언덕, 그리고 도로, 길가와 마을, 읍과 도시의 빈 장소였다

① The term *playground* refers to / all those places / where children gather / to play their free, spontaneous games.
'운동장'이라는 용어는 나타낸다 / 그러한 모든 장소들을 / 아이들이 모이는 / 그들의 자유롭고, 즉흥적인 게임들을 하기 위해

② Only during the past few decades / have children vacated these natural playgrounds / for their growing love affair / with video games, texting, and social networking.
불과 지난 몇 십 년 사이에 / 아이들이 이 자연의 운동장들을 떠나왔다 / 그들의 고조되는 열광으로 인해 / 비디오 게임, 문자와 소셜 네트워크에 대한

③ Even in rural America / few children are still roaming / in a free-ranging manner, / unaccompanied by adults.
심지어 미국의 시골 지역에서도 / 여전히 아이들이 거의 돌아다니지 않는다 / 방목하는 방식으로 / 어른들이 동반하지 않은

④ When out of school, / they are commonly found in neighborhoods / digging in sand, building forts, playing traditional games, climbing, or playing ball games.
학교 밖에 있을 때 / 그들은 흔히 인근에서 발견된다 / 모래를 파거나, 요새를 짓거나, 구식 게임, 등산 또는 구기 게임을 하며

They are rapidly disappearing / from the natural terrain / of creeks, hills, and fields, / and like their urban counterparts, / are turning / to their indoor, sedentary cyber toys / for entertainment.
그들은 급속도로 사라지고 있다 / 자연 지역으로부터 / 시내, 언덕, 그리고 들판의 / 그리고 그들의 도시에 사는 상대방들(아이들)처럼 / 돌아서고 있다 / 그들의 실내의, 주로 앉아서 하는 사이버 장난감들로 / 오락을 위해

해석 역사를 통틀어 아이들의 운동장은 황무지, 들판, 개울과 시골의 언덕, 그리고 도로, 길가와 마을, 읍과 도시의 빈 장소였다. ① '운동장'이라는 용어는 아이들이 그들의 자유롭고, 즉흥적인 게임들을 하기 위해 모이는 그러한 모든 장소들을 나타낸다. ② 불과 지난 몇 십 년 사이에 비디오 게임, 문자와 소셜 네트워크에 대한 그들의 고조되는 열광으로 인해 아이들이 이 자연의 운동장들을 떠나왔다. ③ 심지어 미국의 시골 지역에서도 여전히 아이들이 어른들이 동반하지 않은 방목하는 방식으로 거의 돌아다니지 않는다. ④ 학교 밖에 있을 때, 그들은 흔히 모래를 파거나, 요새를 짓거나, 구식 게임, 등산 또는 구기 게임을 하며 인근에서 발견된다. 그들은 급속도로 시내, 언덕, 그리고 들판의 자연 지역으로부터 사라지고 있고, 그들의 도시에 사는 상대방들(아이들)처럼 오락을 위해 그들의 실내의, 주로 앉아서 하는 사이버 장난감들로 돌아서고 있다.

해설 지문 처음에서 역사를 통틀어 아이들의 운동장이 무엇이었는지 언급한 뒤, ①번에 운동장이 나타내는 것을 설명하고, ②, ③번에서 지난 몇 십 년 사이에 아이들이 자연의 운동장을 떠나왔으며 시골 지역에서도 아이들이 거의 돌아다니지 않는다고 설명하

고 있으므로 모두 첫 문장과 관련이 있다. 그러나 ④번은 아이들이 학교 밖에 있을 때 모래를 파고, 요새를 짓는 등 운동장의 역할을 하는 곳에서 아이들이 시간을 보낸다는 내용으로 지문의 흐름과 반대되는 내용이다. 따라서 ④번이 정답이다.

어휘 wilderness 황무지 stream 개울 spontaneous 즉흥적인
vacate 떠나다, 비우다 rural 시골의, 지방의
roam 돌아다니다, 배회하다 unaccompanied 동반하지 않은
rapidly 급속도로 terrain 지역, 지형 urban 도시에 사는, 도시의
sedentary 주로 앉아서 하는

11 어휘 어휘&표현 engrossed in = preoccupied with 난이도 ★★☆

해석 지루한 오후 강의 동안에는 시간이 느릿느릿하게 흘러가는 듯하고 뇌가 매우 재미있는 무언가에 몰두했을 때는 쏜살같이 가는 듯하다.
① ~에 의해 향상된 ② ~에 무관심한
③ ~에 의해 안정된 ④ ~에 정신이 팔린

어휘 trickle 느릿느릿한 움직임 engrossed in ~에 몰두한
enhance 향상시키다, 강화하다 apathetic 무관심한
stabilize 안정되다, 안정시키다 preoccupied 정신이 팔린, 사로잡힌

👍 이것도 알면 합격!

engrossed in(~에 몰두한)과 유사한 의미의 표현
= engaged in, absorbed in, hard at work with

12 어휘 어휘&표현 keep abreast of = be acquainted with 난이도 ★★★

해석 이러한 일간 업데이트는 정부가 시장을 제어하려고 시도함에 따라 독자들이 시장에 뒤떨어지지 않게 도와주도록 고안되었다.
① ~을 알다 ② ~에 의해 영감을 받다
③ ~을 믿고 있다 ④ ~에 가까이하지 않다

어휘 keep abreast of ~에 뒤떨어지지 않다 attempt 시도하다
keep under control 억제하다

👍 이것도 알면 합격!

keep abreast of(~에 뒤떨어지지 않다)와 유사한 의미의 표현
= stay informed about, stay current with

13 독해 추론 (빈칸 완성 - 단어) 난이도 ★★☆

끊어읽기 해석

In the 1840s, / the island of Ireland suffered famine.
1840년대에 / 아일랜드 섬은 기근에 시달렸다

Because Ireland could not produce enough food / to feed its population, / about a million people died of (A) starvation; / they simply didn't have enough to eat / to stay alive.
아일랜드가 충분한 음식을 생산할 수 없었기 때문에 / 모든 주민에게 공급하기에 / 대략 백만 명의 사람들이 (A) 굶주림으로 죽었다 / 그들은 그야말로 먹을 충분한 양을 가지고 있지 않았다 / 살아가기 위해

The famine caused / another 1.25 million people to (B) emigrate; / many left their island home / for the United States; / the rest went to Canada, Australia, Chile, and other countries.

그 기근은 원인이 되었다 / 또 다른 125만 명의 사람들이 (B) 이주하는 / 많은 사람들은 그들의 고향 섬에서 떠났다 / 미국으로 / 나머지는 캐나다, 호주, 칠레, 그리고 다른 나라들로 갔다

Before the famine, / the population of Ireland was approximately 6 million.
그 기근 전에 / 아일랜드의 인구는 대략 6백만 명이었다

After the great food shortage, / it was about 4 million.
그 엄청난 식량 부족 이후에 / 그것은 대략 4백만 명이었다

해석　1840년대에, 아일랜드 섬은 기근에 시달렸다. 아일랜드가 모든 주민에게 공급하기에 충분한 음식을 생산할 수 없었기 때문에, 대략 백만 명의 사람들이 (A) 굶주림으로 죽었다. 그들은 그야말로 살아가기 위해 먹을 충분한 양을 가지고 있지 않았다. 그 기근은 또 다른 125만 명의 사람들이 (B) 이주하는 원인이 되었다. 많은 사람들은 그들의 고향 섬에서 미국으로 떠났다. 나머지는 캐나다, 호주, 칠레, 그리고 다른 나라들로 갔다. 그 기근 전에, 아일랜드의 인구는 대략 6백만 명이었다. 그 엄청난 식량 부족 이후에, 그것은 대략 4백만 명이었다.

(A)	(B)
① 탈수증	강제 추방되다
② 정신적 외상	이민을 오다
③ 굶주림	이주하다
④ 피로	감금되다

해설　(A) 빈칸 앞 문장에 아일랜드가 모든 주민에게 공급하기에 충분한 음식을 생산할 수 없었다는 내용이 있고, 빈칸 뒤 문장에 그들(주민들)은 살아가기에 충분한 양의 음식을 가지고 있지 않았다는 내용이 있으므로, 빈칸에는 대략 백만 명의 사람들이 '굶주림'으로 죽었다는 내용이 나와야 적절하다. (B) 빈칸 뒤 문장에 많은 사람들이 미국, 캐나다, 호주 등으로 떠났다는 내용이 있으므로, 빈칸에는 또 다른 125만 명의 사람들이 '이주하는' 원인이 되었다는 내용이 나와야 적절하다.
따라서 ③ (A) starvation(굶주림) - (B) emigrate(이주하다)가 정답이다.

어휘　suffer 시달리다　famine 기근　approximately 대략
shortage 부족　dehydration 탈수증, 건조　deport 강제 추방하다
immigrate 이민을 오다　starvation 굶주림　emigrate 이주하다
fatigue 피로　detain 감금하다, 유치하다

14　독해　추론 (빈칸 완성 - 연결어)　난이도 ★★☆

끊어읽기 해석

Today / the technology / to create the visual component / of virtual-reality (VR) experiences / is well on its way to becoming widely accessible and affordable.
오늘날 / 기술은 / 시각적 구성 요소를 만드는 / 가상현실(VR) 체험의 / 거의 널리 이용가능하고 가격이 알맞게 되어간다

But to work powerfully, / virtual reality needs to be / about more than visuals.
하지만 강력하게 작동하기 위해서 / 가상현실은 되어야 한다 / 거의 시각 자료 이상이

(A) Unless / what you are hearing / convincingly matches the visuals, / the virtual experience breaks apart.
(A) 만약 ~이 아니라면 / 당신에게 들리는 것이 / 시각 자료와 납득이 가도록 어울리지 / 그 시각 체험은 끝난다

Take a basketball game.
농구 경기를 예로 들어보자

If the players, the coaches, the announcers, and the crowd / all sound like they're sitting midcourt, / you may as well

watch the game / on television / —you'll get just as much / of a sense / that you are "there."
만약 선수들, 코치들, 해설가들과 관중이 / 모두 그들이 미드코트에 앉아 있는 것처럼 들린다면 / 당신은 그 경기를 보는 것이 낫다 / 텔레비전으로 / 당신은 정확히 동일한 것(느낌)을 받을 것이다 / 느낌과 / 당신이 '거기에' 있다는

(B) Unfortunately, / today's audio equipment and our widely used recording and reproduction formats / are simply inadequate / to the task of re-creating convincingly the sound / of a battlefield on a distant planet, / a basketball game at courtside, / or a symphony / as heard from the first row / of a great concert hall.
(B) 안타깝게도 / 현재의 음향 장비와 우리의 널리 사용되는 녹음과 재생 방식은 / 그야말로 불충분하다 / 소리를 납득이 가도록 재현하는 작업에 / 멀리 떨어져 있는 행성의 전쟁터의 / 코트사이드에서의 농구 경기의 / 혹은 연주회의 / 첫 번째 열에서 듣는 / 정말 좋은 콘서트 홀의

해석　오늘날 가상현실(VR) 체험의 시각적 구성 요소를 만드는 기술은 거의 널리 이용가능하고 가격이 알맞게 되어간다. 하지만 강력하게 작동하기 위해서, 가상현실은 거의 시각 자료 이상이 되어야 한다. (A) 만약 당신에게 들리는 것이 시각 자료와 납득이 가도록 어울리지 않으면, 그 시각 체험은 끝난다. 농구 경기를 예로 들어보자. 만약 선수들, 코치들, 해설가들과 관중이 모두 미드코트에 앉아 있는 것처럼 들린다면, 당신은 그 경기를 텔레비전으로 보는 것이 낫다. 당신은 당신이 '거기에' 있다는 느낌과 정확히 동일한 것(느낌)을 받을 것이다. (B) 안타깝게도, 현재의 음향 장비와 우리의 널리 사용되는 녹음과 재생 방식은 멀리 떨어져 있는 행성의 전쟁터, 코트사이드에서의 농구 경기 또는 정말 좋은 콘서트 홀의 첫 번째 열에서 듣는 연주회의 소리를 납득이 가도록 재현하는 작업에 그야말로 불충분하다.

(A)	(B)
① 만약 ~라면	그와 대조적으로
② 만약 ~이 아니라면	결과적으로
③ 만약 ~라면	유사하게
④ 만약 ~이 아니라면	안타깝게도

해설　(A) 빈칸 앞 문장은 가상현실이 강력하게 작동하기 위해서는 시각 자료 이상이 되어야 한다는 내용이고, 빈칸 (A)가 있는 문장은 들리는 것과 시각 자료가 어떠하게 어울리면 시각 체험이 끝난다는 내용이므로, 빈칸에는 부정적 의미의 조건을 나타내는 연결어인 Unless(만약 ~이 아니라면)가 들어가야 적절하다. (B) 빈칸 뒤 문장은 현재의 음향 장비와 녹음과 재생 방식이 농구 경기장과 연주회의 소리를 납득이 가도록 재현하는 작업에는 불충분하다는 내용이므로, 빈칸에는 유감을 나타내는 연결어인 Unfortunately(안타깝게도)가 들어가야 적절하다.
따라서, ④ (A) Unless(만약 ~이 아니라면) - (B) Unfortunately(안타깝게도)가 정답이다.

어휘　component 구성 요소
be well on the way to -ing ~을 거의 다 이루어가다
convincingly 납득이 가도록　announcer 해설가
equipment 장비　reproduction 재생
inadequate 불충분한, 부적당한　distant 멀리 떨어져 있는

15　독해　논리적 흐름 파악 (문장 삽입)　난이도 ★★☆

끊어읽기 해석

The same thinking can be applied / to any number of goals, / like improving performance / at work.
동일한 생각은 적용될 수 있다 / 몇 개의 목표들에라도 / 성과를 향상시키기와 같은 / 직장에서

The happy brain tends to focus on / the short term.
행복한 뇌는 초점을 맞추는 경향이 있다 / 단기간에

(①) That being the case, / it's a good idea / to consider / what short-term goals we can accomplish / that will eventually lead to accomplishing / long-term goals.
그것이 사실이라면 / 좋은 생각이다 / 고려하는 것은 / 어떤 단기 목표들을 우리가 달성할 수 있는지 / 최종적으로 달성하도록 이끌 / 장기 목표들을

(②) For instance, / if you want to lose thirty pounds / in six months, / what short-term goals / can you associate / with losing the smaller increments of weight / that will get you there?
예를 들어 / 만약 당신이 30파운드를 빼길 원한다면 / 6개월에 / 어떤 단기 목표들을 / 당신은 관련지어 생각할 수 있을까 / 더 적은 양의 증가하는 무게를 빼는 것과 / 당신을 거기(30파운드를 빼는 것)에 도달하게 할

(③) Maybe / it's something / as simple as rewarding yourself each week / that you lose two pounds.
어쩌면 / 그것은 어떤 것이다 / 매주 당신 스스로에게 보상하는 것만큼 간단한 / 당신이 2파운드를 뺀

(④) By breaking the overall goal / into smaller, shorter-term parts, / we can focus on incremental accomplishments / instead of being overwhelmed / by the enormity of the goal / in our profession.
전반적인 목표를 나눔으로써 / 더 작고, 더 단기간의 부분들로 / 우리는 증가하는 성취에 초점을 맞출 수 있다 / 압도되는 대신에 / 목표의 거대함에 의해 / 우리의 직업에서의

해석 행복한 뇌는 단기간에 초점을 맞추는 경향이 있다. 그것이 사실이라면, 최종적으로 장기 목표들을 달성하도록 이끌 어떤 단기 목표들을 우리가 달성할 수 있는지 고려하는 것은 좋은 생각이다. 예를 들어, 만약 당신이 6개월에 30파운드를 빼길 원한다면, 어떤 단기 목표들을 당신을 거기(30파운드를 빼는 것)에 도달하게 할 더 적은 양의 증가하는 무게를 빼는 것과 관련지어 생각할 수 있을까? 어쩌면 그것은 당신이 2파운드를 뺀 매주 당신 스스로에게 보상하는 것만큼 간단한 것이다. ④ 동일한 생각은 직장에서 성과를 향상시키기와 같은 몇 개의 목표들에라도 적용될 수 있다. 전반적인 목표를 더 작고, 더 단기간의 부분들로 나눔으로써, 우리의 직업에서의 목표의 거대함에 의해 압도되는 대신에 우리는 증가하는 성취에 초점을 맞출 수 있다.

해설 지문 처음에서 장기 목표를 달성하도록 이끄는 단기 목표를 고려하는 것은 좋은 것이라고 설명한 뒤, 이어서 몸무게를 줄이는 것을 예로 들고, ④번 뒤 문장에서 목표를 작고 단기간의 부분들로 나눔으로써 직업에서의 목표에 압도되지 않고 성취에 초점을 맞출 수 있다고 설명하고 있으므로, ④번 자리에 동일한 생각(The same thinking)이 직장에서의 목표에도 적용될 수 있다는 주어진 문장이 들어가야 자연스럽게 연결된다. 따라서 ④번이 정답이다.

어휘 improve 향상시키다 accomplish 달성하다
eventually 최종적으로 associate 관련지어 생각하다
increment 증가량, 임금 인상 reward 보상하다
incremental 증가하는 accomplishment 성취, 업적
enormity 거대함, 심각함 profession 직업

16 문법 동사의 종류 난이도 ★☆☆

해설 ③ 타동사의 쓰임 동사(has married) 뒤에 목적어가 없고 marry(결혼하다)가 '~와 결혼한 상태이다'라는 의미로 쓰일 때는 수동태로 쓰이므로 has married를 has been married로 고쳐야 한다.

오답 ① 부사절 접속사 '전화하고 싶은 경우에'는 조건을 나타내는 부
분석 사절 접속사 in case(~의 경우에 대비하여)를 사용하여 나타낼 수 있으므로 just in case you would like to call me가 올바르게 쓰였다.
② 동명사구 관용 표현 '준비하느라 바쁘다'는 동명사구 관용 표현 be busy -ing(-하느라 바쁘다)를 사용하여 나타낼 수 있으므로 I am busy preparing이 올바르게 쓰였다.
④ to 부정사의 쓰임 '내 아들이 읽을 책'을 나타내기 위해 형용사처럼 명사(a book)를 수식할 수 있는 to 부정사 to read가 올바르게 쓰였고, 문장의 주어(I)와 to 부정사(to read)의 행위의 주체가 달라서 to 부정사의 의미상 주어 for my son이 to 앞에 올바르게 쓰였다.

어휘 prepare 준비하다

👍 이것도 알면 합격!

①번 보기의 'in case(~의 경우에 대비하여)와 같이 조건을 나타내는 부사절 접속사들의 의미를 구분하여 알아두자.

• if 만약 ~라면	• unless(= if ~ not) 만약 ~아니라면
• once 일단 ~하자, 일단 ~하면	• as long as ~하는 한, ~하면
• otherwise 그렇지 않으면	• in case ~의 경우에 대비하여
• provided/providing (that) 오직 ~하는 경우에	

17 독해 세부내용 파악 (내용 불일치 파악) 난이도 ★☆☆

끊어읽기 해석

In the nineteenth century, / the most respected health and medical experts all insisted / that diseases were caused by "miasma," / a fancy term for bad air.
19세기에 / 가장 평판 높은 보건의료 전문가들은 모두 주장했다 / 질병들은 '지저분한 공기'에 의해 발생된다고 / 해로운 공기의 근사한 용어인

Western society's system of health / was based on this assumption: / to prevent diseases, / windows were kept open or closed, / depending on / whether there was more miasma / inside or outside the room; / it was believed / that doctors could not pass along disease / because gentlemen did not inhabit quarters / with bad air.
서구 사회의 보건 체계는 / 이 가정에 바탕을 두었다 / 질병들을 예방하기 위해 / 창문들은 열리거나 닫혀 있었다 / ~에 따라서 / 더 많은 지저분한 공기가 있는지 / 실내 혹은 실외에 / 믿어졌다 / 의사들은 질병을 전달할 수 없다고 / 신분이 높은 사람들은 숙소에 살지 않았기 때문에 / 해로운 공기가 있는

Then / the idea of germs came along.
그 후에 / 병균이라는 개념이 생겼다

One day, / everyone believed / that bad air makes you sick.
어느 날 / 모든 사람이 믿었다 / 해로운 공기가 사람을 아프게 한다고

Then, / almost overnight, / people started realizing / there were invisible things / called microbes and bacteria / that were the real cause of diseases.
그러고 나서 / 거의 하룻밤 사이에 / 사람들은 깨닫기 시작했다 / 보이지 않는 것들이 있다는 것을 / 미생물과 박테리아라고 불리는 / 질병들의 진짜 원인이었던

This new view of disease / brought sweeping changes / to medicine, / as surgeons adopted antiseptics / and scientists invented vaccines and antibiotics.
이 질병에 대한 새로운 견해는 / 전면적인 변화들을 가져왔다 / 의학에 / 외과 의사들이 소독약을 썼기 때문이다 / 그리고 과학자들은 백신과 항생제를 발명했다

But, / just as momentously, / the idea of germs / gave ordinary people the power / to influence their own lives.
하지만 / 마찬가지로 중요하듯이 / 병균이라는 개념은 / 일반 사람들에게 힘을 주었다 / 그들 스스로의 생명에 영향을 미치는

Now, / if you wanted to stay healthy, / you could wash your hands, / boil your water, / cook your food thoroughly, / and clean cuts and scrapes / with iodine.
이제 / 당신이 건강을 유지하길 원한다면 / 당신은 손을 씻을 수 있다 / 당신의 물을 끓일 수 있다 / 당신의 음식을 완전히 익힐 수 있다 / 그리고 베인 상처와 긁힌 상처를 소독할 수 있다 / 요오드로

해석 19세기에, 가장 평판 높은 보건의료 전문가들은 모두 질병들은 해로운 공기의 근사한 용어인 '지저분한 공기'에 의해 발생된다고 주장했다. 서구 사회의 보건 체계는 이 가정에 바탕을 두었고, 질병들을 예방하기 위해, 실내 혹은 실외에 더 많은 지저분한 공기가 있는지에 따라 창문들은 열리거나 닫혀 있었다. 신분이 높은 사람들은 해로운 공기가 있는 숙소에 살지 않았기 때문에 의사들은 질병을 전달할 수 없다고 믿어졌다. 그 후에 병균이라는 개념이 생겼다. 어느 날, 모든 사람이 해로운 공기가 사람을 아프게 한다고 믿었다. 그러고 나서, 거의 하룻밤 사이에, 사람들은 질병들의 진짜 원인이었던 미생물과 박테리아라고 불리는 보이지 않는 것들이 있다는 것을 깨닫기 시작했다. 이 질병에 대한 새로운 견해는 의학에 전면적인 변화들을 가져왔는데, 외과 의사들은 소독약을 썼고 과학자들은 백신과 항생제를 발명했기 때문이다. 하지만, 마찬가지로 중요하듯이, 병균이라는 개념은 일반 사람들에게 그들 스스로의 생명에 영향을 미치는 힘을 주었다. 이제, 당신이 건강을 유지하길 원한다면, 당신은 손을 씻고, 당신의 물을 끓이고, 당신의 음식을 완전히 익히고, 베인 상처와 긁힌 상처를 요오드로 소독할 수 있다.

① 19세기에, 창문을 여는 것은 지저분한 공기의 밀도와 무관했다.
② 19세기에, 신분이 높은 사람들은 해로운 공기가 있는 곳에서 살지 않았다고 믿어졌다.
③ 백신은 사람들이 미생물과 박테리아가 질병들의 진짜 원인이라는 것을 깨달은 후에 발명되었다.
④ 상처부위를 소독하는 것은 사람들이 건강을 유지하도록 도울 수 있다.

해설 지문 앞부분에서 19세기에는 질병이 지저분한 공기에 의해 발생된다고 믿었기 때문에 실내 혹은 실외에 더 많은 지저분한 공기가 있는지에 따라 창문들이 열리거나 닫혀 있었다고 했으므로, 19세기에 창문을 여는 것이 지저분한 공기의 밀도와 무관했다는 것은 지문의 내용과 반대이다. 따라서 ①번이 정답이다.

어휘 respected 평판 높은, 훌륭한 miasma (지저분한) 공기, 독기
assumption 가정 prevent 예방하다 inhabit 살다, 거주하다
quarter 숙소, 막사 come along 생기다, 나타나다
invisible 보이지 않는 sweeping 전면적인, 광범위한
antiseptic 소독약, 소독제 antibiotic 항생제
momentously 중요하게도 ordinary 일반적인, 평범한
influence 영향을 미치다 thoroughly 완전히, 철저히 cut 베인 상처
scrape 긁힌 상처 iodine 요오드 irrelevant 무관한, 상관없는
density 밀도

18 독해 세부내용 파악 (내용 불일치 파악) 난이도 ★★☆

끊어읽기 해석

Followers are a critical part / of the leadership equation, / but their role has not always been appreciated.
추종자들은 대단히 중요한 부분이다 / 리더십 균등화의 / 하지만 그들의 역할이 항상 정당하게 평가받은 것은 아니었다

For a long time, / in fact, / "the common view of leadership was / that leaders actively led / and subordinates, / later called followers, / passively and obediently followed."
오랫동안 / 실제로 / "리더십의 보편적인 관점은 ~였다 / 지도자들이 적극적으로 이끌었다는 것 / 그리고 하급자들은 / 이후에 추종자들이라 불린 / 수동적이고 고분고분하게 따랐다"

Over time, / especially in the last century, / social change shaped / people's views of followers, / and leadership theories gradually recognized / the active and important role / that followers play / in the leadership process.
시간이 흘러 / 특히 지난 100년간 / 사회변화는 형성했다 / 사람들의 추종자들에 대한 관점을 / 그리고 리더십 이론들은 점진적으로 인정했다 / 활발하고 중요한 역할을 / 추종자들이 맡는 / 리더십 과정에서

Today / it seems natural / to accept the important role / followers play.
오늘날 / 자연스러운 듯하다 / 중요한 역할을 받아들이는 것은 / 추종자들이 맡는

One aspect of leadership is particularly worth noting / in this regard: / Leadership is a social influence process / shared among all members / of a group.
리더십의 한 가지 측면은 특별히 주목할 가치가 있다 / 이러한 점에서 / 리더십은 하나의 사회적 영향의 과정이다 / 모든 구성원들 사이에 공유된 / 한 집단의

Leadership is not restricted to the influence / exerted by someone / in a particular position or role; / followers are part / of the leadership process, / too.
리더십은 영향에 제한되지 않는다 / 누군가에 의해 행사되는 / 특정한 위치나 역할에 있는 / 추종자들은 일부이다 / 리더십 과정의 / 또한

해석 추종자들은 리더십 균등화의 대단히 중요한 부분이지만, 그들의 역할이 항상 정당하게 평가받은 것은 아니었다. 실제로, 오랫동안, "리더십의 보편적인 관점은 지도자들이 적극적으로 이끌고 이후에 추종자들이라 불린 하급자들은 수동적이고 고분고분하게 따르는 것이었다." 시간이 흘러, 특히 지난 100년간, 사회변화는 사람들의 추종자들에 대한 관점을 형성했고, 리더십 이론들은 추종자들이 리더십 과정에서 맡는 활발하고 중요한 역할을 점진적으로 인정했다. 오늘날 추종자들이 맡는 중요한 역할을 받아들이는 것은 자연스러운 듯하다. 리더십의 한 가지 측면은 리더십이 한 집단의 모든 구성원들 사이에 공유된 하나의 사회적 영향의 과정이라는 점에서 특별히 주목할 가치가 있다. 리더십은 특정한 위치나 역할에 있는 누군가에 의해 행사되는 영향에 제한되지 않는다. 추종자들 또한 리더십 과정의 일부이다.

① 상당한 시간 동안, 리더들은 적극적으로 이끌고 추종자들은 수동적으로 따른다고 이해되었다.
② 하급자들에 대한 사람들의 관점은 사회변화에 의해 영향을 받았다.
③ 추종자들의 중요한 역할은 오늘날에도 여전히 받아들여지지 않는다.
④ 리더들과 추종자들 모두 리더십 과정에 참여한다.

해설 지문 중간에 오늘날 추종자들이 맡는 중요한 역할을 받아들이는 것은 자연스러운 듯하다고 했으므로, 추종자들의 중요한 역할은 오늘날에도 여전히 받아들여지지 않는다는 것은 지문의 내용과 반대이다. 따라서 ③번이 정답이다.

어휘 critical 대단히 중요한 equation 균등화, 동등하게 함
appreciate 정당하게 평가하다 actively 적극적으로, 활발하게
subordinate 하급자, 부하 passively 수동적으로
obediently 고분고분하게, 공손하게 recognize 인정하다
accept 받아들이다, 수용하다 aspect 측면 particularly 특별히
restrict 제한하다 exert 행사하다, 가하다
deny 받아들이지 않다, 인정하지 않다 participate in ~에 참여하다

끊어읽기 해석

Language proper is itself double-layered.
엄밀한 의미의 언어는 그 자체로 두 개의 층을 이룬다

Single noises are only occasionally meaningful: / mostly, / the various speech sounds / convey coherent messages / only when combined into an overlapping chain, / like different colors of ice-cream / melting into one another.
하나뿐인 소음들로는 오직 가끔씩만 의미가 있다 / 주로 / 다양한 언어음들이 / 일관성 있는 메시지들을 전달한다 / 중복된 연속으로 결합될 경우에만 / 다른 색의 아이스크림처럼 / 서로를 향해 녹는

In birdsong also, / individual notes are often of little value: / the sequence is what matters.
새의 지저귐에서 또한 / 개개인의 음들은 보통 가치가 거의 없다 / 연속적인 행동들이 중요한 것이다

In both humans and birds, / control of this specialized sound-system is exercised / by one half of the brain, / normally the left half, / and the system is learned / relatively early in life.
인간과 새 모두에게 / 이 전문화된 소리 체계의 통제는 수행된다 / 뇌의 한쪽 절반에 의해 / 보통 좌뇌인 / 그리고 그 체계는 학습된다 / 상대적으로 젊은 시기에

And just as many human languages have dialects, / so do some bird species: / in California, / the white-crowned sparrow has songs / so different from area to area / that Californians can supposedly tell / where they are / in the state / by listening to these sparrows.
그리고 다수의 인간의 언어들이 방언이 있듯이 / 일부 새 종들도 방언이 있다 / 캘리포니아에서 / 노랑턱멧새는 노래가 있다 / 지역별로 너무 다른 / 그래서 캘리포니아 사람들은 짐작하여 구분할 수 있다 / 그들이 어디에 있는지 / 그 주(캘리포니아)에서 / 그 참새들에게 귀를 기울임으로써

해석 엄밀한 의미의 언어는 그 자체로 두 개의 층을 이룬다. 하나뿐인 소음들로는 오직 가끔씩만 의미가 있다. 주로, 다양한 언어음들이 서로를 향해 녹는 다른 색의 아이스크림처럼 중복된 연속으로 결합될 경우에만 일관성 있는 메시지들을 전달한다. 새의 지저귐에서 또한, 개개인의 음들은 보통 가치가 거의 없다. 연속적인 행동들이 중요한 것이다. 인간과 새 모두에게, 이 전문화된 소리 체계의 통제는 보통 좌뇌인 뇌의 한쪽 절반에 의해 수행되고, 그 체계는 상대적으로 젊은 시기에 학습된다. 그리고 다수의 인간의 언어들이 방언이 있듯이, 일부 새 종들도 방언이 있다. 캘리포니아에서, 노랑턱멧새는 지역별로 너무 다른 노래가 있어서 캘리포니아 사람들은 그 참새들에게 귀를 기울임으로써 그들이 그 주(캘리포니아)에서 어디에 있는지 짐작하여 구분할 수 있다.

① 개개인의 음들은 보통 가치가 거의 없다
② 주기적인 소리는 중요하다
③ 방언들은 대단히 중요한 역할을 한다
④ 어떠한 소리 체계도 존재하지 않는다

해설 빈칸이 있는 문장을 통해 빈칸에 새의 지저귐에서 또한 어떠한지에 대한 내용이 나와야 적절하다는 것을 알 수 있다. 빈칸 앞부분에서 하나뿐인 소음들로는 가끔씩만 의미가 있으며, 다양한 언어음들이 중복된 연속으로 결합될 경우에만 일관성 있는 메시지들을 전달한다고 했고, 빈칸 뒤에서 연속적인 행동들이 중요하다고 했으므로, 새의 지저귐에서 또한, '개개인의 음들은 보통 가치가 거의 없다'고 한 ①번이 정답이다.

어휘 occasionally 가끔 coherent 일관성 있는 combine 결합하다 overlapping 중복된 sequence 연속적인 행동들, 순서 matter 중요하다 specialized 전문화된 relatively 상대적으로 dialect 방언, 사투리 sparrow 참새 note 음 rhythmic 주기적인, 리드미컬한 exist 존재하다

끊어읽기 해석

Nobel Prize-winning psychologist Daniel Kahneman / changed the way / the world thinks about economics, / upending the notion / that human beings are rational decision-makers.
노벨상을 수상한 심리학자인 대니얼 카너먼은 / 방식을 변화시켰다 / 세계가 경제학에 대해 생각하는 / 개념을 뒤집으며 / 인간은 합리적인 의사결정자라는

Along the way, / his discipline-crossing influence / has altered the way / physicians make medical decisions / and investors evaluate risk / on Wall Street.
그 과정에서 / 그의 학문 융합적 영향은 / 방식을 바꾸었다 / 의사들이 의학적 결정을 내리는 / 그리고 투자자들이 위험성을 측정하는 / 월스트리트에서

In a paper, / Kahneman and his colleagues outline a process / for making big strategic decisions.
한 논문에서 / 카너먼과 그의 동료들은 과정의 개요를 서술했다 / 중대한 전략적인 결정들을 내리기 위한

Their suggested approach, / labeled as "Mediating Assessments Protocol," or MAP, / has a simple goal: / To put off gut-based decision-making / until a choice can be informed / by a number of separate factors.
그들의 제안된 방식은 / '조정을 통한 평가 프로토콜' 혹은 MAP라고 불리는 / 간단한 목표가 있다 / 직감에 기반한 의사결정을 미루는 것이다 / 선택의 범위가 통지될 수 있을 때까지 / 많은 독립된 요인들에 의해

"One of the essential purposes of MAP / is basically to delay intuition," / Kahneman said / in a recent interview with The Post.
"MAP의 본질적인 목표 중 하나는 / 기본적으로 직관을 미루는 것입니다" / 카너먼이 말했다 / The Post와의 최근의 인터뷰에서

The structured process calls for / analyzing a decision / based on six to seven previously chosen attributes, / discussing each of them separately / and assigning them a relative percentile score, / and finally, / using those scores / to make a holistic judgment.
그 구조화된 과정은 필요로 한다 / 결정을 분석하는 것을 / 기존에 선택된 6개에서 7개의 특성들에 기반한 / 그것들 각각을 개별적으로 검토하는 것을 / 그리고 그것들에게 상대적인 백분위 점수를 부여하는 것을 / 그리고 마침내 / 그러한 점수들을 사용하는 것을 / 전체적인 판단을 내리기 위해

해석 노벨상을 수상한 심리학자 대니얼 카너먼은 인간은 합리적인 의사결정자라는 개념을 뒤집으며 세계가 경제학에 대해 생각하는 방식을 변화시켰다. 그 과정에서, 그의 학문 융합적 영향은 의사들이 의학적 결정을 내리고 월스트리트에서 투자자들이 위험성을 측정하는 방식을 바꾸었다. 한 논문에서, 카너먼과 그의 동료들은 중대한 전략적인 결정들을 내리기 위한 과정의 개요를 서술했다. '조정을 통한 평가 프로토콜' 혹은 MAP라고 불리는 그들의 제안된 방식은 간단한 목표가 있다. 많은 독립된 요인들에 의해 선택의 범위가 통지될 수 있을 때까지 직감에 기반한 의사결정을 미루는 것이다. "MAP의 본질적인 목표 중 하나는 기본적으로 직관을 미루는 것입니다"라고 카너먼이 The Post와의 최근의 인터뷰에서 말했다. 그 구조화된 과정은 기존에 선택된 6개에서 7개의 특성들에 기반한 결정을 분석하고, 그것들 각각을 개별적으로 검토하고, 그것들에게 상대적인 백분위 점수를 부여하는 것을, 그리고 마침내 그러한 점수들을 전체적인 판단을 내리기 위해 사용하는 것을 필요로 한다.

① 향상시키다
② 미루다
③ 소유하다
④ 용이하게 하다

해설 빈칸이 있는 문장을 통해 빈칸에 MAP의 본질적인 목표 중 하나
가 직관을 어떻게 하는 것인지에 대한 내용이 나와야 적절하다는
것을 알 수 있다. 빈칸 앞 문장에 MAP의 목표는 독립된 요인들에
의해 선택의 범위가 통지될 수 있을 때까지 직감에 기반한 의사결
정을 미루는 것이라고 했으므로, MAP의 본질적인 목표 중 하나는
기본적으로 직관을 '미루는' 것이라고 한 ②번이 정답이다.

어휘 upend 뒤집다 rational 합리적인, 이성적인 alter 바꾸다
evaluate 측정하다 outline ~의 개요를 서술하다, ~의 윤곽을 그리다
strategic 전략적인, 전략상 중요한 label ~라고 부르다
mediate 조정하다, 중재하다 assessment 평가
protocol 프로토콜, 의례 gut 직감, 배짱 inform 통지하다, 알리다
separate 독립된, 별개의 factor 요인 essential 본질적인
intuition 직관, 직감 call for 필요로 하다 analyze 분석하다
attribute 특성 percentile 백분위수의 holistic 전체적인
judgment 판단 possess 소유하다 facilitate 용이하게 하다

14회 | 2018년 지방직 9급

취약영역 분석표

영역	세부 유형	문항 수	소계
어휘	어휘&표현	4	/6
	생활영어	2	
문법	관계절	1	/4
	분사	1	
	가정법	1	
	시제&to 부정사	1	
독해	전체내용 파악	3	/10
	세부내용 파악	1	
	추론	3	
	논리적 흐름 파악	3	
총계			/20

· 자신이 취약한 영역은 '공무원 영어, 이렇게 출제된다!'(문제집 p.8)를 통해 다시 한번 확인하고 학습하시기 바랍니다.

---

01   어휘   어휘&표현   paramount = chief   난이도 ★☆☆

해석   의사의 가장 중요한 의무는 해를 끼치지 않는 것이다. 그 밖의 모든 것들은, 치료조차도 2순위에 있어야 한다.
　　① 가장 중요한 　　　　② 맹세한
　　③ 성공한 　　　　　　④ 신비한

어휘   **paramount** 가장 중요한   **physician** 의사   **do harm** 해를 끼치다
chief 가장 중요한   **sworn** 맹세한   **successful** 성공한
mysterious 신비한

👍 이것도 알면 **합격!**

paramount(가장 중요한)의 유의어
= principal, dominant, foremost

02   어휘   어휘&표현   get cold feet = become afraid   난이도 ★★☆

해석   사람들이 북극으로 여행하는 것에 대해 겁을 먹는 것은 특이한 일이 아니다.
　　① 야망을 가지다 　　② 두려워하다
　　③ 지치다 　　　　　④ 슬퍼하다

어휘   **unusual** 특이한   **get cold feet** 겁을 먹다, 용기를 잃다
ambitious 야심을 품은   **exhausted** 지친, 기진맥진한

👍 이것도 알면 **합격!**

get cold feet(겁을 먹다)과 유사한 의미의 표현
= lose confidence, become anxious, start to worry

03   문법   관계절   난이도 ★☆☆

해석   나는 Mrs. Ferrer의 추천서에 대한 당신의 요청에 응하여 씁니다. 그녀는 내 비서로 지난 3년간 일해 왔고 훌륭한 직원이었습니다. 나는 그녀가 당신의 직무기술서에 언급된 모든 요건들을 충족시키고 실제로 여러 방면으로 그것들을 능가한다고 믿습니다. 나는 그녀의 완벽한 성실을 의심할 이유가 결코 없었습니다. 그러므로 나는 Mrs. Ferrer를 당신이 광고하는 그 직책에 추천합니다.

해설   ④ 관계사 선택   명사 the post를 수식하기 위해 형용사 역할을 하는 관계절이 와야 하므로, 명사절 접속사 what이 아닌 관계대명사가 와야 한다. 선행사 the post가 사물이고, 관계절 내에서 동사 advertise의 목적어 역할을 하므로 명사절 접속사 what을 목적격 관계대명사 which 또는 that으로 고쳐야 한다.

오답 분석   ① 전치사 선택   숫자를 포함한 시간 표현(the last three years) 앞에 와서 '얼마나 오래 지속되는가'를 나타내는 전치사 for(~ 동안)가 올바르게 쓰였다.
② 과거분사   수식받는 명사(all the requirements)와 분사가 '직무기술서에 언급되다'라는 의미의 수동 관계이므로 과거분사 mentioned가 올바르게 쓰였다.
③ to 부정사의 쓰임   '의심할 이유'라는 의미를 표현하기 위해 형용사처럼 명사(reason)를 수식할 수 있는 to 부정사 to doubt가 올바르게 쓰였다.

어휘   **in response to** ~에 응하여   **reference** 추천서   **secretary** 비서
requirement 요건   **job description** 직무기술서   **meet** 충족시키다
integrity 성실, 정직   **post** 직책, 일자리

👍 이것도 알면 **합격!**

to 부정사는 명사처럼 주어, 목적어, 보어 자리에 올 수 있고, ③번에서 쓰인 것과 같이 형용사처럼 명사를 수식할 수 있으며, 부사처럼 목적, 이유, 결과를 나타낼 수도 있다.

04 문법 분사

난이도 ★★☆

해설 ④ 분사구문의 형태 분사구문과 주절의 주어가 일치하지 않으면 분사구문의 주어를 그대로 남겨두어야 하는데, 분사구문의 주어가 날씨를 나타내는 비인칭 주어 it으로 주절의 주어(I)와 일치하지 않으므로 Being cold outside를 It being cold outside로 고쳐야 한다.

오답분석 ① 주어 동사 수 일치 전체를 나타내는 표현(All of)을 포함한 주어는 of 뒤 명사에 동사를 수 일치시켜야 하는데, of 뒤에 불가산 명사 the information이 왔으므로 단수 동사 was가 올바르게 쓰였다.

② 조동사 관련 표현 '더 일찍 사과했어야 했다'는 조동사 관련 표현 should have p.p.(~했었어야 했다)를 사용하여 나타낼 수 있으므로 should have apologized가 올바르게 쓰였다.

③ 과거완료 시제 '영화가 이미 시작한' 것은 '우리가 도착한' 특정 과거 시점보다 명백히 이전에 일어난 일이므로 과거완료 시제 had already started가 올바르게 쓰였다.

어휘 apologize 사과하다 boil 끓이다

👍 이것도 알면 **합격!**

조동사 관련 표현인 should have p.p.(~했었어야 했다)와 must have p.p.(~했음에 틀림없다)의 쓰임을 구별해서 알아두자.

(ex) It's raining. We ~~mustn't~~ have planned to play golf today.
(→ shouldn't)
비가 오고 있다. 우리는 오늘 골프를 치는 것을 계획하지 않았어야 했다.

05 어휘 어휘&표현 intimidating = frightening

난이도 ★☆☆

해석 최첨단의 접근법을 위협적이라고 여기는 학생들은 그 또는 그녀가 예전 방법으로 배웠을지 모르는 것보다 덜 배운다.

① 재미있는   ② 친화적인
③ 편리한   ④ 위협적인

어휘 state-of-the-art 최첨단의 intimidating 위협적인, 겁을 주는 humorous 재미있는 convenient 편리한 frightening 위협적인

👍 이것도 알면 **합격!**

intimidating(위협적인)의 유의어
= threatening, aggressive, terrifying

06 어휘 어휘&표현 make do with

난이도 ★★☆

해석 에어컨들이 현재 수리 중이기 때문에, 사무실 직원들은 오늘 선풍기로 임시변통해야 한다.

① ~을 제거하다   ② ~에서 손을 놓다
③ ~로 임시변통하다   ④ ~와 결별하다

어휘 get rid of ~를 제거하다 let go of ~에서 손을 놓다 make do with ~로 임시변통하다 break up with ~와 결별하다

👍 이것도 알면 **합격!**

make do with(~로 임시변통하다)와 유사한 의미의 표현
= cope with, manage with, improvise with

07 문법 가정법

난이도 ★★☆

해석 ① 제가 지난주에 당신에게 드린 이메일 주소로 저에게 연락해 주세요.

② 만약 물이 없다면, 모든 지구상의 생물들은 멸종될 텐데.

③ 노트북 컴퓨터는 그들의 사무실에서 떨어져 있는 사람들이 일을 계속할 수 있게 한다.

④ 그들이 그들의 실수를 설명하려 더 시도할수록, 그들의 이야기는 더 나쁘게 들렸다.

해설 ② 가정법 과거 if절에 if가 생략된 가정법 과거 관용구문 Were it not for(~가 없다면)가 왔으므로, 주절에도 가정법 과거를 만드는 '주어(all living ~ earth) + would/should/could/might + 동사원형(be)'의 형태인 all living creatures on earth would be extinct가 올바르게 쓰였다.

오답분석 ① 타동사의 쓰임 동사 contact(연락하다)는 전치사(to) 없이 목적어(me)를 바로 취하는 타동사이므로 contact to me를 contact me로 고쳐야 한다.

③ 관계절 수 일치 관계절(who ~ offices) 내의 동사는 선행사 (people)에 수 일치시켜야 하는데, 선행사 people이 복수 명사이므로 단수 동사 is를 복수 동사 are로 고쳐야 한다. 참고로, to 부정사 to continue는 동사 allow의 목적격 보어로 올바르게 쓰였다.

④ 비교급 표현 문맥상 '그들이 그들의 실수를 설명하려 더 시도할수록, 그들의 이야기는 더 나쁘게 들렸다'라는 의미가 되어야 자연스러운데, '더 ~할수록 더 -하다'는 비교급 표현 'The + 비교급(more) + 주어(they) + 동사(attempted) ~, the + 비교급(worse) + 주어(their story) + 동사(sounded) -'의 형태로 나타낼 수 있으므로 최상급 표현 the worst를 비교급 표현 the worse로 고쳐야 한다.

어휘 creature 생물 extinct 멸종된 attempt 시도하다 sound ~하게 들리다

👍 이것도 알면 **합격!**

①번 보기의 contact와 같이 의미상 자동사로 혼동하기 쉬운 타동사를 알아두자.

mention ~에 대해 말하다	oppose ~에 반대하다
discuss ~에 대해 토론하다	reach ~에 도착하다
enter ~에 들어가다	approach ~에 접근하다
resemble ~을 닮다	marry ~와 결혼하다

08 문법 시제&to 부정사

난이도 ★★☆

해설 ① 과거 시제 | to 부정사의 쓰임 과거 시제와 자주 함께 쓰이는 시간 표현 '시간 표현 + ago'(a few days ago)가 왔으므로 과거 시제 동사 went가 올바르게 쓰였다. 또한, '배웅하기 위해'를 나타내기 위해 부사처럼 목적을 나타낼 수 있는 to 부정사구 to see off his friend가 올바르게 쓰였다.

오답분석 ② 숙어 표현 동사 make가 5형식 동사로 쓰일 때 'make + 목적어 + 동사원형'의 형태를 취하지만, 해당 문장에서는 make believe (that)(~인 체하다)라는 숙어 표현으로 쓰였으므로 make it believe를 make believe로 고쳐야 한다.

③ 동명사 관련 표현 '그곳에 가기를 고대하고 있다'는 동명사 관련 표현 'look forward to -ing'(~을 고대하다)로 나타낼 수 있으므로 동사원형 go를 동명사 going으로 고쳐야 한다.

④ 감정동사의 분사 감정을 나타내는 동사(interest)의 경우 수식하는 명사가 감정의 원인이면 현재분사를, 감정을 느끼는 주체이면 과거분사를 써야 하는데, 수식받는 명사(anything)가 '재미있는' 감정의 원인이므로 과거분사 interested를 현재분사 interesting으로 고쳐야 한다.

어휘 see off ~을 배웅하다 spoil 버릇없게 기르다, 망치다
make believe ~인 체하다

👍 이것도 알면 **합격!**

④번 보기의 interested와 같이 감정을 나타내는 동사는 수식하는 명사 및 보충하는 주어, 목적어가 감정의 원인이면 현재분사를, 감정을 느끼는 주체이면 과거분사를 쓴다.

(ex) **exciting** news 신나는 소식 (신나게 만드는 소식)
excited children 신이 난 아이들

---

09 독해 논리적 흐름 파악 (무관한 문장 삭제) 난이도 ★★☆

끊어읽기 해석

The Renaissance kitchen had / a definite hierarchy / of help / who worked together / to produce the elaborate banquets.
르네상스의 부엌에는 있었다 / 명확한 계급제가 / 고용인의 / 함께 일하는 / 정교한 연회를 만들기 위해

① At the top, / as we have seen, / was the *scalco*, or steward, / who was in charge of not only the kitchen, / but also the dining room.
(계급의) 정상에는 / 우리가 보아온 대로 / scalco, 즉 집사가 있었다 / 부엌뿐 아니라 담당했던 / 식당까지도 (담당했던)

② The dining room was supervised / by the butler, / who was in charge of the silverware and linen / and also served the dishes / that began and ended the banquet / —the cold dishes, salads, cheeses, and fruit / at the beginning / and the sweets and confections / at the end of the meal.
식당은 감독되었다 / 급사장에 의해 / 그는 은 식기류와 리넨 천을 담당했다 / 그리고 또한 음식들을 접대했다 / 연회를 시작하고 끝내는 / 차가운 요리, 샐러드, 치즈, 그리고 과일 / 시작에는 / 그리고 디저트들과 과자들 / 식사의 끝에는

③ This elaborate decoration and serving was / what in restaurants is called / "the front of the house."
이 정교한 장식과 접대는 ~이었다 / 식당들에서 불리는 것 / '영업부문'이라고

④ The kitchen was supervised / by the head cook, / who directed the undercooks, pastry cooks, and kitchen help.
부엌은 감독되었다 / 주방장에 의해 / 요리사의 조수들, 페이스트리 전문 요리사들, 그리고 주방 도우미들을 지휘하는

해석 르네상스의 부엌에는 정교한 연회를 만들기 위해 함께 일하는 고용인의 명확한 계급제가 있었다. ① 우리가 보아온 대로 (계급의) 정상에는 scalco, 즉 집사가 있었는데, 그는 부엌뿐 아니라 식당까지 담당했다. ② 식당은 급사장에 의해 감독되었고, 그는 은 식기류와 리넨 천을 담당했고, 그리고 또한 연회를 시작하고 끝내는 음식들을 접대했다. 시작에는 차가운 요리, 샐러드, 치즈, 그리고 과일 그리고 식사의 끝에는 디저트들과 과자들이 있었다. ③ 이 정교한 장식과 접대는 식당들에서 '영업부문'이라고 불리는 것이었다. ④ 부엌은 요리사의 조수들, 페이스트리 전문 요리사들, 그리고 주방 도우미들을 지휘하는 주방장에 의해 감독되었다.

해설 첫 문장에서 '르네상스 부엌의 고용인 계급제'에 대해 언급한 뒤, ①, ②, ④번에서 각각 집사, 급사장, 주방장의 역할을 설명하고

있다. 그러나 ③번은 정교한 장식과 접대가 식당에서 '영업부문'이라고 불리는 것이었다는 내용으로 첫 문장의 내용과 관련이 없다. 따라서 ③번이 정답이다.

어휘 **definite** 명확한 **hierarchy** 계급제 **help** 고용인, 도우미
elaborate 정교한 **banquet** 연회 **steward** (대저택의) 집사, 관리인
in charge of ~을 담당해서 **supervise** 감독하다
butler 급사장, 하인 우두머리 **silverware** 은 식기류
confection 과자 **decoration** 장식 **serving** 접대
front of the house 영업부문(고객이 직접 접하는 서비스 영역)
head cook 주방장 **undercook** 요리사의 조수 **direct** 지휘하다

---

10 독해 전체내용 파악 (요지 파악) 난이도 ★☆☆

끊어읽기 해석

My students often believe / that if they simply meet more important people, / their work will improve.
나의 학생들은 대개 믿는다 / 만약 그들이 더 중요한 사람을 그저 만난다면 / 그들의 성과가 향상될 것이라고

But it's remarkably hard / to engage with those people / unless you've already put something valuable out / into the world.
그러나 몹시 어렵다 / 이러한 사람들과 관계를 맺는 것은 / 당신이 무언가 가치 있는 것을 이미 내놓지 않은 한 / 이 세상에

That's / what piques the curiosity / of advisers and sponsors.
그것은 / 호기심을 돋우는 것이다 / 고문과 후원자의

Achievements show / you have something to give, / not just something to take.
업적은 보여준다 / 당신이 무언가 줄 것을 가지고 있다는 것을 / 그저 무언가 받을 것이 있는 것이 아니라

In life, / it certainly helps / to know the right people.
삶에서 / 그것은 틀림없이 도움이 된다 / 적절한 사람들을 알고 지내는 데

But how hard / they go to bat for you, / how far / they stick their necks out / for you, / depends on / what you have to offer.
그러나 얼마나 열심히 / 그들이 당신을 도와주는지 / 어느 정도까지 / 그들이 위험을 무릅쓰는지 / 당신을 위해 / ~에 달려 있다 / 당신이 제공해야 하는 것

Building a powerful network / doesn't require you / to be an expert / at networking.
영향력 있는 관계를 형성하는 것은 / 당신에게 요구하지 않는다 / 전문가가 될 것을 / 인적 네트워크 형성에 있어서

It just requires you / to be an expert / at something.
그것은 단지 당신에게 요구한다 / 전문가가 될 것을 / 무언가의

If you make great connections, / they might advance your career.
만약 당신이 훌륭한 관계들을 만든다면 / 그들은 당신의 경력을 향상시킬 수도 있다

If you do great work, / those connections will be easier / to make.
만약 당신이 대단한 일을 한다면 / 이 관계들은 더 쉬워질 것이다 / 만들기

Let your insights and your outputs / —not your business cards— / do the talking.
당신의 통찰력과 산물이 ~하게 하라 / 당신의 명함이 아니라 / 대변하게

해석 나의 학생들은 대개 만약 그들이 더 중요한 사람을 그저 만난다면, 그들의 성과가 향상될 것이라고 믿는다. 그러나 이러한 사람들과 관계를 맺는 것은 당신이 이 세상에 무언가 가치 있는 것을 이미 내놓지 않은 한 몹시 어렵다. 그것은 고문과 후원자의 호기심을 돋우는 것이다. 업적은 당신이 그저 무언가 받을 것이 있는 것이 아니라 무언가 줄 것을 가지고 있다는 것을 보여준다. 삶에서

그것은 적절한 사람들을 알고 지내는 데 틀림없이 도움이 된다. 그러나 그들이 당신을 얼마나 열심히 도와줄지, 그들이 당신을 위해 어느 정도까지 위험을 무릅쓸지는 당신이 제공해야 하는 것에 달려 있다. 영향력 있는 관계를 형성하는 것은 당신에게 인적 네트워크 형성에 있어서 전문가가 될 것을 요구하지 않는다. 그것은 단지 당신에게 무언가의 전문가가 될 것을 요구한다. 만약 당신이 훌륭한 관계들을 만든다면, 그들은 당신의 경력을 향상시킬 수도 있다. 만약 당신이 대단한 일을 한다면, 이 관계들은 만들기 더 쉬워질 것이다. 당신의 명함이 아니라 당신의 통찰력과 산물이 대변하게 하라.

① 후원은 성공적인 경력에 필수적이다.
② 좋은 관계를 형성하는 것은 당신의 업적으로부터 출발한다.
③ 영향력 있는 관계는 당신의 업적에 전제 조건이다.
④ 당신의 통찰력과 산물은 당신이 인적 네트워크 형성의 전문가가 되면서 성장한다.

해설 지문 앞부분에서 학생들은 대개 중요한 사람을 만나면 그들의 성과가 향상될 거라고 믿지만, 중요한 사람들과 관계를 맺는 것은 당신이 세상에 무언가 가치 있는 것을 이미 내놓지 않은 한 어렵다고 하고, 이어서 업적은 당신이 무언가 줄 것이 있다는 것을 보여주어 삶에서 적절한 사람들을 알고 지내는 데 도움이 된다고 설명하고 있다. 따라서 이 지문의 요지를 '좋은 관계를 형성하는 것은 당신의 업적으로부터 출발한다'라고 표현한 ②번이 정답이다.

어휘 simply 그저 remarkably 몹시 engage 관계를 맺다
pique 돋우다 certainly 틀림없이 go to bat for ~를 도와주다
stick one's neck out 위험을 무릅쓰다 insight 통찰력
output 산물, 작품, 생산량 business card 명함
do the talking 대변하다 prerequisite 전제 조건; 전제가 되는

11 어휘 생활영어 Try visiting the nearest service center then.
난이도 ★☆☆

해석
> A: 내 컴퓨터가 방금 아무 이유도 없이 꺼졌어. 나는 이걸 다시 켤 수도 없어.
> B: 너 그거 충전해 봤어? 단순히 배터리가 다 된 것일 수도 있어.
> A: 물론, 나는 그걸 충전해 봤어.
> B: 그럼 가장 가까운 서비스 센터를 방문해 봐.
> A: 그렇게 해야 하는데, 나는 너무 게을러.

① 나는 네 컴퓨터를 어떻게 고쳐야 할지 몰라.
② 그럼 가장 가까운 서비스 센터를 방문해 봐.
③ 글쎄, 네 문제들에 대해서는 그만 생각하고 자도록 해.
④ 내 형제는 기술자이기 때문에 네 컴퓨터를 고쳐 주려 할 거야.

해설 A의 컴퓨터가 꺼진 이유가 단순히 배터리가 다 되어서 일 수도 있다는 B의 말에 대해 빈칸 앞에서 A가 배터리를 충전해 봤다고 말하고, 빈칸 뒤에서 다시 A가 I should do that, but I'm so lazy(그렇게 해야 하는데, 나는 너무 게을러)라고 말하고 있으므로, 빈칸에는 '그럼 가장 가까운 서비스 센터를 방문해 봐'라는 의미가 들어가야 자연스럽다. 따라서 ② Try visiting the nearest service center then이 정답이다.

어휘 shut down (컴퓨터를) 끄다 charge 충전하다 lazy 게으른

👍 이것도 알면 합격!

기계나 장치에 문제가 생겼을 때 쓸 수 있는 다양한 표현을 알아두자.
· I don't have Internet access. 인터넷에 접속할 수 없어요.
· The bulb is burned out. 전구가 나갔어요.
· The monitor just went out. 모니터가 그냥 꺼졌어요.

12 독해 전체내용 파악 (글의 감상)
난이도 ★☆☆

끊어읽기 해석

My face turned white / as a sheet. // I looked at my watch.
내 얼굴은 창백해졌다 / 백지장처럼 // 나는 나의 시계를 보았다

The tests would be almost over / by now.
시험은 거의 끝났을 것이다 / 지금쯤

I arrived / at the testing center / in an absolute panic.
나는 도착했다 / 시험장에 / 완전한 공황 상태에 빠져

I tried to tell / my story, / but my sentences and descriptive gestures / got so confused / that I communicated / nothing more than a very convincing version / of a human tornado.
나는 말하려 했다 / 나의 사정을 / 하지만 나의 문장들과 설명적인 몸짓들은 / 매우 혼란스러워서 / 나는 전달했다 / 아주 확실한 형태에 불과한 것을 / 인간 토네이도의

In an effort to curb my distracting explanation, / the proctor led me / to an empty seat / and put a test booklet / in front of me.
나의 산만한 설명을 억제하려는 노력으로 / 시험 감독관은 나를 이끌었다 / 빈 자리로 / 그리고 시험지를 놓았다 / 나의 앞에

He looked / doubtfully / from me to the clock, / and then he walked away.
그는 시선을 돌렸다 / 미심쩍게 / 나에게서 시계로 / 그러고 나서 걸어가 버렸다

I tried desperately / to make up for lost time, / scrambling madly through analogies and sentence completions.
나는 필사적으로 노력했다 / 허비한 시간을 만회하기 위해 / 유추와 문장 완성을 미친 듯이 허둥지둥하면서

"Fifteen minutes remain," / the voice of doom declared / from the front of the classroom.
"15분 남았습니다" / 운명의 목소리가 선언했다 / 교실 앞에서

Algebraic equations, arithmetic calculations, geometric diagrams / swam / before my eyes.
대수 방정식, 산술 계산, 기하학적 도형들이 / 빙빙 도는 것 같이 보였다 / 나의 눈 앞에서

"Time! / Pencils down, please."
"시간이 됐습니다! / 연필을 내려놔 주세요"

해석 내 얼굴은 백지창처럼 창백해졌다. 나는 나의 시계를 보았다. 시험은 지금쯤 거의 끝났을 것이다. 나는 완전한 공황 상태에 빠져 시험장에 도착했다. 나는 나의 사정을 말하려 했지만, 나의 문장과 설명적인 몸짓들은 매우 혼란스러워서 나는 인간 토네이도의 아주 확실한 형태에 불과한 것을 전달했다(토네이도처럼 정리되지 않은 말들을 쏟아 냈다). 나의 산만한 설명을 억제하려는 노력으로, 시험 감독관은 나를 빈 자리로 이끌었고 나의 앞에 시험지를 놓았다. 그는 나에게서 시계로 미심쩍게 시선을 돌렸고, 그러고 나서 걸어가 버렸다. 나는 유추와 문장 완성을 미친 듯이 허둥지둥하면서 허비한 시간을 만회하기 위해 필사적으로 노력했다. "15분 남았습니다," 운명의 목소리가 교실 앞에서 선언했다. 대수 방정식, 산술 계산, 기하학적 도형들이 나의 눈 앞에서 빙빙 도는 것 같이 보였다. "시간이 됐습니다! 연필을 내려놔 주세요."

① 긴장하고 걱정하는　　② 활발하고 쾌활한
③ 차분하고 결연한　　　④ 안전하고 느긋한

해설 지문 전반에 걸쳐 화자가 시험이 거의 끝났을 시간에 공황 상태에 빠진 채 시험장에 도착하여 필사적으로 애쓰며 허둥지둥 시험을 친 일화를 소개하고 있다. 따라서 지문에서 나타난 화자의 심경을 '긴장하고 걱정하는'이라고 표현한 ①번이 정답이다.

어휘 panic 공황 (상태), 극심한 공포 descriptive 설명적인
in an effort to ~하려는 노력으로 curb 억제하다

proctor 시험 감독관   test booklet 시험지   doubtfully 미심쩍게
desperately 필사적으로   make up for 만회하다
scramble through ~을 허둥지둥하다   analogy 유추   doom 운명
algebraic equations 대수 방정식
arithmetic calculations 산술 계산
geometric diagrams 기하학적 도형   swim 빙빙 도는 것 같이 보이다
determined 결연한

13   독해   논리적 흐름 파악 (문단 순서 배열)   난이도 ★★☆

끊어읽기 해석

Devices / that monitor and track your health / are becoming more popular / among all age populations.
장치들은 / 당신의 건강 상태를 체크하고 기록하는 / 더욱 인기 있어지고 있다 / 모든 연령의 사람들 사이에서

(A) For example, / falls are a leading cause of death / for adults 65 and older.
예를 들어 / 넘어짐은 사망의 주된 원인이다 / 65세 이상 성인들의

Fall alerts are a popular gerotechnology / that has been around / for many years / but have now improved.
넘어짐 경보는 대중적인 노인을 위한 양로 기술이다 / 주위에 있어온 / 수년 동안 / 하지만 이제야 개선된

(B) However, / for seniors / aging in place, / especially / those without a caretaker / in the home, / these technologies / can be lifesaving.
그러나 / 고령자들에게는 / 제자리(자신의 집)에서 나이를 먹는 / 특히 / 돌보는 사람 없이 / 집에 / 이 기술들이 / 생명을 구할 수 있다

(C) This simple technology / can automatically alert / 911 or a close family member / the moment a senior has fallen.
이 단순한 기술은 / 자동적으로 알릴 수 있다 / 911 또는 가까운 가족 구성원에게 / 고령자가 넘어진 순간

해석   당신의 건강 상태를 체크하고 기록하는 장치들은 모든 연령의 사람들 사이에서 더욱 인기 있어지고 있다.

(B) 그러나, 특히 집에 돌보는 사람 없이 제자리(자신의 집)에서 나이를 먹는 고령자들에게는 이 기술들이 생명을 구할 수 있다.

(A) 예를 들어, 넘어짐은 65세 이상 성인들의 사망의 주된 원인이다. 넘어짐 경보는 수년 동안 주위에 있어왔지만 이제야 개선된 대중적인 노인을 위한 양로 기술이다.

(C) 이 단순한 기술은 고령자가 넘어진 순간 911 또는 가까운 가족 구성원에게 자동적으로 알릴 수 있다.

해설   주어진 문장에서 건강 상태를 체크하고 기록하는 장치가 모든 연령의 사람들 사이에서 더욱 인기 있어지고 있다고 언급한 뒤, (B)에서 그러나(However) 특히 자신의 집에 돌보는 사람이 없는 고령자들은 이 기술들을 통해 생명을 구할(lifesaving) 수 있다고 이야기하고 있다. 이어서 (A)에서 예를 들어(For example) 넘어짐 경보가 노인을 위한 대중적인 양로 기술이라는 것을 소개하고, (C)에서 이 단순한 기술(This simple technology)이 고령자가 넘어진 순간 911 또는 가까운 가족구성원에게 자동적으로 알릴 수 있다고 구체적인 작동 방법을 설명하고 있다. 따라서 ② (B) - (A) - (C)가 정답이다.

어휘   monitor 상태를 체크하다   track 기록하다, 추적하다   leading 주된
alert 경보   senior 고령자   caretaker 돌보는 사람
lifesaving 생명을 구하는

14   어휘   생활영어   I've always wanted to go there.   난이도 ★☆☆

해석
A: 너는 우리 신혼여행을 어디로 가고 싶어?
B: 우리 둘 다 가본 적 없는 곳으로 가자.
A: 그럼, 우리 하와이로 가는 건 어때?
B: 나는 항상 그곳에 가고 싶었어.

① 나는 항상 그곳에 가고 싶었어.
② 한국은 살기 좋은 곳이지 않아?
③ 좋아! 그곳에서 나의 지난 여행은 굉장했어!
④ 오, 너는 하와이에 이미 다녀왔음이 틀림없어.

해설   신혼여행을 어디로 가고 싶은지 묻는 A의 질문에 대해 B가 둘 다 가본 적 없는 곳으로 가자고 대답하자, 빈칸 앞에서 다시 A가 Then, why don't we go to Hawaii?(그럼, 우리 하와이로 가는 건 어때?)라고 묻고 있으므로, 빈칸에는 '나는 항상 그곳에 가고 싶었어'라는 의미가 들어가야 자연스럽다. 따라서 ① I've always wanted to go there가 정답이다.

어휘   honeymoon 신혼여행

👍 이것도 알면 합격!

여행 계획에 대해 물어보는 다양한 표현을 알아두자.
· Where are you going for vacation? 휴가로 어디에 가나요?
· What do you have in mind for this winter vacation?
  이번 겨울 휴가에 어디로 갈 거예요?
· What's the date of your trip? 여행 날짜가 며칠인가요?

15   독해   추론 (빈칸 완성 - 절)   난이도 ★★☆

끊어읽기 해석

The secret of successful people is usually / that they are able to concentrate / totally on one thing.
성공한 사람들의 비밀은 대개 ~이다 / 그들이 집중할 수 있다는 것이다 / 전적으로 하나의 것에

Even if they have a lot / in their head, / they have found a method / that the many commitments / don't impede each other, / but instead / they are brought into a good inner order.
그들이 많은 것들을 가지고 있다고 할지라도 / 그들의 머릿속에 / 그들은 방법을 찾아왔다 / 많은 책무들이 / 서로 방해하지 않는다 / (~이 아니고) 대신 / 그것들이 적절한 내면의 순서에 이르는

And this order is quite simple: / the most important thing first.
그리고 이 순서는 꽤 간단하다 / 가장 중요한 일이 먼저이다

In theory, / it seems to be quite clear, / but in everyday life / it seems rather different.
이론상 / 이것은 아주 명확한 것처럼 보인다 / 하지만 일상생활 속에서 / 이것은 다소 달라 보인다

You might have tried / to decide on priorities, / but you have failed / because of everyday trivial matters and all the unforeseen distractions.
당신은 노력했을지 모른다 / 우선하는 일들을 결정하려고 / 하지만 당신은 실패해왔다 / 매일의 사소한 문제와 모든 예측되지 않은 집중을 방해하는 것들 때문에

Separate off disturbances, / for example, / by escaping into another office, / and not allowing any distractions to get in the way.
장애물들을 떼어놓아라 / 예를 들어 / 다른 사무실로 달아남으로써 / 그리고 어떤 집중을 방해하는 것들도 방해되지 않게 함(으로써)

When you concentrate / on the one task of your priorities, /

you will find / you have energy / that you didn't even know / you had.
당신이 집중할 때 / 당신의 우선하는 일 중 하나에 / 당신은 알게 될 것이다 / 당신이 힘을 가지고 있다는 것을 / 당신이 알지도 못했던 / 당신이 가지고 있는지

해석　성공한 사람들의 비밀은 대개 그들이 전적으로 하나의 것에 집중할 수 있다는 것이다. 그들이 그들의 머릿속에 많은 것들을 가지고 있다고 할지라도, 많은 책무들이 서로 방해하지 않고, 대신 그것들이 적절한 내면의 순서에 이르는 방법을 찾아왔다. 그리고 이 순서는 꽤 간단하다. <u>가장 중요한 일이 먼저이다.</u> 이론상 이것은 아주 명확한 것처럼 보이지만, 일상생활 속에서 이것은 다소 달라 보인다. 당신은 우선하는 일들을 결정하려고 노력했을지 모르지만, 당신은 매일의 사소한 문제와 모든 예측되지 않은 집중을 방해하는 것들 때문에 실패해왔다. 예를 들어, 다른 사무실로 달아나서 어떤 집중을 방해하는 것들도 방해되지 않게 함으로써, 장애물들을 떼어놓아라. 당신이 당신의 우선하는 일 중 하나에 집중할 때, 당신은 당신이 가지고 있는지 알지도 못했던 힘을 가지고 있다는 것을 알게 될 것이다.

① 빠를수록 더 좋다
② 늦더라도 하지 않는 것보다 낫다
③ 눈에서 멀어지면 마음에서 멀어진다
④ 가장 중요한 일이 먼저이다

해설　빈칸 앞 문장과 빈칸이 있는 문장을 통해 빈칸에 적절한 내면의 순서가 무엇인지에 대한 내용이 나와야 적절하다는 것을 알 수 있다. 지문 중간에서 사소한 문제와 집중을 방해하는 것들로 인해 우선하는 일을 결정하는 데 실패한다고 하고, 지문 마지막에서 우선하는 일 중 하나에 집중할 때 가지고 있는지 알지도 못했던 당신의 힘을 발견할 것이라고 했으므로, '가장 중요한 일이 먼저이다'라고 한 ④번이 정답이다.

어휘　concentrate on ~에 집중하다　commitment 책무
impede 방해하다　inner 내면의, 정신의　order 순서　rather 다소
decide on ~을 결정하다　priority 우선하는 일　trivial 사소한
unforeseen 예측하지 않은　distraction 집중을 방해하는 것
disturbance 장애물　separate 떨어지다
get in the way 방해되다

16　독해　전체내용 파악 (제목 파악)　난이도 ★★☆

끊어읽기 해석

With the help of the scientist, / the commercial fishing industry / has found out / that its fishing must be done / scientifically / if it is to be continued.
과학자의 도움으로 / 상업적인 어업은 / 알게 되었다 / 어획이 행해져야 한다는 것을 / 과학적으로 / 그것(어획)이 계속되려면

With no fishing pressure / on a fish population, / the number of fish will reach / a predictable level of abundance / and stay there.
어획의 압박이 없다면 / 어류 개체군에 대한 / 어류의 수는 이를 것이다 / 예측할 수 있는 과다의 수준에 / 그리고 거기에 머물 것이다

The only fluctuation would be / due to natural environmental factors, / such as availability of food, proper temperature, and the like.
유일한 변동은 ~일 것이다 / 자연 환경적 요인들 때문에 / 식량의 유효성, 적절한 온도 등과 같은

If a fishery is developed / to take these fish, / their population can be maintained / if the fishing harvest is small.
어업이 발달한다면 / 이러한 어류들을 잡도록 / 그것들의 개체군은 유지될 수 있다 / 어획 수확량이 작다면

The mackerel of the North Sea is a good example.
북해의 고등어가 좋은 예이다

If we increase the fishery / and take more fish / each year, / we must be careful / not to reduce the population / below the ideal point / where it can replace / all of the fish / we take out each year.
우리가 어업을 늘린다면 / 그리고 더 많은 어류를 잡는다(면) / 매년 / 우리는 주의해야 한다 / 개체군을 줄이지 않도록 / 이상적인 한도 아래로 / 대체할 수 있는 / 모든 어류를 / 우리가 매년 잡는

If we fish / at this level, / called the *maximum sustainable yield*, / we can maintain / the greatest possible yield, / year after year.
우리가 잡는다면 / 이 수준으로 / '최대 유지 생산량'이라고 불리는 / 우리는 유지할 수 있다 / 최대로 가능한 생산량을 / 해마다

If we catch too many, / the number of fish / will decrease each year / until we fish ourselves out of a job.
우리가 너무 많이 잡는다면 / 어류의 수는 / 매년 줄어들 것이다 / 우리가 스스로를 그 일에서 끄집어낼 때까지

Examples of severely overfished animals / are the blue whale of the Antarctic and the halibut of the North Atlantic.
심하게 남획된 동물들의 예로는 / 남극 지역의 흰긴수염고래와 북대서양의 큰 넙치가 있다

Fishing just the correct amount / to maintain a maximum annual yield / is both a science and an art.
적당한 양의 어획은 / 연간 최대 생산량을 유지하기 위한 / 과학이고 기술이다

Research is constantly being done / to help us better understand / the fish population / and how to utilize it / to the maximum / without depleting the population.
연구는 지속적으로 행해지고 있다 / 우리가 더 잘 이해하도록 돕기 위해 / 어류 개체군을 / 그리고 그것을 이용하는 방법을 / 최대한으로 / 그 개체군을 고갈시키지 않고

해석　과학자의 도움으로, 상업적인 어업은 어획이 계속되려면 그것이 과학적으로 행해져야 한다는 것을 알게 되었다. 어류 개체군에 대한 어획의 압박이 없다면, 어류의 수는 예측할 수 있는 과다의 수준에 이르고 그곳에 머물 것이다. 오직 식량의 유효성, 적절한 온도 등과 같은 자연 환경적 요인들 때문에 변동이 있을 것이다. 이러한 어류들을 잡도록 어업이 발달한다면, 그것들의 개체군은 어획 수확량이 작다면 유지될 것이다. 북해의 고등어가 좋은 예이다. 우리가 어업을 늘리고 더 많은 어류를 매년 잡는다면, 우리는 우리가 매년 잡는 모든 어류를 대체할 수 있는 이상적인 한도 아래로 개체군을 줄이지 않도록 주의해야 한다. 우리가 '최대 유지 생산량'이라고 불리는 이 수준으로 잡는다면, 우리는 해마다 최대로 가능한 생산량을 유지할 수 있다. 우리가 너무 많이 잡는다면, 어류의 수는 우리가 스스로를 그 일에서 끄집어낼 때까지 매년 줄어들 것이다. 심하게 남획된 동물들의 예로는 남극 지역의 흰긴수염고래와 북대서양의 큰 넙치가 있다. 연간 최대 생산량을 유지하기 위한 적당한 양의 어획은 과학이고 기술이다. 연구는 우리가 어류 개체군과 그 개체군을 고갈시키지 않고 최대한으로 그것을 이용하는 방법을 더 잘 이해하도록 돕기 위해 지속적으로 행해지고 있다.

① 상업적인 어업을 거절하라
② 수산업으로 간주되는 양식 어업
③ 어업은 왜 과학을 필요로 하는가?
④ 남획된 동물들: 불법 어업의 사례들

해설　지문 처음에서 상업적인 어업은 어획이 계속되려면 과학적으로 행해져야 한다는 것을 제시하고, 지문 마지막에서 우리가 어류 개체군과 그것을 고갈시키지 않고 최대한으로 이용하는 방법을 더 잘 이해하도록 돕기 위해 연구가 지속적으로 행해지고 있다고 설명하고 있다. 따라서 이 지문의 제목을 '어업은 왜 과학을 필요로

하는가?'라고 표현한 ③번이 정답이다.

어휘 commercial 상업적인 fishing 어업, 어획, 낚시질
population 개체군, 인구 predictable 예측할 수 있는
abundance 과다, 풍부 fluctuation 변동 factors 요인
availability 유효성 proper 적절한 temperature 온도
harvest 수확량 mackerel 고등어 replace 대체하다
the maximum sustainable yield 최대 유지 생산량
fish out 끄집어내다, 빼내다 severely 심하게 Antarctic 남극 지역
halibut 큰 넙치 Atlantic 북대서양 utilize 이용하다
deplete 고갈시키다 sea farming 양식 어업 case 사례

17 독해 추론 (빈칸 완성 - 연결어) 난이도 ★☆☆

끊어읽기 해석

Does terrorism ever work?
테러리즘이 효과가 있던 적 있는가?

9/11 was an enormous tactical success / for al Qaeda, / partly because / it involved attacks / that took place / in the media capital of the world / and the actual capital of the United States, / (A) thereby / ensuring the widest possible coverage / of the event.
9/11은 엄청난 전술적인 성공이었다 / 알 카에다에게 / 부분적으로는 ~ 때문이다 / 그것은 공격을 포함했다 / 일어난 / 세계 대중 매체의 수도에서 / 그리고 미국의 실제 수도에서 / (A) 그렇게 함으로써 / 가장 광범위한 보도를 보장하며 / 그 사건의

If terrorism is a form of theater / where you want / a lot of people watching, / no event in human history / was likely ever seen / by a larger global audience / than the 9/11 attacks.
만약 테러리즘이 연극의 형태라면 / 당신이 원하는 / 많은 사람들이 보기를 / 인류 역사상 어떤 사건도 / 아마 보여지지 않았을 것이다 / 더 많은 전 세계 관중들에게 / 9/11 공격보다

At the time, / there was much discussion about / how 9/11 was / like the attack on Pearl Harbor.
그 당시 / ~에 대한 많은 논의가 있었다 / 어떻게 9/11이 / 진주만 공격과 비슷한지

They were indeed similar / since they were both surprise attacks / that drew America / into significant wars.
그것들은 실제로 비슷했다 / 그것들 모두 기습이기 때문에 / 미국을 끌어들인 / 상당한 전쟁에

But they were also similar / in another sense.
하지만 그것들은 또한 비슷했다 / 또 다른 의미에서

Pearl Harbor was a great *tactical* success / for Imperial Japan, / but it led to a great *strategic* failure : / Within four years of Pearl Harbor / the Japanese empire lay in ruins, / utterly defeated.
진주만은 큰 '전술적인' 성공이었다 / 일본 제국에 / 하지만 그것은 큰 '전략상의' 실패로 이어졌다 / 진주만의 4년 이내에 / 일본 제국은 무너졌다 / 완전히 패배하여

(B) Similarly, / 9/11 was a great tactical success / for al Qaeda, / but it also turned out / to be a great strategic failure / for Osama bin Laden.
(B) 유사하게 / 9/11은 큰 전략적인 성공이었다 / 알 카에다에게 / 하지만 그것 역시 드러났다 / 큰 전략상의 실패인 것으로 / 오사마 빈 라덴에게

해석 테러리즘이 효과가 있던 적 있는가? 9/11은 알 카에다에게 엄청난 전술적인 성공이었는데, 그것은 부분적으로는 세계 대중 매체의 수도와 미국의 실제 수도에서 일어난 공격을 포함했기 때문이었고, (A) 그렇게 함으로써 그 사건의 가장 광범위한 보도를 보장했다. 만약 테러리즘이 당신이 많은 사람들이 보기를 원하는 연극의 형태라면, 아마 인류 역사상 어떤 사건도 9/11 공격보다 더 많은 전 세계 관중들에게 보여지지 않았을 것이다. 그 당시 9/11이 진주만 공격

과 어떻게 비슷한지에 대한 많은 논의가 있었다. 그것들 모두 미국을 상당한 전쟁에 끌어들인 기습이었기 때문에 실제로 비슷했다. 하지만 그것들은 또한 또 다른 의미에서 비슷했다. 진주만은 일본 제국에 큰 '전술적인' 성공이었지만, 그것은 큰 '전략상의' 실패로 이어졌다. 진주만의 4년 이내에 일본 제국은 완전히 패배하여 무너졌다. (B) 유사하게, 9/11은 알 카에다에게 큰 전략적인 성공이었지만, 그것 역시 오사마 빈 라덴에게 큰 전략상의 실패인 것으로 드러났다.

	(A)	(B)
①	그렇게 함으로써	유사하게
②	그런데	그러므로
③	그런데	다행히
④	그렇게 함으로써	그와는 반대로

해설 (A) 빈칸 앞 문장은 9/11이 세계 대중 매체의 수도와 미국의 실제 수도에서 일어난 공격을 포함했다는 내용이고, 빈칸 뒤 문장은 그것이 그 사건의 가장 광범위한 보도를 보장했다는 결과적인 내용이다. 따라서 결과를 나타내는 연결어인 thereby(그렇게 함으로써)가 나와야 적절하다. (B) 빈칸 앞 문장은 진주만이 일본 제국에 큰 전술적인 성공인 동시에 큰 전략상의 실패였다는 내용이고, 빈칸 뒤 문장은 9/11이 알 카에다에게 큰 전략적인 성공이었지만 오사마 빈 라덴에게는 큰 전략상의 실패였다는 내용으로 앞 문장과의 유사점을 설명하고 있으므로, (B)에는 유사성을 나타내는 연결어인 Similarly(유사하게)가 나와야 적절하다.
따라서 ① (A) thereby(그렇게 함으로써) - (B) Similarly(유사하게)가 정답이다.

어휘 tactical 전술적인 partly 부분적으로, 어느 정도
take place 일어나다 ensure 보장하다 coverage 보도, 취재
indeed 정말 surprise attack 기습 sense 의미, 감각
lay in ruins 황폐해지다 strategic 전략상의
turn out ~인 것으로 드러나다 thereby 그렇게 함으로써

18 독해 세부내용 파악 (내용 불일치 파악) 난이도 ★★☆

끊어읽기 해석

We entered a new phase / as a species / when Chinese scientists altered a human embryo / to remove a potentially fatal blood disorder / —not only from the baby, / but all of its descendants.
우리는 새로운 단계에 접어들었다 / 한 생물 종으로서 / 중국의 과학자들이 인간 배아를 개조했을 때 / 잠재적으로 치명적인 혈액 질환을 제거하기 위해 / 그 아기로부터 뿐만 아니라 / 그의 모든 자손들로부터까지

Researchers call / this process / "germline modification."
연구자들은 ~라고 부른다 / 이 과정을 / '생식 계열 수정'

The media likes / the phrase "designer babies."
미디어는 좋아한다 / '맞춤 아기'라는 말을

But we should call it / what it is, / "eugenics."
하지만 우리는 이것을 ~라고 불러야 한다 / 바로 그것인 / '우생학'

And we, the human race, / need to decide / whether or not we want / to use it.
그리고 우리 인류는 / 결정해야 한다 / 우리가 원하는지 원하지 않는지를 / 그것을 이용하길

Last month, / in the United States, / the scientific establishment weighed in.
지난달 / 미국에서 / 과학 기관이 관여했다

A National Academy of Sciences and National Academy of Medicine joint committee / endorsed embryo editing / aimed at genes / that cause serious diseases / when there is "no reasonable alternative."
국립 과학 학회와 국립 의약 학회의 공동 위원회는 / 배아 수정을 지지했

다 / 유전자를 겨냥하는 / 심각한 질병을 일으키는 / '적당한 대안이 아무것도 없을' 때

But it was more wary of editing / for "enhancement," / like making already-healthy children stronger or taller.
하지만 그것은 수정을 더욱 경계했다 / '향상'을 위한 / 이미 건강한 아이를 더 강하고 더 크게 만드는 것과 같은

It recommended a public discussion, / and said / that doctors should "not proceed at this time."
그것은 공공 토론을 권고했다 / 그리고 말했다 / 의사들이 '이 시점에 시작해서는 안 된다'고

The committee had good reason / to urge caution.
위원회는 타당한 이유를 가지고 있었다 / 주의를 촉구할

The history of eugenics is full of oppression and misery.
우생학의 역사는 억압과 고통으로 가득 차 있다

해석　중국의 과학자들이 그 아기로부터 뿐만 아니라 그의 모든 자손들로부터까지 잠재적으로 치명적인 혈액 질환을 제거하기 위해 인간 배아를 개조했을 때, 우리는 한 생물 종으로서 새로운 단계에 접어들었다. 연구자들은 이 과정을 '생식 계열 수정'이라고 부른다. 미디어는 '맞춤 아기'라는 말을 좋아한다. 하지만 우리는 이것을 바로 그것인 '우생학'이라고 불러야 한다. 그리고 우리 인류는 우리가 그것을 이용하길 원하는지 원하지 않는지를 결정해야 한다. 지난달 미국에서 과학 기관이 관여했다. 국립 과학 학회와 국립 의약 학회의 공동 위원회는 '적당한 대안이 아무것도 없을' 때 심각한 질병을 일으키는 유전자를 겨냥하는 배아 수정을 지지했다. 하지만 그것은 이미 건강한 아이를 더 강하고 더 크게 만드는 것과 같은 '향상'을 위한 수정을 더욱 경계했다. 그것은 공공 토론을 권고했고, 의사들이 '이 시점에 시작해서는 안 된다'고 말했다. 위원회는 주의를 촉구할 타당한 이유를 가지고 있었다. 우생학의 역사는 억압과 고통으로 가득 차 있다.
① 의사들은 향상을 위한 배아 수정을 즉시 시작하도록 권장되었다.
② 최근에, 미국의 과학 기관이 우생학에 대한 토론에 참여했다.
③ 중국의 과학자들은 심각한 혈액 질환을 막기 위해 인간 배아를 수정했다.
④ '맞춤 아기'는 생식 계열 수정 과정의 또 다른 용어이다.

해설　지문 중간에서 미국의 과학 기관은 '적당한 대안이 아무것도 없을' 때 심각한 질병을 일으키는 유전자를 겨냥하는 배아 수정을 지지했지만 이미 건강한 아이를 더 강하고 더 크게 만드는 것과 같은 '향상'을 위한 수정을 더욱 경계했다고 했으므로, 의사들이 향상을 위한 배아 수정을 즉시 시작하도록 권장되었다는 것은 지문의 내용과 다르다. 따라서 ①번이 정답이다.

어휘　phase 단계　species 종(種)　human embryo 인간 배아
fatal 치명적인　blood disorder 혈액 질환
germline modification 생식 계열 수정
designer baby 맞춤 아기(선택된 배아를 착상시켜 태어난 아기)
establishment 기관　weigh in 관여하다　joint 공동의
committee 위원회　endorse 지지하다　edit 수정하다, 편집하다
gene 유전자　reasonable 적당한　alternative 대안
wary 경계하는, 주의하는　enhancement 향상, 증진
public discussion 공공 토론　oppression 억압　misery 고통

19 독해 논리적 흐름 파악 (문장 삽입)　난이도 ★★☆

끊어읽기 해석

If neither surrendered, / the two exchanged blows / until one was knocked out.
만약 누구도 항복하지 않는다면 / 둘은 치고 받았다 / 하나가 나가떨어질 때까지

The ancient Olympics provided / athletes / an opportunity / to prove their fitness and superiority, / just like our modern games.
고대 올림픽은 제공했다 / 선수들에게 / 기회를 / 그들의 체력과 우월성을 입증할 / 우리의 현대 경기와 마찬가지로

(①) The ancient Olympic events / were designed / to eliminate the weak / and glorify the strong.
고대 올림픽 종목들은 설계되었다 / 약자를 제거하기 위해 / 그리고 강자를 칭송하기 위해

Winners were pushed / to the brink.
승자들은 밀쳐졌다 / 벼랑 끝까지

(②) Just as in modern times, / people loved / extreme sports.
현대와 마찬가지로 / 사람들은 사랑했다 / 과격한 스포츠를

One of the favorite events was added / in the 33rd Olympiad.
인기 있는 종목 중 하나가 추가되었다 / 33번째 올림픽에서

This was the pankration, / or an extreme mix / of wrestling and boxing.
이것은 판크라티온이었다 / 다시 말하면 극단적인 혼합이었다 / 레슬링과 복싱의

The Greek word *pankration* / means "total power."
그리스 단어 '판크라티온'은 / '총체적 힘'을 뜻한다

The men wore / leather straps / with metal studs, / which could make a terrible mess / of their opponents.
남자들은 착용했다 / 가죽 혁대를 / 금속 징이 달린 / 끔찍하게 엉망으로 만들 수 있었던 / 그들의 상대방을

(③) This dangerous form of wrestling / had no time or weight limits.
이 위험한 형태의 레슬링은 / 시간이나 체급 제한이 없었다

In this event, / only two rules applied.
이 종목에서는 / 오직 두 개의 규칙이 적용되었다

First, / wrestlers were not allowed / to gouge eyes / with their thumbs.
먼저 / 레슬러들은 허락되지 않았다 / 눈을 찌르는 것이 / 그들의 엄지손가락으로

Secondly / they could not bite. // Anything else was considered / fair play.
둘째로 / 그들은 깨물 수 없었다 // 그밖에 다른 것은 여겨졌다 / 정당한 행위로
시합은 결정되었다 / 같은 방식으로 / 복싱 시합과

Contenders continued / until one of the two collapsed.
경쟁자들은 계속했다 / 둘 중 하나가 쓰러질 때까지

(④) Only the strongest and most determined athletes / attempted this event.
가장 힘이 세고 가장 결의가 굳은 선수들만이 / 이 종목에 도전했다

Imagine wrestling "Mr. Fingertips," / who earned his nickname / by breaking his opponents' fingers!
'손가락 씨'와 격투하는 것을 상상해 보라 / 그의 별명을 얻은 / 그의 상대방의 손가락을 부러뜨림으로써!

해석　고대 올림픽은 선수들에게 우리의 현대 경기와 마찬가지로 그들의 체력과 우월성을 입증할 기회를 제공했다. 고대 올림픽 종목들은 약자를 제거하고 강자를 칭송하기 위해 설계되었다. 승자들은 벼랑 끝까지 밀쳐졌다. 현대와 마찬가지로, 사람들은 과격한 스포츠를 사랑했다. 인기 있는 종목 중 하나는 33번째 올림픽에서 추가되었다. 이것은 판크라티온, 다시 말하면 레슬링과 복싱의 극단적인 혼합이었다. 그리스 단어 '판크라티온'은 '총체적 힘'을 뜻한다. 남자들은 금속 징이 달린 가죽 혁대를 착용했는데, 이것은 그들의 상대방을 끔찍하게 엉망으로 만들 수 있었다. 이 위험한 형태의 레슬링은 시간이나 체급 제한이 없었다. 이 종목에서는 오직 두 개의

규칙이 적용되었다. 먼저, 레슬러들은 그들의 엄지손가락으로 눈을 찌르는 것이 허락되지 않았다. 둘째로, 그들은 깨물 수 없었다. 그 밖에 다른 것은 정당한 행위로 여겨졌다. 시합은 복싱 시합과 같은 방식으로 결정되었다. 경쟁자들은 둘 중 하나가 쓰러질 때까지 계속했다. ④ 만약 누구도 항복하지 않는다면, 하나가 나가떨어질 때까지 둘은 치고 받았다. 가장 힘이 세고 가장 결의가 굳은 선수들만이 이 종목에 도전했다. 그의 상대방의 손가락을 부러뜨림으로써 그의 별명을 얻은 '손가락 씨'와 격투하는 것을 상상해 보라!

해설 ④번 앞 문장에서 경쟁자들은 둘 중 하나가 쓰러질 때까지 계속했다고 했으므로, ④번 자리에 '만약 누구도 항복하지 않는다면, 하나가 나가떨어질 때까지 둘은 치고 받았다'라는 주어진 문장이 나와야 지문이 자연스럽게 연결된다. 따라서 ④번이 정답이다.

어휘 surrender 항복하다 exchange blows 치고 받다
knock out 나가떨어지다 athlete 선수 superiority 우월성
eliminate 제거하다 glorify 칭송하다 brink (벼랑, 낭떠러지의) 끝
extreme 과격한 pankration 판크라티온 strap 혁대 stud 징
make a mess of 엉망으로 만들다 gouge 찌르다
contender 경쟁자 collapse 쓰러지다 determined 결의가 굳은

20 독해 추론 (빈칸 완성 - 구) 난이도 ★★★

끊어읽기 해석

In our time / it is not only the law of the market / which has its own life / and rules over man, / but also the development of science and technique.
우리 시대에서 / 시장의 법칙뿐 아니다 / 그것 자체의 생명을 가지는 것은 / 그리고 인류를 지배하는 것은 / 과학과 기술의 발달도 (그렇다)

For a number of reasons, / the problems and organization / of science today / are such that a scientist does not choose his problems; / the problems force themselves / upon the scientist.
많은 이유들에 의해서 / 문제들과 구성은 / 오늘날 과학의 / 과학자가 그의 문제들을 선택하지 않는다는 그런 것이다 / 문제들은 그것들 자체를 강요한다 / 과학자에게

He solves / one problem, / and the result is not / that he is more secure or certain, / but that ten other new problems open up / in place of the single solved one.
그가 해결한다 / 문제 하나를 / 그리고 그 결과는 ~이 아니다 / 그가 더 확고하거나 확신한다는 것 / 열 개의 다른 새로운 문제들이 생겨난다는 것이다 / 해결된 단 하나를 대신해서

They force him / to solve them; / he has to go ahead / at an ever-quickening pace.
그것들은 그에게 강요한다 / 그것들을 해결하도록 / 그는 계속해야 한다 / 빨라지기만 하는 속도로

The same holds true / for industrial techniques.
동일한 것이 들어맞는다 / 산업 기술에

The pace of science forces / the pace of technique.
과학의 속도는 강요한다 / 기술의 속도를

Theoretical physics forces / atomic energy / on us; / the successful production of the fission bomb / forces upon us / the manufacture of the hydrogen bomb.
이론 물리학은 강요한다 / 원자력을 / 우리에게 / 원자 폭탄의 성공적인 생산은 / 우리에게 강요한다 / 수소 폭탄의 제조를

We do not choose our problems, / we do not choose our products; / we are pushed, / we are forced / —by what?
우리는 우리의 문제들을 선택하지 않는다 / 우리는 우리의 생산품들을 선택하지 않는다 / 우리는 밀어붙여진다 / 우리는 강요된다 / 무엇에 의해서?

By a system / which has no purpose and goal / transcending it, / and which makes man its appendix.
시스템에 의해서 / 목적도 목표도 없는 / 그것을 초월하는 / 그리고 인간을 그것의 부속물로 만드는

해석 우리 시대에서 그것 자체의 생명을 가지고 인류를 지배하는 것은 시장의 법칙뿐 아니라 과학과 기술의 발달도 그렇다. 많은 이유들에 의해서 오늘날 과학의 문제들과 구성은 과학자가 그의 문제들을 선택하지 않는다는 그런 것이다. 문제들은 과학자에게 그것들 자체를 강요한다. 그가 문제 하나를 해결하면, 그 결과는 그가 더 확고하거나 확신한다는 것이 아니라 열 개의 다른 새로운 문제들이 해결된 단 하나를 대신해서 생겨난다는 것이다. 그것들은 그에게 그것들을 해결하도록 강요한다. 그는 빨라지기만 하는 속도로 계속해야 한다. 동일한 것이 산업 기술에 들어맞는다. 과학의 속도는 기술의 속도를 강요한다. 이론 물리학은 우리에게 원자력을 강요한다. 원자 폭탄의 성공적인 생산은 우리에게 수소 폭탄의 제조를 강요한다. 우리는 우리의 문제들을 선택하지 않고, 우리의 생산품들을 선택하지 않는다. 우리는 무엇에 의해서 밀어붙여지고 강요되는가? 그것을 초월하는 목적도 목표도 없고 인간을 그것의 부속물로 만드는 시스템에 의해서이다.

① 인간을 그것의 부속물로 만드는
② 안정성에 대한 잘못된 인식을 만드는
③ 인간에게 창의적인 도전을 고취하는
④ 과학자들에게 시장의 법칙을 지배하는 권한을 부여하는

해설 빈칸이 있는 문장과 앞 문장을 통해 빈칸에 우리가 어떤 시스템에 의해 문제를 강요당하는지에 대한 내용이 들어가야 한다는 것을 알 수 있다. 지문 전반에 걸쳐 오늘날 과학의 문제들과 구성은 과학자가 자신의 문제를 선택하는 것이 아니라 문제들이 과학자에게 그것들 자체를 강요하는 것이라고 하고, 지문 뒷부분에서 우리는 우리의 문제들과 생산품들을 선택하지 않고 밀어붙여지고 강요된다고 했으므로, '인간을 그것의 부속물로 만드는' 시스템이라고 한 ①번이 정답이다.

어휘 rule over ~을 지배하다 secure 안정된, 안전한
certain 정확한, 확신하는 open up 생겨나다
in place of ~을 대신해서 go ahead 계속하다
hold true 들어맞다, 유효하다 atomic energy 원자력
fission bomb 원자 폭탄 manufacture 제조
hydrogen bomb 수소 폭탄 product 생산품
transcend 초월하다, 능가하다 appendix 부속물, 부록
inspire 고취하다, 품게 하다 empower 권한을 부여하다

gosi.Hackers.com

서울시 9급 출제 경향

1. 영역별 출제 문항 수 (2017~2019, 2022, 2024)

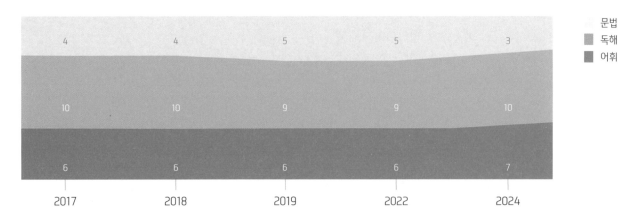

서울시 9급 시험은 2020년부터 인사혁신처에서 출제하여 지방직 9급 시험과 동일한 시험 문제로 시행됩니다. 그렇지만, 서울시에서 자체 출제한 시험 문제에서도 다른 직급/직렬에서 출제되는 문제와 유사한 유형이나 **문법** 포인트 및 **어휘**가 있으므로 함께 학습하는 것이 좋습니다. 최근 서울시 9급 시험의 영역별 출제 문항 수에는 약간의 변동이 있습니다. **독해** 영역은 9~10문항으로 변동이 없으나, 지난 6년간 4~5문항씩 출제되었던 **문법** 영역은 3문항이 출제되었으며, 6문항씩 출제되었던 **어휘** 영역은 7문항이 출제되었습니다.

Part 3
서울시 9급

2. 영역별 최근 출제 경향 및 학습 방법

문법

기출 문법 포인트에 기반한 문제 출제

서울시 9급 시험에서는 최근 5년간 동사의 종류, 관계절, 전치사, 분사 등에 대한 문법 포인트가 매년 반복해서 출제되었습니다.

▶ 최근에 출제되었던 포인트들이 다시 출제될 확률이 높으므로, 최신 기출문제의 문법 포인트를 확실히 정리하는 것이 필수적입니다.

[빈출 포인트] 동사의 종류(9문항) | 관계절(8문항) | 전치사(8문항) | 분사(8문항)

독해

빈칸 완성 유형 중심의 문제 출제

최근 5년간 빈칸 완성 유형의 문제가 높은 비중으로 출제되었으며, 2024년 2월 시행된 시험에는 독해 10문항 중 빈칸 완성 유형의 문제가 4문항 출제되었습니다.

▶ 따라서 빈칸이 있는 문장과 그 주변을 먼저 읽어 빈칸에 어떤 내용이 들어갈지 예상한 뒤 지문의 흐름을 파악하는 전략을 활용하여 시간을 단축해야 합니다.

어휘

높은 난도의 어휘 문제 출제

최근 5년간 perspicuous(명쾌한), pejorative(경멸적인), vigilant(경계하고 있는)와 같은 고난도 어휘가 출제되었습니다.

▶ 따라서 고득점을 위해서는 필수 어휘뿐만 아니라 고난도 어휘까지 꼼꼼히 암기하는 것이 좋습니다.

정답
p.122

01	③ 어휘 - 어휘&표현	11	① 독해 - 논리적 흐름 파악
02	④ 어휘 - 어휘&표현	12	③ 독해 - 세부내용 파악
03	② 어휘 - 어휘&표현	13	③ 독해 - 논리적 흐름 파악
04	④ 어휘 - 어휘&표현	14	③ 독해 - 논리적 흐름 파악
05	① 어휘 - 어휘&표현	15	④ 독해 - 추론
06	② 어휘 - 생활영어	16	② 독해 - 전체내용 파악
07	② 어휘 - 생활영어	17	① 독해 - 전체내용 파악
08	① 문법 - 전치사	18	③ 독해 - 추론
09	② 문법 - 부사절	19	④ 독해 - 추론
10	① 문법 - 수 일치	20	③ 독해 - 추론

취약영역 분석표

영역	세부 유형	문항 수	소계
어휘	어휘&표현	5	/7
	생활영어	2	
문법	전치사	1	/3
	부사절	1	
	수 일치	1	
독해	전체내용 파악	2	/10
	세부내용 파악	1	
	추론	4	
	논리적 흐름 파악	3	
총계			/20

· 자신이 취약한 영역은 '공무원 영어, 이렇게 출제된다!'(문제집 p.8)를 통해 다시 한번 확인하고 학습하시기 바랍니다.

---

01 어휘 | 어휘&표현 spurn = decline
난이도 ★★☆

해석 유명한 회사로부터 매력적인 일자리 제안을 받은 후에, 그녀는 자신의 사업을 시작하겠다는 꿈을 추구하기 위해 결국 그것을 거절하기로 결정했다.

① 숙고하다 ② 연기하다
③ 거절하다 ④ 비난하다

어휘 attractive 매력적인 offer 제안 renowned 유명한
spurn 거절하다, 일축하다 pursue 추구하다
contemplate 숙고하다 postpone 연기하다, 미루다
decline 거절하다 denounce 비난하다, 비판하다

👍 이것도 알면 **합격!**

spurn(거절하다)과 유사한 의미의 표현
= refuse, reject, rebuff, turn down

---

02 어휘 | 어휘&표현 boast = brag
난이도 ★☆☆

해석 1918년에 레드삭스가 베이브 루스를 양키스와 트레이드한 이후로, 보스턴 스포츠 팬들은 좋은 점과 나쁜 점을 함께 받아들이는 법을 배웠다. 그들은 다른 어떤 도시보다 더 많은 농구 선수권 대회를 경험했지만 75년 넘게 월드 시리즈 타이틀을 자랑하지 못했다.

① 포기했다 ② 산출했다
③ 포기했다 ④ 자랑했다

어휘 trade (선수를) 트레이드하다, 교환하다 see 경험하다, 체험하다
championship 선수권 대회 boast 자랑하다
title (스포츠에서) 타이틀 waive 포기하다, 보류하다
yield 산출하다, 내다 renounce 포기하다 brag 자랑하다

👍 이것도 알면 **합격!**

boast(자랑하다)와 유사한 의미의 표현
= show off, bluster, talk big

---

03 어휘 | 어휘&표현 singular = exceptional
난이도 ★☆☆

해석 Nell은 말썽을 피우는 데 뛰어난 재능이 있다. 어느 날 아침에, 그녀는 용케도 다리를 부러뜨리고, 우체국에서 한 여자를 모욕하고, 식료품점에서 달걀을 떨어뜨리고, 침실을 초록색으로 칠하고, 옆집에 사는 이웃의 앞마당에 있는 큰 단풍나무를 베었다.

① 전통적인 ② 뛰어난
③ 호전적인 ④ 복수의

어휘 singular 뛰어난, 단수의 talent 재능 insult 모욕하다
grocery store 식료품점 maple tree 단풍나무
front yard 앞마당 conventional 전통적인, 관습의
exceptional 뛰어난, 예외적인 martial 호전적인, 전쟁의
plural 복수의, 다원적인

👍 이것도 알면 **합격!**

singular(뛰어난)의 유의어
= remarkable, extraordinary, outstanding

---

04 어휘 | 어휘&표현 platitude
난이도 ★★☆

해석 우리에게 현재 다루고 있는 문제에 대한 혁신적인 아이디어를 제시하는 대신, 기조연설자는 장황했던 진부한 이야기를 꺼냈고 우리가 꽤 오랫동안 지루함을 느끼게 했다.

① 브레인스토밍   ② 재담
③ 비문   ④ 진부한 이야기

어휘 innovative 혁신적인, 획기적인 matter 문제
in hand 현재 다루고 있는(일·문제 등)
keynote speaker 기조연설자
bring up (의제·제안·화제 등을) 꺼내다 lengthy 장황한, 긴
tedium 지루함, 단조로움
brainstorming 브레인스토밍(무엇에 대해 여러 사람들이 동시에 자유롭게 자기 생각을 제시하는 방법) witticism 재담, 재치 있는 말
epigraph (건물·동상 등에 새기는) 비문 platitude 진부한 이야기

👍 이것도 알면 **합격!**

platitude(진부한 이야기)의 유의어
= cliché, truism

---

05 **어휘** 어휘&표현 vigilant   난이도 ★★☆

해석 지난 6년 동안 캘리포니아에는 비가 거의 오지 않았기 때문에 산림 경비원들은 산불을 감시할 때 특히 <u>경계하고 있어야</u> 한다.
① 경계하고 있는   ② 느긋한
③ 무관심한   ④ 주의가 산만한

어휘 ranger 경비원, 관리원 especially 특히
vigilant 경계하고 있는, 방심 않는 indifferent 무관심한
distracted 주의가 산만한

👍 이것도 알면 **합격!**

vigilant(경계하고 있는)와 유사한 의미의 표현
= watchful, alert, on the lookout

---

06 **어휘** 생활영어 No need for that. Come at 11:00 and I'll have your documents ready. 난이도 ★★☆

해석
A: 기다리시게 해서 죄송합니다, Krauss 씨.
B: 음, 오늘은 할 일이 많은 것 같군요. 당신을 더 이상 붙잡아 두지 않을게요.
A: 걱정하지 마세요, Krauss 씨. 주문을 제시간에 완료해 드리겠습니다.
B: 제가 전화를 드려야 할까요?
A: <u>그러실 필요 없습니다. 11시에 오시면 서류를 준비해 드리겠습니다.</u>

① 음, 당신은 좋은 고객이시군요. 제가 무엇을 할 수 있는지 알아보겠습니다.
② 그러실 필요 없습니다. 11시에 오시면 서류를 준비해 드리겠습니다.
③ 내일 아침이요? 걱정하지 마세요. 정오 전에 서류를 저에게 가져다주실 수 있나요?
④ 그건 어려울 것 같습니다. 오늘 아침에 완료해야 할 주문이 많습니다.

해설 주문을 제시간에 완료해 주겠다는 A의 말에 B가 전화를 해야 하는지 물었으므로, 빈칸에는 '② 그러실 필요 없습니다. 11시에 오시면 서류를 준비해 드리겠습니다(No need for that. Come at 11:00 and I'll have your documents ready)'가 오는 것이 자연스럽다.

어휘 have a lot on one's plate 해야 할 일이 산더미처럼 있다
order 주문 on time 제시간에 customer 고객 document 서류
no sweat 걱정 마라

👍 이것도 알면 **합격!**

전화할 때 쓸 수 있는 다양한 표현을 알아두자.

- Could you please repeat that?
  다시 한번 말씀해 주시겠어요?
- I'll just put you on hold for a second.
  잠시만 전화를 보류하겠습니다. (잠시만 기다려주십시오.)
- Let me transfer your call to our customer service team.
  저희 고객지원팀으로 전화를 연결해 드리겠습니다.
- May I ask who's calling please?
  전화 주신 분이 누구신지 여쭤봐도 될까요?
- Can you call me back later?
  나중에 다시 전화해 주시겠습니까?

---

07 **어휘** 생활영어 out of the blue   난이도 ★☆☆

해석
A: Emily의 새로 자른 머리 보셨어요?
B: 네, 갑자기 다 잘라버렸더라고요!
A: 정말 깜짝 놀랐어요. 이전이랑 너무 달라요.
B: 그녀는 변화가 필요하다고 말했어요.
A: 음, 확실히 잘 어울려요.
B: 동의해요, 그녀는 멋져요!

① 하늘을 둥둥 떠다니는 듯한
② 갑자기
③ 아직 미정인
④ 몸이 좀 안 좋은

해설 Emily의 새로 자른 머리를 봤냐는 A의 말에 B가 대답하고, 빈칸 뒤에서 A가 I was so surprised(정말 깜짝 놀랐어요)라고 말하고 있으므로, 빈칸에는 '② 갑자기(out of the blue)' 다 잘라버렸다는 내용이 오는 것이 자연스럽다.

어휘 chop 자르다 definitely 확실히 suit 어울리다
over the moon 하늘을 둥둥 떠다니는 듯한(너무나도 황홀한)
out of the blue 갑자기, 난데없이 up in the air 아직 미정인
under the weather 몸이 좀 안 좋은

👍 이것도 알면 **합격!**

색깔이 들어간 다양한 표현을 알아두자.

- green with envy 몹시 샘을 내는
- caught red-handed 현행범으로 잡다
- a little white lie 선의의 거짓말
- once in a blue moon 극히 드물게
- black sheep (집안·조직의) 골칫덩어리, 말썽꾼

---

08 **문법** 전치사   난이도 ★★★

해석 집단 사고에 관한 일관되지 않고 상당히 부족한 실험실 데이터에도 불구하고, 그 이론은 설명적인 잠재력을 가지고 있다고 믿어져 왔다. 이러한 지속적인 확신 중 일부는 의심할 여지 없이 모델의 다양한 가설을 입증하기 위해 발전되어 온 일련의 창의적인 역사적 분석에서 비롯된다. 확실히, 우리는 몇 가지 이유로 그러한 역

사적 분석에 주의해야 하는데, 왜냐하면 우리는 모순되는 사례들이 간과되지 않았다고 확신할 수 없기 때문이다. 그러나, 그러한 사례 연구는 선행 조건이 모델에 의해 필요하다고 여겨지는 조건을 만들 수 있을 만큼 충분히 강했던 사례들을 살펴볼 수 있는 장점이 있다.

해설 ① 전치사 4: 양보 문맥상 '부족한 실험실 데이터에도 불구하고'라는 의미가 되어야 자연스러운데, '~에도 불구하고'는 양보를 나타내는 전치사 Despite를 사용하여 나타낼 수 있으므로 Despite가 올바르게 쓰였다. 또한, 전치사 뒤에는 명사 역할을 하는 것이 와야 하므로 전치사 Despite 뒤에 명사구 the inconsistent ~ regarding groupthink가 올바르게 쓰였다.

오답 분석
② 수량 표현 복수 명사 앞에 쓰이는 수량 표현 a series of(일련의)가 왔으므로 단수 명사 analysis를 복수 명사 analyses로 고쳐야 한다.

③ 능동태·수동태 구별 | 현재완료 시제 주어 contradictory examples와 동사가 '모순되는 사례들이 간과되다'라는 의미의 수동 관계이므로 현재완료 능동태 have not overlook을 현재완료 수동태 have not been overlooked로 고쳐야 한다.

④ 관계부사와 관계대명사 비교 선행사(cases)가 장소를 나타내고 관계사 뒤에 완전한 절(the antecedent conditions ~ by the model)이 왔으므로 불완전한 절을 이끄는 관계대명사 which를 완전한 절을 이끌며 장소를 나타내는 선행사와 함께 쓰이는 관계부사 where로 고쳐야 한다. 참고로 관계부사는 '전치사 + 관계대명사'로 바꾸어 쓸 수 있는데, 문맥상 '사례들에서 선행 조건이 ~ 충분히 강했다'라는 의미가 되어야 자연스러우므로 전치사 in(~에서)이 관계대명사 which 앞에 온 in which로 고쳐도 맞다.

어휘 inconsistent 일관되지 않는 fairly 상당히, 꽤
sparse 부족한, 희박한 laboratory 실험실 regarding ~에 관하여
groupthink 집단 사고(집단 구성원의 토의에 의한 문제 해결법)
explanatory 설명적인, 설명을 위한 potential 잠재력
confidence 확신, 자신감 undoubtedly 의심할 여지 없이
stem from ~에서 비롯되다, ~의 결과로 알게 되다
historical analysis 역사적 분석(과거의 자료를 이용하여 가격이나 추세를 분석하고 예측하는 것) substantiate 입증하다, ~을 구체화하다
hypothesis 가설, 가정 contradictory 모순되는
overlook 간과하다 case study 사례 연구 virtue 장점, 미덕
antecedent 선행하는, 전에 존재하는 condition 조건
deem 여기다, 간주하다

👍 이것도 알면 합격!
전치사 숙어 표현을 추가로 알아두자.

· with no doubt 의심할 바 없이	· absent from ~에 결석한
· with the aim of ~을 목적으로	· identical to ~와 똑같은
· with no exception 예외 없이	· renowned for ~으로 유명한
· against the law 불법인, 법에 저촉되는	

09 문법 부사절
난이도 ★★☆

해석 연구는 차를 마시는 사람들이 어떤 종류의 음료를 선택하든 상관없이 심장병, 암, 그리고 스트레스로부터 더 큰 보호를 누릴 수 있다는 것을 보여준다. 전문가들은 찻잎의 항산화제가 주요한 건강상의 이점을 준다고 말한다. 그것이 우리가 일부 창의적인 요리사들이 컵을 넘어 전채 요리, 식사, 그리고 디저트와 차를 혼합하는 맛있는 방법을 찾아낸 것에 감탄하는 이유이다.

해설 ② 부사절 접속사 3: 복합관계대명사 문맥상 '어떤 종류의 음료를 선택하든 상관없이'라는 의미가 되어야 자연스러운데, '어떤 종류의 음료를 선택하든'은 no matter which(어느 것을 ~하더라도) 또는 no matter what(무엇을 ~하더라도)으로 나타낼 수 있으므로, '아무리 ~하더라도'의 의미를 갖는 no matter how를 no matter which 또는 no matter what으로 고쳐야 한다.

오답 분석
① 비교급 형태 | 병치 구문 문맥상 '차를 마시는 사람들은 더 큰 보호를 누릴 수 있다'라는 의미가 되어야 자연스러운데 1음절 단어는 '원급 + er'의 형태로 비교급을 만들 수 있으므로 greater가 올바르게 쓰였다. 또한, 접속사(and)로 연결된 병치 구문에서는 같은 구조끼리 연결되어야 하는데, and 앞에 명사 disease와 cancer가 왔으므로 and 뒤에도 명사 stress가 올바르게 쓰였다.

③ 관계부사 관계사 뒤에 완전한 절(we admire ~ desserts)이 왔고 문맥상 '그것이 우리가 감탄하는 이유이다'라는 의미가 되어야 자연스러우므로 관계부사 why가 올바르게 쓰였다. 참고로, 관계부사는 선행사의 종류에 따라 선택하는데, 관계부사 why는 선행사와 관계부사 둘 중 하나를 생략할 수 있으므로 선행사(the reason)가 생략된 형태이다.

④ to 부정사의 역할 | 병치 구문 문맥상 '전채 요리, 식사, 디저트와 차를 혼합하는 방법'이라는 의미가 되어야 자연스러우므로 형용사처럼 명사(ways)를 수식하는 to 부정사 to meld가 올바르게 쓰였다. 또한, 접속사(and)로 연결된 병치 구문에서는 같은 구조끼리 연결되어야 하는데, and 앞에 명사 appetizers와 meals가 왔으므로 and 뒤에도 명사 desserts가 올바르게 쓰였다.

어휘 protection 보호 cancer 암 brew (커피 등의) 뜨거운 음료
expert 전문가 antioxidant 항산화제, 산화 방지제
confer 주다, 수여하다 admire 감탄하다, 칭찬하다 meld 혼합하다
appetizer 전채

👍 이것도 알면 합격!
복합관계부사 however(얼마나 ~하든 상관없이)는 형용사나 부사를 수식하며, 주로 'however + 형용사/부사 + 주어 + 동사' 형태로 쓴다는 것을 알아두자.
ex The children had to wait patiently for the bus, however excited they were.
형용사 주어 동사
그들이 얼마나 신이 났든 상관없이, 아이들은 버스를 참을성 있게 기다려야 했다.

10 문법 수 일치
난이도 ★★☆

해석 1910년에서 1930년 사이에 모더니즘 소설과 시의 부흥은 우리가 알고 있는 것처럼 문학 비평의 출현을 수반했다. 이는 비평이 점점 학문적이고 기술적으로 되면서 태도뿐 아니라 직업에 있어서도 19세기에 존재했던 것과는 매우 다른 일종의 문학 비평이다.

해설 ① 주어와 동사의 수 일치 주어 자리에 단수 명사 The rise가 왔으므로 복수 동사 were를 단수 동사 was로 고쳐야 한다. 참고로 주어와 동사 사이의 수식어 거품(of ~ poetry)은 동사의 수 결정에 영향을 주지 않는다.

오답 분석
② 부사절 접속사 2: 기타 문맥상 '우리가 알고 있는 것처럼'이라는 의미가 되어야 자연스러운데, '~처럼'은 부사절 접속사 as를 사용하여 나타낼 수 있고, 부사절 접속사 뒤에는 완전한 절이 와야 하므로 부사절 접속사 as 뒤에 '주어(we) + 동사(know) + 목적어(it)'가 갖추어진 as we know it이 올바르게 쓰였다.

③ **강조 부사 | 부정대명사:** one 강조 부사 very는 보통 형용사 (different)를 앞에서 강조하므로 **very different**가 올바르게 쓰였다. 또한, 대명사가 지칭하는 명사(a kind)가 단수이므로 단수 부정대명사 one이 올바르게 쓰였다.

④ **상관접속사** 문맥상 '태도뿐 아니라 직업에 있어서도'라는 의미가 되어야 자연스러운데, 'A뿐만 아니라 B도'는 상관접속사 not only A but (also) B를 사용하여 나타낼 수 있으므로 **not only in attitude but in vocation**이 올바르게 쓰였다.

어휘 rise 부흥, 출현 novel 소설 poetry 시
accompany 수반하다, 함께 ~하다 literary 문학의
criticism 비평 exist 존재하다 attitude 태도
vocation 직업, 소명 의식, 천직 academic 학문적인
technical 기술적인

👍 이것도 알면 **합격!**

강조 부사를 추가로 알아두자.

• very 매우	• much 너무, 많이
• too (부정적 의미로) 너무	• pretty 꽤, 제법
• quite 꽤, 상당히	• ever 항상, 도대체
• so (긍정적·부정적 의미로) 매우, 너무	
• much/even/still/far/a lot/by far (비교급 앞에서) 훨씬	

---

11 독해 논리적 흐름 파악 (문단 순서 배열) 난이도 ★★☆

끊어읽기 해석

During the first few times / you choose to celebrate / the achievements of members of the group, / you may want to explain / your thinking / behind the small ceremony.
처음 몇 번 동안에는 / 당신이 축하하기로 선택한 / 그룹 구성원의 성취를 / 당신은 설명하는 것이 좋다 / 당신의 생각을 / 작은 의식 뒤에 숨겨진

By simply stating your intention / to thank members of the group / for their courage or hard work, / people become aware / of the meaning of the celebration / and / are less apt to dismiss it.
단순히 당신의 의도를 표명함으로써 / 그룹 구성원들에게 감사하고자 하는 / 그들의 용기나 노고에 대해 / 사람들은 인식하게 된다 / 그 기념행사의 의미를 / 그리고 / 그것을 무시하는 경향이 줄어든다

(A) It is quite possible / as you begin this process / that the member of the group / being honored / will feel self-conscious and awkward.
틀림없이 ~할 수 있다 / 당신이 이 과정을 시작하면서 / 그룹 구성원은 / 영광스러워진 / 남의 시선을 의식하고 어색해할 것이다

(B) Coupled with the fact / that the event being celebrated / is based on authentic achievement, / it is likely / that the members of the group / will feel encouraged / to participate / in future celebrations.
~라는 사실과 더불어 / 기념되고 있는 그 행사가 / 진정한 성취에 기반을 두고 있다는 / ~할 가능성이 높다 / 그룹의 구성원들이 / 격려를 받을 / 참여하도록 / 향후 축하 행사에

(C) This is a natural response, / especially in groups / that do not know each other well / or / in organizations / in which celebration is not a part of the culture.
이것은 자연스러운 반응이다 / 특히 그룹에서 / 서로를 잘 모르는 / 또는 / 조직에서 / 축하가 문화의 일부가 아닌

해석
그룹 구성원의 성취를 축하하기로 선택한 처음 몇 번 동안에는, 작은 의식 뒤에 숨겨진 당신의 생각을 설명하는 것이 좋다. 단순히 그룹 구성원들의 용기나 노고에 대해 감사하고자 하는

당신의 의도를 표명함으로써, 사람들은 그 기념행사의 의미를 인식하게 되고 그것을 무시하는 경향이 줄어든다.

(B) 기념되고 있는 그 행사가 진정한 성취에 기반을 두고 있다는 사실과 더불어, 그룹의 구성원들이 향후 축하 행사에 참여하도록 격려를 받을 가능성이 높다.

(A) 이 과정을 시작하면서 영광스러워진 그룹 구성원은 남의 시선을 의식하고 어색해할 수 있다.

(C) 이것은 특히 서로 잘 모르는 그룹이나 축하가 문화의 일부가 아닌 조직에서 자연스러운 반응이다.

해설 주어진 글에서 그룹 구성원들에게 단순히 감사의 뜻을 표명함으로써 사람들은 기념행사의 의미를 무시하는 경향이 줄어든다고 하고, (B)에서 기념되고 있는 그 행사(the event)가 진정한 성취에 기반을 두고 있다는 사실과 더불어, 그룹 구성원들이 향후 행사에 참여하도록 격려를 받을 가능성이 높다고 설명하고 있다. 이어서 (A)에서 이 과정(this process)을 시작하면서 영광스러워진 그룹 구성원은 남의 시선을 의식하고 어색해할 수 있다고 한 뒤, (C)에서 이것(This)은 자연스러운 반응이라고 설명하고 있다. 따라서 ① (B) – (A) – (C)가 정답이다.

어휘 celebrate 축하하다 achievement 성취, 업적 ceremony 의식
state 표명하다, 분명히 말하다 courage 용기
apt ~하는 경향이 있는 dismiss 무시하다, 일축하다
self-conscious 남의 시선을 의식하는, 자의식이 강한
awkward 어색한 coupled with 더불어
authentic 진정한, 믿을 만한 organization 조직

---

12 독해 세부내용 파악 (내용 불일치 파악) 난이도 ★★☆

끊어읽기 해석

The work of human body's immune system / is carried out / by the body's trillions of immune cells / and / specialized molecules.
인체의 면역체계의 임무는 / 수행된다 / 신체의 수조 개의 면역 세포에 의해 / 그리고 / 특수 분자(에 의해)

The first line of defense / lies in the physical barriers of the skin and mucous membranes, / which block and trap invaders.
첫 번째 방어선은 / 피부와 점막의 물리적 장벽에 있다 / 침입자를 차단하고 가두는

A second, / the innate system, / is composed of cells / including phagocytes, / whose basic job / is to eat the invaders.
두 번째인 / 선천적인 체계는 / 세포로 구성된다 / 포식세포를 포함한 / 이것의 기본적인 임무는 / 침입자를 잡아먹는 것이다

In addition to these immune cells, / many chemical compounds / respond to infection and injury, / move in / to destroy pathogens, / and / begin repairing tissue.
이러한 면역 세포 외에도 / 많은 화학적 화합물들이 / 감염과 부상에 반응하고 / 접근한다 / 병원체를 파괴하기 위해 / 그리고 / 조직을 복구하기 시작한다

The body's third line of defense is / a final, more specific response.
신체의 세 번째 방어선은 / 최종적이고, 보다 구체적인 대응이다

Its elite fighting units / are trained on the job; / that is, / they are created / in response to a pathogen / that the body has not seen before.
그것의 정예 전투 부대는 / 그 일에 대해 훈련을 받는다 / 즉 / 그것들은 생성된다 / 병원균에 대한 반응으로 / 신체가 이전에 본 적이 없는

Once activated / in one part of the body, / the adaptive system / functions throughout, / and / it memorizes the

antigens / (a substance that provokes an immune system response).
일단 활성화되면 / 신체의 한 부분에서 / 적응 체계는 / 전체적으로 기능한다 / 그리고 / 그것은 항원을 기억한다 / (면역체계 반응을 일으키는 물질)

The next time they come along, / the body hits back quicker and harder.
다음번에 그것들이 올 때 / 신체는 더 빠르고 더 세게 반격한다

해석　인체의 면역체계의 임무는 신체의 수조 개의 면역 세포와 특수 분자에 의해 수행된다. 첫 번째 방어선은 침입자를 차단하고 가두는 피부와 점막의 물리적 장벽에 있다. 두 번째인 선천적인 체계는 포식세포를 포함한 세포로 구성되며, 이것의 기본적인 임무는 침입자를 잡아먹는 것이다. 이러한 면역 세포 외에도, 많은 화학적 화합물들이 감염과 부상에 반응하고, 병원체를 파괴하기 위해 접근하고, 조직을 복구하기 시작한다. 신체의 세 번째 방어선은 최종적이고, 보다 구체적인 대응이다. 그것의 정예 전투 부대는 그 일에 대해 훈련을 받는다. 즉, 그것들은 신체가 이전에 본 적이 없는 병원균에 대한 반응으로 생성된다. 일단 신체의 한 부분에서 활성화되면, 적응 체계는 전체적으로 기능하고, 그것은 항원(면역체계 반응을 일으키는 물질)을 기억한다. 다음번에 그것들(병원균)이 올 때, 신체는 더 빠르고 더 세게 반격한다.

해설　지문 중간에서 신체의 세 번째 방어선은 신체가 이전에 본 적이 없는 병원균에 대한 반응으로 생성된다고 했으므로 '③ 면역체계의 세 번째 방어선은 몸에 이전부터 지니고 있던 병원체에 반응한다'는 지문의 내용과 일치하지 않는다.

어휘　immune system 면역체계　carry out 수행하다　trillion 조(兆)
cell 세포　specialize 특수화하다, 전문화하다　molecule 분자
defense 방어, 수비　barrier 장벽　invader 침입자
innate 선천적인, 타고난　compose 구성하다　chemical 화학적인
compound 화합물　infection 감염　injury 부상
move in (무엇을 처리하기 위하여) 접근하다　repair 복구하다, 고치다
tissue 조직　elite 정예의, 선발된　fighting unit 전투 부대
activate 활성화시키다　adaptive 적응하는, 적응할 수 있는
function 기능하다　substance 물질　provoke 일으키다, 유발하다

13　독해　논리적 흐름 파악 (문장 삽입)　난이도 ★★☆

끊어읽기 해석

International management is applied / by managers of enterprises / that attain their goals and objectives / across unique multicultural, multinational boundaries.
국제적 경영은 적용된다 / 기업의 관리자들에 의해 / 그들의 목표와 목적을 달성하는 / 고유한 다문화, 다국적 경계를 넘어

The term management is defined / in many Western textbooks / as the process of completing activities efficiently / with and through other individuals.
관리라는 용어는 정의된다 / 많은 서양 교과서에서 / 효율적으로 활동을 완료하는 과정으로 / 다른 개인들과 함께 그리고 그들을 통해

(①) The process consists of / the functions or main activities / engaged in by managers.
그 과정은 구성된다 / 기능이나 주요 활동으로 / 관리자들이 수행하는

These functions or activities are usually labeled / planning, organizing, staffing, coordinating(leading and motivating), and controlling.
이러한 기능이나 활동은 보통 ~라고 불린다 / 계획, 조직, 직원 채용, 조정(이끌고 동기부여 하는 것), 그리고 통제

(②) The management process is affected / by the organization's home country environment, / which includes / the shareholders, creditors, customers, employees,

government, and community, / as well as technological, demographic, and geographic factors.
관리 과정은 영향을 받는다 / 조직의 본국 환경에 의해 / 그것은 포함한다 / 주주, 채권자, 고객, 직원, 정부, 그리고 지역사회를 / 기술적, 인구 통계학적, 그리고 지리적 요인뿐만 아니라

(③) These business enterprises are generally referred to as / international corporations, multinational corporations(MNCs), or global corporations.
이러한 기업체들은 일반적으로 ~이라고 불린다 / 국제 기업, 다국적 기업 (MNCs), 또는 글로벌 기업

(④) This means / that the process is affected by the environment / where the organization is based, / as well as by the unique culture, / including views on ethics and social responsibility, / existing in the country or countries / where it conducts its business activities.
이것은 의미한다 / 그 과정이 환경에 영향을 받는다는 것을 / 조직이 기반을 두고 있는 / 고유한 문화뿐만 아니라 / 윤리 및 사회적 책임에 대한 견해를 포함한 / 국가나 국가들에 존재하는 / 그것이 사업 활동을 수행하는

해석

> 국제적 경영은 고유한 다문화, 다국적 경계를 넘어 그들의 목표와 목적을 달성하는 기업의 관리자들에 의해 적용된다.

관리라는 용어는 많은 서양 교과서에서 다른 개인들과 함께 그리고 그들을 통해 효율적으로 활동을 완료하는 과정으로 정의된다. (①) 그 과정은 관리자들이 수행하는 기능이나 주요 활동으로 구성된다. 이러한 기능이나 활동은 보통 계획, 조직, 직원 채용, 조정(이끌고 동기부여 하는 것), 그리고 통제라고 불린다. (②) 관리 과정은 조직의 본국 환경에 의해 영향을 받는데, 그것은 기술적, 인구 통계학적, 그리고 지리적 요인뿐만 아니라 주주, 채권자, 고객, 직원, 정부, 그리고 지역사회를 포함한다. (③) 이러한 기업체들은 일반적으로 국제 기업, 다국적 기업(MNCs), 또는 글로벌 기업이라고 불린다. (④) 이것은 그 과정이 사업 활동을 수행하는 국가나 국가들에 존재하는 윤리 및 사회적 책임에 대한 견해를 포함한 고유한 문화뿐만 아니라 그 조직이 기반을 두고 있는 환경에 영향을 받는다는 것을 의미한다.

해설　③번 앞 문장에 관리 과정은 조직의 본국 환경에 의해 영향을 받는다는 내용이 있고, ③번 뒤 문장에 이러한(These) 기업체들은 일반적으로 국제 기업, 다국적 기업, 또는 글로벌 기업이라고 불린다는 내용이 있으므로, ③번 자리에 국제적 경영은 고유한 다문화, 다국적 경계를 넘어 그들의 목표와 목적을 달성하는 기업의 관리자들에 의해 적용된다는 내용의 주어진 문장이 나와야 지문이 자연스럽게 연결된다.

어휘　management 경영, 관리　apply 적용하다　enterprise 기업, 사업
attain 달성하다　objective 목적, 목표　unique 고유한, 독특한
multicultural 다문화의　multinational 다국적의　boundary 경계
term 용어　staffing 직원 채용　coordinate 조정하다, 조직하다
lead 이끌다　motivate 동기부여 하다　shareholder 주주
creditor 채권자　demographic 인구 통계학적인
geographic 지리적인　factor 요인　corporation 기업, 회사, 법인
ethics 윤리　responsibility 책임, 의무
conduct 수행하다, 실시하다

14　독해　논리적 흐름 파악 (문장 삽입)　난이도 ★★☆

끊어읽기 해석

This kind of development / makes us realize / that removing safety hazards is far better / than creating alarms / to detect them.
이러한 종류의 개발은 / 우리가 깨닫게 해준다 / 안전상의 위험을 제거하는

것이 훨씬 더 낫다는 것을 / 경보를 생성하는 것보다 / 그것들을 감지하기 위한

Spinoff technology can help / to make our homes and communities safer and more comfortable places / to live.
스핀오프 기술은 도움이 될 수 있다 / 우리의 집과 지역사회를 더 안전하고 더 편안한 곳으로 만드는 데 / 살기에

Most people are aware / that carbon monoxide(CO) buildup in our homes / can be very dangerous.
대부분의 사람들은 알고 있다 / 우리의 집에 일산화탄소가 축적되는 것이 / 매우 위험할 수 있다는 것을

This may come from / a faulty furnace or fireplace.
이것은 발생할 수 있다 / 결함이 있는 아궁이나 벽난로에서

(①) Consequently, / some people have carbon monoxide detectors / in their homes, but / these detectors only alert them / if the level of carbon monoxide is unsafe.
결과적으로 / 일부 사람들은 일산화탄소 감지기를 가지고 있다 / 그들의 집에 / 하지만 / 이러한 감지기는 경보를 발한다 / 일산화탄소의 수준이 안전하지 않을 때만

(②) However, / using space technology, / NASA developed an air-conditioning system / that can not only detect dangerous amounts of carbon monoxide, / but actually oxidizes the toxic gases / into harmless carbon dioxide.
그러나 / 우주 기술을 사용하여 / NASA는 에어컨 시스템을 개발했다 / 위험한 양의 일산화탄소를 감지할 수 있을 뿐만 아니라 / 실제로 그 유독가스를 산화시키는 / 무해한 이산화탄소로

(③) In addition to helping people / to have clean air, / having access to clean water / is also of major importance / for everyone.
사람들을 돕는 것 외에도 / 깨끗한 공기를 가질 수 있도록 / 깨끗한 물에 접근할 수 있는 것은 / 또한 매우 중요하다 / 모든 사람들에게

NASA engineers have been working with private companies / to create better systems / for clean, drinkable water / for astronauts in space.
NASA 공학자들은 민간 회사들과 협력해 왔다 / 더 나은 시스템을 만들기 위해 / 깨끗하고, 마시기 알맞은 물을 위한 / 우주에 있는 우주 비행사들을 위한

(④) These systems, / which have been developed / for the astronauts, / can quickly and affordably cleanse / any available water.
이러한 시스템은 / 개발된 / 우주 비행사들을 위해 / 빠르고 저렴하게 정화할 수 있다 / 사용 가능한 모든 물을

This is a major advantage / to the people on Earth / who live in remote or developing areas / where water is scarce or polluted.
이것은 주요한 이점이다 / 지구상의 사람들에게 / 외딴곳이나 개발도상국에 사는 / 물이 부족하거나 오염된

해석

이러한 종류의 개발은 우리가 안전상의 위험을 제거하는 것이 그것들을 감지하기 위한 경보를 생성하는 것보다 훨씬 더 낫다는 것을 깨닫게 해준다.

스핀오프 기술은 우리의 집과 지역사회를 살기에 더 안전하고 더 편안한 곳으로 만드는 데 도움이 될 수 있다. 대부분의 사람들은 우리의 집에 일산화탄소가 축적되는 것이 매우 위험할 수 있다는 것을 알고 있다. 이것은 결함이 있는 아궁이나 벽난로에서 발생할 수 있다. (①) 결과적으로, 일부 사람들은 그들의 집에 일산화탄소 감지기를 가지고 있지만, 이러한 감지기는 일산화탄소의 수준이 안전하지 않을 때만 경보를 발한다. (②) 그러나, NASA는 우주 기술을 사용하여 위험한 양의 일산화탄소를 감지할 수 있을 뿐만 아니라, 실제로 그 유독가스를 무해한 이산화탄소로 산화시키는 에어컨 시스템을 개발했다. (③) 사람들이 깨끗한 공기를 가질 수 있도록 돕는 것 외에도, 깨끗한 물에 접근할 수 있는 것 또한 모든 사람들에게 매우 중요하다. NASA 공학자들은 우주 비행사들이 우주에서 마실 깨끗하고, 마시기 알맞은 물을 위한 더 나은 시스템을 만들기 위해 민간 회사들과 협력해 왔다. (④) 우주 비행사들을 위해 개발된 이러한 시스템은, 사용 가능한 모든 물을 빠르고 저렴하게 정화할 수 있다. 이것은 물이 부족하거나 오염된 외딴 곳이나 개발도상국에 사는 지구상의 사람들에게 주요한 이점이다.

해설 ③번 앞 문장에 NASA가 유독가스인 일산화탄소를 무해한 이산화탄소로 산화시키는 에어컨 시스템을 개발했다는 내용이 있고, ③번 뒤 문장에 사람들이 깨끗한 공기를 가질 수 있도록 돕는 것 외에도 깨끗한 물에 접근할 수 있는 것 또한 모든 사람들에게 매우 중요하다는 새로운 주제(깨끗한 물)를 다루는 내용이 있으므로, ③번 자리에 이러한 종류의 개발(This kind of development)은 우리가 안전상의 위험을 제거하는 것이 그것들을 감지하기 위한 경보를 생성하는 것보다 훨씬 더 낫다는 것을 깨닫게 해준다는 내용의 주어진 문장이 나와야 지문이 자연스럽게 연결된다.

어휘 hazard 위험 detect 감지하다 spinoff technology 스핀오프 기술(NASA의 기술이나 전문 지식을 접목해 상용화하는 기술)
carbon monoxide 일산화탄소 buildup 축적, 비축
faulty 결함이 있는 furnace 아궁이, 용광로 fireplace 벽난로
alert 경보를 발하다 oxidize 산화시키다 toxic 유독한
carbon dioxide 이산화탄소 astronaut 우주 비행사
affordably 저렴하게, 감당할 수 있게 remote 외딴, 먼
scarce 부족한, 희귀한 polluted 오염된

---

15 **독해** 추론 (빈칸 완성 - 연결어) 난이도 ★★☆

끊어읽기 해석

Antibiotics are among the most commonly prescribed drugs / for people.
항생제는 가장 흔하게 처방되는 약들 중 하나이다 / 사람들에게

Antibiotics are effective / against bacterial infections, / such as strep throat, / some types of pneumonia, / eye infections, / and ear infections.
항생제는 효과적이다 / 박테리아 감염에 / 패혈성 인두염과 같은 / 일부 유형의 폐렴 / 눈 감염 / 그리고 귀 감염

But / these drugs / don't work at all / against viruses, / such as those that cause colds or flu.
하지만 / 이 약들은 / 전혀 효과가 없다 / 바이러스에 / 감기나 독감을 유발하는 것과 같은

Unfortunately, / many antibiotics / prescribed to people and to animals / are unnecessary.
불행하게도 / 많은 항생제는 / 사람과 동물에게 처방되는 / 불필요하다

(A) Furthermore, / the overuse and misuse of antibiotics / help to create / drug-resistant bacteria.
(A) 게다가 / 항생제의 남용과 오용은 / 생성하는 것을 돕는다 / 약물에 내성이 있는 박테리아를

Here's how that might happen.
그것이 어떻게 일어날 수 있는지는 다음과 같다

When used properly, / antibiotics can help / destroy disease-causing bacteria.
적절하게 사용되면 / 항생제는 도움이 될 수 있다 / 질병을 일으키는 박테리아를 파괴하는 데

(B) However, / if you take an antibiotic / when you have a viral infection / like the flu, / the drug won't affect the viruses / making you sick.
(B) 하지만 / 항생제를 복용하면 / 당신이 바이러스 감염이 있을 때 / 독감과 같은 / 그 약은 바이러스에 영향을 미치지 않는다 / 당신을 아프게 하는

해석 항생제는 사람들에게 가장 흔하게 처방되는 약들 중 하나이다. 항생제는 패혈성 인두염, 일부 유형의 폐렴, 눈 감염, 그리고 귀 감염과 같은 박테리아 감염에 효과적이다. 하지만 이 약들은 감기나 독감을 유발하는 것과 같은 바이러스에는 전혀 효과가 없다. 불행하게도, 사람과 동물에게 처방되는 많은 항생제는 불필요하다. (A) 게다가, 항생제의 남용과 오용은 약물에 내성이 있는 박테리아를 생성하는 것을 돕는다. 그것이 어떻게 일어날 수 있는지는 다음과 같다. 항생제는 적절하게 사용되면 질병을 일으키는 박테리아를 파괴하는 데 도움이 될 수 있다. (B) 하지만, 독감과 같은 바이러스 감염이 있을 때 항생제를 복용하면, 그 약은 당신을 아프게 하는 바이러스에 영향을 미치지 않는다.

	(A)	(B)
①	하지만	대신에
②	게다가	그러므로
③	반면에	예를 들어
④	게다가	하지만

해설 (A) 빈칸 앞 문장은 사람과 동물에게 처방되는 많은 항생제는 불필요하다는 내용이고, 빈칸 뒤 문장은 항생제의 남용과 오용은 약물에 내성이 있는 박테리아를 생성하는 것을 돕는다는 추가적인 내용이다. 따라서 빈칸에는 추가를 나타내는 연결어인 Furthermore(게다가)가 들어가야 한다. (B) 빈칸 앞 문장은 항생제는 적절하게 사용되면 질병을 일으키는 박테리아를 파괴하는 데 도움이 될 수 있다는 내용이고, 빈칸 뒤 문장은 바이러스 감염이 있을 때 항생제를 복용하면 그 약은 바이러스에 영향을 미치지 않는다는 내용으로 앞 문장과 대조적인 내용이다. 따라서 빈칸에는 대조를 나타내는 연결어인 However(하지만)가 들어가야 한다. 따라서 ④ (A) Furthermore(게다가) - (B) However(하지만)가 정답이다.

어휘 antibiotic 항생제, 항균 prescribe 처방하다 effective 효과적인 infection 감염 strep throat 패혈성 인두염 pneumonia 폐렴 overuse 남용 misuse 오용 resistant 내성이 있는, 저항력이 있는 properly 적절하게, 제대로 viral 바이러스의

16 독해 전체내용 파악 (제목 파악) 난이도 ★★★

끊어읽기 해석

The assumption that politics and administration could be separated / was ultimately disregarded / as utopian.
정치와 행정이 분리될 수 있다는 가정은 / 결국 무시되었다 / 비현실적이라고

Wilson and Goodnow's idea / of apolitical public administration / proved unrealistic.
Wilson과 Goodnow의 생각은 / 정파와 관련되지 않은 공공 행정에 대한 / 비현실적인 것으로 판명되었다

A more realistic view / —the so-called "politics school" / —is that politics is very much a part of administration.
더 현실적인 견해는 / 소위 '정치 학파'라고 불리는 / 정치가 행정의 일부라는 것이다

The politics school maintains / that in a pluralistic political system / in which many diverse groups have a voice, / public administrators with considerable knowledge / play key roles.
정치 학파는 주장한다 / 다원적 정치 체제에서 / 다양한 집단이 목소리를 내는 / 상당한 지식을 갖춘 공공 행정가가 / 핵심적인 역할을 한다고

Legislation, / for instance, / is written by public administrators / as much as by legislators.
법령은 / 예를 들어 / 공공 행정가에 의해 작성된다 / 입법자 못지않게

The public bureaucracy / is as capable of engendering support for its interests / as any other participant / in the political process, / and / public administrators / are as likely as any to be part of a policymaking partnership.
공공 관료는 / 자신의 이익에 대한 지원을 발생시킬 수 있다 / 다른 어떤 참여자와 마찬가지로 / 정치 과정의 / 그리고 / 공공 행정가는 / 정책 입안 파트너십의 일부가 될 가능성이 크다

Furthermore, / laws are interpreted / by public administrators / in their execution, / which includes many and often unforeseen scenarios.
게다가 / 법률은 해석된다 / 공공 행정가에 의해 / 그것들이 집행될 때 / 여기에는 많은 그리고 종종 예기치 않은 시나리오가 포함된다

해석 정치와 행정이 분리될 수 있다는 가정은 결국 비현실적이라고 무시되었다. 정파와 관련되지 않은 공공 행정에 대한 Wilson과 Goodnow의 생각은 비현실적인 것으로 판명되었다. 소위 '정치 학파'라고 불리는 더 현실적인 견해는 정치가 행정의 일부라는 것이다. 정치 학파는 다양한 집단이 목소리를 내는 다원적 정치 체제에서 상당한 지식을 갖춘 공공 행정가가 핵심적인 역할을 한다고 주장한다. 예를 들어, 법령은 입법자 못지않게 공공 행정가에 의해 작성된다. 공공 관료는 정치 과정의 다른 어떤 참여자와 마찬가지로 자신의 이익에 대한 지원을 발생시킬 수 있고, 공공 행정가는 정책 입안 파트너십의 일부가 될 가능성이 크다. 게다가, 법률은 집행될 때 공공 행정가에 의해 해석되는데, 여기에는 많은 그리고 종종 예기치 않은 시나리오가 포함된다.

① 정치에서 예측 불가능한 상황에 대처하는 방법
② 공공 행정가의 정치 체제에 대한 놀라운 영향력
③ 정치와 행정을 분리하려는 반복적인 시도
④ 정치와 행정은 분리될 수 없다는 견해의 허점

해설 지문 전반에 걸쳐 정치가 행정의 일부라는 것이 현실적인 견해이며 다원적 정치 체제에서는 공공 행정가가 핵심적인 역할을 한다는 점을 예시를 들어 설명하고 있다. 따라서, '② 공공 행정가의 정치 체제에 대한 놀라운 영향력'이 이 글의 제목이다.

어휘 assumption 가정, 추정 politics 정치 administration 행정, 정부 separate 분리하다 ultimately 결국, 마침내 disregard 무시하다 utopian 비현실적인, 이상적인 apolitical 어떤 정파[정당]와 관련되지 않은 prove 판명하다, 증명하다 unrealistic 비현실적인 so-called 소위 pluralistic 다원적인 diverse 다양한 considerable 상당한 legislation 법령, 입법 legislator 입법자, 법률 제정자 bureaucracy 관료, 관료제 capable ~할 수 있는 engender ~을 발생시키다, 일으키다 policymaking 정책 입안 interpret 해석하다, 판단하다 execution 집행, 실행 unforeseen 예기치 않은, 의외의 cope with ~에 대처하다 unpredictable 예측 불가능한 repetitive 반복적인 attempt 시도 loophole 허점, 빠져나갈 구멍 inseparable 분리할 수 없는

17 독해 전체내용 파악 (제목 파악) 난이도 ★☆☆

끊어읽기 해석

We are living in perhaps the most exciting times / in all human history.
우리는 아마도 가장 흥미로운 시기에 살고 있다 / 인류 역사상

The technological advances / we are witnessing today / are giving birth to / new industries / that are producing / devices, systems, and services / that were once only reflected / in the realm of science fiction and fantasy.
기술 발전은 / 오늘날 우리가 목격하고 있는 / 탄생시키고 있다 / 새로운 산업을 / 생산하는 / 기기, 시스템, 그리고 서비스를 / 한때 반영되었던 / 공상 과학과 판타지의 영역에만

Industries are being completely restructured / to become better, faster, stronger, and safer.
산업은 완전히 재구성되고 있다 / 더 좋고, 더 빠르고, 더 강하고, 더 안전해지기 위해

You no longer have to settle for something / that is "close enough," / because customization is reaching levels / that provide you with / exactly what you want or need.
당신은 더 이상 무언가에 만족할 필요가 없다 / '충분히 가까운' 맞춤화는 수준에 도달하고 있기 때문에 / 당신에게 제공하는 / 당신이 원하거나 필요로 하는 것을

We are on the verge of / releasing the potential of / genetic enhancement, nanotechnology, and other technologies / that will lead to curing many diseases / and / maybe even slowing the aging process itself.
우리는 직전에 있다 / 잠재력을 공개하기 / 유전자 향상, 나노 기술 및 기타 기술의 / 많은 질병을 치료하도록 이끌 / 그리고 / 심지어 어쩌면 노화 과정 자체를 늦추도록 이끌

Such advances are due to discoveries / in separate fields / to produce these wonders.
그러한 발전은 발견에 기인한다 / 별개의 분야에서의 / 이러한 경이로움을 만들어내는

In the not so distant future, / incredible visions of imagination / such as robotic surgeons / that keep us healthy, / self-driving trucks / that deliver our goods, / and / virtual worlds / that entertain us / after a long day / will be commonplace.
그리 머지않은 미래에, / 놀라운 상상의 모습이 / 로봇 외과 의사와 같은 / 우리를 계속 건강하게 해주는 / 자율 주행 트럭 / 우리의 상품을 배달하는 / 그리고 / 가상 세계 / 우리를 즐겁게 해주는 / 긴 하루 끝에 / 흔해질 것이다

If ever there were a time / that we were about to capture perfection, / it is now / —and the momentum is only increasing.
때가 있었다면 / 우리가 완벽함을 정확히 포착하려고 했던 / 그것은 바로 지금이다 / 그리고 그 기세는 점점 더 커지기만 할 뿐이다

해석 우리는 아마도 인류 역사상 가장 흥미로운 시기에 살고 있다. 오늘날 우리가 목격하고 있는 기술 발전은 한때 공상 과학과 판타지의 영역에만 반영되었던 기기, 시스템, 그리고 서비스를 생산하는 새로운 산업을 탄생시키고 있다. 산업은 더 좋고, 더 빠르고, 더 강하고, 더 안전해지기 위해 완전히 재구성되고 있다. 맞춤화는 당신이 원하거나 필요로 하는 것을 정확하게 제공하는 수준에 도달하고 있기 때문에 당신은 더 이상 '충분히 가까운' 것에 만족할 필요가 없다. 우리는 많은 질병을 치료하고 심지어 어쩌면 노화 과정 자체를 늦추도록 이끌 유전자 향상, 나노 기술 및 기타 기술의 잠재력을 공개하기 직전에 있다. 그러한 발전은 이러한 경이로움을 만들어내는 별개의 분야에서의 발견에 기인한다. 그리 머지않은 미래에, 우리를 계속 건강하게 해주는 로봇 외과 의사, 우리의 상품을 배달하는 자율 주행 트럭, 그리고 긴 하루 끝에 우리를 즐겁게 해주는 가상 세계와 같은 놀라운 상상의 모습이 흔해질 것이다. 우리가 완벽함을 정확히 포착하려고 했던 때가 있었다면, 그것은 바로 지금이고, 그 기세는 점점 더 커지기만 할 뿐이다.

① 전례 없는 기술 발전의 시대
② 현대 산업의 불완전한 해결책과의 분투
③ 기술 진보에 대한 역사적 관점
④ 현대 산업의 정체된 상태

해설 지문 전반에 걸쳐 산업은 더 좋고, 더 빠르고, 더 강하고, 더 안전해지기 위해 완전히 재구성되고 있고, 우리가 완벽함을 정확히 포착하려고 했던 때가 있었다면 그것은 바로 지금이라고 설명하고 있다. 따라서 '① 전례 없는 기술 발전의 시대'가 이 글의 제목이다.

어휘 witness 목격하다 reflect 반영하다, 나타내다 realm 영역 science fiction 공상 과학 restructure 재구성하다 settle for ~에 만족하다 customization 맞춤화, 주문에 따라 만듦 on the verge of ~하기 직전에 genetic 유전자의, 유전(학)의 enhancement 향상, 증대 nanotechnology 나노 기술 incredible 놀라운, 믿을 수 없는 vision 모습 surgeon 외과 의사 commonplace 흔한 capture 정확히 포착하다, 포획하다 momentum 기세, 추진력 era 시대 unprecedented 전례 없는 advancement 발전, 진보 imperfect 불완전한 perspective 관점 stagnant 정체된 contemporary 현대의, 동시대의

18 독해 추론 (빈칸 완성 - 단어) 난이도 ★☆☆

끊어읽기 해석

Emotional strength isn't about / maintaining a stiff upper lip, / being stoic / or / never showing emotion / —actually, / it's the opposite.
정서적 힘은 ~에 대한 게 아니다 / 윗입술을 뻣뻣하게 유지하는 것 / 금욕적인 것 / 또는 / 감정을 전혀 나타내지 않는 것 / 사실 / 그 반대이다

"Emotional strength is about / having the skills you need / to regulate your feelings," / says psychotherapist Amy Morin.
"정서적 힘은 ~와 관련이 있다 / 여러분이 필요한 기술을 갖는 것 / 여러분의 감정을 조절하기 위해" / 라고 심리치료사인 Amy Morin이 말한다

"You don't need to chase happiness / all the time.
"여러분은 행복을 좇을 필요가 없습니다 / 항상

Instead, / you can develop the courage you need / to work through uncomfortable feelings, / like anxiety and sadness."
대신에 / 여러분은 필요한 용기를 기를 수 있습니다 / 불편한 감정을 헤쳐 나가기 위해 / 불안과 슬픔 같은"

Someone with emotional strength, / for instance, / will know / when to shift their emotional state, / says Morin.
정서적 힘을 가진 사람은 / 예를 들어 / 알 것이다 / 그들의 감정 상태를 언제 전환해야 하는지 / 라고 Morin은 말한다

"If their anxiety isn't serving them well, / they have strategies they can use / to calm themselves.
"만약 그들의 불안이 그들에게 도움이 되지 않는다면 / 그들은 사용할 수 있는 전략을 가지고 있습니다 / 자신을 진정시키기 위해"

They also have the ability / to tolerate difficult emotions, / but / they do so / by embracing them, / not suppressing them.
그들은 또한 능력을 가지고 있습니다 / 어려운 감정을 견딜 수 있는 / 하지만 / 그들은 그렇게 합니다 / 그것들을 받아들임으로써 / 그것들을 억누르는 것이 아니라

They don't distract themselves / from painful feelings, / like loneliness."
그들은 그들 자신의 주의를 돌리지 않습니다 / 고통스러운 감정으로부터 / 외로움과 같은"

해석 정서적 힘은 윗입술을 뻣뻣하게 유지하는 것, 금욕적인 것, 또는 감정을 전혀 나타내지 않는 것에 대한 게 아니라 사실 그 반대이다. "정서적 힘은 여러분의 감정을 조절하는 데 필요한 기술을 갖는 것과 관련이 있습니다"라고 심리치료사인 Amy Morin이 말한다. "여러분은 항상 행복을 좇을 필요가 없습니다. 대신에, 여러분은 불안과 슬픔 같은 불편한 감정을 헤쳐 나가는 데 필요한 용기를 기를 수 있습니다." 예를 들어, 정서적 힘을 가진 사람은 그들의 감정 상태를 언제 전환해야 하는지 알 수 있을 것이라고 Morin은 말한다. "만약 그들의 불안이 그들에게 도움이 되지 않는다면, 그들은 자신을 진정시키기 위해 사용할 수 있는 전략을 가지고 있습니다. 그들은 또한 어려운 감정을 견딜 수 있는 능력도 가지고 있지만, 그것들을 억누르는 것이 아니라 받아들임으로써 그렇게 합니

다. 그들은 외로움과 같은 고통스러운 감정으로부터 주의를 돌리지 않습니다."

① 과장함
② 추구함
③ 받아들임
④ 무시함

해설 지문 처음에서 정서적 힘은 감정을 전혀 나타내지 않는 것에 대한 게 아니라 사실 그 반대라고 했고, 지문 마지막에서 정서적 힘을 가진 사람은 외로움과 같은 고통스러운 감정으로부터 주의를 돌리지 않는다고 했으므로, 빈칸에는 그들(정서적 힘을 가진 사람들)은 어려운 감정을 견딜 수 있는 능력도 가지고 있지만, 그것들을 억누르는 것이 아니라 '③ 받아들임'으로써 그렇게 한다는 내용이 들어가야 한다.

어휘 **emotional** 정서적인, 감정적인 **strength** 힘, 용기
maintain 유지하다 **stiff** 뻣뻣한 **upper lip** 윗입술 **stoic** 금욕적인
opposite 반대인, 다른 편의 **regulate** 조절하다
psychotherapist 심리치료사 **courage** 용기
work through 헤쳐 나가다 **uncomfortable** 불편한
anxiety 불안 **sadness** 슬픔 **shift** 전환하다, 옮기다 **state** 상태
serve 도움이 되다 **strategy** 전략 **calm** 진정시키다
tolerate 견디다 **suppress** 억누르다 **distract** 주의를 돌리다
loneliness 외로움 **exaggerate** 과장하다
pursue 추구하다, 계속하다 **embrace** 받아들이다 **ignore** 무시하다

19 독해 추론 (빈칸 완성 - 단어) 난이도 ★★☆

끊어읽기 해석

Like many small organisms, / fungi are often overlooked, / but / their planetary significance / is outsize.
많은 작은 유기체와 마찬가지로 / 곰팡이들은 종종 간과된다 / 하지만 / 그것들의 지구상의 중요성은 / 너무나 크다

Plants managed to leave water / and / grow on land / only because of their collaboration with fungi, / which acted / as their root systems / for millions of years.
식물들이 물을 떠난 것은 / 그리고 / 땅에서 자란 것은 / 오직 곰팡이와의 협력 덕분이었다 / 역할을 했던 / 그들의 뿌리 체계의 / 수백만 년 동안

Even today, / roughly 90 percent of plants / and / nearly all the world's trees / depend on fungi, / which supply crucial minerals / by breaking down rock / and / other substances.
심지어 오늘날에도 / 식물의 대략 90퍼센트 / 그리고 / 전 세계의 거의 모든 나무가 / 곰팡이에 의존하고 있다 / 중요한 미네랄을 공급하는 / 암석을 분해함으로써 / 그리고 / 다른 물질들을

They can also be a scourge, / eradicating forests / and / killing humans.
그것들은 또한 재앙이 될 수도 있다 / 숲을 뿌리 뽑는 / 그리고 / 인간을 죽이는

At times, / they even seem to think.
때때로 / 그것들은 심지어 생각하는 것처럼 보이기도 한다

When Japanese researchers released slime molds / into mazes / molded on Tokyo's streets, / the molds found the most efficient route / between the city's urban hubs / in a day, / instinctively recreating / a set of paths / almost identical / to the existing rail network.
일본의 연구원들이 점액 곰팡이를 방출했을 때 / 미로에 / 도쿄의 거리에 만들어진 / 그 곰팡이들은 가장 효율적인 경로를 발견했다 / 도시의 중심지 사이에서 / 하루 만에 / 본능적으로 재현했다 / 일련의 경로를 / 거의 동일한 / 기존의 철도망과

When put in a miniature floor map of Ikea, / they quickly found / the shortest route / to the exit.
이케아의 축소된 평면도에 넣었을 때 / 그것들은 빠르게 발견했다 / 최단 경로를 / 출구로 가는

해석 많은 작은 유기체와 마찬가지로, 곰팡이들은 종종 간과되지만, 그것들의 지구상의 중요성은 너무나 크다. 식물들이 물을 떠나 땅에서 자란 것은 오직 수백만 년 동안 그들의 뿌리 체계 역할을 했던 곰팡이와의 협력 덕분이었다. 심지어 오늘날에도, 식물의 대략 90퍼센트와 전 세계의 거의 모든 나무가 암석과 다른 물질들을 분해함으로써 중요한 미네랄을 공급하는 곰팡이에 의존하고 있다. 그것들은 또한 숲을 뿌리 뽑고 인간을 죽이는 재앙이 될 수도 있다. 때때로, 그것들(곰팡이)은 심지어 생각하는 것처럼 보이기도 한다. 일본의 연구원들이 도쿄의 거리에 만들어진 미로에 점액 곰팡이를 방출했을 때, 그 곰팡이들은 하루 만에 도시의 중심지 사이에서 가장 효율적인 경로를 발견했고, 본능적으로 기존의 철도망과 거의 동일한 일련의 경로를 재현했다. 이케아의 축소된 평면도에 넣었을 때, 그것들은 출구로 가는 최단 경로를 빠르게 발견했다.

① 모이다
② 번식하다
③ 즐기다
④ 생각하다

해설 빈칸 뒤 문장에서 일본의 연구원들이 도쿄의 거리에 만들어진 미로에 점액 곰팡이를 방출했을 때, 그 곰팡이들은 하루 만에 도시의 중심지 사이에서 가장 효율적인 경로를 발견했고, 이케아의 축소된 평면도에 넣었을 때는 출구로 가는 최단 경로를 빠르게 발견했다는 예시를 언급하고 있으므로, 빈칸에는 때때로 그것들(곰팡이)은 심지어 '④ 생각하는' 것처럼 보인다는 내용이 들어가야 한다.

어휘 **organism** 유기체 **fungus** 곰팡이(복수형: fungi)
overlook 간과하다 **planetary** 지구상의, 행성상의
significance 중요성 **outsize** 너무 큰, 특대의
collaboration 협력 **roughly** 대략, 거의 **supply** 공급하다
crucial 중요한, 결정적인 **mineral** 미네랄, 무기물 **substance** 물질
scourge 재앙, 사회악 **eradicate** 뿌리 뽑다, 박멸하다
slime mold 점액 곰팡이 **maze** 미로 **mold** 만들다, 형성하다
urban 도시의 **hub** 중심지 **instinctively** 본능적으로
path 경로, 길 **identical** 동일한 **miniature** 축소된
route 경로, 노선 **gather** 모이다, 수집하다 **breed** 번식하다, 낳다

20 독해 추론 (빈칸 완성 - 절) 난이도 ★★★

끊어읽기 해석

Species (or higher taxa) may go extinct / for two reasons.
종(또는 더 높은 분류군)은 멸종될 수 있다 / 두 가지 이유로

One is "real" extinction / in the sense / that the lineage has died out / and / left no descendants.
하나는 '진짜' 멸종이다 / ~는 의미에서 / 혈통이 사라졌다는 / 그리고 / 후손이 남지 않았다는

For modern species, / the meaning is unambiguous, / but for fossil / real extinction has to be distinguished / from *pseudoextinction*.
현대 종의 경우 / 그 의미는 명확하다 / 하지만 화석의 경우 / 진짜 멸종은 구분되어야 한다 / '유사 멸종'과

Pseudoextinction means / that the taxon appears to go extinct, / but only because of an error or artifact in the evidence, / and not because the underlying lineage really ceased to exist.
유사 멸종은 의미한다 / 분류군이 멸종된 것처럼 보이는 것을 / 하지만 증거의 오류 또는 인공 유물 때문일 뿐 / 근원적인 혈통이 실제로 소멸했기 때문은 아니라는 것을

For instance, / a continuously evolving lineage / may change its taxonomic name.
예를 들어 / 지속적으로 진화하는 혈통은 / 그것의 분류학적 명칭을 바꿀 수도 있다

As a lineage evolves, / later forms may look / sufficiently different from earlier ones / that a taxonomist may classify them / as different species, / even though there is a continuous breeding lineage.
혈통이 진화함에 따라 / 이후의 형태는 보일 수 있다 / 이전의 형태와 충분히 다르게 / 그래서 분류학자들은 그것들을 분류할 수 있다 / 다른 종으로 / 지속적인 번식 혈통이 있음에도 불구하고

This may be because the species are classified phonetically, / or / it may be because the taxonomist only has a few specimens, / some from early in the lineage / and / some from late in the lineage / such that the continuous lineage is undetectable.
이것은 그 종들이 음성학적으로 분류되기 때문일 수도 있다 / 또는 / 분류학자가 몇몇 표본만 가지고 있기 때문일 수도 있다 / 일부는 혈통 초기부터 / 그리고 / 일부는 혈통 후기부터 / 그래서 연속적인 혈통을 찾아낼 수 없다

해석   종(또는 더 높은 분류군)은 두 가지 이유로 멸종될 수 있다. 하나는 혈통이 사라지고 후손이 남지 않았다는 의미에서 '진짜' 멸종이다. 현대 종의 경우, 그 의미는 명확하지만, 화석의 경우 진짜 멸종은 '유사 멸종'과 구분되어야 한다. 유사 멸종은 분류군이 멸종된 것처럼 보이지만, 증거의 오류 또는 인공 유물 때문일 뿐, 근원적인 혈통이 실제로 소멸했기 때문은 아니라는 것을 의미한다. 예를 들어, 지속적으로 진화하는 혈통은 그것의 분류학적 명칭을 바꿀 수도 있다. 혈통이 진화함에 따라, 이후의 형태는 이전의 형태와 충분히 다르게 보일 수 있기 때문에 지속적인 번식 혈통이 있음에도 불구하고 분류학자들은 그것들을 다른 종으로 분류할 수 있다. 이것은 그 종들이 음성학적으로 분류되기 때문일 수도 있고, 분류학자가 일부는 혈통 초기부터, 일부는 혈통 후기부터의 몇몇 표본만 가지고 있어서 연속적인 혈통을 찾아낼 수 없기 때문일 수도 있다.
① 멸종에 대한 단서는 많은 지역에서 발견된다
② 혈통은 화석 기록에서 일시적으로 사라질 수도 있다
③ 지속적으로 진화하는 혈통은 그것의 분류학적 명칭을 바꿀 수도 있다
④ 일부 서로 다른 혈통은 완전히 식별되었다

해설   빈칸 앞 문장에서 유사 멸종은 분류군이 멸종된 것처럼 보이지만 증거의 오류 또는 인공 유물 때문일 뿐, 근원적인 혈통이 실제로 소멸했기 때문은 아니라고 했고, 빈칸 뒤 문장에서 혈통이 진화함에 따라 지속적인 번식 혈통이 있음에도 불구하고 분류학자들은 그것들을 다른 종으로 분류할 수 있다고 설명하고 있으므로, 빈칸에는 '③ 지속적으로 진화하는 혈통은 그것의 분류학적 명칭을 바꿀 수도 있다'는 내용이 들어가야 한다.

어휘   species 종 taxon 분류군(복수형: taxa) extinct 멸종된, 사라진 lineage 혈통, 계통 die out 사라지다, 사멸하다 descendant 후손 unambiguous 명확한, 모호하지 않은 fossil 화석 distinguish 구분하다, 구별하다 pseudoextinction 유사 멸종 artifact 인공 유물 underlying 근원적인 cease to exist 소멸하다 evolve 진화하다 sufficiently 충분히 taxonomist 분류학자 classify 분류하다 continuous 지속적인 breed 번식하다 phonetically 음성학적으로 specimen 표본 undetectable 찾아낼 수 없는 clue 단서 temporarily 일시적으로 divergent 서로 다른, 분기하는 identify 식별하다, 확인하다

정답

p.128

01	① 어휘 – 어휘&표현	**11**	④ 문법 – 능동태·수동태
02	④ 어휘 – 어휘&표현	**12**	③ 독해 – 논리적 흐름 파악
03	② 어휘 – 어휘&표현	**13**	③ 독해 – 논리적 흐름 파악
04	① 어휘 – 어휘&표현	**14**	② 독해 – 전체내용 파악
05	④ 어휘 – 어휘&표현	**15**	④ 독해 – 세부내용 파악
06	④ 어휘 – 생활영어	**16**	③ 독해 – 추론
07	② 문법 – 조동사&병치·도치·강조 구문	**17**	① 독해 – 추론
08	② 문법 – 동사의 종류	**18**	③ 독해 – 논리적 흐름 파악
09	③ 문법 – 형용사와 부사&전치사	**19**	② 독해 – 추론
10	① 문법 – 분사	**20**	③ 독해 – 추론

취약영역 분석표

영역	세부 유형	문항 수	소계
어휘	어휘&표현	5	/6
	생활영어	1	
문법	조동사&병치·도치·강조 구문	1	/5
	동사의 종류	1	
	형용사와 부사&전치사	1	
	분사	1	
	능동태·수동태	1	
독해	전체내용 파악	1	/9
	세부내용 파악	1	
	추론	4	
	논리적 흐름 파악	3	
총계			**/20**

· 자신이 취약한 영역은 '공무원 영어, 이렇게 출제된다!'(문제집 p.8)를 통해 다시 한번 확인하고 학습하시기 바랍니다.

---

01 어휘 | 어휘&표현 renowned = famous 난이도 ★☆☆

해석 로알 아문센이 이끌었던 노르웨이인들은 1911년 1월 14일 남극의 고래만에 도착했다. 한 무리의 개와 함께, 그들은 남극까지 영국인들과 경쟁할 준비를 했다. 유명한 북극 탐험가 프리드쇼프 난센에게서 빌린 아문센의 배 'Fram호'는 그 당시 극지 정예 선박이었다.

① 유명한　　　　　　② 용맹한
③ 초기의　　　　　　④ 악명 높은

어휘 bay 만　race 경쟁하다, 경주하다　loan 빌리다　renowned 유명한
explorer 탐험가　elite 정예의; 엘리트　vessel 선박
intrepid 용맹한　notorious 악명 높은

👍 이것도 알면 **합격!**

renowned(유명한)의 유의어
= well-known, notable, celebrated, famed

---

02 어휘 | 어휘&표현 lucid = perspicuous 난이도 ★★★

해석 발표에서, 그녀는 이 단체의 일원으로서 그녀의 향후 계획에 대해 명쾌한 설명을 할 것이다.

① 수다스러운　　　　② 둔한
③ 차분한　　　　　　④ 명쾌한

어휘 give an account 설명을 하다　lucid 명쾌한, 맑은
loquacious 수다스러운　sluggish 둔한, 부진한
placid 차분한, 잔잔한　perspicuous 명쾌한, 명료한

👍 이것도 알면 **합격!**

lucid(명쾌한)의 유의어
= clear, unambiguous, unequivocal, explicit, plain

---

03 어휘 | 어휘&표현 accumulate 난이도 ★☆☆

해석 사람들은 경쟁력을 가지고 성공하기 위해 그들의 일자리에서 기술을 축적할 필요가 있다.

① 폐지하다　　　　　② 축적하다
③ 약화시키다　　　　④ 분리하다

어휘 competitive 경쟁력을 가진　abolish 폐지하다
accumulate 축적하다, 모으다　diminish 약화시키다, 줄다
isolate 분리하다, 고립시키다

👍 이것도 알면 **합격!**

accumulate(축적하다)의 유의어
= amass, accrue, assemble, collect, develop

---

04 어휘 | 어휘&표현 absence 난이도 ★★☆

해석 맨해튼은 성장할 다른 방향의 결핍으로 인해 하늘을 향해 확장될 수밖에 없었다. 이것(맨해튼이 하늘을 향해 확장된 것)은, 다른 어떤 것보다, 그것의 물리적인 장엄함의 원인이 된다.

① 결핍　　　　　　　② 결정
③ 노출　　　　　　　④ 선택

어휘 compel ~하게 만들다, 강요하다　majesty 장엄함, 폐하
absence 결핍, 부재　exposure 노출

👍 이것도 알면 **합격!**

absence(결핍)의 유의어
= lack, deficiency, nonexistence, dearth, paucity

---

05 어휘 | 어휘 & 표현 plagiarism
난이도 ★★☆

해석 표절은 당신의 글에 다른 사람의 말이나 발상을 그대로 사용하고, 원래 작가나 책, 잡지, 영상, 팟캐스트 또는 당신이 그것들을 발견한 웹사이트의 이름을 밝히지 않는 것이다.
① 인용　　　　　　② 발표
③ 수정　　　　　　④ 표절

어휘 citation 인용　modification 수정, 변경　plagiarism 표절

👍 이것도 알면 **합격!**

plagiarism(표절)의 유의어
= copying, appropriation, infringement, poaching

06 어휘 | 생활영어 OK, I will fix the zipper.
난이도 ★☆☆

해석 ① A: 당신에게 한 가지 부탁할 게 있어요.
　　　　B: 물론이죠, 무슨 일인가요?
② A: 제 계좌를 해지해야 할 것 같아요.
　　　　B: 네, 이 양식을 작성해 주세요.
③ A: 그건 멋진 결혼식이었어요.
　　　　B: 제 말이 그 말이에요. 그리고 결혼하는 커플은 서로에게 아주 잘 어울려 보였어요.
④ A: 저는 지난 월요일에 이 재킷을 샀는데 벌써 지퍼가 고장 났어요. 저는 환불하고 싶어요.
　　　　B: 네, 제가 지퍼를 고칠게요.

해설 ④번에서 A는 B에게 월요일에 산 재킷의 지퍼가 고장 나서 환불을 요청하고 있으므로, 자신이 지퍼를 고치겠다는 B의 대답 '④ OK, I will fix the zipper(네, 제가 지퍼를 고칠게요)'는 어울리지 않는다.

어휘 do a favor 부탁을 들어주다　account 계좌　refund 환불
fix 고치다

👍 이것도 알면 **합격!**

환불이나 수리를 요청할 때 쓸 수 있는 표현
· There's a defect in the shirt I bought here.
　제가 여기에서 산 셔츠에 하자가 있어요.
· I'd like to exchange this blanket. 저는 이 담요를 교환하고 싶어요.

07 문법 | 조동사 & 병치 · 도치 · 강조 구문
난이도 ★★☆

해석 ① 빈곤율은 가족 소득이 절대 수준 이하로 떨어지는 인구의 비율이다.
② 당연히, 어떤 대학 졸업생이라도 경기 위축의 해보다는 경기 팽창의 해에 노동 인구에 들어가는 게 낫다.
③ 사람들은 경제에 대해 최근에 보고된 일부 통계 자료를 보지 않고는 신문을 집어 들기가 어렵다.
④ 비록 평균소득에서 성장이 지속되고 있지만, 빈곤율은 감소하지 않고 있다.

해설 ② 조동사 관련 표현 | 병치 구문 조동사 관련 숙어 would rather(차라리 ~하는 게 낫다) 다음에는 동사원형이 와야 하므로 동사원형 enter가 올바르게 쓰였다. 또한, would rather A than B에서 비교 대상은 같은 구조끼리 연결되어야 하는데, than 앞의 명사구(in a year of economic expansion)가 'in a year

of + 명사'의 형태이므로 than 뒤에도 in a year of economic contraction이 올바르게 쓰였다.

오답 분석 ① 관계대명사 선행사 population이 사람이고, 관계절 내에서 family income이 누구의 가족 소득인지를 나타내므로 목적격 관계대명사 which를 사람을 가리키는 소유격 관계대명사 whose로 고쳐야 한다.
③ 가주어 it | to 부정사의 의미상 주어 문맥상 '사람들은 신문을 집어 들기가 어렵다'라는 의미가 되어야 자연스러운데, that절이나 to 부정사구와 같이 긴 주어가 오면 가주어 it이 진주어인 that절이나 to 부정사구를 대신해서 주어 자리에 쓰이므로 동사원형 pick을 to 부정사 to pick으로 고쳐야 한다. 또한, 문장의 주어(It)와 to 부정사(to pick up)의 행위 주체(people)가 달라서 to 부정사의 의미상 주어 'for + 명사'를 to 부정사 앞에 써야 하므로 명사절 접속사 that을 전치사 for로 고쳐야 한다.
④ 부사절 접속사 2: 양보 문맥상 '비록 ~ 지속되고 있지만'이라는 의미가 되어야 자연스러운데, 두 개의 절을 연결할 수 있는 것은 접속사이므로 전치사 Despite를 부사절 접속사 Although로 고쳐야 한다.

어휘 income 소득　absolute 절대의　labor force 노동 인구
expansion 팽창, 확대　contraction 위축, 수축　statistic 통계 자료
decline 감소하다

👍 이것도 알면 **합격!**

원급 또는 비교 구문에서 비교의 대상은 같은 품사나 구조끼리 연결되어야 한다는 것을 알아두자.
(ex) I prefer to have dinner at home than to eat out.
　나는 저녁을 밖에서 먹기보다는 집에서 먹는 것을 선호한다.

08 문법 | 동사의 종류
난이도 ★★☆

해석 ① 아무것도 남지 않았기 때문에, 그녀는 그녀를 굴복시킨 그것에 매달려야 했을 것이다.
② 그녀에게 그녀의 집이 청소되어야 한다는 말을 전해라.
③ 살아있는 동안, 그녀는 전통이고, 의무이자, 보살핌이었다.
④ 당신은 한 여성을 나쁜 냄새를 풍긴다는 이유로 면전에서 비난할 건가?

해설 ② 5형식 동사 사역동사 have는 목적어와 목적격 보어가 수동 관계일 때 과거분사를 목적격 보어로 취하는 5형식 동사인데, 목적어(her place)와 목적격 보어가 '그녀의 집이 청소되다'라는 의미의 수동 관계이므로 현재분사 cleaning을 과거분사 cleaned로 고쳐야 한다.

오답 분석 ① 분사구문의 관용 표현 | 관계대명사 이유를 나타낼 때는 'with + 명사 + 분사'로 나타낼 수 있는데, 명사(nothing)와 분사가 '아무것도 남아 있지 않다'라는 의미의 수동 관계이므로 과거분사 left가 올바르게 쓰였다. 또한, 선행사(that)가 사물이고 관계절 내에서 동사 had robbed의 주어 역할을 하고 있으므로 사물을 나타내는 주격 관계대명사 which가 올바르게 쓰였다.
③ 부사절 접속사 1: 시간 문맥상 '그녀가 살아있는 동안'이라는 의미가 되어야 자연스러운데, '~하는 동안'은 부사절 접속사 while(~하는 동안)로 나타낼 수 있고, 종속절인 부사절(While she was alive)의 주어가 주절의 주어(she)와 같고 부사절의 동사가 be동사(was)일 경우 부사절 접속사 뒤의 '주어 + 동사'를 생략할 수 있으므로 보어 Alive(살아있는)가 올바르게 쓰였다.

④ 기타 전치사 문맥상 '한 여성을 ~라는 이유로 비난하다'라는 의미가 되어야 자연스러운데, 'A를 B라는 이유로 비난하다'는 전치사 of와 함께 쓰이는 동사 accuse를 사용하여 accuse A of B로 나타낼 수 있으므로 전치사 of가 올바르게 쓰였다.

어휘 cling to ~에 매달리다 rob ~를 굴복시키다, 강도질을 하다
accuse 비난하다, 고소하다

👍 이것도 알면 **합격!**

get, 사역동사, 지각동사는 목적어와 목적격 보어가 수동 관계일 때 목적격 보어로 과거분사를 취할 수 있다. 단, 사역동사 let은 목적어와 목적격 보어가 수동 관계일 때 목적격 보어로 'be + p.p.' 형태를 취한다는 것을 알아두자.

(ex) The city lets the venue be used by nonprofit groups at no
　　　　　　　목적어　　　목적격 보어
charge.
시에서는 그 행사장이 비영리 단체들에게 무료로 사용되도록 허락한다.
→ '사용하다'가 아니라 '사용되다'라는 의미의 수동 관계이므로 사역동사 let의 목적격 보어로 'be + p.p.' 형태(be used)가 온다.

09 문법 형용사와 부사 & 전치사 　　　　난이도 ★★☆

해석 ① 못생기고, 오래되고, 노란 양철통 하나가 난로 옆에 서 있었다.
② 이것은 지금까지 발명된 것 중 가장 완벽한 복사기이다.
③ John은 그녀를 겁먹게 하고 있었다.
④ 그녀는 그가 완전히 바보라고 생각했다.

해설 ③ 강조 부사 | 기타 전치사 동사 frighten(겁먹게 하다)은 전치사 없이 목적어(her)를 바로 취하는 타동사인데, 부사 very는 보통 형용사나 부사를 앞에서 강조하므로 동사(frightening) 앞의 부사 very를 삭제해야 한다. 참고로 형용사 frightening(무서운)은 방향을 나타내는 전치사 for(~에게나 to(~에게)와 함께 쓰여 '~에게 무섭다'라는 의미를 나타낼 수 있으므로 frightening for나 frightening to로 고쳐도 맞다.

오답 ① 전치사 3: 위치 문맥상 '난로 옆에 서 있었다'라는 의미가 되어
분석 야 자연스러운데, '난로 옆에'는 전치사 beside(~ 옆에)로 나타낼 수 있으므로 beside the stove가 올바르게 쓰였다.
② 최상급 문맥상 '발명된 것 중 가장 완벽한 복사기'라는 의미가 되어야 자연스러운데, '가장 ~한'은 최상급 표현 'the + 최상급'의 형태를 사용하여 나타낼 수 있으므로 the most perfect copier가 올바르게 쓰였다.
④ 명사절 접속사 1: that 동사 think(thought)의 목적어 자리에는 명사 역할을 하는 것이 와야 하므로 명사절 접속사 that이 이끄는 명사절(that he was an utter fool)이 올바르게 쓰였다.

어휘 tin 양철 stove 난로 frighten 겁먹게 하다, 놀라게 하다
utter 완전한

👍 이것도 알면 **합격!**

besides(~ 외에)를 beside(~ 옆에)와 혼동하지 않도록 주의한다.
(ex) Besides a short trip to Mexico, I have never left the country.
멕시코로 가는 짧은 여행 외에, 나는 고향을 떠나본 적이 없다.

10 문법 분사 　　　　난이도 ★★☆

해석 사람들은 옷을 입을 때 매일 지속 가능한 방식으로 행동할 기회를 가지고 있고, 패션은 지속가능성에 대한 넓은 이해 안에서 창조될 때 환경뿐만 아니라 사람들을 존재하게 할 수 있다. 사람들은 그들이 구매하는 패션에 대해 사회적으로 책임감 있는 선택을 하고자 하는 욕구가 있다. 패션의 디자이너이자 제품 개발자로서, 우리는 책임감 있는 선택을 제공하는 것에 도전해야 한다. 우리는 현존하는 많은 계층과 복잡성에 변함없이 열려 있기 위해 패션에 대한 인식을 확장할 필요가 있다. 패션을 구현하는 사람, 절차, 그리고 환경도 지속 가능한 새로운 방향을 필요로 하고 있다. 정말 멋진 기회가 기다리고 있다!

해설 ① 분사구문의 형태 주절의 주어(fashion)와 분사구문이 '패션이 창조되다'라는 의미의 수동 관계이므로 현재분사 creating을 과거분사 created로 고쳐야 한다.

오답 ② 부사 자리 형용사를 앞에서 수식하는 것은 부사이므로 형용사
분석 responsible 앞에 부사 socially가 올바르게 쓰였다.
③ 보어 자리 동사 remain은 '변함없이 ~이다'라는 의미로 쓰일 때 주격 보어를 갖는 2형식 동사이고, 보어 자리에는 명사나 형용사 역할을 하는 것이 와야 하므로 형용사 open이 올바르게 쓰였다.
④ 관계대명사 선행사 The people, processes, and environments가 사물이고, 관계절 내에서 동사 embody의 주어 역할을 하므로 주격 관계대명사 that이 올바르게 쓰였다.

어휘 sustainable 지속 가능한 broad 넓은 stretch 확장하다, 뻗다
perception 인식 remain 변함없이 ~이다 embody 구현하다
call for ~을 필요로 하다 fabulous 멋진 await 기다리다

👍 이것도 알면 **합격!**

다음은 보어를 필요로 하는 2형식 동사들이다. 보어 자리에는 명사 또는 형용사 역할을 하는 것이 와야 하므로, 동사나 부사는 올 수 없다는 것을 알아두자.

• look ~처럼 보이다	• taste ~한 맛이 나다
• seem ~처럼 보이다	• sound ~처럼 들리다
• feel ~처럼 느끼다	• become ~이 되다

11 문법 능동태·수동태 　　　　난이도 ★★☆

해석 신문, 학술지, 잡지, TV 및 라디오와 전문 혹은 무역 출판물은 연례 보고서에 제시된 사실이나 보고서가 발간된 이후에 전개된 상황에 관한 사실을 해석하는 데 도움이 될 수 있는 추가적인 정보를 제공한다.

해설 ④ 능동태·수동태 구별 동사 published 뒤에 목적어가 없고, 주어(the report)와 동사가 '보고서가 발간되다'라는 의미의 수동 관계이므로 능동태 published를 수동태 was published로 고쳐야 한다.

오답 ① 주어와 동사의 수 일치 주어 자리에 복수 명사 Newspapers,
분석 journals, ~ trade publications가 왔으므로 복수 동사 provide가 올바르게 쓰였다.
② 불가산 명사 불가산 명사는 부정관사(a/an)와 함께 쓰일 수 없으므로 부정관사 없이 불가산 명사 information이 올바르게 쓰였다.
③ 현재분사 vs. 과거분사 수식받는 명사(the facts)와 분사가 '사실이 제시되다'라는 의미의 수동 관계이므로 과거분사 given이 올바르게 쓰였다.

어휘 *journal* 학술지 *publication* 출판물 *further* 추가적인
interpret 해석하다 *annual* 연례의 *publish* 발간하다

👍 이것도 알면 **합격!**

혼동하기 쉬운 가산 명사와 불가산 명사를 알아두자.

가산 명사	불가산 명사
• a price 가격	• homework 숙제
• a noise 소음	• knowledge 지식
• a result/an outcome 결과	• clothing 의류
• measures 수단, 대책	• furniture 가구
• belongings 소지품	• luggage 수하물, 짐

12 독해 논리적 흐름 파악 (무관한 문장 삭제) 난이도 ★★☆

끊어읽기 해석

Tropical forests are incredibly rich ecosystems, / which provide much of the world's biodiversity.
열대 우림은 믿을 수 없을 정도로 풍부한 생태계이다 / 그리고 이것은 세계의 생물학적 다양성의 많은 부분을 부양한다

① However, / even with increased understanding / of the value of these areas, / excessive destruction continues.
그러나 / 높아진 이해에도 불구하고 / 이러한 지역의 가치에 대한 / 과도한 파괴는 계속되고 있다

There are a few promising signs, however.
그러나, 몇 가지 기대되는 징후가 있다

② Deforestation in many regions is slowing / as governments combat this practice / with intensive tree planting.
많은 지역에서의 삼림 벌채는 느려지고 있다 / 정부가 이 관행에 맞서고 있기 때문에 / 집중적인 나무 심기로

Asia, for example, has gained forest / in the last decade, / primarily due to China's large-scale planting initiatives.
예를 들어, 아시아는 숲을 얻게 되었다 / 지난 10년 동안 / 주로 중국의 대규모 나무 심기 계획으로 인해

③ One part of this challenge is to allow countries / a more equitable share of the revenue / from pharmaceutical products / originating in the tropical forests.
이 도전의 한 부분은 국가들에 허용하는 것이다 / 수입의 더 공평한 몫을 / 제약품에서 나온 / 열대 우림에서 비롯된

Moreover, / the number of reserves designated / for conservation of biodiversity / is increasing worldwide / with particularly strong gains / in South America and Asia.
게다가 / 지정된 보호 구역의 수는 / 생물학적 다양성의 보존을 위해 / 전 세계적으로 증가하고 있다 / 특히 두드러진 증가와 함께 / 남아메리카와 아시아에서

④ Unfortunately, / despite these gains, / the capacity for humans to destroy forests / continues to appear greater / than their ability to protect them.
유감스럽게도 / 이러한 증가에도 불구하고 / 인간이 숲을 파괴하는 능력은 / 계속해서 더 큰 것으로 보인다 / 그것들(숲)을 보호하는 그들의 능력보다

해석 열대 우림은 믿을 수 없을 정도로 풍부한 생태계이고, 이것은 세계의 생물학적 다양성의 많은 부분을 부양한다. ① 그러나, 이러한 지역의 가치에 대한 높아진 이해에도 불구하고, 과도한 파괴는 계속되고 있다. 그러나, 몇 가지 기대되는 징후가 있다. ② 많은 지역에서의 삼림 벌채는 정부가 집중적인 나무 심기로 이 관행에 맞서고 있기 때문에 느려지고 있다. 예를 들어, 아시아는 주로 중국의 대규모 나무 심기 계획으로 인해 지난 10년 동안 숲을 얻게 되었다. ③ 이 도전의 한 부분은 국가들에 열대 우림에서 비롯된 제약

품에서 나온 수입의 더 공평한 몫을 허용하는 것이다. 게다가, 생물학적 다양성의 보존을 위해 지정된 보호 구역의 수는 전 세계적으로 증가하고 있으며, 특히 남아메리카와 아시아에서 두드러진 증가가 있다. ④ 유감스럽게도, 이러한 증가에도 불구하고, 인간이 숲을 파괴하는 능력은 그것들(숲)을 보호하는 그들의 능력보다 계속해서 더 큰 것으로 보인다.

해설 지문 처음에서 열대 우림이 믿을 수 없을 정도로 풍부한 생태계이고 세계의 생물학적 다양성의 많은 부분을 부양한다고 언급하고 있다. ①번에서 그러나(However) 열대 우림의 가치에 대한 높아진 이해에도 불구하고 과도한 파괴가 계속되고 있다고 했지만, 몇 가지 기대되는 징후가 있다고 하며 ②번에서 정부의 집중적인 나무 심기로 인해 느려지고 있는 삼림 벌채를 예시로 들어 설명하고 있다. 이어서 생물학적 다양성의 보존을 위해 지정된 보호 구역의 수가 증가했지만, ④번에서 유감스럽게도(Unfortunately) 이러한 증가(these gains)에도 불구하고 인간이 숲을 파괴하는 능력이 숲을 보호하는 능력보다 계속해서 더 큰 것으로 보인다고 하며 문제점을 지적하고 있다. 그러나 ③번은 열대 우림의 과도한 파괴를 막는 한 부분이 국가들에 열대 우림에서 비롯된 제약품 수입을 공평하게 나누도록 하는 것이라는 내용으로, 열대 우림의 파괴를 줄이고자 하는 전 세계의 노력과 그 한계에 대해 설명하는 지문의 전반적인 내용과 어울리지 않는다.

어휘 *tropical* 열대의 *biodiversity* 생물학적 다양성 *destruction* 파괴
promising 기대되는 *deforestation* 삼림 벌채
initiative 계획, 진취성 *equitable* 공평한
pharmaceutical 제약 *originate* 비롯되다
reserves 보호 구역, 비축물 *conservation* 보존 *capacity* 능력
destroy 파괴하다

13 독해 논리적 흐름 파악 (무관한 문장 삭제) 난이도 ★★☆

끊어읽기 해석

In the early 1980s, / a good friend of mine discovered / that she was dying of multiple myeloma, / an especially dangerous, painful form of cancer.
1980년대 초 / 나의 좋은 친구 하나는 발견했다 / 그녀가 다발성 골수종으로 죽어가고 있다는 것을 / 특히 위험하고 고통스러운 형태의 암인

I had lost elderly relatives and family friends to death / before this, / but I had never lost a personal friend.
나는 나이 든 친척들과 가족의 친구들을 죽음으로 잃은 적이 있었다 / 이보다 전에 / 그러나 개인적인 친구를 잃은 적은 없었다

① I had never watched a relatively young person die / slowly and painfully of disease.
나는 비교적 젊은 사람이 죽는 것을 본 적이 없었다 / 질병으로 천천히 고통스럽게

It took my friend a year to die, / and ② I got into the habit of visiting her every Saturday / and taking along the latest chapter of the novel / I was working on.
나의 친구가 죽기까지 일 년이 걸렸다 / 그리고 나는 토요일마다 그녀를 찾아가는 버릇이 생겼다 / 그리고 소설의 최신 장을 가지고 / 내가 작업하고 있었던

This happened to be *Clay's Ark*.
이것(소설)은 우연히도 『진흙 방주』였다

With its story of disease and death, / it was thoroughly inappropriate / for the situation.
질병과 죽음에 대한 그것의 줄거리 때문에 / 그것은 대단히 부적절했다 / 그 상황에

But my friend had always read my novels.
하지만 나의 친구는 항상 나의 소설을 읽었다

③ She insisted / that she no longer wanted to read this one as well.
그녀는 고집했다 / 그녀가 더 이상 이것(『진흙 방주』)을 읽고 싶지 않다고

I suspect / that neither of us believed / she would live to read it / in its completed form / —④ although, of course, we didn't talk about this.
나는 짐작하고 있다 / 우리 둘 중 누구도 믿지 않았다고 / 그녀가 그것을 읽을 때까지 살 것이라고 / 그것의 완성된 형태로 / 물론, 우리가 이것에 대해 이야기하지는 않았지만

해석 1980년대 초, 나의 좋은 친구 하나는 그녀가 특히 위험하고 고통스러운 형태의 암인 다발성 골수종으로 죽어가고 있다는 것을 발견했다. 나는 이보다 전에 나이 든 친척들과 가족의 친구들을 죽음으로 잃은 적이 있었지만, 개인적인 친구를 잃은 적은 없었다. ① 나는 비교적 젊은 사람이 질병으로 천천히 고통스럽게 죽는 것을 본 적이 없었다. 나의 친구가 죽기까지 일 년이 걸렸고, ② 나는 토요일마다 내가 작업하고 있던 소설의 최신 장을 가지고 그녀를 찾아가는 버릇이 생겼다. 이것(소설)은 우연히도 『진흙 방주』였다. 질병과 죽음에 대한 그것의 줄거리 때문에, 그것은 그 상황에 대단히 부적절했다. 하지만 나의 친구는 항상 나의 소설을 읽었다. ③ 그녀는 더 이상 이것(『진흙 방주』)을 읽고 싶지 않다고 주장했다. ④ 물론, 우리가 이것에 대해 이야기하지는 않았지만, 나는 우리 둘 중 누구도 그녀가 그것을 완성된 형태로 읽을 때까지 살 것이라고 믿지 않았다고 짐작하고 있다.

해설 지문 처음에서 화자는 자신의 친구 중 한 명이 다발성 골수종으로 죽어가고 있다는 것을 발견했다고 하며 개인적인 친구를 잃은 적이 없을 뿐만 아니라 ①번에서 비교적 젊은 사람이 질병으로 천천히 고통스럽게 죽는 것도 본 적이 없음을 설명하고 있다. 이어서 ②번에서 화자는 토요일마다 자신이 작업하던 소설의 최신 장을 가지고 그 친구를 찾아가는 버릇이 생겼다고 하며 그 책이 질병과 죽음에 대한 줄거리 때문에 상황상 부적절했지만 친구가 항상 화자의 책을 읽었다고 한 뒤, ④번에서 서로 이야기하지는 않았지만 둘 중 누구도 그녀가 책을 완성된 형태로 읽을 때까지 살 것이라고 믿지 않았음을 언급하고 있다. 그러나 ③번은 친구가 더 이상 『진흙 방주』를 읽고 싶지 않다고 주장했다는 내용으로, 화자의 아픈 친구가 자신을 위해 화자가 가져오던 소설을 항상 읽었다는 지문 전반의 내용과 어울리지 않는다.

어휘 myeloma 골수종 get into the habit of ~하는 버릇이 생기다
clay 진흙 ark 방주 thoroughly 대단히, 철저히
inappropriate 부적절한 insist 주장하다, 고집하다
suspect 짐작하다, 의심하다

14 독해 전체내용 파악 (요지 파악) 난이도 ★★☆

끊어읽기 해석

From computers to compact-disc players, railway engines to robots, / the origins of today's machines can be traced back / to the elaborate mechanical toys / that flourished in the eighteenth century.
컴퓨터에서 CD 플레이어, 철도 엔진, 로봇에 이르기까지 / 오늘날 기계의 기원은 거슬러 올라갈 수 있다 / 정교한 기계 장난감으로 / 18세기에 번성했던

As the first complex machines / produced by man, / automata represented / a proving ground for technology / that would later be harnessed / in the industrial revolution.
최초의 복합 기계로서 / 인간에 의해 만들어진 / 자동 기계 장치는 나타냈다 / 기술에 대한 검증의 장을 / 훗날 이용될 / 산업혁명에서

But their original uses were rather less utilitarian.
하지만 그것들의 원래 용도는 다소 덜 실용적이었다

Automata were the playthings of royalty, / both as a form of entertainment / in palaces and courts across Europe / and as gifts / sent from one ruling family to another.
자동 기계 장치는 왕족들의 장난감이었다 / 오락의 한 형태일 뿐만 아니라 / 유럽 전역의 궁전과 궁정 내의 / 그리고 선물이기도 한 / 한 지배 가문으로부터 다른 곳에 보내지는

As a source of amusement, / the first automata were essentially scaled-down versions / of the elaborate mechanical clocks / that adorned cathedrals.
오락의 원천으로서 / 최초의 자동 기계 장치는 본래 축소된 형태였다 / 정교한 기계식 시계들의 / 대성당을 장식했던

These clocks provided the inspiration / for smaller and increasingly elaborate automata.
이 시계들은 영감을 주었다 / 더 작고 더욱더 정교한 자동 기계 장치에 대한

As these devices became more complicated, / their time-keeping function became less important, / and automata became first and foremost mechanical amusements / in the form of mechanical theaters or moving scenes.
이러한 장치들이 더 복잡해짐에 따라 / 그것들의 시간 측정 기능은 덜 중요해졌다 / 그리고 자동 기계 장치는 최초이자 가장 중요한 기계로 만든 오락거리가 되었다 / 기계식 극장이나 움직이는 장면의 형태로

해석 컴퓨터에서 CD 플레이어, 철도 엔진, 로봇에 이르기까지, 오늘날 기계의 기원은 18세기에 번성했던 정교한 기계 장난감으로 거슬러 올라갈 수 있다. 인간에 의해 만들어진 최초의 복합 기계로서, 자동 기계 장치는 훗날 산업혁명에서 이용될 기술에 대한 검증의 장을 나타냈다. 하지만 그것들의 원래 용도는 다소 덜 실용적이었다. 자동 기계 장치는 유럽 전역의 궁전과 궁정 내의 오락의 한 형태일 뿐만 아니라 한 지배 가문으로부터 다른 곳에 보내지는 선물이기도 한 왕족들의 장난감이었다. 오락의 원천으로서, 최초의 자동 기계 장치는 본래 대성당을 장식했던 정교한 기계식 시계들의 축소된 형태였다. 이 시계들은 더 작고 더욱더 정교한 자동 기계 장치에 대한 영감을 주었다. 이러한 장치들이 더 복잡해짐에 따라, 그것들의 시간 측정 기능은 덜 중요해졌고, 자동 기계 장치는 기계식 극장이나 움직이는 장면의 형태로 최초이자 가장 중요한 기계로 만든 오락거리가 되었다.

① 기계의 역사는 오락의 원천과 관련이 적다.
② 현대의 기계는 실용적이지 않은 기원을 가지고 있다.
③ 유럽 전역의 왕족들은 장난감 산업에 관심이 있었다.
④ 자동 기계 장치의 쇠퇴는 산업혁명과 밀접하게 연관되어 있다.

해설 지문 처음에서 자동 기계 장치가 훗날 산업혁명에서 이용될 기술에 대한 검증의 장을 나타냈지만, 그것들의 원래 용도는 다소 덜 실용적이었다고 하며 자동 기계 장치가 본래 유럽 전역에서 왕족들의 장난감으로서 대성당을 장식하는 정교한 기계식 시계들의 축소된 형태였다고 설명하고 있다. 따라서 '② 현대의 기계는 실용적이지 않은 기원을 가지고 있다'가 이 글의 요지이다.

어휘 trace back to ~으로 거슬러 올라가다 elaborate 정교한
mechanical 기계의 flourish 번성하다 complex 복합의, 복잡한
automaton 자동 기계 장치(복수형: automata)
represent 나타내다, 대표하다 harness 이용하다, 괴롭히다
utilitarian 실용적인 royalty 왕족 court 궁정, 법정
amusement 오락 scaled-down 축소된 adorn 장식하다
cathedral 대성당 complicated 복잡한 foremost 가장 중요한
have to do with ~과 관련이 있다 decline 쇠퇴, 감소
associated with ~과 연관된

15 독해 세부내용 파악 (내용 불일치 파악) 난이도 ★☆☆

끊어읽기 해석

> When Ali graduated, / he decided / he didn't want to join the ranks of commuters / struggling to work every day.
> Ali가 졸업했을 때 / 그는 결심했다 / 통근자들의 대열에 합류하고 싶지 않다고 / 매일 일하기 위해 고군분투하는
>
> He wanted to set up his own online gift-ordering business / so that he could work from home.
> 그는 자신만의 온라인 선물주문 사업을 차리기를 원했다 / 그래서 그가 집에서 일할 수 있도록
>
> He knew / it was a risk / but felt / he would have at least a fighting chance of success.
> 그는 알았다 / 그것이 모험이라는 것을 / 하지만 생각했다 / 그가 적어도 성공할 가능성이 있을 것이라고
>
> Initially, / he and a college friend planned / to start the business together.
> 처음에 / 그와 대학 친구는 ~할 계획이었다 / 함께 그 사업을 시작할
>
> Ali had the idea / and Igor, his friend, had the money / to invest in the company.
> Ali가 아이디어를 냈다 / 그리고 그의 친구인 Igor는 돈이 있었다 / 회사에 투자할
>
> But then just weeks before the launch, / Igor dropped a bombshell: / he said he no longer wanted / to be part of Ali's plans.
> 하지만 (사업) 개시 몇 주 전에 / Igor는 폭탄선언을 했다 / 그는 더 이상 원하지 않는다고 말했다 / Ali의 계획에 참여하고 싶지 않다고
>
> Despite Ali's attempts / to persuade him / to hang fire on his decision, / Igor said he was no longer prepared / to take the risk / and was going to beat a retreat / before it was too late.
> Ali의 시도에도 불구하고 / 그(Igor)를 설득하려는 / 그(Igor)가 (Ali의 사업에 더 이상 참여하지 않으려는) 그의 결정을 미루도록 / Igor는 그가 더 이상 준비가 되지 않았다고 말했다 / 위험을 감수할 / 그리고 철수할 것이라고 / 너무 늦기 전에
>
> However, two weeks later / Igor stole a march on Ali / by launching his own online gift-ordering company.
> 그러나, 2주 후에 / Igor는 Ali에게 선수를 쳤다 / 자신의 온라인 선물주문 회사를 차려서
>
> Ali was shell-shocked / by this betrayal, / but he soon came out fighting.
> Ali는 어쩔 줄을 몰랐다 / 이 배신에 / 그러나 그는 강하게 반응했다
>
> He took Igor's behaviour / as a call to arms / and has persuaded a bank / to lend him the money he needs.
> 그는 Igor의 행동을 받아들였다 / 적절한 조치를 요구하는 사태로 / 그리고 은행을 설득했다 / 그(Ali)에게 필요한 돈을 빌려주도록
>
> Ali's introduction to the business world has certainly been a baptism of fire, / but I'm sure / he will be really successful / on his own.
> Ali의 재계로의 입문은 분명 힘든 시작이었다 / 하지만 나는 확신한다 / 그가 정말 성공할 것이라고 / 혼자 힘으로

해석 Ali가 졸업했을 때, 그는 매일 일하기 위해 고군분투하는 통근자들의 대열에 합류하고 싶지 않다고 결심했다. 그는 자신만의 온라인 선물주문 사업을 차려서 그가 집에서 일할 수 있기를 원했다. 그는 그것이 모험이라는 것을 알았지만 적어도 성공할 가능성이 있을 것이라고 생각했다. 처음에, 그와 대학 친구는 함께 그 사업을 시작할 계획이었다. Ali가 아이디어를 냈고, 그의 친구인 Igor는 회사에 투자할 돈이 있었다. 하지만 (사업) 개시 몇 주 전에, Igor는 폭탄선언을 했는데, 그는 더 이상 Ali의 계획에 참여하고 싶지 않다고 말했다. 그(Igor)가 (Ali의 사업에 더 이상 참여하지 않으려는) 그의 결정을 미루도록 설득하려는 Ali의 시도에도 불구하고, Igor는 더 이

상 위험을 감수할 준비가 되지 않았고 너무 늦기 전에 철수할 것이라고 말했다. 그러나, 2주 후에 Igor는 자신의 온라인 선물주문 회사를 차려서 Ali에게 선수를 쳤다. Ali는 이 배신에 어쩔 줄을 몰랐지만, 강하게 반응했다. 그는 Igor의 행동을 적절한 조치를 요구하는 사태로 받아들였고 그(Ali)에게 필요한 돈을 빌려주도록 은행을 설득했다. Ali의 재계로의 입문은 분명 힘든 시작이었지만, 나는 그가 혼자 힘으로 정말 성공할 것이라고 확신한다.

해설 지문 뒷부분에서 Ali가 Igor의 배신에 어쩔 줄을 몰랐지만, 이러한 Igor의 행동을 적절한 조치를 요구하는 사태로 받아들여 그(Ali)에게 필요한 돈을 빌려주도록 은행을 설득했다고 했으므로, '④ Ali는 은행을 설득하여 Igor에게 돈을 빌려주게 했다'는 것은 지문의 내용과 다르다.

어휘 rank 대열, 줄 commuter 통근자 risk 모험, 위험
launch 개시; 발사하다 drop a bombshell 폭탄선언을 하다
hang fire (행동을) 미루다 steal a march on ~에게 선수를 치다
shell-shocked 어쩔 줄을 모르는 betrayal 배신
come out fighting 강하게 반응하다
a call to arms 적절한 조치를 요구하는 사태
lend 빌려주다, 대출해 주다 introduction 입문, 도입
baptism of fire 힘든 시작, 첫 경험

16 독해 추론 (빈칸 완성 - 연결어) 난이도 ★☆☆

끊어읽기 해석

> Scientists are working / on many other human organs and tissues.
> 과학자들은 연구하고 있다 / 다른 많은 인간의 장기와 조직에 대해
>
> For example, / they have successfully generated, or grown, / a piece of liver.
> 예를 들어 / 그들은 성공적으로 생성하거나 발달시켰다 / 간의 한 부분을
>
> This is an exciting achievement / since people cannot live without a liver.
> 이것은 흥미진진한 업적이다 / 사람들이 간 없이 살 수 없기 때문이다
>
> In other laboratories, / scientists have created a human jawbone and a lung.
> 다른 실험실에서 / 과학자들은 인간의 턱뼈와 폐를 만들었다
>
> While these scientific breakthroughs are very promising, / they are also limited.
> 이러한 과학적 발전은 매우 기대되지만 / 그것들은 제한적이기도 하다
>
> Scientists cannot use cells / for a new organ / from a very diseased or damaged organ.
> 과학자들은 세포를 사용할 수 없다 / 새로운 장기에 / 매우 병들거나 손상된 장기로부터 나온
>
> **(A) Consequently,** / many researchers are working / on a way to use stem cells / to grow completely new organs.
> (A) 그 결과 / 많은 연구원들은 연구하고 있다 / 줄기세포를 사용하는 방법에 대해 / 완전히 새로운 장기를 만들기 위해
>
> Stem cells are very simple cells / in the body / that can develop into any kind of complex cells, / such as skin cells or blood cells and even heart and liver cells.
> 줄기세포는 매우 단순한 세포이다 / 몸 안의 / 어떤 종류의 복잡한 세포로든 발달할 수 있는 / 피부 세포나 혈액 세포, 그리고 심지어는 심장과 간세포와 같은
>
> **(B) In other words,** / stem cells can grow / into all different kinds of cells.
> (B) 다시 말해서 / 줄기세포는 자랄 수 있다 / 모든 다른 종류의 세포로

해석 과학자들은 다른 많은 인간의 장기와 조직에 대해 연구하고 있다. 예를 들어, 그들은 성공적으로 간의 한 부분을 생성하거나 발달시

켰다. 사람들은 간 없이 살 수 없기 때문에 이것은 흥미진진한 업적이다. 다른 실험실에서, 과학자들은 인간의 턱뼈와 폐를 만들었다. 이러한 과학적 발전은 매우 기대되지만, 그것들은 제한적이기도 하다. 과학자들은 매우 병들거나 손상된 장기로부터 나온 세포를 새로운 장기에 사용할 수 없다. (A) 그 결과, 많은 연구원들은 완전히 새로운 장기를 만들기 위해 줄기세포를 사용하는 방법에 대해 연구하고 있다. 줄기세포는 피부 세포나 혈액 세포, 그리고 심지어는 심장과 간세포와 같은 어떤 종류의 복잡한 세포로든 발달할 수 있는 몸 안의 매우 단순한 세포이다. (B) 다시 말해서, 줄기세포는 모든 다른 종류의 세포로 자랄 수 있다.

	(A)	(B)
①	특히	예를 들어
②	게다가	반면에
③	그 결과	다시 말해서
④	따라서	대조적으로

해설 (A) 빈칸 앞 문장은 과학자들은 매우 병들거나 손상된 장기로부터 나온 세포를 새로운 장기에 사용할 수 없다는 내용이고, (A) 빈칸 뒤 문장은 많은 연구원들이 완전히 새로운 장기를 만들기 위해 줄기세포를 사용하는 방법을 연구하고 있다는 결과적인 내용이므로 (A)에는 Consequently(그 결과)가 나와야 한다. (B) 빈칸 앞 문장에 줄기세포는 어떤 종류의 복잡한 세포로든 발달할 수 있다는 내용이 있고, (B) 빈칸 뒤 문장에 줄기세포가 모든 다른 종류의 세포로 자랄 수 있다고 하며 앞 문장을 다시 설명하는 내용이 있으므로 (B)에는 In other words(다시 말해서)가 나와야 한다. 따라서 ③번이 정답이다.

어휘 tissue (세포들로 이뤄진) 조직 liver 간 laboratory 실험실
lung 폐 promising 기대되는, 장래성 있는 cell 세포 organ 장기
diseased 병든 complex 복잡한

---

17 **독해** 추론 (빈칸 완성 - 단어) 난이도 ★☆☆

끊어읽기 해석

To speak of 'the aim' of scientific activity / may perhaps sound a little (A) naive; / for clearly, different scientists have different aims, / and science itself / (whatever that may mean) / has no aims.
과학 활동의 '목표'에 대해 말하는 것은 / 아마도 약간 (A) 순진하게 들릴지도 모른다 / 왜냐하면 분명히, 서로 다른 과학자들은 서로 다른 목표를 가지고 있기 때문이다 / 그리고 과학 그 자체는 / (그것이 무엇을 의미하든) / 목표가 없다

I admit all this.
나는 이 모든 것을 인정한다

And yet it seems / that when we speak of science we do feel, / more or less clearly, / that there is something characteristic of scientific activity; / and since scientific activity looks pretty much like a rational activity, / and since a rational activity must have some aim, / the attempt to describe the aim of science / may not be entirely (B) futile.
그럼에도 불구하고 ~인 것처럼 보인다 / 우리가 과학에 대해 말할 때 우리는 느낀다 / 다소 분명하게 / 과학 활동 특유의 무언가가 있다는 것을 / 그리고 과학 활동이 이성적인 활동과 거의 비슷해 보이기 때문에 / 그리고 이성적인 활동은 어떤 목표를 가지고 있어야 하기 때문에 / 과학의 목표를 설명하려는 시도가 / 완전히 (B) 헛된 것은 아닐 수도 있다

해석 과학 활동의 '목표'에 대해 말하는 것은 아마도 약간 (A) 순진하게 들릴지도 모르는데, 왜냐하면 분명히, 서로 다른 과학자들은 서로 다른 목표를 가지고 있고, 과학 그 자체는 (그것이 무엇을 의미하든) 목표가 없기 때문이다. 나는 이 모든 것을 인정한다. 그럼에도 불구하고 우리가 과학에 대해 말할 때, 우리는 과학 활동 특유의

무언가가 있다는 것을 다소 분명하게 느끼는 것처럼 보인다. 그리고 과학 활동이 이성적인 활동과 거의 비슷해 보이고, 이성적인 활동은 어떤 목표를 가지고 있어야 하기 때문에, 과학의 목표를 설명하려는 시도가 완전히 (B) 헛된 것은 아닐 수도 있다.

	(A)	(B)
①	순진한	헛된
②	합리적인	유익한
③	혼란스러운	용인되는
④	일관성 있는	버려진

해설 (A) 빈칸이 있는 문장에서 빈칸 앞부분에 과학 활동의 목표에 대해 말하는 것이 어떻게 들릴 수 있는지에 대한 내용이 있고, (A) 빈칸 뒤 문장에 서로 다른 과학자들은 서로 다른 목표를 가지고 있으며 과학 그 자체는 목표가 없다는 내용이 있으므로, (A)에는 naive(순진한)가 나와야 적절하다. (B) 빈칸이 있는 문장에서 빈칸 앞부분에 과학 활동이 이성적인 활동과 거의 비슷해 보이고, 이성적인 활동은 어떤 목표를 가지고 있어야 한다고 하며 과학의 목표를 설명하려는 시도가 어떤 것이 아닐 수 있다고 설명하는 내용이 있으므로, (B)에는 futile(헛된)이 나와야 적절하다. 따라서 ①번이 정답이다.

어휘 aim 목표 admit 인정하다 characteristic 특유의
rational 이성적인 attempt 시도 describe 설명하다, 묘사하다
naive 순진한 futile 헛된 reasonable 합리적인
fruitful 유익한, 생산적인 chaotic 혼란스러운
consistent 일관성 있는 discard 버리다

---

18 **독해** 논리적 흐름 파악 (문단 순서 배열) 난이도 ★★☆

끊어읽기 해석

The child that is born today / may possibly have the same faculties / as if he had been born / in the days of Noah; / if it be otherwise, / we possess no means / of determining the difference.
오늘날 태어나는 아이는 / 같은 능력을 가지고 있을 수도 있다 / 그가 태어났을 때와 같이 / 노아의 시대에 / 만약 그렇지 않다면 / 우리는 방법이 없다 / 그 차이를 판단할

(A) That development is entirely under the control / of the influences / exerted by the society / in which the child may chance to live.
그 발달은 전적으로 통제 하에 있다 / 영향력의 / 사회에 의해 가해지는 / 아이가 우연히 살게 될지도 모르는

(B) If such society be altogether denied, / the faculties perish, / and the child grows up a beast / and not a man; / if the society be uneducated and coarse, / the growth of the faculties is early so stunted / as never afterwards to be capable of recovery; / if the society be highly cultivated, / the child will be cultivated also, / and will show, more or less, through life / the fruits of that cultivation.
만약 그러한 사회가 완전히 부정된다면 / 그 (자연적) 능력은 사라진다 / 그리고 아이는 짐승처럼 자란다 / 인간이 아니라 / 만약 그 사회가 무지하고 열등하다면 / 그 능력의 성장이 일찍이 저해된다 / 그 후로는 결코 회복할 수 없을 만큼 / 만약 그 사회가 대단히 교화되어 있다면 / 그 아이 역시 교화될 것이다 / 그리고 거의 일생 동안 보일 것이다 / 그 교화의 결실을

(C) Hence / each generation receives / the benefit of the cultivation / of that which preceded it.
따라서 / 각 세대는 받는다 / 교화의 혜택을 / 그것(각 세대)에 앞선 세대의

(D) But / the equality of the natural faculties / at starting / will not prevent a vast difference / in their ultimate development.
하지만 / 자연적 능력의 평등은 / 시작에 있어서 / 엄청난 차이를 막지는 못할 것이다 / 그들의 궁극적인 발달에 있어서

해석

> 오늘날 태어나는 아이는 그가 노아의 시대에 태어났을 때와 같은 능력을 가지고 있을 수도 있다. 만약 그렇지 않다면, 우리는 그 차이를 판단할 방법이 없다.

(D) 하지만 시작에 있어서 자연적 능력의 평등은 그들의 궁극적인 발달에 있어서 엄청난 차이를 막지는 못할 것이다.

(A) 그 발달은 전적으로 아이가 우연히 살게 될지도 모르는 사회에 의해 가해지는 영향력의 통제 하에 있다.

(B) 만약 그러한 사회가 완전히 부정된다면, 그 (자연적) 능력은 사라지고, 아이는 인간이 아니라 짐승처럼 자란다. 만약 그 사회가 무지하고 열등하다면, 그 후로는 결코 회복할 수 없을 만큼 그 능력의 성장이 일찍이 저해된다. 만약 그 사회가 대단히 교화되어 있다면, 그 아이 역시 교화될 것이고, 거의 일생 동안 그 교화의 결실을 보일 것이다.

(C) 따라서 각 세대는 그것(각 세대)에 앞선 세대의 교화의 혜택을 받는다.

해설 주어진 글에서 오늘날 태어나는 아이는 그가 노아의 시대에 태어났을 때와 같은 능력을 가지고 있을 수 있다고 언급한 뒤 (D)에서 하지만(But) 시작에 있어서 자연적 능력이 평등하더라도 그들의 궁극적인 발달에 있어서 엄청난 차이를 막지는 못할 것이라고 하고, (A)에서 그 발달(That development)이 전적으로 아이가 살게 될 사회의 영향력의 통제 하에 있다고 설명하고 있다. 이어서 (B)에서 만약 그러한 사회가 완전히 부정된다면 그러한 자연적 능력이 사라져 짐승처럼 자라는 한편, 그 사회가 대단히 교화되어 있다면 그 아이 역시 교화될 것이라고 하며 아이가 살게 될 사회에 따라 아이의 발달이 달라진다는 것을 설명한 뒤, (C)에서 따라서(Hence) 각 세대는 앞선 세대의 교화의 혜택을 받는다고 언급하고 있다.

어휘 faculty 능력 possess 가지다, 소유하다 exert 가하다
chance 우연히 ~하다 deny 부정하다 perish 사라지다
coarse 열등한, 거친 stunt 성장을 저해하다; 곡예
capable of ~을 할 수 있는 recovery 회복
cultivate 교화하다, 경작하다 benefit 혜택 precede ~에 앞서다
vast 엄청난

19 독해 추론 (빈칸 완성 - 구) 난이도 ★★☆

끊어읽기 해석

> It is quite clear / that people's view of what English should do / has been strongly influenced / by what Latin does.
> 꽤 분명하다 / 영어가 무엇을 해야 하는지에 대한 사람들의 관점이 ~라는 것이 / 강하게 영향을 받아 왔다 / 라틴어가 무엇을 하는지에 의해
>
> For instance, / there is (or used to be / —it is very infrequently observed / in natural speech today) / a feeling that an infinitive in English / should not be split.
> 예를 들어 / ~이다(혹은 ~이곤 했다 / 이것은 매우 드물게 관찰된다 / 오늘날 자연스러운 구어에서) / 영어에서 부정사가 ~라는 느낌이 / 나누어지면 안 된다는
>
> What this means is / that you should not put anything / between the *to* / which marks an infinitive verb / and the verb itself: / you should say *to go boldly* / and never *to boldly go*.
> 이것이 의미하는 것은 / 당신이 넣지 말아야 한다는 점이다 / 'to' 사이에 / 부정사를 표시하는 / 그리고 동사 그 자체에 / 당신은 'to go boldly(대담하게 하다)'라고 말해야 한다 / 그리고 결코 'to boldly go'라고 말해선 안 된다
>
> This 'rule' is based on Latin, / where the marker of the infinitive is an ending, / and you can no more split it / from the rest of the verb / than you can split *-ing* / from the rest

of its verb / and say *goboldlying* for *going boldly*.
이 '규칙'은 라틴어에 바탕을 두고 있다 / 여기서 부정사의 표시는 끝이다 / 그리고 그것을 더 이상 나눌 수 없다 / 동사의 나머지 부분으로부터 / 당신이 '-ing'를 분리할 수 있는 것과 같이 / 동사의 나머지 부분으로부터 / 그리고 'going boldly'를 'goboldlying'이라고 말할 수 없다

> English speakers clearly do not feel / that to and go belong together as closely as go and -ing.
> 영어 사용자들은 분명히 느끼지 않는다 / 'to'와 'go'가 'go'와 '-ing'만큼 긴밀하게 짝을 이룬다고
>
> They frequently put words / between this kind of to and its verb.
> 그들은 종종 단어를 넣는다 / 이런 종류의 'to'와 그것의 동사 사이에

해석 영어가 무엇을 해야 하는지에 대한 사람들의 관점이 라틴어가 무엇을 하는지에 의해 강하게 영향을 받아 왔음은 꽤 분명하다. 예를 들어, 영어에서 부정사는 나누어지면 안 된다는 느낌이 있다(혹은 느낌이 있곤 했는데, 이것(느낌)은 오늘날 자연스러운 구어에서 매우 드물게 관찰된다). 이것이 의미하는 것은 당신이 부정사를 표시하는 'to'와 동사 그 자체 사이에 어떤 것도 넣지 말아야 한다는 점이다. 당신은 'to go boldly(대담하게 하다)'라고 말해야 하고 결코 'to boldly go'라고 말해선 안 된다. 이 '규칙'은 라틴어에 바탕을 두고 있는데, 여기서 부정사의 표시는 끝이며, 당신이 동사의 나머지 부분으로부터 '-ing'를 분리하여 'going boldly'를 'goboldlying'이라고 말할 수 없는 것과 같이 더 이상 동사의 나머지 부분으로부터 그것(부정사)을 나눌 수 없다. 영어 사용자들은 'to'와 'go'가 'go'와 '-ing'만큼 긴밀하게 짝을 이룬다고 분명히 느끼지 않는다. 그들은 종종 이런 종류의 'to'와 그것의 동사 사이에 단어를 넣는다.

① ~보다 덜 가까이
② ~만큼 긴밀하게
③ ~보다 더 느슨하게
④ ~만큼 막연하게

해설 빈칸 앞부분에서 영어에서 부정사를 표시하는 'to'와 동사 그 자체 사이에 어떤 것도 넣지 말아야 하고, 동사의 나머지 부분으로부터 '-ing'를 나눌 수 없다고 하며 'to boldly go'와 'goboldlying'과 같은 잘못된 예시를 들어 설명하고 있다. 또한 빈칸 뒤 문장에서 영어 사용자들이 종종 이런 종류의 'to'와 그것의 동사 사이에 단어를 넣는다고 했으므로, 빈칸에는 '② ~만큼 긴밀하게'가 들어가야 한다.

어휘 infrequently 드물게 observe 관찰하다 infinitive 부정사
split 나누어지다, 분리하다 boldly 대담하게
closely 가까이, 밀접하게 loosely 느슨하게, 막연하게

20 독해 추론 (빈칸 완성 - 구) 난이도 ★★☆

끊어읽기 해석

> A company may be allowed / to revalue non-current assets.
> 기업은 허용될 수도 있다 / 비유동자산을 재평가하는 것이
>
> Where the fair value of non-current assets increases / this may be reflected / in an adjustment to the value / of the assets shown / in the statement of financial position.
> 비유동자산의 적정 가치가 증가하는 경우에는 / 이것이 반영될 수도 있다 / 가치 조정에 / 보여지는 자산의 / 재무상태표에
>
> As far as possible, / this should reflect the fair value / of assets and liabilities.
> 가능한 한 / 이것은 적정 가치를 반영해야 한다 / 자산과 부채의
>
> However, / the increase in value of a non-current asset / does not necessarily represent an immediate profit / for the company.
> 하지만 / 비유동자산의 가치 증가가 / 반드시 즉각적인 이익을 나타내는 것은 아니다 / 기업에게

그러나 / 비유동자산의 가치 증가가 / 반드시 당장의 이익을 의미하지는 않는다 / 회사에

A profit is made or realized / only when the asset is sold / and the resulting profit is taken / through the income statement.
수익은 발생하거나 실현된다 / 자산이 매각될 때만 / 그리고 그 결과 발생하는 이익이 취해질 때 / 손익계산서를 통해

Until this event occurs / prudence—supported by common sense—requires / that the increase in asset value is retained / in the balance sheet.
이 일이 일어날 때까지 / 상식에 의해 뒷받침되는 이익에 대한 타산은 필요로 한다 / 자산 가치에서의 증가가 유지되는 것을 / 대차대조표에서

Shareholders have the right to any profit / on the sale of company assets, / so the shareholders' stake (equity) is increased / by the same amount / as the increase in asset valuation.
주주들은 어떤 이익에 대해서든 권리가 있다 / 회사 자산의 매각에 따른 / 그래서 주주들의 지분(자본)은 늘어난다 / 동일한 액수만큼 / 자산 평가에서의 증가액과

A revaluation reserve is created / and the balance sheet still balances.
재평가 적립금이 생성된다 / 그리고 대차대조표는 여전히 잔액이 맞아떨어진다

해석　기업은 비유동자산을 재평가하는 것이 허용될 수도 있다. 비유동자산의 적정 가치가 증가하는 경우에는 이것이 재무상태표에 보여지는 자산의 가치 조정에 반영될 수도 있다. 가능한 한, 이것은 자산과 부채의 적정 가치를 반영해야 한다. 그러나, 비유동자산 가치의 증가가 반드시 회사에 당장의 이익을 의미하지는 않는다. 수익은 자산이 매각되고 그 결과 발생하는 이익이 손익계산서를 통해 취해져야만 발생하거나 실현된다. 이 일이 일어날 때까지, 상식에 의해 뒷받침되는 이익에 대한 타산은 자산 가치에서의 증가가 대차대조표에서 유지되는 것을 필요로 한다. 주주들은 회사 자산의 매각에 따른 어떤 이익에 대해서든 권리가 있기 때문에, 주주들의 지분(자본)은 자산 평가에서의 증가액과 동일한 액수만큼 늘어난다. 재평가 적립금이 생성되고 대차대조표는 여전히 잔액이 맞아떨어진다.

　① 적정 가치
　② 실제 원가
　③ 당장의 이익
　④ 거래의 가치

해설　빈칸 뒤 문장에 수익은 자산이 매각되고 그 결과 발생하는 이익이 손익계산서를 통해 취해져야만 발생하거나 실현되기 때문에 이 일(this event)이 일어날 때까지 자산 가치의 증가가 대차대조표에서 유지되는 것이 필요하다는 내용이 있으므로, 빈칸에는 비유동자산의 가치 증가가 반드시 회사에 '③ 당장의 이익'을 의미하지는 않는다는 내용이 들어가야 한다.

어휘　revalue 재평가하다, 평가 절상하다　non-current asset 비유동자산
statement of financial position 재무상태표　liability 부채
income statement 손익계산서
prudence (이익에 대한) 타산, 신중함　common sense 상식
retain 유지하다　balance sheet 대차대조표
shareholder 주주　stake 지분　equity 자본, 평등
reserve 적립금; 비축하다
balance (잔액이) 맞아떨어지다, 균형을 이루다　transaction 거래

17회 | 2019년 서울시 9급

정답

p.134

01	④ 어휘 – 어휘&표현	11	② 독해 – 전체내용 파악
02	① 어휘 – 어휘&표현	12	③ 독해 – 추론
03	① 어휘 – 어휘&표현	13	① 문법 – 동사의 종류
04	② 어휘 – 어휘&표현	14	③ 독해 – 추론
05	② 어휘 – 어휘&표현	15	④ 독해 – 추론
06	④ 어휘 – 생활영어	16	② 독해 – 추론
07	① 문법 – 전치사	17	④ 독해 – 추론
08	① 문법 – 동사의 종류&능동태·수동태	18	③ 독해 – 논리적 흐름 파악
09	③ 문법 – 수 일치	19	③ 독해 – 논리적 흐름 파악
10	④ 문법 – 병치 구문	20	② 독해 – 논리적 흐름 파악

취약영역 분석표

영역	세부 유형	문항 수	소계
어휘	어휘&표현	5	/6
	생활영어	1	
문법	전치사	1	/5
	동사의 종류&능동태·수동태	1	
	수 일치	1	
	병치 구문	1	
	동사의 종류	1	
독해	전체내용 파악	1	/9
	세부내용 파악	0	
	추론	5	
	논리적 흐름 파악	3	
	총계		**/20**

· 자신이 취약한 영역은 '공무원 영어, 이렇게 출제된다!'(문제집 p.8)를 통해 다시 한번 확인하고 학습하시기 바랍니다.

---

01 어휘 | 어휘&표현 | see eye to eye = agree | 난이도 ★★☆

해석 적어도 고등학교 때 그녀는 마침내 그녀의 부모님과 의견이 일치한 한 가지 결정을 내렸다.
① 언쟁을 벌였다
② 반박했다
③ 헤어졌다
④ 동의했다

어휘 at least 적어도 decision 결정 finally 마침내
see eye to eye 의견이 일치하다 quarrel 언쟁을 벌이다
dispute 반박하다 part 헤어지다 agree 동의하다

👍 이것도 알면 **합격!**

see eye to eye(의견이 일치하다)와 유사한 의미의 표현
= concur, be of the same mind, side with

---

02 어휘 | 어휘&표현 | pejorative = derogatory | 난이도 ★★★

해석 정당화는 누군가 문제의 행동에 대한 책임은 인정하지만 그것과 관련된 경멸적인 속성은 부인하는 말이다.
① 경멸적인
② 외향적인
③ 의무적인
④ 불필요한

어휘 justification 정당화, 변명 account 말, 설명 accept 인정하다
responsibility 책임 in question 문제의, 논의가 되고 있는
deny 부인하다 pejorative 경멸적인 quality 속성, 본질
associated 관련된 derogatory 경멸적인 extrovert 외향적인
mandatory 의무적인 redundant 불필요한, 여분의

👍 이것도 알면 **합격!**

pejorative(경멸적인)의 유의어
= negative, derisive, unpleasant

---

03 어휘 | 어휘&표현 | suspected | 난이도 ★★☆

해석 검사는 황열병의 원인으로 먼지와 열악한 위생 시설을 배제했고, 모기가 의심받는 매개체였다.
① 의심받는
② 미개한
③ 발랄한
④ 자원한

어휘 rule out 배제하다 dirt 먼지 sanitation 위생 시설, 공중 위생
yellow fever 황열병 mosquito 모기 carrier 매개체, 보균자
suspected 의심받는 uncivilized 미개한, 야만적인
cheerful 발랄한

👍 이것도 알면 **합격!**

suspected(의심받는)의 유의어
= believed, alleged, assumed

---

04 어휘 | 어휘&표현 | hover | 난이도 ★★☆

해석 일반적으로 말하면, 2018년에 사는 사람들은 현대 시대를 인류 역사의 전체 규모와 비교했을 때 꽤 운이 좋다. 기대 수명은 약 72세 정도를 맴돌며, 한 세기 전만 해도 널리 퍼져있었고 치명적이었던 천연두와 디프테리아 같은 질병들은 예방 가능하거나 치료할 수 있거나 완전히 근절된다.
① 삭감하다
② 맴돌다
③ 시작하다
④ 악화시키다

어휘 generally speaking 일반적으로 말하면 fortunate 운이 좋은
life expectancy 기대 수명 smallpox 천연두
widespread 널리 퍼진 deadly 치명적인
preventable 예방 가능한 curable 치료할 수 있는
altogether 완전히 eradicate 근절하다 curtail 삭감하다
hover 맴돌다, 배회하다 initiate 시작하다 aggravate 악화시키다

05 어휘 어휘&표현 template 난이도 ★★★

해석 우리의 삶과 결정에 본보기를 제공할 수 있는 과거의 사건들에 구체적인 패턴이 있다고 상상하는 것은 달성할 수 없는 확실성에 대한 희망을 역사에 투영하는 것이다.

① 환영   ② 본보기
③ 조사   ④ 소동

어휘 concrete 구체적인 project 투영하다, 투사하다 certainty 확실성
fulfill 이행하다 hallucination 환영 template 본보기, 원형
inquiry 조사, 연구 commotion 소동, 소란

06 어휘 생활영어 It will take about 45 minutes to get to Boston. 난이도 ★☆☆

해석 ① A: 토요일에 본 영화는 어땠어요?
B: 좋았어요. 저는 정말 재미있게 봤어요.
② A: 안녕하세요. 셔츠 몇 벌이 다림질되었으면 좋겠는데요.
B: 네, 언제까지 이것들이 필요하신가요?
③ A: 싱글룸으로 하시겠습니까, 더블룸으로 하시겠습니까?
B: 아, 저만을 위한 거라서 싱글룸이 좋겠네요.
④ A: 보스턴행 다음 비행기는 몇 시인가요?
B: 보스턴에 도착하는 데 약 45분 정도 걸릴 거예요.

해설 ④번에서 A는 보스턴행 다음 비행기의 출발 시각을 묻고 있으므로, 소요 시간을 알려주는 B의 대답 It will take about 45 minutes to get to Boston(보스턴에 도착하는 데 약 45분 정도 걸릴 거예요)은 어울리지 않는다. 따라서 ④번이 정답이다.

어휘 press 다림질하다 get to ~에 도착하다

07 문법 전치사 난이도 ★★☆

해석 발명가 엘리어스 하우는 재봉틀의 발견을 그가 식인종들에게 붙잡혔던 꿈의 결과로 보았다. 그는 그들이 그의 주위에서 춤을 출 때 창 끝에 구멍이 있다는 것을 알아차렸고, 그는 이것이 그의 문제를 해결하기 위해 그가 필요했던 디자인 특징이라는 것을 깨달았다.

해설 ① 동사 + 전치사 동사 attribute는 전치사 to와 함께 'attribute A(the discovery of the sewing machine) to B(a dream)'(A

를 B의 결과로 보다)의 형태로 쓰이므로 전치사 for를 to로 고쳐야 한다.

오답 분석 ② 전치사 + 관계대명사 관계사 뒤에 완전한 절(he was captured by cannibals)이 왔으므로 '전치사 + 관계대명사' 형태가 올 수 있다. '전치사 + 관계대명사'에서 전치사는 선행사 또는 관계절의 동사에 따라 결정되는데, 문맥상 '꿈에서 식인종들에게 붙잡혔다'라는 의미가 되어야 자연스러우므로 전치사 in(~에서)이 관계대명사 which 앞에 와서 in which가 올바르게 쓰였다.
③ 명사절 접속사 완전한 절(there were ~ spears)을 이끌며 동사(noticed)의 목적어 자리에 올 수 있는 명사절 접속사 that이 올바르게 쓰였다. 참고로, as they danced around him은 동사(noticed)와 접속사(that) 사이에 삽입된 부사절이다.
④ to 부정사를 취하는 동사 동사 need는 to 부정사를 목적어로 취하는 동사이므로 to 부정사 to solve가 올바르게 쓰였다.

어휘 discovery 발견 sewing machine 재봉틀
capture 붙잡다, 포획하다 cannibal 식인종 notice 알아차리다
hole 구멍 tip 끝 spear 창 feature 특징, 특성 solve 해결하다

08 문법 동사의 종류&능동태·수동태 난이도 ★★☆

해석 1955년까지 니키타 흐루쇼프는 소비에트 사회주의 공화국 연방에서 스탈린의 후계자로 부상했고, 그는 (그 정책에 의해) 동서양이 경쟁은 계속되되, 덜 대립적인 방식으로 경쟁할 '평화 공존' 정책에 착수했다.

해설 ① 자동사의 쓰임 | 수동태 동사 emerge(부상하다)는 목적어를 취하지 않는 자동사이므로 수동태로 쓰일 수 없다. 따라서 과거완료 수동태 had been emerged as를 과거완료 능동태 had emerged as로 고쳐야 한다.

오답 분석 ② 시제 | 동사 + 전치사 특정 과거시점을 나타내는 표현(By 1955)이 왔으므로 이미 끝난 과거의 일을 나타내는·과거시제 동사 embarked가 올바르게 쓰였고, 동사 embark는 전치사 on과 함께 embark on(~에 착수하다)의 형태로 쓰이므로 전치사 on이 올바르게 쓰였다.
③ 관계부사의 쓰임 관계사 뒤에 완전한 절(East and West ~ competition)이 왔으므로 선행사의 종류에 관계없이 '~에 의한(by which)' 등의 의미로 관계절을 연결하는 관계부사 whereby가 올바르게 쓰였다.
④ 주어 동사 수 일치 | 대명사 수 일치 접속사 and로 연결된 주어(East and West)는 복수 취급하므로 복수 동사 were가 올바르게 쓰였고, 대명사가 지시하는 명사(East and West)가 복수이므로 복수 소유격 대명사 their가 올바르게 쓰였다.

어휘　emerge 부상하다, 나타나다　successor 후계자
　　　embark on ~에 착수하다　coexistence 공존　competition 경쟁
　　　confrontational 대립적인

👍 이것도 알면 **합격!**

④번 보기에서 be동사 뒤에 보어로 to 부정사가 온 were to continue는 '예정'의 의미를 나타내는 be to 용법으로 쓰인 것이며, be to 용법은 문맥에 따라 '예정, 의무, 가능, 운명, 의도'의 의미를 갖는다.

09　문법　수 일치　난이도 ★★☆

해석　오징어, 문어, 그리고 갑오징어는 모두 두족류 동물의 종류이다. 이 동물들 각각은 피부 아래에 색깔이 있는 액체인 색소가 들어 있는 특별한 세포들을 가지고 있다. 두족류 동물은 이 세포들을 피부 쪽으로 또는 피부로부터 멀어지게 이동시킬 수 있다. 이것은 그것이 외관의 무늬와 색을 바꿀 수 있도록 해준다.

해설　③ 관계절 수 일치　주격 관계절(that ~ liquid) 내의 동사는 선행사(special cells)에 수를 일치시켜야 하는데, 선행사 special cells가 복수 명사이므로 단수 동사 contains를 복수 동사 contain으로 고쳐야 한다.

오답　① 가산 명사의 쓰임　가산 명사 type이 복수형 types로 올바르
분석　　게 쓰였다.
　　　② 수량 표현　문맥상 '이 동물들 각각'이라는 의미로 두족류 동물의 각 개체를 지칭하고 있고, 동사 자리에 단수 동사 has가 왔으므로 단수 취급하는 수량 표현 Each(각각)가 올바르게 쓰였다.
　　　④ 5형식 동사의 쓰임　동사 allow는 to 부정사를 목적격 보어로 취하는 5형식 동사이므로 to 부정사 to change가 올바르게 쓰였다.

어휘　squid 오징어　octopus 문어　cuttlefish 갑오징어
　　　cephalopod 두족류 동물　cell 세포
　　　contain ~이 들어 있다, 포함하다　pigment 색소
　　　colored 색깔이 있는　liquid 액체　pattern 무늬
　　　appearance 외관, 겉모습

👍 이것도 알면 **합격!**

to 부정사를 목적격 보어로 취하는 동사들을 알아두자.

• want 목 to ~이 -하는 것을 원하다	• expect 목 to ~이 -할 것을 기대하다
• ask 목 to ~이 -할 것을 요청하다	• tell 목 to ~에게 -하도록 이야기하다
• cause 목 to ~이 -하게 (원인제공)하다	• allow 목 to ~이 -하게 허락하다
• get 목 to ~이 -하게 시키다	• lead 목 to ~이 -하게 이끌다
• force 목 to ~이 -하게 강요하다	• compel 목 to ~이 -하게 강요하다

10　문법　병치 구문　난이도 ★☆☆

해석　도시를 유지하는 것보다 더 중대한 문제가 있다. 사람들이 혼자 일하는 것을 더 편하게 생각함에 따라, 그들은 덜 사회적이게 될지도 모른다. 편안한 운동복이나 목욕 가운을 입고 집에 머무르는 것이 잇따른 업무 회의를 위해 옷을 차려 입는 것보다 더 쉽다!

해설　④ 병치 구문　비교급 구문에서 비교 대상은 같은 품사나 구조끼리 연결되어야 하는데, than 앞에 to 부정사구(to stay ~ a bathrobe)가 왔으므로 than 뒤에도 to 부정사구가 와야 한다. to 부정사구 병치 구문에서 두 번째 나온 to는 생략될 수 있으므로 동명사 getting을 to 부정사 to get 또는 동사원형 get으로 고쳐야 한다.

오답　① 병치 구문 | 동명사의 쓰임　비교급 구문에서 비교의 대상은 같
분석　　은 품사끼리 연결되어야 하는데, than 앞에 명사 problem이 왔으므로 than 뒤에도 명사가 와야 한다. 따라서 명사 역할을 할 수 있는 동명사 maintaining이 올바르게 쓰였다.
　　　② 비교급 표현　문맥상 '덜 사회적이게 되다'라는 의미가 되어야 자연스러우므로, 부사 little의 비교급 less(더 적게)가 형용사 social(사회적인) 앞에 올바르게 쓰였다.
　　　③ 비교급 표현　비교급 표현은 '형용사/부사의 비교급 + than' 의 형태로 나타내므로 형용사 easy의 비교급 easier가 than 과 함께 올바르게 쓰였다.

어휘　serious 중대한, 심각한　maintain 유지하다
　　　comfortable 편하게 생각하는, 편안한　social 사회적인
　　　bathrobe 목욕 가운　yet another 잇따라, 꼬리를 물고

👍 이것도 알면 **합격!**

to 부정사구 병치 구문에서 두 번째 나온 to는 생략될 수 있다.

(ex) Keith decided to pack up and (to) move to a different hotel. Keith는 짐을 챙겨서 다른 호텔로 옮기기로 결정했다.
It is important to eat sensibly and (to) exercise regularly.
분별 있게 먹고 규칙적으로 운동하는 것은 중요하다.

11　독해　전체내용 파악 (제목 파악)　난이도 ★★☆

끊어읽기 해석

Economists say / that production of an information good involves / high fixed costs but low marginal costs.
경제학자들은 말한다 / 정보재의 생산은 수반한다고 / 높은 고정 비용 그러나 낮은 한계 비용을

The cost of producing the first copy / of an information good / may be substantial, / but the cost of producing(or reproducing) additional copies / is negligible.
초본을 제작하는 비용은 / 정보재의 / 상당할지도 모른다 / 하지만 추가 사본을 제작(또는 복제)하는 비용은 / 무시해도 될 정도이다

This sort of cost structure has / many important implications.
이런 종류의 비용 구조는 가지고 있다 / 많은 중요한 의미를

For example, / cost-based pricing just doesn't work: / a 10 or 20 percent markup / on unit cost / makes no sense / when unit cost is zero.
예를 들어 / 원가 기반 가격은 효과가 없다 / 10퍼센트 또는 20퍼센트 가격 인상은 / 단위 원가에 대한 / 말이 되지 않는다 / 단위 원가가 0일 때

You must price your information goods / according to consumer value, / not according to your production cost.
당신은 당신의 정보재의 가격을 책정해야 한다 / 소비자 가치에 따라 / 당신의 생산비에 따른 것이 아닌

해석　경제학자들은 정보재의 생산은 높은 고정 비용 그러나 낮은 한계 비용을 수반한다고 말한다. 정보재의 초본을 제작하는 비용은 상당할지도 모르지만, 추가 사본을 제작(또는 복제)하는 비용은 무시해도 될 정도이다. 이런 종류의 비용 구조는 많은 중요한 의미를 가지고 있다. 예를 들어, 원가 기반 가격은 효과가 없다. 단위 원가가 0일 때 단위 원가에 대한 10퍼센트 또는 20퍼센트 가격 인상은 말이 되지 않는다. 당신은 당신의 생산비에 따른 것이 아닌 소비자 가치에 따라 당신의 정보재의 가격을 책정해야 한다.

① 저작권을 보호하는 것
② 정보재 가격 책정
③ 지적 재산으로서의 정보
④ 기술 변화의 비용

해설 지문 처음에서 정보재의 초본을 제작하는 비용은 상당할지도 모르지만 추가 사본을 제작하는 비용은 무시해도 될 정도라고 언급한 뒤, 지문의 마지막에서 생산비가 아닌 소비자 가치에 따라 정보재의 가격을 책정해야 한다고 설명하고 있다. 따라서 이 지문의 제목을 '정보재 가격 책정'이라고 표현한 ②번이 정답이다.

어휘 economist 경제학자   production 생산
information good 정보재   fixed cost 고정 비용
marginal cost 한계 비용   substantial 상당한
negligible 무시해도 될 정도의   implication 의미, 암시
markup 가격 인상   unit cost 단위 원가, 제조 단가
make sense 말이 되다, 타당하다   price 가격을 책정하다
copyright 저작권   property 재산

12 독해 추론 (지칭 추론)   난이도 ★★☆

끊어읽기 해석

Dracula ants get their name / for the way / they sometimes drink / the blood of their own young.
드라큘라 개미는 이름을 얻는다 / 방법으로 인해 / 그들이 때때로 마시는 / 자기 새끼의 피를

But / this week, / ① the insects have earned / a new claim to fame.
하지만 / 이번 주에 / ① 이 곤충들은 얻었다 / 새로운 유명한 이유를

Dracula ants of the species *Mystrium camillae* / can snap their jaws / together / so fast, / you could fit / 5,000 strikes / into the time / it takes us to blink an eye.
'Mystrium camillae'종의 드라큘라 개미는 / 그들의 턱을 꽉 물 수 있다 / 함께 붙도록 / 아주 빠르게 / 당신은 들어맞게 할 수 있다 / 5,000번의 타격을 / 시간에 / 우리가 눈을 깜빡이는 데 걸리는

This means / ② the blood-suckers wield / the fastest known movement / in nature, / according to a study / published this week / in the journal *Royal Society Open Science*.
이것은 의미한다 / ② 그 흡혈 동물들이 행사한다는 것을 / 가장 빠르다고 알려진 움직임을 / 자연에서 / 한 연구에 따르면 / 이번 주에 발표된 / 『Royal Society Open Science』지에서

Interestingly, / the ants produce / their record-breaking snaps / simply by pressing their jaws together / so hard / that ③ they bend.
흥미롭게도, / 그 개미들은 만들어 낸다 / 그들의 기록적인 꽉 물기를 / 단순히 그들의 턱을 함께 누름으로써 / 매우 세게 / ③ 그것들이 구부러지도록

This stores energy / in one of the jaws, / like a spring, / until it slides past the other and lashes out / with extraordinary speed and force— / reaching a maximum velocity / of over 200 miles per hour.
이것은 에너지를 저장한다 / 한쪽 턱에 / 용수철처럼 / 다른 쪽 턱을 미끄러지듯이 지나쳐 강타할 때까지 / 놀라운 속도와 힘으로 / 최대 속도에 도달하면서 / 시속 200마일이 넘는

It's kind of like what happens / when you snap your fingers, / only 1,000 times faster.
이것은 일어나는 일과 비슷하다 / 당신이 손가락을 탁 소리가 나도록 재빨리 움직일 때 / 단지 1,000배 더 빠르게

Dracula ants are secretive predators / as ④ they prefer to hunt / under the leaf litter or in subterranean tunnels.
드라큘라 개미는 비밀스러운 포식자들이다 / ④ 그들은 사냥하는 것을 선호하기 때문에 / 낙엽이나 지하 터널 안에서

해석 드라큘라 개미는 그들이 때때로 자기 새끼의 피를 마시는 방법으로 인해 이름을 얻는다. 하지만 이번 주에, ① 이 곤충들은 새로운 유명한 이유를 얻었다. 'Mystrium camillae'종의 드라큘라 개미는 아주 빠르게 그들의 턱을 함께 붙도록 꽉 물 수 있어서, 당신은

5,000번의 타격을 우리가 눈을 깜빡이는 데 걸리는 시간에 들어맞게 할 수 있다. 이번 주에 『Royal Society Open Science』지에서 발표된 한 연구에 따르면, 이것은 ② 그 흡혈 동물들이 자연에서 가장 빠르다고 알려진 움직임을 행사한다는 것을 의미한다. 흥미롭게도, 그 개미들은 ③ 그것들(턱)이 구부러지도록 단순히 그들의 턱을 함께 매우 세게 누름으로써 그들의 기록적인 꽉 물기를 만들어 낸다. 이것은 다른 쪽 턱을 미끄러지듯이 지나쳐 놀라운 속도와 힘으로 강타할 때까지 시속 200마일이 넘는 최대 속도에 도달하면서 용수철처럼 한쪽 턱에 에너지를 저장한다. 이것은 일종의 당신이 손가락을 탁 소리가 나도록 재빨리 움직일 때 일어나는 일과 비슷한데, 단지 1,000배 더 빠른 것이다. ④ 그들은 낙엽이나 지하 터널 안에서 사냥하는 것을 선호하기 때문에 드라큘라 개미는 비밀스러운 포식자들이다.

해설 ①, ②, ④번 모두 드라큘라 개미를 지칭하지만, ③번은 개미의 턱을 지칭하므로 ③번이 정답이다.

어휘 earn 얻다   claim to fame 유명한 이유
snap 꽉 물다, 탁 소리가 나도록 재빨리 움직이다; 꽉 물기   jaw 턱
blink (눈을) 깜박이다   blood-sucker 흡혈 동물   wield 행사하다
record-breaking 기록적인   store 저장하다   spring 용수철
slide 미끄러지듯이 움직이다   lash out 강타하다
extraordinary 놀라운, 대단한   maximum 최대의   velocity 속도
secretive 비밀스러운   predator 포식자   subterranean 지하의

13 문법 동사의 종류   난이도 ★★☆

해석 나는 독일의 기차에서 바닥에 앉아 당신에게 편지를 쓰고 있다. 기차는 붐비고, 좌석은 다 찼다. 그러나, 이미 앉아 있는 사람들이 그들의 자리를 내주도록 하는 '안심 고객'이라는 특별한 등급이 있다.

해설 ① 사역동사의 쓰임 빈칸은 동사 make의 목적격 보어 자리이다. 문맥상 '이미 앉아 있는 사람들이 자리를 내주도록 한다'는 의미가 되어야 자연스러우므로 '(자리를) 차지하다'를 의미하는 take가 쓰인 ②, ④번은 정답이 될 수 없다. 동사 make는 목적격 보어로 원형 부정사를 취하는 사역동사이므로 ① give up이 정답이다.

어휘 crowded 붐비는   give up ~을 내주다, 넘겨주다

👍 이것도 알면 **합격!**

지시대명사 those는 '~한 사람들'이란 뜻으로, 이때 반드시 뒤에서 수식어(전치사구, 관계절, 분사)의 꾸밈을 받는다.

(ex) Only **those** <u>who have registered in advance</u> can attend the seminar.   수식어(관계절)
미리 등록한 사람들만 세미나에 참석할 수 있다.

Those <u>caught stealing</u> will be reported to the police.   수식어(분사)
절도행위로 붙잡힌 사람들은 경찰에 신고될 것이다.

14 독해 추론 (빈칸 완성 - 연결어)   난이도 ★★☆

끊어읽기 해석

A country's wealth plays a central role / in education, / so lack of funding and resources / from a nation-state / can weaken a system.
한 나라의 부는 중심적인 역할을 한다 / 교육에서 / 그래서 자금과 자원의 부족은 / 국가로부터의 / 제도를 약화시킬 수 있다

Governments / in sub-Saharan Africa / spend only 2.4

percent / of the world's public resources / on education, / yet 15 percent / of the school-age population / lives there.
정부들은 / 사하라 사막 이남 아프리카의 / 2.4퍼센트만을 사용한다 / 전 세계 공공 자원의 / 교육에 / 하지만 15퍼센트가 / 취학 연령 인구의 / 그곳에 산다

Conversely, / the United States spends 28 percent / of all the money / spent in the world / on education, / yet it houses / only 4 percent / of the school-age population.
반대로 / 미국은 28퍼센트를 사용한다 / 모든 돈의 / 전 세계에서 지출되는 / 교육에 / 하지만 그것은 수용한다 / 4퍼센트만을 / 취학 연령 인구의

해석 한 나라의 부는 교육에서 중심적인 역할을 해서, 국가로부터의 자금과 자원의 부족은 제도를 약화시킬 수 있다. 사하라 사막 이남 아프리카의 정부들은 전 세계 공공 자원의 2.4퍼센트만을 교육에 사용하지만, 취학 연령 인구의 15퍼센트가 그곳에 산다. 반대로, 미국은 전 세계에서 지출되는 모든 돈의 28퍼센트를 교육에 사용하지만, 그것은 취학 연령 인구의 4퍼센트만을 수용한다.

① 그럼에도 불구하고　　② 게다가
③ 반대로　　④ 비슷하게

해설 빈칸 앞 문장은 사하라 사막 이남 아프리카 정부들은 전 세계 공공 자원의 2.4퍼센트만을 교육에 사용하지만 취학 연령 인구의 15퍼센트가 그곳에 산다는 내용이고, 빈칸 뒤 문장은 미국은 전 세계에서 지출되는 모든 돈의 28퍼센트를 교육에 사용하고 있지만 취학 연령 인구의 4퍼센트만을 수용하고 있다는 대조적인 내용이다. 따라서 대조를 나타내는 연결어인 ③ Conversely(반대로)가 정답이다.

어휘 wealth 부, 재산　central 중심적인, 가장 중요한　education 교육
lack 부족, 결핍　funding 자금　resource 자원
weaken 약화시키다　population 인구　house 수용하다

15 독해 추론 (빈칸 완성 - 구)　난이도 ★★☆

끊어읽기 해석

"Highly conscientious employees do a series of things better / than the rest of us," / says University of Illinois psychologist Brent Roberts, / who studies conscientiousness.
"매우 성실한 직원들은 일련의 업무를 더 잘합니다 / 우리 중 나머지 사람들보다" / 일리노이 대학의 심리학자 Brent Roberts는 말한다 / 성실함을 연구하는

Roberts owes their success / to "hygiene" factors.
Roberts는 그들의 성공을 돌린다 / '위생'요인들의 덕으로

Conscientious people have a tendency / to organize their lives well.
성실한 사람들은 경향이 있다 / 자신의 삶을 잘 정리하는

A disorganized, unconscientious person / might lose 20 or 30 minutes / rooting through their files / to find the right document, / an inefficient experience / conscientious folks tend to avoid.
체계적이지 못하고 불성실한 사람은 / 20분 또는 30분을 허비할지도 모른다 / 그들의 파일들을 뒤지면서 / 알맞은 서류를 찾기 위해 / 비효율적인 경험인 / 성실한 사람들은 피하는 경향이 있는

Basically, / by being conscientious, / people sidestep stress / they'd otherwise create / for themselves.
근본적으로 / 성실해짐으로써, / 사람들은 스트레스를 피한다 / 그렇지 않으면 만들어 냈을지도 모르는 / 그들 스스로

해석 "매우 성실한 직원들은 우리 중 나머지 사람들보다 일련의 업무를 더 잘합니다"라고 성실함을 연구하는 일리노이 대학의 심리학자 Brent Roberts는 말한다. Roberts는 그들의 성공을 '위생' 요인들

의 덕으로 돌린다. 성실한 사람들은 자신의 삶을 잘 정리하는 경향이 있다. 체계적이지 못하고 불성실한 사람은 알맞은 서류를 찾기 위해 그들의 파일들을 뒤지면서 20분 또는 30분을 허비할지도 모르는데, 이것은 성실한 사람들은 피하는 경향이 있는 비효율적인 경험이다. 근본적으로, 성실해짐으로써, 사람들은 그렇지 않으면 그들 스스로 만들어 냈을지도 모르는 스트레스를 피한다.

① 실패를 처리한다
② 빈틈없는 일을 한다
③ 규범을 따른다
④ 스트레스를 피한다

해설 빈칸이 있는 문장을 통해 빈칸에 성실해짐으로써 사람들이 그렇지 않았으면 스스로 만들어 냈을지도 모르는 무엇을 하는지에 대한 내용이 나와야 적절하다는 것을 알 수 있다. 빈칸 앞 문장에서 체계적이지 못하고 불성실한 사람은 알맞은 서류를 찾기 위해 시간을 허비할지도 모르는데, 이것은 성실한 사람들은 피하는 경향이 있는 비효율적인 경험이라고 했으므로, 성실해짐으로써 사람들은 '스트레스를 피한다'라고 한 ④번이 정답이다.

어휘 conscientious 성실한, 양심적인　a series of 일련의
psychologist 심리학자　hygiene 위생　tendency 경향
organize 정리하다, 조직하다　disorganized 체계적이지 못한
root 뒤지다, 파헤치다　inefficient 비효율적인　folk 사람들
avoid 피하다　otherwise 그렇지 않으면　deal with 처리하다
setback 실패, 차질　thorough 빈틈없는, 철저한　norm 규범
sidestep 피하다, 회피하다

16 독해 추론 (빈칸 완성 - 구)　난이도 ★★☆

끊어읽기 해석

Climate change, deforestation, widespread pollution / and the sixth mass extinction of biodiversity / all define living / in our world today / —an era / that has come to be known as "the Anthropocene".
기후 변화, 삼림 파괴, 널리 퍼진 공해 / 그리고 생물 다양성의 여섯 번째 대량 멸종은 / 모두 사는 것을 정의한다 / 오늘날 우리 세계에 / 시대인 / '인류세'라고 알려진

These crises are underpinned / by production and consumption / which greatly exceeds ecological limits, / but blame is far from evenly shared.
이러한 위기들은 뒷받침된다 / 생산과 소비에 의해 / 생태계의 한계를 크게 초과하는 / 하지만 책임은 전혀 균등하게 공유되지 않는다

The world's 42 wealthiest people own / as much as the poorest 3.7 billion, / and they generate / far greater environmental impacts.
세계에서 가장 부유한 42명이 소유하고 있다 / 가장 가난한 37억 명만큼을 / 그리고 그들은 만들어 낸다 / 훨씬 더 큰 환경적인 영향력을

Some have therefore proposed / using the term "Capitalocene" / to describe this era / of ecological devastation and growing inequality, / reflecting capitalism's logic / of endless growth and the accumulation of wealth in fewer pockets.
따라서 어떤 사람들은 제안해왔다 / '자본세'라는 용어를 사용하는 것을 / 이러한 시대를 묘사하기 위해 / 생태계의 황폐화와 증가하는 불평등의 / 자본주의의 논리를 반영하면서 / 끝없는 성장과 더 소수의 주머니로의 부의 축적이라는

해석 기후 변화, 삼림 파괴, 널리 퍼진 공해와 생물 다양성의 여섯 번째 대량 멸종은 모두 '인류세'라고 알려진 시대인 오늘날 우리 세계에 사는 것을 정의한다. 이러한 위기들은 생태계의 한계를 크게 초과하는 생산과 소비에 의해 뒷받침되고 있지만, 책임은 전혀 균등하게 공유되지 않는다. 세계에서 가장 부유한 42명이 가장 가난

한 37억 명만큼을 소유하고 있으며, 그들은 훨씬 더 큰 환경적 영향력을 만들어 낸다. 따라서 어떤 사람들은 끝없는 성장과 <u>더 소수의 주머니로의 부의 축적</u>이라는 자본주의의 논리를 반영하면서 이러한 생태계의 황폐화와 증가하는 불평등의 시대를 묘사하기 위해 '자본세'라는 용어를 사용하는 것을 제안해왔다.

① 여전히 우리가 도달할 수 있는 더 나은 세상
② 더 소수의 주머니로의 부의 축적
③ 기후 변화에 대한 효과적인 대응
④ 더 성공할 수 있는 미래에 대한 불타는 욕망

해설　빈칸이 있는 문장을 통해 빈칸에 끝없는 성장과 어떠한 자본주의의 논리인지에 관한 내용이 와야 한다는 것을 알 수 있다. 지문 중간에서 세계에서 가장 부유한 42명이 가장 가난한 37억 명만큼 소유하고 있다고 설명하고 있으므로 어떤 사람들은 끝없는 성장과 '더 소수의 주머니로의 부의 축적'이라는 자본주의의 논리를 반영하여 '자본세'라는 용어를 사용하는 것을 제안했다고 한 ②번이 정답이다.

어휘　deforestation 삼림 파괴　widespread 널리 퍼진
pollution 공해, 오염　mass 대량의　extinction 멸종
biodiversity 생물의 다양성　define 정의하다　era 시대
crisis 위기　underpin 뒷받침하다　consumption 소비
exceed 초과하다　ecological 생태계의　blame 책임, 탓
far from 전혀 ~이 아닌　evenly 균등하게
generate 만들어 내다, 발생하다　environmental 환경적인
devastation 황폐화　inequality 불평등　reflect 반영하다
capitalism 자본주의　logic 논리　endless 끝없는, 무한한
accumulation 축적　effective 효과적인　viable 성공할 수 있는

17　독해　추론 (빈칸 완성 - 구)　난이도 ★★★

끊어읽기 해석

Ever since the time of ancient Greek tragedy, / Western culture has been haunted / by the figure of the revenger.
고대 그리스의 비극 시대 이후로 / 서양 문화는 시달려왔다 / 복수자의 형상에

He or she stands / on a whole series of borderlines: / between civilization and barbarity, / between <u>an individual's accountability / to his or her own conscience</u> / and the community's need / for the rule of law, / between the conflicting demands / of justice and mercy.
그 또는 그녀는 서 있다 / 모든 일련의 경계선 위에 / 문명과 야만 사이에 / <u>한 개인의 책임</u> 사이에 / <u>그 혹은 그녀 자신의 양심에 대한</u> / 그리고 공동체의 필요 / 법의 지배에 대한 / 상반되는 요구 사이에 / 정의와 자비의

Do we have a right / to exact revenge / against those who have destroyed our loved ones?
우리는 권리를 가지고 있는가 / 복수를 가할 / 우리가 사랑하는 사람들을 파괴한 자들에 대한

Or / should we leave vengeance / to the law or to the gods?
아니면 / 우리는 복수를 맡겨야 하는가 / 법이나 신들에게

And if we do take action / into our own hands, / are we not reducing ourselves / to the same moral level / as the original perpetrator / of murderous deeds?
그리고 만약 우리가 조치를 취한다면 / 스스로 / 우리는 우리 자신을 낮추는 것이 아닌가 / 같은 도덕적인 수준으로 / 원래의 가해자와 / 살인 행위의

해석　고대 그리스의 비극 시대 이후로, 서양 문화는 복수자의 형상에 시달려왔다. 그 또는 그녀는 문명과 야만 사이에, <u>그 혹은 그녀 자신의 양심에 대한 한 개인의 책임</u>과 법의 지배에 대한 공동체의 필요 사이에, 정의와 자비의 상반되는 요구 사이에 있는 모든 일련의 경계선 위에 서 있다. 우리는 우리가 사랑하는 사람들을 파괴한 자

들에 대한 복수를 가할 권리를 가지고 있는가? 아니면 우리는 복수를 법이나 신들에게 맡겨야 하는가? 그리고 만약 우리가 스스로 조치를 취한다면, 우리는 살인 행위의 원래 가해자와 같은 도덕적인 수준으로 우리 자신을 낮추는 것이 아닌가?

① 타락한 상태로부터의 복수자의 구원
② 인간의 잔혹 행위에 대한 신성한 복수
③ 부패한 정치인들의 도덕적 타락
④ 그 혹은 그녀 자신의 양심에 대한 한 개인의 책임

해설　빈칸이 있는 문장을 통해 빈칸에 복수자가 어떠한 것과 법의 지배에 대한 공동체의 필요 사이의 경계선 위에 있는지에 대한 내용이 나와야 적절하다는 것을 알 수 있다. 빈칸 뒤 문장에서 우리에게 사랑하는 사람들을 파괴한 자들에게 복수를 가할 권리가 있는지 아니면 복수를 법이나 신들에게 맡겨야 하는지 묻고 있으므로, '그 혹은 그녀 자신의 양심에 대한 한 개인의 책임'과 법의 지배에 대한 공동체의 필요 사이라고 한 ④번이 정답이다.

어휘　ancient 고대의　tragedy 비극　figure 형상　revenger 복수자
borderline 경계선　civilization 문명　barbarity 야만
conflicting 상반되는　justice 정의　mercy 자비　exact 가하다
vengeance 복수　take action 조치를 취하다　moral 도덕적인
perpetrator 가해자　murderous 살인적인　deed 행위
redemption 구원　depraved 타락한, 부패한
atrocity 잔혹 행위　depravity 타락, 부패　accountability 책임
conscience 양심, 가책

18　독해　논리적 흐름 파악 (무관한 문장 삭제)　난이도 ★★☆

끊어읽기 해석

It seems to me possible / to name four kinds of reading, / each with a characteristic manner and purpose.
나에게는 가능한 것처럼 보인다 / 네 종류의 독서를 이름 짓는 것이 / 각각 독특한 방식과 목적을 가진

The first is reading / for information / —reading to learn / about a trade, or politics, / or how to accomplish something.
첫째는 독서이다 / 정보를 얻기 위한 / 배우기 위해 읽는 것인 / 무역이나 정치에 대해 / 또는 어떤 것을 성취하는 방법

① We read a newspaper / this way, / or most textbooks, / or directions / on how to assemble a bicycle.
우리는 신문을 읽는다 / 이런 식으로 / 또는 대부분의 교과서 / 또는 지시 사항을 / 자전거를 조립하는 방법에 대한

② With most of this material, / the reader can learn / to scan the page quickly, / coming up with what he needs / and ignoring what is irrelevant to him, / like the rhythm of the sentence, or the play of metaphor.
이 자료의 대부분을 가지고 / 독자는 배울 수 있다 / 페이지를 빠르게 훑어보는 법을 / 그가 필요한 것을 찾아내면서 / 그리고 그와 무관한 것을 무시하면서 / 문장의 리듬이나 은유의 유희와 같은

③ We also register / a track of feeling / through the metaphors and associations of words.
우리는 또한 나타낸다 / 감정의 궤적을 / 은유와 단어들의 연관성을 통해

④ Courses in speed reading can help us read / for this purpose, / training the eye / to jump quickly / across the page.
속독 강좌는 우리가 책을 읽는 것을 도와줄 수 있다 / 이러한 목적을 위해 / 눈을 훈련시키면서 / 빠르게 이동하도록 / 페이지 전체에 걸쳐

해석　나에게는 각각 독특한 방식과 목적을 가진 네 종류의 독서를 이름 짓는 것이 가능한 것처럼 보인다. 첫째는 정보를 얻기 위한 독서로 무역이나 정치, 또는 어떤 것을 성취하는 방법에 대해 배우기 위해 읽는 것이다. ① 우리는 이런 식으로 신문이나, 대부분의 교과서,

또는 자전거를 조립하는 방법에 대한 지시 사항을 읽는다. ② 이 자료의 대부분을 가지고, 그가 필요한 것을 찾아내고 문장의 리듬이나 은유의 유희와 같은 그와 무관한 것을 무시하면서 독자는 페이지를 빠르게 훑어보는 법을 배울 수 있다. ③ 우리는 또한 은유와 단어들의 연관성을 통해 감정의 궤적을 나타낸다. ④ 속독 강좌는 페이지 전체에 걸쳐 빠르게 이동하도록 눈을 훈련시키면서 우리가 이러한 목적을 위해 책을 읽는 것을 도와줄 수 있다.

해설   지문 처음에서 정보를 얻기 위한 독서를 언급하고, ①, ②번에서 신문이나, 교과서 등을 이런 식으로 읽고, 이 자료를 가지고 독자는 페이지를 빨리 훑어보는 법을 배울 수 있다고 설명한 뒤, ④번에서 속독 강좌는 눈이 빠르게 이동하도록 훈련 시켜 우리가 이러한 목적(정보 얻기)을 위해 책을 읽는 데 도움을 준다고 했으므로 모두 지문의 흐름과 관련이 있다. 그러나 ③번은 '은유와 단어들의 연관성을 통한 감정 표현'이라는 내용으로 지문 전반의 내용과 관련이 없다. 따라서 ③번이 정답이다.

어휘   characteristic 독특한, 특유의 purpose 목적 information 정보
trade 무역 politics 정치 accomplish 성취하다
direction 지시, 안내 assemble 조립하다 material 자료
scan 훑어보다 ignore 무시하다 irrelevant 무관한, 상관없는
metaphor 은유 register 나타내다, 표하다 association 연관성

특히 집단주의 문화권에서는, 직업은 오히려 더 큰 집단에 대한 의무를 이행하는 것으로 여겨질 수 있다. ③ 이러한 상황에서, 우리는 그 또는 그녀가 속한 직장 조직과 그 조직을 구성하는 사람들을 향한 개인의 사회적 의무 때문에 한 직장에서 다른 직장으로의 더 적은 개인의 이동을 발견할 것을 예상한다. 개인주의 문화권에서는, 직업을 자신으로부터 분리하는 것이 더 쉽기 때문에 한 직장을 떠나 다른 직장으로 가는 것을 고려하는 것이 더 쉽다. 다른 직업도 같은 목표를 쉽게 달성할 수 있을 것이다.

해설   ③번 앞 문장에 집단주의 문화권에서는 직업이 더 큰 집단에 대한 의무를 이행하는 것으로 여겨질 수 있다는 내용이 있으므로, ③번 자리에 이러한 상황(this situation)에서 우리는 직장 조직과 조직의 구성원에 대한 개인의 사회적 의무로 인해 개인의 직장 이동이 더 적을 것을 예상한다는 주어진 문장이 나와야 지문이 자연스럽게 연결된다. 따라서 ③번이 정답이다.

어휘   situation 상황 individual 개인 obligation 의무
organization 조직 comprise 구성하다 manifest 드러내다
aspect 측면 means 수단 accumulate 축적하다
collectivistic 집단주의의 fulfill 이행하다 separate 분리하다
accomplish 달성하다

19 독해 논리적 흐름 파악 (문장 삽입)   난이도 ★★☆

끊어읽기 해석

In this situation, / we would expect to find / less movement of individuals / from one job to another / because of the individual's social obligations / toward the work organization / to which he or she belongs / and to the people / comprising that organization.
이러한 상황에서 / 우리는 발견할 것을 예상한다 / 더 적은 개인의 이동을 / 한 직장에서 다른 직장으로의 / 개인의 사회적 의무 때문에 / 직장 조직을 향한 / 그 또는 그녀가 속한 / 그리고 사람들을 향한 / 그 조직을 구성하는

Cultural differences / in the meaning of work / can manifest themselves / in other aspects as well.
문화적 차이는 / 직업의 의미에 있어서의 / 스스로를 드러낼 수 있다 / 다른 측면에서도

(①) For example, / in American culture, / it is easy / to think of work simply as a means / to accumulate money / and make a living.
예를 들어 / 미국 문화에서는 / 쉽다 / 직업을 단순히 수단으로 생각하기 / 돈을 축적하는 / 그리고 생계를 유지하는

(②) In other cultures, / especially collectivistic ones, / work may be seen / more as fulfilling an obligation / to a larger group.
다른 문화권에서는 / 특히 집단주의 문화권에서는 / 직업은 여겨질 수 있다 / 오히려 의무를 이행하는 것으로 / 더 큰 집단에 대한

(③) In individualistic cultures, / it is easier to consider / leaving one job / and going to another / because it is easier / to separate jobs from the self.
개인주의 문화권에서는 / 고려하는 것이 더 쉽다 / 한 직장을 떠나는 것을 / 그리고 다른 직장으로 가는 것을 / 더 쉽기 때문에 / 직업을 자신으로부터 분리하는 것이

(④) A different job will just as easily accomplish / the same goals.
다른 직업도 쉽게 달성할 수 있을 것이다 / 같은 목표를

해석   직업의 의미에 있어서의 문화적 차이는 다른 측면에서도 스스로를 드러낼 수 있다. 예를 들어, 미국 문화에서는, 직업을 단순히 돈을 축적하고 생계를 유지하는 수단으로 생각하기 쉽다. 다른 문화권,

20 독해 논리적 흐름 파악 (문단 순서 배열)   난이도 ★★☆

끊어읽기 해석

㉠ To navigate in the dark, / a microbat flies / with its mouth open, / emitting high-pitched squeaks / that humans cannot hear.
어둠 속에서 길을 찾기 위해 / 작은 박쥐는 날아간다 / 입을 벌린 채로 / 아주 높은 끼익 하는 소리를 내뿜으면서 / 인간이 들을 수 없는

Some of these sounds / echo off flying insects / as well as tree branches and other obstacles / that lie ahead.
이 소리들 중 일부는 / 날아다니는 곤충들에서 반향한다 / 나무 가지들과 다른 장애물들에서뿐만 아니라 / 앞에 놓여 있는

The bat listens to the echo / and gets an instantaneous picture / in its brain / of the objects / in front of it.
박쥐는 그 메아리를 듣는다 / 그리고 즉각적인 모습을 얻는다 / 그것의 뇌에 / 물체의 / 그 앞에 있는

㉡ Microbats, / the small, insect-eating bats / found in North America, / have tiny eyes / that don't look like they'd be good / for navigating / in the dark / and spotting prey.
작은 박쥐는 / 작고, 곤충을 먹는 박쥐인 / 북미에서 발견되는 / 아주 작은 눈을 가지고 있다 / 좋을 것으로 보이지 않는 / 길을 찾는 데 / 어둠 속에서 / 그리고 먹이를 발견하는 데

㉢ From the use of echolocation, / or sonar, / as it is also called, / a microbat can tell a great deal / about a mosquito or any other potential meal.
반향 정위의 사용으로 인해 / 또는 음파 탐지기 / 그것이 ~라고도 불리는 / 작은 박쥐는 많은 것을 알 수 있다 / 모기나 다른 잠재적인 음식에 대해

With extreme exactness, / echolocation allows microbats to perceive / motion, distance, speed, movement, and shape.
극도의 정확성으로 / 반향 정위는 작은 박쥐가 인식할 수 있게 한다 / 동작, 거리, 속도, 움직임, 그리고 모양을

Bats can also detect and avoid obstacles / no thicker than a human hair.
박쥐들은 또한 장애물들을 발견하고 피할 수 있다 / 사람의 머리카락보다 두껍지 않은

㉣ But, / actually, / microbats can see / as well as mice and other small mammals.
하지만 / 사실 / 작은 박쥐는 볼 수 있다 / 쥐와 다른 작은 포유동물들만큼 잘

해석 ⓒ 북미에서 발견되는 작고, 곤충을 먹는 박쥐인 작은 박쥐는 어둠 속에서 길을 찾고 먹이를 발견하는 데 좋을 것으로 보이지 않는 아주 작은 눈을 가지고 있다.

ⓔ 하지만 사실, 작은 박쥐는 쥐와 다른 작은 포유동물들만큼 잘 볼 수 있다. 박쥐의 야행성 습관은 밤에 먹이를 먹고 날아다니는 것을 누군가 생각하는 것보다 더 쉽게 해주는 특별한 능력인 반향 정위의 힘에 의해 도움을 받는다.

㉠ 어둠 속에서 길을 찾기 위해, 작은 박쥐는 입을 벌린 채로 인간이 들을 수 없는 아주 높은 끼익 하는 소리를 내뿜으면서 날아간다. 이 소리들 중 일부는 앞에 놓여 있는 나무 가지들과 다른 장애물들에서뿐만 아니라 날아다니는 곤충들에서 반향한다. 박쥐는 그 메아리를 듣고 그 앞에 있는 물체의 즉각적인 모습을 그것의 뇌에 얻는다.

ⓒ 반향 정위 또는 음파 탐지기라고도 불리는 것의 사용으로 인해, 작은 박쥐는 모기나 다른 잠재적인 음식에 대해 많은 것을 알 수 있다. 극도의 정확성으로, 반향 정위는 작은 박쥐가 동작, 거리, 속도, 움직임, 그리고 모양을 인식할 수 있게 한다. 박쥐들은 또한 사람의 머리카락보다 두껍지 않은 장애물들을 발견하고 피할 수 있다.

해설 ⓒ에서 작은 박쥐는 어둠 속에서 길을 찾고 먹이를 발견하는 데 좋을 것으로 보이지 않는 작은 눈을 가졌다고 하고, ⓔ에서 하지만(But) 작은 박쥐는 다른 작은 포유동물들만큼 잘 볼 수 있으며 밤에 날아다니는 것을 쉽게 해주는 반향 정위(echolocation)의 도움을 받는다고 설명하고 있다. 이어서 ㉠에서 어둠 속에서 길을 찾기 위해 작은 박쥐는 높은 소리를 내뿜어 반향하는 메아리(echo)를 듣고 앞에 있는 물체의 모습을 얻는다고 반향 정위를 설명한 후, ⓒ에서 반향 정위의 사용은 작은 박쥐가 먹이의 동작, 거리, 속도, 움직임 및 모양을 인식할 수 있게 한다고 알려주고 있다. 따라서 ② ⓒ-ⓔ-㉠-ⓒ이 정답이다.

어휘 navigate 길을 찾다 emit 내뿜다 high-pitched (음이) 아주 높은 squeak 끼익 하는 소리 echo 반향하다; 메아리, 반향 obstacle 장애물 instantaneous 즉각적인, 순간적인 tiny 아주 작은 spot 발견하다, 찾다 prey 먹이 echolocation 반향 정위(박쥐 등이 발사한 초음파의 반향으로 물체의 존재를 측정하는 능력) sonar 음파 탐지기 tell 알다, 판단하다 mosquito 모기 potential 잠재적인 exactness 정확성 perceive 인식하다, 감지하다 motion 동작 shape 모양 detect 발견하다, 알아내다 avoid 피하다 mammal 포유동물 nocturnal 야행성의 aid 돕다 feed 먹이를 먹다

정답

p.138

01	③ 어휘 - 어휘&표현	**11**	④ 어휘 - 어휘&표현
02	① 어휘 - 어휘&표현	**12**	④ 어휘 - 어휘&표현
03	② 어휘 - 어휘&표현	**13**	③ 문법 - 수 일치
04	③ 어휘 - 생활영어	**14**	④ 문법 - 동사의 종류
05	② 문법 - 형용사와 부사	**15**	① 독해 - 추론
06	③ 문법 - 대명사	**16**	③ 독해 - 추론
07	④ 독해 - 추론	**17**	④ 독해 - 세부내용 파악
08	③ 독해 - 세부내용 파악	**18**	① 독해 - 추론
09	④ 독해 - 논리적 흐름 파악	**19**	① 독해 - 추론
10	① 독해 - 추론	**20**	② 독해 - 전체내용 파악

취약영역 분석표

영역	세부 유형	문항 수	소계
어휘	어휘&표현	5	/6
	생활영어	1	
문법	형용사와 부사	1	/4
	대명사	1	
	수 일치	1	
	동사의 종류	1	
독해	전체내용 파악	1	/10
	세부내용 파악	2	
	추론	6	
	논리적 흐름 파악	1	
총계			**/20**

· 자신이 취약한 영역은 '공무원 영어, 이렇게 출제된다!'(문제집 p.8)를 통해 다시 한번 확인하고 학습하시기 바랍니다.

---

01 어휘 **어휘&표현** muzzle = suppress   난이도 ★★☆

해석 인류는 새로운 생각을 억압하려 한 권력자들과 변화를 어리석은 행위라고 선언한 오랫동안 확립된 견해들의 권위에 계속해서 반항해왔다.

① 표현하다   ② 주장하다
③ 억압하다   ④ 퍼뜨리다

어휘 disobedient 반항하는, 복종하지 않는 authority 권력자, 권위
muzzle 억압하다, 입막음하다 declare 선언하다
nonsense 어리석은 행위 assert 주장하다
suppress 억압하다, 진압하다

👍 이것도 알면 **합격!**

muzzle(억압하다)의 유의어
= quiet, restrain, repress

---

02 어휘 **어휘&표현** pompous = presumptuous   난이도 ★★★

해석 거만하게 굴지 마라. 당신은 당신의 글이 너무 비격식적이고 구어적이기를 원하지 않지만, 당신은 또한 당신이 아닌 누군가, 예를 들어 당신의 교수나 상사, 또는 로즈 장학생 조교 같은 인상을 주기를 원하지 않는다.

① 주제넘은   ② 격의 없는
③ 형식적인   ④ 진실한

어휘 pompous 거만한, 과시하는 colloquial 구어의
presumptuous 주제넘은, 건방진 casual 격의 없는, 무관심한
genuine 진실한

👍 이것도 알면 **합격!**

pompous(거만한)의 유의어
= pretentious, self-important, arrogant

---

03 어휘 **어휘&표현** call it a day = finish   난이도 ★☆☆

해석 외과의들은 그 작업에 알맞은 도구들을 찾을 수 없었기 때문에 (일을) 그만 끝낼 수밖에 없었다.

① 시작하다   ② 끝내다
③ 기다리다   ④ 취소하다

어휘 surgeon 외과의 call it a day (일 등을) 그만 끝내다
initiate 시작하다

👍 이것도 알면 **합격!**

call it a day(그만 끝내다)와 유사한 의미의 표현
= stop working, stop and go home, leave it for later

---

04 어휘 **생활영어** Yes, we have risotto with mushroom and cheese.   난이도 ★☆☆

해석 ① A: 저는 내일로 예약하고 싶습니다.
　　 B: 알겠습니다. 몇 시로 하시겠어요?
② A: 주문하시겠어요?
　　 B: 네, 수프 주세요.
③ A: 당신의 리조또는 어떤가요?
　　 B: 네, 저희는 버섯과 치즈가 들어간 리조또가 있습니다.
④ A: 디저트 드시겠어요?
　　 B: 저는 됐어요, 고마워요.

해설 ③번에서 A는 B의 리조또가 어떤지를 묻고 있으므로, 리조또 메뉴를 소개하는 B의 대답 Yes, we have risotto with mushroom and cheese(네, 저희는 버섯과 치즈가 들어간 리조또가 있습니다)는 어울리지 않는다. 따라서 ③번이 정답이다.

어휘 make a reservation 예약하다

👍 이것도 알면 **합격!**

식당에서 쓸 수 있는 다양한 표현을 함께 알아두자.
· Can I make a reservation for two? 2명 예약할 수 있나요?
· Do you have any recommendations? 추천할 만한 메뉴가 있나요?
· What's good here? 여기는 무엇을 잘하나요?
· Could you wrap up the leftovers? 남은 음식을 포장해 주실 수 있나요?

05 문법 형용사와 부사   난이도 ★★☆

해석 1961년의 독립 이후 수년 동안의 그의 생존은 공식적인 방식으로 실제 정책 선택에 대한 논의가 거의 일어나지 않았다는 사실을 바꾸지 않았다. 사실, 니에레레가 NEC(국가행정위원회)를 통해 논의해야 했던 많은 중요한 정책 안건들은 언제나 있어왔다.

해설 ② 이중 부정 부정어 never는 이미 부정의 의미를 포함하고 있는 빈도 부사 hardly(거의 ~않다)와 함께 쓰일 수 없다. 따라서 부정어 never를 부정문에서 강조의 의미를 나타낼 수 있는 부사 ever로 고쳐야 한다.

오답분석 ① 전치사 선택 문맥상 '수년 동안'이라는 의미가 되어야 자연스러우므로 '~동안'이라는 의미를 나타내는 전치사 over가 올바르게 쓰였다.
③ 수량 표현 가산 복수 명사(policy issues)가 왔으므로 가산 복수 명사 앞에 쓰이는 수량 표현 a number of(많은 ~)가 올바르게 쓰였다.
④ 관계사 선택 선행사 policy issues가 사물이고 관계절 내에서 동사 has had to argue의 목적어 역할을 하므로 목적격 관계대명사 which가 올바르게 쓰였다.

어휘 independence 독립 alter 바꾸다 discussion 논의 in a public manner 공식적인 방식으로 occur 일어나다 issue 안건 argue 논의하다

👍 이것도 알면 **합격!**

'거의(좀처럼) ~않다'라는 의미의 부사 hardly, rarely, seldom, scarcely, barely는 이미 부정의 의미를 담고 있으므로 not/never와 같은 부정어와 함께 쓰일 수 없다는 것을 알아두자.

(ex) Rachael is rarely not late for school. (→ is rarely)
Rachael은 좀처럼 학교에 지각하지 않는다.

06 문법 대명사   난이도 ★★☆

해석 지난 3주 동안 주로 홍콩과 베트남에서 150명 이상의 사람들이 병에 걸렸다. 그리고 전문가들은 중국 광동 지방에 있는 또 다른 300명이 11월 중순에 발생한 같은 질병에 걸렸다고 추측했다.

해설 ③ 부정형용사의 쓰임 부정형용사 another(또 다른)는 일반적으로 단수 가산 명사를 수식하지만 특정한 숫자와 함께 오면 복수 명사 앞에 올 수 있으므로, another 뒤에 '수사 + 복수 명사'가 온 형태인 another 300 people이 올바르게 쓰였다.

오답분석 ① 현재완료 시제 현재완료 시제와 자주 함께 쓰이는 시간 표현 'over + 과거시간 표현'(over the past three weeks)이 왔으므로, 현재완료 시제가 쓰여야 한다. 현재완료 시제는 'have/has + p.p.'의 형태로 나타내므로 과거 시제 동사 fell을 과거분사 fallen으로 고쳐야 한다.
② 능동태 vs. 수동태 동사 suspect 뒤에 목적어(that ~ mid-November)가 있고, 주어(experts)와 동사가 '전문가들이 추측하다'라는 의미의 능동 관계이므로 수동태 동사 are suspected를 능동태 동사 suspected로 고쳐야 한다.
④ 분사 자리 주어(another 300 people), 동사(had), 목적어(the same disease)를 모두 갖춘 완전한 절에 또 다른 동사(begin)가 올 수 없고, 문맥상 '11월 중순에 발생한 같은 질병에 걸렸다'라는 의미가 되어야 자연스러우므로 동사 begin을 명사(the same disease)를 수식할 수 있는 분사 beginning으로 고쳐야 한다. 참고로, 수식받는 명사(the same disease)와 분사가 '같은 질병이 발생하다'라는 의미의 능동 관계이므로 현재분사 beginning이 쓰여야 한다.

어휘 fall ill 병에 걸리다 suspect 추측하다 province 지방 begin 발생하다, 나타나다

👍 이것도 알면 **합격!**

③번 보기의 another와 달리 부정형용사 other는 복수 명사를 직접 수식하거나, no, any, some, one, the 등을 동반하여 단수 명사를 수식한다는 것도 알아두자.

(ex) He came up with other ideas. 그는 다른 방안들을 생각해냈다.
I need to go to the hospital today and one other day.
나는 오늘과 또 다른 날에 병원에 가야 한다.

07 독해 추론 (빈칸 완성 - 단어)   난이도 ★★☆

끊어읽기 해석

Social learning theorists offer / a different explanation / for the counter-aggression / exhibited by children / who experience aggression / in the home.
사회 학습 이론가들은 제시한다 / 다른 설명을 / 역공격성에 대한 / 아이들에 의해 나타나는 / 공격성을 경험하는 / 가정에서

An extensive research / on aggressive behavior and the coercive family / concludes / that an aversive consequence may also elicit / an aggressive reaction / and accelerate / ongoing coercive behavior.
광범위한 조사는 / 공격적인 행동과 고압적인 가족에 대한 / 결론을 내린다 / 혐오의 결과가 또한 이끌어 낼 수도 있다 / 공격적인 반응을 / 그리고 촉진할 수도 있다 / 진행하는 고압적인 행동을

These victims / of aggressive acts / eventually learn / via modeling / to initiate aggressive interchanges.
이 희생자들은 / 공격적인 행동들의 / 결국 배운다 / 모델링을 통해 / 공격의 교환을 시작하는 것을

These events perpetuate / the use of aggressive acts / and train children / how to behave / as adults.
이 사건들은 영속시킨다 / 공격적인 행동들의 사용을 / 그리고 아이들에게 가르친다 / 어떻게 행동할지를 / 어른이 되었을 때

해석 사회 학습 이론가들은 가정에서 공격성을 경험하는 아이들에 의해 나타나는 역공격성에 대한 다른 설명을 제시한다. 공격적인 행동과 고압적인 가족에 대한 광범위한 조사는 혐오의 결과가 또한 공격적인 반응을 이끌어 내고 진행하는 고압적인 행동을 촉진할 수도 있다는 결론을 내린다. 이 공격적인 행동들의 희생자들은 결국 모델링을 통해 공격의 교환을 시작하는 것을 배운다. 이 사건들은

공격적인 행동들의 사용을 영속시키고 아이들에게 어른이 되었을 때 어떻게 행동할지를 가르친다.

① 멈추다 　　　　　　② 약화시키다
③ 혐오하다 　　　　　④ 시작하다

해설　빈칸이 있는 문장을 통해 빈칸에 공격적인 행동들의 희생자들이 모델링을 통해 공격의 교환을 어떻게 하는 것을 배우는지에 대한 내용이 나와야 적절하다는 것을 알 수 있다. 빈칸 앞 문장에서 혐오의 결과가 공격적인 반응을 이끌어 내고 진행하는 고압적인 행동들을 촉진할 수도 있다고 했으므로, 희생자들이 결국 공격의 교환들을 '시작하는' 것을 배운다고 한 ④번이 정답이다.

어휘　social learning theorist 사회 학습 이론가　aggression 공격성 exhibit 나타나다　extensive 광범위한　coercive 고압적인 conclude 결론 짓다　aversive 혐오의, 회피적인　elicit 이끌어 내다 accelerate 촉진하다　ongoing 진행하는　victim 피해자 modeling 모델링(개인이 다른 개인을 모방 및 관찰함으로써 학습함) interchange 교환　perpetuate 영속시키다 attenuate 약화시키다　abhor 혐오하다　initiate 시작하다

08　독해　세부내용 파악 (내용 불일치 파악)　난이도 ★☆☆

끊어읽기 해석

Marcel Mauss (1872-1950), / French sociologist, / was born in Épinal (Vosges) in Lorraine, / where he grew up / within a close-knit, pious, and orthodox Jewish family.
마르셀 모스(1872-1950)는 / 프랑스 사회학자 / 로렌 지방의 에피날(보주주)에서 태어났다 / 그가 자란 곳이다 / 유대가 긴밀하고, 신앙심이 깊고, 정통파 유대교인 가정 안에서

Emile Durkheim was his uncle.
에밀 뒤르켐이 그의 삼촌이었다.

By the age of 18 / Mauss had reacted / against the Jewish faith; / he was never a religious man.
18살 때까지 / 모스는 반발했다 / 유대교 신앙에 대해 / 그는 결코 신앙심이 깊은 사람이 아니었다

He studied philosophy / under Durkheim's supervision / at Bordeaux; / Durkheim took endless trouble / in guiding his nephew's studies / and even chose subjects / for his own lectures / that would be most useful to Mauss.
그는 철학을 공부했다 / 뒤르켐의 관리 아래 / 보르도에서 / 뒤르켐은 끝없는 수고를 아끼지 않았다 / 그의 조카의 학업을 지도하는 데 / 그리고 심지어 과목들을 선택했다 / 자신의 강의에 / 모스에게 가장 유용할

Thus / Mauss was initially a philosopher / (like most of the early Durkheimians), / and his conception of philosophy / was influenced / above all by Durkheim himself, / for whom he always retained the utmost admiration.
그러므로 / 모스는 처음에 철학자였다 / (대부분의 초기 뒤르켐주의자들과 마찬가지로) / 그리고 그의 철학 개념은 / 영향 받았다 / 무엇보다도 뒤르켐에 의해서 / 그(뒤르켐)는 언제나 그에 대한 최고의 존경을 간직했다

해석　프랑스 사회학자 마르셀 모스(1872-1950)는 로렌 지방의 에피날(보주주)에서 태어났는데, 그곳은 그가 유대가 긴밀하고, 신앙심이 깊으며, 정통파 유대교인 가정 안에서 자란 곳이다. 에밀 뒤르켐이 그의 삼촌이었다. 18살 때까지 모스는 유대교 신앙에 대해 반발했다. 그는 결코 신앙심이 깊은 사람이 아니었다. 그는 뒤르켐의 관리 아래 보르도에서 철학을 공부했다. 뒤르켐은 그의 조카의 학업을 지도하는 데 끝없는 수고를 아끼지 않았고, 심지어 모스에게 가장 유용할 과목들을 자신의 강의에 선택했다. 그러므로 모스는 (대부분의 초기 뒤르켐주의자들과 마찬가지로) 처음에 철학자였고, 그의 철학 개념은 무엇보다도 뒤르켐에 의해서 영향받았으며, 그는 언제나 그(뒤르켐)에 대한 최고의 존경을 간직했다.

① 그는 유대교의 배경을 가졌다.
② 그는 그의 삼촌에 의해 관리되었다.
③ 그는 교조적인 신앙심을 가졌다.
④ 그는 철학적 배경을 가진 사회학자였다.

해설　지문 중간에서 모스(Mauss)는 유대교 신앙에 반발했으며 결코 신앙심이 깊은 사람이 아니었다고 했으므로, 그가 교조적인 신앙심을 가졌다는 것은 지문의 내용과 반대이다. 따라서 ③번이 정답이다.

어휘　sociologist 사회학자　close-knit 유대가 긴밀한 pious 신앙심이 깊은　orthodox 정통파의 react against ~에 대해 반발하다　faith 신앙 religious 신앙심이 깊은　philosophy 철학　supervision 관리 take trouble 수고를 아끼지 않다　initially 처음에 conception 개념　retain 간직하다　utmost 최고의 doctrinaire 교조적인, 광신적인

09　독해　논리적 흐름 파악 (문단 순서 배열)　난이도 ★★☆

끊어읽기 해석

ⓐ Today, / however, / trees are being cut down / far more rapidly.
오늘날 / 하지만 / 나무들은 베이고 있다 / 훨씬 더 급속히

Each year, / about 2 million acres of forests / are cut down.
매년 / 약 2백만 에이커의 숲들이 / 베인다

That is more than / equal to the area / of the whole of Great Britain.
이것은 ~보다 크다 / 필적하는 면적보다 / 영국 전체에

ⓑ There is not enough wood / in these countries / to satisfy the demand.
충분한 나무가 없다 / 이 나라들에 / 수요를 충족하기에

Wood companies, / therefore, / have begun taking wood / from the forests of Asia, Africa, South America, and even Siberia.
목재 회사들은 / 그래서 / 목재를 들여오는 것을 시작했다 / 아시아, 아프리카, 남아메리카, 그리고 심지어 시베리아의 숲들로부터

ⓒ While there are important reasons / for cutting down trees, / there are also dangerous consequences / for life on earth.
중요한 이유들이 있지만 / 나무를 베는 데는 / 위험한 결과들 또한 있다 / 지구상 생명체에게

A major cause / of the present destruction / is the worldwide demand / for wood.
주요 원인은 / 현재의 파괴의 / 세계적인 수요이다 / 목재에 대한

In industrialized countries, / people are using / more and more wood / for paper.
선진 공업국들에서 / 사람들은 사용하고 있다 / 점점 더 많은 목재를 / 종이를 위해

ⓓ There is nothing new / about people / cutting down trees.
새로운 건 아무것도 없다 / 사람들에 대해 / 나무를 베는

In ancient times, / Greece, Italy, and Great Britain were covered / with forests.
먼 옛날 / 그리스, 이탈리아, 그리고 영국은 뒤덮였었다 / 숲들로

Over the centuries / those forests were gradually cut back.
수 세기에 걸쳐 / 그 숲들은 차츰 축소되었다

Until now / almost nothing is left.
오늘에 이르기까지 / 거의 아무것도 남아 있지 않다

해석　ⓓ 나무를 베는 사람들에 대해 새로운 건 아무것도 없다. 먼 옛날, 그리스, 이탈리아, 그리고 영국은 숲들로 뒤덮였었다. 수 세기

에 걸쳐 그 숲들은 차츰 축소되었다. 오늘에 이르기까지 대부분 거의 남아 있지 않다.

ⓐ 하지만 오늘날, 나무들은 훨씬 더 급속히 베이고 있다. 매년 2백만 에이커의 숲들이 베인다. 이것은 영국 전체에 필적하는 면적보다 크다.

ⓒ 나무를 베는 데는 중요한 이유들이 있지만, 지구상 생명체에게 위험한 결과들 또한 있다. 현재의 파괴의 주요 원인은 목재에 대한 세계적인 수요이다. 선진 공업국들에서 사람들은 종이를 위해 점점 더 많은 목재를 사용하고 있다.

ⓑ 이 나라들에는 수요를 충족하기에 충분한 나무가 없다. 그래서 목재 회사들은, 아시아, 아프리카, 남아메리카, 심지어 시베리아의 숲들로부터 목재를 들여오기 시작했다.

해설 ⓓ에서 나무를 베는 사람들에 대해 새로운 건 아무것도 없으며 수 세기에 걸쳐 숲들이 차츰 축소되었다고 한 뒤, ⓐ에서 하지만 (however) 오늘날에는 나무들이 훨씬 더 급속히 베이고 있다고 하고, ⓒ에서 나무를 베는 것은 지구상 생명체에 위험한 결과를 가져오는데, 파괴의 주요 원인은 선진 공업국들에서 종이를 위해 목재를 사용하는 것이라고 언급하고, ⓑ에서 이 나라들(these countries)은 수요를 충족하기에 충분한 나무가 없어서 아시아, 아프리카, 남아메리카, 심지어 시베리아의 숲들로부터 목재를 들여오기 시작했다고 설명하고 있다. 따라서 ④ ⓓ - ⓐ - ⓒ - ⓑ가 정답이다.

어휘 rapidly 급속히 satisfy 충족시키다 demand 수요, 요구 destruction 파괴 industrialized country 선진 공업국 gradually 차츰 cut back 축소하다, 삭감하다

10 독해 추론 (빈칸 완성 - 연결어) 난이도 ★★☆

끊어읽기 해석

Contemporary art has in fact become / an integral part / of today's middle class society.
현대 미술은 사실 되어왔다 / 없어서는 안 될 부분이 / 오늘날 중산층 사회의

Even works of art / which are fresh from the studio / are met with enthusiasm.
미술 작품들조차도 / 작업실을 갓 나온 / 열광을 받는다

They receive recognition / rather quickly / — too quickly / for the taste of the surlier culture critics.
그것들은 인정을 받는다 / 다소 빠르게 / 너무 빠르게 / 더 불친절한 문화 비평가들의 안목에는

Of course, / not all works of them are bought / immediately, / but there is undoubtedly an increasing number of people / who enjoy buying brand new works of art.
물론 / 그것들(현대 미술 작품들)의 모든 작품이 팔리는 것은 아니다 / 즉시 / 그러나 의심할 여지 없이 사람들의 수가 증가하고 있다 / 새로운 예술 작품들을 구매하는 것을 즐기는

Instead of fast and expensive cars, / they buy / the paintings, sculptures and photographic works / of young artists.
빠르고 비싼 자동차들 대신 / 그들은 구매한다 / 그림들, 조각들, 그리고 사진 작품들을 / 젊은 예술가들의

They know / that contemporary art also adds / to their social prestige.
그들은 안다 / 현대 미술이 또한 기여한다는 것을 / 그들의 사회적 명예에

Furthermore, / since art is not exposed / to the same wear and tear as automobiles, / it is a far better investment.
게다가 / 예술은 노출되지 않기 때문에 / 자동차와 동일한 가치의 저하에 / 이것은 훨씬 나은 투자이다

해석 현대 미술은 사실 오늘날 중산층 사회의 없어서는 안 될 부분이 되어왔다. 작업실을 갓 나온 미술 작품조차도 열광을 받는다. 그것들

은 다소 빠르게, 더 불친절한 문화 비평가들의 안목에는 너무 빠르게 인정을 받는다. 물론, 그것들(현대 미술 작품들)의 모든 작품이 즉시 팔리는 것은 아니지만, 그러나 의심할 여지 없이 새로운 예술 작품들을 구매하는 것을 즐기는 사람들의 수가 증가하고 있다. 빠르고 비싼 자동차들 대신, 그들은 젊은 예술가들의 그림들, 조각들, 그리고 사진 작품들을 구매한다. 그들은 현대 미술이 또한 그들의 사회적 명예에 기여한다는 것을 안다. 게다가, 예술은 자동차와 동일한 가치의 저하에 노출되지 않기 때문에, 이것은 훨씬 나은 투자이다.

① 물론 - 게다가
② 그래서 - 반면에
③ 그래서 - 예를 들어
④ 물론 - 예를 들어

해설 첫 번째 빈칸 앞 문장은 미술 작품들이 빠르게 인정을 받는다는 내용이고, 빈칸 뒤 문장은 그것들(현대 미술 작품들)의 모든 작품이 즉시 팔리는 것은 아니라는 양보적인 내용이므로 양보를 나타내는 연결어인 Of course(물론)가 나와야 적절하다. 두 번째 빈칸 앞 문장은 그들(현대 미술품을 구입하는 사람들)은 현대 미술이 그들의 사회적 명예에 기여한다는 것을 안다는 내용이고, 빈칸 뒤 문장은 예술은 자동차와 동일한 가치의 저하에 노출되지 않기 때문에 훨씬 나은 투자라는 추가적인 내용이므로 추가를 나타내는 연결어인 Futhermore(게다가)가 들어가야 적절하다.
따라서 ① Of course(물론) - Futhermore(게다가)가 정답이다.

어휘 contemporary art 현대 미술 integral 없어서는 안 될 middle class 중산층 recognition 인정 surly 불친절한, 무뚝뚝한 taste 안목, 감상력 undoubtedly 의심할 여지없이 prestige 명예 be exposed to ~에 노출되다 automobile 자동차 wear and tear (사용으로 인한) 가치의 저하, 손상 investment 투자

11 어휘 어휘＆표현 essential ↔ omnipresent 난이도 ★★☆

해석 수정의 필요 조건으로, 수분은 과일과 씨앗용 작물의 생산에 필수적이고 품종 개량을 통해 작물을 개선하기 위해 고안된 프로그램에 중요한 역할을 한다.

① 중대한   ② 필수적인
③ 없어서는 안 되는   ④ 어디에나 있는

어휘 prerequisite 필요 조건 fertilization 수정 pollination 수분 seed crop 씨앗용 작물 breeding 품종 개량 crucial 중대한 indispensable 필수적인 requisite 없어서는 안 되는 omnipresent 어디에나 있는

👍 이것도 알면 합격!

omnipresent(어디에나 있는)의 유의어
= everywhere, ubiquitous, infinite

12 어휘 어휘＆표현 wrong | inconvenient 난이도 ★☆☆

해석 Mr. Johnson은 그 계획에 반대했는데 그것이 잘못된 원칙에 입각해서 만들어졌고 또한 가끔 불편했기 때문이었다.

① 잘못된 - 바람직한
② 필수적인 - 합리적인
③ 순응하는 - 한탄스러운
④ 잘못된 - 불편한

어휘 object 반대하다 proposal 계획 found (~에 입각해서) 만들다 principle 원칙 at times 가끔 faulty 잘못된, 결함이 있는

desirable 바람직한 imperative 필수적인, 중요한
reasonable 도리에 맞는 conform 순응하다
deplorable 한탄스러운 inconvenient 불편한

📱 이것도 알면 **합격!**

wrong(잘못된)의 유의어
= incorrect, false, untrue

inconvenient(불편한)의 유의어
= difficult, troublesome, cumbersome

13 문법 수 일치   난이도 ★★☆

해석 나는 나에게 충분한 옷을 가지고 있다는 것이 만족스럽다. 미국 남
성들은 일반적으로 일본 남성들보다 더 커서 시카고에서 나에게
꼭 맞는 옷들을 찾는 것은 매우 어렵다. 일본에서 중간 사이즈인
것은 여기서는 작은 사이즈다.

해설 ③ 관계절 수 일치 주격 관계절(that fits me)의 동사는 선행사
(clothes)에 수 일치시켜야 하는데, 선행사 clothes가 복수 명사
이므로 단수 동사 fits를 복수 동사 fit으로 고쳐야 한다.

오답
분석 ① 감정동사의 분사 감정을 나타내는 동사(please)의 경우 주어
가 감정의 원인이면 현재분사를, 감정을 느끼는 주체이면 과거
분사를 써야 하는데, 문맥상 '나는 만족스럽다'라는 의미로 주
어(I)가 감정을 느끼는 주체가 되어야 자연스러우므로 과거분
사 pleased가 올바르게 쓰였다.

② 가주어 it to 부정사구(to find ~ me)와 같이 긴 주어가 오면
가주어 it이 진주어(to 부정사구)를 대신해서 주어 자리에 쓰이
므로 it's가 올바르게 쓰였다.

④ 명사절 접속사 주어가 없는 불완전한 절(is a medium size
in Japan)을 이끌면서 문장의 주어 자리에 올 수 있는 명사절
접속사 What이 올바르게 쓰였다.

어휘 please 만족시키다 generally 일반적으로 fit 꼭 맞다

📱 이것도 알면 **합격!**

clothes(옷)는 복수형으로만 쓰이고 clothing(옷)은 불가산 명사로
만 쓰여서, 둘 다 부정관사와 함께(a/an) 단수 형태로는 쓰일 수 없다
는 것을 알아두자.

(ex) A Clothing was expensive in ancient times.
옛날에는 옷이 비쌌다.

14 문법 동사의 종류   난이도 ★★☆

해석 BBC에 의해 제작된 자연 다큐멘터리 '블루 플래닛 II'는 플라스틱
이 바다에 영향을 미치는 정도를 보여준 후 시청자들이 가슴 아픈
상태가 되게 했다.

해설 ④ 타동사의 쓰임 동사 affect(~에 영향을 미치다)는 전치사(on)
없이 목적어를 바로 취하는 타동사이므로 affects on을 affects
로 고쳐야 한다.

오답
분석 ① 과거분사 수식받는 명사 documentary와 분사가 '다큐
멘터리가 제작되다'라는 의미의 수동 관계이므로 과거분사
produced가 올바르게 쓰였다.

② 보어 자리 leave(left)는 목적격 보어를 취하는 5형식 동사로
쓰일 수 있는데, 보어 자리에는 명사나 형용사 역할을 하는 것
이 와야 한다. 따라서 목적어 viewers 뒤에 형용사 역할을 하

는 과거분사 heartbroken이 올바르게 쓰였다.

③ 전치사 + 관계대명사 '전치사 + 관계대명사'에서 전치사는
선행사 또는 관계절의 동사에 따라 결정되는데, 선행사 the
extent는 전치사 to와 함께 짝을 이루어 쓰이므로 to which가
올바르게 쓰였다.

어휘 leave ~한 상태가 되게 하다 heartbroken 가슴 아픈 extent 정도

📱 이것도 알면 **합격!**

분사구문의 뜻을 분명하게 해주기 위해 부사절 접속사가 분사구문 앞
에 올 수 있다.

(ex) (생략) left viewers heartbroken after showing the extent ~
the ocean.   부사절 접속사   분사구문

15 독해 추론 (빈칸 완성 - 절)   난이도 ★★☆

끊어읽기 해석

What became clear / by the 1980s, / however, / as
preparations were made / for the 'Quincentenary Jubilee', /
was / that many Americans found / it hard, / if not
impossible, / to see the anniversary / as a 'jubilee'.
명확해진 것은 / 1980년대에 이르러 / 그러나 / 준비가 갖추어지면서 /
'Quincentenary Jubilee'를 위한 / ~이었다 / 많은 미국인들이 깨달았다
는 것이다 / 어렵다는 것을 / 불가능하지는 않더라도 / 그 기념일을 보는
것이 / '축제'로

There was nothing / to celebrate / the legacy of Columbus.
아무것도 없었다 / 기념할 / 콜럼버스의 업적을

According to many of his critics, / Columbus had been the
harbinger not of progress and civilization, / but of slavery and
the reckless exploitation of the environment.
그의 많은 비평가들에 따르면 / 콜럼버스는 선구자였다 / 진보와 문명이 아
니라 / 노예 제도와 분별없는 환경 개발의

해석 그러나 1980년대에 이르러 'Quincentenary Jubilee'를 위한 준
비가 갖추어지면서 명확해진 것은 많은 미국인들이 그 기념일을
축제로 보는 것이 불가능하지는 않더라도 어렵다는 것을 깨달았다
는 것이다. 콜럼버스의 업적을 기념할 것은 아무것도 없었다. 그의
많은 비평가들에 따르면, 콜럼버스는 진보와 문명이 아니라, 노예
제도와 분별없는 환경 개발의 선구자였다.

① 그의 많은 비평가들에 따르면, 콜럼버스는 진보와 문명이 아니
라, 노예 제도와 분별없는 환경 개발의 선구자였다.

② 1893년 시카고 세계 박람회는 발견과 미국의 진보의 힘 사이
서술적 관련성을 강화했다.

③ 19세기 콜럼버스의 신화에 대한 이 반전은 흥미로운 사실을 드
러낸다.

④ 따라서 콜럼버스는 명백한 사명설에 통합되었는데, 이는 미국
의 발전은 신의 힘으로 정해졌다는 믿음이다.

해설 지문 처음에서 1980년대에 이르러 많은 미국인들은 Quincentenary
Jubilee를 '축제'로 보는 것이 어렵다는 것을 깨달았다고 하고,
빈칸 앞 문장에서 콜럼버스의 업적을 기념할 것이 아무것도 없었
다고 했으므로, '그의 많은 비평가들에 따르면, 콜럼버스는 진보
와 문명이 아니라, 노예 제도와 분별없는 환경 개발의 선구자였
다'라고 한 ①번이 정답이다.

어휘 preparation 준비 celebrate 기념하다 legacy 업적
harbinger 선구자 progress 진보 civilization 문명
slavery 노예 제도 reckless 분별없는 exploitation 개발
reinforce 강화하다 reversal 반전
revealing 흥미로운 사실을 드러내는 integrate 통합하다

Manifest Destiny 명백한 사명설(미국이 북미를 지배할 운명을 갖고 있다는 주장)
divinely 신의 힘으로   ordain 정하다

16 독해 추론 (빈칸 완성 - 단어)   난이도 ★★☆

끊어읽기 해석

Following his father's imprisonment, / Charles Dickens was forced / to leave school / to work at a boot-blacking factory / alongside the River Thames.
그의 아버지의 투옥 후에 / 찰스 디킨스는 강요받았다 / 학교를 떠나도록 / 구두약 공장에서 일하기 위해 / 템즈강 옆에 있는

At the run-down, rodent-ridden factory, / Dickens earned six shillings / a week / labeling pots of "blacking," a substance / used to clean fireplaces.
황폐하고 설치류가 득실거리는 공장에서 / 디킨스는 6실링을 벌었다 / 일주일에 / '흑색 도료'의 통들에 상표를 붙이면서 / 재료인 / 벽난로를 청소하는 데 사용되는

It was the best / he could do / to help support his family.
그것은 최선이었다 / 그가 할 수 있었던 / 그의 가족을 부양하기 위해

Looking back on the experience, / Dickens saw it / as the moment / he said goodbye / to his youthful innocence, / stating / that he wondered / "how he could be so easily cast away / at such a young age."
그 경험을 되돌아보면서 / 디킨스는 그것을 여겼다 / 그 순간이라고 / 그가 작별인사를 한 / 그의 유년기의 순진함에 / 그리고 말했다 / 그는 의아하게 여겼다고 / '그가 어떻게 그토록 쉽게 버려질 수 있었는지' / 그렇게 어린 나이에

He felt abandoned(betrayed, disregarded) / by the adults / who were supposed to take care of him.
그는 버림받았다고(배신당했다고, 외면당했다고) 느꼈다 / 어른들에 의해 / 그를 돌봐야 했던

해석 그의 아버지의 투옥 후에 찰스 디킨스는 학교를 떠나 템즈강 옆에 있는 구두약 공장에서 일하도록 강요받았다. 황폐하고 설치류가 득실거리는 공장에서 디킨스는 벽난로를 청소하는 데 사용되는 재료인 '흑색 도료' 통들에 상표를 붙이면서 일주일에 6실링을 벌었다. 그것은 그의 가족을 부양하기 위해 그가 할 수 있었던 최선이었다. 그 경험을 되돌아보면서, 디킨스는 그것을 그가 그의 유년기의 순진함에 작별인사를 한 순간이라고 여겼고, 그는 '그가 그렇게 어린 나이에 어떻게 그토록 쉽게 버려질 수 있었는지' 의아하게 여겼다고 말했다. 그는 그를 돌봐야 했던 어른들에 의해 버림받았다고(배신당했다고, 외면당했다고) 느꼈다.

① 버림받은   ② 배신당한
③ 지지를 받은   ④ 외면당한

해설 빈칸이 있는 문장을 통해 빈칸에 디킨스가 그를 돌봐야 했던 어른들에 의해 어떻게 되었다고 느꼈는지에 대한 내용이 나와야 적절하다는 것을 알 수 있다. 빈칸 앞 문장에서 디킨스는 그가 그렇게 어린 나이에 어떻게 그토록 쉽게 버려질 수 있었는지 의아하게 여겼다고 했으므로, '지지를 받았다고'(buttressed) 느꼈다는 것은 문맥상 적절하지 않다. 따라서 ③번이 정답이다. 참고로, '버림받은'(abandoned), '배신당한'(betrayed), '외면당한'(disregarded)은 빈칸에 자연스럽게 연결된다.

어휘 imprisonment 투옥 run-down 황폐한 rodent 설치류
ridden 득실거리는 pot 통 youthful 유년기의 innocence 순진함
cast away 버리다 abandoned 버림받은 betray 배신하다
buttressed 지지를 받은 disregard 외면하다

17 독해 세부내용 파악 (내용 일치 파악)   난이도 ★★☆

끊어읽기 해석

A family / hoping to adopt a child / must first select / an adoption agency.
가족은 / 아이를 입양하길 원하는 / 가장 먼저 선택해야 한다 / 입양 기관을

In the United States, / there are two kinds of agencies / that assist with adoption.
미국에는 / 두 종류의 기관이 있다 / 입양을 돕는

③Public agencies generally handle / older children, / children with mental or physical disabilities, / or children / who may have been abused or neglected.
공공 기관은 일반적으로 다룬다 / 나이 많은 아이들 / 정신적 또는 신체적인 장애가 있는 아이들 / 혹은 아이들 / 학대를 당했거나 방치되어왔을지도 모르는

②Prospective parents are not usually expected / to pay fees / when adopting a child / from a public agency.
예비 부모들은 보통 기대되지 않는다 / 돈을 지불할 것으로 / 아이를 입양할 때 / 공공 기관으로부터

Fostering, / or a form of temporary adoption, / is also possible / through public agencies.
위탁 양육(하는 것은) / 즉 일시적인 입양 방식 / 또한 가능하다 / 공공 기관들을 통한

④Private agencies can be found / on the Internet.
사설 기관들은 찾아질 수 있다 / 인터넷에서

They handle / domestic and international adoption.
그것들은 다룬다 / 국내 그리고 국제 입양을

해석 아이를 입양하길 원하는 가족은 가장 먼저 입양 기관을 선택해야 한다. 미국에는 입양을 돕는 두 종류의 기관이 있다. 공공 기관은 일반적으로 나이 많은 아이들, 정신적 또는 신체적인 장애가 있는 아이들, 혹은 학대를 당했거나 방치되어왔을지도 모르는 아이들을 다룬다. 예비 부모들은 보통 공공 기관으로부터 아이를 입양할 때 돈을 지불할 것으로 기대되지 않는다. 공공 기관들을 통한 위탁 양육 즉 일시적인 입양 방식 또한 가능하다. 사설 기관들은 인터넷에서 찾아질 수 있다. 그것들은 국내 그리고 국제 입양을 다룬다.

① 공공 입양 기관은 사설 입양 기관보다 낫다.
② 부모들은 위탁 가정으로부터 아이들을 입양하기 위해 큰 돈을 지불한다.
③ 가난한 아이들은 공공 기관을 통해 입양될 수 없다.
④ 사설 기관은 국제 입양을 위해 연락이 취해질 수 있다.

해설 ④번의 키워드인 international adoption(국제 입양)이 그대로 언급된 지문 주변의 내용에서 사설 기관들은 인터넷에서 찾아질 수 있으며, 국내 그리고 국제 입양을 다룬다고 했으므로, 사설 기관은 국제 입양을 위해 연락이 취해질 수 있다는 것을 알 수 있다. 따라서 ④번이 정답이다.

오답분석 ① 공공 입양 기관이 사설 입양 기관보다 나은지에 대해서는 언급되지 않았다.
② 예비 부모들은 공공 기관으로부터 아이를 입양할 때 돈을 지불할 것으로 기대되지 않는다고는 했지만, 부모들이 위탁 가정으로부터 아이들을 입양하기 위해 큰 돈을 지불하는지는 알 수 없다.
③ 공공 기관은 일반적으로 나이 많은 아이들, 정신적 또는 신체적 장애가 있는 아이들, 학대를 당했거나 방치되어왔을지도 모르는 아이들을 다룬다고는 했지만, 가난한 아이들이 공공 기관을 통해 입양될 수 없는지는 알 수 없다.

어휘 adopt 입양하다 agency 기관 assist 돕다
handle 다루다, 취급하다 disability 장애 abuse 학대하다
neglected 방치된 prospective parent 예비 부모

foster 위탁 양육하다　temporary 일시적인
private agency 사설 기관　domestic 국내의, 가정의
in need 가난한

18 독해 추론 (빈칸 완성 - 단어)　난이도 ★★☆

끊어읽기 해석

Moths and butterflies / both belong to / the order Lepidoptera, / but there are numerous physical and behavioral differences / between the two insect types.
나방과 나비는 / 모두 속한다 / 인시목에 / 그러나 많은 신체의 그리고 행동의 차이점들이 있다 / 두 곤충 종류 사이에

On the behavioral side, / moths are nocturnal / and butterflies are diurnal (active during the day).
행동의 측면에서 / 나방은 야행성이다 / 그리고 나비는 주행성이다 / (낮 동안 활동하는)

While at rest, / butterflies usually fold / their wings / back, / while moths flatten their wings / against their bodies / or spread them out / in a "jet plane" position.
움직이지 않는 동안 / 나비는 대개 접는다 / 그들의 날개를 / 뒤로 / 반면 나방은 그들의 날개를 평평하게 한다 / 그들의 몸에 붙여 / 혹은 펼친다 / '제트기' 자세로

해석　나방과 나비는 모두 인시목에 속하지만, 두 곤충 종류 사이에 많은 신체의 그리고 행동의 차이점들이 있다. 행동의 측면에서, 나방은 야행성이고 나비는 주행성(낮 동안 활동하는)이다. 움직이지 않는 동안 나비는 대개 그들의 날개를 뒤로 접는 반면, 나방은 그들의 날개를 그들의 몸에 붙여 평평하게 하거나 혹은 '제트기' 자세로 펼친다.

① 야행성의　　　② 이성적인
③ 영원한　　　　④ 반원형의

해석　빈칸이 있는 문장을 통해 빈칸에 나비는 주행성이고 나방은 어떠한지에 대한 내용이 나와야 적절하다는 것을 알 수 있다. 지문 처음에서 나방과 나비 사이에 많은 신체의 그리고 행동의 차이점들이 있다고 했으므로, 나방은 '야행성'이라고 한 ①번이 정답이다.

어휘　moth 나방　lepidoptera 인시목　numerous 많은
behavioral 행동의　diurnal 주행성의　flatten 평평하게 하다
spread out 펼치다　nocturnal 야행성의　rational 이성적인
eternal 영원한　semi-circular 반원형의

19 독해 추론 (빈칸 완성 - 구)　난이도 ★☆☆

끊어읽기 해석

The idea of clowns / frightening people / started gaining strength / in the United States.
광대에 대한 생각은 / 사람들을 겁먹게 하는 / 강해지기 시작했다 / 미국에서

In South Carolina, / for example, / people reported / seeing individuals / wearing clown costumes, / often hiding / in the woods or in cities / at night.
사우스캐롤라이나에서 / 예를 들어 / 사람들은 전했다 / 사람들을 보았다고 / 광대 의상을 입은 / 종종 숨은 채였다 / 숲속이나 도시에 / 밤에

Some people said / that the clowns were trying / to lure children / into empty homes or the woods.
몇몇 사람들은 말했다 / 그 광대들이 ~하려고 했다고 / 아이들을 유인하려 / 빈집이나 숲속으로

Soon, / there were reports / of threatening-looking clowns / trying to frighten / both children and adults.
이내 / 소문들이 있었다 / 무섭게 생긴 광대들에 대한 / 겁주려 한 / 아이들과 어른들 모두를

Although there were usually no reports of violence, / and many of the reported sightings were later found / to be false, / this caused a nationwide panic.
비록 일반적으로 폭력에 대한 신고가 없었다 할지라도 / 그리고 많은 알려진 목격이 나중에 판명되었다 (할지라도) / 거짓으로 / 이것은 전국적인 공황을 야기했다

해석　사람들을 겁먹게 하는 광대에 대한 생각은 미국에서 강해지기 시작했다. 예를 들어, 사우스캐롤라이나에서, 사람들은 광대 의상을 입은 사람들을 보았다고 전했는데, 종종 밤에 숲속이나 도시에 숨은 채였다. 몇몇 사람들은 그 광대들이 아이들을 빈집 혹은 숲속으로 유인하려 했다고 말했다. 이내 아이들과 어른들 모두를 겁주려 한 무섭게 생긴 광대들에 대한 소문이 있었다. 비록 일반적으로 폭력에 대한 신고가 없었고, 많은 알려진 목격이 나중에 거짓으로 판명되었음에도 불구하고, 이것은 전국적인 공황을 야기했다.

① 서커스 산업에 이익이 되었다
② 광고에서 광대의 사용을 증진했다
③ 전국적인 공황을 야기했다
④ 행복한 광대의 완벽한 이미지를 형성했다

해석　빈칸이 있는 문장을 통해 빈칸에 폭력에 대한 신고가 없었고 많은 알려진 목격이 거짓으로 판명되었음에도 불구하고 이것이 어떤 결과를 야기했는지에 대한 내용이 나와야 적절하다는 것을 알 수 있다. 지문 처음에서 사람들을 겁먹게 하는 광대에 대한 생각이 미국에서 강해지기 시작했다고 하고, 이어서 무서운 광대에 대한 괴담들을 소개하고 있으므로 이것은 '전국적인 공황을 야기했다'라고 한 ③번이 정답이다.

어휘　lure 유인하다　nationwide 전국적인　panic 공황　sighting 목격
promote 증진하다

20 독해 전체내용 파악 (요지 파악)　난이도 ★★☆

끊어읽기 해석

It is one thing to believe / that our system of democracy is the best, / and quite another / to impose it / on other countries.
믿는 것과 / 우리의 민주주의 체계가 최고라고 / 그리고 상당히 다른 것이다 / 그것을 강요하는 것은 / 다른 나라들에

This is a blatant breach / of the UN policy / of non-intervention / in the domestic affairs / of independent nations.
이것은 뻔뻔스러운 위반이다 / UN 정책에 대한 / 불간섭이라는 / 국내 사건들에 / 독립 국가의

Just as Western citizens fought / for their political institutions, / we should trust / the citizens of other nations / to do likewise / if they wish to.
서구의 시민들이 싸웠던 것처럼 / 그들의 정치적 제도를 위해 / 우리는 믿어야 한다 / 다른 국가들의 시민들이 / 똑같이 할 것을 / 만약 그들이 원한다면

Democracy is also not an absolute term / —Napoleon used elections and referenda / to legitimize his hold on power, / as do leaders today / in West Africa and Southeast Asia.
민주주의는 또한 절대적인 용어가 아니다 / 나폴레옹은 선거와 국민 투표를 사용했다 / 그의 정권 장악을 합법화하기 위해 / 오늘날의 지도자들이 하는 것처럼 / 서아프리카와 동남아시아의

States with partial democracy are often more aggressive / than totally unelected dictatorships / which are too concerned with maintaining order / at home.
부분 민주주의의 나라들은 대개 더 공격적이다 / 전적으로 선출에 의한 것이 아닌 독재 정권들보다 / 질서를 유지하는 것에 매우 관심이 있는 / 본국에서

The differing types of democracy / make it impossible to choose / which standards to impose.
상이한 유형의 민주주의는 / 선택하는 것을 불가능하게 만든다 / 어떤 기준을 적용할 것인지

The U.S. and European countries all differ / in terms of / restraints on government / and the balance / between consensus and confrontation.
미국과 유럽의 국가들은 모두 다르다 / ~의 면에서 / 정부에 대한 규제 / 그리고 균형 / 합의와 대립 사이

해석   우리의 민주주의 체계가 최고라고 믿는 것과 그것을 다른 나라들에 강요하는 것은 상당히 다른 것이다. 이것은 독립 국가의 국내 사건들에 불간섭이라는(간섭하지 않아야 한다는) UN 정책에 대한 뻔뻔스러운 침해이다. 그들의 정치적 제도를 위해 서구의 시민들이 싸웠던 것처럼, 우리는 다른 국가들의 시민들이 만약 그들이 원한다면 똑같이 할 것을 믿어야 한다. 민주주의는 또한 절대적인 용어가 아니다. 나폴레옹은 그의 정권 장악을 합법화하기 위해 오늘날의 서아프리카와 동남아시아의 지도자들이 하는 것처럼 선거와 국민 투표를 사용했다. 부분 민주주의의 나라들은 본국에서 질서를 유지하는 것에 매우 관심이 있는 전적으로 선출에 의한 것이 아닌 독재 정권들보다 대개 더 공격적이다. 상이한 유형의 민주주의는 어떤 기준을 적용할 것인지 선택하는 것을 불가능하게 만든다. 미국과 유럽의 국가들은 정부에 대한 규제와 합의와 대립 사이 균형의 면에서 모두 다르다.

① 울타리 저 편 잔디가 더 푸르다.
② 한 사람에게는 음식인 것이 다른 사람에게는 독이다.
③ 예외 없는 규칙은 없다.
④ 로마에 가면 로마 법에 따르라.

해설   지문 처음에서 우리의 민주주의 체계가 최고라고 믿는 것과 그것을 다른 나라들에 강요하는 것은 상당히 다른 것이라고 언급한 뒤, 이어서 이것은 독립 국가의 국내 사건들에 간섭하지 않아야 한다는 UN 정책에 대한 위반이며, 민주주의는 절대적인 용어가 아니며 국가에 따라 유형이 다를 수 있다고 했으므로, 지문의 내용과 부합하는 속담을 '한 사람에게는 음식인 것이 다른 사람에게는 독이다(한 사람에게는 이로운 것이 다른 사람에게는 독이 될 수 있다)'라고 표현한 ②번이 정답이다.

어휘   impose 강요하다, 적용하다   blatant 뻔뻔스러운
breach 위반, 불이행   non-intervention 불간섭   domestic 국내의
institution 제도, 학회   term 용어   referenda 국민 투표
legitimize 합법화하다   state 나라   aggressive 공격적인
dictatorship 독재 정권   be concerned with ~에 관심이 있다
in terms of ~의 면에서   restraint 규제   consensus 합의
confrontation 대립

19회 | 2017년 서울시 9급

정답

p.143

01	① 어휘 – 어휘&표현	**11**	④ 어휘 – 생활영어
02	② 어휘 – 어휘&표현	**12**	① 독해 – 추론
03	④ 문법 – 수 일치	**13**	④ 독해 – 논리적 흐름 파악
04	③ 문법 – 분사	**14**	① 독해 – 추론
05	③ 어휘 – 생활영어	**15**	④ 독해 – 추론
06	② 독해 – 전체내용 파악	**16**	① 독해 – 추론
07	② 어휘 – 어휘&표현	**17**	② 독해 – 추론
08	② 어휘 – 어휘&표현	**18**	④ 독해 – 논리적 흐름 파악
09	④ 문법 – 분사	**19**	④ 독해 – 세부내용 파악
10	③ 문법 – 동사의 종류	**20**	① 독해 – 전체내용 파악

취약영역 분석표

영역	세부 유형	문항 수	소계
어휘	어휘&표현	4	/6
	생활영어	2	
문법	수 일치	1	/4
	분사	2	
	동사의 종류	1	
독해	전체내용 파악	2	/10
	세부내용 파악	1	
	추론	5	
	논리적 흐름 파악	2	
총계			**/20**

· 자신이 취약한 영역은 '공무원 영어, 이렇게 출제된다!'(문제집 p.8)를 통해 다시 한번 확인하고 학습하시기 바랍니다.

---

01 어휘 어휘&표현 inextricably = inseparably 난이도 ★★☆

해석 리더십과 강인함은 밀접하게 관련되어 있다. 우리는 강인한 사람을 지도자로서 기대하는데, 왜냐하면 그들은 우리 집단을 향한 위협으로부터 우리를 보호할 수 있기 때문이다.

① 불가분하게 　　　② 활기가 없이
③ 헛되게 　　　　　④ 경솔하게

어휘 inextricably 밀접하게, 불가분하게　bind together 관련 짓다
look to 기대하다　inseparably 불가분하게, 밀접하게
inanimately 활기가 없이　ineffectively 헛되게, 무능하게
inconsiderately 경솔하게

👍 이것도 알면 **합격!**

inextricably(밀접하게)의 유의어
= inevitably, intricately, indistinguishably

02 어휘 어휘&표현 transient = momentary 난이도 ★★☆

해석 신중함은 오랫동안 확립된 정부가 사소하고 일시적인 대의명분을 위해 바뀌어서는 안 된다고 확실히 지시할 것이다.

① 투명한 　　　　　② 일시적인
③ 기억에 남는 　　　④ 중대한

어휘 prudence 신중함　indeed 확실히, 정말　dictate 지시하다
established 확립된　transient 일시적인　transparent 투명한
momentary 일시적인　significant 중대한

👍 이것도 알면 **합격!**

transient(일시적인)의 유의어
= temporary, impermanent, fleeting, transitory

03 문법 수 일치 난이도 ★★☆

해석 대학에 접근할 기회(입학할 기회)를 분배하는 데 있어서의 공정성이 대학들이 올바르게 추구하는 바람직한 것과 관계가 있다는 생각은 왜 입학 허가를 파는 것이 부당한지를 설명해준다.

해설 ④ 주어 동사 수 일치 주어 자리에 단수 명사 The idea가 왔으므로 복수 동사 explain을 단수 동사 explains로 고쳐야 한다. 주어와 동사 사이의 수식어 거품(that justice ~ properly pursue)은 동사의 수 결정에 영향을 주지 않는다.

오답분석 ① 전치사 뒤에 올 수 있는 것 전치사(in) 뒤에는 명사 역할을 하는 것이 와야 하므로 동명사 allocating이 올바르게 쓰였다.
② 전치사 뒤에 올 수 있는 것 전치사(with) 뒤에는 명사 역할을 하는 것이 와야 하므로 명사 the goods(바람직한 것)가 올바르게 쓰였다.
③ 주어 동사 수 일치 | 부사의 쓰임 동사 자리에 복수 동사 pursue가 왔으므로 복수 주어 universities가 올바르게 쓰였다. 또한, 동사(pursue)를 앞에서 수식할 수 있는 것은 부사이므로 부사 properly가 올바르게 쓰였다.

어휘 allocate 분배하다, 할당하다
have something to do with ~와 관계가 있다　good 바람직한 것
properly 올바르게, 적당히　pursue 추구하다
admission 입학(허가)　unjust 부당한, 불공평한

👍 이것도 알면 **합격!**

지문의 주어(The idea)와 동사(explains) 사이에 있는 that절(that justice ~ properly pursue)은 동격절이다. that절이 the fact, the idea, the news 등의 명사 뒤에 위치할 경우, 동격절로 쓰일 수 있다는 것을 알아두자.

04 문법 분사

해석 이상하게 보일 수도 있지만, 사하라 사막은 한때 아프리카 평원과 관련된 동물의 생태를 지탱하는 넓게 트인 목초지였다.

해설 ③ 현재분사 vs. 과거분사 수식받는 명사(an expanse of grassland)와 분사가 '넓게 트인 목초지가 지탱하다'라는 의미의 능동 관계이므로 과거분사 supported를 현재분사 supporting으로 고쳐야 한다.

오답 분석
① 부사절 접속사 as가 '비록 ~이지만'이라는 의미의 양보를 나타내는 부사절 접속사로 쓰이고, 양보의 부사절 내의 보어(Strange)가 as 앞에 오는 경우 '보어 + as + 주어 + 동사'의 어순이 되어야 하므로, strange as 뒤에 '주어(it) + 동사(may seem)'가 올바르게 쓰였다.
② 정관사의 쓰임 유일한 것을 나타내는 명사 앞에는 정관사 the가 와야 하므로 the Sahara(사하라 사막)가 올바르게 쓰였다.
④ 현재분사 vs. 과거분사 수식받는 명사(animal life)와 분사가 '동물의 생태와 관련되다'라는 의미의 수동 관계이므로 과거분사 associated with가 올바르게 쓰였다.

어휘 expanse 넓게 트인 지역 grassland 목초지
be associated with ~와 관련되다 plain 평원

👍 이것도 알면 **합격!**

①번 보기처럼 as가 '비록 ~이지만'이라는 의미로 쓰이고, 양보의 부사절 내의 보어나 부사가 as 앞에 와서 '보어/부사 + as + 주어 + 동사' 형태를 이루는 경우, 부사절 접속사 as 대신에 though를 사용할 수도 있다.

(ex) Young **as** Charlie is, he's very mature.
비록 Charlie는 어리지만, 그는 매우 성숙하다.
= Young **though** Charlie is, he's very mature.

05 어휘 생활영어 collateral

해석
A: 당신은 저희가 대출을 받을 수 있다고 생각하시나요?
B: 글쎄요, 그건 상황에 따라 다릅니다. 다른 부동산을 소유하고 계신가요? 주식이나 채권은요?
A: 아니요.
B: 그렇군요. 그렇다면 담보물이 아무것도 없으시네요. 아마도 당신을 위해 대출에 서명해줄 보증인을 구하실 수는 있을 것 같은데요.

① 조사   ② 동물
③ 담보물   ④ 영감

해설 부동산, 주식, 또는 채권을 소유하고 있는지 묻는 B의 말에 대해 빈칸 앞에서 A가 No(아니요)라고 대답하고 있으므로, 빈칸에는 그렇다면 '담보물'이 아무것도 없으시네요라고 말하는 내용이 들어가야 자연스럽다. 따라서 ③ collateral이 정답이다.

어휘 loan 대출 property 부동산 stock 주식 bond 채권
guarantor 보증인 investigation 조사 collateral 담보물
inspiration 영감

👍 이것도 알면 **합격!**

은행 업무를 볼 때 쓸 수 있는 다양한 표현을 알아두자.

- I want to apply for a loan. 대출을 신청하고 싶어요.
- I'd like to withdraw money from my account.
  제 계좌에서 돈을 찾고 싶어요.
- I'd like to open an account, please. 계좌를 개설하고 싶어요.
- What's the interest? 이자율은 어떻게 되나요?

06 독해 전체내용 파악 (주제 파악)

끊어읽기 해석

In 1782, / J. Hector St. John De Crèvecoeur, / a French immigrant / who had settled in New York / before returning to Europe / during the Revolutionary War, / published a series of essays / about life in the British colonies / in North America, / *Letters from an American Farmer*.
1782년에 / 헥터 세인트 존 드 크레브쾨르는 / 프랑스 이민자인 / 뉴욕에 정착했던 / 유럽으로 돌아오기 전에 / 독립 전쟁 동안 / 일련의 수필 시리즈를 출간했다 / 영국 식민지에서의 삶에 대한 / 북미에 있는 / 『미국 농부로부터의 편지』

The book was an immediate success / in England, France, and the United States.
그 책은 즉시 성공을 이루었다 / 영국, 프랑스, 그리고 미국에서

In one of its most famous passages, / Crèvecoeur describes the process / by which people / from different backgrounds and countries / were transformed / by their experiences in the colonies / and asks, / "What then is the American?"
그것의 가장 유명한 구절 중 하나에서 / 크레브쾨르는 과정을 묘사한다 / 사람들이 / 서로 다른 배경과 나라에서 온 / 변화되는 / 식민지에서의 그들의 경험에 의해 / 그리고 묻는다 / '그렇다면 미국인이란 무엇인가?'라고

In America, / Crèvecoeur suggests, / "individuals of all nations / are melted into a new race of men, / whose labors and posterity / will one day cause / great changes in the world."
미국에서 / 크레브쾨르는 주장한다 / '모든 국가의 개인들은 / 새로운 민족의 사람으로 녹아든다고 / 그들의 노동과 후세는 / 언젠가 일으킬 것이다' / 라고 / 세상에 커다란 변화를

Crèvecoeur was among the first / to develop the popular idea / of America / as that would come to be called "melting pot."
크레브쾨르는 최초의 사람 중 하나였다 / 대중적인 개념을 발전시킨 / 미국에 대한 / '용광로'라고 불리게 될

해석 독립 전쟁 동안 유럽으로 돌아오기 전에 뉴욕에 정착했던 프랑스 이민자인 헥터 세인트 존 드 크레브쾨르는 1782년에 북미에 있는 영국 식민지에서의 삶에 대한 일련의 수필 시리즈인 『미국 농부로부터의 편지』를 출간했다. 그 책은 영국, 프랑스, 그리고 미국에서 즉시 성공을 이루었다. 그것의 가장 유명한 구절 중 하나에서 크레브쾨르는 서로 다른 배경과 나라에서 온 사람들이 식민지에서의 그들의 경험에 의해 변화되는 과정을 묘사하며, '그렇다면 미국인이란 무엇인가?'라고 묻는다. 크레브쾨르는 미국에서 '모든 국가의 개인들은 새로운 민족의 사람으로 녹아들며, 그들의 노동과 후세는 언젠가 세상에 커다란 변화를 일으킬 것이다'라고 주장한다. 크레브쾨르는 '용광로'라고 불리게 될 미국에 대한 대중적인 개념을 발전시킨 최초의 사람 중 하나였다.

① 크레브쾨르의 책은 영국에서 즉시 성공을 거두었다.
② 크레브쾨르는 그의 책에서 용광로라는 개념을 발전시켰다.
③ 크레브쾨르는 미국의 개인주의에 대해 묘사하고 논했다.

④ 크레브쾨르는 그의 책에서 미국인들이 어디에서 왔는지 설명했다.

해설　지문 마지막에 크레브쾨르는 그의 책에서 미국에서는 '모든 국가의 개인들이 새로운 민족의 사람으로 녹아든다(are melted)'고 주장하여 용광로(melting pot)라고 불리게 될 미국에 대한 대중적인 개념을 발전시킨 최초의 사람 중 한 명이었다는 내용이 있다. 따라서 지문의 주제를 '크레브쾨르는 그의 책에서 용광로라는 개념을 발전시켰다'라고 표현한 ②번이 정답이다.

어휘　immigrant 이민자　colony 식민지　transform 변화시키다
individual 개인　be melted into ~속으로 녹아들다
posterity 후세, 자손　popular 대중적인
melting pot (많은 사람·사상 등을 함께 뒤섞는) 용광로
individualism 개인주의

07　어휘　어휘&표현　officious　난이도 ★★★

해설　우리는 계속해서 한 때는 좋은 의미로 쓰였으나 현재는 부정적인 의미로 사용되는 단어들을 우연히 발견한다. 18세기 후반까지 이 단어는 '남을 돕기 좋아하는, 호의적인, 아주 공손한 그리고 친절한'을 의미하는 데 사용되었다. 그러나 오늘날 참견하기 좋아하는 사람은 자신의 것이 아닌 일에 참견 잘하는 주제 넘게 나서는 오지랖 넓은 사람을 의미한다.

① 굽실거리는　　　　　② 참견하기 좋아하는
③ 사교적인　　　　　　④ 아부하는

어휘　light on ~을 우연히 발견하다　unfavorable 부정적인, 비판적인
sense 의미, 뜻　serviceable 남을 돕기 좋아하는, 쓸모있는
friendly 호의적인　courteous 공손한, 정중한
obliging 친절한, 도와주는　busy 참견 잘하는, 바쁜
uninvited 주제 넘게 나서는　meddler 오지랖 넓은 사람
servile 굽실거리는, 비굴한　officious 참견하기 좋아하는
gregarious 사교적인, 떼지어 사는　obsequious 아부하는, 아첨하는

👍 이것도 알면 합격!

officious(참견하기 좋아하는)의 유의어
= intrusive, meddlesome, dictatorial, pushy

08　어휘　어휘&표현　avert　난이도 ★★☆

해설　암모니아 또는 식초의 희미한 냄새는 생후 일주일 된 아기들이 얼굴을 찡그리고 고개를 돌리게 만든다.

① 이용하다　　　　　　② 돌리다
③ 감싸다　　　　　　　④ 일으키다

어휘　faint 희미한　odor 냄새　vinegar 식초　infant 아기, 유아
grimace 얼굴을 찡그리다　harness 이용하다
avert (고개를) 돌리다, 피하다　muffle 감싸다, 덮다, (소리를) 죽이다
evoke 일으키다, 자아내다

👍 이것도 알면 합격!

'head'를 포함한 다양한 표현을 함께 알아두자.
• lose one's head 당황하다, 흥분하다
• have one's head in the sand 현실을 외면하다
• come into one's head 머리에 떠오르다

09　문법　분사　난이도 ★☆☆

해석　서유럽의 첫 번째 커피점은 무역이나 상업의 중심지가 아닌 대학가 도시인 옥스퍼드에서 개점했는데, 그곳에서 Jacob이라고 이름 지어진 레바논 사람이 1650년에 가게를 차렸다.

해설　④ 현재분사 vs. 과거분사 수식받는 명사(a Lebanese man)와 분사가 '레바논 사람이 Jacob이라고 이름 지어지다'라는 의미의 수동 관계이므로 현재분사 naming을 과거분사 named로 고쳐야 한다.

오답
분석　① 상관 접속사의 쓰임 문맥상 '무역이나 상업의 중심지가 아닌 대학가 도시인 옥스퍼드에서 개점했다'라는 의미가 되어야 자연스러운데, 'A가 아니라 B'는 상관 접속사 'not A but B'를 사용하여 나타낼 수 있다. 전치사구(in the ~ city) 앞에 but이 나와 있으므로 but과 짝을 이루는 not이 전치사구(in a center) 앞에 올바르게 쓰였다.
② 전치사 뒤에 올 수 있는 것 | 전치사의 쓰임 전치사(in) 뒤에는 명사 역할을 하는 것이 와야 하므로, 전치사 in 뒤에 명사 a center(중심지)가 올바르게 쓰였다. 또한, 문맥상 '무역의 중심지'라는 의미가 되어야 하므로 '~의'라는 의미를 나타내는 전치사 of가 명사 trade(무역) 앞에 올바르게 쓰였다.
③ 전치사 + 관계대명사 관계사 뒤에 완전한 절(a Lebanese man ~ in 1650)이 왔으므로 '전치사 + 관계대명사' 형태가 올 수 있다. '전치사 + 관계대명사'에서 전치사는 선행사 또는 관계절의 동사에 따라 결정되는데, 선행사 Oxford가 장소이고, 문맥상 '옥스포드에서'라는 의미가 되어야 자연스러우므로 전치사 in이 관계대명사 앞에 와야 한다. 따라서 in which가 올바르게 쓰였다. 참고로, in which는 관계부사 where로 바꿀 수 있다.

어휘　commerce 상업　name 이름을 지어주다　set up 차리다, 세우다

👍 이것도 알면 합격!

두 가지의 대상 중 'A가 아니라 B'를 나타내기 위해서는 'not A but B'를 사용하지만, 세 가지 대상 중 'A도 아니고 B도 아니고 C'를 나타내기 위해서는 'not A nor B but C'를 사용한다는 것을 추가로 알아두자.
ex) I'm allergic not to nuts nor to seafood, but to dairy products.
나는 견과류도 아니고 해산물도 아니고 유제품에 알레르기가 있다.

10　문법　동사의 종류　난이도 ★☆☆

해석　① John은 Mary에게 그가 그의 방을 치울 것이라고 약속했다.
② John은 Mary에게 그가 일찍 떠날 것이라고 말했다.
③ John은 Mary가 행복할 것이라고 믿었다.
④ John은 Mary에게 그녀가 그곳에 일찍 도착해야 한다고 상기시켰다.

해설　③ 3형식 동사의 쓰임 문맥상 'John은 Mary가 행복할 것이라고 믿었다'라는 의미가 되어야 자연스럽고, 동사 believe는 that절을 목적어로 갖는 3형식 동사이므로, believe that(~라고 믿다)으로 나타낼 수 있다. 따라서 John believed Mary that she를 John believed that Mary로 고쳐야 한다. 또는 John believed Mary to be happy로 고쳐도 맞다.

오답
분석　① 4형식 동사의 쓰임 that절(that he ~ his room)을 직접 목적어로 갖는 4형식 동사 promise(promised) 뒤에는 전치사 없이 간접 목적어(Mary)가 와야 한다. 따라서 promised Mary that ~ his room이 올바르게 쓰였다.
② 4형식 동사의 쓰임 that절(that he would leave early)을 직접 목적어로 갖는 4형식 동사 tell(told) 뒤에는 전치사 없이

간접 목적어(Mary)가 와야 한다. 따라서 told Mary that ~ early가 올바르게 쓰였다.
④ 4형식 동사의 쓰임 that절(that she ~ early)을 직접 목적어로 갖는 4형식 동사 remind(reminded) 뒤에는 전치사 없이 간접 목적어(Mary)가 와야 한다. 따라서 reminded Mary that ~ early가 올바르게 쓰였다.

어휘 promise 약속하다 remind 상기시키다, 떠오르게 하다

👍 이것도 알면 합격!

that절이나 의문사절을 목적어로 가질 수 있는 3형식 동사와 4형식 동사를 구분하여 기억하자.

3형식 동사	say / mention / announce (~에게) -라고 말하다 explain / describe (~에게) -라고 설명하다 believe -라고 믿다 think -라고 생각하다	(+ to 사람) + that절/의문사절
4형식 동사	tell ~에게 -라고 말하다 convince ~에게 -라고 확신시키다 inform / notify ~에게 -라고 알리다 remind ~에게 -라고 상기시키다	+ 간접목적어(사람) + that절/의문사절

ex I said (to my wife) that I wanted to buy a new car.
나는 (아내에게) 새 차를 사고 싶다고 말했다.

I told my wife that I wanted to buy a new car.
나는 아내에게 새 차를 사고 싶다고 말했다.

---

11 어휘 생활영어 Wish I could but I have another commitment today. 난이도 ★☆☆

해석
A: 오늘은 제가 당신에게 점심을 대접하게 해주는 게 어때요, Mr. Kim?
B: 그럴 수 있으면 좋겠지만, 저는 오늘 다른 약속이 있어요.

① 아뇨, 전 아니에요. 그건 제게 좋은 시간이 될 거예요
② 좋아요. 잊어버리지 않도록 제 달력에 표시해놓을게요
③ 네. 월요일에 당신과 의논할게요
④ 그럴 수 있으면 좋겠지만, 저는 오늘 다른 약속이 있어요

해설 빈칸 앞에서 A가 Why don't you let me treat you to lunch today, Mr. Kim?(오늘은 제가 당신에게 점심을 대접하게 해주는 게 어때요, Mr. Kim?)이라고 말하고 있으므로, 빈칸에는 '그럴 수 있으면 좋겠지만, 저는 오늘 다른 약속이 있어요'라는 의미가 들어가야 자연스럽다. 따라서 ④ Wish I could but I have another commitment today가 정답이다.

어휘 treat 대접하다, 한턱 내다 check with ~와 의논하다
commitment 약속

👍 이것도 알면 합격!

약속을 잡을 때 쓸 수 있는 다양한 표현을 알아두자.

· Only this date works for us. 우리에겐 이 날만 가능하겠네요.
· Tell me what day suits you best.
  언제가 가장 좋은지 저에게 말해 주세요.
· I'm free any time after 6. 6시 이후에는 아무 때나 괜찮아요.

---

12 독해 추론 (빈칸 완성 – 단어&연결어) 난이도 ★★☆

끊어읽기 해석

For centuries, / people gazing at the sky / after sunset / could see thousands of vibrant, sparkling stars.
수 세기 동안 / 하늘을 바라보는 사람들은 / 일몰 후에 / 수천 개의 선명하고 반짝이는 별들을 볼 수 있었다

But these days, / you'll be lucky / if you can view / the Big Dipper.
그러나 요즘에는 / 당신은 운이 좋을 것이다 / 당신이 볼 수 있다면 / 북두칠성을

The culprit: / electric beams / pouring from homes and street lamps, / whose brightness obscures / the night sky.
그 원인은 / 전기 광선들이다 / 집과 가로등에서 쏟아져 나오는 / 이것들의 밝음이 가린다 / 밤하늘을

In the U.S., / so-called light pollution has gotten so bad / that by one estimate, / 8 out of 10 children / born today / will never encounter a sky / dark enough for them to see the Milky Way.
미국에서는 / 이른바 광공해가 너무 심해졌다 / 그래서 한 추정에 따르면 / 아이들 10명 중 8명은 / 오늘날 태어나는 / 하늘을 결코 접하지 못할 것이다 / 그들이 은하수를 볼 수 있을 만큼 충분히 어두운

There is hope, / however, / in the form of astrotourism, / a small but growing industry / centered on stargazing / in the worlds' darkest places.
희망이 존재한다 / 하지만 / 천문관광의 형태로 / 작지만 성장하고 있는 산업이다 / 별을 관찰하는 것에 중점을 두는 / 세상에서 가장 어두운 장소들에서

These remote sites, / many of them in national parks, / offer views / for little more than / the cost of a campsite.
이러한 외딴 장소들은 / 그것들 중 대부분이 국립공원에 있는 / 전망을 제공한다 / 약간 더 많은 비용으로 / 캠프장의 비용보다

And the people / who run them / often work / to reduce light pollution / in surrounding communities.
그리고 사람들은 / 그것들을 운영하는 / 종종 노력한다 / 광공해를 줄이기 위해 / 주변 지역사회의

Although astrotourism may not be as luxurious / as some vacations, / travelers don't seem to mind.
비록 천문관광이 화려하지는 않을 수 있지만 / 일부 휴가들처럼 / 여행자들은 개의치 않는 것 같다

해석 수 세기 동안 일몰 후에 하늘을 바라보는 사람들은 수천 개의 선명하고 반짝이는 별들을 볼 수 있었다. 그러나 요즘에는 당신이 북두칠성을 볼 수 있다면 당신은 운이 좋을 것이다. 그 원인은 집과 가로등에서 쏟아져 나오는 전기 광선들인데, 이것들의 밝음이 밤하늘을 가린다. 미국에서는 이른바 광공해가 너무 심해져서 한 추정에 따르면 오늘날 태어나는 아이들 10명 중 8명은 그들이 은하수를 볼 수 있을 만큼 충분히 어두운 하늘을 결코 접하지 못할 것이다. 하지만 천문관광의 형태로 희망이 존재하는데, 이는 세상에서 가장 어두운 장소들에서 별을 관찰하는 것에 중점을 두는 작지만 성장하고 있는 산업이다. 그것들 중 대부분이 국립공원에 있는 이러한 외딴 장소들은 캠프장의 비용보다 약간 더 많은 비용으로 전망을 제공한다. 그리고 그것들을 운영하는 사람들은 종종 주변 지역사회의 광공해를 줄이기 위해 노력한다. 비록 천문관광이 일부 휴가들처럼 화려하지는 않을 수 있지만, 여행자들은 개의치 않는 것 같다.

① 어두운 – 비록 ~이지만
② 밝은 – 왜냐하면
③ 어두운 – ~이므로
④ 밝은 – ~라는 점에서

해설 첫 번째 빈칸 앞 문장에서 요즘에는 집과 가로등에서 쏟아져 나오

는 전기 광선들의 밝음이 밤하늘을 가리고, 이로 인해 북두칠성을 보기 힘들다고 했으므로, 빈칸에는 오늘날 태어나는 아이들 10명 중 8명은 그들이 은하수를 볼 수 있을 만큼 충분히 '어두운' 하늘을 결코 접하지 못할 것이라는 내용이 들어가야 적절하다. 두 번째 빈칸 뒤에서 여행자들은 개의치 않는다고 했으므로 '비록' 천문관광이 다른 휴가들처럼 화려하지는 않을 수도 '있지만'이라는 내용이 들어가야 적절하다.

따라서 ① dark(어두운) – Although(비록 ~이지만)가 정답이다.

어휘 gaze 바라보다, 응시하다 vibrant 선명한, 활기찬
sparkling 반짝이는 Big Dipper 북두칠성
culprit (문제의) 원인, 범인 beam 광선 street lamp 가로등
obscure 가리다, 흐리게 하다
light pollution 광공해(인공조명이 많아 별빛을 볼 수 없는 것과 같은 상황)
encounter 접하다, 마주치다 Milky Way 은하수
astro tourism 천문관광 stargaze 별을 관찰하다 remote 외딴
campsite 캠프장 luxurious 화려한

13 독해 논리적 흐름 파악 (문단 순서 배열) 난이도 ★★★

끊어읽기 해석

㉠ Millions of people / suffering from / watery and stinging eyes, / pounding headaches, / sinus issues, / and itchy throats, / sought refuge / from the debilitating air / by scouring stores / for air filters and face masks.
수백만 명의 사람들은 / ~으로 고통받는 / 눈물이 나고 찌르는 듯이 아픈 눈 / 지끈거리는 두통 / 부비강 문제 / 그리고 가려운 목구멍 / 피난처를 찾았다 / 심신을 쇠약하게 만드는 공기로부터 / 가게들을 샅샅이 뒤짐으로써 / 공기 정화 장치와 안면 보호용 마스크를 찾아

㉡ The outrage among Chinese residents / and the global media scrutiny / impelled / the government to address / the country's air pollution problem.
중국 거주자들의 분노 / 그리고 세계 언론의 감시는 / 강력히 촉구했다 / 정부가 해결하도록 / 국가의 대기 오염 문제를

㉢ Schools and businesses were closed, / and the Beijing city government warned people / to stay inside their homes, / keep their air purifiers running, / reduce indoor activities, / and remain as inactive as possible.
학교와 기업체는 문을 닫았다 / 그리고 베이징시 당국은 사람들에게 경고했다 / 그들의 집안에 가만히 있으라고 / 공기 청정기를 계속 가동하라고 / 실내 활동을 줄이라고 / 그리고 가능한 한 활동하지 말라고

㉣ In 2013, / a state of emergency in Beijing / resulting from the dangerously high levels of pollution / led to chaos in the transportation system, / forcing airlines to cancel flights / due to low visibility.
2013년에 / 베이징의 비상 사태는 / 위험할 정도로 높은 오염 수준에 의해 야기된 / 운송 시스템의 혼란으로 이어졌다 / 항공사들이 어쩔 수 없이 항공편을 취소하도록 만들었다 / 낮은 가시성(나쁜 시야)으로 인해

해석 ㉣ 2013년에 위험할 정도로 높은 오염 수준에 의해 야기된 베이징의 비상 사태는 운송 시스템의 혼란으로 이어졌고, 낮은 가시성(나쁜 시야)으로 인해 항공사들이 어쩔 수 없이 항공편을 취소하도록 만들었다.
㉢ 학교와 기업체는 문을 닫았으며, 베이징시 당국은 사람들에게 집안에 가만히 있고, 공기 청정기를 계속 가동하고, 실내 활동을 줄이고, 가능한 한 활동하지 말라고 경고했다.
㉠ 눈물이 나고 찌르는 듯이 아픈 눈, 지끈거리는 두통, 부비강 문제 그리고 가려운 목구멍으로 고통받는 수백만 명의 사람들은 공기 정화 장치와 안면 보호용 마스크를 찾아 가게들을 샅샅이 뒤짐으로써 심신을 쇠약하게 만드는 공기로부터 피난처를 찾았다.
㉡ 중국 거주자들의 분노와 세계 언론의 감시는 정부가 국가의 대기 오염 문제를 해결하도록 강력히 촉구했다.

해설 ㉣에서 위험할 정도로 높은 오염 수준에 의해 야기된 2013년의 베이징의 비상 사태에 대해 언급한 후, 이에 대한 결과로 ㉢에서 학교와 기업체는 문을 닫았으며, 베이징시 당국은 사람들이 비상 사태 속에서 어떻게 해야 하는지 경고했다고 언급한다. 뒤이어 ㉠에서 고통받던 사람들이 심신을 쇠약하게 만드는 공기로부터 어떻게 피난처를 찾았는지에 대해 언급한 후, ㉡에서 이에 대한 중국 거주자들의 분노와 세계 언론의 감시가 대기 오염 문제를 해결하도록 강력히 촉구했다고 설명하고 있다. 따라서 ④ ㉣ – ㉢ – ㉠ – ㉡이 정답이다.

어휘 stinging 찌르는 듯이 아픈, 쑤시는
pound (머리가) 지끈거리다, 치다, 쿵쾅거리며 걷다 sinus 부비강
itchy 가려운 refuge 피난처
debilitate 심신을 쇠약하게 하다, 약화시키다
scour 샅샅이 뒤지다 outrage 분노 scrutiny 감시, 정밀한 조사
impel 촉구하다 purifier 청정기, 정화기 inactive 활동하지 않는
chaos 혼란 force 어쩔 수 없이 ~하게 만들다 visibility 가시성, 시야

14 독해 추론 (빈칸 완성 - 연결어) 난이도 ★★☆

끊어읽기 해석

Both novels and romances are works / of imaginative fiction / with multiple characters, / but that's where the similarities end.
소설과 로맨스 모두 작품이다 / 상상력이 만들어낸 허구의 / 많은 등장인물이 있는 / 하지만 유사성은 거기에서 끝난다

Novels are realistic; / romances aren't.
소설은 현실적이다 / 로맨스는 그렇지 않다

In the 19th century, / a romance was a prose narrative / that told a fictional story / dealt with its subjects and characters / in a symbolic, imaginative, and nonrealistic way.
19세기에 / 로맨스는 산문이었다 / 허구적인 이야기를 들려주는 / 그것의 소재와 등장인물을 다루는 / 상징적이고 상상적이며 비현실적인 방식으로

Typically, / a romance deals with / plots and people / that are exotic, / remote in time or place from the reader, / and obviously imaginary.
일반적으로, / 로맨스는 ~을 다룬다 / 줄거리와 사람들 / 이국적인 / 독자로부터 시간이나 장소가 멀리 떨어져 있는 / 그리고 명백히 가상의

해석 소설과 로맨스 모두 많은 등장인물이 있는 상상력이 만들어낸 허구의 작품이지만, 유사성은 거기에서 끝난다. 소설은 현실적이지만 로맨스는 그렇지 않다. 19세기에 로맨스는 그것의 소재와 등장인물을 상징적이고 상상적이며 비현실적인 방식으로 다루는 허구적인 이야기를 들려주는 산문이었다. 일반적으로, 로맨스는 이국적이고, 독자로부터 시간이나 장소가 멀리 떨어져 있으며, 명백히 가상의 줄거리와 사람들을 다룬다.

① 일반적으로 ② 반면에
③ 그럼에도 불구하고 ④ 경우에 따라서는

해설 빈칸 앞 문장은 로맨스가 그것의 소재와 등장인물을 상징적이고 상상적이며 비현실적인 방식으로 다루는 허구적인 이야기를 들려주는 산문이었다는 내용이고, 빈칸 뒤 문장은 로맨스가 이국적이고, 독자로부터 시간이나 장소가 멀리 떨어져 있으며 가상의 줄거리와 사람들을 다룬다는, 앞에서 설명한 로맨스의 일반적인 특성을 설명하는 내용이다. 따라서 일반화를 나타내는 연결어인 ① Typically(일반적으로)가 정답이다.

어휘 fiction 허구 multiple 많은, 다수의 character 등장인물
similarity 유사성 prose narrative 산문 deal with ~을 다루다
symbolic 상징적인 plot 줄거리 exotic 이국적인
obviously 명백히, 분명히 imaginary 가상의, 상상의

15 독해 추론 (빈칸 완성 - 단어) 난이도 ★☆☆

끊어읽기 해석

> Definitions are especially <u>unhelpful</u> / to children.
> 정의는 특히 <u>도움이 되지 않는다</u> / 아이들에게
>
> There's an oft-cited 1987 study / in which fifth graders were given / dictionary definitions / and asked to write their own sentences / using the words defined.
> 자주 인용되는 1987년 연구가 있다 / 5학년생들에게 주어졌던 / 사전적 정의가 / 그리고 자신만의 문장을 써보도록 요청되었던 / 정의된 단어를 사용하여
>
> The results were discouraging.
> 그 결과는 실망스러웠다
>
> One child / given the word erode / wrote / "Our family erodes a lot," / because / the definition given / was "eat out, / eat away."
> 한 아이는 / erode(침식하다)라는 단어를 받은 / 썼다 / '우리 가족은 많이 침식한다'라고 / 왜냐하면 ~ 때문이다 / 주어진 정의가 / 'eat out(외식하다, 침식하다)이었다 / eat away(먹어 치우다, 침식하다)'

해석 정의는 특히 아이들에게 도움이 되지 않는다. 5학년생들에게 사전적 정의가 주어지고 정의된 단어를 사용하여 자신만의 문장을 써보도록 요청되었던 자주 인용되는 1987년 연구가 있다. 그 결과는 실망스러웠다. erode(침식하다)라는 단어를 받은 한 아이는 '우리 가족은 많이 침식한다'라고 썼는데, 왜냐하면 주어진 정의가 'eat out(외식하다, 침식하다), eat away(먹어 치우다, 침식하다)'였기 때문이다.

① 유익한 ② 무례한
③ 도움이 되지 않는 ④ 쉽게 잊혀질

해설 빈칸이 있는 문장을 통해 빈칸에 정의가 특히 아이들에게 어떠한지에 대한 내용이 나와야 적절하다는 것을 알 수 있다. 지문 전반에 걸쳐 어떤 연구에서 아이들에게 사전적 정의를 주고, 그 단어를 이용해 문장을 써보도록 요청했으나 '침식하다'라는 뜻을 사용하여 '우리 가족은 많이 침식한다'는 예문을 만드는 실망스러운 결과가 나왔다는 내용이 있으므로, 정의는 아이들에게 '도움이 되지 않는'다고 한 ③번이 정답이다.

어휘 definition 정의 oft-cited 자주 인용되는
discouraging 실망스러운, 낙담시키는 eat out 외식하다, 침식하다
eat away 먹어 치우다, 침식하다 beneficial 유익한, 이로운
disrespectful 무례한 unhelpful 도움이 되지 않는, 쓸모없는
forgettable 쉽게 잊혀질, 별로 특별할 것 없는

16 독해 추론 (빈칸 완성 - 구) 난이도 ★★★

끊어읽기 해석

> Modern banking has its origins / in ancient England.
> 현대 금융은 그 기원이 있다 / 고대 영국에
>
> In those days / people / wanting to safeguard their gold / had two choices / —hide it under the mattress / or turn it over to someone else / for safekeeping.
> 그 당시에 / 사람들은 / 자신의 금을 보호하고자 하는 / 두 가지 선택권을 가지고 있었다 / 그것을 침대의 매트리스 밑에 숨기는 것이었다 / 또는 그것을 다른 사람에게 넘기는 것이었다 / 보관을 위해
>
> The logical people / to turn to for storage / were the local goldsmiths, / since they had / the strongest vaults.
> 적절한 사람들은 / 보관을 위해 의지할만한 / 그 지역의 금세공인들이었다 / 왜냐하면 그들이 가지고 있었기 때문이다 / 가장 강력한 금고를
>
> The goldsmiths accepted the gold / for storage, / giving the

---

owner / a receipt stating / that the gold could be redeemed / at a later date.
금세공인들은 금을 받아주었다 / 보관을 위해 / 소유자에게 주었다 / 명시하는 영수증을 / 금이 되찾아질 수 있다는 것을 / 나중에

When a payment was due, / the owner went to the goldsmith, / redeemed part of the gold / and gave it / to the payee.
지불일이 되었을 때 / 소유자는 금세공인에게 갔다 / 금의 일부를 되찾았다 / 그리고 그것을 주었다 / 수취인에게

After all that, / the payee was very likely / to turn around / and give the gold back / to the goldsmith / for safekeeping.
그 모든 것 이후에 / 수취인은 가능성이 매우 높았다 / 돌아설 / 그리고 그 금을 다시 맡길 / 금세공인에게 / 보관을 위해

Gradually, / instead of taking the time and effort / to physically exchange the gold, / business people <u>began to exchange</u> / the goldsmith's receipts / as payment.
서서히 / 시간과 노력을 들이는 대신 / 물질적으로 금을 교환하는 데 / 사업가들은 <u>교환하기 시작했다</u> / 금세공인의 영수증을 / 지불금으로

해석 현대 금융은 고대 영국에 그 기원이 있다. 그 당시에 자신의 금을 보호하고자 하는 사람들은 두 가지 선택권을 가지고 있었다. 그것을 침대의 매트리스 밑에 숨기거나 보관을 위해 그것을 다른 사람에게 넘기는 것이었다. 보관을 위해 의지할만한 적절한 사람들은 그 지역의 금세공인들이었는데, 왜냐하면 그들이 가장 강력한 금고를 가지고 있었기 때문이다. 금세공인들은 보관을 위해 금을 받아주었고, 금이 나중에 되찾아질 수 있다는 것을 명시하는 영수증을 소유자에게 주었다. 지불일이 되었을 때, 소유자는 금세공인에게 가서 금의 일부를 되찾고 그것을 수취인에게 주었다. 그 모든 것 이후에 수취인은 돌아서서 보관을 위해 그 금을 다시 금세공인에게 맡길 가능성이 매우 높았다. 물질적으로 금을 교환하는 데 시간과 노력을 들이는 대신, 사업가들은 서서히 금세공인의 영수증을 지불금으로 교환하기 시작했다.

① 금세공인의 영수증을 지불금으로 교환하기 시작했다
② 이 거래에서 수익에 대한 가능성을 보았다
③ 기탁자들에게 그들의 금을 되찾지 말라고 경고했다
④ 요금을 받고 누군가에게 금을 빌려주었다

해설 빈칸이 있는 문장을 통해 빈칸에 물질적으로 금을 교환하는 데 시간과 노력을 들이는 대신, 사업가들은 서서히 무엇을 했는지에 대한 내용이 나와야 적절하다는 것을 알 수 있다. 빈칸 앞에서 금 소유자는 지불일이 되었을 때, 금세공인에게 가서 금의 일부를 되찾은 후 그것을 수취인에게 주었고, 금을 받은 수취인은 돌아서서 그 금을 금세공인에게 다시 맡길 가능성이 매우 높았다고 했으므로, 물질적으로 금을 교환하는 데 시간과 노력을 들이는 대신 사업가들은 서서히 '금세공인의 영수증을 지불금으로 교환하기 시작했다'고 한 ①번이 정답이다.

어휘 banking 금융, 은행업 origin 기원 safeguard 보호하다
safekeeping 보관, 보호 logical 적절한 turn to ~에 의지하다
goldsmith 금세공인 vault 금고 receipt 영수증 redeem 되찾다
payee 수취인 arrangement 거래, 계약 depositor 기탁자, 예금자

17 독해 추론 (빈칸 완성 - 단어) 난이도 ★★☆

끊어읽기 해석

> In some cultures, / such as in Korea and Egypt, / politeness norms require / that when someone is offered / something to eat or drink, / it must be refused / the first time around.
> 일부 문화권에서 / 한국과 이집트 같은 / 공손 규범은 요구한다 / 누군가가 제안받을 때 / 먹을 것이나 마실 것을 / 그것이 거절되어야 한다고 / 처음에는

However, / such a refusal is often viewed / as a rejection of someone's hospitality / and thoughtlessness / in other cultures, / particularly when no <u>excuse</u> is made / for the refusal.
하지만 / 그러한 거절은 보통 간주된다 / 누군가의 친절에 대한 거절로 / 그리고 인정 없음(으로) / 다른 문화권에서는 / 특히 변명을 하지 않을 때 (그러하다) / 거절에 대한

Americans and Canadians, / for instance, / expect / refusals to be accompanied / by a reasonable <u>excuse</u>.
미국인들과 캐나다인들은 / 예를 들어 / 기대한다 / 거절이 수반할 것이라고 / 합당한 <u>변명</u>을

해석 한국과 이집트 같은 일부 문화권에서 공손 규범은 누군가가 먹을 것이나 마실 것을 제안받을 때 그것이 처음에는 거절되어야 한다고 요구한다. 하지만 그러한 거절은 보통 다른 문화권에서는 누군가의 친절에 대한 거절과 인정 없음으로 간주되는데, 특히 거절에 대한 변명을 하지 않을 때 그러하다. 예를 들어, 미국인들과 캐나다인들은 거절이 합당한 변명을 수반할 것이라고 기대한다.

① 역할　　　　② 변명
③ 선택　　　　④ 상황

해설 빈칸이 있는 두 문장을 통해 빈칸에 거절은 다른 문화권에서 특히 무엇을 하지 않을 때 친절에 대한 거절과 인정 없음으로 간주되며, 미국인들과 캐나다인들은 거절이 합당한 무엇을 수반할 것이라고 기대하는지에 대한 내용이 나와야 적절하다는 것을 알 수 있다. 지문 처음에서 한국과 이집트 같은 일부 문화권에서 공손 규범은 누군가가 먹을 것이나 마실 것을 제안받을 때 그것이 처음에는 거절되어야 한다고 요구하지만, 그러한 거절은 보통 다른 문화권에서는 누군가의 친절에 대한 거절과 인정 없음으로 간주된다는 내용이 있으므로, 거절이 합당한 '변명'을 수반할 것이라고 기대한다고 한 ②번이 정답이다.

어휘 politeness 공손(함)　norm 규범　refuse 거절하다　refusal 거절
rejection 거절　hospitality 친절함, 호의
thoughtlessness 인정 없음, 경솔함
be accompanied by ~을 수반하다, 동반하다
excuse 변명, 이유

---

18 독해 논리적 흐름 파악 (문장 삽입)　난이도 ★★☆

끊어읽기 해석

Instead, / these employees spoke first / of the sincerity / of the relationships at work, / that their work culture felt / like an extension of home, / and that their colleagues were supportive.
대신에 / 이 직원들은 먼저 말했다 / 진정성에 대해 / 직장에서의 관계들의 / 그들의 직장 문화가 느껴지는 것(에 대해) / 가정의 연장선처럼 / 그리고 그들의 동료들이 협력적이라는 것(에 대해)

(①) There is a clear link / between job satisfaction and productivity.
명백한 관련성이 있다 / 직업 만족도와 생산성 사이에는

However, / job satisfaction also depends / on the service culture of an organization.
하지만 / 직업 만족도는 또한 달려있다 / 기업의 서비스 문화에

(②) This culture comprises the things / that make a business distinctive / and make the people who work there proud / to do so.
이러한 문화는 것들로 구성된다 / 기업을 특색 있게 만드는 / 그리고 그곳에서 일하는 사람들이 자랑스럽게 만드는 / 그곳에서 일하는 것을

(③) When employees of the "Top 10 Best Companies

to Work For" / were asked / by *Fortune* magazine / why they loved / working for these companies, / it was notable / that they didn't mention / pay, reward schemes, or advancing / to a more senior position.
'일하기 좋은 최고의 10대 기업'의 직원들이 / 질문 받았을 때 / 『포춘』지로부터 / 왜 그들이 좋아하는지 / 이 회사들을 위해 일하는 것을 / 주목할 만했다 / 그들이 언급하지 않았다는 것은 / 급여, 보상제도, 또는 승진하는 것을 / 더 상급직으로

(④)

해석 직업 만족도와 생산성 사이에는 명백한 관련성이 있다. 하지만, 직업 만족도는 또한 기업의 서비스 문화에 달려있다. 이러한 문화는 기업을 특색 있게 만들며 그곳에서 일하는 사람들이 그곳에서 일하는 것을 자랑스러워하게 만드는 것들로 구성된다. '일하기 좋은 최고의 10대 기업'의 직원들이 『포춘』지로부터 왜 그들이 이 회사들을 위해 일하는 것을 좋아하는지 질문 받았을 때, 그들이 급여, 보상제도, 또는 더 상급직으로 승진하는 것을 언급하지 않았다는 것은 주목할 만했다. ④ 대신에, 이 직원들은 직장에서의 관계들의 진정성, 그들의 직장 문화가 가정의 연장선처럼 느껴지는 것, 그들의 동료들이 협력적이라는 것에 대해 먼저 말했다.

해설 ④번 앞 문장에서 '일하기 좋은 최고의 10대 기업'의 직원들이 『포춘』지로부터 왜 그들이 이 회사들을 위해 일하는 것을 좋아하는지 질문 받았을 때, 그들이 급여, 보상제도, 또는 더 상급직으로 승진하는 것을 언급하지 않았다는 것은 주목할 만했다고 했으므로 ④번 자리에 '대신에, 이 직원들은 직장에서의 관계들의 진정성, 그들의 직장 문화가 가정의 연장선처럼 느껴지는 것, 그들의 동료들이 협력적이라는 것에 대해 먼저 말했다'라는 주어진 문장이 나와야 지문이 자연스럽게 연결된다. 따라서 ④번이 정답이다.

어휘 sincerity 진정성　extension 연장선　colleague 동료
supportive 협력적인　productivity 생산성
depend on ~에 달려있다　comprise ~으로 구성되다
distinctive 특색 있는, 뚜렷이 구분되는
notable 주목할 만한, 눈에 띄는　scheme 제도
advance 승진하다, 나아가다　senior 상급의

---

19 독해 세부내용 파악 (내용 일치 파악)　난이도 ★★☆

끊어읽기 해석

Why Orkney / of all places?
왜 오크니인가 / 모든 장소들 중에?

④How did this scatter of islands / off the northern tip / of Scotland / come to be such a technological, cultural, and spiritual powerhouse?
어떻게 이 흩어진 섬들이 / 북쪽 끝에서 떨어져 있는 / 스코틀랜드의 / 그렇게 기술적, 문화적, 그리고 정신적으로 강력한 집단이 되었는가?

For starters, / you have to stop thinking / of Orkney as remote.
먼저 / 당신은 생각하는 것을 멈추어야 한다 / 오크니가 멀리 떨어져 있다고

②③For most of history, / ④Orkney was an important maritime hub, / a place that was on the way / to everywhere.
역사의 대부분 동안 / 오크니는 중요한 해상 중심지였다 / 길에 있는 장소인 / 모든 곳으로 이어지는

①④It was also blessed / with some of the richest farming soils / in Britain / and a surprisingly mild climate, / thanks to the effects / of the Gulf Stream.
그것은 또한 축복받았다 / 가장 비옥한 농사 토양으로 / 영국에서 / 그리고 놀랍도록 온화한 기후(로) / 영향 덕분에 / 멕시코 만류의

해석 왜 모든 장소들 중에 오크니인가? 어떻게 스코틀랜드 북쪽 끝에서 떨어져 있는 이 흩어진 섬들이 그렇게 기술적, 문화적, 그리고 정신적으로 강력한 집단이 되었는가? 먼저, 당신은 오크니가 멀리 떨어져 있다고 생각하는 것을 멈추어야 한다. 역사의 대부분 동안, 오크니는 모든 곳으로 이어지는 길에 있는 장소인, 중요한 해상 중심지였다. 그것은 또한 멕시코 만류의 영향 덕분에 영국에서 가장 비옥한 농사 토양과 놀랍도록 온화한 기후로 축복받았다.

① 오크니 사람들은 많은 사회적, 자연적 불이익을 극복해야 했다.
② 그 지역은 궁극적으로 그곳의 문명을 소멸로 이끌었던 반역의 중심지 중 하나였다.
③ 오크니는 중심지로부터 너무 멀리 떨어져 있었기 때문에 그것의 자원을 최대한 활용하지 못했다.
④ 오크니의 번영은 대체로 그것의 지리적 이점과 천연자원 덕분이었다.

해설 지문 처음에서 어떻게 오크니가 기술적, 문화적, 그리고 정신적으로 강력한 집단이 되었는가 질문하고, 오크니는 모든 곳으로 이어지는 길에 있는 장소인, 중요한 해상 중심지였으며, 가장 비옥한 농사 토양과 놀랍도록 온화한 기후로 축복받았다고 했으므로, 오크니의 번영은 대체로 그것의 지리적 이점과 천연자원 덕분이었다는 것을 알 수 있다. 따라서 ④번이 정답이다.

오답
분석
① 오크니는 멕시코 만류의 영향 덕분에 영국에서 가장 비옥한 농사 토양과 놀랍도록 온화한 기후로 축복받았다고 했으므로, 오크니 사람들은 많은 사회적, 자연적 불이익을 극복해야 했다는 것은 지문의 내용과 다르다.
② 오크니가 중요한 해상 중심지였다고는 했지만 궁극적으로 그곳의 문명을 소멸로 이끌었던 반역의 중심지 중 하나였는지는 언급되지 않았다.
③ 오크니는 역사의 대부분 동안 모든 곳으로 이어지는 길에 있는 장소인 중요한 해상 중심지였다고 했으므로 오크니가 중심지로부터 너무 멀리 떨어져 있었기 때문에 그것의 자원을 최대한 활용하지 못했다는 것은 지문의 내용과 다르다.

어휘 **powerhouse** 강력한 집단, 최강자 **for starters** 먼저, 우선 첫째로
maritime 해상의 **hub** 중심지 **Gulf Stream** 멕시코 만류
rebellion 반역 **annihilation** 소멸, 전멸
make the best of ~을 최대한 활용하다 **prosperity** 번영

20 독해 전체내용 파악 (제목 파악) 난이도 ★★☆

끊어읽기 해석

Initially, / papyrus and parchment were kept / as scrolls / that could be unrolled / either vertically or horizontally, / depending on the direction of the script.
처음에 / 파피루스와 양피지는 보관되었다 / 두루마리로 / 펼쳐질 수 있는 / 수직 또는 수평으로 / 원고의 방향에 따라

The horizontal form was more common, / and because scrolls could be quite long, / a scribe would typically refrain / from writing a single line / across the entire length, / but instead would mark off columns / of a reasonable width.
수평의 형태가 더 일반적이었다 / 그리고 두루마리가 꽤 길어질 수 있었기 때문에 / 필기하는 사람은 일반적으로 삼갔다 / 한 줄로 쓰는 것을 / 전체 길이에 걸쳐 / 하지만 대신에 열을 구별했다 / 적정한 폭으로

That way / the reader could unroll one side / and roll up the other / while reading.
그 방식으로 / 독자는 한 쪽은 펼칠 수 있었다 / 그리고 다른 한 쪽은 말 수 있었다 / 읽는 동안

Nevertheless, / the constant need / to re-roll the scroll / was a major disadvantage / to this format, / and it was

impossible / to jump to various places / in the scroll / the way we skip / to a particular page of a book.
그럼에도 불구하고 / 지속적인 필요성은 / 두루마리를 다시 말아야 하는 / 주요한 단점이었다 / 이 형태의 / 그리고 불가능했다 / 다양한 위치로 건너뛰는 것이 / 두루마리에서는 / 우리가 건너뛰는 방식처럼 / 책의 특정 페이지로

Moreover, / the reader struggled / to make notes / while reading / since both hands (or weights) were required / to keep the scroll open.
게다가 / 독자는 어려움을 겪었다 / 메모를 하는 데 / 읽는 동안 / 양손(또는 추)이 필요했기 때문에 / 두루마리를 계속 펼쳐 놓기 위해

해석 처음에 파피루스와 양피지는 원고의 방향에 따라 수직 또는 수평으로 펼쳐질 수 있는 두루마리로 보관되었다. 수평의 형태가 더 일반적이었고, 두루마리가 꽤 길어질 수 있었기 때문에 필기하는 사람은 일반적으로 전체 길이에 걸쳐 한 줄로 쓰는 것을 삼가고 대신에 적정한 폭으로 열을 구별했다. 그 방식으로 독자는 읽는 동안 한 쪽은 펼치고, 다른 한 쪽은 말 수 있었다. 그럼에도 불구하고 두루마리를 다시 말아야 하는 지속적인 필요성은 이 형태의 주요한 단점이었고, 우리가 책의 특정 페이지로 건너뛰는 방식처럼 다양한 위치로 건너뛰는 것이 두루마리에서는 불가능했다. 게다가, 독자는 두루마리를 계속 펼쳐 놓기 위해 양손(또는 추)이 필요했기 때문에 읽는 동안 메모를 하는 데 어려움을 겪었다.

① 두루마리의 불편함
② 책의 진화
③ 읽는 것과 쓰는 것의 발전
④ 두루마리의 단점을 극복하는 방법들

해설 지문 중간에서 두루마리를 다시 말아야 하는 지속적인 필요성은 이 형태의 주요한 단점이었다고 언급하고, 이어서 두루마리에서는 다양한 위치로 건너뛰는 것이 불가능했고, 독자는 메모를 하는 데 어려움을 겪었다는 추가적인 단점들을 언급하고 있다. 따라서 이 지문의 제목을 '두루마리의 불편함'이라고 표현한 ①번이 정답이다.

어휘 **parchment** 양피지 **scroll** 두루마리 **unroll** 펼치다
vertically 수직으로 **horizontally** 수평으로 **script** 원고
scribe 필기하는 사람, 필경사 **refrain from** ~을 삼가다
mark off 구별하다 **column** 열, 세로줄 **width** 폭, 넓이
struggle 어려움을 겪다, 애를 쓰다 **weight** 추

gosi.Hackers.com

법원직 9급 출제 경향

1. 영역별 출제 문항 수 (2022~2024)

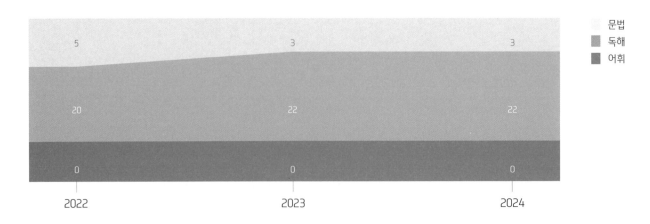

지난 3년간 영역별 출제 문항 수는 거의 동일한 편입니다. **문법** 영역은 3~5문항, **독해** 영역은 20~22문항씩 출제되었습니다. **어휘** 영역에서는 2011년 이후로 문제가 출제되지 않고 있습니다.

Part 4
법원직 9급

2. 영역별 최근 출제 경향 및 학습 방법

문법	**밑줄 친 부분 중 옳지 않은 것을 고르는 유형과 빈칸 안에서 어법에 맞는 것을 고르는 유형 출제** 밑줄 친 부분 중 어법상 옳지 않은 것을 고르는 유형의 문제가 2~3문항씩 꾸준히 출제되고, 빈칸 안에서 어법에 맞는 표현으로 적절한 것을 고르는 문제도 2021년과 2022년에 각각 2문항씩, 2024년에 1문항이 출제되었습니다. ▶ 따라서 밑줄 친 보기나 빈칸을 중심으로 문법 포인트를 확인하고, 밑줄 친 부분이나 빈칸만으로 옳고 그름을 판단할 수 없는 경우에는 주변의 문맥을 통해 파악하는 연습을 하는 것이 좋습니다. [빈출 포인트] 수 일치(4문항) | 명사절(3문항) | 병치·도치·강조 구문(2문항) | 관계절(2문항)
독해	**전체내용 파악, 세부내용 파악, 문단 요약 유형 중심의 문제 출제** 최근 3년간 빈칸 완성 유형의 문제는 2~4문항 수준으로 비교적 적게 출제되었고, 전체내용 파악, 세부내용 파악, 문단 요약 유형의 문제가 주로 출제되었습니다. ▶ 따라서 인칭대명사, 지시대명사, 연결어 등을 통해 지문의 논리적 흐름을 파악하고, 보기의 키워드와 관련된 부분을 지문에서 빠르게 찾아내는 연습을 꾸준히 하는 것이 중요합니다.
어휘	**독해 영역과 연계된 어휘 문제 출제** 2011년 이후 어휘 영역에서는 문제가 출제되지 않고 있습니다. 대신 최근 3년간 '문맥상 적절한/부적절한 어휘 및 표현 고르기' 유형으로 어휘의 의미를 묻는 문제가 매년 1~5문항 출제되었습니다. ▶ 따라서 어휘와 예문을 함께 학습하여 문맥에서 해당 어휘가 어떻게 사용되는지를 확인하는 것이 중요합니다.

정답

p.150

01	④ 독해 - 논리적 흐름 파악	11	② 독해 - 세부내용 파악	21	② 독해 - 추론
02	① 독해 - 추론	12	② 독해 - 논리적 흐름 파악	22	① 독해 - 추론
03	② 독해 - 세부내용 파악	13	② 독해 - 전체내용 파악	23	② 독해 - 전체내용 파악
04	② 독해 - 추론	14	③ 독해 - 논리적 흐름 파악	24	① 독해 - 전체내용 파악
05	④ 독해 - 세부내용 파악	15	① 독해 - 논리적 흐름 파악	25	④ 독해 - 세부내용 파악
06	② 독해 - 추론	16	④ 독해 - 세부내용 파악		
07	④ 독해 - 전체내용 파악	17	② 독해 - 논리적 흐름 파악		
08	④ 독해 - 논리적 흐름 파악	18	② 문법 - 분사&관계절&수 일치		
09	① 독해 - 논리적 흐름 파악	19	② 독해 - 세부내용 파악		
10	③ 문법 - 대명사	20	④ 문법 - 분사		

취약영역 분석표

영역	세부 유형	문항 수	소계
문법	대명사	1	/3
	분사&관계절&수 일치	1	
	분사	1	
독해	전체내용 파악	4	/22
	세부내용 파악	6	
	추론	5	
	논리적 흐름 파악	7	
	총계		**/25**

· 자신이 취약한 영역은 '공무원 영어, 이렇게 출제된다!'(문제집 p.8)를 통해 다시 한번 확인하고 학습하시기 바랍니다.

---

01 독해 | 논리적 흐름 파악 (문단 순서 배열) 난이도 ★★☆

끊어읽기 해석

Now / we stand at the edge of a turning point / as we face / the rise of a coming wave of technology / that includes / both advanced AI and biotechnology.
이제 / 우리는 전환점의 가장자리에 서 있다 / 우리가 직면하면서 / 다가오는 기술 물결의 도래에 / 포함하는 / 첨단 인공지능과 생명공학을 모두

Never before have we witnessed technologies / with such transformative potential, / promising to reshape our world / in ways / that are both awe-inspiring and daunting.
우리는 이전에 기술을 본 적이 없다 / 이렇게 혁신적인 잠재력을 가진 / 우리의 세상을 개조할 것을 보장하는 / 방식으로 / 경외심을 불러일으키고 겁먹게 하는

(A) With AI, / we could create systems / that are beyond our control / and / find ourselves at the mercy of algorithms / that we don't understand.
인공지능으로 / 우리는 시스템을 만들 수 있다 / 우리가 통제할 수 없는 / 그리고 / 알고리즘에 좌우될 수 있다 / 우리가 이해할 수 없는

With biotechnology, / we could manipulate / the very building blocks of life, / potentially creating / unintended consequences / for both individuals and entire ecosystem.
생명공학으로 / 우리는 조작할 수 있다 / 생명의 구성 요소 자체를 / 어쩌면 초래할 수 있다 / 의도되지 않은 결과를 / 개인과 생태계 전체에

(B) With biotechnology, / we could engineer life / to tackle diseases / and / transform agriculture, / creating a world / that is healthier and more sustainable.
생명공학으로 / 우리는 삶을 설계할 수 있다 / 질병과 싸우도록 / 그리고 / 농업을 변화시키도록 / 세상을 만들 수 있다 / 더 건강하고 더 지속 가능한

But / on the other hand, / the potential dangers / of these technologies / are equally vast and profound.
그러나 / 다른 한편으로 / 잠재적인 위험은 / 이러한 기술들의 / 마찬가지로 방대하고 심오하다

(C) On the one hand, / the potential benefits / of these technologies / are vast and profound.
반면에 / 잠재적인 이점들은 / 이 기술들의 / 방대하고 심오하다

With AI, / we could unlock the secrets of the universe, / cure diseases / that have long eluded us / and / create new forms of art and culture / that stretch the bounds of imagination.
인공지능으로 / 우리는 우주의 비밀을 풀 수 있고 / 질병을 치료할 수 있고 / 오랫동안 우리에게 이해되지 않았던 / 그리고 / 새로운 형태의 예술과 문화를 창조할 수 있다 / 상상의 경계를 넓히는

해석

이제 우리는 첨단 인공지능과 생명공학을 모두 포함하는 다가오는 기술 물결의 도래에 직면하면서 전환점의 가장자리에 서 있다. 우리는 이전에 경외심을 불러일으키고 겁먹게 하는 방식으로 세상을 개조할 것을 보장하는 이렇게 혁신적인 잠재력을 가진 기술을 본 적이 없다.

(C) 반면에, 이 기술들의 잠재적인 이점들은 방대하고 심오하다. 인공지능으로, 우리는 우주의 비밀을 풀고, 오랫동안 우리에게 이해되지 않았던 질병을 치료하고, 상상의 경계를 넓히는 새로운 형태의 예술과 문화를 창조할 수 있다.

(B) 생명공학으로, 우리는 질병과 싸우고 농업을 변화시키도록 삶을 설계할 수 있으며, 더 건강하고 더 지속 가능한 세상을 만들 수 있다. 그러나 다른 한편으로, 이러한 기술들의 잠재적인 위험은 마찬가지로 방대하고 심오하다.

(A) 인공지능으로, 우리는 우리가 통제할 수 없는 시스템을 만들고 우리가 이해할 수 없는 알고리즘에 좌우될 수 있다. 생명공학으로, 우리는 생명의 구성 요소 자체를 조작하여, 어쩌면 개인과 생태계 전체에 의도되지 않은 결과를 초래할 수 있다.

해설 주어진 문장에서 우리는 첨단 인공지능과 생명공학을 모두 포함하는 기술 물결의 도래에 직면했는데, 이전에 이렇게 혁신적인 잠재력을 가진 기술을 본 적이 없다고 하고, (C)에서 반면에 이 기술들의 잠재적인 이점들은 방대하고 심오하다고 하면서 인공지능의

장점에 대해 설명하고 있다. 이어서 (B)에서 생명공학으로 우리는 더 건강하고 더 지속 가능한 세상을 만들 수 있지만 이러한 기술들의 잠재적인 위험도 마찬가지로 방대하고 심오하다고 설명하고 있다. 마지막으로 (A)에서 인공지능으로 우리가 통제할 수 없는 시스템을 만들거나 생명공학으로 개인과 생태계 전체에 의도되지 않은 결과를 초래할 수 있다고 하면서 인공지능과 생명공학의 잠재적인 위험에 대해 설명하고 있다. 따라서 ④ (C) - (B) - (A)가 정답이다.

어휘 edge 가장자리 turning point 전환점 biotechnology 생명공학 witness 보다, 목격하다 transformative 혁신적인, 변화시키는 potential 잠재력, 가능성 promise 보장하다, 약속하다 reshape 개조하다, 새 형태로 만들다 awe 경외심, 두려움 at the mercy of ~에 좌우되는, ~의 처분대로 manipulate 조작하다 building block 구성 요소, 필요한 것 potentially 어쩌면, 잠재적으로 unintended 의도하지 않은 consequence 결과 agriculture 농업 sustainable 지속 가능한 vast 방대한, 막대한 profound 심오한, 깊은 bound 경계, 한계 imagination 상상

---

02 독해 추론 (빈칸 완성 - 구) 난이도 ★★☆

끊어읽기 해석

Controversy over new art-making technologies / is nothing new.
새로운 예술 제작 기술에 대한 논란은 / 새로운 것이 아니다

Many painters recoiled / at the invention of the camera, / which they saw / as a debasement / of human artistry.
많은 화가들은 움츠러들었다 / 카메라의 발명에 / 그것은 그들이 본 것이다 / 저하로 / 인간 예술성의

Charles Baudelaire, / the 19th-century French poet and art critic, / called photography / "art's most mortal enemy."
Charles Baudelaire는 / 19세기 프랑스 시인이자 예술 평론가인 / 사진을 불렀다 / '예술의 가장 치명적인 적'이라고

In the 20th century, / digital editing tools and computer-assisted design programs / were similarly dismissed / by purists / for requiring too little skill / of their human collaborators.
20세기에 / 디지털 편집 도구와 컴퓨터 보조 디자인 프로그램은 / 비슷하게 무시되었다 / 순수주의자들에 의해 / 기술을 너무 적게 요구한다는 이유로 / 인간 협력자들의

What makes the new breed of A.I. image generating tools different / is not just that they're capable of / producing beautiful works of art / with minimal effort.
인공지능 이미지 생성 도구의 새로운 유형을 다르게 만드는 것은 / 그것들이 ~할 수 있다는 것만이 아니다 / 아름다운 예술 작품을 생산하는 것 / 최소한의 노력으로

It's how they work.
그것들이 어떻게 작동하는지이다

These tools are built / by scraping millions of images / from the open web, / then teaching algorithms / to recognize patterns and relationships in those images / and / generate new ones / in the same style.
이 도구들은 만들어진다 / 수백만 개의 이미지를 스크랩함으로써 / 오픈 웹에서 / 그다음 알고리즘을 가르침으로써 / 그 이미지들의 양식과 관계를 인식하도록 / 그리고 / 새로운 것들(이미지)을 생성하도록 / 동일한 스타일로

That means / that artists / who upload their works / to the internet / may be unwittingly <u>helping / to train their algorithmic competitors.</u>
이는 의미한다 / 예술가들이 / 자신의 작품을 올리는 / 인터넷에 / 자신도 모르게 도울 수 있다는 것을 / 그들의 알고리즘 경쟁자를 훈련시키는 것을

해석 새로운 예술 제작 기술에 대한 논란은 새로운 것이 아니다. 많은 화가들은 카메라의 발명에 움츠러들었는데, 그것(카메라의 발명)은 그들이 인간 예술성의 저하로 본 것이다. 19세기 프랑스 시인이자 예술 평론가인 Charles Baudelaire는 사진을 '예술의 가장 치명적인 적'이라고 불렀다. 20세기에, 디지털 편집 도구와 컴퓨터 보조 디자인 프로그램은 인간 협력자들의 기술을 너무 적게 요구한다는 이유로 순수주의자들에 의해 비슷하게 무시되었다. 인공지능 이미지 생성 도구의 새로운 유형을 다르게 만드는 것은 그것들이 최소한의 노력으로 아름다운 예술 작품을 생산할 수 있다는 것만이 아니다. 그것들이 어떻게 작동하는지이다. 이 도구들은 오픈 웹에서 수백만 개의 이미지를 스크랩한 다음, 알고리즘에게 그 이미지들의 양식과 관계를 인식하고 동일한 스타일로 새로운 이미지를 생성하도록 가르침으로써 만들어진다. 이는 인터넷에 자신의 작품을 올리는 예술가들이 자신도 모르게 <u>그들의 알고리즘 경쟁자를 훈련시키는 것을</u> 도울 수 있다는 것을 의미한다.

① 그들의 알고리즘 경쟁자를 훈련시키는 것을 돕는
② 인공지능이 만든 예술의 윤리에 대한 논쟁을 촉발하는
③ 디지털 기술을 창의적인 과정의 일부로 수용하는
④ 독창적인 창작물을 만들기 위해 인터넷을 활용하는 기술을 습득하는

해설 빈칸 앞 문장에서 인공지능 이미지 생성 도구는 오픈 웹에서 수백만 개의 이미지를 스크랩한 다음 알고리즘에게 동일한 스타일로 새로운 이미지를 생성하도록 가르친다고 설명하고 있으므로, 빈칸에는 이는 인터넷에 자신의 작품을 올리는 예술가들이 자신도 모르게 '① 그들의 알고리즘 경쟁자를 훈련시키는 것을 도울' 수 있다는 것을 의미한다는 내용이 들어가야 한다.

어휘 controversy 논란, 논쟁 recoil 움츠러들다, 반동하다 debasement 저하, 타락 artistry 예술성 poet 시인 mortal 치명적인 dismiss 무시하다, 일축하다 purist 순수주의자 collaborator 협력자 breed 유형, 품종 generate 생성하다, 발생시키다 spark 촉발하다, 야기하다 ethics 윤리 embrace 수용하다, 포용하다 acquire 습득하다, 얻다 utilize 활용하다 craft 만들다 original 독창적인, 원래의

---

03 독해 세부내용 파악 (내용 불일치 파악) 난이도 ★★☆

끊어읽기 해석

Duke Kahanamoku, born August 26, 1890, near Waikiki, Hawaii, / was a Hawaiian surfer and swimmer / who won three Olympic gold medals / for the United States / and / who for several years / was considered / the greatest freestyle swimmer / in the world.
1890년 8월 26일에 하와이 와이키키 근처에서 태어난 Duke Kahanamoku는 / 하와이의 서퍼이자 수영 선수였다 / 올림픽 금메달 세 개를 획득한 / 미국을 대표해 / 그리고 / 수년 동안 / 여겨진 / 가장 위대한 자유형 수영 선수로 / 세계에서

He was perhaps most widely known / for developing the flutter kick, / which largely replaces / the scissors kick.
그는 아마도 가장 널리 알려져 있을 것이다 / 플러터 킥을 개발한 것으로 / 주로 대체하는 / 시저스 킥을

Kahanamoku set three universally recognized world records / in the 100-yard freestyle / between July 5, 1913, and September 5, 1917.
Kahanamoku는 세계적으로 인정되는 세 개의 세계 기록을 세웠다 / 100야드 자유형에서 / 1913년 7월 5일과 1917년 9월 5일 사이에

In the 100-yard freestyle / Kahanamoku was U.S. indoor champion / in 1913, / and / outdoor titleholder / in 1916-17 and 1920.

1000야드 자유형에서 / Kahanamoku는 미국 실내 챔피언이었다 / 1913년에 / 그리고 / 실외 타이틀 보유자였다 / 1916-17년과 1920년에

At the Olympic Games in Stockholm / in 1912, / he won the 100-metre freestyle event, / and / he repeated that triumph / at the 1920 Olympics in Antwerp, Belgium, / where he also was a member of the victorious U.S. team / in the 800-metre relay race.
스톡홀름 올림픽에서 / 1912년에 / 그는 100미터 자유형 경기에서 우승했다 / 그리고 / 그는 그 승리를 거듭했다 / 1920년 벨기에 앤트워프 올림픽에서 / 그곳에서 그는 우승한 미국 팀의 일원이기도 했다 / 800미터 계주에서

Kahanamoku also excelled at surfing, / and / he became viewed / as one of the icons / of the sport.
Kahanamoku는 서핑에도 뛰어났다 / 그리고 / 그는 여겨지게 되었다 / 우상 중 하나로 / 그 스포츠의

Intermittently from the mid-1920s, / Kahanamoku was a motion-picture actor.
1920년 중반부터 간헐적으로 / Kahanamoku는 영화배우였다

From 1932 to 1961 / he was sheriff / of the city and county of Honolulu.
1932년부터 1961년까지 / 그는 보안관이었다 / 호놀룰루시와 자치주의

He served in the salaried office / of official greeter / of famous personages / for the state of Hawaii / from 1961 until his death.
그는 유급 사무실에서 근무했다 / 공식적으로 맞이하는 / 유명 인사들을 / 하와이주의 / 1961년부터 사망할 때까지

해석 1890년 8월 26일에 하와이 와이키키 근처에서 태어난 Duke Kahanamoku는 미국을 대표해 올림픽 금메달 세 개를 획득하고 수년 동안 세계에서 가장 위대한 자유형 수영 선수로 여겨진 하와이의 서퍼이자 수영 선수였다. 그는 아마도 주로 시저스 킥을 대체하는 플러터 킥을 개발한 것으로 가장 널리 알려져 있을 것이다. Kahanamoku는 1913년 7월 5일과 1917년 9월 5일 사이에 100야드 자유형에서 세계적으로 인정되는 세 개의 세계 기록을 세웠다. 1000야드 자유형에서 Kahanamoku는 1913년에 미국 실내 챔피언이었고, 1916-17년과 1920년에 실외 타이틀 보유자였다. 1912년 스톡홀름 올림픽에서, 그는 100미터 자유형 경기에서 우승했고, 1920년 벨기에 앤트워프 올림픽에서도 그 승리를 거듭했으며, 그곳에서 그는 800미터 계주에서 우승한 미국 팀의 일원이기도 했다. Kahanamoku는 서핑에도 뛰어났고, 그는 그 스포츠의 우상 중 하나로 여겨지게 되었다. 1920년 중반부터 간헐적으로 Kahanamoku는 영화배우였다. 1932년부터 1961년까지 그는 호놀룰루시와 자치주의 보안관이었다. 그는 1961년부터 사망할 때까지 하와이주의 유명 인사들을 공식적으로 맞이하는 유급 사무실에서 근무했다.

해설 ②번의 키워드인 시저스 킥(the scissors kick)과 플러터 킥(the flutter kick)이 그대로 언급된 지문 주변의 내용에서 Duke Kahanamoku는 시저스 킥을 대체하는 플러터 킥을 개발한 것으로 가장 널리 알려져 있을 것이라고 했으므로 '② 그는 플러터 킥을 대체하는 시저스 킥을 개발한 것으로 널리 알려져 있다'는 지문의 내용과 일치하지 않는다.

어휘 freestyle (수영·레슬링 등에서) 자유형 largely 주로, 대부분은
replace 대체하다 triumph 승리 excel 뛰어나다, 두드러지다
motion-picture 영화 salaried 유급의, 월급을 받는
official 공식적인 greeter 맞이하는 사람 personage 인사, 명사

---

04 독해 추론 (빈칸 완성 - 단어) 난이도 ★★☆

끊어읽기 해석

The understandings / that children bring to the classroom / can already be quite powerful / in the early grades.
지식은 / 아이들이 교실에 가져오는 / 이미 꽤 강력할 수 있다 / 저학년 때

For example, / some children have been found / to hold onto their preconception / of a flat earth / by imagining a round earth / to be shaped like a pancake.
예를 들어 / 어떤 아이들은 밝혀졌다 / 그들의 선입견을 고수하는 것으로 / 평평한 지구에 대한 / 둥근 지구를 상상함으로써 / 팬케이크처럼 생겼다고

This construction of a new understanding / is guided / by a model of the earth / that helps the child explain / how people can stand or walk / on its surface.
이러한 새로운 지식의 구성은 / 이루어진다 / 지구의 모형에 의해 / 아이가 설명하는 것을 돕는 / 어떻게 사람들이 서 있거나 걸을 수 있는지를 / 그것의(지구의) 표면에서

Many young children have trouble / giving up the notion / that one-eighth is greater than one-fourth, / because 8 is more than 4.
많은 어린아이들은 어려움을 겪는다 / 개념을 포기하는 데 / 8분의 1이 4분의 1보다 크다는 / 8이 4보다 크기 때문에

If children were blank slates, / just telling them / that the earth is round / or / that one-fourth is greater than one-eighth / would be adequate.
만약 아이들이 백지상태라면 / 단지 그들에게 말하는 것만으로 / 지구가 둥글다고 / 또는 / 4분의 1이 8분의 1보다 크다고 / 충분할 것이다

But / since they already have ideas / about the earth / and / about numbers, / those ideas / must be directly addressed / in order to transform or expand them.
하지만 / 그들은 이미 개념을 가지고 있기 때문에 / 지구에 대한 / 그리고 / 숫자에 대한 / 그 개념들은 / 직접적으로 다뤄져야 한다 / 그것들을 변형하거나 확장하기 위해서는

해석 아이들이 교실에 가져오는 지식은 이미 저학년 때 꽤 강력할 수 있다. 예를 들어, 어떤 아이들은 둥근 지구가 팬케이크처럼 생겼다고 상상함으로써 평평한 지구에 대한 그들의 선입견을 고수하는 것으로 밝혀졌다. 이러한 새로운 지식의 구성은 아이가 어떻게 사람들이 지구 표면에서 서 있거나 걸을 수 있는지를 설명하는 것을 돕는 지구의 모형에 의해 이루어진다. 많은 어린아이들은 8이 4보다 크기 때문에 8분의 1이 4분의 1보다 크다는 개념을 포기하는 데 어려움을 겪는다. 만약 아이들이 백지상태라면, 지구가 둥글다거나 4분의 1이 8분의 1보다 크다고 말하는 것만으로도 충분할 것이다. 하지만 그들은 이미 지구와 숫자에 대한 개념을 가지고 있기 때문에, 그것들을 변형하거나 확장하기 위해서는 그 개념들이 직접적으로 다뤄져야 한다.

① 익숙한
② 충분한
③ 부적절한
④ 무관한

해설 지문 처음에서 아이들이 교실에 가져오는 지식은 이미 저학년 때 꽤 강력할 수 있다고 했고, 빈칸 뒤 문장에서 하지만 그들은 이미 지구와 숫자에 대한 개념을 가지고 있기 때문에 그것들을 변형하거나 확장하기 위해서는 그 개념들이 직접적으로 다뤄져야 한다고 설명하고 있으므로, 빈칸에는 만약 아이들이 백지상태라면 지구가 둥글다거나 4분의 1이 8분의 1보다 크다고 말하는 것만으로도 '② 충분할' 것이라는 내용이 들어가야 한다.

어휘 hold onto 고수하다, 계속 유지하다 preconception 선입견, 편견
flat 평평한 construction 구성, 건설 surface 표면
notion 개념, 생각 blank slate 백지상태, 빈 석판

address 다루다, 해결하다　transform 변형하다, 변화시키다
expand 확장하다, 확대하다　adequate 충분한, 적당한
improper 부적절한　irrelevant 무관한, 부적절한

05 독해 세부내용 파악 (내용 불일치 파악) 난이도 ★★★

끊어읽기 해석

Urban farming, / also known as urban agriculture, / involves growing food / within city environments, / utilizing spaces / like rooftops, abandoned buildings, and community gardens.
도시 농사는 / 도시 농업이라고도 알려진 / 식량을 재배하는 것을 포함한다 / 도시 환경 내에서 / 공간들을 활용하여 / 옥상, 버려진 건물, 그리고 공동체 정원과 같은

This sustainable practice is gaining traction / in cities / across the world, / including New York, Chicago, San Francisco, London, Amsterdam, and Berlin, / as well as in many African and Asian cities / where it plays a crucial role / in food supply and local economies.
이 지속 가능한 관행은 흡입력을 얻고 있다 / 도시들에서 / 전 세계의 / 뉴욕, 시카고, 샌프란시스코, 런던, 암스테르담, 그리고 베를린을 포함한 / 많은 아프리카와 아시아 도시들뿐만 아니라 / 중요한 역할을 하는 / 식량 공급과 지역 경제에서

Urban farming / not only helps reduce carbon footprints / by minimizing transport emissions / but also increases / access to fresh, healthy food / in urban areas.
도시 농사는 / 탄소 발자국을 줄이는 것을 도울 뿐만 아니라 / 운송 배출을 최소화함으로써 / 또한 증가시킨다 / 신선하고 건강한 식량에 대한 접근성을 / 도시 지역에서

It bolsters local economies / by creating jobs / and / keeping profits / within the community.
그것은 지역 경제를 강화시킨다 / 일자리를 창출함으로써 / 그리고 / 이익을 보유함으로써 / 지역 사회 내에

Additionally, / urban farms enhance cityscapes, / improve air quality, / conserve water, / provide educational opportunities, / promote biodiversity, / connect people with nature, / and / improve food security / by producing food locally, / making cities more resilient / to disruptions / like natural disasters.
게다가 / 도시 농장은 도시 경관을 향상시키고 / 대기질을 개선하고 / 물을 보존하고 / 교육 기회를 제공하고 / 생물 다양성을 촉진하고 / 사람들과 자연을 연결하고 / 그리고 / 식량 안정성을 향상시킨다 / 지역에서 식량을 생산함으로써 / 도시를 더 회복력 있게 만든다 / 혼란에 대해 / 자연 재해와 같은

해석 도시 농업이라고도 알려진 도시 농사는 옥상, 버려진 건물, 그리고 공동체 정원과 같은 공간들을 활용하여 도시 환경 내에서 식량을 재배하는 것을 포함한다. 이 지속 가능한 관행은 식량 공급과 지역 경제에서 중요한 역할을 하는 많은 아프리카와 아시아 도시들뿐만 아니라 뉴욕, 시카고, 샌프란시스코, 런던, 암스테르담, 그리고 베를린을 포함한 전 세계의 도시들에서 흡입력을 얻고 있다. 도시 농사는 운송 배출을 최소화함으로써 탄소 발자국을 줄이는 것을 도울 뿐만 아니라 도시 지역에서 신선하고 건강한 식량에 대한 접근성을 증가시킨다. 그것(도시 농업)은 일자리를 창출하고 지역 사회 내에 이익을 보유함으로써 지역 경제를 강화시킨다. 게다가, 도시 농장은 도시 경관을 향상시키고, 대기질을 개선하고, 물을 보존하고, 교육 기회를 제공하고, 생물 다양성을 촉진하고, 사람들과 자연을 연결하고 지역에서 식량을 생산함으로써 식량 안정성을 향상시켜 도시를 자연 재해와 같은 혼란에 더 회복력 있게 만든다.

해설 ④번의 키워드인 '회복력(resilient)'이 그대로 언급된 지문 주변의 내용에서 도시 농장은 생물 다양성을 촉진하고, 지역에서 식량

을 생산함으로써 식량 안정성을 향상시켜 도시를 자연 재해와 같은 혼란에 대해 더 회복력 있게 만든다고 했으므로 '④ 생물 다양성을 촉진하고, 지역에서 식량을 생산함으로써 식량의 안정성을 향상시키나, 자연 재해와 같은 혼란에 대한 도시의 회복력은 약화시킨다'는 지문의 내용과 일치하지 않는다.

어휘 urban 도시의　farming 농사, 농업　agriculture 농업
utilize 활용하다　rooftop 옥상　abandoned 버려진
sustainable 지속 가능한　practice 관행　gain 얻다
supply 공급　carbon footprint 탄소 발자국
emission 배출, 방출　enhance 향상시키다　cityscape 도시 경관
conserve 보존하다　biodiversity 생물 다양성
resilient 회복력 있는, 탄력이 있는　disruption 혼란

06 독해 추론 (함축 의미 추론) 난이도 ★★★

끊어읽기 해석

Ideas or theories about human nature / have a unique place / in the sciences.
인간 본성에 대한 생각이나 이론은 / 독특한 위치를 차지한다 / 과학에서

We don't have to worry / that the cosmos will be changed / by our theories / about the cosmos.
우리는 걱정할 필요가 없다 / 우주가 바뀔 것이라고 / 우리의 이론에 의해 / 우주에 대한

The planets really don't care / what we think / or / how we theorize / about them.
행성들은 상관하지 않는다 / 우리가 무엇을 생각하는지 / 또는 / 우리가 어떻게 이론을 세우는지를 / 그것들에 대해

But / we do have to worry / that human nature will be changed / by our theories / of human nature.
하지만 / 우리는 걱정해야만 한다 / 인간 본성이 바뀔 것이라는 점은 / 우리의 이론에 의해 / 인간 본성에 대한

Forty years ago, / the distinguished anthropologist said / that human beings are "unfinished animals."
40년 전에 / 저명한 인류학자가 말했다 / 인간은 '미완성의 동물'이라고

What he meant is / that it is human nature / to have a human nature / that is very much the product of the society / that surrounds us.
그가 의미한 것은 / 인간 본성이라는 것이다 / 인간 본성을 갖는 것이 / 사회의 산물인 / 우리를 둘러싸고 있는

That human nature is more created / than discovered.
인간 본성은 창조된 것이다 / 발견되었다기보다는

We "design" human nature, / by designing the institutions / within which people live.
우리는 인간 본성을 '설계한다' / 사회 제도를 설계함으로써 / 사람들이 살고 있는

So / we must ask ourselves / just what kind of a human nature / we want to help design.
그러므로 / 우리는 자문해야 한다 / 어떤 종류의 인간 본성을 / 우리가 설계하는 것을 돕고자 하는지

해석 인간 본성에 대한 생각이나 이론은 과학에서 독특한 위치를 차지한다. 우리는 우주에 대한 우리의 이론에 의해 우주가 바뀔 것이라고 걱정할 필요가 없다. 행성들은 우리가 그것들에 대해 무엇을 생각하는지, 또는 그것들에 대해 어떻게 이론을 세우는지를 상관하지 않는다. 하지만 우리는 인간 본성에 대한 우리의 이론에 의해 인간 본성이 바뀔 것이라는 점은 걱정해야만 한다. 40년 전에, 저명한 인류학자가 인간은 '미완성의 동물'이라고 말했다. 그가 의미한 것은 우리를 둘러싸고 있는 사회의 산물인 인간 본성을 갖는 것이 인간 본성이라는 것이다. 인간 본성은 발견되었다기보다는 창

조된 것이다. 우리는 사람들이 살고 있는 사회 제도를 설계함으로써 인간 본성을 '설계한다'. 그러므로 우리는 우리가 어떤 종류의 인간 본성을 설계하는 것을 돕고자 하는지 자문해야 한다.

① 불완전한 발달 단계에 갇혀 있는
② 생물학에 의해 고정된 것이 아니라 사회에 의해 형성된
③ 환경적 맥락으로부터 유례없이 자유로운
④ 동물적인 면과 정신적인 면을 겸비하여 태어난

해설 지문 중간에서 우리는 인간 본성에 대한 우리의 이론에 의해 인간 본성이 바뀔 것이라는 점은 걱정해야만 한다고 했고, 지문 마지막에서 인간 본성은 발견되었다기보다는 창조된 것이며, 우리는 사람들이 살고 있는 사회 제도를 설계함으로써 인간 본성을 설계한다고 설명하고 있다. 따라서 '② 생물학에 의해 고정된 것이 아니라 사회에 의해 형성된'이 밑줄 친 unfinished animals(미완성의 동물)의 의미로 가장 적절하다.

어휘 **theory** 이론, 견해 **unique** 독특한, 특별한 **cosmos** 우주
planet 행성 **distinguished** 저명한, 뛰어난
anthropologist 인류학자 **surround** 둘러싸다
institution 사회 제도, 관습 **biology** 생물학
animalistic 동물적인, 동물성의 **spiritual** 정신적인
aspect 면, 측면

07 독해 전체내용 파악 (문단 요약) 난이도 ★★☆

끊어읽기 해석

Passive House is a standard / and / an advanced method / of designing buildings / using the precision of building physics / to ensure / comfortable conditions / and / to deeply reduce / energy costs.
'패시브 하우스'는 표준이다 / 그리고 / 진보된 방법이다 / 건물을 설계하는 / 건축 물리학의 정밀함을 사용하여 / 보장하기 위해 / 쾌적한 환경을 / 그리고 / 크게 절감하기 위해 / 에너지 비용을

It removes all guesswork / from the design process.
이는 모든 어림짐작을 제거한다 / 설계 과정에서

It does / what national building regulations / have tried to do.
이는 수행한다 / 국가의 건축 규제가 / 하려고 시도했던 것을

Passive House methods don't affect "buildability", / yet / they close the gap / between design and performance / and / deliver a much higher standard / of comfort and efficiency / than government regulations, / with all their good intentions, / have managed to achieve.
'패시브 하우스' 방법은 '시공성'에 영향을 미치지 않는다 / 하지만 / 그것들은 격차를 줄인다 / 디자인과 성능 사이의 / 그리고 / 훨씬 높은 수준을 제공한다 / 쾌적함과 효율성의 / 정부 규제보다 / 그것들의 좋은 의도로 / 간신히 달성하려고 했던

When we use Passive House methods, / we learn / how to use insulation / and / freely available daylight, / in the most sensible way / and / in the right amounts / for both comfort and energy efficiency.
우리가 '패시브 하우스' 방법을 사용할 때 / 우리는 배운다 / 단열재를 사용하는 방법을 / 그리고 / 자유롭게 이용할 수 있는 햇빛을 (사용하는 방법을) / 가장 합리적인 방법으로 / 그리고 / 적절한 양으로 / 쾌적함과 에너지 효율성 모두에

This is, / I believe, / fundamental to good design, / and / is the next step / we have to make / in the evolution / of our dwellings and places of work.
이것이 ~이다 / 내가 믿는 / 좋은 디자인의 기본 / 그리고 / 다음 단계이다 / 우리가 해야 할 / 변화에서 / 우리의 거주지와 일터의

The improvements / that are within our grasp / are potentially transformative / for mankind and the planet.
개선 사항은 / 우리가 이해할 수 있는 / 잠재적으로 변화시킨다 / 인류와 지구를

↓

Passive House utilizes / precise building physics / to ensure comfort and energy efficiency, / (A) surpassing traditional regulations / and / offering transformative potential / for (B) sustainable design.
'패시브 하우스'는 활용한다 / 정밀한 건축 물리학을 / 쾌적함과 에너지 효율성을 보장하기 위해 / 전통적인 규정을 (A) 뛰어넘는다 / 그리고 / 변화시키는 잠재력을 제공한다 / (B) 지속 가능한 설계를 위한

해석 '패시브 하우스'는 쾌적한 환경을 보장하고 에너지 비용을 크게 절감하기 위해 건축 물리학의 정밀함을 사용하여 건물을 설계하는 표준이자 진보된 방법이다. 이는 설계 과정에서 모든 어림짐작을 제거한다. 이는 국가의 건축 규제가 하려고 시도했던 것을 수행한다. '패시브 하우스' 방법은 '시공성'에 영향을 미치지 않지만, 디자인과 성능 사이의 격차를 줄이고 정부 규제가 좋은 의도로 간신히 달성하려고 했던 것보다 훨씬 높은 수준의 쾌적함과 효율성을 제공한다. 우리가 '패시브 하우스' 방법을 사용할 때, 우리는 단열재와 자유롭게 이용할 수 있는 햇빛을 가장 합리적인 방법으로, 그리고 쾌적함과 에너지 효율성 모두에 적절한 양으로 사용하는 방법을 배운다. 이것이 내가 믿는 좋은 디자인의 기본이며, 우리의 주거지와 일터의 변화에서 우리가 해야 할 다음 단계이다. 우리가 이해할 수 있는 개선 사항은 잠재적으로 인류와 지구를 변화시킨다.

'패시브 하우스'는 쾌적함과 에너지 효율성을 보장하기 위해 정밀한 건축 물리학을 활용하여 전통적인 규정을 (A) 뛰어넘고 (B) 지속 가능한 설계를 위한 변화시키는 잠재력을 제공한다.

　　　(A)　　　　　　(B)
① 지속하는　　　　　지속 가능한
② 지속하는　　　　　유지할 수 없는
③ 뛰어넘는　　　　　유지할 수 없는
④ 뛰어넘는　　　　　지속 가능한

해설 지문 중간에서 '패시브 하우스' 방법은 정부 규제가 좋은 의도로 간신히 달성하려고 했던 것보다 훨씬 높은 수준의 쾌적함과 효율성을 제공한다고 했고, '패시브 하우스' 방법을 사용할 때, 단열재와 자유롭게 이용할 수 있는 햇빛을 가장 합리적인 방법으로, 그리고 쾌적함과 에너지 효율성 모두에 적절한 양으로 사용하는 방법을 배운다고 했으므로, 빈칸 (A)와 (B)에는 '패시브 하우스'는 쾌적함과 에너지 효율성을 보장하기 위해 정밀한 건축 물리학을 활용하여 전통적인 규정을 뛰어넘고(surpassing) 지속 가능한(sustainable) 설계를 위한 변화시키는 잠재력을 제공한다는 내용이 들어가야 적절하다. 따라서 ④ surpassing – sustainable 이 정답이다.

어휘 **Passive House** 패시브 하우스(첨단 단열공법을 이용하여 에너지의 낭비를 최소화한 건축물) **standard** 표준, 기준
precision 정밀함, 꼼꼼함 **physics** 물리학 **ensure** 보장하다
guesswork 어림짐작 **regulation** 규제, 규정 **buildability** 시공성
intention 의도 **insulation** 단열재 **daylight** 햇빛, 일광
sensible 합리적인, 현명한 **fundamental** 기본의, 궁극적인
evolution 변화, 진화 **dwelling** 주거(지), 거주
grasp 이해, 확실한 파악 **mankind** 인류, 인간
transformative 변화시키는 **persist** 지속하다, 계속하다
sustainable 지속 가능한 **surpass** 뛰어넘다, 능가하다

08 독해 논리적 흐름 파악 (문맥상 부적절한 어휘) 난이도 ★★★

끊어읽기 해석

Today, / there is only one species of humans, Homo sapiens, left / in the world.
오늘날 / 단 한 종의 인간, 즉 호모 사피엔스만이 남아있다 / 세계에는

But / that one species, / despite the fact / that it is over 99.9 percent genetically ① identical, / has adapted itself / to a wide array of disparate environments.
그러나 / 그 한 종은 / 사실에도 불구하고 / 그것이 유전적으로 99.9퍼센트 이상 ① 동일하다는 / 스스로 적응해 왔다 / 다수의 이질적인 환경에

And / while some degree of human genetic variation / results from each society's adaptation / to its own unique environment, / the cultural adaptations / that each society makes in so adjusting itself will, / in their turn, / exact some further degree of ② variation / on that society's genetic makeup.
그리고 / 어느 정도의 인간 유전의 변이는 / 각 사회의 적응의 결과이지만 / 고유한 환경에 대한 / 문화적 적응은 / 각 사회가 스스로 조정하면서 이루는 / 결국 / 어느 정도 더 많은 ② 변화를 요구할 것이다 / 그 사회의 유전적 구성에

In other words, / we are so entangled with our local ecologies / that not only do we humans ③ transform the environment / as we cull from it / the various resources / upon which we come to depend / but also the environment, / which we have so transformed, / transforms us / in its turn: / at times / exerting upon us profound biological pressures.
다시 말해서 / 우리는 우리 지역의 생태 환경과 너무 얽혀 있다 / 그래서 우리 인간이 환경을 ③ 변화시킬 뿐만 아니라 / 우리가 그것으로부터 뽑아내며 / 다양한 자원을 / 우리가 의존하게 되는 / 하지만 환경도 / 우리가 그렇게 변화시킨 / 우리를 변화시킨다 / 차례로 / 때때로 / 우리에게 지대한 생물학적 압력을 가하면서

In those regions of the world, / for example, / where our environmental exploitation has included / the domestication of cattle / -northern Europe, / for instance, / or / East Africa human populations have ④ reduced / adult lactose tolerance: / the ability to digest milk / past infancy.
세계의 지역들에서는 / 예를 들어 / 우리의 환경 착취가 포함했던 / 소의 가축화를 / 북유럽 / 예를 들어 / 또는 / 동아프리카 인구가 ④ 감소시켰다 / 성인 유당 내성 / 즉, 우유를 소화하는 능력을 / 유아기 이후에

해석 오늘날, 세계에는 단 한 종의 인간, 즉 호모 사피엔스만이 남아있다. 그러나 그 한 종은, 그것이 유전적으로 99.9퍼센트 이상 ① 동일하다는 사실에도 불구하고, 다수의 이질적인 환경에 스스로 적응해 왔다. 그리고 어느 정도의 인간 유전의 변이는 고유한 환경에 대한 각 사회의 적응의 결과이지만, 각 사회가 스스로 조정하면서 이루는 문화적 적응은, 결국 그 사회의 유전적 구성에 어느 정도 더 많은 ② 변화를 요구할 것이다. 다시 말해서, 우리는 우리 지역의 생태 환경과 너무 얽혀 있어서 우리 인간이 우리가 의존하게 되는 다양한 자원을 환경에서 뽑아내며 환경을 ③ 변화시킬 뿐만 아니라, 우리가 그렇게 변화시킨 환경도 때때로 우리에게 지대한 생물학적 압력을 가하면서 차례로 우리를 변화시킨다. 예를 들어, 우리의 환경 착취가 소의 가축화를 포함했던 세계의 지역들, 즉, 예를 들어 북유럽이나 동아프리카에서는, 인구가 성인 유당 내성, 즉 유아기 이후에 우유를 소화하는 능력을 ④ 감소시켰다.

*다섯 번째 문장의 cattle-northern Europe 사이의 하이픈(-)은 이음표(—)로 수정이 필요하며, East Africa 뒤에도 이음표가 빠져 있으므로, 이음표를 넣어 'cattle—northern Europe ~ East Africa—human population'으로 해석했습니다.

해설 지문 전반에 걸쳐 인간이 환경에 적응하며 환경을 변화시킬 뿐만 아니라 환경도 인간을 변화시킨다는 내용에 대해 설명하고 있고, 지문 마지막에서 우리의 환경 착취가 소의 가축화를 포함했던 세

계의 지역들에 대해 언급하고 있으므로, 인구가 성인 유당 내성을 '④ 감소시켰다(reduced)'는 것은 문맥상 적절하지 않다. 주어진 reduced를 대신할 수 있는 어휘로는 '증가시키다'라는 의미의 increased가 있다.

어휘 genetically 유전적으로　identical 동일한, 똑같은　adapt 적응하다　disparate 이질적인, 서로 다른　genetic 유전의, 유전적인　variation 변이, 변화　exact 요구하다, 강요하다　makeup 구성　entangle 얽히게 하다　ecology 생태 환경　transform 변화시키다　cull 뽑아내다, 추려내다　resource 자원　exert 가하다, 영향을 미치다　profound 지대한, 심오한　exploitation 착취, 개발　domestication 가축화, 길들이기　cattle 소　tolerance 내성, 포용력　digest 소화하다　infancy 유아기

09 독해 논리적 흐름 파악 (문단 순서 배열) 난이도 ★★☆

끊어읽기 해석

Briefly consider a metaphor / that plays a significant role / in how we live our daily lives: / Time Is Money.
은유를 잠시 생각해 보라 / 중요한 역할을 하는 / 우리가 일상생활을 어떻게 살아가는가에 / '시간은 돈이다'라는

(A) We often speak of time / as if it were money / —for example, / in everyday expressions / such as / "You're wasting my time," / "This device will save you hours of work," / "How will you spend your weekend?" / and / "I've invested a lot of time in this relationship."
우리는 종종 시간을 이야기한다 / 그것이 마치 돈인 것처럼 / 예를 들어 / 일상적인 표현에서 / ~와 같은 / "당신은 제 시간을 낭비하고 있어요" / "이 기기는 당신의 작업 시간을 절약해 줄 것입니다" / "당신은 주말을 어떻게 보낼 건가요" / 그리고 / "저는 이 관계에 많은 시간을 투자했습니다"

(B) Every metaphor brokers / what is made visible or invisible; / this one highlights / how time is like money / and / obscures ways it is not.
모든 은유는 중개한다 / 눈에 보이게 된 것과 보이지 않게 된 것을 / 이것은 강조한다 / 시간이 돈과 얼마나 같은지를 / 그리고 / 그것이 그렇지 않은 점은 모호하게 한다

Time / thus / becomes something / that we can waste or lose, / and / something that diminishes / as we grow older.
시간은 / 따라서 / 무언가가 된다 / 우리가 낭비하거나 잃을 수 있는 / 그리고 / 줄어드는 것 / 우리가 나이를 먹어 감에 따라

It is abstracted / in a very linear, orderly fashion.
그것은 추상화된다 / 매우 선형적이고, 질서정연한 방식으로

(C) This metaphor, / however, / fails to disclose / important phenomenological aspects of time, / such as how it may speed up or slow down, / depending on our engagement / with what we are doing.
이 은유는 / 그러나 / 밝히지 못한다 / 시간의 중요한 현상학적 측면을 / 시간이 어떻게 빨라지거나 느려질 수 있는지와 같은 / 우리의 참여에 따라 / 우리가 하는 일에 대한

We may instead conceive of time / as quite fluid / —as a stream, for example—/ thought we lose sight of this / to the extent / that we have adopted the worldview of Time Is Money.
대신에 우리는 시간을 생각할 수도 있다 / 매우 유동적이라고 / 예를 들어 물결처럼 / 우리는 이를 놓치고 있긴 하지만 / ~할 정도까지 / 우리가 '시간이 돈이다'라는 세계관을 받아들이는

해석 우리가 일상생활을 어떻게 살아가는가에 중요한 역할을 하는 은유인 '시간은 돈이다'를 잠시 생각해 보라.

(A) 우리는 예를 들어, "당신은 제 시간을 낭비하고 있어요", "이 기기는 당신의 작업 시간을 절약해 줄 것입니다", "당신은 주말을 어떻게 보낼 건가요" 그리고 "저는 이 관계에 많은 시간을 투자했습니다"와 같은 일상적인 표현에서 종종 시간이 돈인 것처럼 이야기한다.

(B) 모든 은유는 눈에 보이게 된 것과 보이지 않게 된 것을 중개하고, 이것은 시간이 돈과 얼마나 같은지를 강조하며 그것이 그렇지 않은(돈과 같지 않은) 점은 모호하게 한다. 따라서 시간은 우리가 낭비하거나 잃을 수 있는 것이 되고, 우리가 나이를 먹어 감에 따라 줄어드는 것이 된다. 그것은 매우 선형적이고, 질서정연한 방식으로 추상화된다.

(C) 그러나, 이 은유는 우리가 하는 일에 대한 우리의 참여에 따라 시간이 어떻게 빨라지거나 느려질 수 있는지와 같은 시간의 중요한 현상학적 측면을 밝히지 못한다. 우리가 '시간이 돈이다'라는 세계관을 받아들일 정도까지 이것(시간의 중요한 현상학적 측면을 밝히지 못하는 것)을 놓치고 있긴 하지만, 대신에 우리는 시간이 예를 들어, 물결처럼 매우 유동적이라고 생각할 수도 있다.

*마지막 문장의 thought는 though의 오타이므로, 원문에 맞춰 해석했습니다.

해설 주어진 문장에서 우리가 일상생활을 어떻게 살아가는가에 중요한 역할을 하는 은유인 '시간은 돈이다'를 잠시 생각해 보라고 하고, (A)에서 우리가 시간이 돈인 것처럼 이야기하는 일상적인 표현들을 예시로 들고 있다. 이어서 (B)에서 모든 은유는 눈에 보이는 것과 보이지 않게 된 것을 중개한다고 하며, 그것은 매우 선형적이고 질서정연한 방식으로 추상화된다고 설명한 뒤, (C)에서 그러나 이 은유는 시간의 중요한 현상학적 측면을 밝히지 못한다고 설명하고 있다. 따라서 ① (A) - (B) - (C)가 정답이다.

어휘 metaphor 은유 invest 투자하다, 투입하다 broker 중개하다 invisible 보이지 않는 diminish 줄어들다, 감소하다 abstract 추상화하다, 요약하다 linear 선형적인 orderly 질서정연한 fashion 방식, 관습 disclose 밝히다, 드러내다 phenomenological 현상학적인 engagement 참여, 개입 conceive 생각하다, 여기다 fluid 유동적인 stream 물결, 흐름 worldview 세계관

10 문법 대명사   난이도 ★★☆

해석 그의 마지막 생각은 그의 아내를 위한 것이었다. "그는 그녀가 그것을 도저히 견디지 못할까 봐 두려워하고 있어요"라고 그가 지난 며칠 동안 그와 함께 있도록 허락받은 주교 Burnet에게 말했다. 그가 그녀에 대해 말했을 때 그의 눈에는 눈물이 고였다. 마지막 날이 왔고, Russell 부인은 아버지에게 영원한 작별 인사를 하기 위해 어린 세 아이들을 데리고 왔다. "Little Fubs"는 겨우 아홉 살이었고, 그의 여동생 Catherine은 일곱 살, 그리고 아기는 세 살이었으며, 그의 죽음을 깨닫기에는 너무 어렸다. 그는 차분하게 그들 모두에게 입을 맞추고, 그들을 돌려보냈다. 그의 아내는 머물렀고 그들은 마지막 식사를 함께했다. 그리고 나서 그들은 침묵 속에서 입을 맞췄고, 그녀는 조용히 그를 떠났다. 그녀가 떠났을 때, Russel 경은 완전히 무너졌다. "오, 그녀는 저에게 정말 축복이었어요!"라며 그는 울부짖었다. "제 아이들을 그런 어머니의 보살핌 속에 맡길 수 있다는 것은 저에게 큰 위로가 됩니다. 그녀는 그들을 위해 그녀 스스로를 돌보겠다고 약속했고, 그녀는 그렇게 할 거예요."라고 그는 단호하게 덧붙였다. Russell 부인은 무거운 마음으로 다시는 그를 맞이하지 않을 슬픈 집으로 돌아갔다. 1683년 7월 21일, 그녀는 과부가 되었고, 그녀의 아이들은 아버지를 여의었다. 그들은 음울한 런던 집을 떠나, 시골의 오래된 수도원으로 갔다.

해설 ③ 재귀대명사 동사구(take care of)의 목적어가 지칭하는 대상

이 문장의 주어(she)와 동일하므로 동사구 take care of의 목적어 자리에 목적격 대명사 her를 재귀대명사 herself로 고쳐야 한다.

오답 분석 ① 빈도 부사 문맥상 '그녀가 그것을 도저히 견디지 못할까 봐'라는 의미가 되어야 자연스러운데, '도저히(거의) ~ 않다'는 빈도 부사 hardly를 사용하여 나타낼 수 있고, 빈도 부사는 보통 조동사 뒤에 오므로 조동사(would) 뒤에 hardly가 올바르게 쓰였다. 참고로, hardly는 부정의 의미를 포함하고 있으므로 not과 같은 부정어와 함께 쓰일 수 없다.

② 부사 자리 동사를 수식할 때 부사는 '동사(kissed) + 목적어(them all)'의 앞이나 뒤에 오므로 kissed them all 뒤에 부사 calmly가 올바르게 쓰였다.

④ 전치사 + 관계대명사 관계사 뒤에 완전한 절(she would ~ him again)이 왔으므로 '전치사 + 관계대명사' 형태가 올 수 있다. '전치사 + 관계대명사'에서 전치사는 선행사 또는 관계절의 동사에 따라 결정되는데, 관계절의 동사 welcome(맞이하다)은 전치사 to와 함께 짝을 이루어 쓰이므로 전치사 to가 관계대명사 which 앞에 온 to which가 올바르게 쓰였다.

어휘 bear 견디다 loss 죽음, 상실 calmly 차분하게 silence 침묵 silently 조용히 blessing 축복 for ones' sake ~을 위해 resolutely 단호하게, 결연히 widow 과부, 미망인 dreary 음울한 abbey 수도원

👍 이것도 알면 합격!

주어나 목적어를 강조할 때 강조하는 대상 바로 뒤나 문장 뒤에 재귀대명사를 쓰며, 이때 재귀대명사는 생략할 수 있다는 것을 알아두자.

ex The musician himself composed the song.
그 음악가는 직접 노래를 작곡했다.

11 독해 세부내용 파악 (내용 불일치 파악)   난이도 ★☆☆

끊어읽기 해석

The gig economy, / referring to the workforce of people / engaged in / freelance and side-hustle work, / is growing rapidly / in the United States, / with 36% of employed participants / in a 2022 McKinsey survey / identifying as independent workers, / up from 27% in 2016.
긱 이코노미는 / 노동 인구를 일컫는 / 종사하는 / 프리랜서와 부업에 / 빠르게 성장하고 있다 / 미국에서 / 고용된 참가자의 36퍼센트가 / 2022 McKinsey 조사에서 / 독립 근로자로 확인되었다 / 이는 2016년의 27퍼센트에서 증가한 수치이다

This workforce includes / a wide range of jobs / from highly-paid professionals / like lawyers / to lower-earning roles / like delivery drivers.
이 노동 인구는 포함한다 / 광범위한 직업을 / 고임금의 전문직 종사자부터 / 변호사와 같은 / 저소득 역할까지 / 배달 기사와 같은

Despite the flexibility and autonomy / it offers, / most independent workers desire / more stable employment; / 62% prefer permanent positions / due to concerns / over job security and benefits.
유연성과 자율성에도 불구하고 / 그것이 제공하는 / 대부분의 독립 근로자는 원한다 / 보다 안정적인 고용을 / 62퍼센트는 정규직을 선호한다 / 우려로 인해 / 고용 안정성과 혜택에 대한

The challenges / faced by gig workers / include / limited access / to healthcare, housing, and other basic needs, / with a significant reliance / on government assistance.
어려움은 / 긱 근로자가 직면한 / 포함한다 / 제한된 접근성을 / 의료, 주택 및 기타 기본 요구 사항에 대한 / 큰 의존과 함께 / 정부 지원에 대한

Technological advancements have facilitated / the rise in

independent work, / making remote and freelance jobs / more accessible and appealing.
기술적인 발전은 촉진했다 / 독립된 근로의 증가를 / 그리고 원격 및 프리랜서 일자리를 만들었다 / 더 쉽게 접근할 수 있고 매력적으로

The trend reflects / broader economic pressures / such as inflation and job market dynamics, / influencing individuals to choose gig work / for survival, flexibility, or enjoyment.
이러한 추세는 반영한다 / 더 광범위한 경제적 압력을 / 인플레이션 및 고용 시장의 역동성과 같은 / 그리고 개인이 긱 근로를 선택하도록 영향을 미친다 / 생존, 유연성, 또는 즐거움을 위해

해석　프리랜서와 부업에 종사하는 사람들의 노동 인구를 일컫는 긱 이코노미는 미국에서 빠르게 성장하고 있으며, 2022년 McKinsey 조사에서 고용된 참가자의 36퍼센트가 독립 근로자로 확인되었는데, 이는 2016년의 27퍼센트에서 증가한 수치이다. 이 노동 인구는 변호사와 같은 고임금의 전문직 종사자부터 배달 기사와 같은 저소득 역할까지 광범위한 직업을 포함한다. 그것(긱 이코노미)이 제공하는 유연성과 자율성에도 불구하고, 대부분의 독립 근로자는 보다 안정적인 고용을 원하며, 62퍼센트는 고용 안정성과 혜택에 대한 우려로 인해 정규직을 선호한다. 긱 근로자가 직면한 어려움은 의료, 주택 및 기타 기본 요구 사항에 대한 제한된 접근성과 정부 지원에 대한 큰 의존을 포함한다. 기술적인 발전은 독립된 근로의 증가를 촉진했고, 원격 및 프리랜서 일자리를 더 쉽게 접근할 수 있고 매력적으로 만들고 있다. 이러한 추세는 인플레이션 및 고용 시장의 역동성과 같은 더 광범위한 경제적 압력을 반영하며, 개인이 생존, 유연성, 또는 즐거움을 위해 긱 근로를 선택하도록 영향을 미친다.

해설　지문 중간에서 긱 이코노미가 제공하는 유연성과 자율성에도 불구하고, 대부분의 독립 근로자는 보다 안정적인 고용을 원한다고 했으므로 '② 대부분의 독립 근로자들은 안정적인 고용보다는 직업이 제공하는 유연성과 자율성을 선호하고 있다'는 지문의 내용과 일치하지 않는다.

어휘　gig economy 긱 이코노미, 임시직 선호 경제(기업들이 정규직보다 필요에 따라 계약직 또는 임시직으로 사람을 고용하는 경향이 커지는 경제 상황) workforce 노동 인구, 노동력　freelance 프리랜서, 자유 계약자 flexibility 유연성　autonomy 자율성　stable 안정적인 employment 고용, 취업　permanent 정규직의 job security 고용 안정, 고용 보장　reliance 의존 facilitate 촉진하다　remote 원격의　accessible 접근할 수 있는 appealing 매력적인　dynamics 역동성, 역학

12　독해　논리적 흐름 파악 (문단 순서 배열)　난이도 ★★☆

끊어읽기 해석

We come to know / and / relate to / the world / by way of categories.
우리는 알게 된다 / 그리고 / 관계를 맺게 된다 / 세상을 / 범주를 통해

(A) The notion of an animal species, / for instance, / might in one setting best be thought of / as described by folklore and myth, / in another / as a detailed legal construct, / and / in another / as a system of scientific classification.
동물 종의 개념은 / 예를 들어 / 어떤 환경에서는 가장 잘 생각될 수 있다 / 민속과 신화에 의해 묘사되는 것으로 / 다른 환경에서는 / 세부적인 법적 구조로 / 그리고 / 다른 환경에서는 / 과학적 분류 체계로

(B) Ordinary communication / is the most immediate expression / of this faculty.
일상적인 의사소통은 / 가장 직접적인 표현이다 / 이 능력의

We refer to things / through sounds and words, / and / we attach ideas to them / that we call concepts.
우리는 사물을 부른다 / 소리와 말을 통해 / 그리고 / 우리는 생각을 거기에 연관시킨다 / 우리가 개념이라고 부르는

(C) Some of our categories remain tacit; / others are explicitly governed / by custom, law, politics, or science.
우리의 범주 중 일부는 암묵적으로 남아있다 / 다른 것들은 명시적으로 지배된다 / 관습, 법, 정치, 또는 과학에 의해

The application of category systems / for the same things / varies / by context and in use.
범주 체계의 적용은 / 동일한 사물에 대한 / 다르다 / 맥락과 용법에 따라

해석　| 우리는 범주를 통해 세상을 알고 관계를 맺게 된다. |

(B) 일상적인 의사소통은 이 능력의 가장 직접적인 표현이다. 우리는 소리와 말을 통해 사물을 부르고, 우리가 개념이라고 부르는 생각을 거기에 연관시킨다.

(C) 우리의 범주 중 일부는 암묵적으로 남아있고, 다른 것들은 관습, 법, 정치, 또는 과학에 의해 명시적으로 지배된다. 동일한 사물에 대한 범주 체계의 적용은 맥락과 용법에 따라 다르다.

(A) 예를 들어, 동물 종의 개념은 어떤 환경에서는 민속과 신화에 의해 묘사되는 것으로 가장 잘 생각될 수 있고, 다른 환경에서는 세부적인 법적 구조로, 그리고 다른 환경에서는 과학적 분류 체계로 가장 잘 생각될 수 있다.

해설　주어진 문장에서 우리는 범주를 통해 세상을 알고 관계를 맺게 된다고 하고, (B)에서 일상적인 의사소통은 이 능력(this faculty)의 가장 직접적인 표현이라고 설명하고 있다. 이어서 (C)에서 우리의 범주 중 일부는 암묵적으로 남아있고, 다른 것들은 관습 등에 의해 지배되는데, 동일한 사물에 대한 범주 체계의 적용은 맥락과 용법에 따라 다르다고 한 뒤, (A)에서 동물 종의 개념은 어떤 환경에서는 민속과 신화에 의해 묘사되는 것으로 생각되고, 다른 환경에서는 세부적인 법적 구조 등으로 가장 잘 생각될 수 있다는 예시를 들고 있다. 따라서 ② (B) - (C) - (A)가 정답이다.

어휘　relate 관계를 맺다, 관련시키다　category 범주　notion 개념, 생각 folklore 민속　myth 신화　legal 법적인　construct 구조 classification 분류　immediate 직접적인, 즉각적인 faculty 능력, 기능　explicitly 명시적으로 govern 지배하다, 통치하다　custom 관습

13　독해　전체내용 파악 (글의 감상)　난이도 ★☆☆

끊어읽기 해석

It's three in the morning, / and / we are making our way / from southern to northern Utah, / when the weather changes / from the dry chill of the desert / to the freezing gales / of an alpine winter.
지금은 새벽 세 시이다 / 그리고 / 우리는 가고 있다 / 유타 남부에서 북부로 / 날씨가 바뀔 때 / 사막의 메마른 쌀쌀함에서 / 얼어붙는 강풍으로 / 고산 겨울의

Ice claims the road.
얼음이 도로를 차지한다.

Snowflakes flick / against the windshield / like tiny insects, / a few at first, / then so many the road disappears.
눈송이가 튄다 / 앞 유리에 / 작은 곤충들처럼 / 처음에는 조금 / 그리고 나서 너무 많아서 도로가 사라진다

We push forward / into the heart of the storm.
우리는 전진한다 / 폭풍의 중심부로

The van skids and jerks.
밴은 미끄러지고 확 움직인다

The wind is furious, / the view out the window pure white.
바람은 맹렬하고 / 창밖의 풍경은 순백이다

Richard pulls over.
Richard는 차를 세운다

He says / we can't go any further.
그는 말한다 / 우리가 더 이상 갈 수 없다고

Dad takes the wheel, / Richard moves / to the passenger seat, / and / Mother lies next to me / and / Audrey on the mattress.
아빠가 운전대를 잡는다 / Richard는 이동한다 / 조수석으로 / 그리고 / 엄마는 내 옆에 누워 있다 / 그리고 / Audrey는 매트리스 위에 있다

Dad pulls onto the highway / and / accelerates, / rapidly, / as if to make a point, / until he has doubled / Richard's speed.
아빠가 고속도로로 차를 몬다 / 그리고 / 가속한다 / 빠르게 / 마치 주장을 입증하려는 듯 / 두 배가 될 때까지 / Richard의 속도의

"Shouldn't we drive slower?" // Mother asks.
"우리 더 천천히 운전해야 하지 않을까요?" // 엄마가 물어본다

Dad grins. // "I'm not driving faster than / our angels can fly."
아빠가 웃는다 // "나는 더 빨리 운전하지 않고 있어요 / 우리 천사들이 날 수 있는 것보다"

The van is still accelerating. // To fifty, / then to sixty.
밴은 여전히 가속하고 있다 // 50까지 / 그다음에는 60까지

Richard sits tensely, / his hand clutching the armrest, / his knuckles bleaching / each time the tires slip.
Richard는 긴장한 채로 앉아 있다 / 그의 손은 팔걸이를 움켜쥐고 / 그의 손가락 마디가 하얗게 변한다 / 타이어가 미끄러질 때마다

Mother lies on her side, / her face next to mine, / taking small sips of air / each time the van fishtails, / then / holding her breath / as Dad corrects / and / it snakes back into the lane.
엄마는 옆으로 누워 있다 / 내 얼굴 옆에 / 그리고 공기를 조금씩 들이킨다 / 밴의 뒷부분이 좌우로 미끄러질 때마다 / 그리고 / 숨을 참는다 / 아빠가 바로잡을 때 / 그리고 / 차가 차선으로 다시 구불구불 들어올 때

She is so rigid, / I think she might shatter.
그녀는 너무 경직되어 있다 / 나는 그녀가 산산이 부서질 수도 있다고 생각한다

My body tenses with hers; / together we brace a hundred times / for impact.
내 몸은 그녀와 함께 긴장한다 / 우리는 함께 백 번의 준비를 한다 / 충격에 대해

해석 지금은 새벽 세 시이고, 날씨가 사막의 메마른 쌀쌀함에서 고산 겨울의 얼어붙는 강풍으로 바뀔 때, 유타 남부에서 북부로 가고 있다. 얼음이 도로를 차지한다. 눈송이가 작은 곤충들처럼 앞 유리에 튀기는데, 처음에는 조금 그리고 나서 너무 많아서 도로가 사라진다. 우리는 폭풍의 중심부로 전진한다. 밴은 미끄러지고 홱 움직인다. 바람은 맹렬하고, 창밖의 풍경은 순백이다. Richard는 차를 세운다. 그는 우리가 더 이상 갈 수 없다고 말한다. 아빠가 운전대를 잡고, Richard는 조수석으로 이동하고, 엄마는 내 옆에 누워있고, Audrey는 매트리스 위에 있다. 아빠가 고속도로로 차를 몰고, 마치 주장을 입증하려는 듯, Richard의 속도의 두 배가 될 때까지 빠르게 가속한다. "우리 더 천천히 운전해야 하지 않을까요?"라고 엄마가 물어본다. 아빠가 웃는다. "나는 우리 천사들이 날 수 있는 것보다 더 빨리 운전하지 않고 있어요." 밴은 여전히 가속하고 있다. 50까지, 그다음에는 60까지. Richard는 긴장한 채로 앉아 팔걸이를 손으로 움켜쥐고, 타이어가 미끄러질 때마다 손가락 마디가 하얗게 변한다. 엄마는 내 얼굴 옆에 옆으로 누워 밴의 뒷부분이 좌우로 미끄러질 때마다 공기를 조금씩 들이키고, 아빠가 바로잡아 차가 차선으로 다시 구불구불 들어올 때 숨을 참는다. 그녀는 너무 경직되어 있어서 나는 엄마가 산산이 부서질 수도 있다고 생각한다. 내 몸은 그녀와 함께 긴장하고, 우리는 함께 충격에 대해 백 번

의 준비를 한다.
① 신이 나고 아주 흥분한
② 불안하고 두려운
③ 신중하지만 안정된
④ 편안하고 느긋한

해설 지문 전반에 걸쳐 화자가 유타 북부로 가는 길에 길이 얼어서 밴이 미끄러지는데 운전대를 잡은 아빠가 빠르게 가속하여 밴의 뒷부분이 좌우로 미끄러질 때마다 긴장하고, 충격에 대해 준비를 한다고 이야기하고 있으므로, '② 불안하고 두려운'이 이 글에 나타난 화자의 심경으로 적절하다.

어휘 chill 쌀쌀함, 냉기 alpine 고산의 flick 튀기다, 튀겨 날리다 windshield 앞 유리 insect 곤충 furious 맹렬한, 사나운 pull over 차를 세우다 accelerate 가속하다 grin 웃다 tensely 긴장한 채로 clutch 움켜쥐다 armrest 팔걸이 knuckle 손가락 마디 bleach 하얗게 되다 slip 미끄러지다 lane 차선 rigid 경직된 shatter 산산이 부서지다 tense 긴장하다 brace 준비하다 impact 충격

14 독해 논리적 흐름 파악 (문장 삽입) 난이도 ★☆☆

끊어읽기 해석

However, / there are now a lot of issues / with the current application / of unmanned distribution.
그러나 / 현재 많은 문제가 있다 / 현행 적용에는 / 무인 유통의

The city lockdown policy / during COVID-19 / has facilitated / the rapid growth of / numerous takeaways, / vegetable shopping, / community group buying, / and / other businesses.
도시 봉쇄 정책은 / 코로나19 동안의 / 촉진했다 / ~의 급속한 성장을 / 수많은 테이크아웃 전문점 / 채소 쇼핑 / 지역사회 공동 구매 / 그리고 / 기타 사업의

(①) Last-mile delivery / became an important livelihood support / during the epidemic.
최종 단계의 배송은 / 중요한 생계 지원이 되었다 / 그 전염병 동안

(②) At the same time, / as viruses can be transmitted / through aerosols, / the need for contactless delivery / for last-mile delivery / has gradually increased, / thus / accelerating the use / of unmanned logistics / to some extent.
동시에 / 바이러스가 전파될 수 있기 때문에 / 에어로졸을 통해 / 비접촉 배송의 필요성이 / 최종 단계의 배송을 위한 / 점차 증가했다 / 그래서 / 사용이 가속화되었다 / 무인 물류의 / 어느 정도

(③) For example, / the community space is not suitable / for the operation / of unmanned delivery facilities / due to the lack / of supporting logistics infrastructure.
예를 들어 / 공동체 공간은 적합하지 않다 / 운영에 / 무인 배송 시설의 / 부족 때문에 / 물류 인프라 지원의

(④) In addition, / the current technology is unable to complete / the delivery process / and / requires the collaboration / of relevant space / as well as personnel / to help dock unmanned delivery nodes.
또한 / 현재 기술로는 완료할 수 없다 / 배송 과정을 / 그리고 / 협조가 필요하다 / 관련 공간의 / 인력뿐만 아니라 / 무인 배송 중심점의 도킹을 도울

해석 그러나, 현재 무인 유통의 현행 적용에는 많은 문제가 있다.

코로나19 동안의 도시 봉쇄 정책은 수많은 테이크아웃 전문점, 채소 쇼핑, 지역사회 공동 구매 및 기타 사업의 급속한 성장을 촉진했다. (①) 최종 단계의 배송은 그 전염병 동안 중요한 생계 지원

이 되었다. (②) 동시에, 바이러스가 에어로졸을 통해 전파될 수 있기 때문에, 최종 단계의 배송을 위한 비접촉 배송의 필요성이 점차 증가하여, 무인 물류 사용이 어느 정도 가속화되었다. (③) 예를 들어, 공동체 공간은 물류 인프라 지원이 부족하여 무인 배송 시설 운영에 적합하지 않다. (④) 또한, 현재 기술로는 배송 과정을 완료할 수 없으며 무인 배송 중심점의 도킹을 도울 인력뿐만 아니라 관련 공간의 협조가 필요하다.

해설 ③번 앞 문장에 바이러스가 에어로졸을 통해 전파될 수 있기 때문에 비접촉 배송의 필요성이 증가하여 무인 물류 사용이 가속화되었다는 내용이 있고, ③번 뒤 문장에 예를 들어 공동체 공간은 물류 인프라 지원이 부족하여 무인 배송 시설 운영에 적합하지 않다는 내용이 있으므로, ③번 자리에 그러나 현재 무인 유통의 현행 적용에는 많은 문제가 있다는 내용의 주어진 문장이 나와야 지문이 자연스럽게 연결된다.

어휘 current 현행의, 현재의 application 적용, 응용, 활용
unmanned 무인의 distribution 유통, 분배 lockdown 봉쇄
facilitate 촉진하다 rapid 급속한 numerous 수많은
takeaway 테이크아웃 전문점(다른 데서 먹을 수 가지고 갈 수 있는 음식을 파는 식당) livelihood 생계, 민생
epidemic 전염병, 유행병 transmit 전파하다, 전염시키다
aerosol 에어로졸(대기 중 부유하는 고체 및 액체 입자)
contactless 비접촉의 logistics 물류, 화물
to some extent 어느 정도는, 다소 suitable 적합한
operation 운영 infrastructure 인프라, 기반, 시설
collaboration 협조, 협동 relevant 관련 있는 personnel 인력
dock (하역·승하선하기 위해) 도킹하다, 정박하다
node 중심점, 교점

15 독해 논리적 흐름 파악 (문단 순서 배열) 난이도 ★★★

끊어읽기 해석

People are too seldom interested / in having a genuine exchange of points of view / where a desire to understand / takes precedence / over the desire to convince / at any price.
사람들은 거의 관심이 없다 / 진정한 관점의 교환에 / 이해하려는 욕구가 / 우선하는 / 설득하려는 욕구에 / 어떤 대가를 치르더라도

(A) Yet / conflict isn't just an unpopular source of pressure / to act.
그러나 / 갈등은 단지 압력의 인기 없는 원천이 아니다 / 행동하라는

There's also a lot of energy inherent to it, / which can be harnessed / to create positive change, / or, / in other words, / improvements, / with the help of a skillful approach.
그것에는 또한 많은 에너지가 내재되어 있다 / 이는 활용될 수 있다 / 긍정적인 변화를 창출하는 데 / 또는 / 다른 말로 / 개선을 (창출하는 데) / 능숙한 접근법의 도움을 통해

Basically, / today's misery / is the starting shot / in the race / towards a better future.
기본적으로 / 오늘의 고통은 / 출발점이다 / 경주의 / 더 나은 미래를 향한

(B) A deviating opinion / is quickly accompanied / by devaluation, denigration, insults, / or / even physical confrontations.
일탈적인 의견은 / 곧 동반한다 / 평가절하, 명예훼손, 모욕 / 또는 / 심지어 물리적인 대립을

If you look at the "discussions" taking place / on social media networks, / you don't even have to look / to such hot potatoes / as the refugee crisis / or / terrorism / to see a clear degradation / in the way people exchange opinions.
당신이 벌어지는 '토론'을 보면 / 소셜 미디어 네트워크에서 / 당신은 볼 필

요도 없다 / 뜨거운 감자를 / 난민 사태와 같은 / 또는 / 테러(와 같은) / 확연히 저하되는 모습을 보기 위해 / 사람들이 의견을 교환하는 방식이

(C) You probably know this / from your own experience, too, / when you have succeeded / in finding a constructive solution / to a conflict / and, / at the end of an arduous clarification process, / realize / that the successful outcome / has been worth / all the effort.
당신은 이것을 알고 있을 것이다 / 당신의 경험을 통해서도 / 당신이 성공했을 때 / 건설적인 해결책을 찾는 데 / 갈등에 대한 / 그리고 / 몹시 힘든 설명의 과정 끝에서 / 깨달았을 때 / 성공적인 결과가 / 가치가 있었다는 것을 / 모든 노력의

해석
> 어떤 대가를 치르더라도 이해하려는 욕구가 설득하려는 욕구에 우선하는 진정한 관점의 교환에 사람들은 거의 관심이 없다.

(B) 일탈적인 의견은 곧 평가절하, 명예훼손, 모욕, 또는 심지어 물리적인 대립을 동반한다. 소셜 미디어 네트워크에서 벌어지는 '토론'을 보면, 사람들이 의견을 교환하는 방식이 확연히 저하되는 모습을 보기 위해 난민 사태나 테러 같은 뜨거운 감자를 볼 필요도 없다.
(A) 그러나 갈등은 단지 행동하라는 압력의 인기 없는 원천이 아니다. 그것에는 또한 많은 에너지가 내재되어 있으며, 이는 능숙한 접근법의 도움을 통해 긍정적인 변화, 즉, 개선을 창출하는 데 활용될 수 있다. 기본적으로, 오늘의 고통은 더 나은 미래를 향한 경주의 출발점이다.
(C) 당신이 갈등에 대한 건설적인 해결책을 찾는 데 성공하고 몹시 힘든 설명의 과정 끝에서 성공적인 결과가 모든 노력의 가치가 있었다는 것을 깨달았을 때의 당신의 경험을 통해서도 이것을 알고 있을 것이다.

해설 주어진 문장에서 이해하려는 욕구가 설득하려는 욕구에 우선하는 관점의 교환에 사람들은 거의 관심이 없다고 하고, (B)에서 일탈적인 의견은 곧 평가절하 등을 동반한다고 하며 소셜 미디어 네트워크에서 벌어지는 토론을 예시로 들고 있다. 이어서 (A)에서 그러나(Yet) 갈등은 단지 행동하라는 압력의 원천이 아니며, 긍정적인 변화를 창출하는 데 활용될 수 있다고 하고, (C)에서 갈등에 대한 건설적인 해결책을 찾는 데 성공했을 때의 경험을 통해서 이것(this)을 알고 있을 것이라고 설명하고 있다. 따라서 ① (B) - (A) - (C)가 정답이다.

어휘 seldom 거의 ~ 않다 genuine 진정한 point of view 관점
desire 욕구 precedence 우선, 선행 convince 설득하다
at any price 어떤 대가를 치르더라도 conflict 갈등
inherent 내재된 harness 활용하다 misery 고통, 불행
deviate 일탈하다, 벗어나다 accompany 동반하다, 수반하다
devaluation 평가절하, 가치 하락 insult 모욕
physical 물리적인, 신체적인 confrontation 대립, 대결
hot potato 뜨거운 감자, 어려운 문제 refugee 난민
crisis 사태, 위기 degradation 저하, 붕괴, 하락
constructive 건설적인 clarification 설명, 해명

16 독해 세부내용 파악 (내용 불일치 파악) 난이도 ★☆☆

끊어읽기 해석

Belus Smawley grew up / on a farm / with his parents and six siblings.
Belus Smawley는 자랐다 / 농장에서 / 그의 부모님과 여섯 명의 형제들과

In his freshman years, / he was tall / and / able to jump / higher than any other boy, / trying to improve his leaping

ability / by touching higher and higher limbs / of the oak tree / on their farm.
그가 1학년 때 / 그는 키가 컸다 / 그리고 / 뛸 수 있었다 / 다른 어떤 소년보다 더 높이 / 그의 도약 능력을 향상시키려고 노력했다 / 더 높은 가지를 만지면서 / 참나무의 / 그들의 농장에 있는

This is where his first jump shot attempt is said to have taken place.
이곳이 그의 첫 번째 점프 슛 시도가 있었던 곳이라고 한다

When Belus Smawley started using his shot / regularly, / he became the leading scorer.
Belus Smawley가 그의 슛을 사용하기 시작했을 때 / 정기적으로 / 그는 최고 득점자가 되었다

At the age of 18, / he got accepted for a position / on an AAU18 basketball team.
18세에 / 그는 자리에 합격했다 / AAU18 농구팀의

He finished high school / afterwards / and / got an All-American athletic scholarship / for Appalachian State University / (majoring in history and physical education).
그는 고등학교를 마쳤다 / 그 후에 / 그리고 / 전미 체육 장학금을 받았다 / 애팔래치아 주립대학교에서 / (역사와 체육 교육 전공)

He became player-coach / until he went to the Navy.
그는 선수 겸 코치가 되었다 / 그가 해군에 입대할 때까지

He started playing in their basketball team / and / refined his jump shot.
그는 그들의 농구팀에서 뛰기 시작했다 / 그리고 / 그의 점프 슛을 다듬었다

He got married / and / either worked as a high school teacher and basketball coach / or / further pursued his NBA basketball career / playing fulltime / for several teams.
그는 결혼했다 / 그리고 / 고등학교 교사 및 농구 코치로 일하거나 / 또는 / NBA 농구 경력을 계속했다 / 풀타임으로 뛰면서 / 여러 팀에서

Eventually / he focused on family and his teaching career, / becoming the principal / of a junior high school.
마침내 / 그는 그의 가족과 교사 경력에 집중했다 / 교장이 되었다 / 중학교의

해석 Belus Smawley는 그의 부모님과 여섯 명의 형제와 함께 농장에서 자랐다. 그가 1학년 때, 그는 키가 컸고, 다른 어떤 소년보다 더 높이 뛸 수 있었는데, 그는 농장에 있는 참나무의 더 높은 가지를 만지면서 도약 능력을 향상시키려고 노력했다. 이곳이 그의 첫 번째 점프 슛 시도가 있었던 곳이라고 한다. Belus Smawley가 그의 슛을 정기적으로 사용하기 시작했을 때, 그는 최고 득점자가 되었다. 18세에, 그는 AAU18 농구팀의 자리에 합격했다. 그는 그 후에 고등학교를 마쳤고 애팔래치아 주립대학교(역사와 체육 교육 전공)에서 전미 체육 장학금을 받았다. 그는 해군에 입대할 때까지 선수 겸 코치가 되었다. 그는 그들의 농구팀에서 뛰기 시작했고 그의 점프 슛을 다듬었다. 그는 결혼하여 고등학교 교사 및 농구 코치로 일하거나 여러 팀에서 풀타임으로 뛰면서 NBA 농구 경력을 계속했다. 마침내 그는 그의 가족과 교사 경력에 집중하면서 중학교의 교장이 되었다.

해설 지문 마지막에서 Belus Smawley는 결혼하여 여러 팀에서 풀타임으로 뛰면서 NBA 농구 경력을 계속했다고 했으므로 '④ 결혼 후 NBA 농구 선수로서 한 팀에서 활동했다'는 지문의 내용과 일치하지 않는다.

어휘 sibling 형제 freshman 1학년, 신입생 leap 도약하다, 뛰어오르다
limb (나무의) 가지, 팔다리 oak tree 참나무 attempt 시도
athletic 체육의, 운동의 scholarship 장학금
refine 다듬다, 정제하다

끊어읽기 해석

It might be understandable, / then, / for us to want to expect / something similar / from our machines: / to know / not only what they think they see / but where, / in particular, / they are looking.
이해할 수 있을 것이다 / 그렇다면 / 우리가 기대하고 싶어 하는 것은 / 비슷한 것을 / 우리의 기계로부터 / 아는 것이다 / 그것들이 무엇을 본다고 생각하는지 뿐만 아니라 / 어디를 / 특히 / 그들이 보고 있는지를

Humans, / relative to most other species, / have distinctly large and visible sclera / —the whites of our eyes / — and as a result / we are uniquely exposed / in how we direct our attention, / or / at the very least, / our gaze.
인간은 / 대부분의 다른 종과 비교했을 때 / 확연히 크고 눈에 보이는 공막을 가지고 있다 / 즉, 눈의 흰자를 / 그리고 그 결과 / 우리는 유일하게 노출된다 / 우리가 어떻게 주의를 집중하는지가 / 또는 / 최소한 (어떻게) 우리의 시선(을 집중하는지가)

(①) Evolutionary biologists have argued, / via the "cooperative eye hypothesis," / that this must be a feature, / not a bug: / that it must point to the fact / that cooperation has been uncommonly important / in our survival / as a species, / to the point that the benefits of shared attention outweigh / the loss / of a certain degree / of privacy or discretion.
진화 생물학자들은 주장했다 / '협력적 눈 가설'을 통해 / 이것은 특징임이 틀림없다고 / 오류가 아니라 / 즉, 사실을 지적해야 한다는 것이다 / 협력이 몹시 중요했다는 / 우리가 생존하는 데 / 하나의 종으로서 / 공유된 주의력의 이점이 더 크다는 점에서 / 잃는 것보다 / 어느 정도의 / 사생활이나 신중함을

(②) This idea in machine learning / goes by the name of "saliency": / the idea is that if a system is looking at an image / and / assigning it to some category, / then / presumably / some parts of the image / were more important or more influential / than others / in making that determination.
기계 학습에서 이 개념은 / '중요점'이라는 이름으로 통한다 / 즉, 시스템이 이미지를 본다면 / 그리고 / 그것을 어떤 범주에 할당한다면 / 그러면 / 아마도 / 이미지의 어떤 부분이 / 더 중요하거나 더 영향력이 있었을 것이라는 것이다 / 다른 부분보다 / 그러한 결정을 내리는 데

(③) If we could see / a kind of "heat map" / that highlighted these critical portions / of the image, / we might obtain / some crucial diagnostic information / that we could use / as a kind of sanity check / to make sure / the system is behaving / the way we think it should be. (④)
우리가 볼 수 있다면 / 일종의 '열 지도'를 / 이러한 중요한 부분을 강조하는 / 이미지의 / 우리는 얻을 수 있을 것이다 / 몇 가지 중요한 진단 정보를 / 우리가 사용할 수 있는 / 일종의 온전성 점검으로 / 확인하기 위한 / 시스템이 작동하는지 / 우리가 생각하는 방식으로

해석
> 그렇다면 우리가 기계로부터 비슷한 것을 기대하고 싶어 하는 것은 이해할 수 있을 것이다. 즉, 그것들이 무엇을 본다고 생각하는지 뿐만 아니라, 특히 어디를 보고 있는지를 아는 것이다.

인간은 대부분의 다른 종과 비교했을 때, 확연히 크고 눈에 보이는 공막, 즉, 눈의 흰자를 가지고 있으며, 그 결과 우리는 어떻게 주의를 집중하는지, 또는 최소한 어떻게 시선을 집중하는지가 유일하게 노출된다. (①) 진화 생물학자들은 '협력적 눈 가설'을 통해, 이것이 오류가 아니라 특징임이 틀림없다고 주장했다. 즉, 공유된 주의력의 이점이 어느 정도의 사생활이나 신중함을 잃는 것보다 더 크다는 점에서, 우리가 하나의 종으로서 생존하는 데 협력이 몹시 중요했다는 사실을 지적해야 한다는 것이다. (②) 기계 학습에서 이 개념은 '중요점'이라는 이름으로 통한다. 즉, 시스템이 이

미지를 보고 그것을 어떤 범주에 할당한다면, 아마도 이미지의 어떤 부분이 그러한 결정을 내리는 데 다른 부분보다 더 중요하거나 더 영향력이 있었을 것이라는 것이다. (③) 우리가 이미지의 이러한 중요한 부분을 강조하는 일종의 '열 지도'를 볼 수 있다면, 우리는 시스템이 우리가 생각하는 방식으로 작동하는지 확인하기 위한 일종의 온전성 점검으로 사용할 수 있는 몇 가지 중요한 진단 정보를 얻을 수 있을 것이다. (④)

해설 ②번 앞 문장에 공유된 주의력의 이점이 어느 정도의 사생활이나 신중함을 잃는 것보다 더 크다는 점에서 우리가 생존하는 데 협력이 몹시 중요했다는 사실을 지적해야 한다는 내용이 있고, ②번 뒤 문장에 기계 학습에서 이 개념은 '중요성'이라는 이름으로 통한다는 내용이 있으므로, ②번 자리에 '중요성'이라고 불리는 개념에 대한 설명으로 우리가 기계로부터 비슷한 것을 기대하고 싶어 하는 것은 이해할 수 있을 것이며, 그것은 그것들이 무엇을 본다고 생각하는지 뿐만 아니라 어디를 보고 있는지를 아는 것이라는 내용의 주어진 문장이 나와야 지문이 자연스럽게 연결된다.

어휘 distinctly 확연히, 뚜렷하게　white (눈의) 흰자
uniquely 유일하게, 독특하게　gaze 시선, 응시
evolutionary 진화의, 진화론적인　argue 주장하다, 논쟁하다
cooperative 협력적인　hypothesis 가설　feature 특징, 기능
bug 오류, 버그, 결함　uncommonly 몹시, 현저하게
assign 할당하다, 부여하다　presumably 아마도, 추정하건대
influential 영향력 있는　determination 결정　portion 부분, 일부
diagnostic 진단의, 진단상의　sanity 온전성, 분별

18　문법　분사&관계절&수 일치　난이도 ★★☆

해석 관개된 평야의 기후는 벽화에서 엿볼 수 있다. 여름의 태양이 단단한 땅 위에 내리쬐고, 왕 본인에게도 커다란 우산으로 그늘이 드리워져 있다. 종종 존재하는 전쟁도 생생한 세부 양식으로 새겨져 있다. 기원전 878년쯤에는, 세 명의 남자가 아마도 함락되었을 것으로 추정되는 도시로부터 도망치는 모습이 묘사되어 있다. 긴 옷을 입은 그들은 유프라테스강으로 뛰어들고, 그곳에서 한 사람은 수영하고 다른 사람들은 구명부표를 가슴에 껴안는다. 긴 베개처럼, 구명부표는 공기로 부풀려진 동물의 피부로 이루어진다. 난민들의 손이 부풀려진 구명부표를 움켜쥐고 있고, 그들의 숨 중 대부분은 그 안에 공기를 불어 넣는 데 쓰이기 때문에, 그들은 다리로 수영해야만 물 위에 떠 있을 수 있다. 그들이 반대편 해안에 도달했는지 여부는 결코 알 수 없을 것이다.

해설 (A) 현재분사 vs. 과거분사　주어(three men)와 분사가 '세 명의 남자가 도망치다'라는 의미의 능동 관계이므로, 과거분사 fled가 아닌 현재분사 fleeing이 와야 한다.
(B) 관계부사와 관계대명사 비교　관계사 뒤에 완전한 절(one is ~ their chests)이 왔으므로 관계대명사 which가 아닌 관계부사 where가 와야 한다.
(C) 주어와 동사의 수 일치　주어 자리에 복수 명사 the hands가 왔으므로 단수 동사 is가 아닌 복수 동사 are가 와야 한다.
따라서 ② (A) fleeing – (B) where – (C) are가 정답이다.

어휘 climate 기후　irrigate 관개하다, 물을 대다
glimpse 엿보다, 흘끗 보다　mural 벽화　shade ~을 그늘지게 하다
carve 새기다, 조각하다　vivid 생생한
detail (그림 등의) 세부 양식, 디테일　depict 묘사하다, 표현하다
flee 도망치다, 탈출하다　capture 함락시키다, 포획하다
robe 옷, 가운　lifebuoy 구명부표　chest 가슴　pillow 베개
inflate 부풀리다　refugee 난민　clutch 움켜쥐다
expend 쓰다, 소비하다　afloat 물 위에 떠서　shore 해안

이것도 알면 합격!

관계부사는 '전치사 + 관계대명사'로 바꾸어 쓸 수 있다는 것을 알아두자.

관계부사	전치사 + 관계대명사
where	in/on/at/to + which
when	in/on/at/during + which
why	for + which
how	in + which

19　독해　세부내용 파악 (내용 불일치 파악)　난이도 ★★☆

끊어읽기 해석

When the Dutch arrived in the 17th century / in what's now New York City, / their encounters / with the indigenous peoples, / known as the Lenape, / were, at first, mostly amicable, / according to historical records.
네덜란드인들이 17세기에 도착했을 때 / 지금의 뉴욕시인 곳에 / 그들의 만남은 / 원주민들과의 / 르나페로 알려진 / 처음에는 대부분 우호적이었다 / 역사적 기록에 따르면

They shared the land / and / traded guns, beads and wool / for beaver furs.
그들은 땅을 공유했다 / 그리고 / 총, 구슬 그리고 양모를 교환했다 / 비버의 모피와

The Dutch even "purchased" / Manahatta island / from the Lenape / in 1626.
네덜란드인들은 심지어 '구매했다' / Manahatta 섬을 / 르나페로부터 / 1626년에

The transaction, / enforced by the eventual building of wall / around New Amsterdam, / marked the very beginning / of the Lenape's forced mass migration / out of their homeland.
이 거래는 / 결국 장벽이 건설되면서 시행된 / 뉴 암스테르담 주변에 / 시작을 나타냈다 / 르나페가 강제로 대량 이주하는 것의 / 그들의 고향에서

The wall, / which started showing up / on maps / in the 1660s, / was built / to keep out / the Native Americans and the British.
그 장벽은 / 나타나기 시작한 / 지도에 / 1660년대에 / 세워졌다 / 막기 위해 / 북미 원주민과 영국인들을

It eventually became Wall Street, / and / Manahatta became Manhattan, / where part of the Lenape trade route, / known as Wickquasgeck, / became Brede weg, / later Broadway.
그것은 결국 월스트리트가 되었다 / 그리고 / Manahatta는 맨해튼이 되었다 / 그곳에서 르나페 무역로의 일부는 / Wickquasgeck으로 알려진 / Brede weg가 되었다 / 나중에 브로드웨이가 된

The Lenape helped / shape the geography / of modern-day New York City, / but / other traces of their legacy / have all but vanished.
르나페는 도움을 주었다 / 지형을 형성하는 데 / 현대 뉴욕시의 / 하지만 / 그들의 유산에 대한 다른 흔적들은 / 거의 사라졌다

해석 역사적 기록에 따르면, 네덜란드인들이 17세기에 지금의 뉴욕시인 곳에 도착했을 때, 르나페로 알려진 원주민들과의 만남은 처음에는 대부분 우호적이었다. 그들은 땅을 공유했고 총, 구슬 그리고 양모를 비버의 모피와 교환했다. 네덜란드인들은 심지어 1626년에 르나페로부터 Manahatta 섬을 '구매했다'. 뉴 암스테르담 주변에 결국 장벽이 건설되면서 시행된 이 거래는, 르나페가 강제로 그들의 고향에서 대량 이주하는 것의 시작을 나타냈다. 1660년대에 지도에 나타나기 시작한 그 장벽은 북미 원주민과 영국인들을 막기 위해 세워졌다. 그것은 결국 월스트리트가 되었고, Manahatta

는 맨해튼이 되었는데, 그곳에서 Wickquasgeck으로 알려진 르나 페 무역로의 일부는 나중에 브로드웨이가 된 Brede weg가 되었다. 르나페는 현대 뉴욕시의 지형을 형성하는 데 도움을 주었지만, 그들의 유산에 대한 다른 흔적들은 거의 사라졌다.

해설 지문 중간에서 네덜란드인들은 1626년에 르나페로부터 Manahatta 섬을 구매했는데, 이 거래는 뉴 암스테르담 주변에 장벽이 건설되면서 시행되었다고 했으며 르나페가 강제로 그들의 고향에서 대량 이주하는 것의 시작을 나타냈고, 그 장벽은 북미 원주민과 영국인들을 막기 위해 세워졌다고 했으므로 '② 이후에 월스트리트가 된 지역에 지어진 벽은 르나페 원주민이 영국인을 막기 위해 세웠다'는 지문의 내용과 일치하지 않는다.

어휘 Dutch 네덜란드인, 네덜란드의 encounter 만남; 만나다, 마주치다
indigenous 원산의, 토착의 amicable 우호적인
transaction 거래 enforce ~을 강제하다, 시행하다
mark ~을 나타내다, 표시하다 migration 이주, 이동 trace 흔적
legacy 유산 vanish 사라지다

20 문법 분사 난이도 ★★☆

해석 오늘날, 우리는 미디어와 그것이 유지하는 유명인 문화가 새로운 형태의 공공성을 만들어 냈으며, 이를 통해 우리가 한 번도 만난 적 없는 사람들과 친밀한 관계를 맺을 수 있다는 것을 당연하게 여긴다. 미디어 기술 덕분에 우리는 유명인에게 훨씬 더 가까워지게 되고, 그들과 친밀감을 느끼는 환상을 즐길 수 있다. 어느 정도, 우리는 유명인을 내면화하고, 무의식적으로 마치 그들이 사실은 우리의 친구인 것처럼 우리 의식의 일부로 만들었다. 유명인들은 우리의 몽상과 환상의 중심이 되고, 행동과 야망의 지침이 되면서 우리 내면의 삶에서도 영구적인 거처를 차지한다. 이제, 정말로, 우리 중 많은 사람들이 그들, 그들의 특성, 그리고 그들과의 관계를 우리의 정신적 짐의 일부로 가지고 다니기 때문에, 유명인 문화는 영구적으로 우리의 감성의 일부가 될 수 있다.

해설 ④ 분사구문의 형태 문장 내에 이미 동사(take up)가 있으므로 부사절 역할을 하는 분사구문이 쓰여야 하는데, 주절의 주어 (Celebrities)와 분사구문이 '유명인들이 우리의 몽상과 환상의 중심이 되고, 행동과 야망의 지침이 된다'라는 의미의 능동 관계이므로, 동사원형 become을 현재분사 becoming으로 고쳐야 한다.

오답 ① 전치사 + 관계대명사 관계사 뒤에 완전한 절(we might ~
분석   never met)이 왔으므로 '전치사 + 관계대명사' 형태가 올 수 있다. '전치사 + 관계대명사'에서 전치사는 선행사 또는 관계절의 동사에 따라 결정되는데, 문맥상 '새로운 형태의 공공성을 통해 우리가 한 번도 만난 적 없는 사람들과 친밀한 관계를 맺을 수 있다'라는 의미가 되어야 자연스러우므로 전치사 through(~을 통해)가 관계대명사 which 앞에 온 through which가 올바르게 쓰였다.
② 능동태·수동태 구별 주어(we)와 동사가 '우리는 가까워지게 된다'라는 의미의 수동 관계이므로 수동태 are brought가 올바르게 쓰였다.
③ 기타 가정법 문맥상 '마치 그들이 사실은 우리의 친구인 것처럼 우리 의식의 일부로 만들었다'라는 의미가 되어야 자연스러운데, '마치 ~인 것처럼'은 As if 가정법을 사용해 나타낼 수 있으므로 '주어(they) + 과거 동사(were)' 앞에 as if가 올바르게 쓰였다.

어휘 take for granted ~을 당연하게 여기다 celebrity 유명인
publicness 공공성 intimate 친밀한, 가까운 illusion 환상, 착각
internalize 내면화하다 unconsciously 무의식적으로
consciousness 의식, 정신 take up 차지하다

permanent 영구적인 residence 거처, 주거 ambition 야망
sensibility 감성, 정서

과거	주어 + 동사 + as if/as though + 주어 + 과거 동사	마치 ~인 것처럼
과거완료	주어 + 동사 + as if/as though + 주어 + had p.p.	마치 ~이었던 것처럼

21 독해 추론 (빈칸 완성 - 구) 난이도 ★★☆

끊어읽기 해석

Festivals are significant cultural events / that showcase / tradition, heritage and community spirit / globally.
축제는 중요한 문화 행사이다 / 보여주는 / 전통, 유산 그리고 공동체 정신을 / 전 세계적으로

They serve as platforms / to celebrate diversity, / with each festival / reflecting unique traditions / like Brazil's Carnival or India's Diwali.
그것들은 플랫폼 역할을 한다 / 다양성을 기념하는 / 각 축제는 / 독특한 전통을 반영한다 / 브라질의 카니발이나 인도의 디왈리와 같은

Festivals also commemorate / historical moments, / such as Independence Day in the US / or / Bastille Day in France.
축제는 또한 기념한다 / 역사적인 순간을 / 미국의 독립 기념일과 같은 / 또는 / 프랑스의 혁명 기념일(과 같은)

Additionally, / they preserve customs and rituals / that strengthen personal and cultural identity, / while fostering / strong community ties / through shared activities.
또한 / 그것들은 관습과 의식을 보존한다 / 개인적, 문화적 정체성을 강화하는 / 형성하는 동시에 / 강력한 공동체 유대를 / 공유된 활동을 통해

Festivals reflect societal values, / promote local crafts and arts, / enhance spirituality, / and / attract tourism, / which facilitates / cultural exchange and understanding.
축제는 사회적 가치를 반영하고 / 지역 공예와 예술을 장려하며 / 영성을 강화하고 / 그리고 / 관광을 유치한다 / 이는 촉진한다 / 문화 교류와 이해를

Seasonal festivals, / like Holi in India, / align with natural cycles, / celebrating times of renewal.
계절 축제는 / 인도의 홀리와 같은 / 자연의 순환에 맞춰 / 재생의 시기를 기념한다

Ultimately, / participating in festivals / reinforces community and individual identity, / contributing to a global narrative / that values diversity / and / encourages mutual respect and understanding.
궁극적으로 / 축제에 참여하는 것은 / 공동체와 개인의 정체성을 강화한다 / 그리고 세계적인 서사에 기여한다 / 다양성을 중시하는 / 그리고 / 상호 존중과 이해를 장려하는

해석 축제는 전 세계적으로 전통, 유산 그리고 공동체 정신을 보여주는 중요한 문화 행사이다. 그것들은 다양성을 기념하는 플랫폼 역할을 하며, 각 축제는 브라질의 카니발이나 인도의 디왈리와 같은 독특한 전통을 반영한다. 축제는 또한 미국의 독립 기념일이나 프랑스의 혁명 기념일과 같은 역사적인 순간을 기념한다. 또한, 그것들은 개인적, 문화적 정체성을 강화하는 관습과 의식을 보존하는 동시에 공유된 활동을 통해 강력한 공동체 유대를 형성한다. 축제는 사회적 가치를 반영하고, 지역 공예와 예술을 장려하며, 영성을 강화하고, 관광을 유치하는데, 이는 문화 교류와 이해를 촉진한다. 인도의 홀리와 같은 계절 축제는 자연의 순환에 맞춰 재생의 시기를 기념한다. 궁극적으로, 축제에 참여하는 것은 공동체와 개인의

정체성을 강화하여 <u>다양성을 중시하고 상호 존중과 이해를 장려하</u>는 세계적인 서사에 기여한다.

① 참가자들이 일상의 걱정과 고통을 잊게 만드는
② 다양성을 중시하고 상호 존중과 이해를 장려하는
③ 사람들이 사생활과 사회생활의 연결을 끊게 하는
④ 축제가 사람들이 자신에 대해 어떻게 생각하는지 결정하지 못하게 하는

해설 지문 처음에서 축제는 전 세계적으로 공동체 정신 등을 보여주는 중요한 문화 행사라고 했고, 지문 중간에서 축제는 공유된 활동을 통해 강력한 공동체 유대를 형성한다고 했으므로, 빈칸에는 축제에 참여하는 것은 공동체와 개인의 정체성을 강화하여 '② 다양성을 중시하고 상호 존중과 이해를 장려하는' 세계적인 서사에 기여한다는 내용이 들어가야 한다.

어휘 significant 중요한, 상당한 showcase 보여주다, 전시하다 heritage 유산 spirit 정신 platform 플랫폼, 발판, 기반 diversity 다양성 preserve 보존하다 custom 관습 ritual 의식 identity 정체성 foster 형성하다, 증진하다 tie 유대, 관계 enhance 강화하다, 높이다 spirituality 영성, 숭고함 align 맞추다 reinforce 강화하다 contribute 기여하다, 공헌하다 narrative 서사 value 중시하다 mutual 상호의, 서로의 determine 결정하다

22 독해 추론 (함축 의미 추론) 난이도 ★★☆

끊어읽기 해석

Life is full of its ups and downs.
인생은 기복으로 가득 차 있다

One day, / you may feel like / you have it all figured out.
어느 날 / 당신은 느낄지도 모른다 / 당신이 모든 것을 다 이해했다고

Then, / in a moment's notice, / <u>you've been thrown a curve ball</u>.
그런 다음 / 곧바로 / 당신에게 변화구가 던져졌다

You're not alone / in these feelings.
당신만 있는 것이 아니다 / 이러한 감정 속에

Everyone has to face / their own set of challenges.
모든 사람은 직면해야 한다 / 자신만의 어려움에

Learning / how to overcome challenges / will help you / stay centered / and / remain calm / under pressure.
배우는 것은 / 어려움을 극복하는 방법을 / 당신에게 도움이 될 것이다 / 중심을 유지하는 데 / 그리고 / 침착함을 유지하는 데 / 압박감 속에서도

Everyone has their own preferences / for how to face a challenge / in life.
모든 사람은 자신만의 선호가 있다 / 어려움에 직면하는 방법에 대해 / 인생에서

However, / there are a few good tips and tricks / to follow / when the going gets tough.
그러나 / 몇 가지 좋은 팁과 요령이 있다 / 따라야 할 / 상황이 어려워질 때

There's no need / to feel ashamed / for asking for help.
필요가 없다 / 부끄러워할 / 도움을 요청하는 것을

Whether you choose to rely on / a loved one, a stranger, a mentor, or a friend, / there are people / who want to help you succeed.
당신이 의존하기를 선택하든 간에 / 사랑하는 사람, 낯선 사람, 멘토, 또는 친구에게 / 사람들이 있다 / 당신이 성공하는 것을 돕고 싶어 하는

You have to be open / and / willing to accept support.
당신은 개방적이어야 한다 / 그리고 / 기꺼이 지원을 받아들여야 한다

People who come to your aid / truly do care about you.
당신을 도우러 오는 사람은 / 진심으로 당신에게 마음을 쓰고 있다

Be open to receiving help / when you need it.
도움을 받을 수 있도록 열려 있어라 / 당신이 도움이 필요할 때

해석 인생은 기복으로 가득 차 있다. 어느 날, 당신은 모든 것을 다 이해했다고 느낄지도 모른다. 그런 다음, 곧바로, 당신에게 <u>변화구가 던져졌다</u>. 당신만 이러한 감정 속에 있는 것이 아니다. 모든 사람은 자신만의 어려움에 직면해야 한다. 어려움을 극복하는 방법을 배우는 것은 당신이 중심을 유지하고 압박감 속에서도 침착함을 유지하는 데 도움이 될 것이다. 모든 사람은 인생에서 어려움에 직면하는 방법에 대해 자신만의 선호가 있다. 그러나, 상황이 어려워질 때 따라야 할 몇 가지 좋은 팁과 요령이 있다. 도움을 요청하는 것을 부끄러워할 필요가 없다. 당신이 사랑하는 사람, 낯선 사람, 멘토, 또는 친구에게 의존하기를 선택하든 간에, 당신이 성공하는 것을 돕고 싶어 하는 사람들이 있다. 당신은 개방적이어야 하고 기꺼이 지원을 받아들여야 한다. 당신을 도우러 오는 사람들은 진심으로 당신에게 마음을 쓰고 있다. 도움이 필요할 때 도움을 받을 수 있도록 열려 있어라.

해설 지문 처음에서 어느 날 당신은 모든 것을 다 이해했다고 느낄지도 모른다고 하고, 지문 중간에서 모든 사람은 자신만의 어려움에 직면해야 한다고 설명하고 있으므로, '① 어려운 상황에 직면하다'가 밑줄 친 you've been thrown a curve ball의 의미로 가장 적절하다.

어휘 ups and downs 기복, 오르내림 figure out 이해하다, 알아내다 curve ball 변화구, 책략 overcome 극복하다, 이겨내다 preference 선호 ashamed 부끄러운

23 독해 전체내용 파악 (문단 요약) 난이도 ★★★

끊어읽기 해석

Social dominance / refers to situations / in which an individual or a group / controls or dictates / others' behavior / primarily / in competitive situations.
사회적 지배는 / 상황을 나타낸다 / 개체나 집단이 / 통제하거나 지시하는 / 다른 개체들의 행동을 / 주로 / 경쟁 상황에서

Generally, / an individual or group / is said to be dominant / when "a prediction is being made / about the course of / future interactions / or / the outcome of competitive situations".
일반적으로 / 개체나 집단은 / 지배적이라고 한다 / '예측이 이루어지고 있을' 때 / 과정에 대한 / 미래의 상호 작용 / 또는 / 경쟁 상황의 결과에 대한'

Criteria for assessing and assigning / dominance relationships / can vary / from one situation to another.
평가하고 지정하는 기준은 / 지배 관계를 / 다를 수 있다 / 상황마다

It is difficult / to summarize / available data / briefly, / but / generally / it has been found / that dominant individuals, / when compared to subordinate individuals, / often have more freedom of movement, / have priority of access to food, / gain higher-quality resting spots, / enjoy favorable grooming relationships, / occupy more protected parts of a group, / obtain higher-quality mates, / command and regulate the attention / of other group members, / and / show greater resistance / to stress and disease.
어렵다 / 요약하기는 / 이용 가능한 자료를 / 간략하게 / 하지만 / 일반적으로 / 밝혀졌다 / 지배적인 개체는 / 하위 개체와 비교했을 때 / 종종 이동에 대한 더 많은 자유를 가지고 / 음식에 대한 접근의 우선권을 가지며 / 더 높은 수준의 휴식 공간을 얻고 / 유리한 몸단장 관계를 누리고 / 집단에서 더 많이 보호받는 부분을 차지하고 / 더 높은 지위의 짝을 얻고 / 주의를 끌고 규제하며 / 다른 집단 구성원들의 / 그리고 / 더 큰 저항을 보인다 / 스트레스와 질병에

Despite assertions / that suggest otherwise, / it really is not clear / how powerful the relationship is / between an individual's dominance status / and / its lifetime reproductive success.
주장에도 불구하고 / 그렇지 않다고 시사하는 / 실제로 명확하지 않다 / 관계가 얼마나 강력한지는 / 개체의 우세 상태 사이의 / 그리고 / 평생 번식 성공

해석 사회적 지배는 주로 경쟁 상황에서 개체나 집단이 다른 개체들의 행동을 통제하거나 지시하는 상황을 나타낸다. 일반적으로, 개체나 집단은 '미래의 상호 작용 과정이나 경쟁 상황의 결과에 대한 예측이 이루어지고 있을' 때 지배적이라고 한다. 지배 관계를 평가하고 지정하는 기준은 상황마다 다를 수 있다. 이용 가능한 자료를 간략하게 요약하기는 어렵지만, 일반적으로 지배적인 개체는 하위 개체와 비교했을 때, 종종 이동에 대한 더 많은 자유를 가지고, 음식에 대한 접근의 우선권을 가지며, 더 높은 수준의 휴식 공간을 얻고, 유리한 몸단장 관계를 누리고, 집단에서 더 많이 보호받는 부분을 차지하고, 더 높은 지위의 짝을 얻고, 다른 집단 구성원들의 주의를 끌고 규제하며, 스트레스와 질병에 대한 더 큰 저항을 보이는 것으로 밝혀졌다. 그렇지 않다고 시사하는 주장에도 불구하고, 개체의 우세 상태와 평생 번식 성공 사이의 관계가 얼마나 강력한지는 실제로 명확하지 않다.

해설 지문 중간에서 지배 관계를 평가하고 지정하는 기준은 상황마다 다를 수 있다고 하고, 지문 마지막에서 개체의 우세 상태와 평생 번식 성공 사이의 관계가 얼마나 강력한지는 실제로 명확하지 않다고 설명하고 있으므로, '② 개체의 우세 상태와 평생 번식 성공 사이의 관계는 다면적이며 명확하게 정립되어 있다고 할 수는 없다'가 이 글에서 설명된 사회적 지배력과 번식 성공 사이의 관계를 가장 잘 요약한 것으로 가장 적절하다.

어휘 dictate 지시하다, 명령하다 primarily 주로, 우선
competitive 경쟁의, 경쟁적인 prediction 예측, 추정
course 과정 interaction 상호 작용 outcome 결과
criterion 기준(복수형: criteria) assess 평가하다
assign 지정하다, 할당하다 summarize 요약하다
subordinate 하위의, 종속하는 favorable 유리한, 호의적인
groom 몸단장하다 occupy 차지하다, 점령하다
obtain 얻다, 획득하다 mate 짝, 친구
command (주의를) 끌다, 명령하다 regulate 규제하다, 조절하다
resistance 저항(력), 반항 assertion 주장 status 상태, 지위
reproductive 번식의, 생식의

24 독해 전체내용 파악 (주제 파악)   난이도 ★☆☆

끊어읽기 해석

While mindfulness meditation is generally safe, / concerns arise / from its side effects / like panic attacks and psychosis, / which are seldom reported / and / poorly understood / in academic studies.
마음 챙김 명상은 일반적으로 안전하지만 / 우려가 발생한다 / 그것의 부작용으로 인해 / 공황 발작과 정신 질환 같은 / 이것은 거의 보고되지 않는다 / 그리고 / 잘 이해되지 않는다 / 학계 연구에서

Critics argue / the rapid adoption of mindfulness / by organizations and educational systems / may inappropriately shift / societal issues / to individuals, / suggesting that personal stress is due to a lack of meditation / rather than addressing / systemic causes / like environmental pollution / or / workplace demands.
비평가들은 주장한다 / 마음 챙김의 빠른 채택이 / 조직과 교육 시스템에 의한 / 부적절하게 옮길 수 있다고 / 사회 문제를 / 개인에게 / 개인적인 스트레스가 명상의 부족 때문이라고 시사한다 / 해결하기보다는 / 체계적

인 원인을 / 환경 오염과 같은 / 또는 / 직장의 요구(와 같은)

Critics like Professor Ronald Purser suggest / that mindfulness may make individuals / more compliant / with adverse conditions / instead of empowering them / to seek change.
Ronald Purser 교수와 같은 비평가들은 시사한다 / 마음 챙김이 개인들을 만들 수 있다고 / 더 순응하게 / 불리한 조건에 / 그들에게 권한을 부여하는 대신 / 변화를 추구하도록

Despite these concerns, / the critique isn't against mindfulness itself / but / against its promotion / as a universal solution / by entities / resistant to change.
이러한 우려에도 불구하고 / 비평은 마음 챙김 그 자체에 반대하는 것이 아니다 / 하지만 / 그것의 홍보에 반대하는 것이다 / 보편적인 해결책으로서의 / 주체들에 의한 / 변화에 저항하는

For a more thorough understanding / of mindfulness' benefits and risks, / long-term and rigorously controlled studies / are essential.
보다 철저한 이해를 위해서는 / 마음 챙김의 유익성과 위험에 대한 / 장기적이고 엄격하게 통제된 연구가 / 필수적이다

해석 마음 챙김 명상은 일반적으로 안전하지만, 공황 발작과 정신 질환 같은 부작용으로 인한 우려가 발생하는데, 이것(부작용)은 학계 연구에서 거의 보고되지 않고 잘 이해되지 않는다. 비평가들은 조직과 교육 시스템에 의한 마음 챙김의 빠른 채택이 사회 문제를 개인에게 부적절하게 옮길 수 있다고 주장하며, 개인적인 스트레스는 환경 오염이나 직장의 요구와 같은 체계적인 원인을 해결하기보다는 명상의 부족 때문이라는 점을 시사한다. Ronald Purser 교수와 같은 비평가들은 마음 챙김이 개인에게 변화를 추구하도록 권한을 부여하는 대신 불리한 조건에 더 순응하게 만들 수 있다고 시사한다. 이러한 우려에도 불구하고, 비평은 마음 챙김 그 자체에 반대하는 것이 아니라 변화에 저항하는 주체들에 의한 보편적인 해결책으로서의 그것의 홍보에 반대하는 것이다. 마음 챙김의 유익성과 위험에 대한 보다 철저한 이해를 위해서는, 장기적이고 엄격하게 통제된 연구가 필수적이다.

① 마음 챙김 명상의 광범위한 채택의 안전성과 사회적 영향에 관한 비판
② 개인적인 스트레스를 해소하고 사회적, 문화적 혼란을 예방하기 위해 취해지는 사회적, 국가적 조치
③ 개인의 문제보다는 사회적 문제의 해결에 선행되어야 하는 마음 챙김의 기본 요소들
④ 부적절하게 수행된 명상과 명상 부족으로 인해 개인과 사회가 직면하는 불이익

해설 지문 처음에서 마음 챙김 명상은 일반적으로 안전하지만 부작용으로 인해 우려가 발생한다고 하고, 지문 전반에 걸쳐 마음 챙김의 빠른 채택은 사회 문제를 개인에게 부적절하게 옮길 수 있으며, 개인들이 불리한 조건에 더 순응하게 만들 수 있는 등의 위험이 존재하기 때문에 비평은 변화에 저항하는 주체들에 의한 보편적인 해결책으로서의 마음 챙김의 홍보에 반대한다고 하고 있다. 따라서 '① 마음 챙김 명상의 광범위한 채택의 안전성과 사회적 영향에 관한 비판'이 이 글의 주제이다.

어휘 mindfulness 마음 챙김 meditation 명상
panic attack 공황 발작 academic 학계의, 학업의
critic 비평가 adoption 채택, 채용 organization 조직, 단체
inappropriately 부적절하게 shift 옮기다, 전환하다
address 해결하다 systemic 체계적인 adverse 불리한, 부정적인
empower 권한을 부여하다 promotion 홍보, 촉진
universal 보편적인 entity 주체, 실체 resistant 저항하는
rigorously 엄격하게, 엄밀히 essential 필수적인, 본질적인
implication 영향, 의미 widespread 광범위한
precede 선행하다 resolution 해결 improperly 부적절하게

끊어읽기 해석

A man of few words and great modesty, / Mike Mansfield often said / he did not want to be remembered.
말수가 적고 매우 겸손한 사람이었던 / Mike Mansfield는 종종 말했다 / 그는 기억되고 싶지 않다고

Yet, / his fascinating life story / and / enormous contributions / are an inspiration / for all / who follow.
하지만 / 그의 매혹적인 인생 이야기 / 그리고 / 엄청난 공헌은 / 영감을 준다 / 모든 사람들에게 / 그의 뒤를 잇는

Mike Mansfield was born / in New York City / on March 16, 1903.
Mike Mansfield는 태어났다 / 뉴욕시에서 / 1903년 3월 16일에

Following his mother's death / when Mike was 7, / his father sent him and his two sisters / to Great Falls, Montana, / to be raised / by an aunt and uncle / there.
그의 어머니가 돌아가신 후에 / Mike가 7살이었을 때 / 그의 아버지는 그와 두 명의 여동생을 보냈다 / 몬태나주 Great Falls로 / 자라게 하기 위해 / 숙모와 삼촌 밑에서 / 그곳에서

At 14, / he lied about his age / in order to enlist in the U.S. Navy / for the duration of World War I.
14살에 / 그는 그의 나이를 속였다 / 미 해군에 입대하기 위해 / 제1차 세계 대전 동안

Later, / he served in the Army and the Marines, / which sent him / to the Philipines and China, / awakening a lifelong interest in Asia.
그 후 / 그는 육군과 해병대에서 복무했다 / 그곳에서 그를 파견했다 / 필리핀과 중국으로 / 그리고 아시아에 대한 평생의 관심을 일깨웠다

Mike Mansfield's political career was launched / in 1942 / when he was elected / to the U.S. House of Representatives.
Mike Mansfield의 정치 경력은 시작되었다 / 1942년에 / 그가 당선되었을 때 / 미국 하원의원으로

He served five terms / from Montana's 1st District.
그는 다섯 번의 임기를 수행했다 / 몬태나주의 제1구역에서

In 1952, / he was elected to the U.S. Senate / and / reelected / in 1958, 1964 and 1970.
1952년에 / 그는 미국 상원의원으로 당선되었다 / 그리고 / 재선되었다 / 1958년, 1964년 그리고 1970년에

His selection as Democratic Assistant Majority Leader / was followed by election in 1961 / as Senate Majority Leader.
그가 민주당 다수당 원내대표로 선출된 것은 / 1961년의 선출로 이어졌다 / 상원 다수당 원내대표로의

He served in that capacity / until his retirement from the Senate / in 1977, / longer than any other Majority Leader in history.
그는 그 직위를 역임했다 / 그가 상원에서 은퇴할 때까지 / 1977년에 / 이는 역사상 그 어떤 다른 다수당 원내대표보다 더 오랜 기간이다

해석   말수가 적고 매우 겸손한 사람이었던 Mike Mansfield는 종종 기억되고 싶지 않다고 말했다. 하지만, 그의 매혹적인 인생 이야기와 엄청난 공헌은 그의 뒤를 잇는 모든 사람들에게 영감을 준다. Mike Mansfield는 1903년 3월 16일에 뉴욕시에서 태어났다. Mike가 7살이었을 때 어머니가 돌아가신 후에, 그의 아버지는 그와 두 명의 여동생을 몬태나주 Great Falls로 보내 그곳에서 숙모와 삼촌 밑에서 자라게 했다. 14살에, 그는 제1차 세계 대전 동안 미 해군에 입대하기 위해 그의 나이를 속였다. 그 후, 그는 육군과 해병대에서 복무했고, 그곳에서 그를 필리핀과 중국으로 파견하여 아시아에 대한 평생의 관심을 일깨웠다. Mike Mansfield의 정치 경력은 그가 1942년에 미국 하원의원으로 당선되었을 때 시작되었다.

그는 몬태나주의 제1구역에서 다섯 번의 임기를 수행했다. 1952년에, 그는 미국 상원의원으로 당선되었고, 1958년, 1964년 그리고 1970년에 재선되었다. 그가 민주당 다수당 원내대표로 선출된 후 1961년에 상원 다수당 원내대표로 선출되었다. 그는 1977년에 상원에서 은퇴할 때까지 그 직위를 역임했는데, 이는 역사상 그 어떤 다른 다수당 원내대표보다 더 오랜 기간이다.

해설   지문 중간에서 Mike Mansfield가 1942년에 미국 하원의원으로 당선되어 몬태나주의 제1구역에서 다섯 번의 임기를 수행했다고 했으므로 '④ 상원의원에 5번 당선되었으며 가장 긴 다수당 원내대표를 역임했다'는 지문의 내용과 일치하지 않는다.

어휘   **of few words** 말수가 적은   **modesty** 겸손
enormous 엄청난, 거대한   **contribution** 공헌, 기여
inspiration 영감   **enlist** 입대하다   **marine** 해병대
awaken 일깨우다, 각성하다   **lifelong** 평생의
political 정치의, 정치적인   **term** 임기   **capacity** 직위, 자격
retirement 은퇴, 퇴직

정답

p.163

01	③ 독해 – 세부내용 파악	11	④ 독해 – 논리적 흐름 파악	21	③ 독해 – 논리적 흐름 파악
02	② 문법 – 수 일치	12	② 독해 – 논리적 흐름 파악	22	③ 독해 – 추론
03	③ 독해 – 세부내용 파악	13	③ 독해 – 세부내용 파악	23	① 독해 – 논리적 흐름 파악
04	① 독해 – 추론	14	④ 독해 – 전체내용 파악	24	④ 독해 – 전체내용 파악
05	② 독해 – 전체내용 파악	15	④ 독해 – 논리적 흐름 파악	25	③ 독해 – 세부내용 파악
06	③ 문법 – 관계절	16	③ 독해 – 논리적 흐름 파악		
07	③ 독해 – 논리적 흐름 파악	17	① 문법 – 주어·동사/목적어·보어/수식어		
08	③ 독해 – 논리적 흐름 파악	18	② 독해 – 전체내용 파악		
09	④ 독해 – 세부내용 파악	19	④ 독해 – 세부내용 파악		
10	② 독해 – 논리적 흐름 파악	20	③ 독해 – 전체내용 파악		

취약영역 분석표

영역	세부 유형	문항 수	소계
문법	수 일치	1	/3
	관계절	1	
	주어·동사/목적어·보어/수식어	1	
독해	전체내용 파악	5	/22
	세부내용 파악	6	
	추론	2	
	논리적 흐름 파악	9	
총계			/25

· 자신이 취약한 영역은 '공무원 영어, 이렇게 출제된다!'(문제집 p.8)를 통해 다시 한번 확인하고 학습하시기 바랍니다.

---

01 독해 세부내용 파악 (내용 불일치 파악)   난이도 ★★☆

끊어읽기 해석

Henry Molaison, a 27-year-old man, / suffered from debilitating seizures / for about a decade / in the 1950s.
27세의 Henry Molaison은 / 쇠약하게 하는 발작으로 고통을 겪었다 / 약 10년 동안 / 1950년대에

On September 1, 1953, / Molaison allowed surgeons to remove a section of tissue / from each side of his brain / to stop the seizures.
1953년 9월 1일에 / Molaison은 외과의사들이 조직의 한 부분을 제거하는 것을 허락했다 / 그의 뇌의 양쪽에서 / 발작을 멈추기 위해

The operation worked, / but Molaison was left / with permanent amnesia, / unable to form new memories.
그 수술은 효과가 있었다 / 그렇지만 Molaison은 가지게 되었다 / 영구적인 기억상실증을 / 새로운 기억을 형성할 수 없는

This tragic outcome led to one of the most significant discoveries / in 20th century brain science: / the discovery that complex functions like learning and memory are linked / to specific regions of the brain.
이 비극적인 결과는 가장 중요한 발견 중 하나로 이어졌다 / 20세기 뇌 과학에서 / 이는 학습이나 기억과 같은 복잡한 기능들이 연결되어 있다는 발견이다 / 뇌의 특정 영역과

Molaison became known as "H.M." in research / to protect his privacy.
Molaison은 연구에서 'H.M.'으로 알려지게 되었다 / 그의 사생활을 보호하기 위해

Scientists William Scoville studied Molaison and nine other patients / who had similar surgeries, / finding that only those who had parts of their medial temporal lobes removed / experienced memory problems, / specifically with recent memory.
과학자인 William Scoville은 Molaison과 9명의 다른 환자들을 연구하

였다 / 비슷한 수술을 받은 / 내측 측두엽의 일부가 제거된 사람들만이 ~이라는 것을 발견했다 / 기억력 문제를 경험했다는 것을, / 특히 최근의 기억력의

He discovered / that a specific structure in the brain / was necessary for normal memory.
그는 발견했다 / 뇌의 특정한 구조가 / 정상적인 기억을 위해 필수적이라는 것을

Molaison's life was a series of firsts, / as he couldn't remember anything / he had done before.
Molaison의 인생은 처음의 연속이었다, / 그가 어떤 것도 기억할 수 없었기 때문에 / 그가 전에 했던

However, / he was able to acquire / new motor skills / over time.
하지만, / 그는 습득할 수 있었다 / 새로운 운동 기술을 / 시간이 지나면서

Studies of Molaison allowed neuroscientists / to further explore the brain networks / involved in conscious and unconscious memories, / even after his death in 2008.
Molaison에 대한 연구는 신경과학자들에게 허용했다 / 뇌 네트워크를 더 탐구하도록 / 의식적이고 무의식적인 기억과 관련된 / 2008년 그의 죽음 이후에도

해석 27세의 Henry Molaison은 1950년대에 약 10년 동안 쇠약하게 하는 발작으로 고통을 겪었다. 1953년 9월 1일에 Molaison은 발작을 멈추기 위해 외과의사들이 그의 뇌의 양쪽에서 조직의 한 부분을 제거하는 것을 허락했다. 그 수술은 효과가 있었지만, Molaison은 새로운 기억을 형성할 수 없는 영구적인 기억상실증을 가지게 되었다. 이 비극적인 결과는 20세기 뇌 과학에서 가장 중요한 발견 중 하나로 이어졌는데, 이는 학습이나 기억과 같은 복잡한 기능들이 뇌의 특정 영역과 연결되어 있다는 발견이다. Molaison은 그의 사생활을 보호하기 위해 연구에서 'H.M.'으로 알려지게 되었다. 과학자인 William Scoville은 Molaison과 비슷한 수술을 받은 9명의 다른 환자들을 연구하여 내측 측두엽의 일부가 제거된 사람들만이 기억력 문제, 특히 최근의 기억력 문제를 경

험했다는 것을 발견했다. 그는 뇌의 특정한 구조가 정상적인 기억을 위해 필수적이라는 것을 발견했다. Molaison은 그가 전에 했던 어떤 일도 기억할 수 없었기 때문에, 그의 인생은 처음의 연속이었다. 하지만, 그는 시간이 지나면서 새로운 운동 기술을 습득할 수 있었다. Molaison에 대한 연구는 신경과학자들이 2008년 그의 죽음 이후에도 의식적이고 무의식적인 기억과 관련된 뇌 네트워크를 더 탐구하도록 허용했다.

해설 지문 마지막에서 Molaison은 그가 전에 했던 어떤 일도 기억할 수 없었기 때문에 그의 인생은 처음의 연속이었지만 시간이 지나면서 새로운 운동 기술을 습득할 수 있었다는 내용이 있으므로, '③ 살아가면서 이전에 한 일을 조금씩 기억할 수 있었지만, 시간이 지나면서 운동 능력이 약화되었다'는 것은 지문의 내용과 일치하지 않는다.

어휘 suffer from ~으로 고통을 겪다 debilitating 쇠약하게 하는
tissue 조직 operation 수술 permanent 영구적인
region 영역, 지역 acquire 습득하다 motor 운동의
conscious 의식적인

02 문법 수 일치 난이도 ★★☆

해석 인간은 우리가 살고 있는 생물군계의 미생물, 식물, 그리고 동물로부터 얻을 수 있는 가시적인 이익을 넘어서는 자연에 대한 선천적인 친밀감을 가지고 있다. 풍경, 식물, 그리고 동물의 형태로 이루어진 자연이 우리의 행복에 좋다는 생각은 오래되었고 찰스 다윈이나 그 이전으로 거슬러 올라갈 수 있다. 이 생각은 심리학자 Erich Fromm에 의해 녹색 갈증(생물애)이라고 불렸고 하버드 개미 생물학자 Edward O. Wilson 과 Steven Kellert에 의해 연구되었다. 1984년에, Willson은 『녹색 갈증』을 출판했고, 이어서 1995년에 Kellert와 Willson이 편집한 또 다른 책인 『녹색 갈증 가설』을 출판했다. 그들의 녹색 갈증 가설은 인간이 자연 환경에 있고 싶어 하는 보편적인 욕망을 가지고 있다는 것이다.

해설 ② 주어와 동사의 수 일치 주어 자리에 단수 명사 nature가 왔으므로 복수 동사 are를 단수 동사 is로 고쳐야 한다. 참고로 주어와 동사 사이의 수식어 거품(in ~ animals)은 동사의 수 결정에 영향을 주지 않는다.

오답 분석
① 전치사 + 관계대명사 관계사 뒤에 완전한 절(we live)이 왔으므로 '전치사 + 관계대명사' 형태가 올 수 있다. '전치사 + 관계대명사'에서 전치사는 선행사 또는 관계절의 동사에 따라 결정되는데, 문맥상 '우리가 생물군계에서 살고 있다'라는 의미가 되어야 자연스러우므로 전치사 in(~에서)이 관계대명사 which 앞에 와서 in which가 올바르게 쓰였다.
③ 현재분사 vs. 과거분사 수식받는 명사(another book)와 분사가 '또 다른 책이 편집되다'라는 의미의 수동 관계이므로 과거분사 edited가 올바르게 쓰였다.
④ 명사절 접속사 1: that 완전한 절(humans have ~ natural settings)을 이끌면서 be동사(is)의 보어 자리에 올 수 있는 명사절 접속사 that이 올바르게 쓰였다.

어휘 inborn 선천적인 go beyond ~을 넘어서다
tangible 가시적인, 만질 수 있는 derive benefit 이득을 취하다
trace 거슬러 올라가다 biophilia 녹색 갈증(생물애(愛); 자연과 생명에 대한 인간의 본능적인 사랑을 의미하는 말) universal 보편적인
desire 욕망

03 독해 세부내용 파악 (내용 불일치 파악) 난이도 ★★☆

끊어읽기 해석

Life on Earth / faced an extreme test of survivability / during the Cryogenian Period, / which began 720 million years ago.
지구상의 생명체들은 / 생존 가능성에 대한 극단적인 시험에 직면했다 / 크라이오제니아기 동안 / 그것은 7억 2천만 년 전에 시작되었다

The planet was frozen / over most of the 85 million-year period.
이 행성은 얼어 있었다 / 8천 5백만 년의 대부분의 기간 동안

But life somehow survived / during this time / called "Snowball Earth".
하지만 생명체는 어떻게든 살아남았다 / 이 시기에 / '눈덩이 지구'라고 불리는

Scientists are trying / to better understand / the start of this period.
과학자들은 노력하고 있다 / 더 잘 이해하려고 / 이 시기의 시작을

They believe / a greatly reduced amount of the sun's warmth / reached the planet's surface / as its radiation bounced / off the white ice sheets.
그들은 믿는다 / 크게 감소된 태양의 온기의 양이 / 그 행성의 표면에 닿았다고 / 그것의 방사선이 반사되면서 / 흰 빙상에서

Also, / they said / the fossils found in black shale / and identified as seaweed / are a sign / that livable water environments were more widespread / at the time / than they once believed.
또한, / 그들은 말했다 / 검은 셰일에서 발견된 화석들이 / 그리고 해조류로 확인된 / 흔적이라고 / 살기에 적합한 물의 환경이 더 널리 퍼져 있었다는 / 그 당시에 / 그들이 한때 믿었던 것보다

The findings of some research / support the idea / that the planet was more of a "Slushball Earth" / with melting snow.
일부 연구 결과는 / 생각을 뒷받침한다 / 이 행성이 '슬러시볼 지구'에 더 가까웠다는 / 눈이 녹고 있는

This enabled / the earliest forms of complex life / to survive in areas / once thought to have been frozen solid.
이것은 가능하게 했다 / 복잡한 생명체의 가장 초기의 형태가 / 지역에서 생존하는 것을 / 한때 고체로 얼어 있었다고 생각되었던

The researchers said / the most important finding / was that ice-free, open water conditions existed in place / during the last part / of so-called "the Ice Age".
연구원들은 말했다 / 가장 중요한 발견은 / 얼음이 없는 개방된 물 조건이 존재했다는 것이라고 / 마지막 부분 동안 / 소위 '빙하 시대'의

The findings demonstrate / that the world's oceans were not completely frozen.
이 연구 결과는 보여준다 / 세계의 바다가 완전히 얼지 않았었다는 것을

It means / areas of habitable refuge existed / where multicellular organisms could survive.
그것은 의미한다 / 거주 가능한 피난처가 존재했다는 것을 / 다세포 생물이 생존할 수 있는

해석 지구상의 생명체들은 크라이오제니아기 동안 생존 가능성에 대한 극단적인 시험에 직면했는데, 그것은 7억 2천만 년 전에 시작되었다. 이 행성은 8천 5백만 년의 대부분의 기간 동안 얼어 있었다. 하지만 생명체는 '눈덩이 지구'라고 불리는 이 시기에 어떻게든 살아남았다. 과학자들은 이 시기의 시작을 더 잘 이해하려고 노력하고 있다. 그들은 태양의 방사선이 흰 빙상에서 반사되면서 크게 감소된 그 온기의 양이 그 행성의 표면에 닿았다고 믿는다. 또한, 그들은 검은 셰일에서 발견되고 해조류로 확인된 화석들이 그 당시에 살기에 적합한 물의 환경이 그들이(과학자들이) 한때 믿었던 것보다 더 널리 퍼져 있었다는 흔적이라고 말했다. 일부 연구 결과는 이 행성이 눈이 녹고 있는 '슬러시볼 지구'에 더 가깝다는 생각을 뒷받침한다. 이것은 한 때 고체로 얼어 있었다고 생각되었던 지역에서 복잡한 생명체의 가장 초기의 형태가 생존하는 것을 가능하게 했다. 연구원들은 가장 중요한 발견은 소위 '빙하 시대'의 마지막 부분 동안 얼음이 없는 개방된 물 조건이 존재했다는 것이라고 말했다. 이 연구 결과는 세계의 바다가 완전히 얼지 않았었다는 것을 보여준다. 그것은 다세포 생물이 생존할 수 있는 거주 가능한 피난처가 존재했다는 것을 의미한다.

해설 ②번의 키워드인 "눈덩이 지구"(Snowball Earth)가 그대로 언급된 지문 주변의 내용에서, 과학자들은 태양의 방사선이 흰 빙상(얼어 있던 지구)에서 반사되면서 크게 감소된 그 온기의 양이 그 행성(지구)의 표면에 닿았다고 믿는다고 했으므로, '② 과학자들은 "눈덩이 지구" 기간 동안에도 지구의 표면에 다다른 태양의 온기가 크게 감소하지 않았다고 믿고 있다'는 것은 지문의 내용과 일치하지 않는다.

어휘 face 직면하다 survivability 생존 가능성 radiation 방사선
bounce off ~에서 반사하다 fossil 화석
shale 셰일, 이판암(얇은 층으로 되어 있어 잘 벗겨지는 퇴적암)
seaweed 해조류 livable 살기에 적합한, 살 만한 solid 고체의
demonstrate 보여주다, 입증하다 habitable 거주 가능한
refuge 피난처 multicellular 다세포의

04 독해 추론 (빈칸 완성 - 구) 난이도 ★★☆

끊어읽기 해석

As global temperatures rise, / so do sea levels, / threatening coastal communities / around the world.
지구 기온이 상승함에 따라 / 해수면도 상승하여 / 해안 지역 사회를 위협하고 있다 / 전 세계의

Surprisingly, even small organisms like oysters <u>can come to our defense.</u>
놀랍게도, 굴과 같은 작은 유기체들도 <u>우리의 방어물이 될 수 있다</u>

Oysters are keystone species with ripple effects / on the health of their ecosystems and its inhabitants.
굴은 파급효과가 있는 중심종이다 / 생태계와 서식 동물들의 건강에

Just one adult oyster can filter / up to fifty gallons of water / in a single day, / making waterways cleaner.
성체 굴 한 마리만으로도 여과할 수 있다 / 최대 50갤런의 물을 / 하루에 / 수로를 더 깨끗하게 만든다

Healthy oyster reefs also provide a home / for hundreds of other marine organisms, / promoting biodiversity and ecosystem balance.
건강한 굴 암초는 또한 집을 제공한다 / 수백 개의 다른 해양 생물들에게 / 생물 다양성과 생태계 균형을 촉진하면서

As rising sea levels lead to pervasive flooding, / oyster reefs act as walls / to buffer storms / and protect against further coastal erosion.
해수면 상승이 만연하는 홍수로 이어질 때 / 굴 암초는 벽의 역할을 한다 / 폭풍을 완충하고 / 추가적인 해안 침식으로부터 보호하는

해석 지구 기온이 상승함에 따라 해수면도 상승하여 전 세계 해안 지역 사회를 위협하고 있다. 놀랍게도, 굴과 같은 작은 유기체들도 <u>우리의 방어물이 될 수 있다</u>. 굴은 생태계와 서식 동물들의 건강에 파급효과가 있는 중심종이다. 성체 굴 한 마리만으로도 하루에 최대 50갤런의 물을 여과할 수 있고, 이는 수로를 더 깨끗하게 만든다. 건강한 굴 암초는 또한 생물 다양성과 생태계 균형을 촉진하면서 수백 개의 다른 해양 생물들에게 집을 제공한다. 해수면 상승이 만연하는 홍수로 이어질 때, 굴 암초는 폭풍을 완충하고 추가적인 해안 침식으로부터 보호하는 벽의 역할을 한다.

① 우리의 방어물이 될 수 있다
② 비상식량이 될 수 있다
③ 미세 플라스틱에 의해 오염될지도 모른다
④ 지역 주민들의 수입을 증가시킬 수 있다

해설 지문 처음에 지구 기온이 상승함에 따라 해수면도 상승하여 전 세계 해안 지역 사회를 위협하고 있다는 내용이 있고, 빈칸 뒤 문장에서 굴이 생태계와 서식 동물들의 건강에 파급효과가 있는 중심종이라고 하면서 지문 전반에 걸쳐 굴이 생태계 파괴와 자연 재해로부터 생태계를 보호하는 역할을 한다고 설명하고 있으므로, 빈칸에는 굴과 같은 작은 유기체들도 '① 우리의 방어물이 될 수 있다'는 내용이 들어가야 한다.

어휘 temperature 기온, 온도 threaten 위협하다 coastal 해안의
oyster 굴 keystone 중심, 중추 inhabitant 서식 동물, 주민
filter 여과하다, 거르다 reef 암초 promote 촉진하다
biodiversity 생물 다양성 pervasive 만연한, 퍼지는
buffer 완충하다 erosion 침식

05 독해 전체내용 파악 (문단 요약) 난이도 ★★☆

끊어읽기 해석

The myth of the taste map, / which claims that different sections of the tongue are responsible / for specific tastes, / is incorrect, / according to modern science.
맛 지도의 신화는 / 혀의 서로 다른 부분이 책임이 있다고 주장하는 / 특정한 맛에 / 부정확하다 / 현대 과학에 따르면

The taste map originated from the experiments / of German scientist David Hänig / in the early 1900s, / which found that the tongue is most sensitive to tastes / along the edges / and not so much at the center.
맛 지도는 실험에서 비롯되었는데, / 독일 과학자 David Hänig의 / 1900년대 초에 / 그것은 혀가 맛에 가장 민감하다는 것을 발견했다 / 가장자리를 따라서 / 가장 중심은 별로 그렇지 않고

However, / this has been misinterpreted / over the years / to claim that / sweet is at the front of the tongue, / bitter is at the back, / and salty and sour are at the sides.
그러나, / 이것은 잘못 해석되어 왔다 / 수년간 / ~라고 주장하는 것으로 / 단맛이 혀의 앞쪽에 있고, / 쓴맛이 뒤쪽에 있으며, / 짠맛과 신맛이 양쪽에 있다고

In reality, / different tastes are sensed / by taste buds / all over the tongue.
실제로는, / 다양한 맛이 감지된다 / 미뢰에 의해 / 혀 전체에 있는

Taste buds work together / to make us crave or dislike certain foods, / based on our long-term learning and association.
미뢰는 함께 작용한다 / 우리가 특정 음식을 간절히 원하거나 싫어하도록 만들기 위해 / 우리의 오랜 학습과 연상에 근거하여

For example, / our ancestors needed fruit / for nutrients and easy calories, / so we are naturally drawn to sweet tastes, / while bitterness in some plants / serves as a warning of toxicity.

예를 들어, / 우리의 조상들은 과일을 필요로 했다 / 영양소와 쉽게 얻을 수 있는 칼로리를 위해 / 그래서 우리는 자연스럽게 달콤한 맛에 끌린다 / 반면, 어떤 식물의 쓴맛은 / 독성에 대한 경고로 작용한다

Of course, / different species in the animal kingdom / also have unique taste abilities: / carnivores do not eat fruit / and therefore do not crave sugar / like humans do.
물론, / 동물계의 다른 종들도 / 독특한 맛 능력을 가지고 있는데, / 육식동물들은 과일을 먹지 않는다 / 그렇기 때문에 설탕을 갈망하지 않는다 / 사람들이 그러는 것처럼

해석 현대 과학에 따르면, 혀의 서로 다른 부분이 특정한 맛에 책임이 있다고 주장하는 맛 지도의 신화는 부정확하다. 맛 지도는 1900년대 초 독일 과학자 David Hänig의 실험에서 비롯되었는데, 그것은 혀가 가장자리를 따라서 가장 맛에 민감하고 중심은 별로 그렇지(민감하지) 않다는 것을 발견했다. 그러나, 이것은 단맛이 혀의 앞쪽에 있고, 쓴맛이 뒤쪽에 있으며, 짠맛과 신맛이 양쪽에 있다고 주장하는 것으로 수년간 잘못 해석되어 왔다. 실제로는, 다양한 맛이 혀 전체에 있는 미뢰에 의해 감지된다. 미뢰는 우리의 오랜 학습과 연상에 근거하여 우리가 특정 음식을 간절히 원하거나 싫어하도록 만들기 위해 함께 작용한다. 예를 들어, 우리의 조상들은 영양소와 쉽게 얻을 수 있는 칼로리를 위해 과일을 필요로 했기 때문에, 우리는 자연스럽게 달콤한 맛에 끌리는 반면, 어떤 식물의 쓴맛은 독성에 대한 경고로 작용한다. 물론, 동물계의 다른 종들도 독특한 맛 능력을 가지고 있는데, 육식동물들은 과일을 먹지 않기 때문에 사람이 그러는(갈망하는) 것처럼 설탕을 갈망하지 않는다.

> 혀의 서로 다른 부분이 특정한 맛에 책임이 있다는 주장은 현대 과학에 의해 (A) 거짓인 것으로 입증되었고, 맛 선호도는 (B) 진화론적인 역사의 영향을 받는다.

	(A)		(B)
①	옳은	…	진화론적인
②	거짓인	…	진화론적인
③	거짓인	…	심리학적인
④	옳은	…	심리학적인

해설 지문 처음에서 현대 과학에 따르면 혀의 서로 다른 부분이 특정한 맛에 책임이 있다는 주장은 부정확하다고 하고, 지문 중간에서 실제로는 다양한 맛이 혀 전체의 미뢰에 의해 감지되는데 이것은 우리의 오랜 학습과 연상에 근거하여 우리가 특정 음식을 원하거나 싫어하도록 만들기 위해 함께 작용한다고 했으므로, 빈칸 (A)와 (B)에는 혀의 서로 다른 부분이 특정한 맛에 책임이 있다는 주장은 현대 과학에 의해 거짓인(false) 것으로 입증되었고, 맛 선호도는 진화론적인(evolutionary) 역사의 영향을 받는다는 내용이 와야 적절하다. 따라서 ② false – evolutionary가 정답이다.

어휘 myth 신화 claim 주장하다 tongue 혀
originate 비롯되다, 유래하다 experiment 실험
sensitive 민감한, 세심한 edge 가장자리, 모서리
misinterpret 잘못 해석하다 bitter 쓴 sour 신
crave 간절히 원하다 association 연상, 연관성 nutrient 영양소
carnivore 육식동물 preference 선호도
evolutionary 진화론적인 psychological 심리학적인

06 문법 관계절
난이도 ★★☆

해석 언어는 사람들이 서로 의사소통하는 주요한 수단이다. 비록 대부분의 생물들이 의사소통을 하지만, 인간의 말은 다른 동물들의 의사소통 시스템보다 더 복잡하고, 더 창의적이며, 더 광범위하게 사용된다. 언어는 인간이 되는 것이 무엇을 의미하는지에 대한 필수적인 부분이며 모든 문화의 기본적인 부분이다. 언어 인류학은 언어와 그것의 문화와의 관계를 이해하는 것과 관련이 있다. 언어는 우리가 당연하게 여기는 놀라운 것이다. 우리가 말할 때, 우리는 가지각색의 음색과 음높이의 소음을 내기 위해 폐, 성대, 입, 혀, 그리고 입술과 같은 우리의 몸을 사용한다. 그리고, 어떻게든, 우리와 다른 사람들이 함께 이것을(말을) 할 때, 우리는 서로 의사소통을 할 수 있지만, 우리가 같은 언어를 사용할 때만 가능하다. 언어 인류학자들은 언어 간의 차이와 언어가 어떻게 구조화되고, 학습되고, 사용되는지 이해하기를 원한다.

해설 ③ 관계절 자리와 쓰임 | 관계대명사 that 선행사(an amazing thing)가 사물이고, 관계절 내에서 동사 take의 목적어 역할을 하므로 명사절 접속사 what을 사물을 가리키는 목적격 관계대명사 that으로 고쳐야 한다. 참고로, 명사절 접속사 what이 이끄는 명사절은 문장 내에서 명사처럼 주어, 목적어, 보어 자리에 오므로, 명사(an amazing thing) 뒤에서 수식하는 형용사처럼 쓰일 수 없다.

오답 ① 전치사 + 관계대명사 '전치사 + 관계대명사'에서 전치사는 선
분석 행사 또는 관계절의 동사에 따라 결정되는데, 문맥상 '사람들이 언어로 서로 의사소통하다'라는 의미가 되어야 자연스러우므로 수단을 나타내는 전치사 by(~으로)가 관계대명사 앞에 온 by which가 올바르게 쓰였다.
② 능동태·수동태 구별 주어 human speech와 동사가 '인간의 말이 더 광범위하게 사용되다'라는 의미의 수동 관계이므로 be동사(is) 뒤에서 수동태를 완성하는 과거분사 used가 올바르게 쓰였다.
④ 주어와 동사의 수 일치 주어 자리에 복수 명사 we and others가 왔으므로 복수 동사 do가 올바르게 쓰였다.

어휘 primary 주요한 communicate 의사소통하다
extensively 광범위하게 essential 필수적인
linguistic anthropology 언어 인류학 relation 관계
take A for granted A를 당연히 여기다 lung 폐 vocal cord 성대
varying 가지각색의, 변화하는 structure 구조화하다

👍 이것도 알면 합격!

능동태 문장의 목적어가 수동태 문장의 주어가 되므로, 목적어를 취하지 않는 자동사는 수동태로 쓸 수 없다.

ex He was sneezed(→ sneezed) suddenly, catching everyone by surprise.
그는 갑자기 재채기를 해서 모두를 놀라게 했다.

07 독해 논리적 흐름 파악 (문장 삽입)
난이도 ★☆☆

끊어읽기 해석

Healthcare chatbots have been purposed / to solve this problem / and ensure proper diagnosis and advice for people / from the comfort of their homes.
건강관리 챗봇은 의도되었다 / 이 문제를 해결하도록 / 그리고 사람들이 적절한 진단과 조언을 받는 것을 보장하도록 / 그들의 집에서 편안하게

People have grown hesitant / to approach hospitals or health centers / due to the fear of contracting a disease / or the heavy sum of consultation fees.
사람들은 망설이게 되었다 / 병원이나 보건소에 가는 것을 / 질병에 걸리는 것에 대한 두려움으로 인해 / 또는 상담비의 가혹한 액수로

(①) This leads them to self-diagnose themselves / based upon unverified information sources / on the Internet.
이것은 그들로 하여금 자가 진단을 하게 한다 / 검증되지 않은 정보원을 기반으로 / 인터넷상의

(②) This often proves harmful effects / on the person's mental and physical health / if misdiagnosed and improper medicines are consumed.
이것은 종종 해로운 영향을 끼친다는 것을 증명한다 / 사람의 정신적, 신체적 건강에 / 오진되거나 부적절한 약이 섭취되는 경우

(③) Based upon the severity of the diagnosis, / the chatbot prescribes over the counter treatment / or escalates the diagnosis / to a verified healthcare professional.
진단의 심각성에 따라 / 챗봇은 처방전 없이 처방하거나 / 진단을 확대시킨다 / 검증된 건강관리 전문가에게

(④) Interactive chatbots that have been trained / on a large and wide variety of symptoms, risk factors, and treatment / can handle user health queries with ease, / especially in the case of COVID-19.
훈련된 대화형 챗봇은 / 광범위하고 다양한 증상, 위험 요소 및 치료에 대해 / 사용자의 건강 문의를 쉽게 처리할 수 있다 / 특히 코로나 19의 경우에

해석　사람들은 질병에 걸리는 것에 대한 두려움 또는 상담비의 가혹한 액수로 인해 병원이나 보건소에 가는 것을 망설이게 되었다. 이것은 그들로 하여금 인터넷상의 검증되지 않은 정보원을 기반으로 자가 진단을 하게 한다. 이것은 종종 오진되거나 부적절한 약이 섭취되는 경우 사람의 정신적, 신체적 건강에 해로운 영향을 끼친다는 것을 증명한다. ③ 건강관리 챗봇은 이 문제를 해결하고 사람들이 그들의 집에서 편안하게 적절한 진단과 조언을 받는 것을 보장하도록 의도되었다. 진단의 심각성에 따라, 챗봇은 처방전 없이 처방하거나 검증된 건강관리 전문가에게 진단을 확대시킨다. 광범위하고 다양한 증상, 위험 요소 및 치료에 대해 훈련된 대화형 챗봇은 특히 코로나 19의 경우에 사용자의 건강 문의를 쉽게 처리할 수 있다.

해설　③번 앞 문장에 병원에 가는 것을 망설이는 것이 사람들로 하여금 자가 진단을 하게 하고, 이것이 오진되거나 부적절한 약이 섭취되는 경우 사람의 정신적, 신체적 건강에 해로운 영향을 끼친다는 것을 증명한다는 내용이 있다. 또한 ③번 뒤 문장에 진단의 심각성에 따라 챗봇이 처방전 없이 처방하거나 전문가에게 진단을 확대시킨다는 내용이 있으므로, ③번 자리에 건강관리 챗봇이 이 문제(오진이나 부적절한 약 섭취가 사람에 끼치는 해로운 영향)를 해결하고 사람들이 적절한 진단과 조언을 받는 것을 보장하도록 의도되었다는 주어진 문장이 나와야 지문이 자연스럽게 연결된다.

어휘　healthcare 건강관리의, 의료의
chatbot 챗봇(사람과 대화할 수 있는 대화형 메신저 프로그램)
purpose 의도하다　diagnosis 진단　hesitant 망설이는
contract (병에) 걸리다　self-diagnose 자가 진단하다
unverified 검증되지 않은　improper 부적절한　severity 심각성
prescribe 처방하다　over the counter 처방전 없이
escalate 확대하다　symptom 증상　query 문의

08　독해　논리적 흐름 파악 (문단 순서 배열)　난이도 ★★☆

끊어읽기 해석

Sports fan depression is a real phenomenon / that affects many avid sports fans, / especially during times of disappointment or defeat.
스포츠 팬들의 우울증은 실제적인 현상이다 / 많은 열심인 스포츠 팬들에게 영향을 미치는 / 특히 실망이나 패배의 시기에

(A) Fans may experience / a decrease in mood, appetite, and sleep quality, / as well as an increase in stress levels and a heightened risk of developing anxiety or depression.
팬들은 경험할지도 모른다 / 기분, 식욕, 수면의 질에서의 저하를 / 뿐만 아니라 스트레스 수준의 증가와 불안이나 우울증을 발생시킬 증가된 위험을

There are many factors / that can contribute to sports fan depression, / including personal investment in a team's success, / social pressures to support a particular team, / and the intense media coverage and scrutiny / that often accompanies high-profile sports events.
많은 요소들이 있다 / 스포츠 팬들의 우울증에 기여할 수 있는 / 한 팀의 성공에 대한 개인적인 투자를 포함하여 / 특정 팀을 지지해야 하는 사회적 압력, 그리고 집중적인 언론 보도와 정밀 조사를 / 종종 유명한 스포츠 행사에 수반되는

(B) For many fans, / their emotional investment in their favorite teams or athletes / can be so intense / that losing or failing to meet expectations / can lead to feelings of sadness, frustration, and even depression.
많은 팬들에게, / 그들이 가장 좋아하는 팀이나 운동선수들에 대한 그들의 감정적인 투자는 / 너무 강렬할 수 있어서 / 패배하거나 기대를 충족시킬 수 없게 되는 것은 / 슬픔, 좌절, 그리고 심지어 우울증의 감정으로 이어질 수 있다

Research has shown / that sports fan depression can have a range of negative effects / on both mental and physical health.
연구는 보여주었다 / 스포츠 팬들의 우울증이 다양한 부정적인 영향을 미칠 수 있다는 것을 / 정신적, 신체적 건강 모두에

(C) To mitigate the negative effects of sports fan depression, / it's important for fans / to maintain a healthy perspective on sports / and remember that they are ultimately just games.
스포츠 팬들의 우울증의 부정적인 영향을 완화하기 위해서는 / 팬들에게 중요하다 / 스포츠에 대한 건강한 관점을 유지하고 / 그것들이 궁극적으로 단지 게임이라는 것을 기억하는 것이

Engaging in self-care activities / such as exercise, / spending time with loved ones, / and seeking support from a mental health professional / can also be helpful.
자기 관리 활동에 참여하는 것은 / 운동과 같은 / 사랑하는 사람과 시간을 보내는 것, / 그리고 정신 건강 전문가에게 도움을 청하는 것 / 또한 도움이 될 수 있다

해석
스포츠 팬들의 우울증은 특히 실망이나 패배의 시기에 많은 열심인 스포츠 팬들에게 영향을 미치는 실제적인 현상이다.

(B) 많은 팬들에게, 그들이 가장 좋아하는 팀이나 운동선수들에 대한 그들의 감정적인 투자는 너무 강렬할 수 있어서 패배하거나 기대를 충족시킬 수 없게 되는 것은 슬픔, 좌절, 그리고 심지어 우울증의 감정으로 이어질 수 있다. 연구는 스포츠 팬들의 우울증이 정신적, 신체적 건강 모두에 다양한 부정적인 영향을 미칠 수 있다는 것을 보여주었다.

(A) 팬들은 기분, 식욕, 수면의 질에서의 저하를 경험할 뿐만 아니라 스트레스 수준의 증가와 불안이나 우울증을 발생시킬 증가된 위험을 경험할지도 모른다. 한 팀의 성공에 대한 개인적인 투자, 특정 팀을 지지해야 하는 사회적 압력, 그리고 종종 유명한 스포츠 행사에 수반되는 집중적인 언론 보도와 정밀 조사를 포함하여 스포츠 팬들의 우울증에 기여할 수 있는 많은 요소들이 있다.

(C) 스포츠 팬들의 우울증의 부정적인 영향을 완화하기 위해서는, 팬들이 스포츠에 대한 건강한 관점을 유지하고 그것들이 궁극적으로 단지 게임이라는 것을 기억하는 것이 중요하다. 운동, 사랑하는 사람들과 시간을 보내는 것, 그리고 정신 건강 전문가에게 도움을 청하는 것과 같은 자기 관리 활동에 참여하는 것도 도움이 될 수 있다.

해설　주어진 문장에서 스포츠 팬들의 우울증은 실제적인 현상이라고 하고, (B)에서 많은 팬들에게 그들이 가장 좋아하는 팀이나 운동선수들에 대한 감정적인 투자가 너무 강렬할 수 있어서 패배하거나

기대를 충족시킬 수 없게 되는 경우 우울증으로 이어질 수 있고 이 우울증은 정신적, 신체적 건강 모두에 부정적인 영향을 미칠 수 있다고 설명한다. 이어서 (A)에서 팬들에게 발생하는 신체적, 정신적인 부정적 영향의 예시를 설명하고, (C)에서 이러한 스포츠 팬들의 우울증이 미치는 부정적 영향을 완화하기 위한 방법에 대해 설명하고 있다. 따라서, ② (B) - (A) - (C)가 정답이다.

어휘 **depression** 우울증 **phenomenon** 현상 **disappointment** 실망 **defeat** 패배 **mood** 기분 **appetite** 식욕 **heighten** 증가시키다 **anxiety** 불안 **media coverage** 언론 보도 **scrutiny** 정밀 조사 **accompany** 수반하다 **investment** 투자 **intense** 강렬한 **meet** 충족시키다 **frustration** 좌절 **mitigate** 완화시키다 **perspective** 관점 **ultimately** 궁극적으로 **engage in** ~에 참여하다 **seek** 청하다, 찾다

09 독해 세부내용 파악 (내용 불일치 파악) 난이도 ★☆☆

끊어읽기 해석

Roald Dahl (1916-1990) was born / in Wales / of Norwegian parents.
로알드 달(1916-1990)은 태어났다 / 웨일즈에서 / 노르웨이인 부모 사이에서

He spent his childhood in England / and, at age eighteen, / went to work / for the Shell Oil Company in Africa.
그는 어린 시절을 영국에서 보냈다 / 그리고, 18세의 나이에 / 일을 하러 갔다 / 아프리카에 있는 셀 오일 회사로

When World War II broke out, / he joined the Royal Air Force / and became a fighter pilot.
제2차 세계 대전이 발발했을 때, / 그는 영국 공군에 입대했다 / 그리고 전투기 조종사가 되었다

At the age of twenty-six / he moved to Washington, D.C., / and it was there / he began to write.
26살의 나이에 / 그는 워싱턴 D.C로 이사했다 / 그리고 바로 그곳이었다 / 그가 글을 쓰기 시작했던 곳이

His first short story, / which recounted his adventures in the war, / was bought by *The Saturday Evening Post*, / and so began a long and illustrious career.
그의 첫 번째 단편 소설은 / 전쟁에서의 그의 모험을 이야기한 /「The Saturday Evening Post」에 의해 구입되었다 / 그리고 그렇게 길고 빛나는 경력을 시작했다

After establishing himself as a writer for adults, / Roald Dahl began writing children's stories in 1960 / while living in England with his family.
어른들을 위한 작가로 자리매김한 후, / 로알드 달은 1960년에 어린이 이야기를 쓰기 시작했다 / 그의 가족과 함께 영국에서 사는 동안

His first stories were written / as entertainment for his own children, / to whom many of his books are dedicated.
그의 첫 번째 이야기는 쓰여졌고, / 그의 아이들을 위한 읽을거리로 / 그의 책들 중 많은 것들이 그들(그의 아이들)에게 헌정되었다

Roald Dahl is now considered / one of the most beloved storytellers / of our time.
로알드 달은 현재 여겨진다 / 가장 소중한 이야기꾼 중 한 명으로 / 우리 시대의

해석 로알드 달(1916-1990)은 웨일즈에서 노르웨이인 부모 사이에서 태어났다. 그는 어린 시절을 영국에서 보냈고, 18세의 나이에 아프리카에 있는 셀 오일 회사로 일을 하러 갔다. 제2차 세계 대전이 발발했을 때, 그는 영국 공군에 입대했고 전투기 조종사가 되었다. 26살의 나이에 그는 워싱턴 D.C로 이사했으며, 그가 글을 쓰기 시작했던 곳이 바로 그곳이었다. 전쟁에서의 그의 모험을 이야기한 그의 첫 번째 단편 소설은 「The Saturday Evening Post」에 의해

구입되었고, 그렇게 길고 빛나는 경력을 시작했다. 어른들을 위한 작가로 자리매김한 후, 로알드 달은 1960년에 그의 가족과 함께 영국에서 사는 동안 어린이 이야기를 쓰기 시작했다. 그의 첫 번째 이야기는 그의 아이들을 위한 읽을거리로 쓰여졌고, 그의 책들 중 많은 것들이 그들(그의 아이들)에게 헌정되었다. 로알드 달은 현재 우리 시대의 가장 소중한 이야기꾼 중 한 명으로 여겨진다.

해설 지문 마지막에서 로알드 달이 어른들을 위한 작가로 자리매김한 후 그의 가족과 함께 영국에서 사는 동안 어린이 이야기를 쓰기 시작했다고 했으므로 '④ 성인을 위한 작가가 된 뒤 영국에서 가족과 떨어져 혼자 살면서 글을 썼다'는 것은 지문의 내용과 일치하지 않는다.

어휘 **break out** 발발하다, 발생하다 **recount** 이야기하다, 자세히 말하다 **illustrious** (행위 등이) 빛나는, (사람이) 유명한 **establish** 자리매김하다, 확립하다 **entertainment** 읽을거리, 오락물 **dedicate** 헌정하다, 바치다 **beloved** 소중한, 가장 사랑하는

10 독해 논리적 흐름 파악 (무관한 문장 삭제) 난이도 ★★☆

끊어읽기 해석

One of the most interesting discoveries / in the field of new sources of sustainable energy / is bio-solar energy from jellyfish.
가장 흥미로운 발견 중 하나는 / 지속 가능한 에너지의 새로운 원천 분야에서 / 해파리의 바이오 태양 에너지이다

Scientists have discovered / that the fluorescent protein in this animal / can be used to generate solar energy / in a more sustainable way / than current photovoltaic energy.
과학자들은 발견했다 / 이 동물의 형광 단백질이 / 태양 에너지를 생산하는 데 사용될 수 있다는 것을 / 더 지속 가능한 방법으로 / 현재의 광전기성 에너지보다

How is this energy generated?
이 에너지는 어떻게 생성될까?

① The process involves / converting the jellyfish's fluorescent protein / into a solar cell / that is capable of generating energy / and transferring it to small devices.
그 과정은 포함한다 / 해파리의 형광 단백질을 변환하는 것을 / 태양 전지로 / 에너지를 생성할 수 있는 / 그것을 작은 장치로 전달하고

② There has been constant criticism / that the natural environment is being damaged / by reckless solar power generation.
지적이 끊이지 않고 있다 / 자연환경이 훼손되고 있다는 / 무분별한 태양광 발전으로 인해

③ The main advantage of using these living beings / as a natural energy source / is that they are a clean alternative / that does not use fossil fuels / or require the use of limited resources.
이 생물들을 사용하는 것의 주된 장점은 / 천연 에너지원으로 / 그것들이 깨끗한 대안이라는 것이다 / 화석 연료를 사용하지 않거나 / 제한된 자원을 사용할 필요가 없는

④ Although this project is still currently in the trial phase, / the expectation is that this source of energy will be able to be expanded / and become a green alternative / for powering the type of small electronic devices / that are becoming more and more common.
비록 이 프로젝트가 현재 아직 시험 단계에 있지만, / 이 에너지원이 확대될 수 있을 것이라고 기대한다 / 그리고 녹색 대안이 될 수 있을 것이라고 / 소형 전자 장치 유형에 전력을 공급하기 위한 / 점점 더 보편화되고 있는

해석 지속 가능한 에너지의 새로운 원천 분야에서 가장 흥미로운 발견 중 하나는 해파리의 바이오 태양 에너지이다. 과학자들은 이 동물

의 형광 단백질이 현재의 광전기성 에너지보다 더 지속 가능한 방법으로 태양 에너지를 생산하는데 사용될 수 있다는 것을 발견했다. 이 에너지는 어떻게 생성될까? ① 그 과정은 해파리의 형광 단백질을 에너지를 생산하고 그것을 작은 장치로 전달할 수 있는 태양 전지로 변환하는 것을 포함한다. ② 무분별한 태양광 발전으로 인해 자연환경이 훼손되고 있다는 지적이 끊이지 않고 있다. ③ 이 생물들을 천연 에너지원으로 사용하는 것의 주된 장점은 그것들이 화석 연료를 사용하지 않거나 제한된 자원을 사용할 필요가 없는 깨끗한 대안이라는 것이다. ④ 비록 이 프로젝트가 현재 아직 시험 단계에 있지만, 이 에너지원이 확대될 수 있을 것이며, 점점 더 보편화되고 있는 소형 전자 장치 유형에 전력을 공급하기 위한 녹색(환경을 생각하는) 대안이 될 수 있을 것이라고 기대한다.

해설 지문 처음에서 지속가능한 에너지의 새로운 원천 분야에서 가장 흥미로운 발견 중 하나는 해파리의 바이오 태양 에너지라고 하고, 지속 가능한 방법으로 태양 에너지를 생산할 수 있는 이 에너지가 어떻게 생성되는지에 대해 ①번에서 설명하고 있다. 이어서 ③번에서 이 에너지원의 장점에 대해 설명하고, ④번에서 이 에너지원의 전망에 대해 설명하고 있다. 그러나 ②번은 무분별한 태양광 발전으로 인해 자연이 훼손되고 있다는 지적이 끊이지 않고 있다는 내용으로, 해파리의 바이오 태양 에너지와 그 장점 및 전망에 대해 설명하는 지문 전반의 내용과 관련이 없다.

어휘 sustainable 지속 가능한 jellyfish 해파리 fluorescent 형광의
protein 단백질 generate 생산하다 convert 변환하다
transfer 전달하다, 옮기다 reckless 무분별한, 난폭한
alternative 대안 trial 시험의 phase 단계, 국면
expand 확대시키다, 팽창하다

11 독해 논리적 흐름 파악 (문단 순서 배열) 난이도 ★★★

끊어읽기 해석

On the human level, / a cow seems simple.
인간의 수준에서, / 소는 단순해 보인다

You feed it grass, / and it pays you back with milk.
당신이 풀을 먹이면, / 그것은 우유로 보답한다

It's a trick / whose secret is limited to cows and a few other mammals (most can't digest grass).
그것은 속임수이다 / 소와 몇몇 다른 포유동물(대부분 풀을 소화할 수 없음)에게만 국한된 비밀이 있는

(A) A cow's complexity is even greater.
소의 복잡성은 훨씬 더 크다

In particular, / a cow (plus a bull) can make a new generation of baby cows.
특히, / 소(그리고 황소)는 새로운 세대의 새끼 소를 만들 수 있다

This is a simple thing / on a human level, / but inexpressibly complex / on a microscopic level.
이것은 단순한 것이다 / 인간 수준에서는 / 하지만 표현할 수 없을 정도로 복잡하다 / 미시적 수준에서는

(B) Seen through a microscope, / though, / it all gets more complicated.
현미경으로 보면, / 하지만, / 모든 것이 더 복잡해진다

And the closer you look, / the more complicated it gets.
그리고 당신이 더 면밀히 볼수록, / 그것은 더 복잡해진다

Milk is not a single substance, / but a mixture of many.
우유는 하나의 물질이 아니다 / 하지만 여러 물질의 혼합물이다

Grass is so complex that we still don't fully understand it.
풀은 너무 복잡해서 우리는 아직도 완전히 이해하지 못하고 있다

(C) You don't need to understand the details / to exploit the

process: / it's a straightforward transformation / from grass into milk, / more like chemistry — or alchemy — than biology.
당신은 세부 사항을 이해할 필요가 없다 / 그 과정을 활용하기 위해 / 그것은 직접적인 변환이다 / 풀에서 우유로의 / 생물학보다는 화학이나 연금술에 가깝다

It is, in its way, magic, / but it's rational magic that works reliably.
그것은 그것 나름대로 마법이다 / 하지만 신뢰할 수 있게 작동하는 합리적인 마법이다

All you need is some grass, a cow and several generations of practical knowhow.
당신이 필요한 것은 약간의 풀, 소, 그리고 여러 세대에 걸친 실용적인 노하우뿐이다

해석 인간의 수준에서, 소는 단순해 보인다. 당신이 풀을 먹이면 그것은 우유로 보답한다. 그것은 소와 몇몇 다른 포유동물(대부분 풀을 소화할 수 없음)에게만 국한된 비밀이 있는 속임수이다.

(C) 그 과정을 활용하기 위해 당신이 세부 사항을 이해할 필요는 없다. 그것은 풀에서 우유로의 직접적인 변환이며, 생물학보다는 화학이나 연금술에 가깝다. 그것은 그것 나름대로 마법이지만, 신뢰할 수 있게 작동하는 합리적인 마법이다. 당신이 필요한 것은 약간의 풀, 소, 그리고 여러 세대에 걸친 실용적인 노하우뿐이다.

(B) 하지만, 현미경으로 보면, 모든 것이 더 복잡해진다. 그리고 당신이 더 면밀히 볼수록, 그것은 더 복잡해진다. 우유는 하나의 물질이 아니라 여러 물질의 혼합물이다. 풀은 너무 복잡해서 우리는 아직도 완전히 이해하지 못하고 있다.

(A) 소의 복잡성은 훨씬 더 크다. 특히, 소(그리고 황소)는 새로운 세대의 새끼 소를 만들 수 있다. 이것은 인간 수준에서는 단순하지만, 미시적 수준에서는 표현할 수 없을 정도로 복잡한 것이다.

해설 주어진 문장은 인간의 수준에서 소는 단순해 보이고, 당신이 풀을 먹이면 그것은 우유로 보답한다고 한 뒤, (C)에서 그 과정(the process)을 활용하기 위해 세부 사항을 이해할 필요는 없고, 그것은 풀에서 우유로의 직접적인 변환이며, 필요한 것은 약간의 풀, 소, 그리고 실용적인 노하우뿐이라고 설명하고 있다. 이어서 (B)에서 하지만(though) 현미경으로 보면 모든 것이 더 복잡해진다고 하고, (A)에서 소의 복잡성은 훨씬 더 크다고 설명하고 있다. 따라서 ④ (C) - (B) - (A)가 정답이다.

어휘 mammal 포유동물 digest 소화하다 complexity 복잡성
bull 황소 inexpressibly 표현할 수 없을 정도로
microscopic 미시적인, 미세한 microscope 현미경
complicated 복잡한 substance 물질
exploit 활용하다, 이용하다 straightforward 직접의
transformation 변환 chemistry 화학 biology 생물학
rational 합리적인 reliably 신뢰할 수 있게

12 독해 논리적 흐름 파악 (문장 삽입) 난이도 ★★☆

끊어읽기 해석

But here it's worth noting / that more than half the workforce has little or no opportunity for remote work.
그러나 여기에서, 주목할 가치가 있다 / 노동력의 절반 이상이 원격 근무를 할 기회가 거의 또는 전혀 없다는 점에

COVID-19's spread flattened the cultural and technological barriers / standing in the way of remote work.

코로나19의 확산은 문화적, 기술적 장벽을 허물었다 / 원격 근무를 가로막는

One analysis of the potential for remote work to persist showed that / 20 to 25 percent of workforces in advanced economies could work from home / in the range of three to five days a week.
원격 근무의 지속 가능성에 대한 한 분석에 따르면 / 선진국 노동력의 20에서 25퍼센트가 집에서 일할 수 있었다 / 일주일에 3일에서 5일의 범위에서

(①) This is four to five times more remote work / than pre-COVID-19.
이는 4배에서 5배 더 많은 원격 근무이다 / 코로나19 이전보다

(②) Moreover, / not all work that can be done remotely should be; / for example, / negotiations, brainstorming, and providing sensitive feedback are activities / that may be less effective / when done remotely.
게다가, / 원격으로 할 수 있는 모든 업무가 원격으로 이루어져야 하는 것은 아니다 / 예를 들어, / 협상, 브레인스토밍, 그리고 민감한 피드백 제공은 활동이다 / 덜 효과적일 수 있는 / 원격으로 수행될 때

(③) The outlook for remote work, / then, / depends on the work environment, job, and the tasks at hand, / so hybrid work setups, / where some work happens on-site and some remotely, / are likely to persist.
원격 근무에 대한 전망은, / 그러면, / 업무 환경, 직업, 그리고 당면한 과업에 달려있다 / 따라서 혼합 근무 구성이 / 일부 업무는 현장에서 수행되고 일부는 원격으로 수행되는 / 지속될 가능성이 높다

(④) To unlock sustainable performance and well-being in a hybrid world, / the leading driver of performance and productivity / should be the sense of purpose work provides to employees, / not compensation.
혼합의 세계에서 지속 가능한 성과와 복지를 실현하려면, / 성과와 생산성의 주요 동인은 / 업무가 직원에게 제공하는 목적 의식이어야 한다 / 보상이 아니라

해석 코로나19의 확산은 원격 근무를 가로막는 문화적, 기술적 장벽을 허물었다. 원격 근무의 지속 가능성에 대한 한 분석에 따르면 선진국 노동력의 20에서 25퍼센트가 일주일에 3일에서 5일의 범위에서 집에서 일할 수 있었다. 이는 코로나19 이전보다 4배에서 5배 더 많은 원격 근무이다. ② 그러나 여기에서, 노동력의 절반 이상이 원격 근무를 할 기회가 거의 또는 전혀 없다는 점에 주목할 가치가 있다. 게다가, 원격으로 할 수 있는 모든 업무가 원격으로 이루어져야 하는 것은 아니다. 예를 들어, 협상, 브레인스토밍, 그리고 민감한 피드백 제공은 원격으로 수행될 때 덜 효과적일 수 있는 활동이다. 그러면, 원격 근무에 대한 전망은 업무 환경, 직업, 그리고 당면한 과업에 달려있으므로, 일부 업무는 현장에서 수행되고 일부는 원격으로 수행되는 혼합 근무 구성이 지속될 가능성이 높다. 혼합의 세계에서 지속 가능한 성과와 복지를 실현하려면, 성과와 생산성의 주요 동인은 보상이 아니라 업무가 직원에게 제공하는 목적 의식이어야 한다.

해설 ②번 앞 문장에 선진국 노동력의 20에서 25퍼센트가 일주일에 3일에서 5일의 범위에서 집에서 일할 수 있었는데, 이는 코로나19 이전보다 4배에서 5배 더 많은 원격 근무라는 내용이 있고, ②번 뒤 문장에 게다가(Moreover), 원격으로 할 수 있는 모든 업무가 원격으로 이루어져야 하는 것은 아니라는 내용이 있으므로, ②번 자리에 노동력의 절반 이상이 원격 근무를 할 기회가 거의 또는 전혀 없다는 점에 주목할 가치가 있다는 주어진 문장이 들어가야 지문이 자연스럽게 연결된다.

어휘 note 주목하다 workforce 노동력 remote work 원격 근무
flatten 허물다, 깨부수다 barrier 장벽 analysis 분석
potential 가능성 persist 지속되다 negotiation 협상
sensitive 민감한 outlook 전망 at hand 당면한

setup 구성 unlock 실현하다, 드러내다 driver 동인
productivity 생산성 compensation 보상

13 독해 세부내용 파악 (내용 불일치 파악) 난이도 ★★☆

끊어읽기 해석

Sigmund Freud was a doctor of psychology in Vienna, Austria / at the end of the nineteenth century.
Sigmund Freud는 오스트리아 빈의 심리학 박사였다 / 19세기 말에

He treated many patients / with nervous problems / through his "talk cure."
그는 많은 환자들을 치료했다 / 신경질환의 / '담화 치료'를 통해

For this type of treatment, / Freud simply let his patients talk to him / about anything that was bothering them.
이러한 유형의 치료를 위해, / Freud는 단순히 환자들이 그에게 이야기하도록 했다 / 그들을 괴롭히는 모든 것에 대해

While treating his patients, / he began to realize that / although there were events in a patient's past that she or he might not remember consciously, / these events could affect the person's actions in her or his present life.
환자들을 치료하는 동안, / 그는 깨닫게 되었다 / 환자의 과거에 그나 그녀가 의식적으로 기억하지 못할지도 모르는 사건이 있었더라도, / 이러한 사건들은 현재 삶에서의 그나 그녀의 행동에 영향을 미칠 수도 있다는 것을

Freud called the place / where past memories were hidden / the unconscious mind.
Freud는 장소를 ~라고 불렀다 / 과거의 기억이 감춰진 / 무의식적 마음이라고

Images from the unconscious mind might show up / in a person's dreams or through the person's actions.
무의식적 마음의 이미지는 나타날 수 있다 / 사람의 꿈이나 행동을 통해

Freud wrote a book about his theories / about the unconscious mind and dreaming in 1899.
Freud는 그의 이론에 대한 책을 썼다 / 1899년에 무의식적 마음과 꿈에 관한

The title of the book was "The Interpretation of Dreams"
그 책의 제목은 『꿈의 해석』이었다

해석 Sigmund Freud는 19세기 말 오스트리아 빈의 심리학 박사였다. 그는 '담화 치료'를 통해 많은 신경질환 환자들을 치료했다. 이러한 유형의 치료를 위해, Freud는 단순히 환자들이 그들을 괴롭히는 모든 것에 대해 그에게 이야기하도록 했다. 환자들을 치료하는 동안, 그는 환자의 과거에 그나 그녀가 의식적으로 기억하지 못할지도 모르는 사건이 있었더라도, 이러한 사건들은 현재 삶에서의 그나 그녀의 행동에 영향을 미칠 수도 있다는 것을 깨닫게 되었다. Freud는 과거의 기억이 감춰진 장소를 무의식적 마음이라고 불렀다. 무의식적 마음의 이미지는 사람의 꿈이나 행동을 통해 나타날 수 있다. Freud는 1899년에 무의식적 마음과 꿈에 관한 그의 이론에 대한 책을 썼다. 그 책의 제목은 『꿈의 해석』이었다.

해설 지문 중간에서 Freud는 환자의 과거에 그나 그녀가 의식적으로 기억하지 못할지도 모르는 사건이 있었더라도, 이러한 사건들은 현재 삶에서의 그나 그녀의 행동에 영향을 미칠 수도 있다는 것을 깨닫게 되었다고 했으므로, '③ 기억이 나지 않는 과거는 환자에게 영향을 미치지 못한다고 주장했다'는 지문의 내용과 일치하지 않는다.

어휘 psychology 심리학 treat 치료하다 patient 환자
nervous 신경의 bother 괴롭히다 consciously 의식적으로
affect 영향을 미치다 unconscious 무의식
interpretation 해석

끊어읽기 해석

All emotions tell us something / about ourselves and our situation.
모든 감정은 우리에게 알려준다 / 우리 자신과 우리의 상황에 대해

But sometimes / we find it hard to accept / what we feel.
그러나 때때로 / 우리는 받아들이기가 어렵다는 것을 알게 된다 / 우리가 느끼는 것을

We might judge ourselves for feeling a certain way, / like if we feel jealous, for example.
우리는 특정한 방식으로 느끼는 것에 대해 자신을 판단할 수 있다 / 예를 들어, 질투심을 느끼는 것과 같이

But / instead of thinking we should not feel that way, / it's better to notice how we actually feel.
하지만 / 그렇게 느껴서는 안 된다고 생각하기보다는 / 우리가 실제로 어떻게 느끼는지 알아차리는 것이 더 낫다

Avoiding negative feelings / or pretending we don't feel the way we do / can backfire.
부정적인 감정을 피하는 것 / 또는 우리가 느끼는 방식대로 느끼지 않는 척하는 것은 / 역효과를 낼 수 있다

It's harder / to move past difficult feelings / and allow them to fade / if we don't face them and try to understand / why we feel that way.
더 어렵다 / 어려운 감정이 지나가고 / 그것들이 사라지도록 하기가 / 우리가 그것들을 직시하고 이해하려고 노력하지 않으면 / 왜 그렇게 느끼는지

You don't have to dwell / on your emotions / or constantly talk about / how you feel.
곱씹을 필요는 없다 / 당신의 감정을 / 또는 끊임없이 이야기할 필요는 없다 / 당신이 어떻게 느끼는지

Emotional awareness simply means recognizing, respecting, and accepting your feelings / as they happen.
정서 인식이란 단순히 당신의 감정을 인식하고, 존중하고, 받아들이는 것을 의미한다 / 그것들이 발생할 때

해석 모든 감정은 우리에게 우리 자신과 우리의 상황에 대해 알려준다. 그러나 때때로 우리는 우리가 느끼는 것을 받아들이기가 어렵다는 것을 알게 된다. 우리는, 예를 들어 질투심을 느끼는 것과 같이, 특정한 방식으로 느끼는 것에 대해 자신을 판단할 수 있다. 하지만 그렇게 느껴서는 안 된다고 생각하기보다는, 우리가 실제로 어떻게 느끼는지 알아차리는 것이 더 낫다. 부정적인 감정을 피하거나 우리가 느끼는 방식대로 느끼지 않는 척하는 것은 역효과를 낼 수 있다. 우리가 어려운 감정을 직시하고 왜 그렇게 느끼는지 이해하려고 노력하지 않으면 그것들이 지나가고 사라지도록 하기가 더 어렵다. 당신의 감정을 곱씹거나 당신이 어떻게 느끼는지 끊임없이 이야기할 필요는 없다. 정서 인식이란 단순히 당신의 감정이 발생할 때 인식하고, 존중하고, 받아들이는 것을 의미한다.

해설 지문 중간에서 우리가 질투심 같은 감정을 느껴서는 안 된다고 생각하기보다는 실제로 어떻게 느끼는지 알아차리는 것이 더 낫다고 언급하고 있고, 지문 마지막에서 정서 인식이란 단순히 감정이 발생할 때 인식하고, 존중하고, 받아들이는 것을 의미한다고 설명하고 있으므로, '④ 우리의 감정을 인식하고 존중하며 그대로 받아들여야 한다'가 이 글의 요지이다.

어휘 emotion 감정 accept 받아들이다 judge 판단하다
certain 특정한 jealous 질투하는 notice 알아차리다
avoid 피하다 pretend ~인 척하다 face 직시하다
dwell on ~을 곱씹다 constantly 끊임없이 awareness 인식
recognize 인식하다

끊어읽기 해석

At the level of lawmaking, / there is no reason / why tech giants should have such an ironclad grip / on technological resources and innovation.
입법 차원에서, / 이유는 없다 / 기술 거대 기업이 왜 그토록 철통같은 지배력을 가져야 하는지 / 기술 자원과 혁신에 대해

(A) As the Daily Wire's Matt Walsh has pointed out, / for example, / if you don't buy your kid a smartphone, / he won't have one.
<Daily Wire>의 Matt Walsh가 지적했듯이, / 예를 들어, / 당신이 자녀에게 스마트폰을 사주지 않으면, / 그는 스마트폰을 갖지 못할 것이다

There is no need to put in his hand a device / that enables him to indulge his every impulse / without supervision.
장치를 그의 손에 쥐어 줄 필요는 없다 / 그의 모든 충동을 탐닉할 수 있게 하는 / 감독 없이

(B) At the private and personal level, / there's no reason / why they should have control of your life, either.
사적이고 개인적인 차원에서도, / 이유가 없다 / 그들이 왜 당신의 삶을 통제해야 하는지

In policy, politics, and our personal lives, / it should not be taken as "inevitable" / that our data will be sold to the highest bidder, / our children will be addicted to online games, / and our lives will be lived in the metaverse.
정책, 정치, 그리고 우리의 개인적인 삶에서, / '불가피한' 것으로 받아들여서는 안 된다 / 우리의 자료가 최고 입찰자에게 팔리고, / 우리 아이들이 온라인 게임에 중독되고, / 우리의 삶이 메타버스에서 살게 되는 것을

(C) As a free people, / we are entitled to exert *absolute* control / over which kinds of digital products we consume, and in what quantities.
자유인으로서, / 우리는 '절대적인' 통제권을 행사할 자격이 있다 / 우리가 소비하는 디지털 제품들의 종류와 양에 대해

Most especially, / parents should control / what tech products go to their kids.
특히, / 부모는 통제해야 한다 / 자녀에게 제공되는 기술 제품을

해석
입법 차원에서, 기술 거대 기업이 기술 자원과 혁신에 대해 그토록 철통같은 지배력을 가져야 할 이유는 없다.

(B) 사적이고 개인적인 차원에서도, 그들이 당신의 삶을 통제해야 할 이유가 없다. 정책, 정치, 그리고 우리의 개인적인 삶에서, 우리의 자료가 최고 입찰자에게 팔리고, 우리 아이들이 온라인 게임에 중독되고, 우리의 삶이 메타버스에서 살게 되는 것을 '불가피한' 것으로 받아들여서는 안 된다.

(C) 자유인으로서, 우리는 우리가 소비하는 디지털 제품들의 종류와 양에 대해 '절대적인' 통제권을 행사할 자격이 있다. 특히, 부모는 자녀에게 제공되는 기술 제품을 통제해야 한다.

(A) 예를 들어, <Daily Wire>의 Matt Walsh가 지적했듯이, 당신이 자녀에게 스마트폰을 사주지 않으면 그는 스마트폰을 갖지 못할 것이다. 감독 없이 그의 모든 충동을 탐닉할 수 있게 하는 장치를 그의 손에 쥐어 줄 필요는 없다.

해설 주어진 문장에서 입법 차원에서 기술 거대 기업이 기술 자원과 혁신에 대해 그토록 철통같은 지배력을 가져야 할 이유는 없다고 한 뒤, (B)에서 사적이고 개인적인 차원에서도 그들(기술 거대 기업)이 당신의 삶을 통제해야 할 이유가 없다고 언급하고 있다. 이어서 (C)에서, 우리는 우리가 소비하는 디지털 제품들의 종류와 양에 대해 '절대적인' 통제권을 행사할 자격이 있으며, 특히 부모는 자녀에게 제공되는 기술 제품을 통제해야 한다고 이야기하고 있다. 뒤이어 (A)에서 그 예시로, 당신이 자녀에게 스마트폰을 사주지

않으면 그는 스마트폰을 갖지 못할 것이라고 설명하고 있다. 따라서 ② (B) - (C) - (A)가 정답이다.

어휘   lawmaking 입법 giant 거대 기업 ironclad 철통같은, 엄격한
       grip 지배력 innovation 혁신 point out 지적하다 device 장치
       enable 할 수 있게 하다 indulge 탐닉하다 impulse 충동
       supervision 감독 policy 정책 politics 정치
       inevitable 불가피한 bidder 입찰자
       be entitled to ~을 할 자격이 있다 exert 행사하다
       absolute 절대적인 consume 소비하다

16 독해 논리적 흐름 파악 (문장 삽입) 난이도 ★★★

끊어읽기 해석

> These may appear as challenges / which may be impossible to address / because of the uncertainty in our ability to predict future climate.
> 이것들은 과제로 보일 수 있다 / 해결이 불가능할 수 있는 / 미래 기후를 예측하는 우리의 능력에 대한 불확실성 때문에

Global warming is a reality man has to live with.
지구 온난화는 인간이 함께 살아가야 하는 현실이다

(①) This is a very important issue to recognize, / because, / of all the parameters that affect human existence, / on planet earth, / it is the food security / that is of paramount importance / to life on earth / and which is most threatened by global warming.
이것은 인식해야 할 매우 중요한 문제이다 / 왜냐하면, / 인간의 존재에 영향을 미치는 모든 변수 중에서 / 지구상에서 / 식량 안보이다 / 가장 중요한 것은 / 지구상의 생명체에게 / 그리고 지구 온난화에 의해 가장 위협받는 것은

(②) Future food security will be dependent / on a combination of the stresses, both biotic and abiotic, / imposed by / climate change, / variability of weather within the growing season, / development of cultivars / more suited to different ambient conditions, / and, the ability to develop effective adaptation strategies / which allow these cultivars to express their genetic potential / under the changing climate conditions.
미래의 식량 안보는 달려 있을 것이다 / 생물적 및 비생물적 압박의 조합에 / ~에 의해 부과된, / 기후 변화, / 생장기의 날씨 변동성, / 품종의 개발, / 다양한 주변 환경에 더 적합한 / 그리고 효과적인 적응 전략을 개발할 수 있는 능력 / 그들의 유전적인 잠재력을 표현할 수 있게 하는 / 변화하는 기후 조건 하에서

(③) However, / these challenges also provide us the opportunities / to enhance our understanding / of soil-plant-atmosphere interaction / and how one could utilize this knowledge / to enable us achieve / the ultimate goal of enhanced food security / across all areas of the globe. (④)
그러나, / 이러한 과제는 또한 우리에게 기회를 제공한다 / 우리의 이해를 높이는 / 토양-식물-대기 간 상호작용에 대한 / 그리고 이 지식을 어떻게 활용할 수 있을지에 대한 / 우리가 달성하는 / 강화된 식량 보장이라는 궁극적 목적을 / 전 세계 모든 지역에서의

해석   지구 온난화는 인간이 함께 살아가야 하는 현실이다. 이것은 인식해야 할 매우 중요한 문제인데, 왜냐하면, 지구상에서 인간의 존재에 영향을 미치는 모든 변수 중에서 지구상의 생명체에게 가장 중요하고 지구 온난화에 의해 가장 위협받는 것은 식량 안보이기 때문이다. 미래의 식량 안보는 기후 변화, 생장기의 날씨 변동성, 다양한 주변 환경에 더 적합한 품종의 개발, 그리고 이러한 품종들이 변화하는 기후 조건 하에서 그들의 유전적인 잠재력을 표현할 수 있게 하는 효과적인 적응 전략을 개발할 수 있는 능력에 의해 부과

된 생물적 및 비생물적 압박의 조합에 달려 있을 것이다. ③ 이것들은 미래 기후를 예측하는 우리의 능력에 대한 불확실성 때문에 해결이 불가능할 수 있는 과제로 보일 수 있다. 그러나, 이러한 과제는 또한 우리에게 토양-식물-대기 간 상호작용과 전 세계 모든 지역에서의 강화된 식량 보장이라는 궁극적인 목적을 달성하는데 이 지식을 어떻게 활용할 수 있을지에 대한 이해를 높이는 기회를 제공한다.

해설   ③번 앞 문장에서 미래의 식량 안보는 기후 변화, 생장기의 날씨 변동성 등에 의해 부과된 생물적 및 비생물적 압박의 조합에 달려 있을 것이라고 언급하고 있고, ③번 뒤 문장에서 그러나(However) 이러한 과제는 또한 우리에게 토양-식물-대기 간 상호작용과 전 세계 모든 지역에서의 강화된 식량 보장이라는 궁극적인 목적을 달성하는데 이 지식을 어떻게 활용할 수 있을지에 대한 이해를 높이는 기회를 제공한다고 설명하고 있으므로, ③번 자리에 이것들(These)은 미래 기후를 예측하는 우리의 능력에 대한 불확실성 때문에 해결이 불가능할 수 있는 과제로 보일 수 있다는 주어진 문장이 들어가야 지문이 자연스럽게 연결된다.

어휘   address 해결하다 uncertainty 불확실성 predict 예측하다
       parameter 변수 existence 존재 food security 식량 안보
       paramount 가장, 다른 무엇보다 중요한 combination 조합
       stress 압박 impose 부과하다 variability 변동성
       growing season 생장기 adaptation 적응 genetic 유전적인
       potential 잠재력 enhance 높이다 utilize 활용하다
       ultimate 궁극적인

17 문법 주어·동사/목적어/보어/수식어 난이도 ★★☆

해석   인류학자 Paul Ekman은 1970년대에 인간이 분노, 두려움, 놀람, 혐오, 기쁨, 슬픔의 여섯 가지 기본 감정을 경험한다고 제시했다. 그러나, 감정의 정확한 수에 이의가 제기되었는데, 일부 연구원들은 단지 네 개만 있다고 제안하고, 다른 연구원들은 27개까지 세고 있기 때문이다. 또한, 과학자들은 감정이 모든 인간 문화에 보편적인지 또는 우리가 감정을 가지고 태어나는지 아니면 경험을 통해 학습하는지에 대해 논쟁한다. 이러한 이견에도 불구하고, 감정은 뇌의 특정 영역에서의 활동의 분명한 산물이다. 편도체와 섬 또는 대뇌 피질은 감정과 가장 밀접하게 연결된 두 가지 대표적인 뇌 구조이다. 뇌 깊숙이 있는 한 쌍의 아몬드 모양 구조인 편도체는 감정, 감정적 행동, 그리고 동기를 통합한다. 그것은 두려움을 해석하고 친구와 적군을 구별하는 데 도움을 주며, 사회적 보상과 그것들을 얻는 방법을 식별한다. 섬은 혐오의 근원이다. 혐오의 경험은 당신이 독이나 상한 음식을 섭취하지 않도록 보호할 수 있다.

해설 ① 동사 자리 동사 자리에 '-ing'의 형태는 올 수 없고, 주어(the exact number ~ emotions)와 동사가 '감정의 정확한 수에 이의가 제기되다'라는 의미의 수동 관계이므로 수동태가 쓰여야 한다. 따라서, 현재분사 disputing을 수동태 동사 is disputed로 고쳐야 한다.

오답
분석 ② 전치사 자리 문맥상 '이러한 이견에도 불구하고'라는 의미가 되어야 자연스럽고, 전치사의 목적어 자리에는 명사 역할을 하는 것이 와야 하는데 뒤에 명사구(these disagreements)가 왔으므로, 전치사 Despite이 올바르게 쓰였다.

      ③ 부사 자리 형용사(linked)를 수식할 수 있는 것은 부사이므로, 부사 closely가 올바르게 쓰였다. 참고로, 부사가 동사 이외의 것을 수식할 때 부사는 수식받는 것 앞에 온다.

      ④ 인칭대명사 대명사가 지시하는 명사가 복수 명사 social rewards(사회적 보상)이므로 복수 인칭대명사 them이 올바르게 쓰였다.

anthropologist 인류학자 **propose** 제시하다, 제안하다
disgust 혐오 **dispute** 이의를 제기하다 **universal** 보편적인
disagreement 이견 **insula** (뇌·췌장의) 섬
representative 대표적인 **structure** 구조 **integrate** 통합하다
motivation 동기 **interpret** 해석하다 **distinguish** 구별하다
foe 적(군) **identify** 식별하다 **ingest** 섭취하다 **spoil** 상하다

👍 이것도 알면 **합격!**

진행형·완료형·수동형 동사를 수식할 때, 부사는 '조동사 + -ing/ p.p.' 사이나 그 뒤에 온다.

· [조동사 + 동사] 사이

(ex) The laptop has **unexpectedly** crashed.
　　　　　　조동사　　　　　　　　　p.p.
노트북이 예기치 못하게 작동을 멈추었다.

· [조동사 + 동사] 뒤

(ex) The curious cat is **playfully** chasing its tail.
　　　　　　　　　조동사　　　-ing
호기심 많은 고양이가 장난스럽게 꼬리를 쫓고 있다.

---

18 독해 전체내용 파악 (주제 파악)　　난이도 ★★☆

끊어읽기 해석

Do you want to be a successful anchor?
성공적인 앵커가 되고 싶은가?

If so, / keep this in mind.
그렇다면, / 이것을 명심하라

As an anchor, / the individual will be called upon / to communicate news and information to viewer / during newscasts, special reports and other types of news programs.
앵커로서, / 개인은 요청받을 것이다 / 시청자에게 뉴스와 정보를 전달하도록 / 뉴스 방송, 특별 보도, 그리고 다른 유형의 뉴스 프로그램 중에

This will include / interpreting news events, / adlibbing, / and communicating breaking news effectively / when scripts are not available.
이것은 포함할 것이다 / 뉴스 사건 해석, / 애드리브, / 그리고 속보를 효과적으로 전달하는 것을 / 대본을 입수할 수 없을 때

Anchoring duties also involve gathering and writing stories.
뉴스를 진행하는 임무는 이야기를 수집하고 작성하는 것도 포함한다

The anchor must be able to deliver scripts clearly and effectively.
앵커는 대본을 명확하고 효과적으로 전달할 수 있어야 한다

Strong writing skills, solid news judgement and a strong sense of visual storytelling are essential skills.
유능한 작문 기술, 확실한 뉴스 판단력 및 유능한 시각적 스토리텔링 감각은 필수적인 기술이다

This individual must be a self-starter / who cultivates sources and finds new information / as a regular part of job.
이 개인은 일을 자발적으로 하는 사람이어야 한다 / 자료를 개척하고 새로운 정보를 찾는 / 일상적인 업무의 일부로써

Live reporting skills are important, / as well as the ability to adlib and describe breaking news as it takes place.
실시간 보도 기술은 중요하다 / 애드리브를 하고 속보가 발생하는 대로 설명하는 능력뿐만 아니라

해석 성공적인 앵커가 되고 싶은가? 그렇다면, 이것을 명심하라. 앵커로서, 개인은 뉴스 방송, 특별 보도, 그리고 다른 유형의 뉴스 프로그램 중에 시청자에게 뉴스와 정보를 전달하도록 요청받을 것이다. 이것은 뉴스 사건 해석, 애드리브, 그리고 대본을 입수할 수 없을 때 속보를 효과적으로 전달하는 것을 포함할 것이다. 뉴스를 진행

하는 임무는 이야기를 수집하고 작성하는 것도 포함한다. 앵커는 대본을 명확하고 효과적으로 전달할 수 있어야 한다. 유능한 작문 기술, 확실한 뉴스 판단력 및 유능한 시각적 스토리텔링 감각은 필수적인 기술이다. 이 개인은 일상적인 업무의 일부로써 자료를 개척하고 새로운 정보를 찾는 일을 자발적으로 하는 사람이어야 한다. 애드리브를 하고 속보가 발생하는 대로 설명하는 능력뿐만 아니라 실시간 보도 기술도 중요하다.

① 실시간 뉴스 제작의 어려움
② 뉴스 앵커가 되기 위한 자격
③ 언론인의 사회적 역할의 중요성
④ 올바른 여론 형성의 중요성

해설 지문 처음에서 성공적인 앵커가 되고 싶은지 묻고, 지문 전반에 걸쳐 유능한 작문 기술, 확실한 뉴스 판단력 및 유능한 시각적 스토리텔링 감각 등 성공적인 앵커가 되기 위해 갖춰야 할 기술과 능력에 대해 설명하고 있으므로, '② 뉴스 앵커가 되기 위한 자격'이 이 글의 주제이다.

어휘 **anchor** 앵커 **newscast** 뉴스 방송
adlib 애드리브를 하다, 즉흥적으로 말하다 **breaking news** 속보
duty 임무 **judgement** 판단력 **visual** 시각적인
essential 필수적인
self-starter 일을 자발적으로 하는 사람, 능동적인 사람
cultivate 개척하다 **qualification** 자격 **journalist** 언론인
public opinion 여론

---

19 독해 세부내용 파악 (내용 불일치 파악)　　난이도 ★☆☆

끊어읽기 해석

Modern sculpture is generally considered / to have begun with the work of French sculptor Auguste Rodin.
현대 조각은 일반적으로 여겨진다 / 프랑스 조각가 오귀스트 로댕의 작품으로 시작되었다고

Rodin, often considered a sculptural Impressionist, / did not set out to rebel against artistic traditions, / however, / he incorporated novel ways of building his sculpture / that defied classical categories and techniques.
종종 조각의 인상파 화가로 여겨지는 로댕은, / 예술적 전통에 반항하는 것을 시도하지 않았다 / 하지만, / 그는 조각품을 만드는 새로운 방법을 통합했다 / 고전적인 범주와 기법을 거부하는

Specifically, / Rodin modeled complex, turbulent, deeply pocketed surfaces into clay.
구체적으로, / 로댕은 복잡하고, 격동적이며, 깊게 패인 표면을 점토로 만들었다

While he never self-identified as an Impressionist, / the vigorous, gestural modeling he employed in his works / is often likened to the quick, gestural brush strokes aiming to capture a fleeting moment / that was typical of the Impressionists.
그가 절대로 자신을 인상파라고 정의한 적이 없지만, / 그가 그의 작품에 사용한 활기차고 몸짓적인 모형 제작술은 / 종종 덧없는 순간을 포착하기 위한 빠르고 몸짓적인 붓놀림에 비유된다 / 인상파에게 전형적이었던

Rodin's most original work departed from traditional themes of mythology and allegory, / in favor of modeling the human body with intense realism, / and celebrating individual character and physicality.
로댕의 가장 독창적인 작품은 신화와 우화라는 전통적인 주제에서 벗어났다 / 강렬한 사실주의로 인체의 모형을 만드는 것을 지지하여 / 그리고 개별적인 성격과 신체적 특질을 칭송하는 것을

해석 현대 조각은 일반적으로 프랑스 조각가 오귀스트 로댕의 작품으로 시작되었다고 여겨진다. 종종 조각의 인상파 화가로 여겨지는

로댕은, 예술적 전통에 반항하는 것을 시도하지 않았지만, 고전적인 범주와 기법을 거부하는 조각품을 만드는 새로운 방법을 통합했다. 구체적으로, 로댕은 복잡하고, 격동적이며, 깊게 패인 표면을 점토로 만들었다. 그가 절대로 자신을 인상파라고 정의한 적이 없지만, 그가 그의 작품에 사용한 활기차고 몸짓적인 모형 제작술은 종종 인상파에게 전형적이었던 덧없는 순간을 포착하기 위한 빠르고 몸짓적인 붓놀림에 비유된다. 로댕의 가장 독창적인 작품은 강렬한 사실주의로 인체의 모형을 만들고, 개별적인 성격과 신체적 특질을 칭송하는 것을 지지하며 신화와 우화라는 전통적인 주제에서 벗어났다.

해설 지문 중간에서 로댕은 절대로 자신을 인상파라고 정의한 적이 없다고 했으므로, '③ 로댕은 자신을 인상파라고 밝히며 인상파의 전형적인 붓놀림을 보여주었다'는 지문의 내용과 일치하지 않는다.

어휘 modern 현대의 sculpture 조각 generally 일반적으로
impressionist 인상파 화가 rebel 반항하다
incorporate 통합하다, 도입하다 novel 새로운
defy 거부하다, 저항하다 turbulent 격동적인 vigorous 활기찬
gestural 몸짓적인 employ 사용하다 liken 비유하다, 비교하다
capture 포착하다 fleeting 덧없는 typical 전형적인
original 독창적인 depart 벗어나다 mythology 신화
intense 강렬한 realism 사실주의 celebrate 칭송하다
physicality (신체적) 특질

20 독해 전체내용 파악 (주제 파악) 난이도 ★★☆

끊어읽기 해석

Cosmetics became so closely associated with portraiture / that some photography handbooks included recipes for them.
화장품은 인물 묘사와 매우 밀접하게 연관되었다 / 그래서 일부 사진 안내서는 그것(화장품)의 사용법을 포함했다

American photographers also, / at times, / used cosmetics / to retouch negatives and prints, / enlivening women's faces with traces of rouge.
미국의 사진작가들도, / 때때로, / 화장품을 사용했다 / 음화와 인화된 사진을 수정하기 위해 / 여성들의 얼굴에 약간의 볼 연지로 생기를 불어넣었다

Some customers with dark skin requested photographs / that would make them look lighter.
어두운 피부를 가진 일부 고객들은 사진을 요청했다 / 그들을 더 밝게 보이게 만드는

A skin lightener advertisement that appeared in an African American newspaper in 1935 referenced this practice / by promising that its product could achieve the same look produced by photographers: / a lighter skin Cop free of blemishes.
1935년에 아프리카계 미국 신문에 등장한 피부 미백제 광고는 이 관행을 증명했다 / 자사 제품으로 사진작가들에 의해 만들어진 것과 같은 모습을 얻을 수 있다고 약속함으로써 / 잡티 없는 더 밝은 피부색을 얻을 수 있다고

By drawing attention to the face and encouraging cosmetics use, / portrait photography heightened the aesthetic valuation of smooth and often light-colored skin.
얼굴에 주의를 끌고 화장품 사용을 장려함으로써, / 인물 사진은 매끄럽고 종종 밝은색인 피부의 미적 가치를 높였다

해석 화장품은 인물 묘사와 매우 밀접하게 연관되어 일부 사진 안내서에는 그것(화장품)의 사용법을 포함했다. 미국의 사진작가들도, 때때로, 음화와 인화된 사진을 수정하기 위해 화장품을 사용했고, 여성들의 얼굴에 약간의 볼 연지로 생기를 불어넣었다. 어두운 피부를

가진 일부 고객들은 그들을 더 밝게 보이게 만드는 사진을 요청했다. 1935년에 아프리카계 미국 신문에 잡티 없는 더 밝은 피부색을 얻을 수 있다며 등장한 피부 미백제 광고는 자사 제품으로 사진작가들에 의해 만들어진 것과 같은 모습을 얻을 수 있다고 약속하며 이 관행을 증명했다. 얼굴에 주의를 끌고 화장품 사용을 장려함으로써, 인물 사진은 매끄럽고 종종 밝은색인 피부의 미적 가치를 높였다.

① 화장품 과다 사용의 부작용
② 사진작가에 의해 홍보된 화장품의 남용
③ 얼굴을 보기 좋게 하기 위한 적극적인 화장품 사용
④ 사진의 발달로 인한 화장품 사용의 감소

해설 지문 처음에서 미국의 사진작가들이 때때로 음화와 인화된 사진을 수정하기 위해 화장품을 사용했고, 여성들의 얼굴에 약간의 볼 연지로 생기를 불어넣었다고 언급했으며, 지문 마지막에서 얼굴에 주의를 끌고 화장품 사용을 장려함으로써 인물 사진은 매끄럽고 종종 밝은색인 피부의 미적 가치를 높였다고 설명하고 있으므로, '③ 얼굴을 보기 좋게 하기 위한 적극적인 화장품 사용'이 이 글의 주제이다.

어휘 cosmetics 화장품 associate 연관시키다 portraiture 인물 묘사 handbook 안내서 retouch 수정하다
negative 음화(촬영한 피사체를 현상한 후 피사체의 색과 반대되는 보색을 얻는 방법) enliven 더 생기 있게 하다 trace 약간의, 미량의
rouge 볼(입술) 연지 reference 증명하다 practice 관행
heighten 높이다 aesthetic 미적 valuation 가치
side effect 부작용 excessive 과다한 overuse 남용
promote 홍보하다 active 적극적인 advance 발달

21 독해 논리적 흐름 파악 (문맥상 부적절한 어휘) 난이도 ★★★

끊어읽기 해석

"Play is something done for its own sake." / says psychiatrist Stuart Brown, author of "Play,"
"놀이는 그 자체를 위해 하는 것이다." / 라고 『놀이』의 저자인 정신과 의사 Stuart Brown은 말한다

He writes: / "It's voluntary, it's pleasurable, it offers a sense of engagement, it takes you out of time.
그는 기술한다 / "그것은 자발적이고, 유쾌하고, 참여의 감각을 제공하고, 시간 가는 줄 모르게 한다

And the act itself is more important than the outcome."
그리고 행위 자체가 결과보다 더 중요하다."라고

With this definition in mind, / it's easy to recognize play's potential benefits.
이 정의를 염두에 두면, / 놀이의 잠재적 이점을 인식하는 것은 쉽다

Play ① nurtures relationships with oneself and others.
놀이는 자신과 타인과의 관계를 ① 길러준다

It ② relieves stress and increases happiness.
그것은 스트레스를 ② 해소하고 행복을 증진시킨다

It builds feelings of empathy, creativity, and collaboration.
그것은 공감, 창의성, 그리고 협력의 감정을 형성한다

It supports the growth of sturdiness and grit.
그것은 강건함과 기개의 성장을 지원한다

When children are deprived of opportunities for play, / their development can be significantly ③ enhanced.
어린이들이 놀 기회를 박탈당하면, / 그들의 발달은 상당히 ③ 향상될 수 있다

Play is so important that the United Nations High Commission on Human Rights declared it a ④ fundamental right of every child.

놀이는 매우 중요해서 유럽 연합 인권 위원회는 그것을 모든 어린이의
④ 기본적인 권리라고 선언했다

Play is not frivolous.
놀이는 하찮지 않다

It is not something to do after the "real work" is done.
그것은 '실제 작업'이 끝난 후에 할 일이 아니다

Play is the real work of childhood.
놀이는 어린 시절의 진정한 일이다

Through it, / children have their best chance / for becoming whole, happy adults.
그것을 통해, / 어린이들은 최고의 기회를 갖게 된다 / 온전하고 행복한 어른이 될 수 있는

해석　『놀이』의 저자인 정신과 의사 Stuart Brown은 "놀이는 그 자체를 위해 하는 것이다."라고 말하며, 그는 "그것은 자발적이고, 유쾌하고, 참여의 감각을 제공하고, 시간 가는 줄 모르게 한다. 그리고 행위 자체가 결과보다 더 중요하다."라고 기술한다. 이 정의를 염두에 두면, 놀이의 잠재적 이점을 인식하는 것은 쉽다. 놀이는 자신과 타인과의 관계를 ① 길러준다. 그것은 스트레스를 ② 해소하고 행복을 증진시킨다. 그것은 공감, 창의성, 그리고 협력의 감정을 형성한다. 그것은 강건함과 기개의 성장을 지원한다. 어린이들이 놀 기회를 박탈당하면, 그들의 발달은 상당히 ③ 향상될 수 있다. 놀이는 매우 중요해서 유럽 연합 인권 위원회는 그것을 모든 어린이의 ④ 기본적인 권리라고 선언했다. 놀이는 하찮지 않다. 그것은 '실제 작업'이 끝난 후에 할 일이 아니다. 놀이는 어린 시절의 진정한 일이다. 그것을 통해, 어린이들은 온전하고 행복한 어른이 될 수 있는 최고의 기회를 갖게 된다.
*2번째 줄의 author of "Play" He writes는 author of "Play," he writes의 오타이므로, 원문에 맞춰 해석했습니다.

해설　지문 전반에 걸쳐 어린이들에게 놀이가 갖는 중요성에 대해 설명하고 있다. 지문 중간에서 놀이는 자신과 타인과의 관계를 키워주고, 스트레스를 해소하고, 행복을 증진시키고 공감, 창의성, 그리고 협력의 감정을 형성하며, 강건함과 기개의 성장을 지원한다고 하고 있으므로, 어린이들이 놀 기회를 박탈당하면 그들의 발달은 상당히 '③ 향상될(enhanced)' 수 있다는 것은 문맥상 적절하지 않다. 주어진 enhanced를 대신할 수 있는 어휘로는 '줄이다'라는 의미의 diminished가 있다.

어휘　for one's own sake ~자체를 위해　psychiatrist 정신과 의사
voluntary 자발적인　pleasurable 유쾌한　engagement 참여
outcome 결과　definition 정의　recognize 인식하다
potential 잠재적인　nurture 기르다, 키우다　relieve 해소하다
empathy 공감　collaboration 협력　grit 기개　deprive 박탈하다
significantly 상당히　enhance 향상하다　commission 위원회
declare 선언하다　right 권리

22　독해　추론 (빈칸 완성 - 단어)　난이도 ★★☆

끊어읽기 해석

Lewis Pugh is a British endurance swimmer, / who is best known for his long-distance swims / in cold and open waters.
Lewis Pugh는 영국의 지구력 수영 선수이다 / 장거리 수영을 하는 것으로 가장 잘 알려진 / 차갑고 탁 트인 바다에서

He swims in cold places / as a way to draw attention to the urgent need / to protect the world's oceans and waterways / from the effects of climate change and pollution.
그는 차가운 곳에서 수영한다 / 긴급한 필요성에 주의를 끌기 위해 / 세계의 바다와 수로를 보호할 / 기후 변화와 오염의 영향으로부터

In 2019, / Pugh decided to swim in Lake Imja, / which is

---

located in the Khumbu region of Nepal, near Mount Everest.
2019년에, / Pugh는 Imja 호수에서 수영하기로 결정했다 / 에베레스트산 근처의 네팔 Khumbu 지역에 위치한

After a failed first attempt, / Lewis had a debrief / to discuss the best way to swim at 5,300 meters above sea level.
실패한 첫 번째 시도 이후, / Lewis는 평가회의를 했다 / 해발 5,300미터에서 수영하는 가장 좋은 방법에 대해 논의하기 위해

He is usually very aggressive when he swims / because he wants to finish quickly and get out of the cold water.
그는 보통 수영할 때 매우 공격적이다 / 그가 빨리 끝내고 차가운 물에서 벗어나고 싶어하기 때문에

But this time / he showed humility and swam slowly.
그러나 이번에는 / 그는 겸손함을 보이며 천천히 수영했다

해석　Lewis Pugh는 차갑고 탁 트인 바다에서 장거리 수영을 하는 것으로 가장 잘 알려진 영국의 지구력 수영 선수이다. 그는 기후 변화와 오염의 영향으로부터 세계의 바다와 수로를 보호해야 할 긴급한 필요성에 주의를 끌기 위해 차가운 곳에서 수영한다. 2019년에, Pugh는 에베레스트산 근처의 네팔 Khumbu 지역에 위치한 Imja 호수에서 수영하기로 결정했다. 첫 번째 시도에서 실패한 후, Lewis는 해발 5,300미터에서 수영하는 가장 좋은 방법에 대해 논의하기 위해 평가회의를 했다. 그는 보통 빨리 끝내고 차가운 물에서 벗어나고 싶어하기 때문에 수영할 때 매우 공격적이다. 그러나 이번에는 겸손함을 보이며 천천히 수영했다.

① 슬픔
② 분노
③ 겸손함
④ 자신감

해설　빈칸 앞 부분에서 실패한 첫 번째 시도 이후, Lewis는 해발 5,300미터에서 수영하는 가장 좋은 방법에 대해 논의하기 위해 평가회의를 했다고 했고, 그는 보통 빨리 끝내고 차가운 물에서 벗어나고 싶어하기 때문에 수영할 때 매우 공격적이라고 했으므로, 빈칸에는 그러나 이번에는 '③ 겸손함'을 보이며 천천히 수영했다는 내용이 들어가야 한다.

어휘　endurance 지구력　urgent 긴급한　waterway 수로, 항로
attempt 시도　aggressive 공격적인　grief 슬픔
humility 겸손함

23　독해　논리적 흐름 파악 (무관한 문장 삭제)　난이도 ★★☆

끊어읽기 해석

Fast fashion is a method / of producing inexpensive clothing at a rapid pace / to respond to the latest fashion trends.
패스트 패션은 방식이다 / 빠른 속도로 저렴한 의류를 생산하는 / 최신 패션 경향에 대응하기 위해

With shopping evolving into a form of entertainment / in the age of fast fashion, / customers are contributing to / what sustainability experts refer to as a throwaway culture.
쇼핑이 오락의 형태로 진화함에 따라 / 패스트 패션 시대에 / 소비자들은 ~에 기여하고 있다 / 지속 가능성 전문가가 그냥 쓰고 버리는 문화라고 말하는 문화에

This means / customers simply discard products / once they are deemed useless / rather than recycling or donating them.
이는 의미한다 / 소비자들이 제품을 단순히 폐기하는 것을 / 그것들이 쓸모없다고 여겨지면 / 그것들을 재활용하거나 기부하는 대신

① The consumers are generally satisfied / with the quality of fast fashion brand clothing.

소비자들은 일반적으로 만족한다 / 패스트 패션 브랜드 의류의 품질에

② As a result, / these discarded items add a huge burden to the environment.
결과적으로, / 이러한 버려진 물건들은 환경에 막대한 부담을 준다

③ To resolve the throwaway culture and fast fashion crisis, / the concept of sustainability in fashion is brought to the spotlight.
그냥 쓰고 버리는 문화와 패스트 패션의 위기를 해결하기 위해, / 패션의 지속 가능성 개념이 부각되고 있다

④ Sustainable fashion involves apparel, footwear, and accessories / that are produced, distributed, and utilized as sustainably as possible / while taking into account socio-economic and environmental concerns.
지속 가능한 패션은 의류, 신발, 그리고 액세서리를 포함한다 / 가능한 한 지속 가능하게 생산, 유통, 그리고 활용되는 / 사회 경제적, 그리고 환경적 관심을 고려하면서

해석 패스트 패션은 최신 패션 경향에 대응하기 위해 빠른 속도로 저렴한 의류를 생산하는 방식이다. 패스트 패션 시대에 쇼핑이 오락의 형태로 진화함에 따라, 소비자들은 지속 가능성 전문가가 그냥 쓰고 버리는 문화라고 말하는 문화에 기여하고 있다. 이는 제품이 쓸모없다고 여겨지면 소비자들이 제품을 재활용하거나 기부하는 대신 단순히 폐기하는 것을 의미한다. ① 소비자들은 일반적으로 패스트 패션 브랜드 의류의 품질에 만족한다. ② 결과적으로, 이러한 버려진 물건들은 환경에 막대한 부담을 준다. ③ 그냥 쓰고 버리는 문화와 패스트 패션의 위기를 해결하기 위해, 패션의 지속 가능성 개념이 부각되고 있다. ④ 지속 가능한 패션은 사회 경제적, 그리고 환경적 관심을 고려하면서 가능한 한 지속 가능하게 생산, 유통, 그리고 활용되는 의류, 신발, 그리고 액세서리를 포함한다.

해설 지문 처음에서 패스트 패션은 그냥 쓰고 버리는 문화에 기여하고 있다고 언급한 뒤, ②번에서 이렇게 버려진 물건들은 환경에 막대한 부담을 준다고 설명하고, 이어서 ③번과 ④번에서 그냥 쓰고 버리는 문화와 패스트 패션의 위기를 해결하기 위해 패션의 지속 가능성 개념이 부각되고 있다고 설명하고 있다. 그러나 ①번은 소비자들이 일반적으로 패스트 패션 브랜드 의류의 품질에 만족한다는 내용으로, 패스트 패션의 위기와 그 해결에 관한 지문 전반의 내용과 관련이 없다.

어휘 rapid 빠른 pace 속도 latest 최신의 evolve 진화하다
age 시대 contribute 기여하다 sustainability 지속 가능성
expert 전문가 throwaway (값싸게 만들어져) 그냥 쓰고 버리는
discard 폐기하다 deem 여기다 useless 쓸모없는
donate 기부하다 crisis 위기 apparel 의류 distribute 유통하다
utilize 활용하다 take into account ~을 고려하다
socio-economic 사회경제적인 concern 관심, 우려

24 독해 전체내용 파악 (요지 파악)   난이도 ★☆☆

끊어읽기 해석

Wrinkles are a sure sign of aging, / and may also hint that bone health is on the decline.
주름은 노화의 확실한 징후이다 / 그리고 뼈 건강이 쇠퇴하고 있음을 암시할 수도 있다

Researchers at Yale School of Medicine found / that some women with deepening and worsening skin wrinkles also had lower bone density, / independent of age and factors known to influence bone mass.
예일 의과대학교의 연구원들은 발견했다 / 피부 주름이 깊어지고 악화되는 일부 여성들이 골밀도도 낮다는 것을 / 연령과 골수에 영향을 미친다고 알려진 요인과 관계없이

Skin and bones share a common building-block protein, type 1 collagen, / which is lost with age, / says study author Dr. Lubna Pal.
피부와 뼈는 공통 구성 요소 단백질인 1형 콜라겐을 공유한다 / 이는 나이가 들면서 손실된다 / 연구 저자 Lubna Pal 박사는 말한다

Wrinkles between the eyebrows / — the vertical lines above the bridge of the nose / — appear to be the strongest markers of brittle bones, she says.
눈썹 사이의 주름 / 즉 콧대 위의 수직선은 / 잘 부러지는 뼈의 가장 강력한 지표인 것처럼 보인다고 그녀는 말한다

Long-term studies are needed, / but it appears the skin reflects / what's happening at the level of the bone, / says Pal.
장기적인 연구가 필요하다 / 하지만 피부는 반영하는 것으로 보인다 / 뼈 수준에서 일어나는 일을 / Pal은 말한다

해석 주름은 노화의 확실한 징후이며, 뼈 건강이 쇠퇴하고 있음을 암시할 수도 있다. 예일 의과대학교의 연구원들은 피부 주름이 깊어지고 악화되는 일부 여성들은 연령과 골수에 영향을 미친다고 알려진 요인과 관계없이 골밀도도 낮다는 것을 발견했다. 피부와 뼈는 공통 구성 요소 단백질인 1형 콜라겐을 공유하며, 이는 나이가 들면서 손실된다고, 연구 저자 Lubna Pal 박사는 말한다. 그녀는 눈썹 사이, 즉 콧대 위의 수직선은 잘 부러지는 뼈의 가장 강력한 지표인 것처럼 보인다고 말한다. 장기적인 연구가 필요하지만, 피부는 뼈 수준에서 일어나는 일을 반영하는 것으로 보인다고 Pal은 말한다.

해설 지문 처음에서 주름은 노화의 확실한 징후이며, 뼈 건강이 쇠퇴하고 있음을 암시할 수도 있다고 언급하고 있고, 지문 마지막에서 피부는 뼈 수준에서 일어나는 일을 반영하는 것을 보인다고 하고 있으므로, '④ 주름은 단지 피부 노화와만 연관된 것이 아니라 뼈 건강 상태와도 연관이 있다'가 이 글의 요지이다.

어휘 wrinkle 주름 decline 쇠퇴하다 density 밀도
independent of ~과 관계없이 factor 요인 bone mass 골수
building-block 구성 요소 protein 단백질 vertical 수직의
reflect 반영하다

25 독해 세부내용 파악(내용 불일치 파악)   난이도 ★★☆

끊어읽기 해석

Meditation can improve your quality of life / thanks to its many psychological and physical benefits.
명상은 당신의 삶의 질을 향상시킬 수 있다 / 그것의 많은 심리적, 신체적 이점 덕분에

Mindfulness-based interventions, such as meditation, have been shown to improve mental health, / specifically in the area of stress, / according to a study in the Clinical Psychology Review.
명상과 같은 마음 챙김 기반 중재는 정신 건강을 개선하는 것으로 나타났다 / 특히 스트레스 영역에서 / 「Clinical Psychology Review」의 연구에 따르면

When faced with a difficult or stressful moment, / our bodies create cortisol, / the steroid hormone responsible for regulating stress and our natural fight-or-flight response, / among many other functions.
어렵거나 스트레스가 많은 순간에 직면했을 때, / 우리의 몸은 코르티솔을 생성한다 / 스트레스와 우리의 자연스러운 투쟁 및 도피 반응을 조절하는 것을 담당하는 스테로이드 호르몬인 / 다른 많은 기능 중에서

Chronic stress can cause sustained and elevated levels of cortisol, / which can lead to other negative effects on your health, / including cardiovascular and immune systems and gut health.

만성 스트레스는 지속적이고 고조된 코르티솔 수준을 유발할 수 있다 / 이는 당신의 건강에 다른 부정적인 영향을 미칠 수 있다 / 심혈관계 및 면역 체계와 장 건강을 포함하여

Meditation, which focuses on calming the mind and regulating emotion, / can help to reduce chronic stress in the body / and lower the risk of its side effects.

마음을 진정시키고 감정을 조절하는 데 중점을 둔 명상은 / 신체의 만성적인 스트레스를 줄이는 데 도움이 될 수 있다 / 그리고 부작용의 위험을 낮추는 데

해석 명상은 많은 심리적, 신체적 이점 덕분에 당신의 삶의 질을 향상시킬 수 있다. 「Clinical Psychology Review」의 연구에 따르면, 명상과 같은 마음 챙김 기반 중재는 특히 스트레스 영역에서 정신 건강을 개선하는 것으로 나타났다. 어렵거나 스트레스가 많은 순간에 직면했을 때, 우리의 몸은 다른 많은 기능 중에서 스트레스와 우리의 자연스러운 투쟁 또는 도피 반응을 조절하는 것을 담당하는 스테로이드 호르몬인 코르티솔을 생성한다. 만성 스트레스는 지속적이고 고조된 코르티솔 수준을 유발할 수 있는데, 이는 심혈관계 및 면역 체계와 장 건강을 포함하여 당신의 건강에 다른 부정적인 영향을 미칠 수 있다. 마음을 진정시키고 감정을 조절하는 데 중점을 둔 명상은 신체의 만성적인 스트레스를 줄이고 부작용의 위험을 낮추는 데 도움이 될 수 있다.

① 명상은 우리에게 정신적으로, 육체적으로 유익하다.
② 코르티솔은 스트레스 상황에서 분비된다.
③ 스트레스는 대개 우리의 심혈관계에 영향을 미치지 않는다.
④ 명상은 신체의 만성 스트레스를 낮추는 데 도움이 될 수 있다.

해설 지문 마지막에서 만성 스트레스는 지속적이고 고조된 코르티솔 수준을 유발할 수 있고, 이는 심혈관계 및 면역 체계와 장 건강을 포함하여 당신의 건강에 다른 부정적인 영향을 미칠 수 있다고 했으므로, '③ 스트레스는 대개 우리의 심혈관계에 영향을 미치지 않는다'는 것은 지문의 내용과 일치하지 않는다.

어휘 meditation 명상 psychological 심리적인 physical 신체적인
mindfulness 마음 챙김 intervention 중재 regulate 조절하다
flight 도피 sustain 지속하다 elevate 고조시키다
immune 면역의 gut 장, 소화기관 chronic 만성적인
side effect 부작용 mentally 정신적으로

정답

p.175

01	① 문법 - 수 일치 & to 부정사 & 관계절	**11**	① 문법 - 명사절 & 시제 & 능동태 · 수동태	**21**	③ 독해 - 논리적 흐름 파악
02	① 독해 - 전체내용 파악	**12**	③ 독해 - 추론	**22**	② 독해 - 전체내용 파악
03	① 독해 - 전체내용 파악	**13**	① 독해 - 논리적 흐름 파악	**23**	③ 독해 - 전체내용 파악
04	③ 독해 - 논리적 흐름 파악	**14**	② 독해 - 논리적 흐름 파악	**24**	② 독해 - 세부내용 파악
05	④ 독해 - 세부내용 파악	**15**	④ 문법 - 수 일치	**25**	③ 독해 - 세부내용 파악
06	④ 독해 - 추론	**16**	② 독해 - 전체내용 파악		
07	① 독해 - 세부내용 파악	**17**	③ 독해 - 추론		
08	③ 독해 - 논리적 흐름 파악	**18**	① 문법 - 병치 · 도치 · 강조 구문		
09	③ 독해 - 전체내용 파악	**19**	① 문법 - 조동사		
10	④ 독해 - 논리적 흐름 파악	**20**	② 독해 - 추론		

취약영역 분석표

영역	세부 유형	문항 수	소계
문법	수 일치 & to 부정사 & 관계절	1	/5
	명사절 & 시제 & 능동태 · 수동태	1	
	수 일치	1	
	병치 · 도치 · 강조 구문	1	
	조동사	1	
독해	전체내용 파악	6	/20
	세부내용 파악	4	
	추론	4	
	논리적 흐름 파악	6	
	총계		/25

· 자신이 취약한 영역은 '공무원 영어, 이렇게 출제된다!'(문제집 p.8)를 통해 다시 한번 확인하고 학습하시기 바랍니다.

---

01 문법 수 일치 & to 부정사 & 관계절 난이도 ★★☆

해석 일이나 직무에 적합한 보호복의 선택은 보통 야기되는 위험에 대한 분석 또는 평가에 의해 좌우된다. 노출의 빈도와 유형에 더하여 착용자에게 예상되는 활동이 이 결정에 입력되는 전형적인 변수이다. 예를 들어, 소방관은 다양한 연소 물질에 노출된다. 따라서 특수한 여러 겹의 직물 조직이 야기되는 열 문제에 대처하기 위해 사용된다. 이것은 보통 상당히 무겁고 어떤 화재 상황에도 대비하여 근본적으로 최고 수준의 보호를 제공하는 보호 장비가 된다. 대조적으로, 돌발적인 화재의 가능성이 있는 지역에서 일해야 하는 산업 근로자는 매우 다른 일련의 위험 요소와 필요 조건을 갖게 될 것이다. 많은 경우에, 면으로 된 작업복 위에 착용하는 방염 작업복은 충분히 위험에 대처할 수 있다.

해설 (A) 주어와 동사의 수 일치 주어 자리에 단수 명사 The selection이 왔으므로 단수 동사 is가 쓰여야 적절하다.
(B) to 부정사의 역할 문맥상 '대처하기 위해'라는 의미가 되어야 자연스러우므로 부사처럼 목적을 나타낼 수 있는 to 부정사 to meet이 쓰여야 적절하다.
(C) 관계부사와 관계대명사 비교 관계사 뒤에 완전한 절(the possibility ~ requirements)이 왔으므로 관계대명사 which가 아닌 관계부사 where가 와야 한다.
따라서 ① (A) is – (B) to meet – (C) where가 정답이다.

어휘 **appropriate** 적합한 **dictate** ~을 좌우하다 **assessment** 평가
hazard 위험 (요소) **present** (문제 등을) 야기하다, 제시하다
frequency 빈도 **exposure** 노출 **typical** 전형적인
variable 변수 **meet** 대처하다, 만나다 **protective** 보호의, 방어적인
fairly 상당히, 꽤 **flash fire** 돌발적인 화재
flame-resistant 방염의, 내염성의(불에 잘 타지 않는)

👍 이것도 알면 **합격!**

관계부사(when, where, why, how)는 '전치사 + 관계대명사'의 형태로 바꾸어 쓸 수 있고 뒤에는 완전한 절이 온다는 것을 알아두자.

ex The protesters weren't entirely clear about the reasons why (= for which) they were demonstrating.
그 시위자들은 왜 그들이 시위에 참여하고 있는지 완전히 분명하지 않았다.

---

02 독해 전체내용 파악 (문단 요약) 난이도 ★★☆

끊어읽기 해석

In India, / approximately 360 million people / —one-third of the population— / live in or very close to the forests.
인도에서는 / 약 3억 6천만 명이 / 인구의 3분의 1인 / 숲속이나 숲과 매우 가까이에 살고 있다

More than half of these people / live below the official poverty line, / and consequently / they depend crucially / on the resources / they obtain from the forests.
이러한 사람들 중 절반 이상이 / 공식적인 빈곤선 이하에서 살고 있다 / 그리고 그 결과 / 그들은 결정적으로 의존한다 / 자원에 / 그들이 숲에서 얻는

The Indian government now runs / programs aimed at improving their lot / by involving them / in the commercial management of their forests, / in this way / allowing them to continue / to obtain the food and materials / they need, / but at the same time / to sell forest produce.
인도 정부는 현재 운영한다 / 그들 지역의 가치를 높이는 것을 목적으로 하는 프로그램을 / 그들을 참여시킴으로써 / 숲의 상업적 관리에 / 이 방식으로 / 그들이 계속 ~하는 것을 가능하게 한다 / 필요한 식량과 재료를 얻는 것을 / 그들이 필요한 / 그러나 동시에 / 임산물을 판매하는 것을

If the programs succeed, / forest dwellers will be more prosperous, / but they will be able to preserve / their

traditional way of life and culture, / and the forest will be managed sustainably, / so the wildlife is not depleted.
만약 그 프로그램이 성공하면 / 숲에 사는 사람들은 더 부유해지겠지만 / 그들은 보존할 수 있을 것이고 / 그들의 전통적인 생활양식과 문화를 / 그리고 숲이 지속 가능하게 관리되어서 / 야생동물은 대폭 감소하지 않을 것이다

해석 인도에서는, 인구의 3분의 1인 약 3억 6천만 명이 숲속이나 숲과 매우 가까이에 살고 있다. 이러한 사람들 중 절반 이상이 공식적인 빈곤선 이하에서 살고 있고, 그 결과 그들은 그들이 숲에서 얻는 자원에 결정적으로 의존한다. 인도 정부는 현재 그들을 숲의 상업적 관리에 참여시킴으로써 그들 지역의 가치를 높이는 것을 목적으로 하는 프로그램을 운영하는데, 이 방식으로 그들이 필요한 식량과 재료를 계속 얻게 하면서 동시에 임산물을 판매하는 것을 가능하게 한다. 만약 그 프로그램이 성공하면, 숲에 사는 사람들은 더 부유해지겠지만, 그들은 그들의 전통적인 생활양식과 문화를 보존할 수 있을 것이고, 숲이 지속 가능하게 관리되어서, 야생동물은 대폭 감소하지 않을 것이다.

⇒ 인도 정부는 숲을 (B) 파괴하는 것 없이 숲 근처에 사는 가난한 사람들의 삶을 (A) 개선하려 하고 있다.

　　　　(A)　　　　　(B)
① 개선하다　　　파괴하는 것
② 통제하다　　　보존하는 것
③ 개선하다　　　제한하는 것
④ 통제하다　　　확대하는 것

해설 지문 중간에 인도 정부가 숲이나 그 근처에 사는 사람들을 숲의 상업적 관리에 참여시킴으로써 그들 지역의 가치를 높이기 위한 프로그램을 운영한다는 내용이 있고, 지문 마지막에 그 프로그램이 성공한다면 숲에 사는 사람들이 더 부유해지면서도 숲이 지속 가능하게 관리되어 야생동물이 대폭 감소하지 않을 것이라는 내용이 있으므로, (A)와 (B)에 인도 정부는 숲을 파괴하는 것(ruining) 없이 숲 근처에 사는 가난한 사람들의 삶을 개선하려(improve) 하고 있다는 내용이 와야 적절하다. 따라서 ① improve – ruining이 정답이다.

어휘 poverty line 빈곤선(빈곤의 여부를 구분하는 최저 수입)
depend 의존하다 obtain 얻다 aim at ~을 목적으로 하다
lot 지역, 다량 forest produce 임산물
dweller ~에 사는 사람, 거주자 prosperous 부유한
preserve 보존하다 sustainably 지속 가능하게
deplete 대폭 감소시키다, 고갈시키다 ruin 파괴하다, 망치다
enlarge 확대하다

03 **독해** 전체내용 파악 (문단 요약)　　난이도 ★★☆

끊어읽기 해석

In the absence of facial cues or touch / during pandemic, / there is a greater need / to focus on other aspects of conversation, / including more emphasis on tone and inflection, / slowing the speed, / and increasing loudness / without sounding annoying.
얼굴을 사용하는 신호나 접촉이 없어서 / 팬데믹 중에는 / 필요성이 더욱 크다 / 대화의 다른 측면들에 집중할 / 어조와 억양을 더 강조하는 것을 포함하여 / 속도를 낮추는 것 / 음량을 높이는 것 / 성가시게 들리지 않게

Many nuances of the spoken word / are easily missed / without facial expression, / so eye contact will assume / an even greater importance.
구어의 많은 뉘앙스는 / 놓치기 쉬워서 / 얼굴 표정이 없으면 / 눈맞춤이 나타낼 것이다 / 더욱 큰 중요성을

Some hospital workers / have developed innovative ways / to try to solve this problem.
일부 병원 근로자들은 / 혁신적인 방법을 개발했다 / 이 문제를 해결하려고 시도하기 위해

One of nurse specialists was deeply concerned / that her chronically sick young patients / could not see her face, / so she printed off a variety of face stickers / to get children to point towards.
전문 간호사들 중 한 명은 깊은 관심을 가졌다 / 그녀의 만성적으로 아픈 어린 환자들이 / 그녀의 얼굴을 볼 수 없다는 것에 / 그래서 그녀는 다양한 얼굴 스티커를 인쇄했다 / 아이들이 가리키게 하기 위해

Some hospitals / now also provide their patients / with 'face-sheets' / that permit easier identification / of staff members, / and it is always useful / to reintroduce yourself and colleagues / to patients / when wearing masks.
일부 병원들은 / 오늘날 또한 환자들에게 제공한다 / '페이스 시트'를 / 더 쉬운 신원 확인을 가능하게 하는 / 직원의 / 그리고 그것은 항상 유용하다 / 당신 자신과 동료들을 다시 소개하는 데 / 환자들에게 / 마스크를 착용하고 있을 때

해석 팬데믹 중에는 얼굴을 사용하는 신호(표정)나 접촉이 없어서, 어조와 억양을 더 강조하는 것, 속도를 낮추는 것, 성가시게 들리지 않게 음량을 높이는 것을 포함하여 대화의 다른 측면들에 집중할 필요성이 더욱 크다. 구어의 많은 뉘앙스는 얼굴 표정이 없으면 놓치기 쉬워서, 눈맞춤이 더욱 큰 중요성을 나타낼 것이다. 일부 병원 근로자들은 이 문제를 해결하려고 시도하기 위해 혁신적인 방법을 개발했다. 전문 간호사들 중 한 명은 그녀의 만성적으로 아픈 어린 환자들이 그녀의 얼굴을 볼 수 없다는 것에 깊은 관심을 가졌고, 그래서 그녀는 아이들이 가리키게 하기 위해 다양한 얼굴 스티커를 인쇄했다. 오늘날 일부 병원들은 또한 환자들에게 직원의 더 쉬운 신원 확인을 가능하게 하는 '페이스 시트'를 제공하고 있는데, 그것은 마스크를 착용하고 있을 때 환자들에게 당신 자신과 동료들을 다시 소개하는 데 항상 유용하다.

일부 병원과 근로자들은 팬데믹 중에 환자들과의 대화를 (B) 보완하기 위한 (A) 대안적인 방법들을 찾고 있다.

　　　(A)　　　　(B)
① 대안적인　―　보완하다
② 성가신　　―　분석하다
③ 효과적인　―　방해하다
④ 방해하는　―　개선하다

해설 지문 중간에서 전문 간호사들 중 한 명이 환자들이 자신의 얼굴을 볼 수 없다는 것에 깊은 관심을 가지게 되어 환자들이 가리킬 수 있는 얼굴 스티커를 인쇄했다고 하였고, 오늘날 일부 병원들은 마스크를 착용하고 있을 때 환자가 직원을 쉽게 확인할 수 있도록 '페이스 시트'를 제공한다고 설명하고 있으므로, (A)와 (B)에 일부 병원과 근로자들은 팬데믹 중에 환자들과의 대화를 보완하기(complement) 위한 대안적인(alternative) 방법들을 찾고 있다는 내용이 와야 적절하다. 따라서 ① alternative – complement가 정답이다.

어휘 in the absence of ~이 없어서, ~이 없을 때 cue 신호, 단서
pandemic 팬데믹(전 세계적인 유행병) inflection 억양, 굴절
annoying 성가신 assume (특질 등을) 나타내다, 추정하다
chronically 만성적으로 permit 가능하게 하다
identification 신원 확인, 인지 alternative 대안적인
complement 보완하다 bothering 성가신 analyze 분석하다
hinder 방해하다 disturb 방해하다, 불안하게 하다

04 독해 논리적 흐름 파악 (문단 순서 배열) 난이도 ★★☆

끊어읽기 해석

> Once they leave their mother, / primates have to keep on making decisions / about whether new foods they encounter / are safe and worth collecting.
> 일단 그들이 어미 곁을 떠나면 / 영장류는 계속 결정해야 한다 / 그들이 접하게 되는 새로운 음식이 ~인지에 대해 / 안전하고 채집할 가치가 있는
>
> (A) By the same token, / if the sampler feels fine, / it will reenter the tree / in a few days, / eat a little more, / then wait again, / building up to a large dose slowly.
> 같은 이유로 / 만약 그 시식자가 괜찮다고 느낀다면 / 그것은 다시 나무에 들어갈 것이다 / 며칠 내로 / 좀 더 먹고 / 그 후 다시 기다린다 / 많은 양으로 천천히 늘려가면서
>
> Finally, / if the monkey remains healthy, / the other members figure / this is OK, / and they adopt the new food.
> 마침내 / 그 원숭이가 건강을 유지하면 / 다른 구성원들은 생각한다 / 이것이 괜찮다고 / 그래서 그들은 그 새로운 음식을 채택한다
>
> (B) If the plant harbors / a particularly strong toxin, / the sampler's system will try / to break it down, / usually making the monkey sick / in the process.
> 만약 그 식물이 숨기고 있는 경우 / 특히 강한 독소를 / 그 시식자의 몸은 시도할 것이다 / 그것을 분해하려고 / 보통은 그 원숭이를 병들게 한다 / 그 과정에서
>
> "I've seen this happen," / says Glander.
> "저는 이것이 일어나는 것을 본 적이 있습니다" / 라고 Glander는 말한다
>
> "The other members of the troop are watching / with great interest / —if the animal gets sick, / no other animal / will go into that tree.
> "무리의 다른 구성원들은 지켜보고 있습니다 / 아주 흥미롭게 / 만약 그 동물이 병든다면 / 다른 어떤 동물들도 / 그 나무로 가지 않으려 할 것입니다
>
> There's a cue being given / —a social cue."
> 거기에는 주어진 신호가 있습니다 / 바로 사회적 신호입니다"
>
> (C) Using themselves / as experiment tools / is one option, / but social primates have found a better way.
> 그들 스스로를 사용하는 것은 / 실험 도구로 / 하나의 선택지이다 / 하지만 사회적인 영장류는 더 나은 방법을 찾았다
>
> Kenneth Glander calls it "sampling."
> Kenneth Glander는 그것을 '샘플링'이라고 부른다
>
> When howler monkeys move / into a new habitat, / one member of the troop will go to a tree, / eat a few leaves, / then wait a day.
> 짖는원숭이가 이동할 때 / 새로운 서식지로 / 무리의 한 구성원이 나무로 갈 것이다 / 약간의 이파리를 먹는다 / 그 후 하루를 기다린다

해석

> 영장류는 일단 어미 곁을 떠나면 그들이 접하게 되는 새로운 음식이 안전하고 채집할 가치가 있는지에 대해 계속 결정해야 한다.

(C) 그들 스스로를 실험 도구로 사용하는 것도 하나의 선택지이지만, 사회적인 영장류는 더 나은 방법을 찾았다. Kenneth Glander는 그것을 '샘플링'이라고 부른다. 짖는원숭이가 새로운 서식지로 이동할 때, 무리의 한 구성원이 나무로 가서 약간의 이파리를 먹은 후 하루를 기다릴 것이다.

(B) 만약 그 식물이 특히 강한 독소를 숨기고 있는 경우, 그 시식자의 몸은 그것을 분해하려고 시도할 것이고, 보통은 그 과정에서 그 원숭이를 병들게 한다. "저는 이것이 일어나는 것을 본 적이 있습니다"라고 Glander는 말한다. "무리의 다른 구성원들은 아주 흥미롭게 지켜보고 있습니다. 만약 그 동물이 병든다면, 다른 어떤 동물들도 그 나무로 가지 않으려 할 것입니다.

거기에는 주어진 신호가 있는데, 바로 사회적 신호입니다."

(A) 같은 이유로, 만약 그 시식자가 괜찮다고 느낀다면, 그것은 며칠 내로 다시 나무에 들어가서 좀 더 먹은 후 많은 양으로 천천히 늘려가면서 다시 기다릴 것이다. 마침내, 그 원숭이가 건강을 유지하면 다른 구성원들은 이것이 괜찮다고 생각해서 그 새로운 음식을 채택한다.

해설 주어진 문장에서 영장류가 어미 곁을 떠나면 그들이 접하게 되는 음식이 안전하고 채집할 가치가 있는지를 계속 결정해야 한다고 한 뒤, (C)에서 사회적 영장류가 그들 스스로를 실험 도구로 사용하는 것보다 더 나은 방법인 '샘플링'이라는 방법을 사용한다고 설명하면서 짖는원숭이가 서식지를 이동할 때 한 구성원이 약간의 이파리를 먹고 하루 지켜보는 것을 예시로 들고 있다. 이어서 (B)에서 만약 원숭이가 먹은 그 식물(the plant)이 독소를 숨기고 있어 시식자인 그 원숭이가 병든다면 다른 동물들도 그 나무로 가지 않으려 할 것이라고 하며 이것이 바로 사회적 신호라고 설명한 뒤, (A)에서 이와 같은 이유로(By the same token) 만약 시식자가 건강을 유지하면 다른 구성원들도 이것이 괜찮다고 생각하여 그 새로운 음식을 채택하게 된다고 결론짓고 있다.

어휘 primates 영장류 encounter 접하다
by the same token 같은 이유로 dose 양 harbor 숨기다, 품다
toxin 독소 break down 분해하다, 부수다 troop 무리, 부대
cue 신호 experiment 실험 habitat 서식지

05 독해 세부내용 파악 (내용 불일치 파악) 난이도 ★★☆

끊어읽기 해석

> Following Japan's defeat / in World War II, / the majority of ethnic Koreans (1-1.4 million) left Japan.
> 일본의 패배 후 / 제 2차 세계대전에서의 / 한국 교포(100에서 140만 명) 대다수가 일본을 떠났다
>
> By 1948, / the population of ethnic Koreans settled / around 600,000.
> 1948년까지 / 한국 교포 인구는 정착했다 / 약 60만 명이
>
> These Koreans and their descendants are commonly referred to as Zainichi / (literally "residing in Japan"), / a term that appeared / in the immediate postwar years.
> 이 한국인들과 그 후손들은 흔히 Zainichi라고 일컬어진다 / (문자 그대로 '일본에 거주하는') / 이 용어는 나타났다 / 종전 직후에
>
> Ethnic Koreans / who remained in Japan / did so / for diverse reasons.
> 한국 교포들은 / 일본에 남은 / 그렇게 했다 / 여러 가지 이유로
>
> Koreans / who had achieved successful careers / in business, the imperial bureaucracy, and the military / during the colonial period / or who had taken advantage of economic opportunities / that opened up immediately / after the war / —opted to maintain / their relatively privileged status / in Japanese society / rather than risk returning / to an impoverished and politically unstable post-liberation Korea.
> 한국인들은 / 성공적인 경력을 쌓아온 / 기업, 제국의 관료 체제와 군대에서 / 식민지 시대에 / 또는 경제적 기회에 편승한 / 즉시 열린 / 전후에 / 유지하는 것을 선택했다 / 그들의 상대적으로 특권이 있는 지위를 / 일본 사회에서의 / 돌아가는 위험을 무릅쓰기보다는 / 빈곤하고 정치적으로 불안정한 해방 후의 한국으로
>
> Some Koreans / who repatriated / were so repulsed / by the poor conditions / they observed / that they decided to return / to Japan.
> 몇몇 한국인들은 / 본국으로 송환된 / 매우 혐오감을 느껴서 / 열악한 환경에 / 그들이 본 / 그들은 돌아가기로 결심했다 / 일본으로
>
> Other Koreans / living in Japan / could not afford the train

fare / to one of the departure ports, / and among them / who had ethnic Japanese spouses / and Japanese-born, Japanese-speaking children, / it made more sense / to stay in Japan / rather than to navigate the cultural and linguistic challenges / of a new environment.

또 다른 한국인들은 / 일본에 살고 있던 / 기차 요금을 낼 여유가 없었다 / 출국항 중 하나로 가기 위한 / 그들 사이에서 / 일본인 배우자를 두거나 / 일본에서 태어난, 일본어를 하는 자녀를 둔 / 더 타당했다 / 일본에 머무르는 것이 / 문화 및 언어적인 문제를 처리하는 것보다 / 새로운 환경의

해석 제 2차 세계대전에서의 일본의 패배 후, 한국 교포(100에서 140만 명) 대다수가 일본을 떠났다. 1948년까지, 한국 교포 인구는 약 60만 명이 정착했다. 이 한국인들과 그 후손들은 흔히 Zainichi(문자 그대로 '일본에 거주하는')라고 일컬어지는데, 이 용어는 종전 직후에 나타났다. 일본에 남은 한국 교포들은 여러 가지 이유로 그렇게 했다. 식민지 시대에 기업, 제국의 관료 체제와 군대에서 성공적인 경력을 쌓아 왔거나, 전후 즉시 열린 경제적 기회에 편승한 한국인들은 빈곤하고 정치적으로 불안정한 해방 후의 한국으로 돌아가는 위험을 무릅쓰기보다는 일본 사회에서의 상대적으로 특권이 있는 지위를 유지하는 것을 선택했다. 본국으로 송환된 몇몇 한국인들은 그들이 본 열악한 환경에 매우 혐오감을 느껴 일본으로 돌아가기로 결심했다. 일본에 살고 있던 또 다른 한국인들은 출국항 중 하나로 가기 위한 기차 요금을 낼 여유가 없었고, 그들 사이에서 일본인 배우자나 일본에서 태어난, 일본어를 하는 자녀를 둔 이들은 새로운 환경의 문화 및 언어적인 문제를 처리하는 것보다 일본에 머무르는 것이 더 타당했다.

해설 지문 마지막에서 일본에 살고 있던 또 다른 한국인들은 출국항으로 가기 위한 기차 요금을 낼 여유가 없었고, 그들 사이에서 일본인 배우자나 일본에서 태어난 자녀를 둔 이들은 일본에 머무르는 것이 더 타당했다고 했으므로, '④ 한국으로 돌아갈 교통비를 마련하지 못한 사람들은 일본인과 결혼했다'는 것은 지문의 내용과 일치하지 않는다.

어휘 defeat 패배 ethnic Koreans 한국 교포 settle 정착하다
descendant 후손 refer to as ~라고 일컫다
reside 거주하다, 살다 postwar 종전 후 imperial 제국의
bureaucracy 관료 체제 colonial period 식민지 시대
take advantage of ~에 편승하다 opt to ~하기로 선택하다
privileged 특권이 있는 impoverished 빈곤한
unstable 불안정한 post-liberation 해방 후
repulse 혐오감을 주다 fare 요금 departure port 출국항
spouse 배우자 navigate 처리하다, 항해하다

06 독해 추론 (빈칸 완성 - 구) 난이도 ★★☆

끊어읽기 해석

There are a few jobs / where people have had to develop their signing / a bit more fully.
몇몇 직업이 있다 / 사람들이 손짓 언어를 개발해야 하는 / 좀 더 충분히

We see referees and umpires / using their arms and hands / to signal directions / to the players / —as in cricket, / where a single finger upwards means / that the batsman is out / and has to leave the wicket.
우리는 (농구, 축구 등의) 심판과 (테니스, 야구 등의) 심판을 본다 / 팔과 손을 사용하는 것을 / 방향을 제시하기 위해 / 선수들에게 / 크리켓에서처럼 / 여기에서(크리켓에서) 한 손가락을 위로 향하는 것은 의미한다 / 타자가 아웃이 된 것을 / 그리고 삼주문(투구장)을 떠나야 한다는 것을

Orchestra conductors control the musicians / through their movements.
오케스트라 지휘자는 연주자들을 통제한다 / 그들의 동작을 통해

People working at a distance / from each other / have to invent special signals / if they want to communicate.
멀리 떨어져서 일하는 사람들은 / 서로 / 특별한 신호를 만들어야 한다 / 그들이 의사소통하고 싶은 경우

So do people working in a noisy environment, / such as in a factory / where the machines are very loud, / or lifeguards around a swimming pool / full of school children.
시끄러운 환경에서 일하는 사람들도 그렇게 한다(특별한 신호를 만들어 의사소통한다) / 공장에서처럼 / 기계 소리가 매우 시끄러운 / 또는 수영장 주변의 안전요원들도 / 학생들로 가득 찬

해석 손짓 언어를 좀 더 충분히 개발해야 하는 몇몇 직업이 있다. 우리는 크리켓에서처럼 (농구, 축구 등의) 심판과 (테니스, 야구 등의) 심판이 선수들에게 방향을 제시하기 위해 팔과 손을 사용하는 것을 보는데, 여기에서(크리켓에서) 한 손가락을 위로 향하는 것은 타자가 아웃이 되어 삼주문(투구장)을 떠나야 한다는 것을 의미한다. 오케스트라 지휘자는 그들의 동작을 통해 연주자들을 통제한다. 서로 멀리 떨어져서 일하는 사람들은 의사소통하고 싶은 경우 특별한 신호를 만들어야 한다. 기계 소리가 매우 시끄러운 공장에서처럼, 시끄러운 환경에서 일하는 사람들이나 학생들로 가득 찬 수영장 주변의 안전요원들도 그렇게 한다(특별한 신호를 만들어 의사소통한다).

① 부모와 아이들을 지원하다
② 완전히 새로운 근무 방식에 적응하다
③ 기본적인 인권을 위해 법정에서 싸우다
④ 손짓 언어를 좀 더 충분히 개발하다

해설 지문 전반에 걸쳐 크리켓의 심판, 오케스트라 지휘자, 공장과 같은 시끄러운 환경에서 일하는 사람 등을 예시로 들며 몇몇 직업을 가진 사람들은 의사소통을 위해 특별한 신호를 만들어야 한다고 설명하고 있으므로, 빈칸에는 '④ 손짓 언어를 좀 더 충분히 개발하다'가 들어가는 것이 적절하다.

어휘 referee (농구, 축구 등의) 심판 umpire (테니스, 야구 등의) 심판
conductor 지휘자 adapt to ~에 적응하다

07 독해 세부내용 파악 (내용 불일치 파악) 난이도 ★★☆

끊어읽기 해석

Opponents of the use of animals / in research / also oppose use of animals / to test the safety / of drugs or other compounds.
동물을 사용하는 것을 반대하는 사람들은 / 연구에서 / 동물을 사용하는 것 또한 반대한다 / 안전성을 검사하기 위해 / 약물이나 다른 화합물의

Within the pharmaceutical industry, / it was noted that / out of 19 chemicals / known to cause cancer in humans / when taken, / only seven caused cancer / in mice and rats / using standards / set by the National Cancer Instituted / (Barnard and Koufman, 1997).
제약 업계 내에서는 / ~라는 점이 주목되었다 / 19개의 화학 물질 중 / 인간에게 암을 유발하는 것으로 알려진 / 섭취되었을 때 / 오직 7개만이 암을 유발했다는 것이 / 생쥐와 쥐에게 / 기준을 사용했을 때 / 미국 국립 암 연구소에 의해 정해진 / (1997년 Barnard와 Koufman이 설립)

For example, / and antidepressant, nomifensin, / had minimal toxicity / in rats, rabbits, dogs, and monkeys / yet caused liver toxicity and anemia / in humans.
예를 들어 / 항우울제인 노미펜신은 / 아주 적은 독성을 가지고 있었다 / 쥐, 토끼, 개, 그리고 원숭이에게는 / 그러나 간독성과 빈혈을 유발했다 / 인간에게는

In these and other cases, / it has been shown that / some compounds have serious adverse reactions / in humans /

that were not predicted by animal testing / resulting in conditions / in the treated humans / that could lead to disability, / or even death.
이와 다른 경우에는 / ~인 것으로 보인다 / 일부 화합물에 심각한 부작용이 있다는 / 인간에게 / 동물 실험에서는 예측할 수 없었던 / 상태를 초래한다 / 치료 받은 인간에게 / 장애에 이를 수 있는 / 심지어 죽음에까지

And researchers / who are calling for an end / to animal research / state that they have better methods available / such as human clinical trials, / observation aided by laboratory of autopsy tests.
그리고 연구자들은 / 중단을 요구하고 있는 / 동물 연구에 대한 / 더 나은 방법이 있다고 말한다 / 인간의 임상 실험처럼 / 해부 검사 실험실의 도움을 받는 관찰

해석 연구에서 동물을 사용하는 것을 반대하는 사람들은 약물이나 다른 화합물의 안전성을 검사하기 위해 동물을 사용하는 것 또한 반대한다. 제약 업계 내에서는, 섭취되었을 때 인간에게 암을 유발하는 것으로 알려진 19개의 화학 물질 중 오직 7개만이 미국 국립 암 연구소(1997년 Barnard와 Koufman이 설립)에 의해 정해진 기준을 사용했을 때 생쥐와 쥐에게 암을 유발했다는 점이 주목되었다. 예를 들어, 항우울제인 노미펜신은 쥐, 토끼, 개, 그리고 원숭이에게는 아주 적은 독성을 가지고 있었지만 인간에게는 간독성과 빈혈을 유발했다. 이와 다른 경우에는, 일부 화합물에 동물 실험에서는 예측할 수 없었던 심각한 부작용이 있는 것으로 보이며, 이는 치료 받은 인간에게 장애나 심지어 죽음에까지 이를 수 있는 상태를 초래할 수 있다. 그리고 동물 연구에 대한 중단을 요구하고 있는 연구자들은 인간의 임상 실험이나 해부 검사 실험실의 도움을 받는 관찰 등 더 나은 방법이 있다고 말한다.
*세 번째 문장의 and는 an의 오타이므로, 해석하지 않았습니다.

해설 지문 처음에서 섭취되었을 때 인간에게 암을 유발하는 것으로 알려진 화학 물질 19개 중 오직 7개만이 미국 국립 암 연구소에 의해 정해진 기준을 사용했을 때 생쥐와 쥐에게 암을 유발했다는 점이 제약 업계에서 주목되었다고 했으므로, '① 한 기관의 실험 결과 동물과 달리 19개의 발암물질 중에 7개는 인간에게 영향을 미쳤다'는 것은 지문의 내용과 일치하지 않는다.

어휘 opponent 반대하는 사람 compounds 화합물
pharmaceutical 제약의 chemicals 화학 물질 standard 기준
antidepressant 항우울제 toxicity 독성
adverse reaction 부작용 disability 장애 call for ~을 요구하다
aid 돕다 autopsy 해부, 부검

08 독해 논리적 흐름 파악 (문맥상 부적절한 어휘) 난이도 ★★☆

끊어읽기 해석

Cold showers are any showers / with a water temperature below 70°F.
찬물 샤워는 모든 샤워이다 / 화씨 70도 이하 온도의 물로 하는

They may have health benefits.
그것들에는 건강상의 이점이 있을지도 모른다

For people with depression, / cold showers can work / as a kind of gentle electroshock therapy.
우울증이 있는 사람들에게 / 찬물 샤워는 작용할 수 있다 / 일종의 가벼운 전기 충격 요법으로서

The cold water sends many electrical impulses / to your brain.
차가운 물은 많은 전기적 자극을 보낸다 / 당신의 뇌에

They jolt your system / to ① increase / alertness, clarity, and energy levels.
그것들(전기적 자극)은 당신의 몸이 갑자기 덜컥 움직이게 한다 / ① 향상시키도록 / 각성도, 명확성과 활력 수준을

Endorphins, / which are sometimes called happiness hormones, / are also released.
엔도르핀 / 때때로 행복 호르몬이라고 불리기도 하는 / 또한 방출이 된다

This effect leads to / feelings of well-being and ② optimism.
이 효과는 이어진다 / 행복감과 ② 낙관주의로

For people that are obese, / taking a cold shower / 2 or 3 times per week / may contribute / to increased metabolism.
비만인 사람들에게 / 찬물 샤워하는 것은 / 일주일에 두세 번 / 기여할지도 모른다 / 신진대사 향상에

It may help fight obesity / over time.
그것은 비만과 싸우는 데 도움이 될지도 모른다 / 시간이 지남에 따라

The research about / how exactly cold showers help people / lose weight / is ③ clear.
~에 대한 연구는 / 정확하게 어떻게 찬물 샤워가 사람들을 돕는지 / 체중 감량을 하도록 / ③ 분명하다.

However, / it does show / that cold water can even out certain hormone levels / and heal the gastrointestinal system.
그러나 / 그것은 보여준다 / 찬물이 특정 호르몬 수준을 안정되게 할 수 있다는 것을 / 그리고 위장계를 치료하는 것을

These effects may add / to the cold shower's ability / to lead to weight loss.
이러한 효과들이 증가시키는 것일지도 모른다 / 찬물 샤워의 능력을 / 체중 감량으로 이어지는

Furthermore, / when taken regularly, / cold showers can make our circulatory system / more efficient.
게다가 / 정기적으로 (찬물 샤워가) 행해진다면 / 찬물 샤워는 우리의 순환계를 만들 수 있다 / 더욱 효율적으로

Some people also report / that their skin looks better / as a result of cold showers, / probably because of better circulation.
어떤 사람들은 또한 전한다 / 그들의 피부가 더 보기 좋아졌다는 것을 / 찬물 샤워의 결과로 / 이는 아마도 더 나은 혈액 순환 때문일 것이다

Athletes have known this benefit / for years, / even if we have only ④ recently seen data / that supports cold water / for healing after a sport injury.
운동선수들은 이 장점을 알고 있었다 / 몇 년 전부터 / 우리는 불과 ④ 최근에 자료를 봤지만 / 찬물을 지지하는 / 스포츠 부상 이후의 치료를 위한

해석 찬물 샤워는 화씨 70도 이하 온도의 물로 하는 모든 샤워이다. 그것들에는 건강상의 이점이 있을지도 모른다. 우울증이 있는 사람들에게, 찬물 샤워는 일종의 가벼운 전기 충격 요법으로서 작용할 수 있다. 차가운 물은 당신의 뇌에 많은 전기적 자극을 보낸다. 그것들(전기적 자극)은 당신의 몸이 각성도, 명확성과 활력 수준을 ① 향상시키도록 갑자기 덜컥 움직이게 한다. 때때로 행복 호르몬이라고 불리기도 하는 엔도르핀 또한 방출이 된다. 이 효과는 행복감과 ② 낙관주의로 이어진다. 비만인 사람들에게, 일주일에 두세 번 찬물 샤워하는 것은 신진대사 향상에 기여할지도 모른다. 그것은 시간이 지남에 따라 비만과 싸우는 데 도움이 될지도 모른다. 정확하게 어떻게 찬물 샤워가 사람들의 체중 감량을 돕는지에 대한 연구는 ③ 분명하다. 그러나, 그것은 찬물이 특정 호르몬 수준을 안정되게 해서 위장계를 치료할 수 있다는 것을 보여준다. 이러한 효과들이 체중 감량으로 이어지는 찬물 샤워의 능력을 증가시키는 것일지도 모른다. 게다가, 정기적으로 (찬물 샤워가) 행해진다면, 찬물 샤워는 우리의 순환계를 더욱 효율적으로 만들 수 있다. 어떤 사람들은 또한 그들의 피부가 찬물 샤워의 결과로 더 보기 좋아졌다고 전하는데, 이는 아마도 더 나은 혈액 순환 때문일 것이다. 우리는 스포츠 부상 이후의 치료를 위한 찬물을 뒷받침하

는 자료를 불과 ④ 최근에 봤지만, 운동선수들은 몇 년 전부터 이 장점을 알고 있었다.

해설 지문 중간에 일주일에 두세 번의 찬물 샤워가 신진대사 향상에 기여할지도 모르며, 그것이 시간이 지남에 따라 비만과 싸우는 데 도움이 될지도 모른다는 내용이 있고, ③번 뒤 문장에 그러나 (However) 찬물이 특정 호르몬 수준을 안정되게 해서 위장계를 치료할 수 있다는 것은 보여준다는 내용이 있으므로, 정확하게 어떻게 찬물 샤워가 사람들의 체중 감량을 돕는지에 대한 연구가 '③ 분명하다(clear)'는 것은 문맥상 적절하지 않다. 주어진 clear를 대신할 수 있는 어휘로는 '불분명하다'라는 의미의 unclear 등이 있다.

어휘 temperature 온도 depression 우울증 electroshock 전기 충격
impulse 자극 alertness 각성도 clarity 명확성
optimism 낙관주의 obese 비만인, 뚱뚱한
contribute to ~에 기여하다 metabolism 신진대사
even out 안정되다 heal 치료하다 circulatory system 순환계
efficient 효율적인

09 독해 전체내용 파악 (문단 요약) 난이도 ★★☆

끊어읽기 해석

Researchers have been interested / in the habitual ways / a single individual copes with conflict / when it occurs.
연구원들은 흥미를 느껴왔다 / 습관적인 방법들에 / 한 개인이 갈등에 대처하는 / 그것이 발생했을 때

They've called this approach / conflict styles.
그들은 이 접근법을 불러왔다 / 갈등 방식이라고

There are several apparent conflict styles, / and each has its pros and cons.
몇 가지 분명한 갈등 방식이 있다 / 그리고 각각 장단점이 있다

The collaborating style tends / to solve problems / in ways that maximize the chances / that the best result is provided / for all involved.
협력 방식은 경향이 있다 / 문제를 해결하는 / 가능성을 최대화하는 방식으로 / 최상의 결과가 제공될 / 관련된 모두에게

The pluses of a collaborating style include / creating trust, maintaining positive relationship, and building commitment.
협력 방식의 이점은 포함한다 / 신뢰를 형성하는 것, 긍정적인 관계를 유지하는 것, 그리고 참여를 만들어 내는 것을

However, / it's time consuming / and it takes a lot of energy / to collaborate with another / during conflict.
그러나 / 그것은 시간이 걸린다 / 그리고 많은 에너지를 필요로 한다 / 다른 사람과 협력하는 것은 / 갈등 중에

The competing style may develop hostility / in the person / who doesn't achieve their goals.
경쟁 방식은 적대감이 생기게 할 수도 있다 / 사람에게 / 목표를 달성하지 못한

However, / the competing style tends / to resolve a conflict quickly.
그러나 / 경쟁 방식은 경향이 있다 / 갈등을 빠르게 해결하는

해석 연구원들은 갈등이 발생했을 때 한 개인이 그에 대처하는 습관적인 방법들에 흥미를 느껴왔다. 그들은 이 접근법을 갈등 방식이라고 불러왔다. 몇 가지 분명한 갈등 방식이 있으며, 각각 장단점이 있다. 협력 방식은 관련된 모두에게 최상의 결과가 제공될 가능성을 최대화하는 방식으로 문제를 해결하는 경향이 있다. 협력 방식의 이점은 신뢰를 형성하는 것, 긍정적인 관계를 유지하는 것, 그리고 참여를 만들어 내는 것을 포함한다. 그러나, 그것은 시간이 걸리고 갈등 중에 다른 사람과 협력하는 것은 많은 에너지를 필요

로 한다. 경쟁 방식은 목표를 달성하지 못한 사람에게 적대감이 생기게 할 수도 있다. 그러나, 경쟁 방식은 갈등을 빠르게 해결하는 경향이 있다.

협력 방식은 (A) 상호 이해에 큰 가치를 부여하는 사람에 의해 사용될 수 있는 반면, (B) 시간 효율을 선호하는 사람은 경쟁 방식을 선택할 것이다.

	(A)	(B)
①	재정적 능력	상호작용
②	시간 절약	평화로움
③	상호 이해	시간 효율
④	유효성	일관성

해설 지문 중간에 협력 방식은 관련된 모두에게 최상의 결과가 제공될 가능성을 최대화하는 방식으로 문제를 해결하는 경향이 있다는 내용이 있고, 지문 후반에 다른 사람과 협력하는 데는 시간이 걸리고 많은 에너지가 필요하며, 경쟁 방식이 갈등을 빠르게 해결하는 경향이 있다는 내용이 있으므로, (A)와 (B)에 협력 방식은 상호 이해(mutual understanding)에 큰 가치를 부여하는 사람에 의해 사용될 수 있는 반면, 시간 효율(time efficiency)을 선호하는 사람은 경쟁 방식을 선택할 것이라는 내용이 와야 적절하다. 따라서 ③ (A) mutual understanding – (B) time efficiency 가 정답이다.

어휘 habitual 습관적인 cope with ~에 대처하다 conflict 갈등
apparent 분명한 pros and cons 장단점 collaborate 협력하다
maximize 최대화하다 plus 이점 maintain 유지하다
commitment 참여, 약속 time consuming 시간이 걸리는
compete 경쟁하다 hostility 적대감, 적의 prefer 선호하다
interaction 상호작용 mutual 상호의, 서로의
efficiency 효율, 능률 effectiveness 유효성
consistency 일관성

10 독해 논리적 흐름 파악 (문단 순서 배열) 난이도 ★★★

끊어읽기 해석

The historical evolution of Conflict Resolution / gained momentum / in the 1950s and 1960s, / at the height of the Cold War, / when the development of nuclear weapons and conflict between the superpowers / seemed to threaten human survival.
'분쟁 해결'의 역사적 발전이 / 탄력을 받게 되었다 / 1950년대와 1960년대에 / 냉전이 한창이었던 / 그 당시에는 핵무기 개발과 초강대국 간 분쟁이 / 인류의 생존을 위협하는 것처럼 보였다

(A) The combination of analysis and practice / implicit in the new ideas / was not easy / to reconcile with traditional scholarly institutions / or the traditions of practitioners / such as diplomats and politicians.
분석과 실천의 조합은 / 그 새로운 발상에 내재된 / 쉽지 않았다 / 전통적인 학술기관과 조화시키기가 / 혹은 전문직 종사자들의 관례와 / 외교관 및 정치인과 같은

(B) However, / they were not taken seriously / by some.
그러나 / 그들은 진지하게 받아들여지지 않았다 / 일부 사람들에게

The international relations profession had its own understanding / of international conflict / and did not see value / in the new approaches / as proposed.
국제 관계 전문가는 고유한 이해를 갖고 있었다 / 국제 분쟁에 대한 / 그리고 가치를 찾지 못했다 / 새로운 접근법에서 / 제안된 것과 같은

(C) A group of pioneers / from different disciplines / saw the value of studying conflict / as a general phenomenon, / with similar properties, / whether it occurs / in international

relations, domestic politics, industrial relations, communities, / or between individuals.
선구자 집단은 / 서로 다른 학문의 / 분쟁을 연구하는 것의 가치를 이해했다 / 일반적인 현상으로써 / 유사한 특성들을 갖는 / 그것(분쟁)이 발생하는지와 관계없이 / 국제 관계, 국내 정치, 산업 관계, 지역사회 / 또는 개인들 사이에

해석 냉전이 한창이었던 1950년대와 1960년대에 '분쟁 해결'의 역사적 발전이 탄력을 받게 되었는데, 그 당시에는 핵무기 개발과 초강대국 간 분쟁이 인류의 생존을 위협하는 것처럼 보였다.

(C) 서로 다른 학문의 선구자 집단은 그것(분쟁)이 국제 관계, 국내 정치, 산업 관계, 지역사회, 또는 개인들 사이에 발생하는지와 관계없이 분쟁을 유사한 특성들을 갖는 일반적인 현상으로써 연구하는 것의 가치를 이해했다.

(B) 그러나, 그들은 일부 사람들에게 진지하게 받아들여지지 않았다. 국제 관계 전문가는 국제 분쟁에 대해 고유한 이해를 갖고 있었고 제안된 것과 같은 새로운 접근법에서 가치를 찾지 못했다.

(A) 그 새로운 발상에 내재된 분석과 실천의 조합은 전통적인 학술 기관이나 외교관 및 정치인과 같은 전문직 종사자들의 관례와 조화시키기가 쉽지 않았다.

해설 주어진 문장에서 냉전이 한창이던 1950년대와 1960년대에 '분쟁 해결'의 역사적 발전이 탄력을 받게 되었다고 한 뒤, (C)에서 서로 다른 학문의 선구자 집단이 분쟁을 일반적인 현상으로써 연구하는 것의 가치를 이해했다고 하면서 분쟁에 관한 새로운 발상을 설명하고 있다. 이어서 (B)에서 그러나(However) 그들(they)이 일부 사람들에게는 진지하게 받아들여지지 않았다고 하며 국제 관계 전문가들은 그러한 새로운 접근법에서 가치를 찾지 못했다고 한 뒤, (A)에서 그 새로운 발상에 내재된 내용은 전통적인 학술기관이나 외교관 및 정치인과 같은 전문직 종사자들의 관례와 조화시키기가 쉽지 않았다고 하며 분쟁에 관한 새로운 발상이 직면하게 된 문제를 설명하고 있다.

어휘 resolution 해결 momentum 탄력, 가속도
at the height of ~이 한창일 때 superpower 초강대국
threaten 위협하다 combination 조합 analysis 분석
implicit 내재된, 암시된 reconcile 조화시키다, 화해시키다
scholarly 학술의, 학문적인
practitioner 전문직 종사자, 실천하는 사람 diplomat 외교관
pioneer 선구자 disciplines 학문 phenomenon 현상
properties 특성, 성질 domestic 국내의

11 문법 명사절&시제&능동태·수동태 난이도 ★★☆

해석 경제학을 이해하는 비결은 항상 의도하지 않은 결과가 있다는 것을 받아들이는 것이다. 사람들이 자신만의 타당한 이유들로 취하는 행동들은 그들이 상상하지 못하거나 의도치 않은 결과를 낳는다. 지정학에 있어서도 마찬가지이다. 기원전 7세기에 확장을 시작한 로마의 마을이 500년 이후의 지중해 권역 정복에 관한 기본 계획을 가지고 있었는지는 의문이다. 하지만 인근 마을에 대해 그곳의 주민들이 취했던 가장 첫 번째 행동은 현실에 제약받았을 뿐만 아니라 의도치 않은 결과로 가득 찼던 과정을 촉발했다. 로마는 계획되지 않았고, 그저 우연히 일어난 것 또한 아니었다.

해설 (A) what vs. that 완전한 절(there are ~ consequences)을 이끌면서 동명사 accepting의 목적어 자리에 올 수 있는 명사절 접속사 that을 써야 한다.
(B) 과거 시제 문맥상 '로마의 마을이 기본 계획을 가지고 있었는지'라는 의미가 되어야 자연스럽고 특정 과거 시점을 나타내

는 표현(in the seventh century BC)이 왔으므로 과거 동사 had를 써야 한다.
(C) 능동태·수동태 구별 동사 filled 뒤에 목적어가 없고, 관계절의 선행사(a process)와 동사가 '의도치 않은 결과로 가득 찬 과정'이라는 의미의 수동 관계이므로 be동사(was) 뒤에서 수동태를 완성하는 과거분사 filled를 써야 한다.
따라서 ① (A) that – (B) had – (C) filled가 정답이다.

어휘 key 비결, 열쇠 unintended 의도하지 않은 consequence 결과
envision 상상하다 expansion 확장 conquer 정복하다
Mediterranean 지중해의 inhabitant 주민, 거주자
set in motion 촉발하다, 움직이게 하다
constrain 제약하다, 제한하다

👍 이것도 알면 합격!

능동태 문장의 목적어가 수동태 문장의 주어가 되므로, 목적어를 갖지 않는 자동사는 수동태가 될 수 없다.

ex An ominous set of storm clouds was appeared (→ appeared) on the horizon last week.
불길한 폭풍우 구름 떼가 저번 주 지평선 위에 나타났다.

12 독해 추론 (빈칸 완성 - 구) 난이도 ★★☆

끊어읽기 해석

Water and civilization go hand-in-hand.
물과 문명은 밀접하게 관련되어 있다

The idea of a "hydraulic civilization" argues / that water is the unifying context and justification / for many large-scale civilizations / throughout history.
'수력학의 문명'이라는 발상은 주장한다 / 물이 통합적인 배경이자 타당한 이유라는 것을 / 많은 대규모 문명에 대한 / 역사를 통틀어

For example, / the various multi-century Chinese empires survived / as long as they did / in part / by controlling floods / along the Yellow River.
예를 들어 / 여러 세기에 걸친 다양한 중국 제국은 살아남았다 / 그들이 그랬던 만큼 오래 / 부분적으로 / 홍수를 제어함으로써 / 황하를 따라

One interpretation of the hydraulic theory / is that the justification / for gathering populations / into large cities / is to manage water.
수력학 이론 중 한 가지 해석은 / 타당한 이유가 ~라는 것이다 / 인구를 모으는 것에 대한 / 대도시로 / 물을 관리하기 위해서다

Another interpretation suggests / that large water projects enable / the rise of big cities.
또 다른 해석은 시사한다 / 대규모 치수 사업이 가능하게 한다는 것을 / 대도시들의 발생을

The Romans understood / the connections between water and power, / as the Roman Empire built / a vast network of aqueducts / throughout land they controlled, / many of which remain intact.
로마인들은 이해하고 있었다 / 물과 권력의 관련성을 / 로마 제국이 건설했다는 점에서 / 송수로의 광활한 망을 / 그들이 지배하는 땅의 도처에 / 그것들(송수로)의 대부분은 온전히 남아 있다

For example, / Pont du Gard in southern France stands today / as a testament to humanity's investment / in its water infrastructure.
예를 들어 / 프랑스 남부에 있는 가르 수도교는 오늘날 세워져 있다 / 인류의 투자의 증거로서 / 그것의 물 기반 시설에 대한

Roman governors / built roads, bridges, and water systems / as a way of concentrating and strengthening / their authority.

로마의 지배자들은 / 도로, 다리, 그리고 상수도를 건설했다 / 집중하고 강화하는 방법으로서 / 그들의 권한을

해석 물과 문명은 밀접하게 관련되어 있다. '수력학의 문명'이라는 발상은 물이 역사를 통틀어 많은 대규모 문명에 대한 통합적인 배경이자 타당한 이유라고 주장한다. 예를 들어, 여러 세기에 걸친 다양한 중국 제국은 부분적으로 황하를 따라 홍수를 제어함으로써 그들이 그랬던 만큼 오래 살아남았다. 수력학 이론 중 한 가지 해석은 대도시로 인구를 모으는 것에 대한 타당한 이유가 물을 관리하기 위해서라는 것이다. 또 다른 해석은 대규모 치수 사업이 대도시들의 발생을 가능하게 한다는 것을 시사한다. 로마 제국이 그들이 지배하는 땅의 도처에 송수로의 광활한 망을 건설했다는 점에서, 로마인들은 물과 권력의 관련성을 이해하고 있었던 것이고, 그것들(송수로)의 대부분은 온전히 남아 있다. 예를 들어, 프랑스 남부에 있는 가르 수도교는 오늘날 그것(인류)의 물 기반 시설에 대한 인류의 투자의 증거로서 세워져 있다. 로마의 지배자들은 <u>그들의 권한을 집중하고 강화하는</u> 방법으로서 도로, 다리, 그리고 상수도를 건설했다.

① 젊은이들을 교육하는 데 초점을 맞추는
② 현지 시장에서 자유 무역을 금지하는
③ 그들의 권한을 집중하고 강화하는
④ 다른 나라들에 그들의 토지를 넘겨주는

해설 지문 중간에서 수력학 이론의 또 다른 해석은 대규모 치수 사업이 대도시들의 발생을 가능하게 한다는 것이라는 것을 시사한다고 하며 로마 제국이 지배하는 땅의 도처에 송수로의 광활한 망을 건설했다는 점에서 로마인들이 물과 권력의 관련성을 이해하고 있었던 것이라고 설명하고 있으므로, 빈칸에는 로마의 지배자들이 '③ 그들의 권한을 집중하고 강화하는' 방법으로서 도로, 다리, 그리고 상수도를 건설했다는 내용이 들어가야 적절하다.

어휘 civilization 문명 go hand-in-hand 밀접하게 관련되어 있다
unify 통합하다, 통일하다 justification 타당한 이유, 정당화
interpretation 해석 gather 모으다 intact 온전한
Pont du gard 가르 수도교(프랑스 남부에 있는 고대 로마의 수도교)
testament 증거 infrastructure 기반 시설
governor 지배자, 통치자 prohibit 금지하다
concentrate 집중하다 strengthen 강화하다 authority 권한
give up ~을 넘겨주다 property 토지, 소유지

13 독해 논리적 흐름 파악 (문단 순서 배열) 난이도 ★★☆

끊어읽기 해석

Ambiguity is so uncomfortable / that it can even turn / good news into bad.
모호함은 매우 불쾌해서 / 심지어 바꿀 수 있다 / 좋은 소식을 나쁜 소식으로

You go to your doctor / with a persistent stomachache.
당신은 의사에게 간다 / 계속되는 복통으로

Your doctor can't figure out / what the reason is, / so she sends you / to the lab for tests.
당신의 담당 의사는 알아내지 못한다 / 이유가 무엇인지를 / 그래서 그녀는 당신을 보낸다 / 검사를 위해 연구실로

(A) And what happens?
그리고 어떤 일이 일어날까

Your immediate relief may be replaced / by a weird sense of discomfort.
당신의 즉각적인 안도감이 대체될지도 모른다 / 이상한 불편함으로

You still don't know / what the pain was!
당신은 아직도 모른다 / 그 고통이 무엇이었는지

There's got to be an explanation / somewhere.
설명이 있어야만 한다 / 어딘가에

(B) A week later / you're called back / to hear the results.
일주일 후 / 당신은 다시 호출된다 / 결과를 듣기 위해

When you finally get into her office, / your doctor smiles / and tells you the tests were all negative.
마침내 그녀의 진료실에 들어섰을 때 / 당신의 의사는 웃는다 / 그리고 검사 결과가 모두 음성이었다고 당신에게 말한다

(C) Maybe it is cancer / and they've just missed it.
어쩌면 암일지도 모른다 / 그리고 그것들이(검사 결과) 그것을 놓쳤다

Maybe it's worse. // Surely / they should be able to find a cause.
더 나쁠 수도 있다 // 분명 / 그것들은 원인을 찾을 수 있어야만 한다

You feel frustrated / by the lack of a definitive answer.
당신은 좌절감을 느낀다 / 명확한 답이 없는 것에

해석 |모호함은 매우 불쾌해서 심지어 좋은 소식을 나쁜 소식으로 바꿀 수 있다. 당신은 계속되는 복통으로 의사에게 간다. 당신의 담당 의사는 이유가 무엇인지를 알아내지 못해서, 그녀는 검사를 위해 연구실로 당신을 보낸다.|

(B) 일주일 후 당신은 결과를 듣기 위해 다시 호출된다. 마침내 그녀의 진료실에 들어섰을 때, 당신의 의사는 웃으면서 검사 결과가 모두 음성이었다고 당신에게 말한다.
(A) 그리고 어떤 일이 일어날까? 당신의 즉각적인 안도감이 이상한 불편함으로 대체될지도 모른다. 당신은 아직도 그 고통이 무엇이었는지 모른다! 어딘가에 설명이 있어야만 한다.
(C) 어쩌면 암일지도 모르고 그것들이(검사 결과) 그것을 놓쳤을지도 모른다. 더 나쁠 수도 있다. 분명 그것들은 원인을 찾을 수 있어야만 한다. 당신은 명확한 답이 없는 것에 좌절감을 느낀다.

해설 주어진 글에서 모호함은 매우 불쾌해서 심지어 좋은 소식을 나쁜 소식으로 바꿀 수 있다고 하며 계속되는 복통으로 의사에게 갔지만 의사가 이유를 알아내지 못해 검사를 위해 연구실로 보내는 상황을 예시로 들고 있다. 이어서 (B)에서 일주일 후 결과를 듣기 위해 다시 호출되었고 의사를 만나 검사 결과가 음성이었다는 이야기를 듣는 상황을 설명한다. 뒤이어 (A)에서 그리고(And) 어떤 일이 일어날지 물어보면서 안도감이 이상한 불편함으로 대체된다고 한 뒤, (C)에서 어쩌면 암일지도 모르는 것을 검사 결과가 놓쳤을지도 모른다고 하며 당신은 명확한 답이 없는 것에 대해 좌절감을 느끼게 된다고 설명하고 있다.

어휘 ambiguity 모호함 persistent 계속되는 stomachache 복통
lab(=laboratory) 연구실 immediate 즉각적인
replace 대체하다 weird 이상한 discomfort 불편함
explanation 설명 negative 음성의 cancer 암
frustrated 좌절감을 느끼는 definitive 명확한, 결정적인

14 독해 논리적 흐름 파악 (문장 삽입) 난이도 ★☆☆

끊어읽기 해석

The effect, however, was just the reverse.
그러나, 효과는 그 반대였다

How we dress for work / has taken on a new element of choice, / and with it, new anxieties.
우리가 일할 때 어떻게 옷을 입을 것인가 하는 것은 / 새로운 선택 요소를 띠게 되었다 / 그리고 그로 인해, 새로운 불안감을 떠안게 되었다

(①) The practice of having a "dress-down day" or

"casual day," / which began to emerge / a decade or so ago, / was intended to make life easier / for employees, / to enable them to save money / and feel more relaxed / at the office.

'자유 복장으로 근무하는 날'이나 '평상복의 날'의 관행은 / 그것이 부각되기 시작했던 / 10여 년 전 / 생활을 더 편안하게 하기 위해 의도되었다 / 직원들이 / 돈을 절약할 수 있게 하도록 / 그리고 더 편안함을 느낄 수 있도록 / 사무실에서

(②) In addition to the normal workplace wardrobe, / employees had to create / a "workplace casual" wardrobe.

표준적인 직장 옷뿐만 아니라 / 직원들은 만들어 낼 필요가 있었다 / '직장 평상복' 옷을

(③) It couldn't really be the sweats and T-shirts / you wore around the house / on the weekend.

그것이 운동복이나 티셔츠였을 리는 없다 / 당신이 집안에서 입던 / 주말에

(④) It had to be a selection of clothing / that sustained a certain image / —relaxed, but also serious.

그것은 엄선된 옷이어야 했다 / 특정 이미지를 유지하는 / 편안하지만 진지하기도 한

해석 우리가 일할 때 어떻게 옷을 입을 것인가 하는 것은 새로운 선택 요소를 띠게 되었고, 그로 인해 새로운 불안감을 떠안게 되었다. 10여 년 전 부각되기 시작했던 '자유 복장으로 근무하는 날'이나 '평상복의 날'의 관행은 직원들이 돈을 절약할 수 있게 하고 사무실에서 더 편안함을 느낄 수 있도록 하여 생활을 더 편안하게 하기 위해 의도되었다. ② 그러나, 효과는 그 반대였다. 표준적인 직장 옷뿐만 아니라, 직원들은 '직장 평상복' 옷을 만들어 낼 필요가 있었다. 그것이 주말에 당신이 집안에서 입던 운동복이나 티셔츠였을 리는 없다. 그것은 편안하지만 진지하기도 한 특정 이미지를 유지하는 엄선된 옷이어야 했다.

해설 ②번 앞 문장에 10여 년 전 '자유 복장으로 근무하는 날'이나 '평상복의 날'의 관행이 직원들의 생활을 더 편안하게 하기 위해 의도되었다는 내용이 있고, ②번 뒤 문장에 표준적인 직장 옷뿐만 아니라, 직원들은 '직장 평상복' 옷을 만들어 낼 필요가 있었으며 그것은 편안하지만 진지하기도 한 특정 이미지를 유지하는 엄선된 옷이어야 했다는 처음 의도와 반대되는 내용이 있으므로 ②번 자리에 그러나(however) 효과는 그 반대였다는 주어진 문장이 들어가야 지문이 자연스럽게 연결된다.

어휘 reverse 반대 take on (특질·모습 등을) 띠다, (책임 등을) 떠맡다
anxiety 불안감, 염려 practice 관행, 관습
emerge 부각되다, 부상하다 intend 의도하다, 작정하다
wardrobe 옷, 옷장 sustain 유지하다, 지탱하다

15 문법 수 일치 난이도 ★★☆

해석 당신은 당신이 원하는 결과에 가장 적합한 연구 방법을 선택해야 한다. 당신은 수많은 사람들에게 질문하고 보고서 형식으로 완전한 분석을 할 수 있게 하는 온라인 설문을 진행할 수 있으며, 아니면 당신은 일대일로 질문을 하는 것이 더 적은 시험 선발 인원으로부터 당신이 필요한 답변을 얻기 위한 더 좋은 방법이라고 생각할 수도 있다. 당신이 어느 방법을 선택하든, 동일한 것끼리 비교해야 한다. 사람들에게 동일한 질문을 하고 답을 비교하라. 유사점과 차이점을 모두 찾아라. 양식과 추세를 찾아라. 데이터를 기록하고 분석하는 방법을 결정하는 것은 중요하다. 스스로 작성한 간단한 스프레드시트라면 기본적인 조사 데이터를 기록하는 데 아마도 충분할 것이다.

해설 ④ 주어와 동사의 수 일치 동명사(Deciding) 주어는 단수 취급하므로 복수 동사 are를 단수 동사 is로 고쳐야 한다. 참고로 주어

와 동사 사이의 수식어 거품(on ~ the data)은 동사의 수 결정에 영향을 주지 않는다.

오답 ① 관계대명사 that 선행사(the research method)가 사물이고
분석 관계절 내에서 동사 suits의 주어 역할을 하므로 주격 관계대명사 that이 올바르게 쓰였다.
② 주격 관계절의 수 일치 주격 관계절(provides ~ format)의 동사는 선행사(a survey)에 수 일치시켜야 하는데, 선행사가 단수 명사이므로 단수 동사 provides가 올바르게 쓰였다. 참고로, 해당 문장은 관계대명사 that 뒤에 주격 관계절이 접속사 and로 연결된 병치 구문이다.
③ 명사절 접속사 4: 복합관계대명사 복합관계형용사를 쓸지 의문사를 쓸지는 문맥에 따라 결정되는데, 문맥상 '당신이 어느 방식을 선택하든'이라는 의미가 되어야 자연스러우므로 명사 way를 수식하는 복합관계형용사 Whichever가 올바르게 쓰였다.

어휘 suit 적합하다 compare 비교하다 analyse[analyze] 분석하다

👍 이것도 알면 합격!

주어와 동사 사이의 수식어 거품은 동사의 수 결정에 영향을 주지 않는다는 것을 알아두자.

ex The song playing on the radio was my favorite when I was
    단수 주어   수식어 거품   단수 동사
growing up.
라디오에서 흘러나오는 그 노래는 내가 자랄 때 가장 좋아했던 노래이다.

16 독해 전체내용 파악 (요지 파악) 난이도 ★☆☆

끊어읽기 해석

Some criminal offenders may engage in illegal behavior / because they love the excitement and thrills / that crime can provide.
일부 범죄자들은 불법 행위에 관여할지도 모른다 / 흥분과 스릴을 대단히 즐기기 때문에 / 범죄가 줄 수 있는

In his highly influential work Seductions of Crime, / sociologist Jack Katz argues / that there are immediate benefits / to criminality / that "seduce" people / into a life of crime.
그의 매우 영향력 있는 작품인 『범죄의 유혹』에서 / 사회학자 Jack Katz는 주장한다 / 즉각적인 이익이 있다는 것을 / 범행들에 / 사람들을 '유혹' 하는 / 범죄의 삶으로

For some people, / shoplifting and vandalism are attractive / because getting away with crime is a thrilling demonstration / of personal competence.
일부 사람들에게 / 물건을 훔치는 것과 기물 파손은 매력적이다 / 이는 범죄를 저지르고도 처벌을 모면하는 것이 스릴 있는 증명이기 때문이다 / 개인 능력의

The need for excitement may counter / fear of apprehension and punishment.
흥분에 대한 욕구는 역행할지도 모른다 / 불안과 형벌에 대한 두려움에

In fact, / some offenders will deliberately seek out / especially risky situations / because of the added "thrill".
실제로 / 일부 범죄자들은 의도적으로 추구할 것이다 / 특히 위험한 상황을 / 더해진 '스릴'로 인해

The need for excitement is a significant predictor / of criminal choice.
흥분에 대한 욕구는 중요한 예측 변수이다 / 범죄 선택의

해석 일부 범죄자들은 범죄가 줄 수 있는 흥분과 스릴을 대단히 즐기기 때문에 불법 행위에 관여할지도 모른다. 사회학자 Jack Katz는 그

의 매우 영향력 있는 작품인 『범죄의 유혹』에서 사람들을 범죄의 삶으로 '유혹'하는 범행들에는 즉각적인 이익이 있다고 주장한다. 일부 사람들에게, 범죄를 저지르고도 처벌을 모면하는 것이 개인 능력의 스릴 있는 증명이기 때문에 물건을 훔치는 것과 기물 파손은 매력적이다. 흥분에 대한 욕구는 불안과 형벌에 대한 두려움에 역행할지도 모른다. 실제로, 일부 범죄자들은 더해진 '스릴'로 인해 특히 위험한 상황을 의도적으로 추구할 것이다. 흥분에 대한 욕구는 범죄 선택의 중요한 예측 변수이다.

해설 지문 처음에서 일부 범죄자들은 범죄가 줄 수 있는 흥분과 스릴을 대단히 즐기기 때문에 불법 행위에 관여할지도 모른다고 한 뒤, 지문 전반에 걸쳐 범죄자들이 흥분에 대한 욕구로 범죄를 저지르는 것에 대해 설명하고 있으므로, '② 범죄 행위에서 생기는 흥분과 쾌감이 범죄를 유발할 수 있다'가 이 지문의 요지이다.

어휘 criminal offender 범죄자 engage in ~에 관여하다
illegal 불법의 seduction 유혹
shoplifting 물건을 훔치는 것, 좀도둑질
get away with 처벌을 모면하다, ~을 잘 해내다
demonstration 증명, 증거 competence 능력
counter ~에 역행하다 apprehension 불안, 우려
deliberately 의도적으로 predictor 예측 변수, 예언자

17 독해 추론 (빈칸 완성 - 단어) 난이도 ★☆☆

끊어읽기 해석

In one classic study / showing the importance of attachment, / Wisconsin University psychologists Harry and Margaret Harlow investigated the responses / of young monkeys.
한 고전적인 연구에서 / 애착의 중요성을 보여주는 / 위스콘신 대학의 심리학자 Harry와 Margaret Harlow는 반응을 조사했다 / 어린 원숭이들의

The infants were separated / from their biological mothers, / and two surrogate mothers were introduced / to their cages.
새끼들은 분리되었다 / 그것들의 생모로부터 / 그리고 두 명의 대리모가 놓여졌다 / 그것들의 우리에

One, the wire mother, / consisted of a round wooden head, / a mesh of cold metal wires, and a bottle of milk / from which the baby monkey could drink.
하나는 철사 어미이다 / 둥근 나무 머리로 이루어진 / 차가운 금속 철사 그물망 그리고 우유병으로 / 새끼 원숭이가 마실 수 있는

The second mother was a foam-rubber form / wrapped in a heated terry-cloth blanket.
두 번째 어미는 스펀지 고무 형태였다 / 데워진 테리 직물 담요로 감싸진

The infant monkeys went to the wire mother / for food, / but they overwhelmingly preferred / and spent significantly more time / with the warm terry-cloth mother.
새끼 원숭이들은 철사 어미에게 갔다 / 먹을 것을 찾아 / 그렇지만 그것들은 (따뜻한 테리 직물 어미를) 압도적으로 선호했다 / 그리고 더 많은 시간을 보냈다 / 따뜻한 테리 직물 어미와

The warm terry-cloth mother / provided no food, / but did provide comfort.
따뜻한 테리 직물 어미는 / 먹이를 주지는 않았다 / 그렇지만 안락함을 주었다

해석 애착의 중요성을 보여주는 한 고전적인 연구에서, 위스콘신 대학의 심리학자 Harry와 Margaret Harlow는 어린 원숭이들의 반응을 조사했다. 새끼들은 그것들의 생모로부터 분리되었고, 두 명의 대리모가 우리에 놓여졌다. 하나는 철사 어미로, 둥근 나무 머리, 차가운 금속 철사 그물망, 그리고 새끼 원숭이가 마실 수 있는 우유병으로 이루어졌다. 두 번째 어미는 데워진 테리 직물 담요로 감

싸진 스펀지 고무 형태였다. 새끼 원숭이들은 먹을 것을 찾아 철사 어미에게 갔지만, 그것들은 (따뜻한 테리 직물 어미를) 압도적으로 선호했고 따뜻한 테리 직물 어미와 더 많은 시간을 보냈다. 따뜻한 테리 직물 어미는 음식을 제공하지는 않았지만, 안락함을 주었다.

① 일   ② 약물
③ 안락함   ④ 교육

해설 지문 전반에 걸쳐 생모로부터 분리된 새끼 원숭이들이 우유병을 가진 철사 어미보다 따뜻한 테리 직물 담요로 감싸진 스펀지 고무 형태의 어미를 압도적으로 선호했고 더 많은 시간을 보냈다고 하며 애착의 중요성을 보여주는 한 연구 결과에 대해 설명하고 있으므로, 빈칸에는 따뜻한 테리 직물 어미는 음식을 제공하지는 않았지만 '③ 안락함'을 주었다는 내용이 들어가야 적절하다.

어휘 attachment 애착 investigate 조사하다 infant 새끼, 유아
separate 분리하다 biological mother 생모 wire 철사
consist of ~으로 이루어지다 mesh 그물망
foam-rubber 스펀지 고무 wrap 감싸다
terry-cloth 테리 직물(일반적으로 타월이라고 불리는 면직물)
overwhelmingly 압도적으로 prefer 선호하다 comfort 안락함

18 문법 병치·도치·강조 구문 난이도 ★★☆

해석 나는 입양을 위해 내 친부모로부터 포기되었고, 내 인생의 첫 10년을 보육원에서 보냈다. 나는 나에게 뭔가 문제가 있다고 생각하며 몇 년을 보냈다. 만약 나의 부모님이 나를 원하지 않았다면, 누가 그러겠는가(원하겠는가)? 나는 내가 무엇을 잘못했고 왜 그렇게 많은 사람들이 나를 쫓아 보냈는지 알아내려고 노력했다. 만약에 내가 그렇게 하면(친해지면) 그들이 나를 떠날지도 모르기 때문에 나는 지금 그 누구와도 친해지지 않는다. 나는 어렸을 때 살아남기 위해 나 자신을 감정적으로 고립시켜야 했고, 여전히 내가 어렸을 때 했었던 가정을 가지고 행동한다. 나는 버림받는 것이 너무 무서워서 모험을 하지 않을 것이고 최소한의 위험도 감수하지 않을 것이다. 나는 지금 40살이지만, 아직 아이인 것처럼 느낀다.

해설 ① 병치 구문 접속사(and)로 연결된 병치 구문에서 같은 품사끼리 연결되어야 하고, 이때 동사끼리 수·시제가 일치해야 하므로 현재 시제 동사 spend를 과거 시제 동사 spent로 고쳐야 한다.

오답
분석 ② 명사절 접속사 3: 의문사 목적어가 없는 불완전한 절(I had done wrong)을 이끌며 전치사 out 뒤의 목적어 자리에 올 수 있는 명사절 접속사 what이 올바르게 쓰였다.
③ 재귀대명사 동사(isolate)의 목적어가 지칭하는 대상이 문장의 주어(I)와 동일하므로 동사 isolate의 목적어 자리에 재귀대명사 myself가 올바르게 쓰였다.
④ 부사절 접속사 2: 기타 문맥상 '나는 버림받는 것이 너무 무서워서 ~하지 않을 것이다'라는 의미가 되어야 자연스러우므로 부사절 접속사 so ~ that(매우 ~해서 -하다)가 와야 한다. 따라서 부사절 접속사 that이 올바르게 쓰였다.

어휘 release 포기하다, 방출하다 adoption 입양 orphanage 보육원
send away 쫓아 보내다 assumption 가정 deserted 버림받은
venture 모험하다

👍 이것도 알면 합격!

병치 구문에서는 같은 구조끼리 연결되어야 한다는 것을 알아두자.
ex Please set the table and arrange the decorations.
                동사구   동사구
식탁을 차리고 장식물을 배치해주세요.

19 문법 조동사

해석 음악은 일상생활에 전할 수 있는 심리 요법의 효과를 가져올 수 있다. 많은 학자들은 사람들에게 음악을 심리 요법의 동인으로 사용할 것을 제안했다. 음악 요법은 '개인의 심리적, 신체적, 인지적, 또는 사회적 기능을 높이기 위한 치료나 재활의 부가물로서의 음악의 사용'으로 널리 정의될 수 있다. 음악으로부터의 긍정적인 감정의 경험은 치료 과정을 개선해서 전통적인 인지적/행동적 방법과 일상 목표로의 이전을 강화할 수도 있다. 이것은 부분적으로는 음악과 일상적인 행동에 의해 유발되는 감정의 경험이 긍정적인 감정과 자극을 담당하는 서로 중복되는 신경학적 경로를 공유하고 있기 때문일 수도 있다.

해설 ① 조동사 should의 생략 문맥상 '많은 학자들이 ~ 제안했다'라는 의미가 되어야 자연스럽고 제안을 나타내는 동사 suggest가 주절에 나오면 종속절에 '(should +) 동사원형'의 형태가 와야 하므로 to 부정사 to use를 (should) use로 고쳐야 한다. 참고로 동사 suggest는 that절을 목적어로 취하는 3형식 동사이므로 5형식 동사와 같이 '목적어 + 목적격 보어'를 취할 수 없다.

오답분석 ② 목적어 자리 동사 enhance의 목적어 자리에 올 수 있는 것은 명사 역할을 하는 것이므로 동명사 functioning이 목적어 자리에 올바르게 쓰였다.
③ 병치 구문 접속사(and)로 연결된 병치 구문에서는 같은 구조끼리 연결되어야 하는데 and 앞에 동사구(improve ~ process)가 왔으므로 and 뒤에도 동사구(strengthen ~ goals)를 이끄는 동사 strengthen이 올바르게 쓰였다.
④ 주어와 동사의 수 일치 주어 자리에 복수 명사(emotional experiences)가 왔으므로 복수 동사 share가 올바르게 쓰였다. 참고로, 주어와 동사 사이의 수식어 거품(elicited by ~ behaviors)은 동사의 수 결정에 영향을 주지 않는다.

어휘 transfer 전하다, 이동하다
agent 동인(사물을 발동하여 일으키게 하는 원인) define 정의하다
adjunct 부가물, 부속물 rehabilitation 재활 enhance 높이다
therapeutic 치료(상)의 strengthen 강화하다
behavioral 행동적인, 행동의 partially 부분적으로
elicit 유발하다, 끌어내다 overlap 중복되다, 겹치다
neurological 신경학적인, 신경학의 pathway 경로, 길

👍 이것도 알면 **합격!**

주절에 아래와 같은 제안·의무·요청·주장을 나타내는 동사나 형용사가 나오면, 종속절에는 '(should +) 동사원형'이 와야 한다는 것을 알아두자.

동사	require 요구하다	request 요청하다
	suggest 제안하다	recommend 추천하다
	order 명령하다	insist 주장하다
	demand 요구하다	move 제의하다
형용사	necessary 필수적인	imperative 필수적인
	essential 필수적인	important 중요한

20 독해 추론 (빈칸 완성 - 단어)

끊어읽기 해석

Cultural interpretations are usually made / on the basis of prejudice / rather than measurable evidence.
문화적 해석은 대개 만들어진다 / 편견을 토대로 하여 / 측정 가능한 증거보다는

The arguments / tend to be circular.
그 주장들은 / 순환적인 경향이 있다

People are poor / because they are lazy.
사람들은 가난하다 / 그들이 게으르기 때문에

How do we "know" / they are lazy? // Because they are poor.
우리가 어떻게 '알까' / 그들이 게으르다는 것을 // 왜냐하면 그들이 가난하기 때문이다

Promoters of these interpretations / rarely understand / that low productivity results / not from laziness and lack of effort / but from lack of capital inputs / to production.
이러한 해석의 옹호자들은 / 좀처럼 이해하지 못한다 / 낮은 생산성이 온다고 / 게으름과 노력의 부족에서가 아니라 / 자본 투입의 부족에서 / 생산에 대한

African farmers are not lazy, / but they do lack / soil nutrients, tractors, feeder roads, irrigated plots, storage facilities, / and the like.
아프리카 농부들은 게으르지 않다 / 하지만 그들은 정말 부족하다 / 토양 영양분, 트랙터, 지선 도로, 관개된 토지, 저장 시설 / 같은 것들이

Stereotypes / that Africans work little / and therefore are poor / are put to rest immediately / by spending a day in a village, / where backbreaking labor by men and women is the norm.
고정관념은 / 아프리카 사람들이 일을 거의 하지 않는다는 / 그래서 가난하다는 / 즉시 잠재워진다 / 마을에서 하루를 보냄으로써 / 남성과 여성의 몹시 힘든 노동이 일반적인

해석 문화적 해석은 대개 측정 가능한 증거보다는 편견을 토대로 하여 만들어진다. 그 주장들은 순환적인 경향이 있다. 사람들은 그들이 게으르기 때문에 가난하다. 그들이 게으르다는 것을 우리가 어떻게 '알까'? 왜냐하면 그들이 가난하기 때문이다. 이러한 해석의 옹호자들은 낮은 생산성이 게으름과 노력의 부족에서가 아니라 생산에 대한 자본 투입의 부족에서 온다는 것을 좀처럼 이해하지 못한다. 아프리카 농부들은 게으르지 않지만, 그들은 토양 영양분, 트랙터, 지선 도로, 관개된 토지, 저장 시설 같은 것들이 정말 부족하다. 아프리카 사람들이 일을 거의 하지 않아서 가난하다는 고정관념은 남성과 여성의 몹시 힘든 노동이 일반적인 마을에서 하루를 보냄으로써 즉시 잠재워진다.

① 통계
② 편견
③ 겉모습
④ 환경

해설 지문 처음에 밑줄이 있는 문장에서 문화적 해석이 대개 측정 가능한 증거보다는 다른 어떤 것을 토대로 만들어진다는 내용이 있고, 지문 전반에 걸쳐 가난한 사람들이 게으르기 때문에 가난하다는 해석을 옹호하는 사람들에 대해 아프리카 농부들을 예시로 들며 그들이 일을 거의 하지 않기 때문에 가난하다는 고정관념(stereotype)은 몹시 힘든 노동이 일반적인 마을에서 하루를 보냄으로써 즉시 잠재워진다고 설명하고 있다. 따라서 빈칸에는 '② 편견'이 들어가야 적절하다.

어휘 interpretation 해석 on the basis of ~를 토대로 하여
measurable 측정 가능한 circular 순환적인 lazy 게으른
promoter 옹호자, 기획자 capital 자본 soil 토양
tractor 트랙터(견인차) irrigate 관개하다(토지에 물을 대다)
plot 토지, 작은 땅 조각 storage 저장 facility 시설
stereotype 고정관념 put to rest 잠재우다
backbreaking 몹시 힘든, 고된 statistics 통계 prejudice 편견
appearance 겉모습 circumstance 환경, 상황

끊어읽기 해석

> But the demand for food isn't elastic; / people don't eat more / just because food is cheap.
> 하지만 음식에 대한 수요는 탄력적이지 않다 / 사람들은 더 많이 먹지 않는다 / 그저 음식이 싸다고 해서

> The free market has never worked / in agriculture / and it never will.
> 자유 시장은 결코 잘 된 적이 없다 / 농업에서 / 그리고 앞으로도 그럴 것이다

> (①) The economics of a family farm are very different / than a firm's:
> 가족 농장의 경제는 매우 다르다 / 회사의 그것과

> When prices fall, / the firm can lay off people / and idle factories.
> 가격이 떨어지면 / 회사는 사람들을 해고할 수 있다 / 그리고 공장을 놀게 한다

> (②) Eventually the market finds a new balance / between supply and demand.
> 결국 시장은 새로운 균형을 찾는다 / 수요와 공급 사이의

> (③) And laying off farmers doesn't help / to reduce supply.
> 그리고 농부들을 해고하는 것은 도움이 되지 않는다 / 공급을 줄이는 데

> (④) You can fire me, / but you can't fire my land, / because some other farmer / who needs more cash flow / or thinks he's more efficient / than I am / will come in and farm it.
> 당신은 나를 해고할 수는 있다 / 하지만 당신은 나의 땅을 해고할 수는 없다 / 왜냐하면 다른 어떤 농부가 / 더 많은 현금 유동성이 필요한 / 또는 그 자신이 더 효율적이라고 생각하는 / 내가 그러한 것보다 / 와서 농사를 지을 것이기 때문이다

해석   자유 시장은 농업에서 결코 잘 된 적이 없으며 앞으로도 그럴 것이다. 가족 농장의 경제는 회사의 그것과 매우 다르다. 가격이 떨어지면, 회사는 사람들을 해고하고 공장을 놀게 할 수 있다. 결국 시장은 수요와 공급 사이의 새로운 균형을 찾는다. ③ 하지만 음식에 대한 수요는 탄력적이지 않은데, 사람들은 그저 음식이 싸다고 해서 더 많이 먹지 않는다. 그리고 농부들을 해고하는 것은 공급을 줄이는 데 도움이 되지 않는다. 당신은 나를 해고할 수는 있지만 나의 땅을 해고할 수는 없는데, 왜냐하면 더 많은 현금 유동성이 필요하거나 내가 그러한 것보다 그 자신이 더 효율적이라고 생각하는 다른 어떤 농부가 와서 농사를 지을 것이기 때문이다.

해설   지문 처음에 농업에서는 자유 시장이 잘 된 적이 없다고 하며 가족 농장과 회사의 경제가 다르다는 내용이 있다. ③번 앞부분에 회사는 가격이 떨어지더라도 해고를 하거나 공장을 멈춰서 시장이 수요와 공급 사이의 새로운 균형을 찾는다는 내용이 있고, ③번 뒤 문장에 그리고(And) 농부들을 해고하는 것은 공급을 줄이는 데 도움이 되지 않는다는 내용이 있으므로, ③번 자리에 하지만(But) 음식에 대한 수요는 탄력적이지 않다고 하며 자유 시장이 농업에서 실패하는 이유에 대한 주어진 문장이 들어가야 지문이 자연스럽게 연결된다.

어휘   demand 수요   agriculture 농업   firm 회사   lay off 해고하다   idle (노동자 등을) 놀게 하다   supply 수요   reduce 줄이다   cash flow 현금 유동성   efficient 효율적인

끊어읽기 해석

> Daily training creates special nutritional needs / for an athlete, / particularly the elite athlete / whose training commitment is almost a fulltime job.
> 매일의 훈련은 특별한 영양적 필요를 만들어낸다 / 운동선수에게 / 특히 선발된 운동선수에게 / 훈련에 전념하는 것이 거의 전업인

> But even recreational sport will create nutritional challenges.
> 하지만 오락적인 스포츠조차도 영양 문제를 일으킬 것이다

> And whatever your level of involvement in sport, / you must meet these challenges / if you're to achieve the maximum return / from training.
> 그리고 스포츠에 대한 당신의 관여 수준이 어느 정도이든 / 당신은 이러한 도전들을 반드시 잘 대처해야 한다 / 만약 당신이 최대한의 이익을 얻고자 한다면 / 훈련으로부터

> Without sound eating, / much of the purpose of your training might be lost.
> 건강한 식사 없이는 / 당신 훈련 목적의 상당 부분을 잃게 될 수도 있다

> In the worst-case scenario, / dietary problems and deficiencies / may directly impair / training performance.
> 최악의 경우 / 식습관 문제와 영양 부족은 / 직접적으로 손상시킬 수도 있다 / 훈련 성과를

> In other situations, / you might improve, / but at a rate / that is below your potential / or slower than your competitors.
> 다른 상황에서 / 당신은 향상될 수도 있다 / 하지만 속도로 / 당신의 잠재력보다 낮은 / 또는 당신의 경쟁자보다 느린

> However, / on the positive side, / with the right everyday eating plan / your commitment to training will be fully rewarded.
> 그러나 / 긍정적인 측면에서 / 매일 올바른 식사 계획과 함께 / 훈련에 대한 당신의 전념은 충분히 보상받을 것이다

해석   매일의 훈련은 운동선수, 특히 훈련에 전념하는 것이 거의 전업인 선발된 운동선수에게 특별한 영양적 필요를 만들어낸다. 하지만 오락적인 스포츠조차도 영양 문제를 일으킬 것이다. 그리고 스포츠에 대한 당신의 관여 수준이 어느 정도이든, 만약 당신이 훈련으로부터 최대한의 이익을 얻고자 한다면 당신은 이러한 문제를 반드시 잘 대처해야 한다. 건강한 식사 없이는, 당신의 훈련 목적의 상당 부분을 잃게 될 수 있다. 최악의 경우, 식습관 문제와 영양 부족은 훈련 성과를 직접적으로 손상시킬 수 있다. 다른 상황에서, 당신은 실력이 향상될 수도 있지만, 당신의 잠재력보다 낮거나 당신의 경쟁자보다 느린 속도로 향상될 수도 있다. 하지만, 긍정적인 측면에서, 매일 올바른 식사 계획과 함께 훈련에 대한 당신의 전념은 충분히 보상받을 것이다.

① 신체의 유연성을 향상시키는 방법
② 운동에서 잘 먹는 것의 중요성
③ 과도한 식사로 인해 발생하는 건강 문제
④ 지속적인 훈련을 통한 기술 향상

해설   지문 전반에 걸쳐 운동선수뿐만 아니라 오락적인 스포츠를 하는 경우에도 특별한 영양적 필요가 발생한다고 하며 건강한 식사 없이는 훈련 목적의 상당 부분을 잃게 될 수 있고 식습관 문제와 영양 부족은 훈련 성과를 직접적으로 손상시킬 수 있다고 설명하고 있다. 또한, 지문 마지막에서 매일 올바른 식사 계획을 하는 것의 중요성에 대해 언급하고 있다. 따라서 '② 운동에서 잘 먹는 것의 중요성'이 이 글의 주제이다.

어휘   nutritional 영양적인   athlete 운동선수   elite 선발의   commitment 전념, 헌신   recreational 오락적인

involvement 관여, 몰두 **sound** 건강한; 소리
dietary 식습관의, 음식물의 **deficiency** 영양 부족, 결함
impair 손상시키다, 해치다 **rate** 속도, 비율 **potential** 잠재력
reward 보상하다

23 독해 전체내용 파악 (주제 파악) 난이도 ★☆☆

끊어읽기 해석

A very well-respected art historian / called Ernst Gombrich /
wrote about something / called "the beholder's share".
매우 존경받는 미술사가는 / 에른스트 곰브리치라는 이름의 / 무언가에 대
해 썼다 / '관람자의 몫'이라고 불렸던

It was Gombrich's belief / that a viewer "completed" the
artwork, / that part of an artwork's meaning came / from
the person viewing it.
그것은 곰브리치의 믿음이었다 / 보는 사람이 미술작품을 '완성'한다는 /
미술작품의 의미 중 일부는 나온다는 / 그것을 관찰하는 사람으로부터

So you see— / there really are no wrong answers / as it is
you, / as the viewer / who is completing the artwork.
알다시피 / 오답은 정말로 없다 / 당신이기 때문에 / 관찰자로서의 / 미술
작품을 완성하는

If you're looking at art / in a gallery, / read the wall text / at
the side of the artwork.
만약 당신이 미술품을 보고 있다면 / 갤러리에서 / 벽의 글을 읽어 보아라 /
미술작품의 측면에 있는

If staff are present, / ask questions. // Ask your fellow visitors /
what they think.
만약 직원이 있다면 / 질문을 하라 // 동행한 방문객들에게 물어보아라 /
어떻게 생각하는지

Asking questions is the key / to understanding more / —and
that goes for anything in life— / not just art.
질문을 하는 것은 비결이다 / 더 많은 것을 이해하는 / 인생의 어떤 것이라
도 해당되는 / 미술(을 이해하는 것)뿐만이 아니라

But above all, / have confidence / in front of an artwork.
하지만 무엇보다도 / 자신감을 가져라 / 미술작품 앞에서

If you are contemplating an artwork, / then you are the
intended viewer / and what you think matters.
만약 당신이 미술작품을 감상하고 있다면 / 당신은 의도된 관찰자이며 /
당신의 생각이 어떤지가 중요하다

You are the only critic / that counts.
오직 당신만이 비평가이다 / 중요한

해석 에른스트 곰브리치라는 이름의 매우 존경받는 미술사가는 '관람자
의 몫'이라고 불렸던 무언가에 대해 썼다. 그것은 보는 사람이 미술
작품을 '완성'한다는, 즉 미술작품의 의미 중 일부는 그것을 관찰
하는 사람으로부터 나온다는 곰브리치의 믿음이었다. 알다시피 미
술작품을 완성하는 것은 관찰자로서의 당신이기 때문에 오답은 정
말로 없다. 만약 당신이 갤러리에서 미술품을 보고 있다면, 미술작
품의 측면에 있는 벽의 글을 읽어 보아라. 만약 직원이 있다면, 질
문을 하라. 동행한 방문객들에게 어떻게 생각하는지 물어보아라.
질문을 하는 것은 미술(을 이해하는 것)뿐만이 아니라 인생의 어떤
것에라도 해당되는, 더 많은 것을 이해하는 비결이다. 하지만 무엇
보다도, 미술작품 앞에서 자신감을 가져라. 만약 당신이 미술작품
을 감상하고 있다면, 당신은 의도된 관찰자이며 당신의 생각이 어
떤지가 중요하다. 오직 당신만이 중요한 비평가이다.

해설 지문 처음에서 존경받는 미술사가인 곰브리치가 미술작품의 의미
중 일부는 그것을 관찰하는 사람으로부터 나온다는 믿음을 가졌
다고 했고, 지문 마지막에서 만약 미술작품을 감상하고 있다면 당
신은 의도된 관찰자이며, 당신의 생각이 어떤지가 중요하다고 언

급하면서 오직 당신만이 중요한 비평가라고 했으므로, '③ 미술작
품은 감상하는 사람으로 인하여 비로소 완성된다'가 이 글의 주제
이다.

어휘 well-respected 존경받는 **beholder** 관람자, 구경꾼
share 몫, 지분 **fellow** 동행하는, 동료의
contemplate 감상하다, 곰곰이 생각하다 **intend** 의도하다, 작정하다
matter 중요하다 **critic** 비평가 **count** 중요하다

24 독해 세부내용 파악 (내용 불일치 파악) 난이도 ★★☆

끊어읽기 해석

Argentina is the world's eighth largest country, / comprising
almost the entire southern half / of South America.
아르헨티나는 세계에서 여덟 번째로 큰 나라이다 / 거의 남쪽 전체를 차지
하는 / 남아메리카의

Colonization by Spain began / in the early 1500s, / but in
1816 Jose de San Martin led the movement / for Argentine
independence.
스페인에 의한 식민지화는 시작되었다 / 1500년대 초반에 / 하지만 1816년
에 호세 데 산 마르틴이 운동을 이끌었다 / 아르헨티나 독립을 위한

The culture of Argentina / has been greatly influenced / by
the massive European migration / in the late nineteenth and
early twentieth centuries, / primarily from Spain and Italy.
아르헨티나의 문화는 / 크게 영향을 받아 왔다 / 유럽인들의 대규모 이주
로 인해 / 19세기 후반과 20세기 초에 있었던 / 주로 스페인과 이탈리아로
부터의

The majority of people are at least nominally Catholic, / and
the country has the largest Jewish population (about 300,000)
/ in South America.
대다수의 사람들은 적어도 명목상으로는 가톨릭 신자이다 / 그리고 그 나라
는 가장 많은 유대인 인구(약 30만 명)를 가지고 있다 / 남아메리카에서

From 1880 to 1930, / thanks to its agricultural development, /
Argentina was one of the world's top ten wealthiest nations.
1880년부터 1930년까지 / 농업 개발 덕분에 / 아르헨티나는 세계에서 가
장 부유한 10개 국가 중 하나였다

해석 아르헨티나는 남아메리카의 거의 남쪽 전체를 차지하는 세계에서
여덟 번째로 큰 나라이다. 스페인에 의한 식민지화는 1500년대 초
반에 시작되었지만, 1816년에 호세 데 산 마르틴이 아르헨티나 독
립을 위한 운동을 이끌었다. 아르헨티나의 문화는 19세기 후반과
20세기 초에 있었던 주로 스페인과 이탈리아로부터의 유럽인들의
대규모 이주로 인해 크게 영향을 받아 왔다. 대다수의 사람들은 적
어도 명목상으로는 가톨릭 신자이고, 그 나라는 남아메리카에서
가장 많은 유대인 인구(약 30만 명)를 가지고 있다. 1880년부터
1930년까지, 농업 개발 덕분에, 아르헨티나는 세계에서 가장 부유
한 10개 국가 중 하나였다.

해설 지문 중간에서 아르헨티나의 문화는 19세기 후반과 20세기 초에
있었던 주로 스페인과 이탈리아로부터의 유럽인들의 대규모 이주
로 인해 크게 영향을 받아 왔다고 했으므로, '② 북미 출신 이주민
들이 그 문화에 많은 영향을 끼쳤다'는 것은 지문의 내용과 일치
하지 않는다.

어휘 comprise 차지하다, 구성하다 **entire** 전체의, 완전한
colonization 식민지화 **massive** 대규모의, 대량의
migration 이주, 이동 **primarily** 주로 **nominally** 명목상으로
Jewish 유대인인 **agricultural** 농업의

끊어읽기 해석

Sonja Henie is famous / for her skill into a career / as one of the world's most famous figure skaters / —in the rink and on the screen.
소냐 헤니는 유명하다 / 경력에서 그녀의 기술로 / 세계에서 가장 유명한 피겨 스케이팅 선수 중 한 명으로서 / 스케이트장과 스크린에서

Henie, winner of three Olympic gold medals / and a Norwegian and European champion, / invented a thrillingly theatrical and athletic style of figure skating.
올림픽 금메달 3관왕인 헤니는 / 그리고 노르웨이와 유럽 챔피언인 / 황홀하게 극적이며 활발한 스타일의 피겨 스케이팅을 만들어냈다

She introduced / short skirts, white skates, and attractive moves.
그녀는 도입했다 / 짧은 치마, 하얀 스케이트와 매력적인 동작들을

Her spectacular spins and jumps raised the bar / for all competitors.
그녀의 화려한 스핀과 점프는 기대치를 높였다 / 모든 경쟁자들에 대한

In 1936, / Twentieth-Century Fox signed her / to star in One in a Million, / and she soon became / one of Hollywood's leading actresses.
1936년에 / 20세기 폭스는 그녀와 계약했다 / 「One in a Million」에 출연시키기로 / 그리고 그녀는 곧 되었다 / 할리우드의 주연 여배우들 중 한 명이

In 1941, / the movie 'Sun Valley Serenade' received three Academy Award nominations / which she played as an actress.
1941년에 / 영화 「Sun Valley Serenade」는 아카데미상 후보에 세 번 올랐다 / 그녀가 여배우로 연기한

Although the rest of Henie's films were less acclaimed, / she triggered a popular surge / in ice skating.
비록 헤니의 나머지 영화들은 덜 칭송받았지만 / 그녀는 대중적인 급증을 일으켰다 / 아이스 스케이팅의

In 1938, / she launched extravagant touring shows / called Hollywood Ice Revues.
1938년에 / 사치스러운 투어 쇼를 시작했다 / 'Hollywood Ice Revues'라고 불린

Her many ventures made her a fortune, / but her greatest legacy was inspiring little girls / to skate.
그녀의 많은 모험들은 그녀가 부자가 되게 했다 / 하지만 그녀의 가장 큰 유산은 어린 소녀들에게 영감을 준 것이었다 / 스케이트를 타도록

해석 소냐 헤니는 세계에서 가장 유명한 피겨 스케이팅 선수 중 한 명으로서 스케이트장과 스크린에서의 경력에서 그녀의 기술로 유명하다. 올림픽 금메달 3관왕이자 노르웨이와 유럽 챔피언인 헤니는, 황홀하게 극적이며 활발한 스타일의 피겨 스케이팅을 만들어냈다. 그녀는 짧은 치마, 하얀 스케이트와 매력적인 동작들을 도입했다. 그녀의 화려한 스핀과 점프는 모든 경쟁자들에 대한 기대치를 높였다. 1936년에, 20세기 폭스는 그녀를 「One in a Million」에 출연시키기로 계약했고, 그녀는 곧 할리우드의 주연 여배우들 중 한 명이 되었다. 1941년에, 그녀가 여배우로 연기한 영화 「Sun Valley Serenade」는 아카데미상 후보에 세 번 올랐다. 비록 헤니의 나머지 영화들은 덜 칭송받았지만, 그녀는 아이스 스케이팅의 대중적인 급증을 일으켰다. 1938년에, 그녀는 'Hollywood Ice Revues'라고 불린 사치스러운 투어 쇼를 시작했다. 그녀의 많은 모험들은 그녀가 부자가 되게 했지만, 그녀의 가장 큰 유산은 어린 소녀들에게 스케이트를 타도록 영감을 준 것이었다.

해설 지문 뒷부분에서 1941년에 그녀가 여배우로 연기한 영화 「Sun Valley Serenade」는 아카데미상 후보에 세 번 올랐다고 했으므로, '③ 출연한 영화가 1941년에 영화제에서 3개 부문에 수상했다'는 것은 지문의 내용과 일치하지 않는다.

어휘 rink 스케이트장   invent 만들어내다, 발명하다   theatrical 극적인   athletic 활발한   spectacular 화려한, 장관의   raise the bar 기대치를 높이다   competitor 경쟁자   nomination 후보   acclaim 칭송하다   trigger 일으키다   surge 급증, 쇄도   launch 시작하다, 개시하다   extravagant 사치스러운, 낭비하는   make a fortune 부자가 되다, 재산을 모으다   legacy 유산   inspire 영감을 주다

gosi.Hackers.com

국회직 9급 출제 경향

1. 영역별 출제 문항 수 (2021~2023)

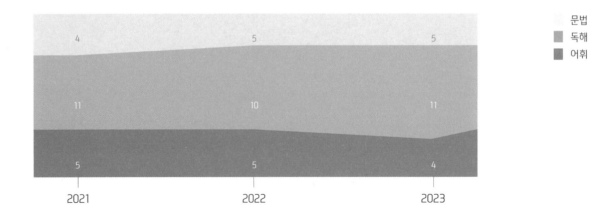

지난 3년간 영역별 출제 문항 수는 거의 동일한 편입니다. **문법** 영역은 4~5문항, **독해** 영역은 10~11문항, **어휘** 영역은 4~5문항 수준으로 출제되었습니다.

Part 5
국회직 9급

2. 영역별 최근 출제 경향 및 학습 방법

문법	**밑줄 친 부분 중 옳지 않은 것을 고르는 유형과 빈칸에 적절한 것 고르기 유형의 문제 출제** 밑줄 친 부분 중 옳지 않은 것을 고르는 유형이 2~3문항씩 꾸준히 출제되었고, 2022년과 2023년에는 빈칸에 적절한 것 고르기 유형의 문제도 출제되어, 문제 유형이 다양해지는 추세입니다. ▶ 따라서 빈출 포인트에 유의하여 밑줄을 확인하면서 오답 보기를 소거하고, 문장 전체의 구조를 파악한 후 빈칸이 문장 내에서 하는 역할을 확인하여 정답을 고르는 연습을 해야 합니다. [빈출 포인트] 관계절(5문항) | 시제(5문항) | 수 일치(5문항) | 비교 구문(5문항)
독해	**추론 유형 중심의 문제 출제** 최근 3년간 독해 문제 대다수를 빈칸 완성(추론) 유형 중심의 문제가 차지하고 있으며, 2023년 시험에도 독해 문제 10문항 중 빈칸 완성(추론) 유형이 5문항 출제되었습니다. ▶ 따라서 빈칸에 필요한 정보를 파악하고, 문맥을 통해 정답을 고르는 연습을 하는 것이 좋습니다.
어휘	**유의어 찾기 문제와 고난도 어휘 출제** 2023년 시험에서는 유의어 찾기 유형이 3문항, 빈칸에 들어갈 어휘 고르기 유형이 1문항 출제되었으며, resilience (회복력), flippancy(경솔한 언행) 등의 고난도 어휘가 출제되었습니다. ▶ 따라서 유의어를 포함한 폭넓은 어휘 학습을 해야 하며, 고난도 어휘까지 꼼꼼히 암기하는 것이 좋습니다.

정답

p.188

01	② 어휘 - 어휘 & 표현	11	③ 독해 - 세부내용 파악
02	① 어휘 - 어휘 & 표현	12	⑤ 독해 - 추론
03	① 어휘 - 어휘 & 표현	13	④ 문법 - 분사
04	③ 문법 - 시제&능동태·수동태	14	③ 독해 - 추론
05	④ 문법 - 전치사	15	② 어휘 - 어휘 & 표현
06	④ 문법 - 주어/동사/목적어·보어/수식어&관계절	16	④ 독해 - 전체내용 파악
07	③ 독해 - 전체내용 파악	17	② 독해 - 추론
08	② 독해 - 논리적 흐름 파악	18	③ 독해 - 추론
09	⑤ 독해 - 세부내용 파악	19	⑤ 독해 - 세부내용 파악
10	④ 문법 - 능동태·수동태&전치사	20	② 독해 - 추론

· 자신이 취약한 영역은 '공무원 영어, 이렇게 출제된다!'(문제집 p.8)를 통해 다시 한번 확인하고 학습하시기 바랍니다.

취약영역 분석표

영역	세부 유형	문항 수	소계
어휘	어휘&표현	4	/4
문법	시제&능동태·수동태	1	/5
	전치사	1	
	주어·동사/목적어·보어/수식어&관계절	1	
	능동태·수동태&전치사	1	
	분사	1	
독해	전체내용 파악	2	/11
	세부내용 파악	3	
	추론	5	
	논리적 흐름 파악	1	
총계			/20

---

01 어휘 어휘&표현 resilience = elasticity   난이도 ★★☆

해석 이 앱은 사용자가 그들의 심장 리듬과 정신 건강을 조절하여 스트레스 감소, 증진된 회복력, 더 나은 전반적인 정서적 건강을 특징으로 하는 '일관성' 상태를 달성할 수 있게 고안되었다.

① 자비심　　　　　② 탄력성
③ 억압　　　　　　④ 증진
⑤ 경험

어휘 regulate 조절하다 achieve 달성하다, 성취하다
coherence 일관성 resilience 회복력 overall 전반적인
benevolence 자비심, 선의 elasticity 탄력성
suppression 억압, 억제

👍 이것도 알면 **합격!**

resilience(회복력)의 유의어
= fortitude, perseverance

02 어휘 어휘&표현 inevitably = necessarily   난이도 ★★☆

해석 수요가 반드시 활발하게 반등하며, 향후 브렌트유와 서부 텍사스산 중질유의 가격을 상승시킬 것이라고 생각하는 것은 타당하다.

① 반드시　　　　　② 상당히
③ 기적적으로　　　④ 완전히
⑤ 엄청나게

어휘 demand 수요 rebound 반등하다, 제자리로 돌아오다
briskly 활발하게 Brent (oil) 브렌트유(유럽과 아프리카 지역에서 거래되는 원유 가격을 결정하는 기준 원유)
WTI(West Texas Intermediate) 서부 텍사스산 중질유(미국산 원유의 표준 유종) substantially 상당히 utterly 완전히

👍 이것도 알면 **합격!**

inevitably(반드시)의 유의어
= unavoidably, naturally

03 어휘 어휘&표현 flippancy = disrespect   난이도 ★★☆

해석 2학년 학생들의 경솔한 언행은 임시 교사가 참을 수 있는 것 이상에 가까웠다.

① 실례되는 말　　　② 유머가 없음
③ 심각함　　　　　④ 봉급
⑤ 가장자리

어휘 flippancy 경솔한 언행, 경박
substitute teacher 임시 교사, 대체 교사 stand 참다, 견디다
disrespect 실례되는 말, 무례 stipend 봉급, 장학금
verge 가장자리

👍 이것도 알면 **합격!**

flippancy(경솔한 언행)의 유의어
= irreverence, frivolousness, impertinence

04 문법 시제&능동태·수동태   난이도 ★☆☆

해석 지역의 기업 지도자들이 조직하고 후원하는 모금 캠페인인 '다정한 이웃'은 지난 일요일에 칼라마주 병원을 위한 첫 번째 자선 행사를 시작했다. 칼라마주 컨벤션 센터에서 열린 이 행사는 800명이 넘는 후원자들의 활기찬 군중을 끌어모았다.

해설 ③ 과거 시제 | 능동태·수동태 구별 특정 과거 시점을 나타내는 표

현(this past Sunday)이 왔고, 주어(Kind neighbors)와 동사가 ''다정한 이웃'이 자선 행사를 시작했다'라는 의미의 능동 관계이므로, 과거 시제 능동태 jump-started를 써야 한다.

어휘 fund-raising 모금, 자금 조달 sponsor 후원하다
corporate 기업의 jump-start 시작하다

👍 이것도 알면 **합격!**

능동태 문장의 목적어가 수동태 문장의 주어가 되므로, 목적어를 취하지 않는 자동사는 수동태로 쓸 수 없다는 것을 알아두자.

(ex) Only three cookies ~~are remained~~ (→ remain) in the jar.
세 개의 쿠키만이 병 안에 남아있다.

05 문법 전치사   난이도 ★★☆

해석 17세기와 18세기는 공공 재정의 현대로의 전환이었다. 처음에는 영국과 네덜란드에서 그리고 나서 그 밖의 다른 곳에서, 투자자들은 주권자의 자의적인 행동으로부터 보호를 확보했다. 그들은 주의 재정 정책에 대해 조언하고 동의하기 위해 채권자들이 대표되는 입법부와 의회를 설립했다. 견제와 균형이 마련되면서, 금리는 내려갔고, 대출은 더 쉬워졌다. 이러한 추가적인 재정 및 행정 자원의 획득은 더 큰 영토의 형성을 가능하게 했고, 이는 현대 국가 시스템의 출현을 이끌었다. 공공부채는 민족 국가의 출현과 빈 조약 이후 19세기에 국가 간 분쟁 사건의 감소에 상당한 역할을 했다. 공공부채 시장을 일찍부터 발전시킨 두 나라인 영국과 네덜란드가 이 과정의 선두에 있었던 것은 우연이 아니다.

해설 ④ 전치사 2: 시점 문맥상 '빈 조약 이후'라는 의미가 되어야 자연스럽고, 문장에 동사(played)가 이미 쓰였으므로 과거분사 followed를 '~ 후에'라는 의미를 갖는 전치사 following으로 고쳐야 한다.

오답
분석
① 전치사 + 관계대명사 관계사 뒤에 완전한 절(creditors were represented)이 왔으므로 '전치사 + 관계대명사' 형태가 올 수 있다. '전치사 + 관계대명사'에서 전치사는 선행사 또는 관계절의 동사에 따라 결정되는데, 문맥상 '입법부와 의회에서 채권자들이 대표되다'라는 의미가 되어야 자연스러우므로 전치사 in(~에서)이 관계대명사 which 앞에 온 in which가 올바르게 쓰였다.
② 분사구문의 관용 표현 문맥상 '견제와 균형이 마련되면서'라는 의미가 되어야 하는데 이유를 나타낼 때는 분사구문 관용 표현인 'with + 명사 + 분사'로 나타낼 수 있고, 분사구문에서 being은 생략될 수 있으므로, '명사(checks and balances) + 분사(being)' 앞에 With가 올바르게 쓰였다. 참고로, in place는 형용사 역할을 하는 전치사구로, being의 보어 자리에 올바르게 쓰였다.
③ 분사구문의 형태 | 자동사 주절의 주어(Acquisition ~ resources)와 동사가 '획득이 이끌었다'라는 의미의 능동 관계이므로 현재분사가 와야 하고, 자동사 lead(이끌다)는 전치사 to와 함께 쓰여 '~을 이끌다'라는 의미를 나타내므로 leading to가 올바르게 쓰였다.
⑤ 가짜 주어 구문 that절(that ~ this process)과 같이 긴 주어가 오면 진짜 주어인 that 절을 맨 뒤로 보내고 가주어 it이 주어 자리에 대신해서 쓰이므로 진짜 주어 자리에 that절을 이끄는 that이 올바르게 쓰였다.

어휘 transition 전환, 변환 investor 투자자 secure 확보하다
arbitrary 자의적인, 임의의 sovereign 주권자; 주권의, 독립의
establish 설립하다, 확립하다 legislature 입법부
parliament 의회, 국회 creditor 채권자 consent 동의하다

fiscal 재정의 check and balance 견제와 균형
interest rate 금리 borrowing 대출, 차용
acquisition 획득, 습득 administrative 행정의
formation 형성, 구성 territory 영토 emergence 출현
debt 부채 substantial 상당한, 중대한 advent 출현, 도래
nation-state 민족 국가 interstate 국가 간
coincidence 우연의 일치 vanguard 선두, 선봉

👍 이것도 알면 **합격!**

분사구문 관용 표현을 추가로 알아두자.

- according to ~에 따르면
- generally speaking 일반적으로 말하면
- providing/provided (that) 만일 ~이라면
- depending on ~에 따라
- considering ~을 고려해 보면
- supposing/suppose (that) 만일 ~이라면
- concerning ~에 관하여
- granting/granted (that) 설사 ~이라 하더라도

06 문법 주어·동사/목적어·보어/수식어&관계절   난이도 ★★☆

해석 유기 분자들은 30억 년 이상 전에 물이 많은 호수였을지도 모르는 넓은 지역인 화성의 게일 분화구에서 발견되었다. NASA의 핵동력 탐사차인 '큐리오시티'는 그 지역으로부터 추출된 암석들에서 분자의 흔적들과 마주쳤다. 그 암석들은 또한 황을 함유하고 있는데, 과학자들은 그것(황)이 그 암석들이 행성의 표면에 있는 혹독한 방사능에 노출되었을 때도 그 유기물들을 보존하는 데 도움을 준다고 추측한다. 과학자들은 분자들이 살아있지 않은 과정에 의해 형성되었을 수도 있기 때문에 이러한 유기 분자의 존재가 화성의 고대 생명체에 대한 충분한 증거가 아니라고 신속히 표명한다. 하지만 그것은 여전히 가장 놀라운 발견 중 하나이다.

해설 ④ 동사 자리 | 주격 관계절의 수 일치 동사 자리에 '-ing'의 형태는 올 수 없고, 주격 관계절(which ~ the planet)의 선행사가 단수 명사(sulfur)이므로 현재분사 helping을 단수 동사 helps로 고쳐야 한다.

오답
분석
① 관계대명사 선행사 a large area가 사물이고 관계절 내에서 동사 may have been의 주어 역할을 하므로 주격 관계대명사 that이 올바르게 쓰였다.
② 현재분사 vs. 과거분사 수식받는 명사 rocks와 분사가 '암석들이 추출되다'라는 의미의 수동 관계이므로 과거분사 extracted가 올바르게 쓰였다.
③ 관계대명사 선행사 sulfur가 사물이고, 관계절 내에서 동사 helps의 주어 역할을 하므로 주격 관계대명사 which가 올바르게 쓰였다. 참고로, 계속적 용법으로 쓰인 관계절에는 관계대명사 that이 올 수 없다.
⑤ 부사절 접속사 2: 이유 문맥상 '분자들이 형성되었을 수도 있기 때문에'라는 의미가 되어야 자연스러우므로 이유를 나타내는 부사절 접속사 as(~이기 때문에)가 올바르게 쓰였다.

어휘 organic 유기적인, 유기체의 molecule 분자 watery 물이 많은
rover 탐사차, 탐사선 encounter 마주치다, 만나다 trace 흔적
extract 추출하다 contain 함유하다, 포함하다 sulfur (유)황
speculate 추측하다 preserve 보존하다 expose 노출하다
radiation 방사능 presence 존재 sufficient 충분한
evidence 증거 ancient 고대의 astonishing 놀라운

07 독해 전체내용 파악 (요지 파악) 난이도 ★★☆

끊어읽기 해석

Maps are imperfect projections / of a three-dimensional globe / onto a two-dimensional surface.
지도는 불완전하게 투사하는 것이다 / 3차원의 지구를 / 2차원의 표면에

Similarly, / a mapmaker superimposes / his own point of view / upon the world he is visualizing.
비슷하게 / 지도 제작자는 겹쳐 놓는다 / 그의 관점을 / 자신이 시각화하고 있는 세계에

What he presents / may seemingly appear objective, / but / it is to a considerable extent / a product of his own cultural and political proclivities / —and even of his imagination.
그가 제시하는 것은 / 겉보기에는 객관적으로 보일지도 모른다 / 하지만 / 그것은 상당한 정도는 / 그 자신의 문화적, 정치적 성향의 산물이다 / 그리고 심지어 그의 상상력의 (산물이다)

The cartographer's projection / of the outer world / is therefore dependent / on his own inner psychological state / as his maps are based / on an "act of seeing" rather than on "what was seen."
지도 제작자의 투사는 / 외부 세계에 대한 / 그러므로 의존한다 / 그 자신의 내면 심리 상태에 / 그의 지도가 기초하기 때문에 / '보는 행위'에 / '보였던 것'보다

Geographical maps reflect / perceptions of space / that are socially conditioned, / and / they are basically mental.
지리적 지도는 반영한다 / 공간에 대한 인식을 / 사회적으로 조정된 / 그리고 / 그것들은 기본적으로 관념적이다

They are "mediators" / between a person's inner world and the physical world, / and / they "construct" the world / rather than "reproduce" it.
그것들은 '매개자'이다 / 한 사람의 내면 세계와 물리적 세계 사이의 / 그리고 / 그것들은 세계를 '건설한다' / 그것을 '재생산하기'보다는

People tend to see / what they describe, / rather than vice versa.
사람들은 보는 경향이 있다 / 그들이 묘사하는 것을 / 반대의 경우보다는

Conceptual categories, / such as continents or oceans, / emanate from the cartographer's intellect / and are then applied to his maps / just as constellations are formulated / to provide a systematic vision / of the skies.
개념상의 범주들은 / 대륙이나 해양과 같은 / 지도 제작자의 지성에서 나온 것이다 / 그리고 그의 지도에 적용된다 / 마치 별자리들이 형성된 것처럼 / 체계적인 시각을 제공하기 위해 / 하늘에 대한

해석　지도는 2차원의 표면에 3차원의 지구를 불완전하게 투사하는 것이다. 비슷하게, 지도 제작자는 자신이 시각화하고 있는 세계에 자신의 관점을 겹쳐 놓는다. 그가 제시하는 것은 겉보기에는 객관적으로 보일지도 모르지만, 상당한 정도는 그 자신의 문화적, 정치적 성향과 심지어 그의 상상력의 산물이다. 그러므로 지도 제작자의 외부 세계에 대한 투사는 그의 지도가 '보였던 것'보다 '보는 행위'에 기초하기 때문에 그 자신의 내면 심리 상태에 의존한다. 지리적 지도는 사회적으로 조정된 공간에 대한 인식을 반영하고, 그것들은 기본적으로 관념적이다. 그것들은 한 사람의 내면 세계와 물리적 세계 사이의 '매개자'이고, 그것들은 세계를 '재생산하기'보다는 '건설한다'. 사람들은 반대의 경우(그들이 묘사하는 것을 보지 않

는 경우)보다는 그들이 묘사하는 것을 보는 경향이 있다. 대륙이나 해양과 같은 개념상의 범주들은 지도 제작자의 지성에서 나온 것이고, 마치 별자리들이 하늘에 대한 체계적인 시각을 제공하기 위해 형성된 것처럼 그의 지도에 적용된다.

해설　지문 중간에서 지도 제작자가 제시하는 것은 겉보기에는 객관적으로 보일지도 모르지만, 상당한 정도는 그 자신의 문화적, 정치적 성향과 심지어 그의 상상력의 산물이라고 설명하고 있으므로, '③ 지도는 제작자의 문화적·정치적 성향과 상상력의 산물이다'가 이 글의 요지이다.

어휘　imperfect 불완전한　projection 투사, 전망　dimensional 차원의
globe 지구, 세계　superimpose 겹쳐 놓다, 포개놓다
point of view 관점　visualize 시각화하다　objective 객관적인
considerable 상당한　extent 정도, 범위　proclivity 성향, 기질
cartographer 지도 제작자　state 상태　geographical 지리적인
perception 인식, 지각　condition 조정하다, 조절하다
mental 관념적인, 정신의　mediator 매개자, 중재인
construct 건설하다, 구성하다　reproduce 재생산하다
vice versa 반대로, 반대의 경우도 마찬가지
conceptual 개념상의, 개념의　continent 대륙
emanate 나오다, 발산하다　intellect 지성　constellation 별자리
formulate 형성하다, 만들어내다　systematic 체계적인

08 독해 논리적 흐름 파악 (무관한 문장 삭제) 난이도 ★★☆

끊어읽기 해석

According to Sigmund Freud, / the Id, Ego, and Superego / are the three components / of personality.
지그문트 프로이트에 따르면 / 이드, 자아, 그리고 초자아는 / 세 가지 구성 요소이다 / 성격의

He contended / that people are born with the Id.
그는 주장했다 / 사람들이 이드를 가지고 태어난다고

① The Id contains / basic human drives / like hunger and thirst.
이드는 포함한다 / 인간의 기본적인 욕구를 / 배고픔과 목마름 같은

It cares for nothing / except that its needs are met / immediately.
그것은 아무것도 신경 쓰지 않는다 / 그것의 욕구가 충족된다는 것 외에는 / 즉시

It does not even care / whether those needs are rational or harmful.
그것은 심지어 신경 쓰지 않는다 / 그러한 욕구들이 이성적인지 해로운지도

② Therefore, / it is closely associated / with the reality principle.
따라서 / 그것은 밀접하게 연관되어 있다 / 현실 원리와

③ In contrast, / the Ego develops / as a person grows / after birth.
이에 반해 / 자아는 발달한다 / 사람이 성장함에 따라 / 태어난 후

The Ego realizes / that other people have needs as well.
자아는 깨닫는다 / 다른 사람들도 욕구를 가지고 있다는 것을

④ It seeks to satisfy the Id's instinctual needs / in realistic ways / while simultaneously weighing / those of other people.
그것은 이드의 본능적인 욕구를 충족시키려고 한다 / 현실적인 방법으로 / 신중히 고려하는 동시에 / 다른 사람들의 그것(본능적인 욕구)을

Last to develop is the Superego.
마지막으로 발달하는 것은 초자아이다

The Superego functions / as an individual's conscience.
초자아는 기능한다 / 개인의 양심으로서

⑤ It distinguishes / between what is right and wrong.
그것은 구분한다 / 무엇이 옳고 그른지를

해석 지그문트 프로이트에 따르면, 이드, 자아, 그리고 초자아는 성격의 세 가지 구성 요소이다. 그는 사람들이 이드를 가지고 태어난다고 주장했다. ① 이드는 배고픔과 목마름 같은 인간의 기본적인 욕구를 포함한다. 그것은 그것의 욕구가 즉시 충족된다는 것 외에는 아무것도 신경 쓰지 않는다. 그것은 심지어 그러한 욕구들이 이성적인지 해로운지도 신경 쓰지 않는다. ② 따라서, 그것은 현실 원리와 밀접하게 연관되어 있다. ③ 이에 반해, 자아는 사람이 태어난 후 성장함에 따라 발달한다. 자아는 다른 사람들도 욕구를 가지고 있다는 것을 깨닫는다. ④ 그것은 다른 사람들의 본능적인 욕구를 신중히 고려하는 동시에 현실적인 방법으로 이드의 본능적인 욕구를 충족시키려고 한다. 마지막으로 발달하는 것은 초자아이다. 초자아는 개인의 양심으로서 기능한다. ⑤ 그것은 무엇이 옳고 그른지를 구분한다.

해설 ②번 앞 문장에서 이드는 욕구들이 이성적인지 해로운지도 신경 쓰지 않는다고 했으므로 그것(이드)이 현실 원리와 밀접하게 연관되어 있다는 내용의 ②번 문장은 글의 흐름상 적절하지 않다.

어휘 Id 이드(인간의 원시적·본능적 요소가 존재하는 무의식 부분) Ego 자아
Superego 초자아, 상위 자아 component 구성 요소
personality 성격 contend 주장하다 drive 욕구, 동인
rational 이성적인, 합리적인 instinctual 본능적인
weigh ~을 신중히 고려하다 function 기능하다, 작용하다
conscience 양심 distinguish 구분하다, 분간하다

---

09 **독해** 세부내용 파악 (내용 불일치 파악)　난이도 ★★★

끊어읽기 해석

Leucippus and Democritus taught / that everything is composed of / elementary objects / in constant movement.
레우키포스와 데모크리토스는 가르쳤다 / 모든 것이 구성되어 있다고 / 기본적인 물체들로 / 일정한 운동을 하는

This proposal did not meet with the approval / of Plato or Aristotle, / for / if everything is made of / corpuscles in motion, / why are the forms of things / so well preserved?
이 제안은 승인을 얻지 못했다 / 플라톤이나 아리스토텔레스의 / 그렇다는 것은 / 만약 모든 것이 구성되어 있다면 / 움직이는 기본 개체들로 / 왜 사물들의 형태는 / 그렇게 잘 보존되어 있을까

The atomic theory could not account for / the stability of nature / or / for the reappearance of organic forms / generation after generation.
원자론은 설명할 수 없었다 / 자연의 안정성을 / 또는 / 유기적인 형태가 다시 나타나는 것을 / 세대를 거듭할수록

All in all, / atoms appeared / to be a rather mechanical explication.
대체로 / 원자는 ~처럼 보였다 / 다소 기계적인 설명(처럼)

This certainly did not appeal / to those Greek philosophers / who envisioned a world / of underlying forms and ideals.
이것은 확실히 매력적이지 않았다 / 그리스 철학자들에게 / 세계를 상상했던 / 근원적인 형태와 이상의

All in all / the Greeks preferred / their elements.
대체로 / 그리스 사람들은 선호했다 / 그들의 원소를

These were not actual physical substances / —such as real fire or real water/ —but rather, / nonmaterial essences / out of which the whole world was created.
그것들은 실제의 물질적인 물질이 아니었다 / 실제 불이나 실제 물과 같은 / 차라리 / 비물질적인 본질이었다 / 온 세계가 창조된

Such ideas persisted / in the West / for well over 2,000

---

years, / and, / with the rise of alchemy, / new principles, / or elements, / were added.
그러한 생각들은 지속되었다 / 서양에서 / 2,000년이 훨씬 넘는 세월 동안 / 그리고 / 연금술의 등장과 함께 / 새로운 원리 / 즉 원소들이 추가되었다

The spirit Mercury, / for example, / is present in all / that is volatile.
수성의 기운은 / 예를 들어 / 모든 것에 존재한다 / 휘발성이 있는

Salt, / which is unchanged by fire, / represents that which is fixed, / while sulfur is the principle of combustion.
소금은 / 불에 의해 변질되지 않는 / 고정된 것을 나타낸다 / 황은 연소의 원리인 반면

해석 레우키포스와 데모크리토스는 모든 것이 일정한 운동을 하는 기본적인 물체들로 구성되어 있다고 가르쳤다. 이 제안은 플라톤이나 아리스토텔레스의 승인을 얻지 못했는데, 그렇다는 것은 만약 모든 것이 움직이는 기본 개체들로 구성되어 있다면, 왜 사물들의 형태는 그렇게 잘 보존되어 있을까? 원자론은 자연의 안정성이나 세대를 거듭할수록 유기적인 형태가 다시 나타나는 현상을 설명할 수 없었다. 대체로, 원자는 다소 기계적인 설명처럼 보였다. 이것은 근원적인 형태와 이상의 세계를 상상했던 그리스 철학자들에게는 확실히 매력적이지 않았다. 대체로 그리스 사람들은 그들의 원소를 선호했다. 그것들은 실제 불이나 실제 물과 같은 실제의 물질적인 물질이 아니라, 차라리 온 세계가 창조된 비물질적인 본질이었다. 그러한 생각들은 2,000년이 훨씬 넘는 세월 동안 서양에서 지속되었고, 연금술의 등장과 함께 새로운 원리, 즉 원소들이 추가되었다. 예를 들어, 수성의 기운은 휘발성이 있는 모든 것에 존재한다. 황은 연소의 원리인 반면, 불에 의해 변질되지 않는 소금은 고정된 것을 나타낸다.

해설 지문 중간에서 대체로 그리스 사람들은 그들의 원소를 선호했는데, 그것들은 실제 불이나 실제 물과 같은 실제의 물질적인 물질이 아니라, 온 세계가 창조된 비물질적인 본질이었다고 설명하고 있으므로, '⑤ 당대의 그리스 철학자들은 세계가 창조된 물질적 본질을 선호했다'는 지문의 내용과 일치하지 않는다.

어휘 compose 구성하다 elementary 기본적인, 기본의
constant 일정한, 지속적인 proposal 제안 approval 승인
corpuscle 기본 개체, 미립자 preserve 보존하다 atomic 원자의
account for 설명하다, 차지하다 stability 안정성
reappearance 다시 나타나는 것, 재현 mechanical 기계적인
explication 설명, 해석 envision 상상하다, 마음에 그리다
substance 물질 essence 본질 persist 지속하다
alchemy 연금술 principle 원리 spirit 기운, 정신
volatile 휘발성의 combustion 연소, 발화

---

10 **문법** 능동태·수동태 & 전치사　난이도 ★★☆

해석 학교 자체가 어느 정도 다르게 준비될 때까지, 우리는 학교에서 사회생활에 대한 그리고 학생들에게 사회적 관점을 가르치고 사회적 동기와 목적을 제공하기 위한 충분한 준비를 할 수 없다. 사회적 정신과 동기는 사람들이 함께 살고 어떤 일을 공동으로 하고, 그들이 공통의 목표와 목적이 있기 때문에 서로의 활동과 서로의 경험을 공유하는 것의 산물이다. 사람들에게는 그들에게 흥미롭고 그들 모두를 동일하게 유지하고, 각자가 기여하게 하는 일이 있기 때문에 사람들에게 진정한 사회적 정신이 스며들게 되는 것이다.

해설 ④ 3형식 동사의 수동태 | 전치사 3: 방향 감정을 나타내는 동사(interest)의 경우 주어가 감정의 원인이면 현재분사를, 감정을 느끼는 주체이면 과거분사를 써야 하는데, 문맥상 '그들에게 흥미로운 일'이라는 의미로 주어(something)가 감정을 일으키는 주

체이므로 과거분사 interested를 be 동사(is) 뒤에서 능동태를 완성하는 현재분사 interesting으로 고쳐야 한다. 또한, 문맥상 '~에게 흥미롭다'라는 의미가 되어야 자연스러우므로, '~에게'의 의미를 나타내는 전치사 to가 올바르게 쓰였다.

오답 분석
① 전치사 자리 전치사(for) 뒤에는 명사 역할을 하는 것이 와야 하므로 동명사 instilling이 올바르게 쓰였다.

② 전치사 2: 시점 문맥상 '학교 자체가 어느 정도 다르게 준비될 때까지'라는 의미가 되어야 자연스러우므로 특정 시점까지 어떤 행동이나 상황이 계속되는 상황을 나타내는 전치사 until (~까지)이 올바르게 쓰였다.

③ 부사 자리 문맥상 '어떤 일을 공동으로 하다'라는 의미가 되어야 자연스러운데 동사(doing)를 수식할 수 있는 것은 부사이므로, 부사 역할을 하는 전치사구 in common이 올바르게 쓰였다.

⑤ 보어 자리 | 현재분사 vs. 과거분사 주격 보어를 취하는 동사 become의 보어 자리에는 명사나 형용사 역할을 하는 것이 와야 하는데, 주어(people)와 분사가 '사람들이 스며들게 되다'라는 의미의 수동 관계이므로 형용사 역할을 하는 과거분사 permeated가 올바르게 쓰였다.

어휘 adequate 충분한, 적당한 preparation 준비
instill 가르치다, 주입시키다 pupil 학생 furnish 제공하다
motive 동기, 의도 equip 준비하다, 갖추다 end 목표, 목적
contribution 기여 permeate 스며들다, 퍼지다

👍 이것도 알면 합격!

시점을 나타내는 전치사를 추가로 알아두자.

· since ~ 이래로	· from ~부터	+ 시점
· until/by ~까지	· before/prior to ~ 전에	
· after/following ~ 후에		

---

11 독해 세부내용 파악 (내용 일치 파악) 난이도 ★★☆

끊어읽기 해석

①The system / in which men have more value / and / more social and economic power / than women / is found / throughout the history of the world.
체계는 / 남성이 더 많은 가치를 갖는 / 그리고 / 더 많은 사회적, 경제적 힘을 (갖는) / 여성보다 / 발견된다 / 세계의 역사 곳곳에서

②Women suffer / both from structural oppression and from individual men.
여성은 고통을 받는다 / 구조적 억압과 남성 개인들 모두로부터

③Too many movements / for social justice / accept the assumptions of male dominance / and / ignore the oppression of women, / but / ④patriarchy pervades / both our political and personal lives.
너무 많은 운동들은 / 사회적 정의를 위한 / 남성 지배의 가정을 받아들인다 / 그리고 / 여성에 대한 억압을 무시한다 / 하지만 / 가부장제는 널리 퍼져 있다 / 우리의 정치적 삶과 개인적 삶 모두에

⑤Feminism recognizes / that no pattern of domination is necessary / and / seeks to liberate / both women and men / from the structures of dominance / that characterize patriarchy.
여성주의 운동은 인식한다 / 어떤 양식의 지배도 필요하지 않다는 것을 / 그리고 / 해방하고자 한다 / 여성과 남성 모두를 / 지배의 구조로부터 / 가부장제를 특징짓는

해석 남성이 여성보다 더 많은 가치와 더 많은 사회적, 경제적 힘을 갖는 체계는 세계의 역사 곳곳에서 발견된다. 여성은 구조적 억압과

남성 개인들 모두로부터 고통을 받는다. 사회적 정의를 위한 너무 많은 운동들은 남성 지배의 가정을 받아들이고 여성에 대한 억압을 무시하지만, 가부장제는 우리의 정치적 삶과 개인적 삶 모두에 널리 퍼져 있다. 여성주의 운동은 어떤 양식의 지배도 필요하지 않다는 것을 인식하고 가부장제를 특징짓는 지배의 구조로부터 여성과 남성 모두를 해방시키고자 한다.

해설 지문 중간에서 사회적 정의를 위한 너무 많은 운동들은 남성 지배의 가정을 받아들이고 여성에 대한 억압은 무시한다고 했으므로, '③ 사회적 정의를 추구하는 역사적 운동들도 여성 억압 현상을 경시했다'는 지문의 내용과 일치한다.

오답 분석
① 역사적으로 동양 여성들이 서양 여성들보다 더 많이 억압받아 왔는지에 대해서는 언급되지 않았다.
② 두 번째 문장에 여성은 구조적 억압과 남성 개인들 모두로부터 고통을 받는다고 언급되었지만, 여성에 대한 구조적 억압이 남성 개인들에 의한 억압보다 더욱 심각한 문제인지에 대해서는 언급되지 않았다.
④ 세 번째 문장에 가부장제는 우리의 정치적 삶과 개인적 삶 모두에 널리 퍼져 있다고 언급되었지만, 가부장제가 개인적 삶보다 정치적 삶에 더 많이 퍼져 있는지에 대해서는 언급되지 않았다.
⑤ 마지막 문장에서 여성주의 운동은 가부장제를 특징짓는 지배의 구조로부터 여성과 남성 모두를 해방시키고자 한다고 언급되었으므로 지문의 내용과 다르다.

어휘 suffer 고통을 받다, 겪다 structural 구조적인, 구조의
oppression 억압, 탄압 social justice 사회적 정의
assumption 가정, 추측 dominance 지배 patriarchy 가부장제
pervade ~에 스며들다, 널리 퍼지다
liberate 해방시키다, 자유롭게 하다

---

12 독해 추론 (빈칸 완성 - 단어) 난이도 ★★☆

끊어읽기 해석

Over the past four decades / a fundamental shift has been occurring / in the world economy.
지난 40년간 / 근본적인 변화가 일어나고 있다 / 세계 경제에

We have been moving away / from a world / in which national economies were relatively self-contained entities, / (A) isolated from each other / by barriers to cross-border trade and investment; / by distance, time zones, and language; / and by national differences / in government regulation, culture, and business systems.
우리는 멀어지고 있다 / 세계에서 / 국가 경제가 상대적으로 자립적인 주체였던 / 서로 (A) 고립되어 / 국경 간 무역과 투자에 대한 장벽으로 인해 / 거리, 시간대, 그리고 언어로 인해 / 그리고 국가적 차이로 인해 / 정부의 규제, 문화, 그리고 비즈니스 시스템의

We are moving toward a world / in which barriers to cross-border trade and investment are (B) declining; / perceived distance is shrinking / due to advances in transportation and telecommunications technology; / material culture is starting to look similar / the world over; / and national economies are merging / into an interdependent, integrated global economic system.
우리는 세계로 나아가고 있다 / 국경 간 무역과 투자의 장벽이 (B) 낮아지고 / 인식되는 거리가 줄어들고 / 교통과 원격 통신 기술의 발전으로 인해 / 물질문화가 비슷해 보이기 시작한다 / 전 세계적으로 / 그리고 국가 경제가 융합되는 / 상호 의존적이고, 통합적인 세계 경제 체계로

The process / by which this transformation is occurring is / commonly referred to as globalization.
과정은 / 이러한 변화가 일어나는 / 흔히 세계화라고 불린다

해석 지난 40년간 세계 경제에 근본적인 변화가 일어나고 있다. 우리는 국경 간 무역과 투자에 대한 장벽으로 인해, 거리, 시간대, 그리고 언어로 인해, 그리고 정부의 규제, 문화, 그리고 비즈니스 시스템의 국가적 차이로 인해 서로 (A) 고립되어 국가 경제가 상대적으로 자립적인 주체였던 세계에서 멀어지고 있다. 우리는 국경 간 무역과 투자의 장벽이 (B) 낮아지고, 교통과 원격 통신 기술의 발전으로 인해 인식되는 거리가 줄어들고, 물질문화가 전 세계적으로 비슷해 보이기 시작하고, 국가 경제가 상호 의존적이고, 통합적인 세계 경제 체제로 융합되는 세계로 나아가고 있다. 이러한 변화가 일어나는 과정은 흔히 세계화라고 불린다.

	(A)		(B)
①	~에 도입되는	-	충족시키는
②	~을 돌보는	-	확대되는
③	~와 통합되는	-	감소하는
④	~을 사로잡는	-	단호한
⑤	~로부터 고립되는	-	낮아지는

해석 (A) 빈칸 앞부분에서 우리는 국가 경제가 상대적으로 자립적인 주체였던 세계에서 멀어지고 있다고 설명하고 있고, 빈칸 뒷부분에서 국경 간 무역과 투자에 대한 장벽, 거리, 시간대, 그리고 언어와 같은 장벽들에 대해 설명하고 있으므로, (A)에는 우리는 서로 '고립되어(isolated from)' 국가 경제가 상대적으로 자립적인 주체였던 세계에서 멀어지고 있다는 내용이 들어가야 한다. (B) 빈칸 앞부분에서 국경 간 무역과 투자의 장벽에 대해 언급하고 있고 빈칸 뒷부분에서 인식되는 거리가 줄어들고, 물질문화가 전 세계적으로 비슷해 보이기 시작한다는 내용을 언급하고 있으므로, (B)에는 국경 간 무역과 투자의 장벽이 '낮아진다(declining)'는 내용이 들어가야 한다. 따라서 ⑤ (A) isolated from(~로부터 고립되는) - (B) declining(낮아지는)이 정답이다.

어휘 fundamental 근본적인 shift 변화 occur 일어나다, 발생하다 relatively 상대적으로 self-contained 자립적인, 독립의 entity 주체, 실체 barrier 장벽 cross-border 국경 간의, 국경을 넘는 trade 무역 investment 투자 distance 거리 regulation 규제 perceive 인식하다, 인지하다 shrink 줄어들다, 감소하다 telecommunication 원격 통신 material 물질의 merge 융합하다, 합병하다 interdependent 상호 의존적인 integrate 통합하다, 융합하다 converge 통합하다 unfaltering 단호한

13 문법 분사
난이도 ★★☆

해석 가장 많이 논의된 탈산업화의 원인 중 하나는 새로운 산업화 국가로의 일자리 이동이었다. 이것은 더 오래된 산업 도시 내부 지역의 생산 기능이 능가하게 된 새로운 국제적 노동 분업의 출현을 나타낸다는 것이 주장되어 왔다. 이 이론은 다수의 주요한 전 세계적 경제 발전을 설명할 수 있다. 이것들은 서구 도시들의 탈산업화, 새로운 산업화 국가들의 성장과 상호 연결된 세계 경제의 통제와 지휘 본부로서의 세계적인 도시들의 성장을 포함한다. 그러나, 그럼에도 불구하고, 이 이론의 설명 범위는 틀리지는 않지만 제한적이다. 예를 들어, 경제적 과정에 너무 과하게 의존함으로써 경제 변화와 명백하게 관련된 도시들의 사회적 지형에 대해서는 거의 말할 수 없다. 이 이론은 경제 변화와 도시화 사이의 관계에 대한 단방향적인 설명만을 제공할 수 있다.

해석 ④ 분사구문의 형태 '틀리지는 않지만'이라는 의미를 나타내기 위해 분사구문을 써야 하는데 분사구문을 만들 때는 부사절의 동사를 분사 형태로 바꾸어야 하고, 주절의 주어(the explanatory scope of this theory)와 분사가 '이 이론의 설명 범위는 틀리지는

않다'라는 의미의 능동 관계이므로 to 부정사 to be를 현재분사 being으로 고쳐야 한다. 참고로, 분사구문의 의미를 분명하게 하기 위해 부사절 접속사(while)가 분사구문 앞에 올 수 있으며, 분사구문의 부정형을 쓸 때는 분사 앞에 not을 붙인다.

오답 분석

① 현재완료 시제 | 능동태·수동태 구별 문맥상 '주장되어 왔다'라는 과거에 시작된 일이 현재까지 영향을 미치는 상황을 표현하고 있으므로 현재완료 시제가 와야 하고, 주어(this)와 동사가 '이것은 ~ 주장되어 왔다'라는 의미의 수동 관계이므로 현재완료 수동태를 완성하는 과거분사 argued가 올바르게 쓰였다.

② 주어와 동사의 수 일치 주어 자리에 복수 명사(the manufacturing functions)가 왔으므로 복수 동사 have가 올바르게 쓰였다. 참고로, 주어와 동사 사이에 온 수식어 거품(of ~ cities)은 동사의 수 결정에 영향을 주지 않는다.

③ 자동사 문맥상 '이 이론은 설명할 수 있다'라는 의미가 되어야 하는데 '~을 설명하다'라는 의미의 자동사 account는 전치사 for와 함께 쓰이므로 account for가 올바르게 쓰였다.

⑤ 강조 부사 강조 부사 so(매우)는 보통 형용사나 부사를 앞에서 강조하므로 부사 heavily(과하게) 앞에 강조 부사 so가 올바르게 쓰였다.

어휘 cause 원인 de-industralisation 탈산업화 migration 이동, 이주 emergence 출현, 등장 division 분업, 분할 labour 노동, 근로 manufacturing 생산, 제조업 surpass 능가하다, 넘어서다 theory 이론 account for 설명하다 command 지휘; 지휘하다 interconnected 상호 연결된 explanatory 설명적인 scope 범위 geography 지형 one-directional 단방향적인 urbanization 도시화

👍 이것도 알면 합격!

enough는 동사와 형용사를 뒤에서 강조한다는 것을 알아두자.

(ex) The playground is safe enough for children to play in.
그 놀이터는 아이들이 놀기에 충분히 안전하다.

14 독해 추론 (빈칸 완성 - 단어)
난이도 ★★☆

끊어읽기 해석

Usually / you will find / that each scene / in a fictional narrative film / uses an establishing shot; / that is / a shot that gives the setting / in which the scene is to take place / and / enables the viewer / to establish the spatial relationships / between characters / involved in the scene.
보통 / 여러분은 발견할 것이다 / 각 장면이 / 허구적인 이야기 영화의 / 설정 샷을 사용한다는 것을 / 그것은 / 배경을 제공하는 샷이다 / 장면이 발생할 / 그리고 / 시청자가 ~할 수 있게 해주는 / 공간적 관계를 확립하게 / 등장인물들 사이의 / 장면과 관련된

But, / although this is what might be known / as the Hollywood standard / and / was certainly the expected norm / throughout the period of Classical Hollywood, / the practice of using an establishing shot / has not always been followed / by filmmakers.
그러나 / 이것이 알려져 있을 수도 있는 것이지만 / 할리우드의 표준이라고 / 그리고 / 확실히 기대되는 표준이었지만 / 고전 할리우드 시대 내내 / 설정 샷을 사용하는 관행이 / 항상 따라졌던 것은 아니다 / 영화 제작자들에 의해

By omitting an establishing shot / the viewer is put in the position / of struggling to make sense of the relationship / between the characters shown.
설정 샷을 생략함으로써 / 시청자는 위치에 놓이게 된다 / 관계를 이해하기 위해 고군분투하는 / 보여지는 등장인물들 사이의

We are effectively disorientated / and / this will be part / of what the filmmakers are attempting to achieve; / as well as perhaps defying the expected filmic norm / and / thereby challenging any presumption / that there are certain correct (and therefore, certain incorrect) ways / of making films.

우리는 사실상 방향 감각을 상실했다 / 그리고 / 이것은 일부일 것이다 / 영화 제작자들이 성취하려고 시도하는 것의 / 또한 아마도 기대되는 영화적 표준을 거부한다 / 그리고 / 어떤 가정에도 도전할 수 있다 / 특정한 정확한 (따라서, 특정한 잘못된) 방법이 있다는 / 영화를 만드는

해석 보통 여러분은 허구적인 이야기 영화의 각 장면이 설정 샷을 사용한다는 것을 발견할 것이다. 그것은 장면이 발생할 배경을 제공하고 시청자가 장면과 관련된 등장인물들 사이의 공간적 관계를 확립할 수 있게 해주는 샷이다. 그러나, 이것이 할리우드의 표준이라고 알려져 있을 수도 있는 것이고 고전 할리우드 시대 내내 확실히 기대되는 표준이었지만, 설정 샷을 사용하는 관행이 영화 제작자들에 의해 항상 따라졌던 것은 아니다. 설정 샷을 생략함으로써 시청자는 보여지는 등장인물들 사이의 관계를 이해하기 위해 고군분투하는 위치에 놓이게 된다. 우리는 사실상 방향 감각을 상실했고 이것은 영화 제작자들이 성취하려고 시도하는 것의 일부일 것이다. 또한, 아마도 기대되는 영화적 표준을 거부하고 영화를 만드는 특정한 정확한 (따라서, 특정한 잘못된) 방법이 있다는 어떤 가정에도 도전할 수 있다.

① 과소평가함
② 유발함
③ 생략함
④ 유지함
⑤ 통제함

해설 지문 처음에서 설정 샷은 장면이 발생할 배경을 제공하고 시청자가 장면과 관련된 등장인물들 사이의 공간적 관계를 확립할 수 있게 해주는 샷이라고 설명하고 있고, 지문 중간에서 설정 샷이 기대되는 표준이었지만 설정 샷을 사용하는 관행이 영화 제작자들에 의해 항상 따라졌던 것은 아니라고 설명하고 있으므로, 빈칸에는 설정 샷을 '③ 생략함'으로써 시청자는 보여지는 등장인물들 사이의 관계를 이해하기 위해 고군분투하는 위치에 놓이게 된다는 내용이 들어가야 한다.

어휘 fictional 허구적인, 소설의 narrative 이야기
establishing shot 설정 샷(다음 사건이나 장면의 배경을 설정하는 장면)
setting 배경 take place 발생하다 enable ~을 할 수 있게 하다
spatial 공간적인 standard 표준 norm 표준, 규범
practice 관행, 관습 effectively 사실상, 효과적으로
disoriented 방향 감각을 상실한, 혼란에 빠진 attempt 시도
defy 거부하다 presumption 가정, 추정 omit 생략하다, 제외하다

---

15 어휘 어휘&표현 collaborative 난이도 ★★☆

해석 언어가 없다면, 개인이나 개인들의 집단은 다른 사람들에게 그것들을 설명하거나, 공동의 목표를 향하는 협력적 기업에서 참가자들의 행동을 지시할 방법이 없을 것이다.

① 포괄적인
② 협력적인
③ 의미가 없는
④ 경쟁적인
⑤ 해로운

어휘 participant 참가자 enterprise 기업 common 공동의
comprehensive 포괄적인 collaborative 협력적인

 이것도 알면 **합격!**

collaborative(협력적인)의 유의어
= cooperative, collective, synergetic

---

16 독해 전체내용 파악 (요지 파악) 난이도 ★★☆

끊어읽기 해석

The naive listener might assume / a life story / to be a truthful, factual account / of the storyteller's life.
순진한 청자는 가정할지도 모른다 / 전기를 / 진실되고, 사실적인 설명으로 / 작가의 삶에 대한

The assumption is / that the storyteller has only to penetrate the fog / of the past / and / that once a life is honestly remembered, / it can be sincerely recounted.
그 가정은 / 작가는 안개를 뚫고 나가기만 하면 된다는 것이다 / 과거의 / 그리고 / 일단 삶이 정직하게 기억되면 / 그것은 진심으로 이야기될 수 있다는 것이다

But / the more sophisticated listener understands / that no matter how sincere the attempt, / remembering the past cannot render it / as it was, / not only because memory is selective / but because the life storyteller is a different person now / than he or she was ten or thirty years ago; / and / he or she may not be able to, / or even want to, / imagine that he or she was different then.
그러나 / 더 정교한 청자는 이해한다 / 시도가 아무리 진실되더라도 / 과거를 기억하는 것이 그것을 만들 수 없다 / 원래대로 / 기억이 선택적일 뿐만 아니라 / 전기 작가가 지금은 다른 사람이기 때문에 / 그나 그녀가 10년이나 30년 전보다 / 그리고 / 그나 그녀는 할 수 없을지도 모른다 / 또는 하지 않고 싶을지도 모른다 / 그나 그녀가 그때는 달랐다고 상상하는 것을

The problem of how much a person may change / without losing his or her identity / is the greatest difficulty / facing the life storyteller, / whose chief concern, / after all, / is to affirm his or her identity / and / account for it.
한 사람이 얼마나 많이 변할 수 있는가의 문제는 / 그나 그녀의 정체성을 잃지 않고 / 가장 큰 어려움이다 / 전기 작가가 직면하는 / 그들의 주된 관심사가 / 결국 / 그나 그녀의 정체성을 확인하는 것인 / 그리고 / 그것을 설명하는 것인

So / life storytelling is a fiction, a making, an ordered past / imposed by a present personality / on a disordered life.
따라서 / 전기는 허구, 제작물, 질서 있는 과거이다 / 현재의 인격에 의해 부과되는 / 무질서한 삶에

해석 순진한 청자는 전기를 작가의 삶에 대한 진실되고, 사실적인 설명으로 가정할지도 모른다. 그 가정은 작가는 과거의 안개를 뚫고 나가기만 하면 되고 일단 삶이 정직하게 기억되면, 그것은 진심으로 이야기될 수 있다는 것이다. 그러나 시도가 아무리 진실되더라도, 기억이 선택적일 뿐만 아니라 전기 작가가 지금은 10년이나 30년 전과는 다른 사람이기 때문에, 그리고 그나 그녀는 자신이 그때는 달랐다는 것을 상상할 수 없거나, 상상하고 싶지 않기 때문에 과거를 기억한다고 해서 그것을 원래대로 만들 수는 없다는 것을 더 정교한 청자는 이해한다. 그나 그녀의 정체성을 잃지 않고 한 사람이 얼마나 많이 변할 수 있는가의 문제는 결국 자신의 정체성을 확인하고 그것을 설명하는 것이 주된 관심사인 전기 작가가 직면하는 가장 큰 어려움이다. 따라서 전기는 현재의 인격에 의해 무질서한 삶에 부과되는 허구, 제작물, 질서 있는 과거이다.

해설 지문 중간에서 기억은 선택적일 뿐만 아니라 작가가 과거를 기억한다고 해서 그것을 원래대로 만들 수는 없다고 설명하고 있고, 지문 마지막에서 전기는 현재의 인격에 의해 무질서한 삶에 부과

되는 허구, 제작물, 질서 있는 과거라고 설명하고 있으므로, '④ 전기(傳記)는 무결(無缺)하지 않은 작가에 의해서 기록된 일종의 픽션이다'가 이 글의 요지이다.

어휘 **naive** 순진한, 고지식한 **assume** 가정하다, 추정하다
factual 사실적인, 사실에 입각한 **account** 설명
penetrate 뚫고 나가다, 관통하다 **sincerely** 진심으로
recount 이야기하다, 묘사하다 **sophisticated** 정교한, 복잡한
render ~을 만들다, 되게 하다 **identity** 정체성 **face** 직면하다
impose 부과하다, 적용하다, 강요하다

---

17 독해 추론 (빈칸 완성 - 구)   난이도 ★★☆

끊어읽기 해석

The problems which have preoccupied / recent social anthropology / are rather different / to those which interested Herodotus and Tacitus.
사로잡은 문제들은 / 최근의 사회 인류학을 / 다소 다르다 / 헤로도토스와 타키투스의 관심을 끌었던 것들(문제들)과는

They were first formulated / during the Enlightenment.
그것들은 처음으로 만들어졌다 / 계몽주의 시대에

Theories which attempt to resolve these problems were established / at the same time.
이 문제들을 해결하려고 시도하는 이론들은 수립되었다 / 동시에

Until the seventeenth and eighteenth centuries, / European kings had been believed / to rule by Divine Right, / and / human society was supposed to reproduce, / on a lower scale, / the Divine society / of Heaven.
17세기와 18세기까지 / 유럽의 왕들은 믿어졌다 / 신수 왕권으로 통치한다고 / 그리고 / 인간 사회는 재생산해야 했다 / 더 낮은 규모에서 / 신 사회를 / 천국의

These assumptions were questioned / during the Enlightenment.
이러한 가정은 의문이 제기되었다 / 계몽주의 시대에

Once people considered themselves free / to decide for themselves / what was, or was not, proper social behaviour / according to natural / rather than divine law / it became possible / to ask / both how actual societies might be improved, / and / how present societies had diverged / from the natural, or original human condition.
일단 사람들이 그들 스스로가 자유롭다고 생각하게 되면서 / 그들 스스로 결정하는 것이 / 무엇이 적절한 사회적 행동이었는지 아닌지를 / 자연법에 따라 / 신성한 법이 아닌 / 가능하게 되었다 / 묻는 것이 / 어떻게 실제 사회가 개선될 수 있는지 / 그리고 / 어떻게 현재 사회가 벗어났는지 / 자연적인, 또는 본래의 인간 조건으로부터

Both the European past and more exotic but living, human societies / were seen / as sources of information / that could help / answer these questions.
유럽의 과거와 더 이국적이지만 살아있는 인간 사회 모두 / 여겨졌다 / 정보의 원천으로 / 도움을 줄 수 있는 / 이러한 질문들에 대답하는 데

해석 최근의 사회 인류학을 사로잡은 문제들은 헤로도토스와 타키투스의 관심을 끌었던 문제들과는 다소 다르다. 그것들은 계몽주의 시대에 처음으로 만들어졌다. 이 문제들을 해결하려고 시도하는 이론들은 동시에 수립되었다. 17세기와 18세기까지, 유럽의 왕들은 신수 왕권으로 통치한다고 믿어졌고, 인간 사회는 더 낮은 규모에서 천국의 신 사회를 재생산해야 했다. 이러한 가정은 계몽주의 시대에 의문이 제기되었다. 일단 사람들이 신성한 법이 아닌 자연법에 따라 그들 스스로 무엇이 적절한 사회적 행동이었는지 아닌지를 결정하는 것이 자유롭다고 생각하게 되면서 어떻게 실제 사회가 개선될 수 있는지, 그리고 어떻게 현재 사회가 자연적인, 또는

본래의 인간 조건으로부터 벗어났는지를 묻는 것이 가능하게 되었다. 유럽의 과거와 더 이국적이지만 살아있는 인간 사회 모두, 이러한 질문들에 대답하는 데 도움을 줄 수 있는 정보의 원천으로 여겨졌다.

① 이러한 사회적 문제의 기저에 있는 가정의 진실
② 무엇이 적절한 사회적 행동이었는지 아닌지
③ 정부 형태의 사회주의적 종류
④ 시민과 왕 사이의 갈등
⑤ 사회가 어떻게 타락했는지

해설 빈칸 뒷부분에 사람들이 신성한 법이 아닌 자연법에 따른다는 것과 어떻게 실제 사회가 개선될 수 있는지, 그리고 어떻게 현재 사회가 자연적인, 또는 본래의 인간 조건으로부터 벗어났는지를 묻는 것이 가능하게 되었다는 내용이 언급되었으므로, 빈칸에는 그들 스스로 '② 무엇이 적절한 사회적 행동이었는지 아닌지'를 결정하는 것이 자유롭다고 생각하게 되었다는 내용이 들어가야 한다.

어휘 **preoccupy** 사로잡히다, 몰두하다 **anthropology** 인류학
Herodotus 헤로도토스(그리스의 역사가)
Tacitus 타키투스(로마의 역사가) **formulate** 만들어내다, 형성하다
Enlightenment 계몽주의 **resolve** 해결하다
Divine Right 신수 왕권 **reproduce** 재생산하다 **scale** 규모
diverge 벗어나다, 갈라져 나오다 **exotic** 이국적인 **proper** 적절한
socialistic 사회주의적인 **conflict** 갈등 **degenerate** 타락하다

---

18 독해 추론 (빈칸 완성 - 구)   난이도 ★★☆

끊어읽기 해석

Hunting big game / would have likely been a dangerous activity / in early times, / especially before the invention / of throwing spears / about half a million years ago.
큰 사냥감을 사냥하는 것은 / 위험한 활동이었을 가능성이 높다 / 초기에 / 특히 발명 이전에는 / 투창의 / 약 50만 년 전

Prior to this, / hunting even small and medium-size game / likely depended on / thrusting spears / (i.e., held in the hands / while thrusting into the animal).
이 이전에는 / 심지어 작거나 중간 크기의 사냥감을 사냥하는 것조차도 / ~에 달려있었을 가능성이 높다 / 찔러 넣는 창에 / (즉, 손에 쥐어진 / 동물에게 찔러 넣는 동안)

Some have suggested / that hunting may have occurred / by chasing animals / until they died / from exhaustion.
어떤 사람들은 말했다 / 사냥이 이루어졌을 수도 있다고 / 동물들을 쫓아다니면서 / 그들이 죽을 때까지 / 지쳐서

This technique is called / persistence hunting / and / essentially means / that a small group of people / would simply chase a selected animal, / perhaps for days, / until the animal died / from exhaustion.
이 기술은 불린다 / 지속 사냥이라고 / 그리고 / 본질적으로 의미한다 / 작은 무리의 사람들이 / 단지 선택한 동물을 쫓는 것을 / 어쩌면 며칠 동안 / 그 동물이 죽을 때까지 / 지쳐서

This makes sense to some / since, / while most game animals are quite quick / over short distances, / they usually cannot maintain the quickness / over long distances.
일부에게는 이것이 타당하다 / 왜냐하면 / 대부분의 사냥감 동물들은 꽤 빠르지만 / 짧은 거리에서는 / 그들은 보통 빠름을 유지할 수 없다 / 긴 거리에서는

Bipedalism in humans, / on the other hand, / leads to extended endurance.
인간의 두 발 보행은 / 반면에 / 연장된 지구력으로 이어진다

People may not be as quick as some animals / over

short distances, / but / they can outlast them / over long distances.
사람들은 일부 동물들만큼 빠르지 않을지도 모른다 / 짧은 거리에서는 / 하지만 / 그들(사람들)은 그들(일부 동물들)보다 오래 지속될 수 있다 / 긴 거리에서는

해석　초기에 큰 사냥감을 사냥하는 것은, 특히 약 50만 년 전 투창의 발명 이전에는 위험한 활동이었을 가능성이 높다. 이 이전에는, 심지어 작거나 중간 크기의 사냥감을 사냥하는 것조차도 찔러 넣는 창(즉, 동물에게 찔러 넣는 동안 손에 쥐어진)에 달려 있었을 가능성이 높다. 어떤 사람들은 동물이 지쳐서 죽을 때까지 그들을 쫓아다니면서 사냥이 이루어졌을 수도 있다고 말했다. 이 기술은 지속 사냥이라고 불리고 본질적으로 작은 무리의 사람들이 선택된 동물이 지쳐서 죽을 때까지, 어쩌면 며칠 동안, 단지 그 동물을 쫓는 것을 의미한다. 일부에게는 이것이 타당한데, 대부분의 사냥감 동물들은 짧은 거리에서는 꽤 빠르지만, 긴 거리에서는 보통 빠름을 유지할 수 없기 때문이다. 반면에, 인간의 두 발 보행은 연장된 지구력으로 이어진다. 사람들은 짧은 거리에서는 일부 동물들만큼 빠르지 않을지도 모르지만, 긴 거리에서는 그들보다 오래 지속될 수 있다.

① 기력 소진
② 상대적 열세
③ 연장된 지구력
④ 팀플레이
⑤ 지연된 공격

해설　빈칸 뒤 문장에서 사람들은 짧은 거리에서는 일부 동물들만큼 빠르지 않을지도 모르지만 긴 거리에서는 그들보다 오래 지속될 수 있다고 설명하고 있으므로, 빈칸에는 인간의 두 발 보행은 '③ 연장된 지구력'으로 이어진다는 내용이 들어가야 한다.

어휘　game 사냥감　throwing spear 투창(창을 던짐)　thrust 찔러 넣다
exhaustion 지침, 소진　persistence 지속, 끈기
essentially 본질적으로　maintain 유지하다
bipedalism 두 발 보행　outlast 오래 지속되다
comparative 상대적인　extend 연장하다
endurance 지구력, 인내

19　독해　세부내용 파악 (내용 불일치 파악)　난이도 ★★☆

끊어읽기 해석

Weather forecasts, market reports, cost-of-living indexes, and the results of public opinion polls / are good examples.
일기예보, 시장 보고서, 소비자 물가 지수, 그리고 여론 조사 결과들은 / 좋은 예시이다

Statistical methods are employed extensively / in the preparation of such reports.
통계학적 방법은 광범위하게 활용된다 / 이러한 보고의 준비에

Reports / that are based / on sound statistical reasoning / and / the careful interpretation of conclusions / are truly informative.
보고는 / ~에 기초한 / 완전한 통계적 추론에 / 그리고 / 결론의 신중한 해석에 / 진정으로 유익하다

Frequently, / however, / the deliberate or inadvertent misuse of statistics / leads / to erroneous conclusions / and / distortions of truth.
종종 / 그러나 / 의도적이거나 무심코 한 통계의 오용은 / 이어진다 / 잘못된 결론으로 / 그리고 / 진실의 왜곡으로

For the general public, / the basic consumers of these reports, / some idea of statistical reasoning / is essential / to

properly interpret the data / and / evaluate the conclusions / that are drawn.
일반 대중에게 있어서 / 이러한 보고의 기본 소비자인 / 통계적 추론의 어떤 아이디어는 / 필수적이다 / 자료를 적절하게 해석하기 위해서 / 그리고 / 결론을 평가하기 위해서 / 도출되는

Statistical reasoning provides criteria / for determining the conclusions / that are actually supported / by data / and / those that are not.
통계적 추론은 기준을 제공한다 / 결론을 결정하는 / 실제로 뒷받침되는 / 자료에 의해 / 그리고 / 그렇지 않은 것을

해석　일기예보, 시장 보고서, 소비자 물가 지수, 그리고 여론 조사 결과들은 좋은 예시이다. 통계학적 방법은 이러한 보고의 준비에 광범위하게 활용된다. 완전한 통계적 추론과 결론의 신중한 해석에 기초한 보고는 진정으로 유익하다. 그러나, 의도적이거나 무심코 한 통계의 오용은 종종 잘못된 결론과 진실의 왜곡으로 이어진다. 이러한 보고의 기본 소비자인 일반 대중에게 있어서, 자료를 적절하게 해석하고 도출되는 결론을 평가하기 위해서 통계적 추론의 어떤 아이디어는 필수적이다. 통계적 추론은 자료에 의해 실제로 뒷받침되는 결론과 그렇지 않은 것을 결정하는 기준을 제공한다.

해설　지문 중간에서 의도적이거나 무심코 한 통계의 오용은 종종 잘못된 결론과 진실의 왜곡으로 이어진다고 설명하고 있으므로, '⑤ 정확한 통계 자료는 실수에 의해서만 잘못된 결론으로 이어진다'는 것은 지문의 내용과 일치하지 않는다.

어휘　cost-of-living index 소비자 물가 지수
public opinion poll 여론 조사　statistical 통계(학)상의, 통계적인
method 방법　employ 활용하다　extensively 광범위하게
preparation 준비　sound 완전한, 건전한　reasoning 추론
interpretation 해석　informative 유익한　deliberate 의도적인
inadvertent 무심코 한, 우연한　misuse 오용
erroneous 잘못된, 틀린　distortion 왜곡　essential 필수적인
evaluate 평가하다　draw 도출하다, 끌어내다　determine 결정하다
support 뒷받침하다

20　독해　추론 (빈칸 완성 - 단어)　난이도 ★★☆

끊어읽기 해석

Text representations / must be built up / sequentially.
텍스트 표현은 / 구축되어야 한다 / 순차적으로

It is not possible / psychologically / to construct and integrate / a text representation / for a whole book chapter / or / a whole lecture.
가능하지 않다 / 심리적으로 / 구성하고 통합하는 것은 / 텍스트 표현을 / 전체 책의 장에 대한 / 또는 / 전체 강의(에 대한)

The chapter and the lecture / have to be processed / word by word / and / sentence by sentence.
장과 강의는 / 처리되어야 한다 / 단어별로 / 그리고 / 문장별로

As each text segment is processed, / it is immediately integrated with / the rest of the text / that is currently being held / in working memory.
각 텍스트 부분이 처리됨에 따라 / 그것은 즉시 통합된다 / 텍스트의 나머지 부분과 / 현재 보관되어 있는 / 작업 기억에

The immediate processing hypothesis / generally holds, / at least for lower-level processes / in comprehension.
즉각 처리 가설은 / 일반적으로 유지된다 / 적어도 하위 수준 단계에 대해서는 / 이해의

Occasionally, / however, / readers use delay strategies / when dealing / with potentially ambiguous syntactic constructions / or / they continue reading / when

constructing a situation model / when they do not understand something, / in the hope / that the succeeding text / will clarify their problem.
때때로 / 하지만 / 독자들은 <u>지연</u> 전략을 사용한다 / 다룰 때 / 잠재적으로 모호한 통사적 구조를 / 또는 / 그들은 계속해서 읽는다 / 상황 모델을 구축할 때 / 그들이 무언가를 이해하지 못하는 경우에 / 바라면서 / 다음 텍스트가 / 그들의 문제를 명확하게 해주기를

But / in general / information in a text / is processed / as soon as possible.
그러나 / 일반적으로 / 텍스트 안의 정보는 / 처리된다 / 가능한 한 빨리

In the model / this means / that as each text element is processed / and / a new proposition is added / to the text representation, / it is immediately integrated / with the text representation.
그 모델에서 / 이것은 의미한다 / 각 텍스트 요소가 처리되면 / 그리고 / 새로운 명제가 추가되면 / 텍스트 표현에 / 그것이 즉시 통합된다는 것을 / 텍스트 표현과

해석　텍스트 표현은 순차적으로 구축되어야 한다. 전체 책의 장 또는 전체 강의에 대한 텍스트 표현을 구성하고 통합하는 것은 심리적으로 가능하지 않다. 장과 강의는 단어별, 문장별로 처리되어야 한다. 각 텍스트 부분이 처리됨에 따라, 그것은 현재 작업 기억에 보관되어 있는 텍스트의 나머지 부분과 즉시 통합된다. 즉각 처리 가설은 일반적으로 적어도 이해의 하위 수준 단계에 대해서는 유지된다. 하지만, 때때로, 독자들은 잠재적으로 모호한 통사적 구조를 다룰 때 지연 전략을 사용하거나 그들이 무언가를 이해하지 못하는 경우에 상황 모델을 구축할 때, 다음 텍스트가 그들의 문제를 명확하게 해주기를 바라면서 계속해서 읽는다. 그러나 일반적으로 텍스트 안의 정보는 가능한 한 빨리 처리된다. 그 모델에서 이것은 각 텍스트 요소가 처리되고 텍스트 표현에 새로운 명제가 추가되면, 그것이 텍스트 표현과 즉시 통합된다는 것을 의미한다.

① 사회적
② 지연
③ 설명
④ 회상
⑤ 보상

해설　빈칸 앞부분에서 각 텍스트 부분이 처리됨에 따라, 그것은 현재 작업 기억에 보관되어 있는 텍스트의 나머지 부분과 즉시 통합된다고 설명하고 있고, 빈칸이 있는 문장에 '하지만(however)'이라는 역접의 의미를 갖는 연결어가 사용되었으며 독자들은 그들이 무언가를 이해하지 못하는 경우에 상황 모델을 구축할 때 다음 텍스트가 그들의 문제를 명확하게 해주기를 바라면서 계속 읽는다는 설명이 있으므로, 빈칸에는 때때로 독자들은 잠재적으로 모호한 통사적 구조를 다룰 때 '② 지연' 전략을 사용한다는 내용이 들어가야 한다.

어휘　representation 표현, 표상　sequentially 순차적으로, 연속적으로
psychologically 심리적으로　construct 구성하다
integrate 통합하다　process 처리하다　segment 부분, 부문
immediately 즉시　hypothesis 가설　comprehension 이해
occasionally 때때로　ambiguous 모호한　syntactic 통사적
succeeding 다음의, 이어서 일어나는　proposition 명제
retrospection 회상　compensation 보상

정답

p.196

01	③ 어휘 – 어휘 & 표현	11	① 독해 – 세부내용 파악
02	① 어휘 – 어휘 & 표현	12	④ 독해 – 논리적 흐름 파악
03	⑤ 어휘 – 어휘 & 표현	13	③ 독해 – 추론
04	② 어휘 – 어휘 & 표현	14	② 독해 – 추론
05	① 어휘 – 어휘 & 표현	15	⑤ 문법 – 대명사 & 관계절 & 형용사와 부사
06	③ 문법 – 시제 & 능동태·수동태	16	⑤ 독해 – 전체내용 파악
07	② 문법 – 비교 구문	17	③ 독해 – 세부내용 파악
08	④ 문법 – 관계절	18	④ 독해 – 논리적 흐름 파악
09	④ 문법 – 수 일치	19	① 독해 – 추론
10	② 독해 – 논리적 흐름 파악	20	⑤ 독해 – 추론

취약영역 분석표

영역	세부 유형	문항 수	소계
어휘	어휘 & 표현	5	/5
문법	시제 & 능동태·수동태	1	/5
	비교 구문	1	
	관계절	1	
	수 일치	1	
	대명사 & 관계절 & 형용사와 부사	1	
독해	전체내용 파악	1	/10
	세부내용 파악	2	
	추론	4	
	논리적 흐름 파악	3	
총계			/20

· 자신이 취약한 영역은 '공무원 영어, 이렇게 출제된다!'(문제집 p.8)를 통해 다시 한번 확인하고 학습하시기 바랍니다.

---

01 어휘 어휘&표현 erupt = explode
난이도 ★☆☆

해석 그들이 폭발할 때, 그들은 대기 중으로 많은 양의 이산화탄소를 방출하여, 그것을 따뜻하게 한다.
① 해결하다
② 감소하다
③ 폭발하다
④ 견디다
⑤ 숙고하다

어휘 address 해결하다 endure 견디다, 지속하다 ponder 숙고하다

👍 이것도 알면 합격!

erupt(폭발하다)와 유사한 의미의 표현
= blow up, outbreak, burst

02 어휘 어휘&표현 sanction = embargo
난이도 ★★☆

해석 독일에서 만난 G7 선진국 지도자들은, 우크라이나가 이번 주 전쟁에서 승리할 수 있도록 지원하겠다는 그들의 약속을 다시 한번 강조했으며, 러시아 석유 수출 가격 상한선을 포함하여 러시아에 대한 새로운 제재를 추가했다.
① 제한
② 제공
③ 상품
④ 약속
⑤ 참여

어휘 reiterate 다시 한번 강조하다 commitment 약속 sanction 제재 cap 상한선, 한도 embargo 제한, 금지 provision 제공

👍 이것도 알면 합격!

sanction(제재)의 유의어
= restriction, penalty, injunction

03 어휘 어휘&표현 antagonistic = hostile
난이도 ★★★

해석 일반적으로, 젊은 사람들은 성적 경쟁을 할 때 종종 서로에 대해 적대적인 감정을 갖는다.
① 사치스러운
② 공감하는
③ 견딜 수 없는
④ 원래의
⑤ 적대적인

어휘 antagonistic 적대적인 extravagant 사치스러운 sympathetic 공감하는 unbearable 견딜 수 없는 aboriginal 원래의, 토착의 hostile 적대적인

👍 이것도 알면 합격!

antagonistic(적대적인)의 유의어
= adversarial, combative, conflictual

04 어휘 어휘&표현 at odds with = incongruent with
난이도 ★★☆

해석 과학자들은 구어에 대한 인간의 능력을 매우 중요시한다. 하지만 우리는 또한 이에 상응하는 방식인 비언어적 의사소통 방식도 가지고 있으며, 그러한 메시지들은 우리가 신중하게 선택한 단어들보다 더 많은 것을 드러낼 수도 있고 때로는 그것들과 상충될 수도 있다.
① ~과 조화하여
② ~과 일치하지 않는
③ ~에 필수적인
④ ~에 무관심한
⑤ ~에 우호적인

어휘 attach importance to ~을 중요시하다 capacity 능력 parallel ~에 상응하는 track 방식, 방법 nonverbal 비언어적인 at odds with ~과 상충하여 incongruent 일치하지 않는 indispensable 필수적인 indifferent 무관심한

이것도 알면 **합격!**

부사 still은 비교급을 뒤에서도 수식할 수 있다.
(ex) The author's new novel is good, but the previous one is better still.
그 작가의 새 소설도 좋지만, 이전 것이 훨씬 더 좋다.

---

05 어휘 어휘&표현 profanity 난이도 ★★★

해석 성인 관객들에게 '제한된' 영화들은 'R' 등급을 받고 노출과 성교 장면들을 포함한다. 이러한 영화들의 언어는 <u>비속어</u>를 포함하고, 보여지는 폭력은 보통 피와 다른 불쾌한 특수 효과로 촬영되어 매우 사실적일 수 있다.

① 비속어   ② 지침
③ 처벌   ④ 경고
⑤ 진부한 표현

어휘 nudity 노출 graphic 사실적인, 생생한 disturbing 불쾌한
profanity 비속어, 불경스러운 것 cliché 진부한 표현

이것도 알면 **합격!**

profanity(비속어)의 유의어
= obscenity, vulgarity, curse

---

06 문법 시제&능동태·수동태 난이도 ★★☆

해석 지금까지, 약 130명의 학생들이 정학 조치를 받았는데, 이것은 그들이 30일까지 도서관을 이용할 수 없다는 것을 의미한다.

해설 ③ 현재완료 시제 | 능동태·수동태 구별 문맥상 '지금까지 약 130명의 학생들이 정학 조치를 받았다'라는 과거에 시작된 일이 현재까지 영향을 미치는 상황을 표현하고 있으므로 현재완료 시제가 와야 하고, 주어(around 130 students)와 동사가 '정학 조치를 받다(주어지다)'라는 의미의 수동 관계이므로 현재완료 수동태 have been given이 들어가야 적절하다.

어휘 suspension 정학

이것도 알면 **합격!**

완료진행 시제(have/has/had been + -ing)는 기준 시점 이전에 시작된 일이 기준 시점까지 계속 진행 중임을 표현한다.
(ex) He has been playing the violin since this morning.
그는 오늘 아침부터 바이올린을 켜고 있다.

---

07 문법 비교 구문 난이도 ★★☆

해석 이러한 이유로, 드론은 전통적인 항공기보다 훨씬 더 작고 더 조작하기 쉬울 수 있다.

해설 ② 비교급 강조 표현 | 비교급 형태 문맥상 '전통적인 항공기보다 훨씬 더 작고 더 조작하기 쉬운'이라는 의미가 되어야 자연스러우므로 비교급 표현 '형용사/부사의 비교급 + than'으로 나타낼 수 있다. 비교급(smaller)을 강조하기 위해 비교급 표현 앞에 강조 표현 much가 올 수 있고, -able로 끝나는 3음절 이상의 형용사(maneuverable)는 'more + 원급'의 형태로 비교급을 나타내므로, much smaller and more maneuverable로 나타낸 ②번이 정답이다. 부사 very는 비교급을 강조하는 표현으로 쓸 수 없으므로, ①, ⑤번은 정답이 될 수 없다.

---

08 문법 관계절 난이도 ★★☆

해석 다른 세계의 생명체에 대한 모든 문제는 다음과 같은 질문을 던진다. 생명이란 무엇이며, 우리는 그것을 어떻게 인식할 것인가? 확실히, 생명체는 세포들(또는 한 개의 세포)로 이루어져 있으며 그들을 살아있게 하는 세 가지 중요한 과정을 공유한다. 그들은 에너지를 섭취하고, 폐(廢) 에너지를 방출하며, 번식을 통해 그들의 유전자를 물려준다. 하지만 그들은 또한 그들의 환경에 반응한다. 그들은 항상성, 즉 내부 균형을 유지한다. 그들은 진화하고 적응한다. 어떤 생명체들은 심지어 그들이 걸을 수 있고 그들을 둘러싸고 있는 우주에 대해 생각할 수 있는 지점까지 진화했다. 우리는 말 그대로 우주의 산물이다. 우리 몸에 있는 대부분의 원자와 분자는 별의 동력에서 만들어졌고, 우리가 받아서 생명을 가능하게 하는 에너지는 우리의 별인 태양으로부터 온다.

해설 ④ 관계부사와 관계대명사 비교 선행사(the point)가 장소를 나타내고 관계사 뒤에 완전한 절(they can ~ them)이 왔으므로 관계대명사 which를 장소를 나타내는 선행사와 함께 쓰이는 관계부사 where로 고쳐야 한다.

오답분석 ① 주어와 동사의 수 일치 주어 자리에 단수 명사(The whole issue)가 왔으므로 단수 동사 begs가 올바르게 쓰였다. 참고로, '주어와 동사 사이에 온 수식어 거품(about ~ worlds)은 동사의 수 결정에 영향을 주지 않는다.
② 보어 자리 동사 make는 목적격 보어를 갖는 동사인데, 보어 자리에는 명사나 형용사 역할을 하는 것이 와야 하므로 형용사 alive(살아 있는)가 올바르게 쓰였다.
③ 자동사 동사 respond는 전치사(to) 없이는 목적어를 취할 수 없는 자동사이므로 목적어(their environment)앞에 전치사 to(~에)가 올바르게 쓰였다.
⑤ 주어와 동사의 수 일치 주어 자리에 단수 명사(the energy)가 왔으므로 단수 동사 comes가 올바르게 쓰였다. 참고로, 주어와 동사 사이에 온 수식어 거품(we ~ life)은 동사의 수 결정에 영향을 주지 않는다.

어휘 recognize 인식하다 cell 세포 critical 중요한 ingest 섭취하다
excrete 방출하다 reproduction 번식 maintain 유지하다
homeostasis 항상성 internal 내부의 evolve 진화하다
adapt 적응하다 surround 둘러싸다 literally 말 그대로
atom 원자 molecule 분자 enable 가능하게 하다

이것도 알면 **합격!**

'전치사 + 관계대명사' 뒤에는 완전한 절이 온다.
(ex) The city in which <u>he was born</u> is a popular tourist destination.
그가 태어난 도시는 인기 있는 관광지이다.

(상단 좌측)

이것도 알면 **합격!**

at odds with(~과 상충하여)와 유사한 의미의 표현
= in conflict with, in disagreement with, inconsistent with

09 문법 수 일치   난이도 ★★☆

해석 타당성은 시험 평가에서 가장 중요한 고려 사항이다. 이 개념은 시험 점수에서 도출된 특정한 추론의 적절성, 의미성, 그리고 유용성을 나타낸다. 시험 타당성 검증은 그러한 추론을 뒷받침하기 위해 증거를 축적하는 과정이다. 주어진 시험에서 도출된 점수로 다양한 추론이 이루어질 수 있으며, 특정한 추론을 뒷받침하는 증거를 축적하는 많은 방법이 있다. 그러나, 타당성은 단일한 개념이다. 비록 증거가 여러 방법으로 축적될 수 있을지라도, 타당성은 항상 그 증거가 점수로부터 도출된 추론을 뒷받침하는 정도를 나타낸다. 시험 그 자체가 아니라, 시험의 특정한 용도에 관한 추론이 검증된다.

해설 ④ **주격 관계절의 수 일치** 주격 관계절(that ~ scores) 내의 동사는 선행사(the inferences)에 수 일치시켜야 하므로 단수 동사 is를 복수 동사 are로 고쳐야 한다.

오답 분석 ① **현재분사 vs. 과거분사** 수식받는 명사 the specific inferences와 분사가 '시험 점수에서 특정한 추론이 도출되다'라는 의미의 수동 관계이므로 과거분사 made가 올바르게 쓰였다.
② **현재분사 vs. 과거분사** 수식받는 명사 test와 분사가 '시험이 주어지다'라는 의미의 수동 관계이므로 과거분사 given이 올바르게 쓰였다.
③ **to 부정사의 역할** 문맥상 '특정한 추론을 뒷받침하는 증거'라는 의미가 되어야 자연스러우므로 형용사처럼 명사(evidence)를 수식할 수 있는 to 부정사를 완성하는 동사원형 support가 to 뒤에 올바르게 쓰였다.
⑤ **전치사 4: ~에 관하여** 문맥상 '시험의 특정한 용도에 관한 추론이 검증된다'라는 의미가 되어야 자연스러운데, '특정한 용도에 관한'은 '~에 관하여'라는 의미의 전치사 regarding을 사용하여 나타낼 수 있으므로 regarding이 올바르게 쓰였다.

어휘 validity 타당성 appropriateness 적절성 inference 추론 validation 타당성 검증 accumulate 축적하다 unitary 단일의

👍 **이것도 알면 합격!**

주어가 아래 접속사들로 연결된 경우, B에 동사를 수 일치시킨다.

Not A but B A가 아니라 B	either A or B A 또는 B 중 하나
neither A nor B A도 B도 아닌	not only A but (also) B A뿐만 아니라 B도

10 독해 논리적 흐름 파악 (문맥상 부적절한 어휘)   난이도 ★★☆

끊어읽기 해석

Databases provided / an ① efficient way / to store and search for data.
데이터베이스는 제공했다 / ① 효율적인 방법을 / 자료를 저장하고 검색하는

Organized into fields of information, / the database enabled marketers / to rank or select / various groups of individuals / from its master list of customers / —a practice called "modeling."
정보 분야로 조직된 / 데이터베이스는 마케터들이 할 수 있게 해 주었다 / 순위 매기거나 선택하는 것을 / 다양한 개인들의 그룹을 / 고객들의 주요 목록에서 / 이는 '모델링'이라고 불리는 행위이다

Through this process, / ② more mailings or calls needed to be made, / resulting in a higher response rate and lower costs.
이 과정을 통해, / ② 더 많은 우편물 발송이나 전화 통화가 필요하게 되었다 / 이는 더 높은 응답률과 더 낮은 비용을 낳았다

In addition to isolating a company's most ③ profitable customers, / marketers studied them, / profiled them, / and then used that profile / to find ④ similar customers.
회사의 가장 ③ 수익성 있는 고객들을 분리하는 것 외에도, / 마케터들은 그들을 연구하고, / 그들의 자료 수집을 하고, / 그런 다음 그 분석표를 사용했다 / ④ 유사한 고객들을 찾는 데

This, of course, required / not only information / about existing customers, / but the collection of data / about ⑤ prospective customers / as well.
이것은 물론 ~을 필요로 했다 / 정보뿐만 아니라 / 기존 고객들에 대한 / 자료 수집도 / ⑤ 잠재 고객들에 대한 / ~ 또한

해석 데이터베이스는 자료를 저장하고 검색하는 ① 효율적인 방법을 제공했다. 정보 분야로 조직된 데이터베이스는, 마케터들이 고객들의 주요 목록에서 다양한 개인들의 그룹을 순위 매기거나 선택할 수 있게 해 주었는데, 이는 '모델링'이라고 불리는 행위이다. 이 과정을 통해, ② 더 많은 우편물 발송이나 전화 통화가 필요하게 되었고, 이는 더 높은 응답률과 더 낮은 비용을 낳았다. 마케터들은 회사의 가장 ③ 수익성 있는 고객들을 분리하는 것 외에도, 그들을 연구하고, 자료 수집을 한 다음 그 분석표를 ④ 유사한 고객들을 찾는 데 사용했다. 이것은 물론, 기존 고객들에 대한 정보뿐만 아니라 ⑤ 잠재 고객들에 대한 자료 수집 또한 필요로 했다.

해설 지문 처음에서 데이터베이스가 자료를 저장하고 검색하는 효율적인 방법을 제공했다고 했고, 정보 분야로 조직된 이 데이터베이스는 마케터들이 고객들의 주요 목록에서 다양한 개인들의 그룹을 순위 매기거나 선택할 수 있게 해주었다고 했으며 지문 중간에서 그 과정을 통해 더 높은 응답률과 더 낮은 비용을 낳았다고 했으므로, 더 많은(more) 우편물 발송이나 전화 통화가 필요하게 되었다는 것은 문맥상 적절하지 않다. 따라서 ② more가 정답이다. 참고로, 주어진 more를 대신할 수 있는 어휘로는 '더 적은'이라는 의미의 less가 있다.

어휘 master 주요한 isolate 분리하다 profitable 수익성이 있는 profile 자료 수집을 하다; 분석표 prospective 잠재의, 장래의

11 독해 세부내용 파악 (내용 불일치 파악)   난이도 ★☆☆

끊어읽기 해석

Despite such losses, / Germany as a country is rich, / but a recent study from the European Central Bank suggests / that the typical German household is not.
그러한 손실에도 불구하고, / 한 국가로서의 독일은 부유하다 / 하지만 유럽 중앙은행의 최근 연구는 시사한다 / 일반적인 독일 가구는 그렇지 않다는 것을

Astonishingly, / the median household's net assets, / at €51,400, / are less than / those of the typical Italian, Spanish or even Greek household.
놀랍게도, / 중위 가구의 순자산은 / 51,400유로로, / ~보다 더 적다 / 일반적인 이탈리아, 스페인, 또는 심지어 그리스 가구의 그것들(순자산)보다

These figures need / careful interpretation.
이 수치들은 필요하다 / 신중한 해석이

Households in Germany are / smaller than in those countries, / and their average is / dragged down by the east, / where 20 years ago / no one had any assets to speak of.
독일의 가구들은 / 그 나라들(이탈리아, 스페인, 그리스)보다 더 작다 / 그리고 그들의 평균은 / 동부에 의해 끌어내려진다 / 이곳은 20년 전에 / 아무도 말할 자산이 없었다

Moreover, / the figures do not include / pension promises.
게다가, / 그 수치는 포함하지 않는다 / 연금 보장을

But / the main reason / for the poor showing is / that far fewer

people than in other European countries / own their homes.
하지만 / 주된 이유는 / 나쁜 성과의 / 다른 유럽 국가들보다 훨씬 더 적은
사람들이 / 집을 소유하고 있기 때문이다

Most households rent, / and the housing stock is / owned by
a relatively small number of people, / so Germany ends up
with / the most unequal distribution of household wealth / in
the euro zone.
대부분의 가구가 임대한다 / 그리고 주택 재고는 / 상대적으로 적은 수의
사람들이 소유한다 / 따라서 독일은 결국 ~가 되었다 / 가계 부(富)의 분배
가 가장 불평등한 국가가 / 유로존에서

해석 그러한 손실에도 불구하고, 한 국가로서의 독일은 부유하지만, 유
럽 중앙은행의 최근 연구는 일반적인 독일 가구는 그렇지 않다는
것을 시사한다. 놀랍게도, 중위 가구의 순자산은 51,400유로로, 일
반적인 이탈리아, 스페인, 또는 심지어 그리스 가구의 그것들(순자
산)보다 더 적다. 이 수치들은 신중한 해석이 필요하다. 독일의 가
구들은 그 나라들(이탈리아, 스페인, 그리스)보다 더 작고, 그들의
평균은 동부에 의해 끌어내려지는데, 이곳은 20년 전에 아무도 말
할 만한 자산이 없었다. 게다가, 그 수치는 연금 보장을 포함하지
않는다. 하지만 나쁜 성과의 주된 이유는 다른 유럽 국가들보다 훨
씬 더 적은 사람들이 집을 소유하기 때문이다. 대부분의 가구가 임
대하고, 주택 재고는 상대적으로 적은 수의 사람들이 소유하고 있
기 때문에, 독일은 결국 유로존(유로화를 통화로 사용하는 유럽 연
합 국가들)에서 가계 부(富)의 분배가 가장 불평등한 국가가 되었
다.

해설 지문 처음에 한 국가로서의 독일은 부유하지만, 유럽 중앙은행의
최근 연구는 일반적인 독일 가구는 그렇지 않다는 것을 시사한다는
내용이 있으므로, '① 전형적인 독일 가구가 부유하다는 최근 연구
결과가 있다'는 지문의 내용과 일치하지 않는다.

어휘 median 중위의, 중간의 household 가구, 가정
net asset 순자산 figure 수치 drag down ~을 끌어내리다
pension 연금 showing 성과, 실적 rent 임대하다
stock 재고 unequal 불평등한 distribution 분배

12 독해 논리적 흐름 파악 (무관한 문장 삭제) 난이도 ★★★

끊어읽기 해석

Now that we have some understanding of / how language
works, / we can go back / and try and answer the question
of / whether any animals have a true language.
우리가 ~에 대해 어느 정도 이해하므로 / 언어가 어떻게 작동하는지 / 우
리는 돌아갈 수 있다 / 그리고 ~에 대한 질문을 시도하고 대답할 수 있다 /
동물들이 진정한 언어를 가지고 있는지

① According to many leading scientists in the field, / the
answer is: maybe.
그 분야의 많은 선도적인 과학자들에 따르면, / 대답은 '아마도'이다

Most scientists agree / that human language is clearly
the most complex, / and that no other animal / has a
communication system that comes close.
대부분의 과학자들은 동의한다 / 인간의 언어가 분명히 가장 복잡하다는
것에 / 그리고 어떤 다른 동물도 / 비슷한 의사소통 체계를 가지고 있지 않
다는 것에

② Many forms of animal communication / do have some of
the elements of human language.
많은 형태의 동물 의사소통은 / 인간 언어 요소들의 일부를 가지고 있다

Some scientists believe that / certain animals, / such as
primates and marine mammals, / do use a type of language.
일부 과학자들은 ~을 믿는다 / 특정한 동물들이 / 영장류와 해양 포유류와
같은 / 일종의 언어를 사용한다고

③ For example, / vervet monkeys have / different sounds
for different predators.
예를 들어, / 버빗 원숭이들은 가지고 있다 / 서로 다른 포식자들을 위한
서로 다른 소리들을

When an alarm call is given, / the monkeys know / whether
they should be on the lookout / for an eagle, leopard, or
snake.
경보가 주어지면, / 그 원숭이들은 안다 / 그들이 경계해야 하는지 / 독수
리, 표범, 또는 뱀을

④ Monkeys aren't the only land mammals / that have a
complex communication system / with elements of human
language in it.
원숭이들은 유일한 육지 포유류가 아니다 / 복잡한 의사소통 체계를 가진 /
인간 언어의 요소가 포함된

⑤ These monkeys / are using arbitrary sounds / that have
agreed-upon meanings.
이 원숭이들은 / 임의의 소리를 사용하고 있다 / 합의된 의미를 가진

This is a key element of language.
이것은 언어의 핵심 요소이다

해석 우리는 언어가 어떻게 작동하는지에 대해 어느 정도 이해하게 되
었으므로, 우리는 돌아가서 동물들이 진정한 언어를 가지고 있는
지에 대한 질문을 시도하고 대답할 수 있다. ① 그 분야의 많은 선
도적인 과학자들에 따르면, 대답은 '아마도'이다. 대부분의 과학자
들은 인간의 언어가 분명히 가장 복잡하고, 어떤 다른 동물도 비슷
한 의사소통 체계를 가지고 있지 않다는 것에 동의한다. ② 많은
형태의 동물 의사소통은 인간 언어 요소들의 일부를 가지고 있다.
일부 과학자들은 영장류와 해양 포유류와 같은 특정한 동물들이
일종의 언어를 사용한다고 믿는다. ③ 예를 들어, 버빗 원숭이들은
서로 다른 포식자들을 위한 서로 다른 소리들을 가지고 있다. 경보
가 주어지면, 그 원숭이들은 독수리, 표범, 또는 뱀 중 어느 것을 경
계해야 하는지 안다. ④ 원숭이들은 인간 언어의 요소가 포함된 복
잡한 의사소통 체계를 가진 유일한 육지 포유류가 아니다. ⑤ 이
원숭이들은 합의된 의미를 가진 임의의 소리를 사용하고 있다. 이
것은 언어의 핵심 요소이다.

해설 지문 처음에서 우리는 동물들이 진정한 언어를 가지고 있는지에 대
한 질문을 시도하고 대답할 수 있다고 하고, ①번에서 그 질문에 대
한 과학자들의 대답은 '아마도'라고 하고 있다. 이어서 과학자들은
인간의 언어가 가장 복잡하다는 것에 동의한다고 언급한 뒤, ②번
에서 많은 형태의 동물 의사소통이 인간 언어 요소의 일부를 가지
고 있다고 설명하고, ③, ⑤번에서 이것에 대한 예시인 버빗 원숭
이들이 가진 소리에 대해 설명하고 있다. 그러나 ④번은 원숭이들
이 인간 언어의 요소가 포함된 복잡한 의사소통 체계를 가진 유일
한 육지 포유류가 아니라는 내용으로, 인간의 언어가 가장 복잡하
며 버빗 원숭이와 같은 일부 동물들은 인간 언어 요소의 일부를 가
지고 의사소통 한다고 설명하는 지문 전반의 내용과 관련이 없다.

어휘 leading 선도적인 element 요소 primate 영장류
mammal 포유류 lookout 경계 arbitrary 임의의

13 독해 추론 (빈칸 완성 - 연결어) 난이도 ★★☆

끊어읽기 해석

A 'cover' is typically defined / as a recording of a song / that
was first recorded by someone else.
'커버'는 일반적으로 정의된다 / 곡의 녹음으로 / 다른 사람에 의해 처음 녹
음되었던

Something like this / is given in many dictionaries and by
some scholars.

이와 같은 것은 / 많은 사전과 일부 학자들에 의해 주어진다

(A) For example, / Albin Zak provides a glossary entry / defining a 'cover version' / as "a recording of a song that has been recorded previously by another artist."

(A) 예를 들어, / Albin Zak은 용어 풀이 표제어를 제공한다 / '커버 버전'을 정의하는 / '이전에 다른 예술가에 의해 녹음되었던 곡의 녹음'이라고

Don Cusic writes, / "the definition of a 'cover' song is / one that has been recorded before."

Don Cusic은 쓴다 / '커버' 곡의 정의는 / 이전에 녹음되었던 적이 있는 곡이라고

Consider the song 'Let It Be,' / written by John Lennon and Paul McCartney.

<Let It Be>라는 곡을 생각해 보라 / John Lennon과 Paul McCartney에 의해 쓰인

Their band, the Beatles, had a hit with it / when they released their version / in 1970.

그들의 밴드인 비틀즈는 그것으로 히트를 쳤다 / 그들의 버전을 발표했을 때 / 1970년에

(B) However, / the first released recording of the song / —by a few months— / was by Aretha Franklin.

(B) 하지만, / 이 곡의 최초로 발표된 녹음은 / 몇 달 전에 / Aretha Franklin에 의해 이루어졌다

A website / which generates its descriptions automatically / labels the Beatles' version / as a cover of Franklin's, / and that is just what the usual definition would suggest.

웹사이트는 / 그것의 설명을 자동으로 생성하는 / 비틀즈의 버전을 분류한다 / Franklin의 커버로 / 그리고 그것이 바로 일반적인 정의가 시사하는 바일 것이다

해석 '커버'는 일반적으로 다른 사람에 의해 처음 녹음되었던 곡의 녹음으로 정의된다. 이와 같은 것은 많은 사전과 일부 학자들에 의해 주어진다. (A) 예를 들어, Albin Zak은 '커버 버전'을 정의하는 용어 풀이 표제어를 '이전에 다른 예술가에 의해 녹음되었던 곡의 녹음'이라고 제공한다. Don Cusic은 "커버" 곡의 정의는 이전에 녹음되었던 적이 있는 곡'이라고 쓴다. John Lennon과 Paul McCartney에 의해 쓰인 <Let It Be>라는 곡을 생각해 보라. 그들의 밴드인 비틀즈는 1970년에 그들의 버전을 발표했을 때 그것으로 히트를 쳤다. (B) 하지만, 이 곡의 최초로 발표된 녹음은 몇 달 전에 Aretha Franklin에 의해 이루어졌다. 설명을 자동으로 생성하는 웹사이트는 비틀즈의 버전을 Franklin의 커버로 분류하는데, 그것이 바로 일반적인 정의가 시사하는 바일 것이다.

	(A)	(B)
①	예를 들어	그러므로
②	게다가	그럼에도 불구하고
③	예를 들어	하지만
④	예를 들어	결과적으로
⑤	게다가	하지만

해설 **(A)** 빈칸 앞부분은 '커버'에 대한 정의가 많은 사전과 일부 학자들에 의해 주어진다는 내용이고, (A) 빈칸 뒤에 '커버'를 정의하는 Albin Zak과 Don Cusic의 예시가 나오고 있으므로 (A)에는 For example(예를 들어)이 들어가야 한다. **(B)** 빈칸 앞부분은 비틀즈가 1970년에 <Let It Be>에 대한 그들의 버전을 발표했을 때 히트를 쳤다는 내용이고, (B) 빈칸 뒤 문장은 이 곡(Let It Be)의 최초로 발표된 녹음은 몇 달 전에 Aretha Franklin에 의해 이루어졌다는 대조적인 내용이므로, (B)에는 However(하지만)가 들어가야 한다. 따라서 ③번이 정답이다.

어휘 **typically** 일반적으로 **scholar** 학자 **glossary** 용어 풀이 **entry** 표제어 **previously** 이전에 **release** 발표하다 **generate** 생성하다 **description** 설명 **automatically** 자동으로

---

14 **독해** 추론 (빈칸 완성 - 단어) 난이도 ★★☆

끊어읽기 해석

As the scale of economic activity has proceeded steadily upward, / the scope of environmental problems / triggered by that activity / has transcended / both **(A)** geographic and **(B)** generational boundaries.

경제 활동의 규모가 꾸준히 증가함에 따라, / 환경 문제의 범위는 / 그 활동에 의해 촉발된 / 넘어섰다 / (A) 지리적이고 (B) 세대적인 경계를 모두

When the environmental problems were smaller in scale, / the nation-state used to be a sufficient form of political organization / for resolving them, / but is that still the case?

환경 문제의 규모가 더 작았을 때, / 민족 국가는 충분한 정치적 조직의 형태였다 / 그것들을 해결하기 위한 / 하지만 그것이 여전히 사실인가?

Whereas each generation used to have the luxury / of being able to satisfy its own needs / without worrying about the needs of generations to come, / intergenerational effects are now more prominent.

각 세대가 사치를 누렸던 반면에 / 자신의 요구를 충족시킬 수 있는 / 미래 세대의 요구에 대해 걱정하지 않고 / 이제는 세대 간 영향이 더 두드러진다

Solving problems / such as poverty, climate change, ozone depletion, and the loss of biodiversity / requires international cooperation.

문제들을 해결하는 것은 / 빈곤, 기후 변화, 오존 고갈, 그리고 생물 다양성의 상실과 같은 / 국제적인 협력을 필요로 한다

Because future generations cannot speak for themselves, / the current generation / must speak for them.

미래 세대가 스스로를 대변할 수 없기 때문에 / 현세대가 / 그들을 대변해야 한다

Current policies / must incorporate our obligation to future generations, / however difficult or imperfect that incorporation might prove to be.

현재의 정책은 / 미래 세대에 대한 우리의 의무를 포함해야 한다 / 통합이 어렵거나 불완전한 것으로 판명될 수 있더라도

해석 경제 활동의 규모가 꾸준히 증가함에 따라, 그 활동에 의해 촉발된 환경 문제의 범위는 (A) 지리적이고 (B) 세대적인 경계를 모두 넘어섰다. 환경 문제의 규모가 더 작았을 때, 민족 국가는 그것들을 해결하기 위한 충분한 정치적 조직의 형태였지만, 여전히 그것이 사실인가? 각 세대가 미래 세대의 요구에 대해 걱정하지 않고 자신의 요구를 충족시킬 수 있는 사치를 누렸던 반면, 이제는 세대 간 영향이 더 두드러진다. 빈곤, 기후 변화, 오존 고갈, 그리고 생물 다양성의 상실과 같은 문제들을 해결하는 것은 국제적인 협력을 필요로 한다. 미래 세대가 스스로를 대변할 수 없기 때문에, 현세대가 그들을 대변해야 한다. 현재의 정책은 통합이 어렵거나 불완전한 것으로 판명될 수 있더라도, 미래 세대에 대한 우리의 의무를 포함해야 한다.

	(A)	(B)
①	문화 간의	경제적인
②	지리적인	세대적인
③	정치적인	사회 문화적인
④	생태학적인	도덕의
⑤	환경적인	행동의

해설 지문 처음에서 환경 문제의 규모가 더 작았을 때, 민족 국가는 그것들을 해결하기 위한 충분한 정치적 조직의 형태였지만, 여전히 그것이 사실인지 의문을 제기하고 있고, 지문 중간에서 각 세대가 미래 세대의 요구에 대해 걱정하지 않고 자신의 요구를 충족시킬 수 있는 사치를 누렸던 반면, 이제는 세대 간 영향이 더 두드러진다고 설명하고 있으므로 빈칸에는 경제 활동에 의해 촉발된 환경 문제의 범위는 '지리적', '세대적' 경계를 모두 넘어섰다는 내용이 들어가야 적절하다.

따라서 ② (A) geographic(지리적인) - (B) generational(세대적인)이 정답이다.

어휘 steadily 꾸준히 trigger 촉발하다 transcend 넘어서다 boundary 경계 nation-state 민족 국가 sufficient 충분한 resolve 해결하다 prominent 두드러진 poverty 빈곤 depletion 고갈 biodiversity 생물 다양성 cooperation 협력 incorporate 통합하다 obligation 의무 imperfect 불완전한 geographic 지리적인 ecological 생태학적인

15 문법 대명사&관계절&형용사와 부사 난이도 ★★★

해석 의사 전달 소리가 진화하는 데 그렇게 오래 걸린 이유는 무엇인가? 박테리아와 단세포 생명체는 알려진 소리 신호 없이 30억 년 동안 존재했다. 비록 이 모든 세포들이 물의 움직임과 진동을 감지할 수 있었지만, 아무것도 소리로 다른 것들에게 접근하지 않았다. 처음 3억 년 동안의 동물 진화 역시, 어떠한 의사 전달의 신호도 없었던 것으로 보인다. 이 시기에 알려진 어떤 화석도 거친 소리나 다른 소리 생성 구조를 가지고 있지 않다. 내가 조언을 구한 전문적인 고생물학자들은 모두 최초의 귀뚜라미와 매미와 같은 곤충이 진화하기 전까지는 동물의 소리 생성 구조에 대한 물리적 증거를 알지 못했다고 말했다. 물론, 화석 기록은 불완전하고 물고기의 부레와 같은 일부 소리 생성 구조들은 바위에 흔적을 거의 또는 아예 남기지 않아서, 우리는 이 거대한 시간의 기간에 걸쳐 불완전하게 듣는다.

해설 (A) 부정대명사: other 부정형용사 other(다른)은 명사 없이 전치사(to)의 목적어 자리에 올 수 없고, 문맥상 '다른 것들에게'라는 의미가 되어야 자연스러우므로 부정대명사 others가 들어가야 적절하다.
(B) 관계대명사 선행사(The expert paleontologists)가 사람이고, 관계절 내에서 advice가 누구의 조언인지를 나타내므로 사람을 가리키는 소유격 관계대명사 whose가 들어가야 적절하다.
(C) 수량 표현 문맥상 '일부 소리 생성 구조들은 바위에 흔적을 거의 남기지 않는다'라는 의미가 되어야 자연스러우므로, '거의 없는'이라는 의미의 수량 표현 little이 들어가야 적절하다.
따라서 ⑤번이 정답이다.

어휘 evolve 진화하다 single-celled 단세포의 sonic 소리의 motion 움직임 vibration 진동 reach out 접근하다 paleontologist 고생물학자 cricket 귀뚜라미 cicada 매미 swim bladder 부레 trace 흔적

👍 이것도 알면 합격!

each other, one another은 '서로서로'라는 뜻으로 쓰인다.
(ex) The team members supported **one another** throughout the project.
그 팀 구성원들은 프로젝트 내내 서로서로 도왔다.

16 독해 전체내용 파악 (제목 파악) 난이도 ★★☆

끊어읽기 해석

Eating at home / is the norm for most people on most days, / yet traditions of eating out / go back centuries, / and the practice is typical.
집에서 식사하는 것은 / 대부분의 날에 대부분의 사람들에게 표준이다 / 하지만 외식의 전통은 / 수 세기 전으로 거슬러 올라간다 / 그리고 그 관습은 전형적이다

The French / do not eat outside of the home / as frequently

as residents of some nations / with a comparable standard of living, / such as the United Kingdom.
프랑스인들은 / 집 밖에서 식사를 하지 않는다 / 일부 국가의 거주민들만큼 자주 / 비슷한 생활 수준을 가진 / 영국과 같이

Nonetheless, / the trend to take meals outside of the home / increases perceptibly / in France, / if not as quickly as in some affluent nations.
그럼에도 불구하고, / 집 밖에서 식사를 하는 경향이 / 눈에 띄게 증가한다 / 프랑스에서 / 일부 부유한 나라들만큼 빠르게는 아니더라도

Between 1970 and 1990, / household spending on eating out / increased 0.25 percent, / and expenditure for food to be eaten at home / fell by a full 7 percent.
1970년과 1990년 사이에, / 외식에 대한 가계 소비는 / 0.25퍼센트 증가했다 / 그리고 집에서 먹을 음식에 대한 지출은 / 7퍼센트 감소했다

An estimate from 2004 / calculated / 9 billion meals out taken annually.
2004년의 추정치는 / 계산했다 / 연간 90억 번의 외식이 이루어졌다고

Of these people / ate 3.7 billion meals in cafeterias and other collective settings / and 4.6 billion in commercial restaurants, / from fine restaurants to fast-food restaurants and chains.
이 사람들 중 / 37억 명이 식당과 다른 공동의 장소에서 식사를 했다 / 그리고 46억 명이 상업적인 식당에서 (식사를 했다) / 고급 레스토랑에서 패스트푸드점과 체인점에 이르기까지의

해석 집에서 식사하는 것은 대부분의 날에 대부분의 사람들에게 표준이지만, 외식의 전통은 수 세기 전으로 거슬러 올라가며, 그 관습은 전형적이다. 프랑스인들은 영국과 같이 비슷한 생활 수준을 가진 일부 국가의 거주민들만큼 자주 집 밖에서 식사를 하지 않는다. 그럼에도 불구하고, 일부 부유한 나라들만큼 빠르게는 아니더라도, 프랑스에서 집 밖에서 식사를 하는 경향이 눈에 띄게 증가한다. 1970년과 1990년 사이에, 외식에 대한 가계 소비는 0.25퍼센트 증가했고, 집에서 먹을 음식에 대한 지출은 7퍼센트 감소했다. 2004년의 추정치는 연간 90억 번의 외식이 이루어졌다고 계산했다. 이 사람들 중 37억 명이 식당과 다른 공동의 장소에서 식사를 했고, 46억 명이 고급 레스토랑에서 패스트푸드점과 체인점에 이르기까지의 상업적인 식당에서 식사를 했다.

① 유럽의 화려한 식당
② 프랑스의 패스트푸드 체인점
③ 프랑스의 전통음식
④ 전형적인 프랑스 음식
⑤ 프랑스에서의 외식

해설 지문 전반에 걸쳐 프랑스에서 집 밖에서 식사를 하는 경향이 눈에 띄게 증가한다는 것에 대해 설명하고 있으므로, '⑤ 프랑스에서의 외식'이 이 글의 제목이다.

어휘 norm 표준, 기준 tradition 전통 practice 관습 resident 거주민 comparable ~과 비슷한, 비교할 만한 standard 수준, 기준 perceptibly 눈에 띄게 affluent 부유한 expenditure 지출 estimate 추정치 annually 연간 collective 공동의, 집단적인

17 독해 세부내용 파악 (내용 일치 파악) 난이도 ★☆☆

끊어읽기 해석

①Glass Beach was created by accident.
Glass Beach는 우연히 만들어졌다

Beginning in 1906, / people were permitted to throw away their garbage / in the ocean near the city.
1906년부터, / 사람들은 쓰레기를 버리는 것이 허용되었다 / 도시 근처의 바다에

People threw away glass bottles, appliances, and even cars.

사람들은 유리병, 가전제품, 심지어 자동차까지 버렸다

②In 1967, / the local government / made it illegal / to throw away trash in the water.
1967년에, / 지방 정부는 / 불법으로 만들었다 / 쓰레기를 물에 버리는 것을

③After this, / there were many cleanup efforts / to recycle the metal and the other non-biodegradable waste.
이후, / 많은 정화 노력이 있었다 / 금속과 다른 비(非)생분해성 폐기물을 재활용하기 위한

However, / most of the glass / had already been broken into tiny pieces.
하지만, / 대부분의 유리는 / 이미 아주 작은 조각들로 깨져 있었다

④The glass was too difficult to remove, / so it was left in the water.
그 유리는 제거하기가 너무 어려웠다 / 그래서 물속에 남겨졌다

Over time, / the pounding waves / caused the rough pieces of glass to become smooth.
시간이 지나면서, / 파도의 타격이 / 거친 유리조각들을 매끄러워지게 만들었다

⑤These green, white, and brown pieces of smooth glass / began washing up on shore, / creating Glass Beach.
이 녹색, 흰색, 그리고 갈색의 매끄러운 유리조각들이 / 해안가로 씻겨 내려오기 시작했다 / 그리고 Glass Beach를 만들었다

해석 Glass Beach는 우연히 만들어졌다. 1906년부터, 사람들은 도시 근처의 바다에 쓰레기를 버리는 것이 허용되었다. 사람들은 유리병, 가전제품, 심지어 자동차까지 버렸다. 1967년에, 지방 정부는 쓰레기를 물에 버리는 것을 불법으로 만들었다. 이후, 금속과 다른 비(非)생분해성 폐기물을 재활용하기 위한 많은 정화 노력이 있었다. 하지만, 대부분의 유리는 이미 아주 작은 조각들로 깨져 있었다. 그 유리는 제거하기가 너무 어려워서, 물속에 남겨졌다. 시간이 지나면서, 파도의 타격이 거친 유리조각들을 매끄러워지게 만들었다. 이 녹색, 흰색, 그리고 갈색의 매끄러운 유리조각들이 해안가로 씻겨 내려오기 시작했고, Glass Beach를 만들었다.

해설 ③번의 키워드인 금속(the metal)이 그대로 언급된 지문 주변의 내용에서 지방 정부가 쓰레기를 물에 버리는 것을 불법으로 만든 이후, 금속과 다른 비(非)생분해성 폐기물을 재활용하기 위한 많은 정화 노력이 있었다고 했으므로, '③ 금속 폐기물을 재활용하기 위한 노력이 있었다'는 지문의 내용과 일치한다.

오답 분석
① 첫 번째 문장에서 Glass Beach는 우연히 만들어졌다고 했으므로, 지문의 내용과 다르다.
② 네 번째 문장에서 1967년에 지방 정부가 쓰레기를 물에 버리는 것을 불법으로 만들었다고 했으므로, 지문의 내용과 다르다.
④ 일곱 번째 문장에서 작은 조각들로 깨진 유리는 제거하기가 너무 어려워서 물속에 남겨졌다고 했으므로, 지문의 내용과 다르다.
⑤ 마지막 문장에서 매끄러운 유리조각들이 해안가로 씻겨 내려오기 시작했고, Glass Beach를 만들었다고는 했지만, 거대한 유리조각들이 Glass Beach를 관광명소로 만들었는지는 알 수 없다.

어휘 by accident 우연히 permit 허용하다 appliance 가전제품 biodegradable 생분해성의 remove 제거하다 shore 해안가

18 독해 논리적 흐름 파악 (문단 순서 배열) 난이도 ★★☆

끊어읽기 해석

Some visual displays / are meant only for members / of an animal's own species.
일부 시각적 표시는 / 구성원들만을 위한 것이나 / 동물들의 같은 종의

These include / mating rituals and signals / that tell a group when to move to a new location.
이것들은 포함한다 / 짝짓기 의식과 신호를 / 무리에게 새로운 장소로 언제 이동해야 하는지를 알려주는

Have you ever noticed / that when a flock of birds takes off, / they often all leave together?
알아차린 적이 있는가 / 한 무리의 새들이 날아오를 때, / 그들이 종종 모두 함께 떠난다는 것을

(A) The only difference is / that instead of using sound, / one of the more dominant birds / will signal to the rest of the birds / using an action / called an intention movement.
유일한 차이점은 / 소리를 사용하는 대신에, / 더 우세한 새들 중 하나가 / 나머지 새들에게 신호를 보낼 것이라는 것이다 / 행동을 사용하여 / 의도 행동이라고 불리는

(B) In a typical "take off" signal, / one bird will raise its wings / and lift off the ground a few inches.
일반적인 '날아오르기' 신호에서, / 한 마리의 새가 날개를 들 것이다 / 그리고 땅에서 몇 인치 날아오를 것이다

(C) It's almost as if / one of them said, "Let's go."
이것은 마치 ~인 것 같다 / 그들 중 한 마리가 "가자"라고 말한

In fact, / this is exactly what happens.
사실, / 이것이 정확히 일어나는 일이다

Seeing this, / the birds around it / will pick up the signal / and pass it / to the other members of the group.
이것을 보고, / 주변의 새들이 / 그 신호를 포착할 것이다 / 그리고 그것을 전달할 것이다 / 무리의 다른 구성원들에게

Within a few seconds, / the whole flock / lifts off and heads into the sky.
몇 초 안에, / 전체 무리는 / 하늘로 날아오른다

해석
일부 시각적 표시는 동물들의 같은 종 구성원들만을 위한 것이다. 이것들은 짝짓기 의식과 무리에게 새로운 장소로 언제 이동해야 하는지를 알려주는 신호를 포함한다. 당신은 한 무리의 새들이 날아오를 때, 그들이 종종 모두 함께 떠난다는 것을 알아차린 적이 있는가?

(C) 이것은 마치 그들 중 한 마리가 "가자."라고 말한 것 같다. 사실, 이것이 정확히 일어나는 일이다.

(A) 유일한 차이점은 소리를 사용하는 대신에, 더 우세한 새들 중 하나가 의도 행동이라고 불리는 행동을 사용하여 나머지 새들에게 신호를 보낼 것이라는 것이다.

(B) 일반적인 '날아오르기' 신호에서, 한 마리의 새가 날개를 들고 땅에서 몇 인치 날아오를 것이다.

이것을 보고, 주변의 새들이 그 신호를 포착하고 그것을 무리의 다른 구성원들에게 전달할 것이다. 몇 초 안에, 전체 무리는 하늘로 날아오른다.

해설 처음에 주어진 글에서 한 무리의 새들이 날아오를 때, 그들이 종종 모두 함께 떠난다고 한 뒤, (C)에서 이것이 마치 그들 중 한 마리가 "가자."라고 말한 것 같으며, 정확히 일어나는 일이라고 설명하고 있다. 이어서 (A)에서 소리를 사용하는 대신에 더 우세한 새들 중 하나가 나머지 새들에게 신호를 보낼 것이라고 하고, (B)에서 일반적인 '날아오르기' 신호에서, 한 마리의 새가 날개를 들고 땅에서 몇 인치 날아오를 것이라고 설명하고 있다. 뒤이어 마지막에 주어진 글에서 이것(this)을 보고 주변의 새들이 그 신호를 포착하고 그것을 무리의 다른 구성원들에게 전달할 것이라고 설명하고 있다. 따라서 ④ (C) – (A) – (B)가 정답이다.

어휘 mating 짝짓기 ritual 의식 flock 무리, 떼 take off 날아오르다 dominant 우세한 intention 의도 lift off 날아오르다, 이륙하다

끊어읽기 해석

> What counts / as private information or as intrusion / can vary / among cultures / and even within subcultures of a particular society.
> 간주되는 것은 / 개인 정보 또는 침범으로 / 다를 수 있다 / 문화마다 / 그리고 심지어 특정 사회의 하위문화 내에서도
>
> Whether an act is regarded / as intrusion or comfortable familiarity / depends on / <u>the circumstances and shared understandings of those involved</u>.
> 어떤 행동이 여겨지는지는 / 침범 아니면 편안한 친숙함으로 / ~에 달려 있다 / <u>상황과 관련된 사람들의 공유된 합의에</u>
>
> For example, / knocking on doors / and waiting to be granted permission to enter / is one way / that privacy is respected / in some cultures.
> 예를 들어, / 문을 두드리는 것은 / 그리고 들어갈 허락을 받는 것을 기다리는 것은 / 한 가지 방법이다 / 사생활이 존중되는 / 일부 문화에서
>
> In other cultures, / it is acceptable / for people / to walk unannounced through entranceways / or to enter a friend's or family member's home / without knocking.
> 다른 문화에서는, / ~이 받아들여진다 / 사람들에게 / 예고 없이 입구를 통과하는 것이 / 또는 친구나 가족의 집에 들어가는 것이 / 노크 없이

해석 개인 정보 또는 침범으로 간주되는 것은 문화마다 다를 수 있으며 심지어 특정 사회의 하위문화 내에서도 다를 수 있다. 어떤 행동이 침범으로 여겨지는지 아니면 편안한 친숙함으로 여겨지는지는 <u>상황과 관련된 사람들의 공유된 합의</u>에 달려 있다. 예를 들어, 문을 두드리고 들어갈 허락을 받는 것을 기다리는 것은 일부 문화에서 사생활이 존중되는 한 가지 방법이다. 다른 문화에서는, 사람들에게 예고 없이 입구를 통과하거나 친구나 가족의 집에 노크 없이 들어가는 것이 받아들여진다.

① 상황과 관련된 사람들의 공유된 합의
② 사생활과 관련된 권리와 책임
③ 간섭받지 않고 삶을 살 수 있는 사람들의 능력
④ 개인 정보에 대한 개인의 통제
⑤ 사생활을 보호하기 위한 법의 효력

해설 빈칸 뒤 문장에서 일부 문화에서는 문을 두드리고 들어갈 허락을 받는 것을 기다리는 것이 사생활이 존중되는 한 가지 방법이고, 다른 문화에서는 사람들에게 예고 없이 출입구를 통과하거나 친구나 가족의 집에 노크 없이 들어가는 것이 허용된다고 하며 어떤 행동이 침범이나 편안한 친숙함으로 여겨지는 것은 상황이나 공유된 합의에 달려있다는 것에 대한 예시를 들고 있다. 따라서, 빈칸에는 어떤 행동이 침범으로 여겨지는지 아니면 편안한 친숙함으로 여겨지는지는 '① 상황과 관련된 사람들의 공유된 합의'에 달려 있다는 내용이 들어가야 한다.

어휘 intrusion 침범, 침입　vary 다르다, 달라지다　subculture 하위문화　particular 특정한　familiarity 친숙함　grant 부여하다, 허가하다　acceptable 받아들일 만한　unannounced 예고 없이　entranceway 입구, 통로　circumstance 상황　understanding 합의, 이해　associated with ~과 관련된　interfere 간섭하다, 방해하다　efficacy 효력

끊어읽기 해석

> Researchers at Princeton University and the University of California, Los Angeles, found / that students who handwrote lecture notes / rather than typing them out /

> retained more of the information precisely / because they were slowed down.
> 프린스턴 대학교와 캘리포니아 대학교 로스앤젤레스 캠퍼스의 연구원들은 발견했다 / 강의 노트를 손으로 쓴 학생들이 / 그것들을 타이핑하기보다는 / 더 많은 정보를 정확하게 보유했다 / 그들의 속도가 느려졌기 때문에
>
> A quick keyboard transcription / doesn't require critical thinking.
> 빠른 키보드 필사는 / 비판적인 사고를 필요로 하지 않는다
>
> The slower process of handwriting means / not everything will be captured verbatim; / instead, / the brain is forced to exert more effort / to capture the essence of what's important, / thus <u>committing the information</u> / <u>more effectively</u> / <u>to memory</u>.
> 손으로 쓰는 것의 더 느린 과정은 의미한다 / 모든 것이 글자 그대로 포착되지는 않을 것이라는 것을 / 대신에, / 뇌는 더 많은 노력을 해야 한다 / 중요한 것의 본질을 포착하기 위해 / 따라서 <u>정보를 남긴다</u> / <u>더 효과적으로</u> / <u>기억에</u>
>
> Slowing down / doesn't mean being slow; / it just means / taking a few minutes / to absorb / what we are seeing.
> 속도를 늦추는 것은 / 느리다는 것을 의미하는 것이 아니다 / 단지 의미한다 / 몇 분이 걸린다는 것을 / 흡수하는 데 / 우리가 보고 있는 것을
>
> Details, patterns, and relationships / take time to register.
> 세부 정보, 양상, 그리고 관계는 / 기억하는 것에 시간이 걸린다
>
> Nuances and new information can be missed / if we rush past them.
> 뉘앙스와 새로운 정보를 놓칠 수 있다 / 우리가 그것들을 서둘러 지나치면

해석 프린스턴 대학교와 캘리포니아 대학교 로스앤젤레스 캠퍼스의 연구원들은 강의 노트를 타이핑하기보다는 손으로 쓴 학생들이 속도가 느려졌기 때문에 더 많은 정보를 정확하게 보유했다는 것을 발견했다. 빠른 키보드 필사는 비판적인 사고를 필요로 하지 않는다. 손으로 쓰는 것의 더 느린 과정은 모든 것이 글자 그대로 포착되지는 않을 것이라는 것을 의미한다. 대신에, 뇌는 중요한 것의 본질을 포착하기 위해 더 많은 노력을 해야 하고, 따라서 <u>정보를 더 효과적으로 기억에 남긴다</u>. 속도를 늦추는 것은 느리다는 것을 의미하는 것이 아니라, 단지 우리가 보고 있는 것을 흡수하는 데 몇 분이 걸린다는 것을 의미한다. 세부 정보, 양상, 그리고 관계는 기억하는 것에 시간이 걸린다. 우리가 서둘러 지나치면 뉘앙스와 새로운 정보를 놓칠 수 있다.

① 더 많은 정보에 대한 우리의 주의를 산만하게 한다
② 상상의 모든 과정의 속도를 높인다
③ 우리의 정신적 자원을 다양한 과업에 할당한다
④ 너무 많은 정보로 기억을 범람시킨다
⑤ 정보를 더 효과적으로 기억에 남긴다

해설 빈칸 앞부분에 강의 노트를 손으로 쓴 학생들이 속도가 느려졌기 때문에 더 많은 정보를 정확하게 보유했다는 연구 결과에 대해 설명하고 있고, 빈칸 뒷부분에 세부 정보, 양상, 그리고 관계는 기억하는 것에 시간이 걸리며, 우리가 그것들을 서둘러 지나치면 뉘앙스와 새로운 정보를 놓칠 수 있다는 내용이 있다. 따라서 빈칸에는 뇌는 중요한 것의 본질을 포착하기 위해 더 많은 노력을 해야 하고, 따라서 '⑤ 정보를 더 효과적으로 기억에 남긴다'는 내용이 들어가야 적절하다.

어휘 retain 보유하다　precisely 정확하게　transcription 필사, 전사　critical 비판적인　verbatim 글자 그대로, 말 그대로　exert 노력하다, 분투하다　essence 본질　absorb 흡수하다　register 기억하다, 알아채다　assign 할당하다　inundate 범람시키다　commit (기록·기억 등에) 남겨두다

정답

p.203

01	④ 어휘 – 어휘&표현	11	⑤ 어휘 – 어휘&표현
02	③ 어휘 – 어휘&표현	12	⑤ 어휘 – 어휘&표현
03	④ 문법 – 시제	13	③ 독해 – 추론
04	① 독해 – 추론	14	③ 문법 – 관계절
05	⑤ 독해 – 추론	15	④ 독해 – 논리적 흐름 파악
06	② 독해 – 세부내용 파악	16	① 독해 – 추론
07	② 문법 – 능동태·수동태	17	② 독해 – 전체내용 파악
08	③ 독해 – 논리적 흐름 파악	18	① 문법 – 수 일치
09	⑤ 독해 – 추론	19	④ 어휘 – 어휘&표현
10	① 독해 – 추론	20	⑤ 독해 – 논리적 흐름 파악

취약영역 분석표

영역	세부 유형	문항 수	소계
어휘	어휘&표현	5	/5
	생활영어	0	
문법	시제	1	/4
	능동태·수동태	1	
	관계절	1	
	수 일치	1	
독해	전체내용 파악	1	/11
	세부내용 파악	1	
	추론	6	
	논리적 흐름 파악	3	
총계			/20

· 자신이 취약한 영역은 '공무원 영어, 이렇게 출제된다!'(문제집 p.8)를 통해 다시 한번 확인하고 학습하시기 바랍니다.

---

01 | 어휘 | 어휘&표현 | inimical = harmful
난이도 ★★☆

해석 이러한 경제 정책들은 사회의 이익에 해롭다.
① 잘 받아들이는
② 고된
③ 유리한
④ 해로운
⑤ 적절한

어휘 inimical 해로운 amenable 잘 받아들이는 arduous 고된
favorable 유리한, 호의적인 harmful 해로운 pertinent 적절한

👍 이것도 알면 **합격!**

inimical(해로운)의 유의어
= detrimental, injurious, deleterious, unfavorable, adverse

---

02 | 어휘 | 어휘&표현 | dissipate = scatter
난이도 ★★☆

해석 한 원자의 집단이 외부의 에너지원에 의해 움직이고 열원에 둘러싸여 있을 때, 그것은 대개 점점 더 많은 에너지를 방산하기 위해 점진적으로 스스로를 재구성한다.
① 보존하다
② 만들다
③ 확산하다
④ 확보하다
⑤ 활용하다

어휘 atom 원자 heat bath 열원 restructure 재구성하다, 개조하다
dissipate 방산하다, 낭비하다 conserve 보존하다
scatter 확산하다, 흩뿌리다 secure 확보하다; 안전한
utilize 활용하다

👍 이것도 알면 **합격!**

dissipate(방산하다)의 유의어
= disperse, strew, distribute, spray

---

03 | 문법 | 시제
난이도 ★★☆

해석 ① 어제 의회에서 논의된 문제는 새로운 세금에 관한 것이었다.
② 빨간 조끼를 입은 한 남자가 롤러스케이트를 신고 가만히 서 있다.
③ 그들은 딸과 사귀고 있던 남자를 알고 있었다.
④ 그 목록은 그 소유자에게 속한 모든 항목을 보여 준다.
⑤ 당국은 진실을 알고 있는 사람들을 두려워한다.

해설 ④ 현재진행 시제 상태를 나타내는 동사 belong(~에 속하다)은 진행 시제로 쓸 수 없으므로 현재진행 시제 are belonging to를 현재 시제 belong to로 고쳐야 한다.

오답
분석 ① 현재분사 vs. 과거분사 | 주어와 동사의 수 일치 수식받는 명사 (The question)와 분사가 '문제가 논의되다'라는 의미의 수동 관계이므로 과거분사 debated가 올바르게 쓰였다. 또한, 주어 자리에 단수 명사 The question이 왔으므로 단수 동사 was가 올바르게 쓰였다. 참고로, 주어와 동사 사이의 수식어 거품(debated ~ yesterday)은 동사의 수 결정에 영향을 주지 않는다.
② 현재분사 vs. 과거분사 | 현재진행 시제 수식받는 명사(A man)와 분사가 '남자가 입다'라는 의미의 능동 관계이므로 현재분사 wearing이 올바르게 쓰였고, 문맥상 '한 남자가 서 있다'라는 의미가 되어야 자연스러우므로 현재진행 시제 is standing이 올바르게 쓰였다.
③ 관계대명사 | 주격 관계절의 수 일치 선행사(the man)가 사람이고 관계절 내에서 동사(was)의 주어 역할을 하므로 사람을

가리키는 주격 관계대명사 who가 올바르게 쓰였다. 관계절의 동사는 선행사에 수 일치해야 하는데 선행사 the man이 단수 명사이므로 단수 동사 was가 올바르게 쓰였다.

⑤ 전치사 자리 | 현재분사 vs. 과거분사 전치사 뒤에는 명사 역할을 하는 것이 와야 하므로, 전치사 of 뒤에 명사 people(사람들)이 올바르게 쓰였다. 수식받는 명사(people)와 분사가 '사람들이 알다'라는 의미의 능동 관계이므로 현재분사 knowing이 올바르게 쓰였다.

어휘 debate 논의하다 Parliament 의회, 국회 still 가만히 있는, 고요한 article 항목

👍 이것도 알면 합격!

진행 시제로 쓸 수 없는 동사들도 알아두자.

감정	like 좋아하다 prefer 선호하다 hate 싫어하다
상태	be ~이다 owe 빚지다 consist 구성하다
인지	believe 믿다 know 알다 realize 깨닫다
감각	sound ~하게 들리다 seem ~인 것 같다
기타	need 필요하다 want 원하다

04 독해 추론 (빈칸 완성 - 절)   난이도 ★★☆

끊어읽기 해석

Obviously, / the educational process for jurors needs to be improved, / and judges and lawyers need to become active participants / in this educational process.
분명히 / 배심원들을 위한 교육 과정은 개선되어야 한다 / 그리고 판사와 변호사들은 적극적인 참여자가 되어야 한다 / 이 교육 과정에서

They need to take the responsibility for informing jurors / about the relevant legal issues / in each case.
그들은 배심원들에게 알리는 것에 대한 책임을 져야 한다 / 관련된 법률적 쟁점 사항들을 / 각각의 사건에

They must educate jurors / on the rules of law / applicable to the cases at hand / and in language / they can understand.
그들은 배심원들을 교육해야 한다 / 법규에 대해 / 당면한 사건에 적용되는 / 그리고 언어로 / 그들이 이해할 수 있는

Some may argue / that this system may be abused / by lawyers / who want to bias a jury / in their favor.
어떤 사람들은 주장할지도 모른다 / 이 제도가 남용될 수도 있다고 / 변호사들에 의해 / 배심원을 편향시키고 싶어 하는 / 그들에게 유리하게

This is, of course, possible.
이것은, 물론 가능하다

But one must realize / that juries are inherently biased.
그러나 깨달아야 한다 / 배심원들은 본질적으로 편향되어 있다는 것을

Each juror walks in / with his or her own distinct set of values and beliefs.
각각의 배심원들은 걸어 들어온다 / 자신만의 독특한 가치관과 신념을 가지고

The lawyers are always trying to influence them / to see their side.
변호사들은 항상 영향을 미치려고 한다 / 그들(배심원들)이 그들(변호사들) 편을 들게끔

I would argue, however, / that it is better to risk the possibility / of some additional bias / in order for the juries to be better informed.
그러나, 나는 주장할 것이다 / 가능성을 감수하는 것이 더 낫다고 / 어느 정도의 부가적 편견의 / 배심원들이 더 잘 알 수 있도록

It is more desirable to have a knowledgeable jury, / even at the risk of some bias, / rather than to have a jury / that

---

is totally in the dark about the legal issues / surrounding a particular case.
아는 것이 많은 배심원을 두는 것이 더 바람직하다 / 어느 정도의 편견의 위험을 무릅쓰고라도 / 배심원을 두는 것보다는 / 법률적 쟁점 사항에 대해 완전히 아무것도 모르는 / 특정 사건을 둘러싼

해석 분명히, 배심원들을 위한 교육 과정은 개선되어야 하며, 판사와 변호사들은 이 교육 과정에서 적극적인 참여자가 되어야 한다. 그들은 배심원들에게 각각의 사건에 관련된 법률적 쟁점 사항들을 알리는 것에 대한 책임을 져야 한다. 그들은 당면한 사건에 적용되는 법규에 대해 그들이 이해할 수 있는 언어로 배심원들을 교육해야 한다. 어떤 사람들은 이 제도가 배심원을 그들에게 유리하게 편향시키고 싶어 하는 변호사들에 의해 남용될 수도 있다고 주장할지도 모른다. 이것은, 물론 가능하다. 그러나 배심원들은 본질적으로 편향되어 있다는 것을 깨달아야 한다. 각각의 배심원들은 자신만의 독특한 가치관과 신념을 가지고 걸어 들어온다. 변호사들은 항상 그들(배심원들)이 그들(변호사들) 편을 들게끔 영향을 미치려고 한다. 그러나, 나는 배심원들이 더 잘 알 수 있도록 어느 정도의 부가적 편견의 가능성을 감수하는 것이 더 낫다고 주장할 것이다. 특정 사건을 둘러싼 법률적 쟁점 사항에 대해 완전히 아무것도 모르는 배심원을 두는 것보다는 어느 정도의 편견의 위험을 무릅쓰고라도 아는 것이 많은 배심원을 두는 것이 더 바람직하다.

① 배심원들은 본질적으로 편향되어 있다
② 배심원들은 결코 그들의 마음을 바꾸지 않을 것이다
③ 판사는 항상 공정하다
④ 변호사들은 배심원단을 설득하는 것을 좀처럼 성공하지 못한다
⑤ 판사들이 법정에 영향을 끼칠 가능성이 있다

해설 빈칸 앞부분에 배심원들을 위한 교육 과정이 배심원 자신들에게 유리하게 편향시키고자 하는 변호사들에 의해 남용될 수 있다는 내용이 있고, 지문 뒷부분에 아무 것도 모르는 배심원을 두는 것보다는 어느 정도의 편견의 위험을 무릅쓰고라도 아는 것이 많은 배심원을 두는 것이 더 바람직하다는 내용이 있다. 따라서 빈칸에는 그러나(But) '① 배심원들은 본질적으로 편향되어 있다'는 것을 깨달아야 한다는 내용이 들어가야 적절하다.

어휘 juror 배심원 judge 판사
take the responsibility for ~에 대한 책임을 지다
relevant 관련된 applicable 적용되는 at hand 당면한
abuse 남용하다; 남용 bias 편향시키다, 편견 risk 감수하다
informed 잘 아는 desirable 바람직한
knowledgeable 아는 것이 많은 in the dark 아무것도 모르는
inherently 본질적으로 impartial 공정한
dictate 영향을 끼치다, 명령하다 court 법정

05 독해 추론 (빈칸 완성 - 구)   난이도 ★★☆

끊어읽기 해석

One useful guideline / for differentiating a dialect from a language / is that different languages are not mutually intelligible, / whereas different dialects generally are.
유용한 한 가지 지침은 / 방언과 언어를 구별하는 데 / 서로 다른 언어들은 상호 간에 이해할 수 없다는 점이다 / 서로 다른 방언들은 일반적으로 그렇다는(상호 간에 이해할 수 있다는) 반면

For example, / if you are a monolingual speaker of Mandarin Chinese / and you encounter a monolingual speaker of Cantonese Chinese, / the two of you will have a great deal of difficulty communicating / through language alone, / since Mandarin and Cantonese are two different languages.
예를 들어 / 만약 당신이 표준 중국어 하나만 사용하는 사람이라면 / 그리고 당신은 광둥어 하나만 사용하는 사람과 마주친다 / 당신 두 사람은 의사

소통하는 데 많은 어려움을 겪을 것이다 / 언어만으로 / 이는 표준 중국어와 광둥어가 두 개의 서로 다른 언어이기 때문이다

On the other hand, / if you are a native Dane / and you encounter a native Norwegian, / the similarities between your linguistic systems will far outweigh any differences; / you will have little trouble communicating / with each other, / since Danish and Norwegian represent two different dialects / of a single language.
반면에 / 만약 당신이 덴마크 출신인 사람이다 / 그리고 당신은 노르웨이 출신인 사람을 만난다 / 당신들의 언어 체계 사이의 유사성이 모든 차이보다 훨씬 더 클 것이다 / 당신들은 의사소통하는 데 거의 문제가 없을 것이다 / 서로 / 이는 덴마크어와 노르웨이어가 두 가지 서로 다른 방언에 해당하기 때문이다 / 한 언어의

해석 방언과 언어를 구별하는 데 유용한 한 가지 지침은 서로 다른 언어들은 상호 간에 이해할 수 없는 반면, 서로 다른 방언들은 일반적으로 그렇다는(상호 간에 이해할 수 있다는) 점이다. 예를 들어, 만약 당신이 표준 중국어 하나만 사용하는 사람이고 광둥어 하나만 사용하는 사람과 마주친다면, 당신 두 사람은 언어만으로 의사소통하는 데 많은 어려움을 겪을 것인데, 이는 표준 중국어와 광둥어가 두 개의 서로 다른 언어이기 때문이다. 반면에, 만약 당신이 덴마크 출신인 사람이고 노르웨이 출신인 사람을 만난다면, 당신들의 언어 체계 사이의 유사성이 모든 차이보다 훨씬 더 클 것이다. 당신들은 서로 의사소통하는 데 거의 문제가 없을 것인데, 이는 덴마크어와 노르웨이어가 한 언어의 두 가지 서로 다른 방언에 해당하기 때문이다.

① 같은 민족적 배경을 가진
② 문화적으로 이해할 수 있는
③ 어느 나라에서 공식적으로 사용되는
④ 같은 방법으로 배운
⑤ 상호 간에 이해할 수 있는

해설 빈칸 뒤 문장에서 표준 중국어만 사용하는 사람과 광둥어만 사용하는 사람은 두 언어가 서로 다른 언어이기 때문에 의사소통하는 데 어려움을 겪는 반면, 덴마크인과 노르웨이인은 덴마크어와 노르웨이어가 한 언어의 방언이기 때문에 의사소통에 거의 문제가 없다는 예시를 들고 있다. 따라서, 빈칸에는 서로 다른 언어들은 '⑤ 상호 간에 이해할 수' 없는 반면, 서로 다른 방언들은 일반적으로 상호 간에 이해할 수 있다는 내용이 들어가야 한다.

어휘 differentiate 구별하다　dialect 방언
monolingual 한 가지 언어를 사용하는　Mandarin 표준 중국어
Cantonese 광둥어　Dane 덴마크인　linguistic 언어의
outweigh ~보다 더 크다

06　독해　세부내용 파악 (내용 불일치 파악)　난이도 ★☆☆

끊어읽기 해석

Do dragons really exist? // In Indonesia they do.
용은 정말 존재할까 // 인도네시아에서는 그렇다

Called Komodo dragons, / they are the largest living members / of the lizard family.
코모도왕도마뱀이라고 불리는 / 그것들은 현존하는 가장 큰 일원이다 / 도마뱀과의

They grow up to 10 feet long.
그것들은 10피트 길이까지 자란다

They are part of a group of lizards / known as monitors.
그것들은 도마뱀과 일원이다 / 왕도마뱀이고 알려진

According to legend, / these lizards get the name "monitor" / because they warn of the presence of crocodiles.

전설에 따르면 / 이 도마뱀들은 'monitor'라는 이름을 얻게 되었다 / 그것들이 악어의 존재를 경고하기 때문에

Coincidentally, / Indonesians call Komodo dragons "land crocodiles."
동시에 / 인도네시아인들은 코모도왕도마뱀을 '육지 악어'라고 부른다

They have armor-plated heads, thick forked tongues, claws / that are sharp and long, / and strong skin / that looks like polished gravel.
그것들은 장갑을 두른 머리, 두툼하고 갈라진 혀, 발톱을 가지고 있다 / 날카롭고 긴 / 그리고 강한 피부를 / 윤이 나는 자갈처럼 보이는

They don't breathe fire / like the mythical dragons of European lore.
그것들은 불을 내뿜지 않는다 / 유럽 구비 설화의 신화 속에 나오는 용들처럼

But neither do they sit on logs all day / sunning themselves / like some lizards.
하지만 하루 종일 통나무 위에 앉아 있는 것도 아니다 / 햇볕을 쬐면서 / 일부 도마뱀들처럼

During the hottest hours of the day, / the giant lizards rest in caves / that they've dug, / storing up their energy for hunting / in the evening and early morning.
하루 중 가장 더운 시간 동안 / 그 거대한 도마뱀들은 동굴 속에서 휴식을 취한다 / 그것들이 파놓은 / 사냥을 위한 에너지를 비축하면서 / 저녁과 이른 아침의

Their hunting tactics are a lot like a cat's.
그것들의 사냥 전술은 고양이의 것과 많이 유사하다

After hiding in a bush, / they lunge at and surprise their prey, / which includes deer, wild pigs, and even water buffalo.
덤불 속에 숨은 다음 / 그것들은 사냥감에 달려들어 놀라게 한다 / 이것은 사슴, 멧돼지, 심지어는 물소도 포함한다

If carrion (the rotting flesh of dead animals) presents itself, / they'll choose it over animals / they have to kill themselves.
만약 죽은 동물의 고기(죽은 동물의 썩어가는 고기)가 나타나면 / 그것들은 동물보다 그것을 선택할 것이다 / 그것들이 직접 죽여야 하는

해석 용은 정말 존재할까? 인도네시아에서는 그렇다. 코모도왕도마뱀이라고 불리는 그것들은 도마뱀과의 현존하는 가장 큰 일원이다. 그것들은 10피트 길이까지 자란다. 그것들은 왕도마뱀이라고 알려진 도마뱀과의 일원이다. 전설에 따르면, 이 도마뱀들은 악어의 존재를 경고하기 때문에 'monitor'라는 이름을 얻게 되었다. 동시에, 인도네시아인들은 코모도왕도마뱀을 '육지 악어'라고 부른다. 그것들은 장갑을 두른 머리, 두툼하고 갈라진 혀, 날카롭고 긴 발톱, 그리고 윤이 나는 자갈처럼 보이는 강한 피부를 가지고 있다. 그것들은 유럽 구비 설화의 신화 속에 나오는 용들처럼 불을 내뿜지 않는다. 하지만 일부 도마뱀들처럼 하루 종일 햇볕을 쬐면서 통나무 위에 앉아 있는 것도 아니다. 하루 중 가장 더운 시간 동안, 그 거대한 도마뱀들은 저녁과 이른 아침의 사냥을 위한 에너지를 비축하면서 그것들이 파놓은 동굴 속에서 휴식을 취한다. 그것들의 사냥 전술은 고양이의 것과 많이 유사하다. 덤불 속에 숨은 다음, 그것들은 사냥감에 달려들어 놀라게 하는데, 이것은 사슴, 멧돼지, 심지어는 물소도 포함한다. 만약 죽은 동물의 고기(죽은 동물의 썩어가는 고기)가 나타나면, 그것들은 직접 죽여야 하는 동물보다 그것을 선택할 것이다.

해설 지문 중간에서 코모도왕도마뱀은 두툼하고 갈라진 혀를 가지고 있다고 했지만, 그것의 피부는 윤이 나는 자갈처럼 보인다고 했으므로, '② 두껍고 갈라진 혀를 가지고 있으며 피부 표면이 거칠어 보인다'는 것은 지문의 내용과 다르다.

어휘 lizard 도마뱀　family (동식물 분류상의) 과
monitor 왕도마뱀, 감시자　coincidentally 동시에
armor-plated 장갑을 두른　forked (두 갈래로) 갈라진　claw 발톱

polished 윤이 나는   gravel 자갈   mythical 신화 속에 나오는
lore 구비 설화, 구전 지식   log 통나무   dig 파다
store 비축하다, 저장하다   tactic 전술
carrion (죽은 동물의) 고기   rot 썩다   flesh 고기, 살
choose A over B B보다 A를 선택하다

07 문법 능동태·수동태   난이도 ★★☆

해석 대부분의 사람들은 스톡홀름 증후군이라는 단어를 그것이 인용되어 왔던 세간의 주목을 받은 납치와 주로 여성이 관련된 인질 사건들 때문에 알고 있다. 그 용어는 1974년 혁명 무장군에 납치된 캘리포니아지의 상속녀 패티 허스트와 가장 관련이 있다. 그녀는 납치범들에게 동정심을 갖게 된 듯했고 그들과 함께 강도질을 했다. 그녀는 결국 잡혔고 징역형을 받았다. 하지만 허스트의 피고 측 변호인인 Bailey는 그 19세 소녀(허스트)가 세뇌되어 '스톡홀름 증후군'을 앓고 있다고 주장했는데, 이는 납치범에 대한 일부 인질들의 명백히 비이성적인 감정을 설명하기 위해 최근에 만들어진 용어이다.

해설 ② 능동태·수동태 구별 주어(The term)와 동사가 '그 용어가 관련이 있다(관련되다)'라는 의미의 수동 관계이므로 능동태 most associates with를 수동태 is most associated with로 고쳐야 한다.

오답
분석 ① 전치사 + 관계대명사 '전치사 + 관계대명사'에서 전치사는 선행사 또는 관계절의 동사에 따라 결정되는데, 선행사 cases는 전치사 in과 함께 짝을 이루어 '사건들에서'라는 의미로 사용되므로 in which가 올바르게 쓰였다.
③ 수동태로 쓸 수 없는 동사 동사 appear(~인 듯하다)는 목적어를 갖지 않는 자동사이고 수동태로 쓸 수 없으므로 능동태 appeared가 올바르게 쓰였다.
④ 과거완료 시제 '허스트가 세뇌된' 것은 'Bailey가 주장한' 특정 과거 시점보다 이전에 일어난 일이므로 과거완료 시제 had been brainwashed가 올바르게 쓰였다.
⑤ 부사 자리 동사 이외의 것을 수식할 때 부사는 수식받는 것 앞에 오므로 부사 apparently가 형용사 irrational 앞에 올바르게 쓰였다.

어휘 syndrome 증후군   high-profile 세간의 주목을 받는
kidnapping 납치   hostage 인질   cite 인용하다
associate with ~와 관련 짓다   sympathy 동정심
captor 납치범, 포획자   robbery 강도질   defense 피고 측, 방어
claim 주장하다   coin 만들다, 주조하다   irrational 비이성적인
captive 인질

👍 이것도 알면 **합격!**

'전치사 + 관계대명사' 뒤에는 완전한 절이 온다는 것을 알아두자.
(ex) We visited the cottage in which my parents used to live.
우리는 나의 부모님이 살았었던 오두막을 방문했다.

08 독해 논리적 흐름 파악 (문장 삽입)   난이도 ★★☆

끊어읽기 해석

Similarly, / television gave rise to televise, / double-glazing preceded double-glaze, / and baby-sitter preceded baby-sit.
마찬가지로 / 'television'(텔레비전)은 'televise'(텔레비전으로 방송하다)가 생기게 했다 / 'double-glazing'(이중 유리창)은 'double-glaze'(이중 유리를 끼우다)보다 먼저 생겼다 / 그리고 'baby-sitter'(아이를 돌봐주는 사람)가 'baby-sit'(아이를 돌봐주다)보다 먼저 생겼다

It is common in English / to form a new lexeme / by adding a prefix or a suffix to an old one.
영어에서는 흔하다 / 새로운 어휘소를 형성하는 것이 / 기존의 것(어휘소)에 접두사나 접미사를 추가하여

From happy we get unhappy; / from inspect we get inspector.
우리는 'happy'(행복한)에서 'unhappy'(불행한)를 얻는다 / 'inspect'(조사하다)에서 'inspector'(조사관)를 얻는다

(①) Every so often, however, / the process works the other way round, / and a shorter word is derived from a longer one / by deleting an imagined affix.
그러나, 이따금 / 그 과정은 반대로 작용한다 / 그래서 짧은 단어가 긴 단어에서 파생된다 / 가상의 접사를 삭제함으로써

(②) Editor, for example, looks / as if it comes from edit, / whereas the noun was in the language first.
예를 들어, 'editor'(편집자)는 보인다 / 'edit'(편집하다)에서 나온 것처럼 / 하지만 명사가 먼저 언어에 있었다

(③) Such forms are known as 'back-formations'.
이러한 형식을 '역성어'라고 한다

Each year sees a new crop of back-formations.
매년 잇단 새로운 역성어들을 볼 수 있다

(④) Some are coined / because they meet a real need, / as when a group of speech therapists in the 1970s felt / they needed a new verb / to describe what they did / —to therap.
어떤 것들은 만들어진다 / 그것들이 진정한 필요를 충족시키기 때문에 / 1970년대의 언어치료사들의 한 집단이 느꼈을 때처럼 / 새로운 동사가 필요하다고 / 그들이 한 일을 묘사하기 위해 / 'therap'(치료하다)

Some are playful formations, / as when a tidy person is described / as couth, kempt, or shevelled.
어떤 것들은 장난스러운 형태이다 / 깔끔한 사람이 묘사되는 것과 같이 / 'couth'(예의 바른), 'kempt'(깔끔한), 혹은 'shevelled'(단정한)로

(⑤) Back-formations often attract criticism / when they first appear, / as happened in the late 1980s / to explete ('to use an expletive') and accreditate (from accreditation).
역성어는 종종 비판을 불러일으킨다 / 그것들이 처음 등장할 때 / 1980년대 후반에 일어난 일처럼 / ('expletive(비속어)'를 쓰다를 뜻하는) 'explete'와 ('accreditation'(승인)에서 온) 'accreditate'(승인하다)에

해석 영어에서는 기존의 것(어휘소)에 접두사나 접미사를 추가하여 새로운 어휘소를 형성하는 것이 흔하다. 우리는 'happy'(행복한)에서 'unhappy'(불행한)를 얻고, 'inspect'(조사하다)에서 'inspector'(조사관)를 얻는다. 그러나, 이따금 그 과정은 반대로 작용해서, 가상의 접사를 삭제함으로써 짧은 단어가 긴 단어에서 파생된다. 예를 들어, 'editor'(편집자)는 'edit'(편집하다)에서 나온 것처럼 보이지만, 명사가 먼저 언어에 있었다(명사인 editor가 먼저 존재했다). ③ 마찬가지로, 'television'(텔레비전)은 'televise'(텔레비전으로 방송하다)가 생기게 했고, 'double-glazing'(이중 유리창)은 'double-glaze'(이중 유리를 끼우다)보다 먼저 생겼으며, 'baby-sitter'(아이를 돌봐주는 사람)가 'baby-sit'(아이를 돌봐주다)보다 먼저 생겼다. 이러한 형식을 '역성어'라고 한다. 매년 잇단 새로운 역성어들을 볼 수 있다. 1970년대의 언어치료사들의 한 집단이 그들이 한 일을 묘사하기 위해 새로운 동사 즉, 'therap'(치료하다)가 필요하다고 느꼈을 때처럼, 어떤 것들은 그것들이 진정한 필요를 충족시키기 때문에 만들어진다. 어떤 것들은 깔끔한 사람이 'couth'(예의 바른), 'kempt'(깔끔한), 혹은 'shevelled'(단정한)로 묘사되는 것과 같이 장난스러운 형태이다. 역성어는 1980년대 후반 ('expletive'(비속어)를 쓰다를 쓰다를 뜻하는) 'explete'와 ('accreditation'(승인)에서 온) 'accreditate'(승인하다)에 일어난 일처럼, 그것들이 처음 등장할 때 종종 비판을 불러일으킨다.

해설 ③번 앞부분에 이따금 가상의 접사를 삭제함으로써 짧은 단

어가 긴 단어에서 파생된다고 하며, 'editor'가 'edit'보다 먼저 언어에 존재했었다는 예시를 드는 내용이 있으므로, ③번에 'television'은 'televise'가 생기게 했고, 'double-glazing'은 'double-glaze'보다 먼저 생겼다고 하며 짧은 단어가 긴 단어에서 파생된 추가적인 예시를 설명하는 내용의 주어진 문장이 들어가야 지문이 자연스럽게 연결된다.

어휘　give rise to ~이 생기게 하다　televise 텔레비전으로 방송하다
precede 먼저 생기다, 우선하다　common 흔한, 공통의
lexeme 어휘소　prefix 접두사　suffix 접미사　inspect 조사하다
the other way round 반대로　derive 파생하다, 유래하다
affix 접사　a crop of 잇단　therapist 치료사　tidy 깔끔한
couth 예의 바른　kempt 깔끔한　shevelled 단정한
attract (어떤 반응을) 불러일으키다, 마음을 끌다
expletive (화나거나 아플 때 뱉는) 비속어　accreditation 승인

09　독해　추론 (빈칸 완성 - 절)　난이도 ★★☆

끊어읽기 해석

Issues seem to become more and more complex / as the world becomes more complex.
문제들이 점점 더 복잡해지는 것 같다 / 세상이 더 복잡해짐에 따라

In an interview, / the actress Susan Sarandon, / who has always been engaged with social issues, / stated / that in the mid- to late 1960s, / when she was in college, / the issues seemed simpler, more black and white.
한 인터뷰에서 / 여배우 수잔 서랜던은 / 항상 사회적 문제에 관여해 온 / 말했다 / 1960년대 중후반에 / 그녀가 대학을 다니고 있었을 때 / 문제들이 더 단순하고 뚜렷해 보였다고

The issues at that time, / for example, centered on civil rights and the Vietnam War.
그 당시의 문제들은 / 예를 들어, 시민권과 베트남 전쟁에 집중하고 있었다

"We were blessed with clear-cut issues," / she says.
"우리는 명백한 문제들을 누리고 있었어요." / ~라고 그녀는 말한다

"We were blessed with clear-cut grievances.
"우리는 명백한 고충들을 누리고 있었죠.

Things were not as gray as they are now."
상황이 지금처럼 애매하지는 않았어요."

해석　세상이 더 복잡해짐에 따라 문제들이 점점 더 복잡해지는 것 같다. 한 인터뷰에서, 항상 사회적 문제에 관여해 온 여배우 수잔 서랜던은 1960년대 중후반, 그녀가 대학을 다니고 있었을 때, 문제들이 더 단순하고, 뚜렷해 보였다고 말했다. 예를 들어, 그 당시의 문제들은 시민권과 베트남 전쟁에 집중하고 있었다. "우리는 명백한 문제들을 누리고 있었어요."라고 그녀는 말한다. "우리는 명백한 고충들을 누리고 있었죠. 상황이 지금처럼 애매하지는 않았어요."
　　① 문제들은 그것들이 (오늘날) 그런 것처럼 결코 분명하지 않았다.
　　② 우리는 정치에 대해 오늘날보다 더 자주 얘기했었다.
　　③ 우리는 지금 터널 끝의 빛을 보고 있다.(길고 힘든 시기가 거의 끝나간다.)
　　④ 진정으로, 모든 구름의 뒤편은 은빛으로 빛난다.(괴로움 뒤에는 기쁨이 있다.)
　　⑤ 상황이 지금처럼 애매하지는 않았다.

해설　빈칸 앞부분에서 1960년대 중후반에는 문제들이 더 단순하고 뚜렷해 보였고, 명백한 문제들과 고충들을 누리고 있었다는 한 여배우의 인터뷰를 인용하고 있으므로, 빈칸에는 '⑤ 상황이 지금처럼 애매하지는 않았다'가 들어가야 적절하다.

어휘　complex 복잡한　engage with ~에 관여하다, ~을 다루다

---

black and white 뚜렷한, 흑백의　center on ~에 집중하다
bless with ~을 누리다, ~의 축복을 베풀다　clear-cut 명백한
grievance 고충, 불만
the light at the end of the tunnel 길고 힘든 시기 끝에 보이는 광명
every cloud has a silver lining 모든 구름의 뒤편은 은빛으로 빛난다(괴로움 뒤에는 기쁨이 있다)　gray 애매한, 특징이 없는

10　독해　추론 (빈칸 완성 - 연결어)　난이도 ★★☆

끊어읽기 해석

Child psychologist Jean Piaget was one of the first / to study questions of moral development.
아동 심리학자 장 피아제는 최초의 사람 중 한 명이다 / 도덕적 발달에 대한 의문을 연구한

He suggested / that moral development, like cognitive development, proceed in stages.
그는 시사했다 / 인지 발달과 같은 도덕적 발달이 단계적으로 진행된다고

The earliest stage is a broad form of moral thinking / he called heteronomous morality, / in which rules are seen / as invariant and unchangeable.
가장 초기 단계는 도덕적 사고의 광범위한 형성이다 / 그가 타율적 도덕성이라고 부르는 / 그리고 이 안에서 규칙은 간주된다 / 변함없고 바꿀 수 없는 것으로

During this stage, / which lasts from about age 4 to age 7, / children play games rigidly, / assuming that there is one, and only one, way / to play / and that every other way is wrong.
이 단계 동안 / 약 4세부터 7세까지 지속되는 / 아이들은 융통성 없이 놀이를 한다 / 유일한 단 한 가지 방법만 있다고 가정하면서 / 놀이를 하는 / 그리고 다른 모든 방법이 틀렸다고

At the same time, though, / preschool-age children may not even fully grasp game rules.
그러나, 동시에 / 미취학 아동들은 놀이 규칙을 완전히 이해하지 못할 수도 있다

(A) Consequently, / a group of children may be playing together, / with each child playing / according to a slightly different set of rules.
(A) 그 결과 / 아이들 무리는 함께 놀고 있는 것일지도 모른다 / 각각의 아이가 노는 상태로 / 약간 다른 규칙들에 따르며

Nevertheless, / they enjoy playing with others.
그럼에도 불구하고 / 그들은 다른 사람들과 노는 것을 즐긴다

Piaget suggests / that every child may "win" such a game / (B) because winning is equated with having a good time, / as opposed to truly competing with others.
피아제는 시사한다 / 모든 아이들이 이러한 놀이에서 '이길' 수 있다고 / 이기는 것은 즐거운 시간을 보내는 것과 같기 (B) 때문에 / 진정으로 다른 사람들과 경쟁하는 것이 아니라

해석　아동 심리학자 장 피아제는 도덕적 발달에 대한 의문을 연구한 최초의 사람 중 한 명이다. 그는 인지 발달과 같은 도덕적 발달이 단계적으로 진행된다고 시사했다. 가장 초기 단계는 그가 타율적 도덕성이라고 부르는 도덕적 사고의 광범위한 형성이며, 이 안에서 규칙은 변함없고 바꿀 수 없는 것으로 간주된다. 약 4세부터 7세까지 지속되는 이 단계 동안, 아이들은 놀이를 하는 유일한 단 한 가지 방법만 있고 다른 모든 방법이 틀렸다고 가정하면서 융통성 없이 놀이를 한다. 그러나, 동시에 미취학 아동들은 놀이 규칙을 완전히 이해하지 못할 수도 있다. (A) 그 결과, 아이들 무리는 각각의 아이가 약간 다른 규칙들에 따르며 노는 상태로 함께 놀고 있는 것일지도 모른다. 그럼에도 불구하고, 그들은 다른 사람들과 노는 것을 즐긴다. 피아제는 이기는 것은 진정으로 다른 사람들과 경쟁하

는 것이 아니라 즐거운 시간을 보내는 것과 같기 (B) 때문에 모든 아이들이 이러한 놀이에서 '이길' 수 있다고 시사한다.

	(A)	(B)
①	그 결과	~ 때문에
②	예를 들어	비록 ~일지라도
③	사실은	반면에
④	하지만	~할 무렵에
⑤	게다가	~하는 경우에 대비해서

해설 (A) 빈칸 앞부분은 약 4세부터 7세까지의 아이들은 놀이를 하는 유일한 단 한 가지 방법만 있고 다른 모든 방법이 틀렸다고 가정하면서 융통성 없이 놀이를 하고, 놀이 규칙을 완전히 이해하지 못할 수도 있다는 내용이고, (A) 빈칸 뒤 문장은 아이들 무리가 각자 약간 다른 규칙들에 따르며 함께 놀고 있는 것일지도 모른다는 결론적인 내용이므로, (A)에는 Consequently(그 결과)가 들어가야 한다. (B) 빈칸이 있는 문장에서 (B) 빈칸 앞부분은 이러한 놀이에서는 모든 아이들이 '이길' 수 있다는 내용이고, (B) 빈칸 뒷부분은 이기는 것이 진정으로 다른 사람들과 경쟁하는 것이 아니라 즐거운 시간을 보내는 것과 같다고 하며 그 이유를 설명하는 내용이므로, (B)에는 because(~ 때문에)가 들어가야 한다. 따라서 ①번이 정답이다.

어휘 moral 도덕적인 cognitive 인지의 proceed 진행되다
broad 광범위한, 넓은
heteronomous morality 타율적 도덕성(도덕적 판단의 기준을 부모와 같은 권위자에게서 받아들이는 도덕 발달단계의 일종)
invariant 변함없는 last 지속되다 rigidly 융통성 없이
assume 가정하다 grasp 이해하다, 움켜쥐다 slightly 약간
be equated with ~와 같다

11 어휘 어휘&표현 apathy = indifference 난이도 ★★☆

해석 그는 새로운 COVID-19 무리의 출현을 초래한 대중의 무관심에 안타까워했다.

① 분노
② 염려
③ 동요
④ 무질서
⑤ 무관심

어휘 lament 안타까워하다, 한탄하다 apathy 무관심
emergence 출현 cluster 무리, 떼
commotion (마음의) 동요, 소란 disorder 무질서
indifference 무관심

👍 이것도 알면 합격!

apathy(무관심)의 유의어
= disinterest, unconcern, detachment, insensitivity, lethargy

12 어휘 어휘&표현 altruistic = unselfish 난이도 ★☆☆

해석 이타적인 사람들은 당신의 피부색이나 당신의 은행 계좌에 얼마나 많은 돈이 있는지를 신경 쓰지 않는다.

① 쾌활한
② 흉악한
③ 욕심 많은
④ 편협한
⑤ 이타적인

어휘 altruistic 이타적인 ferocious 흉악한, 사나운 greedy 욕심 많은
intolerant 편협한, 견딜 수 없는 unselfish 이타적인, 헌신적인

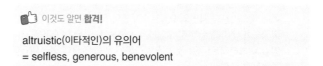 이것도 알면 합격!

altruistic(이타적인)의 유의어
= selfless, generous, benevolent

13 독해 추론 (빈칸 완성 - 절) 난이도 ★☆☆

끊어읽기 해석

The slippery-slope fallacy is a scare tactic / that suggests / that if we allow one thing to happen, / we will immediately be sliding down the slippery slope to disaster.
미끄러운 경사면의 오류는 위협 전술이다 / 암시하는 / 만약 우리가 한 가지 일이 벌어지도록 내버려 둔다면 / 우리가 즉시 참사로 가는 미끄러운 경사면을 미끄러져 내려갈 것임을

This fallacy is sometimes introduced / into environmental and abortion issues.
이 오류는 때때로 도입된다 / 환경 및 낙태 문제에

If we allow loggers to cut a few trees, / we will soon lose all the forests.
만약 우리가 벌목꾼들에게 몇 그루의 나무를 베도록 허락한다면 / 우리는 곧 모든 숲을 잃게 될 것이다

Or if a woman is required to wait twenty-four hours / to reconsider her decision to have an abortion, / soon there will be so many restrictions / that no one will be able to have an abortion.
또는 만약 한 여성이 24시간 동안 대기하는 것을 요구 받는다면 / 낙태를 하기로 한 그녀의 결정을 재고하도록 / 곧 너무 많은 제약이 생길 것이다 / 아무도 낙태를 할 수 없게 될 것이다

This fallacy is similar to the saying / about the camel that gets into its nose in the tent.
이 오류는 속담과 비슷하다 / 코를 천막에 들이미는 낙타에 관한

If we permit the nose today, we have the whole camel to deal with tomorrow.
만약 오늘 우리가 그 코를 내버려 둔다면, 우리는 내일 낙타 전체를 상대해야 한다

It is better not to start because disaster may result.
참사가 발생할 수도 있기 때문에 시작하지 않는 것이 좋다

해석 미끄러운 경사면의 오류는 만약 우리가 한 가지 일이 벌어지도록 내버려 둔다면, 우리가 즉시 참사로 가는 미끄러운 경사면을 미끄러져 내려갈 것임을 암시하는 위협 전술이다. 이 오류는 때때로 환경 및 낙태 문제에 도입된다. 만약 우리가 벌목꾼들에게 몇 그루의 나무를 베도록 허락한다면, 우리는 곧 모든 숲을 잃게 될 것이다. 또는 만약 한 여성이 낙태를 하기로 한 그녀의 결정을 재고하도록 24시간 동안 대기하는 것을 요구 받는다면, 곧 너무 많은 제약이 생겨나 아무도 낙태를 할 수 없게 될 것이다. 이 오류는 코를 천막에 들이미는 낙타에 관한 속담과 비슷하다. 만약 오늘 우리가 그 코를 내버려 둔다면, 우리는 내일 낙타 전체를 상대해야 한다. 참사가 발생할 수도 있기 때문에 시작하지 않는 것이 좋다.

① 비록 우리가 안전하게 지내기 위해 할 수 있는 모든 것을 한다 해도
② 비록 우리가 끝이 좋으면 다 좋다고 믿는다고 해도
③ 만약 우리가 한 가지 일이 벌어지도록 내버려 둔다면
④ 만약 우리가 다른 사람들을 겁주려고 한다면
⑤ 만약 우리가 우리 자신을 보호하기 위해 아무것도 하지 않는다면

해설 지문 뒷부분에서 코를 천막에 들이미는 낙타에 관한 속담을 예시로 들며 오늘 낙타의 코를 내버려 둔다면 내일은 낙타 전체를 상대해야 하는 참사가 발생할 수 있다고 설명하고 있다. 따라서 빈칸에는 미끄러운 경사면의 오류는 '③ 만약 우리가 한 가지 일이 벌어지도록 내버려 둔다면' 우리가 즉시 참사로 가는 미끄러운 경사면을 미끄러져 내려갈 것임을 암시하는 위협 전술이라는 내용이 들어가야 적절하다.

어휘 **slippery** 미끄러운 **slope** 경사면 **fallacy** 오류 **tactic** 전술
suggest 암시하다, 시사하다 **introduce** 도입하다 **abortion** 낙태
logger 벌목꾼 **saying** 속담 **camel** 낙타
permit 내버려 두다, 허용하다 **deal with** ~을 상대하다

14 문법 관계절   난이도 ★★☆

해석 의문을 제기하고 만족스러운 정보를 얻는 것을 배우는 것은 아동 발달에 있어 중요한 사회적 경험일 뿐만 아니라 지적 경험이다. 이 단계에서 성공적인 경험이 없는 아이들, 즉, 경험이 좌절되거나 그르쳐진 아이들은 학습 과정에 참여하는 것을 멈춘다. 그들은 그들의 의문을 표현하는 것을 멈추고, 결국 그것들(의문)을 생각해 내는 것을 멈출지도 모른다.

해설 ③ 관계대명사 선행사(Children)가 사람이고, 관계절 내에서 experience가 누구의 경험인지를 나타내므로 주격 관계대명사 who를 사람을 가리키는 소유격 관계대명사 whose로 고쳐야 한다.

오답 분석
① to 부정사의 역할 '의문을 제기하는 것을'이라는 의미를 표현하기 위해 명사처럼 동명사(Learning)의 목적어 자리에 올 수 있는 to 부정사구를 완성하는 pose questions가 올바르게 쓰였다.

② 주어와 동사의 수 일치 | 명사를 수식하는 여러 요소들의 어순 동명사 주어는 단수 취급하므로 단수 동사 is가 올바르게 쓰였다. 여러 품사가 함께 명사(experience)를 수식하는 경우 '관사(a) + 형용사(key social as well as intellectual) + 명사(experience)'의 어순이 되어야 하므로 a key social이 올바르게 쓰였다.

④ 동명사와 to 부정사 둘 다 목적어로 취하는 동사 동사 stop은 '~하는 것을 멈추다'라는 의미의 타동사로 쓰일 때 동명사를 목적어로 취하는데, 문맥상 '참여하는 것을 멈추다'라는 의미가 되어야 자연스러우므로 동명사 participating이 올바르게 쓰였다.

⑤ 혼동하기 쉬운 어순 '동사(think) + 부사(up)'로 이루어진 구동사는 목적어가 대명사(them)이면 '동사 + 대명사 + 부사'의 어순으로 쓰이므로 thinking them up이 올바르게 쓰였다. 참고로, 동사 stop 뒤에 동명사 thinking이 목적어로 쓰인 형태이다.

어휘 **pose** (위협·문제 등을) 제기하다 **satisfying** 만족스러운
intellectual 지적인 **pervert** 그르치다, 왜곡하다
think up 생각해 내다

👍 **이것도 알면 합격!**

구동사의 목적어가 명사인 경우, '동사 + 부사 + 명사' 혹은 '동사 + 명사 + 부사' 순으로 모두 쓸 수 있다.
(ex) We turned on some music(= turned some music on).
우리는 음악을 틀었다.

15 독해 논리적 흐름 파악 (무관한 문장 삭제)   난이도 ★★☆

끊어읽기 해석

Although parent-child conflicts are found / in every culture, / there does seem to be less conflict / between parents and their teenage children / in "traditional," preindustrial cultures.
비록 부모와 자녀 간 갈등이 발견되지만 / 모든 문화에서 / 갈등이 덜한 것 같다 / 부모와 그들의 십대 자녀들 사이에 / 산업화 이전의 '전통적인' 문화에서는

① Teens in such traditional cultures also experience / fewer mood swings and instances of risky behavior / than do teens / in industrialized countries.
그러한 전통적인 문화의 십대들은 또한 경험한다 / 더 적은 감정 기복과 위험 행동의 사례를 / 십대들이 그러한 것보다 / 산업화된 나라의

② Why? // The answer may relate to the degree of independence / that adolescents expect and adults permit.
왜 그럴까 // 그 답은 독립성의 정도와 관련이 있을 수 있다 / 청소년들이 기대하고 어른들이 허용하는

In more industrialized societies, / in which the value of individualism is typically high, / independence is an expected component of adolescence.
더 산업화된 사회에서 / 개인주의의 가치가 일반적으로 높은 / 독립성은 청소년기에 기대되는 요소이다

③ Consequently, / adolescents and their parents must negotiate the amount and timing / of the adolescents' increasing independence / —a process that often leads to strife.
결과적으로 / 청소년과 그들의 부모는 정도와 시기를 의논해서 결정해야 한다 / 청소년의 늘어나는 독립성의 / 이 과정이 종종 불화로 이어진다

④ Parent-child conflicts are more likely to occur / during adolescence, / particularly / during the early stages.
부모와 자녀 간 갈등은 발생할 가능성이 더 높다 / 청소년기에 / 특히 / 초기 단계에서

In contrast, / in more traditional societies, / individualism is not valued as highly, / and therefore adolescents are less inclined to seek out independence.
대조적으로 / 더 전통적인 사회에서는 / 개인주의가 높게 평가되지 않는다 / 그래서 청소년들은 독립성을 추구하는 경향이 덜하다

⑤ With diminished independence-seeking / on the part of adolescents, / the result is less parent-child conflict.
독립성 추구가 감소함에 따라 / 청소년들의 / 그 결과는 더 적은 부모와 자녀 간 갈등이 된다

해석 비록 모든 문화에서 부모와 자녀 간 갈등이 발견되지만, 산업화 이전의 '전통적인' 문화에서는 부모와 그들의 십대 자녀들 사이에 갈등이 덜한 것 같다. ① 그러한 전통적인 문화의 십대들은 또한 산업화된 나라의 십대들이 그러한 것보다 더 적은 감정 기복과 위험 행동의 사례를 경험한다. ② 왜 그럴까? 그 답은 청소년들이 기대하고 어른들이 허용하는 독립성의 정도와 관련이 있을 수 있다. 개인주의의 가치가 일반적으로 높은 더 산업화된 사회에서, 독립성은 청소년기에 기대되는 요소이다. ③ 결과적으로, 청소년과 그들의 부모는 청소년의 늘어나는 독립성의 정도와 시기를 의논해서 결정해야 하는데, 이 과정이 종종 불화로 이어진다. ④ 부모와 자녀 간 갈등은 청소년기, 특히 초기 단계에서 발생할 가능성이 더 높다. 대조적으로, 더 전통적인 사회에서는 개인주의가 높게 평가되지 않아서, 청소년들은 독립성을 추구하는 경향이 덜하다. ⑤ 청소년들의 독립성 추구가 감소함에 따라, 그 결과는 더 적은 부모와 자녀 간 갈등이 된다.

해설 지문 처음과 ①번에서 산업화 이전의 전통적인 문화에서는 부모와 십대 자녀 간 갈등이 덜하고 십대들이 더 적은 감정 기복과 위

험 행동의 사례를 경험한다고 한 뒤, ②번에서 그 원인이 독립성의 정도와 관련이 있을 수 있다고 언급하고 있다. 이어서 ③번, ⑤번에서 각각 산업화된 사회와 전통적인 사회에서 청소년기 자녀의 독립성에 대한 태도 차이를 설명하고 있다. 그러나 ④번은 부모와 자녀 간 갈등이 주로 발생하는 시기에 관한 내용으로, 산업화된 사회와 전통적인 사회에서의 부모와 자녀 간 갈등 양상에 대해 설명하는 지문 전반의 내용과 관련이 없다.

어휘 conflict 갈등 preindustrial 산업화 이전의
mood swing 감정 기복 risky 위험한 independence 독립성
adolescent 청소년 individualism 개인주의 component 요소
negotiate 의논해서 결정하다, 협상하다
inclined to ~하는 경향이 있는 seek out ~을 추구하다
diminish 감소시키다, 줄어들다

---

16 **독해** 추론 (빈칸 완성 - 구) 난이도 ★★☆

끊어읽기 해석

Two kinds of evidence show / that much of the behavioral differences among groups are not genetic.
두 가지 종류의 증거는 보여준다 / 집단 간의 행동 차이 중 많은 부분이 유전적이지 않다는 것을

First, / individual cross-cultural adoptees behave / like members of their adopted culture, / not the culture of their biological parents.
첫째로 / 각각의 다문화 입양인들은 행동한다 / 입양된 문화의 구성원처럼 / 그들 친부모의 문화가 아니라

Second, / groups of people often change behavior / much more rapidly / than natural selection could change gene frequencies.
둘째로 / 사람들의 집단은 종종 행동을 바꾼다 / 훨씬 더 빠르게 / 자연선택이 유전자 빈도를 바꿀 수 있는 것보다

These data are far too coarse to prove / that there are no genetic differences / between human groups, / but we believe the evidence is sufficient to conclude / that the cultural differences between groups are much larger / than any genetic variation that might exist.
이 자료들은 너무 정확하지 않아서 증명할 수 없다 / 유전적 차이가 없다는 것을 / 인간 집단 사이에 / 하지만 우리는 그 증거가 결론을 내리기에 충분하다고 믿는다 / 집단 간의 문화적 차이가 훨씬 더 크다는 것을 / 존재할 수 있는 어떤 유전적 변이보다

해석 두 가지 종류의 증거는 집단 간의 행동 차이 중 많은 부분이 유전적이지 않다는 것을 보여준다. 첫째로, 각각의 다문화 입양인들은 그들 친부모의 문화가 아니라 입양된 문화의 구성원처럼 행동한다. 둘째로, 사람들의 집단은 종종 자연선택이 유전자 빈도를 바꿀 수 있는 것보다 훨씬 더 빠르게 행동을 바꾼다. 이 자료들은 너무 정확하지 않아서 인간 집단 사이에 유전적 차이가 없다는 것을 증명할 수 없지만, 우리는 그 증거가 집단 간의 문화적 차이가 존재할 수 있는 어떤 유전적 변이보다 훨씬 더 크다는 결론을 내리기에 충분하다고 믿는다.

① 유전적이지 않은
② 인간 고유의
③ 생물학적 특성과 관련이 있는
④ 진화의 관점에서 설명되는
⑤ 알 수 없는

해설 빈칸 뒤 문장에서 각각의 다문화 입양인들이 친부모의 문화가 아니라 입양된 문화의 구성원처럼 행동하는 것과 사람들의 행동이 자연선택으로 유전자 빈도가 바뀌는 것보다 훨씬 더 빠르게 바뀌어서 집단 간의 문화적 차이가 존재할 수 있는 어떤 유전적 변

이보다 훨씬 더 크다고 믿는 것에 대해 설명하고 있으므로, 빈칸에는 두 가지 종류의 증거가 집단 간의 행동 차이 중 많은 부분이 '① 유전적이지 않다'는 것을 보여준다는 내용이 들어가야 한다.

어휘 cross-cultural 다문화의 adoptee 입양인, 양자
natural selection 자연선택(자연계에서 그 생활 조건에 적응하는 생물은 생존하고, 그러지 못한 생물은 저절로 사라지는 일)
frequency 빈도 coarse 정확하지 않은, 열악한 genetic 유전의
variation 변이

---

17 **독해** 전체내용 파악 (주제 파악) 난이도 ★★☆

끊어읽기 해석

Think about how you feel / if somebody cuts you off, / or makes an illegal left turn / in front of you.
당신의 기분이 어떨지 생각해 보아라 / 만약 누군가가 당신의 말을 끊는다면 / 혹은 불법 좌회전을 한다면 / 당신 앞에서

If you are like most people / you get annoyed, / perhaps very annoyed, / and want to punish the rule breaker, / even though you know / you'll never see the person again.
만약 당신이 대부분의 사람들과 같다면 / 당신은 짜증이 난다 / 아마도 매우 짜증이 날 것이다 / 그래서 규칙을 어기는 사람을 처벌하고 싶어할 것이다 / 당신은 알면서도 / 그 사람을 다시는 볼 수 없다는 것을

Or, think about how you feel / when someone cuts in line / while you wait for a movie.
아니면, 당신의 기분이 어떨지 생각해 보아라 / 누군가가 새치기했을 때 / 당신이 영화를 기다리는 동안

Most people get quite angry, / even if they are near the front of the line / and are sure to get a good seat.
대부분의 사람들은 꽤 화를 낸다 / 비록 그들이 줄의 거의 앞에 있다 할지라도 / 그래서 좋은 자리를 확실히 얻는다

Such emotions can give rise / to voluntary, informal punishment of people / who break social rules.
그러한 감정은 초래할 수 있다 / 사람들에 대한 자발적이고 비공식적인 처벌을 / 사회 규칙을 어기는

But in complex societies, / it's hard to know / whether such punishment plays a significant role / in maintaining social norms / because police and courts also act / to punish rule breakers.
하지만 복합 사회에서는 / 알기 어렵다 / 그러한 처벌이 중요한 역할을 하는지 / 사회 규범을 유지하는 데 / 경찰과 법원이 행동하기 때문에 / 규칙 위반자들을 처벌하기 위해

Many simple societies lack formal legal institutions, / so the only kind of punishment is informal and voluntary.
많은 단순 사회는 공식적인 법적 제도가 없다 / 그래서 유일한 종류의 처벌이 비공식적이고 자발적인 것이다

In small-scale societies, / considerable ethnographic evidence suggests / that moral norms are enforced by punishment.
소규모 사회에서는 / 상당한 민족지학적 증거가 암시한다 / 도덕적 규범이 처벌에 의해 강제된다는 것을

해석 만약 누군가가 당신의 말을 끊거나 당신 앞에서 불법 좌회전을 한다면 당신의 기분이 어떨지 생각해 보아라. 만약 당신이 대부분의 사람들과 같다면, 당신은 짜증이 날 것이고, 아마도 매우 짜증이 나서 당신은 그 사람을 다시는 볼 수 없다는 것을 알면서도 규칙을 어기는 사람들을 처벌하고 싶어할 것이다. 아니면, 당신이 영화를 기다리는 동안 누군가가 새치기했을 때 당신의 기분이 어떨지 생각해 보아라. 대부분의 사람들은 비록 그들이 줄의 거의 앞에 있어서 좋은 자리를 확실히 얻는다 할지라도, 꽤 화를 낸다. 그러한 감정은 사회 규칙을 어기는 사람들에 대한 자발적이고 비공식적인

처벌을 초래할 수 있다. 하지만 복합 사회에서는, 경찰과 법원이 규칙 위반자들을 처벌하기 위해 행동하기 때문에 그러한 처벌이 사회 규범을 유지하는 데 중요한 역할을 하는지 알기 어렵다. 많은 단순 사회는 공식적인 법적 제도가 없기 때문에, 유일한 종류의 처벌이 비공식적이고 자발적인 것이다. 소규모 사회에서는, 상당한 민족지학적 증거가 도덕적 규범이 처벌에 의해 강제된다는 것을 암시한다.

① 공식적 처벌의 이점과 불리한 점
② 처벌과 사회의 규모 사이의 관계
③ 도덕규범과 그것이 사회에 미치는 영향
④ 가혹한 처벌이 반사회적 행동에 미치는 영향
⑤ 국가 안보를 지키는 법률 제도의 역할

해설 지문 뒷부분에 복합 사회에서는 경찰과 법원이 규칙 위반자들을 처벌하기 때문에 사회 규칙을 어기는 사람들에 대한 자발적이고 비공식적인 처벌이 사회 규범을 유지하는 데 중요한 역할을 하는지 알기 어렵지만, 단순 사회는 공식적인 법적 제도가 없어서 유일한 종류의 처벌이 비공식적이고 자발적인 것이라는 내용이 있다. 또한 소규모 사회에서는 상당한 민족지학적 증거가 도덕적 규범이 처벌에 의해 강제된다는 것을 암시한다는 내용이 있으므로, '② 처벌과 사회의 규모 사이의 관계'가 이 글의 주제이다.

어휘 cut somebody off ~의 말을 끊다 cut in line 새치기하다
give rise to ~을 초래하다 voluntary 자발적인
informal 비공식적인
complex society 복합 사회(여러 개의 단순 사회가 모여 이루어진 사회)
play a role in ~에 역할을 하다 norm 규범, 기준
simple society 단순 사회(아직 사회적 분업이나 분화가 되지 않아 개인의 기능이 분화되지 않고, 필요한 모든 기능이 전체 속에서 수행되는 사회)
lack ~이 없다, 부족하다 institution 제도, 기관 scale 규모
ethnographic 민족지학적인 enforce 강제하다, 시행하다

---

18 **문법** **수 일치** 난이도 ★★☆

해석 ① 인간의 평균적인 신장은 지난 백만 년 동안 계속 변화해 왔다.
② 내가 무엇을 할지 결정하기 전에, 나는 모든 대안을 따져 보았다.
③ Tom은 연주를 너무 잘해서 청중들로부터 기립박수를 받았다.
④ 지방 정부는 그 주의 영양실조 문제에 대해 고심하고 있다.
⑤ 모든 회원은 클럽 규정을 준수하는 데 동의해야 한다.

해설 ① 주어와 동사의 수 일치 주어 자리에 단수 명사(The average size)가 왔으므로 복수 동사 have를 단수 동사 has로 고쳐야 한다. 참고로, 주어와 동사 사이의 수식어 거품(of humans)은 동사의 수 결정에 영향을 주지 않는다.

오답 ② 과거완료 시제 문맥상 '내가 모든 대안을 따져 본' 것은 '내가
분석 무엇을 할지 결정한' 특정 과거 시점보다 이전에 일어난 일이므로 과거완료 시제 had weighed가 올바르게 쓰였다.
③ 부사절 접속사 2: 기타 문맥상 '연주를 너무 잘해서 ~ 받았다'라는 의미가 되어야 자연스러운데 '매우 ~해서 ―하다'는 부사절 접속사 so ~ that으로 나타낼 수 있으므로 so well that he received ~가 올바르게 쓰였다.
④ 타동사 동사 address는 '~에 대해 고심하다'라는 의미로 쓰일 때 전치사 없이 바로 목적어(the problems)를 취하는 타동사이므로 addresses the problems가 올바르게 쓰였다.
⑤ 기타 전치사 동사 abide는 전치사 by와 함께 abide by(~을 준수하다)의 형태로 자주 쓰이므로 전치사 by가 올바르게 쓰였다.

어휘 fluctuate 계속 변화하다, 변동하다 weigh 따져 보다, 무게가 ~이다

---

standing ovation 기립박수
address (문제 등에 대해) 고심하다, 다루다 malnutrition 영양실조
abide by ~을 준수하다

👍 이것도 알면 **합격!**

보기 ②번처럼 '의문사 + to 부정사'는 명사절 자리에 오며, '의문사 + 주어 + should + 동사원형'으로 바꿀 수 있다.
(ex) Not knowing **where to go**(=where I should go), I got lost in the mountains.
어디로 가야 할지 모른 채로, 나는 산에서 길을 잃었다.

---

19 **어휘** **어휘＆표현** indignation = resentment 난이도 ★★★

해석 대학에 다닐 나이인 자녀들의 삶에 지나치게 관여하는 부모들은 우리가 비웃기 좋아하는 사람들이다. 기사와 블로그 게시물들의 끊임없는 흐름은 사소한 문제로 학장에게 전화를 하는 아빠들이나 우리가 생각하는 것보다 학생들의 연애에 대해 더 많이 알고 있는 엄마들에 대한 분노로 가득 차 있다.

① 논쟁
② 사색
③ 인내
④ 분노
⑤ 탐구

어휘 involve in ~에 관여하다 folk 사람들 scorn 비웃다, 경멸하다
steady 끊임없는 stream 흐름, 개울
bristle with ~으로 가득 차 있다 dean 학장 trivial 사소한
argumentation 논쟁, 논증 contemplation 사색, 명상
indulgence 인내, 방종 resentment 분노 quest 탐구, 탐색

👍 이것도 알면 **합격!**

indignation(분노)의 유의어
= anger, rage, outrage, fury, exasperation

---

20 **독해** **논리적 흐름 파악 (문단 순서 배열)** 난이도 ★★☆

끊어읽기 해석

Dottie and I entered 1966 / expecting another good year, / but as it turned out, / that was not to be, / as our parents were hurting.
Dottie와 나는 1966년에 들어섰다 / 또 다른 좋은 한 해를 기대하며 / 하지만 나중에 밝혀진 것처럼 / 그것은 그렇지 않았다 / 우리 부모님께서 편찮으셨기 때문이다

(A) We flew to Wichita / and were met by my sisters.
우리는 Wichita로 비행기를 타고 갔다 / 그리고 언니들을 만났다

By the time we got to the hospital, / Dad was responding to some new medicine.
우리가 병원에 도착했을 때 / 아버지는 어떤 새로운 약에 차도를 보이고 있었다

He recovered / and was able to go home / in a couple of weeks.
그는 회복했다 / 그리고 집에 갈 수 있었다 / 2주 만에

(B) We made some changes / in his care, / and after a couple of days, / he was beginning to recover.
우리는 어느 정도의 변화를 만들었다 / 그의 치료에 / 그리고 며칠 후 / 그는 회복되기 시작했다

We then received the call / that Dad had gotten worse, / his remaining kidney had stopped functioning, / he had fallen into a coma, / and that we should come.
그리고 나서 우리는 전화를 받았다 / (나의) 아버지가 악화되었다는 / 그의 남은 신장이 기능을 멈췄다는 / 그가 혼수상태에 빠졌다는 / 그래서 우리가 와야 한다고

(C) Mother had fallen and hurt her leg; / then, in April, / Dad had a kidney removed / due to a tumor.
어머니는 넘어져 다리를 다쳤다 / 그 후 4월에 / 아버지는 신장을 제거했다 / 종양 때문에

At the same time, / Dottie's father became very sick, / and we flew to Tucson / to be with him.
동시에 / Dottie의 아버지가 매우 편찮아지셨다 / 그리고 우리는 Tucson 으로 비행기를 타고 갔다 / 그와 함께 있기 위해

해석

Dottie와 나는 또 다른 좋은 한 해를 기대하며 1966년에 들어섰지만, 나중에 밝혀진 것처럼, 그것은 그렇지 않았는데, 우리 부모님께서 편찮으셨기 때문이다.

(C) 어머니는 넘어져 다리를 다쳤고, 그 후 4월에, 아버지는 종양 때문에 신장을 제거했다. 동시에, Dottie의 아버지가 매우 편찮아지셨고, 우리는 그와 함께 있기 위해 Tucson으로 비행기를 타고 갔다.

(B) 우리는 그(Dottie의 아버지)의 치료에 어느 정도의 변화를 만들었고, 며칠 후, 그는 회복되기 시작했다. 그리고 나서 우리는 (나의) 아버지가 악화되어, 그의 남은 신장이 기능을 멈췄고, 그가 혼수상태에 빠졌으며, 그래서 우리가 와야 한다는 전화를 받았다.

(A) 우리는 Wichita로 비행기를 타고 가서 언니들을 만났다. 우리가 병원에 도착했을 때, 아버지는 새로운 약에 차도를 보이고 있었다. 그는 회복했고 2주 만에 집에 갈 수 있었다.

해설 주어진 문장에서 1966년에 필자의 부모님이 편찮으셨다고 한 뒤, (C)에서 필자의 부모님이 편찮으신 동시에 Dottie의 아버지도 매우 편찮아지게 되어서 Dottie와 필자가 그와 함께 있기 위해 Tucson으로 간 것을 설명하고 하고 있다. 이어서 (B)에서 그의 치료(his care)에 변화가 있었고 Dottie의 아버지가 회복하기 시작하고 나서는 필자의 아버지의 상태가 더 악화되어 다시 돌아가야 한다는 전화를 받았다고 하고, (A)에서 우리(We)가 Wichita 의 병원에 도착했을 때 필자의 아버지가 새로운 약에 차도를 보여 결국 퇴원할 수 있었음을 언급하고 있다.

어휘 turn out 밝혀지다 respond 차도를 보이다 recover 회복하다
get worse 악화되다 kidney 신장
fall into a comma 혼수상태에 빠지다 remove 제거하다
tumor 종양

MEMO

MEMO

MEMO

2025 대비 최신개정판

해커스공무원

7개년 기출문제집
영어

개정 11판 1쇄 발행 2024년 9월 2일

지은이	해커스 공무원시험연구소
펴낸곳	해커스패스
펴낸이	해커스공무원 출판팀

주소	서울특별시 강남구 강남대로 428 해커스공무원
고객센터	1588-4055
교재 관련 문의	gosi@hackerspass.com
	해커스공무원 사이트(gosi.Hackers.com) 교재 Q&A 게시판
	카카오톡 플러스 친구 [해커스공무원 노량진캠퍼스]
학원 강의 및 동영상강의	gosi.Hackers.com

ISBN	979-11-7244-263-7 (13740)
Serial Number	11-01-01

공무원 교육 1위,
해커스공무원 **gosi.Hackers.com**

해커스공무원

· **해커스공무원 학원 및 인강**(교재 내 인강 할인쿠폰 수록)
· 어휘 잡는 **핵심 기출 단어암기장** 및 다회독에 최적화된 **회독용 답안지**
· 내 점수와 석차를 확인하는 **모바일 자동 채점 및 성적 분석 서비스**
· 해커스 스타강사의 **공무원 영어 무료 특강**

공무원 합격의 비밀!

해커스공무원 **단기 합격생**이 말하는

해커스공무원과 함께라면
다음 합격의 주인공은 바로 여러분입니다.

대학교 재학 중,
7개월 만에 국가직 합격!

김*석 합격생

영어 단어 암기를 하프모의고사로!

하프모의고사의 도움을 많이 얻었습니다. 모의고사의
5일 치 단어를 일주일에 한 번씩 외웠고, 영어 단어
100개씩은 하루에 외우려고 노력했습니다.

가산점 없이
6개월 만에 지방직 합격!

김*영 합격생

국어 고득점 비법은 기출과 오답노트!

이론 강의를 두 달간 들으면서 **이론을 제대로 잡고 바로
기출문제로 들어갔습니다.** 문제를 풀어보고 기출강의를
들으며 **틀렸던 부분을 필기하며 머리에 새겼습니다.**

직렬 관련학과 전공,
6개월 만에 서울시 합격!

최*숙 합격생

한국사 공부법은 기출문제 통한 복습!

한국사는 휘발성이 큰 과목이기 때문에 **반복 복습이
중요하다고 생각**했습니다. 선생님의 강의를 듣고 나서
바로 **내용에 해당되는 기출문제를 풀면서 복습**
했습니다.
